1 MONTH OF
FREE
READING

at

www.ForgottenBooks.com

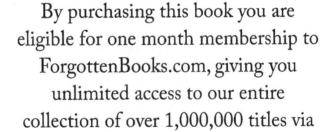

By purchasing this book you are eligible for one month membership to ForgottenBooks.com, giving you unlimited access to our entire collection of over 1,000,000 titles via our web site and mobile apps.

To claim your free month visit:

www.forgottenbooks.com/free830510

ISBN 978-0-484-39578-6
PIBN 10830510

HISTORICAL MANUSCRIPTS COMMISSION.

(ELEVENTH REPORT, APPENDIX, PART IV.)

THE

M A N U S C R I P T S

OF THE

MARQUESS TOWNSHEND.

𝕻𝖗𝖊𝖘𝖊𝖓𝖙𝖊𝖉 𝖙𝖔 𝖇𝖔𝖙𝖍 𝕳𝖔𝖚𝖘𝖊𝖘 𝖔𝖋 𝕻𝖆𝖗𝖑𝖎𝖆𝖒𝖊𝖓𝖙 𝖇𝖞 𝕮𝖔𝖒𝖒𝖆𝖓𝖉 𝖔𝖋 𝕳𝖊𝖗 𝕸𝖆𝖏𝖊𝖘𝖙𝖞.

LONDON:
PRINTED FOR HER MAJESTY'S STATIONERY OFFICE,
BY EYRE AND SPOTTISWOODE,
PRINTERS TO THE QUEEN'S MOST EXCELLENT MAJESTY.

And to be purchased, either directly or through any Bookseller, from
EYRE AND SPOTTISWOODE, EAST HARDING STREET, FLEET STREET, E.C.; and
32, ABINGDON STREET, WESTMINSTER, S.W.; or
ADAM AND CHARLES BLACK, 6, NORTH BRIDGE, EDINBURGH; or
HODGES, FIGGIS, & Co., 104, GRAFTON STREET, DUBLIN.

1887.

[C.—5060.-III.]   *Price 2s. 6d.*

INTRODUCTION.

THE following account of the vast collection of papers accumulated at Raynham by successive generations of the family of the Marquis Townshend is by no means to be considered exhaustive. The papers here described were selected from thirty or forty large boxes chiefly filled with early deeds, accounts, surveys, rentals, &c. relating to the family estates, which would be of great interest and importance to the Norfolk antiquary; and it is possible that in going through such a mass of material some documents of historical value may have escaped notice. Moreover, previous to the examination of the collection, a selection had been made by Lord Townshend's agent, the late Mr. William Ansell Day (whose kind assistance to and hearty interest in the work of the Commissioners cannot be too warmly acknowledged by them), from the letters, &c. of the Elizabethan and Jacobean periods, with a view to publication. The majority of these letters formed the correspondence of Sir Nathaniel Bacon, half-brother to the Lord Chancellor, whose estates and papers came by marriage to the Townshend family. The lamented death of Mr. Day has suspended for the present the intended publication, though great progress was made with the arrangement and transcription of the documents; but the Commissioners hope that before long some steps will be taken to make this interesting portion of the Raynham collection of manuscripts also available for historical purposes.

The Elizabethan papers removed to London for examination by the Commissioners, and noticed in the subsequent report are comparatively few in number. They include a few news-letters from Sir Francis Wyndham; some commissions and council letters illustrating Norfolk affairs; a copy of the will of Sir Nicholas Bacon, the Lord Keeper; and a list of persons implicated in the Earl of Essex's rebellion, showing the prison in which each one was confined. Early in the seventeenth century is a letter from the Norfolk justices to the Council, urging that in that time of plenty places abroad with which England is in amity are the only market for the summer corn, and praying for liberty to ship away barley, malt, peas, and beans, and also beer; the country being so emptied of money that, unless this prayer be granted, it cannot meet the payments demanded for her Majesty's service. Licences appear to have been granted to export corn and beer from Lynn shortly after this. A series of college bills show the cost of living and tuition at Cambridge between the years 1605 and 1610; an apothecary's bill of some ten years later in date is another curious illustration of prices at that time. There are also three or four good news-letters from Roger Townshend and N. Bacon. Of the Civil Wars and the Commonwealth there is hardly a trace among these manuscripts of any value. The papers of the time of Charles II. are more numerous, but their bearing upon public and county affairs is not marked enough to require special notice here, with the exception of a very lengthy document headed " Some particular matters of fact relating to the administration of affairs in Scotland under the Duke of Lauderdale," and addressed to the King ; it is a very severe indictment of that Duke's government. A bundle of " Warrants of Commitment to the Tower " in the years 1675, 1676, and 1677 is useful as evidence of the incarceration of many noted pesrons at that time on various grounds. There is also a large collection of songs, lampoons, &c., belonging to the latter part of the seventeenth and the beginning of the eighteenth centuries, of which it has only appeared necessary to quote a specimen relating to Lord Wharton and Bishop Burnet.

Among the State Papers and Despatches of the time of Queen Anne and later, we find many addressed to, or concerning, the second Viscount Townshend during his embassy to the Hague in the years 1709, 1710, and 1711. The English agents at Turin, Florence, Milan, Hamburgh, and other places were among his regular correspondents, and their letters give many details of the diplomatic and martial preparations in various courts of Europe during Marlborough's successful campaigns. Some of the letters are addressed to Horatio Walpole, afterwards Lord Walpole of Wolterton, who was attached to Lord Townshend's embassy. There is a good letter from Lord Stair at Warsaw, written in March 1710, referring to the difficulties created by the erratic Charles XII. ; and another of about the same date by Stephen Poyntz, referring to the extreme want of the French army " insomuch that in several places their leathern shoes were taken ,from them in the winter " [lest they should eat them, we may suppose the writer means] " and locked up till the opening of the campaign, and wooden shoes given them in the meantime ; and every post we hear of their plundering bakers' shops." One correspondent tells Horatio Walpole in June 1710 of the " late sudden illness called " Collero Morbus " of his brother Robert, which had nearly put an early period to the career of the then rising statesman; and another friend James Craggs, when with the English army in Spain, writes to him about the battle of Almenara and other matters. Among other letter writers are the Earl of Peterborough and Lord Raby, afterwards Earl of Strafford, who succeeded Lord Townshend as Ambassador at the Hague. After Townshend became Secretary of State in 1715, we find a capital series of despatches from Admiral Sir John Norris, when in command of the expedition sent to the Baltic to protect British commerce, and to demand satisfaction from the King of Sweden for the losses inflicted on our merchants by the confiscation of their ships and cargoes. Other letters of this time in the collection, notably some from Lord Bolingbroke when in Paris, and of Sir Robert Walpole, were allowed to be used by Archdeacon Coxe, and printed in his Memoirs of Sir Robert Walpole. The correspondence for the year 1725 of Horatio Walpole when Minister in Paris, bound in four folio volumes, and many loose letters of his from Paris of earlier and later date were also examined by Coxe. In a long communication dated in January 1727, Sir Charles Wager, the Admiral, gives his "private opinion of the Russians," and their inclinations towards England. The series of notes which passed between George II., in his own handwriting, and Lord Townshend, on various public matters between 1728 and 1730, printed in Coxe's Walpole, are still preserved at Raynham. The last diplomatic letter of importance, dated 3rd November 1735, is from Thomas Robinson, afterwards Lord Grantham; in it he refers to his six years' residence at the Imperial Court, and earnestly desires to be removed from Vienna.

Passing by many petitions and memorials dated in the earlier half of the eighteenth century, which are chiefly of personal interest, we reach the next division of this collection which is that of the Jacobite Papers, ranging in date between 1703 and 1727. The most important in number and interest relate to 1715 and succeeding years, when Viscount Townshend was Secretary of State. Among these are reports from the country of local riots (including a notable one from Oxford in December 1715), and on the state of public feeling; information supplied by spies at various places abroad as to the intentions of the Pretender; many intercepted Jacobite letters; Privy Council minutes by Lord Townshend on the steps to be taken against the rebels and suspected persons; and copies of Jacobite proclamations. Lord Carlisle and James Craggs write from Preston and Wigan on the proceedings against the prisoners taken in Lancashire, and make some interesting references to

Lord Derwentwater, and to others still remembered for their share in the rebellion. There is a good letter, too, from General George Carpenter, dated at Nottingham on the 23rd November 1715, detailing his own services during a month's chase of the rebels, and complaining of their inadequate recognition by the authorities. Copies of despatches to the Duke of Argyll, when commanding the expedition to Scotland against the Earl of Mar, from Lord Townshend and Secretary Stanhope, are also among these Jacobite papers, and the extracts given from them in the following report are of great interest. The first despatch is dated 1st September 1715, and the series is continued at intervals of a few days until 21st February in the year following. Of later date are some curious papers bearing on a project for " disarming the Highlands," and a very long letter from General Wade, showing the manner in which that part of the kingdom could in his opinion be made secure against future attempts to disturb its peace.

Of a totally different character are the letters and accounts formerly belonging to the Earl of Wilmington. The Earl, when Mr. Spencer Compton, was treasurer to Prince George of Denmark, and he held in later years a similar post with regard to the Prince of Wales, afterwards George II. The papers and accounts relating to these positions have more personal than historical interest, but they will be found not unworthy of the space given them in the report. Passing by some details of the cost of regimental clothing and the like, we come upon a long inventory of the personal effects of Prince George, a valuation of his breeding mares, stallions, coach horses, hunters, and "padds," and of his plate, guns, and pistols; the last article included in the list being a twelve-oared barge. Perhaps the most noticeable fact about this property is that most of it was claimed by various officers of the late Prince's household as their fees and perquisites; thus certain plate fell to the share of Lord Delawarr as Groom of the Stole, all the coaches and horses (the latter valued at 992l.) were given up to Lord Bridgewater as Master of the Horse, and the barge to the bargemaster of the Prince. Some letters concerning the Duchy of Cornwall are best worth attention among the evidences of Compton's second term of office.

Some papers relating to the Tower of London, chiefly between 1712 and 1715, when the Earl of Northampton was Governor of the Tower, next fall under notice. Among them are documents showing the privileges claimed by the inhabitants of the Tower Hamlets, and some curious petitions, notably one from a poor man who claims relief for having been shot by a sentinel

under peculiar circumstances. There are also many orders from
the council for the great guns to be fired on certain memorable
occasions.

Following these are some private letters addressed to Elizabeth, Countess of Northampton, dated between 1713 and 1737.
These are chiefly of domestic interest, but are not without
reference to public affairs. Thus the satirical Lady Ferrers
writes a few days after the death of Queen Anne, "he
[George I.] is very stately, and everything must be very fine;
he speaks neither French nor English; he won't be very good
company to these Kings [the Lords Justices] when he comes.
. . . . . . The little Duke of Kent has gained three inches; I
have seen one of them [the Kings aforesaid], but he doesn't
speak to subjects." The majority of Lady Northampton's correspondents are of her own sex, and their epistles, though doubtful
in their orthography even for that lax age, are usually amusing
if not always instructive. Almost her only male correspondent
was one Nicholas Guillibeau, who appears to have kept a select
young gentlemen's academy at Fulham, whence he dates his
reports on the progress of her young son, Lord Compton, in his
studies.

Of far wider interest is the section of the report under which
is grouped the numerous papers relating to the American plantations, &c. during the first 40 years or so of the last century.
These, like other portions of the Townshend collection already
noted, seem to have been brought together by Lord Wilmington,
who between the years 1731 and 1743 held the position of President of the Council. The majority of the letters are addressed
to him. Some of them give glimpses of the condition of Carolina and the difficulties which beset its Lords Proprietors: the
letters of Governor Gabriel Johnston, three or four of which are
given at full length, together with some petitions and other
letters from Charles Town, will be found of marked value for
the history of that colony. The Governor of Georgia about the
same time was the celebrated General James Oglethorpe, of
whom is preserved a letter wth two very curious reports of his
interviews with the Chiefs of the Chicksaw Indians at Savannah.
The papers relating to Massachusetts (1730–1742) are equally
numerous and important, the majority of them being letters and
reports from Governor Jonathan Belcher; a memorial signed by
eight pastors of churches in Boston, Roxbury, and Cambridge,
and a letter from Governor W. Shirley, who succeeded Belcher,

should also be noticed. Of all these letters the most striking is
a private one written by Belcher to his brother-in-law, Richard
Partridge, who lived in London, setting forth the difficulties
which surrounded his governorship. Other interesting papers
in this section relate to New Jersey, New York, Connecticut
Newfoundland, Nova Scotia, and Jamaica.

George Townshend, afterwards fourth Viscount and first
Marquis, was a brigadier-general early in the year 1759, when
he was sent to Canada with the expedition under General
Wolfe. On Wolfe's death, at the capture of Quebec, he succeeded to the command. Many letters, of both public and
private character, relating to this expedition are preserved at
Raynham, and have been printed in this report. Roger Townshend, younger brother of George, was a colonel in the same
expedition, and died from wounds received at the siege of
Tyconderago a few weeks before the fall of Quebec; a letter
from him to Lady Ferrers (wife of his brother George), dated from
the Camp at Fort Edward, June 7, 1759, gains additional interest
on that account. The most important official documents are
some "rough notes" relating to the siege of Quebec, and a copy
of Townshend's long despatch to Pitt describing the operations
and the capture ; among the private ones the brigadier's letters to
his wife are noticeable. In the first quoted he writes :—" General
Wolf's (*sic*) health is but very bad. His generalship in my
poor opinion is not a bit better, this only between us. He never
consulted any of us till the latter end of August, so that we have
nothing to answer for, I hope, as to the success of this campaign."
Passages in other letters cast a doubt on Wolfe's military skill,
though, happily, his character as a hero remains undisturbed ;
thus, about three weeks after his death, Brigadier James Murray
writes to Townshend that Wolfe's " orders throughout the campaign show little stability, stratagem, or fixed resolution ; I wish
his friends had not been so much our enemies, his memory
would probably have been dearer to his country than now it
can be. We are acting on the defensive ; you have the execution of the plan, and I am well persuaded you will manage it·
with as much tenderness to the memory of the poor general as
the nature of things will admit of."

The concluding portion of the report contains notices and
copies of miscellaneous letters and papers covering in date
nearly the whole of the eighteenth century. Many of them
have little interest except as autographs of persons of more or

less distinction. Among the remainder the following may be
selected for mention:—a letter from Horatio Walpole to his
brother Robert in August 1727 referring to a conversation he had
had with Cardinal Fleury about the intention to send the young
Lord Chesterfield as minister to Paris; one from Colonel John
Harbord describing an attack by a French privateer in August
1710 on the packet boat in which he crossed from Holland;
Lord Findlater's account of an election of representative peers
for Scotland in June 1721; two letters from Charles Compton,
Consul-General in Portugal, to Lord Wilmington in 1731 and
1732; a letter written on the coast of Guinea to a Norwich alderman in 1737, urging the fine prospects of a profitable trade with
that country which lie open to enterprise; a few chatty letters
of Lord Hervey, and of his sons George and Augustus, afterwards Earls of Bristol, to Lady Townshend; one from General
John Campbell, afterwards Duke of Argyll, describing his pursuit of the Young Pretender; a curious agreement between Lord
Townshend and Lord Weymouth in 1765 about the borough of
Tamworth, besides letters concerning other elections at different
dates; a letter of Viscount Clare, member for Bristol, on the
linen manufacture in Ireland in 1770. Among the latest in
date is a note of the Chevalier D'Eon.

Scattered among the above in their chronological order are
many letters of the most brilliant member of the family whose
papers are being described, the statesman Charles Townshend.
One of them is as early in date as September 1735, when the writer
was but ten years old; the next was written ten years later,
from Scarborough, in which he gives his conviction that his
illnesses have no other source than constitutional weakness;
three years later he is again at Scarborough, looking forward to
a seat at the Board of Trade, as well as for the borough of
Yarmouth; and other letters to his mother give glimpses of his
domestic life and character. The most important political
document is the copy of a long letter he wrote to the Duke of
Newcastle, April 30, 1764, suggesting the steps to be taken to
strengthen the opposition to the government of that day.

A singular contribution to the history of the study of political
economy will be found in the lengthy correspondence which
passed in 1752 between the third Lord Townshend and the Rev.
Josiah Tucker, afterward Dean of Gloucester; and in the many
letters, with their replies, written by the same Lord two or
three years later to the authorities of Cambridge University,
relative to his proposal to give a prize of twenty guineas each
to the two best dissertations " upon subjects included within the

theory of trade." After much discussion the proposal was accepted, and the prizes awarded, but the subjects chosen were so little to his lordship's taste that he declined the offer made by the Vice-Chancellor to send the two winning dissertations for his perusal.

Fortunately for historical and literary students, the present noble owner of Raynham has not placed such restraint upon the use of his manuscript treasures there as his ancestor, the third Viscount, thought fit to do. In May 1752 Horatio Walpole asked permission of this nobleman to have a sight of those letters which Lord Townshend's father "wrote and received while he was ambassador in Holland in the late Queen Anne's reign, because I have under my consideration some Posthumous Works of the late Lord Bolingbroke, and the sight of your father's papers might be of service to set in a true light the false and scandalous misrepresentations of the transactions in which Lord Townshend had been greatly concerned." There is no record of any answer whatever having been made to this application, and more than two years later, in October 1754, Walpole repeats his application, with a reference to his previous letter. The rough draft of Lord Townshend's reply to this, from Raynham, deserves quoting at length. It runs thus :—" My father did during his retirement here in the country in the latter part of his life determine to write a history of his own times, which he had entered upon, and though he died soon after, yet as he had resolved rather to take the trouble on himself of drawing up this historical account than to leave it to any other hand, I think that he has by such his resolution plainly signified to me his inclination and desire that these papers which he has left in my custody should not be perused or made use of by any other hand. I should otherwise have been glad to have complied with your request."

The portion of the following report which deals with the Townshend papers previous to 1700 was drawn up by Mr. W. O. Hewlett; the papers of the last century were examined and calendared by the late Mr. H. Barr Tomkins. Upon the death of the last-named gentleman, while his calendar was still in manuscript, Mr. Hewlett undertook the revision of the whole report.

THE MANUSCRIPTS OF THE MARQUESS TOWNSHEND, AT RAYNHAM HALL, CO. NORFOLK.

I.—LETTERS AND PAPERS BEFORE 1600.

MARQUESS
TOWNSHEND
MSS.

Besides those set out below there are numerous letters between the following persons.

Amy Bedingfeld (1591) ; Sir Nathaniel Bacon of Stifkey, *passim ;* Sir Drew Drury (1597) ; Sir Roger Townshend of Rainham (1577 *et passim*) ; Sir Edward Clere of Blickling (1582) ; William Townshend (1587) ; Sir Nicholas Bacon Lord Keeper (1569 *et passim*) ; John Dychfield, mayor of Lyme Regis (1577) ; Edward Walpole (1588) ; Sir Francis Wyndham Justice of the Common Pleas in 1579 (1576 *et passim*) ; Nicholas Bacon son of the Lord Keeper (1572) ; and many others of less note.

N.D. Old memorandum book in parchment covers, with no name or date. It appears to have been made about the beginning of the 16th century, and contains a number of rough notes, written frequently in Norman French, all relating to the Townshends. It contains (*inter alia*) (1) notes *tempore* Henry VII. of payments of money, delivery of deeds, and of places where deeds and writings are to be found ; (2) Extracts from the wil lof a Lady Townshend, name not mentioned, who died 8th Hen. 7. 1492-3 (possibly Ann daughter of Sir William de Brewse wife of Sir Roger Townshend), the bequests are chiefly plate furniture and linen ; (3) Similar extracts from the will of a Sir R. Townshend Chivalier, appointing chaplains at his various houses and detailing their duties. "And the sayd 2 prests to say at every of ther masses after the Gospell, *de Profundis* with a speciall colect for my father's soule, my moder's soule, my soule, my wyff's soule, and all our aunceters' and frends' soules, and principally for all the soules that I and my wyff be bounden to pray for, and for all the soules that we have had eny good and not deserved of ageyn consciens ; and for all cristen soules ;" (4) Notes of leases made by Dame Eleanor Townshend daughter of Sir John Heydon and wife of Sir John Townshend of Brampton ; (5) Notes headed "Consideracons that ther was never lawful bergayn between William Paston the younger and Jan Mariot and John her son," being apparently legal notes of some law suit then pending ; (6) Extract from a will, (testator not mentioned) mentioning John Townshend, Robert Townshend, George Townshend ; (7) Notes headed "Valor maneriorum terrarum et tenementorum Rogeri Townshend." There are many other rough notes, domestic, and estate accounts, many of which are dated. These dates range from 15th to 17th Hen. VII. 1449-1502.

1572. Oct. 13th. Sir Francis Wyndham * to Nathaniel Bacon. " Newes here be none but that the Quene's Majesty is very well recovered agayne.

---

* Sir Francis Wyndham was son of Sir Edmund Wyndham, sheriff of Norfolk, by Susan daughter of Sir Roger Townshend of Rainham. He married Jane, daughter of Sir Nicholas Bacon, the Lord Keeper,' and was thus brother-in-law of Sir Nathaniel Bacon. He was elected recorder of the City of Norwich in 1576, and was a judge of the Court of Common Pleas in 1579.

The newes in Flanders grow now contrarye to the successe of that contrye reported in Norffolk. For I thynke you have hard that Mowntz ys geven over by Counte Lodwicke unto the Duke of Alva: that the Counte by composition ys passed with bagge and haggadge, and that the Prynce of Orenge ys retyred to Mecklyn, he groweth weake as ys feared thorough want of payment to his sowldyars."

N.D. Nov. 4th. Sir Francis Wyndham to Nathaniel Bacon. The first part of business matters. "Flushyng begynneth to feare by reason of the sowldyers will skale (? sail) now awaye shortly and therefor yt ys sayd that they of the towne do make awaye their goods. All the townes revolted from the Duke of Alva are retorned to hym agayne, but Mecklyn hath bene spoyled by the sayd Duke. It begynneth now to be in whysperyng of our league to be renewed with Kyng Philip and that embassadors shall be sent enterchangeably for the purpos."

1576. Oct. 8th. "Goramburye." Copy Royal Commission under the Great Seal, headed "A comission within the county of Norfolk touching restraint of transportacon of corne and grayne and other victuall beyond the seas, and for furnishinge of the merkets ; and also to enquire of regrators." The commission is directed to Sir Christopher Heydon, Sir William Butts, Robert Bell, Drew Drewry, Henry Wood-howse, Raphe Shelton, William Heidon, Nathaniel Bacon and Thomas Barroughe Esquires. It sets out that it is evident to her Majesty and her Council that "the prises of corne and grayne, and other victuall without any naturall or evident just cause do begynne to ryse and increase only (as it seameth) by reason that divers couetous gready and evill disposed farmors and other ingrossors and badgers inhabitinge within divers counties of this our realme havinge greate quantitie of grayne in their hands, and myndinge for their owne private lucre and gaine to make a greate scarcitye thereof, not without some expectacon by some occations of secret transportacon of grayne and other victualls owt of the realme by reason of the great prises of the same in forraine partes growne by the inward trobles ther ; and so havinge great store of corne and grayne in their hands and possessions they will kepe and withehold the same from the markets by unlawfull confederacies amongest themselves to the intente only to kepe the same at very excessyve prises. By reason whereof and by false rumors and reporte divised for that purpose as we ar enformed, all manner of corne and grayne and other victualls and especially wheate and rye, barley malte and otes, and also butter and chease have not only been but also do yet continewe at very greate and extreme prises, and greater is like to doe yf some speady remeadye for the dewe cor-rection of such offendors and the staye of such practises of ingrossors and badgers be not had and provided." The Commissioners are therefore required and empowered to find out by examination of wit-nesses and other means, (1) all persons in the County of Norfolk who commit the above practices, and the magnitude of their offences and all other necessary particulars concerning them and their transactions ; (2) the names of all engrossers of corn and other provisions ; and (3) full particulars of all persons who in any way, by their dealings, tend to enhance the prices of corn and other victuals. They are further re-quired to enjoin all farmers having corn to sell that they bring to the market such quantity only as they shall be empowered to do by the Commissioners and "to sell the same at reasonable prices without any fraud, covin or delaye" power being given to the Commissioners to commit to gaol any such who transgress these regulations.

MARQUESS
TOWNSHEND
MSS.

No corn, grain, butter, cheese or other victual is to be transported abroad on pain of imprisonment, but under strict supervision of the customs' officers, it may be carried between English ports and harbours.

1576. Oct. 19th. Hampton Court. Letter signed W. Burghley, T. Sussex, A. Warwyk, F. Bedford, R. Leycester, F. Knollys, James Croft, Fra. Walsyngham. To the Sheriff and Justices of Norfolk on the prevailing scarcity of corn and the means to be adopted for remedying it. Forbidding the exportation of corn abroad, &c.

1577. Jan. 1st. Emblem beautifully sketched in ink of a man on horseback and a man about to mount a bare backed colt. Above is written " *Aliquando tamen proficit qoo sero sapit.*" Then beneath follow the lines :

> Before the sturdye colte will byde the bytt,
> He beares oftymes the broont of many blowes,
> But when at laste he letts his ryder sytt,
> He learns to rayne, and forwarde then he goes.
> Some men be coltes : they friske and flynge at first,
> Yett (onse well broke) suche men prove not the worste.

To the righte Honorable Sir Nycholas Bacon Knighte, Lorde Keeper of the Greate Scale, good newe yeare and many to God's good pleasure. My verie favorable good Lorde.

Being latelye receavede into Her Majestie's service (wherein I hope to recover my decayede estate) I devisede to presente all my lordes and good frendes in Courte with certayne emblems for their new yeres gyftes, an exercyes, (as I judge) neyther unplesante nor unproffitable. Att leaste my meaninge is thereby to showe proofe that my penn cann as well be paynfull in moral poetrie, as itt hathe bene hetherto over curious in expressinge of lighte affections.

And my resolutione beinge suche, I coulde not chuse but proffer your Lordship the lyke presennte, an objecte not altogether corespondente to the gravite of your judgmente, and yett voyde of any vanitie which may justlie offende your honorable disposicon and in full hope thereof I have put in hazarde to send you the same, beseachinge your Lordship thus to understande I kept my koltish tricks much longer then was eyther for my credytte, or for my proffytte, I friskede, I flange, I refused the brydell of discretione, and ran still at lardge in the fenns of sondrye follyes. At last it hath pleasede God to make reasone my ryder, and he haveinge firste corectede me, nexte enstructede me, and laste of all encouragede and coyed me. I begyne to beare the brydle pretelye well and hope so to goe forwards as I may deserve in thende to be well placed in a prynce's stable.

But (my goode Lord) my colltyshe and jadishe tricks have longe sythens broughte me oute of ffleashe as withowte some spedye provysione of good provender I shall never be able to endure a longe jorneye and therefor am enforcede to neye and braye unto your good Lordship and all other which have the keye of her Majesties storehouses . beseaching righte humblie that you will voutchsaffe to reamember me with some extreordynarye allowaunce when it fallethe. God preserve your Lordship to the common proffyte and my perticuler comforte this firste of January 1577 and ever your Lordship's redye at comaunde.

G. Le Gascoigne.

1577. May 31st. Greenwich. The Lords of the Privy Council. Lords Burghley, Lincoln, Sussex, Leicester, Sir Francis Knollys, Sir Francis Walsingham and James Croftes to the Justices of Norfolk, with regard to the injury done to the wool trade and to the customs by

A 2

certain persons who buy up all the wool and sell it again at what price they choose; enclosing a list of such persons, and requiring the Justices to compel them in a bond of 100*l.* each only to buy such wool every year "as they by themselves and ther apprentices shall yerelie make or do to be maid and wrought in ther mantion howses in things used to be maid of wolle and mixed with wolle within this realme. And further they shall not buye anie to sell the same backe in whole againe to anie other." The list of persons who are to give bonds follows on another page.

1577. July 20ᵗʰ. "From the Court at Richemond." Copy letter signed "W. Burghley," "Edward Lyncolne," "T. Sussex," "F. Knolles," ".Ja Crofts," & "F. Walsingham," but unaddressed, requiring a return of all the inns, taverns, and alehouses, on which a small tax is to be levied to raise money for the improvement of the port of Dover.

1578. April 27ᵗʰ. Greenwich. Copy letters signed by Lords Burghley, Lincoln, Sussex, Warwick, and Hunsdon, Sir F. Knollys, Sir Christopher Hatton, Sir Francis Walsingham, and others, directed to the Sheriff and Justices of the Peace of the County of Norfolk as to the training of the militia in shooting.

1589. Aug. 20ᵗʰ. "The Court at Otelandes." Copy letter from the Council to the Lord Lieutenant of Norfolk as to the levying of a loan on the County.

1578. Dec. 23ʳᵈ.   Copy Will of SIR NICHOLAS BACON, Lord Keeper
of the Great Seal.

In the name of God Amen.   The thre and twentithe daie of December in the yere of our Lord God a thousand fyve hundredthe seaventye and eighte and in the one and twentithe yere of the reigne of our Sovereigne Laydie Elizabethe by the Grace of God Queene of England Fraunce and Ireland Defendor of the Faithe etc. [I] Sir Nicholas Bacon Knighte Lord Keper of the Greate Seale of England beynge of whole mynde and memorie doe make this my present testament in manner and forme followynge revokynge all former wills and testaments made by me before the date hereof.

First.   I comyte my sowle to the hands of Almightie God whoe of his omnipotencie did create yt and of his infinite mercie redemed yt and nowe as my undoubted hope ys by the same mercifull redemcon will glorifie yt and save yt.

My desier ys to be buried at Pawles where my tombe is.   And because I geve noe blackes to the riche that have noe neede therefore I geve to the poore that have neede fyve hundredthe marks to be distributed accordynge as by a sedule subscribed wythe my hand dothe appeare.   I will notwithstandyng blackes be geven to my housholde folkes both at London and Gorhamburie and to all my childeren their husbands and wiffes.

Item I geve to my deare and welbeloved wiefe one thowsande fyve hundredthe ounces of my plate whereof thone haulfe guylte and thother haulfe parcel guylte and white, to be chosen by hir oute of all my plate excepte soutche parcels as I geve awaye by speciall name.

I give hir also all my lynen, naperie, hangynges, coches, lytters, and all other my howshold stufe and howsholde stoore remayninge at London excepte my readie money, plate and armor and excepte suche evidence as apperteyne to eny lands or hereditaments as be assigned to eny of my children by my former wief, and excepte suche things as remayne in my studie and suche things as I geve awaye by

MARQUESS
TOWNSHEND
MSS.

speciall woordes requyringe my wief in consideracon of the same provision and stoore to kepe so many of my howsholde together at her charges durynge a monethe after my deathe as will tarrie so longe for the better doinge whereof I give hir in readie money c^{li}. I give hir also suche jewells and golsmythes worke (excepte plate) as remaynethe with hir. I will also to my said wief all my horses and geldyngs And also all my intereste in all my stockes of sheepe goynge at Ingham or Tymwoorthe or within eny of my sheepe courses there To possesse and use durynge hir life uppon condicon that within one yeare nexte after my decease and before her mariage agayne she become bounde to my executors in the some of twoo hundredthe pounds that at the tyme of her deathe she shall leave to suche person or persons as oughte then to possesse the same mannor and stocke of sheepe goynge uppon the same mannor and within the said sheepe courses of like goodnes and of as greate a nomber as she shall receave.

And this is donne because I ame bownde uppon covenaunts of marriage of my eldest sonne to leave suche a stocke after the deathe of my said wief And I will that the stockes letten with Stifkey goe as the lands is there appoynted to goe and remayne And I will that the one haulfe of all the howsholde stufe that shall remayn at Gorhamburie at the tyme of my deathe (except my plate, tent and pavylion) to Anthonie at thage of 24 years And if he die before then to Frauncis at the same age And thother haulfe I will to Anthonie after the deathe of my wief And in the meanetyme my wief to have the use of it. To whome also I geve all my greene store of howseholde remayninge either at Redburn or Windridge and all my other goodes and cattalls remayninge there (except my plate and money and other things before geven or excepted).

Item I will that all that my lease of Aldenham and all copiehold lands or tenements lyinge in the parrishes of Sainte Michall or Sainte Stephens nighe Saint Albones or joyninge to any lands of Westwicke, Gorhamburie or Praye shall remayne and goe accordynge as my howse of Gorhamburye is appoynted to goe and remayne.

Item I geve to my said wief all my intereste in Yorke Howse in consideracon of which legacies and in consideracon of suche assurances of mannors lands and tenements as I have assuered unto my said wief and for all loves that have benne betwene us I desier her to see to the well bringing upp of my twoo sonnes Anthonie and Frauncis that are nowe left poore orphans without a father.

And further I will and bequethe to the said Anthonie my sonne all that my lease and tearme of yeres and all my intereste and demaunde which I have of or in all those woodes comonly knowne or called by the name or names of Brittetfirth alias Brighteighfirthe alias Brighteighe woode and Burnet Heathe lyinge and beynge in the parrish of Sainte Stephens in the countie of Hertforde And also all that yerely reute of £26 13 4 due and payable for the said woodes And also all my righte tittle and possession which I have of and in eny lands tenements and heriditamentes assuered to my said [son] Sir Nicholas for the true payment of the said rente of £26 13 4 And also all that my lease and tearme of yeres and all my tittle and intereste and demaunde which I have of or in the fearme of Pynner Parke lying in the parrishe of Harrowe in the County of Middlesex. And also of and in all my other landes tenements and heriditaments lying in the said parrishe of Harrowe To have and to houlde to the said Anthonie the said woodes lying within the said parrishe of Sainte Stephens And all the said fearme called Pynner Park and all the said landes and heriditaments in Harrowe for and duryinge so maney yeres as yt shall happen the said Anthonie to live. And if yt shall fortune the said Anthonie to die before the full ende and expiracon or determinacon of the said leases and tearmes of yeares therein contained then my will and intent is that the eldeste sonne of the bodie of the said Anthonie for the tyme beynge and the heyres mayles of his bodie for the tyme boynge shall have houlde occupie and enjoye successively during their severall lyves all the said woodes and fearme and other the premysses before bequeathed to the said Anthonie for so maney yeres as the said eldeste sonne of the said Anthonie for the time beinge or the heyres males of the bodie of the said eldeste sonne shall severallye and successivelie fortune to live and yf it fortune the said Anthonie and his said eldeste sonne and the heyres males of the said eldest sonne and everie of them to die without issue male of their bodies and of the body of every of them before the full ende and determination of the saide leases and termes of yeares therein contayned, then my will and full meanynge is further that Frauncis my sonne shall have houlde occupy and enjoye the said woodes fearme and other the premysses before bequeathed to the said Anthonie. To hym the said Frauncis his executors and assignes for ever.

Item I geve also to my eldeste sonne and his heyres all my fearmes in Mildenhall and of Langerfearme and of the lands and tenementes in Ilketeshall and of my howse in Silver Streete that I have of the House of Westminster and of my fearme of Dullyngbams.

And further I will to my said heyre my tent and pavilyon remayninge at Gorhamburie and all my apparrell armor and weapon re-maininge eyther at Redgrave or at any howse in London and all my howshoulde stufe stocke stoore and other goodes remayning at Redgrave, and all things remayninge in my studie at London excepte suche as be geven awaye by speciall wordes.

Item I geve to Roberte Blackeman my nephewe all my intereste in the lease of the meadowes and grounde at Hame.

And to Nathaniell my sonne towardes the buildynge of his howse at Stifkey twoo hundredthe poundes and besides all my lease of the lands in Stifkey and my stocke of sheepe goeing uppon them.

Item I give to the Master and Fellowes of Bennet Colledge in Cambridge to the building of a chappell there cc^{li}.

And I geve to every of my freendes and to my servantes and suche other person as be named in a pagyne hereafter followynge subscribed with my hand all suche thyngs and somes of money as beeue in the same appoynted.

Provided alwayes that iff Ann my said wief doe not make or cause to be made within one yere next after my decease and before she be maried agayne to everie of my sonnes Nicholas, Nathaniell, Edwarde, Anthonie and Frauncis, a sufficient release in lawe of all her right tittle intereste and demaundes of dower of and in all the mannors landes tenements and hereditamentes whereof by reason of my seysin she is or then shalbe dowable and deliver or cause to be delivered to everie of my said sonnes one suche release within the said yere and before she be maried, then I will all my legacies guifts and bequestes to her made shalbe voied and then I will the same together with the rest of my goodes debtes and cattalles after my debtes paied funeralls discharged and legacies performed to my eldeste sonne Nicholas.

Item I will that the hundrethe poundes stocke remayninge with the Mayor of Sainte Albones and his brethern's handes for the settinge of the poore of woorke be continued in their handes so longe as they per-ferme the covenauntes agreed uppon betweene them and me otherwise that my wief or heyres to Gorhamburie receave and kepe the same.

MARQUESS
TOWNSHEND
MSS

And of this my will I make my executors Sir Nicholas Bacon Knyghte and Nathanyell Bacon, and overseer my Lorde Treasorer my brother in lawe to whom I geve a standynge cuppe with a cover garnyshed with christall weighing 53 ounces 3 quarters, and to my Ladie Burghleye my sister in lawe a deepe bowle with a cover haveyng my cognizaunce weighing 21 ounces and a half.

To Anthonie my jewell that I weare and to my daughter Bacon my eldeste sonne's wief my cheaste in my study made by Albert and my little boxe with ringes and to Mistress Butts my ringe with the beste turquois.

In wittnes whereof I have subscribed everie pagyne of this my will with myne owne hande and set to my seale the daie and yere firste above written.

1578. The names of the poorest prisoners in the comon gayle in the Kinges Benche who this 6th of Marche received the som of foure pownds as the legacye of the ryght honorable Sr Nicholas Bacon Knyght decessyd late Lord Keper of the Great Seale of England by thands of Hugh Morgan grocer and Thomas Awdeley skynner.

Endorsed : Prisoners acquittances.

1579. June 12th. "St Kateryns." Nicholas Mynne to Nathaniel Bacon. News of the town. The Bishop of York just dead. The Queen has been "syckly" but is now better.

1579. Aug. 19th. "From the Court at Nonsuch." Copy letter signed by Sir Thomas Egerton, Sir W. Knowles, Sir Robert North, Sir Robert Cecil, Lords Hunsdon and Buckhurst, to whom does not appear, " After our hartie comendacons, we have receaved a letter from Sir Henry Woodhouse by which we perceave that som of you the Comyssioners have not only taken from him the charge which longe tyme was comytted unto him, but have of late appointed him againe to attend the defence of Yarmouth not allowing him those forces that have benne by former direccon appointed for that purpose. Theis courses seminge straunge unto us that you should proceed in such sorte with a gente of reputacon and good service, we canne do no lesse then requier you to yeeld us a reason and accompt of your doeings in that behalf, and what moved you to take those unfreindly courses with a gente of his sorte."

1579 [about]. Paper headed " The charge of the buryall in Paules," and endorsed "The verger's bill, to the ryght worshipfull Sir Nicholas Bacon Knight and other the executors of my Lord Keper." It probably refers to the burial of Sir Nicholas Bacon Lord Keeper of the Great Seal, who died in 1579. It gives an estimate (which comes to 18l. 4s. 4d.) of the cost of a funeral at St. Paul's and is signed " Alexander Nowell, deane, Jo: Mullins, Jo: Walker."

1581. March 11th. Blickling. Sir Edward Clere to Nathaniel Bacon, enclosing a copy of a letter from the Privy Council relating to some wax come ashore by reason of a wreck to which certain persons, living near the coast, lay claim. It is her Majesty's pleasure that ten thousand weight of the said wax be delivered to her messenger on her behalf.

1582. Nov. 16th. Sir Edward Clere to Nathaniel Bacon, concerning injuries inflicted on Sir Edward by his "cousin Heidon," forcibly entering Saxlingham House, killing and impounding his cattle, assaulting his servants, &c.

1583. Paper headed "The oryginall of the falling out of Mʳ Thomas Cooper and Mʳ Robert Markham the younger at Sowthwell the 12ᵗʰ of Maye 1583 in the presence of Mʳ Thomas Locke Mʳ William Sutton the younger and Mʳ Marshall brother in law to Mʳ Markham."

1587. Nov. 22ⁿᵈ. Sir Francis Wyndham to Nathaniel Bacon. "The opportunytye of this berer together with the freshenes of occurrents here, moveth my wrytynge at this present. Here is very fresh newes and that dyversely confyrmed, that there be at Dunkyrke of late ccme 12000 Italyan sowldyers, but whither they shall be sent ys dowbted. Some saye into Praunce, some feare into Scotlande, or yf hither or not ys unknowen. But upon this, though there have bene a great calme and stylues in not executynge soch preparatyon as was publyshed in the Star chamber should be made at everye hande as well by sea as by lande, yet even now upon advertisement that came but yesterdaye upon conference by the Privye Cownsell yt ys sayd to be resolved that my Lord Admyrall shall presently go to the sea with a great navye. And this daye came there letters from my Lorde of Hunsden that the Scotts have fayled of kepynge of the dayes of trewce at which was promised restytution of and amends for the great spoyles of late taken by the Scotts. Whereupon my Lord of Hunsden in person hath entered into Scotlande and hath taken a great botye there to satysfie the partyes afore spoyled. The Kynge there hath a great power up and in redynes. He geveth owt that he ys dryven for his owne safetye agaynst some of his own subiects to provyde his power for his owne defence. But yt ys not beloved, for rather yt ys thought that he maketh hymselfe redye to joyne with forren forces to invade us, and therfore his excuses begyn not to be trusted nor belened. Here ys other good newes even yesterday advertysed hither   That there be 12 hulkes laded with cordadge (which ys cables and soch lyke furniture for ships) by tempest of wether dryven into Plymowthe haven in the west contrye, which by the helpe of two or three shypps beyng then nere upon the coast helped them to be kept and stayed there, though they moch resisted the same. They came from Hanboroughe (Hamburgh) and were goyng to Lyseburne (Lisbon) as a provision made for the Kynge of Spayne's navye. But by God's providens more then by humayne foresyght they be stayed to do us good to unfurnyshe the adversarye. And so we may see how moch we are bound to God if we wold be thankefull."

1590. Jan. 9ᵗʰ. "The Courte at Richmonde. Letter signed "Chr. Hatton, *Canc*," "W. Burghley," "Hounsdon," "T. Howard," "T. Heneage," "J. Fortescue," "J. Wolley," and "F. Cobham" to Nathaniel Bacon, Esq., appointing him collector of a loan about to be raised in the county of Norfolk.

1591. March 1ˢᵗ. "A certificat touching divers persons who have had privie scales delivered unto them for the loane of money within the Countie of Norfolk." Lists of persons who have furnished money on loan for the Queen's service; of persons who the justices consider have not lent enough; of persons certified to be too poor to lend any thing; and of persons who are able to lend, but whose names have been omitted.

1592. Oct. Copy of a long letter (in Sir Nathaniel Bacon's writing) from the Justices of Norfolk and Suffolk, probably to the Privy Council, as to a grant made to two persons named William Garton and Robert Kyrke of the profits of the forfeiture of a penal statute for the sowing of flax and hemp in Norfolk and Suffolk. In a letter from their Lord-

MARQUESS TOWNSHEND MSS.

ships the Justices were required to call before them the patentees and other witnesses and to certify to the Council the correctness or non-correctness of their accounts. This has been done, though the patentees, when summoned, neglected to appear, and the accounts have been proved to be false. The patentees appear to have been under a contract to construct a pier at Sheringham in Norfolk from the proceeds of the grant of the forfeitures, and the Justices had been further required to view and report upon the progress and value of the pier. In this letter they state that they have viewed the pier and have heard the testimony of local men on its value, which is not considered great, and the letter concludes with suggestions that the present pier shall be discontinued and in part pulled down and the timber applied to the building of jetties in front of the town of the merits of which the local fishermen and shippers have a higher opinion.

1596. Feb. 18th. Sir Francis Wyndham to Nathaniel Bacon. "I am sorry I have not suffycyent tyme to wryte so largely unto you as the circumstances of matters do requyre; for fyrst you shall understande that within these three or four dayes my Lord Canterbury in the presens of the Counsell (except my Lord Treasorer who was sicke) dyd delyver to her Majestie that her Government by her ecclesiastical courts were like cleane to be otherthrowen by reason of a charge geven by me and Mr Cocke at Sessions vidz. that ther ordynarye cowld not cyte men to appere pro salute anime to awnswer upon oathe, the rumour whereof hath bred a scruple to all the byshops in Englande, that they dowbt how to procede in theyr cowrts, for that they have ever synce the Conquest used no other cowrse. With this her Majestie was greatly grieved with me and sayd that she wold have all the Counsell calle all the judges together before theyr cyrcuyte to comand them not to geve yt any more in chardge. And then dyd my Lord Chamberlayne take opportunytie to exasperat the Quenes Majestie further agaynst me saying also that I dyd impugn her Majestie's comissions and other her prerogatyves and procedyngs in her seryice in Norffolke, which complaynt the Cownsell was lykewyse comanded to call me to awnser. So as this daye my Lord of Canterburye my Lord Chancelor, my Lord Admyrall, my Lord Chamberlayne, my Lord Cobbham, and my Lord of Buckherst were assembléd at my Lord Chancelor's howse where all the judges were appoynted to hear her Majestie's pleasure before we went in cyrcuyt. So at our beyng there my Lord shewed her Majestie's myslyke that the judges as she harde were not all of one mynde towchinge the offence of the Martynists and some favored them which yf she knewe she wold remove from theyr places, and then as to the charge geven towchinge the oathes in spyrytuall courts we were comanded from her Majestie to forbeare to geve yt any further till more consultatyon were had theref. Then my Lord shewed further her Majestie's pleasure towchinge such as were convicted of the Martynists. That yf they wold not submytt themselves accordyng to a draft made thereof that they shuld be executed ! So the judges departed, but myselfe. And then my Lord Chamberlain (withowt callynge Sir Arthur in) dyd hymselfe informe agaynst me, that I sought to dyscontenans hys Lordship in his lieftenancy in that shyre ; that I impugned her Majestie's commission and all other her service there for levyeng of money, and then he fell to partycularities of baylyng of   which I justyfyed, and so to other thyngs as well towchinge yourselfe and Drurye whom he will send for presently, and chardged me he should be forthcomynge, and I sayd his servants had made him forthcomying. He sayd he deserved yt well and how yt was but that one of his men dyd mete hym and asked hym whether he did not speke certen words of my Lord Chamberlain, which he confessed he dyd and thereupon he brake his heade with his dagger. So then I shewed the whole facts which he denyed and sayd further that I bare hym' and all his mallyce for that he was honest agaynst my brother for the Scotts." Sir Francis relates several other charges preferred against him by the Lord Chamberlain and his answers thereto " and so when all this was done the dynner was redye and my Lord Chamberlaine sayd he had xx^{ty} other matters I should awnswer hereafter and so I departed."

1598. April 30th. Stifkey. Paper in Sir Nathaniel Bacon's writing headed "A warrant to be sent to all the C. Con. (*sic*) in Norffolk," requiring that all persons who advanced money to the Crown on loan, should defer seeking repayment for six months. Giving below the names of all those in the several districts of the County to whom this warrant is to be communicated.

1599. July 19th. Norwich. Paper headed " Matters agreed upon at Norwich in execution of the Councell's letters of the 3rd of May, for musters in the Countie of Norfolk." The orders are signed by Sir Christopher Heydon, Sir Philip Woodhouse and Sir Nathaniel Bacon.

N.D. [but about 1600]. Paper giving a list of persons implicated in the Essex rebellion, and stating where they were imprisoned.

" In the Toweare.

Earlle of Essex.
Earlle of Rutland.
Earlle of Sowthamton.
Lord Saundes.
Lord Mountegello
Lord Cromwell.
Ser Charlles Davies.
Ser Christopher Blonte.

In Newe Gaite.

Ser Jhon Davies.
Ser Gillam Merricke.
Sir Hinerie Carie.
Mr Treshame.
Mr Doweall.

In the Gard House.

Ser Jhon Hadame.
Ser Robarte Veron.
Ser Christopher Laydon.

In the Marshallseas.

Ser Edward Myckilborn.
Mr Bushell.
Mr Cosnall.
Mr Bucke.

In the Flete.

Ser Charles Perce.
Ser Jhon Perce.

Ser Edward Banshaind.
Ser Edward Letilltowne.
Mr Fraunces Maneres.
Mr Gregorie Brigge.
Mr Cas^te.

In the Counter in Wodstret.

Mr Thomas West.
Mr Man.
Mr Foster.
Mr Addine.
Mr Dasoune.
Mr Compton.
Mr Arwell.
Mr Elleap Jonnes.
Mr Jhon Laid.
Mr Lawsonne.
Mr Richard Herferd.

In the Counter in the Poultrie.

Mr Raphe Smeth.
Mr Williame Parratt.
Mr Thomas Blondall.
Mr Praunces Kinersleaye.
Mr Williame Grauntam.
Mr Edward Harte.
Mr Edward Harber.
Mr Richard Chamley.
Mr Auntheny Rouse.
Mr Jhon Ardinge.
Mr Jhon Trimpe.
Mr Fraunces Lenster.

MARQUESS
TOWNSHEND
MSS.

Mr Thomas Sandall.
Mr Thomas Tippinges.
Ser William Constabill.
Mr Peter Redall.
Mr Williame Orrme.
Mr Jhon Morries.
Mr John Parmell.
Mr Robarte Coote.
Mr John Binbrigge.
Mr Gregorie Sissill.
Mr Alexander Greshim.
Mr Jhon Robartes.

In Ludgaite Feloninge.

Mr Jhon Wheller.
Mr Thomas Wheeler.
Mr Thomas Medley.
Mr William Liane.
Mr Jhon Grainte.
Mr Jhon Wright.
Mr Christopher White.

The Lorde of Sussiex in bould at Ser Jhon Stannope's.   The Lorde
of Bedford in houlld at Alldermane Holidaie's.
Captine Sallesberie slaine in Essiexe house."

N.D. Ann Lady Gresham to her nephew Nathaniel Bacon respecting
the sale of some land.

N.D. March 11th. Lady Gresham to her nephew Nathaniel Bacon
relating to the sale of some of her property.

II.—LETTERS AND PAPERS FROM 1600 TO 1660.

Among the letters of no importance save to the correspondents are
some between ;
Henry Earl of Northampton (1611) ; Sir Horace Townshend afterwards the 1st Lord Townshend of Lyme Regis *passim;* Sir Roger
Townshend his father, *passim;* Henry Curzon (1624) ; Mildmay 2nd
Earl of Westmoreland who married the widow of Sir Roger father of
the first Lord Townshend (S.D.) ; Anne wife of Sir John Townshend
and daughter of Sir Nathaniel Bacon (1614 *et passim*) ; Elizabeth
Knyvet (1626) Dorothy wife of Sir Nathaniel Bacon of Stifkey (S.D.) ;
Nathaniel Knyvet (1634) ; Sir Nathaniel Bacon of Stifkey (1614 *et
passim*) ; Sir Philip Wodehouse of Kimberley (1612) ; Lady Townshend wife of Horace 1st Lord Townshend (1654) ; Sir Hamon Le
Strange (1623) ; and many others from and to members of the Townshend and Bacon families.

1600. Jan. 20th. Copy declaration signed Christopher Heydon,
Myles Corbett, Na. Bacon, Thomas Knyvett, Edm. Mundeford, W.
Welby, Rich. Stubbe, and Mathew Gamble Commissioners appointed for
settling a controversy which had arisen as to what towns should contribute to the repair of the banks of the township of Terrington, stating
that the townships of Wiggenhall, Tylney, and Clendwarton are not
liable to contribute.

1600. July 7th. Lynn. The Mayor and Corporation of Lynn to
Nathaniel Bacon High Sheriff of Norfolk, Sir John Townshend, Sir
Christopher Heydon, and Sir Philip Woodhouse, claiming an exemption
from musters outside their town, by charter.

1600. Dec. Copy interrogatories and answers thereto relating to the
repair of the sea walls of Marshland in Norfolk and as to what townships are liable to defray the expences of the same.

1601. April. Copy letter from the Justices of Norfolk to the Lords of the Privy Council as to a recent order prohibiting the carrying of corn from port to port, requesting that this order may be rescinded, as there is now no scarcity of corn, and on account of petitions they have received to that effect from shipowners who go to get coals from Newcastle and who have been accustomed to carry on their way thither corn &c. for the northern markets.

1601. May 24th. Greenwich. Copy letter from the Privy Council to the Commissioners for the Musters in Norfolk, for reducing the numbers in each trainband of the militia, so that no man should have command of more than two hundred men.

1601. July 15th. Norwich. The Justices of the Peace of Norfolk to the Privy Council, giving the names of the gentlemen appointed to view the decays of the sea bank at Terrington and to estimate the charge of repairing it.

1601. Nov. 30th. Whitehall. Copy letter from the Privy Council signed Tho. Egerton; T. Buckhurst; Nottingham; E. Worcester; W. Knollys; J. Stanhope; Ro. Cecyll; Jo. Fortescue; Jo. Popham; J. Herbert; to the Commissioners of Sewers for the County of Norfolk, as to the repair of the sea walls of Torrington and what townships in Marshland are liable to help defray the cost thereof.

1602. March. Letter in Sir N. Bacou's writing, from the Justices of Norfolk to the Privy Council (probably, but it is not addressed) "The transportacon beyonde the seas to places in amity with her Majesty being the onely markett for our somer corne in this tyme of plentie, doth so much import the state of our contrey here in Norffolk, as wee are bold to crave your honour's favours, that it would please you to give direccon wherby warrants maie be sent to the officers of our ports for libertie to shippe away barley, malt, peas, and beanes and also beere, payeing her Majesty's custome, according to the Statute. The reasons which move us to be suitors herin be especially these. First our experience letteth us see that our contrey is so emptied of money, as a nomber of persons within the same when thei are demaunded to make payment towards sondrie charges of her Majesty's service and the realme, are to seake, and do praie a staye, untill thei mai sell that wherewith thei maie gett money." Now that corn is more plentiful (barley is stated to be at 10s. per quarter) the writers beg that permission for its transportation may be allowed, as benefitting growers, sailors, and her Majesty's Customs.

1602. March 15th. The court at Richmond. Copy letter from the Privy Council to Sir Arthur Hevenyngham Knight High Sheriff of Norfolk, Sir Philip Woodhouse, Sir Bassingbourne Gawdy, Nathaniel Bacon, and others, in answer to a letter from them to the Justices of Norfolk, of March 1602 (see above) stating that they will give licences to a limited extent to persons in the county to export corn and beer beyond the seas.

1602. May 1st. Copy letter unsigned and unaddressed, but the person written to is styled "My Lord," and the letter mentions "this port of Lynn." It relates to the question of exportation of corn and grain, which is forbidden by statute, and requests that, as there is a very plentiful supply this year, exportation may be permitted.

1603. Feb. 15th. "At the Court." Thomas Lord Buckhurst to Nathaniel Bacon Steward of the King's manors of West Walton, Walso-

MARQUESS
TOWNSHEND
MSS.

ken, Emeth and Tylney, requiring him not to grant admittances or receive surrenders of any tenants of those manors until further notice, and to send a certificate of the value of the said manors.

1603. July 5th. Lord Buckhurst and others to the officers of the port of Lynn, forbidding strictly the exportation of corn or beer beyond the seas except to Scotland.

1603. Sept. 23rd. Norwich. Draft letter in Sir Nathaniel Bacon's writing, from the Justices of Norfolk, to the Earl of Northampton Lord Lieutenant of the County, on the subject of the musters.

1606–1609. "M^r. William Smith's charges uppon his beinge at Cambridge.

Michaelmas quarter 1605.—For Mr. Percivall and the Schoolmaster's charges to Cambridge about his admittance - - - - -	xxxviij^s
Christmas quarter 1605.—For seeleing a chamber in Trinity Colledge - - - - -	iiij^{li}
For a yeares rent from Michaelmas 1605 -	liij^s iiij^d
Geven Mr. William in money - -	x^s
For a violl - - - - -	l^s
Summa - -	xi^{li} xi^s iiij^d

"Lady quarter 1606.—For Seton's logicke and paper	xvi^d
For a truncke and porter - -	xix^s x^d
Geven him when he went to Cambridge -	xxx^s
For apparrell for him to Mr. Anguishe -	iiij^{li} xvii^s vi^d
For the schoolmaster and 2 men's charges with him to Cambridge - - - -	xlix^s iiij^d
For poynts - - - -	ij^s
To Mr. Aldrich his tutor to defray his charges 27th May - - - -	xx^{li}
Summa - -	xxix^{li} xix^s x^d

"Midsomer quarter 1606.—For a pott given the Colledge - - - - - -	v^{li} vi^s x^d
To Mr Smith - - -	v^s
Geven Mr Aldrich by my Lady Bacon -	l^s
Added geven to officers and servants there -	xiij^s
For my Ladie's charges to Cambridge to see her sonne - - - -	vij^{li} xviij^s x^d
Geven to Mr William Smith - -	v^s
Geven by my Ladie to schollers -	iiij^s vj^d
Added geven to the wayter at Cambridge -	ij^s vj^d

li   s   d
16 2 10   Summa   -   xv^{li} vij^s iiij^d

"Michaelmas quarter 1606.—To Mr. Buckworth the tutor by Thurlow 24th October - -	x:iij^{li} vj^s viij^d
For carriage of the same to Cambridge -	iij^s iiij^d
For a paire of garters - - -	viij^s
Sent him - - - -	v^s
For cambricke for ruffs - - -	viij^s
Summa - -	xiiij^{li} xi^s

Summa pagine 71^l 9^s 6^d

" Christmas quarter 1606.—To his tutor Mr Buckworth 2nd January - - - -	lvi
For tuition then - - -	xx
To him 18th January - - -	x^{li}
To Mr Smith - - -	x^s
For a paire of pantofles - -	iij^s
To him at Stewkey 2nd January - -	xxx^s
For his expenses at Falsham - - -	iij^s vj^d
For a paire of shoes - - -	iij^s vj^d
To him at his returne to Cambridge - -	x^s
For his expences upon his returne to Cambridge - - - -	xxxv^s xj
For cambricke - - - -	viij^s
Added For a sword and dagger, girdle and spurres -	lviij^s ij^d
Ladie quarter 1607.—To Mr Buckworth 6 Aprill -	x^{li}
To him 20th Junü - - -	x^{li}
Midsomer quarter 1607.—To Mr Smith 12th August	v^{li}
To him 17th September - - -	l^s
For lawne for him - - -	v^s viij^d
For shoes - - - -	iij^s vi^d
To him at Stewkey - - -	x^s
For gloves - - -	vj^s
To him more - - -	xx^s
For his charges from Cambridge to Stewkey and upon his goeing againe thether -	lvij^s iiij^d
Sent him to Cambridge - - -	x^s
To Mr Kempe upon a bill for apparrell -	vij^{li} xij^s
For shoes viij^s viij^d. Sent him x^s - -	xviij^s viij^d
My ladie's charges at Cambridge - -	ix^{li} xvj^s
Michaelmas quarter 1607.—To Mr Burckworth 16th October - - - - -	x^{li}
To him 19th December - - -	x^{li}
For porter of the money - - -	xij^d
For knitting a paire of stockings - -	xx^d
Summa pagine -	90^{li} 11^s 1^d

Added to Mr Smyth at diverse tymes in the holly dayes - - - - -	xlv^s
Christmas quarter 1607.—To Mr Buckworth 25th Jan.	x^{li}
To him in February - - -	x^{li}
For shoes - - -	iij^s vi^d
For his charges from Cambridge to Stewkey -	xxix^s vij^d
For shoes - - - -	xiij iiij^d
To him when he returned - -	xx^s
To him more - - -	x^s
Added for a saddle bridle and furniture - -	xx^s
For his charges upon his goeing againe to Cambridge - - - - -	xxxij^s x^d
For porter of money to the carrier - -	ij^s
xxviij^{li} xvij^s iij^d Summa -	- xxv^{li} xij^s lij^d

Ladie quarter 1608.—To Mr. Buckworth 18th Junii - - - - -	x^{li} }	x^{li} xij^d
Added for portage - - -	xij^d }	

MARQUESS TOWNSHEND MSS.

Midsomer quarter 1608.—To him 5th August x^{li} ⎫
For carriage of money   -   -   xij^d ⎬ x^{li} xij^d

Summa   -   -   -   x^{li} xij^d

Michaelmas quarter 1608.—To him 27th October   -   x^{li}
Sent him to Cambridge with xij^d to the porter   xi^s
For apparrell provided at London by M^r
   Kempe   -   -   -   -   - viij^{li} vij^s viij^d
Geven him money   -   -   -   -   xx^s
Added to him 3rd December for expences   -   -   xxx^s
For a hatt   -   -   -   -   -   vij^s vi^d
Added to him for expences   -   -   -   v^s
For boots and shoes   -   -   -   xvij^s x^d

xxij^{li} xix^s   Summa   -   xx^{li} iiij^s

Christmas quarter 1608.—To Mr Buckworth in full - xvij^{li} j^s iiij^d
To Mr Smith at Stewkey   -   -   -   xx^s
For a paire of pantofles   -   -   -   iij^s iiij^d
For apparrell   -   -   -   iiij^{li} xviij^s

xxij^{li} ij^s viij^d   Summa   -   - xxij^{li} xij^s viij^d

And in this tyme he Summa of the charges dureing ⎫
came often into the his being at Cambridge ⎪
cuntrey and staide longe before he went to London ⎬ ccl^{li} x^s vj^d
with Mr Stanhope ac- being from our Lady 1606 ⎪
companinge him and his till February 1609 aboute ⎪
man. 3 yeares ⎭

li   s   d   l   s   d
250   10   6   Summa pagine   -   88   9   11

Mr WILLIAM SMITH's EXPENSES after his goeing to the INNES of COURT.

Christmas quarter 1608.—For his expences up to
  London with Mr Stanhope and his man   -   -   iij^{li} vj^s
For his diett and horsemeate at London   - xxxviij^s ix^d
For his horses backe   -   -   -   -   xvj^s iij^d
To him for the quarter ending at our Lady
  1609   -   -   -   -   -   xx^{li}
For the lease of a chamber and furnishing it - xxvj^{li} v^s vj^d
For a gowne   -   -   -   -   v^{li} xij^s x^d
For lace for a suite   -   -   -   xix^s viij^d

Summa   -   -   -   108^{li} 19^s 0^d

Lady quarter 1609.—To Mr Smith 23rd Martii   -   xx^{li}
For carriage of a truncke   -   -   -   iii^s iij^d
To Mr Kempe for interest for lx^{li} laide out for
  the lease of the chamber   -   -   -   iiij^{li} xij^s
To the taylor for making his apparrell   -   xl^s
For a close stole   -   -   -   -   vij^s vj^d
Paied uppon a bill for apparrell   -   - xiiij^{li} xvij^s v^d

Summa   -   -   -   42^{li} 2^s 5^d

Midsomer quarter 1609.—To Mr Smith 17th Junii ·   **xx^{li}**
         To him xith July -   -   -   ·   **xx ^{li}**
         For garters and poynts   -   -   -   **xvi^s xiij^d**
         Delivered him in money this quarter more - **iiij^{li}**

                Summa   -   ·   **43^l 16^s 8^d**

Michaelmas quarter 1609.—For a liverie cloake for his
   man -   -   -   -   -   -   **xxxv^s iij^d**
         To himselfe in money   -   -   -   **xxvij^s iij^d**

Mr WILLIAM SMITH'S CHARGES at CAMBRIDGE upon his last returne thether.

Added expences for Mr Smythe's returne to Cam-
    bridge -   -   -   -   -   -   **xxvi^s viij^d**
           Paid him xith October   -   -   **x^{li}**
           Paid to Mr Anguish for his apparrell - **iiij^{li} xv^s**

            Summa 17^l 17^s 6^d   19^l   4^s   2^d
            Summa pagine 212^l 15^s 7^d
         For a sword -   -   -   -   **xxxv^s**
        ⎧ Lent him 13th Aprill -   -   **iij^{li} v^s**
        ⎪ More lent 24th Aprill -   -   **v^{li}**
Paid to   ⎪ More 13th May -   -   -   **xi^{li}**
M^r   ⎨ For grogarine -   -   -   **v^{li} xji^s**
Kempe   ⎪ For glaseing a paire of stockings - **ij^s**
        ⎪ For an ell of cambricke -   -   **x^s**
        ⎩ For interest -   -   -   **xv^s**
         To Mr Smith 6th November -   -   **x^{li}**

                Summa -   ·   **37^{li} 19^s 0^d**

Christmas quarter 1609.—For shoes -   -   **vij^s**
         To Mr Smith 29th January -   -   **x^{li}**
         To him   6th February -   -   **x^{li}**
         For a hatt -   -   -   -   **xii^s iiij^d**
Middsummer quarter 1610.—Disbursed (as appear- ⎫
   eth in Midsomer quarter 1610) -   -   - ⎬   **vij^{li} vj^s vi^d**
   For a remainder of debt for apparrell - ⎭

                Summa -   ·   **28^l 5^s 10^d**

Summa pagine 66^l 4^s 10^d
     Summa laid out from Christmas 1608 till
       Febr. 1609 -   -   -   **cclxxix^{li} v^d**
            Summa total is · -   -   **cxxix^{li} x^s xi^d**

Endorsed. Particulers of Mr William Smythe's expences butt nott the particulers proved.

The following entries relating to Mr. William Smith's education occur in the " Particular disbursements by Sir Nathaniel Bacon sumed upp" as Executor of Mr William Smyth the Father.

   Item geven to the College librarie in books -   **xx^{li}**

MARQUESS
TOWNSHEND
MSS

Education of William and Owyn Smyth in the howse.

Item for Mr William Smythe's and Sir Owyn Smythe's
charges of lodginge, apparrell, dyett, scoolinge, and attendance for viij yeares and a halfe in Sir Nathaniel
Bacon's howse att cc^{li} per ann. amounting *in toto* for
that tyme to -   -   -   -   -   - $\begin{array}{c} c \\ xvij^{li} \end{array}$

Expenses by Mr. William Smyth att Cambridg and Grayes Inne for 4
yeares.

Item for Mr William Smythe's expences and mayntenance
att Cambridge and Grayes Inne for fower yeares or
thereabouts as by particulers in Sir Nathaniel's Booke of
receipts and payments appeareth viz. from our Ladye   *l. s. d.*
1606 untill February 1609 *in toto* -   -   - 529–10–11

*Expences for mayntenance of Sir Owyn Smyth att Stewkye and Cam-
bridge.*

Item for Sir Owyn Smythe's mayntenance and expenses att
Stewkye and Cambridge for 4 yeares or thereabouts viz.
from our Ladye 1606 untill the death of his brother M^r c
William Smyth in February 1609 *in toto* at c^{li} per ann.   iiij^{li}

The whole charge of the profits of Mr William Smythe's lands re-
ceived by Sir Nathaniel Bacon Knight A.D. 1597 to 1609.
          Sum total -   -   - £6669. 15. 5¼.
Particular account of the disbursements by Sir Nathaniel Bacon.
A.D. 1547 to A.D. 1609.
For the Lady Bacon's debts due by her before Sir Nathaniel's mar-
riage with her.
For debts of Mr William Smith the Lady Bacon's first husband.
For jewels bought and other extraordinary charges expended for the
Lady Bacon before and after marriage.
For fines paid to the Lady Bacon for admittances within Mr Smith's
manors.
For the education of Mr William Smyth (who died in February 1609)
and Sir Owen Smyth (at Stewkey and Cambridge) by Sir Nathaniel Bacon
for or concerning them or their estate or estates during the time they
were in his tuition education and government.
For the purchase of lands in Irmingland and for the building and
finishing of the house there.
Excess of disbursements over receipts £4734. 7. 9½ and half farthing.

1606. June 10th. Wyssett. The inhabitants of the town of Wyssett
to Sir Nathaniel Bacon and Lady Dorothy his wife requesting them to
appoint Mr Swallow to the living as minister in succession to his brother
recently dead.

1607. Jan. 9th. Letter in Sir Nathaniel Bacon's writing, unaddressed, but probably to the Privy Council, announcing the decision
come to by the Justices of the Peace of the County of Norfolk in a
case which had been referred to them, between Henry Clifton, Esq.
plaintiff and John, Henry, and Robert Kempe defendants, relating to the
defendants' lands lying in the plaintiff's fold-course.

1607. Sep. 21st. Feltwell. Sir Edward Moundeford to " the Steward
of the Courte of his Majestie's maner of Methwold," concerning a procla-

mation to be made at the next court by order of Sir John Fortescue Chancellor of the Duchy of Lancaster concerning the "breakeinge & spoylinge the Kinge's soyle and destroyinge of his shepe's course ther by digginge flagges and turffes ther." The letter goes on to specify the exact places where the damages complained of have been committed.

1608. Sep. 21st. Burnham. Petition signed by the inhabitants of Burnham to the Justices of the Peace of Norfolk complaining of one Henry Hopkins for bad behaviour and "all lewdnes" and praying he may be proceeded against. On the other side is a statement signed by Sir Nathaniel Bacon, of charges proved against Hopkins.

1609. June 16th. Serjeants Inn. Copy letter signed Tho. Fleming; Edw. Fenner; Chr. Yelverton; Da. Williams; and Jo. Crooke to whom is not stated, probably to the Justices of Norfolk. Many prisoners have lately been set free by forged writs of *Habeas Corpus :* the writers require for the future that, upon receipt of a writ of *Habeas Corpus* to bring any prisoner into the Court of King's Bench or before any Judge, the said prisoner be conveyed safely guarded to the place directed by the writ, and not to be set at liberty.

1609. Octr 21st. Letter from Henry (Howard) Earl of Northampton to Sir Henry Gawdy, Sir Arthur Heveningham, Sir Philip Woodhouse, and Sir Nathaniel Bacon, Knights, Deputy Lieutenants in the County of Norfolk, touching the proportion of the muster-master's allowance.

1610. Dec. 21st. "This Saint Thomasses day" Ann Lady Townshend (wife of Sir John Townshend and daughter of Sir Nathaniel Bacon) to Mr Mason. Sending "2 turkyes and a pheasant, 7 brace of partrige and halfe a dosen greene plover . . . . . also a fewe puddings . . . . for a breakfast to my brother Sir Robert, yourselfe and my sunn Roger ; I wish them worthy your eatinge."

1611. July 8th. Northampton House (Copy). Henry Earl of Northampton to Sir Philip Woodhouse, Sir Charles Cornwallys, Sir Henry Gawdy, Sir Henry Heveningham, Sir Henry Bedingfield, and Sir Nathaniel Bacon, deputy lieutenants of Norfolk, on the subject of the musters. No muster has been held until this year, since 1591, and Lord Northampton is amazed to see that this year the horse are 500 fewer than they were in 1591. This he attributes to the negligence of the deputy lieutenants and he therefore requires them to hold musters of all the forces every year and to raise them to the 1591 establishment.

1612. June 29th. "Articles agreed upon at Norwich signed by Sir Philip Wodehouse and Sir Nathaniel Bacon, relating to the mustering of the militia bands.

1613. Nov. 15th. London. Sir Ralph Cave, Sir Henry Bedingfield, Sir Henry Spelman and others to Sir Nathaniel Bacon. A letter has been received by the writers from the Privy Council directed as well to them as to Sir Nathaniel and other Norfolk justices, requiring them to survey the damage made by the sea on the district called Marshland, appointing a time to meet at Stowbridge to survey the said damages.

1613. Dec. 10th. Whitehall. The Privy Council to the Justices of Norfolk enclosing His Majesty's directions to be observed in the keeping of Lent.

1614. July 16th. Whitehall. Letter signed "T. Suffolke" "-Gilb. Shrewsbury," "E: Worcester," "W. Knollys" "Ralphe Winwood"

"Jul. Cæsar" and "Tho : Lake" directed to "the Heigh Sheriffe for the time being of the Countie of Norfolk Sir Phillip Woodehowse Knight and Barronnett Sir Henry Gawthey Sir Arthur Heveningham Sir Thomas Hobbart Sir Hamon L'Estrange Sir Nathaniel Bacon and Sir Henry Bedingfield King's Justices of the Peace of the said Countie." Appointing them Commissioners for musters in the County of Norfolk "to cause generall veiwes and musters to be taken of all the forces in that countie boeth of horse and foote."

1614. July 18th. Whitehall. Same to Same. On the same subject directing the Commissioners not to remove any officers at present holding commissions and expressing a high opinion of Mr Curson muster-master of the county.

1614. August 3rd. Extracts from the rolls of the Court Leet of the Manor of Fakenham, Norfolk.

1614. Sep. 17th. Whitehall. Copy letter from the Privy Council to the Sheriff and Justices of Norfolk, as to a benevolence to be levied in the county to supply his Majesty's urgent necessities at home and abroad. "For ye cannot but understand that the Marquesse Spinola hath amassed togither a stronge and powerfull army which sometime he pretendeth to have don under the charge of the Archduke, sometime under the name of the King of Spayne, sometime as best may serve for his advantage under the comand of the Emperor. Whereby we may conclude that thei all thre are combined togithei, and [he] hath caried all the townes in the coun‐ tries of   and Cleves scituate upon the tract of the Rhyne, wherby not onely the Elector of Brandenburg is deprived of the posses-sion of those townes, which he 'or many years peacebly enioyed, whose right his Majestie is bound to defend by vertue of the treaties contracted between him and the Princes of the Uuyon in Germany, but the per-sons and States of the Elector Palatine, and the Princesse his lady, his Majesty's only and deerest daughter, environed on all sides by divers armyes are at this present endangered."

1614. Dec. 29th. Eccles. Thomas Barsham to Sir Nathaniel Bacon, on local matters of no great importance. "Sir Phillipp Knevet is tra-vayled beyond the seas; his lady remaynes at Buckenham Castell. Sir Frauncis Lowell keepeth a great house at Harlinge where the poore hath good releife, and so doth Sir Thomas Hollande at Quiddenham to whome I am much bounden for his kindnes especially for suppressinge of ale-houses in Eccles, who hath promised me to licence none without my con-sent. We have no need of any, for we are poore enough already."

1615. Aug. 7th. Northampton House. Thomas (Howard)(1st) Earl of Suffolk, Sir Fulke Grevyll, and Sir Thomas Parry (Chancellor of the Duchy of Lancaster) to Sir Nathaniel Bacon "farmour of the perquisitts of the Manor of Methwold in the County of Norffolk" The writers are the King's Commissioners for selling his Majesty's copyhold property and are charged to inform themselves of the true yearly value of all the copy-holds belonging to the King, requiring Sir Nathaniel not to hold any court for the admitting of tenants, but to order the Steward to refuse the surrender of any tenants, and to prepare a true rental of the manor.

1619. April 16th. Wivenhoe. A petition from many of the inhabi-tants of Wivenhoe to the patron of the Church and Lord of the Manor, Sir Roger Townshend, asking him to take some steps to stop the "des-perate distempers" and "implacable contentions" that have arisen in the parish.

1619. June 24th. Paper endorsed "The Apothycarie's bill." Sir Roger Townshend's account.　Among the items are:

"Grene ginger"	-	-	- 7ᵃ
Tabacco	-	-	- 2ᵃ
Grene ginger	-	-	- 8ᵃ
A masse of pills	-	-	- 5ᵃ
An electuarye	-	-	- 3ᵃ 6ᵈ

Under the name of Mr Stanhope Townshend 12th September 1618 are

"A clyster"	-	-	- 3ᵃ 4ᵈ
A julep	-	-	- 3ᵃ
A cordiall with behoardston (*sic*)	-	3ᵃ
The cordiall julep	-	-	- 3ᵃ
Hearbs for brothe	-	-	- 4ᵈ
Rose water	-	-	- 6ᵈ
A suppositorye	-	-	- 6ᵈ
Another suppositorye	-	-	- 6ᵈ
An unguent	-	-	- 3ᵈ
A purge	-	-	- 3ᵃ
Purgeing pills	-	-	- 2ᵃ 6ᵈ

1620. July 12th. Whitehall. The Privy Council to the Justices of Norfolk directing them to impress 80 seamen in their county to go in the expedition his Majesty is preparing for the suppression of piracy.

1620. August. Norwich. Copy Letter unsigned and unaddressed, headed "Letters to the Captain of Foote." Probably a circular to be sent to all the Captains of militia regiments in Norfolk, requiring them to prepare for a general muster on the 15th September next, and giving other instructions.

1622. April 14th. Sir Nathaniel Bacon to his son-in-law Sir Roger Townshend. "I have lately received from our High Sheriff a coppie of the Counsell's letters about a voluntary contribucon without the name of benevolence to the Kinge, for the recovery of the Palatinat, and all our Justices of Peace are to labour therein, first in setting ther owne somes thei will give, next to call befor them all subsidy men and others of value, and privatly to deale with one by one apart from another, and so to persuade them to give. It will be some labour to effect this yf it be performed accordingly."

1622. Aug. 31st. Roger Townshend to his father Sir Roger Townshend. "Here is much uncertaine newes from the Low Countries; sometymes wee have the day, then they, but certaine much loss on both sides. The towne stands yett firm; Count Mansfield is now certainely come into Brabant and hath taken Marie Mount, hath done much spoile to the country, and wee heare in comming to joyne with his Excellencye hath received a blow, but the contrary is reported too, so that I know not what you may beleave more certaine then that they are dayly in action, and much slaughter on both sides. The King is at Windsor whither he hath summoned all the Councell; most say it is about the marriage which is now afresh againe, and the dispensation certainely come, but others think it is about the Palatinat which is now in great distresse, for there is onely 3 townes left, at least threescore thousand of the enemyes in the country; more expected. They have cutt of all meanes of supply of victualls, and notwithstanding all treaties proceed in a hostile manner, for they took a towne there by composition, yett putt all to the sword. They have put garisons in Spire and Wormes, imperiall townes, and soe racke the Protestants in them, as they feare a sacke. Yet the King promisethe a redeliverye of all againe. Thus they stand abroad ; at home we are feasting. Great intertainement in Sussex by my Lord Thresorer at his new howse which he bought of Sir Thomas Sherley, where was my Lord of Buckingham and his dependents. From thence they went to Petiworth to my Lord of Northumberland where there hapened a difference betwene his two sonnes in law, my Lord of Doncaster and my Lord Lisle. I cannot tell you the particulars, but they were at blowes, and parts taken. But my Lord of Buckingham being there made a peace for the tyme."

1622. Nov. 5th. Paper headed " The King of Spain's letter, Phillip the 4th to his favorite the Count d'Olivares."

" The King my father declared at his death that his intention never was to marrie my sister Donna Maria with the Prince of Wales which your uncle Don Balthasar understood ; so treated this match ever with an intent to delay it. Notwithstanding it is now so far advanced that (considering withall the aversenes unto it of the Infanta) it is time to seeke by some meanes to divert the treatie which I would have you finde out and I will make it good whatsoever it be. But in all other things procure the satisfaction of the King of Great Brittaine who hath deserved verio much and it shall content me so it be not in the matche."

1623. Jan. 27th. Maningeton. John Potts, to whom does not appear. Relating an election contest at which Sir John Corbett backed by Sir Hamon Le Strange and the writer, Sir John Holland, and Sir Robert Gawdye were candidates. Sir John Corbett was declared by the Sheriff to have been elected, but the party of Sir Robert Gawdy carried him and his son " downe into the markett place in triumph, from thence downe to the Maid's heade, where they drew a cartell (signed principally by the mutineers, Urber, Stileman, Parr, Tubbinge, &c. besides many others ignorant of their designe) to traduce our election. Notwithstandinge that all the Knights, justices and gentlemen of quality (even of Gawdye's partye) approved the sentence and sealed the indentures with the shreife."

1623. Jan. 27th. Sir Hamon Le Strange to Sir Roger Townshend, on election matters. Mentions Sir John Corb[et] Sir Thomas Holland, Sir Roger Gawdy. (Seal.)

[1624-5.] Jan. 3rd. London. Roger Townshend to his father Sir Roger Townshend. " Here hath bene an addition of the Duke of Brunswick, who came on Christmas Eve, was conducted presently to St James's and that night fetched by the Prince to the King, who made him sett by him in a chair, would have had him put on his hatt, acknowliged a greater bond to him then to any Prince in Christendome in the love shewed to his daughter, promised a requitall, and so sent him back to St James's where he was lodged in the Prince's owne bedd, and the same servis in state, till he was weary of it, and desired to be freed of the solitude of eating alone, or he would take a lodging some where els. So he was, and afterwards feasted in divers places, as my Lord of Mountgomery, the Countess of Bedford, the Lady Hatton. His intertainments otherwise were only playes, and running at the ring he was but a spectator. On New Yeare's Eve he had the Garter and my Lord of Salisbury with him, and my Lord of Carleile by a deputye ; there were some cerimonyes in the chappell for it, and that night he tooke his leave, and went awaye the next morning, and the French Embassador the day before him . . . . . .

There is no stay of the match with France, that wee heare of, there is articles abroad of very hard conditions but wee say they are false, and that the Pope hath sent a dispensation without any conditions at all, for which the King of Spaine hath taken exceptions against him, and nothing is like to come of it, for there is hope of theire reconsiliation."

[Before 1628]. Oct. 22⁰ᵈ Grays Inn. N. Bacon to his uncle Sir Nathaniel Bacon. "For Bohemia the newes is verrie uncertaine as allsoe for Hungaria, but sure it is that Count Mansfeildt having payed his soldiers with forrage heretofore in Bavaria standeth now in neede of another manner of treasurie, and bathe sent over to our King Mr Ramsey who vexeth the King with importunitie and vowes he will not returne from the King without a satisfactorie answere.

The report is suddaine and late that the Turke hathe overthrowne the Polonian ; that the King and his sonne are bothe slaine with manie thousands more ; that our supplies that were sent over at the request of the Polonian are staied by the way by the King of Denmark under shew of feare least they should be imployed against the King of Sweden.

The Palatinate after the loss of Heydleberg is now rocked asleepe with a halfe yere's truce. The English are well in Mayuheim, Franken-dale, and another towne all wel fortified although all of them have had theire severall assalts with shame and loss to the enimie. Gulick is yet begirt with a seege by Spinola ; the Prince of Orange lieth within 4 miles of the towne. It is hoped cold wether will coole theire courages ; other remedie is hardlie to be expected. The King of Bohemia is comme back againe to the Hage, being resolved to forgoe not a title that he hath allreadie gotten.

Sluice is aymed at ; the enemie are building a fort near it, yet the haven is open and free and it's evident, notwithstanding, they meane to beseege it. The affaires of France are somewhat better. The King is (if not latelio comme awaie) before Montauban ; the town holds out resolutlie, having caused to be sett over the gate of theire town in large letters : *Roy sans foy, et peuple sans peure*, a faithlesse King and fearelesse people. They were in greate want, but the Duke of Roan with 4000 men in the face of the campe releved them though with loss of nere 100 men. The report is that the Duke d'Espernon is latelie dead of sicknesse before Rochell. The King to block up theire haven had sent thither 30 shipps whoe were set uppon by 20 Rochellers and were scattered, 9 of them being taken and sunk, and the next day 2 shipps more coming with provision for the King's fleete fell into the Rochellers' power while they supposed them to be the King's shipps and were taken by them. They had a greate quantitie of powder and store of corne. The Pope bathe sent a lettre to the King of admirable commendations and praises and in the end of all his apostolick benediction.

Since Sir Robert Mansel's returne the pyrates have taken above 40 of our shipps, the gennerall report is 57, in severall places being most fisher men of small burthen belonging to other havens in the west and east parts, none belonging to London but 2 ; I feare Linne or Yermouth have theire shares in the loss . . . . For ourselves the Lord Archbishop as yet stands in uncertaintie ; the Commissioners have not done with him, it is feared he shall hardlie escape a faver by it . . . . . . The Marquis Hamilton is going or is gone from the Court, allsoe Mr Thomas Murrie secretary to the Prince, and Mr Fullerton bothe religious honest gentlemen are putt from theire places : they say Coddington shall succede the secretarie's place. This Coddington was legier in Spaine. The Court speakes Spanish, Councel Spanish, Clergie

Spanish, why should not all the countrie be Spanish at lengthe? The match they saie is concluded, a high alter making at St. James's and a sylver crucifix, and gentlewomen are suters to the Spanish embassadot for places of attendance under her. I leave it to your discretion to beleve or not, for my part I shall tell you more when I see these things fulfilled. But enough for this time."

1628. May 6th. Copy Order of the Court of Chancery in a suit of Sir Roger Townshend and others v. Harris and others. Signed Washington.

1629. March 31st. Whitehall. The Privy Council to the Commissioners for the subsidies in Norfolk. (Copy.) As to a subsidy to be assessed on those that can best afford to be taxed and who in the former assessment were too much undervalued.

[Before 1636]. John Yates to Sir Roger Townshend on election matters. Sir Roger has been elected with Sir Robert Bell for the county in spite of his determination expressed that he would not stand. The writer begs him to alter his determination.

1659. Jan. 23rd. Sir William Doyly to Sir Horace Townshend that he is willing to meet Sir Horace at the time he wishes and to do anything requisite for the " Country's peace, ease of grevances and settlement of the nation."

1659. Feb. 11th. Whitehall. Copy letter headed " Lord Generall Monck and the officers here to the several and respective regiments and other forces in England Scotland and Ireland " recommending, as a means of further establishing and strengthening the Commonwealth, the readmission to the House of Commons of the secluded members, the legal dissolution of Parliament and the issue of writs for a future full representation of the whole commonwealth of England Scotland and Ireland. The writers are confident that the present Parliament if the secluded members are admitted will not repeal any of the Acts and orders for supplies or public disposition of lands, &c.

" And if any disafected persons shal hereby take occasiou to make disturbance of the peace of the Commonwealth either in favour of Charles Stuart or any other pretended authority we desire you to secure them til the pleassure of the Parliament, or Counsell of State be knowne in that behalfe."

1659. " Charles R. (autograph) Charles by the Grace of God King of England Scotland France and Ireland Defender of the faith, &c. to our trusty and welbeloved · (sic) greeting. Wee do by these presents constitute and appoint you to be Governor of (sic) and to put such a garrison of horse and foote therein as you judge necessary for the defence of the same against the rebells and to command the said garrison as Governor thereof, and to do all things necessary for the preservation of the said place for which this shall be your warrant. Given at our Court at Bruxelles the 6th day of March 1659 in the eleventh yeare of our reigne."

Sealed with the Royal Arms.

[1617-36.] April 8th. Thomas Godsalve to his cousin Sir Roger Townshend. The writer is in prison on a false accusation of having attempted to escape, and "for want of paying for my chamber, I am cast downe into the lower ward;" begging Sir Roger to write to Sir John Corbet asking him to talk with Mr Weekes the gaoler on his behalf.

MARQUESS
TOWNSHEND
MSS.

N.D. [1648–1660]. Draft Petition of the gentry of Norfolk to Sir William Lenthall speaker of the House of Commons "Wee the gentry of the County of Norfolk and County and City of Norwich being deeply affected with the sence of our sad distractions and divisions both in church and State and wearied with the misery of an unnatural civill warre, the too frequent interruptions of Government, the impositions of severall heavy taxes, and the loud outcryes of multitudes of undone and almost famished people, occasioned by a generall decay of trade which hath spread itselfe throughout the whole nation and these countyes in particular; and haveing mett together and consulted what may best remedy and remove our and the nation's present grevances and distractions, doe humbly conceive that the chiefe expedient will be the recalling of those members that were secluded in 1648 and sntt before the force put upon the Parliament (wee of this county of Norffolk being by such seclusion deprived of any person to represent us in Parlament) and alsoe by filling upp the vacant places therof and all to be admitted without any oathe or ingagement previous to there entrance, which being done wee shalbe ready to acquiesce and submitt in all things to the judgment and authority of Parliament, without which authority the people of England cannot be obliged to pay any taxes."

N.D. [temp. Interregnum] Copy "petition of the barronets, knights, esquires, gentlemen, ministers, and others of the County of Norfolke" to the Parliament, complaining of the state of their county which they ascribe to its not being represented in Parliament.

Praying that such of their members as have not forfeited their rights may be summoned to come and sit in Parliament.

N. D. Dorothy Lady Bacon to her grandson Sir Roger Townshend. Unimportant. The postscript is, "O Sir lett me say as I dare speake my mind if I had you privatt. My mallencaly sonne hath within this few weekes so groved my selfe and him selfe as it wear strang to tell you ondly because hee can not indevar but to lede a singell life, and a travelling life. Alas what shall I saye; I cannot indevar him once more to ventar all the chellderen I have in this world, but this must not be knowen it came from me."

N.D. Dorothy Lady Bacon to her daughter-in-law Lady Townshend on private family affairs; mentions her daughter Knyvett.

N.D. Sep. 11th. London. Roger Townshend to his mother Lady Townshend. Mentions his cousin Stanhope.

N.D. Ann Corbett to Sir Roger Townshend. Acknowledging a loan of £200.

N.D. Ann Townshend to her sister (name not given) on family and domestic matters. Mentions her cousin Robin Bacon, and her cousin Hungat.

N.D. Nicholas Le Strange to Sir Roger Townshend asking him to be godfather with Sir H. Spelman to his infant son who is to be baptised at Hunstanton.

N.D. Paper unsigned in Lady Anne Townshend's writing beginning "Mr Manu" relating to Sir Roger Townshend and her son whose tutor Mr Mann appears to be.

N.D. [temp. Interregnum]. Copy petition to Lord Fairfax requesting him to take steps as suggested at the foot of the petition to secure the lasting peace of the County, the punishment of rebels and enemies, and the prevention of the liberties of the County being further endangered.

N.D. " To the townsmen of Helloughton and Martin Raynham. Sir Horatio Townshend Baronet sendeth greeting.

As 'tis the duty of all Christian people fearing the Lord, to keepe the unity of the Spirit in the bond of peace, soe theese are to will and require you the townsmen aforesaid to live in a peaceable and quiet manner with your minister that soe al divisions and differences being laid aside ye may follow after peace and holines without which noe man shall see the Lord."

III—Letters and Papers, 1660–1700.

Letters between the following persons are not of sufficient importance to be set out at length :

Horatio Lord Townshend and Charles Viscount Townshend *passim* ; Lord Richardson (1661) ; Charles Spelman (1661 etc.) ; Sir Philip Wodehouse of Kimberley (1663) ; Gilbert Archbishop of Canterbury holograph (1663) ; Sir Jacob Astley (1663) ; Sir Robert Kemp (1663 *et seq.*) ; Sir Joseph Paine (1664) ; Hugh Morrell (1664) ; Sir Henry Bedingfeld (1664) ; Sir John Holland (1674) ; Ann Lady Townshend (1675) ; Lord Arlington (1677 etc.) ; Christopher Bedingfeld (1679) ; Sir Peter Glean of Norwich (1680, etc.) ; Sir John Holland (1681 *et seq.*) ; W. Harbord (1681) ; Sir Christopher Calthorpe (1681) ; Thomas Townshend (1681–2) ; Sir William Jones (1682) ; Sir R. Potts (1682); James Fountain (1682) ; The Earl of Rochester (1685) ; Thomas Warde (1686) ; The Bishop of Hereford (1686) ; The Duke of Beaufort (1686).

1660. Nov. 5th. Paper headed " an inventory of what cloathes are in my keepeinge " and " an inventory of what boots and shoos are in my keepeinge " same date. Endorsed by Lord Townshend.

1661. Feb. 3rd. Robert Reade to Charles Spellman. " Att the right honourable my Lord Townshend's in the old Palace Yard Westminster." The writer says that he has as yet received no command from Mr Spellman or from Lord Townshend, " nor do I wonder at it, because the flying post lay drunke last Friday at Fakenham (being the day that he should have binn at Thetford to take those letters then there which he should bring hether on Saterday) and had not changed his quarter yesterday as I am informed by one of Scott's men who saw him pittyfully drunke. The cuntry complaines of him."

1661. Mar. 22nd. London. Nathaniel Norcrosse to " his loveing friend Mr Keimar these at Wells." A letter from one Puritan to another on religious matters, containing no information. The postscript, however, is " as for newes we are expecting to have the bill of Conformity to come forth. It will silence all ministers that will not conforme, and suppresse all meeteings that yet wee enjoy through mercy."

1661 to 1667. A Schedule comprising the names times and causes of commitments of all the prisoners in the gaol belonging to the County of Norfolk, excepting those that are in for debt.

1662. March 16th. Heigham. The Bishop of Norwich to Lord Townshend. Apologizes for his long absence from the House of Lords owing to his wife's severe illness, and thanks Lord Townshend for having excused him there. The Bishop of Worcester has his proxy. (Seal.)

1662. June 12th. Norwich. Sir John Pettus to Lord Townshend enclosing " A narrative concerning the proceedings upon an order of the House of Lords bearing date the 26th Feb. 1661 wherein the determination of admeasuring seaven miles from the Crane Key in Yarmouth towards Laystoffe is referred to the two severall and respective sheriffes of Suffolk and Norfolk," relating what took place on the measurement being made, and speaking of the opposition of the sheriffs to its being done.

1663. May 13th. Lynn. Laurence Withers to Horatio Lord Townshend asking him for the place of one Mr Bromley, against whom certain charges have been made, should it be vacated by him.

1663. Aug. 5th. Whitehall. Original note signed : Clarendon, Albemarle, Lindsey, Manchester, Anglesey, Ashley, Carbery, Middleton, W. Compton, Will. Morice, Henry B——, and Richard Browne to Lord Townshend, Lord Lieutenant of Norfolk, recommending to his Lordship the speedy establishment of the militia of the County as the best means for checking and preventing the assemblies and conventicles of the disaffected in that part of the country, and stating what extra pay can be given to officers and men under the provisions of a recent Act intituled " An additional Act for the better ordering the forces in the severall counties of this kingdome."

1663. Sep. 2nd. Whitehall. Copy (signed Richard Browne) of a letter unsigned and unaddressed, requiring that the militia of the County (Norfolk) shall be put into such a position as shall enable them to suppress the assemblies, meetings, and conventicles of the disaffected in the County and specifying the sums to be paid to them for such extra duty, out of the money received of the month's tax of 70,000l. levied by a late Act intituled " An Act for ordering the forces of the several Counties of this kingdome."

1664. Mar. 22nd. Copy " *Significavit*" under Sign Manual addressed to the Lord Treasurer and Chancellor of the Exchequer to grant to Horatio Lord Townshend the two-thirds belonging to the Crown in Marshlands in Walton, Walsoken, Walpole, Tyd St Mary's, Wisbich, Leverington, Newton, and Tyd St Giles, in the Counties of Cambridge, Lincoln, and Norfolk.

1664. Ap. 29th. Lynn. Laurence Withers to Sir Ralph Hare Baronet requesting the office of King's Searcher should it be vacated by the present occupant Mr Bromley against whom several charges are about to be brought. (Seal.)

1664. May. 2nd. A letter signed " M. M." unaddressed, but as it commences " My Lord " and deals with questions affecting the government of Norwich, is probably to Lord Townshend, on some matter of a charter sought by the Mayor of Norwich, to which the writer is strongly opposed.

1664. Oct. 29th. Sir William Doyly to Lord Townshend indignantly denying some charges brought by Lord Townshend against him relative to the government of the town of Yarmouth.

1664. Oct. 31st. Norwich. John Gladman to Lord Townshend. The writer has incurred Lord Townshend's displeasure owing to his having written something to the Duke of Albemarle without first shewing it to his Lordship, and writes to explain his conduct in the affair.

MARQUESS TOWNSHEND MSS.

1664. Nov. 2nd. Yarmouth. Sir Thomas Medowes to Lord Townshend, Lord Lieutenant and Vice-Admiral of Norfolk, as to the impressing of men for service in the Navy.

1664. Nov. 23rd. Ovington. Mr T. Felton to Lord Townshend. Would have written to his Lordship before but "was stopped by a very great snow and the waters which were so upp as there was no travelling, and when I returned thence to Apleton the waters were so up as I was stayed there 7 or 8 days togeather before I could pass thence." The letter relates to Lord Townshend's mineral property.

1664. Dec. 12th. Raynham. Charles Spelman to Lord Townshend chiefly on the affairs of his Lordship's Norfolk property "Here is nothing new here that wee wonder att but 2 millions and an halfe, and the new blasing starr that poynts his beard to the new world where most matter for money is to be had. These mistye nights has much perplexed Mr Clarke whoe, hearing on Monday last that there was such a thing as a comett, has broake his sleepe all this weeke, nor could he take sight of any till this morne, which has a little appeased him after he had roused his wholl family to pertake of the prodigie."

1665. Ap. 26th. Lynn Regis. Thomas Greene Mayor of Lynn to Lord Townshend, complaining of the injury done to the traders of the town by "sea pirates, and forreigne men of warr" and asking for a convoy for their vessels to and from Newcastle and other northern ports.

1666. May 5th. "Royal Charles in the Buoy of the Nore" The Duke of Albemarle to whom does not appear (probably to Lord Townshend) asking assistance to the ketch of Sir Edward Spragge commanding the Triumph to impress some seamen for the King's service. (Seal.)

1666. Sep. 7th. Whitehall. Lord Arlington to Lord Townshend on business relating to the County of Norfolk, acknowledging three letters from Lord Townshend the first two being on County business "the third takeing notece of the unhappy fire fallen here and desireing to know his Majesty's pleasure to you in this great exegency. To which his Majesty bids me answer, that seeing it hath pleased God miraculously to extinguish this rageing fire, and that it hath not been accompanyed with any of those troublesome consequences from the desaffected party which wee might reasonably have apprehended, there will be no need for the present of your Lordshipp's assembleing any part of the meletia or further troubleing the country there, unlesse your Lordshipp sees cause for it. If any appears here, your Lordshipp shall be timely advertised thereof. Which is all I have leasure now to say to you."

1667. June 16th. "Cockpitt" The Duke of Albemarle to Lord Townshend asking him to send two or three companies of the regiment, which he had raised, into Yarmouth, for the safety of that town.

1667. July 11th. Whitehall. Lord Arlington to Lord Townshend "I did not cohtend with your Lordshipp that Cromen was an honest man, but an Irish man, and if your lordshipp find him otherwise in either of these qualities I am farre from desiring his release.

1669. Sep. 14th. Sir Francis Bacon to "Mr Townshend" enclosing a copy of Mr Justice Rainsford's opinion on the case of a man named Blancher who was convicted at the Norwich Assizes of killing two men named Cooke and Hendry.

1670. Mar. 30th. London. Lord Townshend to the Mayor of Norwich to be communicated to the Aldermen of the City. Acknowledges receipt of their letter of the 9th March. He has never failed to assist them with the King. Desires to know wherein he has failed towards them. Refers to those employed in the present concern with the Corporation of Great Yarmouth to say whether he has been wanting in his endeavour to serve them in that matter.

1671. June 19th. Copy abstract of a docquet appointing Sir Robert Long Baronet Treasurer and Receiver General of the Revenues late in jointure to the late Queen Dowager in the place of Sir Henry Wood. Signed : " Ashley " and " J. Duncombe."

1673. Feb. 19th. Warrant signed " Charles R. " and countersigned " Arlington " for the disbanding of Lord Northampton's regiment.

1674. May 22nd. Quidenham. Sir John Holland to Lord Townshend. Concurs with his Lordship's opinion of Sir Robert Kemp. Thanks him for acquainting him with his Lordship's intention of setting him up to supply the vacancy in Parliament by the death of Lord Rychardson. Will support him.

N. D. (1674). Letter unaddressed and signed " T."—from Lord Townshend—beginning " my Lord " asking for assistance to further Sir Robert Kemp's election as M.P. for the County of Norfolk.

1674. July 2nd. Lord Yarmouth to Lord Townshend promising his assistance to Sir Robert Kemp in the forthcoming election for Norfolk.

1676. July 23rd. Quidenham. Sir John Holland to Lord Townshend. Congratulates him on the verdict and damages given him by the jury at Norwich. He intends to go to Norwich to-morrow and to visit the Judge, whom he has told that he did not at all doubt but he should yet live to be better understood by his Majesty's great ministers and so to be restored to his Majesty's good opinion and favour which was all the ambition he had.

1676. Aug. 6th. Quidenham. Letter from Sir John Holland to Lord Townshend. Has been to Norwich where he met the Lord Marshall and visited the Judge. The Lord Marshall blamed him for deserting the King's service in the militia and told him that the Lord Chancellor had said that he had refused to serve the King in his Lieutenancy under Lord Yarmouth though he had done it under Lord Townshend, and that such refusal was a kind of warring against the King. That he replied that that was one of the Lord Chancellor's rhetorical expressions to satisfy the Lord Treasurer and that he was very well content with his present condition.

" Since the verdict passed all things are and will be improved to your prejudice. To meet and prevent the ill consequences of this, your Lordship should frequently impress by your friends at Court the constancy of your loyal and faithful affections towards his Majesty in his person and Government, and that no disobligations shall or can make you depart from your duty."

1676. Oct. 24th. Deposition of the defendant in an action of trespass Horace Lord Townshend v. Dr. Owen Hughes.

1676. Nov. 12th. Copy letter from Lord Townshend to Sir John Duncombe. Enclosing opinion of Sir Robert Sawyer upon Lord Townshend's

MARQUESS
TOWNSHEND
MSS.

Patent of the sea coal rents dated 21st March 19 Charles II. 1667, and upon further Letters Patent dated 26th May 1676 granted to Sir John Duncombe of the rent of £1000 reserved by the above Letters Patent.

1677. Mar 12th. Norwich. Letter signed by the Mayor of Norwich and many others, to Lord Townshend, praying his Lordship's influence in Parliament " in preventinge the Corporation of Yarmoth from obteyninge any aditional time granted in Parliament to levie monie upon the Counties of Norffolk Suffolk and this citie towards the repaire of their haven and peeres, they haveinge alreadie received nere £12000 to that purpose." (Corporation Seal.)

N.D. [but about 1677]. Sir John Holland to Lord Townshend as to a motion (the nature of which does not transpire) the writer intends to make in the House of Commons and asking Lord Townshend's support. Inclosed is a copy of some correspondence Sir John has had with the Lord Chamberlain, Lord Arlington, on the same subject :

1677. Jan. 29th. Sir John Holland to Lord Arlington, stating that he intends to make a complaint in the House of Commons against a person who has misrepresented him to the King, and asking Lord Arlington's permission to make use of his name as his Lordship was his informant of the name of the person who so misrepresented him.

1677. Jan. 29th. Lord Arlington to Sir John Holland in answer to the above, begging Sir John not to mention his name in the complaint he intends making.

1678. March 28th. Deed signed and sealed by James Calthorpe acknowledging the receipt of £550 from Horatio Lord Townshend paid to him after the death of Lady Townshend wife of the said Lord Townshend in accordance with a bond signed and sealed by his Lordship.

1679. April 5th. Norwich. Letter signed with a monogram—apparently S. T.—to Lord Townshend on election and other local matters. Endorsed by Lord Townshend, " This letter concerns the Bishop and Mr Turguinton's being turned out of his surrogate's place." Mentions Sir H. B[edingfeld], Lord Shaftesbury, Sir Francis Winnington, and Sir T. Hare.

1680. June 25th. Sir John Hobart to Lord Townshend. Endorsed by Lord Townshend, " Sir John Hobart's answer to mien of the 24 of June 1680. This letter must be keept." The letter is on election matters and relates to Lord Townshend's having said he would withdraw his interest from Sir John's side in consequence of some difficulty which had arisen in reference to the election expenses.

1681. May 2nd. Melford. Sir Robert Kemp to Lord Townshend on election matters. Mentions Sir P. G[leane], Sir John Cordil, Mr Wyndham. (Seal.)

1631. May 16th. Sir Peter Gleane to Lord Townshend in answer to one of his Lordship's of 11th May, announcing his intention not to stand at the next election.

1681. June 28th. John Stewart to Mr Rudding (a tenant of Lord Townshend's) written at Lord Townshend's desire relating to the destruction by fire of Mr Rudding's dairy, stating that, if Mr Rudding rebuilds the dairy and all other destroyed buildings, Lord Townshend, if he approves of the work, "is like to bee kinde" to him.

1682. March 11th. Lord Townshend to Thomas Townshend, endorsed:—"My answer to Sir Peter Gleane's letter to my cossen Thomas Townshend dated the 11th of March '81-2" on election matters. Sir Peter appears to claim money from Lord Townshend on behalf of his election expences on the score of service done to his Lordship; Lord Townshend repudiates the services and refuses to pay the money, but is willing to refer the matter to arbitrators. The writer is evidently very angry with Sir Peter Glean. " For his wound if hee have received any I cannot but bee sorry for it, though ignorant of any, but what hee hath now given himselfe in this affaire. As to his pleasure or easie travile, I thinko noe furder worth my taking notice of then only to tell him, that I have knowne fortie pounds buy a paire of naigs (if one will not doe) that hath draged as weighty a man, from head to taile, as Sir Peter Gleane, and to more freinds then hee will leave himselfe, unless hee useth them better than hee hath done mee. As for his service to mee my wife and children, though he bee not ashamed to present it, yett I am, and they shall bee soe for my sake to receive it upon the tearms it is tendered."

1682–4. Rough notes in Lord Townshend's writing of sums of money received and expended by him, the receipts amounting to £3147-8-11 in 1684.

1683. Sep. 10th. Sir John Holland to Lord Townshend. Relative to the differences and unhappy divisions which have arisen among the chief gentlemen in the country through contested elections and submitting to his Lordship certain proposals relative thereto, which he intended to make to some in his neighbourhood.

Paper endorsed
" Sir John Holland's speeches made in '75 "
The paper contains (*a*) a long speech apparently upon the King's Speech on the question of Supply. (*b*) A speech upon reading the Order for the House to take into consideration what is to be done in the matters of dispatch with the Lords. (*c*) A speech upon the 2nd reading of the Bill for the repealing of the Act passed in the beginning of the Long Parliament for the continuation of that Parliament and the calling of future Parliaments.

1684–5. Mar. 17th. Copy Letter from Lord Townshend to the Earl of Rochester. Relative to the attendance of himself and his wife at the Coronation of the King and Queen.

N.D. " Some particular matters of fact relating to the administration of affaires in Scotland under the Duke of Lauderdale, humbly offered to your Majestie's consideration in obedience to your Royal commands.
1st The Duke of Lauderdale did grosly misrepresent to your Majestic the condicon of the western counties as if they had beene in a state of rebelion though there never had been any opposicon made to your Majestie's authority, nor any resistance offered to your fforces nor to the execucon of the lawes, but hee purposeing to abuse your Majestic that soe hee might carry on his sinister designes by your authority advised your Majestic to raise an army against your peaceable subjects, at least did frame a letter to be sent to your Majestic to bee signed by your Royall hand to that effect, which being sent downe to your Councell orders were there-

MARQUESS
TOWNSHEND
MSS.

upon given out for the raiseing an army of 8 or 9000 men the greatest parte whereof were Hylanders, and notwithstanding that to avert this threatning the nobility and gentry of that country did send to Edenburgh and for the security of the peace did offer to engage, that whosoever should bee sent to put the lawes in execucon should meet with noe affront and that they would become hostages for their safety : yett this army was marched into a peaceable country and did take free quarters according to their comissions and in most places leavyed great sumes of money under notion of dry quarters and did plunder and robb your subjects of which noe redresse could bee obtained though complaynts were frequently made.

2. All which were expressly contrary to the lawes of the kingdome. In these quarterings it was apparent, that regard was only had to that Duke's private animosityes, for the greatest part of these places that were mostly quartered on, and destroyed had not been guilty of any the feild conventicles complayned of, and many of the places that were most guilty were spared upon private consideracons.

3. The subjects at that tyme were required to subscribe an exorbitant and illegall bond which was imposible to bee performed by them (viz.) that they their wives and children and servants, their tenants ard their wives children and servants should live orderly according to law, not goe to conventicles or entertaine vagrant preachers and severall other particulars. By which bond those which syned it were made lyable for every man's fault that lived upon the grounds.

4. Your subjects were charged with laborrowes, denounced rebells, and captions were issued out for seizeing their persons upon there refuseing to signe the aforesaid bond, and the nobility and gentry there who have been ever faithfull to your Majesty and had appeared in armes for suppressing the last rebellion were disarmed upon oath, a proclamacon was also issued forbidding them upon great penaltyes to keepe any horses above 4l. 3s. 4d. price :

5. The nobility and gentry of the Shire of Ayre were also indicted at the instance of your Majestie's Advocate of very high crimes and mismeanors whereof some did import treason. These indictments were delivered them in the evening to bee answered by them next morning upon oath, and when they did demand two or three dayes' tyme to consider of their indictments and make the bencfitt of lawyers to advise within matters of soe high concernment and also excepted to their being put to sweare against themselves in matters that were capitall, which was contrary to all law and justice, those their desires were rejected though the like had never been done to the greatest malefactor in the Kingdome, and it was told them, they must either sweare instantly or they would repute them guilty and proceed accordingly :

6. The noblemen and gentlemen knowing themselves inocent of all that had been surmised against them did purge themselves by oath of all the particulars that were objected to them and were thereupon acquitted, and tho' the Comitte of the Councell used the severest maner of enquiry to discover any seditious or treasonable designes which were pretended as the grounds of leading in that army into those countryes yett nothing could ever bee proved, soe false was that sugestion concerning a rebellion then designed that was offered to your Majestic and prevayled with you for sending the afore mentioned letter.

7. The oppressions and quarterings still continuing, the noblemen and gentlemen of those countyes went to Edenburgh to represent to your Councills the heavy pressure that they and their people lay under, and were ready to offer to them all that in law or reason could bee required of them for securing the peace, the Councill did imediately upon their appearing sett forth a proclamation requiring them to depart the town

within three dayes upon all highest paines, and when the Duke of Hamilton did petition for leave to stay two or three dayes longer for some very urgent affaires, that was refused him.

8. When some persons of quality had declared to the Duke of Lauderdale, that they would goe and represent their conditions to your Majestie, if they could not have justice from your ministers, for preventing that a proclamacon was sett forth forbidding all the subjects to depart the kingdome without lycence, that soe your majestie might not bee acquainted with the said condicon of your subjects a thing without all president or law for putting of your subjects from makeing their application to your majestie noo less contrary to your majestie's true interest (who must alwayes bee the refuge of your people) then to the naturall right of the subject :

> The former particulars relate to the invasion of the rights of great numbers of your subjects all at once; what followe, have indeed only fallene on some single persons yett are such that your whole people apprehend that they may bee upon the slightest occasions brought under the like mischiefes.

The Councill hath upon many occasions proceeded to a new kinde of punishment of declareing men incapable of all publique trust, concerning which your majestie may remember what complaints the said Duke made when dureing the Earle of Midleton's administracon hee himselfe was put under and incapacitated by an Act of Parliament ; The words of his paper against the Earle of Middleton are uncapacitating (*sic*) was to whipp with scorpions, a punishment to robb men of their honour and to lay a lasting stayne upon them and their posterity, and if this was complayned of when done by the high court of Parliament your Majestie may easily conclude it cannot bee done in any lower court. But that notwithstanding it is become of late yeares an ordinary sentence in Councill when the least complaints are brought against any with whom the Duke of Lauderdale and his brother are offended :)

Instances of these are :

The declaring twelve honest worthy cittizens of Edenburgh incapable of publique trust against whome noe complaint was ever made to this day as your Majestie will percive more fully by a paper concerning that affaire. The true cause of it was, that those men being in the magistracy, the Duke and his brother could not gett a vast bribe from them out of the towne's money which was afterwards obtayned when they were removed.

The Provosts of Glasgow, Aberdeen and Jadburgh were put under the same sentence for signing a letter to your Majestie in that Convencon of the buroughs with the rest of that body, which letter was advised by him whoe is now your Majestie's Advocate, as that which had nothing in it which could bring them under any guilt, and yett these three were singled out of the whole number and incapacitated, besides an high fine and a long imprisonment as your Majestie will moore fully percive by another paper.

Sir Patrick Home of Polworth being sent by the sbeire of Berwick to complaine of some illegall proceedings, and to obtain a legall remedy to them which hee did only in the comon forme of law was alsoe declared uncapable of publique trust besides many months of imprisonment.

The Provost of Linlithgoe being complained of for not furnishing some of your forces with baggage horses was called before the Councill, and because hee said that they were not bound in law to furnish horses in such maner, hee was immediately declared incapable of publique trust and was both fined and imprisoned. There were also fifty of the towne of St Johnston's incapacitated upon a very slight pretence, soe that it is now impossible for them to finde a sufficient number of citizens for the ma-

MARQUESS
TOWNSHEND
MSS.

gistracy of that towne. Your subjects are sometymes upon slight and sometymes upon noe grounds imprisoned, and often kept prisoners many months and yeres nothing being objected to them, and are required to enter themselves prisoners which is contrary to law. It was in the former articles expressed that many of the persons declared incapable of publique trust did alsoe suffer imprisonment; and besides those instances Levetennant Generall Drumond (whose eminent loyalty and great services are well knowne to your Majestie) was required to enter himselfe prisoner in the Castle of Dumbarton where hee was keept one yeare and a halfe and was made a close prisoner for nine mcnths of that tyme and yett nothing was ever objected to him to this day to justifie that usage.

The Lord Cardross, whoe was for his Lady's keeping two conventicles in her owne house (at which hee was not present) fyned £11,000, and hath been now keept four yeares prisoner in the Castle of Edenburgh where he still remaines, although he hath often peticoned for his liberty: And Sir Patrick Holme hath been now a second tyme almost one yeare imprisoned and nothing is yett laid to his charge.

Besides these illegall imprisonments the officers of your Majestie's forces carry frequently warrants with them for the apprehending persons that are under noe loyall censure, nor have been soe much as cyted to appeare, which hath putt many of your subjects under great feares especially upon what was done in Councill three yeares agoe (viz.)

Captaine Carstaires (a man now well enough knowne to your Majestie) did entrap one Kirkton, an outed minister, into his chamber at Edenburgh and did violently abuse him, and designed to have extorted some money from him. The noise of this coming to the ears of one Bayly, brother in law to the said Kirkton, hee came to the house, and heareing him cry "murther, murther," forced open the chamber doore, where hee found his brother in law, and the Captaine grapling. The Captaine pretended hee had a warrant against Kirkton, and Bayly desired him to show it, and promised that all obedience should bee given to it, and that hee himselfe would assist him in the executing of it, but the Captaine refusing to doe it, Kirkton was rescued. This was only delivering of a man from the hands of a robber, which nature obligeth all men to doe, especially when joyned with soe neare a relation. The Captaine complayned of this to the Councill and the Lord Hatton with others were appointed to examine the witnesses; and when it was brought before the Councill the Duke of Hamilton, Earles of Morton, Dumfrize, and Kingcarding the Lord Cocheren and Sir Archibald Primrose then Lord Register, desired that the report of the examinacon might bee read, but that not serveing their ends was denyed, and thereupon those Lords declaired their opinion, that since Carstaires did not shewe any warrant nor was cloathed with any publique character, it was noe opposeing of your Majestie's authority in Bayly soe to rescue the said Kirkton, yett Bayly was for this fined in 6000 markes and kept long a prisoner.

These Lords were upon that soe repreeented to your Majestie that by the Duke of Lauderdale's procurement they were turned out of the Councill and all comand of the militia, and it can bee made appeare that the Captaine had at that tyme noe warrant at all against that Kirkton, but procured it after the violence comitted and it was antedated on designe to serve a turne at that time This maner of proceeding hath ever since put your subjects under sad apprehensions.

There is one particular further offered to your majestie's consideracon concerning their way of useing prisoners. There were fourteen men taken at a feild conventicle, whoe without being legally convict of that

U 24953.

C

or any other cryme were secretly and in the night taken out of prison upon a warrant signed by the Earl of Linlithgoe and the Lord Hatton and Collington and were delivered to Captaine Maitland, whoe had been paige to the Duke of Lauderdale but was then a French officer, and was makeing his leavyes in Scotland and were carryed over to the service of the French King in the yeare 1676.   The Councell hath upon many occasions proceeded to most unreasonable and arbitrary fynes, either for slight offences or for offences where the fine is regulated by law which they have never considered when the persons were not acceptable to them, soe the Lord Cardross was fined in £11,000—for his ladye's keeping two conventicles in his house and christning a child by an outed minister without his knowledge.   The Provost formerly menconed, and Bayly with many more were also fined without any regard to law.   The Councill hath at severall tymes proceeded to the takeing of gentlemen's dwelling houses and putting garisons in them which in tyme of peace is contrary to law.   In the yeare 1675 it was designed against twelve of your majestie's subjects and put in execucon in the houses of the Earle of Callender, the Lord Cardrosse, the Lady Lumsdon &c. and was againe atempted in the yeare 1678.   The houses belonging to the Leards of Cosnok, Blagand, and Rowalland were possessed by souldiers and declaired garrisons nor did it rest there, but orders were sent from the Councill requiring the countrye about those houses to furnish them for the souldiers use and to supply them with necessaries much contrary to law. ، It was against this that Sir Patrick Home came to desire a remedy, and comon justice being denyed him hee used a legall protestation in the ordinary forme of law, whoe was thereupon kept many months a prisoner and declared incapable of all publique trust.

There is another particular which because it is soe odious is unwillingly touched yett it is necessary to informe your majestie about it for there by it will appeare that the said Duke of Lauderdale and his brother have in a most solemn maner broken the publique faith which was given in your Majestie's name.   One Mitchell being put in prison upon great suspition of his haveing atempted to murther the late Archbishopp of St Andrewes and there being noe other evidence against him, warrant was given by the Duke of Lauderdale (then your Majestie's Commissioner and your Councill to promise him his life if he would confess, whereupon he did confess and yett some yeares after, that person (who indeed deserved many deaths if there had been any evidence against him) was upon that confession convicted of the cryme, and the Duke of Lauderdale and his brother being put to it by him did sweare that they neither gave nor knew of any assurance of life given him, and when it was objected that the promise was upon record in the Council bookes, the Duke of Lauderdale did in open court (where hee was present only as a wittness and soe ought to have been silent) threaten them if they should proceed to the examinacon of that act of Councill which (as hee then said) might inferre perjury on them that had sworne and soe did cutt off the proofe of that defence which had been admitted by the court as good in law and sufficient to save the prisoner if proved. Thus was that man hanged upon that confession only though the promise that drew it from him doth appeare upon record, and can bee proved by good and cleare evidence, and from this your Majestie may judge what credditt may bee given to such men.

Wee doe not at present enlarge upon other particulars though of great importance, such as monopolies, selling of places and honours, turning men of knowne integrity out of their imployments to which they had a good and just right during their lives, the profitts of one of the most considerable of those being sequestred for some tyme and applyed for

MARQUESS
TOWNSHEND
MSS

the Dutchess of Lauderdale's use the treating about and receiving of great bribes by the Duke and Duchess of Lauderdale and the Lord Hatton and particularly from the townes of Edinburgh, Aberdeen, Linlithgoe, and many others, for procuring from your Majestie's Warrants for illegall imposicons within those townes to the manifest and publique perverting of justice besides, the most signall abuses of the mint and copper coyne that are most grevious to all your subjects but the number of those is soe great and they will require soe many witnesses to bee brought hither for proving the same that wee feare it would too much trouble your Majestie now to examine them all but your Majestie shall have a full account of them afterwards.

One thing is humbly offered to your Majestie as the roote of these and many other oppressions which is that the method of governing that nation for severall yeares hath been that the Lord Hatton and his adherants, frame any letter that they desire from your Majestie to your Councill and sends it to the Duke of Lauderdale, who returns it signed, and this is brought to the Councill upon which if a debate at any tyme arises concerning the matter of the letter as being against or without law and when it is proposed that a representacon of it should bee made to your Majestie then the Lord Hatton in his insolent way calls to have it putt to the question, as if it were a cryme to have any warrant either debated or represented to your Majestie which is procured by the Duke of Lauderdale or himself, and this is ecchoed by his party, and by this meanes any further debate is stopt.

There are some other particulars relating to these heads that are to bee offered to your Majestie in other papers which are not added now least your Majestie should now bee troubled with too long a paper.

1685. Oct. 1st. Letter from Lord Townshend unaddressed. It is written to a gentleman who has disagreed with Lord Townshend about magisterial business in Norfolk.

1687–8. March 20th. Discharge, signed "·James R.," by King James II. to Sir Peter Apsly and Sir Benjamin Bathurst the treasurers and Receivers General of his Majesty's revenue before his accession, of a debt of 600l. on their account which had since been paid.

1689. Nov. 5th. Letter (in French) unsigned ; headed " Lettre escritte à Monseigneur L'Evesque de Salisbury par le Secretaire Chouet. The writer mentions "notre république," and the letter deals with its diplomatic relations with France. Mentions that Monsieur des Marais who had been destined by the French King to go there as ambassador, was much objected to by the inhabitants of the writer's "town" (name not given).

1696. April 18th. Sir James Calthorp to Viscount Townshend. "The late horrid plot of assassinating the King, and encouraging an invasion from France has filled the goales with prisoners ; three have been executed for the assassination, all papists ; two gentlemen Sir John Freind and Sir William Parkins for being ready to joyn with K[ing] J[ames] upon his landing with a French force. Three more condemned his week upon the same account, the witness a partye to the plott. This gives occasion to greater severity in the severall countryes, and all non-jurors are called upon to take the oathes; in our County Sir N. L. and Sir C. amongst many others. Though most papist, Sir N. has given bale to appear at the next assises, and to be upon his good behaviour till then, when the oathes are to be rendred to him again. Sir C. chose rather to endure the penalty of six moneths imprisonment, after which he is discharged by law according to the late Act, but this Parliament have made a new one that all non-jurors shall be reputed as Papists convict which is forfeiture of two-thirds of their estates."

N. D. [after 1660]. Copy Petition to the House of Lords in an appeal now before them in which Edward Birmingham and others, some of " the officers and soldiers who reduced Ireland in 1641 " are appellants, and Henry Earl of Shelburn, George Lord Carbery and others, trustees for the appellants, are respondents, praying that their Lordships will order the said appeal to be set down for hearing.

[After 1661.] Draft letter from Horatio first Lord Townshend to whom is not stated, but to an aunt of the writer's, respecting the proposal of a marriage of his " niece Cartwright " to one Mʳ Papillon, to which Lord Townshend is strongly opposed.

N. D. Apethorpe. March 23ʳᵈ. Lord Westmoreland to his son-in-law Lord Townshend. Relating to the placing of the writer's proxy in the House of Lords as he is too unwell to attend. " Your mother entertained a clowd of sorrow and melancholly for the death of one of your sister Cartwright's children, else she is much after the old manner never perfectly well. So like Bausis and Philemon we two owld acquaintances sit cherishing one the other in the chimney corner hawking and coughing like mad, but least you deem me so indeed I forbear all farther trouble saving to kiss my pretty lady's little fine hand." In a postscript " Pray remember me kindly to Hare and mind him of Ogleby's Homer ; what would I give that the Lady had leverets in her belly, and yours another such like blessing."

N. D. Aug. 27ᵗʰ. Anthony Bishop of Norwich to Lord Townshend. " In pursuance of your Lordship's reference to me and generous offer to accept what I should approve in Dʳ Hugh's case, I have under my hand recomended to your Lordship a submission made to me by the Dr. which he will present to your Lordship as soon as his health permits. I cannot say it merits your acceptance, I am sure it canot, but finding your Lordship so charitably inclined. I canot but hope that your Lordship will admit both it and him to receive your pardon for which noble favour and admitting me to be the instrument under your Lordship of so pious and charitable a work, I shall give your Lorddship my hearty thanks as now I do for your late noble present."

N. D. Francis Barber to Lord Townshend. The writer is a clergyman holding two livings, and has been threatened by Lord Townshend that he shall be procceded against under a recent act for some Ecclesiastical offence, praying his lordship to allow him to retain his benefices until further crder be taken and pointing out words in the act which will warrant his Lordship in doing so.

N. D. A MS, apparently a case for opinion of counsel, relating to the estate of Sir Edward Lewkener grandfather of Lady Townshend the wife of Sir Horace Townshend, containing a great deal of genealogical information. The case states that said Sir Edward Lewkener died leaving a son Edward and three daughters ; by his will he devised certain property to his wife for life, remainder to his heir, and in case his wife should die leaving the heir a minor he conveyed the property to trustees during such minority on trust to raise portions for the daughters. Edward Lewkener the son married Elizabeth daughter of Sir William Russell of Chippenham, and died three weeks before he was 21, leaving one child, the present Lady Townshend, an infant only a few months old ; Lady Lewkener mother of the said Edward received all the profits of the estate of her son and had his wife's marriage portion—£5000; two of the daughters married, and had their portions assigned to them under the will of their father, one to Sir Nicholas Le Strange, the other to Mr Calthorpe and was since a widow; the youngest was 40 years old and unmarried, and also had a portion on her reaching the age of 21; then Lady Lewkener died leaving her daughters her executors.

Sir Horace Townshend married Mary the only daughter and heir of the said Edward Lewkener after Lady Lewkener's death, and settled a jointure upon her. Afterwards Sir Nicholas Le Strange, Mr Calthorpe and Miss Lewkener filed a bill in Chancery against Sir Horace Townshend and his wife "to bee releeved for the meane profitts of all the lands demised by Sir Edward Lewkener to the trustees during the minority of his heir.'' The paper goes on to state the questions that arise on this suit

N.D. Draft letter in the writing of Horace Lord Townshend, to whom does not appear; the letter commences "My Lord." He hears that the Lord Lieutenants and deputies take it ill, that he has taken into his hand the book of the proceedings during the time he was Lord Lieutenant of Norfolk, explaining his reason for doing so, and ascribing the King's displeasure with him to the slanders of his enemies.

N.D. Lord Townshend to whom is not stated. Draft letter beginning "My Lord" and written on a piece of paper addressed to Lord Townshend and sealed with a shield bearing three demi-lions, two and one, surrounded by the garter, and surmounted with an earl's coronet. The letter is an answer to an intimation that the King is willing to restore Lord Townshend to favour, and is written in a dignified strain, the writer hinting at the King's ingratitude for his past services in the rebellion, and denying that he has anything to be forgiven except speaking his mind when questioned by his Majesty, fearlessly and boldly.

IV.—UNDATED AND MISCELLANEOUS PAPERS BEFORE 1700.

1584. 27 Elizabeth. Nov. 10th. Lease from William Heygate to Roger Townshend of East Rayneham of the Mansion house called Ludgreves and premises thereunto belonging containing 100 acres, from Michaelmas then last past for three years at the yearly rent of 52l. per annum.

1613. Letters and particulars relating to lands and sheep pastures in East Rudham belonging to the Lady Berkeley and to the manor of West Rudham St Faythe.

1614. May 10th. Portion of the will of Sir Nathaniel Bacon devising lands in Stifkey, Long Merston and other towns adjoining. Mentions his daughter Lady Anne Townshend, his grandchild Roger Townshend, his second daughter Lady Elizabeth Knyvett, his third daughter Lady Winifryd Gawdie, and his brother Edmund Bacon.

1617. A view of the estate of Sir Roger Towneshend's manors lands and possessions in the counties of Norfolk Essex and Middlesex and in London.

1617. April 17th. " A note of the payments to the Kinge and of all the fees and charges payed upon passage of the Patent of Baronetshipp for Sir Roger Towneshend Baronett."

MARQUESS
TOWNSHEND
MSS.

Inprimis to Mr Morgan my Lord Treasorer's Secretarye for his paynes in renewing of the Commission three peeces - - - - - - - £3 6ˢ 0ᵈ

Item to the then Attorney's man Yonge for drawinge and ingrossing of the Commission and first patent—three peeces - - - - - - - £3 6ˢ 0ᵈ

Item geven to Mr Finche for drawinge of the seconde Patent, two peeces - - - - - 44ˢ

Item, to his clerke for coppying thereof - - - 11ˢ

Item to Mr Finche more for goinge to Mr Attorney Yelverton aboute some points altered by him in the saide draught - - - - - 22ˢ

Item to Mr Calvert the Clerke of the Councell for the Lords' Warrant to Mr Attorney, and to his clerke for writinge thereof - - - - - 44ˢ

Item to Mr Attorney for his fees for perusinge and certifyinge of the Patent - - - - £5 10ˢ

Item geven to Mr Attorney's clerke for his fees for the same - - - - - - 55ˢ

Item to his man that engrossed the Patent - - 11ˢ

Item to Mr Attorney's doorekeeper - - 11ˢ

Item to the Clerke of the Councell for gettinge of the Comissioners' hands to the Patent - - - 22ˢ

Item payde in to the Receipte xi Aprilis 1617 for the first payment to the King ut patet by talley - - £365

Item payde then to Mr Rowdon for fees in that office uppon payment of the said money - - - 20ˢ

Item payde for the fees of the talley - - 10ˢ

Item payde for the makinge and enrolment of two bonds for the other two payments to the Kinge at viˢ viijᵈ apeece 13ˢ 4ᵈ

Item payde to Mr Watson for his certificate of the first payment of the money and of the tallinge of the bonds 40ˢ

Item payde to Mr Benbowe for the fees of the Clerks of the Signet and Privye Seale, the Clerke of the Crowne, and the Heralds in toto - - - £8

Item payde to him more of the vellum flourishing and strings for the Patent - - - - 12ˢ

Item payde to him more for the fayre writinge of the patent & for the clerk's paynes - - - 40ˢ

Item payde to him more for the docquett - - 5ˢ

Item payde to him more for the enrolment and dividend - 40ˢ

Item payde to him more for the fees at the Seale - 41ˢ 8ᵈ

Item payde to him more for the Sealer and Chafewax - 6ˢ 8ᵈ

Sum total £407 10ˢ 8ᵈ.

Whereof in money payde to the Kinge for the first payment of the fyne - - - - £365

And in fees payde ut patet supra - - - £42 10ˢ 8ᵈ

1624. May 25th. Agreement made by the inhabitants of West Raynham for the Cow pasture and New Close and Hearth Moore.

1661. April 20th. Paper endorsed "Warrants for creations."

"It is his Majestie's pleasure that the noblemen to be created meet at a Chamber that will be provided at the lower end of the banquetting house on Satterday the 20th of Apprill 1661 at 2 of the clocke in the afternoone precisely.

The Barons to provide a surcoate.

A Baron is to carry a mantle.

And 2 Barones are to support him.

The Baron to bee created is to goe in his surcoate, and atter hee is presented to the King by his 2 supportors uppon theire knees, they rise upp leaveinge the Baron to be created in that posture during the reading of his Pattent, and at the word *Creamus* the Baron whoe carrys the mantle presents it to his Majestie who (the King laying his hand uppon it) with the helpe of the 2 supports, putts it on, then the Patent being read'out, and delivered by his Majestie to the new created Baron hee gives his Majestie humble thanks for that greate honor and then ariseth."

Note. This Warrant is for the creation of Sir Horatio Townshend as Baron Townshend of Lynn Regis by Letters Patent dated the 20th of April 1661.

Fees for passing a Patent for a Baron, Viscount, & Earl.

	£	s.	d.
Secretary's fee for the warrant - -	6	0	0
For enteringe it - - - -	0	5	0
Attorney-General fees £30 10s. for each -	30	10	0
To the Secretary for signing the bill when it's brought back - - - - -	6	0	0
Signett for each - - - -	6	13	4
Privy Seal the like for each - - -	6	13	4
Crown Office, Hanaper Office, &c. - -	135	0	0
King's servants.			
For an Earl - - - - -	206	10	0
For a Viscount - - - -	167	9	4
For a Baron - - - - -	135	5	4
Lord Chancellor's Secretary. For the *Recepi* -	5 guineas.		
For a Baron in all - - - -	246	14	6
For a Viscount - - - -	288	17	10
For an Earl - - - - -	332	18	6

Fees due to his Majestie's Servants, Hanaper Office, Crowne Office, and Great Seale for the Lord Towneshend's Dignity of Viscount.

	£	s.	d.
To his Majestie's Servants - - -	175	9	4
Hanaper Office - - - - -	34	13	4
Lord Chancellor's Grant of the Divident -	3	13	4
For signeing the Docquett - - -	1	0	0
Flourisht guilt skynne with gould and silver strings - - - - -	12	0	0
To the Clerke of the Crowne - - -	8	10	0
Clerk of the Crowne's Deputy and clerks -	4	6	8
Lord Chancellor's Gentleman of the Chamber -	6	10	0
Under Officers of his Lordshipp's House -	4	10	0
Sealers and Chafewax - - - -	5	10	0
Clerke of the Hanaper's Deputy and clerk -	3	13	4
Private Seale and attendance - - -	3	0	0
	90	6	8
	175	9	4

sic 266

The Charge of passing the **Right** Honourable the Lord Townshend's Dignity of a Viscount.

	£	s.	d.
To the Secretary for the King's Warrant and his Majestie's signeing the Bill - - -	32	5	0
Mr. Attorney, fee for the Bill - - -	30	10	0
Signet and Privy Seal - - - -	17	0	0
Docquets 3 guinnies - - - -	3	4	6
For a private Seal - - - -	2	0	0
Lord Chancellor's *Recepi* 5 guinees - -	5	7	6
Great Seal, and to the King's servants at Whitehall, Hanaper, Crowne Office, and Lord Chancellor's servants *in toto* - - -	266	0	0
To under Officers - - - -	7	5	0
For a box - - - -	1	0	0
To the Solicitor for passing the Patent, tenn guinnies - - - - - -	10	15	0
Totall -	375	7	0

1661. Oct. 20ᵗʰ. List of the officers of the several regiments of the militia of the County of Norfolk by John Kendall muster master.

N. D. Similar list and Proclamation relative to the Act for better ordering of the militia and service thereunder.

1664. Nov. 3ʳᵈ. " Letter Office London." A copy of a letter to Mʳ Salterton the Postmaster from the Post officers. "In answer to what you write concerning Mʳ Kendall's demanding money of you for expresses sent by him to the Lord Townshend the like hath uot been demanded from this office nor any postmaster that I ever yet heard of. Therefore you may give Mʳ Kendall so much to understand that you cannot allow it without order The Post Master General is not obliged to carry any letters or pacquets free but such as come to these persons of honor, viz., The Lord High Admiral of England, Lord Chancellor, Lord Treasurer and his Majestie's two principal Secretaries of State ; except by particular order under the King's hand, Duke of Ormond, Duke of Albermarle and the Lord Lowtherdale, Lord Secretary of Scotland could not have their letters and despatches free until they sent His Majesty's warrant for the same. And if my Lord Townshend please to procure the like order under His Majesty's royal hand for his own and Mʳ Kendall's letters and pacquetts passing free, his Honor and Mʳ Kendall will receive the benefit of it. Until that be obtained the office cannot pass them to His Majesty's accompt, nor can the Postmaster General bear the loss for many reasons, and this is all the answer to be given you at present."

ACCOUNT touching the Lord Townshend's defalcations from 1674 to Lady day 1680 (amounting with interest to £10110 6s 5½d.,) under his Majesty's grant of the coal farm — to be made up out of the growing reserved rent or otherwise as His Majesty shall think fit.

N. D. Draft for the conditions of a bond for 200l. relative to the sum of £100 bequeathed to the townsmen of Denham in the County of Suffolk by the Lady Mary Townshend, wife of Horatio Lord Townshend, Baron of King's Lynn.

MARQUESS
TOWNSHEND
MSS.

Undated. Temp. Charles II. Sir John Knyvett's list of officers of Sir John Holland's regiment with his owne troope of Volunteers.

Undated. Temp. Eliz. Paper relative to the enforcement of certain orders of the Privy Council for stay of the dearth of corn and the prevention of a rise in the price thereof.

Sentences printed in the Lord Keeper's gallerie at Gorambury and selected by him out of divers authors and sent to the good Lady Lumley at her desire.

N.D. "Articles obiected against Thomas Beckham touchinge his begettinge of a basterd child of the bodie of Katthryne Pallmer."

N.D. Paper signed Hugh Morrell and headed "Sundry overtures (in all humility) to the Right honorable the Lord Townsend for improving the exportacon of our sea coales to all forraigne princes dominions and plantacons in Christendome."

N.D. Paper endorsed "Case of Bewdley election, Herbert and Winnington," containing a narrative of the proceedings at an election of a burgess to sit in Parliament for the borough of Bewdley, contested by Mr Winnington a burgess of the borough and Mr Herbert. A dispute arose as to whether Mr Herbert not being a burgess could be elected, and the Town Clerk thinking he could not, took down only the names of those who voted for Mr Winnington and declared him duly elected, although a majority of the burgesses polled for his opponent.

N.D. Case and petition of Valentine Knightley Esquire claiming the Barony of Fitz Warine.

N.D. Fragment of a book (commencing at p 25.) containing a list of officers in the Royal Household with their salaries, a list of the castles, parks &c. belonging to the Crown and other information. No date is given, but the Earl of Salisbury and Lord Elphinstone are returned as Principal Secretaries, John Lord Stanhope as Master of the Posts, and the Earl of Worcester Master of the Horse.

N.D. Letter from the Justices of the Peace in the County of Norfolk to Lord Townshend the Lord Lieutenant, on the subject of the militia of the County.

N.D. Petition (to whom is not stated; possibly to the Privy Council) from the Mayor and Corporation of King's Lynn setting forth the losses their town has suffered of late years at the hands of the Dutch and that they are unable to supply the two ships of war which they have been commanded to furnish to the fleet now preparing in consequence of the depression and injury done to their trade, praying to be excused from furnishing the ships.

N.D. Papers unsigned relative to providing a house for the poor of Aylysham and the opposition to the proposal offered by Sir Christopher Heydon.

N.D. An undated memorandum.
"That the Dutchess of Queensberry is surprized and well pleased that the King hath given her soe agreeable a comand as to stay away from Court where she never came for diversion; but to bestow a greater civility upon the King and Queen. She hopes by such an unpresedented order as this that the King will see as few as he wishes att his Court

(perticularly such as dare to thinke or speake truth). I dare not doe other ways and ought not nor could not have imagined that it would not have been the highest compliment that I would possibly pay the King to endeavour to support truth and innocence in his house. Particularly when the King and Queen had both told me that they had not read Mr Gay's Play. I have certainely done right then to stand to my own word rather than his Grace of Grafton's who hath neather made use of truth, judgment, or honour through this whole affaire either for himselfe or his freinds.

" C. QUEENSBURRY."

N.D. Letter unsigned and unaddressed beginning "Dear Cosin," relating to the Norwich petition which has been "dismissed without anything being done upon it." The arbitrary proceedings of the Mayor, the writer thinks, deserve the severest punishment the Privy Council can inflict. The present action of the Council will be a great encouragement to the Mayor.

N. D. Temp. James II. Petition of the House of Commons to the King. Thanking his Majesty for his great care in the suppression of the late rebellion which threatened "the utter extirpation of our religion as by law established which is most dear unto us and which your Majesty has been pleased to give us repeated assurances you will always defend and support which with all gratefull hearts wee shall ever acknowledge." The King's recent speech has been considered "and as to that part of it relating to the officers in the army, not qualified for theire employments according to an Act of Parliament made in the 25th year of the reigne of your Majestie's royal brother of blessed memory, entituled An Act for preventing dangers which may happen from Popish Recusants, wee doe out of our bounden duty, humbly represent unto your Majesty that those officers cannot by law bee capable of theire employments, and that the incapacityes they bring upon themselves thereby, can no wayes bee taken off, but by an Act of Parliament." Therefore a bill is now being prepared for the Royal assent to indemnify these officers, and the petitioners beg that pending the new act they may be removed from their posts.

The King's answer is: " I did not expect such an adresse from this House of Commons, after haveing soe lately recommended to your consideration the great advantages a good understanding between us had procured in a very short time, and giving you warning of fears and jealousies amongst ourselves. I had reason to hope that the reputation God hath blessed me with in the world would have created and confirmed a greater confidence in you of me and of all I say to you. But however you proceed on your part, I will bee steady in all the promises I have made you and bee very just to my word in everyone of my speeches."

N.D. A dialogue in verse between "The Lord R's Ghost and Dr C. Dean of Can." A rather scurrilous production of which the meaning is very obscure.

Lord R. calls the Dean a rebel, whereupon the Dean answers

> D. " Rebell, my Lord, that's too severe
>   I did give way, comply and sweare
>   Sure that admitts a softer name
> G. To praise it when 'tis done's the same
>   *   *   *   *   *
>   Besides you've sworn i' th' face of the nation
>   For to support the usurpation

Since this no doubt must be the sence
Of swearing to another Prince,
Because in any elce 'twould bee
Nothing to his security
*   *   *   *   I can tell
It is the comon talke of H—ll
That you more instrumentall was
In bringing matters to this pass
Than either Danby or Delamere
Or he who did the Jack boot weare
Or e'n that curst false Scotch Apostle
Who so much in the cause did bustle
Nor were by one halfe soe serviceable
As you to raise the headstrong rabble.
    *   *   *   *   *

But now the stars become less bright
And I must goe before 'tis night.
D. I wish your Lordship may get home well
G. What! Nothing to your uncle Cromwell
D. Yes, duty, and his paines to soften
    Tell him the newes
G.   I'll see you often."

N.D. (latter end of 17th century). General instructions of a mother to a daughter (named Julia) for her conduct in life.

Ends: "Thus, my dearest Julia, have I led you through the different stages of human life, and hope, when you read this, you'll rather think it came from a friend whose tenderness endeavoured to make you perfect than from a mother grown severe by age; and do not enquire whether she who gave you these lessons, observed them herself, only think that she who could give them was capable of following them; others' faults do not lessen ours, but ought to serve as examples to deter others from them. I flatter myself from the observations I have made on your temper that this abridgment of your conduct may be serviceable to you in all instances of your life, on which I beseech the Divine Being to pour His Holy Blessing."

BUNDLE marked "WARRANTS OF COMMITMENT TO THE TOWER."

1675. Jan. 16th. Warrant under the Sign Manual to the Constable of the Tower to take into his custody Colonel Henry Danvers committed for treasonable practices against the King and the State.

1675. Feb. 27th. Warrant under the Sign Manual to the Constable of the Tower to take into his custody Robert Cobbett committed for treasonable practices against the King and the State.

1675. Sept. 22nd. Warrant signed by "Finch C." "Danby," "Carbery," "Newport," "H. Coventry," "Tho. Chicheley," "R. Carr" (?), "Edw. Walker" to the Earl of Northampton, Constable of the Tower, to take into his custody Colonel Philip Warner for the murder of his own brother, in commission from his Majesty and some Indians in friendship with the English.

1675. Oct. 21st. Warrant signed by Edward Seymour Speaker of the House of Commons, to the Earl of Northampton, Constable of the Tower, to take into his custody Lord Cavendish for his breach of the privilege of the House of Commons in prosecuting a quarrel against M[r] Thomas Howard whilst the matter was depending before the said House.

1675. Oct. 22ⁿᵈ. A like warrant for the discharge of the said Lord Cavendish.

1675. October 26ᵗʰ. Warrant signed by Edward Seymour Speaker of the House of Commons, to the Constable of the Tower to take into his custody Mʳ Thomas Howard for being the author, promoter, and disperser of a paper signed T. Howard of Richmond and Carlisle, voted by the House to be a scandalous paper and a breach of the privilege of the said house.

1675. Nov. 8ᵗʰ. A like warrant for the discharge of the said Mʳ Thomas Howard.

1676. Feb. 7ᵗʰ. Order of the House of Lords to the Constable of the Tower to receive into his custody George, Duke of Buckingham for his high contempt committed against the House.

1676. Feb. 9ᵗʰ. Warrant signed by " Finch C." " Danby," " Ormonde," " Lindsey." " H. Coventry," " J. Williamson," " Robert Southwell " to the Constable of the Tower to receive into his custody Dʳ Nicholas Cary for publishing a scandalous and seditious libel to the dishonor of the King's Majesty and his Government, and in which libel it is most falsely affirmed and by many feigned reasons endeavoured to be proved that the present Parliament is dissolved.

1676. Feb. 16ᵗʰ. Order of the House of Lords to the Constable of the Tower to receive James, Earl of Salisbury, Anthony Ashley, Earl of Shaftesbury, and Philip, Lord Wharton—for their high contempts committed against the House.

1676. Feb. 17ᵗʰ. Order to the Earl of Northampton Constable of the Tower, for strengthening the guard in the Tower, signed ' Monmouth.'
                                                            Seal.

1676. Feb. 21ˢᵗ. Warrant under the sign manual for Mʳˢ Amée Cary to visit her husband.

1676. Mar. 1ˢᵗ. Order of the House of Lords that Dʳ Cary be fined 1,000l. and remain a prisoner until he have paid the same.

1676. Mar. 28ᵗʰ. Warrant under the Sign Manual to the Constable of the Tower to send Colonel Philip Warner on board the *Phœnix* to be transported to the Island of Barbados.

1676. April 28ᵗʰ. Warrant under the Sign Manual to the Constable of the Tower for Colonel Henry Danvers' discharge.

1676. May 4ᵗʰ. Warrant under the Sign Manual to the Constable of the Tower for Major Cobbett's discharge.

1676. May 12ᵗʰ. Warrant signed by " Anglesey," " Worcester," " Finch C." " Peterborow," " J. Bridgwater," " W. Maynard," " J. Williamson," " Edw. Walker " to the Earl of Northampton, Constable of the Tower, to take into his custody John Freake of the Middle Temple Esq. for dispersing a seditious libel called the Chronicle of which he is presumed to be the Author.

1676. May 19ᵗʰ. Warrant signed by " Finch C.," " Worcester," " C. Craven," " J. Bridgwater," " H. London," " H. Coventry," " J. Williamson," " J. Erule," and " Edw. Walker " to the Constable of the Tower to take into his custody John Radford committed for high treason.

MARQUESS
TOWNSHEND
MSS.

1676. May 28th. Warrant under the Sign Manual to keep Mr. Freake a close prisoner, being committed for high treason.

1676. June 21st. Warrant under the Sign Manual to the Constable of the Tower to take into his custody Charles Lord Cornwallis, committed for being indicted for murder.

1676. July 5th. Warrant signed by " Finch C.," " Anglesey," " Danby," " Ormonde," " J. Ernle," " J. Williamson," " John Nicholson," to the Constable of the Tower to take into his custody Sir Philip Monckton, knight, for writing a seditious and scandalous letter to defame the Government and the Lords of his Majesty's Privy Council and to raise groundless jealousies and fears among the people tending to public disturbance.

1676. July 22nd. Warrant under the sign manual to permit the Duke of Buckingham to have his liberty unto the 22nd August next.

1677. Jan. 2nd. Warrant under the Sign Manual to James Earl of Northampton, Constable of the Tower, to take into his custody Philip Earl of Pembroke and Montgomery, committed for speaking blasphemy and other misdemeanours.

1677. June 1st. Warrant under the sign manual to the Constable of the Tower to permit the Earl of Salisbury to go to Hatfield to remain until the 30th June.

1677. June 29th. Similar warrant, enlarging the time to 31st July.

1677. July 23rd. Similar warrant, discharging him from imprisonment, he having expressed his extreme trouble for having offended the King and House of Peers by what he owned to have unadvisedly said concerning the late Prorogation.

1677. July 29th. A similar warrant for the discharge of Philip Lord Wharton.

1677. July 20th. Warrant under the sign manual to the Constable of the Tower to permit any person signified by a Secretary of State to have access to Anthony Earl of Shaftesbury.

1677. July 2nd. Warrant signed by Sir Joseph Williamson principal Secretary of State, to the Constable of the Tower, to receive George Bullen on board the ship *John*, and convey him to the Tower, being committed for dangerous words by him spoken against his Majesty on board the ship called the *John*.

1677. Aug. 26th. Secretary Coventry's letter to the Earl of Northampton to permit Richard Lucy to have access to the Earl of Shaftesbury.

1677. Dec. 5th. Warrant signed by " Finch C.," " Danby," " Anglesey," " W. Maynard," " J. Ernle," " J. Williamson," " Thomas Dolman," to the Earl of Northampton, Constable of the Tower, to take into his custody the Lord Purbeck for carrying and delivering a challenge to the Heer Van Benting, Chamberlain to the Prince of Orange, in the Palace of St James's and for other misdemeanours.

1677. Dec. 29th. Warrant to the Constable of the Tower to recruit the three Companies in the Tower and to admit and entertain such recruits.

N.D.—Draft appointment by James Earl of Northampton, Constable of the Tower, of Sir John Robinson, Knight and Baronet, as his Deputy Constable of the Tower.

BUNDLE marked "PETITIONS."

N.D. Petition of Robert Perkins, "lying under sentence of death," to Charles Viscount Townshend, praying his Lordship to procure his pardon.

N.D. Petition (in French) of the Duchess of Grafton to the King, on behalf of Sir Henry Bombury accused of high treason for having franked a seditious letter of one Captain White. The Duchess alleged, in excuse of Sir Henry, that it was the custom for members of Parliament (who had the privilege of franking letters) to give blank envelopes ready franked to their servants to be used on occasion, and that one of these had been given to White and used by him to convey a treasonable letter. She prays the clemency of the King on behalf of Sir Henry.

N.D. Petition of Sir Humfrey Ferrers Knight to the King, stating that certain manors in Essex Bucks and Derbyshire had been granted to his ancestor Sir Henry Ferrers : that these manors had come into the hands of the Crown by reason of the minority of one of the petitioner's predecessors in title and that they have never since been recovered for various causes; praying a restoration of them to him.

N.D. Petition to the King of the Mayor and burgesses of Thetford, imprisoned for contempt of the King and of Lord Townshend his Lord Lieutenant of Norfolk, making apology and submission and praying thereupon their release.

There is a large collection (marked "Verses") of fugitive songs, poems ballads, squibs, lampoons &c. of no particular interest.

The following is amusing, and a fair sample of the remainder.

1.

A wicked old Peer
And a Bishop I hear
About going to Hell made a rout
They both had observed
'Twas what they deserved
But which should go first was the doubt.

2.

That, swore and lyed
This, hypocrisy tryed
'Twas hard to say which was the worst,
Give the Devil his due,
Two worse he ne're knew
But however the Bishop went first.

3.

Affronted in Hell
At what I can't tell
He sat musing, nor opened his mouth
But soon the bright M——s,
Who now in the dark is,
As usual began with an oath.

MARQUESS
TOWNSHEND
MSS.

4.

Wh—–n   G—d d—mn ye old Nick,
           We'll shew you a trick,
           We Monarchy always have hated,
           We both will disown
           Your right to the Throne
           And swear you have abdicated.

5.

S—r——m   Right Marq—s of W——n
           'Tis what I first thought on
           His title nor you nor I know
           'Twould be a fine thing
           If horns made a king,
           I'm sure he is not *jure divino.*

6.

           But straightway the D——
           Grown wondrous civil
           At the sayings of each hopeful imp
           Cryed hold up your faces,
           Ye both shall have places
           S——m my porter, and W——n my pimp.

7.

           They bowed and went on
           But whispered the throng
           Now we're in, of our time we'll make use,
           We'll maul the old whelp
           If you'll lend us your help
           And who knows but all Hell may break loose

8.

           Then W——n did say
           If we can't get away
           For one thing we'll give you our words
           Here will be by and by
           With S——m & I,
           Two thirds of the Bishops and Lords.

9.

           With these helps I hope
           Spite of D——l and P—pe
           If the honest damned will come over
           My friend's zeal and mine
           To the Protestant line
           Will bring in the House of H———r.

There is a bundle of letters marked on the outside " Letters to Mr.
Titley." These are of the years 1692 and 1693 and are from various

servants, bailiffs, and agents of Lord Townshend to Mr. Titley, who appears to have been his Lordship's chief agent in London, on various matters, such as sending down wigs, boots, shoes, saddles, wine, clothes &c. for Lord Townshend's use. Several letters are from Mrs. Ann Newborough the dame of Lord Townshend's sons, Roger and Horace, at Eton.

STATE PAPERS, DESPATCHES, ETC.

1702–1742.

170⅔. March 3rd. Copy of a letter " for his Maties Service," addressed to the County Magistrates of Norfolk ; directing them to carry out the Council Order of Feby 19th, 1701, relating to the impressment of seamen. Dated at Norwich Castle and signed by, " yor very loving Friends, Edward Ward, Arthur Windham, and John Harbord, Deputy Lieutenants of the County of Norfolk."

. . . . . You are by His Maties especiall Directions to issue out yor Wa^{tts} forthw^{th} to the Chief Constables w^hin yor Divisions, to send out their War^{tts} forthw^{th} to the Petty Constables w^hin their Limitts, that they may make exact Lists of the Names of all Seamen, comprehending also Boatmen, Bargemen, Watermen, & Fishermen, as inhabit w^hin their respective Parishes, wth an Account of their severall Ages, & Conditions, according to the Forme and Scheme which is hereunto annexed . . . . . that the s^d Chief Constables may transmitt the same to Mr. Edward L'Estrange, Clerke to the Lieutenancy of Norfolke, ... that soe he may give his L^dship, the Lord Viscount Townshend an Acc^o thereof . . . . . .

1702. May 16th. Sir Charles Hedges, Secretary of State, to Lord Townshend (Lord Lieutenant of Norfolk). Dated at Whitehall and stating that the Queen wishes the Privy Council Letters for procuring Seamen to be carried out forthwith in the most effectual manner.

1702. Dec. 5th, N.S. Copy of a Memorial of Alexander Stanhope, British Minister at the Hague, in reply to a Memorial of the States General dated $\frac{16th}{27th}$ November. 2 pp.

170⅔. March 16th. " Extract of a Letter from Mr. Stanyan, Her Ma^{tys} Envoy in Swisserland, to the Earl of Sunderland." About the territory of Tockenbourg in Switzerland, which is subject to the Abbots of St. Gall, and is in danger of losing its privileges through the bribery and intrigues of the latter. 5 pp.

1709. April 10th. Baron Schutz, Hanoverian Minister in London, to Secretary Boyle, " to have France's acknowledging the Electorate of Hanover made a Preliminary of the Treaty." In French. Dated at St. James's Square. 1½ pp.

1709. April 17th Copy of Monsr Schutz's Scheme of a Barrier for the Empire. In French. 3¼ pp.

1709. April —. Copy of a letter, in French, " on behalf of the Protestants at the Treaty of Peace." Dated at the Hague and unsigned. 8 pp.

1709. May 2nd. Copy of Lord Townshend's Credentials to the States General. In French. 1½ pp.

Same date. Court at St. James's. The Queen's "Private Instructions for D. of Marlborough and Lord Townshend."

"Whereas it is expected that several towns now belonging to, and in the hands of France should be given up, and yeilded by the Treaty of Peace to be garrisoned by the Forces of the States General, for the security of their Barrier. If therefore the Revenews of such towns, their Dependencies, and Territorys, so deliver'd up, and garrisoned, be nott found sufficient to answer the necessary expences to be made for that Service, in such case you have liberty to consent to the adding such further Sum, or Sums, as shall be thought requisite and reasonable for that purpose, out of the Incomes, and Reveneues, arising in general from the Spanish Low Countries."

A. R.

[No date.] "A List of Treaties that are in Mr. Secretary Boyle's Office." 18½ pp.

This list commences with the Emperor's Ratification of King William's Accession to the Treaty made between the Emperor and the States General at Vienna,—12th May 1689; and it ends with the Elector Palatine's Ratification of the Convention between her Majesty and the States General, and his Electoral Highness, at the Hague,—17th May 1703.

1709. May 10th. Whitehall. George Tilson to Horatio Walpole. Written in great haste.

. . . . . "We have directions for 7 Lieut⁸ Genˡ, Stanhope, Mordant, Farrington, Howe, Cadogan, Meredyth, Palmes. You see we make provision for War, whatever the Fr[ench] may think of peace " . . . .

1709. May 13th. Christopher Tilson "To his Excellency the Lord Viscount Townshend, Ambassador Extraordinary and Plenipotentiary from the Queen of Great Britain to the States Genˡ of the United Provinces." Dated at the Treasury Chambers.

. . . . "The Privy Seal for Your Lordp̄s allowances is passed and at my Lord Treas̄rs return from New Markett, wᶜʰ wilbe tomorrow, I hope to obtaine his Warrant to the Excheqʳ for your Lordp̄s Equipage money wᶜʰ is 1500ˡⁱ, and for three months advance on your Entertainmᵗ of 100ˡⁱ ℘ weeke ; that being done your Lordship may please to value your selfe on me for 2700ˡⁱ or thereabᵗ."

1709. May 14th. Monsʳ Schutz to Secretary Boyle. "Concerning the Barrier and the affair of Religion." Copy. In French. 2 pp.

1709. May 15th. Copy of a letter from Frederick Augustus, Elector of Saxony and King of Portugal, to Queen Anne. In Latin with the following translation :—

We Friderick Augustus, by the Grace of God King, Duke of Saxony, &c., To the most Serene and most Potent Princess, Anne, by the same Grace, Queen of Great Britain France and Ireland &c., Greeting. Friderick Khune Our Subject has humbly represented in a memorial offered to Us, that his Brother Rudolph formerly Closet Keeper to the late King William of pious Memory died at Kensington in Septʳ 1707, having left a Will, whereby he made Martin Christian his Brother's Son his Heir. And tho' there was no such Person in being, so that upon Default of the said Heir, the Will became void, and the Estate was to devolve to the next of kin to the Intestate, among whom is the said Friderick Khune, yet his Share of the Inheritance is contested by the Sons of another Brother of the deceased, upon a Pretence that the whole belonged of right to One of them ; wherefore he has humbly & earnestly desired Us to recommend his Case to Your Ma[jes]ty. And indeed We could not easily deny him Our Letters to Your Ma[jes]ty in his favour, not only as he thought Our Recommendation would be of great Advantage to him, but also as it seemed just & reasonable to Us that the Lawfull Successors should have their Right preserved to them intire. And as We are persuaded Your Ma[jes]ty's great Justice will incline you to be of the same Opinion, We make it Our Brotherly Request, that You would please to vouchsafe Your Royal Favour to the said Kuhne Our Subject, and interpose Your Authority in this unjust Controversy carrying on against him, that he may possess his just Right of Inberitance without any Vexation or Trouble. Which will not only be a great Addition to the Character of Your Ma[jes]ty's Justice so well known in the World, but will also be a particular favour done to Us, when We find we have so successfully interested Ourself in this Matter. As to what remains, May Your Ma[jes]ty long enjoy your health, & promise to Yourself every thing that can be expected from a Prince, who has so true a Respect and Value for the British Name.

Given at Dresden the 13th day of May 1709.

Your Majesty's
Good Brother and
Cousin,
AUGUSTUS REX.

1709. May 15th. Copy of a resolution of the States General in behalf of the French Protestants.

[No date.] A Memorial in French, endorsed :—" The Guaranty of the Kings of England for the treatys between the Protestants and the King of France." 7 pp.

[No date.] A Memorial [in French] concerning the Protestants in France. 8 pp.

[No date.] Raisons pourquoi Sa Majesté la Reine de la Grande Brettagne & les Seigneurs Etats Gen[erau]x des Provinces Unies peuvent avec justice demander en depost la Ville de Strasbourg avec le Haute et Basse Alsace et les moyens comment y parvenir. [Unsigned and unaddressed.] 3¼ pp.

1709. May 24th. Christopher Tilson to Lord Townshend. Dated at the Treasury Chambers and addressed as before.

. . . . . "touching your Lor[p]s money at the Excheq[r] I have now nothing to repeat to your Lord[p] but that I have actually received the same ; and have obtained also from my L[d] Chamb[er]l[ai]n W[arran]ts for the nec[essa]rys following Vizt, for 5893 oz. White Plate & 1066 oz. guilt Plate, For a State [Coach] with the other nec[essa]rys attending it, For an Altar Cloth, Books & other Chaple necessarys, For the Queen's Picture at Length and Frame & Case ; I am now going to acquaint my Lady (who is now is Towne,) with these things, expecting her Ladyship has your Lordships particular directions about them. I am with all imaginable respect " etc.

1709. May ¹⁷th/₂₈th. John Robinson to the same. Hamburgh.

The writer suggests that France should be obliged to discharge all foreigners serving in its armies.

[No date.] Plan d'une Barriere pour l'Empire. Unsigned. Endorsed "Rec[d] from Baron Schutz." 3¼ pp.

[No date.] The projects of the States General and the British Ambassadors compared. In parallel columns in the handwriting of Horatio Walpole. A preamble and 22 Articles.

MARQUESS
TOWNSHEND
MSS.

[No date.] Draught of the 26th Article of the Preliminaries relating to the French King acknowledging the Elector of Hanover —
"Sa Majesté reconnoistra dès la Signature de ces Preliminaires la dignite Electorale de son Altesse Electorale de Brounsvic Luneebourg et son Office d'Architresorier de l'Empire qui y est attaché."

1709. May 28th. Articles preliminaires pour servir aux traitez de la Paix Generale. Signed at the Hague at this date. 40 Articles. 14 pp. [copy]. The signatories were [Prince] Eugene of Savoy, Philippe Louis Comte of Sinzendorf, the Prince and Duke of Marlborough, [Viscount] Townshend, J. de Welderen, L. B[aron] de Reede, A. Heinsius, [Baron] Coninck, F. Baron de Reede de Renswoode, S. V[on] Goslinga, Van Ittersum, W. Wickers, Willem Buys, and P_t V[an] Dussen.

Same date. John Wich, Envoy at Hamburg, to Lord Townshend.
. . . . "This Town will have an occasion to lay themselves att your Excellencie's feett, and implore Your Protection, when the grand & alluring Topick of Trade may come to be handled . . . ."

Same date. The same to Horatio Walpole.
Is sending by Mr Statton "a box in which are five gold meddalls, however I tell him 'tis some of the Duke of Cells powder, so famous on all occasions you wrote for." . . . .

1709. June $\frac{3rd}{14th}$. John Robinson to the same. From Hamburgh.
The writer hears that the King of Sweden gained a great victory about the end of March.

1709. June 4th. The same to the same.
Will send a translation of the requests of the Town of Dantzig.

1709. June 6th. Minutes of a Conference between the Ministers of the Allies and Monsr de Rouille. In French. $5\frac{1}{3}$ pp.

1709. June 7th. Resolution of the States General upon the Report of the Conference between the Ministers of the Allies and Monsr de Rouille, in reference to the French King's refusal of the Preliminaries. In French. 4 pp.

Same date. John Chetwynd to Lord Townshend. From Turin.
. . . . "I beg to congratulate your Ex^{cy} upon the good choice wch the Queen hath made of you to manage her affaires in so nice a conjuncture, & I heartily wish your Ex^{cy} may meet with good Success in your Negotiations. If what our last letters bring us be true, you have already gon a good way in your great worck, so far, that we expect a Courier here from the Duke of Savoy's Minister every moment, with the news of y^{re} haveing adjusted the preliminarys of Peace, or that you have dismissed the Marq^s de Torcy. The Duke of Savoy's Courier is just now arrived with the news of your haveing signed the Preliminarys, I have been at Court, and have seen the Duke's letters from his Ministers, as well as from my Ld Duke [of Marlborough] & Prince Eugene; H.R.H. seems pritty well satisfied with what you have don for him, & I must own, I am very well pleased to see things in so fair a way" . . . . .

Same date. John Robinson to Horatio Walpole. From Hamburgh.
It is reported the King of Sweden with his Army has passed the River Dnieper without any hindrance from the Muscovites.

D 2

1709. June 11th. John Wich to Lord Townshend.

"The King of Danemarck is expected in Holstein very suddainly, and then wee may hear a little what passed at that magnificent interview" . . . .

Same date. The same to Horatio Walpole.

. . . "I am and always was of the Opinion that His Grace [the Duke of Marlborough] will gett much better and more advantageous conditions with the Sword drawn, then in suffering the Ribaldrye of three or four French slaves, and Sycophants to be whisper'd about the World as a sort of a Preliminary" . . . .

Same date. A diary of the affairs of Hamburg (from May 13th, 1708, to May 3rd, 1709). Enclosed in Mr. Wych's letter of this date. In French. 11½ pp.

Same date. Dr Henry Newton to Lord Townshend. From Florence.

. . . . . . "The Pope has not yet acknowledgd King Charles the Third, in hopes that a Generall Peace may take of from him the Envy & the Hazard of such an Act, & so upon one pretence or another, temporizes betwixt the contending powers, & delayes to make good the late Treaty with the Emperr in that Part. Hee fears the Two Crowns, loves not the House of Austria, & at present suffers by them all: no mony being now returnd to Rome from Naples or Millain, & as little at present likewise to be expected from Spain: so that the Cardinalls are not able to keep up their usuall Port at Rome, most of their Revenews as likewise of the Apostolic Chamber arising from those parts. Here in Tuscany the Succession of the Family being in danger, since there is now no Likelihood, that either of the two Princes, the Sons of the G[rand] Duke, should have any issue, the Court has at last resolvd that the Cardinall of Medices shall marry with the second Daughter of the Duke of Guastalla, with whom all things are now said to be adjusted, & that we may expect the Bride in a few dayes at Florence . . . . Tis thought Cardinall Medices's Cap will be bestowd upon the Abbat Salviati, Brother to the Duke of that name in this Citty & is at present Nuncio at Paris for the carrying the Consecrated Blanketts from the Pope to the Duke of Britanny; wch at Rome will bee reckned for an Honr doné by them to that Court." . . . . . .

1709. June 12th. The same to the same. From Turin.

. . . . . . I had the honour to write to Lord Sunderland in favour of the exiled Protestants in the Valley of Perouse . . . . I flatter myself that her Majty will be pleased to approove of what I have had the honour to write in their favour, & I hope your Exey will allso grant them your protection, when the Treaty with the Duke of Savoy shall be concluded. . . . . . The Dutch Envoy at this Court hath wrote to his Masters to this purpose, we allways act in concert in things of this nature.

1709. June 14th. Christian Cole to the same. From Venice.

. . . . . Two Brittish Merchants, Messr Boddington & Colebrooke set out from hence for Holland by the post. I have charged them with some Pamphletts newly published, and relating to the present differences, lately half adjusted at Rome. . . . Since the departure of the Germans for Pie[d]mont every thing is hush in Italy, and I cannot send your Lordship any news of moment. . . . . .

MARQUESS
TOWNSHEND
MSS.

1709. June $\frac{14th}{25th}$. John Robinson to Lord Townshend. From Hamburgh.

The writer hears from Poland and Saxony that King Augustus is resolved to return to Poland and to endeavour to regain that Crown.

1709. June 18th. John Wich to Horatio Walpole. From Hamburgh.

You will have seen the propositions this poor Town has made to England towards being restor'd to the same priviledges of Trade with [as] the Hollanders. I must beg you to recommend their miserable case on all hands to his Excellence . . . .

1709. June 18th. Draft of a letter from Horatio Walpole to M[r] Secretary Boyle.

1709. June 24th. Draft of a letter, the same to the same.

1709. June 25th. John Robinson to Horatio Walpole.

The writer objects to a Squadron being sent into the Sound to intercept Corn Ships going to France since no force can be used there without a violation of the King of Denmark's neutrality.

1709. June 28th. The same to the same.
Enclosing a paper which has become separated.

Same date. John Wich to the same.
About the plans of King Augustus.

1709. July 6th. John Chetwynd to the same. Dated at Turin.

"Last Thursday Mar[sh]all Dawn reviewd the Imperiall and Piedmontese horse at Orbassano consisting of about ten thousand. The Infantry w[th] a Detachment of 600 horse, have begun their march, and are to be at the foot of mount Cenis tomorrow when the Mar[sh]al designs to join them, an the 9[th] Inst. they will begin to climb up that Mountain.

Two thousand Pioneers or more w[th] some Infantry have been employed ever since the 2[d] Ins[t] to make a way over Mount Cenis to facilitate the passage of our heavy Artillery in case Mar[sh]all Dawn should have occasion for any, to force some of the Enemies Posts in Savoy or make a Siege on that Side.

Besides the Army w[ch] marches with Mar[sh]all Dawn over Mount Cenis, Gen[ll] Rehbinder is detached w[th] 16 Batt. to observe the Enemies at Briancon where we are informed they have 30 Battallions.

Letters from Paris say that they are under great Consternation there & apprehensive of an Action in Flanders. Mons[r] de Roclore Govern[r] & M[r] de Baville Intendant of the Sevennes, have sent Courier upon Courier to the Court of France to demand a speedy Succour from the King to endeavour to extinguish the fire w[ch] kindles there. The number of those who have taken up Arms is considerable and encreases daily, these are both Roman Catholics and Protestants. This being so near the Fronteer, to be favoured by the Duke of Savoys designs, gives great uneasiness to the Court of France.

They talk in France that all their Troops are recalled from Spain, & that their design Seems to be to have an army in the Kingdom to curb the people in the severall Provinces, who begin to mutiny, rather than to send Succours to the Armies in Flanders and Dauphiné as the Court gives out.

Mr. Palmes went from hence yesterday for Milan to wait the Arrivall of Count Slick or what other Minister the Emp[r] will be pleased to send to see and adjust the differences betwixt his Impll Maj[ty] and the Duke of

Savoy who seems resolved not to take the field till he get Satisfaction
from the Court of Vienna, as to the entire execution of his Treaty.

The Duke of Savoy has given leave to Prince Emmanuel & P. Eugene
of Soisons, nephews to P. Eugene of Savoy to make the Campain with
Mar[sh]all Dawn, and they will leave this place to join the Army
tomorrow.

His R.H. having sent all the Troops that he possibly could into the
field, we have nothing but the Militia left for the guard of this place."

1709. July 9th. Florence. Dr. Henry Newton to Lord Townshend.
The Peace of Italy has made us here but empty of News at present.
The Pope's health declines, and the recognition of King Charles the
Third's stile delay'd, wch upon the News of the Preliminaryes at Rome
wanted but little of being complyd with. Wee are like to have a very
extraordinary Harvest in these parts, after all the fears they had of a bad
one ; Wee expect to heare every houre of the arrivall of the Princesse
Guastalla here to consumate the marriage with the Prince Francesco
Maria (for that is the name the late Cardinall Medici goes by) who is
now upon the road with his Nephew, the youngest Prince, to meet and
conduct her hither. I had my first Audience on the 6th instant of that
Prince, hee being no longer now Protector of the Two Crowns ; to congratulate him upon the occasion of his Marriage; there being no hope
left, of keeping up the Succession of the Family, and consequently of
securing on this Side the quiet of Italy . . . . .

1709. July 10th. Milan. General Francis Palmes to the same.
Att my Arrival att Turin from the Court of Venice I found the
news of the treaty of Peace being broke of wch made me believe that
y^r Excellency would have returned from thence for London, but since
I find that y^w are like to continue att the Hague sometime I desire
leave to pay my respects to y^r Excellency and att the same time to
communicate to y^w what passes in my station where I hope to be very
soon. I have been here these three or four days expecting the
Emperors Minister who is to be sent hither in order to adjust the
differences between his R. Highnesse the Duke of Savoye and that
Court, who I fear will not when he does come settle those affairs
altogether to his R : H : Satisfaction . . . . .

I doe with all my heart congratulate y^r Lord^p being employed by
her Maty to put an honorable end to a tedious and just warr, wch I hope
will give a happy and lasting peace to Old England, and quiet and
honor to all those who contributed to bring its Enemys to reason.

1709. July 12th. John Wich to Horatio Walpole.

Enclosing a statement in French of the proceedings of the "Commission Imperiale" from May 3rd to July 9th.

1709. July 14th. Mr. David Flotard's Proposal to support and assist
the rising in the Vivares and the Cevennes. Dated at Amsterdam.
In French. 3 pp.

[No date.] A Memorial of Mr. Flotard enclosed in the last and
addressed to Queen Anne and the Allies. In French. 3 pp.

1709. July 20th. James Cockburn to Horatio Walpole. From
Turin.

"Marshall Dawn arrived at Ossois the 14th Inst., from whence he
detached the Count de la Rogue with 5000 Men to drive the Enemies
from the Tarentaise, where they have 8 Battalions, a Regiment of
Dragoons and part of a regiment of horse. General Schulenberg who

comands in the Valley D'Aoust is to advance on that Side to assist Count la Roque. The Mareschall designed to march from Ossois the 18th & was to be last night at Modane or Aurelle.

Our Letters from Paris of the 3rd Inst. and from Lyons of the 7th assure that the french King has sent orders to countermand the retreat of his Troops from Spain, and that the Mar[sh]all Bezons is to assemble the Army of the two Crowns with all possible diligence near Lerida in order to enter Catalonia. The Paris letters are full of the change of the Ministry, and say that the King has left the management of affairs wholly to the Dauphine. The Camisars continue to encrease, the last letters bring nothing particular from them.

. . . . We are informed that the Enemies Army is in such great want of Corn, that they subsist only of what they can get daily from the neighbouring marketts and Villages part of wch they buy & part they take by force, and not only the Deserters who come daily in great numbers, but likewise all the advices from Lions & the frontiers say that they want money so much, that the Soldiers have received no Subsistance money for a considerable time " . . . . . .

1709. July 23rd. Dr Henry Newton to the same. From Florence. . . . . the Subsidyes demanded here of the people, wch the Contributions required by the Germans have in a great measure given rise to, cause no little discontent & murmurings amongst them: & in Naples they are every day in apprehensions of a Tumult upon the accompt of the new Gabells; wch has obliged Cardinall Grimani the Viceroy, to call thither the greater part of the Horse in this Kingdome, for his own & the Governments Security. Matters are not yet settled at Millain to the Content of the D. of Savoy: & the Pope's decaying & broken health makes it very probable, that there may bee a Conclave yet before the end of the Yeare. Before wch time too I hope my Lord Townshend may yet again Successfully assist in the procuring a Generall Peace for Christendome. . . . . .

1709. July 26th. John Wich to Lord Townshend. . . . . "The Emperor's Commissioner here has given a wonderfull offence to the Priesthood, and last Sunday he was declaimed against in every Pulpitt in this Citty [Hamburgh]. He has taken two children from their Friends who design'd to breed 'em up Lutherans and on Prætext that their Mother was a Portugaise and a Catholick keep 'em in his own House and has Jesuits over 'em " . . . .

1709. July 30th. The same to the same. Mentions a reported victory of the Russians over the Swedes and encloses an extract in French from a severe paper by Count Schönborn against those ministers who animadverted in their sermons upon the case of the Schlebush children.

1709. Augt. 9th. Nicholas Clignet to the same. From Leyden. In French. Enclosing the accounts of the Marquis D'Arseiller against the British Government.

1709. Augt. 13th. John Wich to the same. The Plague is at Dantzig. The accounts concerning the Defeat of the Swedes and the Death of their King continue the same.

1709. Augt. 23rd. The same to Horatio Walpole. There is no doubt of the entire Victory gained by the Muscovite. " We begin to be a little upon the muddle in the commission."

MARQUESS TOWNSHEND MSS.

MARQUESS
TOWNSHEND
MSS.
___

The two main Machines being at present absent. The Em[pero]rs
and Ele[cto]rs Ministers, however I shall keep them at play, tho but at
a small game.

1709. Augt. 26th. General Palmes to Lord Townshend. From the
Camp at Faverges.

. . . . . . "Our Army reaches from Conflans to Annecy and wants
for nothing, and in a few days we expect our field Artillery here. The
Enemy are very strongly intrenchd at Montmeillan, and have severall
posts between that place and Chamberry, they have also a considerable
Number of Militia, and five Regiments of Dragons on the Rhone, being
very apprehensive that the Mareschall should attempt to pass that
River with a Body of Horse.

Lt Gen^{ll} Baron de St Rhemy of H.R.H.^{s} troops march'd the 24th with
3,000 foot to the Chartreuse not farr from the left of the Enemys Camp
to see what posture they are in on that Side.

The Enemy are daily reinforced by the troops that came out of Spain,
and the Roussillon so that we count them at present 100 battalions,
and 45 Squadrons on this side of the Rhone. I am obliged to y^r Excellency for y^r letter of the 30th of July and could wish I could send y^w
such news from hence as would facilitate y^r negotiations when they
begin att the Hague, however I doe not thinke the Army on this side
nor the Expences can be called uselesse since we employ the enclosed
number of the Enemys troopes and hope we shall oblige more of em to
march as these wch otherwise must augment their forces against my
Lord Marlborough who hitherto has been our Sheet Anchor and where
our greatest hopes lye.

His R.H. [the Duke of Savoy] has hitherto shown very great zeal
for the success of the Campagne and great attention for the providing
the army wth necessarys wch I can assure y^r Lord'p in this difficult
country is both chargeable and painful, considering the superiority the
Duke of Berwyck has in foot and the good measures he has hitherto
taken I believe a strong diversion will be the utmost of our hopes on
this side. I have etc."

Enclosed is a list of the 97 Batallions and the 19 Squadrons under
the orders of the Duke of Berwick.

1709. Augt. 31st. James Cockburn to Horatio Walpole. From
Turin.

. . . . . "As on one side Marshall Dawn endeavours to bring the
French to an action, so on the other Gen^{ll} Rehbinder who was left in the
lines of Exiles wth 12 Batt^s was ordered to advance towards Briançon,
he is allready passed Mount Genevre & attacked the Enemies at Pont
la Vachette, & beat them from thence with the loss of 120 or 130 men
and if he had been strong enough might have taken possession of some
posts near the Town " . . . .

1709. Sept. 7th. The same to the same. From Turin. Dated at
Turin.

. . . . . "Genl Rehbinder has been ordred to detach two of the Batt^s
under his comand to join Marshall Dawn and they are marched over
Mount Cenis.

. . . . . . The Duke of Savoy having appointed the 8th Inst. to be
observed as a Generall Day of Thanksgiving in all Piedmont for the
happy delivery of this Town, His R. H. designs to hold a chappell of
the Knights of the Order of the Anuntiade to hear Te Deum sung, and
afterwards make a Solemn Procession with the Princes and rest of the
Nobility of both Sexes."

1709. Sept. 10th. John Wich to the same.
The King of Sweden lives but whether he will do well the writer cannot tell.

Same date. The same to Lord Townshend.
The Accounts are that the King is well and perfectly recovered of his Wound, that His Majesty after an incredible March of several Days through the Deserts got safe to the Banks of the Boristhenes with three or four hundred Horse; That finding the River vastly broad and the Transports few, he was obliged to send over to Oczakow for assistance. The Officer there not daring to do any thing without leave of the neighbouring Basha kept that unfortunate Prince on the other side four and twenty hours before any boats could be order'd him, which arriving at last, came just time enaugh to save His Majesty and some few of his retinue, the rest being all taken prisoners by a Party of Muscovites who were sent in his pursuit.

1709. Sept. 11th. A letter from the Protestant Ministers at the Diet of Ratisbon to Queen Anne, on behalf of the Protestant Religion. In Latin. 4 pp.
Enclosing a Declaration in French, signed by Charles Whitworth and dated at Ratisbonne 15th March 1703, of the Queen's intention to use her utmost endeavours in support of the Protestant Religion.

1709. Sept. 17th. John Wich to Horatio Walpole.
. . . . "I am full of Transport [at the victory of Malplaquet] and like the Bowle which I shall this Evening consecrate to their Healths, runne over with Joy and Sattisfaction. Whilst you are drawing towards a Peace, Wee here are preparing for Blood and Slaughter. Danemarck resolved to make a huge Bustle" . . . .

1709. Sept. 28th. James Cockburn to the same. From Turin.
. . . . . "Our Army is now on their Retreat from Savoy the last of them was to be on this side Mount [St] Bernard yesterday, so we shall soon have them all in the plain at Ivrea. We expect Mr Palmes here every moment. Tomorrow we are to sing Te Deum here for the Reduction of Tournay & the great Victory the Duke of Marlborough & P. Eugene obtained [at Malplaquet] in Flanders the 11th Inst." . . . .

1709. Sept. 30th. John Laws to the same. From Brussels. Misdated "30th October 1709."
. . . . . . At the opening of the Trenches before Mons on the 25th [Sept. 1709] Lieut. General Cadogan was wounded by a Shot in the Neck . . . . .

1709. Oct. 1st. John Wich to the same.
"The Sweeds have got together 16000 men in Schonen and have already fitted out fourteen Men of War. Their Ministers begin to talk as if they would be glad to have a peace with the Czar and suffer King Augustus to be dethroned upon certain conditions."

1709. Oct. 3rd. John Laws to the same. From Brussels.
. . . . . . "Lieut. General Cadogan is in a fair way of Recovery, the Ball not having Lodged. His Aide de Camp Foxen is dead, of a shott he receiv'd in the head at the same time."

1709. Oct. 8th. John Wich to the same.
[I] intend to settle this winter here betwixt a Rummer of Rhenish, and a smart jole of Stergeon.

Same date. Stephen Poyntz to Thomas Ward. Dated at the Hague and addressed "For Mr. Ward at Raynham Hall in Norfolk— By Swaffham Post." Franked "R. Walpole."

. . . . . . "We hope to hear some good news fro' Spain."

1709. Oct. 12th. James Cockburn to Horatio Walpole. From Turin.

"Marshall Dawn with most of the Generall Officers of our Army have been here some days. The Enemies having reinforced their posts about Briancon & on that frontier his R. H. has thought fitt to order 15 Batt[s] to be detached from our grand Army w[ch] is now encamped near to Ivrea to reinforce the body under Gen[ll] Rehbinder & these Troops are allready marched towards Suze under the comand of Gen[ll] S[t] Remy " . . . . .

1709. Oct. 18th. John Wich to the same.

Enclosing a Memorial in French from the Bishop of Lubec on the case of the Princess of Gottorp, and giving General Meyerfeld's account of the affairs of the King of Sweden.

It concludes: " For God's sake where is Lord Raby ? "

1709. Oct. 12th, N.S. Daniel Pulteney, Envoy at Copenhagen, to the same.

Enclosing an extract from his despatch of this date to M[r] Secretary Boyle informing him that the King of Denmark has fully resolved to attack Sweden. It concludes . . . " New difficulties seem to arise every day ; I am almost tempted to believe all will come to nothing at least for this Year."

1709. Oct. 29th. The States Rough Draft of the Barrier Treaty. [In French 11¼ pp. Together with] A Separate Article of the same Treaty. [2½ pp.]

1709. Oct. 30th. General Francis Palmes to Lord Townshend. From Turin. Giving the movements and winter quarters of the Imperial Troops.

1709. Nov. 1st, N.S. Stephen Poyntz to Thomas Ward. From the Hague.

. . . . . No talk of a Peace till Spring. The D. of Marlborough will be here on Sunday.

1709. Nov. 1st. A Memorial about appointing a Person to examine the Interests of the Protestant Churches. Enclosed in Mr. Boyle's letter of the date. 4 pp.

[No date.] Directions for Mr. Hales, a Special Commissioner to the Protestant Courts and States on behalf of the Oppressed Protestants. Unsigned, 4 pp.

1709. Nov. 15th, N.S. Stephen Poyntz to Thomas Ward. From the Hague.

. . . . Mr. Hor[ace] Townshend is not yet come, but expected daily.

1709. Nov. 27th. King of France's Answer to Mons[r] Petkum's proposals. In French, 1½ pp.

1709. Nov. 29th. John Wich to Lord Townshend.

The writer is forwarding a copy of his despatch, of the same date, to the Secretary of State, in which he mentions that the marriage of the Czar's son with the Princess of Wolffenbuttel is a good as concluded and that the Princess has set out for Dresden where the Czar's son is to wait on her. "It is stipulated among the Articles that his Czaarish Majestye is to purchase such Lands in Silesia, as may be a competent jointure hereafter in Case the Prince should dye, which some people think is little less then admitting the Muscovite into Germany."

Same date. Earl of Sunderland, Secretary of State, to John Chetwynd, Envoy Extraordinary at Turin.

This is a despatch enclosing Orders from the Lords of the Admiralty to the Mediterranean Fleet, which was never forwarded.

The seal on its cover bears the arms of Lord Sunderland, but his Signature is written by a Secretary.

His Lordship informs Mr Chetwynd that by Her Majesty's Command he is sending him Orders from the Lords Commissioners of Admiralty to the Mediterranean Fleet, to seize all Genoese ships unless the Genoese immediately cease exporting corn to France. It goes on : "The Dutch Envoy will receive the like from his Masters, and You in conjunction and concert with him are to acquaint the Republick of Genoa that You have such Orders, which You are comanded by Your respective Masters to send forthwith to their Admirals and Commanders in the Mediterranean, to putt a Stop to this carrying of Corn into France, and no fair words without the real doing of it will be accepted by the Queen and States, and if they should upon this new Representation putt a Stop to it for a while, & then begin it again, you are not to fail to send the Orders to the Fleet . . . . "

[P.S.] " Her Ma^{ty} thinks that when You and the Dutch Envoy notify this to the Republick of Genoa, it will have the greater effect if it be done in the most formal manner, & therefore Her Ma^{ty} would have You go with the Dutch Envoy Yourselves to Genoa rather than do it only by Letter."

The Admiralty Orders enclosed in the above despatch are signed by Lord Orford [Edward Russell], [Sir] George Byng, George Doddington, Paul Methuen, and J[osiah] Burchett [Secretary to the Board] ; They are addressed : " To Sr John Norris Kn^t, Adm^{ll} of the Blew Squadron of Her Majesty's Fleete, and Adm^l & Comander in chiefe of Her Ma^{tys} Ships in the Mediterranean ; Or to the chiefe Flag Officer, or Commander in chiefe of her Ma^{tys} Ships employed in the Mediterranean for the time being."

The Orders after reciting that the Genoese have for some time furnished France with corn, notwithstanding the representations of the Queen's Envoy at Genoa [William Chetwynd] go on :—

" You are therefore hereby required & directed, forthwith upon your receipt hereof, to give strict & effectual Orders to the respective Capt^s of her Majesty's Ships which are or shall be under your Command, to seize all Shipps belonging to the Republick of Genoa, in pursuance of Her Majesty's pleasure as aforesayd. For which this shall be Your Warrant : Given etc."

1709, Dec. 13th. Copy of a letter from the Ministers of the Reformed Religion assembled at Ratisbon, 23rd Nov. 1709. Enclosed in Mr. Boyle's letter of this date. In Latin, 3 pp.

1709, Dec. 14th. Copy of the Resolution of the States General upon the French King's answer to Petkum. In French, 9¼ pp.

[No date.] Etat du Rapport des Contributions, sauvegardes &c. de 16 de Mai 1703 jusque 15 de Mai 1709.

[No date.] Etat General de la Depense des Provinces Unies pour l'annee 1710.

[No date.] Enumeration of the troops of the United Provinces from the Peace of Ryswick to 1710. In French, 7½ pp.

Note. In the latter year the total force is stated as 142,185.

[No date.] A memorandum in French requesting Passports from Her Britannic Majesty for three vessels, lying at Amsterdam, which have been built for subjects of her Majesty, viz., the Amsterdam of 900 tons, Captain Samuel Adams ; the Devonshire of 700 tons, Capt. Richard Horswell ; and the Portsmouth of 700 tons, Capt. David Setter.

1709–1710. A bundle of " Papers relating to the King of Prussia's Pretensions at a Treaty of Peace."

1709–1710. Extracts from the Despatches of the Hon. Henry Boyle, Secretary of State, to the Duke of Marlborough and Lord Townshend, the British Plenipotentiaries at the Hague, from 5th April 1709 to 8th August 1710. In an official hand on folio sheets numbered I. to LIV. The sheets numbered II., and X. to XVI., are missing.

1709–1710. A bundle of rough drafts and fair copies of despatches from the Duke of Marlborough and Lord Townshend to Mr. Secretary Boyle, from 23rd July 1709 to 25th April 1710.

1709–1710. A memorandum of the official corresponence, between the Foreign Office and the British Plenipotentiaries, from 21st March 170⁹⁄₁₀ to 8th August 1710. 4 sheets.

1709–1710. Mr. Secretary Boyle's despatches to Lord Townshend, from 13th May 1709 to 30th August 1709; and from 4th April 1710 to 19th September 1710.

1709–1710. A bundle of letters and despatches from Daniel Pulteney, Envoy at Copenhagen, to Lord Townshend and Horatio Walpole, from 19th November 1709 to 16th September 1710.

1710, Jan. 7th, N.S. Stephen Poyntz to Thomas Ward   From the Hague.

. . . . " There is no likelyhood of a Peace this winter, however the Gardiner may sow what he thinks fitt, since it will be better to have the garden stocked tho' my L^d should not come, than to run the hazard of finding it empty.

The family continues well God be praised."

1710, Jan. 29th, N.S.   John Chetwynd to Lord Townshend.   From Turin.

. . . . . " I observe with pleasure the good dispositions of the States-Genll to have every thing ready to open the Campain early. I wish I could send your Ex^cy the like good news from hence, instead of telling you that his R. H. hath his differences with the Impu Court so much at heart, that he openly prefers their adjustement to any other view. Mr Palmes is gon from hence very well instructed with his R. H.^s reasons and he is so sensible of the necessity of satisfying this Prince, that I am perswaded he will leave no stone unturned to compass so great a worck. On the other hand, the resolution of the States Gen^ll after the Conference wth y^r Ex^cy, C^t Zinzendorf, &c., joined to the orders wch the Queen will probably give on the same head, will, I hope, have a good effect at Vienna, as that we shall see them disposed to make an end of this difference."

1710, Feb. 7th.   John Wich to the same.   From Hamburgh.

. . . "a title once in a family is hereditarye to the Children, therefore the son of Sr Peter Wich is call'd Chevalier.

MARQUESS
TOWNSHEND
MSS.

. . . . I am afraid the Elector of Hannover will hardly be persuaded to make the next campagne. I hear My Lord Staires could gett no positive Answer from his Highness " . . . .

1710, Feb. $\frac{9th}{20th}$. Extract from a letter of Charles Whitworth to Secretary Boyle. From Moscow. In French, 1½ pp.

1710, Feb. 10th. General Palmes to Lord Townshend. From Vienna.
. . . . " I fear 'tis not the intention of this Court to execute the treaty without being very much pushed to it by the Queen and the States " . . . .

Same date, N.S. James Cockburn to the same. From Turin.
. . . . . " all the letters from France assure that we have accepted the last offers & that two Deputies are gon from the Hague to meet the Mar[sh]all D'Uxelles & the Abbé de Polignac at Moredike, but we do defer our belief of this news till we have it confirmed from the Hague.

1710, Feb. 11th. Stephen Poyntz to Thomas Ward. From the Hague.
. . . . . " Something relating to the Peace has been in Agitation lately, but the French King not being yet brought to reason, 'tis gone off again except he thinks fitt to renew the Negotiation by accepting of the terms proposed in the Preliminary Treaty ; wch pehaps he may still do before the opening of the Campn . . . . . .
. . . . . Mr. Townshd is like to stay here all the Winter. The Pears &c. are come but all rotten."

1710, Feb. 13th. Monsr Petkum's letter to the Marquis de Torcy. In French. 1¼ pp.

1710, Feb. 28th. Stephen Poyntz to Thomas Ward. From the Hague.
. . . . . " The French Ministers are expected somewhere near Breda by the 5th or 8th of next month, in order to try if an Exped[ien]t can be found out for qualifying the 37th Article of the Preliminarys, the French King having consented to all the rest. But whether these Conferences will introduce the General Treaty or not is as yet very uncertain, tho' I believe it is thought by most here that when once the Fr[ench] Ministers are come they will hardly go back again without making the Peace. If so I hope we may be able to see Norfolk some time this Summer, or at least to return to London by the beginning of Winter."
" His Excy has sent over for the two little Masters from Mrs Windham's.
I desire the favour of you to present my humble service to Mr Prestland, and to lett him know that our friend Dr. Hare is married. I wish the good examples of this kind wch our College have sett might influence him to do the same. Mr Horace Walpole is expected here soon, by whose coming I shall be eased from that weight of business wch I have had upon me for some time, and shall oftener find myself at liberty to write both to him and you. The whole family enjoy their health rather better here than in England."

Same date. John Wich to Lord Townshend.
The writer encloses a Memorial (in French) from the Minister of Holstein in Hamburgh, and an " Extract of the Right Honourable

M[r] Secretary Boyl's Letter. Whitehall Feb[y] 17$\frac{09}{10}$" directing him to
follow instructions received from Lord Townshend without waiting to
receive particular directions from Whitehall.

1710, March 3rd. Copy of Instructions to M[r] Envoy Palmquist.
Dated at Stockholm, 6½ pp.

1710, March 7th.   John Wich to Lord Townshend.
Enclosing a memorial from Baron Goertz and a copy of a letter to
M[r] Secretary Boyle.

1710, March 14th.   The same to Horatio Walpole.
. . . " I'le answer Y[rs], Dear Sir, next Post, in the mean time I recommend you to Madamoselle Czarenburg's whale bone Petticot. The Danes
are beaten. Make Peace and Peace hereafter. Our Northern Bullys
begin to cock their Crests. The King of Sweden has at last wrote
himself to the Government of Stat Pomern and Stockholm. When he
heard the Danes had invaded him, He laught and said, My Subjects
know how to defend themselves. The Cloud is gathering."

1710, March 27th.   John Laws to the same. From Brussels.
"I beg leave to congratulate your coming on this side, and to renew
my correspondence . . . . .
. . . . . The Marechal de Villars is daily expected at the French
Camp near Cambray. Some Letters say he is arriv'd there. The
Maison du Roy is in march towards the frontier having receiv'd orders
to leave Paris without being pass'd in review by the King upon the
news [of] the precipitate Success of the Allies."

1710, March 29th.   The Earl of Stair to Lord Townshend. Dated
at "Warshaw" and unaddressed.
My Lord,—I have little to trouble y[r] Excellency wth at this time,
having upon the 27 given a full account to my Lord Duke of Marlborough of the situation of things in this country. The King obliges
himself not to invade Pomerania nor to march his troops through
the Empire, upon condition that the Swedes doe not march out of
Pomerania, nor reinforce their corps that is there, w[ch] his Majesty
conceives can be done wth no other view than that of invading the
Empire or returning into Poland. I dont at all question but there will
be care taken that the Sweedes in Pomerania dont move, for if they
should it will be impossible to prevent all Germany's being in a flame,
and I conceive it to be of very great importance that exact measures be
taken that the corps in Pomeraina be not reinforced, for when the
Campagne is once begun and the Muscovites employ'd in the siege of
Rog[n], if the King of Sweeden returns and puts himself at the head of
his troops in Pomerania w[ch] it will not be a hard matter to reinforce w[th]
8000 or 10000 foot if the war in Schonen is at an end, I say I doe not
see w[t] hinders him to march into the heart of the Empire he understands the secret of getting money there, and when he has that men
wont be wanting. I believe w[t] he did formerly will not be a very
sufficient pledge of his moderation at this time & in no other place
but Pomerania he can pretend to have an army capable to act, in
Pomerania there is actually remaining a body of five thousand horse.
The Danish Minister here makes strong instances for the march of
the Succours or the invasion of Pomerania, the king seems to think the
case is not yet arrived in w[ch] he is obliged to furnish the Succours the
Danes not being attackt but he promises to invade Pomerania the
minute the Sweedes moves towards Holsteyn. Orders are given to

make magazines upon the frontier, an express from [the] Empress
is sent to the Czar at Petersbourg.

My Lord I must beg y^r Excellency will be pleased to speak a word
to Monsr de Starembourg who is president of the committee de Raaden,
the Pensionary must be spoke too because it must pass in the States of
the Province, to obtain a prolongation of Leave for Capt. Kennedy who
is along wth mee, he is Capt. in Brigadier Douglas his Regiment. I have
wrote to Monsr de Wissenbourg wch I take the liberty to send under y^r
Lo^{ps} cover. I am wth very great respect and Esteam my Lord,

y^r Excellency's
most obedient
humble Servant

STAIR.

1710, April 1st, N.S. Stephen Poyntz to Thomas Ward. From the
Hague.

...... " The French Ministers continue still at Gertruydenberg,
and the last Courier they sent to Versailles is now returned, but what he
has brought is not yet made publick. Their design seems to be to amuse
and disunite the Allys, and to retard the preparations for the Campain,
and they have made no new proposals except some relating to a Partition
wch are not likely to be accepted ; so that I believe we must give them
another blow before they will hear reason. Prince Eugene is expected
here the 3rd & the D. of Marlborough setts out for Flanders the 12th.
The Magazins are all ready and the Army very well cloathed & re-
cruited, while that of the Enemy is in extreme Want, insomuch that in
sev^l places their Leathern Shoes were taken from them in the winter
and locked up till the opening of the Campⁿ, & wooden Shoes given
them in the mean time ; and every post we hear of their plundering
Bakers' shops &c^a.

I hope there have been no disturbances in Norfolk on acc^t of D^r
Sachev[ere]l's Tryal ......

[P.S.] The 2 little Masters are arrived in good health."

1710, April 4th. William Penn to Lord Townshend.

Dated " 4. 2^{mth} (Ap.) 1710 " and unaddressed. Endorsed " April
ye 4.—Rec^d Aprill 22 N.S. 1710."

" My Noble Friend,
There being Fifty or Sixty Swissers, called Menonists comeing
for Holland in order to goe for PennSylvania, It is feard the States of
Holland will stop them being well to pass for as much as one Mitchell,
their Agent has contracted wth m[e] for them, for lands &c. : I humbly
beg that If the States should stop them, It would please thee, as for the
Queen's Interest & Service, It may be taken off or prevented, & thou
wilt much oblige

Thy very re-
spectf^{ll} Friend

WM. PENN.

Menonists or Menist[s] are Annabaptists here."

1710, April —. Etats de Fourages necessaires pour pouvoir former
une Armée aux environs de Tournay et de Lille Vers le 15me ou 20me
d'Avril 1710. 4 pp.

1710, April 16th. John Chetwynd to Horatio Walpole. From
Turin.

Details the movements of some of the French and Imperial Troops,
and states that H.M.'s Ships Dartmouth, Gosport and Ludlow Castle

MARQUESS
TOWNSHEND
MSS.

arrived at Genoa the previous week having left Sir John Norris with
his Squadron at Port Mahon.

1710, April 23rd.   John Cockburn to the same.   From Turin.

. . . . "By our last letters from Genoa we are informed that a Genoese
ship was arrived there from Cadix having on board 500ᵐ p[iece]s of
eight of the money lately come by the Flotille, wᶜʰ the Genoese Captain
assures [us] to be richer than any arrived for some time.

. . . . The Earle of Rochford went from this on Munday last for
Genoa to wait Mʳ Stanhope's arrivall there " . . . .

1710, April 25th, N.S.   Stephen Poyntz to Thomas Ward.   From
the Hague.

. . . . . . "I suppose you will have recᵈ before this can reach you the
joyful news of the Duke of Marlborough's and Prince Eugene's having
passed the French Lines in two different places without opposition,
upon which fortunate opening of this early Campain I congratulate you
the more heartily because if the future successes are but answerable to
this beginning I shall hope to see you next Spring in Norfolk.   It is
thought the Army will immediately lay siege to Douay, and though I
know we are often too hasty in computing the time that a Town can
hold out, yet it is confidently reported here that it cannot defend it self
above 10 days or a fortnight, that I could not but let you know it.

His Exᶜʸ is extremely glad to hear that there have been no rebellious
riots within his Lieutenancy upon the account of the late Tryal; which
good disposition I hope will extend it self so far as to keep all parts of
Norfolk from attempting to imitate the Gloucestershire address, and to
disturb the peace of Her Maᵗʳˢ happy reign by unseasonable professions
of duty and Loyalty.   Which humour is so like that of the times of the
late Rebellion that every good subject ought to check it for fear of the
consequences . . . . . .

1710, May 3rd.   John Chetwynd to Lord Townshend.   From Turin.
Enclosing a Despatch for Lord Sunderland under a flying seal.

1710, May $\frac{5th}{16th}$.   Copy of a letter from Mʳ Rosencrantz to Mʳ
Secretary Boyle about renewing the Treaty of Alliance with Denmark
In French.   2 pp.

1710, May 6th.   Lord Drummond to Horatio Walpole.   From
Amsterdam.

Is sending 51 flasks of Claret to Lord Townshend.   There is a
rumour that the Duke has arrived with a Peace signed in his pocket.

1710, May 10th.   Monsieur de Quesne to the same.   In French.
Dated at Geneva.

The envoy Stanian has received no orders, and there does not seem
to be any one charged with the commission entrusted to the Marquis
d'Arzeliers . . . .   We hear that the French are in consternation through
fear lest they fail to secure a peace.   The flight of the Duke d'Ossuna
and the imprisonment of the Duke de Medina Celi make one believe
that there is some disorder at the Court of Madrid.   God grant that
profit may be made of circumstances favourable to the [Protestant].
Religion.

1710, May $\frac{7th}{18th}$.   Charles Whitworth to the Duke of Marlborough.
From Stolpe in Pomerania.   Copy.

Stating the views of the Czar as to his joining the Grand Alliance.

Same date. The same to Lord Townshend. From Stolpe. Enclosing the last.

. . . . " I have had hitherto the most fatiguing Voyage imaginable which has not a little impaired my health, however I shall make what diligence I can to the Hague " . . . .

1710, May $\frac{18\text{th}}{24\text{th}}$. The same to the same. From Berlin.

Enclosing two letters from the Swedish Secretary Mons* Caderhielm who was taken prisoner with Count Piper. . . . " I suppose the formal siege of Riga will now be begun very suddenly, according to the resolution taken before the Czar and his Court left Mosco[w] but I don't hear that any of the Saxon Troops will be employed in that expedition; on which occasion I am obliged to acquaint you that the Czar has no manner of Confidence in King Augustus, & will not give his Majesty or the Polish Troops any footing in Riga during this war " . . . .

1710, May 15th. John Laws to Horatio Walpole. From Brussels.

. . . . " Letters from Madrid of the 28th confirm the close Emprisonment of the Duke of Medina Celi but we have yet here no certain advices of the reason of it.

. . . . I see you have sent back the French Ministers, unless this last Courrier brings something new to stopp them. I suppose you hear the Duke of Burgundy [is] grown very clamorous at their coming back, and at the successes of the Allies."

1710, May 16th. Monsieur Clignet to Lord. Townshend. In French. From Leyden.

If the slightest change is made in the preliminaries the French ought to be made to surrender Upper Alsace and Strasbourg together with the fortresses in their present state . . . . and they should give security for their debts and plunder and the money they took by force from the good families of Strasbourg.

1710, May 19th. Anthony Corbiere to Horatio Walpole. In French. From London.

The writer thought that the affairs of Capt Caries would have been finished before he wrote but will not delay sending his grateful compliment.

1710, May 21st. John Chetwynd to the same. From Turin.

" Marshall Dawn arrived here last Saturday from Vienna & went to wait on his R. H. [the Duke of Savoy] to . . . . concert the necessary dispositions for assembling our Army . . . & its hoped before the end of next month, that they will be all encamped at the foot of the mountains . . . .

M* Stanhope sailed the 16th inst from Finall with three of the Queens ships of war for Barcelona . . . . tho' M* Stanhope designed when I left him to stay at Genoa till such time as the 3000 Germans, with the rest of the recruits designed for Catalonia, had been ready to embark wch will be about the beginning of next month, he hath however carried along with him all the recruits wch were ready at Finali, and a considerable Sum of money." . . .

" His R. H. received a courier the other day from the Hague with letters of the 10th inst by which we find that you have sent the French Ministers about their business."

Same date. " Copy of M* Pultney's Memorial to the Danish Ministers " in relation to the instructions given by that Court to its Privateers. In French. 1½ pp.

U 24953. E

1710, May 26th. "Extract of Mr Secretary Boyle's letter of the 26th May 1710, O.S.," to Lord Townshend.

"I send your Excellency by Her Majesty's order a great bundle of papers concerning two Spanish ships that had Her Majesty's passes to go from Passage in Biscay to Buenos Ayres in America, and return from thence to any Port in Spain. The said Ships sailed from Cadiz the 25th of March last under protection of the said passes and were the next day mett by three Dutch ships of warr, which carried them as prize into Lisbon, and when they are brought to Holland the captors will endeavour to have them condemned. Your Ex^cy has all the materials in the enclosed papers to support those passes which you can be furnished with from hence ; and you will be pleased to inform the pensionary with what is most effectual in them to exempt this capture from being adjudged lawful prize. But before you make any representation to the States in this matter in Her Maties name Her Ma^ty would be willing to learn what his thoughts are of those passes, and what success she is like to meet with in maintaining the validity of them."

—, 1710. A bundle of papers relating to the above-mentioned Spanish ships.

1710, May 28th.   John Chetwynd to Horatio Walpole.   From Turin.

"Thursday last we received advice by an express from Genoa of Sir John Norris being arrived at Vado with the fleet under his command " . . . .

1710, June 3rd.   Copy of a Memorandum signed by Lord Townshend at the Hague.

"Monsieur le Baron de Schmettau Plenipotentiaire de Sa Ma^te le Roy de Prusse ayant declaré au nom de sadite Mat^e au sujet du renouvellement de la convention regardant le corps de troupes de Sa dite Ma^te faisant en Italie qu'en attendant que Sa Ma^te Imperiale, Sa Ma^te la Reine de la Grande Bretagne, et leurs Hautes Puissances Messrs les Etats G[e]n[er]aux des Provinces Unis puissent adjouster et convenir des conditions dudit renouvellement, ledit Roy son maitre est content que ledit corps en Italie continue de rendre les mêmes services qu'il a rendus les campagnes precedentes sur le pied de la derniere convention du 31e de Mars 1709 pourvû que le dit corps tant de la part de S. M. I^le et de S. M. B^r que de L^s. H^s. P^a soit traité sur le pied de la dite convention aussi bien à l'egard du payement exact des subsides que du fournissement des autres douçeurs y stipulées ;

"Sa Majesté la Reine de la Grande Bretagne ayant appris avec plaisir la resolution prise par S. Majesté Prussienne pour qu'en attendant que l'on s'explique sur le projet presenté au nom de Sa dite Majesté son dit corps de troupes continue sur le pied des années precedentes, et concoure à agir pour le bien de la cause commune, a autorisé le sousigné Ambassadeur Extraordinarie et Plenipotentiaire de Sa Majesté de declarer au nom de Sa Majesté Britannique qu'en attendant qu'on se puisse expliquer sur le projet susdit elle veut bien continuer la dernière convention regardant ce corps de troupes Prussiennes et Italie faite le 31e de Mars 1709, tant à l'egard du payement de sa part des subsides que des autres points y contenus.

                    " Signé   TOWNSHEND."

Same date.   Dr Henry Newton to Lord Townshend. Dated Rome May 31st and Florence June 3rd.

". . . They are here much dissatisfied with the carriage of the Court of France, their Courrier having returned from thence without any

satisfactory answer for the restoring the Dutch marchant man which
was lately taken by Monsr L'aigle a French privateer under the guns
of one of the G. Duke's [the Grand Duke of Tuscany] forts at Leghorn
and afterwards carryed by him to Toulon . . . . the ship being to the
value of about 150,000 peices of eight . . . . ."

1710, June 4th. John Chetwynd to Horatio Walpole. From Turin.
"Upon Sr John Norris arrival at Vado I sent an express to Marshall
Dawn to hasten the march of the two Imperiall regiments designed for
Catalonia with the remainder of the recruits for the German and Italian
troops in Spain . . . . .

"The Earle of Rochford's Regiment of Dragoons which are to em-
barck at the same time, are on their march to the sea side and being to
pass thro part of the Duke of Savoy's country, I sollicited his R : H :
for a march route with orders for the necessary furrage, carriages &c:
which his R : H : was pleased not only to grant me but also [to] send
orders to all the places through which they are to pass belonging to
his State to furnish them with forrage, oats and carriages gratis . . . ."

1710, June 7th. Daniel Pulteney to Lord Townshend. From
Copenhagen.
Enclosing a copy of a despatch to Mr Secretary Boyle and pointing
out the difference between the writer's instructions and those of the
Dutch envoy.

1710, June 11th. James Cockburn to Horatio Walpole. From
Turin.
" . . . By an express which we received yesterday from Vado we
have advice that they had begun to embark the troops designed for
Spain, and that it was hoped all would be on board and the fleet ready
to saill by the 14th Ins^t . . . ."

1710, June 14th. James Pelham to the same. Dated " At the Camp
before Douay."
Begging Mr Walpole to secure Lord Townshend's influence in procuring the writer the vacant troop in Lieut. Genl Rosse's Regiment.

1710, June 15th. The same to the same. Dated : "before Douay."
Recapitulating what the writer wrote the day before in case the former
letter should be lost.

1710, June 16th. James Taylor to the same. Dated at Whitehall.
" I am desired to put the enclosed letter under your cover for the
Lord Lonsdale and am very sorry to tell you by this post that on
Wednesday last the Earl of Sunderland delivered up his Seals and the
Lord Dartmouth succeeds him which was a surprise upon every body.
This had liked to' have had such a blow upon credit that yesterday
some of the Dons of the City and Bank were to wait on her Majesty.
I do not yet find if we are to have a new Parliament or not ; that doubt
once cleared for the negative people's minds will be pretty well satisfyd.
I must tell you that the discourses of the changes has so filled our
ears that we talk no more of peace or the taking of Doway or any thing
else relating to the warr. Your brother my very good Master is very
well recovered from his late sudden illness call'd Collero Morbus which
put all about him under dreadfull apprehensions for 4 hours. I hope
effectual methods will be taken to prevent the like for the future. I
thank God he is brave and well, and may be long continue so is my daily
prayer. I am ever etc."

Same date. Sir William Hodges to the same. Dated in London.
About two Spanish ships which had been taken by the Dutch.

Same date. James Craggs to the same. Dated at the Camp at Portella. The writer, who says it is his first opportunity of writing since he arrived in Spain, begs Mr Walpole, if he has not received some money for him, to be so kind as to forward enclosed bills to Cardonnel the first time he writes to him.

1710, June 17th. A project for the passage of English letters through Denmark to Sweden. Undated but enclosed in Mr Pulteney's letter to Lord Townshend of this date. In French. 1½ pp.

1710, June 18th. John Chetwynd to Horatio Walpole. From Turin. "By our last letters from Genoa we have advice that Sir John Norris sailed the 12th inst from Vado, with the two German regiments and other recruits . . .

"Last Sunday Mar[sh]all Dawn arrived here from Milan. All the German troops which are to compose our army here are arrived at their respective quarters, but the march of the Prussian troops has been countermanded upon some new difficulties the Imperiall Comissariat has raised, about the payment of what is due to these troops.

". . . . . I have said all I can think of to perswade his R. H. [the Duke of Savoy] to take the field and convince him of the unreasonableness in making his best friends suffer as he doth for his ill humour ag^t the Imp^ll Court, but all I can say is not of weight enough to make him change . . . ."

1710, June 22nd, N.S. James Craggs to the same. Dated at the Camp at Portella.
The writer acknowledges the receipt of Mr Walpole's letter of May 6th and thanks him for recovering his desperate debts. " Our Master [the Duke of Marlborough] is very well. I hope if we send you no great news this Campaign we may at least assure you, you will not hear of any great misfortune befallen us." . . . .
The following postscript is dated " Barcelona the 26th June 1710."
" Dear Horace, Since I writ this letter it has been judged necessary for me to come here to concert the operations of the Fleet with Admiral Norris. I have met yours of the 23rd of May and returne you my hearty thanks for the measures you have taken about my mouey. I have nothing to add but that since I have learn't we are come to our old Camp at Balaguer I will tell you in private that we shall doe nothing this Campaign and that our fine hopes are entirely vanished, 'tis what I desire you to acquaint my Lord Townshend with and believe me entirely y^r.

"J. C."

Same date. John Laws to the same. From Ghent.
". . . . . . All letters from the Camp agree that Douay is agonizing . . . . . Tis probable the return of the Dutch Deputies from Tournay will bring Mr Cadogan hither with them . . . . ."

1710, June 26th. Lieutenant General Charles Rosse to Lord Townshend. Dated at the Camp near Douay. Explaining that the vacant troop that Mr Pelham had desired to obtain had been given by the Duke of Marlborough to the writer's nephew Mr Rosse.

1710, June 27th. Copy of Mr Pultney's letter to Mr Schlestadt, with reference to forwarding of English letters to Sweden. Enclosed in the writer's letter of the same date to Mr Walpole. In French. 2¼ pp.

1710, June 28th. Mr Pultney's Reflections upon the Danish Declaration about allowing the passage of English letters to and from Stockholm. Enclosed in Mr Pulteney's letter of the same date to Secretary Boyle. 2½ pp.

MARQUESS
TOWNSHEND
MSS.

1710, June 30. Sir William Hodges to Horatio Walpole.

The writer is grateful to Lord Townshend for so heartily espousing the unfortunate case of the two Spanish ships and their cargoes and humbly prays the continuance of his favours and protection.

1710, July 1st. James Pelham to the same. Dated "before Douay."

The writer after having explained that he would not have troubled Lord Townshend in the matter of the troop without Mr Cardonell's direction, writes : "You know we are in possession of the town and fort, I don't hear what is to be done next, 'tis thought our regiment will be sent to garrison being very much shatterd at the siege. I intend to stay in the field as a volunteer the remaining part of the campaigne . . . . I beg the favour of you when you write to Spain to forward the inclosed to my Coz. Mountagu."

1710, July 5th. John Chetwynd to Lord Townshend. From Turin.

". . . . his R. H. [Prince Eugene] having been ill for these ten dayes, I have not had the honour to see him . . . . so that the Dutch Envoy or I have not been able to renew our sollicitations for his takeing the field, on which head I have so oftnen alledged all the reasons I could think of, to so little purpose that I quite dispair of meeting with the least Success till the Court of Vienna shew more inclination to do him justice . . . . . his R. H.'s distemper which was thought a malignant feavour hath prooved the meazles, which have been of so ill a sort, that he will not be able to stir out of his chamber these 8 or ten dayes yet . . . ."

1710, July 8th. Copy of a letter in French from Messrs. Buys and Vander Dussen to Marshal D'Uxelles and the Abbé Polignac. Dated at the Hague, and minuted "Received in Lord Townshend's letter to Mr Boyle of the 8th July 1710 N.S." ¾ p.

1710, July 9th. Copy of a letter in French from Marshal D'Uxelles and the Abbé Polignac to Messieurs Buys and Vander Dussen, in reply to the last. Dated at Gertrudenberg, and minuted "Received in Lord Townshend's letter to Mr. Boyle of the 11th July 1710 N.S." 1½ pp.

1710, July 12th. John Chetwynd to Horatio Walpole. From Turin.

". . . . . . All our Royall familly expect [except] his R. H. are well again ; he is much better, but so weak that his phisitians do not think it adviseable for him to see company or meddle with any business, so our visits have been very short, without any conversation for above this fortnight.

"Mar[sh]all Dawn left this place yesterday to put himself at the head of our army and I propose to follow him in a day or two . . . ."

1710, July 18. Christian Cole to the same. From Venice.

"This letter will be given you by my Lady Richelieu, Dutches of Aguillon. I begg, and conjure you to give her all the assistance she may desire of you. I have a very great and just esteem for this lady, and doe assure you she does not deserve the anger of the nation. I begg you would recommend her affaires to my Lord Townshend, and I shall ever be, etc."

1710, July 20th. John Chetwynd to the same. From the "Camp at la maison de meane—in sight of Arches." Received August 7th.

Describing the operations of the allied forces. Marshall Dawn "declares that he will give them no quarter, however I do not believe we shall be so cruell, or that they will yield their post till our cannon obliges them, though it seems something strange that so small a body should stop our army."

1710, July 25. The same to the same. From Arches in Spain. Received August 13th.

Describing the capture of Arches, etc.

". . . . If we should not succeed I do not know which way we may steer our course, neither shall I dare to hope for any great advantage dureing the rest of our Campain, seeing the enemies will be in a better condition every day then other to oppose us, now that they see our whole force in these valleys. A good peace would be agreable news here, that we might bid adieu to the terrible mountains which we are forced to climb every day like so many goats . . . ."

1710, July 25th, N.S. Stephen Poyntz to Thomas Ward. From the Hague.

". . . . I have no news to send you but that the peace is at a stand at present. The late change and the divisions in England having encouraged the French to talk very high, which has made the Allies resolve not to send their Deputies any more till they come to more reasonable terms. We have some hopes given us that the Parliament will not be dissolv'd which perhaps may humble them again."

1710, July 30th. Lord Stair to Lo   Townshend. Dated at the "Camp at Vilers Brulin," and addre   to "My Lord Ambassadour Townshend." 7¼ pp.

The writer details his views as to the affairs of Poland and the North and begs to be informed of what is doing at the Hague. He mentions his secretary Mr Mackenzie and General Count Fleming prime minister of the King of Poland, ... "the takeing of Wybourg and the falling of Riga into the Czar's hands which in all probability has happen'd already, or must happen very soon, will diminish the apprehensions the K. of Poland has of the K. of Sweeden's return, but at the same time will be a reason to the allys to give the Princes concerned in the northern war against Sweeden no ground of offence, which may serve them for a pretext for entering into measures to our disadvantage, to recall their troops or to ask greater conditions. If the war should continue I believe it would be no hard matter to prevail with the Czar to lett the Allys have ten thousand foot for their bread and their forrage . . . . ."

[P.S. Dated August 4th.] "My Lord, I give you a thousand thanks for your obtaining another forloff for Captain Kennedy.

"Everything in the Army goes as wee could wish, so that I think there is a morall certainty of procuring very soon a solid and a lasting peace, if we continue the way wee are in; which I hope is sufficient to prevent any changes which may discourage our friends and incourage our ennemys.

Your Lordship will see by the date that what is above was writt before the French made their last movement: which is certainly a disadvantage to us. My opinion is that the strength of the argument taken from the ill prospect of our affairs lyes for venturing whilst wee have so good an Army rather than against it. I wish we mayn't have occasion to repent our letting the French nestle where they are now intrenched.

"Since that time wee have likewise the certain account of Rega's being taken, that will make the Princes of the North more ticklish, and will make it more necessary to give them no offence especially the Czar with whom I think it absolutely necessary wee should have a Minister. I wonder the States doe not suit Monsieur de Crauenburgh. I am etc."

No date. A resumé of the Conferences at Gertrudenberg (being extracts from the British Ambassadors' letter to Mr. Secretary Boyle) from 12th March 1710 to 25th July 1710. 30 pp.

[1710, Augt..] A few concluding lines of a letter from General James Stanhope relating to the battle of Almenara. The postscript is as follows:—

" List of English Officers killed and wounded at Almanira the 27th July 1710 N.S.
"Killed Lord Rochford [and] Count Nassau, Brigadiers Lt Col. Trevor, Captn La Porie, Cornet Carson, Cornet Webb.
" Wounded Lt Col. Bland, Lt Col. Montgomery (Aide de Camp to Genl Stanhope) Capts Ravanel, Wills, Moor, Naison, Lts Neville, Paterson, Jobber, Nieron, Wood, Cornets Wildgoose, Du Casse, Quarter Master Smith."

1710, Augt. 3rd. John Chetwynd to Horatio Walpole. From Foglioso. "Received August 20th."
Describing the further operations of the Allies in Italy, etc It concludes :—
" Sir John Norris being gon with a small body of troops to make a descent upon the coast of Languedoc to favour and succour the Cevennois I hope we shall soon receive some good news from him and that this expedition will cause a considerable diversion in our favour."

Same date. James Cockburn to the same. From Foglioso.
Enclosing, by the Envoy's [Mr Chetwynd's] orders, an extract from a letter in French cautioning the latter against a certain Monsieur Dupuis, a Burgundian, who has long intrigued at the Hague in the interests of France.

1710, Augt. 10th. John Chetwynd to the same. From Turin.
". . . . Our friend Mr Stanhope hath had a considerable advantage over a body of the Enemies horse near to Lerida, of which I have as yet received no other particulars then that of our haveing got the better, with the loss of Count Nassau and Lord Rochford who were cut in pieces.
" I am to acknowledge the receipt of your letters of the 22 and 25th inst by which I find that your negotiations for peace are very near being interrupted, if not allready broke off."

[1710], Aug. 10th. Copie d'une lettre de Monsieur le Marq[ui]s de Torcy ce 10me d'Aoust." Unaddressed.
" J'ai receu Monsieur les lettres que vous avez pris la peine de m'ecrire le 24 et le 31 Juillet. Lorsque les Conferences, ont commencé les affaires d'Angleterre se brouilloient déjà, et celles du Nord n'etoient pas moins agitées qu'elles le sont aujourdhuy puis que les Danois avoient une armée dans la province de Schone. Ces considerations n'ont pas empeché le Roy d'envoyer Messieur les Plenip[otentiaire]s à Gertruyd[enber]g et de faire par eux des offres plus amples que sa Ma[jes]té ne les avoit jamais faites. Il ne faut pas donc dire que l'esperance des nouveaux évènements que ces divisions pouvent produire ayant obligé la France à s'éloigner la paix. La reponse dont vous avez été le porteur et que Messieurs les Deputés ont confirmée dans la dernière Conference n'a fait voir que trop clairem[en]t à qui la rupture en devoit être attribuée. Vous savés de quelle manière j'ay toujours pensé sur la droiture et sur les bonnes intentions de Monsieur le Pensionaire, mais en verité je me trouve bien seul presentem[en]t dans mon opinion ; et comme je n'en ay pas encore changé, je comprens plus que personne, combien il doit être sensible à la rupture de la Negotiation.
" On donne plusieurs autres causes au chagrin de M. le Duc de Marlborough et à son inquietude, mais il n'est guère vraysemblable que les Anglois osent et qu'ils puissent se passer de luy tant que la guerre durera.

" Quant a Mi Lord Townshend si l'on croit les avis de l'Angleterre il sera incessamment rappellé, et je croy que la perte du poste qu'il occupoit luy sera sensible principalement s'il retourne en Angleterre dans un temps ou le parti de Thorris[Tories]aura la superiorité. Monsieur le Comte de Sinz[endorf] n'aura pas été faché de retourner à Vienne à l'exercise de sa charge, et l'Hollande à s'épuiser encore pour soutenir la querelle de l'Emp[ereu]r et qu'il s'est conduit en Ministre habile, et que ce n'est pas peu que d'avoir obligé deux Nations eclairées à demander opiniatrement une condition qui rendit la paix impossible. Quoy qu'il ne soit plus question de negotiation, vous me ferez plaizir de continuer la correspondance avec moy et de croire que je suis très veritablem[en]t entièrement à vous."

1710, Augt. 17th. James Craggs to Horatio Walpole. From Genoa. Enclosing an account of the battle of Almenara and a list of British cavalry officers killed and wounded in that engagement.

1st enclosure [3¼ pp.]. An account of the battle dated " From the Camp at Almenara the 31th of July 1710." It concludes as follows :—
" Our great loss and such a one as is regretted by the whole army is the want of Lord Rochfort and Count Nassaw who both dyed upon the spott, the killed & wounded on our side are not above 400 men the half of which are English . . . . . the account we have of the loss of the enemy is . . . . . 300 men prisoners, and killed and wounded they have about 1500. Mr Stanhope [General James Stanhope who was in command of the British Cavalry] received a contusion by a dead ball and Genl Carpenter has a slight cutt. Tho' the night preventing us from reaping a greater advantage from this overthrow it is no small benefitt wee have gott that wee are undeceived in the opinion of their horse, which hitherto has kept us in great awe, but since 16 squadrons have been sufficient to beat 42, wee may reasonably hope to deal with them at any time . . . . . The sixteen squadrons that did engage were six English vizt 2 of Harvey's 2 of Nassaw's 2 Rochfort, 4 Dutch and 6 Palatines and the Generals with Mr Stanhope were Lieutenant General Carpenter, Major General Trancherberg of the Palatines, and Major General Pepper."

2nd enclosure. " A list of officers and men killed or wounded in the Brittish Brigade of Horse July 17th O : S : 1710."

1710, Augt. 19th. The same to the same. From Turin.
" . . . . I cannot tell you the Mar[sh]all's reasons for marching thro' the plains of Piedmont . . . . I cannot help looking upon our Campain as ended. I heartily wish I may be mistaken . . . . "

1710, Augt. 29th. Sir William Hodges " To Horasio Walpole Esqre—Secretary to the Embassy of Her Majesty of Great Britain &c.—at the Hague."

" Sir—I have not very lately troubled you with any of my lines, nor should not have done it now, but to thank you again for the continuance of your favour and good offices, which the Spaniards there and all the concerned in the two unfortunate B[uenos] A[yres] ships are very sencible of. Also of my Lord Ambassador's endeavours for some good success in that unfortunate affaire. My honoured friend your brother was pleased some dayes since to promise me to mention me in his letter to you. One of the two Spaniards which remained here is gone over with Mr Secretary Boyle's pass, and will waite on you with the others already there. Pray favour me to give my humble duty to his Excy and believe me to be etc."

NOTE.—From later papers it appears that the States General carried Resolutions on the 15th, and 21st, of November, 1710, directing the

College of the Admiralty of Amsterdam to suspend their proceedings for the condemnation of the two Spanish ships until further orders.

1710, Augt. 30th. Alexander Cunningham to the same. Dated at Berlin and addressed "A Monsieur Monsieur Horace Walpoole Secritaire del Ambassade, Chez My Lord Tounsend à la Hay, Holland.

" . . . . I return you thanks particularlie for the letters you sent me by Mr. Chittey which I received. We intend to leave this place in two days and are to goe into Italie by the way of Tirol, if there come to your hands any letters for my Lord Lonsdale or me, please to direct them for me at Samuel Williams' house at Venice, for we shall not make a long stay at any place now till we come to Padua.

" Yesterday we had the news of my Lord Tr[easure]r's breaking his staff, and that his place is put in Comissiou. Why my Lord L[onsdale] should be concerned for it I know not, I wish it may be for the publick good and to you much joy of your new Masters. . . . . . . Yesterday the K. was taken ill at table, but was perfectlie well in half an hour. The Prince Royal is a keen Whig and cals the Torys rogues etc., but perhaps a short time will make him change his thoughts, as I expect [it] will doe to most of the new violent Whigs, who they say are all going over with Jack Smith at their head, if so I hope you will not be among the last, unless you think constancie is a vertue which I fancie Mademoiselle Dorp herself will scarce allow, 'tis well the Duke of Marlborough is content to stay at the head of the armie, better half loaf than none at all, others will be of his mind, but they are not to be received by mother church as they say, soe had better goe out with a good grace, if the experiment be not dangerous. . . . . ."

1710, Augt. 31st. John Chetwynd to the same. Dated at Oulx.

" . . . . the enemies have ordered some redouts to be made betwixt Foglioso and Larche to hinder our penetrating that way another time.

" We shall sing Te Deum here tomorrow for the redition of Douay."

1710, Sept. 1st. John Lawes to the same. From Brussels.

" Yesterday we received here the capitulation of Bethune, by which the garrison was to march out that day with the usual marks of honour, and to be conducted to Saint Omer. Monsieur Keppel brother to the Earl of Albemarle is made Governor of Bethune. . . . .

" Yesterday we rejoiced for the late victory in Spain. Having been at Gand some days with Mr Cardonel, I did not trouble you last week. He is so well recovered that he thinks of setting out on Wednesday next for the army."

1710, Sept. 1st. Lord Stair to the same. Dated at the "Camp at Vilers Brulin." 4 pp. on the balance of power in the North.

The same to the same. Dated, "Fryday 10 a clock."

" Sir,

Here are Sir Richard Temple and I so intent on the wind that wee dare not allow ourselves the pleasure of waiting on my Lord Townshend and your honour, wee shall much repent it if the wind continues obstinate. You'll doe us a great deall of pleasure it you'll lett us know how the world goes I am his Excellency's most faithful servant, and yours with all my heart.

"STAIR."

[P.S.] " Don't forget the article of England, for our letters I'm afraid are not to be come at here."

The seal on this letter is curious. It represents a female figure, standing in the foreground, towards whom a Cupid is rowing in a small boat. The motto on the seal is "Seguardo non arivo."

1710, Sept. 5th. James Taylor to the same. From Whitehall.

". . . . take Leave to congratulate you on our great success in Spain and are impatient for the particulars but wee have no reason to doubt the truth of it since France owns it . . . . . Enclosed you have the Queries Nº 2 and the Earl of Clarendon's Opinion about the dissolution of the Parliament Anno 1640 very apropos to this time . . . . This day's Tatler being a good one I send you that also . . . ."

1710, Sept. 8th. John Laws to the same. From Brussels.

. . . . I heartily congratulate you on this glorious success [near Sarragossa on August 20th].

1710, Sept. 9th. Thomas Willymott to the same. Dated at Doctor's Commons, and addressed " To the Honorble Horatio Walpoole att his Excellency's the Lord Townsend's att the Hague Holland.—These."

The writer asks Mr Walpole to interest himself in the case that Mr. Robert Breame, master of the ship Mary and Elizabeth, has pending at the Court of Holland.

1710, Sept. 10th. Monsieur Charion to Lord Townshend. In French. From Berne.

Congratulations on the two victories in Spain (Almenara and Saragossa). It concludes:—" so long as Joshua shall be at war with Amalek I shall have my hands stretched out towards the Heavens."

1710, Sept. 23rd. J. Macky to Horatio Walpole. From Ostend.
Recommending an officer for promotion but not naming him.

1710, Oct. 7th. Henry Hale to the same. From Amsterdam.

". . . . Tomorrow departs from hence our great Gouvernr Pitt and [he] will be sure to wait on my Lord Townshend . . . . ."

1710, Oct. 8th. General Palmes to the same. Dated at Vienna and unaddressed.

" Sr—I am infinitely obliged to you for your constant correspondence . . . . . can send you nothing in return from here, most of our Ministers being in the country, and little more to be effected in the Duke of Savoy's affaires til we have his answer to the last dispatches we sent from here.

The Count de K—— who is to assist as plenipotentiary att Milan in case his R. H. consents to a conference upon the resolutions of this Court is ordered to come hither to receive the instructions in order to it, and if his R. H. accepts of that I shall according to the orders I have formerly received goe thither, I have not as yet signify'd her Majestie's desires to the Court relating to the Hungarians, expecting the return of the Ministers from their country houses, but I am humbly of opinion it will be of little purpose, however I shall give you an account of it . . . . . ."

1710, Oct. 13th. A Camp Circular. Unsigned. Dated at the " Camp before Aire the 13th Octobr 1710."

Describing the siege operations from October 10th.

1710, Oct. 16th. Dr Francis Hare to Horatio Walpole. From the Camp at St Andre.

" Dear Horace,

I had a letter from Mr Naylor by the last mail, desiring me to send him a Certificate, if Jemmy Pelham was alive the ninth of September O.S. his name being concerned in some of Mr Naylor's writings. Jemmy being from the army I can't do what he desires, but believe you may ; the Captain having been, if I am not mistaken, with you at the Hague since that time . . . . I hear by the last letters, you are eased of the trouble of serving two masters . . . . ."

1710, Oct. 20th. John Drummond to the same. From Amsterdam.

. . . Mr Stawell my Lord Stawell's brother entreats his Excellency's pass to go for England, he has not his health very well and goes direct to Rotterdam, if you please to direct Mr Forbes to send his Excellency's pass for him and his servant to Mr Black's at Rotterdam, I hope to be with you on Saturday evening, and shall pay Mr Forbes the dues, I thinke his name is Edward Stawell . . . . ."

1710, Oct. 24. Count Stadion to Lord Townshend. In French. From Mayence.

The Elector fears lest the troubles in the United Kingdom and the change of Parliament may not import some change into affairs, and the writer hopes that, if the allies continue to be blessed with success in Spain, France will think more seriously, and with better intentions, of Peace.

1710, Oct. 27th. Henry St John, Secretary of State, to Horatio Walpole. From Whitehall.

" Sir,
I hope you will attribute it to the hurry I have lately been in to take care of my elections, and I have not answered sooner your congratulations upon her Ma^{tys} having honoured me with this Employment. I shall be very glad to make use of it upon all occasions.

After what I write to my Lord Townshend I can have no further directions to send to you ; but I don't question your diligence in sending all such advices as may be for her Ma^{tys} service, which will be always acceptable to

" S^r your most humble servant
" H. St JOHN."

1710, Nov. 3rd. Copy of a letter, in French, dated at the Camp before Aire, from the Duke of Marlborough to the Count of Colmenero. The Duke enquires if the latter had written to him on the 22nd of October as he had received a letter bearing the Count's signature but doubted its authenticity.

1710, Nov. 24th. James Taylor to Horatio Walpole. Dated at the Horse Guards.

". . . . . your brother came to towne last night and is this day much pesterd with company and tomorrow our new sennators meet which prevents his writing to you by this post. . . . . . Enclosed you have two Medlys which are esteemed very good and very apropôs. . . ."

1710, Nov. 27th. Alexander Cunningham to the same. From Padua.

" Worthy Sir,
I had the favour of yours of September the 9th, just as I was entering the Lazaretto the 4th of November we stayed there 14 days during which time I could make no return to you, being then buried in Lazarus's house, but now being risen as it wer from the dead I can assure you that my dutie to you is one of the first things that I call to mind and [I] shall be proud of all opportunitys of entertaining friindship with a person of your merit. I thank you for the care you have had of my letters, and desire you would be soe kind as to put forward the enclosed to Mr Wortley Montague who I believe would see you in his return to England. The measures taken latelie in England surprise all that doe not know us, they think 'tis odd a bruer should set up against a General, but you know the merit of brewers better, soe it seems the new brooms sweep clean.

I would not have thought that they would have, gone soe far, but they know best what they are doing, I wish they take care of the poor foolish nation and not put all in danger. The Church is in none unless it be of one that's much prouder than herself. They ask me here what's Dr Sacshevral's religion, for my part I know not, but pray ask and let me know, for they tell me here he is of theirs, only the Germans are sorrie that he should disturb the alliance, others think he has pretensions on the Crown and that he may set up for himself, I'm amased to see what notions people has of us. As for what you say of yourself I'm sorrey to hear it, that you must perish 'with' those you are imbarked with, constancy makes a man cheap as you well observed in Lovers. As for those that are gone out instead of going over I fancie some of them have mistaken their way, however betwixt you and me they have this comfort, they goe not out soe poor as they came in. Of all things I wonder most of Mr B[oy]l's being out for he was obnoxious to none, I hope the Whigs will think of travelling, if they'l come thus far I shall be glad to see them, they'l find friends among the fair here, but I leave politicks knowing I'm never to be at the helm.

My Lord Lonsdale gives his humble service to his Excellencie and your self, he has bought a Horace for love of you, and studys now [to make up] for his idleness at the Hague, he has laid all politicks aside since his friends have done the same, now he reads incessantlie. We shall be here till Christmas, then will go to Venice to refresh our selves with Operas and other interluds. Tell Mr Peryra that in the Lazaretto I have converted two Jews to Whigrie but they'l be old Whigs, they not being for Places or preferment.

My dear Mr Walpool I shall be glad of your Commands alsoe, your news, save your self if you can, your sins are only venial yet, and the Whig's can't blame you for occasional conformitie. Operas bals and the like is our business, my Lord [Lonsdale] is a mightie hopefull youth, soe that 'tis a pleasure to me to be abrode at this time. Give my most humble services to his Exely and I am etc.''

'' [P.S.] Direct yours to me under a cover to Messrs Samel Williams and Smith Marchants at Venice.''

1710, Nov. 29th. Monsieur Charion to Lord Townshend. In French from Berne on the prospects of the War and the chances of Peace.

1710, Dec. 1st. A letter from Count de Valdenz, Governor of the Castle of Milan, to Lord Townshend. In Italian. 3 pp.

About certain Spanish fiefs of the Emperor.

1710, Dec. 7th, N.S. John Molesworth to Horatio Walpole. From Wesel.

'' . . . All my letters go through Mousr Clignet's hands : I mean him who is Postmaster at Leyden. . . .

'' I shall stay some days at Dusseldorpf, and from thence proceed to Francfurt, where I should be mighty glad that the frosts would overtake me, for the roads we have allready past are but a bad sample of what we are to expect especially in the Westerwalt, which am affraid is allmost impassable.

'' [P.S.] I have made bold to trouble you with a lettor to Mr Stanhope, not knowing any safer way of conveying it to him.''

1710, Dec. 10th. James Cockburn to the same. From Turin.

'' During Mr Chetwynd's absence . . . . . I will take the liberty to trouble you when we have any news here worth your attention . . . .
. . . . They continue to mention the enemies fitting out 18 or 20 men of war at Toulon. . . . .

MARQUESS
TOWNSHEND
MSS.

" Last week a Brittish Man of War arrived at Genoa, with advice that Sr John Norris with the fleet, was gone out from Port Mahon to cruise for two months."

1710, Dec. 10th. Admiral Sir John Norris to Lord Townshend. Endorsed " Duplicate To the R^t Honble Lord Townshend." Dated on board the Ranelagh, at Port Mahon. The writer reports the movements of his ships and of the Turkish convoy.

1710, Dec. 24th. From Turin. James Cockburn to Horatio Walpole.
" . . . . By letters of the 20th from Genoa we have an acct that Genll Wade was arrived there from Spain being sent into England by Mr Stanhope. Our Army is still near Toledo, but it is feared we shall be obliged in a little time to return to the fronteers of Arragon, by reason that the Portuguese would not join us & that the Spaniards seem against us in Castile. . . . . . .
" The ship which the Enemies have fitted out from Toulon to the number of 37 are gone towards the Straits near Cartagena ; Sir John Norris being likewise that way I hope he will have the good fortune to meet with some of them . . . . . ."

1710, Dec. 25th, O.S. Geoffrey Walpole to the same. From Port Mahon.
" Dr Brother,
I have been favoured with yours & am glad to hear of your continuing still at the Hague, our success here in cruising has been very bad all this winter, the enemy having fitted out such a number of ships in these parts as has obliged us to keep in a body ; since the late misfortune of Gen : Stanhope the King has pressed our going up to Italy for the troops that are there ready to embark for Spain, for which Service we now a fitting out with all expedition ; I have spoken to Sr J^{no} Norris in behalfe of Mr Goddard but do not find that there is any likelyhood of succeeding, the usuall answer is that he has obligations to provide for several others who came abroad with him, which he shall not be able to do, before the arrivall of Sir J^{no} Jennings who is dayly expected here to relieve him, & to whome I believe it will not be improper for my L^d [Townshend] to recommend Mr Goddard to, he having served some time under his command ; we expect to be in Italy by the middle of next month where I beg you let me hear from you, 'tis reported here that my brother Walpole is out of his employment as treasurer of the Navy, but we do not hear who has succeeded him, I wish it may prove otherwise ; the arrivall of Sr J^{no} Jennings in these parts I'm in hopes will give me a greater prospect of Success by cruising than hitherto I've had, I am
Dear Brother
most affectionatly yours
G. WALPOLE."

[P.S.] " I'm afraid we have had no success
in the lottery by your silence.

1710, ——. Copy of a Memorial from the States General to Prince Eugene. In French. 15½ pp.

1710–1711. Copies of forty-six " Letters from Ld Townshend to Mr Secretary St John." From Novr 4th 1710 to March 27th 1711. In a cardboard cover.

1710–11. Twenty-one letters, in French, from Isaac D'Alais, Secretary at Hanover, to Lord Townshend and Horatio Walpole. From March 28th 1710 to March 27th 1711.

In a postscript to the latest of these letters the writer says that Lord Raby is expected to arrive in Hanover the same evening.

1710 to 1719.   Miscellaneous letters and papers from Feby 8th 1710 to Augt 4th 1719.   In a cardboard cover.

1711, Jan. 9th.   A Discourse on the affairs of Portugal.   Unsigned. 17½ pp.

1711, Jan. 16th.   An unsigned police advertisement.   Dated at Rotterdam.   It runs as follows :—

"AVERTISEMENT.—Le Sieur Devisseau est party aujourdhuy par le Bateau D'Anvers, il a bien dit qu'il devoit revenir icy dans 7 à huit jours, mais comme c'est un fin Je ne say sy on doit y ajouter foy, il doit loger à Anvers au Grand Laboureur.   C'est un homme de moyenne taille, agé de 60 à 64 ans, le Cou courte, une mechante perruque blonde, sy on est dans le Dessin de l'arrester, on aura tout le temps necessaire parce que le Batteau est beaucoup charge & que le Vent luy est contraire."

1710, Jan. 21st.   James Cockburn to Horatio Walpole.   From Turin.
". . . . things are not so bad as the Enemies gave out; tho' the misfortune of the English troops being made prisoners is great enough . . . . . . "
"We have no news of Sr John Norris, but expect him every day at Vado."

1711, Jan. 30th.   Abraham Stanyan to Lord Townshend.   From Berne.
Recommending the bearer, Monsr Le Camus a French Officer, to his Lordship's protection.

1711, Feb. 4th.   Monsr de St Saphorin to the same.   From Berne. In French.
Explaining the writer's views on a projected alliance with the Protestant Cantons of Switzerland.

[No date.]   "Projet d'une Alliance deffensive entre Sa Ma^{té} Brit[annique] et L[eurs] H[autes] P[uissance]s d'un côté et la Suisse Protestante de l'autre."   Unsigned.   Perhaps enclosed in the last.   17½ pp.

1711, Feb. 9th.   James Taylor to Horatio Walpole.   From the Horse Guards.
"Enclosed you have the Medley of Munday last and the Examiner of yesterday which is more scurrilous than any I have yet seen except N° 4 in which he calls his Grace [the Duke of Marlborough] a Cataline at the head of a Mercinary Army.   I am astonish'd at the Liberty the Author takes, and more at those who protect him.   There was a very great shew on Tuesday last at Court everybody vying who should be finest 'tis said my Lord Duke will be going hence in a few days.   God send him good Success.   As for Mony wee are yet in the dark and the Spring advanceing very forward gives us but a very melancholly prospect of a good Champaigne.   I hear there are several parties in the house & one in particular call'd the October Clubb consisting of 64.   The Malt Act is pass'd & I am told not £10,000 lent upon it, wee live in hopes that Credit will be better, your Brother [Robert] is very well & thank God is yet Treasurer of the Navy."
[P.S.]   "His Grace came to Towne from Woodstock a Wednesday Night last."

1711, Feb. 10th.   Lord Peterborough to Lord Townshend.   From Frankfort.
"After a most wretched journey I am come well to Frankfort, the Ice was too strong to force, & too weak to bear, so that I stuck one whole night in the Road.

"I find the confirmation of raising the Siege of Gironne upon the Road from all parts which makes me conclude 'tis true, the Warr in Catalonia had been impracticable if that place had been lost.

"As soon as I come to Vienna I will give your Lordship an account of what Success my endeavours may have in that terrible Court & I return you my most humble thanks for all your favours att the Hague."

Same date. Daniel Pulteney to Horatio Walpole. From Copenhagen. About affairs at the Danish Court. 5 pp.

1711, Feb. 13th. Adam Cardonnel to the same. From Westminster.

". . . . [I] am now in a hurry preparing to' hasten over to you, our Baggage is gone on board Cap[t] Sanderson this afternoon, and he is to saile to morrow for Harwich whether we shall be hastening in three or four Days in order to embark.

"Lord Orrery is to be with my Lord Duke [of Marlborough] this evening and I hope we shall leave matters here pretty easy. . . ."

Same date. Duke of Queensberry to the same.

Enclosing a letter to be forwarded to Mr Jefferyes who has left no directions in his grace's office how his letters may be addressed to him while he is on his way to Bender.

1711, Feb. 19th. Lord Peterborough to Lord Townshend. From Lintz.

"After a most uneasy journey I'am come as far as Lintz & have the mortification to be stop'd within a day & a half of Vienna. The Snow is melted & the Rivers impassable by Land, & the Ice prevents the passage by the Danube.

". . . I fear our affairs in Spain are in an ill Condition, in a few days I shall give you the best account I can of affairs in these parts . . ."

Same date. John Laws to Horatio Walpole. From Brussels.

"Our freshest letters from Paris are of the 13th . . . . . . We are still without any accompt of what has passed at Girona since the Capitulation of the Town on the 25th of January . . . . . There is nothing material from the Enemies Frontier on this side except that the great want of money still continues among their Troops.

"The 17th being Her Majesty's Birthday it was celebrated here by firing the Cannon, with all other usual Rejoicings, and the greatest marks of Zeal and Affection were shown on this Occasion by the Government and People, in acknowledgement of the good effects they receive from Her Majesty's gracious Protection . . . . ."

1711, Feb. 20th. James Taylor to the same. From the Horse Guards.

". . . The Lottery Act will pass in a very few days, and consequently very soon wee shall know if the People like the proposition, I wish they may with all my heart for the Money wee want very much. My Lord Duke [of Marlborough] left the Towne a Sunday Morning last for Holland. I wish him a good Voyage & good Success this Summer. Wee are here under some apprehensions that Barcelona will be beseiged."

1711, Feb. 24th, N.S. James Jefferyes to Lord Townshend. From Hanover.

Enclosing a despatch under a flying seal for his Lordship's perusal.

1711, Feb. 27th. James Taylor to Horatio Walpole. From the Horse Guards.

"I forgott to tell you in my last that the house of Lords had passd the Qualification Bill which I hear by a Computation will throw out above two hundred Members (at the next Election for a new Parliament) of the present house. The Duke of Argyll will be setting out for Spain in about 8 or ten days."

Same date. Lord Townshend's Letters of Recall. Dated at St. James's. Signed and sealed by Queen Anne, and countersigned by Henry St. John.

1711, Feb. 28th. Lord Peterborough to Horatio Walpole. Dated at Vienna and addressed to "Monsieur Walpool" and "Mr Wallpool."

The writer is hoping to send accounts from Vienna that may not be disagreeable. The news from Spain is very mortifying.

Same date. Lord Raby to the same. From Berlin.

". . . I know before yours [came to band] that my Reg^t was taken, seeing my agent writ me very lately word that he had received a letter from my major Coll. Benson at Burgos in Spain, but by yours I am informed that King Charles has raized up a Reg^t of Dragoons which is cal'd the Royall which I thought was attributed to mine & am obliged to you for your information. This Court is in great hopes now of an accomodation with the Prince of Frieze & and if the conclusion is intirely made perhaps you may see our Court with you in the spring.

"I do assure you I am very glad the Duke of Marlborough is like to command again, I shall win 10 pistoles by it which I laid with the Prince Royall in November last . . . . I have very great hopes the War in Hungary is ended by Prince Ragotzys making his peace with the Emperor."

[P.S.] "The affair of the Elector of Hanover's taking the Bishoprick of Hildesheim continues to make a great noys here but the quarels o these German Princes are allways ended by a paper war at Ratisbone."

1711, March 2nd. James Taylor to the same. From the Horse Guards.

"I am sorry to hear that your Revocation was sent a Tuesday Night last . . . . . expecting now to have the Pleasure of seeing you in England I am etc."

1711, March 6th. Robert Mann to the same. From London.

. . . . "I have taken the liberty to order Mr Davis of Rotterdam to send you a small parcell of Silk for hancercheifs which I desire your Care of when you come for England and beg you'l buy me a peace of lace not two fine for Shirts and not quite so broad as your uncle's . . ."

1711, March 7th. General Francis Palmes to the same. From Vienna.

Explaining a projected interim settlement of the dispute between the Emperor and the Duke of Savoy as to the right of the latter to certain fiefs in Montferrat, and mentioning that the Elector of Mayence, uncle of the Vice Chancellor of the Empire, has agreed to furnish four batallions which the States General are to send into Spain.

1711, March 10th. John Wich to Horatio Walpole. From Hamburgh.

". . . . The King of Sweden's Declaration, I had two or three days before, and find the Vandall's wandering blood is in him and that the Goth will sooner leave his Cittyes, and Dominions, then the pleasure of rambling at randome I am affraid, wee shall have the Devill to do with him, for in all his proceedings Revenge is his most Christian attribute, and he is made of such Mold that he must have a magicall wheele that puts him into any shape, but what bee'l bare himself. You must be speedy in what you do one way or other, for you have now to do with a Man, I mean Generall Governour Welling, Who is the most retir'd, cunning Polititian, at least Intriguer, on earth, and one who is no less then a Swedish Caper in the very Midelle of a French Soop. Putt him into a Limbeck, and when the Sueed is Evaporated the Spiritt will be *un cordial pour le Roy de France* . . . ."

1711, March 11th. Josiah Burchett, Secretary to the Admiralty Board, to Lord Townshend. From the Admiralty Office.

"I send your Lordship herewith an Order from the Lords Comm^rs of the Admiralty directing one of the Captains of the Yachts now in Holland to bring your Excellency to England. There are now at Rotterdam severall of her Maj^te Ships under the Command of Captain Scott of the Romney, who is ordered to convoy your Lordship to England if you can be timely ready, otherwise the Deptford a Ship of 50 Gunus is ordered from the Downes to Holland to attend on your Excellency."

Same date. Abraham Stanyan to Horatio Walpole. From Berne.

Referring to a Col. Bugnot's proposal to "debauch 7 or 8000 men from the Enemy's Army, it would be methinks a piece of Service that deserves Encouragement."

1711, March 13th. John Wich to the same. From Hamburgh.

A hurried line requesting Mr Walpole to give the enclosed to Mr Cardonnell. "I wish you a bumper, and a good night."

Same date. A News-letter from Paris. In French.

The king last Tuesday reviewed his two regiments of French and Swiss Guards, which cannot set out so soon as was intended on account of the rains having rendered the roads impassable.

In connection with this review they tell rather a curious story, which is mortifying for the Duke de Guiche. As colonel of the King's Guards he went to Versailles to learn on what day it pleased the King to hold the review, and he enquired where it should be held, seeing that it could not well be held as usual on the Plain of Grenelle, near the Invalides, which was still under water from the inundation of the Seine. To this enquiry the King replied that it would be no great harm if they were all drowned . . . . . .

Same date. George Tilson to Horatio Walpole. From Whitehall.

"D[ear] S^r—I am now much tired at near three in the morning and cannot do any more than acknowledge yours . . . . . I did not deliver your first letter wth any ceremony to Mr Sec^y [St John] since your last ended with that request, however I put it into his hands that he might see how desirous you were of his Protection. We have not a farthing from Ireland yet. When it comes I shall be mindfull of your just Pretensions. I hope our Lottery will make a great Sound abroad. It has surpass'd every body's imagination. I have lost a Guinea upon it, besides being excluded, but the Parl^t wants more, and may get it by this method which seems so agreable.—I am D^r S^r—Y^rs &c. G. T."

1711, March 14th. Lord Raby to the same. From Berlin. Endorsed "Lord Raby's Circular of March 14, 1711."

It begins :—Having receiv'd my letters of revocation Sunday last, I would have taken my Audience of leave immediately, but the King having a mind I shou'd have a publick one, desired me to defer it till Tuesday next, & told me at the same time he would dine with me the day before."

Same date. Daniel Pulteney to the same. From Copenhagen.

F

About the Swedish Declaration against the neutrality &c. [5¼ pp.]
and enclosing an extract from a letter to the Duke of Queensberry on
the same subject [2¼ pp.].

1711, March 15th. Lord Raby to the same. From Berlin.

" . . . the Declaration of the Swedes was general as you will see by
what I sent formerly to his Excellence my Lord Townshend, & it can't
but extreemly embarrase all the Powers concerned in the Guaranty.
. . . . I hope soon to have the honour of waiting on him myself at
the Hague . . . . . . tho' I dread the roads . . . . . . I hope to be
setting out from hence before the end of next week."

1711, March 16th. George Tilson to the same. From Whitehall.

" Dr Sr—Since last Post I have had the favour of yours of the 20th

" I put my Bror [Christopher] in mind to sollicit for money for Ld
Townshend upon Mr Secrys letter, but I fear the Trea[su]ry bears
dunning very well, if I could forward it more [expeditiously] I would
do my utmost. I sent your good News to Sr W. Hodges who by his
Son has let me know, how much satisfied they are to have come off so
well. They ought surely to own your hearty Pains in this matter with
great thankfullness.—[The Marquis' de] Guiscard we believe will dye,
it is not his wounds that prove mortal, they are all well, but the Messengers & others when they got him down bruised him horribly; they
were fain to make an Inciston yesterday, & above a quart of Sanies, or
bruised blood came out. If he dyes he will save us the trouble of straining
hard with the Laws to hang him ; 'tis wretched to see how difficult it is
to come at the life of a Vilain by Law. I am told the Lords have passed
the Wine Bill with an Amendment which the Commons have agreed to,
so people hope to have good wine here, tho' not much cheaper; & as we
must have it, our Merch¹ˢ may do it as well as others. The over-filling
the Lottery causes a great Confusion in the City. I think they have
agreed to compute, & deduct proportionally from every one to reduce it
to the sum they want, & those who won't take their money back in proportion, may take the Law of the Bank if they please. I hear one Blunt
who put in above 100 m. li. [£100,000] is very resty & untractable. I waited
on Mr. Boyle this morning before he went out of Town, & he bid me
desire that you would add to the Com[issio]n you have already from him
half a hogshead of the best Hermitage wine you can get. I thank you
for your readiness as to my Shirts and Lace. We find by this Post
that Lord Peterborow has executed his Com[issio]n very vigorously. I
hope we shall see good effects of it. I think it is our Sheet Anchor.
Were the Hungerian trouble finished we might be more easy as to the
pernicious projects of the Swedes. Mor Steinghens seems to think his
Master too generous; 'tis seldome that German Princes' generosity hurts
them.—I am ever—Dr Sr, Yrs G. T."

1711, March 17th. George Mackenzie to the same. From Dresden.

" . . . . what you wrote me in Cyphers by the last of the 10th Instant
was very acceptable to me . . . . such are my orders to make as little
use of numbers as possible. 'tis to no purpose to me to alledge prudence
will have it otherwise, because I must hold that obedience is better
than Sacrifice."

Same date. Daniel Pulteney to the same. From Copenhagen.

About the Swedish declaration against the neutrality, etc. 5¼ pp.

Same date. Copy of an unsigned letter in French. Dated at Geneva
and unaddressed. Enclosed in Mr. Stanyan's letter to Horatio Walpole
of March 28th.

" L'on a fait courir un bruit sourd à Paris, que Milor Duc de Marl·
borough étoit mort subitement en Angleterre d'un Mal qui n'avoit dure
que 18 heures, l'on ma assuré que M^r d'Yberville avoit écrit ici cette
Nouvelle . . . . .

" On se previent en France que S. M. Britannique pourra etre bien tôt
détrônée, et que l'Angleterre ayant un Roy entierement devoüe au sien,
elle se trouvera bientôt triomphante, et au dessus de tous ses ennemies,
auxquels elle se trouvera pour lors en état de pouvoir faire absolument
la Loy. Il est certain qu'en général en France l'on donne fort à present
dans ces sortes d'idées. C'est ce que j'ay peu reconnoitre.

" Les Dommages qu'on à receus par l'enflure extraordinaire de la Seine
sont considerables, tout fois l'incommodite et la crainte en a été
beaucoup plus grande que le Mal.

" Le Rhône a été aussi débordé, et en general plusieurs Provinces du
Royaume ont souffert par ces Debordem^{ts} extraordinaires.

" Pour peu qu'on reflechisse la dessus, on jugera bien que les pertes
considerables arrivées ainsi à une partie des Peuples de France, ne
peut en ce tems ci que causer une fort grande breche aux recettes
du Roy, et faire qu'il trouvera infiniment plus de difficultés à recouvrer
les fonds qui lui seroient necessaires pour le Soutien de cette guerre."

1711, March —. A Memorandum of letters written by Lord Townshend
and Mr Walpole on March 10th, March 13 & March 17th, 1711, N.S., and
part of a rough draft of a letter in the handwriting of Mr Walpole.

1711, March 18th. James Jefferyes to Horatio Walpole. From
Vienna.

" . . . . . I am sorry your stay at the Hague is like to be of so
short continuance . . . . . The French, Poles and Swedes opposed
with all their power the mission of the Turkish envoy to this court,
but he is expected in a few days. The Turks reckon they shall have
80,000 fighting men, besides those designed for the fleet. There is little
appearance of their doing any great mischief, especially if they do not
succeed in their first fury.

" The horse tail's not yet expo^ed among them."

[P.S.] " Your commands will come safe to my hands if you address
them to Mr Fury, Agent for the Turkish Merch^{ts} at this Place."

1711, March 20th. George Tilson to the same. From Whitehall.

" Dear Sir—Now you have put off your Ministerial Airs, perhaps even
the shortest of my letters may be important to you, but almost two in the
morning will not suffer me to be long. You needed no Apology to
Mr Sec^{ry} [Boyle] for my Lord Townshend's Mem[oria]ll, which came at
the same time with the letters. Mr Boyle is out of Town, so I could
only forward your letter to him by this Post, but I told his servant, who
is here, that he should look out sharp, as soon as the Rotterdam Fleet
arrives. I wish you a good voyage expecting to see you now with the
first easterly wind.

" I am ever D^r S^r—Y^{rs} &c. G.T."

Same date. John Wich to the same. From Hamburgh.

" . . . . . Whensoever, or Wheresoever I can serve dear Mr Walpole, I'le do it with a Freindship becoming a Man of Honour, and hope
I may now and then have the same satisfaction by the [Packett] Boat, I
have had by the Post. Pray lett my Lord Ambassadour carrye with him
from the Hague a good impression of me. . . . . ."

Same date. George Mackenzie to the same. From Dresden.

Alludes to misunderstandings and explanations and expresses great
regard for Mr Walpole. Sends humblest services to Colonel Cathcart
and to Mr Envoy Chetwynd "when he shal arryve on this Side."

Same date. Alexander Cunningham to the same. From Venice.
Addressed " A Monsieur, Monsr Ho^{ne} Walpoole Secretaire de Sa Maj^{tie}
Britannique chez My Ld Tounsend à la Hay, Holland."

" Dear S^r—I did not intend to trouble you this post, but being to goe
from hence to Rome the morrow and having had yours this morning I
can't leave this place without expressing the horror I conceive at my
Ld Tou[nshen]d's leaving the Hague, I see it likewise in print, and all
are amazed with the news, what's the meaning of it God knows, L^d
Lon[s]d[a]le is heartilie concerned and hopes we shall all meet, and will
now pass the time in Italie that he intended to have stayed at the
Hague next winter. The acc^{ts} we have from Engl^d are odd, soe I'm more
virtuoso than ever, and for my own happiness will shut my eyes henceforth from all news and fortifie my incredulitie and not think the
Islel[an]d is to be ruined before 'tis ruined. The French here tell me
the secrets of our cabinet, I looked on their acc^{ts} as Romance or Com-
medie, but I find them some thing else, and can assure you they laugh
at all your preparations against Spain, nay they rejoyce at 'em ; Italie is
much influenced by Vienna at present, and if the Great Duke should
chance to dye now, the fate of his Cuntrey is in the hands of the Emp^r.
However the French faction, tho' quiet at present, is numerous and
busie under hand, they heave [have] Abbatours among our travellers,
and I expect to see more of that where I'm going, but I shall shut
my eyes, as others did on me. The Doge of the Nicolotti is dead
and the watermen are cabaling as much against the time of electing
a new Doge as our parteys doe for a Speaker or a Secretary of
State. Mr Newton is gone from Rome having got the Pope's Medals
and other marks of Esteem from the Virtuosi, the book he has
printed makes him famous with the learned, I have not yet seen it,
but belive it must be weel done, and heave that pleasure yet to
come. We hear nothing from Mr Molesworth since he left this place,
but I know he's safe arrived at Florence. If My Ld Amb^{dr} have
any Com^{ds} for me he knows how much I'm his serv^t and shall receive 'em with particular pleasure, I shall write to him verie soon.
My Ld Lonsdale gives his heartie service to his Exc^{ly}, and all the
adversitys of his friends don't in the leest alter him ; he travells with
reputation wherever he goes and I must say he's one of the hope-
fullest young Gen^t I have ever known, he has a particular kindness
for you and gives his service to you and 'tis with the greatest respect
that I am etc."

1711, March 21st. Daniel Pulteney to the same. From Copenhagen
Besides the six Norway ships taken by the Swedes eleven more have
been taken, some of them by French Privateers sailing under Swedish Commissions. Mr Jackson Her Majesty's Resident at Stockholm writes that
" no more Zimtouns of the Plague had appeared " there since the early
part of February.

Same date. Lord Raby to Lerd Townshend. From Berlin.
" . . . . . Our good fortune is, the conjunctures are such in these
parts that the King's best Game is certainly continuing firm with the
allies, & all the offers of France are not to be relyd on, which they are
sencible of here, tho' the Divel can't hinder them from nibbling at the
baite. . . . . . "

17$\frac{10}{11}$, March 23rd. Sir William Hodges to the Same. Dated in London and addressed "To his Ex^{cy} the Lord Townshend. Her Maj^{ty} of Great Britain's Ambassador & Plinipotentiary at the Hague—Present."

The writer thanks his Excellency for having procured, through his interest with the States General, the restoration of two Buenos Ayres ships and their cargoes.

Same date. The same "To Horatio Walpole Esqr att his Ex^{cies} the Lord Townshend her Maj^{ty} of Great Britain's Ambass^{or} & Plenipotentiary—At the Hague."

On the same matter as the last which was enclosed in this. It goes on :—

. . . . . the Spanyards have a great many excellent Proverbs and one is, Medio pan e mejor que innguno. [Half a loaf is better than no bread]
. . . . . . I have presumed to write his Ex^{cy} a few lines of thankes for the hon^r he hath been pleased to do me and the [persons] concerned, which letter goes inclosed, so pray favor me to deliver it, and [this] is all I can say till I shall have the hon^r to waite on his Ex^{cy} & to see you in England, which I hope shortly to do, interim I tender you all due respects and am etc. WM. HODGES."

1711, March 24th. Lord Raby to Horatio Walpole. From Berlin.

The writer is setting out for the Hague the next day.

1711, March 25th. Admiral Sir John Norris to Lord Townshend. Dated on board the Ranelagh in Vaia Bay. Reports an engagement between three of the writer's ships and four French ships. The names of the English ships are the Severn, the Lyme, and the Lyon. Captain Pudner commands the Severn. Captain Strickland commands the Nassau. Captain Walpole has lost his right arm by a cannon ball.

1711, March 26th. John Wich to Horatio Walpole. From Hamburgh.

Regrets at Mr Walpole's departure for England and compliments.

1711, March 27th. William Gibson to the same. From Rotterdam. Addressed "To Horatio Walpole Esqr Secretary to his Excellence the Lord Townshend, Tot, St Gravenhage. Enclosing a "bill of Loading" for two casks of wine shipped on board "the Martha, Richd Perkins master."

1711, March 28th. Abraham Stanyan to Lord Townshend. From Berne.

"My Lord,—Not knowing how long your Ex^{cy} may continue at the Hague, I take this Opportunity of returning my most humble thanks to your Lordp. for the many favours I have received from you both during my Stay at the Hague and since, begging leave to assure you that I shall always retain a gratefull sense of them, and think myself very happy, if I can ever find an Opportunity of shewing my gratitude. It is not for me to judge of the reasons which prevailed with your Lordp. to quitt your Embassy, I doubt not but they are good as to your own particular, but I don't know whether you can so well justify them to the publick, since all the letters from Holland, as well as the persons I meet with that come from thence, speak with great regret of your Ex^{cys} leaving that Countrey. However it be, since it has been your Choice I heartily wish it may prove to your Satisfaction, and beg leave to assure you, that wherever you are, I shall always be with the utmost respect—My Lord—Your Ex^{cys} most faithfull & most humble servant.

"A : STANYAN."

Same date. The same to Horatio Walpole. From Berne.

"I have no news to send you but the Copy of a letter I have seen from a General Officer in the D. de Noailes's army in Catalonia which you will find here annexed.

"The letters from Milan of the 20th inst. say that they had yet no News of the Arrival of our Fleet at Vado, but that it was expected every day, and that the Troops would embark for Catalonia as soon as it arrived.

"Pray can you tell me what is become of Mr Stanhope? & since I am making enquiry I desire you would let me know whether I must lose you with my Lord Townshend, or whether you stick to the Embassy and not to the Ambr. Wherever you are I shall always be very heartily—Dear Sr—Your etc."

As a postscript to this letter is a copy of a letter in French from a General Officer in the army of the Duc de Noailes, dated March 15th.

1711, March 30th. Les Plaintes du Roy de Prusse contre les Etats G[e]n[er]aux. Dated at the Hague and unsigned. 8 pp.

[No date.] Les demandes faites à l'Empereur, outre celles qui sont faites cy dessus aux Etats Generaux. 3 pp. This paper is appended to the last.

1711, March 31st, N.S. George Mackenzie to Lord Townshend. Dated at Dresden.

"My Lord,—I received yesterday the honour of the letter that your Excellency had been pleas'd to write to me of the 24th Just., and sincerely beg leave to assure Your Lordship, that I am too sensibly touch'd with the loss I must make, to've receiv'd with indifference the notice you've thereby given me of your Excie's purpose to return into England . . . . I must presume that Your Lordp's remembrance of the plainness and fullness with which I have faithfully ever acquainted you, with all that past in these parts, will continually be such proofs of my unbounded Confidence in, and of the attachment I really conserve for Your Lordp, that if hereafter any thing offer wherein I may be usefull, that at least I may still promise myselfe the Satisfaction of your Excie's commands.

"I am with a most profound respect—My Lord—Your Excellencie's most obedient, most faithfull, & humblest Servt

"GEORGE MACKENZIE."

Same date. The same to Horatio Walpole. Dated as the last.

"Sir,—I ingenously receiv'd with the deepest regrait the notice you had been pleas'd to give me of the 24th Instant, that you are at same time with My Lord Townshend to return into England. I'm very sensible that your own personal Merit as well as other advantageous Circumstances will still make every Situation easie to you, but as I cannot promise myselfe the like happiness with any by the freedom and Confidence that I used [to receive from] and repos'd in you, I presume you will forgive me to be sensibly affected with what may be my highest misfortune : I hope you have had some demonstrations of my soundness and Sincerity, and therefore may be persuaded I shal never be very diffuse in Protestations ; but as you cannot doubt, that I have the due Sentiments I ought, of the many and signal obligations you've done me, in the Course of your Residence & Negotiations ; I presume you'le give me leave to assure you, that I will in all time comeing very gladely embrace every opportunity that can contribute to your Satisfaction and my acknowledgments.

". . . . . I presume you are more generous, than [to] deny me the complacency I shal ever receive, to effectually declare that I am with the utmost Sincerity & cordial respect—Dr Sir—Your most obedient & most humble Servant,

"GEORGE MACKENZIE."

1711, April 6th. Mons. Thomas Laurens to the same [?] Dated at Briel and unaddressed.

".... Je suis informé que les vaisseaux de guerre resteront en mer sans entrer à Goree, pour attendre Son Excellence Mylord Townshend. . . . ."

1711–1712. Copies of six letters from Lord Peterborough. From 1st September 1711 to 12th August 1712. Dated at Venice.

1713, Jan. 9th. "To The R^t Honble the Lord Visc^t Townshend at Rainham Hall near Swaffam—Norfolk –Free." In an official hand and unsigned. Dated in London.

"My Lord—From the Hague [we hear] that the main Point in Question between Prince Eugine and Villars is about a safe Barrier for the Empire with the latter as yet is far from yeilding and insists not only on the entire Soveraignty of Strasburg and Alsace, but alsoe of the Country quite down to Germersheim inclusive which it's beleived the Emperor neither will or can agree to, meantime the States are very uneasy least France should stipulate something from his Imp^{ll} Maj^{ty} to their Prejudice touching the Barrier in the Netherlands, have ord^{rc} the Comanders of the Frontier Provinces and Towns to repaire to their sev^{ll} Gov^{rm}^{ts} and double their usuall Guards.

"From Hamborough [we hear] that the King of Denmark has given leave for Provisions to be brot in every Fortnight into Touinghen on condition the Congress be held the 24th at Brunswick to accomodate differences between the Northern Princes, and that the house of Mr. Roberts the Brittish Consull at Elsnore was lately burnt but (sic) a sudden Fire and all his Papers consum'd, among them a Packet from England directed to Stockholme and another from thence to England.

"Charles Vivian Esqr is made a Com^r of the Stamp office in the room of Capt Steele who some time since resign'd.

"This Day's Dutch Post advises from Vienna that sev^{ll} Imperiall Regiments in Hungary have orders to march for Italy where new Troubles are expected from the King of Sicily.

"From Strasburgh [there is news] of the 1st, That a detachm^t of the Garrison of Friburgh have taken the Pass of Newstadt 4 Leagues from Villinghen and thereby opened a way on that side into the Black Forrest.

"From Paris [we hear] that their Sea Armament is very great haveing 12,000 Landmen on board and all Materialls of Warr in order as they give out to assist the Spaniards in [the] Conquest of Sardinia.

"And from the Hague [we hear] that on the 13th the 2 Dutch Ambassad^{rs} set out for Paris and on the 15th that [the Ambassador] of France made his publick Entry at the Hague."

1714, Oct. 12th, O.S. Copy of a letter from Lord Townshend to Monsr Vandenberg. From Whitehall. In French.

His Lordship returns thanks for congratulations on his appointment as Secretary of State, and will contribute as far as lies in his power to maintain a good understanding and friendship between Great Britain and Holland. .

1714, Oct. 29th. A letter from the Avoyer and Council of Berne to Lord Townshend on politics and local disputes. In German. 4 pp.

1714, Dec. 6th. "Baron Schack's new Letter of Credence," from Peter the Great, "rec⁴ from Sir Clement Cottrel 30ᵗʰ April 1715." In Latin. Dated at Sᵗ Petersburg. 1 p.

1714 --. "A Narrative of Mʳ R. A['s] Correspondence with the House of Hanover." From Augᵗ 1712 to Novʳ 1714. In a parchment cover, 41 pp. Eight more pages have been destroyed. Printed copies of the Queen's Speeches of 6ᵗʰ June 1712 and 2ⁿᵈ March 1713, and also a copy of the "Post-Boy" of 3rd July 1714, are bound up with this MS.

1714–1717. Letters from Lᵈ V[iscount] Townshend, Lᵈˢ Stanhope, Sunderland, and others, belonging to Marquis Townshend. [In a cardboard cover.]

1715, March 9th. Copy of a letter from the Emperor Charles VI. to King George I., on the Affair of the Barrier. Dated at Vienna. In French. 7 pp.

1715, March 14th. "Abstract of a letter from Bilbao about a Spanish Ship fitting out for Newfoundland to demand and assert their Right pursuant to the 15 Article of the treaty att Uttrich [Utrecht]."

1715, March 16. Copy of a letter from the Emperor to King George I., acknowledging a letter of Janʳ 15ᵗʰ received at the hand of Lieut. General Cadogan.

It concludes : " Je ne dois pas oublier de donner ici au'Zôle particulier & à la dexterité de Mʳ Cadogan à menager et à finir sa Commission, les louanges qu'il merite, étant etc."

[No date.] A Memorial in French showing how the Emperor could attach to his interests the League of the Grisons and thereby establish an easy communication between the States of the Empire and the Duchy of Milan. 11 pp.

1715, April 1st. Translation of a letter from Peter the Great to King George I., congratulating the latter on his accession.

1715, July 10th. Monsieur Baruer to Lord Townshend. In French. Dated at Vienna and unaddressed.

The writer sends compliments and would much like to come to England" . . . . . Madᵉˡˡᵉ d'Appermont has the small pox ; if our hero [the Prince Eugene] escapes [it] the mother and daughter may go to Brabant whither the Prince who has been appointed governor will shortly go too. . . . ."

[1715, August.] Marquis de Rochegude to the same. In French. Undated and unaddressed. Written "at the Hand and Pen, in Panton Street near Leicester Square."

Enclosing a copy of the writer's recent despatch to the Protestant Cantons of Switzerland, and begging a continuance of his Lordship's favour.

1715, Augt. 12th. The copy of the despatch just mentioned. In French. Dated in London.

It begins :—"Great and sovereign Lords the good resolutions of Parliament sustained by the levy of 8 or 10 thousand men have arrested the Pretender on his road . . . . "

1715, Augt. 13ᵗʰ⁄24ᵗʰ. Monsieur Petkum to Lord Townshend. In French. Dated in London and unaddressed. Endorsed : " Mr. Petticū 13 Aug."

The writer complains that he has not as yet received any satisfaction for the offence done to him in the King's Chamber at the Palace by Mr Graham, in violation of the Law of Nations ; and he begs his Lordship to obtain for him speedy redress.

MARQUESS TOWNSHEND MSS.

1715, Aug. 27th. Extract from a letter in Italian. Unsigned and unaddressed. Dated at Paris and describing the last hours of Louis XIV.

[Circ. 1715.] An anonymous undated letter addressed "To the Right Honble Lord Viscount Townsend, Principall Minister of State, Albemarle Street."

"My Lord —— As your Lordpp is generally knowne [as] a great Benefactor to your Country in all your Eminent Stations ; I made bold to intimate to your Ldpp that I could discover a gang of Rogues, some high way men, who have beene out very lately a month [ago] ; and by some undoubted Circumstances brought home great booty. I am a stranger to them and to all ill practice, the Intelligence came to me by chance, and I inferr from makeing a discovery of the house they resort to ; if I am known to be the discoverer, my life incurrs great danger ; to serve my Country is my sole motive, notwithstanding if it prove true, I expect £300 : your Ldpp's word I and the world can depend on : if it be approved off I will proceede to my uttmost to serve my Country, but I will not be knowne to any such rogues who [I] am told are notorious ones. I beg your Ldpp's pardon your obet ser^t. a.b : ooo.

" [P.S.] in the flying post, if occation be I expect to hear further."

1715, Sept. 1st. Chidly Pigott to Lord Townshend.

The writer prays his Lordship to recover from one Mr Beak a petition that the King had referred to his Lordship's Committee.

No date. " Deduction de ce qui s'est passé à l'egard de la demolition de Dunkerque depuis la Signature de la Paix à Utrecht jusqu'à la mort de la feüe Reyne." 18 pp.

1715-1716. Letters from Horatio Walpole to Lord Townshend. Dated at the Hague from the 8th February 1715 N.S. to 23rd October 1716. A thick bundle in a cardboard cover.

1715-1716. Despatches of Admiral Sir John Norris from 13th May 1715 to 4th November 1716.

1715, May 10th. Copy of a despatch from the Lords of the Admiralty to Lord Townshend.

Enclosing a copy of "Instructions for Sir John Norris for his proceeding to and from the Baltic with the Squadron of his Matie Ships under his Command." Signed by Sir George Byng, George Dodington, Sir John Jennings, George Baillie, Sir Charles Turner, and Abraham Stanyan.

To these instructions are appended "A List of his Majesties Ships, designed to proceed to the Baltic under your Command," and "A List of Ships Employ'd by the underwritten Merchants to import Hemp from Petersbergh for his Majesties service, Anno 1715."

From the second of these lists it appears that the number of ships placed under the command of Sir John Norris—was four third-rate, fifteen fourth-rate, and one sloop.

The Merchant ships were the America, Thomas Pickarden ; the Adventure, John Smith ; the Three Martins, Robert Tomson ; the Mary & Elizabeth, Samuel Cont ; the Hannah, Ralph White ; the Benjamin, John Hooper ; the Thomas & Henry, Nicholas Constant ; the Plym Stock, Capt. Harrison ; the Dorothy, Adam Abbot ; and the Friend's Adventure, Alexander Long.

The names of the owners of these vessels (so far as they are given),
are [Sir] Randolph Knipe, [Sir] Godfrey Webster, Jos. Martin, William
Astell, Charles Goodfellow, and George Morley Jnʳ.

1715, May 13th. Sir John Norris, on board the Cumberland at the
Nore, to Lord Townshend.

The writer is delayed as he is waiting for some of the Merchant Ships
and for Naval Stores. He concludes " I shall not loose one moment of
time in proceeding from hence as soon as in the power of My Lord.—
Your Lordships most Obedᵗ faithful Serᵗ.

" JN : NORRIS."

[1715.] " Draught of a lettʳ to be writt by Sʳ Jⁿ Norris to His Maᵗʸˢ
Ministers at Stralsund & Stockholm." Undated.

" Pursuant to the Instructions I have received from His Majesty ; I am
to acquaint you that I am arrived here with a Squadron of Men of war,
and a fleet of Merchant men under my Convoy, as well for the Security
& protection of the Commerce in the Baltick Sea, as to demand of the
King of Sweden reparation and satisfaction for the great losses wᶜʰ the
British Merchants have sustained of late years, in having great number
of their ships taken and confiscated with their Cargo's by the Swedes
without any just reason or pretence whatsoever, and also to require an
abrogation of the Edict relating to Privateers published by the King of
Sweden at Stralsund the 19ᵗʰ February last ; I must therefore desire you
to' lose no time after the receipt of this to represent to his Swedish
Majesty the occasion of my arrival with the fleet under my Command in
these Seas ; and that the King my master having nothing more at heart
than the preservation of the antient Friendship between the two Crowns,
is very much concerned that the behaviour of the Swedes in taking and
confiscating contrary to some treaties still in force the ships and effects
belonging to His subjects, and the denyall of satisfaction & redress to
them notwithstanding the repeated instances made by you as well as by
Mr Jackson on that account has obliged His Majesty to send me with
a naval force to protect His subjects in carrying on their lawful trade
to the Baltick ports, and to demand of the King of Sweden immediate
reparation for the losses sustained by the British Merchants (an account of which is here annexed) and also an abrogation of the aforesaid
unjustifyable Edict relating to Privateers, which renders the Commerce
to these parts impracticable contrary to the Treaties still subsisting between the two Crowns ; and lastly to insist that the freedom of trade
to the ports of the Baltick may be immediately restored to His Majesties
Subjects, and preserved for the future without any interruption or
molestation whatsoever.

" You will at the same time let His Swedish Majesty know for these
reasons I am directed to stop all such ships that I shall meet with which
shall belong to him, or to his subjects, or that carry his Commission,
and to detain them, untill I shall receive from you the King of Sweden's
full complyance to these demands ; which are so agreable to justice and
reason, that I cannot doubt but His Swedish Majesty out of his known
love and regard to both will grant a ready and favourable answer ; but
if contrary to all expectations he shall continue to refuse complying
with what is desired in the name of the King my master, I shall then be
obliged to [take] such ships as I shall intercept belonging to him or to
his subjects, or carrying his Commission, as just reprizalls for the
damages sustained by the British subjects, and carry them with me as
such into England."

[No date.] " Copic. Conte Specifique des pertes et domages qu'ont
faites les Sujets Britanniques par la Saisie et Confiscation de Vaisseaux

et Marchandises sous mentionnées dans la Suède." Fourteen claims the total of which amounts to £65,449. Perhaps enclosed in the last. 6¼ pp.

1715, June 23rd. Copy of Minutes of Council of War, held on board the Cumberland at Revel. Enclosed in the next letter.

Present : Sir John Norris, Admiral of the Blue, &c. ; Sir Thomas Hardy, Rear Admiral of the Blue ; Captains Edward Hopson, Charles Strickland and Thomas Smith ; Monsr L. du Neth, Rear Admiral of Holland, and Captains Jolle Jolles and John Taatman.

The decision come to at this Council of War was to set sail for Dorwind, for the protection of the trade of Riga, so soon as the four ships daily expected from the Island of Hoghland should return ; to call for despatches at Dantzick ; and to hold a fresh Council of War to determine the proper time for returning with the Fleet to Revel in order to convoy the Trade to England and Holland.

With the above paper was also enclosed in the next letter a " List of the Czar's Fleet as they are disposed in a Line of Battel."

1715, June 24th. Sir John Norris to Lord Townshend. Dated, on board the Cumberland, at Revel.

The writer sent away the Trade bound to Petersburgh with four men-of-war to see them as far as the Island of Hoghland. On the 23rd he held a Council of War, " so we may put to Sea again so soon as the said four Ships have rejoin'd us." Has had the good Fortune to prevail with the Dutch Admiral to join with him " in such a Cruise as will not only serve for the Security of our Commerce, but also enable me to answer the other purposes of his Majty. so far as the time will allow. . . . . . . The people here are stil in dayly expectation of the Czar's Arrival with his Fleet from Crouslot but we have not received any Account of his leaving that Place."

[P.S.] 25th June.

" The Post not going away yesterday I have an Opportunity to acquaint your Lordp that last night I had a letter from the Czar by his private Secretary, by which and what that Gentn had orders to tell me I find his Majty is very desirous of my stay till he arrives with his Fleet from Cronslot, which his Secy assures me will be in a day or two . . . . I have inclos'd the Muscovite Line of Battel, and can tell your Ldp our Trade is got safe to Petersburgh. I sailed this morning from the Road of Revel and anchord off Nargan. Your Ldp will pardon the Liberty I take of putting my Family's Letters under your Cover."

1715, July 8th. The same to the same. Dated on board the Cumberland at Revel. Enclosing " Lists of the Danish and Sweedish Fleets," and " a State of Provisions on board his Majesty's Ships in the Baltick under the Command of Sr Jn Norris."

The writer has striven to persuade the Dutch Rear Admiral to act with him offensively against the Swedes, but the latter says that he cannot join in any offensive action until he receives such orders from the States, or advice from their Minister, Mr. Lentilo. " I have also received a second letter from the King of Prussia, wherein he acquaints me the Danish Fleet is retired, being too weak for the Swedes, and presses me immediately to endeavour to join the Danes . . . . if your Lordship shall send any orders for me at Copenhagen, we may attempt to put them in execution in conjunction with the Danes, as far as our provisions and the season of the year will admit, which are both pretty far spent . . . . ."

"P.S. His Czarian Majesty has ordered Gen¹ Prince Galexin to make a descent with 60 Gallies from Neustadt or Wassaw, on the coast of Finland in the North Bodom, upon the opposite coast where they can land best, in order to burn the country and divert the Swedes from transporting any troops to Pomerania. The Czar's troops designed for Pomerania are in motion, and I am told he designs to go thither in person.

"I enclosed yᵣ Lᵈship the copy of a List I have just had from the Czar of the Danish and Swedish fleets said to be at Sea and of the Danish Flotilla."

1715, July 13th. The same to the same. Dated on board the Cumberland at Dantzick.

". . . . . We sailed from thence [Nargan] the 28th, and meeting variable winds we came upon the coast of Windaw the 5th of this month, and being informed there that the Men of War and Trade at Riga were not molested by any Cruisers, we came from that coast, and arrived at Dantzick the 10th, and I am informed here by Mr. Beaumont and Mr. Hopman that they received a packet from your Ldship for me, but had forwarded the same to Revel . . . . . the Dutch Rear Admiral is informed from the Prints of his Country which he has seen here, that the States have lately declared that their order to him is to keep an exact neutrality, and therefore he cannot joyn with me in any case to act offensively against the Swedes and there being but 14 English Men of War with me, and by letters I have met with here from Mr. Jackson he sends me a List of the Swedish fleet now together, which is 26 sail, and 21 of them are of the Line . . . . . considering that by the last of this month our trade at Petersburgh will be ready, and that from that time we must be gathering up the Commerce to return down the Baltick, yᵣ Lᵈsp will expect no further of us than a proceeding with our Trade, unless the Swedes will seek an occasion ; but if it happen that we get down with them to Elsenure in any short time, where they will be free from any apprehension of the Swedes, if His Majesty be pleased that I have any further Orders to act with the Men of War, I shall very faithfully endeavour to obey his commands, which I beg your Lᵈship will answer for me.

"Here is two Merchant Men come to this place, whose Masters I have examined, and they give so odd a relation of the Swedish and Danish fleets, that if I had not examined them myself and found them ready to deliver wᵗ they said on oath, I should hardly have related it to your Lᵈship. One of them says that on the 8th instant near Bornholm, he was carried into the Swedish fleet by one of their Cruizers, that they were in all 35 sail, whereof 21 were of the Line, that while he was with them, they discovered the Danish fleet to Leeward and bore down to them, who he says were also 35 sail, and 21 of them in a line to receive the Swedes, that when the Swedes were near the Danes about 30 Cannons were fired from the Swedes at the Danes who made no return ; after wᶜʰ the Danes bore away and the Swedes kept their wind and so separated, and this man coming on his voiage hither saw no more of their proceedings. The other Master says that on the 9th he was likewise in the Swedish fleet near Bornholm, and saw them in sight of the Danes ; that the Swedes had the Wind of them, that he saw some few guns fired from the Swedes, after which the Swedes tacked and stood towards the Island of Bornholm and the Danes towards Fosterburn. . . .''

1715, July 16th. The same to the same. Dated on board the Cumberland at Dantzick.

Sir John encloses a copy of the resolutions come to at a Council of War two days before, and will pursue them if the post brings him nothing to the contrary.

In the Council of War it was decided that the fleet should proceed to Revel "and dispatch four ships from thence to Hoghland, to fetch the trade from Petersburgh to Revel, and that when they shall have rejoyned the fleet there, it be considered in another Council of War in what manner 'twill be best to take up the rest of the trade of both nations to proceed down the Baltick in order to return to our Countrys."

MARQUESS TOWNSHEND MSS.

1715, Augt. 2nd.   Lord Townshend to Sir John Norris.   From Whitehall.   Copy.   3 pp.

His Majesty entirely approves Sir John's conduct ; thinks it is of the last consequence to the nation that the merchant men who are now upon their return from the Baltic should be conducted home in safety—since if they should miscarry such a scarcity of naval stores must ensue as would disable him from fitting out a Fleet next Spring—and therefore orders Sir John to convey them home with all convenient speed. As, by returning home with his whole squadron and the merchant ships under convoy, Sir John will probably have no opportunity of making reprizals on the Swedes, he is instructed to leave behind him in the Baltic eight of his ships "under the command of some discreet Officer that is not a Flag," to act in concert with the Danish fleet, to compel the Swedes to make reparation for the damages they have done to his Majesty's subjects during the last two years, and to compel the King of Sweden to revoke the unjustifiable Edict lately published.

1715, Sept. 3rd.   Sir John Norris to Lord Townshend.   Dated at Copenhagen.

"My Lord—Since my last to your Lord^p from Dantzick, I am to acquaint you that I sail'd from thence the 25th of August, and anchor'd off Bornholm the 27th by reason of contrary Winds. I sail'd from thence the 1st of this Month and yesterday arrived with all our fleet in the Bay of Knyke, where I found the Danish fleet, whose Admiral sent me by a Frigat, Your Lord^{p's} Orders of the 2^d of August, upon wch I immediately came to an Anchor in that Road, and pursuant to your Commands made a detachment of eight of the best of our Ships under the Command of Captain Hopson, to join the Danish fleet and act according to your Lord^{p's} directions ; and have drawn from our other Ships what provisions they can possibly spare, to enable them to continue on the said service. After they seperated from me this Morning, I sail'd with the rest of our Ships and pass'd the Grounds of Elseneur, and am just come a shoar to this place to adjust with the Ministers for such further Provisions as shall be wanted for the service of the said eight Ships, but as the Post is now going and I have not opportunity to acquaint your Lord^p with any thing further, I shall not fail of taking particular Care to do it by the next," etc.

1715, Sept. 5th.   The same to the same.   Dated at Copenhagen. A signed duplicate, enclosed from Elseneur in the next letter.   3 pp.

The writer has arranged terms with the King of Denmark's Ministers for the provisioning of the squadron that he is to leave behind him in the Baltic. He hopes [very shortly] to have all our Trade clear'd at Elseneur and to be ready to sail by the first Opportunity to our Country. Is going to Fredricksberg tomorrow, to receive the Queen of Denmark's Commands, and from thence to Elseneur to our ships. The Danish Magazines have neither hemp, cordage, masts nor yards, sufficient for their own ships whence his Lordship will see that in case of difficulty they will not be able to supply our squadron.

Enclosed in the above letter are the three following papers.

1. Sir John Norris's Instructions to Capt. Hopson, Commander of his

Maj^re Ship the Burford.   Dated "aboard the Cumberland off Draco this
3ᵈ Sepʳ 1715."   4¾ pp.

2. State of the Provisions of the 8 Ships under the Command of
Captain Hopson in the Baltick.   ½ page.

3. Rates to be paid for Provisions that shall be taken up at Copenhagen for the Squadron in the Baltick, and charge of putting Men into
the Danish Hospitals &c.

The last-mentioned paper which illustrates prices and exchange, and
weights and measures, is as follows :—

"At what Rates such Provisions are to be paid for, as the eight Men
of War left in the Baltick have occasion to be supply'd with from
Copenhagen (Vizᵗ)

			li.	*s.*	*d.*	
Bread (of the King's sort)	} 2 Danish Schillings, or		0	0	1	sterling per pound.
Beer	112	,, ,,	0	4	8	{ per Danish tun said to contain 34 English Gallons.
Beef (salt)	4	,, ,,	0	0	2	} per pound.
Pork (salt)	7	,, ,,	0	0	3½	
Oatmeal	480	,, ,,	1	0	0	{ per Danish Ton said to contain 36 Eng. Gall.
Butter	10	,, ,,	0	0	5	} per pound.
Cheese	6	,, ,,	0	0	3	

" The Bills given for the said Provisions, are to be drawn according to
the printed Course of Exchange when the Provisions are deliver'd.

" If any Sea Men be put into the King of Denmark's Hospitals, the
Charge will be three Rixdollers per Man per Mensem, and five such
Dollers are accounted equal to a pound Sterling.

"1715, Sept. 10th. Sir John Norris to Lord Townshend. Dated on
board the Cumberland at Elseneur.

" My Lord—Herewith is the Duplicate of what I had the honour to
write to you from Copenhagen the 5th. After I had adjusted every
thing then with the Danish Ministers relating to the eight Ships wᶜʰ
stay under the Command of Capⁿ Hopson, I went to Fredricksburg,
where I had the honour of waiting upon the Queen of Denmark and all
that Royal Family. Her Majesty was pleased to command me to make
her Compliments to the King and Prince and Princess of Wales, and
commanded me to dine at her table, when she was pleas'd to drink their
Healths and Prosperity, as did all the Royall Family. I came that night
to our fleet, and we now only wait a fair wind to sail, wᶜʰ I shall be
carefull to do the first opportunity that shall present. I am, etc."

1715, Sept. 13th. The same to the same. Dated on board the
Cumberland at Elsenure.

" My Lord—Since my last to your Lᵈsp I have only to acquaint you
that by contrary winds I am still [kept here with the fleet, and the
shortness of our provisions has obliged me to endeavour the procuring
some at this place, the account of wᶜʰ I shall take care be regularly
sent to the Commissʳ of the Victualling at the cheapest rates I am
able, and pray the Lᵈship to move His Majesty that Admiralty may
order the bills my Secretaries shall draw on the Victualling be regularly
complyed with. I am, etc."

1715, Sept. 26th. Captⁿ Edward Hopson, R.N., "From on board
the Burford in Ruyck Bay," to Lord Townshend. In a clerk's hand;
unaddressed, and signed E. Hopson. 2 pp.

" My Lord—In Obedience to the Orders I receiv'd from Sir John Norris, I joyn'd the Danish Fleet with the Squadron of his Majesty's Ships under my Comand, at this Place the 4th instant, where we have continued ever since without any Motion towards proceeding any further. . . . .

" Count Geldenlew came on board and took the Command of the Danish Fleet two days since.

". . . . . The small quantity of Provisions which was demanded to compleat our ships to Twelve Weeks at Short Allowance, and but half Allowance of Beer is not yet all delivered . . . . . . should we want a further Supply, I fear it will be very difficult to get. As for Naval Stores by what I can learn they have not any in their Magazines should we be in want thereof. All these things considered, as well as the Season of the Year far advance'd, I don't see we shall be able to remain in these Seas longer than about the Tenth of October; but my Instructions directing me to consider that at a Council consisting of the Captains of the Squadron, I shall act accordingly, and shall not omit giving your Lordship an Account of our Proceedings as often as Opportunity shall offer, and pray leave to subscribe myself, etc.

" P.S. Just now I received a Message from Count Geldenlew that he had receiv'd the King's Orders, and design'd to sail the next morning by Day light, towards Rugen, I shall accompany him with my Squadron, being willing to promote the Publick Service, but am a little surprized at his giving me no other Intimation of his Intention."

1715, Sept. 27th. Copy of a despatch from Lord Townshend to Captn Hopson. Dated at Whitehall.

". . . . the King being acquainted that the Ministers of Denmark have agreed to furnish you wth provisions at the same Rates as his Danish Majesty is obliged to pay, and that you have a quantity sufficient to serve you till the 10th of October, about wch time Sr John Norris supposes you may be preparing to return home; I am commanded by his Majty to acquaint you that he thinks the interests of his Subjects, and his own Honour too much concern'd to support the particular points mention'd in the instructions Sr John Norris has given you; that it is therefore his pleasure that you should not think of leaving those seas with the Squadron under you Command untill your shall receive the King's speciall orders for that purpose . . . . . ."

1715, Oct. 17th. Sir John Norris to Lord Townshend. Dated on board the " Cumberland near the mouth of the Thames."

" My Lord,—I sailed with the fleet from Elseneur the 29th of the last month, and the 30th the wind coming contrary [we] were obliged to anchor off the Island of Lesson, where we rid till the 2d instant, and then having a favourable Easterly wind, we sailed out of the Categat, and passed the Schaw with all the fleet in the afternoon. That night came on a violent storm of wind from the South to the South West which dispersed the fleet so, that on the 3rd having hard gales and thick weather, we could not see, besides our own Men of War, and three Dutch, above 40 sail . . . .

" The Swallow and Moor, who were ordered to keep in the rear of the fleet were separated from us the night of the Gale.

" The 7th, three Dutch Men of War and some Merchant men parted from us for their Country . . . . . ."

" Captn Finbo will have the honour of delivering this letter to your Ldp. He is a very worthy Gentleman . . . . . I pray leave to recommend him to your Ldship's favour, and hope soon to be permitted the honour of waiting upon you, and am " etc.

1715, Nov. 5th. "Traduction d'une lettre du Commissariat de l'estat de la Marine, au Conseil, à Copenhagen." Signed Rantzau, Seckman, and Lassen. (1 page.) To which is appended a statement " Des provisions que l'Admiral le Chevalier John Norris a demandé pour l'Escadre Angloise qui est avec la flotte Danoise, et des provisions receues là-dessus, selon le poid et mesure de Dannemarc." 1 page.

The letter expresses surprise at complaints that the English ships had failed to obtain the provisions promised them, and calls the Council's attention to the accompanying extract which shows how the provisions have been supplied, in payment for which at present the commissariat have not touched a sou, though the commissariat had to advance money for the purchase of the provisions at considerable inconvenience.

[1716]. A list of the Swedish Ships which engaged the Danes on the 28 July 1715, and ought to be expected at Sea this year. Unsigned and undated.

[The total number of ships in this List is 21, and of their guns is 1366, and the proposals that follow seem to have been drawn up by Sir John Norris.]

" . . . . . Besides the above-mentioned ships the Swedes have at Gottenberg ten sail from 28 to 50 guns, which are in condition for the Sea and were out the 1st of last year.

" The aforesaid Account is the whole number of ships the Swedes had at Sea last year.

" If the King have Occasion for his fleet to proceed up the Baltick, the Danes, not being in a condition, or it not being for their interest to go above the Island of Bornholm, the English should have an equal number of guns in their fleet to the Swedes, to expect the success of a battle in case Occasion offer.

" If the English be only to joyn the Danes and act in conjunction with them, as much less a number as may be reasonably supposed the Danes shall joyn them with, to give the success to a battel in case of an engagement may suffice.

" The Swedes have a much greater number of Men than the English, insomuch that the Adml's ship of Sweden will have 1,100 men, and the English Admiral but 470, and a proportional difference between all the ships of the two nations; wherefore 'tis proposed that the English Ships may be allowed the same complement of Men they have in War.

The English ships are now ordered only the allowance of ammunition at home in time of Peace, which is but 40 Charges for each Canon, and in case they have an engagement, that will be neither sufficient to conquer their Enemies nor defend themselves; it is therefore proposed they be allowed the same proportion of Ammunition they carry aboard in time of War, together with 20 rounds of pound-shot, for the Danish Magazines are in so ill a condition, that they cannot supply the English in case of necessity.

" The English were, last year, victualled with four months provision at whole allowance, but if more had not been procured abroad, the ships had not been able to return, and yet, with that help, they were obliged to live some time at half allowance, wch in sharp weather men are not able to bear; and it is therefore proposed, they carry out with them a greater proportion of provisions.

" It is likewise proposed the fleet be allowed a fifth Rate Frigat, and two Sloops or sixth-rates, to assist in the useful parts of Sounding before the fleet, or helping any Ship that may be distressed by running aground, and also that an Hospital Ship may be allowed for the reception of sick or hurt seamen from the Men of War.

MARQUESS
TOWNSHEND
MSS.

" The Government of England has allowed 16,000 Seamen for this year, and if 7,000 of them be employed to the Baltick, it will be very little or no more charge to England than if they were all kept in the Channel."

1716, May 10th. Instructions for Sir John Norris. Given at the Court at St. James's at this date. $5\frac{3}{4}$ pp.

The instructions recite the grievances of the British Crown and Merchants against the Swedes. The King of Sweden "is now endeavouring to make himself Master of Norway, the reduction of wch Kingdome we look upon, besides the loss of the trade of Great Britain thither, to be the most ready way both to enable him to cut off entirely the Commerce of our Subjects to the Baltick, and to afford him greater opportunitys of carrying on those projects, which from good grounds we cannot but apprehend he is forming against the Peace and Safety of our Kingdomes."

Then follow specific instructions to Sir John Norris with regard to the reparation he is to demand and to the measures he is to take to enforce it. If he shall judge the King of Sweden's answer to be full and satisfactory, he must then "use all possible instances to divert the Danes from making an Invasion upon Schonen, and from carrying on any hostile attempt against any other the Territories of Sweden."

1716, May 11th. Lord Townshend to Sir John Norris. From Whitehall.

Requesting Admiral Norris to carry the bearer to the Sound and set him ashore at Elsingburg, and on his return to take him on board again and have him landed somewhere near Lubec.

1716, May 12th. Lord Townshend to Sir John Norris, and to Robert Jackson, British Resident at Stockholm. Dated at Whitehall. Copies of two letters (on the same sheet) enclosing duplicate drafts of the memorial (in French) which Sir John Norris was to send by express to the King of Sweden. Mr. Jackson is desired to form a memorial upon the same plan and to the same purpose, to deliver it to the Senate at Stockholm, and then to transmit to Lord Townshend with all convenient speed an account of the proceedings thereon, and of the answer he receives.

1716, May 17th. Sir John Norris to Lord Townshend. Dated on board the Cumberland at the Nore.

The writer hopes the Hampshire will join him to-morrow from Sheerness, and will take the first opportunity of wind to sail on his voyage. The Muscovite ships sailed the day before he came here.

1716, May 18th. Lord Townshend to Sir John Norris. From Whitehall. Copy.

" The King desires that Sir John will sail at the very first opportunity, and further that, if during his stay in the Baltick, application should be made to him by the Court of Denmark or by any of His Ministers abroad for granting a Convoy to ships carrying provisions for the Garrison at Wismar, he should comply therewith and see the said ships safe to Wismar."

1716, June 5th. Sir John Norris to Lord Townshend. Dated on board the Cumberland at Elseneur.

" . . . . . I waited on his Danish Maj^{ty} at Fredricksberg and made him our Master's compliments. His Ma^{ty} was pleased to receive me very favourably, and in discourse with me ask'd if he might know the purport of my Express to the King of Sweden. I told him 'twas by the command of the King to press his Swedish Maj^ty in the strictest manner to desist from his Enterprises in Norway, and for the Freedom of our Trade in the Baltick, and that I expected a favourable answer . .

. . . . if the King of Sweden should be so unreasonable as not to permit any answer to come to me, I shall be in want to know from your Lord^p how his Maj^ty will please to have me behave myself.

" Mr. Püchler tells me he has writ to England that the Court of Denmark intends a Descent upon Schonen with 20,000 Men who are to intrench themselves there till Troops can be got to strengthen them. . . . .

" I trouble your Lord^p with the inclosed Petition of the Master of one of our Merch^t Ships wch have been detained at Copenhagen by the Danes. I have made application to the Ministers for his Discharge, and they have promised me to be favourable to him. . . . ."

1716, May 30th. Copy of the humble petition of Robert Curson. Enclosed in the last. 1¾ pp.

The petitioner is master of the Adventure of Wells which is principally owned by himself and Mr. John Buckler of Wells. Last March when bound from Coningsberg to London the said ship was taken by a Swedish Privateer. It was recaptured by a Danish Frigate and carried to Copenhagen where it has been detained ever since because he refuses to pay the Danes one fourth of the value of the ship and cargo as salvage. Wherefore he humbly begs " that he may have liberty to prosecute his voyage without being obliged to answer the demand above-mentioned, since our Royal Master is at peace both with the King of Denmark and Sweden."

1716, June 11th. Copy of a letter in French from Monsr de Puckler to Admiral Norris. Dated at Copenhagen and enclosed " In Sir John Norris's of 1st June 1716."

The writer, on behalf of the King of Denmark, wishes the British Admiral to station his squadron between Carlscrona and Bernholm, or between Maën and Dornsbusch, so as to protect the vessels that are coming from Pomerania Mecklenbourg and Holstein. Their arrival is much needed both for fitting out the fleet, and for victualling the fleet and Copenhagen.

1716, June 13th. Robert Jackson to Sir John Norris. Dated at Stockholm. Copy 1½ pp.

" . . . . . . On Monday morning last the Holstein Privy Councillor Count Vander Nath arrived here in town from Wennersborg, a place about 20 Leagues from the King of Sweden's Camp at Swinesund, and I chanced to meet him the same Afternoon at Court, where after the usual Civility I inquired if he had not seen Monsr Stambke, when he made no difficulty to own that he left him at Wennersberg this day se'night, and seemed to believe he might still be att the same place, for he told me that while Baron Gortz the Holstein Treasurer and himself were regulating some matters at Wennersbourg, which the said Count Vander Nath went down on purpose to confer with him about, Monsr Stambke came to the same place in his way to the King of Sweden's Camp, and getting notice of their being there he immediately came to them, and acquainted Baron Gortz of his having some Letters to the King from you, when the said Baron demanding to see the Copys, and Monsr Stambke telling him he had received none from you, the Baron would not suffer him to proceed any further, but told him that as he was himself returning the same Day to the King of Sweden, he would let him know as soon as possible when it might be his Maj^s pleasure to permit him to come to him, so that I cannot but conclude Mr. Stambke will be some time detained, and consequently that you will not see him so very suddenly."

1716, June 15th. Lord Townshend to Sir John Norris. Copy. 1¼ pp.

Lord Townshend expresses the King's approval of Sir John's having strictly followed his instructions and states that in the King's opinion he should station his squadron at Bornholm or some other place near Carlscroon so as to have a watchful eye on the Swedish Fleet and enable the Dutch Squadron to proceed securely up the Baltic with the Trade.

1716, June 19th. Sir John Norris to Lord Townshend. Dated on board the Cumberland at Elseneur. A signed Duplicate. 4 pp.

"My Lord —— I recᵈ a Letter from his Danish Majᵗˢ Secʸ of State, Mʳ Schesledt, desiring me to attend his Majᵗʸ at Fredricksburg the 18ᵗʰ which I accordingly did, and acquainted him that I had recᵈ Letters from Mr. Jackson, and was in hopes, since the Swedes permitted them to come to me, soon to receive some Answer from his Swedish Majᵗʸ to the Memorial. But the King of Denmark believing the Swedish Fleet at Sea press'd very much that I wou'd, in the meantime, move with the Squadron towards the Bay of Ruyke and the Meun; in order to be a Countenance to his Men of War, who could then cruise, and secure the bringing his Troops and Provisions to the Island of Zeeland for the intended descent upon Schonen, which they are earnestly desirous to put in execution as soon as possible. I made as civil an excuse as I could; telling his Majᵗʸ that while I waited for the King of Sweden's Answer, I could not remove from where I ride, unless the Swedes made any Attack upon his Countries which should require my Assistance in his Defence. This did not satisfie the King, who told me he had been given to understand I was to assist as well as to defend him . . . . ."

1716, June 23rd. Copy of a Statement of Thomas Hall, Master of the Ship Prosperity of Hull, made on board the Cumberland at Elseneur. Enclosed in the next.

"Captain Hall states that he left Stockholm ten days ago, that 'twas reported there the Swedes were preparing to send an Army into Schonen, and that he saw three Regiments of Horse on their way thither," etc.

1716, June 26th. Sir John Norris to Lord Townshend. Dated on Board the Cumberland at Elseneur.

". . . . . I sent to the Governour of Elsinburg a letter for Mr. Jackson, importing only the recᵗ of his, desiring it might go by that day's post to Stockholm. The Governour received the letter, and sent me his assurances he would forward it, and that there was no answer come from the King of Sweden to the memorial, but [he] would not let any Officer land, but talked to him at the Boat, and said it was the King of Sweden's orders so to do. . . . . . ."

1716, June 30th. The same to the same. Dated on board the Cumberland at Elseneur. 2¼ pp.

". . . . . The Danes and Muscovites have nothing so much to wish for, as that we may be engaged alone with the Swedes; in wᶜʰ action let the advantage be as it will, we shall be both so disabled, as that after it they will be entire masters of these seas and have their own advantage to pursue it at pleasure . . . . . I have not any return to the Memorial, and every body here is of opinion, the King of Sweden will not come to any terms . . . ."

1716, July 3rd. Copy of a despatch from Lord Townshend to Sir John Norris. Unsigned. 1¾ p.

". . . . The King has ordered me to let you know that in case the Swedish fleet be out of port, or in such a station as may endanger the Trade, then you are to joyn 'such a detachment of your squadron with the Dutch, as you shall judge sufficient to oppose any attempt of the Swedes upon our Merchant men ; and since upon detaching a squadron of such a Force as may be requisite to protect our Commerce, you will be so much weakened, that your lying longer in the Sound may expose you to Insults from the Swedes, the King thinks it best you should go with the rest of his fleet to the Bay of Kiog or to such other station as you shall judge convenient and secure to wait for the King of Sweden's answer. And in case you have any apprehension of danger to the Squadron remaining with you from the superior strength of the Swedes, it is His Majestie's pleasure that you should joyn the fleet of Denmark for your better security. And as the King of Sweden has hitherto protracted his returning an answer, and probably will not give any, his Majesty therefore directs that you should not give any hindrance to the Danes in their descent upon Schonen either by representations or otherwise."

Same date. The same to the same. Copy 3 pp.

". . . . His Maj'y is well assured that the Swedish Minister at Paris has concluded a Treaty with the Rebels in France, by which they are to be admitted into the service of the Kg of Sweden in the same rank and Station as they enjoyed respectively under the Pretender . . . . it is his pleasure that in case the Fleet of Sweden should advance to attack that of Denmark, or otherwise to defeat the descent on Schonen, you should join with the Danes in giving them Battle, and in opposing their designs by all means possible. His Matys intentions being that you should observe no measures towards Sweden in any case where the assistance of his Fleet shall be necessary to deprive them of any signal advantage, or where your joyning the Danes may procure them some signal advantage over Sweden. But without one or the other of these two cases you are not to give the Danes such a degree of assistance a me be interpreted to amount to an open rupture with Sweden. I am," &c.

1716, July $\frac{13th.}{24th}$ Copy of Additional Instructions to Sir John Norris. "Given at our Court at Osnaburg." Docqueted "In Mr. Stanhope's of 21 July, 1716." 3½ pp.

These instructions are, concert with the Dutch squadron to convoy the merchant men so far to the eastward of the Swedish fleet that they may safely reach their destinations under a detachment sufficient to protect them from Capers and other Frigates, and then with the main body of the joint fleet to watch the Swedish fleet and to execute reprisals Further to request the King of Denmark to order a strong squadron of his ships to join the joint fleet and to give him assurances of being ready to act in concert with the Danish Squadron to oblige the Swedish fleet to retire into their ports.

1716, Nov. $\frac{2nd}{13th}$. Sir John Norris "to Mr. Secy Schestedt." Copy. Dated at Copenhagen and enclosed in Sir John's letter to Lord Townshend on the following day.

" Sir—My Royal Master having commanded me to put a Squadron of his ships in a Condition to remain in these parts some time longer, and finding it absolutely necessary for that End, that a Quantity of Bread, besides other Provisions should be provided, I directed our Commissary to endeavour to procure the same. He has accordingly ingag'd two hundred barrels of Wheat flower, but as he informs me he is unable to bring it into Copenhagen without paying a Duty, I humbly request you will be pleas'd to represent the same to his Majty, and as it is not for Merchandizing but the Use of my Master's ships, he will be pleas'd to grant that the said flower, as well as what other Provisions it may be necessary to procure for that Squadron while in these parts, may be free of any Duty or Douaine; the like flower [? favour] having been always granted by the Crowns of Spain and Portugal when our fleets were useful there. And for avoiding any fraud to the Crown of Denmark by this favour, I have given directions by our Commissary, Mr. Vere who is the Bearer of this Letter to give you what Testimony you please, either upon his honour or Oath, that whatever Provisions he shall procure will be only for our Master's Service, and Mr. Clevland who has the honour to command in chief the said Squadron will likewise assure you of the same from time to time as it shall be necessary. I am &c. J. N."

MARQUESS TOWNSHEND MSS.

1716, Nov. $\frac{3rd}{14th}$. Sir John Norris to Secretary Stanhope. Dated at Copenhagen. Copy. Enclosed in the next. 2¾ pp.

"Since my last of the 30ᵗʰ October, the Dutch Men of War with all their Trade arrived here, and all the Merchant Men will be clear'd by tomorrow at Elseneur for leaving this Country and I shall accordingly take the first opportunity of Wind to sail to ours.

"I have not been favoured with any of yours since that of the fourteenth last Month, but Mr. Bothmar having shewn me his Letters, that you would send me his Majᵗˢ Commands by Major Finbo for leaving six Ships under Captain Clevland in these Seas for some time longer, I shall perform the same tho' your Orders do not come to my hands, and if his Majᵗʸ will permit me humbly to name a time proper for their return from these parts, I believe the 20ᵗʰ of December will be as long as they can well stay for the Ice . . . . .

"P.S.—I have only time to acquaint you Major Finbo is just arrived, and that by next Post I shall send you an Account of all our Proceedings. I have likewise received a Message from Mʳ Sehestedt that their Court has consented to my request of the Provisions."

Same date. Sir John Norris to Lord Townshend. Dated at Copenhagen.

"My Lord—I had the honour of writing to your Lᵈᵖ the 28ᵗʰ of last Month, and came to this place with our Men of War and Trade next day, when I received the favour of your Letter of the 9ᵗʰ past, and am very glad my behaviour has met with his Royal Highness's approbation.

"For the present State of our Affairs here I pray leave to refer your Lordᵖ to the enclos'd copies of what I write Mr. Secʸ Stanhope by this Post, and am with the greatest Respect etc.

"Jⁿ. Norris."

1716, Nov. 4th. The same to the same. Dated "off Copenhagen."

"My Lord I have only to trouble your Ldp with the inclosed copy of my letter of this date to Mr. Secʳʸ Stanhope of my orders to Captain Clevland, and to acquaint you I am now under sail in order to make the best of my way for England. I am with great respect, etc.

"John Norris."

Same date. The same to Secretary Stanhope. Dated at Copenhagen. Enclosed in the last. Copy, 1½ pp.

Enclosing the writer's Instructions for Capt. Clevland and begging
that further instructions may be sent to the latter to rectify whatever
the writer may have omitted.

Same date. Copy of Instructions from Sir John Norris Admiral of
the Blue, etc. "To William Clevland, Esq., Command^r in Chief of
the Squadron of his Majestic's ships to be employed upon the Coast of
Norway." Enclosed with the last. 2½ pp.

These orders are ; To wait at Copenhagen till the 30th of Novr for
his Majesty's commands ; to inform Mr. Stanhope of this, and to obey
the instructions he will send, to open despatches arriving for Sir John
Norris, and communicate them to Lord Polwarth and Mr. Bothmar, etc

17$\frac{15}{16}$, Jan. 9th. William Thomson, Recorder of London, to Lord
Townshend.

"My Lord,
I am obliged to trouble your Lordship once more on the
behalf of John Wild who was reprieved to wensday next. He persisted
in his innocence to the last not knowing of his repreive, I presume your
Lordship will please to mention it to the King that he may be repreived
till further orders, and that you will please to signifie his Majesty's
intentions to the Sheriffs or myself in a letter to that purpose. I am" etc.

17$\frac{15}{16}$, March 8th. Walter Etherington to Lord Townshend. "Principal Secretary of State."

The writer has brought Lieut. Cunningham to make affidavit against
Francis Hamond, Governor of Landguard Fort, and Mathew Draper his
Deputy, who put him under arrest for 24 hours for drinking the health
of the Duke of Marlborough on the 31st of December last.

[1716, July.] Proposed alterations in the Cabinet. In French and
undated. The Duke of Devonshire to be President of the Council with
the salary of 3500 pounds sterling a year which ought to be drawn in
part from the pension of the Duke of Argyle and in part from the
profits of the Privy Seal which Lord Sunderland is willing to surrender
for this purpose.

Lord Sunderland to be Keeper of the Privy Seal without Salary and
to have sole charge as Vice Treasurer of Ireland.

The Duke of Kent to be Lord Steward of the Household [Grand
Maitre] in the place of the Duke of Devonshire.

The Duke of Kingston to be Master of the Horse [Grand Ecuyer].

Mr. [Francis] Negus to be Master of the Horse under the Duke of
Kingston.

Mr. [Conyers] Darcy to be Master of the Buckhounds.

The Duke of Montrose to be Lord Clerk Register [Greffier] to Scotland, in the place of Lord Isla.

Lord Tankerville to be a Lord in Waiting [Seigneur de la chambre
du Roy] in the place of the Duke of Kent.

Lord Leicester to be a Lord in Waiting in the place of Lord Orrery.

Lord Haversham to be Keeper of the King's Forests south of Trent,
in the place of Lord Tankerville.

Lord Cobham to be Constable of Windsor Castle, in the place of the
Duke of Kent.

1716, July 22nd. A letter to Monsr d'Ibberville from the Conseil de
Marine " wth a Memorial on the Insults they say the English Fishermen
on the Coasts of France and England do the French Fishermen on the
afores^d Coasts." In French. 1 page.

1716, Nov. 11th. Lord Sunderland to Lord Townshend. Dated at MARQUESS
TOWNSHEND
MSS. Gohre in Holland and unaddressed.

"My Lord—My giving your Ld^p this trouble, is occasion'd by Mr Stanhop's having shewn me, a letter he has writt to you, by the King's express Command, upon the subiect of the French Treaty, and the delays in the signing of it. Your Lord^p may remember that at the beginning of this negotiation with France I was very much against it, apprehending it was an artifice onely of the French Party in Holland, to avoid the Treaty with the Emperour, and to sow disunion among the Allies, however when I left England, I saw plainly the Torrent was for carrying on the negotiation ; I knew no more till I came hither of this affair, butt what I had from common news, and reports in the Low Countries, and therefore upon the same generall notion, I writt my opinion to your Ld^p in generall still to the same effect, whilst I was at Aix. Butt upon my arrivall here, and Mr Secretary Stanhop's having acquainted me with the Treaty itself, and every step that had been taken in it; I was entirely convinc'd that no negotiation had ever been managed with more pains and prudence, nor no Treaty ever brought to a Conclusion more glorious, nor more advantageous to the King and England ; especially under the circumstances Europe is like to be in, by these proceedings of the Czar, the King of Prussia, &c. which very probably may make France, take a pretence from these delays, to avoid signing at last, and what is more yett is, that the occasions of this delay, leave it in the power of France to say it is not their fault. I am sincerely concern'd at any thing that may be preiudiciall to the King's service, and particularly at any thing that happens that may nott rightly be understood among those in his service, that allways have, and allways ought to act cordially together; and that is the single reason why I say any thing upon so unpleasant a subiect. I must therefore be so plain as to tell you that I never saw the King resent any thing so much as this affair, in which he thinks, nott only Mr Secretary Stanhope butt himself nott well us'd ; and indeed I think, it wants to be explain'd ; I must nott omitt too acquainting your Ld^p that the King is very much surpris'd at the strange notion that seems at present to prevail, as if the Parliament was not to concern themselves in any thing that happens in these parts of the world, which he looks upon, nott onely as exposing him to all kind of affronts, but even to ruine ; and indeed this notion is nothing butt the old Tory one, that England can subsist by itself, whatever becomes of the rest of Europe, which has been so iustly exploded by the Wigs, ever since the Revolution. I am very sensible, that upon many accounts it might have been more prudent in me nott to have mention'd these things, butt the King's service, and the supporting the right interest, and the union of those in his service depend so much upon these things being rightly understood, that I could nott have answer'd it to my self, if I had nott troubled you a[bout] this,—you will take it is, I am sure [mos]t sincerely meant, by him that is with [the] greatest truth and respect—My Lord—y^r Ld^{ps}— Most obedient humble servant

"SUNDERLAND."

[1716.] "Copy of the K^{gs} lett^r to the Prince [of Wales] containing the restrictions laid upon him in his Regency." [In French. 6½ pp.]

1716. [Draft] Letters from Lord Townshend to [the Pensionary] Mr Secretary Stanhope, Horatio Walpole, &c., from Jany 10th, 17$\frac{15}{16}$ to Decr 11th 1716. [In a card board cover.]

The latest of these letters is addressed to Secretary Stanhope and encloses a letter in French, for him to hand to the King, in which Lord Townshend accepts his dismissal and declines the Lord Lieutenantship of Ireland.

1716-1717. "Copies of letters relating to the change of Ministry in 1716-1717, from Lord Townshend, Mr. Walpole, &c." In book form. On the cover is the following memorandum :—" I know this to be in the handwriting of the Revd Thos Patrick Young who was a Prebendary of Westminster and Rector of North Church Herts— TOWNSHEND & LEICESTER—April 1808."

1716-1724. A packet of ten letters described on their cover as " Curious letters from Lord Bolingbroke to Lords Townshend & Harcourt—belonging to the Marquis Townshend."

These letters have been printed by Archdeacon Coxe in his Memoirs of Sir Robert Walpole.

1. The first is undated, unsigned, and unaddressed, and is apparently in a Secretary's handwriting. 1¼ pp.

2. "Paris le 16 Mars 1716." In French. Unsigned and unaddressed. 1 p.

3. "Paris Dec : the 17th 1723." Probably to Lord Harcourt. Unaddressed. 4 pp.

4. "Paris Dec : the 28th 1723." Unsigned and unaddressed. Endorsed, "From Lord Bolingbroke to Ld Harcourt." 6¼ pp.

5. "Dec. 29 1723." Unsigned and unaddressed. In the same handwriting as the 1st letter. 3 pp.

6. "Paris Dec : the 29th 1723." Address obliterated. Signed " B." Lord Bolingbroke to *Lord Townshend?* 2 pp.

7 and 8. "30 Dec 1723." Unsigned and unaddressed, with cipher names and cipher figures. Lord Bolingbroke to *Lord Harcourt.* It is accompanied by a deciphered rendering in the same handwriting as the letters 1 and 5. 2 pp.

9. "Jan. 12, 1724." Unsigned and unaddressed. In cipher. 8¾ pp.

10. "Feb. 3, 1724." Unsigned and unaddressed. In cipher. 6 pp.

1717, April 9th. General Stanhope, Secretary of State, to Lord Townshend. Dated at the Cockpitt.

" My lord—the King judging it for his service to dispense with your lordship's service as lord lieut^t of Ireland I am commanded to signifie his Maties pleasure to your lordship upon it, his Ma^ty is sorry that many circumstances render this alteration necessary at present he commands me to assure your lordship that he will never forget your past services and you'l give me leave to say that I shall be very gladd of an occation of writing to your lordship upon a more agreable subject as being with great respect—my lord—your lordship's most humble and most obedient servant

" JAMES STANHOPE."

[1720.] The extract of a Project sent by Count Bernsdorf to Count Zinzendorf. [Undated.]

" The disgusted Whiggs have endevoured to convince his Majesty that the Cabal designe to alter the Constitution, to destroy the present Establishment and the Quadruple Alliance, which was formed for the Security of both, but it seems now they intend that Allians[e] only to secure themselves in their Places, the better to enable them to run the Nation into an Aristocracy as appears by the Frame of the South Sea Bill.

" That the Cabal designe to amuse his Majesty with a Peace in the South in the same Manner as they have done that of the North, but in the end will order it so as to establish themselves, and be able for the future to give Laws to the King and his Son, and even to remove him when they shall think Proper.

" That they will be condescending to France and Spain the better to secure the Intrest of those two Crowns by whose Power they intend to keep the Czar from a Peace in the North till such time as they can be in a Condition to enable him to disturbe the Peace of the Empire.

"The disgusted Party offer to countermine the designes of the Caball after [*sic*] the following method.

"To give good Termes to Spain by which means they hope to secure the South Sea Trade the better to enable that Company to furnish his Majesty with two or three Millions independent of Parliament if his affairs abroad should require it.

"By this means his Majesty may bring the Czar and other Northern Princes to be at his Devotion and keep them in his Intrest.

"To secure the Peace of the North and the Empire for the future they propose to advance Money to King Augustus to buye off the Crown Generall and some other considerable Palatines in order to make Poland Hereditary by which means they would also be able to keep the Power of France within bounds.

"That it would be more for the Intrest of his Majesty and the Nation to make an Addition to his German Dominions by the Purchase of some Country contiguous to his present Teritories which would enable him to hold the Ballance between the Northern Powers better then by sending a Fleet yearly to the Baltick which gives umbrage to the People.

"France will undertake no new Warr during this Minority, consequently his Majesty in conjunction with his Imperial Majesty may the easier put these Scheams in execution.

"As the present Cabal is made up of two Classes of Men entirely resigned to the will and direction of two or three at most, and as the one class are men of birth but no experience all miscarriages may be laid at their dore, and the lat[t]er being men of some experience but no birth there can be no difficulty to bring them to Justice to make an attonement to the People, that when their indirect practices and miscarriages are laid open it is presumed none either at home or abroad will appear in their favour.

"It is conceaved his Majesty must not delay long to give attention to this Scheame because to defer it to the next Sessions will be dangerous.

"Your Excellency may see that it is the opinion of most of our friends as well as our owne that there is a necessity to chaing[e], and as the persons that offer this project are of consequence, and promise sincerely to stand by his Majesty he may safely give into them. It is true the regent may be dubious, but as he has Views of his owne he will at least stand neuter, however I am certain that his Majesty will be much better in the hands of these new projectors then where he is at present.

"The King must dissemble and take no notice of their proceedings towards us which will give us the better opertunity to provide ourselves with honest men, probably the measurs that was formed against us may be improved to our advantage. This somer will in all likelyhood be spent in Treaties (you know our mouthes are shutt up,) therefore it would be very proper to hasten an Imperial Minister here to observe their motions, and to find out what Clandestin measurs may be carried on with France which if not timely discovered may tend to the prejudice of both our Mastiers, you are sencible how dangerous 'tis to trust Ministers abandoned to their pleasurs for such have more then once been corrupted by France.

"Thank God we have persons that will counterpoyse and assist the King to disapoynt them.

"Instead of performing their promise to push forwards and to assist the King to cutt of[f] all dependance they relent, and in all likelyhood will spend eight monthes time doing that which might be done in three, however I hope their designes will be brought to light and the

eyes of the People will be opened, which will give the King an opertunity to part with them with honour and Reputation to himselfe, by
substituting the following persons :

> Sr Peter King Lord Keeper
> Duke of Somersett Master of the Horse
> Duke of Devonshire Groom of the Stole
> Duke of Rutland Master of the Householbl
> Duke of Chandois first Lord of the Treasury
>   or in case he refuses Ld Pembrook
> Lord Orford in his former Place
> Lord Couper President of the Councill
> Lord Stanhop[e] Privy Seale or Generall of the Horse
> Mr Methwin Secretary of State
> Lord Carlton Secretary of State
> Lord Sunderland Ld Livetenant of Ireland
> Lord Townshend in Lord Linco[l]n's place
> Mr Walpole Chancelor of the Exchequer
> Duke of Argile may keep his place or cho[o]se to be Generall of
>   the Foot.

There will be rome left for 5 or 6 of the leading county Tories to
come in for the rest of the places and in case they refuse the other
country gentlemen of god esteame and estates, that will accept of the
King's Favours.

"D. C. [DAVID CRAWFORD?]"

1720–1729. Miscellanies of Foreign Correspondence from the 14th
Novr 1720 to 8th Novr 1729. In a cardboard cover.

[After 1720]. "List of the Attendance of the R^{bt} Honble the late
Earl of Stanhope on his Journey, and during his Residing at Hannover."
[Undated 3½ pp.]

17$\frac{20}{21}$, Jan. 4th. Lord Irwin to George Treby. Dated "Whensday
Morning" and enclosed in the next. Endorsed "Ld Irwin to Secry at
War in his of 6 Jan."

The writer states that he is sending papers to justify the action of
Quartermaster Thompson, and he concludes : "I had waited on you my
self but am not yet able to walke. I'm S^r—Your verry humble and
obediant Servant.

"IRWIN."

[P.S.] "the Quarter Master is a relation of Mr Methuen's and I doe assure you of as good a charrecter as any young fellow in the Kings serviss.
I send you likewise Mr Taylor's letter desireing such a force which I
beg you will not loose."

17$\frac{20}{21}$, Jan. 6th. George Treby to the R^t Honble James Craggs. From
Whitehall. Endorsed "Secretary at War—with an acc^t of what was
done by Ld Irwin's Dragoons in assisting the Custome Officers at Weymouth."

17$\frac{20}{21}$, Feb. 9th. Lord Townshend to Colonel William Stanhope, afterwards Earl of Harrington. From Whitehall. "Sir—The King having
been pleas'd to honour me with the Seals I can with great truth assure
you that it is a very great mortification to me to find my self under a
necessity of beginning our correspondence by condoleing with you on the
death of Lord Stanhope. You have lost in him a very kind and sincere
friend and relation, and the King an able and faithfull servant at a juncture when he had great occasion for his help and assistance. I heartily

wish I could say anything to you upon this melancholy occasion that might give you ease and relief under your present affliction, for tho' I have not the happiness of being personally acquainted with you, yet your character and the services you have done the King in the stations you are in are so well known to me, that I can without flattery assure you that you may upon all occasions command my best services. It is a great addition to our present misfortune that Mr Craggs is fall'n ill of the small pox and I fear is in some danger. I have not seen your last letters; I am told they are before the King from whom I have nothing in particular at present in command for you, but believe I shall dispatch a messenger to you in a few days. I have therefore now nothing further to add but only to lett you know that His Ma^{ty} is resolvd to pursue the same measures and to support steadily all the engagements he is entred into, and you may assure both the Marq^s Scotti and Monsr Grimaldi that His Ma^{ty} will persevere in the same favourable intentions towards his Catholick Ma^{ty} and wishes most earnestly to see a firm and lasting friendship and correspondence settled between the two crowns. I am with the greatest respect etc.

"TOWNSHEND."

1721, Feb. 14th. Copy of a letter from the Emperor Charles VI. to King George I. Dated at Vienna. In German. 8 pp.

1721, March $\frac{7}{18}$th. Copy of a letter from King George I. to the Emperor Charles VI. In German. 10 pp.

1721, March 15th. Bill of extraordinary expenses of Robert Jackson, Envoy to Sweden. From December 25th 1720 to March 25th 1721. Dated at Stockholm.

The amount claimed is £99 of which £30 is for postage.

Minuted at foot " Whitehall, 6 June 1721—I allow this Bill.

"TOWNSHEND."

1721, April 1st. Translation of Mr Renard's Letter to my Lord Townshend. Dated at Amsterdam. 3 pp.

The writer forwards a list of the effects of the late Directors of the South Sea Company that he has seized as his Majesty's Agent, viz. :—In the hands of George Clifford & Company 243,540 Florins in divers bonds upon Silesia, and a year's interest thereon at 8 per cent., due to Sir Theodore Jansen, Sir Lambert Blackwell, Charles Joye, Robert Knight, Richard Horsey, and John Gore . . . Andrew Pels and Company declare that Sir Theodore Janssen has transferred to them 10,000^{li} South Sea Stock which they are to restore him . . . . Henry Termitten declares that Sir Theodore Janssen has transferred for his account to Mr Christopher Van Brants 4,400^{li} South Sea Stock . . . . Mark Cocky declares that Sir Theodore Janssen has transferred to him 9000^{li} South Sea Stock, and 3000^{li} more of the said Stock, for his account, to Nicholas Dirckens ; but that Sir Janssen has laid hold of 103,900 Florins belonging to him, Mark Cocky, as a deposit for the said Stock.

" . . . . here is an instance of what passes in relation to the Quarantaine of Ships that come from France. A French ship from Bayonne bound for Amsterdam put into Ireland and there received on board five men, the King's subjects, who were to search this ship and remain on board during the Quarantaine ; but the French Captain being unwilling to wait so long, would have sent the Irish on shore, where their countrymen refused to admitt them ; so that these five men were obliged to reimbark in the French vessel, which brought them hither and here they landed without performing any Quarantaine. These poor people came to me to help them to a passage home. I sent them to the Resident Dayrolle at the Hague, to be examined.

"One sees by this instance that Quarantaine is better observed in Great Britain than here."

1721, May 19th. "Le Rev^de Monsr de Choisy" to Lord Townsend. Addressed "A Monseigneur—Monseigneur le Comte de Townsend premier Secretaire d'Estat, at his house in Albemarle Street, near Picadili."

"Monseigneur—Comme depuis longtemps, les pauvres Ministres Refugiez n'ont rien reçéu des trois années, et un mois de pension, qui nous sont maintenant déuës pour ce regne; et comme cela est cause qu'enfin, avec une santé fort mauvaise, je suis deplus dans un tres pressant besoin, manquant mesme des choses les plus necessaires pour la vie; vous me permettrez, Monseigneur, de vous le representer par cette lettre, espérant que vous aurez quelque compassion d'un Ministre de l'Evangile qui bier que dans un Royaume Protestant, se voit néanmoins reduit à un estat si deplorable, je vous en seray extrèmement obligé, et en attendant, je demeure, avec tout le respect possible,—Monseigneur—Vostre très humble, et tres obéissant serviteur

"De Choisy."

"Le 19me de May, 1721,
     At the Seven Stars
          in King Street, Covent Garden."

1721, July 22nd. George Tilson to the same. Dated at Whitehall and unsigned.

A memorandum about some despatches. It concludes :—"I sent your Lo^p last night a draught to the Archbishop of Cambray [Fenelon] Perhaps there may be too much flourish in it but to a French man I thought something of that sort not amiss."

1721, Sept. 16th. The same to the same. Dated at Whitehall.

". . . . Lord Cartaret still finds more convincing reasons to believe the business of the partition real; I had a short letter from M^r de St Saphorin of the 10th wherein he says nothing but that the Germans are passive in the business of making new grandees which he looks on as an ill sign for the congress, and a mark of the prevalency of the Spaniards. Lord Whitworth . . . . thinks he has found great benefit by the baths; he is preparing to return to the Hague and from thence to Berlin. . . ."

1721, Sept. 25th. The Archbishop of Canterbury (Dr Wake) to Lord Townsend. Signed "W. Cant."

Enclosing two papers in Latin reporting the Evangelical Conference held at Ratisbon on the 16th of the previous month, and relating to the affairs of the Protestants and the reformed religion in Germany.

The Archbishop begs Lord Townshend and Lord Sunderland to consider these papers; and, if they shall judge proper, mention the matter to the King, and obtain his favour on behalf of the Reformed. He hopes to be at Lambeth at the end of the week for the whole winter, and will then enquire what is thought tit to be done in this matter, so that he may return some answer to our friends abroad.

1721 to 1730. Copies and drafts of Lord Townshend's depatches from 9th Feby 17 21/22 to 12th May 1730. In cardboard cover.

[1722?] An undated Address to the King "from the Protestant Dissenting Ministers of the three denominations in and about the Cities of London and Westminster."

This address expresses the loyalty of the Dissenters and their hopes for the full detection of traiterous designs of the King's Enemies.

1722, Oct. 31st. Count Walleurodt to Lord Townshend. In French. Dated in London and unaddressed.

The writer reminds his Lordship of his promises to Mʳ Dayrolles at the Hague about an arrangement with the House of Nassau, and also to send orders to Mʳ [James] Scot at Berlin as to the Conferences set on foot in favour of the poor Protestants of Poland.

172$\frac{2}{3}$, March 8th. Copy of the King's letter to the Duke of Orleans.

" Mon Frère et Cousin, Les égards que J'ay pour les contesses de Holderness et Deguenfeld, m'obligent de m'interesser aupres de vous en leur faveur. Je vous prie de permettre que le Chevalier Schaub ait l'honneur de vous representer l'affaire, qui les regarde, à l'occasion de laquelle Je me flatte, que vous voudrez bien, à ma recommendation, leur temoigner quelque bienveillance. C'est en quoy vous me ferez un sensible plaisir, et Je vous assure, que Je n'en auray pas moins, de pouvoir vous en marquer ma reconnoissance, et l'attachment sincère, avec le quel Je suis,

" Mon Frere et Cousin
" À Sᵗ James le 8ᵉ   Votre bien bon Frère et
de Mars 172$\frac{2}{3}$ Cousin
" À Mon Frère e[t] Cousin   " GEORGE R."
le Duc d'Orléans."

1723, May 15th. Copy of a letter from the Duke of Modena to Monsʳ Riva. In Italian, and partly in cipher numbers. 7 pp.

1723. A packet of letters which have been printed by Archdeacon Coxe in his " Memoirs of Sir Robert Walpole." (Vol. II. p. 294 et seq.)

1723, Oct. 1st. Whitehall. Robert Walpole to Lord Townshend Unsigned. 12 pp.

1723, Oct. 11th. Whitehall. The same to the same. " Private." 4 pp.

1723, Oct. 18th. Whitehall. The same to the same. " Private.' 6½ pp.

1723, Oct. 26th. Houghton. The same to the same. 3 pp.

1723, Nov. 1st. Claremont. Duke of Newcastle to the same. 10 pp.

1723, Nov. $\frac{19\text{th}}{30\text{th}}$. Whitehall. Robert Walpole to the same. Enclosing a memorandum endorsed " Bishop of London's paper relating to the Deanery of Rochester.'

1723–1727. A bundle of despatches (in a cardboard cover) selected and copied by Archdeacon Coxe.

These despatches are dated and addressed as follows :—

1723, Sept. 24th. N. S. Lord Townshend to Mr. Secretary Walpole. From Hanover. " Private." 11 pp.

1723, $\frac{\text{Oct. 21st}}{\text{Nov. 1st}}$. Horatio Walpole to Lord Townshend. From Paris. 18½ pp. The latter part of this letter is dated $\frac{\text{Oct. 23}}{\text{Nov. 3}}$, 1723.

Same date. The same to the same. From Paris. 14½ pp. foolscap.

1723, Nov. 8th, 9th, and 10th, N.S. The same to the same. From Paris. 13½ pp.

1723, Nov. $\frac{9th}{20th}$. The same to the same. From Paris. 26½ pp.

1723, Nov. $\frac{11th}{22nd}$. The same to the same. Unsigned and unaddressed. Mostly in cipher numbers which are deciphered between the lines. About the marriage of the Countess of Platen's daughter. 1 p.

1723, Nov. $\frac{16th}{27th}, \frac{18th}{29th}$. The same to the same. Unsigned and unaddressed. A cipher letter on the same subject as the last. 1 p.

1723, Nov. 27th. Lord Townshend to Horatio Walpole. Unsigned draft.

1723, Nov. ——. Draft of "Instructions [from the King] sent to Mr. Secretary Walpole for Mr. Horatio Walpole relating to the marriage of the Countess of Platen's daughter. Referred to in Mr Secretary Walpole's private letter of the 19th of Novembr 1723."

1723, Dec. 1st. Horatio Walpole to Lord Townshend. From Paris. "Private." 7 pp.

Same date. The same to the same. From Paris. 15½ pp.

1723, Dec. 8th. The same. "To the Rt Honble Robert Walpole Esqr." From Paris. Copy. 3½ pp.

1723, Dec. 10th, N.S. The same to George Tilson. From Paris. Unaddressed, partly in cipher. 2 pp.

Same date. The same to Lord Townshend. From Paris. 2 pp.

1723, Dec. 15th, N. S. The same to Robert Walpole. From Paris. 16½ pp.

1723, Dec. $\frac{11th}{22nd}$. The same to the same. From Paris. 5½ pp.

172¾, Jan. 29th, Lord Townshend to Horatio Walpole. Draft. 2½ pp.

1724, Sept. 27th. Horatio Walpole to George Tilson. Unaddressed. Dated at Fontainebleau. Endorsed "Recd by Stone [the messenger] 21 [Sept. O. S]." 2 pp.

1725, April 21st. The same to Lord Townshend. From Paris. 2 pp.

1725, July 20th. Lord Townshend to Stephen Poyntz. From Pyrmont. "Very private and to yourself alone." Copy 4 pp.

1725, Augt. $\frac{16th}{27th}$. The same to Horatio Walpole. From Hanover. "Very private." Copy. 18½ pp.

1725, $\frac{\text{Augt. 30th}}{\text{Sept. 10th}}$. The same to Horatio Walpole. From Fontainebleau. "Very private." 19 pp.

1726, March 19th. Count de la Lippe Shaumbourg to George Tilson. From Manheim. In French. Unaddressed. 1 p.

1726, April 10th. Horatio Walpole to George Tilson. From Paris. Unaddressed. 1 p.

1726, May 6th, N. S. The same to the same. From Paris. Unaddressed. 4 pp.

1726, July 12th. Lord Townshend to Stephen Poyntz. From Whitehall. Unaddressed. "Very private and to yourself alone." Copy. 4 pp.

1726, August 25th. The same to Horatio Walpole. From Whitehall. Draft. 5½ pp.

1726, Augt. 27th. The same to the same. "Private." Draft.
1½ pp.

1726, Sept. 1st. Horatio Walpole to Stephen Poyntz. From Fontainebleau. Copy sent "with Mr. Walpole's of the 2 Septr 1726." 4 pp.

1726, Sept. 2nd. The same to George Tilson. From Fontainebleau.
Unaddressed. 3 pp.

172$\frac{4}{5}$, $\frac{\text{Jan. 25th}}{\text{Feb. 5th}}$ to $\frac{\text{Sept. 23rd}}{\text{Oct. 4th}}$ 1726. Extracts from Mr. Stanhope's
letters. [9 sheets foolscap.]

1726, Dec. 11th. Horatio Walpole to George Tilson. Unaddressed.
1 p. The writer will set out for Calais to-morrow.

1726, — Dec. Projet des propositions à faire a l'Empereur et a
l'Espagne. Draft in French. 3½ sheets.

1727, Jan 11th, N. S. Thomas Robinson to George Tilson. From
Paris. 2½ pp.

1727, Jan. 13th. Copy of the letter of Cardinal de Fleury to Mr.
Walpole. In French. 3¼ pp.

1727, Feb. 15th. Thomas Robinson to George Tilson. From Paris.
1 p.

1727, March 12th, N.S. Horatio Walpole to the same. From Paris.
Unaddressed. 3 pp.

1727, March $\frac{\text{2nd}}{\text{13th}}$. The same to the same. From Paris. Unaddressed.
2 pp.

1727, March $\frac{\text{4th}}{\text{15th}}$. The same to the same. From Paris. 1 p.

1727, March $\frac{\text{16th}}{\text{27th}}$. The same to the same. From Paris. 2 pp.

1727, April 3rd. A copy of Mr. Walpole's letter to Mr. Finch.
From Paris. Enclosed in the next. 3 pp.

1727, April 6th. Horatio Walpole to George Tilson. From Paris.
Unaddressed. 3 pp.

1727, April 15th. Lord Townshend to Horatio Walpole. Unsigned
draft. "Very private."

"The King expects France to use its utmost efforts against the
Emperor, and is very little concerned for their making any vigorous
attack upon Spain, there being no fear of the Spaniards taking Gibraltar which is plentifully supplied with men and necessaries and our
strength at sea being so much superior to theirs—." 3 pp.

1727, April 22nd. Copy of the reply of Cardinal de Fleury to Mr.
Walpole. From Versailles. In French. 1¼ pp.

1727, April 28th, N.S. Extract of Mr. Walpole's letter to the Duke
of Newcastle. From Paris. 7 pp.

1727, April 30th. Horatio Walpole to George Tilson. From Paris.
Unaddressed. 2 pp.

1727, May $\frac{\text{4th}}{\text{15th}}$. The same to the same. From Paris. Unaddressed.
5 pp.

1727, May 5th, N.S. The same to William Finch. From Paris. Copy. 2 pp.

1727, May 9th, N.S. The same to the Duke of Newcastle. From Paris. "Private" copy. 5 pp.

Same date. The same to George Tilson. From Paris. Unaddressed. 2 pp.

1727, May 11th. The same to the same. From Paris. 3 pp.

1727, May —. George Tilson to Horatio Walpole. "Draft of letter in reply to Mr. Walpole's letter to the Duke of Newcastle of May 9th."

1727, May $\frac{13th}{2 \frac{nd}{3}}$. Copy of a letter from Messrs Walpole and Armstrong to the Duke of Newcastle. From Paris. 5¼ pp.

1727, May 24th. Horatio Walpole to George Tilson. From Paris 2 pp.

1727, May 27th. Lord Townshend to Horatio Walpole. From Whitehall. "Private." Draft. 7 pp.

1727, May 28th. Horatio Walpole to George Tilson. From Paris. 5 pp.

Same date. The same to the Duke of Newcastle. From Paris. [3 pp.] Enclosing preliminary articles [12 articles in Latin] for a general peace in Europe.

1727, May 30th, N. S. The same to the same. From Paris. Copy. 12 pp.

1727, June 1st. The same to George Tilson. From Paris. Unaddressed 1 p.

1727, June 4th. The same to the same. From Paris. Unaddressed. 1½ pp.

1727, June 8th. The same to the same. From Paris. Unaddressed. 1½ pp.

1727, June 15th. The same to William Finch. From Paris. 2¼ pp.

1727, June 17th. The same to Lord Townshend. From Paris. "Private." [5 pp.] Enclosing advices from the camp before Gibraltar which state that the siege has been turned into a blockade.

Same date. The same to the same. From Paris. "Very private." [4 pp.] Enclosing a "Copy of the separate and secret article of the particular peace between France and Spain concluded at Buenretiros March 23, N. S. 1721."

Same date. The same to the same. From Paris. [6 pp.] Enclosing a copy of a letter, in French, from Cardinal de Fleury, dated at Versailles June 14th, 1727.

1727, June 20th, N. S. The same to George Tilson. From Paris. 1½ pp.

1727, June 22nd. The same to the same. From Paris. Unaddressed. 2 pp.

Same date. The same to Lord Townshend. From Paris [6½ pp.] Enclosing :—

1. Copy of a letter, in French, from Monsr Vandermeer to Monsr Boreel; dated at Madrid, June 9th, 1727. 4½ pp.

2. Copy of a letter, in French, from the Duke de Richelieu to Horatio Walpole; dated, at Vienna, June 14th, 1727, N. S. 2 pp.

3. Copy of a letter, in French, from Monsr de Morville to Horatio Walpole ; dated, at Versailles, June 21st, 1727, N.S. 1 p.

4. Copy of a letter, in French, from Horatio Walpole to Monsr Van de Meer ; dated, at Paris, June 22nd, 1727.

Same date. The same to the same. From Paris. "Private." [2 pp.] Enclosing copy of a letter, in French, from Cardinal de Fleury to Horatio Walpole, and a copy of a project with respect to the Princes of Germany.

1727, July 16th. Thomas Robinson to George Tilson. From Paris. 1 p.

1727, July 26th. Horatio Walpole to the same. From Paris. Unaddressed. 4 pp.

1727, $\frac{\text{July 22nd}}{\text{Augt. 2nd}}$. Cardinal de Fleury to Horatio Walpole. From Versailles. In French. 1½ pp.

1727, Augt. 9th. Horatio Walpole to George Tilson. From Paris. 3 pp.

1797, Aug. 21st. Lord Townshend to Horatio Walpole. From Whitehall. "Very private." 3 pp.

1727, Sept. 3rd. Horatio Walpole to George Tilson. From Paris. Unaddressed. [1 p.] Enclosing copy of a letter, in French, from Monsr Kli——n to Monsr G[edda ?]; dated, at Berlin, August 20th, 1727.

1727, Sept. 6th. N. S. The same to the same. From Paris. Unaddressed. "Part in the Old Cypher." 1½ pp.

1727, Sept. 30th. N. S. The same to the Duke of Newcastle. From Fontainebleau. "Very private." Describing the writer's interviews and correspondence with the Sicilian Priests who had been the King of Spain's advisers, and what he had heard from them about the secret articles of the Treaty of Vienna. Copy. 8 pp.

Enclosure (1.) "Translation of the answer from the Sicilian Abbots to Mr. Walpole." Undated. 1½ p.

Enclosure (2.) "Translation of a Note of 26 Septr 1727 from the Sicilian Abbots to Mr. Walpole." 4 lines.

1727, Oct. 2nd. Horatio Walpole to William Finch. From Fontainebleau. [Copy 3½ pp.] Enclosed in the next.

1727, Oct. 3rd. The same to George Tilson. From Fontainebleau. 2 pp.

1727, Oct. 12th. George Tilson to Horatio Walpole. From Whitehall. Unsigned and unaddressed. [Draft 4½ pp.]

Enclosure (1). Copy of a letter, in French, from Baron Dehn to the Duke of Wolfenbuttel; dated, at Vienna, Sept. 24th 1727, with a "Postscriptum Secretum." 1¼ pp.

Enclosure (2). Extract from a letter, in French, from Schleunitz to Baron Dehn ; dated at Brunswick, October 3rd 1727. 2 pp.

Enclosure (3). Draft of letter, in French, from Lord Townshend to Prince Keurakin ; dated, at Whitehall, Oct. 12th 1727, and offering condolences on the death of the Prince's father. 2 pp.

1727, Oct. 21st. Horatio Walpole to George Tilson. From Fontainebleau. Unaddressed. 4 pp.

1727, Oct. 31st. The same to the same. From Fontainebleau.

Unaddressed. A few lines to say that the letter and its enclosures of Oct. 12th never came to hand.

1727, Oct. —. Daniel Preveran to the same. Undated. The writer forwarded the packets of letters on the 12th with several other letters .in a basket directed to Mr Walpole, and will not fail to write to him by the next post to know if he received it.

1727, Nov. 3rd. Horatio Walpole to Benjamin Keene. From Fontainebleau. In French. Copy. 15½ pp.

1727, Nov. 4th. The same to George Tilscn. From Fontainebleau. Unaddressed. 4 pp.

1727, Dec. 13th. Lord Townshend to Horatio Walpole. From Whitehall. Unsigned draft. 4½ pp.

1727, Dec. 25th. Horatio Walpole to George Tilson. From Paris. Unaddressed. 2 pp.

172$\frac{4}{5}$. Jan. $\frac{12th}{23rd}$, Lord Marchmont and Charles Whitworth to Lord Townshend. Dated at Cambray and unaddressed. "Private. My Lord . . . . . Your Lordship may be sure that we shall not make the least step in the important affairs which are now depending, till we have His Majesty's further instructions.

"When Mr. Rondeau was in England, having occasion to speak to your Lordship concerning the manufacture of cambrick, which is in a great measure carried on by Protestants at the town of St Quentin; your Lordship thought it might be of great advantage to Great Britain if such a manufacture could be set up in it and brought to bear.

"Mr. Rondeau, since he came over, has been at St Quentin, and taken pains to be informed how that matter can be brought about. Your Lordship will see by the inclosed project how that can be done, and will judge if it may be advantageous to Great Britain, and what may be further adviseable to be done in it.

"We have sent this by Mr Smith the messenger to Calais. We are my Lord with the greatest respect etc.

"MARCHMONT,
"C. WHITWORTH."

[1725.] An undated proposal for the revival of the Order of the Knights of the Bath, with a list of the proposed Knights, and with marginal notes in the handwriting of John Austis, Garter King of Arms. 4 pp.

This scheme was carried out and the first Knights of the revived Order were installed on June 17th 1725.

1725. Correspondence of Horatio Walpole whilst British Minister in Paris in this year. Bound in four volumes folio.

172$\frac{5}{6}$, Feb. 8th. Copy of His Majesty's letter to the Duke of Bourbon, and the Duke of Bourbon's Answer, 13th March, 1726, N.S.

"Mon Cousin, L'Affection que J'ay avec beaucoup de raison pour le Duc de Devonshire President de mon Conseil m'engage à recommander à votre protection un procès qu'il a au conseil de mon bon frère le Roy Très Chrétien pour le succession du feu Comte de Gallway. Sa cause me paroit si juste que Je me persuade que vous ne trouverés nulle difficulté à la favoriser, dont Je vous auray une obligation toute particulière. Je suis avec l'estime et l'affection les plus sincères,

Mon Cousin
Votre bon Cousin,
"GEORGE R."

"À St James le 8e
Fevrier 172$\frac{5}{6}$.
"À Mon Cousin
le Duc le Bourbon."

[The Answer of the Duke of Bourbon :—]
" Sire,
J'ay receu la lettre que Votre Mat^e m'a fait l'honneur de m'écrire
en faveur de Monsr le Duc de Devonshire. J'ay donné ordre qu'on in-
struise exactement l'affaire qui l'interesse, et lorsqu'elle sera en état
d'être rapportée au Roy j'y donnerai l'attention le plus particulière, et je
serai ravi de pouvoir faire connoitre en cette occasion à Votre Maj^{té} la
disposition où je serai toujours de lui marquer l'attachement respectueux
avec lequel Je suis

" Sire,
" À Versailles le 13e   De Votre Maj^{té} [votre]
   Mars 1726.   Très humble et très
" Au Roy de la Grande Bretagne."   Obéissant Serviteur "
                                   [BOURBON.]

1726, March 4th. Copy of Admiralty orders to Admiral Hosier, Vice
Admiral of the Blue Squadron of his Mat^{y's} Ships employed and to be
employed in the West Indies, to take sink burn or otherwise destroy
any Ships of War, or Privateers, or Merchant Ships or Vessels, belonging
to the King of Spain or his subjects, the Spaniards having acted
hostilities against His Majesty's Subjects at Gibraltar.
Signed by, John Cockburne, William Chetwynd, [Sir] John Norris,
and J[osiah] Burchett.

1726, March 28th. Copy of a letter from the King to the Governor
of Barbadoes.
Enjoining the latter to give every assistance in his power to Admiral
Hosier.
Given at St James's, signed by the King and countersigned by the
Duke of Newcastle.
" Memd^m a like letter was wrote to the Duke of Portland and to the
Governor of the Leeward Islands. Dated ut supra."

1726, May 4th. Copy of His Majesty's Letter to the Duke of
Bourbon.
Mon Cousin, La memoire que Je conserve du mérite du feu Comte
de Stanhope et des services qu'il m'a rendu, particulièrem^t en ayant con-
tribué à l'établissement de l'Union intime dans laquelle Je suis avec mon
bon Frère le Roy trés Chrétien m'engage à vous recommander les in-
terêts de sa famile. Une grande partie de l'héritage qu'il laissa à ses
orphelins consistoit en une somme de Cent Quarante Trois Mille
Livres en Billets de Banque convertis ensuite en nouveau Comte de
Banque [sic], qui furent remis[es] entre les mains du feu Cardinal du
Bois à dessein de distinguer cette affaire des autres de même nature,
mais les papiers s'ètant perdus entre les mains du Cardinal, il est arrivé
que ce qu'on faisoit pour y donner un tour favourable l'a envelopée dans
des difficultés, lesquelles si on peut lever par votre interposition Je vous
en auray beaucoup d'obligation. Je suis très sincèrement,
" À St James le 4e   Mon Cousin
   de May 1726.   Votre bon Cousin
" À Mon Cousin   " GEORGE R."
   le Duc de Bourbon."

1726, June 12th. F. c. d. S. M. [Marshal Sandroski ?] to——. Unaddressed. A letter in French enclosed in two covers: the inner one
addressed to " Monsieur le Comte de Sandroski Mareschal des Camps
et armées de S[a] M[ajesté] C[atholique] et Commandant la Cavalerie

à Barceloune," and the outer one addressed in Spanish to Don Phelipe
de Sabula &c. Knight of the Order of St. Lago at Madrid.

The letter contains polite excuses for not having written sooner etc.

1726, Nov. 11th.   Colonel Richard Kane to [George Tilson] ? Dated
at Gibraltar and unaddressed.

When the King had apprehensions in July 1725 that some design was
formed against Gibraltar, Lord Townshend dispatched one of his
Majesty's Messengers from Pyrmont to Minorca with the King's Commission and Orders for the writer to come from thence and take the
Command of that Garrison.   Upon his arrival there, in expectation of
a blockade, the writer ordered a ship-load of coals for which he desires
£235 may be paid to Mr Henry Neale and be deducted from the remittance of contingencies.

1726, Dec. 27th.   Jasper Clayton to the same? Dated at Portsmouth,
unaddressed.

The writer thinks it ill timed of Colonel Kane to be anticipating the
contingencies when Gibraltar is threatened with a seige.

The soldiers are all on board and the writer hopes they may arrive in
good time to support the Garrison his Majesty has been pleased to
honour him with the charge of, and which he will defend to the utmost
of his power.

17$\frac{26}{27}$, Feb. 7th, N.S.   Richard Polcy to George Tilson.   Copy.
Dated at the Hague.

" . . . I have read with a true pleasure His Majesty's speech and the
two addresses, which I am persuaded will be no very welcome pieces at
Rome, Vienna, or Madrid.   I find the House of Commons don't want Sr
Robert Neufville's spur.

1726, June 25th.   Copy of Vice Admiral Hosier's Letter to the
Duke of Newcastle.—Dated at Bastinentoes. $\frac{1}{2}$ page.

Enclosing an account of the Admiral's proceedings since writing from
Tiberoon Bay.   This account is dated " On board the Bredah at the
Bastimentoes the 28th June 1726."   5 pp.

1726, July 28th.   " Copie de la declaration du Sieur Diego Ramos par
devant les Alcaldes ordinaires de la Ville de la Trinité de Cuba le
28 Juillet 1726."   4 pp.

1726, Augt. 8th.   Copie d'une lettre du Chef d'Escadre Antoine
Seranno; écrite de la Havane le 8e Août 1726."   1$\frac{1}{2}$ pp.

172$\frac{6}{7}$, Jan. 1st.   Sir Charles Wager, R.N., to Lord Townshend.
Dated on board the " Kent at Spithead," and unaddressed.

" My Lord—I beg leave, before I go away, to give your Lordship my
private opinion of the Russians : By all that I could perceive, the
Russian nation in general, as well as the officers of their Navy, have no
inclination at all to have a warr with England, but would much rather
choose to have a free commerce, and a better friendship with us, they
having no trade by sea with any nation but us and the Dutch, at least
not anything considerable : and, by the way, we should be much put to
it for hemp, if a warr should break out with them, having no hemp for
the Navy, at least very little, but what we have from them; and what
we have in store would be exhausted in one year, as Sr Jacob Acworth
the Survey[o]r, can inform you.   Perhaps the Dutch, who cannot subsist
without trade, may be suffer'd to carry on a trade, even tho' there
should be warr, and it might be refus'd to us : the consequence of that
would be, that we must buy our hemp of them, which would raise the
clamour of the disaffected at home and be a real prejudice to us.   The

Court of Russia, are, no doubt, intent upon the interest of the Duke
of Holstein, but when they find their schemes miscarry I think they
would easily be perswaded to come into more reasonable ones with a
little encouragement in them, for the Duke of Holstein, knowing very well
that it is not the interest of the Russian nation to come into a warr for the
Duke of Holstein's sake only, who perhaps, will be no relation of theirs
when the Czarina is dead ; and there are none of the Russians so blind as
not to see that, and therefore I have allways thought since I saw any thing
of that country, that a little friendly invitation would bring them into
his Maj[esty]'s schemes which are so much for the quiet and peace of
Europe. The Swedes would not then be so backward in coming into
the Treaty of Hanover, or need be so dearly bought. Besides, the
Russians should, I think be perswaded, by all means to look upon themselves as Protestants, least if Religion should once come to be the dispute they should take the wrong side. I think their dominions are far
too extended, as well for their own safety as the quiet of their neighbours, and in a warr I think they would be more like to loose ground
than gain [any] for both Livonia and Finland on the other side of the
gulph tho' not theirs yet are so depopulated that if armys should come
into them againe, they would soon be a desart, and therefore I think it
very much the interest of Russia to have peace especially with England, and Holland, but if that cannot be, all trade with Petersburgh
should be prevented if possible, but I fear that the Dutch must be permitted it, and that we shall want Hemp, tho' I hope we shall have
enough to hang such as shall appear enemys to their Country. But
your Lordship may very justly bid me mind my own business ; and I am
sorry to find that some of the Flota are arriv'd, and I fear the rest by
favour of the bad weather, will escape too ; so that part of my business,
I doubt, will be over before I come to my Station. But I hope I shall
soon see what the Spaniards are doing, either at Gibraltar or Cadiz : I
think the time of year will not admit their making any hasty progress
in any of their enterprizes, and therefore hope they will be timely prevented and nip'd in the bud, though I would have them be at as much
expence about them as possible, that with the help of the Emperor, the
Flota that does arrive may be soon unloaded and the mony gone.

" I doubt not but Admiral Hosier will have intelligence of the sailing
of the Flota from the Havana, and then he will have nothing to do but
watch the Galleons.

" I shall allways be glad to receive your Lordships Commands, and
hope you will pardon the liberty I take in writing so long a letter with
so little in it. I am—your Lordship's most obedient Servt

"CHA : WAGER."

" P.S. 2^d Jan^y : The wind is come again to SSW : so that I can not
sail."

1727, Jan. 8th. Copy of Letters of Credence from the Elector for
John James Zamboni, Envoy to England. Dated at Warsaw. In Latin.
3 pp.
The Elector signs as Augustus the Second, King of Poland.

[No date.] An Oath of Allegiance to be sworn by all Bishops in the
United Kingdom. 1¼ pp.

[No date.] " Copy of the Emperor's answer ab^t Meclenbourg.—Sent
to the Cardinal by a Courier from Vienna." In the handwriting of Mr.
Tilson. 2 pp.

[No. date.] A paper endorsed, in the handwriting of Mr. Tilson,
" Drat of a Declar^n on the Conversation with the L[andgrave] of H[esse]
Cassell." 2 pp.

[No date.] " Copie des raisons faites par Mr Hugetan pour soutenir la defense du Commerce avec la France et la Holland." 12¼ pp.

[No date.] Plan d'une Alliance defensive entre S.M. Britannique et S.M. Czarienne. Addressed to Monsr Bernstorff and unsigned. 5 pp.

1727, June $\frac{13th}{24th}$. Lord Townshend to King George the Second. Dated at " Osnabrug," two days after the King's accession. Copy in the handwriting of the writer's son Thomas.

" May it please Your Ma^{ty},
     At the same time that I take the liberty of condoling with your Ma^{ty} upon the unspeakable loss of your late Royal Father, I beg leave humbly to assure your Ma^{ty} that you have no subject in all your Dominions who wishes more cordially than I do, that your reign may be as prosperous and as glorious as that of any of your greatest and most renown'd predecessors. I came hither hoping I might be of some use to your Ma^{ty}'s service, and being likewise desirous to pay this mark of respect to my deceased sovereign. I shall return to England with all expedition, in order to lay myself at your Ma^{ty}'s feet, being with the utmost duty and veneration

                    " Your Ma^{ty}'s most dutifull
                         most obedient and most
                         faithfull servant and
                         subject
                                   " TOWNSHEND."

1727, July 25th. Earl of Orford (Admiral Russell) to Lord Townshend. Dated at Chippenham and unaddressed. Written by an amanuensis, and signed by Lord Orford.

" My Lord—I was this morning honour'd with a letter from your Lords^p in which you was pleas'd to tell me that it was the King's commands that I shou'd serve him as one of the Commissioners of the Admiralty, but it is my misfortune that from old age and infirmities I am wholly incapable of doing that service which I well know that employment requires. I must therefore desire the favour of your Lords^p to acquaint his Majesty that I have the deepest sense of duty and acknowledgment for the honour he is pleased to do me, in thinking me capable of performing so great a trust, and believing me a man perfectly attach'd to his interest and service, which I ever was and ever shall be, but that I beg His Majesty in his Goodness will please to excuse me, because 'tis not in my power, from my present want of health, to serve him as I would, and as I ought, and rather accept that which is in my power, the integrity of my heart, and unshaken duty, and my prayers to God for all blessings that may make His Majesty and his family happy and prosperous.
" I am—My Lord—Y^r Lordship's—most obedient humble Servant
                                   " ORFORD."

1727, July 30th. Extract from a letter from Vienna of this date relating what had passed at the Conference held between Count Ziuzendorff, the Duke of Bournonvill, and Mons. Hamel Bruyninx on July 26th. In French. 4 pp.

1727, July 31st. Letter of credence from Charles Landgrave of Hesse to H. B. M. in behalf of Lieut. General Diemar. Dated at Cassel. In Latin. 2 pp

MARQUESS
TOWNSHEND
MSS.

1727, Augt. 8th.   Richard Manning to Lord Townshend.
Enclosing a copy of a memorial which the writer is about to present
to the King.

1727, Sept. 19th.   Copy of a letter to the King, on his Accession,
from the States General?   [Unsigned]. · In French.   2 pp.

[1727.] "Secret Articles concluded at Vienna [in 1725] between the
Emperor and the King of Spain."   Five Articles (4 pp.), together with
"Reasons that were given against the said Articles" (43½ pp.).   The
whole stitched, in book form, and endorsed "Translation of the paper
recᵈ from the Sicilian Abbots concerning the Secret Treaty between the
Emperor and the K. of Spain."
The contracting parties :—
1°. Guarantee each other's dominions.
2°. The Emperor obliges himself to press England to restore Gibraltar
to Spain.
3°. "If the King of France dies without leaving a son the Emperor will
assist with all his force the King of Spain's right to the Crown of
France ; or, if the other Powers set the Duke of Orleans on the throne
of France, the Emperor will take the French Low Countries, Alsace,
and the Franche-Comté of Burgundy, and the King of Spain would
unite to the Spanish Monarchy Roussillon, French Cerdaigne, Lower
Navarre, and the other countries he might conquer " on the part of the
Pirenean Mountains."
4°. Contracts a marriage between the Infante Don Carlos and the
eldest Arch Duchess, and the King of Spain obliges himself to maintain
the Pragmatic Sanction.
5°. "Their Cesarean & Catᑫᵘᵉ Majᵗʸˢ foreseeing that the King of
England will oppose the execution of such designs as well in regard to
his particular interests, as not to loose his Umpireship in Europe, for
which reason he will undoubtedly engage the English Nation, and unite
the Dutch and other Princes in his League, they oblige themselves to
seek all methods to restore the Pretendᵣ to the Throne of G. Britain ; to
which end the Cat[holic] King was to make use of the pretence of the
restitution of Gibraltar, which he was to demand immediately as soon as
the Peace of Vienna was published."

1727 —. The concluding part of a detailed statement of the strength
of the Prussian Army in this year.   From Paris.   In French.   4 pp.
Note.—The total strength is stated to have been 63,932 men.

1728, March 1st.   Baron Munchhausen to Lord Townshend [?]   Un
addressed.   Dated at Ratisbon, and signed G. A. de Munchhausen.
A letter of compliments 3½ pp.

1728, March 16th.   Extract from a Latin Protocol, signed by
Waldstettin, stipulating that there shall be a re-investiture of certain
Spanish fiefs belonging to the Emperor.

1728, May 5th.   The Marquis of Monteleone to Lord Peterborough.
From Venice.   In French.   Unaddressed and enclosed in the next.   6 pp.
. . . . Has written from Florence to Lord Townshend and is writing
to the Duke of Newcastle, begging them both to make the South Sea
Company promptly pay his appointments, which were charged by the
King his Master on the Assiento, and entreats Lord Peterborough to
hasten the payment.
". . . . Today's news is that the Pretender arrived here last night
incognito, without the republic being in any way mixed up with his
coming ; there is no mystery, he only comes to see the City and the
Church ceremonies on Ascension Day. . . ."

1728, May 20th.   Lord Peterborough to Lord Townshend. Dated at Bath.

" My Lord,
          I thought the best way was to send to your Lordship the Marquis of Monteleoni's letter, I have taken the liberty to tell him I was well assured, that no sollicitations were necessary on his behalf either to Sir Robt Walpole or yourself.

" I wish our pacifick endeavors may procure quiet to the world, I am tould our Spanish friends comply very awkwardly and with much unwillingnesse, but give me leave to assure your Lord^p that the King and my friends shall have my best assistance either in peace or war.

                    " My Lord
                    Your most faithfull and affectionate
                              Servant
                              " PETERBOROW."

1728, Nov. $\frac{13th}{24th}$.   Horatio Walpole to Charles Delafaye. Dated at Paris, and unaddressed. In the handwriting of George Tilson, and noted by him "Cop: Mr Walpole's to Mr Delafaye."

" Dear Sir—I have received your favour of the 6th O. S. by Whiggs the Messenger on Monday in the afternoon, and last night that of the 7th by the Post. Mr Poyntz has been with us these two or three days in expectation of a Courier from Spain ; but he returns this morning with Mr Sta Cruz to Soissons, to come hither again with that Gentleman upon the arrival of any Courier from Spain with an account of Mr Bournonville's negociation there. In the mean time the Spanish Amb^rs have received one with letters dated the 14th and orders to congratulate their Ma^tys here on the recovery of the French King's health ; and they accordingly went yesterday to Versailles for that purpose ; so that now the Court of Spain is freed from all uneasiness and agitation on account of this extraordinary event. It is not doubted but they will seriously consider of the negociations depending, and which were certainly suspended untill the fate of this important Crisis was over.

" Mr. Stanhope and I shall go tomorrow to Versailles ; and upon our return shall send you a Messenger with an answer to the D. of Newcastle's last dispatches of the 6th, and with an account of what news may have come by the last Courier from Spain. I am &c.
                              " H. WALPOLE "

1728-1729. Despatches of Horatio Walpole from Paris. In cardboard cover.

1728 - 1730. A collection of notes from Lord Townshend to the King. In a card board cover. They have been printed by Archdeacon Coxe in his " Memoirs of Sir Robert Walpole" pp. 520-543. The earliest of these notes is dated " 2 July 1728," and the latest " 6 May 1730." On the 8th of May 1730 Lord Townshend surrendered the secretaryship to Lord Harrington. Archdeacon Coxe writes, " It is remarkable that not one of these notes is in the handwriting of Lord Townshend," and he suggests " the reason probably was because the handwriting of Lord Townshend was very indifferent and sometimes almost illegible." The King's replies are uniformly in his own handwriting, and are generally written on the same paper as Lord Townshend's notes.

1729, May 15th. St. James's. Copy of the King's Letter to His most Christian Majesty.

MARQUESS
TOWNSHEND
MSS.

"Monsieur mon Frère. Le Colonel Douglas s'en retournant en France pour soliciter ses prétensions à votre Cour, je le recommande à votre protection, vous priant d'ordonner qu'on luy fasse droit, selon ce qui est stipulé par la Traité d'Utrecht sur les terres en fonds qu'il reclame. Je recevray comme une marque de votre amitié pour moy cette justice que vous luy rendrés, et Je vous prie d'être persuadé que Je me serviray toujours avec plaisir des occasions de vous donner des preuves de l'estime et de l'affection avec laquelle Je suis.

"Monsieur Mon Frère
Votre bon Frère
"GEORGE R."

1729, Nov. 4th. Claudio Francesco Re to Signor Como. Dated at Paris, and endorsed, "Copie d'une lettre de Mr Re, a Mr Como." In Italian, to the following effect:—We are expecting news next week from Seville about the great matters, although we calculate that Mr. Stanhope may have reached there the 23d or 24th of the past month. Things remain as they were, and there is nothing new here except that yesterday five Ministers of the Hanoverian Allies gave the Imperial Ministers their reply on the point of the guarantee of the Austrian Succession. It is said that the reply which was given viva voce, contained neither 'yes' nor 'no.' Politicians here say that it ought to conclude with a 'No' and not with a 'Yes.' This is all the current news to-day.

This letter is subscribed:—"mi ratificio con tutto l'animo.
"CLAUDIO FRANCo RE."

1729, Dec. 12th. Copy of a letter from the Marquis D'Aix to the King of Sardinia. In French. 2 pp.

1729, Dec. 22nd. The Duc de Broglie to Lord Townshend. In French. Dated in London and unaddressed.

Asking for information as to the reply his Brittanic Majesty has sent to his ministers in Paris touching the guarantee of the succession to the Empire, and asking for an appointment for an interview the next day.

1729, Dec. 23rd. John Couraud to ——. Unaddressed.

"Dear Sir—Mr Delafaye having acquainted me that my Lord Townshend desired to have all the Drats of his Lops Letters to France and Spain during my Lord Duke's absence in Sussex, I send you herewith several, which with those that his LoP has already had are all, I think, that were wrote in that time. I am &c."

1729–1730. Letters from Messrs Stanhope, Poyntz, Keen, &c. In cardboard cover.

17$\frac{29}{30}$, Jan. 11th. Robert Daniel to George Tilson. Dated at Brussels.

". . . . It is current here that the prevailing party in the United Provinces is for abandoning the Barrière Towns whence some infer there must be *some considerable change in agitation* [interlined in another hand over the cipher figures 864. 875. 640. 516. 419. 320. 650] this they interpret *in favour of a younger Infant of Spain* [interlined over 14. 419. 735. 814. 911. 124. 47. 500. 567. 364. 814. 960] since nothing else could make the Barrière useless . . . . . The Princess de Ligne was on the 7th delivered of a daughter, which baulked for the second time the hopes of a son in that Family . . . ."

17$\frac{29}{30}$, Jan. 27th. Charles Delafaye to the same. Unaddressed. Endorsed by Mr Tilson, "Mr Delafaye—abt the Spanish Men of Warr."

" Dear George,—Here is what we can readily find. The remainder of your history must be made out by letters from the governor of Port Mahon or of Col. Stanhope, which I doubt are not in our hands, for my Lord Cartaret took most of his papers with him. What I have from Lord Carpenter is, that the Ships were first sold to the Emperor, and put into the possession of his Commissarys at Port Mahon ; that the Spanish Commissary came thither, and would not receive them in the Condition they were in ; And then the Empr's Commissary gutted them, and the Ships being at last so spoiled that they were ready to sink and spoil the Harbour, the Governor had them towed out to Sea in shoal water and there sunk where they now lye not worth the weighing.

" Yours ever,   C. D."

" [P.S.] Are you forestalling the liquidation of the affair wch is referred to Commissarys ?"

173$\frac{2}{3}$, March 17th. James Evelyn to Lord Townshend. Dated in Duke Street and unaddressed.

" . . if the persons, who have complain'd to your Lordship, will give us an account of what they have paid on account of fees [for Debentures on the exportation of silk manufactures] we shall be very ready to examine whether the Custom house officers have here taken more than the Law allows . . . ."

173$\frac{4}{5}$, March 14th. A detailed scheme of the arrangements made for the procession which was to be formed the following day on the marriage of the Princess Royal. 10 pp.

1734, July 18th. An Agenda paper for the Privy Council meeting of this date. Noted by Lord Wilmington with the business disposed of. 1$\frac{1}{4}$ pp.

1734, July 20th.   Copy of a grant from the King to the Duke of Richmond, Duke of Montagu, Duke of Portland, Earl of Loudoun, and Sir Conyers Darcy, of " all that piece or parcel of Land . . . in the Privy Garden within the precinct of Our Palace of Whitehall . . . . containing in length from North to South three hundred and seventy one Feet and in breadth from East to West one hundred and fifty one feet *abutting to the West on a piece of wast Ground reserved to erect and build some publick offices upon for Our use if occasion be* and on the street leading from Whitehall Gate to Westminster Hall, and on the garden of Mrs. Jane Lowther, South on an area or open space of ground granted or intended to be granted to the said Earl of Loudoun, Nathaniel Gould Esqr and the said Jane Lowther, East on ground in the possession of the said Charles Duke of Richmond John Duke of Montagu and Sir Conyers Darcy, and on a piece of wast ground there, and North on the area before the Banquetting house in Our said Palace . .   ."

" N.B. This is conceiv'd to be an engagement from the Crown to use the above reserved piece of ground for no other purpose but to erect a Publick Office thereon if need be."

Endorsed : " Grant of part of the Privy Garden to the D. of Richmond &c. July 20th 1734."

1735, Nov. 3rd.   Thomas Robinson, afterwards Lord Grantham, to Horatio Walpole.   From Vienna.

" Sir.—If the true explication of things has not come not sooner than by this messenger, I cannot well attribute so late a communication of them but to the decay of my credit here, nor that decay to any thing but to the more or less part I may have had in the suggestion of the expedient of the marriage. If it was not the first opening of that matter as of myself in the month of July, it was however the proposal which I made on the 5th of August, that threw me entirely out of my seat. Bartenstein has the sole power here. Upon the Bishop of Bamberg's telling him in a conference *que ce n'étoit pas à luy à y parler, mais à écrire seulement*, his highness was forced to quit the Vice-presidentship of the Council of war to be *Grand Maître* to the Empress, and that for having desired the Emperor in a letter from Italy *de se fier plutôt dans les affaires de la guerre à ses Generaux qu'à un Ecrivain*. The Prince of Savoy himself is piqued against Bartenstein, who however does and will maintain himself. I must therefore be humbly desiring that your Excellency will in time think of withdrawing me from hence. I do not repine as long as it shall be thought for the King's service to have me at this Court, and tho' my principal object in view is to get home and to endeavour to think for myself at this time of day in the *quiet* manner which I have formerly had the honour to explain to your Excellency, yet for the sake of leaving this place with a less appearance of discredit, I could almost be bold enough to show some desire of being employed in the future congress, if there should be an occasion for more then one, and you should be at the head of the Embassy. In an old letter from Mr Pelham, and written with your knowledge, he says " the Duke [of Newcastle] was pleased to express the greatest affection and freindship for me, and was ever ready to support in the strongest manner, as were Sr Robert and M[r Horatio] Walpole, any thing that might be proposed for my honour and credit at Vienna, or for my future ease and satisfaction, that my conduct met with approbation, and my lot consequently to remain here." You know, Sir with what resignation I have been contented with that lot, while it was thought that my being here could be of immediate service ; but without supposing that my continuing here may perhaps prove disserviceable, if circumstances however are such, that I can be equally serviceable to the King in another employment, be it never so much superior to my expectations or even desires, it would be, I thought, inexcusable in me not to put myself, as the occasion may offer, in a way which by withdrawing me from hence with *honour and credit*, may also lead to my *future ease and satisfaction*. And *this last* I can assure Your Excellency will be always so moderate, as never to give rise to the question. *What shall we do with him afterwards?* The Peace that is to be made with the Empire will authorise the employing of one, who has lived near six years at the Imperial Court, and tho' I may be thought to aspire to something much beyond my sphere, yet it is in fact looking out for an employment, which in all probability will not be of long duration, and must naturally, if there should be any occasion at all for it, be given to one or other of my foreign Colleagues, amongst whom of the same rank, not one will be found, whose fortune it will have been to have born[e] the heat of the day with more zeal and industry than I have done.

" I beg leave to entrust this affair with Your Excellency singly, and for God's sake, Sir, stifle the thing in its very infancy, if out of your goodness for me, you find it improper for me even to have thought of it, but should there happen to be room for a second or third person in the ensuing Congress, and Your Excellency should think from my known attachment to you personally, that particularly during your occasional attendance in Parliament, you cannot in any respect leave one that can be more your self, that is, who can more faithfully enter into and carry on your thoughts, I will be bold to say you may throw your eyes upon persons of greater distinction and fortune, but not upon one that can be with a truer and profounder respect than that which makes me more and more every day of my life—Sir—Your most obedient and most humble servant.

"T. ROBINSON."

[P.S.] Vienna. 1735 [Nov.] 5ᵗʰ N.S.

" I had written this letter on Thursday morning while I was expecting at leisure to be called to a conference ; but however true the contents of it are as to my situation here, I little thought that the very paper, which according to the inclosed copy of the letter written this day to Your Excellency in cypher I have treated as a modification of my orders of the 13ᵗʰ past should have fournished so much matter for nourishing Mr. Barteustein's spleen.

" C[oun]t Konigseck was declared *Grand Maître* yesterday but with a view, as it is generally thought to take from him in time the Vice presidentship of the Council of war. What is at least certain, the command of an army is incompatible with his new post.

"T. R."

1737, May 14th. Sir William Thomson, Baron of the Exchequer, to Lord Wilmington [?] Dated in Bloomsbury Square and unaddressed.

" My Lord—Your Lordship having done me the honour to enquire concerning the power of trying the person convicted last sessions for a murder in Newfoundland, I not being then apprised of the Case, could not give your Lordship a satisfactory answer. But as I find the fact was done upon the Land, and not in any harbour or haven (though thrown into the water there after the death). He was tryed by virtue of a clause in the 10ᵗʰ & 11ᵗʰ of K. Wᵐ the third, Cap, 25. sect. 13, which gives power to try murders in that country of Newfoundland upon the land & on the Islands belonging to it—within any County in England, as if committed within this Realm. But if the fact had been done in any harbour or haven on the water, it would have been otherwise.

" I take the liberty of assuring your Lordship, that I have the honour to be with the highest respect, My Lord, *etc.*

" Wᴹ THOMSON."

1738, July 20th. An Agenda Paper for the Privy Council meeting of this date, with notes on the handwriting of Lord Wilmington. 2½ pp.

1738, July 27th. A List of Papers referred at the last Council and other business for the Committee. Noted by Lord Wilmington. 2½ pp.

1739, June 25th. Thomas Skottowe to Edward Weston "at the Secretary's Office, London."

". . . . . I have transcribed his Lordship's [Lord Wilmington's] letter to D[epu]ty L[ieutenan]ts and the Order of Council and have sent them to the only three acting Deputy Lᵗˢ here (Mʳ Le heup being in London) viz.: Harbord Harbord, Lee Warner, Ja : Host Esqʳˢ.

" Sir Edmᵈ Bacon tho' he appear[s] every Sessions would not put pen o paper as a Dᵗʸ Lᵗ but tell[s] me he have paid for his Commission which perhaps many others have not. I have been the less obliged to an old acquaintance . . . . . "

1739, July 15th. Lord Cobham to Lord Wilmington [?] Dated at Stowe and unaddressed.

" My Lord,
     Your Lordship will find by the enclosed the necessity of an election of Jurats in Jersey and that they themselves cannot agree

were it left to their choice whether they would have all or part. I
need not observe to your Lordship that as little harmony subsists
amongst them at present as formerly; the petition of Badinel the Viscount and the Judgment of the King and Council upon it is too plain
a proof that six will act illegally and arbitrarily as well as twelve.
I shall therefore humbly offer it as my opinion that they may be authorized to proceed to Election to compleat the number of the Royal Court
. . . . .'

1739, July —. The Earl of Malton to Lord-Wilmington. Undated
and unaddressed. Enclosing the next. Endorsed " July 1739."

1739, July 21st. The same to Sir Walter Calverley, Bart., and Mr
Horton, with reference to an Order in Council about sea-faring men.
Dated at Wentworth House.

1739, Augt. 17th. Dr Edward Chandler, Bishop of Durham, to Lord
Wilmington.
" My Lord,
In obedience to the commands I had the honor to receive from
some of the Lords of His Majesty's Privy Council in their letter for
taking up men for the sea service, I enclose a list of two of His Majesty's
Justices of Peace for this County, of persons sent by them and received
by the collector of Sunderland. I believe had the ship continued here,
sent down by the Admiralty, many more might have been taken up
here and about Newcastle, and delivered aboard, but there is no detaining
men in expectation [of a ship]. . . . . all I know of certainty is that
I have the honor to be with a firm attachment My Lord,
" Yor Obedient humble servt
" E. DURESME."

1740, Jan. 18th. John Strange (afterwards Attorney General)
to Lord Wilmington [?] Unaddressed.
" My Lord.—In my Lord Coke's 4 Institute cap. 77 pag[e] 362 there
is nothing said in the text of the book by way of exposition of the
words the King's nephew in the 31 H. 8 c. 10. But by a reference
to the margin they are explained, i e. the King's grandchilde. But in
the lower part of the page which I have marked with a ☞ there is a
reference to some Parliament Rolls which he says are full of notable
precedents concerning precedency both in respect of the blood royal and
otherwise, for which reason I have troubled your Lordship with the
book itself.
" If I can be of any further service to your Lordship I hope you will
honour me with your commands to your etc. J. STRANGE."

1740, April 9th. An Agenda paper for the Privy Council meeting
of this date. Noted by Lord Wilmington. 1 p.

1742, April 10th. J. Gore to Lord Wilmington. Dated in Bishops-
gate Street.
Showing how the remittance of £200,000 to Genoa, and £300,000 to
Vienna, for the Queen of Hungary's Service, in bills, would derange
the exchanges, and recommending that a Man of War be sent to carry
gold from Lisbon to Trieste. 4 pp.

1742, April 17th. A letter from Monsr Du Plan to the King on
behalf of the Protestant cause. 4 pp.

1742, May 4th. London. Baron de Wasner, Hungarian Minister
in London, to Lord Wilmington. Unaddressed.

" My Lord—Vous scavez, my Lord, la situation pressante où S. M^{té} la Reyne ma très gracieux maitresse se trouve, et combien il importe de ne pas perdre un moment de tems pout lui mettre en état de soutenir les efforts des ennemys qui n'ont pas moins la ruine de sa maison que cette de la liberté de l'Europe pour objet. Dans cette considération je prends la liberté de vous prier, my Lord, de vouloir bien donner vos ordres, pourquoi la somme accordée par le Parlement à Sa Maj^{té} le Roy pour sad[i]te Maj^{té} la Reyne puisse m'être payée au plustôt.

" Votre zèle si connu pour le bien de votre patrie et de la cause commune me laisse d'autant moins lieu de douter de la promptitude et de la facilité, que vous voudrez bien y apporter, que my Lord Carteret m'a fait l'honneur de me repéter encore avant hier, que cet argent étoit prêt et que je trouve beaucoup de difficultés à faire le remises avec promptitude et avantage tant que cette Somme n'est pas payée.

" Si vous permettez my Lord j'aurai l'honneur de vous aller rendre mes respects ce matin pour vous en parler conjointement avec Mr Gore; et pour vous réiterer de vive voix les assurances de la plus parfaite veneration, avec la quelle je serais à jamais—My Lord—Votre très-humble et très-obéissant serviteur.

"DE WASNER."

1742, May 7th. R. Salter to the same. Enclosing a scheme for a lottery.

[1742]. " An Account of his Majesty's Ministers to Foreign Princes, States, &c., with the expence of each particular, and the amount of the whole for one year." Undated.

Given in a tabular form, from which the following rates of pay and allowances are extracted.

Earl of Stair. Ambassador Extraordinary and Plenipotentiary to the States General, £100 per week with an extraordinary allowance of £1600 per annum.

Envoys Extraordinary and Plenipotentiaries: Thomas Robinson (afterwards Lord Grantham) at Vienna, and the Earl of Hyndford in Prussia, each £8 per diem, with extra allowances of £600 and £400 respectively.

Envoys Extraordinary: Thomas Villiers (afterwards Earl of Clarendon) in Poland; the Hon. Charles Compton in Portugal; Walter Titley in Denmark; Sir Cyril Wich in Russia; the Hon. Robert Trevor (afterwards Lord Hampden) to the States General; and Melchior Guy-Dickens in Sweden;—each £5 per diem, with extra allowances of from £300 to £600.

Arthur Villetes, Envoy at Turin; Horatio Mann, Envoy at Florence; and James Cope, Envoy to the Hanse Towns; each £3 per diem with allowance of £300 or £400.

Commissary, James Porter at Vienna £3 per diem.

Secretaries: Onslow Burrish at Antwerp, and Anthony Thompson at Paris, each 40^s per diem.

Consuls: Ambrose Stanyford in Algiers, £600 per ann. with £500 extraordinary allowance; William Reade at Tripoli, £380 per ann. with £250 allowance; William Latton at Tetuan, £250 per ann.; John Deane in Flanders, £200 per ann.; John Burn-Parker at Oporto, £500 per ann.; William Cayley at Faro. £200 per ann.

Ministers of divers natures: John Lay, Resident at Dunkirk, 20^s per diem; Charles Hozendorff, and for services, £400 per ann.; Brinley Skinner, till provided for, 30^s per day; Robert Daniel, Agent in the Low Countries, £100 per ann.

PETITIONS, MEMORIALS, ETC.

1701–1771.

1701, Dec. 6th.　Agreement between the several candidates for the next election for the County of Norfolk.　Signed by J. Houghton for Mr. Townshend; J. Holland and Jacob Astley.　1 page.

1705, Oct. 2nd.　Copy of an " Order for discommoning several persons of the Corporation of Cambridge."　Signed by Sir John Ellys, Vice-Chancellor of the University.　The persons discommoned " for violating the rights and priviledges thereof," are the Mayor, Mr. James Fletcher, Aldermen Daniel Dove, and Francis Percy, and the Deputy Recorder John Welbore.

1705 ——.　The Case of the Corporation of Cambridge.　3 pp.

1705, Dec. 24.　Abstract of the late Earl of Romney's title to [be Keeper of the Palace and Park of] Greenwich, &c.　[3 pp.]

1706 to 1711.　A collection of undated petitions (many of them in French) referred by the Queen and the Treasury to Spencer Compton as Treasurer of the Queen's Bounties.　Some of these petitions are noticed further on.

1709, Nov. 25th.　A report of the Board of Trade, on the Petition of Sir William Hodges, setting forth that there is " a debt of $80,839\frac{1}{2}$ peices of 8 or Dollars (which at 4s. 6d. each is 18,188l. 16s. sterling) " due to him and his partners from the Crown of Portugal, and praying that the same may be stopped out of what shall become due from his Majesty to that Crown, or that he may be otherwise relieved. Dated at Whitehall and signed by the Earl of Stamford, Lord Dartmouth, Philip Meadows, J. Pulteney, and R. Monckton.

" A true copy—WM. POPPLE."

To this paper is appended a " Mémoire touchant l'affaire de Guillaume Hodges Chevalier Barron et Marchand de Londres et ses Associés," dated 11th Oct. 1709, and witnessed as " a true copy—

CHARLES DELAFAYE."

1709, Dec. 14th.　Rev. Dr John Robinson, Dean of Windsor, to Spencer Compton, at Whitehall.　Dated in London.

" Sr—At the earnest request of Mademoiselle Lapie I take leave to acquaint you that I have seen attestations setting forth that her father was formerly a Secretary at the Court of France, and that her self fled thence for religion.　I also know that she was for several years at Stockholm, and went under the character of a religious and virtuous woman and has been oft recommended to me as such, by persons of distinction in that place, in order to procure her some relief here, which I verily believe she much wants ; and that if it please Her Majty to extend her charity to the said Mrs Lapie it will not be misplac'd.—I am with great respect—Sir—your most humble and obedt servant,

[No date.]　　　　　　　　　　　" J. ROBINSON."

The petition of Marie Lapie.　Undated and unsigned.

" À la Reyne.

" Madame—Marie Lapie fille d'un Sécretaire du Roy de France, remontre très humblement a vostre Maiesté, quelle est sortie de Paris, lieu de sa naissance, depuis vingt cinq ans pour cause de religion, et que depuis ce temps elle a vescu avec deux de sa sœurs qu'elle a attiré auspres d'elle de l'ouvrage de ses mains, sans avoir jamais receu aucun secours de personne, mais comme à present, a force de travailler, sa veue est tout à fait affoiblie, et qu'elle se trouve dans une extrème necessité, elle se jette a vos pieds Madame pour supplier Votre Maiesté de vouloir jetter un regard de compassion sur son estat qui est des plus triste, et d'ordouner qu'elle soit au nombre des pensionaires qui subsistent par vos beneficiences Royalles, et elle continuera ses voeus pour la conservation de vostre personne sacrée."

1709, Dec.—. A list of the several regm^ts of British forces according to seniority. Endorsed "List of the British Forces.—Decr 1709." 3½ pp.

[170$\frac{9}{10}$.] Petition of the Governor and Company of Adventurers of England trading into Hudson's Bay. Undated, and endorsed "Hudson's Bay Company's Petition to her Ma^ty. Enclosed in their letter of the 17th Feb^ry 17$\frac{09}{10}$."

The petition details French aggressions on the territories of the Company from the year 1682 and concludes as follows :—

"The premises considered, when your Majesty in your high wisdome shall think fitt to give peace to those enemys whome your victorious armes have so reduced and humbled and when your Majesty shall judge it for your people's good to enter into a treaty of peace with the French King your petitioners pray that the said Prince be obliged by such treaty to renounce all right of 'pretensions to the Bay and Streights of Hudson to quitt and surrender all ports and settlements erected by the French or which are now in their possession as likewise not to saile any shipp or vessell within the limitts of the Company's Charter and to make restitution of the £108,514. 19. 8, of which they robb'd and dispoyled you[r] petitioners in times of perfect amity between the two kingdomes.

"And yor pet^rs as in duty bound shall ever pray, &c."

[1710, March 7th]. An undated paper headed "Dr Sacheverell— Extract." 5½ pp.

This is a condensed report of a portion of Dr Sacheverell's speech in his defence before the House of Lords at this date.

1710, March 14th, N.S. Adam Cardonnel and Horatio Walpole to Spencer Compton (as Treasurer or the Queen's Bounties). Dated at the Hague and unaddressed.

"Sir—Here is a poor gentlewoman M^rs Le Bas a vertuous good woman, who it is certain has quitted a reasonable subsistance in France for the sake of her religion, she had a small pension of 15 p^ds a year in the late reign as you will see by her Petition, it would be a real act of charity if you would take a fitting opportunity of laying her case favourably before my L^rd Treasurer that she may be restored to her 15l. a year to find her bread ; we should likewise take it as a particular obligation. We are with great truth and esteem—Sir—Your most faithfull and obed^t servants.

"AD. CARDONNEL.
"H. WALPOLE."

1710, July 4th, O.S. "Sr William Hodges and several other merch^ts of London to my Lord Townshend, in behalf of the two Spanish Ships going to Buenos Ayres, and taken by the Dutch men of war.

"May it please your Ex^cy—Wee the subscribers, in behalfe of ourselves and many others of Her Maj^tie's subjects trading to Spaine, do render your Ex^cy our most humble thankes for so heartily espousing our interest, and that of the Spaniards, and others concerned in the two unfortunate Spanish ships, which sayled from Cadiz for the Buenos Ayres, and were taken by the Dutch and carried to Holland, without any regard to her Maj^{tie's} passes, which were granted for reasons wee shall not now trouble your Ex^{cy} with, knowing that you have had them and all other papers relating to this matter, from the Right Honble Mr Secretary Boyle, and directions to reclaime the said ships and cargoes; in which the hon^r of her Maj^{ties} passes, and that branch of our trade (so beneficial to this Kingdome) is so much concerned; besides the ill consequences that may attend the latter if restitution be not made.

" We therefore humbly pray your Ex^{cie's} favor and protection in this case, which will infinitely oblidge—My Lord—Yo^r Ex^{cy's}—most obedient and most humble servants—Jno Houblon, William Hodges, P. Porreel, Christop Hayne, Ferd. Mendes, Anthony da Costa, Rog. Braddyll, P. & F. H. . . . . , Jos. Hodges, E. Terrell, Ben. Ash, Robt Hull, Lw^s de Dorpere, Thos Herne, Fran. Beuzelin, Jno Love, Fran. Trobridge, Jno Fellowes, Jno Radburne, Peter Lepipre, John Lambert, John Edmonds, Moses Carñon.

" [P.S.] My Lord—If there be no other remedy wee will hope the Dutch will admitt of a favourable composition for the Spanyards and others."

1710, Dec. 8th. Dr John Robinson, Bishop of Bristol, to Spencer Compton. Unaddressed and endorsed " M^e La Pie."

" Sir—Her Maj^{ty} has been pleas'd to order me to putt into your hands the enclosed note, which I read to Her Maj^{ty} this morning, being the name of the poor French woman, who has troubled you so long with her solicitations ; it being Her Maj^{ty's} intention, that she may be added to the list of those, to whom Her Maj^{ty} is graciously pleased to extend her charity, as upon-mention thereof I hope you will find—I am *etc.*

" JOH. BRISTOL."

1711, June 13th. William Lowndes "To Spencer Compton Esqr Paymaster of Her Ma^{tys} annuall and other pencoñs and bountys.—These."

Transmitting by order of the Lord High Treasurer (Harley Earl of Oxford and Mortimer) a petition from Margaret Countess Dowager of Marlborough.

Within is a memorandum that the Countess never had any annual pension, though she had received 400*l.* in several sums by Warrants of Bounty.

17$\frac{11}{12}$, Jan. 7th. Dr Compton, Bishop of London, "To the Honourable Spencer Compton Esq.—These." Dated at Fulham, and signed for the writer.

" Dear Nephew—Let me trouble you on behalf of this bearer Mr. Charles L'ogle Minister of the French Church in Wapping establish't by her Majesty's especial command; for the cure of wch she was pleased to appoint forty pounds a year, wch was paid · to Mr Carron whom this bearer hath succeeded. : . . . . . .

" H. LONDON."

[P.S.] " My hand is yet so lame, that I am not able to write myself."

[Circa. 1713.] Draft report of Spencer Compton to the Lord Treasurer [the Earl of Oxford], on Mr Pauncefort's memorial relating to Mr Guy Palmes. [Undated].

" . . . . . . Guy Palmes Esqr having been app^{ted} one of the Tellers of the Exchequer by their late Maj^{tys}, did in the year 1698 assign and make over the said office to Thomas Gibson for a term of 12 years in trust that the said Thomas Gibson should out of the profits of the said office pay to the said Guy Palmes £200 per ann. and discharge several debts due to divers persons named in the said assignment. And whereas

Wm Palmes Esq. father to the said Guy Palmes did pay or satisfie the greatest part of the said debts amounting to £14,500 ; therefore the said Thomas Gibson by the direction of the said Guy Palmes did in the year 1700 assign the residue of the said term to Bennet Sherrard Esq. in trust that the said B. S. should pay 800 per ann. to the said William Palmes and the overplus to the said Guy Palmes. . . . . . . I further humbly certify to your Lord^p that her present Majesty was graciously pleased to grant by Letters Patent dated August 4th 1702, £1000 per ann. out of the Post Office during her Majesty's pleasure to the said Guy Palmes in consideration of his losses in the said office of Teller."

[Temp. Anne.] "The Case of John Evans Merchant and his wife, Dame Mary Hussey, late widow and relict of Sr William Hussey who was Ambassador Extraordinary from King William to Vienna and Constantinople to mediate a Peace between the Emperor and his Allys, and the Grand Signior in 1690 and 1691."

The petitioners claim £10,863 12s. as Extraordinary Expenses due to the late Sir William Hussey.

[Temp. Anne.] Lady Killigrew to Lord Godolphin [or the Earl of Oxford]. Undated and unaddressed. Endorsed "Lady Killigrew's Letter to my Lord Treasurer."

" My Honoured Lord, if I cou'd by any means keep my selfe, and my poor daughter from starving, I wou'd not importune your Lordship, but what can a woman of eighty due, without y^r Honour will save me, in my great distress, my humble Petition is that you wou'd graciously please to give me as a private favour the half yeare which is due of my pention ; before the rest have theirs, it shall not be a pressident for others to solicite, for I will pray for you in humble silence, I have exhausted all my creditt, nor have a possibility of living but by your Lordship's favour ; upon my old knees I beg you wou'd order me the half year, for a quarter will not clear me of half I owe ; I am, my Lord, your Lordship's most dutifull and most obedient servant, BARBARA KILLIGREW.

[Circ. 1714.] Two undated identical petitions to the House of Commons, from the freeholders and inhabitants of the Parishes of Maresfield and Uckfield, near East Grinstead in the County of Sussex. In favour of a Road-Bill, with many signatures appended.

[1715.] An undated petition to Lord Townshend as Secretary of State from " the Stewards of the Protestants of Ireland for the celebration of their Anniversary meeting in London, in memory of their deliverance from a generall massacre begun in that Kingdom by the Irish Papists in the yeare 1641, and appointed by Act of Parliament there." It concludes:—

" The Reverend Mr Jonathan Smedley Preacher to the Protestants of Ireland for this present year 1715, having signalized himself for adhereing to the interest of the succession of the House of Hanover for severall years last past, and having suffer'd in his fortune for the same, the above-mentioned Stewards in respect of those circumstances, and of his excellent and seasonable discourse preached before them at this time, as well as in regard to his being a person of known abilities . . . . do beg leave to present the said Mr Smedley as a person fit to be encouraged by your Lords^p and worthy of his Maties notice and favour."

[Signed.] " MEATH ; MOUNTJOY ; CASTLECOMER ; S. MOLYNEUX ; ROB^r FINLAY ; [and] RICHARD STEELE."

1715, Augt. 23rd. George Townshend to Lord Townshend. Dated in Lincoln's Inn and unaddressed.

The writer solicits his Lordship's interest in behalf of his son who is anxious to be appointed an Extraordinary Clerk of the Council, in the room of Mr James Vernon who is also one of the Commissioners of the Excise and is dying if not dead.

Note. George Townshend was a Commissioner of Excise from 1699 to 1726, and James Vernon from 1710 to 1756.

1715, Sept. 6th. Rev. R. Davies to Spencer Compton. Unaddressed Endorsed by Mr. Compton " Mr. Davies petition for a prisoner."

" Honoured Sir—I beg leave to make application to you in favr of a poor prisoner in the Marshalsea who is under sentence of death. The crime for which he is condemn'd is the stealing of a horse, which he says he himself did not do, but had the horse from another, that stole him. . . you will do a very good deed, in being instrumental in procuring his pardon. I therefore beg in this poor man's behalf that you wou'd be pleas'd to make application for him to my Ld Townshend. He was condemned at Kingston Assizes, his name is —— Gascoyne, or Gaskin, his first name I have forgot. . . . . . My humble service to my Lady Phillips. I am, *etc.* R. DAVIES."

[P.S.] " If you should think it requisite to write to me any thing in answer to this, it will be sufficient to direct to me in Christ Church, Southwark."

1715, 19th Sept. Walter Etherington to Lord Townshend. Addressed " To The Rt Honrble The Lord Townshend Secretary of State —These humbly prsent."

The writer encloses the following Petition and Information, and begs his Lordship to dismiss the said Mr Hamond, Governor of Landguard Fort, and to put in a just person in his room.

First enclosure :—

" The humble petition of Sampson Seagoe and sixty others, all Masters of shipps tradeing to Newcastle, and other parts—To the King's most Excellent Majesty." 1 page.

The petitioners pray to be relieved from the oppressions of Mr Hamond the Governor of Landguard Fort, and that the salute of the said fort may be ascertained by the firing of [a] gun as is usual to other forts.

Second enclosure attached to the last :—

" The sworn information of Sampson Seagoe, of Great Yarmouth Master of the good Shipp called the William and Mary of Yarmouth of the burthen of two Hundred and Sixty tunns, laden with coales from Newcastle; that this morning when sailing out of the harbour of Harwich, his ship was fired at by the Governour of Landguard Fort, ... Sworn Sept. 2nd, 1715, before Samuell Lucas, Mayor (of Harwich) and Daniell Smyth." 1 page.

Note. From the printed Calendar of Treasury Papers, it appears that a Capt. Francis Hamon was Lieut. Governor of Landguard Fort in 1702.

[1715, Sept.] Complaint agst the " Governr of Landguard Fort." Addressed.—" To The Rt Honrble Viscount Townshend, Lumbly prsent." In the handwriting of Walter Etherington, and signed by Henry Townshend

It begins and ends as follows :—

" My Lord,—The subscriber, Mr. Henry Townshend, Master of the good Shipp called the Lake of Wisbitch is redy and willing to make

affidavitt that Mr Hamond Governer of Landguard Fort fired a gunn
at him."

[P.S.] "Allso Mr Thomas Murfort paid Thirteen Shillings and 4^d
and was without the harbour, witnes my hand, THOMAS MORFORT."

1715, Oct. 1st. Dr Smallridge, Bishop of Bristol, to Lord Townshend. Dated at Bristol, and unaddressed.

"My Lord—Yo^r L^p was pleas'd at my request to interest your self so
far in obtaining from his Ma^ty directions for the payment of the 2,000*l.*
given by the late Queen to the poor, that when I came out of town a
month ago, I had reason to hope it would be immediately paid, and
therefore left with the Sub-almoner a list of persons to whom it should
be distributed. I hear from him that the Warrant for payment of it is
not yet sign'd by his Ma^ty, and that the poor gentleman is afraid of
being torn to pieces by those who have long with great impatience waited
for it. I must therefore entreat your lordship's farther favour in prevailing with Mr Wortley Montague, in whose hands I understand the
Warrant is, to lay it before His Ma^ty, which act of charity will entitle
your L^p to the blessings of the poor as well as to the thanks of their
importunate sollicitour — Your L^ps most humble and most obedient
servant, GEO. BRISTOL."

1716, July 6th. An Order of Council, dated at the Court at S^t
James's and sealed with the Council wafer-seal.

"Present—The King's Most Excell^t Ma^ty
Archb^p of Canterbury, *etc.*

"The Right Honourable Spencer Compton Esqr Speaker of the House
of Commons having been this day by his Majesty's Command sworne of
his Majesty's Most Honourable Privy Councill, took his place at the
Board accordingly.

"EDWARD SOUTHWELL."

To the above Order is attached by the Council Seal the following form
of oath :—

"The oath of a Privy Councillor taken by the R^t Honble Spencer
Compton Esqr the 6th of July 1716.

"You shall swear to be a true and faithfull servant unto the King's
Majesty as one of His Maj^ties Privy Council you shall not know or
understand of any manner of thing to be attempted done or spoken
against His Majesty's person, honour, crown, or dignity royal, but
you shall lett and withstand the same to the uttermost of your power,
and either cause it to be reveal'd to His Majesty himself, or to such of
his Privy Council as shall advertise his Majesty of the same. You
shall in all things to be moved, treated and debated in Council, faithfully
and truly declare your mind and opinion according to your heart and
conscience, and shall keep secret all matters comitted and revealed
unto you, or that shall be treated of secretly in Council. And if any of
the said Treaties or Councils shall touch any of the Councillors, you
shall not reveal it unto him but shall keep the same until such time as by
the consent of His Majesty or of the Council, publication shall be made
thereof. You shall to your uttermost bear faith and allegiance unto
the King's Majesty and shall assist and defend all jurisdictions pre-
heminences and authority's granted to His Majesty and annexed to the
Crown by Act of Parliament or otherwise against all foreign Princes,
Persons, Prelates, States, or Potentates. And generally in all things
you shall do as a faithfull, and true servant ought to do to His Majesty.

"So help you God, and the holy contents of this Book."

With the above papers is the following :—

" Note of fees for swearing the R^t Honble Spencer Compton Esqr, Speaker of the House of Commons, of the Privy Council.

	£	s.	d.
To the Clerks of the Council - - -	10	0	0
To the under Clerks - - - -	4	0	0
To the Keeper of the Records - -	6	0	0
To the Keepers of the Council Chamber -	5	0	0
To the Under Chamber Keeper - -	1	0	0
	£26	0	0
To the Messenger [a guinea]. -	1	1	6
	27	1	6 "

[The last item, and the total, are in Spencer Compton's handwriting.]

[1716]. Two copies of a petition, of which one is endorsed " Copy— East India Comp^y Pet^n to the King—about ships going from Ostend &c^a to the East Indies ; " and the other is endorsed " Petition from the E. India Comp. Inclos'd in L^d T's to Ld Cadog^n & Mr Walpole. 5th Octr 1716."

The petitioners, after reciting the Acts of Parliament, complain that several of his Majesty's subjects have presumed to trade into and visit the said East Indies and in hopes to evade the law have contriv'd to purchase Commissions from Foreign States and Potentates, which may be gotten at easy rates, hoping under colour thereof to screen themselves from the prohibitions and penalties contained in the said Act.

" . . . . . On the 15th of the preceeding October arriv'd at Surat Bar the ship Victoria of Ostend, burden 240 Tons with 70 men, Captn Haver Sandfield an Irishman commander, under the Emperor's colours . . . . . they had received a letter from the Company's factors at Callicut on the Mallabar coast dated the 5th of said January [17$\frac{15}{16}$] which informs of two large ships from Ostend under the Emperor's colours being arriv'd, one at Surat, the other at Callicut, commanded by Monsr Sarsfield both intending to load home from those places directly . . . . the Petitioners have very great reason to apprehend that Captain John Opie an Englishman who went several months since from London to Leghorne is gone from thence to the East Indies on the like design . . . . .

" The Petitioners do therefore most humbly intreat Your Majesty will be graciously pleas'd to take the premisses into your royal consideration and to apply such a remedy for checking in its infancy this practice so many ways destructive to this considerable branch of the trade of Great Britain as to your Majesty's great wisdom shall seem meet.

" And the Pet^{rs} as in duty bound shall ever pray &c."

[circ. 1716.] The humble address of thanks from the Chancellor, Masters and Scholars of the University of Cambridge—To the King's Most Excellent Majesty. Undated. 1 page.

" Humbly thanking his Majesty for the gracious mark of royall favour which he has bestowed on his ancient University of Cambridge in presenting to it the noble collection of books and manuscripts gathered in many years by the great industry and accurate judgement of the late Bishop of Ely." [Dr Moore.]

[1717 ?] Petition to the King from Sir John Wittewrong Bart. In French. Unsigned and undated. 1 page.

The petitioner has always supported the Protestant Succession and his Majesty's interest for which he has spent great sums in the County of Bucks. Has served as a Member of Parliament for more than twelve years, and is still a member.

During the last Ministry much injustice was done him and he rejected several advantageous offers as his principles prevented his entering into the measures that were then on foot.

He has had the honour to serve as a Colonel of Infantry and he would rather be cashiered than sell out.

· Notwithstanding such a character and his zeal for his Majesty, he has had the misfortune to be excluded from the new levies, several colonels of less standing than him have been preferred, and many persons have had civil employments without any one having the least regard for the petitioner.

He therefore humbly prays for the command of a regiment or to be put on the Excise Commission, or in such other employment as his Majesty shall think fit, so that the petitioner's enemies cannot have occasion to say that he is entirely neglected.

1719, —. [Copy of a] petition to the King in Council of Samuel Tatem, Richard Reeve, Lawrence Ingoldsby, and others, Merchants of London traders to the Porte of Bilbao in Spain. Undated and without signatures. Endorsed by Spencer Compton " Petition of Sam¹ Tatem &c. Merchants, trading to the Port of Bilboa—1719." 1 page.

The petitioners pray for passes for two Spanish ships laden with wool and iron to come to the Port of London as was practised in the late war with Spain.

1719, April —. Copy of a humble representation addressed by the same London merchants to the Commissioners for Trade and Plantations in support of their petition to the Privy Council. Undated and without signatures. Endorsed by Spencer Compton " In Mr. Wace's hands in Lᵈ Harrington's office, Apr. 1719. Passes granted and dated May 12ᵗʰ do." 2 pp.

The merchants represent that "Spanish wool is absolutely necessary to the makeing our superfine cloth and the lessening the consumption of that wool in the manufactoring of the cloth debasses its qualitie and will if practiced bring it into disreputation in forreign marketts. Iron is allso necessary for the use of his Majesty's Navy as well as to all other shiping perticularly large ships for their anchors chain plates, and the like great work . . . . . . During the late war this practice of granting passes was indulged perticularly to Bilbao by which means we were constantly furnished with a suply of Spanish wool as our occations required but now by the interruption of commerce their remains no door open for that trade. . . . .

" Nevertheless some of our manufactories have been exported to Spain by way of Holland and other nutral portes to suply their demand and prevente the disuse of our manufactories at that markett tho' loaded with the Aditional charge of two freights commission and customes in and out which we have been obliged to pay in Holland as some of us has lately experienced . . . . . . "

1721, April 22. A curious petition to the King at Bordeaux, and subscribed :—" Le très humble très obéissant très fidelle suject Gauien de Valois de Terrefort prince du sang Cardinal."

" C'est d'une très profonde soumission que j'ose avoir l'honeur de m'adresser au roy de la grande bretaigne non comme on faisoit vers les roys de perse qu'on n'osoit leur parler moins encore les aprocher, mais

comme à un roy graciux, riche, puissant, inmance, décoré des qualités à
un si grand prince, car quel plus grand et plus auguste roy puist être
miux que votre Maiesté, Sire le digne subject de mes louanges si
j'étois capable d'en faire le gloriux panégirique ; l'hurux souvenir des
graciuses faveurs que le feu roy Guillaume prince d'orange m'honora à
la prière du feu roy de France et mon devoir, m'oblige de prier le roy
d'Angleterre avoir agréable la démission que j'ay, l'honeur de faire à sa
Majesté de l'archevêché de Cantorbery primat du royaume que le roy
Guillaume m'avoit pourveu, il m'honora aussi de plusieurs lettres pour
m'obliger d'aler remplir cette haute dignité que l'on a teneu putêtre
secret au roy qui est une recompence à favoriser le sujet le plus fidelle à
sa Majesté, mes bules sont dans les argives du conseil d'Angleterre que
le prince me promit faire conserver avec soin, la persone qui jouit de ce
grand benefice est mon coadjuteur, le titre de cet illustre prélat avec
mes bules que j'ay l'honeur d'indiquer sont des temoignages fidèles de la
verité que j'ay l'honeur d'avancer au roy, mes incomodités, la pauvreté, la
peine que je ressans par le malheur que j'eus d'encourir la disgrace du
feu roy de France peu de tems après la mort du prince Maurice, m'a
mis hors d'état d'exercer aucun des nombrux emplois desquels j'avois
eu l'honeur d'être graciosé par le roy Louis Quatorse et par le roy
Guillaume qui sont les plus grands et les plus eminents dans le monde
et dans l'église : si la relation de ma vie n'étoit enuyuse à votre Majesté
Sire, jaurois l'honeur d'en faire icy un détail ; mais je n'ose exiger une
longue attantion de la generosité du roy.　Son altesse serenissime le duc
de Florance à qui j'eus l'honeur d'éviter une surprise qu'on vouloit luy
faire où il s'agissoit de la perte de ses états, puit assurer le roy que tout
mon malheur depand d'être issu du sang de Valois : je prie sa Majesté
de vouloir être memoratif qu'àprès la mort du prince Maurice, je fus
receu et recognu héritier a touts les biens honeurs et dignités de ce
prince par le roy de France la famille royale et par le conseil d'état, en
consequance et par la grace de Dieu, j'eus l'honeur d'être couroné, du
diadème que je remis au roy de France àprès luy avoir fait démission
des droits que j'avois sur la courone qui consistent a la moitié du
royaume de France, les portes fermées ; àprès avoir enrichi le roy de
France mon maitre et avoir eu le bonheur d'hurusement sauver la vie
aux très dignes altesses mes seigneurs le Dauphin de Vienois et le Duc
de Bourgoigne, sachant que les intantions du roy de France me devien-
droit prejudiciables, leurs tres hautes altesses par le suport d'une
reconoissante tandresse aydèrent a mon creasion.　Depuis ce tems
malhurux je suis errant dans le monde, pardon grand roy de ma trop
grande liberté mais animé d'une noble ardeur, me sentant encore honoré
d'un des bienfaits du roy Guillaume en l'election qu'il luy plût faire
de ma persone, pour que mon nom fut inseré au nombre des très illus-
tres et très honorables chevaliers de la jaretière. Je prie a main jointe le
roy avoir agréable mes tres profondes soumissions, qu'il plaise a sa
Majesté Bretanique me faire la grace de me remetire les·bules de
L'archeveché de Cantorberi qui ont resté dans les argives d'Angleterre,
qui sont inutiles pour d'autres persones, et permetre que j'aye l'honeur
d'être continué dans l'ordre de la jaretière même de la porter ce que
j'espère recevoir de la bienveillance du roy, par surabondance d'une
très grande marque d'honeur de triomphe a ma famille ; je promets
garder ce preciux trésor avec tout le soin la precaution et l'ordre neces-
sere, en memoire des très hautes très dignes très graciuses faveurs des
roys de la Grande Bretaigne. Le roy de France avant son décès me fit
la grace de m'acorder une amnistie qui me remet dans mes biens
honeurs et dignités renouvelée par le roy à present regnant, mais mes
biens particuliers ayant été distribués aux plus grands du royaume

Monsieur le regent jouissant d'une partie, je ne panse plus qu'à mourir en répos dans mon indigence ne mangeant que du pain vivant de charité, il ne me reste plus Sire pour la tranquilité de mon esprit qu'à avoir l'honeur de me demetre comme j'ay l'honeur de faire par ces présentes de l'archêveché de Cantorbery en faveur du roy d'angleterre, que j'espère être agréable à sa Majesté brétanique, et à la faveur de son inmance protection royale que j'ay l'honeur de reclamer a main jointe, mes penes seront adoucies, mon nom ne sera pas divulgué, sous cet hureux apui j'entreprans d'un cœur généreux la liberté que je prans, parceque sa bonté royale m'attire et m'engage d'avoir l'honeur de me presanter à ses pieds sous les auspices d'un grand roy pour qu'il plaise à sa plus qu'impériale Majesté m'octroyer les très nobles demnndes que j'ay l'honeur de faire : ce sont les graces, faveurs inmances que jay l'honeur d'attendre et espère recevoir de très grand très auguste très puissant roy de la Grande Bretaigne priant sa Majesté d'être assuré que j'ay toujours esté inviolablement comme j'ay l'honneur d'être d'une très profonde soumission des roys d'angleterre et de votre Majesté, &c.

"Le Duc de Barwic qui comande en cette ville m'est suspect."

1721, July 28th. Sir William Thompson, ex-Solicitor General, and afterwards a Baron of the Exchequer, to Lord Townshend.

"My Lord—I presume to trouble your Lordship with the enclosed memorial, and beg your perusal of it and that your Lordship will be so good as to alter it where you are pleased to think it wanting, and I shall esteem it an honour to be allow'd a few moments of your Lordship's time as soon as it may be convenient.—I am, etc."

The enclosed memorial is in French and is addressed to the King.

The writer represents that he has been Recorder of Ipswich and Member of Parliament for about fourteen years, and Recorder of London for nearly seven years.

That he has always been attached to his Majesty both in Parliament, in the Courts of Justice, and in the other public assemblies of the London Magistrates.

That he was one of those appointed by the lower house to conduct the prosecution of Dr. Sacheverel when the Protestant Succession was in danger, and was consequently very illused by the last ministry of Queen Ann, etc.

In conclusion the writer represents that he has the mortification of having no marks of his Majesty's approbation, which greatly diminishes his credit, and also his authority against his Majesty's enemies. Wherefore he very humbly prays his Majesty not leave him longer under so painful a discouragement.

[1721?] An undated petition to the King from Charlotte, widow of Capt. Rycaut, daughter of Sir Gilbert Gerrard, and granddaughter of the late Bishop of Durham [Lord Crew]. Praying for a pension upon the Irish Establishment to enable her to maintain and educate her five children.

[1721?] An undated petitition to the King from Viscount Gage. In French. Praying for the payment of the balance of the £5000 promised to the petitioner out of the sale of some timber in the Forest of Dean. It concludes:—

"The petitioner will try to render himself more capable to serve his Majesty in getting himself elected Member of Parliament in the place of [Nicholas Lechmere recently created] Lord Lechmere."

1722, March 28th. An unsigned paper giving a list of some Election returns up to date, and addressed "For my Lord Townshend's Office— These."

Most of the names mentioned are marked with a (+) or a (—), and it would appear that the latter mark was employed to distinguish supporters of the Ministry. The list is as follows:—

Wednesday the 28th March, 1722.

B[isho]ps Castle. Bowater Vernon —. Wᵐ Peer Williams+.
Welby. Serjᵗ Birch —. Nicholas Philpott —.
Derby. Lᵈ [James] Cavendish —. [Thomas] Bayley+.
Cricklade. Sʳ Thoˢ Reed —. [Thomas] Gore.
County of Essex. [William] Harvey+. [Robert] Honeywood—.
Preston. Thoˢ Hescoth+. Daniel Poulteny —.
Thetford. Sʳ Edmund Bacon. Robt Jacombe.
East Redford. Thomas White—. [Patrick] Chaworth+.
Shaftsbury. Sʳ Edwᵈ Desbouverie—. Edward Nich[o]las+.
Eye. Spencer Compton —. Edward Hopkins —.
Dartmouth. Collº George Treby —. Thomas Martin —.
Bridport. Sʳ Dewey Bulkeley —. Peter Walter —.
Edinburgh. John Campbell—.
Newark. Brigadʳ [Richard] Sutton —. James Pelham —-.
Barnstaple. Sʳ Hugh Ackland+. Genl [Thomas] Witham — [a mistake for Wetham.
Haslemere. [James] Oglethorpe+. [Peter] Burrell (a false return—Lᵈ Blundell and Mr Molineux) [*Note.* This appears to have been stated in error], and the error is repeated in a note at the foot of the paper].
Highworth [? Malmesbury]. Lᵈ Hilsborough—. Sʳ John Rushworth [a mistake for Sir John Rushout.] Collº [Giles] Earle — Collº [John] Farmer [a mistake for Fermor].—a double return.
A note at the foot of this paper adds:—" N.B. [James] Oglethorpe [and Peter] Burrell, are false returned for Haslemere," but the election return does not seem to have been challenged and those gentlemen represented Haslemere in this and the next four parliaments.

1722, April 27th. Horatio Walpole to Lords Townshend and Carteret. Unaddressed.

My Lords—I having by the consent of my late lord Stanhope and Mʳ Secretary Craggs received the principall fees for Irish Commissions sign'd during their time in the Secretary of State's Office upon my notification amounting to the sum of 213–10–10 I beg leave to lay before your Lʳᵈᵖˢ an account of what fees have since accrued in your offices on the same account to the time of my Lʳᵈ Lievtᵗᵃ [the Duke of Grafton's] departure into Ireland when I resigned my employment as Secretary to his Grace *etc*."

The above letter is written on the fly leaf of a List—(2 pp. and 58 names of officers, with the fees they paid for their commissions being drawn) headed "Principal Fees for Irish Commissions received in the Right Honoᵇˡᵉ the Lord Townshend and Lord Carteret's offices from the 4th of March 17²⁰⁄₂₁ to the time of the Lord Lieutᵗᵃ departure in September following under the notification of Horº Walpole Esqʳᵉ Secʳy to Lord Lieutᵖ"—and it is endorsed with the following minutes:—

"I allow the repayment of the proportion received by me of the fees within mentioned—TOWNSHEND,"
and "I allow the same—CARTERET."

The following receipt is also endorsed upon this letter:—Received this 14th day of June 1722 for the use of Horatio Walpole Esq. late

Secretary to his Grace the Lord Lieut of Ireland, of the Right Honoᵇˡᵉ the Lord Viscoᵗ Townshend by the hands of John Wace Esqᵣᵉ the Sum of one hundred and eight poundsand fifteenth shillings being his Lordships proporčon of the principal fees of Irish comicons received in his office from the 4ᵗʰ of March 173̸0 to Sepʳ following being the time he resigned that employment which his Lordship was pleased to give and allow to the sᵈ Horᵉ Walpole according to the within written accompt—I say received by me—PETER LEHEUP—£108 : 15.

1722, Aug. 11th. George Treby, Secretary at War, to the " Rᵗ Honᵇˡᵉ Spencer Compton Esqᵣ Paymaster Generall of his Majesty's Forces." Dated at Whitehall.

" Sir—His Majesty having been pleased by a sign manual to constitute you together with—

  The Rᵗ Honᵇˡᵉ the Earl of Cadogan.
  Rᵗ Honᵇˡᵉ Robert Walpole Esqᵣ.
  Rᵗ Honᵇˡᵉ Lord Viscount Cobham.
  Lieutenᵗ Genˡˡ [George] Macartney.
  Major Genˡˡ [Williams] Tatton.
  Major Genˡˡ [Joseph] Wightman.
  Brigadier [Richard] Russell.
  Brigadier [Andrew] Bisset.
  Brigadier [Phineas] Bowles.
Comptrollers of the Accounts of the army.

And myself a Board to examine the reduced officers of his land Forces and Marines upon the Establishment of Half Pay in Great Britain ;

I am to desire you will meet the said Commissioners in the Great Room at the Horse Guards on Tuesday the 14ᵗʰ Instant at ten of the clock in the forenoon in order to hear the Warrant read, and to proceed upon the said Examination, I am" etc.

1722, Augt. 10th. The Case of Capt. John Welbe, addressed with a Petition to Lord Townshend as Principal Secretary of State. In book form 32½ pp.

" The humble Petition of Capt John Welbe sheweth —

That Your Petitioner has been confined a prisoner in the King's Bench prison above six months, on accᵗ of unjust sutes of William Adye a packer, and Capt Nicholas Mandell and others, who have vowed revenge for his discovering their unlawfull practices and testifying the truth against them, at two tryalls before the Lord Cheife Justice King at Guild Hall in June last was a twelvemonth. And attending severall tryalls before the Lord Cheife Justice Pratt likewise relating to the wilful destruction of the ship Riga merchant in Port Mahone on purpose to defraud the insurers, And particularly William Adye who has sworn never to dye in peace till he has ruind your Petitioner, the particulars of which may be seen in Your Petitioner's Case.

That there is another Conspiracy against Your Petitioner by Mᵣ Edward Morgan a Roman Catholick liveing in Bloomsbury Square who was round the globe with Capt Dampire the same voyage that Your Petitioner was and was the death of the first Lievetennant by turning him most barbarously ashore at the Island of Sᵗ Jago, where he miserably ended his days with hunger and greife, and the said Morgan was afterwards the ruin of the said expedition, and now endeavours to ruin Your Petitioner, and thereby overthrow his intended discovery, in concert with others, and Mᵣ Gregson Mᵣ Richᵈ Cambridge's attorney and Tho[s] Burtt a nonjuror one of Ormes's congregation and book-keeper to M[r] Rich[d] Cambridge, who were your petitioner's bail, and surrendered Your Petitioner after they had confounded his mony, and trickt him out of all that he had, by encouraging sham actions, and given them the advantage in the law against Your Petitioner designedly, by latting judgements goe by default, and bringing writts of errors, and suffering *non pross* upon the errors, for want of paying the transcript &c. Some particulars of which may be seen in the inclosed copy of Your Petitioners letter to Mr Tho[s] Burtt.

That Your Petitioner was under some apprehention in the month of March last was a twelvemonth, of the designed barbarous usage that Your Petitioner was to expect from William Adye, Capt Nicholas Mandell and others, and therefor presented a Petition to Your Lordship dated the 13th of March 1720 a copy whereof is hereunto annext, And in the Month of June following presented a Petition to His Majesty likewise, dated the 18th of the said month, relating to the barbarous usage Your Petitioner then expected from Mr. Richard Cambridge, Tho[s] Burtt his book-keeper, Mr Edward Morgan, and M[r] Gregson their attorney, and others, And the consequence thereof is hereunto annext likewise.

That the usage Your Petitioner meets with, is a conspiracy against the interest of His Majesty, and the whole nation, as well as against Your Petitioner, which Your Petitioner will undertake to prove before the Parliament, when they meet, the concequence and views of which, may be seen in the annext copy of Your Petitioners Petition to his Majesty, dated the 18th of June 1721.

> Therefore Your Petitioner humbly Prays that Your Lordships woud be pleased to Order Your Petitioner some releife till the Parliament meets, And thereby defeat the designs of the enemies of His Majesty, and the nation.
>
> And Your Lordships Petitioner Shall pray &c.

King's Bench Prison,
August the 10th 1723."

The Case of Capt John Welbe [24 pp.].

1. Containing a copy of a letter to the Right Hon[ble] Robert Walpole Esq[r].

2 His Case and Petition to the R[t] Hon[ble] the L[d] Viscount Townshend.

3. A copy of his Affidavit made before M[r] Delafay (Under Secretary of State) relating to the designed destruction of his Majesty's Fleet under the command of Sir George Bing then in the Mediteranian, and the wilful destruction of the merchant ships on purpos to defraud the Insurers.

4. A list of severall persons who in their own and other names have prosecuted the said Capt Welbe for making such affidavit with an account of disbursements ocationed thereby.

5. Two copies of letters to Gov[r] Pitt thereupon.

6. Instructions to discover the several frauds in the said Affidavit mentioned.

7. A copy of a Petition to His Majesty in Council relating to the establishment of a South Land Company [*i.e.* a chartered company, with a capital of three millions sterling, for colonizing, and trading with, Australia, " and for working the gold and silver mines which there abound "].

MARQUESS TOWNSHEND MSS.

8. A copy of an Order [of the King in Council, dated Decr 14th 1720] of refference to to the Lords Commissioners of Trade and Plantations thereupon.

9. A copy of a Petition to the Lords Commissioners of Trade and Plantations relating to the same.

10. A copy of a Petition to His Majesty relating to the barbarous and unjust usage that the said Capt hath met with for detecting treasonable and fellonius practices and offering to undertake to discharge the nations debts and inrich the nation upwards of one hundred millions sterling.

11. Reasons humbly offerd by the said Capt for granting a Charter for establishing a South Land Company.

All which is humbly offer'd to the consideration of the Honble House of Commons by

CAP^T JOHN WEBBE.

[1722]. Copy of the Petition of Richard Cambridge and others to Lord Townshend, Principal Secretary of State.

"Sheweth: That of late great demands have been made upon Your Petitioners and several other merchants for losses of divers ships which Your Petitioners and other merchants had insured and which have been wilfully and designedly lost, particularly the Diligence, Jeremiah Finch, Master, the Riga, merchant, John Cattell, master, and Capt John Welbe hath discovered these unlawfull practices, which tend to the ruin of the insurers, upon whose hazard and adventure the trade of the nation very much depends.

That in order to oppress Capt Welbe, many actions have been brought at law against him, and he has been frequently arrested, and put to great expense, and trouble, by persons whome your Petitioners have great reason to believe were concerned in such the said evil practices, and he has therefore been obstructed from attending the defence of sutes presented against several of the insurers, to the great disadvantage of Capt Welbe, and the loss and hazard of the insurers.

Your Petitioner therefore humbly prays that Your Lordships would be pleased to grant to the said Capt Welbe, such protection, and encouragement, as may defeat the designes of such evil disposed persons, and enable the said welbe to assist Your Petitioner in the further discovery of the said evil practices, and in prosecuting the offenders. And Your Petitioners Shall pray, &c."

1722, Augt. 22. A copy of a letter to Mr Burtt, bookkeeper to Mr Richard Cambridge. "Mr Burtt,—I Remember when you carryed me to the Fleet to surrender to those actions in the Common Pleas, that you and your master's friends were bail for you told me that you would move me from thence to the King's Bench to surrender to those actions that you and your Master's friends were bail for me likewise, that my bail might be intirely discharged, And that then you would get me the liberty of the rules of the King's Bench and supply me with money weekly till I could be in a capacity by chymistry to maintain my self and which I proposed to doe in a few months it requiring about three months to prepare my medicines &c. in which time you promised to allow me fifteen shillings a week subsistance besides a certain sume for erecting a small labaratory of about three or four furnaces and materials &c. At that time I little expected that you woud have used me thus barbarously as you have don, especially considering

MARQUESS
TOWNSHEND
MSS.

that the whole overthrow of my affair is intirely owing to the usage that I have mett with from you, for Mr Gregson, Morgan, Adye, nor Mandell nor any of the rest could not have ruined me had it not been for you, and for which you must expect to answer either in this world or the next, Some particulars of which I have thought fit to remind you of (viz.) in the first place all those actions were ocationed by my discovering the wilfull loss of the Riga, merchant in Port Mahone, and being a witness for your Master relating to the same, who had underwritt about six hundred pound on the said ship and therefore became my bail, and you told me your self that your Master promised to spend a thousand pound in my defence, before I should be wronged, 2^ly you employed Mr Gregson on that acct he being your Master's attorney, 3^ly I proposed the inditing of them, and told you that there woud be no end of their actions. But you and Mr Gregson refused saying that your Master was not willing to hang them but would take care they should not ruin me, 4^ly you know Mr Gregson had instruction for a Bill in Chancery severall termes by him but would not file the Bill, but let judgements goe by default and brought writts of errors, and suffer'd a *Nonpross* for want of paying the transcrip and 5^ly at the first generall meeting you came and told the gentlemen that your Master could not come but gave his service to them, and what they concluded on he woud agree to, And said your Master desired them to have regard to Mr Morgan's caractor, and not speak disrespectfully of him &c. altho' you knew he was a Roman Catholick, and had ruind Capt Dampire's Expedition, and was then endeavouring to ruin mine, 6^ly After I had found out Mr Morgan's designes against me, you came in a coach to my house, on purpose to hinder my going to St James's with a Petition to His Majesty, relating to the said affair, and swore that if I did I should ruin it, so that neither Mr Morgan, nor I should get the Charter, and 7^ly when you sent for me in order to surrender me about April last was twelvemonth I told you that I had acquainted the Board of Trade and Secretary of State that you had a design to Surrender me, and that therefore you could not alledge any just reason for the same I being reddy at your pleasure, upon which you altered your resolution, and then concluded on sumonsing 40 merchants to a meeting to advance a sume of money for my defence and to enable me to carry on the said affair, you being in hopes at the same time that I could not prevail on them to advance any money, haveing your self made a party against me which you depended on to oppose it, and when the gentlemen mett, your Master did not come but you came in his stead at last when the gentlemen were reddy to conclude, and when you found that I had in your absence, prevaild on the gentlemen to advance me two hundred pound, you undertook to gather the money for me, by which you got it in your power, to keep me out of the same, whereby you have ruind me, I could remind you of a great many more particulars, but hope this is sufficient to touch your concience, if you have any, that you may have some remorse, and not murder me, by keeping me in a prison, without money, after you had been one of the cheife instruments of confounding all that I had in the world, therefore [I] desire to speak with you, that I may know what to depend on, after all this barbarous usage &c.

I am, as I am used,

JNO. WELBE."

King's Bench Prison,
August the 22^d 1722.
P.S. What doe you think of a fiery tryall &c.

1724, May 15th. Copy of a report from the Committee of Council in Ireland. Dated in the "Council Chamber Dublin" and unaddressed.

May it please your Excell^{cys} and Lordships.—In obedience to your Exellencys and Lordships Order of re-reference of a report signed the sixth day of May pursuant to His Grace [the Duke of Grafton] the then Lord Lieut and Council's Order dated the 27th day of April last, requiring us to consider what is proper to be done to allay and quiet the great fears of the people of this kingdom occasioned by the apprehensions under which they are of William Wood's copper half-pence and farthings becoming current among them, we have met and considered the same, and are of opinion that for allaying and quieting the great fears of the people upon the occasion it will be proper that an humble Address be made to His Majesty in order to obtain from his royal wisdom and goodness such remedy as may be fitting to avert the great evil that we apprehend would unavoidably befall this kingdom in case the said half-pence and farthings should become current among us, a draught of which Address is hereunto annex'd and humbly submitted to your Excellencys and Lordships by,

> Edward [Singe Archbishop of] Tuam, [The Earl of] Abercorn, [Lord] Mountjoy, Santry Tullamoore, Ralph Gore, [The Earl of] Meath, Gust[avus] Hume, Edw[ard] Crofton, Oliver St George, R. Tighe, Marm[aduke] Coghill.
>
> (A true Copy)
> ED. DERING,
> Dep. Cler. Con. Priv. [Hib.]"

1725, Jan. 18th. Count de Broglio to Count de Morville. Copy of a letter, in French, dated in London.

[Translation] . . . . The Princess of Wales has forwarded to me a petition, which has been sent her by [a] galley slave who entreats her to intercede with the King [of France] for his pardon, and she has expressed a wish that I should write to the Court. As the galleys are in the Department of the Count of Maurepas I have sent him the petition, and have explained to him how anxious she is that it may be granted . . . .

1725, May 29th. A Privy Council Report addressed to the King from the Council Chamber at Whitehall, and endorsed in a clerk's hand "Copy of Committee Report for issuing a Special Commission to try Capt [Robert] Elston for the Murder of two of his ships crew beyond the seas [on the coast of Guinea].

1st June 1725, read and approved, and Lord Chancellor ordered to issue a Special Commissⁿ accordingly.

"Mem^d. The Act of Parliament upon which the Commissⁿ was founded, was past in the 33^d of Henry Eighth chap. 23^d, Entituled An Act to proceed by Commission of Oyer and Terminer agst such Persons as shall confess Treason &c^a. without remanding the same to be tried in the shire where the offence was committed."

1725, Oct. 28th. F[rances?] Killigrew to Sir Spencer Compton? Dated in Church Street, Soho, and unaddressed.

"Sir—Your great compassion and good nature upon all ocations encourages me to take this liberty. Mrs. Howard has informed me that His Royal Highness is determined to give no pensions and the misfortune I am in oblidges me to trespas upon your great goodness to beg that you woud recomende me to His Royal Highness for part of his

bounty: I dare say if his Royal Highness knew the distres I am in MARQUESS TOWNSHEND MSS.
that he woud be so charitable as to condicende to think of me; I have
no meritt to pleade in excuse for troubling you but my misfortunes
which are very great and too many to repeat. I am, Sir, with great
respect your most obedient and most humble servant,

F. KILLIGREW."

1725–26, Jan. 23. Edward Stables, Clerk-Assistant to the House of
Commons, to Spencer Compton. Unaddressed.

"Sir—I beg leave with a heart filled the deepest sense of duty and
gratitude, to return my most humble thanks for your honor's great
goodness, in again interposing between me and death, hastening upon
me, by overmuch fatigue in the service of the publick; as these
are beyond expression, I humbly hope you will be pleased to accept,
on all occasions, the utmost returns of gratitude in my power, long
since a duty upon me, far above any ability of mine to answer, and
will ever be so, tho' alwaies attempting to be acknowledged, and
repaid, with the greatest pleasure.

Upon my present recollection I was thus admitted Clerk Assistant in
December 1710 when Mr [Culverwell] Needler and Myself had
agreed, (he being disabled by palsie) Mr. [Paul] Jodrell [Clerk of the
House of Commons] and he waited on Mr. Bromley (then Speaker)
and acquainted him therewith, and Mr. Jodrell proposing me to succeed
Needler, Mr. Bromley asked him who he thought was to name the
Clerk-Assistant, Mr. Jodrell insisted, himself, as his Clerk; Mr.
Bromley denyed that, as not being Clerk to the Clerk, but a distinct
and proper Clerk of the House, to be appointed by the House, as their
Clerk-Assistant and a check upon the Clerk of the House appointed
by the Crown, and that, at most, Mr. Jodrell could only propose, but
that the nomination, or approbation, was in the House, and that no
such officer could be admitted without a que[sti]on; and this was the
opinion of Sr John Trevor, the Ma[ste]r of the Rolls: (In conversation).

I had the good fortune to be well spoken of to Mr. Bromley and he
received me in the most generous, and ready manner, he acquainted
the House with Mr. Needler's disability, and that a proper person had
been considered of to succeed him, and giving a recommendatory
character of me (according to his goodness, which I was alwaies very
sensible of) he put the qu[est]ion for calling me in, which was done,
without more ado; but Mr. Jodrell entred nothing of this upon the
Journal.

Give me leave, Sir, to conclude with my humble thanks also for
your great indulgence to me, on this occasion, for time to recover my
health, which I hope will be very soon, and I hope I shall alwaies
make use of it to testify, with as gratefull a heart as ever filled
mortal breast, the greatest duty to your honor most justly owing from
Sir—your—Honors most obliged and most obed't humble serv't

E. STABLES."

1717, Sept. 26th. An Order in Council, dated at the Court at
Kensington, and sealed with the Council Wafer-seal.

Present—The King's most Excellt Majesty in Council.

This day the Right Honourable Sir Spencer Compton Knight of the
Bath was by his Majesty's command sworn of his Majesty's most
Honourable Privy Council and took his place at the Board accordingly.

ROBERT HALES.

17—, Nov. 3rd. [Date torn.] A paper endorsed "Judges opinion
[in favour of] the Prince of Wales chusing his own servants." It is

signed by [Sir] Robert Raymond, William P. Williams, and Samuel Mead.

Note.—The endorsement is inexact as there were no judges named Williams and Mead on the Bench at the same time, during the reigns of George the First and George the Second. Sir Robert Raymond was Attorney-General from 1720 to 1723, and a Justice of the King's Bench from 1723 to 1733.

[1727?]. The humble Petition of Mary o'Brine widow—To the Right Honble Spencer Compton Barronet [sic] Speaker to the House of Commons. Undated.

" Sheweth—That your Petitioner's first husband Thomas Evans was a Captain of a Man of War in King William's time, and was killed by the French on board the ship he comanded in New found Land the same year his husband King William dyed, that her husband John o'Brine was L[ieu]t of Granadiers in Colonl Molsworth's Regiment and was kill'd at Prats del Roy in Spain, That in consideration of her last husband's faithfull service, the Government was pleased to allow her a pension, which she enjoyed for some time, untill one Thomas Fox and his wife falsely swore her out of it, because she would not allow him ten pounds in hand and six pounds per annum, and has served several honest widows the same way to their utter ruine, under pretence of being an evidence for the King, which in effect was only to extort money from the poor widows, That your Peticoner had him taken up and tryed at the Old Baily for robbing of her and extorting a note of ten pounds, That then he the said Fox receiv'd his sentence to be whipt from Newgate to Tyburn, fifty pounds fine, and two years imprisonm^t who after receiving this, his sentence, made escape from justice, but is now coming to ruin what he did not before, That his wife gives out that your hon^r will give him a protection to appear again in order to ruin your Peticoner and the said widows, That your Peticoner and her family are utterly ruin'd through his means, and beside is afr[a]ide of her life wch his wife strove to take away before.

Therefore your poor Peticoner most humbly begs that your Hon^r would be pleased to grant her a hearing to satisfie your hon^r further and she as in duty bound will ever pray."

1728, May 4th. [Copy of.] " The humble Address of the General Assembly of the Church of Scotland.—To the King's Most Excellent Majestie." Dated at Edinburgh and subscribed, on behalf of the Assembly, by William Wishart, Moderator. A loyal and pious address congratulating the King upon his accession. The following is a specimen of its wording :—

" The death of our late Gracious Sovereign, Your Majestie's Royal Father of glorius memory, whom God made the instrument of so great Blessings to us, and to all Europe, was so sensible and heavy a stroke to us, that we should have been inconsolable under it, if so great a loss had not been made up to us, by Your Majestie's most peaceable and happie accession to the throne.

Permitt us, then, Great Sir, to congratulate Your Majestie upon Your ascending the throne of Your royal ancestors with the joyful acclamations of all Your dutiful subjects. We can never cease to bless Our Gracious God, when we think of his setting a King over us, whose royal qualities do so brightly adorn the throne upon which he sits," etc.

[1729?]. Copy of a very loyal Address from the Commons to the King. Undated and signed by Edward Stables, Clerk of the House of Commons.

1730, Dec. 31st. An Order of Council, dated at the Court of St James's and sealed with the Council Wafer-seal.

Present—The King's most Excellent Majesty, Duke of Newcastle etc.

His Majesty in Councill was this day pleased to declare the Right Honourable Spencer Earl of Wilmington, Lord President of his Majesty's Most Honourable Privy Councill, and His Lordship took his place at the Board accordingly.

JA. VERNON.

[Circ. 1730.] An undated petition to the King from John Carter under sentence of death for robbery. Signed by Edmund Waller M.P., and John Clavering M.P., [Members for Great Marlow from 1727 to 1734], Sir John Etheredge, George Bruere, and other inhabitants of Great Marlow.

[Circ. 1730.] Petition in French to King George II. from Louis Bernard of Lezan in the Diocese of Nismes, a French Protestant convict on board the Invincible galley.

The Petitioner who has been condemned to the galleys for life has already spent 14 years in chains and implores the King's protection, the promise of which was renewed in the year 1729.

1730–31, Jan. 4th. Thomas Tomkyns to the Earl of Wilmington. Dated in the Poultry Compter and unaddressed.

" My Lord—When I reflect on the frequent trouble I have given your Lordship already in this way I can't refrain [from] being ashamed at the thought of it; and yet my unhappy circumstances are such as urge me nevertheless to the farther trespass.

It is now two years and a half since my being confined upon an Extent, without being able, as yet, to regain my liberty, notwithstanding my having compleated a discovery, that by competent judges is thought to be worth a million sterling to the nation : upon this foundation I am, at present, seeking my releasm[en]t, and in order there to, have lodgd a Petition to His Majesty praying the same.

What I have therefore now to entreat of your Lordship (as apprehending your being lately appointed President) is, that you would be so good as to order my petition to be read [at] your next generall Council, and to contribute to its being referred to a Committee of Council."

. . . .

1731, Jan. 12th. Memorial to the King about an Establishment for the relief of the widows of poor officers in the Navy. Dated at the Admiralty and unsigned. 4½ pp.

The memorial proposes that three pence in the pound should be stopped out of all naval pay and half-pay for the relief of the widows in question.

[1731.] Proposed heads of [a Scheme for] an Establishment for the relief of the widows of poor officers in the Navy. Unsigned and undated. Enclosed in the last ten clauses. 7 pp.

The Scheme proposes the formation of a charitable Corporation, with a Board of Governors and a Court of Assistants, to administer the funds subscribed. It also proposes the names of many naval men (from the Lords of the Admiralty down to Warrant Officers,) to be the first Governors of the proposed Corporation.

1731, Feb. 8th. Extract from the Minutes of the House of Commons. Dated " Lunæ 8° die Februarij 1730–1."

Resolved, **That an humble Address be presented to His Majesty that**
He will be graciously pleased to give directions, that an account be
laid before this House of what proceedings have been had for the
establishing a Civil Government at Gibraltar, and for declaring the same
a free Port, since the last application of this House to His Majesty for
that purpose.

1731, June 9th.   Thomas Tomkins to Lord Wilmington.   Unaddressed. "My Lord—Upon a Petition lately presented to the Treasury
praying my liberty, having been informed, that, under my present circumstances, the proper application for it, is to His Majesty in Council I
have therefore prepared the inclosed in order to be lodged forthwith, in
hopes that your Lordship will be so good as to order it to be read at the
next general Council.

To succour the distressed is an action expressive of humanity and
great goodness; and if from an inclination of that kind, you shall be
induced to contribute to a favourable issue of this my intended application, it shall always be remembered with the utmost gratitude by him,
who is, with the greatest submission and respect—My Lord--Your
Lordships most obedient and most humble servant.

THOMAS TOMKINS."

[1731.]   The humble Petition of Thomas Tomkyns now a prisoner in
the Poultry Compter upon an Extent.—" To the King's most Excellent
Majesty in Council assembled." Unsigned and undated. Enclosed in
the last.

The petitioner prays for his enlargement from prison, on parole or
otherwise, that he may put in practice his invention for making cast
iron malleable with sea or pit coal.

1732, July 20th.   An undated Petition (to the King) of the widow
of Robert Gregon, late Office Keeper and servant to his Majesty's Council
Chamber.

Humbly shewing.   That it hath been usual for the Crown on the
death of such under officers of the Council Chamber to allow their
widows some small pension for the support of themselves and family.

That the poor Petitioner being left with two children destitute of the
common necessarys of life some time since made her humble application
to His Majesty for such pension proved unsuccessful therein in regard
Mrs. Holland the widow of the former Office Keeper was at that time
alive and receiving a pension of twenty pounds p annum.

That being lately informed the said widow Holland is now dead and
the said pension void.

The Peititoner in consideration of her husband's long & faithful services
to the Crown, and she being in a starving condition and grown past her
labour, prays that the like small pension may be granted to her as was
enjoyed by the said Mrs. Holland.

Certified at foot under the above date as follows :—
" We the Clerks of His Majesty's most Honourable Privy Council
hereunder written do certify the contents of this Petition to be true and
do believe the Petitioner to be an object of great charity.

JAS. VERNON,   W. SHARPE,
TEMPLE STANYON,   CH. DELAFAYE."

1735, Nov. 28th.   Copy of a letter from the Russia Company to
Claudius Rondeau Esquire, English Resident at the Russian Court.
Dated at London and Signed S. Holden.   2 pp.

This letter encloses an undated Petition, addressed to the Privy
Council, signed by Joseph Chitty, a Russian merchant, and also a copy

MARQUESS
TOWNSHEND
MSS.

of a letter (translated out of High Dutch), from Baron Peter von Shaffiroff to Mr. Bardewick (the Agent for the Petitioner in Russia), dated at St. Petersburg, July 25th 1735.

The Petition relates to an alleged purchase, from the Czarina, of Rhubarb to the value of £2,500, and also to the alleged refusal of Mr. Rondeau to render the petitioner's agent any assistance in enforcing the said contract.

1735, Dec. 27th. Copy of a letter from Claudius Rondeau to Samuel Holden, Governor of the Russia Company. Dated at St. Petersburg. 7 pp.

This letter controverts the statement that the above-mentioned contract had been entered into; and the writer further asserts that he offered to speak to the Czarina's Ministers on behalf of Mr. Bardewick, and has done his utmost to maintain a good harmony and understanding among the gentlemen of the English factory in St. Petersburg.

Same date. Copy of a letter from Claudius Rondeau. Dated at St. Petersburg and unaddressed.

With reference to Mr Chitty's Memorial explaining that neither the Senate nor the College of Commerce (at St. Petersburg) had authority to conclude any such contract without a possible order from the Czarina or her Cabinet Ministers.

1736, Aug. 12th. Abstract of the Return of the Secretary to the Governors of Queen Anne's Bounty to an Order of the Committee of Council of the 12th of August 1736:—

The total number of livings augmented from the beginning of the Corporation to the 1st of January 1735—

				£
	⌈ 220	not exceeding	10	p ann.
		209	-	- 20
By Joint Benefactions	⟨ 176	-	- 30
		161	-	- 40
	⌊ 137	-	- 50

903

By the Bounty alone   234 not exceeding 10 p ann.

In all 1137—Of which 517 have been augmented with purchase of real estates with the whole money appropriated for that purpose, 23 Livings with part of the money, and 597 remain for which no purchases have been made.

Total number of Livings which remain under the yearly values of £10 £20 £30 £40 and £50, vizt—

					£
694	-	-	-	not exceeding	10
1139	-	-	-	„	20
1095	-	-	-	„	30
1161	-	-	-	„	40
1329	-	-	-	„	50

In all 5418 Livings.

1738, April 4th. Memorial from the Lords Commissioners of the Admiralty, praying His Majesty's Orders for issuing Warrants to impress seamen. Dated at the Admiralty Office and signed by Sir Charles Wager, Sir Thomas Lyttelton and Sir Thomas Frankland. 1 page. Endorsed with a Minute "6th April 1738.—Read and approved.— L^ds Ad^ty to issue Warrants accordingly."

1738, July 26th. Representations of the Lords Commissioners of the Admiralty praying directions may be given for the speedy manning of the Fleet. Dated at the Admiralty Office and signed by Sir Charles Wager, Sir Thomas Frankland, Thomas Clutterbuck, and Lord Vere Beauclerk. 5½pp.
Endorsed with a Minute "31st July 1738.—Read and app[rove]d and Orders to be issued accordingly."

[1738 ?] An undated paper in the handwriting of Lord Wilmington, being a list of British ships captured by the Spaniards, with some memoranda as to documents relating to their capture :—

St James of Bristol, [Capt] Cartis, bound from Cork to Jamaica, taken the 12th of May. Carried to a Bay in Puerto Rico, Order on the 22nd, d° to carry the s^d Ship to St Johns, arriv'd there the 25th, d° part of the Provisions sold to the St Juan, a Spanish Man of War.

Prince William, [Capt.] Kinselagh, from St Kits to London, taken the 24th of March, 250 Leagues to the Eastward of Bermudas, having Brazletto Wood on Board, was sent to Havanna.

[Capt.] Kinselagh['s Letter] to Isaac Pero, July 27th.
Do. to Wilks and Berian, July 28th.

Certificate from St Kits that the Brasiletto was imported from Providence.

Brigantine George, [Capt.] Ware, from Jamaica to Bristol, taken the 21st May.

Affidavit of Harris and Jenkins.

Loyall Charles, [Capt.] Way; Dispatch, [Capt.] Delamotte, from Jamaica to London, Spaniards told [Capt.] Griffin of the Seahorse, that these two ships were condemned at Havanna, the latter for having logwood on board.

Two Sisters Brigantine, [Capt.] Gardner, taken in 1732 at the Tortugas.

Eight Ships taken in 1734.

Friends Adventure, Sloop Johannah, fired at, not taken, Endeavour and Friendship, Bermudas Sloop.

Sloop Carac, [Capt.] Donaldson, from St Kits to Curaçao [Capt.] Donaldson['s letter] to Somers.

Sloop Thomas, [Capt.] Keeling, taken April 3rd 1734, bound from Curaçao to Virginia.

Protest at St Kits and Certificate of the Deputy Govern^r of Virginia.

Prince William, [Capt.] Ivy, from Virginia to Jamaica, 1731, taken plundered and let go.

Mr William Coventry.

Sloop from New-York, [Capt.] Wolf, from Madeira to Curaçao and Jamaica. July, 1736, carried to Camina.

Another Vessel, [Capt] Walters, from North Carolina to Curaçao, taken plundered and then discharg'd.

Another Vessel 3 Months ago.

Captain Playter.
Neptune Snow, [Capt.] Playter, 12th July last plundered.

15th d° rummaged again.

MARQUESS
TOWNSHEND
MSS.

Nicholas Forster, mate.

Carried on Board the Spanish ship, saw a great number of English sailors, who had been prisoners two years aboard. [The Spanish] Captain inquired what ships were coming from Jamaica, &c.

Richmond, [Capt.] Halifax, in 1729–30 went from London to St Kits, 14th Apl. 1730, carried to St Jago de Cuba.

Pheasant, [Capt.] Wilson, carried to Puerto Rica, stript and plundered, bound from Barbadoes to S. Carolina.

1739, Aug. 2nd. The humble Petition of the United Company of Merchants of England trading to the East Indies—To the King's most Excellent Majesty in Council. [Undated, but endorsed by Lord Wilmington, President of the Council. "Copy of the Pe[titi]on of the United Company of Merchants of England trading to the East Indies —Augst 2^d 1739."

[The Petition] "SHEWETH—That in order to protect the trade in the East Indies, your Petitioners maintain a considerable naval force, and large garrisons at their own expence.

That in the late war in the reign of Queen Anne, several privateers were fitted out from Europe to cruize in India upon your Petitioners Ships.

That your Petitioners' Governours there would have fitted out a naval force in order to take or destroy them, but upon considering they had sufficient powers for that purpose, they were obliged to desist, whereby your Petitioners trade was exposed to the enemy and several ships were taken, and the ship Marlborough, Captain Matthew Martin, valued at upwards of one hundred and fifty thousand pounds was attack'd, but by the bravery and conduct of the Captain and officers she got clear from them, after a fight of several days.

That your Petitioners are apprehensive that attempts of the like kind may now be made, and that with sufficient powers vested in the Governors at Bombay, Fort St George and Bengal their trade may be greatly prejudiced.

Your Petitioners therefore most humbly beseech your Majesty to take their case into consideration, and that your Majesty will be graciously pleased to grant to Stephen Law Esq. Governour of Bombay, Richard Benyon Esq. Governor of Fort St George, and Thomas Braddyll Esq. Governor of Fort William in Bengal, and to the Governors of the time being, such or the like powers as are given to your Majestys Governours in the West Indies, to enable them to grant Letters of Marque and Reprizal in such manner as your Majesty may think proper, or such other relief as your Majesty in your great wisdom shall think fitt.

And your Petitioners shall ever pray &c.

Signed by Order of the Court of Directors of the said United Company.

CHRIST[OPHER] MOLE,
Secr^y."

1740, June 26th, Aug. 16th, and Aug. 20th. Robert Robinson to Lord Wilmington. Dated in Lincoln's Inn and unaddressed.

These three letters relate to their writer's appointment as Chief Justice of Gibraltar. On the fly leaf of the earliest of them are "Some Minutes or Memorandums relating to Gibraltar," and with them are preserved two undated papers relating to the same matter; viz., "The Humble Memorial of Robert Robert Robinson, Esqr, To the right Honourable Sir Robert Walpole and the rest of the Lords Commissioners of his Majesties Treasury," and " A few Minutes for Lord Wilmington's inspection with relation to what appointments [are] to be allowed the Judge at Gibraltar.

In his Memorial Mr. Robinson prays the Treasury that his salary may be fixed at £1,000 a year ; that he may have a suitable provision for Out-set Money, and for erecting Courts; and that he may have the house which was late in the possession of General [Francis] Columbine etc.

1740–41, Jan. 5th. Letter of Henry Mauger to Lord Wilmington. Dated in Guernsey and addressed to the President of the Council. 3 pp. Under cover of Peter Dobree, of Monument Yard, London, dated Jany 13th 1741.

The writer who has for seventeen years been the King's Attorney and Solicitor in Guernsey, informs the Council as to an intricate dispute which has been for long on foot between the Crown and the Jurats of Guernsey.

1742, June 16th. Copy of a Memorial from the Commissioners of the Customs, to the Lords of the Treasury, in favour of appointing Mr. Francis Hurdd to an office in the Customs. Signed by Richard Chandler, John Evelyn, Brian Fairfax, and Isaac Leheup.

Enclosed is Mr. Robert Paul's Report to the Commissioners of Customs, as to the services of the said Francis Hurdd, which is dated May 20th 1742. 2½ pp.

1742, Nov. 9th. Francis Hurdd to Lord Gower, Lord Privy Seal.

The writer (" a considerable dealer in haberdashery Wares ") prays his Lordships' favour and interest in procuring him an appointment under the Commissioners of the Customs.

His statement of his claims proceeds as follows :—

. . . . "On the 12th of April 1739 I waited on Mr. [John] Hill one of the Commissioners of the Customs, and represented to him that vast quantities of goods were run at Hull and other outports to the very great loss of the revenue as well as prejudice to the fair trader . . . . By my instructions this clandestine trade has in a great measure been prevented. . . . . I had the thankes of the Commissioners for this service with an assurance of being recommended to the Lords of the Treasury for a suitable post . . . . The Earl of Orford when at the head of the Treasury was made acquainted with these particulars and promised all due encouragement : but the elections then coming on, it was defer'd til the 30th of June 1741, when it was referred to the Commissioners of Customs for them to report the true state of the case, and what they thought proper to be done thereon. Here also by one occurrence or other intervening it was protracted till June last, and the post which was then vacant being supplyed before their Honours' Memorial came to the Treasury; nothing has yet been done. I have the vanity to think my services may be thought worthy a superior post than that, and do most humbly pray your Lordship's favour and interest in behalf of your Lordship's," *etc.*

[1742 or 1743]. The Memorial of James Cockburn to the Right Honble the Earl of Wilmington First Lord Commissioner of the Treasury. [Undated.]

Humbly sheweth—That by the accompts of his late Majesty's household (delivered into the Treasury) from the 30th June 1726 to the 11th of June 1727, there is

MARQUESS
TOWNSHEND
MSS.

	£	s.	d.
due to the said James Cockburn to clear the accompts of wines bought by him, for his said Majesty's service, the sum of	375	4	11
That there is likewise due to him for the purveyance of charcoal, furnish'd at the contract price and for wages within the said time the sum of -	1,230	14	6¼
	£1,605	19	5¾

. . . . . . " He therfore most humbly prays your Lordship will be pleas'd to give directions, when any money comes in upon his late Majesty's accompt, that it may be issued to the cofferer towards discharging the said debt of £1,605 19 5¾.

Or in case there be not now any great likelyhood of any more money coming into the Excheq^r for his late Majesty's arrears, that your Lordship will be pleas'd to take him into your compassionate consideration, and favour him with such other relief as your Lordship out of your great goodness shall think fit.

And he is in duty bound shall ever pray &c^a."

[1742 or 1743.] The Memorial of John Earl of Loudoun, addressed to Lord Wilmington as First Commissioner of the Treasury etc. Undated.

The Petitioner prays that the arrears of the pension of £500 per annum granted to him in 1733 may be paid to him before the troops go abroad there being two years due to him.

[1745.] The memorial of Sir Robert Munro, Lieut. Colonel in Lord Sempill's Regiment [the 42nd foot]. Unsigned, undated, and unaddressed. It sets out the dates of the Commissions of the Memorialist, who was killed at the Battle of Falkirk in the following year, when Colonel of the 37th Foot.

1753, Oct. 3rd. The Petition of Henry Spelman Gent. to the Honourable George Townshend Esqre (M.P. for Norfolk). Dated at Norwich. 3½ pp.

The Petitioner after setting forth at considerable length his descent from Sir Henry Spelman the Antiquary, and also the careers of his father and his uncles, concludes thus :—

" That your Petitioner is the only survivor of the senior branch of Spelman, being the son of John Spelman abovementioned . . . . . in the year 1737 became a Voluntier in His Majesty's Own Regiment of Horse [the 1st Dragoon Guards], then commanded by the Right Honble the Earl of Pembroke, wherein he continu'd to serve for some time in England, and during the severall Campaigns in Germany and Flanders, in hopes of being preferr'd, but not having the good fortune to succeed and the regiment returning to England in 1746 by the good offices of some friends and there being then a vacancy he purchased a Warrant and was appointed a Quartermaster in the said regiment, but the change of the Establishment thereof, from Horse to Dragoons taking place the Xmas following, he thereby became greatly affected in his circumstances and by means of the great reduction of his subsistance, and meeting with considerable losses and disappointments in his private affairs, was reduced to the necessity of disposing of his Warrant in 1748 in order to extricate himself from the many difficulties and incumbrances he then labour'd under, as many more particularly appear by his Certificate from the said regiment, to which he craves leave to referr. And having ever since labour'd under the misfortunes of poverty and [being] intirely destitute of employment [he] is now reduced to great distress.

He therefore prays such favour, recommendation or relief in the premises as to your great wisdom humanity and compassion shall seem meet.

And your Petitioner shall ever pray.

HENRY SPELMAN."

[No date]. Copy Certificate of Service of Henry Spelman, Gent. [Enclosed in the list].

THESE are to certifie That the bearer Mr. Henry Spelman hath serv'd for the space of ten years, private and corporal in his Majesty's Own late regiment of Horse commanded by General Sir Philip Honywood, and in my troop: four years of which he served abroad in the late war with approbation.

That he serv'd eight months as Quarter Master, till the establishment of the said regiment was chang'd from Horse to Dragoons.

That he likewise serv'd after the change of the establishment, two years and a quarter as Quarter Master in the said regiment, during all which time, of about thirteen years he distinguish'd himself, by honestly and faithfully discharging ev'ry trust repos'd in him as became a good soldier, and subject, but by the unforeseen disappointments and misfortunes in his private affairs, was obliged to obtain leave to sell his Warrant, to extricate himself from the difficulties and incumbrances he then labour'd under.

Given under my hand and regimental Seal in London this 12th day of March 1749-50.

T. CARR, L^t. Coll.

A true Copy. The Original of the above Certificate was sign'd and seal'd, at the time mention'd, by me.   T. CARR, Lt. Coll.

NOTE.—From recitals in the petition of Henry Spelman it appears that his father, John Spelman, who died in 1741, had been Clerk and Surveyor in the "Hand in Hand" Fire Insurance Office, which was founded by his uncle Henry Spelman of Wickmer, Esq., and was called the Friendly Society; had been afterwards a Volunteer in the 2nd Foot Guards, then Surveyor of the duty on printed calicoes, and lastly, a Land Carriage Waiter in the Port of London, to which post he was appointed by Sir Robert Walpole in 1735. It also appears that the Petitioner's grand father was the Rev. Charles Spelman, Vicar of Congan, and that the latter sold the family's Norfolk estates on the death of his father, Sir John Spelman, who was the eldest son of Sir Henry Spelman the Antiquary.

1771, May 7th. Capt. Daniel Shaw of the 62nd Reg^t. "To John Lees, Esqre, Private Secretary to His Excellency the Lord Lieutenant of Ireland." This letter is dated at Kinsdale, and endorsed "Capt. Shaw to Sir Geo. Macartney."

"Dear Sir—About five weeks agoe I did presume to apply to His Excellency the Lord Lieutenant to succeed the Ensign of my Company lately deceased in England.

I once in my life had an oppertunity of exerting my self by going beyond the proper distance from my guard to rendre some small service to the present Lord Lieutenant of this Kingdom the day after the Battle of Lafelt, when he was the Honble Captain Townshend and aide des camp to His late Royall Highness the Duke of Cumberland.— Notwithstanding it happened so long agoe I should imagine His Excellency may recollect the circumstance. In my last to His

Excellency I made bold to mention the afair but never will any more. The multiplicity of State afairs I fear much will injure my application in feavor of my dear and most deserving young lad just in his sixteenth year well grown and properly educated, how happy I should be to have him in my own company; Inclosed you have a detail of my services which ought to have some weight."

. . . . .

The enclosure above referred to is as follows :—

A detail of Captain Shaw's service.

1744. — Joined the armie in Flanders a Volunteer in the 42nd Regiment.

1745.—Left the 42nd Regimt and joined Lord Crawford's Corps a Volunteer. Was in the Battle of Fontenoia [Fontenoy]; the latter part of that day remained on the field of Battle to the very last, acted as aide des camp. Delivered his Lordship's orders to different Regiments in retreating particularly to the 42nd regiment which can avouch the same.

1747.—Was by the Duke of Cumberland's recommendation with fourteen or fifteen more Volunteers from the British armie appointed Ensigns in the Dutch service with a promise from His Royall Highness to be recalled whenever an oppertunity offered to be provided for in His Majestie's service.

1756.—Was recalled by order of the Duke of Cumberland and appointed first Lieutenant in the 34th Regiment with rank from the date of my Commission in the Dutch service.

1761.—Was offered a Company in the new raised levies but preferred going on the Expedition against the Havanna which will appear by a letter from the Right Honable Charles Tounshend Esqr the Secretary at War.

1762.—Was appointed Captain of a Company in the 42nd Regiment.

1763.—Was put on half pay when the second Battalion was reduced.

1768.—Was appointed to a Company in the 62nd Regiment where he is at present one cf the oldest officers in that Corps.

Captain Shaw was at the Battles of Fontenoia and Lafelt—was at the seige cf Bergen op Zoom where he was stormed—was at the burning of the shipping at St Malo—takeing of Cherburgh at St Cas—was at the Siege of the Muro [the Moro Fort near Havanna] and reduction of the Havanna.

JACOBITE PAPERS AND LETTERS, 1703–1727.

1703. Papers relating to the Scottish Conspiracy of this year, viz. :—

1. "An account of the Conspiracy in Scotland." Unsigned and undated. 13 pp.

2. "The Substance of Sir John McLean's discovery to the Earl of Nottingham, No. 4." 5¼ pp.

3. "The Duke of Queensbury's paper delivered to Her Majesty on Jan. 14th 170¾, No. 14." 6 pp.

4. "The Duke of Queensbury's paper delivered to Her Majesty on Jany 10th 170¾, No. 15." 5¼ pp.

NOTE.—These four papers are printed in extenso in the House of Lords' Journals of Feby 8th 170¾, with the above titles. On the 15th of the same month the Lords moved an Address to the Queen for the production of further papers relating to the Conspiracy, amongst which they specified certain "Letters written in a Gibberish Language." The

Earl of Nottingham on Feb. 19th, when he produced the papers that had been moved for, stated that Her Majesty thought it for the Public Service not to take any further notice of these letters. The Lords, however, entered them in their Journals on the following day, and on Feb. 23rd presented an Address to the Queen praying her to issue a Proclamation promising a pardon and a reward of £500 to whomever should " make known to . . . . the Lords' Committees appointed to examine into the Scottish Conspiracy (of whom Lord Townshend was one) the Key or Cipher whereby the four letters written in Gibberish Language may be fully explained." Amongst these MSS. are copies in the handwriting of the 2nd Viscount Townshend of three of the Gibberish Letters with the interlinear translations given below. The three copies are dated March 4th 1703–4 and March 5th 1703–4, on which days, perhaps, the originals were translated to the Lords' Committee by some person acquainted with the key to them. The language of the translations would make it appear as if the informer were a foreigner.

March 4th 1703–4. Translation, under this date, of the Gibberish Letter dated June 1st. 1703, and addressed " To My Ld 7."

" My Ld,—I send by this *gondellion* an account of Lord   three of the good luck when he had last remonstrance and particular account of the managements of this affair which at present, God be praised, to so happy an event is brought that we have all belief of speedy helps after long expectation of so many years, nothing now ruin hope but disagreement only yourselves by which will give distrust to the most timorous in the universe, and force these less forward in venturing on the bottom when they may fear it uncertain if not they do find unanimity. They hope of your in all counsells, and chiefly the Parliament present on which the eyes of Europe are fix'd. The Votes and resolutions will determine in everything whether any expectations are left of the return of your antient and ruined family, your resolves in asserting rights your against pretended authority of false Parliament that the people Scotch will assure not so altogether corrupted without keeping some sense of their antient vertue of fidelity and honour and yet gold English so often disposed to dazzle eyes their, both in the last reigns and this not so can overcome just sense of duty toward God fidelity towards naturall Prince and affection towards native country which debauch'd by the example of the English did forget to be Scotch ; as for succession of Hannover and also the abjuration we apprehend no at all *dues pligadunes* two points about which not we doubt that a party the greater to venture too much *fortindi* to yield any compliance at that rate, too much fatal wou'd be a backsliding such after promises so many only they can affaires nothing to destroy and to loose good opinion which long they have taken pains to give the court French, of party honest in Scotland, not I mean this *V: Mo* [your Lordship] whose fidelity just from we depend but since it might be convenient to communicate this letter to others who have not your probity so perfect, I am willing these to shew what is expected from them, at the same time to shew the rocks upon which they may so good a course to split as was never more happy a juncture, so the French court never did shew greater inclination of supporting our interest present good endeavour of the noble rich and considerable Scotch and universal ferment (or *disposition*) in that Kingdome, too much they are conspicuous not to make clear sighted men to see his own interest and to graspe so happy a conjuncture of disengaging themselves from these difficulties in which they are entangl'd by breaking *Zunamento* armed his dispaire and conscience of guilt thus present happy prospect of their

affaires at this time will give power of making good all promises and
assurances of late made, the conjunction with Bavaria which here is
thought a matter so well concerted, as to leave no room of miscarriage
will give so fatall a blow to the confederacy little *revicuda* empire as
to capacitate the French to impose laws to others, and to bring *Badafes*
to points his own who are too much thoughtfull not to see his
own proper advantage and to consult his interest, the game of the
B[avarians] falling off French will be able to dispute with the English
all on the sea, which point is not only credible beyond Tweed then
amongst English, but upon it depend thus they will be able if they
succeed to exert their generosity and us to help, if they miscarry in this
great affaire them will force to cast eyes upon Scotland and to endeavour
a chain there to break considerablle diversion thus I did give *V: Mor:*
[your Lordship] an acount particular of affaires present so that I have
nothing besides with which to trouble *V: Mor:* [your Lordship] but
to beseech you [you] will exert usuall your vigour and wisdome in carrying
on affaires of our session appearing [approaching ?] and honour me to do
answer speedy.   I am Morion [my Lord] *Vo: Mor:* [your Lordship's].
June 1st 1703.   FIGILLISSIMO.

1703, March 5th.   To Philotheus.   No date to this letter.

" Sr,—Brought yours all satisfaction which is wonted when the I have to
receive commands yours, also I must me confess apart some men did give
me not small dissatisfaction to find some so senceless as not to be
satisfyed except all things be carryed in a manner their own proper,
I did expect the last promise which we made might give satisfaction
entire to people all I w'd desire them sensible that we have severall parties
to satisfye who sh'd be distinguished only by their merit and forwardness
in our service.   I know that there are some chief (or forward) men whose
little conscience of their own crimes too much did influence others,
these beleiving that never they cou'd pardon deserve, they did not know
the hereditary goodness [of] this family, which is not only to pardon but
them to reward if it they shall deserve, they may depend upon such
solemn assurances as were given, and as more conscious of guilt they
are than others, they must endeavour by more timely penitence and zeal
in the cause to obliterate the memory of crimes their, not I must think
again they may play the old game as by the treaty of Breda, not we are
God be thank'd in so bad circumstances as Charles the Second at this
time it is better still to starve and be precarious then to obtain bread upon
such barbarous and termes unreasonable, as ourselves, in better circumstances we are so they may reflect that they are in much worse themselves then ancestours their half an age of years past, at that time was
to be feared a vast majority in this country and all things did govern
whereas the affair now is altered and who are willing us to serve by
inclination are most considerable in all respects if they shall not act
upon principall we must consult interest our and we may declare for the
strongest but ought to take care never to appear too late, our King
young as he is is father of all Universally will extend as before I did
observe his protection to people all who shall lay hold on it, and as he
will endeavour to bring to good subjects satisfaction universall in all
reasonable [things] so on the other hand not will be imposed upon and
tied up from rewarding the most faithfull and the antient friends, his
behaviour already fatall too much hath been to fanily his, and at this
time not w'd want this help, when he ask'd people his if that his father
and uncle not had follow'd this advice curse[d].   I desire that these
gentlemen w'd consider that it will be very well if after reconciliation

they are upon equall foot with them who never did fall but to engrosse every and to exclude them who we have merit constant is most unreasonable and also barbarous imposition, which *Zungi* imposed necessities of Princes was made in Scotland, and not offered in other country, I am willing such temper to keep my, this affair as if your own sentiments were; without exposing this letter which *Ventuni* them sh'd exasperate by appearing from us, well I am assured of your inclination to serve so good cause and of your interest and power them among when always you supported them by necessary friendship which not was contrary to this strict probity which most justly did bring respect from all good but none more particularly then from *V: M—.*you Lordship's —.]"

1703-4, March 5th. "To the late Queen at St. Germain."
"Madam—In obeying the orders of *V: M:* [your Majesty] pressing the point to the gentleman *V: M:* did appoint me so that according to thought mine I did find at first much unwilling and shy which proceed's from timourousness of his nature and no want of obligation or affection towards *V: M: &* his Prince his service all satisfaction I cou'd from him gain is that whenever the King shall appear with power sufficient to protect his friends not will fail to have all in his power to serve the interest but as to that surrender of the place trusted to his charge me he did tell not he cou'd promise a thing which not night be in power his [to] perform, him I did tell that it was most absolute necessary that our friends sh'd possess any a port otherwise never we may venture a fleet on our coast yᵗ assurances of having harbour only c'd engage France to a powerfull prosecution of affairs our ; he did reply that he cou d do no more say,that he w'd do all in his power, but as to giving anything under hand he thought it most unreasonable to be hoped for, when him I did speak that paper blanc [carte blanche] he sh'd have, most generously he did reply that he w'd make no termes to those to whom there was obligation them to serve, that might (or c'd) engage thoughts of rewards to the goodness and bounty of *V: M:* after so generous a declaration I did think not it fitt him to press home any more in an affair which him had made uneasie he is without doubt a man of honour & upon whom *V: M:* with confidence may depend, I required my Lᵈ *Momerion* the rest *anhortiden* [to exhort ?] our that from [from that hour ?] I have no more to trouble *V:M:* but to conjure in consideration to take these alterations which were requir'd little last *gondellion* [courier ?], which will procure only satisfaction entire [to the] well inclined party of subjects your to give and fix the King's cause [in a] faithful [sure] way of success of which the accomplishment is the daily wish *V:M: Figellissimo omilindi Sugnon ei aden Esclavansi* [of your Majesty's faithful humble —— and servant.]
London Oct. 8-19 [1702]. PHILARCHUS.

170¾, March 20th. Rough notes on seven sheets, in the handwriting of Lord Townshend, reporting the examination of certain witnesses by the Lords' Committee on the Scottish Conspiracy.
The evidence here preserved is that of the following witnesses on the following dates, and it agrees with the Committee's report to the House of Lords as printed in the House of Lords Journals :—
Colin Campbell, Thomas Clarke, Keith and Mʳˢ Fox, on Feb. 23ʳᵈ.
Sir John Maclean and Colin Campbell, on Feb. 24ᵗʰ.
Colin Campbell, on Feb. 25ᵗʰ.
Sir John Maclean, on 25ᵗʰ, 26ᵗʰ, and 28ᵗʰ.
Sir Thomas Stewart and Furguson, on March 7ᵗʰ.
Campbell and Keith, on March 8th.

1711, Jan. 17th.   Colonel A[dolphus] Oughton to Horatio Walpole.
From Bruges.

"I have hitherto heard no news of the arrival of Seaton and am perfectly perswaded he is not as yet in this town . . . a Scotch man who had been taken prisoner on board the Salisbury at the time of the intended descent, came here about three months since, and after haveing had frequent conferences for about ten days together with several suspected persons here particularly those of his own country, went from hence to Antwerp where he made a stay of about three weeks, and afterwards returned hither in his way to Paris . . . . this may be the very person in question, although at the time of his being here he went by the name of Cambell and pretended to be a chirurgeon. My Lord Drummond receives almost every day letters from France, Some of which I can easily have intercepted, if you think it proper to proceed in that manner . . . . meantime I shall continue my endeavours to inform my self more particularly of his behaviour. . . . . . . Major Erwyn is just arrived and desired me to assure you of his most humble respects."

1714, Augt. 24th.   Dr Bernard Gardiner to Dr Smallridge Bishop of Bristol.   Dated at Oxford and addressed "For the R^t Reverend Father in God the Lord Bishop of Bristol near the new Chappell, Westminster."

Complaining of the conduct of the soldiers recruiting in Oxford. . . . . "This day the Serjeant who makes the speech for the Volunteers to come in, after that is ended, adds words to this effect, that the people would come in to serve King George, and not be governed by those who *have a Pope in their belly*. . . . .'

1715, March 3rd.   Lord Islay to Lord Townshend.   From Edinburgh.

The writer promises to get the best information he can relative to the steps which the enemies to his Majesty's Government are making.

1715, March 5th.   Matthew Price to the same.   Addressed "To the Right Honble the Lord Viscount Townshend Principall Secretary of State."

Intelligence about a secret Jacobite assembly.   The place where it met is not specified and no names are given.   The writer gives his address as "Matthew Price, Callico Officer att Mr. E. Graftons—By the Horse Ferry att Chelsea."

1715, May 10th.   Nouvelles de Paris le 10 May 1715.

Mil[ord] Bullingbrock part pour aller faire sa residence dans le Lionnois à portée de Genève, muni d'une bonne lettre de crédit sur le Chevallier Richard Cantellon Irlandois, banquier en cette ville et Chevallier de la façon du Prétendant. Il reconnoit à présent le mauvais tour, que luy a joué le C[omte] d'Oxford, en se cachant dans sa Province, et faisant repandre le bruit, qu'il s'estoit sauvé, à dessein de faire peur à Mil[ord] Bullingbrock, et luy faire prendre le parti qu'il a pris. Il reconnoit aussy, que le Prétendant a rendu un grand service au Roy George, en parlant dans son Manifeste de l'intelligence qui estoit entre luy, et la feuë Reine Anne. Que par la mesme raison il avoit aussy ruiné tous ceux, qui avoient dans ce pays eté dans ses interests asseurant, qu'il n'y en avoit plus un seul qui désormais vouloit entendre parler de luy. Il a adjouté, dit-on, sans que je sache, si ce n'est pas une charité, qu'on luy prête, que cette seule démarche du Prétendant suffisoit de convaincre tout le monde, qu'il estoit vray fils de son pére.

1715, May 18th.   Monsr Gullman to Lord Townshend.   From Frankfort.   In French.

The writer wishes the British Government to employ as their Agent in Lorraine a certain honest man who had served King William, of glorious memory, both by sea and land, in his tenderest youth. This person is anxious to be employed to go to Bar le Duc, whence he will render an exact and faithful account of the Pretender, and of all the faces at his Court.

1715, July 9th. James Blakeway, John Hill, Jonathan Scott, Edward Jones, and Samuel Thomas to "The R.t Honorble the Earl of Bradford att his house in Soehoe Square — London." Dated at "Salop."

A letter signed by the above-named members of the corporation of Shrewsbury describing "a most notorious riott that hath happened in this Corporation," in which a meeting house was wrecked and the "goal" broken into. The riot commenced by "some few drunken idle boys . . . . crying out down with the round heads, noe Duke of Marlbrô, Ormond for ever."

1715, July 18th. "The Information of Samuel Mence and Samuel Yardley of the City of Worcester, taken upon oath before the worship-full Benjamin Mence Esqr Mayor of the City aforesaid and Philip Bearcroft one of the aldermen and Justices of Peace of the said City."

This Information states that the Mayor and Alderman Bearcroft having on July 12th committed one Henry Weeke for riot and high treason, Mr. Benjamin Pearks, one of the aldermen, to encourage the rioters, said that none but a parcell of [those] that would swear anything would swear against him and that he was an honest fellow and that he would bail him out on the morrow morning, or words to that effect.

1715, July 22nd. Thomas Horsley to Lord Townshend. Dated at Conway.

Information received from "one Samuel Webber who was in the time of the last fatal M[inistr]y, a Messenger to her late Majesty, and who was very frequently sent with dispatches to France to the Duke of Shrowsbury," that he informed the late ministry of a plot to bring in the Pretender and that they would pay no attention to him as "they were so well paid with French money."

Same date. Draft of a letter from Lord Townshend to Monsr Slingelandt, and a translation of the same into French. Unsigned.

"Sir—You will have seen by the publick prints that His Majesty has rec.d certain advices from abroad of an invasion designed in favour of the Pretendr and though the vigorous resolutions of the Parliamt and the dispositions that are making on this occasion give reason to hope that this enterprise may end in the confusion of those by whom it was sett on foot, without troubling the State[s General] for any assistance, yet as it is impossible to foresee at once how far the contagion may spread, and since the Duke of Ormonde's flight may to[o] probably be in order to putt himself at the head of this attempt, His Majesty knowing how zealously the Pens[iona]ry and you are concerned for the inseparable interests of the two nations has commanded me to let you know in confidence that he hopes that in case the provision of Forces made by Parliament should not be sufficient he hopes he may depend upon the States [General] letting him have 5 Regiments of the Scotch his subjects which are now in their service. His Majesty chose rather to make this overture to you and to the Pensionary than to write to the States upon this subject at first, as well to avoid the alarm such a step might cause as to prevent that delay and opposition which might be raised by the friends of France if such a proposition were brought into the States directly without any previous deliberation. His Majesty desires to receive your answer with all possible speed, and promises himself that in case of need there will be no difficulty to grant this assistance.

1715, July 23rd. George Lucy to Colonel Oughton. Dated at Warwick. . . . . . . "The Posse mustered at Warwick near 300 men with such firelocks as could be gott, I hope suffitient to dislodge the rioters . . . . you will observe by the Journall our intentions of approaching Birmingham about Tuesday." . . . . .

1715, July 27th. A letter signed by the Earl of Sutherland, A. Grant, John Forbes, J. Campell, William Gordon and Robert Munro and addressed "To The Right Honble The Viscount Tounsend principall Secretary of State"; begging the favour of an appointment for an interview with him on a subject of great moment for his Majestie's service.

1715, July 30. Major J. Wyvill to the same. Dated at Manchester. Since writing three days before there have been no riots. Lieut. Colonel Holley, Major to Genl Carpenter's Dragoons, arrived yesterday, and attempted to supersede the writer in the command of the King's troops at Manchester but the writer threatened to put him in arrest till Lord Townshend's commands were known.

1715, Aug. 1st. Monsr Gullmann to the same. Dated at Frankfort. In French. . . . . . To-day our man writes me from Bar le Duc (under date the 26th) that the Pretender was there with his pretended mother, and their suite who were about 50 persons, all well affectioned for him. That the Pretender was preparing to start two days later for Nancy with Queen Mary to try to dispell the vexation they felt at the ill success of their affairs. That courriers reached them every day but that for lack of sufficient means he had not attempted to learn the contents of their despatches which were kept very secret. That he (the Pretender) had returned some time from Nancy and from Luneville. As for the current report that someone had attempted his life it was only- a false alarm which laid hold of them for the following reason; an English priest having arrived at Bar le Duc was at the Pretender's Palace when he said that he wished to speak to him immediately. From the suspicions they had of him because he would not unburden himself to any one but the Pretender they imagined that he sought the latters life and that he was sent by his enemies to rob him of it; that his servants thereupon closed the doors and the priest was threatened with the severest tortures. However it appeared, after a severe examination, that he was a courrier, despatched by his friends in England, and that he brought good news, which made the Pretender's people change their tone and flattered him so much that he presented him with five or six hundred crowns.

1715, Augt. 19. Dr. Trimnell, Bishop of Norwich, to the same. The writer understands that Lord Townshend has heard from Mr. Turretin from Geneva to beg his good offices with the King for the recovery of a young gentleman out of the hands of the priests in the dominions of the King of Sicily. There is a fresh Alarm there about the Pretender but we are in a better condition to receive him than we were some time ago.

1715, Aug. 20th. ———— to ————. In French dated at the Hague, and endorsed "Mr S." The writer learns that the States General have determined that the two vessels that were equipping at Ostend for the Pretender (as is supposed) shall be detained until their destination be known. At

Versailles they say the King has been ill from a surfeit and that the Pretender's project got wind by being communicated to the English Court by the French Ministers.

1715, Augt. 25th. William Eden to Lord Townshend. Dated at Birmingham.

"Since the arrival of the King's messengers all things have been very quiet . . . . the Eyes of many of his majestie's poor mislead subjects begin to be opened since that grand incendiary Dr Sacheverell is removed from amongst us . . . . . I am assured the person in theire [the Messengers'] Custody will make a discovery to yor Lordshipps satisaction."

1715, Augt. 27th. A paper dated at Hereford, and endorsed "Return of the Dep[uty] Lieut[enant]s relating to Papists, Non Jurors, &c." It is signed by Thomas Wilkinson, Mayor, and by Benjamin Phillips, Jonah Taylor, Richard Poole, John Morse and Thomas ——, Aldermen.

1715, Sept. 1st. The Earl of Sutherland to Lord Townshend.

"My Lord,—I have all this day been preparing my self for my voyage, if the ship were come to the Nore and had I those things soc very necessary for the King's service which I gave your Lordship a memorandum of, I shall be ready to goe and putt the country in as good a posture as I can for his Majesty's service, and venture my life in the good old cause, I doubt not but your Lordship has gott that affair of the Chamberlane of Ross done for my son Strallinaver after the same manner the Earl of Cromarty had it, favor me with anything extraordinary either from Scotland or France, being just now about my letters to North Britain, I am," etc.

1715, Sept. 5th. From —— to ——. A Jacobite letter, unsigned and unaddressed. Begins "My dear Kinsman" and ends "My Dearest Cosin Yours."

. . . . . "The old bully left every thing uncertain, and the young one is resolved to take care of himself in the first place. . . . . . The Duke of Powis as innocent and as harmless a man as any that suffer'd in the Popish Plot, is already taken up. The Duke of Argyle goes for Scotland next Tuesday and divers other Scotch Lords. Sir G. Bing is sail'd for the Irish Coast where he is to ly to prevent any succours to be sent to that Kingdom. Lord Oxford has given us his answer which is very full, very bold, and very fine. Mr Ford is return'd from France where he left Lord B[olinbroke] and the D. of O[rmond] in good health : He brings no news but that our apprehensions here of an invasion are groundless, and yet we proceed as if they were real. Walpole is to be at the head of the Treasury, and his brother Horace Paymaster in trust. The feuds at Court run high. I long to see you and will do it very soon, if nothing happens to intercept me. Take care of yourself. Liberty is as precious as life. . . . . ."

1715, Sept. 6th. Duke of Argyll to Lord Townshend.

I was this moment at the Treasury where I was told that the ten thousand pound credit is not yet gon to Scotland, and the thousand pound I was to receive is not to [be] had to day, by this your Lordship will see that I may be detained here and I not be in fault.

1715, Sept. 9th. Copy of the Earl of Mar's call to arms : addressed "To the Baillie and the rest of the Gentlemen of the Lordship of Kildrummy.—Given at Braemar."

On the same sheet is a copy of the following letter, of the same date, from the Earl of Mar to John Forbes of Inereran. Dated at Invercauld "at night."

"Jocke,—Ye was in the right not to come with the 100 men ye sent up to night, when I expected four times the number. It is a prettie thing when all the highlands of Scotland are now riseing upon their King and countrey's accompt, as I have accompts from them since they were with me, and the Gentlemen of our neighbouring Lowlands expecting us down to joyn them, that my men should be only refractory. Is not this the thing we are now about, which they have been wishing these six and twenty years—and now when it is come and the King and countrey's cause at stake will they for ever sitt still and see all perish.

I have used gentle means too long, and see I'll be forced to put other orders and I have in execution. I have sent you inclosed an order for the Lordship of Kildrummie which you are immediately to intimat to all my vassals If they give ready obedience it will make some amends, and if not ye may tell them from me that it will not be in my power to serve then (were I willing) from being treated as enemies by those who are ready soon to joyn me, and they may depend on it, that I will be the first to propose and order their being so. Particularly let my own tennants in Kildrummy know that if they come not forth with their best arms that I will send a party immediately to burn what they shall miss taking from them, and they may believe this not only a threat, but by all that's sacred I'll put it in execution, let my loss be what it will that it may be example to others. You are to tell the Gentlemen that I'll expect them in their best accoutrements on horse back and no excuse to be any let off. Goe about this with all diligence and come your self and let me know your having done so, all this is not only as ye will be answerable to me but to your King and country."

Your assured freind and servant,
Sic subscribitur MARR.

1715, Sept. 15th. James Anderson <i>to Lord Townshend?</i> From Edinburgh. Unaddressed . . . . . "I had advices from Perth and Dundee both of yesterday's date. That from Perth bears that the Quality and Gentry in the north are gathering about Blairgowry, Couper of Angus &c. And are about 4 or 500 Horsemen who that night or too morrow were to come there and proclaim the Pretender and to overturn the Magistracy there and settle new ones of their own appointing. Mar nor any other fool had not yet joined them and that the disaffected there were very uppish. From Dundee that they daily expect 100 Horse there to proclaime the pretender and that it was talked confidently they wou'd be there tomorrow . . . . That it was talkt there that D[uke of] Berwick was landed . . . . . . Tis also reported that some of Mar's vassalls refuse to rise with him and that he threatens them with fire and sword.

Yesterday afternoon the Dukes of Argyll and Roxburgh arrived safe here; and yesternight Brigadier Grant was ordered to take care of the Castle where the prisoners of the tolbooth here that were taken the night of the design upon that are carried to this evening. This day ane express was sent to Newcastle to the commanding officers of Carpenter and Ker's Dragoons to hasten their march hither and such directions I hear are given as 'tis hoped we shall have here very soon a handsome army" . . . . . .

1715, Sept. 17th. ——— to ———. Unsigned and unaddressed.

" I would write to you oftner if any thing occurred worth troubling the Post Masters in the first place with reading, and afterwards yourself.
. . . . . . The public prints have sent Charles Kainard into France;

I really thought him all this while in the Highlands . . . . . Carteret and Boscawen are gone post into Cornwall, upon what arrand the Lord knowes, for if we are to believe what we are told all prospect of a disturbance is over."

This, and the similar letter of Sept. 5th, are endorsed "Copies of letters taken upon Sr Wm Wyndham."

1715, Sept. 18th.   Charles Lovell *to the Lords in Council?* From Dover.   Unaddressed.

"Right Honourable Sirs . . . . last night at eight came over Mr Barton (of late one of the King's messengers) who went for London immediately, he could tell me no news.

Mas[te]r Browne who was principally intended to have been taken up by my Lord Townshend's Warrant which Mr Wilcox came down with is now come from Holland and is in towne here . . . . I believe 'twill not be possable to come at any wrightings of his because (but by what means I know not) I hear he's apprised of his being designed to have been taken up with Driscall " . . . . .

1715, Sept. 21st.   Colonel the Hon. Hatton Compton, Lieutenant of the Tower, to Lord Townshend.   Dated in the Tower.

"My Lord—This morning at six a'Clock I received an order from the Privy Councill, and since that I have the honour of another letter from your Lord$\overline{pp}$. both directing without loss of time my regulating the Militia of the Tower Hamletts, to be in readiness to march when-ever His Majesty's service shall require ; this is to acquaint your Lord$\overline{pp}$ that there is no Horse belonging to the Tower Hamlets but two very strong Regiments of Foot ; and [they] are ready to march when His Majesty pleases.   I am *etc.*

[P.S.] This morning early I gave orders for the searching for, and seizing all Papists, Jacobites, and Non-Jurors, according to orders."

Same date.   Lord Dupplin to the same.   Dated in Leicester Fields "a quarter after seven in the morning " and unaddressed.

"My Lord—Mr Nightingale is here with your Lordship's Warrant to bring me to your Lordship.   I'm ready to wait upon your Lordship whenever you please.   I only beg the favour of your Lordship that the messenger may have orders to stay here with me, till your Lordship is ready to examine me, My wife is just now in labour, which makes me give you this trouble.   I am," *etc.*

1715, Sept. 23rd.   Council Minutes, in the handwriting of Lord Townshend, dated at Whitehall :—

[That] an extract of Lord Hay's letter relating to the ships who are cruising on the coast of Scotland be sent to the Admiralty for their opinion and to desire in case they approve of what is therein propose[d] they wou'd send directions accordingly.

to thank the Mayor of Glascow.

that the Lord Hay be removed out of his house by the messenger into custody.

A Councill [must be held] for [drawing up] a Proclamation for the apprehending Sir William Wyndham.

1715, Sept. 30th.   Lord Carteret to Spencer Compton.   Dated at Stowe and unaddressed.

"Sir—I still persist in my opinion that there will be no troubles in the West ; notwithstanding there are many people in very ill humour, the design being so happily discover'd, that disaffected persons are so dampt, that they rather strive to smother their own contrivance than to bring it to bear.   If any insurrection shou'd be in this country, we are in a bad posture of defence.   I sent a messenger last Wednesday to Mr. Boscowen,

who lives fifty miles westward from me, that if there shou'd be any
occasion, we may take the best means we can. The county about me·
has been alarm'd by a flying report that the Tinners are in arms upon the
account of Sir Richard Vivyian's being in custody, but nothing of it
was true when it was said, and I have not heard anything these two days ;
however severall gentlemen have been here begging my protection, and
assuring me that they will follow me for the King's service, if any rebellion
shou'd break out here. I heartily wish that all things here may be quiet ;
the observation I make is, that the discontented people are rather cold to
the present government, than dispos'd to venture any thing against it. I
know you will do me the justice to thinke that I will do all I can for the
best ; and I will have the vanity to say, that not one of the Kings subjects
is ready to hazard more in his service, than I, to the utmost of my mean
abilities, will be. I thank you for your second letter and am sorry to find
so near [a] kindsman as Sir William Wyndham is to me so deeply
engaged. If any thing happens within my knowledge—you shall have
a speedy account of it. I am, yours,

CARTERET."

MARQUESS
TOWNSHEND
MSS.

1715, Oct. 31st. Monsr H. de Caris to Lord Townshend. In French.
Dated at Ostend and unaddressed.
  The writer explains the precautions he is taking to prevent the em-
barkation of the Pretender from Ostend or its environs.

  1715, Oct. 7th. "Nouvelles de Paris." In French. Unsigned.
  . . . . . "The adherents of the Pretender whose numbers are much
increased for some months past no longer conceal that they have a revolt
all ready to break out in England in favour of that of Scotlnnd, but
notwithstanding their entreaties the Pretender postpones his departure
from time to time, and one sees sufficiently clearly that he thinks he
would expose himself too much as yet if he were to cross over to
England " . . . . . .

  [1715 ?], Oct. 10th. Council Minutes in the handwriting of Lord
Townshend. Endorsed "Oct. 10th. Minutes : "—
  To seize Row a Dyer at the Elephant and Castle in Drury Lane and
search his house for one Painter and one Rowe his brother.
  That the western waggons be searched at the several inns for arms.
  To refer the informations sent by Mr Boscowen to the Attorney
[General] in order to have indictments prepared against as many as
there are two witnesses against for H[igh] Treason, in order to have the
said indictments proved at the first opportunity.
  That there be an advertisement in the Gaz[ette] promising a reward of
100^{li} to any one that shall discover so as to bring to justice any of the
persons mentioned in the said informations.

  1715, Oct. 11th. "Nouvelles de Paris." In French. Unsigned.
  . . . . . "The revolt of the Scotch makes much noise here, and the
adherents of the Pretender say out loud that there is a considerable one
[preparing] in England which must break out shortly, and as the Duke
of Ormond has disappeared for the last two days it is believed he has
left to put himself at the head of that party, and it is asserted that
many persons of consideration are mixed up with it.
  . . . . . There is positive news that the Pretender was still at Bar le
Duc, and that he always refused to leave before seeing more daylight in
his hopes " . . . . . .

  1715, Oct. 17th to Oct. 27th. Copies of four letters from the Earl of
Mar, dated at Perth and Aucherarder, and addressed to Lord Kenmure
and to Mr. Thomas Forster (M.P. for Northumberland) who is addressed

MARQUESS
TOWNSHEND
MSS.

as ' Mr Forrester.' Each of these letters is endorsed " Received from Major Browne—Jo. Micklethwaite."

1715, Oct. 18th. Michael Pallister to the Honorable General Wills at Preston. Endorsed: "Received 26th Novb^r 1715—from Major Browne—Jo: Micklethwait."

" Sir,—I have sent you a list of those gentlemen that joined the rebels about Lancaster and Preston as i have the account from a neighbor of this place." . . . . .

The list, which is headed " Lancaster Papists," is as follows :—

My Lord Mollineux of Bardsey, Mr Walton of Windermore, Mr Hodgson of Leighton, Mr Carns of Halton, Mr Dalton of Thurnham, Mr Butler of Rawcliffe, Mr Leyborn of Naleby, Mr Cliftons of Lytham, Mr Westbys of Bourne, Mr Tyldesleys of Lodge, Mr Whittingham of Whittingham, Mr Threlfall of Ashes, Mr Shuttleworth of Brookside, Mr Shuttleworth of Turnover, Mr Plesington of Dimples, Mr Hesketts of Goosnargh, Mr Townley of Townley, Mr Brockholes of Claughton, H^r Winckley of Banister hall, Mr Walmsley of Showley, Sr Francis Anderton of Lostock.

1715, Oct. 23rd. Copy of a letter from Francis Campbell and A. Campbell "to Glengary and the Capt of Clanronald."

" Wee send the bearer to you that you may lett us knowe what further damage has come to your knowledg, wee will as soon as wee can make a strict and impartial enquiery into it, and as you desire in your letter will send after you, with a line to one of you two with ane account of it and wee are," etc.

No date. Copy of a memorandum, in the same handwriting as the last. Signed by Alex^r Macdonald and headed "Declaration of Glengary."

It states that in Oct. 1715 at Inveray the Earl of Yla appointed Clanronald and Glengary to treat with Sir Duncan Campbell of Lochnell and Lt Coll Campbell of Finah on the part of General Gordon, and it was agreed that Gordon and his people should abandon Argyllshire and compensate the poor people for their losses, and on the other hand that the Hanoverian troops should not molest the clans. It was after this treaty that the Earl of Broadalbin [Breadalbane] and his men were allowed to make their escape out of Argyllshire. Most of the tenants of the Duke of Argyll on his lands of Morvene were in arms at Sheriffmuir with Lochiel, and though Lochiel had with him all of the Camerons from the Marquis of Huntley's property in Lochaber it was by the positive orders of the Marquis. The money that was promised as a pension to the Clans by the late Queen Anne " of which latter they did never gett any " was for the readily assisting her Majesty against all her enemies at home or abroad.

The last two papers are endorsed " Inf[ormatio]ns relating to the D[uke] of A[rgyll]."

1715, Oct. 24th. "Instructions given by the Earl of Mar to a certain person to be communicated to the King's friends be south Forth."

An endorsement in nearly the same words gives the name of the person to whom these instructions were sent as Mrs Miller, and it bears a further endorsement: " Received 26th 9ber 1715—from Major Browne, —Jo: Micklethwait."

1715, Oct. 28th. A Memorandum, in French, endorsed " Avis de Mr de Pettecu[m] 28 Oct. 1715."

It is headed [in French] " Secret advice as to the designs of the Pretender on the Kingdoms of Great Britain which I have had the 28th of October 1715."

MARQUESS
TOWNSHEND
MSS.

The Pretender is immediately about to start for Scotland, Lord Bolinbroke will remain in France to hasten the execution of the Secret Treaty concluded between the [ex]Queen of England in the name of the Pretender with the Regent of France, by virtue of which France will assist with money and arms. A separate article in the treaty stipulates for the marriage of the Pretender with the second daughter of the Duke of Orleans.

The Duke of Ormond as soon as he lands in Scotland will advance to the frontiers of England to encourage a general rising to compel his Majesty to divide his forces and to prevent his sending more troops into Scotland, of which country Lord Mar will try to render himself the master.

The Pretender on his arrival in Scotland will summon a Parliament to regulate the succession to the Crown and to denounce as traitors the adherents of his Majesty, and will publish a new Manifesto inviting the nation to submit itself, in which he will promise to make no changes in Religion and to have Mass only said for him in his chamber. The Catholics in England furnish every month a sum of money for this enterprise and the Court of Rome has promised fifty thousand crowns a month.

The Duke of Berwick who has received letters from the Pretender has been to see the ex-Queen. He has given orders to prepare his equipage which is to leave in a vessel from Brest. He is about to ask the Regent for permission to serve his King which will probably be refused but nevertheless he will follow the Pretender.

The Pretender has not chosen to hazard himself rashly on the assurances that have reached him from England and Scotland, and he will not be decided to start without being sure of external assistance. He will embark in Normandy on board of a vessel he has purchased.

At the instigation of the Court of France he has sent a confidential agent to Madrid to beg his Catholic Majesty to fulfil his promises and assist him to mount the throne of his ancestors.

By the same advice he has applied to the King of Sicily, to whom it is represented that he is interested through relationship (being the next heir to Great Britain should the Pretender die childless) and besides that he ought to fear a close union between the Emperor and the King of Great Britain.

Those who have pressed the Pretender to undertake this enterprise assure him that all Scotland will declare for him immediately he lands, and that the discontent in England is so general that there will be a rising in every county. That the army itself is divided and that the King cannot trust it. That both officers and men are equally disgusted with the Dutch troops being brought over. A certain Ecclesiastic has written to one of his friends in France that the Pretender has no need of troops to defeat the English Army. His presence alone will suffice, and a single pathetic address would make them throw down their arms.

France to deprive the King of foreign assistance will foment the war in the North and encourage, by subsidies, certain princes of the Empire to aid the King of Sweden.

Up to the present time those who are opposed to the Ministry in England have not declared themselves for the Pretender. The Duke of Ormond and Lord Bolingbroke hold out hopes that they will do so so soon as the Pretender shall land and shall have regulated and confirmed the liberties of the Church of England and of the Nation.

1715, Nov. 1st. From ——— to ———. Unsigned and unaddressed. Endorsed " Received 26th Novb : 1715—from Major Browne,—Jo. Micklethwait."

The writer gives an account of the mutiny of some Highlanders at Langholme. for want of pay, when ordered to march to England.

Same date. John Campbell to Lord Townshend. Dated at Edinburgh. Unaddressed. . . . . . . " Wee are all soe sensible of the great service the Duke of Argyll did to this town, in preventing the danger it was in, of falling into the hands of the enemie, and how absolutelie necessary it is for the King's service to preserve it, that wee have been at the expence of making such works at all the avenues of it, as may render it defencible ; without giveing his Grace the trouble of a detachment from the little army he has to employ against the designs of the enemy at Perth, which your Lordship will judge is of as great importance as Stirling to his Majestie's service.

I am sorry to fynd both from the printed papers and private letters that soe bad acc^{ts} of our affairs are sent to London. . . . . Since I began to write this letter I have advice that the three regim^{ts} of Claytone, Marsone and Egertone, are landed from Ireland, Egerton's with 2 companies of Clayton's wer last night at Glasgow, the rest are on ther march. I shall not pretend to give your lordship any account of the rebels at Perth since by this express the Duke of Argyll writes to your lordship or Mr Stanhope. And as for those in the south wee have noe certain accounts of them since they arrived at Howick wher they were in great confusione onlie that some of the Highlanders were come back to Selkirk which I beleive may be deserters from them, I am not affraid that the Highlanders will ever attempt goeing to England unless joyned by a considerable more number which I hope now is prevented since these three Regim^{ts} are landed. I am, etc.

[P.S.]   The Inclosed copie of a letter from Jedburgh will show your lordship the disorder these Rebels are in."

1715, Nov. 2nd.   General Cadogan (afterwards Lord Cadogan) to ——.   Dated at Brussels and unaddressed.

" This minute Monsr Plessen is arrived here from Nancy, and has brought the particulars contained in the enclosed relation of the Pretender having left Commercy early on Wednesday last, in order to go through France into England . . . . the Barrier Treaty will I hope be signed on Thursday next.   I have. etc.,
                                 WILLIAM CADOGAN."

1715, Nov. 5th.   Two Informations sworn before Tobias Paine, Mayor of Oxford, and William Wright, J.P., by Daniel Houghton and Mathew Wisdom ; relative to the finding of a large number of swordblades, etc., in the house of one George Vincent, a cutler.

1715, Nov. 6th.   Sir Jonathan Trelawney, Bishop of Winchester, " To the Lord Bishop of Norwich Clerk of the Closet to the King at his bous in Stretton Street neare Devonshire hous Westminster."
Endorsed.   " B^p Winchester upon signing the Declarat^n."

" MY VERY GOOD LORD,

I RECEIV'D the expresse fryday at night, and having sign'd it with both my long names at length to shew I did it heartily. I forwarded it to our brother of Oxon, tis admirably well drawn, and I wish it had been sooner thought on ; and why is it not forthwith printed ? it will doe more to quashing the rebellion than an army, at least a Scotch one can, or will.

I am with greate respect and affection
              Your most faithful servant
                     and loving brother
                         JONATHAN WINCHESTER."

Same date. An anonymous letter of advice from Oxford. Unaddressed.

" My Most Honored Lord,—The Soldiers keep us here in good order at night. We have scarce had any tumults except on Monday night some scholars in Catstreet met a file of soldiers, and after they had pass'd them they cry'd out an Ormond and a Bolingbroke and the Pretender. Upon which two musquetts were fir'd after them, but without doing hurt. This hap'ning the first night has struck such a terror, that I believe will contribute much to our future peace. Many of the scholars had form'd a design to corrupt the soldiers by giving them money, and entertaining them in their butteries and kitchins, but the officers have had timely notice of this ; and on Fryday two soldiers run the gantlope for drinking Ormond and Bolingbroke's healths, and confusion to their officers. This fact hap'ned at Wadham Coll[ege], and the soldiers were seduc'd to it by four scholars, who were conven'd before the Vice-Ch[ancello]r, but the proofs being not full enough, the Vice-Ch[ancello]r thought fit to dismiss them without punishment.

On Fryday in the evening the officers search'd for arms, and at Vincent the cutler's, they seiz'd 120 large cutting swords. About 10 at night the Coll[onel] sent for me and acquainted me with the success he had at Vincent's, but Ethersey and the rest had convey'd away their arms, having had suspicion of a search. Upon perusal of Vincent's books which were seiz'd I found a Memorand[um] which I believe will be of use to the Government.

The Memorand[um] was this

Mr Vicery	-	6^d	} A mercer in town.
Mr Vicery	-	3	
Mr Jones	-	6	Of All Souls I believe.
Mr Thatcher	-	6	A Baker.
Mr Sherwin	-	6	A Milliner.
Mr Greenway	-	2	A Quarter-M[aste]r in the Militia under Lord Abington.

Now all these persons are violent Jacobites ; and that Jones of All-Souls is meant by *Jones* I have reason to think, because he was the person hinted at in my first letter, who was seen at Vincent's the day Coll[onel] Pepper search'd for Owen, and it is more than probable the letter *d* at the head of the numbers signifies dozens, and what these dozens should be besides swords which are lodg'd with these persons I can't imagine. It appears likewise by the books some swords have been delivered to Bayly the Cheshire Carrier. I had very little time to look into the books, or else I believe further discoveries might have been made. I design to get them privately into my chamber, with one of the officers, and then your Lorddship will hear further from me.

Yesterday we kept here with due solemnity (illuminations excepted). Bells were rung, and bonfires made in most parishes without disturbance. I hope to hear the same good order was preserv'd in London and Westminster, tho' I was inform'd, that the Tory mob had given a challenge to the Whigs and were resolv'd to engage them last night.

We have lately had two or three robberies committed in the London road near the town. The persons are known to the Buckingham-shire men, but are not yet taken.

Lord H. is very well and gives his service.

Mr Talbot I hear is in town, but I have not yet seen him.

I am with all duty, my Lord,—

Your Lordship's most obedient and H : Servt."

1715, Nov. 9th. A list of signatures dated at Preston, and endorsed, " Received 26th Novbr 1715—from Major Browne— J : Micklethwait."

This list is headed " All Gentlemen who are come to this place to serve his Majesty are desir'd to set their names to this paper, and such as have been in the army to mention the post in which they served."

The signatures are : Robert Cotton, John Trafford, Richard Towneley, Richard Gascoigne, Robert Scarisbrick, Jordan Langdale " served two years under Coll. Sheldon and three years under Coll. Dorington," Hugh Anderton, Charles Chorley, William Nelson " serv'd under Captin Eccleston as Quarter Master of Horse," Richard Chorley " Ensign in Coll. Gage's Regiment," Alexander Osbaldiston, John Cotton, Francis Anderton, Roger Diccinson " Lieutnt under Coll : Gage and town Major of Chester," Francis Legh " Capt : of a Man of War," Lionel Walden, John Leyburne " Lieutenant," Cuthbert Hesketh, Richard Chattesworth of Brockside " sub-brigadier in the Guards under the Duke of Berwick," Thomas Carus, Albert Hodshon, Edward Howard of Norfolk, Ralph Standish, Thomas Stanley, and Ralph Grappe.

[No date.] The following Jacobite Proclamation is endorsed :— " Received 26th 9ber 1715—from Major Browne—Jo : Micklethwait."

BY THE KING. A PROCLAMATION.—JAMES REX.

WHEREAS by the Laws and Constitution of these Realms our native born Prince James the Third immediately upon his fathers demise had the sole unquestionable right to these his paternall hereditary dominions and our Gratious Soveraign now coming to assert his own right and relieve his Kingdoms from the tyranicall oppression arbitary power and foreign yoke under which they groan THEREFORE WE NOBLEMEN Gentlemen and others his Majesty's faithfull subjects being now met together in obedience to his royall commands and being fully resolv'd to spend our lives and fortunes in his Majestie's service for the promoting his happy restoration the reestablishment of the Constitution in Church and State and the deliverance of our native county Do hereby unanimously and in concert with others his dutifull subjects in many different parts of these Realms with heart and voice proclaim notifie and declare to all men that the most august and high born Prince James the third by the grace of God King of England &c : Defender of the Faith is the only rightfull and lawfull Soveraign of the Realms to whome alone we acknowledge our allegience and subjection to be due inviting hereby all his Majestie's faithfull and loyall subjects of both nations to join with us in his service and promising to stand by them in the prosecuting of these glorious ends.

GOD SAVE THE KING.

1715, Nov. 10th. E. Francke " To the Rt Honble the Earl of Darwentwater." Endorsed :—" Received 26th Novb. 1715—from Major Browne—Jo. Micklethwait."

The writer, who is in confinement on suspicion of concealing arms, begs his Lordship to use his interest for his enlargement, and explains that the arms in question were delivered to Sir Henry Houghton, who was Colonel of the Militia of the Hundred from which he is writing.

1715, Nov. 11th. The Parole signed by Thomas Wybergh, a prisoner in the hands of the Jacobite General Forster at Preston in Lancashire, under which he undertakes to get himself exchanged within twenty days for Allen Ascough, Esqre, a prisoner in the hands of the Governor of Carlisle, or else to return to the said General Forster's army and continue his prisoner during his pleasure.

Endorsed as the last.

1715, Nov. 15th. Lord Carlisle to Lord Townshend. Unaddressed. Dated at Preston.

" MY LORD,
THE Expresse sent yesterday morning by Mr Wills [General Willes] would acquaint your Lordship that the rebells have surrender'd at discretion. . . . . I being particularly well acquainted with my Lord Darwentwater and my Lord Witherington (and they being at this time under great dejection of mind) I thought this might be a proper time to trye if they were disposed to make a confession. I therefore lay'd before them in the best manner I could the little reason they had to expect the King's mercy unless they did some thing very material of this kind to deserve it. I asked them several questions, and particularly I told them they must know what part Sir William Blackett, my Lord Downe and some Bishopbrig Gentlemen had in this undertaking. . . . . I am really of opinion that they do not know much, I believe they had promised Mr Forster, whenever he called upon them they would rise and that they were so simple as to do it, and to believe him when he told them, that all England would do the same.

I have adviced Mr Wills to call upon Mr Forster to refund all the publick money he obliged the King's officers to pay in the places through which he marched. I have likewise desired him to take particular care, that no innocent person be carryd away when the prisoners are removed, for I am afraid several of the country people were in the disorder and confusion hurried into the church, with the rebells, that being the place where they are at present secured.

I shall return home tomorrow with great ease of mind hopeing weè may live quietly now if good care be taken of my Lord Marr.

[P.S.] Allmost all the Roman Catholicks of Northumberland, and of this county are now in your power."

1715, Nov. 22nd. James Craggs to the same. Dated at Preston and unaddressed.

" My Lord, I had stopd Major Brown whom Mr Wills [General Willes] was dispatching to London till I receiv'd the letter your Lordship was pleased to write me last Saturday. It came to my hands this minute, and thô I could wish my powers had been somewhat fuller, I don't despair of making such a use of it as may answer your Lordship's expectations, for by what I understand of Mr Forster's behaviour he seems to think himself that this will be the only means to preserve his life and family, thô in his professions he has said he was ready to doe any thing becoming a man of honour so that I cannot judge how he will understand that to be effected by my propositions till I come to talk with him. He is certainly the man that can speak to some purpose if he pleases. I may also as I see occasion try my Lords Derriugwater and Widdington. I hear the first seems most desirous to doe somewhat to save his life, the latter's conduct has been sensible and in his priuciple more steddy, saying that he had no other encouragem^t to take arms, but that he thought he should make a bad figure with his religion and his opinion to sit still in this cause when his neighbours and so many others had. That he had first propos'd to surrender and by that means sav'd many of his subjects lives, which if he could obtain he would deserve it by his future conduct. These are the only men one can hope any good from. And your Lordship will find Mr Wills had sent them two days agoe to Wigan, where they are followed this morning by the rest of the prisoners in their way to London. However I thought it proper to come on to this place, I shall goe there again tomorrow morning and stay as long as I judge it to any purpose, from whence I will send your Lordship punctuall accounts of what passes, thô I hope after a day or two's residence to bring you my accounts myself.

The powers for holding Court Martials being only directed to Genll Carpenter, Mr Wills does not think himself authorised to execute the half pay officers and other deserters. He sends up .to Majr Brown the lists of the prisoners and other intercepted letters of DerringWater Widdrington and Forster.

I find this expedition was as fortunate for the conjuncture as any other circumstance because the rebells in two or three days would certainly have been joyned by as many thousands well armed and mounted, but now one would wonder where all these disaffected people are gone, for you meet thrô all these countrys with none that are not ready to live and dye by King George and the Government.

1715, Nov. 23rd. The same to the same, from Preston.

" My Lord, This is only to rectify a mistake in my letter of yesterday, Major Brown being detained by Genll Wills till this morning, that went by the post, and he will set out with the lists of prisoners and their papers this morning, I am also going to Wigan three hours hence, from whence I will trouble your Lordship but with one letter, and follow it very close my self ; My Lord Orkney has sent an express here to Mr Wills with a letter to intercede for Lord Ch. Murray, his nephew a son of Lord Bazil Hamilton, and an officer in his own Regim{t} one Dalzell. He says he has spoke to the King and the Duke of Marlbro who bid him send. Wills has lost the letter or I would send it your Lordship.

This morning Collo Killigrew is march'd into quarters at Lancaster with Dormer's regim{t} and part of the prisoners to be put into the Goal. The Brigadier is in a fair way of recovery. I am," etc.

Same date. General George Carpenter to——. Dated at Nottingham and unaddressed.

" Sir,—Having writt to you of my coming to this place, I was in hopes to find your commands here. I had a letter from Mr Pulteney telling me onely, that his Majesty judg'd itt necessary for his service I should continue here till a more perfect account of affaires from Scotland ; so tis likely I may be sent there, having offered my self lately ; as I did before to follow the rebells with fresh troops in case they should have gott by me northward.

Sir, after having chac't the rebells a month, with unusuall difficultys and fatigue, saving Newcastle by dilligence, and att last driving them into the nett, where I was present and commanding att taking them ; tis a great mortification that Mr Will's who march't but two days and made a rash attack, highly blameable, by loosing so many men to no purpose, (of which you will hear more) except to serve his ambition by ending itt before I came up should have friends to magnify what he did so as to prevail on his Majesty to make him Lieut. Genl for his good services ; and no notice taken of me nott so much as a compliment. This is very unequall treatment, and a great discouragement to me, having serv'd well, and with success ; for the cheif prisoners assur'd me and others that as soon as they saw my detachment from the steeple the Lord Widdrington who was in the churchyard said very loud before their men that they were all undone, and upon that they consulted to ask termes, which they did in 4 houres after my arrivall, thô nott yeilded till next morning. Twas I that insisted that Lord Darwentwater and one of the Makintoches should come out hostages, and was with them arguing their having no termes ; thô I have good reason to believe Wills assumes to have done all himself. One very great fault I committed, viz. just as wae were mounting to go into the towne Mr Wills was taking on him great command, att which I us'd him very ffreely, and was going to putt him in arrest, butt my Lord Carlisle who was present, and Lord Lumley begg'd me nott to do itt, and indeed att that instant itt might have proved fatall to his Majesty's Service, for the rebells had yet possession of their armes and the towne ; and Wills was likely enough to have call'd the troops that came with him to support him. So I did not do itt ; and when in the towne I made another false step very unthinkingly. For seeing there would nott be cover for half the forces, out of pitty and care of those barass't troops that came with me, I sent them away to good quarters att Wigan, and so on to these they are now in, which I after imagin'd took the command from me, when none of my troops were there; so could not putt him in arrest, thô he deserved itt. I find the prints give him all the power and applause, I suppose by his own or some friends direction, and I fear his Majesty may be under that mistake also, which makes me desirous to come to London, otherwise no busyness or ease should hinder my pressing to go on service, thô a winter's campagne in Scotland, which however I am willing to do, provided I have justice done me in this affair, for itt must be sett right. I desire your friendship in reading over this letter again with attention, and then I know your justice is so great, that I shall nott suffer in my reputation or any other respect by my absence. I intreat the favour of a line in answere, and am, etc.

[P.S.] I have writt to the Duke of Marlborough and referr'd his Grace to this letter which please to shew him."

1715, Nov. 24th. James Craggs to Lord Townshend. Unaddressed. Dated at Wigan.

"My Lord—I arrived here last night and had Mr Forster to sup with me, I told him in the best manner I could the reason why I desired his company, and the behaviour by which he might deserve the King's mercy. He answer'd me that if he were to declare all he knew it would come far short of what he believ'd might be expected from him and then he doubted he should not be thought to deserve his pardon when he had no more to say. All the information I could get from him amounted to this, that he had promis'd the Duke of Ormond to rise whenever he should land, but was precipitated into it sooner by the order to seize him, that he came out of town when the Duke made his escape. He does not own any concert with other people, but says in general he look'd on the whole body of the Torys to be in it. That he has indeed been in companys where their King's health has been drunk but unless he had his pardon does not see to what purpose he should be more particular, for he imagines he should be suppos'd to know a great deal more. So we have parted on these terms, that if when he comes to London he thinks I may be of any service to him, which I can only be by his putting it in my power, I shall be very ready to wait on him and intercede for him. So we have parted with this only and no promise of my side, and I would observe to your Lordship that the same thing as to my part has concluded my conferences with every one to whome I have spoke. The next was my Lord Derringwater; he swears he was in no secret himself but will be very ready to relate any former passages he can recollect and promises on the road to make it his

business to get what information he can from the other prisoners and
acquaint me with it at London. My Lord Widdrington says the same
thing as to his own ignorance of what measures were intended and
promises but with more reserve than the former that if he can persuade
any of them to tell any thing material they know to save their lives he
will use his utmost endeavour, but thinks he cannot betray anything
they should say without their consent. I have also discours'd one Gascoigne and a gamester who had fled with the Mac Donalds and others
from the Bath, and fell into this gang by chance. He tells me he was
in no deep secret, but understood there Sir W. Wyndh[am] Sir W.
Carew and Sir Copplest[one] Banfield were to rise, that he had been
told my Lord Gore was in it, but it was in a genu way of talking
amongst the Jacobites and he could not be more particular, only they
were drunk with an opinion their game was secure. The last man I
entertain'd is one Tunstall a R[oman] Catholick who has been very
active, but he seems also as determin'd, and rejects with great contempt the character of an informer. In all these conversations I had
the assistance of Coll° Neist who had had the chiefs at his quarters at
Preston, and in case they will or can make any new discovery at London
would be very usefull, for he's a very sensible man and has been very
civill to them. I am afraid this will not appear to your Lordship a very
great piece of service, but as I could doe no more I intend after having
tryed this day if I can get any thing else amongst 'em, to set out to
morrow for London where I propose to be on Monday morning next to
give your Lordship a more distinct acco^t of this treaty between the rebels
and me and assure you no body is more what I am," etc.

1715, Dec. 13th. Lord Nairne to the same. Dated in the Tower
of London and unaddressed.

" My Lord—If your Lordship will be pleased to be so good as to forgive
what I have either omited or neglected in answering to your Lordships
queries by reason of a deafness I have had the misfortune to labour under
these severall years, it will be ane obligation I shall never forget and I hop
for forgiveness from the rest of your august assembly for any disorder or
confusion I have been in when I had the honour to apear befor them.
I'm sure it was my duty as well as inclination to behave my self with
all due respect to your high carectars; if I durst presume to beg pardon
for my life and that only, at the King's hands I shall throw my self at
his feet for mercy and I'm sure I will not want Inglish as well as Scots
friends to answer for me. I shall ever prove as gratefull ane object
of it as any. I with all humilytie press this no less for my poor wife's
sake and 12 children then my own, if this can bo graciously obtain'd,
may the never failing mercies of Almighty God reward His Majesty,
offspring, and councilors shall be ever the earnest wishes of him whô is
with all profound respect My Lord " etc.

[No date.] Richard Lluellin to the same. Addressed " To the
Right.-Honourable The Ld Viscount Townsend one of His Majesty's
Principall Secretary[s] of State."

" My Lord, In obedience to your commands I came to London last
Saturday with Mr Nightingall.

And thô I am now a prison^r I woud prefer an honourable way of
making my application the most agreably to your Lordship, before the
loss of business in my profession, or the loss of my liberty.

For two reasons, I dare not press for a speedy examination, thô
never guilty of any crime against his present Majesty, or Ministry.

The First is : least it may be suggested that I did it, to prevent some
future, some more materiall evidence.

The second because your Lordship's hours are taken up with persons of greater figure and more weighty affairs.

These being my real thoughts: if your Lordship wou'd be so generously kind to allow the following persons (all unexceptionable in your interest) free access to me twou'd make my confinement more easy, and lay the greatest

obligation upon, My Lord, your " etc.

The names appended to this letter are as follows :—

Mr Justice Saintloe
Mr Row Secretary to the Councill of the Prince
Mr Parsons of Charter-house-Yard
Mr Russen and ⎫ Aldermen of High Wicomb.
Mr Shrimpton ⎭

[No date.] Copy of a petition to the King in favour of Lord Lovat. Endorsed " Petⁿ and Security for the Ld Lovat," and minuted at foot, in Lord Townshend's handwriting, " Sign'd by some members of Parliament and near 80 Gentlemen zealous for his Majesty King George."

It concludes: " we are so sensible not only of his power, but of his sincere intentions to joyn with us in the supporting inviolably the authority of your Majestie's Government in the North of Scotland that if we can be so happy as to obtain the royal favour for him we humbly make offer to become bound for his loyal faithful and dutiful behaviour to your Majesty in whatever sum your Majesty shall be graciously pleased to appoint."

1715–1716. Copies of Despatches to the Duke of Argyll, whilst he was commanding the troops in Scotland employed in the suppression of Mar's Rebellion.

1715, Sept. 1st, Whitehall. Lord Townshend encloses a Warrant for the disposal of the arms and ammunition in the Castle of Edinburgh and informs his Grace that the Treasury will lodge at Edinburgh a credit of £10,000 for His Majesty's service to be employed as he shall appoint.

1715, Sept. 13th, Whitehall. Secretary Stanhope writes about the pay of a recent addition to the garrison to Edinburgh Castle, and adds " I am also to signify to your Grace His Majesty's pleasure that you give orders for seizing the Laird of Borlum younger and for securing him in the safest way till His Majesty's further pleasure shall be known. The charge of the additional men in the Castle, is to be supplied out of that money which is lodged at Edinburgh, to be disposed of by your Grace."

1715, Sept. 15th, Whitehall. From Lord Townshend.

" I had yesterday morning the honour of your Grace's letter from Burrowbridge, of the 12th by the flying Packet, which brought us an account of the attempt made to surprise the Castle of Edinburgh. I heartily congratulate your Grace on the failing of this design, which we hope will be no small discouragement to the enemies, who probably were to form their measures by the success of the enterprise. I have laid your Grace's letter before the King, and His Majesty is very much dissatisfied with the slow motions of the Regiments of Carpenter and Ker which we were in hopes might have been in Scotland as soon as your Grace. The Secretary at War has received directions to hasten their march with all possible expedition.

My Lord, after writing what is above, a flying Packet brings letters from Edinburgh of the 12th giving an account of the marching from

several places of the Highlands, of the enemy, to the places of general
rendezvous near to Perth, with further particulars of the disappointment and discouragement they meet with from the bad success of their
attempt against the Castle of Edinburgh. We hope they will be soon
convinc'd they are to have no support nor assistance from abroad, for
by an Express arrived yesternight from the Earl of Stair. we understand that an embargo is laid on the ships at Havre de Grace, and
indeed on all ships in any ports of France, that have on board any
counterband goods. That the Duke of Orleans has refused to see the
Duke of Ormond and Lord Bolingbroke, and that the Marquis de
Torcy is laid aside. All which we reckon the foundation of such a
good understanding between this Court and that of France, as to leave
us under no apprehensions of our ennemies receiving any support from
thence. I am &c.
P.S. [Signed by James Stanhope.] My Lord, Since writing what is
before, the King having received some information touching the Lieu^t.
Governour of the Castle of Edinburgh, hath thought it proper to remove
him, and to grant a Commission of Lieutenant Governour to Brigadier
Preston who carries this Dispatch."

1715, Sept. 24th, Whitehall. Lord Townshend excuses himself for
not having written himself in reply to the Duke's last letter.—" I am now
to acquaint your Grace that whatever you have writ hath been faithfully
and punctually communicated to His Majesty .   .   .   and it is with
very great pleasure I obey His Majesty orders, in assuring your Grace
that he is entirely satisfied with your Grace's conduct, and with every
step you have made. .   .   .   .   The situation of our affairs here
is such as makes it impracticable to spare any more regular troops
from hence. .   .   .   .   Your Grace may be sure that the Government is not idle, and we hope to come to the bottom of the matter, and
to learn who are embarq'd in it, as your Grace may judge by the orders
that have been already given, for the seizing of several persons. Sir
Wm Wyndham has indeed made his escape after he was once taken,
but has left some papers behind him which we judge of consequence "

. . . . .

1715, Sept. 26th, Whitehall. From Secretary Stanhope.
.   .   .   .   .   " The very day that we received your Grace's letter of
the 15th it was laid before the King, who immediately dispatched Maj^r
General Evans to you, and orders to Ireland for his Regiment to join
your Grace with all possible dispatch. .   .   .   .   Every advice
we have here, both from home, and abroad, and particularly the two last
letters from my Lord Stair, make it evident that a general insurrection
is intended to be begun at the same time in several counties of England.
Bristol is to be their place of arms. They reckon themselves sure of all
the West, of Wales, of Staffordshire, Worcestershire, Derbyshire,
Lancashire. Whether the seizing some of their chiefs will disconcert
their measures, a little time will show. The same advices, and particularly those from my Lord Stair, do represent their hopes of success
to be grounded upon the prospect they have that a great number of
forces would be sent to Scotland; the confessions of some who are
taken up, confirm the same thing. Our last letters from Edinburgh
assure us, that the Jacobites there, give out that there is to be a rising
in England, and particularly that a considerable body of horse of the
English rebells is to join the Earl of Mar; I may further tell your
Grace that by papers under the hand of one of the chief conspirators,
found about Sir Wm Windham, not only the same is confirmed, but
further, that it was immediately expected to break forth. After all this

My Lord I submit it to your Grace whether the King's Ministers will not be justify'd before God and ·man, if they advise the King, to keep this nation in some posture of defence; and give me leave, My Lord, to offer you truly my poor opinion, that nothing will so much dishearten the rebells in Scotland, as to find themselves disappointed of the hopes which had been given them from hence.

. . . . . If your Grace will be pleased to suggest to me any particular in which you would require orders, I shall not fail to receive his Majesty's commands in it. I am My Lord &c.,

JAMES STANHOPE.

[P.S.] Beating orders are issued for filling up Grant's Regiment to the same complement with the others."

1715, Sept. 29th, Whitehall. From Secretary Stanhope.

"Your Grace's letter to my Lord Townshend of the 24th instant, hath been laid before His Majesty who hath given orders that some battalions do immediately pass from Ireland to the River Clyde. . . . . As to what your Grace mentions concerning positive orders, how far your Grace is to risque the King's troops, His Majesty relyes entirely upon your conduct, and your doing every thing that shall be most for his service, and does not think it practicable at this distance, to give positive directions how to act against an enemy whose circumstances may alter every day. · And your Grace may, as I told you in my last, be very secure of his Majesty's approving your best endeavours for his service.

The King approves of altering the Lieutenant of Lord Wm Hay, as is proposed by your Grace. Whether a Commission from hence, will be requisite, your Grace will please to inform me. . . . .

Letters from France, come by an Express this day, confirm every thing I told you in my last, but its to be hoped, the seizing of their freinds here, will at least occasion some delay in their attempts."

1715, Oct. 4th, Whitehall. From Lord Townshend.

. . . . "His Majesty does entirely approve of your conduct . . . all is left to your Grace's own management. . . . Very probably your Grace judges right that little dependence is to be made upon the informations and advices you receive from the Duke of Atholl considering how he is beseiged. . . . .

Your Grace knows with what unwearied application our enemies have endeavoured to poyson the people and to alienate their effections from his Majesty and his Government, and therefore if upon the first advices given of that spirit of rebellion which has since appeared in your parts and which I may freely say, has been more or less, every year since the Revolution, His Majesty had proposed the augmenting of his forces, I leave it to your Grace to judge what use would have been been made of it when . . . even honest and well meaning people, were drawn into believe the whole a sham and a pretext for a standing army. . . . .

His Majesty approves very much of your Grace's design of leaving 200 of the Militia of Glasgow in Stirling Castle, when you remove your Camp in that place, that being a place of consequence, and which ought by all means to be secured." . . .

1715, Oct. 4th, Whitehall. From Lord Townshend.

"Since writing my other letter of this date, having laid before his Majesty what your brother has represented to me of the bad state of the Castle of Edinburgh as to its provisions, His Majesty has ordered me to direct My Lord Justice Clerk, in regard of My Lord Hay's being out

of town immediately to cause lay in three months provisions for which he
is to draw bills which will be answered." . . . .

1715, Oct. 11th, Cockpit. From Secretary Stanhope.
 . . . "We shall be impatient of hearing the Regiments from Ireland
landing with you. Some Squadrons will be ordered immediately to the
North of England, which is hoped will have a good effect. We begin
to hope that the troops which have marched towards the West will
check the rebellion which was certainly ready to break out there." . .

1715, Oct. 27th, Whitehall. From Secretary Stanhope.
"By the flying Pacquett which arrived last night I received the honour
of your Grace's of the 21st inst by which I perceive neither my Lord
Townshend's of the 4th nor mine of the 11th were then come to hands ;
they have probably been intercepted by the rebels, which in all appearance has likewise been the fate of some of your Grace's . . . .
His Majesty has observed with some concern, how weak the Regimts
of Foot with your Grace appeared by the last returns notwithstanding
the orders for increasing the numbers, as likewise money for the said
augmentation, have been issued long since . . . Lieutenant Genl
Carpenter with the Regiments under his command has positive orders to
pursue and attack the rebels of Northumberland who have now joyned
those of your country ; by a letter we received from him this night he
promises not to lose an hour in getting up with them." . . . .

1715, Nov. 2nd, Whitehall. From Lord Townshend and Secretary
Stanhope.
"The same Express having brought to each of us a letter from your
Grace, the one of the 18th and the other of the 19th inst. you will allow us
to answer them together in one letter.
We did immediately upon receipt of them get them translated into
French for His Majesty's perusall and we are commanded by his Majesty
to tell your Grace very plainly, that he was not a little surprised at some
expressions in them . . . . His Majesty is surprised to find that
you treat these orders as bills on Terra Incognita ; how becoming
your Grace's reflections touching the necessary precautions, which
have been taken to prevent a rebellion in England, are, your Grace
upon reflection will your self best judge. His Majesty hath had and has
good reasons, for all the resolutions he has taken, which a very little
time may possibly demonstrate, and however your Grace may please to
treat his Ministers, certainly some respect is due to the resolutions of
the King. We submit it to your Grace, whether it is not possible
there should be many grounds of apprehension, which it is not
proper to publish, especially when so many of our letters are intercepted. . . . .
We hope, my Lord, that the Irish Regiments will have joined you
before now, that Mr. Carpenter will likewise be in Scotland, and that
your Grace will give us an opportunity of laying before the King
accounts from you more acceptable ; we do assure your Grace, that we
most sincerely wish it, not only for the King's and our country's
service but for that of your Grace &ca."

1715, Nov. 4th, Whitehall. From Lord Townshend.
 . . . . . "I am by His Majesty's order to acquaint your Grace, that
as to the troops, which were ordered for Newcastle, your Grace must be
sensible that they advanced to that place with all the haste, the distance
of the quarters they were in, and the badness of the roads at that time
could possibly allow of, and that after their arrival at Newcastle, not
one moment's time has been lost in the pursuit of the rebels, Carpenter

being got by a very extraordinary expedition within 7 or 8 miles of them, so that whatever design the rebels might have to return to Edinburgh, His Majesty hopes that is prevented, and that Mr Carpenter will keep so close to them, that they will not have it in their power to give your Grace any disturbance. I hope this situation will give your Grace much ease, by delivering you from the care of the town of Edinburgh, and leave you at liberty to employ all the troops as your Grace shall judge best for His Majesty's service. . . . . .

. . . . Your Grace will easily imagine, what acceptable service it would be, if the countys which have sent out their Militia so frankly, could be prevailed with to keep them up for some time longer at their own expense . . . . you here set them a very good example by the great expense you have put your self to, in Argyleshire in keeping up the Militia of that country, of which his Majesty is highly sensible, and [he] ordered me to return your Grace thanks for this singular mark of your zeal for his service. His Majesty hopes this will influence other countys, and the rather that they must be sensible, from what extravagant contributions they are exempted, to which the countys which are in the possession of the rebels are exposed.

By the last letter your Grace had from Mr. Secretary Stanhope and me, we acquainted you, that the Pretender had set out from Bar le Duc and was come to Chateau Thierry. The Earl of Stair by his letter of the 9th N.S. writes that having represented this to the Regent, His Highness had directed the Duke De Guiche to give order to Major Genl Coulade to carry the Pretender back to Lorrain and for that end to use force if necessary, and Coulade was gone from Paris to put his orders in execution. We have as yet no certain accounts of the Duke of Ormonde. The Lords Justices of Ireland have by their letter of the 26th to Mr. Secretary Stanhope writ that Morrison's and Clayton's Regim^{ts} had sailed that afternoon, having been embarked some days before but detained by contrary winds, and that Edgerton's and one troop of Evans' sailed on the 23rd from Donachadee for Port Patrick, so we hope all these may be by this time have joined your Grace, of which His Majesty will be very glad to hear " . . . .

1715, Nov. 8th, Whitehall. From Lord Townshend.

. . . . . I must own I have not taken notice of any thing in the publick prints that reflects on your Grace's conduct . . . . as your Grace may very well judge from what particular views and selfish designs such insinuations may proceed you will know how little weight ought to be laid on them . . . . .

Your Grace need not doubt of His Majesty's approving your design of attacking the enemies if they attempt to pass the Forth ; their getting between you and England being, as your Grace observes, of too great consequence, not to be prevented if it can be done.

His Majesty approves of your Grace's sending back E[arl]Mar's trumpet without giving him any answer, and His Majesty being determined that he and all with him shall be treated as rebels, your Grace will take notice of this, and regulate your self by it, in all matters of this kind.

. . . . . I am further to tell your Grace in confidence, that for a considerable time His Majesty has had good ground to suspect the conduct of the Regent, which our last accounts from the Earl of Stair do very much confirm, it being certain that the Pretender is on the coast of Normandy, and very probable that the Duke of Ormonde is landed in England, and that Dillon is gone to Ireland. So that it appears the Court of France designs to foment a rebellion in all His Majesty's Dominions.

His Majesty has agreed to what your Grace proposes for Mᵣ Neill Campbell, to be Minister of Renfrew, and has ordered a presentation to be prepared, which will be ready to be sent down by the next occasion." 1715, Nov. 14th, Whitehall. From Lord Townshend.

. . . . . " His Majesty approves of your conduct, which ought to make you easy whatever reflections private persons from their own particular views may think fit to make upon it.

. . . . His Majesty who has had under consideration what your Grace has so fully represented in relation to the circumstances of your troops under your command, and observing you are of opinion that by the disposition your Grace has made of these troops, they will be as ready for action as if they continued in their tents, and that the lodging them in Stirling and the other places mentioned, will be very much for their ease and conveniency, His Majesty does approve of what your Grace has done in this particular " . . . .

1715, Nov. 15th, Whitehall. From Lord Townshend.

. . . . . " as it appears by the intelligence your Grace has had of the Earl of Marr's advancing with the rebels to Auchterarder that he may design to pass the Forth, your Grace needs not doubt of His Majesty's impatience to have your next accounts " . . . . .

Same date. Whitehall. From the same.

" I despatch this by a flying Pacquett to communicate to your Grace, and to congratulate with you, on the good newes we received this morning from Lancashire. We have accounts that on Saturday morning, Major Gen¹ Willis having intelligence that the Lords Derwentwater and Widringtoun with the Northumberland and Scots rebels, and such as had joined them in Lancashire, making in all between 4 and 5000 men, were at Preston he marched from Wigan, to attack them, with the Regiments of horse and Dragoons of Pitt, Winne, Honywood, Dormer, Munden, and Stanhope, and Preston's Regiment of foot. He had left Col¹ Newtoun's Regim¹ of Dragoons at Manchester, to prevent the disaffected in that town from stirring as they had promised. About one in the afternoon, he arrived at the bridge of Ribble, and found there, about 2 or 300 of the Rebells horse, and foot, who upon the approach of his Majesty's troops withdrew with precipitation into the town, at the entrance of which they had made a strong barricade, The Maj: Gen¹ ordered Preston's Regiment to attack it, which they did with great bravery, and at the same time ordered the whole town to be surrounded to the right and left, by the horse and Dragoons. The rebells having the advantage of being very well posted at the barricade, Preston's Regiment sustained some loss, and the Maj: Gen¹ having effectually secured all the avenues, about the town, ordered the foot to make a lodgement. The horse and Dragoons continued at their horses heads all that night. On Sunday morning about nine aclock Lien¹ General Carpenter joined him with the three Regiments of Dragoons of Cobham, Churchill, and Molesworth. About one the rebells began to parley, and after several messages agreed to surrender themselves prisoners at discretion. On Monday morning at seven aclock, they had laid down their arms, and the King's troops were preparing to march into the town. Brigadᵣ Dormer and the Lord Forrester were wounded in this action. Of which we hourly expect further particulars, as also the list of the Lords and other persons of note, who are prisoners. All the troops express'd great zeal and resolution on this occasion, and the new Regiments appeared in perfect good order.

MARQUESS
TOWNSHEND
MSS.

I hope, my Lord, we may flatter ourselves that by this action, the rebellion here is supprest, and that it may have no small influence. On your parts, it has this advantage, that it leaves His Majesty at liberty to order the 3000 of the Dutch troops that were at first designed for the Firth of Forth, to proceed thither. I wrote to your Grace, that upon the motions of the rebells in Lancashire, they were directed to the Humber, but having been forced by a violent storm, to put into Harwich, which has disabled them so much, it is found absolutely necessary they should land soon. Your Grace may depend upon it they will be ordered to Scotland with all possible expedition."

1715, Nov. 19th, Whitehall. From Lord Townshend.

This Evening Mr Harrison arrived and brought me your Grace's of the 11th inst which was immediately laid before the King, who has ordered me to return you his hearty thanks for the good service you have done His Majesty and your country by this victory you have obtained over the rebels, the good consequence of which His Majesty doubts not will appear every day, and your Grace must allow Mr Secretary Stanhope and me to congratulate you on this good success, which we do both very sincerely. I have also His Majesty's orders to desire your Grace to give thanks in his name to all the officers and others under your Grace's command, who have on this occasion given proof of their bravery and fidelity. His Majesty was very much concerned to hear of My Lord Hay's being wounded but glad, as are all his servants, to find by your Grace's that you do not apprehend him to be in great danger. You need not doubt but all here regret very much poor Lord Forfar's fate. My Lord, as soon as we had the news of the suppressing the rebels in Lancashire His Majesty ordered the 3000 Dutch which were designed to put into the Humber to proceed to the Firth of Forth, but by a violent storm with which they were overtaken, they have been so disperst and not only the transport ships but the convoys so disabled that they could not possibly keep at sea. But I have His Majesty's orders to assure your Grace that no time shall be lost in falling upon the most expeditious way for these troops to take in order to join your Grace. Some of the Transports have put into the river of Thames, some to Harwich, some to Yarmouth, so that it must be some time before they can be got together, but your Grace may depend upon it, all possible care shall be taken to reinforce you as soon as possible."

1715, Nov. 22nd, Whitehall. From Secretary Stanhope.

. . . . "My Lord Townshend has already acquainted your Grace that upon suppressing the rebels in Lancashire directions were given for the 3000 Dutch troops that were ordered to the Humber, to proceed to the Firth of Forth, but upon what your Grace has represented in your last letters, His Majesty has come to a resolution of sending the whole 6300 to joyn your Grace. . . . . As these troops with those already under your Grace's command, will make a considerable body, and such as may well require two Lieut Genls under your Grace, and as the Dutch are commanded by a Lieut Genl Vander Beck His Maty thinks it very reasonable in case by any accident your Grace should be hindred from being your self at the head of the troops, that there should be a British Lieut Genl elder than Vander Beck, to take the command upon him, and for this purpose His Majesty has pitched upon Mr Cadogan as the person who is the best acquainted with the Dutch Troops, and who His Majesty judges will be most acceptable to your Grace."

1715, Nov. 26th, Whitehall. From Lord Townshend.

. . . . . "It is with great concern that His Majesty observes the

M 2

uneasiness you are under, notwithstanding the repeated assurances which have been given you of His Majesty's approbation of your conduct, and of his relying intirely upon it. I think your Grace must be convinced, that nothing has been wanting on the part of the Governm' to give your Grace all the assistance, the circumstances of Affairs here could possibly allow of . . . . .

. . . . . His Majesty cannot think of your Grace's withdrawing from his service or imploying any other to command his army. I am sure there is nothing your Grace can desire of me, in which I will not most heartily serve you, except in this particular, which in my opinion is absolutely inconsistent with the good of His Majesty's service and with the interest of my country."

1715, Nov. 27th, Whitehall. From Lord Townshend.

" M' Cadogan will have your honour to deliver this to your Grace. His Majesty has appointed him to serve under you as Lieu' Gen' of his forces judging it absolutely necessary for his service, that there should be a British Lieut Gen' older than Vanderbeek. . . . . Mr. Secretary Stanhope and I have by our former letters acquainted your Grace with the directions given for reinforcing the army under your command part of which from Yarmouth and Hull, we hope may be in the Firth of Forth this day, neither shall I trouble you with any particulars in relation to His Majesty's further views, as to what operations may be further neces-sary in your parts, which M' Cadogan will fully explain to you, and therefore I take the liberty to referr your Grace to him."

1715, Nov. 30th, Whitehall. From Lord Townshend.

" I have received the honour of your Grace's of the 25th which I have laid before the King, who has commanded me to acquaint your Grace, that from the representations you have made of the state of affairs since the battle, as well as from the repeated advices he has had of the Pretender's being sailed for Scotland, His Majesty is very apprehensive, that his service may suffer by your absence; however he is so unwilling to refuse your Grace any request that is not directly inconsistent with his interest and service, that he leaves it intirely to you to come hither for the time you mention, in case you think the enemy will make no advantage of your leaving the army at this juncture."

1715, Dec 3rd, Whitehall. From Lord Townshend.

. . . . . "in relation to the offer made by Mar. . . . His Majesty looks upon this as a matter of the very last consequence to his service . . . as soon as I receive His Majesty's directions upon it I shall not fail to transmit them to your Grace.

His Majesty read with very much concern what your Grace writes the Earl of Forfar, and exprest himself with so much affection and regard to that poor Earl, that what your Grace mentions as his request for his aunt M Lockhart, I believe you need not doubt but it will be complyed with." . . . . .

1715, Dec. 6th, Whitehall. From Lord Townshend.

His Majesty observes with satisfaction and approves very much of your declining to enter into any treaty on the proposals made by [Mar] Huntley and others till you had his further orders . . . . neither does His Majesty think that in the present situation and circumstances of affairs, it is consistent with the honour of his Governm' or the future peace and quiet of his good subjects, that the rebels should be admitted to any terms but those of surrendering their persons, and intirely submitting to His Majesty's pleasure.'

1715, Dec. 15th, Whitehall. From Lord Townshend.

. . . . " Your Grace seems to think the Pretender may still land, and if he should, that he may soon be at the head of 20000 men, but I must acquaint your Grace, that by our freshest advices from France, we have good ground to think, he is still there, neither is it probable, that after the great checks and disappointments, his partisans have met with both here and from your Grace, he will think of making any further attempt, but should he land and even find that assistance your Grace apprehends, His Majesty does not doubt but that providence which has hitherto so visibly blessed the justice of his cause will continue to do it, to the distruction of his enemies, and to the rooting out of the very seeds of this rebellion.

. . . . you should as soon as you are joined by that reinforcement, which has been ordered, and which we hope will be soon with you, march without loss of time against the rebels and endeavour to dislodge them from Perth, and even follow them amongst the hills, if they shall seek their shelter there." . . . . .

1715, Dec. 23rd, Whitehall. From Lord Townshend.

. . . . . . " His Majesty continues firm in his sentiments of not entring into treaty with any of the rebels, on other terms then these of their surrendering themselves, and submitting intirely to His Majesty's pleasure . . . . it appears by Sir Robert [Gordon]'s own letter, that he is gone North, it is not proper any other step should be made in relation to him, till he first comply with what His Majesty proposes, and surrender himself to your Grace on these terms." . . . . .

1715, Dec. 27th, Whitehall. From Lord Townshend.

. . . . . . " My Lord the King is very sensible of the good services the Lord Lovat has done, at this time, and tho' I cannot, by this Post, give your Grace those assurances you desire of his pardon, yet I am sure nothing can give him so just a title to it as his continuing to serve with that zeal he has hitherto done, and ingaging his dependents and friends to the like. . . . . .

Mr. Secretary Stanhope and I had both of us letters of the 19th from Lieut. Genl Cadogan, with which he transmitted a plan of such operations as appeared necessary for reducing the rebels, and as he writes that the same had been approven of by your Grace, they have been laid before the King, and I am by His Majesty's order to acquaint your Grace, that he does intirely approve of the project . . . . His Majesty leaves it to your Grace to consider whether a part of the forces may not be sufficient to attacque the rebels at Perth, especially if this great frost continues, which by the freezing of the river must necessarily make one half of the town defenceless. . . . . . My Lord, His Majesty judges the execution of this project of the very last consequence to his service, and the rather that by the letters we have from France we have received this day, we have reason to believe the Pretender may be in Scotland before this reach your Grace, which makes it absolutely necessary that the rebels be dislodged from Perth, and deprived of that hold which has been of so great use to them, and without which it is scarce possible for them to keep together a great body."

17$\frac{15}{16}$, Jan. 3rd, Whitehall. From Lord Townshend.

. . . . . " His Majesty is sensible that a winter campaign will be of great expences, for the reasons your Grace takes notice of in your letter, but at the same time His Majesty looks upon it of such consequence to his service, and so absolutely necessary for the suppressing of this rebellion, that it must not either on that or any other consideration

whatsoever, be laid aside, and therefore as soon as the Dutch troops
have joined your Grace, His Majesty is persuaded you will without loss
of time, pursue the instructions you have received on this head. . . . . .
My Lord, to the following the rebels amongst the bills, in case they
retire from Perth, His Majesty never intended that the whole army shall
be imployed to follow them. . . . . .

As your Grace is pleased to renew your request to return, I am
ordered to tell you, His Majesty consents to your Grace's coming hither
whenever you please. . . . . .

Upon what your Grace represents to Mr Evans' indisposition, His
Majesty allows him to go to Bath or where he thinks fit for his recovery ;
tho' at the same time sorry for the occasion of it. His Majesty and all his
serv^{ts} being sensible of that gentleman's merit, and of the loss it may
be to His Majesty's service that he should be absent."

17½⅔, Jan. 6th, Whitehall.   From Lord Townshend.
. . . . . . "Your Grace might very well presume that you are to
answer such rebels as apply to you that His Majesty expects they shall
surrender themselves to your Grace and submit intirely to his pleasure,
this being as I have often repeated to your Grace, what His Majesty
judges [necessary] both for the honour and security of his Governm^t and
it is by this your Grace is to regulate your self with relation to the
Laird of Methven, or any other who shall make the like proposal to your
Grace, as he has done.

I have also in Command from His Majesty to repeat by this occasion to
your Grace, what I wrote in my letter of the 27th for putting in execution, without the least loss of time, the project I there mention, the
copy whereof had been transmitted by Lieu^t Genl Cadogan. . . . . .

Tho' the advices of the Pretender's being landed do not seem to be
such as to be absolutely depended upon, yet as the thing is very probable His Majesty is so far from thinking it should retard the execution
of the project, and of the attempt against Perth, that I am ordered to
make use of it, as a motive for your Grace's forwarding the expedition
as much as possibly can be.   His Majesty approves of your Grace's
causing take possession of the Castles of the Earl of Broadalbin, and
likewise of your Grace's supplying Tinah, in the way you mention, to
enable him to keep possession of these places." . . . . .

17½⅕, Jan. 10th, Whitehall.   From Lord Townshend.
" I am to acknowledge your Grace's of the 3^d, which I have laid before
the King who was very much surprized to find your Grace attribute the
continuance of the rebellion to the orders His Majesty has thought fit to
send you, as not having given you sufficient power, till you received
mine of the 27th past.

His Majesty was from the beginning of this rebellion of our opinion,
that he could not either in honour or conscience go into any measures
in relation to the rebels, but such as would effectually secure the future
peace and quiet of his faithfull subjects, and your Grace was therefore
impower'd by your instructions, which were drawn, as you must well remember, by your self, to give assurances of His Majesty's mercy and
favour to such only, as should by submitting themselves, to His Majesty
and by making early discoveries, or doing some other signal services, merit
them.   His Majesty has since several times repeated these orders to
your Grace, that before any of the rebels could expect favour, they
should surrender themselves to your Grace, and my letter of the 27th of
Decr can be understood in no other sence, and His Majesty having carefully reviewed all your Grace's letters, cannot find in them one instance

where any of the Rebels have offered to comply with those terms, except Lord Rollo and [the] Master of St Clare.

His Majesty observes the offers which have been made by Marr, Huntley and others have been made only to seperate themselves from the body of the rebels, without any offer of coming to your Grace, and bringing their followers with them, or making any Discovery as to the Lord Rollo and [the] Master of St Clare, tho' your Grace in your Letter of the 30th Novr mentions their offering to joyn your Grace with the Fife Squadron, yet, besides that in your preceeding letter, which was of the 27th and to which I gave a return by mine of the 6th Decr your Grace only speaks of their offering to seperate themselves from the rest of the rebels, His Majesty would have thought it very hard, but these persons should be the first objects of his royal clemency, who had most signalized themselves in the ravaging and destroying of their country, and in the harrassing and pillaging of His Majesty's faithfull subjects, as by particular advices, His Majesty is informed, the Lord Rollo and [the] Master of St Clare, did with the Fife Squadron, and particularly in a most barbarous and inhumane manner against the Earl of Rothes, who, besides his being of one of the first and best families of the Kingdom, has at this time distinguished himself by his singular zeal in His Majesty's and his country's service.

Upon the whole His Majesty is persuaded, that your Grace, when you have seriously reflected on and considered this whole transaction, will in justice rather impute the contrivance of this rebellion to the obstinacy of the rebels, or to some other cause, than to any defect in his orders, or to the want of powers, and since they have put the nation to such vast expence and obliged the King to call for the assistance of foreign troops, the greater the preparations are for the suppressing of this rebellion the less reason there is for listening to any offers of the rebels, but such as carry with them evident advantages to His Majesty's Service, are absolutely consistent with the honour of his Government, and tending to the future quiet and security.

My Lord, if in my letter to your Grace of the 27th I mentioned that project sent up by Lieut Genl Cadogan, as his, it was because it was transmitted by him to Mr. Secretary Stanhope, and your Grace was not pleased in your two first letters, after it came, to take any notice of it. As to the alterations which may be thought necessary to make in the scheme, His Majesty leaves that intirely to your Grace, not doubting, but they will be such, as will be no obstruction to the execution of the project, and the attempting the expedition against Perth, and that the want of artillery, by reasons of the ships being detained by contrary winds, may be as well supplyed, as possibly may be. Orders are sent by his Grace the Duke of Marlborough to Berwick for furnishing your Grace, with what that place affords, of canon, ball and other stores, and what else may be fit for the train, as your Grace shall call for them, Tho' if the frost be such in your parts, as it is here at present, we presume your Grace will have little occasion for them.

Tho' your Grace mentions the arrival of the Pretender, as not absolutely certain, in yours of the 3d which is the last I have received from you, yet from all our advices from France, as well as from Scotland, by letters of the 5th the King has no reason to doubt, but that he is landed in Scotland. I am therefore by his particular command to let you know, that he thinks it of the last Consequence to his service, that no time should be lost in marching to the enemy, the least delay of that kind, at this juncture, may be dangerous, and grow every day, as your Grace most justly observes, more difficult. I am &ca.

TOWNSHEND."

17$\frac{1}{16}$, Jan. 23rd, Whitehall.   From Lord Townshend.

. . . . . . " His Majesty hopes to hear very soon of your Grace's putting the project against Perth in execution, the inconveniencys your Grace apprehended from Mr Burrows' absence, and I hope sufficiently supplyed. . . . . .

His Majesty is very well pleased that Mr Evans's health is such as will allow him to continue there, I shall not fail when there is any alteration in the Establishment of the General Officers to do him justice, by putting His Majesty in mind of his pretentions, I shall also take the first opportunity to receive His Majesty's directions in relation to Cap^n Stewart, whom your Grace has recommended in two of your letters."

17$\frac{1}{6}$, Jan. 31st, Whitehall.   From Lord Townshend.

. . . . . . " His Ma^{ty} is extreamly well pleased to find your Grace has made a disposition of every thing so as to be in readiness to march as on Saturday last, His Majesty hopes the returning of the frost, which we have now here to as great a degree as ever, will render your enterprize the more practicable, I need not tell your Grace of how great importance it is to His Majesty's Service, the reduction of Perth, and obliging the rebels to betake themselves to the hills, when it will be impossible for them to keep together in a body. . . . . .

As to what Your Grace mentions of the Earl of Rothes's censuring your conduct, it is what I do assure you, I am wholly a stranger to, having never corresponded with any but your Grace, except on some few occasions with His Majesty's servants at Edinburgh, when the exigencies of his affairs required it.

. . . . . His Majesty does not think it consistent either with the honour of his Government or the interest of his service, that there should be any cartel made with the rebels; but if your Grace can fall on any way of having the prisoners who are of any consequence released, as the gentlemen of Sturler's Regiment, you mention, the Laird of Gilkindie or any such, your Grace may fairly do it and depend upon His Majesty's approbation of it. I have by His Majesty's order put into the hands of the Secretary at Warr, the Memorial your Grace transmitted from Colonel Hawley and shall on his report receive His Majesty's further directions.

As to what I have said above, in relation to the exchange of prisoners, there was a method found out to exchange them in Flanders during the last warr with France, when there was no cartel settled, and if your Grace can find any such expedient, His Majesty will approve of it rather than let those who served him faithfully suffer in the hands of the rebels."

17$\frac{1}{6}$, Feb. 4th, Whitehall.   From Lord Townshend.

. . . . . " It was very agreeable to His Majesty to hear that the army was at Dumblain, and that your Grace had made all the necessary dispositions for its marching the next day to Ardoch, and His Majesty doubt not but your Grace will as far as possible by your care and conduct overcome the difficulties occasioned by the barbarities of the rebels, and other accidents and that we shall soon hear of your being before Perth . . . . .

. . . . . I have further in Comand from His Majesty to acquaint your Grace that there being good ground to believe that upon the Pretender's going to Scotland, there was a design laid for a rebellion in Ireland, to be carried on in concert with that in North Britain, and for raising of which no endeavours are still wanting, His Majesty judges it absolutely necessary for his service, that your Grace should establish, in the most expeditious and safe way you can possibly, a constant correspondence with the Lords Justices of Ireland " . . . . .

17$\frac{15}{16}$, Feb. 6th, Whitehall. From Lord Townshend. ·

" I received by Mr Stewart your Aide de Camp, the honour of your Grace's letter of the 31st past which I immediately laid before the King. His Majesty received it with very great satisfaction the news of your Grace's having advanced so farr with the army, and of the rebels having abandoned Perth. His Majesty returns your Grace thanks for your good conduct on this occasion and approves intirely of your Grace's resolution of following the rebels whatever way they take." . . . .

17$\frac{15}{16}$, Feb. 10th, Whitehall. From Lord Townshend.

"I received yesterday morning by a flying Pacquet the honour of your Grace's letter of the 2^d from Erroll, and by another in the afternoon, that of the 4th from Dundee, both which have been laid before the King, who was extreamly well pleased to hear of the army's being in such close pursuit of the rebels. . . . . . His Majesty is of opinion that no Quarters can be settled for them till this rebellion is wholy at an end, by the rebels being disarmed, their chiefs in custody, and the Highlands reduced intirely to the King's obedience.

His Majesty is of your Grace's sentiment that it may be very necessary to reinforce the garrison of Fort William, that they may be in a condition to act offensively against the rebels in that neighbourhood. . . . . .

Before the Address which your Grace mentions to have been transmitted, in behalf of the Lord Lovat, came to hands, His Majesty was so sensible of the good services of that Lord, at this juncture upon the representations of the Earl of Southerland, who has not failed to do him justice, that he thought fit that the Earl of Southerland should be impowered to assure the Lord Lovat of His Majesty's pardon, and I can now tell your Grace that I have His Majesty's order to prepare it, in which no time shall be lost.

[P.S.] Since writing what is above I have a fresh occasion of congratulating your Grace on the news we have received by letter of the 5th of the Pretender's imbarking in great precipitation at Montrose, and of Sir John Jennings being in pursuit of him."

17$\frac{15}{16}$, Feb. 17th, Whitehall. From Lord Townshend.

" I have received the honour of your Grace's of the 8th which I have laid before the King, with the letters from the Earl of Southesk and others, but have no commands for your Grace in relation to the submission they offer, that matter being under His Majesty's consideration. . . . ·

Your Grace may remember that by my former letter you were, at your own desire, at liberty to leave Scotland, as soon as you could do it without prejudice to His Majesty's affairs, and now that you are pleased to repeat the same request, and His Majesty's affairs being as your Grace observes, on such a foot as that they cannot suffer by your absence, your Grace has not only His Majesty's leave, but I have his orders to tell you that he thinks your presence here very much for his service, and therefore desires you would return as soon as conveniently you can."

. . . .

17$\frac{15}{16}$, Feb. 21st, Whitehall. From Lord Townshend.

" I have by two different flying Pacquets received the honour of your Grace's letters of the 12th & 13th from Aberdeen, with the letters and other papers referred to in them, all which have been laid before the King.

His Majesty approves of the answer your Grace has given to the Marquis of Huntley and such as have made the like offer as he has done. As to Major Urquhart, tho' His Majesty upon inquiry finds that ·

what he alledges is true, and that therefore he is not to be considered as a diserter; yet it is His Majesty's pleasure that he should be kept in custody till further orders.

The King is not as yet come to a resolution as to the disposal of the troops into quarters, which, as I wrote to your Grace by my letter of the 10th, His Majesty thinks cannot be settled this rebellion is wholly at an end. . . . . .

I should very heartily have concurred with my good offices, in prometing what your Grace has proposed for the Earl of Deloraine, but before your letter came to hand, His Majesty had declared his resolution to bestow the government of Stirling Castle on the Earl of Rothes.

As I suppose this may find your Grace at Edinburgh, or on the road hither, that Lieut Genl Cadogan may be apprized of what is in this letter which concerns His Majesty's service, I have by His Majesty's order sent him a copy of it and have nothing further to trouble your Grace with." . . . .

1716, March 2nd. Copy of a despatch from the Marquis d'Uxelles to Mons. d'Iberville, In French—and chiefly in cipher numbers. Dated at Paris, and indorsed " Mr d'Iberville du M[arech]al d'huxelles—Most in cypher—& 2 paragraphs abt My Ld Stairs." 12½ pages on 13 sheets stitched.

The two paragraphs referring to Lord Stair are as follows :—

" Il est vray que l'on ne peut point espérer de concilier les Esprits pendant que le Roy d'Anglet^re se servira de M. le Comte de Stairs. Il a si clairem^t fait conoitre en toute occasion qu'il ne vouloit rien pour faire naistre des sujets de defiance et il a affecté avec tant da soin de garder le silence sur ce qu'il a vue par luy meme de la sincerité des intentions de Monseigneur le duc d'Orleans qu'il n'est pas possible que l'on puisse jamais prendre confiance en luy ; cependant le Roy n'a pas voulu faire de plainte formelle de sa conduit et Sa Majesté a cru qu'elle devoit la dissimuler afin de ne pas donner lieu de dire qu'il voulut demander le rappel d'un homme actif et éclairé qui pust être témoin de ce qui se passoit.

Il n'y a rien de plus faux que ce que vous a été raporté d'un pré-tendu discours de Monseigneur le Duc d'Orleans à M. le Comte de Staire. S.A.R. luy a bien dit que ce n'estoit pas sa faute si le Roy d'Anglet^re n'avoit pas accepté l'offre qu'elle luy avoit faite au nom de Sa Majesté de former une Alliance entre la France l'Angleterre et la Hollande qui auroit levé toutes sortes d'ombrages et de soupçons mais jamais elle ne luy a pu dire que par rette caison elle ne fut pas en état d'empecher que le Prétendant ne tirast des secours du Royaume. Elle l'a empeshé autant qu'il a esté en son pouvoir et c'est une de ces inventions que le party qui veut le renovellement de la guerre . . . . [two or three words are here illegible from decay of the MS.] de vraisemblance aussy bien que de verité et qu'il sontient parce qu'elle convient à ses vües. Je vous prie d'être persuadé que je suis très veritablem^t Monsr entierem^t à vous le M^{al} d'HUXELLES."

1716, May 16th. The last statement of Richard Gascoigne, a Catholic Jacobite, lying under sentence of death in Newgate. 3 pp.

[1716]. An undated letter from the same to Sir Roger Bradshaw, Baronet, begging the latter to appear and give evidence on behalf of the writer at his approaching trial.

[1716]. A Memorandum, signed by the same, and dated in Newgate " Friday Morning, betwixt 9 and 10.":—

" All that was contain'd in my paper yesterday was true and as I shall and am obliged to day when I leave the world to declare, itt is soe and

I bless my God as I wou'd not tell an untruth for the world att any time, soe much less, when in a few minutes I expect to appear before the tribunal of our good God.

Itt wou'd be an instance of mercy and charity, if I cou'd be allowed some few days longer, for I was ill of a feavour. Many of those I have pass'd since my condemnation. If itt can be obtain'd, my poor prayers shall be offer'd for them that doe itt, who ever they are, I am heartily their well wisher both of soul and body."

1716, July 9th. Draft of a Council Minute. In Lord Townshend's handwriting.

. . . . Sir David Dalrymple and Sir James Stuart being heard upon the letters from Scotland giving an account of the endeavours used by the rebels who are prisoners there to obtain their liberty by applying to the Justiciary Court, they were ordered to prepare a letter with directions how to prevent their being released before they are brought to a legal tryal the draught of the letter to be laid before the Lords to merrow night.

1716, July 12th. Draft of a Council Minute. In Lord Townshend's handwriting.

To approve what Mr Wich has done in relation to Lord Duffus and to order him to thank the Magistrates for the assistance they gave him upon this occasion . . . . . . to [write to] Mr Stanhope that H.R.H. is of opinion if his Majesty approve it, that care sh'd be taken to secure Lord Duffus in safe custody and that he sh'd be sent over hither.

[1716.] A petition to the King from John Gordon, condemned for High Treason and a prisoner in Newgate, imploring his Majesty's clemency and mercy. Two copies, on the same sheet, one in French and one in English. Undated. Signed by the petitioner.

The petitioner states that his father, the late Patrick Gordon of Duumeath in the County of Banff, and his uncle Sir George Gordon of Edenglassie—the Sheriff Principal in the same county, were early concerned in the happy Revolution in favour of which they both distinguished themselves.

[1716.] A copy of the above petition addressed "to the Lord Viscount Townshend His Majestie's Principall Sec^y of State." Undated, and signed by the Petitioner.

[1716 ?] "Memorandum of the Duke of Montrose to my Lord Townshend with relation to the following persons, in case there should be any application made to their prejudice.

Mr Walter Stirling, Keeper of the Wardrobe, he was my tutor till I went abroad.

Sir Gilbert Kennedy, Under-Falconer, a very honest gentleman upon half-pay, and a friend of My Lord Stair's.

Mr Henry Graham of Braikness, Chamberlain for the Bishoprick of Orkney ; a namesake of mine, very well affected, and was recommended by the honest people in those parts.

Mr Mungo Graham of Gorthie, Receiver General of the Customs, who executes that office with so much care and integrity, that I doubt not but he will always deserve your Lordships particular favour and protection."

[1716.] Three undated papers in the same clerk's hand which seem to have been dictated by Horatio Walpole.

1. A Memorial, in French, endorsed by Horatio Walpole "1st Project of a Memoriall." 6 pp.
2. A similar Memorial, in French, endorsed by Horatio Walpole, "2^d Project of a Memoriall." 5 pp.

3. An undated "Memoriall to be delivered in a Conference with the Deputys for Foreign affairs " of the States General.

These three memorials are to the same effect, and the last of them, which is in English, commences as follows :—

"The King my Master being firmly persuaded that his own interest and security is inseparable from that of the States . . . . . has commanded me to acquaint you that notwithstanding the Rebells have been entirely suppressed in England and their army defeated in Scotland yett the person commonly called the Pretender has by the encouragement of some conspirators against their lawfull sovereign and country and by other ennemys to the publick tranquility of Europe dared to invade his Majesty's dominions. . . . . . And although the precautions his Majesty has already taken, the assistance of the brave troops which the States have been pleased to lend him and the vigorous and unanimous Resolutions of his loyall Parliament will in all probability by the blessing of God enable him soon to put an end to this unnaturall rebellion and entirely to baffle the hopes of success that his ennemys may have vainly imagined to find within his own Dominions, yett as on the other side the Pretender and his adherents flatter themselves with certain assurances of the assistance and support of a foreign power and as it is notorious that notwithstanding the repeated promises given by the Court of France that the Treaty of Utrecht should be strictly observed, and that no officers soldiers arms and ammunition should be permitted to goe from any Port of France for the service of the Pretender and that positive orders had been given in all the Ports of France for that effect, yett great numbers of officers etc. doe constantly pass into Scotland for the service of the sayd Pretender from most of the Ports of France without the le[a]st opposition from the Governours there and particularly the Commandant of Calais . . . when Mr Moore an Englishman did on the part of my Lord Stair acquaint him that severall hundreds of persons were ready to embark from thence to go to the Pretender . . . . . instead of giving a civill answer to Mr Moore threatned to make him leave the town, and accordingly the sayd officers sayled the 30th of January at midnight in four vessels fitted out for that purpose." . . . . .

This memorial goes on to insist upon the importance to the Dutch republic of the Protestant succession to the Crown of Great Britain, and concludes by urging the States General, in concert with the King, to "invite other Princes and States to join his Majesty and this Republiek for their common security and defence in order to " discourage " and distresse by all possible means any Power that shall endeavour to violate the peace which Europe now enjoys or to give any succour or assistance to the sayd Pretender."

The following Postscript to the above memorial is in the handwriting of Horatio Walpole :—

" The army of the rebells being put to flight, and the Pretender obliged to leave Holland since this Memoriall was drawn it will be easy to make the alterations which these incidents require."

1717, Dec. 6th. Copy of a Jacobite letter with names in cipher. Unsigned and unaddressed :—

"Doubtless you heard of the alterations at South's house ; you might have heard on't long ago had Moulsworth and his gang made use of the fair handles given 'em from time to time, but as Rog[e]rs had reason to suppose the sd Moulsw[orth] was willing to live upon the spoil us long as he cou'd, took a resolution with himself to strain a point so as to bring matters to an open rupture.

MARQUESS
TOWNSHEND
MSS.

He happened to discourse over a bottle a fast friend of Hall's that he knew formerly in Gerard's house, and finding [him] uneasy at Hall's management, saying that he was blind and stupid and was in hands that wou'd treat him as they did the late Mr Kemp, I agreed with him, on which he drew a paper out of his pocket which he said [he] was to give to Mr Hall the day follow^g and was to tell him withal that if he didn't change hands and take in some of the leading and moderate ones of the Waggs and Tanners he was an undone man.

The paper contained in substance that he should forthwith reduce Allen, give a free protection to Overbury and those with Mr Ken not to meddle in Egleton's quarrel, to bring Segrave, Beaumont and several others of the gang to be his mates, to give free access to all Tanners and others, and equal encouragem^t with the Wags. I told him this wou'd be a means to rivet him in Hall's affections, and his family in the copyhold ; as soon as I parted from him I put all this suggestion into an order, sent it to Scogel by an old friend and acquaintance of Moulsworth, Scog[el] shew'd it to Moulsworth on sight, and as he came back to my friend he ask't if he wou'd make good what he said : my friend answer'd he would be ready to do it on occasion, and wou'd wait on old Hall when he desir'd him. On inquiry I found Scogel made nothing of the matter for a while to see what Hall wou'd do, and find out his natural bent and inclination, upon which I made some of the Waggs and Cope's partners acquainted with all this matter, and convinc't them Hall wou'd drop them in a little time. They answered they wou'd put it out of his power. They made a noise and a splutter and blamed Cotton and Moulsworth as well as Hall saying if he wou'd not be their tool they shou'd not be his tools, and wou'd have no motly mates. This frightened him and his mates and [I] was obliged to shew a steadiness to them, but I found this wou'd not do. I went to a person that waits on Mr Hall, and told her that Moulsworth wou'd lay hold on this occasion of the child's christening to affront her, and if he got one point of her or her husband she must give up all other points, to ingratiate herself with her mistress. She improved it to advantage, telling her withal old Hall's supposed wife and mistress was at the bottom on't. I found after Arbuthnet influenced them, and spurr'd them on against Moulsworth and Hall who has consign'd himself over to the former, being the only person now in the Keeper[s] that can aesist him against Knell and Treyton, therefore he will sacrifice all his friends and family to preserve his quart[e]rs in Gerard's house. None now can so well do as Moulsworth and the present mates, 'twill be his ruin in the end, for he and all the Gerardins are too much govern'd by passion and interest that 'twould be an easy matter to run 'em aground had the Tanners or Moulsworth a true love for their country or Mr Kenedy. I must confess Segrave and Overton have been the main occasion that the Tanners are so backward, buzzing in their ears the power of the patron and Finch's House ; now they see they can't do anything without Otway or Knell the latter will do nothing for them but with assistance of the former.

If Hall or his family were beloved, this last proceeding of his would inflame the 3 Keepers, if Arberthnet and his friends can but get young Hall to declare in Holt's house that the partners of Hungate is now illegal, it will produce some good effect ; and reconcile all the Waggs to your interest, or at least be passive. In the mean time don't doubt but the present proceeding will have some good effect or other ; 'twill encourage the Tanners, discourage the moderate Waggs,and forward the Registerious and Cope's partners to proceed with more violence, and oblige Hall to reduce Allen to the same state Quaint left it, if so you'l find work that will please you.

MARQUESS
TOWNSHEND
MSS.
—

I have no news to send you but that the P[rince] & P[rin]c[e]ss of Wales that were banisht the Court are going to live at the D[uke] of Devonshire's house till matters are made up with the King. They are now indispos'd, and 'tis hop'd they'll be better in a few days; at least I hope so, and that they will be reconcil'd to the King. You know I can't be but sorry for this difference. So will Mr. Ken and you.

I hope and don't doubt but Mr. Kirk will be at Evlin's honse by Easter; if a project Rogers has in hand succeeds he is in a way to serve Rion and his cause. He'll spurr 'em on. Otway may be convinc't is nor will be in any power to withstand him or his Allen if he comes his late [sic]. A gentl[eman] was acquainted with the scheme Rog[e]rs laid for these proceed[in]gs and seemed well pleased with it. He thought me too daring."

1721, June 10th. Report by Anthony Cracherode on the Case of James Gartside. In reference to the Information laid by the latter against Captain James Leonard whom the informant alleged to have committed High Treason at Calais in December 1716.

[1722.] The following copies of Jacobite letters seem to have been made for the Privy Council, and to be connected with Layer's Conspiracy. The contents of these letters are very similar to those printed in " Reports from Committees of the House of Commons; which have been printed by Order of the House and are *Not* inserted in the Journals."

[No date.] Londres, Jeudy. À Mi Lord Mar à Paris sous l'addresse de Monsieur D'Hubert chez Monsr Waters banquier à la Rue Dauphine à Paris.

1722, April 23rd. To Capt Volnson—N or X—under the cover of Mr Francia at Calais. Signed Goodwin.

1722, May 10th. N.S. Copy of a Letter from Mr Blunt To Mr. N—X under the cover of Mr. Francia at Calais. Dated in London and signed Blunt.

[No date] Received 3d June.—Copy of a letter from Robert Brown directed to [the writer's cousin], Mr. Hary Blair,Writer [to the Signet] at his house in Allan's Close opposite to the Cross Edinburgh North Brittain." Without date.—This letter came by the French Mail 3rd June 1722, and is an answer to a letter of the 4th May signed Walter Grahame and directed à Monsr Collins chez Monsr Waters, Banquier à Paris.

1722, June 20th. T. J. To Mr. Jno Paterson; in the care of Mrs Alexander in the Canon Gate, Edinburgh.

1722, June 21st. Copy of an unsigned letter dated at Castle Howard and addressed, under cover to Mr. Walters at Paris, to Madame D'Hubert.

" My Dear Sister, I received a letter from you last Post which was much long'd for—My Lord Carlisle is the most agreeable in his own house that's possible, there is one thing that surprises me much to find both my Lord Car[lisle] and Lord Irwin quite brock with Lady Lechmer and Lady Mary hears of her seldom in great dryness. I know the opinion you have of her which I must always think she deserves it. . . . I heard today [from] Mrs. Harvey she complains sadly of never hearing from you, and has done so in every letter I've had from her."

[1722], Augt. 4th. To Mr Chauncey at Mr Chesshyres in Devonshire Square near Bishop's Gate. [Unsigned.]

1792, Aagt. 13th. Dated Dieppe. To the Revd Dr Hunt head of Baliol Colledge in Oxford. By a person who subscribes himself Alexr

Richmond. Another Letter from the same Alex^r Richmond of the like date directed to Wm Phips Esqre at the Honble Sir Constantine Phips in Ormond Street.

1722, Augt. 13th and Aug. 16th. Two letters addressed from London. "A Monsr Francois Bernard chez Mr Tuillies tapissier, rue de St Pere près la Charité Faubourg St Germain à Paris."

1722, Augt. 15th. To Mr. David Wilkins at Wills Coffee house near Covent Garden London.

1722, Augt. 18th. To Mrs. Draycott to be left at Mr Glasco's on Arrars Key Dublin.

1722, Augt. 19th. For M^r La Fontaine at Clare's Coffee house in Conduit Street near Hannover Square.

Same date. For Mr. Spencer at Old Man's Coffee house, Charing Cross. From Paris.

1722, Augt. 24th. To Mr. Wilkins at Mrs Brydges at the Lumber House in Duke Street Westminster.

1722, Augt. 25th. Extract of a Letter to The Lord Garlies ; to the care of the Post Masters of Edinburgh and Wigton Scotland. The author signs C. S. with a flourish.

1722, Augt. 29th. "For Mr. Wilkins" etc. as above. It begins "My dearest dear," and is subscribed "your for ever—LE BRUNE."

1722, Sept. 3rd. An anonymous letter addressed to Monsr Evans chez Monsr Waters, Banq^r rue Christine Fauxbourg St Germains.

1722, Sept. 7th. To Robert Dillon Esqr at his house in Latins Court Dublin.

1722, Sept. 10th. To Mr. Shortip at his house the lower end of Norfolk Street in the Strand. Dated at Dunkirk and signed Tho. Smith.

1722, Oct. 6th. À Milord le Vis-Conte de Bolingbrook under a blank Cover to Monsr de L'Orme chez Monsr de Blissy Commissaire des Poudres rue des Minimes à Orleans. In English ; unsigned.

" I write this upon my birthday, and am now come to that age of man which according to the Scripture is the uttermost extent of life.

I am sorry to hear you have bin ill if you apprehend any thing of the palsy, or rheumatism and that your lameness continues, I should think that the waters of Aix La Chapelle, or Barage, very proper for you ; we see many every year who come to our Bath, supported with sticks, and crutches that return leaving both behind them.

We have had so fine an autumn that I hope it has made amends for the badness of the summer and that you will have a good vintage and we good wine.

I hear poor Jo : Whiteman is dead suddingly of an apoplex at the Bath ; well at Lyndsey's a tuesday night, and dead a few hours after. Lord Hinchinbrook is likewise dead there.

The King is come to town and the Parlim^t meets on tuesday, we shall leave this place about the 18th inst.

Pray make my wife and daughters complim^{ts} to Mad^m La Marq^{se} and my service in particular.

All mine are Yours—Adieu.

[P.S.] I am glad to hear you have had no hand in this dirty work, you have run hazards enough already for the party which you and your family will feel to its great loss if not to its ruin."

1722, Oct. 10th. John Colebrooke to Mr. William Lock in Exchange Ally, London.

[1722], Oct. 17th. For James Fountaine E·q^r [from R. Eustace]. To be left at Howel's Coffee House in Great Wild Street, London. This letter is supposed to be design'd for the person, who writes from hence and who commonly signs Rogers, or sometimes Richards.

[1722], Oct. 18th. To Mr. Louis Clement at Mr Charie at the sign of the Dog and Duck in St James's Street, London. From Ronen. In French, signed C. C.

[1722], Oct. 19th. To Mr. Floyd at Mrs Wild's in Bennet Street St James. Cette lettre est marquée sur l'addresse par la poste, estre de Rouen.

1722, Oct. 21st. To Mr. Martin at the hat and Beavor, a Hatter's near the new Exchange in the Strand.

1722, Oct. 24th. To Mr. Wye in Wine Office Court, Fleet Street. N.B. this letter is by the same hand that signs Quittwell &c^a. Dated at Paris and signed Dorval.

1722, Oct. 26th. A Monsr La Tour chez Monsr Brailli chez un tapissier vis à vis St Joseph rue Mon Martre à Paris.

[No date.] For Mr Wilkins at Mrs. Brydges House at the Lumber House in Duke Street Westminster. Weds^d morn. 10 a Clock. Unsigned.

1722, June 29th. The examination of Walter Steeres gentleman taken [and sworn] before John Parnell Esqr one of the Judges of his Majesty['s] Court of King's Bench [in Ireland]. 3¼ folio pages.
The information is to the effect that in the previous July one John Steers an attorney living near Lincoln's Inn Fields, proposed to Major William Crosby, Gentleman of the Horse to the Duke of Chandos, to kill the King, and asked him what was the best method they should take to murder him *etc.*

[1722, July 28th]. Council Minutes in the handwriting of Lord Townshend. Undated.
[Present] Ld President—Ld Privy Seal—Duke [of] Roxburgh—Mr Walpole—Ld Cadogan.
That the visitours [Lady Bellew and others] who were seized with M^r [Dennis] Kelly this morning be discharged there being no papers of a treasonable nature found upon them.
Mr Mills the merchant who shipt the goods and [was] formerly in custody and Mr Drycote.
That a guard be placed at the house where Kelly is in custody.
Mr. Draycott [to be] examined and remanded into custody.
That the persons that were taken on board the ship and in Mark Lane be brought hither by water with their baggage and that they be here by ten of the clock in the morning.
Nothing to be stirred out of the ship.

1722, Augt. 20th. Hon. Edward Carteret, the Post Master General, to Lord Townshend. Dated at the G[eneral] P[ost] Office.
" My Lord—I have met with the enclos'd letter this afternoon amongst the letters which came into the office today from the country, which I thought it might not he a miss to send you, that you might have the perusal of it. It is dated from Billinsgate a place in the country not known in our office, Thursday last the 16th, and in the letter, says that Mr. Rogers and he went this morning to the mercer, whom he mentions to live beyond Hanover Square. The mention of the name of Rogers and the oddness of the letter induces me to send it you, and if it he of no consequence you will I doubt not have the goodness to excuse the

trouble, and return it me by the messenger, and I will forward it to night for France. I am " etc.

1722, Sept. 1st. An unsigned MS. of nine pages in book form, endorsed in Mr. Tilson's hand "Informations about designes &c." It begins :—"The person that communicated his observations last year has continued to have a watchful eye stil upon some particular persons, from whom he has made some discoverys, which would have been sent sooner if thought necessary : but such as they are you have them now." And ends :—" All matters seem to be at a stand but the papists [are] no ways baulked, tho' they think things will not be ripe before spring, at least they *seem* to think so."

[1722]. Extracts from Jacobite letters of this year. 9 pp.

[1722]. An alphabetical key to the cyphered names in the Jacobite Correspondence. 16¼ pp.

[1722]. Lists of Jacobite letters-that had been signed. 14 pp.

[1722]. Cypher keys to Jacobite names. 4 pp.

May 11th, 1723. "Le Connû" (a Government spy in Holland) to *George Tilson or to Anthony Corbiere?* In French. Unaddressed. [Translation]. "Sir,—I have the honour of your letter of April 26th. My enclosure to his Excellency contains one of those foreign letters, the contents of which have always been obscure to me, that it may well be that he is not too skilful, or that not having a high character he has no occasion to show his 'sçavoir faire.'

Here are two extracts from letters of Walkinshaw. In that from the Hague there was a song of which you have a copy here annexed. To-day Walkinshaw sent a copy of it to Hugh Paterson at Boulogne in France, he has also sent an abstract-copy to a certain Mr Waddel a Scotch student, and according to my opinion to have it printed there. "*I did destroy the paper with my own hand*" this is [i.e. refers to] that paper which Walkinshaw had tried to get printed here, and which I suspect to be concerning that sample.

In order to prevent those sort of papers being printed Mr D'Ayrolle [Dayrolles] would have nothing to do but to mention in conversation to the Deputy of the town of Leyden, in the Committee of the Dutch Raad, that one knew that ill-intentioned persons would try to get printed at Leyden pieces odious to the Government and in favour of the Pretender, and that they might be prevented if the Magistrats served orders on all the printers not to print in English flying sheets like this one, or at least not till they had shown the original to Mr Gouwan, the English Minister here, that he might see and examine it before hand. This Minister is a perfectly honest man and of the best intentioned for the Government, for I believe that he prints many little flying sheets in this country, and that they are sent into England to be dispersed there.

I am very respectfully—Sir—Your humble and very obedient servant.
LE CONNÛ "

The following copies, in Le Connû's handwriting, of two intercepted Jacobite letters were enclosed in the above.

(1). Extract. De Paris, 3 May 1723.—" I am sorry that the disappointments of these paper affairs should deprive us of the pleasure of seeing you here. I shall inform my self more particularly as to the affairs of the Canal and advise you and I am not without hopes of recovering your other affair. Mr Dundass his business with L: M : [*the Earl Marshal?*] goes but very slowly the people believe they will be able to clear all in time.

De   £1200 à 1205.   A. Alexander."

(2.) à Mr Walkinshaw.   Hague the 8th May 1723.

" Dr Sir—If this comes time enough to hand take care that Willie Hay may be as right as Kaperdish can make him and I shall repay you the favour at meeting. You can [ken] my meaning.

I did destroy the paper with my own hand and had all the others you sent for which I most heartily thank you, the inclosed will make amend for all my neglects. My good wishes to Mr Maul Mr Cunningham and Mr Morrow from—Your &c.

                          James Hamilton."

1724, July 4th. Petition of William Downham, of Bristol, to Lord Townshend Secretary of State ; recommended to his Lordship by Sir Abraham Elton and Henry Walter. .

[1724 ?] An undated petition of Jonathan Kelly of Dartmouth, and William Downham of Bristol, to George Prince of Wales. 16 pp.

The petitioners represent that they were the principal agents in discovering to Lord Townshend certain details (which they minutely specify) of " the late horrid bloody and unnatural conspiracie," and that they have only received a reward of £600 etc.

The last paragraph commences as follows :—

" That not being provided for his Majesty's service as was often really promised us, we are therefore brought under great inconveniences, only pityed by our friends and flouted at by the Jacobites. That being become their scorn and derision we cannot expect nothing else (some time or other) but to fall a Sacrifice to the furie of them. But our trust is in the God of Heaven who has hitherto defended Our Majestie King George and his Kingdom, from the vile attempts, and secret conspiracies of the Pope and a Popish Pretender, and we hope ever will. And as we are true subjects of his Majestic King George (the best of Kings) we doubt not but our actions will be duly considered, and countenanced, knowing his Majestic to be the great example of Europe in incouraging good actions."

1724-5, Jan. 14th. "A Memorial concerning the Highlanders Sheriefships Vassalages &c. of Scotland." Dated at Edinburgh and unsigned. Numbered (1). 7½ pp.

1724-5, Jan. 15th. A Memorial etc. with the same title, and in the same handwriting as the last. Dated at Edinburgh and numbered (3). 13 pp.

[No date.] A memorial entitled " Proposall ab^t the Highlanders." 5½ pp.

To the proposal are appended the following lists :—

(1.) Clans or tribes [that] were engag'd in the late Rebellion. Most of them are arm'd and committ depredations.

(2.) Clans belonging to superiours well affected to his Majesty. The Athol men, 2000, [and] The Broadalbin men, 1000, went into the Rebellion in 1715 without their superiours.

(3.) Clans in the late Rebellion and suppos'd still to be disaffected to his Majesty.

(4.) Roman Catholics in the Highlands.

(5.) List of the most considerable gentlemen who are well affected to His Majesty's Government.

(6.) Gentlemen inhabiting the Highlands of the Shire of Inverness said to be proper persons for executing the office of Justice of the Peace.

[1725.] Copy of a " Proposal for disarming the Highlands of Scotland." Unsigned and undated. 8 pp.

To this proposal is appended the following papers. The first is headed "Provision of money will be wanting for the purposes undermentioned," and endorsed "Services to be performed in the Highlands in the years 1725 and 1726." 1 p. The second is headed "Numbers of the Highlanders as they were estimated [in] 1715. At a mean calculation partly from the numbers actually in Rebellion and partly from different informations." This paper is as follows :—

In Argylshire including Lord Breadalbin's and the Laird of Calder's men (chiefly whig) about 4000.

Macleans in the Isle of Mull : the land belongs to the Duke of Argyl, the men for the most part Tory 600.

Stewart of Appin attainted, the land belonging to the Duke of Argyl, the men Tory 200.

Mackdonald of Glencoe, Torie 100.

Mackdonald of Keppock attainted, the men Torie 200.

Mackdonald of Glengarie, Torie 500.

Mackdonald of Klenronald attainted and the land belonging to the Duke of Argyl (Tories) 600.

Camerons belonging to Lochiel, in several places, Tories 800.

Mackleods Tories 600.

Seafort's Mackenzies Tories 1500.

Lovat and his Frazers whigs 600.

Grant and his followers at present Tories 800.

carried over 10500

Duke of Gordon and his followers Papists 1500.

Mackintoshes Tories 500.

Mackfersons Tories 400.

Duke of Athol, his followers and the Robertson Tories 1500.

Mackniel of Ranny Papists 100.

Mackinnon Tories 150.

Rosse's mixt Whigs and Tories 500.

Kilrawack and his Rosses, Whigs 200.

Munroe's Whigs 300.

Lord Rea 300.

Lord Sutherland 500.

[total] 16450.

Mem. There are several other Gentlemen on the borders of the Highlands who can influence a small number of men.

Earl Breadalbin in Perthshire 500.

Total according to this gross computation 16950

No date. " A projected Act abt [disarming] the Highlands." In 3 clauses. 4 pp.

No date. A Memorial concerning prosecutions begun in Scotland relating to what passed in September last in the towns of Dingwal and Nairn. 4 pp.

It begins :—" There being several contests at the late elections for Magistrates of the towns which are now represented in Parliament by

Colonel Monroe and William Stewart Esq."——and concludes, after
mentioning that Lord Lovat is likewise in the Indictments branded with
the imputation of several crimes without so much as being made a party
to the suit, by submitting that it would be for His Majesty's service if
His Majesty's Advocate should waive his suit by (as it is called in the
Law of Scotland) deserting the Diet simpliciter.

1726, April 22nd. Substance d'un projet qui fut donnée au Duc de
Riperda le mois de Fev^r dernier 1726. Endorsed " Substance d'un
projet pour le Prétendant. Madrid 22^d Av^l 1726, in Mr Stanhope's
$\frac{1}{2}\frac{1}{2}$ Ap^l." Unsigned and undated. The following translation accompanies this paper.

Substance of a project given to the Court of Spain in February
1726, N.S.

" After having reflected on the project which has been formed and
communicated to me, to burn the English men of war at Chatham, I
find many inconveniencys in the execution of it; and even thô it were to
succeed, yet it would have no effect for the advantage of the Pretender ;
because as there are at Chatham but part of the ships of England, the
rest being dispersed in the several Ports of that Kingdom, besides that,
by the Union subsisting between the King and the States General,
another fleet would soon be provided, such an expedition would only
serve to alarm all England, give them warning there to be more upon
their gard, and prevent the making any enterprise hereafter in favor of
the Pretender. I have another project to offer, which will infallibly
have the success of placing the Pretender upon the English throne, if
it be sure that the Emperor will sincerely join with the King; and this
is the substance of it.

1°. Instead of sending troops into Galicia, as was proposed, which
indeed would not fail to give uneasiness, by reason of the little need there
is of troops in that country, where there never used to be above two or
three battallions ; 12,000 men should be sent into Navarre out of such
Regiments as shall be chosen, and of which I shall give the names,
under pretence of providing for the security of the frontiers on that
side. These troops would be within reach of Guipuscoa, where
transport ships might be easily had, and the two men of war lately
built at Orogua might join the said transports in order to convoy them,
and on board of these I would put some arms, as knowing where they
are to be had.

2. I take it upon me to get six men of war armed in several Ports of
Brittany, provided with all necessary stores, men, provisions, &c.,
reserving to myself the naming of the officer that shall command that
Squadron. These ships shall be joined by those that shall go from the
Ports of Guipuscoa with the troops, and the whole shall be commanded
by the Duke of Ormond; I also offer myself to serve in that expedition
if the King thinks proper to employ me in it.

3°. The Emperor must have 6000 men ready to be embarked at
Ostend ; I shall take the necessary measures for their embarkment.
This matter must be kept very secret; and in order to prevent or retard
the discovery of this enterprise, as soon as the troops shall march to be
embark't, the letters must be stop't for two Posts together, and very
strict orders given on the frontier not to suffer any person to pass, nor
any courrier to go from Madrid.

4°. Two ships may likewise be sent away from Cadiz, on board of
which the Earl Marshall may go with arms which I shall put in those
ships. He shall go to Scotland, where the best part of the troops will,

MARQUESS
TOWNSHEND
MSS.

without doubt, be ordered to march into England, upon the first alarm occasioned by the descent; and then he will land with his arms and infallibly find the people ready to receive him.

5°. The Pretender must set out from Rome to Vienna to go to Ostend, and there go on board of one of the six ships which I shall have provided in Brittany. If his project be relished, and approved by the King of Spain, I shall propose the several means of putting it into practice, so as to make it succeed infallibly, &c.

6°. The three Mascovite ships, which- are now at St. Ander, may be employed in this expedition."

[1726?]. Project du Duc de Wharton pour rétablir le Prétendant. Unsigned and undated. The following translation accompanies this paper :—

The Duke of Wharton project to restore the Pretend[e]r.

The Pretender must go from Rome to Vienna *incognito*, and make a secret treaty with the Emperor and the King of Spain to give Minorca and Gibraltar to the latter, as soon as he shall be in possession of Great Britain ; and he shall not only guarantee to the Emperor the Ostend trade, but grant him the trade to the English Colonies, as well in the East as West Indies. From Vienna the Pretender shall go to Petersbourg, the Czarina being absolutely resolved to assist him. From thence he shall go to Archangel to be transported into G[reat] Britain with ten or twelve thousand men. The King of Spain must land 8000 men in England and make himself master of a Port, and that the Emperor shall send all the troops that shall be thought fit from the Port of Ostend, and shall, at the same time, march more troops into the Low-Countrys to hinder the Dutch from sending any assistance into England. The affair must be begun in Scotland which will quickly be in arms, the Pretender having arms in Spain, Britany, Holland ; and 2 millions of pounds sterling are ready in the hands of his friends in England, where they only wait for the Pretender's order to begin a general insurrection as well in England as in Scotland; and it is assured that in Scotland almost every body is in the Pretender's interest and ready to rise on his first order. The landing must be executed when the English Squadrons shall be abroad, and in case that opportunity cannot be laid hold of, it must be done in winter time when the ships are laid up.

April 10th, 1727. General (afterwards Field Marshall) Wade to Lord Townshend. In a secretary's hand, and signed by the General. Slightly torn. Dated in London and unaddressed.

"My Lord,—As you have been pleased to allow me the liberty to represent to your Lordship what I conceive to be necessary for His Majesty's service in North Britain, for securing the present peace of the Highlands on a solid and lasting foundation ; and to frustrate the designs of His Majesty's enemys who for the future may attempt to disturb the present tranquility of that part of the Kingdom.

Nothing can more effectually contribute to those ends than the proposals I had the honour to make of erecting new forts and barracks at Inverness and Killitruiman ; which His Majesty was graciously pleas'd to approve of. But I am sorry to acquaint your Lordship that notwithstanding my repeated representations of the necessity of carrying on these works, and of repairing the Castle of Edinburgh, and other fortresses in the South of Scotland, nothing has yet been effectually done (either in the one or the other) but repairing the old Castle of Inverness. . . . .

I hope your Lordship will likewise procure His Majesty's consent that an allowance may be made out of the contingencys of the army as was [done] the last year for carrying on the roads of communication. The great military way through the centre of the Highlands extending from Fort William to Inverness (50 miles in length) is now almost finished and made practicable for the march of troops, canon or other wheel carriage, and may be continued to Perth at a very moderate expence by the Regiments quartered in those parts.

I formerly took the liberty to represent to your Lordship that it would be of use if a small man of war were ordered to cruise on the West Coasts of Scotland, for if the Pretender should ever attempt to land arms or forces in that part of the Kingdom it will probably be on the West Coasts, which by my last intelligence has been already surveyed by a sea officer in the Spanish service sent thither for that purpose.

I had the honour to acquaint your Lordship by letter from Edinburgh the last year that I had information that four persons attainted for High Treason were returned to Scotland, viz' John Stuart of Innernitty, Alex' Robinson [sic for Robertson] of Strowan, Sir David Trepland of Fingask, and John Walkinshaw of Scots Town, in hopes of being permitted to make their submissions to His Majesty. . . . . . But if His Majesty does not see fit to receive their submissions and grant them his royal pardon, proper measures should be taken to chase them out of the country.

I begg leave to observe to your Lordship that as the Governour and Lieu' Governour of Edinburgh Castle are generally absent the Earl of Orkney by his attendance on His Majesty, and Brigadier Preston by his ill state of health, occasioned from the wounds he received [in] the last warr, the highest officer resident there is the Fort Major, who though an experienced officer is often indisposed by sickness and [is] decayed in his constitution. I therefore am humbly of opinion that it would contribute to the security of that important place if His Majesty would please to constitute a Deputy Lieu' Governour of known zeal and experience who would constantly reside in the Castle. The person who I should recommend as most proper for that employment is one Major Hardine formerly Major to Sir Charles Hotham's Regiment and who was Major to the Castle of Allicant when besciged by the Spaniards in 1708, which he defended with great resolution after the Governour and other his superior officers were blown up by the springing the mine of 1500 harrells of powder. This gentleman is now in Loudon, and has offerr'd to serve as Deputy Lieu' Governour without any sallary provided he may have the promise of succeeding Brigadier Preston in the Lieu' Government of the Castle when it may happen to become vacant.

I take the liberty likewise to recommend Coll° Cunningham as a proper person to be made Lieu' Governour of the Castle of Inverness ; he served with reputation in all the Campains of the two last wars in Flanders, but is now out of employment ; he is willing to reside constantly at Inverness where there has been no Governour since Col[onel] Clayton's departure to Gibraltar. An officer of experience will be usefull, in that part of the Highlands, as well to keep the country in a due subjection to His Majesty, as to forward the fortifications and barracks intended to be executed erected there.

I must likewise put your Lordship in mind of two persons I had the honour to mention to you, the one is the Lord John Murray, the eldest son of the Duke of Athol by his second marriage; he has been educated in England, is a youth of good parts, very desirous to serve in the army, and would be very well pleased with a Colours in the Foot Guards having very little to depend on. The other is the nephew and heir to the Laird of McIntosh, and will succeed him as Chief of that Clan; he has served for some years as Quarter Master in Coll^o Kerr's Dragoons who gives him a good character as well for his diligence in his station as for zeal he has allways shown to His Majesty and Government, and if he were encouraged (by being made Lieutenant of Foot) to continue in His Majesty's service he would in time be able to work a great alteration in the minds of that Clan whose disaffection has been so notorious.

When I had the honour to be last with your Lord[ship I took] the liberty to inform you, that the Moderator by order of [the *National*?] Assembly of the Kirk of Scotland had wrote a letter to [His Majesty forwar]ding the Petition of the Inhabitants of Maryburgh w[ho request that] his Majesty will be graciously pleased to allow them a sallary for the maintenance of a Minister to perform Divine service, and to educate their children. If His Majesty is pleased to grant their request 50^li per annum will be sufficient for that purpose, and if no other fund can be found to defray that charge it may be allowed out of His Majesty's annual bounty to the Kirk of Scotland for the support of itinerant ministers.

I have only to acquaint your Lordship that the Highlands continue in perfect quiet. The garrison Companys, as also those raised for [the service of the Highlands have been compleat ever since the 24th of February last, since which time the latter have been assembled at proper Stations, and ready to march to any part of the sea coasts, if occasion shall require. I am—My Lord—your Lordship's must humble and most obedient servant.

GEORGE WADE."

1727, May 16th. Copy of advices from the Camp before Gibraltar. In French. Unsigned. It concludes:—

" The day before yesterday the Duke of Wharton insisted on going to a Battery to show his Garter-Riband crying out a thousand times " Long live the Pretender," and using a quantity of bad language. They represented to him repeatedly that he ought to withdraw, but he refused to do so. At last he was struck by a piece of a shell on the toe. He had been drinking brandy, otherwise perhaps he would have been wiser. . . . . . If the English do not have pity on us we shall all have our beards grey before Gibraltar is taken. Plenty of persons have engaged to write otherwise but I would rather hold my tongue than write falsehoods."

1727, August 18th. Mons. La Roche to *Horatio Walpole*? Endorsed :—" In Mr Walpole's to Sr Robert Walpole." In French.

[Translation.] " Sir—I believe that you are sufficiently persuaded that there is nothing on foot in favour of the Pretender. The Bishop and O'Brien have both told me that there was some appearance that he would go to make a tour in Spain. There were frequently councils at the Bishop's where Mr Ruth always assisted and about three weeks ago the Bishop passed a whole day and night at Mr Ruth's. It is this which has given rise to someone belief that an interview with the Pretender took place—O'Brien also being absent for some days. O'Brien told me yesterday that there is a treaty concluded between Spain and France, and that the affairs of Europe were about to change

their aspect a good deal. I do not think that few persons are informed
of the place where the Pretender is. I believe that he has been at
Cologne and at Liege, and I am persuaded that he has been at
Connonges at Mʳ O'Roark's or at Commersi, and that so much the
more probable that I am persuaded that the journey of Mʳ Roark
to Vienna is [undertaken] on that subject, for he is one of the
most zealous Jacobites in the world, and one of the best fitted for
negotiations.

I have seen my Lord Blandford very often for a month past and
he continues to have his head very confused with all those affairs, and he
no longer thinks of returning to England. I supped last evening with
the Duke of Beauford and Lord Blandford and it seems that those two
Lords wish to make a grand intrigue together, for they often enough
have secret " teste à teste " conferences, and I find that Lord Blandford
is very pleased with the Duke.

The chief rumour current among the Jacobites is that Spain is
preparing an armament in favour of the Pretender. There are some
people here who affirm this with great positiveness but I believe it
would be unreasonable to pay the least attention to it: Above all [to]
a piece of news which took its origin in the head of the Chevalier Toby
Burck.

I hope, Sir, that I have not had the misfortune to displease you. The
apprehension that I have done so has given me all imaginable paine.
However I take the liberty to assure you that I act with zeal in this
affair and that I have neglected no occasion of arriving at a knowledge
of the things that I have thought useful to be known and to be communicated. I am resolved whatever happens always to continue to do
so. I commend myself to your goodness and protection and entreat
you to believe me with very profound respect—Sir—Your very humble
and obedient servant.

LA ROCHE."

" à Paris ce 18 d'Aoust 1727 a l'hotel d'hausbac [*Anspach ?*] rue
Jacobe."

1727, Augt. 19th. An Affidavit made by George McCaines at Portsmouth.

George McCaines Master of the Catherine of London this day arrived
from Havre de Grace in France, which place he left on Tuesday last,
who says it was there reported by people of good credit, that the Pretender in company with the German Embassador lately went to Versailes
and that the Pretender was two hours in private with the King of France,
after which he immediately took post chaise and in company with the
said Embassador went for Brussels.

Jurat' *etc.* Jnº Norris.   [Signed]   GEORGE MCAINES.

ACCOUNTS, ETC., FORMERLY BELONGING TO THE EARL OF
WILMINGTON.

1705–1728.

1705, Nov. 30th. A copy of a Warrant, from Prince George of
Denmark to his Treasurer and Receiver General Edward Nicholas, to
pay to Sir Isaac Newton and others a sum not exceeding £1100.

It begins :—" Whereas I have thought fitt to appoint the Honᵇˡᵉ
Francis Roberts Esqʳ, Sir Isaac Newton Kᵗ President of the Royall

Society, Sir Christopher Wren K^{nt} Her Majesties Surveyor Generall, M^{r}
John Arbuthnot and Mr David Gregory Professor of Astronomy in the
University of Oxon, to oversee and take care of the printing and
publishing of the observations of the Heavens for thirty years last
[past] by Mr. John Flamstead, with power to contract for printing and
publishing the same at my expense " . . . . .
This warrant is noted at foot :—" 25 Apr. 1707. Paid to Sir Isaac
Newton in part £375*l*. and incident charges, £9 7*s*. 6*d*.—£384 7*s*. 6*d*."

1705–1709. A bundle of Accounts, Inventories, and Valuations,
etc., formerly belonging to the Hon. Spencer Compton as Treasurer to
Prince George of Denmark. Some of these are quoted further on.

1707, March 17th. A coppy of the Warrant of His Royall Highness
Prince George of Denmark to Spencer Compton Esqre, Treasurer and
Receiver General of his Household and Revenue, to pay the Duke of
Argyle £431 for Colours drummers' coats &c.
" I doe hereby direct and require you that out of such moneys as are or
shall come to your hands by the receipt of any Revenue you pay or
cause to be paid to the Duke of Argyle or his assignes the sume of
four hundred thirty one pounds according to the bill hereunto
annexed. For which this with the acquittance of the said Duke of
Argyle or his assignes shall be your warrant. Given &c."
Same date. The Duke of Argyle's bill for the use of His Royal
Highness Prince George of Denmark's Regiment of Foot :—

	li.	*s.*	*d.*
For 26 drummers coats, wascoats and briches, stockings, shoes, shirts and cravatts 15^{li} each, 3 pair of Colours at 10^{li} each - - - -	420	0	0
Incidental charges -	11	0	0
[Total £] -	431	0	0

170$\frac{7}{8}$, March 12th. Major William Churchill to Spencer Compton.
" Sir—inclosed are the reasons which induced [the] Duke of Marl-
borough Duke of Argyle and Genl Churchill to beg his Royal Highness's
favour to his Regim^{t}, the Duke of Argyle is very uneasy till 'tis granted.
I this morning received the inclosed from his agent. I beg pardon for
this trouble and am " *etc.*
" State of the Prince's Regiment." Enclosed in the above letter.
" That upon the Revolution in 1688, the regiment of your Royal
Highness, late commanded by Gen^{ll} Churchill, now by his Grace the
Duke of Argyle, did most of them desert with new cloathing, which
upon their recruiting, being forced to be new cloath'd, occasion'd two
new whole cloathing in one year.
That when it came to Gen^{ll} Churchill it was left by Sir Theoph[ilus]
Oglethorpe above 500*l*. in debt.
That in Ireland there was 400 draughted from them with their new
cloathing, for which the said Regim^{t} was never reimbursed.
That during the time of small money, and the great deficiency on
tallies, the Regim^{t} being alwayes on service, the cloathing exceeded
the off reckonings in 5 years above 4000*l*.
That at the Battles of Landen and Hoghstet, the Regiment was almost
destroy'd being new cloathed.
These misfortunes occasion'd a great debt on the Regim^{t}, which by
management is above half of it reduced.

MARQUESS
TOWNSHEND
MSS.
—

But Her Majestic having been pleas'd to appoint a new method of clothing for the future, which cannot be comply'd with by his Grace of Argyle, without running the Regiment further in debt, unless Her Majestic, or your Royal Highness will be pleas'd to shew some favour to it.

'Tis therefore humbly pray'd your Royal Highness will be pleas'd to bestow on the said Regiment, the favour annually (till the Regiment is out of debt, which will be in three years) that your Royal Highness used to grant to Gen¹¹ Churchill every other year.

All which is humbly submitted."

PAPERS relating to the personal effects of the late Prince George of Denmark.

1709, June 9th. A Memorandum, signed by Lord De La Warr, Groom of the Stole to Prince George.

"There was alsoe taken out of the Prince's pocketts, vizt.:

A gold watch and seals, a gold tooth pin case, a gold tuisar case and 20 guineas. All these things were put into the Prince's scrutore that stood in the closett att Kensington, and I delivered both the key of the closett & scrutore to the Queen.

There was alsoe put into this scrutore att that time, a pair of diamond shoe buckles, and a diamond hat buckle.

There was also 2 diamond Georges and a gold George put into the Prince's strong box and his collar of SS with his enamelled George.

There was also 2 gold headed canes in his closett at Kensington.

There was alsoe 2 pair of diamond buttons which he constantly wore in his shirt sleeves which I delivered to the Queen.

There was alsoe 2 pair more of diamond buttons for his shirt which were in the Prince's own custody either in the scrutore or strong box as Mʳ Buckholt Informed me.

The was 2 Boxes of guilt dressing plate brought from Denmark whereof one was presented to the Queen, when Princess, the other was kept for his own use in his Bedchamber, when his Royal Highness was in health, & used to dress in his own side. This box consists of 24 pieces which was always kept by Mʳ Buckholt only, as being first barber, and when he att any time held the Prince's leave to goe to Denmark he delivered it over to Mr. Laroch as the Prince's second barber with a list."

1709, June 21st. A Memorial delivered to Queen Anne by [the Rᵗ Honᵇˡᵉ John Smith Esqʳᵉ and the Rᵗ Honᵇˡᵉ Sir Charles Hedges] the Administrators to his late Royall Higuness.

With this memorial are preserved the following exhibits :—

An appraismeut of the horses and mares of his late Royall Highness Prince George of Denmark, the 20ᵗʰ of June 1709. [Signed by John Willis and Robert Simcoke.] :—

Breeding mares.

					Prized at		
					li.	s.	d.
Grey Webb	-	-	-	-	30	0	0
Chesnutt Webb -	-	-	-	-	10	0	0
Charming Jenny has now 2 bone spavins				-	20	0	0
Pope Bess	-	-	-	-	25	0	0
Chesnutt Ramsdon	-	-	-	30	0	0
Bay Courant	-	-	-	-	50	0	0
Bay Scratch	-	-	-	-	35	0	0
A Bay filley 4 years old		-	-	-	12	0	0
Chesnutt Spot good for nothing -		-	-				

MARQUESS
TOWNSHEND
MSS.

Stallions.

Leeds	-	-	-	-	-	80	0	0
Dunn Arabian	-	-	-	-	-	60	0	0
Black Arabian	-	-	-	-	-	43	0	0
Honey Wood	-	-	-	-	-	30	0	0

Coach horses.

Sett of 7 Black Danish horses and I gelding (1 blind, 1 spavin'd, 1 bad eyes, 1 broken winded & good for little. The whole set at -	170	0	0
The sett of Danish bay mares and geldings (3 spavin'd, 2 blind.) The whole Set at	50	0	0
The leading set of English horses being 8	143	11	0
Three chaise horses - - - -	40	0	0

Hunters.

The brown Welley mare	-	60	0	0
A little Barb Stone horse, 23 guis	-	24	14	6
A little Barb nag - -	-	20	0	0

Padds.

A dunn padd - - -	-	7	0	0
The Doctor's nagg - -	-	12	0	0
One gray padd - -	-	29	0	0
The old dunn padd ⎫				
The Chiddle padd ⎬ - -	-	10	15	0
Old Ormond padd ⎭				

	Total	-	992	0	6

Valuation of the coaches. [Signed by Francis Kitson and Timothy Budworth.]

	li.		*d.*
His Royall Highness Body coach out of mourning valued at - - -	150	00	00
And old coach put into mourning for a Body coach valued at - - - -	40	00	00
The three end leading coach in mourning: and an old velvitt lining and a scatt cloth belonging to it valued at - - -	55	00	00
The chariott in mourning valued at - -	30	00	00
The old chaise in second mourning lin'd with a grey cloth valued at - -	10	00	00
The three old wagins valued at - -	15	00	00
The old sashmere valued at - -	06	00	00
The old chair valued at - - -	20	00	00

The valuation of the Prince's silver plate. [Signed by Richard Adams and Pierre Platel.]

Note. The total weight is stated as 10329 oz. 12 dwt., and the total value at £2681 17*sh.* 5½*d.* The highest value set on any pieces being 5*sh.* 4½*d.* per oz., and the lowest 4*sh.* per oz.

Arms belonging to his late Royall Highness valued the eighth day of June 1709 by Thomas Wright, Master of the Gunmakers' Company, Francis Phillipps, Warden, John Shaw sen^r and Andrew Dolep.

	£		
Item. Twenty pair of pistolls valued at three pounds a pair - - - -	60	0	0
Item. Ten pair of pistolls at one pound a pair -	10	0	0
Item. Four pair of pistolls at seven shillings and sixpence a pair - - - -	1	10	0
Item. Eight mortar peices at one pound a peice -	8	0	0
Item. Fifteen wheellock guns at one pound a piece - - - - -	15	0	0
Item. Sixteen bullet guns at one pound fifteen shillings apeice - -	28	0	0
Item. Eighteen ordinary guns at one pound five shillings apeice - -	22	10	0
Item. Six double guns at ten pounds apeice	60	0	0
Item. Two wind guns at five pounds apeice -	10	0	0
Item. Twenty four guns at three pounds ten shillings apeice - - -	84	0	0
	£299	0	0

A barge belonging to his late Royall Highness deceased valued the 16th day of June 1709 by John Loftus and Robert Mason.

Item a twelve oar'd barge and glasses and oares -   130   0   0.

Item. These exhibitants declare that the plate belonging to the bed chamber of his late Royal Highnes and which was in constant use there was appraised at 93. 5. 9¾. but was claimed by the R^t Honble the Lord Delawarr who was Groome of the Stole to his late Royall Highnes as a fee and perquisite of his office and as such was delivered to him.

Item. These exhibitants declare that the coaches chaises carriages chaires saddle and coach horses, breeding mares and stallions and all other things belonging to his late Royall Highnes's stable were claimed by the R^t Honble the Earl of Bridgewater who was Master of the Horse to his late Royall Highnes as a fee and perquisite of his office and as such have been delivered to him.

Item. These exhibitants do declare that the barge belonging to his late Royall Highnes was claimed by Christopher Hill who was Barge-master to his late Royall Highnes as a fee and perquisite of his place and as such was delivered to him.

[1709 ?]. Duke of Argyll to Spencer Compton. Unaddressed and undated.

" Sir—You know when I came to command his late Royall Higness Prince George's regiment of foot [the 3rd Buffs] the board of gen^{ll} officers found that Gen^{ll} [Charles] Churchill had left the regim^t £3858 in that debt to Major [William] Churchill and Mr Harnege on the clothing acc^t. The Duke of Marlborough was acquainted with it and for accommodating the matter on their application his Royall High-ness was pleased in place of the £200 he gave yearly for clothing the drums and hautboys of his regim^t in his livery to allow £430 p annum for that untill the above mentioned sum of £3858 should be paid the regim^t being to be clothed new and the first £430 being paid from your office last year I desire you'l oblige me by acquainting my Lord Treasurer herewith and pray the favour of him to speak to Her Majesty to ordere the paym^t of the £430.

Your favour herein in will oblige Sir &c.

ARGYLL."

1712, March 31st. Sir John Stanley to Spencer Compton. Dated at the Cockpit, and unaddressed.

" Sir,—Her Majestie having been pleased to referr my Lord Chamberlain the inclosed peticon of Mr Hill, master of the barges to his late Royall Highness [Prince George of Denmark], his Grace desires you to inform him what allowance was made to Mr Hill out of your office for repairs of the barges, barge-house, &c., and to what time paid. Also to inform him whether the Prince's barges do now belong to her Majestie, or [can be] claimed as a fee by any of his officers, or any other person. I am with respect—Sir—your most obedient and most humble serv^t

J. STANLEY."

1715-1723. Abstract of the expences of His R. Highness [the Prince of Wales'] Household [for every month] from Oct. 1st 1715 to Septr 30th 1722. On a sheet in tabular form.

A similar abstract from 1st Oct. 1715 to 1st Oct. 1723.

With the above abstracts are several other papers and accounts, most of which are undated and of no great interest, relating to the Prince of Wales' Household.

In an undated paper headed " An Establishment for Richmond House," which begins " Mr Carter the gardner for the whole charge of the gardens 210*li* p aun.," there is entered " The Black [a] Moor in the menagery 8*li* p ann. [and] 6*s.* board wages' p week. Totall 23. 12. p ann."

From another paper it appears that Mrs Margarett Purcell in 1718 was housekeeper of His Royal Highness's House in Leicester Fields at a salary for herself and her servants of £100.

1720–1722. Accounts of [and letters to] Spencer Compton as Treasurer to the Prince of Wales.

1723-1728. The following papers relate to the Duchy of Cornwall, and formerly belonged to Mr. Compton as Treasurer of the Duchy.

1723, April 16th. Edward Trelawny to *Capt. Rogers ?* Unaddressed and apparently a copy in a clerk's hand.

" Sir,—Haveing the hon^r to dine with the Judges at your Assizes, I took that oppertunity to more my Lord Eyres for a farm [*qu.* a lease of mining rights ?] in fav^r of the tinners; his lordship seemed very well pleased with it, and with an uncommon earnestness encourag'd me to endeavour a petition in order thereunto from the tinners, saying it was not theires but our business to petition which if I would forward in the contrary [*sic*], his lordship assured me, he would promote it above with his utmost interest, and doubted not of bringing it to a happy conclusion.

Soon after I did my self the honour to write to my Lord Falmouth [Lord Warden of the Stanneries] in it, for his lordship's direction; whose answer now lies before me in these words. I am very well pleased, that you or any other gentleman, should use their utmost endeavours for a farm; which no man living more earnestly desires than my self.

I need not tell you how hardly the tinners are dealt with by the merchants; and you are so much interested in this affair, and have the interest of your contrary [sic] so much at heart, that I flatter my self, you will not only approve of my endeavours for the common good, but will promote it among your neighbours with your utmost zeal.

I therefore make it my request to you, that you would give me your opinion (who have been so lon[g] experienc'd in forwarding farms for many yeares last past) whether this will be most properly promoted by a generall meeting of the best adventurers; or by a Petition drawn in form and circulated through the county for subscriptions; which together with your pardon for this trouble, will be very welcome to Sir —Your humble serv[t],

ED. TRELAWNY."

1723, April 22nd. William Pendarves "To the Hon[rd] Col. Godolphin Member [of] Parl[t] at his house in Scotland Yard—Whitehall." Dated at Pendarves.

" Hon[rd] Sir—Thursday last at our half Quarter Sessions at Penzance a letter was there communicated to us by Cap[t] Rogers a coppy of which is inclosed. We came to the resolution that we would make application to some of the Prince's Councell to know ir what manner his Royal Highness will be address; whither by the Lord Warden [of the Stanneries] or any other way, if you would give your self the trouble to ask the Speaker his thoughts thereon, and let me know them it will be a great obligation on this country, and if we can bring it to a conclusion, will rivet his Highness['s] int[erests] so in the hearts of our country men; as no other favour can parcel. If for any reason you do not think fit to grant this request, you may please to communicate to any [of] our country men (the enclosed) who you may perchance meet.—I am—Sir your obliged humble servant

WILL PENDARVES.

[P.S.] Pay the inclosed to my wife."

1723, April 27th. Colonel Sidney Godolphin to Spencer Compton. Dated at Whitehall and unaddressed. Endorsed in Spencer Compton's hand " Sidney Godolphin—Apl. 27th 1723—Tin-Farm."

" Sir—I beg leave to trouble you with the inclosed, and that I may wayte on you at your coming to towne to receive your commands I am—Sir—Your most obedient servant

S. GODOLPHIN."

1723, Sept. 25th. The most humble Petition of William Munday —To the High and Mighty Prince George Prince of Wales Duke of Cornwall &c :—

Sheweth—That your Petitioner hath been Chief Clerk in your Royal Highnesses Auditor Gen[ls] Office ever since the establishment thereof, And was many years before in the Auditor's Office for your Dutchy of Cornwall, and was sworne Deputy therin at your Highnesses new granting the said office to M[r] Bertie. And your Petitioner hath likewise acted in your Survey[r] Gen[ls] Office as Chief Clerk, all the time that M[r] [Samuel] Travers [late M.P. for S[t] Mawes] held the same, and is now continued by Mr. [Walter] Cary the present Surveyor Gen[l] . . . . .

That for all these services your Pet[r] doth not receive from your Royal Highness any salary or yearly fee whatsoever, nor from any of his principals, but M[r] Bertie, who pays him 40[li] p ann. only : And his perquisites are so small in all the said Offices, that your Petitioner is

unable to support himself and family without your Royal Highnesses
bounty towards him, *etc.*

Endorsed : " Referr'd to his Royal Highness's Council the 25th Septr
1723," and minuted at foot:—It is his Royal Highnesses pleasure that
this Petition be referr'd to the consideration of his Royal Highness's
Council ; and that they do report their opinion to his Royal
Highness what gratification it may be reasonable to allow for the
extraordinary services mentioned therein.

S[AMUEL] MOLYNEUX.

1724, April 29th. The Memorial of Wm Munday Deputy Auditor of
the Dutchy of Cornwall relating to the Accounts of Robert Corker Esqr
Receiver General thereof. Addressed " To the Rt Honble Spencer
Compton Esqr His Royal Highnesses Treasurer and Receiver General."
2 pp.

From this Memorial it appears that " the Ipsum " of the Dutchy Receiver's Account for the year ended at Michelmas was £21,807. 12. 5¼.

1724, May 18th. The second Memorial of Wm Munday Deputy
Aud[ito]r of the Dutchy of Cornwal relating to the Accounts of
Robert Corker Esqr Rec[eive]r Gen[era]l thereof.

. . . . . "The remains of the Ipsum of his Accounts to and for
the Year ended at Michaelmas 1721, according to my former state is
3,257l. 12s. 6½d."

" In all in the Recr Genl's hands due to his Royal Highness to
Michaelmas last 16,884l. 10s. 11¾d."

" 1724, Dec. 16th. Nicholas Vincent to Spencer Compton. Dated at
Chelsea and unaddressed. Endorsed by the Speaker " Mr Vincent's
letter relating to the Sheriff of Cornwall."

The writer states that he has received a letter from Mr Samuel
Philips complaining of ill health, and begs Mr Compton to prevail with
his Royal Highness to name Thomas Long of Penheale his Sheriff
of Cornwall, for the ensuing year, instead of Mr Philips.

1725, April 7th.—Monsr Bruuand to " The Right honourable Spencer
Compton Treasurer to his Royal Highness the Prince of Wales—In St
James—London." Dated at Bordeaux.

The writer advises his Highness's Treasurer as to drafts he has drawn
for wines bought for the Prince's use. From his figures it appears that
the then rate of exchange between England and France was then about
3s. 2d. per écu of 3 francs.

" £200 at 37¾ p. v. making in French money frs. 3814·10." The
letter concludes :—

" I did not draw all at once as Mr Powell writes me you wished I had
done but I durst not do it before the wines were ready to go aboard.
However [I] am glad that what remained to draw was but little at this
high rate of exchange, it being started up in one post from 37¾ to 38⅝
& ½ yeasr 38¾ never have I seen the like, nor monneys so scarce ;
that we may thank the famous system of Mississippi for. I subscribe
[myself] with submission " *etc.*

1725, July 3rd. J. Collier " To The Right Honourable Sir Spencer
Compton Speaker of the House of Commons." Sir—I have sent the
farther bill to Mr Andrews for your honor—and would humbly presume
to begg your Honor's favourable recomandation of the item in my former
bill which is left in blank. I am sure from your owne justice and
generosity considering my Extroadnary paines and service in the affair
there is noe occation to mention it but that it may not slipp your mind,
I am Sr—Yor honors most obedient humble servt,—J. COLLIER."

1725, Oct. 9th, N.S.   William Rollinson to Sir Spencer Compton. Dated at Bordeaux and unaddressed. 3 pp.

The writer discusses the merits of various wines and the prospects of the approaching vintage. Begs his correspondent's acceptance of a barrell of grapes which he is sending by Capt⁰ Henry Beach of the Bordeaux Merchant. " Twenty-four hours more wet before the grapes are cut must infalibly spoil the whole sans resource. I am therefore so far at present from saying what sorts may be most proper this year for His Royal Highness, that 'tis impossible for me to imagine whether any wine in this province can be found worth bringing into England. . . . . I have this day drawn upon you for 2903 : 1 : Livres, at 38⅞ per French Crown, £156. 14. 11. sterling, payable to the order of Mʳ Robert Gordon at two [months ?] usance, being the amount of five tons of wine according to the enclosed invoice . . . . . ."

Note.—From this letter it appears that the claret supplied to the Prince of Wales's household cost about thirty guineas a tun, that the value of the French *livre* at this date was nearly thirteen pence, and that the exact value of the French *écu* of three livres was 38⅞ pence.

1725, Dec. 13th.   Nicholas Vincent, " To William Munday Esq. at his House in Grovesnor Street near Hanover Square—London." Dated at Truro.

" Mr. Munday—I receiv'd yours last Saturday, and though I have no objection to the characters of the persons whose names you sent me, yet I think it would be more for the service of the Government, that John Collins of Treworgan Esqʳᵉ should be appointed Sheriff for the ensuing year, and therefore hope he will be nominated accordingly. I desire you will present my humble service to that Gentleman who commanded you to write the letter and am—your friend and servant,

                                              Nic. Vincent."

1726, April 17th.   Sidney Godolphin to Sir Spencer Compton.— Dated at Thames Ditton in Surry, and unaddressed.

" Sir, Haveing (beyond expectation) survived the winter I am not without hopes of liveing a little longer, in order to which I don't know anything that can contribute more effectually then his Royall Highnesses's grace and favour.

I am told Mʳ Vincent (if liveing) is in a verry ill state of health. Upon Mr. Godolphin's death be succeeded him in the place of scymaster [? Assay-master] of the stannerys. I did then with all humility address my self to your Honour (who I am proud to call my Patron) to recomend me to the Prince's favour on that ocation which I now again do if you approve of this the most humble request of— Your most faithfully devoted and obedient servᵗ.

                                              S. Godolphin."

1726, July 1st.   Lord Falmouth, Lord Warden of the Stannaries, to Sir Spencer Compton. Dated in London and unaddressed.

" Sir—I take the liberty to lett you know, that att two this morning Mʳ Vincent dyed, by whose death the office of essny master is vacant in the gift of His Royall Highness. If itt would be His Royall Highnesse's pleasure to bestow that office on Samuel Foot Esq., who lives constantly in the Country, is knowing in these affairs, and has ever been steady to the interest of the royall fameleye itt would allsoe enable me to be very usefull, in severall corporations, which to be permitted to be (to His Royˡ Highness) is my utmost ambition, but this must be as (he pleases) and it must be told Him or not as you please, att least you will pardon this, from him that is most truly Sir—Your very scall [? speciall] humble servant.

FALMOUTH."

172⅖, Feb. 2nd. Robert Mann "To Mr Andrews at the Right Honble Sr Spencer Compton's—These."

" Sir—A vacancy being likely to happen in a very little time here, I think it my duty to let my great Master know it, and being confin'd to my room, where I have been more then ten dayes, thought none so proper to tell him of it as yourself—'tis Mr Astells [Post of] Controller of the cole yard ; the sallery 30ll pr ann, diet coles and candles, with a pretty little lodgeing fit indeed only for a single man. He sells the College coles by contract and delivers out all candles and by that means serves all the offices with both cole and candle. In a word in my opinion 'tis to a man that will be here and mind his business a good 100ll a year. Formerly the Wardrobe was enext to this and Pope the present Wardrobe Keeper is in a very bad way and had he dy'd first Astall was to have had both (as I have heard) and then it would be twice as good and two very good lodgeings, and indeed the first establishment runs for one man to both places, and since my time one Heeler had them both. If you please to let his Honor know this and with humble duty, you'l oblege me. I don't Care to pressume to write this bussey time to him, but you'l believe me—Sir your most humble servant.

ROB. MANN."

[P.S.] Interest is making by some [who] will make the Speaker believe its worth a very triffle but mine is a true state of the matter.

PAPERS RELATING TO THE TOWER OF LONDON.
1712 to 1719.

.1712, April 1st. Petition of Thomas Cornelius, Master Gunner of the Town to the Earl of Northampton. Assigned and Endorsed " Capt Cornelius's Petition."
The petitioner thinks it his duty to acquaint his lordship that yesterday when putting the guns in order on Evan's Battery Mr Eustace, Mr Gibson, and Mr Musgrove that assists the Surveyor came there and "without any provocation the said Mr Musgrove grew very passionate and did not only villifie and degrade your petitioner with very bad language but also struck your petitioner severall times while upon his post and duty as aforesaid and the other two held your petitioner that he could not defend nor helpe himself " etc.

[1712.] Another Petition of the same to the same; unsigned and dated.
Humbly Sheweth.—That it hath been an antient custome for the Master Gunner of the said Tower to be empowered by Warrant from the Rt Honrtl the Constable of the said Tower to demand and receive a smale matter of money for tole or warffidg for landing of goods at and carrying goods from Iron Gates stayres adjoining to Tower Wharff in the Tower liberty . . . . .
Humbly prayes your Lordshipp will please to graunt your petitioner the like Warrant.

1712, April 2nd. Humphry Brent "To the Rt Honble George Earl of Northampton att his house in Bloomsbury Square." Franked " Walpoole," and bearing the impressed Post Office stamp " Post-payd,

Peny." Endorsed " Mr Brent's Letter concerning the Commissioners of Sewers."

" My Honoured Lord . . . . . . I have acted as Clerk of the Sewers for about seven years . . . . about four months agoe there was a Petition lodged att my Lord Keeper's (which still lyes before him) under the hands of the Sheriffe Cass, Mr Justices [i.e. Deputy Lieut^s of the Tower Hamletts] Tyssen Brattle Frampton Johnson Kyrby and others. With the list of Commissioners [of Sewers] which my Lord Abingdon was so kind to deliver for me to my Lord Rivers, the same having been first approved of by the Sheriffe and Mr Baron [Robert] Price [of the Exchequer] who had sent me before to renew the Commission as being much concerned himselfe to have it done, because his estate at Wapping which is considerable (as well as the estate of many others) suffers very much by the foulness of the Sewers in those parts, But my Lord Rivers being expected to be moved from his Government of the Tower 'twas thought adviseable to defur renewing the Commission till that Post was filled . . . . . . I humbly beg your Lordship's pardon for this trouble as well as leave [to] subscribe myselfe (with the utmost defference and respect)—My honoured Lord, etc.

HUMPH: BRENT."

1712, April 11th. John Hales and David Crauford (two of the Commissioners of Chelsea Hospital) to the Earl of Northampton. Dated at Chelsea.

The writers beg that the bearer, Mr Crispe, may be continued as agent for the 3 Invalids Companies in the Tower, to which post he was appointed by his Lordship's predecessor, the Earl Rivers.

1712, June 7th. Sir Stephen Fox " To the R^t Honble the Earl of Northampton. Dated at Chiswick, and endorsed " Sir St. Fox's letter recomending Henry Bowman."

" My noble Lord,

I was earnestly desired to put this Petition into your Lordship's hands by a person that was recommend'd to me very earnestly and by his stern look [he] seems very fitt f,r the imployment he desires, there will be good security given for his faithfull performance of that office the Petitions for which I leave to your Lordship's judgement and remain,

My noble Lord,
Your Lordship's
Most affectionate and humble servant,
ST^E: Fox."

[1712]. The Earl of Northampton's case as to the Custos Rotulorum of the Tower Hamletts. Undated.

The Tower and Liberty and Precinct thereof hath an antient Court of Record for tryall of all actions there, and a Court Leet, and by a Charter in King James the 2^d there are Justices and Sessions of the Peace peculiarly and restrictive from those of Middlesex.

The Hamletts of the Tower are not in the Liberty or Precincts but are in the County of Middlesex and the inhabitants have bin formerly by orders of Councell exempted from appearing at the Sessions for the county in respect of their duty to attend and guard the Tower when required and the Trained Bands of the Hamletts were antient and their rights are reserved in the Militia Act of 13, 14, 15 Car. 2^d from which time the Chiefe Governo^r of the Tower hath bin. (by Comission) Lord Leut^t of the Hamletts and all other places incorporated and priviledged within the limitts and Precincts of the Tower or Hamletts and hath made Deputy Lieuf^ts as in other countys.

The Earl of North[amp]ton's Comissions of Lieuftenancy and Custos Rotulorum are of the Hamletts of the Tower and place incorporated and priviledged within the limitts or Precincts of the Tower or Hamletts with a clause in the Comission of Custos to return to the Sessions of Peace of the Tower Liberty, all writts precepts processes and indictm^ts there to be determined.

But there are noe particular Comissions, Sessions or Clerke of the Peace for all the Hamletts as there are for the Liberty and tho' the Earle of North[amp]ton be Custos Rotulor[um] of both Hamletts and Liberty, yet the Justices and Clerke of the county continue to execute their Office in the Hamletts as in the other parts of the county. Soe that at p^rsent his Lordship's grant of Custos Rotulor[um] of the Hamletts is of noe use to him.

1712, June 13th. A list of the new Commissioners of Sewers [for the Tower Hamlets]. In duplicate, in the handwriting of Humphrey Brent. One copy is endorsed " List of the Commissioners of Sewers for the Tower Hamlets," and the other is endorsed " List of the Commissioners of Sewers given to my Lord Keeper. June 13th 1712."

The R^t Honble Simon Lord Harcourt, Baron of Stanton Harcourt, Lord Keeper of the Great Seal of Great Brittain : The R^t Honble Robt Earl of Oxford and Mortimer, Lord High Treasurer of Great Brittaine : The R^t Honble George Earl of Northampton Constable of her Majesties Tower of London : The R^t Honble Richard Earl Rivers, Master of the Ordnance : The R^t Honble Montagu Earl of Abingdon : The R^t Honble Mr Baron Price : Sir Edward Northey her Majesties Attorney generall ; Sir Robert Raymond her Majesties Solicitor Generall : The Honble James Bertie Esqre [and] Hugh Smithson Esqre [M.P.'s for Middlesex] : Sir Samuel Garrard, Sir William Leman, [and] Sir Nathaniel Barnadiston, Bar^ts : Sir John Lake, Sir Henry Johnson, Sir John Parsons, Sir Jonathan Andrews, Sir Thomas Davall, Sir Edward Betenson, Sir William Benson, [and] Sir James Etheridge, Kn^ts : [Alderman] John Cass, William Gore, Francis Tyssen, John Ward, William Johnson, Alexander Peudarvis, Uvedale Price, William Bridges, Simon Harcourt (Clerk of the Crowne), Thomas Chamber, William Parker of Hackney, William Northey, Daniel Brattell, Paul Dockmanique, Samuel Benson, Thomas Frampton, Bastwick Johnson, Robert Kyrby, Alexander Ward, Sherman Godfrey, Robert Thornhill sen^r, Robert Thornhill jun^r, Nathaniel Manlove, Charles Cæsar, Thomas Blackmore, Joseph Short, Felix Feast, John Metcalfe, Ephraim Beauchamp, Henry Hunt, Samuel Brewster, Joseph Moxon, Edward Ambrose, Joseph Jorye, Alexander Pitfield, Robert Doyley, John Dorrell, Humphrey Parsons, Samuel Twinn, Richard Beauvoir, John Smart, Daniel King, William King, James Walker, Clare Windham, Thomas Wright, and William Wright, Esquires : Dr Richard Welton, [Rev.] John Wright Cler[k], Dr Richard Mead, Peter Monger, Edmond Noble, John Silk, Thomas Bacon, William Jewell, William Blakewey, Edward Lee, John Goreum, Richard Byrom, Capt John Hazelwood of Wapping, Henry Mulcaster, Henry Whitehand, John Warner of Spittlefeilds, Philip Shepheard, Stephen Hall, Charles Boone, John White, Thomas Bateman, Timothy Thornbury, John Bateman, Robert Dennett, Henry Marshall, William Benwes, Capt John Merry, Thomas Preston, Samuel Skinner, John Blackhall, Alexander Weller, John Kirby, Robert Bird, Richard Mount, Thomas Sargeaunt, Ralph Harwood, John Hawkins, Capt Thomas Wharton, Joseph Wilmot, Capt John Haselwood of St Barthol[omew] the Great. — [All the above gentlemen are] off the Quorum.

[Those whose names follow are] not of the Quorum—James Spagg, Daniel Taylor, Thomas Webb, Samuel Groome, Robert Stephens, Massey Owen, John Elderton, Thomas Cooke, Charles Venner and Art[hur] Stephens, gent[lemen.]

1712, June 17th. J. D. Crispe (Secretary to the Commissioners of Chelsea Hospital) to the Earl of Northampton. Dated at the Royal Hospital near Chelsea.

The writer encloses a copy of her Majesty's instructions to the Lords and others Commissioners of Chelsea Hospital.

[1712, June]. The humble Petition of Henry Bowman to Sir Stephen Fox. Undated.

The place of goal-keeper of the Tower-Court being in the gift of the Earl of Northampton, and not in the gentleman porter of the Tower, and Mʳ Steward [Robert] Thornhill having regulated many abuses committed by the Deputy-goaler, who is not duely admitted to the said Imployment, the Petitioner begs the favour of a recommendation to the Earl of Northampton to admit him into that office.

[1712, June]. The humble Memorial of the same to the same. Undated.

SHEWETH—That he having humbly petitioned your Honoᵣ to present him to the Right Honoᵇˡᵉ the Earl of Northampton, to be goale-keeper of the prison bolden for the Tower Court . . . long since informed relating to that station that goale-keeper, and returne-brevium, is one and the same place: returning all the process sent by the Sherriff, when executed in his Lordship's Precincts.—Therefore most humbly prays your Honoᵣˢ farther favour to prevaile with his Lordship to gran̄. his Warrant directed to Robert Thornhill Esqᵣ, Steward of the Court for the Tower Liberty: that your Petitioner may be settled in the said imployment.—And as in duty bound, etc.

1712, July 26th. J. Blount to Humphrey Brent. Endorsed " Copy of Blount's letter to Mᵣ Brent to go with the Deputy Lieuˡᵗ to Windsor."

" Sir,—Since we parted I have hired 2 three end coaches with 6 horses each at 2ˡⁱ each coach. I have paid 10ₛ. earnest and the rest to be paid after the journey is perform'd. The man's name is Blunt and [he] lives at the upper end of the Hay Market Pickadily. The coaches will be at the Exchange at the hour appointed but my Lord being determin'd to go out of town to-morrow I am oblig'd to wait upon his Lordship into the country so cannot attend the Lieutenancy to Windsor so must desire you will defray all the charges as I should have done had I been there. I am &c.

                                                                            J. B.

        To Mᵣ Brent."

1712, July 26th. Humphrey Brent " To Mr. Blunt or in his absence to Mᵣ Hewett att the Rᵗ Honᵇˡᵉ the Earl of Northampton's in Blooms-bury Square. Endorsed " Mᵣ Brent's letter in ansᵣ to Blount that he could not do as desired."

" Sir—I do not intend to returne from Windsor with the coaches but to hire a chaise to carry me directly to Reading tomorrow night and to further [sic] in Berkeshire to bring up my spouse who is there. So that I must desire you to order Mᵣ Hewitt or some other person to discharge the coach-hire which has been always done by the Clerk and for which you have an order. This Charge as well as other incident

MARQUESS
TOWNSHEND
MSS.

charges will be satisfyed out of the first trophy money collected. I can't tell how you can excuse yourselfe from going this journey, for you know the gentlemen must be provided for, when they come to Windsor, and I am sure you'd not think it either reasonable or proper for me to be concerned in this affaire since I am not as yett so much as appointed Deputy Clerk nor do I know whether I ever shall [be], and besides the care of this affaire was left you know wholly to you by the gentlemen which I doubt not on a second thought you'l take care not to sufferr any failure in I am—Sir—

Your most humble serv
H. BRENT."

1712, Oct. 21st. Humphrey Brent to the Earl of Northampton. Addressed " To the Rt Honble George Earl of Northampton—Present," and endorsed " Mr Brent's letter with excuses for not going with the Deputy Lieuts to Windsor."

The writer expresses his regrets that he should have fallen under his Lordship's displeasure, either from a letter he wrote to Mr Blunt [on July 26th] or from not sooner paying his duty to his Lordship. He prays for forgiveness and explains his inadvertency. The letter concludes:—

" From all which, my Lord, I beg leave to say that I do not so much sollicite your Lordship for the Deputy Clerkeship of the Lieutenancy (tho' I should even in that post be proud of serving your Lordship and the gent[lemen]) as to reconcile myselfe to your Lordship's favour, which if you please to grant me will not only be an argument of your Lordship's great lennity and goodness; but of convincing me how much I am.—My honoured Lord.—Your Lordship's most dutifull and most obliged humble servt.

HUMPH. BRENT."

1712, Oct. 22nd. Minutes taken by Humphrey Brent " Att a Court of Lieutenancy held for the Tower Hamletts att the Rummer Taverne in Whitechappell on the 22d day of October Anno Domini 1712 " :—

Present—Sir John Cass Knt, William Northey Esqre, Thomas Hardwick Esqre, Thomas Frampton Esqre, Edmond Noble Esqre, John Blackhall Esqre, John Elderton Esqre, Thomas Blackmore Esqre, Sir Samuel Clerke Knt., Robert Kirby Esqre, William Nicholas Esqre, Samuel Skinner Esqre, Thomas Preston Esqre, Peter Monger Esqre, George Tourville Esqre, Stephen Hall Esqre. [Deputy Lieutenants].— In the chair Sir John Cass Knt.

THE Rt Honble George Earl of Northampton Lord Lieutenant of the said Hamletts having this day by Sir John Cass Knt recomended to this Court Humphrey Brent Gentleman to officiate as Clerk in the absence of Mr Hewett Clerk to the Lieutenancy the said Humphrey Brent was accordingly unanimously elected and declared Clerk and is appointed by this Court to officiate as Clerk in the said Mr Hewett's absence.

ORDERED that the severall Companyes of the two regiments of the Militia for the Tower Hamletts which are at present commissioned be forthwith ticketted and that the rolls of each Company together with a duplicate of the same be brought in by the severall Captains to the next Lieutenancy to be holden at the place abovesaid on Monday next att two of the Clock in the afternoon in order to be approved off and signed by them and that Major Thomas Hardwick and Major Thomas Kemp do forthwith give the necessary orders to the severall Captains of their respective Regiments accordingly.

ORDERED that all such orders as shall from time to time be issued forth by authority of this Court to the respective Majors of the two regiments be signed by three of the Deputy Lieutenants att least.

ADJOURNED to the place abovesaid to
Monday next att two a clock.

[1712?]. Petition of Ellinor Calverly to the Earl of Northampton. Unsigned and undated.

Sheweth—That your Petitioner hath given credit to the men doing duty here, the sum of seven hundred pounds : the officers haveing receiv'd no pay (although haveing done twelve months duty) your Petitioner being involv'd in dept and brought to the last extreamity by giveing credit to above halfe the garrison wee all expecting your Lordship's takeing possession of the garrison, do hope for your Lordship's favour in this our deplorable condition. Otherwise both officer, soldier and sutler must come to utter ruine.—Your Petitioner most humbly prays your Lordshipp will be pleas'd to give us your letters to the Lord High Treasurer, and that the Company's doing duty here may be establish't and paid, whereby the officers may be kept from starving as well as the men and sutlers from goales, and falling into utter destruction.

[1712?]. Petition of Peter Steward to the same.

The Petitioner is one of his Lordship's tenants as a sutler in the Tower, in the house where Eaton lately lived and he prays that his Lordship will "let him continue in the said business or otherwise your Lordship's poore old petitioner and wife must unavoidably perrish."

[Circ. 1713.] The humble Petition of Charles Wills quiltmaker in Buckle Street in Whitechappel and Headborough for the Upper Precinct.—To the Right Honorable the Earle of Northampton Constable of her Majestie's Tower of London :—

Humbly Shewith—That on Thursday the 19th instant about 3 and 4 a clock in the afternoon he having finished the collection of a brief for building the church of Burton upon Trent was goeing to Tower Street upon business and having a sudden occasion he went donne to the side of the Tower Dock near the rayl that goes donne from the turn pike to ease himself. Whilst he was there he was shott by the centenell upon or about Leg's Mount with pease or small shott in about 60 places that the blood followed and near 40 of them on his right thigh and 20 in his right leg and 6 in his cod which beat him downe and [he] was taken up senceless by Capt Bolton and other gentlemen who were passing by who led him to the Czar of Muscovy's Head in Tower Street . . . . . . a surgeon being brought he order'd some plaisters and oyntment and that he should goe home where he has continued ever since in great paine not being able to follow his trade to his detrimt having a wife and 3 children to maintain. The persons that took him up saw a serjeant and soldiers of the garrison and which were upon the hill when he was taken up s[ai]d that the centenells had orders from the Gover[no]r to shoote at all persons that eased themselves there.

WHEREFORE Your Petitioner humbly prays your Lordship wilbe pleased to take his condition into your consideration and give him such relief as in your Lordship's great wisdome shall think propper.

And your Petitioner shall ever pray &c.

[Circ. 1713]. Petition of Thomas Glover for, and on behalfe of, his Father Richard Glover, to the same. Unsigned and undated.

SHEWETH—That your Petitioner's brother Richard Glover was by your Lordship's Comission in Feby last admitted one of the Yeomen

Waiters att the Tower, under your Lordship's Command, and paid for the said place 250^{li} being all his substance: that his said brother left an ancient father and six children to maintaine in a low condicion, and before his death desired that an Humble Memoriall might be presented to your Lordship of his hard case—AND most humbly pray'd your Lordship that his said father or your Petitioner for him, might be admitted to the said place, or otherwise that your Lordship would be pleased to grant his said father such reliefe upon the admittance of any other in consideration of the great loss, as your Lordship of your wisdome and goodness shall think fitt; hee being an object of your Lordship's pitty, as will bee certifyed to your Lordship by Mr Foley of Stoake Hall, in Herefordshire, Richard Hopton Esqr, Robert Unit Esqr and others there."

[Circ. 1713]. Petition of Elizabeth Eades to the same. Unsigned and undated.

The Petitioner, a widow, who for several years has had the use of a cellar near Traytor's Gate has lately been locked out of it by the orders of Colonel Pendlebury, and begs that she may have the use of it as formerly.

[Circ. 1713]. "The humble petition of the Inhabitants of the North and West sides of Tower hill" to the same. Undated.

The petitioners beg his Lordship's permission "to plant a row of trees before their dwelling houses which they humbly conceive may be an ornament to the hill and no manner of ill conveniency," etc.

Signed by Tho. Andrews, Harcourt Master, J. Hunt, John Gore, Sam^{ll} Percivall, P. Cranke, Wm Baynes. Sprig Manesty, Richard Harris, and Benjamin Fowler.

[1713]. The humble address (To the Queen's Most Excellent Majesty (of the R^t Hono^{ble} the Lord Lieuten^t and Custos Rotulorum, and of the Deputy Lieutenants, and Justices of the Peace, and Militia Officers of the Tower Hamletts. Endorsed "copy of an Address to Her Majesty, from the Tower Hamletts." No signatures:

" Most Gracious Sovereign
We your Majesty's most dutiful and loyal subjects humbly crave leave to approach your royal person with hearts full of gratitude for your princely care and steddy resolution in procuring a peace [at Utrecht] not only for your own subjects but for your allies, notwithstanding the utmost efforts that have been used to obstruct it.

The overcoming so many difficulties in the course of the negotiations is a manifest proof of your Majesty's wisdom in the choice of your Ministers, and of their faithfulness and abilities in discharge of the great trust repos'd in them.

" We can't be sufficiently thankful to your Majesty for securing the Protestant Succession in the House of Hanover and establishing a perfect friendship with that illustrious family which has effectually disappointed the malice of your enemies, and put it out of their power to divide your interests.

" We beg leave to assure your Majesty that we m our several stations will diligently use our constant endeavours to promote and preserve the publick peace, to defend your sacred person, our happy constitution both in Church and State, and to shew ourselves loyall and dutiful subjects to the most indulgent and best of princes."

1713, Jan. 2nd. Sir William Windham to Lord Northampton. Dated at Whitehall, and endorsed " Sr William Windham's about changing the garrison at the Tower.—Ans^d Jany 5th 17$\frac{12}{13}$."

1713, Feb. 2nd. The same to the same. Dated as the last and endorsed " Sr Wm Windham about disbanding the 3 companys of invalides, that did duty at the Tower."

1713, March 3rd. A burial certificate from St Andrew's, Holborn. " These are to certifie that Robert Gill Esqre [Keeper of the lyons in the Tower] from his house in the great street in Hatton Garden was bu[rie]d the 29th of March 1673, as by our Reg^r Book appears. Witness my hand this 3^d day of March 1713. WILLIAM CHARLES P^{ish} Clerk."

1713, March 25th. The humble petition of Richard Heaton late one of the Sutlers in her Majesty's Tower of London—to the same. Undated, but endorsed " Richard Heaton petition—Read the 25th March 1713—Ordered that Mr Heaton do bring a certificate of his good behaviour.—Q[uery] if Kettleby had a legall warr^t for what he did " :—

" HUMBLY SHEWETH—That your peticoner about June 1707 became a Sutler at the Punch Bowl in the Tower and at his coming in besides the vallue of the household goods and drink gave the widdow Mayes twenty pounds over and above for her good will and paid the rent of 12^h per annum for about two yeares to the order of Gen^{ll} Cadogan, but a dispute ariseing between the said Cadogan and Coll. Farwell then Dep^{ty} Governor the rent lay for about a yeare and half in your petitioner's hands when Farwell having inform'd your petitioner that he had a right to the rent and could indempnifie your petitioner for paying the rent to him, your petitioner applyed to Mr Pearce secretary to Cadogan (to whom he paid his rent before) and informed him of what Farwell had said who told him he must then pay it to Farwell.

" When Farwell disposed of his Commission to Coll. Pendlebury your petitioner then paid his rent to the said Pendlebury as he demanded it, and soe continued till Christmas 1711 about which time the Tower was garreson'd by Invalids who not being upon the establishm^t of Guards and garrisons your petitioner did subsist them upon his creditt and trusted those of Capt Hide's company to the vallue of 100^{li}. Some few days before Christmas last when the year's rent would be due, Coll. Pendlebury by his serv^t demanded the rent, which your petitioner could not then pay by reason of his having disburs'd soe much money to subsist the Invalids.

" About the 3^d day of February last your petitioner had his goods seized and body arrested by Kettleby (on the suit of Coll. Pendlebury) who put severall persons imediately into possession of your petitioner's house and would have carryed your petitioner to prison tho' the goods seized were of much more valine then the debt and tho' he offered substantiall bayle, unless he gave him 8^s 9^d. Upon which he permitted your petitioner to have his liberty tho' he imediately [ap]praised his goods, at which time there was between 30^h and 40^{li} due to your petitioner for subsising the Invalids above [mentioned]. But your petitioner owing money to his brewer and other tradesmen was for fear of other actions forced to leave his habitation and obscond without having any consideration from Coll. Pendlebury (who then put a serv^t of his into the house) for the 20^h he had paid to the widow Mayes which with the money due from the Invalids (which was paid in [a] few days after) and the vallue of the goods seized would have amounted to more then would have paid all your petitioner's debts by a considerable sume.

" Wherefore your petitioner humbly prays your Lordship to consider the oppression he has had in this matter and the deplorable condition he and his family is thereby reduced to, and wilbe graciously pleas'd to restore him to his employment as a Sutler in the Tower under your Lordship's

MARQUESS
TOWNSHEND
MSS.

command or to order he may have some allowance for the 20ᵗⁱ paid at his coming in and for the damage disgrace and ruin that is brought upon him and his family.

" And your petitioner shall ever pray &c."

1713, April 3rd. Lord Dartmouth to Lord Northampton. Dated at Whitehall, and endorsed " Lord Dartmouth's letter for fireing the Tower guns upon the peace being concluded at Utrecht."

1713, April 18th. A certificate from the Commissary's office (signed by J. Crawford) "that the Rᵗ Honᵇˡᵉ Robert Lord Lucas was mustered as Chief Governor of the Tower both before and after the Treaty of Reswick."

1713, April 20th. Two certificates from the Paymaster's office, signed by James Moody Deputy Auditor.

From the first it appears that by the accounts of the Earl of Rane-lagh, late Paymaster General, that the pay of Lord Lucas, as Chief Governor of the Tower, was at the rate of 38s. 4¼d. per diem, from 1ˢᵗ April 1692 to 24ᵗʰ June 1702.

From the second certificate it appears that the pay of the garrison of the Tower, from 25ᵗʰ June 1702 to 24ᵗʰ Oct. 1702, was paid to the Rᵗ Honᵇˡᵉ Montague Earl of Abingdon.

1713, May 4th. Lord Dartmouth, Secretary of State, to Lord North-ampton, from Whitehall; acquainting his Lordship by the Queen's commands that she has ordered proclamation of the Peace to be made the next day and that it is her pleasure that the Tower Guns should be fired as usual.

1713, June 25th. The same to the same, from Whitehall.

" My Lord—Her Majesty commands me to acquaint your Lordship that when the French Ambassador makes his publick entry, it is her pleasure that he should be treated with all the marks of respect that are usually shewn to persons of his character on the like occasion."

1713, July 6th. The same to the same, from Whitehall.

" My Lord — I am commanded by the Queen to acquaint your Lordship that Her Majesty does not go to Sᵗ Paul's Church tomorrow, but both Houses of Parliament being to be there it is Her Majesty's pleasure that the guns of the Tower should be fired at the singing of the Te Deum as has been usual at times of publick thanksgivings in that place."

1713, July 21st. The Duke of Ormonde, Commander in Chief, to the same, from the Cockpit.

" My Lord—The third regiment of Foot Guards being to be re-viewed on Thursday next, I desire your Lordship will give orders for such of that Regiment as are now in the Tower, to march out tomorrow morning, and to be reliev'd by such others of the Foot Guards as shall be appointed for that service according to Her Majestie's pleasure signifyd to me thereupon."

1713, July 28th. William Nicholas to the same. Endorsed :—" Mʳ Nicolas letter about my being muster'd and appointing an Agent."

1713, Augt. 1st. The same to the same. Endorsed : — " Mʳ Nicholas's letter upon his being made Agent to the Tower Garrison."

1713, Augt. 3rd. The Duke of Ormonde to the same. Dated at Sᵗ James's.

" My Lord — I am inform'd your Lordship is plac'd on the estab-lishment of guards and garrisons for the more regular payment of your appointment as Constable of the Tower, but I must at the same time acquaint your Lordship that it is not the Queen's intention, the

privileges which the Lieutenant has by custom enjoy'd should be thereby any way lessen d, either in regard to the agency or any thing else."

1713, Augt. 3rd. Sir William Wyndham, Secretary at War, to Hatton
Compton Esqr [Lieutenant General in the army and Lieutenant of the
Tower]. Dated at London, and enclosed in the next.

" Sir—I have received yours with the copy of a letter from Mr Wm
Nicholas, and an extract of your patent. My Lord Northampton is att
his request placed on the establishment and ordered to be mustered, he
desiring rather to be paid on the military list than the civil where the
Constable used to be paid. When Her Majesty complied with that
request of his Lordship's I am satisfied she never meant to make any
alteration in the power or authority of that post much less to take
away any from yours as Lieutenant which is conferred by patent."

1713, Augt. 4th. Hatton Compton to Lord Northampton. Dated at
Fulham, and endorsed :—" Lt Genll Compton's letter."

" My Lord—When first I hear'd of your Lordship's being upon the
establishment I reioyced extremly knowing 'twas your own request and I
hoped you would a stoped there ; but last Saturday night I received a very
pert letter from your agent as he calls himself : which allarumed me that
your Lordship was taking what of right belongs to me : whereupon I made
my applycation to my Lord Treasurer [Lord Oxford and Mortimer] his
grace of Ormonde and the Secretary of Warr ; the first spoke to the
said secretary in my hearing a sunday night to the same purpose which
is hoped will satisfie your Lordship since the other two have writ the
inclosed to convince you so far as to recall what orders you have given
to your clarke or agent for I have got the Muster stoped to avoid disputes
untill I receive your Lordship's comands : which I desire next post.
Now I humbly beg leave to give my poor opinion : viz. : that by being
musterd you brought yourself to be one of the 8000 men and consequently under whosoever commands the army, which I fear lessens
the grandure of the Constable ; I still hope 'twill not be in the power
of little underhand people to create any misunderstanding betwixt your
Lordship and him that ever was and is " etc.

1713, Augt. 4th. William Nicholas to the same.

" . . . . . I cannot learn why the Muster was putt off till Friday
. . . I have provided the Muster Rolls so every thing will be
ready for Friday."

1713, Augt. 6th. The same to the same.

My Lord—I have onely to acquaint your Lordship that the Lieutenant
has sent a lettr to the Tower wch Major D'Oyly shewed me this day in
these words : " These are to acquaint you that the Muster is putt off
till a further day, of which you shall have timely notice from &c. The
lettr was directed to Coll. Pendlebury . . . ."

1713, Augt. 6th. Lord Northampton to the Lieutenant of the Tower.
Endorsed—" Copy of my letter to Generall Compton."

" — I received your letter and am surprised you should be so much dissatisfied with my being putt at the head of the Muster Roll and at my
appointing an agent, which I take to be the regular way and shall not recall any orders I have given having writt by this post to the D. of
Ormond. As to any misunderstanding between us I know of none nor
of any person that endeavours to promote it, but if there should be any
it will be wholy owing to yourself, for I am as I have always been."

1713, Augt. 6th. The same to Lord Oxford and Mortimer. Dated
at Ashby, and addressed " Copy of my Letter to Lord Treasurer."

" My Lord, I hear the Lieutenant of the Tower hath been with your Lordship upon my being placed on the establishment of guards, and garrisons and upon my appointing an agent which of right belongs to him that is at the head of the Muster Roll ; it was by your Lordship's favour I was made Constable and also putt upon this establishment, which makes me hope for your protection in maintaining me in my just rights . . . . ."

1713, Augt. 6th. The same to the Duke of Ormonde. Dated at Ashby, and endorsed—" Copy of my letter to the D. of Ormond." To the same effect as the last.

[1713]. " The Case relating to the Power of the Constable of the Tower in appointing an agent for that garrison when upon the establishm^t for guards and garrisons."

1713, Augt. 8th. William Nicholas to Lord Northampton. Endorsed — " Mr Nicholas with answers to Querys concerning an agent."

1713, Augt. 11th. The same to the same. Endorsed—" Mr Nicholas concerning the appointing an agent."

1713, Augt. 12th. The same to the same. Endorsed—" Mr Nicholas concerning an agent."

1713, Sept. 3rd. Samuel Lynn to the same. From Whitehall.
" My Lord—Her Majesty having order'd the Third Reg^t of Foot Guards in the Tower Hamletts and on duty at the Tower to march from thence, being first relieved by a detachment from the other reg^ts of Foot Guards in the said Tower duty, I am comanded in the absence of M^r [Francis] Gwyn [Secretary at War] to acquaint your Lordship therewith that you may please to permit the said relief to be made accordingly . . . ."

1713, Oct. 6th. Lord Northampton. " To the Right Honble M^r [John] Hill Lieu^t Generall of the Ordnance."
" Sir,—There being a vacancy of one of the garrison gunners under my command by the death of Danl Thorp, this is to desire you will please to give the necessary orders for Rob. Trimble to have a warrant to succeed him. I doubt not but he will be the more acceptable he having served in the Royall Artillery in Flanders till it was broke and he allso having assured me he will reside in the Tower the better to do his duty which I shall for the future expect from the garrison gunners."

[1713]. " Extract[s] of sev[era]l patents [temp. Jac. I., and Car. L] of the office of keeping the lyons in the Tower."

[1713.] John Martin to Lord Northampton. Undated and unaddressed.
" My Lord,—The grant of the said lyon office is most humbly desired for the term of forty years or any other term that may be readily granted, by—My Lord—Your Lordship's most humble and obedient servant, JNO MARTIN."

[1713]. " Establishment of the Tower of London for 184 days, from the 24th June inclusive to the 24th December inclusive."
NOTE.—From this paper it appears that the pay, per diem, of the Constable is 2l. 14s. 9½d.; of the Lieutenant 1l. 18s. 4½d.; of the Deputy Lieutenant 16s. 5¼d. ; of the Chaplain 6s. 8d. ; of the Tower Major 4s.; of the Surgeon 2s. 6d. ; of the Master Gunner 2s.; of four other Gunners 1s. 2d. each; of the Gentleman Porter 1s. 4d.; of 40 Yeomen

Warders 1*s*. 2*d*. each; of the Physician 1*s*. 1½*d*.; of the Apothecary 6½*d*.; and of the Gentleman Gaoler 1*s*. 1½*d*.

1714, Feb. 27th. William Bromley, Secretary of State, to Lord Northampton. Dated at Whitehall, and addressed to the Earl "at his house at Castle Ashby."

"My Lord—The Queen having this day received the ratifications of the Treatys of peace and commerce between her Majesty and the King of Spain, I am commanded to signify the same to Your Lordship, that you may immediately order the Tower guns to be discharged as has been usual on such extraordinary occasions."

Same date. The same to the same. Dated at Whitehall.

"My Lord,—Her Majesty being pleased to order that the [Treaty of] peace and comerce between Her and the King of Spain be proclaimed next Monday at twelve of the clock in the forenoon, I am to acquaint your Lordship therewith that you may give directions for firing the great guns in the Tower on occasion of that solemnity.

1714, July 30th. Lord Bolingbroke to the same. Dated at Kensington.

"My Lord,—The Queen has been taken very ill this morning, and the Lords of the Councill who are now assembled here upon that occasion, have commanded me to write to your Lordship that you do without loss of time come up to town to attend in your post, and to take care of the Tower in this juncture."

[P.S.] "I am too much in haste to use my own hand."

Same date. Francis Gwyn, Secretary at War, to the same. Dated at Whitehall.

"My Lord—I am commanded by his Grace the Duke of Ormonde, [Commander in Chief] to acquaint you that you are forthwith to repair to the garrison under your command, and that you take care that all the officers thereunto belonging do likewise attend their duty."

1714, Aug. 1st. "Letter from the Privy Councell for proclaiming his Majesty King George at the Tower." Addressed "To our very good Lord George Earl of Northampton Chief Governor of the Tower of London" and endorsed "2ᵈ Augᵗ 1714. There is a meeting of [the] Council appointed at Sᵗ James's at ten a clock this Day."

"After our very hearty comendations to yoʳLordship. It haveing pleased Almighty God this day to take to his mercy out of this troublesome life our late sovereign Lady Queen Anne of blessed memory and thereupon his royall Majesty King George being here proclaim'd according to the tenor of the proclamation signed by us herewith sent to your Lordshipp forthwith to cause the said Proclamation to be proclam'd and published in the usual places within your jurisdiction with the solemnities and ceremonies accustomed on the like occasion, so not doubting of yoʳ ready complyance herein we bid your lordship very heartily farewell, from the Council Chamber at Sᵗ James's the first Day of August 1714.

Your Lordships very Loving Friends.

[Signed by John Duke of] BUCKINGHAM [President of the Council; William Earl of] DARTMOUTHE [Lord Privy Seal; Simon Lord] HARCOURT [Lord Chancellor; Charles Duke of] SHREWSBURY [Lord High Treasurer, Lord Chamberlain, and Lord Lieutenant of Ireland; George Duke of] NORTHUMBERLAND, [James Duke of] ORMONDE; [James Earl of] FINDLATER; [Hugh Earl of] LOUDOUN; [Charles Bodville Earl of] RADNOR; [John Earl] POULETT [Lord Steward of the Household; Heneage Lord] G[U]RRNSEY; and WILLIAM BROMLEY [Secretary of State].

Same date. An Order of Council—Dated at the Court of St James, and signed by Edward Southwell.

It directs the Earl of Northampton to give directions for firing the Tower Guns at 12 Clock being the time appointed for proclaiming King George.

1714, Augt. 3rd. William Bromley to Lord Northampton from Whitehall.

"My Lord—Since the City of London enjoys a perfect Tranquility, & there is no just Cause to apprehend that any Designs are carrying on to disturb the Publick Peace, their Excellencies the Lords Justices think fit that the Militia of the Tower Hamlets be forthwith dismissed. I am with the greatest Respect,"

Same date. Francis Gwyn, Secretary at War, to the same, from Whitehall.

"My Lord—I am to desire your Lop will cause an accot to be returned to me what Number of Men the Barracks in the Tower of Londo will contain, and in what condition they are at present."

1714, Augt. 5th. A Sealed Order in Council. Dated at the Council Chamber St James', and signed by Edward Southwell.

It directs that Particular Care be taken that during the Proceeding of her late Majts Funerall from Kensington to Westminster Abby, and untill Her Majts Body be interred, a Gun be fired at the Tower every Minute.

1714, Augt. 15th. Thomas Gwyn to Lord Northampton. Dated at Whitehall.

"My Lord—The Lords Justices having ordered seven Battallions of Foot to be brought over from Flanders to England some of which are already Arriv'd and the rest hourly Expected, I am therefore to Signify their Excellency's Command to your Lordship, that as any of the said Batallions shall be brought up the River of Thames, You permitt them to land at the Tower Wharfe in order to follow the Route given them to their intended Quarters."

1714, Augt. 17th. A sealed Council Order. Dated at the Council Chamber, St James, and signed by Christopher Musgrave. Endorsed:—

"Order of Council for firing a Gun at the Tower every Minute on Sunday Night next while her Majesties Funerall is proceeding from the Princes Lodgings to the Abby at Westminster and till Her Majestie is interr'd."

1714, Augt. 25th. The humble Petition of Thomas Cable to the same. Undated, but endorsed "The petition of Thomas Cable—25th August 1714—To succeed his Father in ringing the bell in the Tower":—

SHEWETH—That your Petitioner's Father Thomas Cable after haveing ruugg a Bell wch goes at Half an Hour after Nine a Clock at Night in the Tower for Twelve Years, and upwards, died Yesterday (the 24th of this instant August) his Wife haveing also departed this life the 28th of July last, and have left behind them, ten Fatherless and Motherless Children, six of whom are not able to do any thing for a Liveing; and being left in miserable poor Circumstances wthout any manner of Dependance for their Support, but the Charity of well despos'd people.

Wherefore and in regard to his Fathers long and Faithfull Service, your Petitioner Humbly prays you'l be pleasd to bestow on him his Fathers said Benefitt of ringing the Bell (wch will be a most charitable Act and enable him to maintain his poor Brothers and Sisters).

Your Petitioner as in Duty Bound shall ever pray &c.

THOS CABLE.

1714, Sept. 6th, Whitehall. Francis Gwyn to Lord Northampton.

"My Lord—A Detachment of Two hundred Men and Officers proportionable of Lieut Genl [John Richmond] Webb's Regiment [the 8th Foot] being order'd to march and releive the Detachment of the Foot Guards now doing Duty at the Tower of London the Day before His Majesty's coming from Greenwich to St James's, It is the Lords Justices Direction that upon the Arrival of the said Detachment of Lt General Webb's Regiment Your Lordship do permit the said Releif to be made accordingly."

1714, Sept. 8th. A Sealed Council Order. Dated at the Council Chamber, St James's, and signed by Edward Southwell. Endorsed :—

"Order of Councill for firing the Gun's at the Tower 1st wn the King Lands at Greenwich ; 2. wn the King setts out on the day of his Entry ; 3. wn His Majtie & all his Guards shall have pass'd ovr Londn Bridge."

1714, Sept. 16th. Francis Gwyn to Lord Northampton. Dated at Whitehall, and endorsed :—

"Lettr from Francis Gwyn Secy of War that the Detachmt of Guards [at the Tower] be forthwith retired by the Detachmt of Genl Webbs Regiment."

1714, Sept. 27th. William Pulteney to the same. Dated at Whitehall, and endorsed :—

"A Letter from Wm Pulteney Esqr Secretary at War, for permitting Genl Webbs Regmt to be relieved by a Detachment of the 3 Regimts of Foot Guards."

1714, Oct. 14th. The same to the same. Dated at Whitehall, and endorsed :—

"William Pulteney Secretary at War That a List of the Commission[ed] Officers in the Tower be sent to him."

1714, Oct. 19th. Lord Townshend to the same. Dated at Whitehall, and endorsed :—

"Letter from my Ld Townshend Secry of State to fire the Guns as usual [tomorrow] on the Day of His Majesties Coronation."

Same date. William Pulteney to the same. Dated at Whitehall, and endorsed :—

"Order for firing the Tower Guns for His Majesty's Coronation."

1714, Oct. 26th. The Board of Ordnance to the same. Dated at the Office of Ordnance, and signed by C[harles] Musgrave (Clerk of the Ordnance) the Hon Dixie Windsor (Storekeeper of the Ordnance), and Rupert King.

"My Lord—We desire your Lordship will be pleased to give directions, that the person who has the Key of the House belonging to this Office on the East end of Tower Wharfe (which was lent for the Guard to do duty when doubled on the demise of her late Majesty) do forthwith deliver the said Key to Mr Farmer Messenger to this Office."

1715, Jan. 7th. The same to the same. Dated at the Office of Ordnance, and signed by Edward Ashe (Clerk of the Ordnance), James Craggs (Clerk of the Deliveries of the Ordnance), Major General

Michael Richards (Surveyor General of the Ordnance), and John Armstrong (afterwards Surveyor General).

" My Lord—We writt to your Lordᵖ the 26ᵗʰ of October last to desire you to give directions for delivering the Keys of the House on the East end of Tower Wharfe (which was lent for the Guard to do duty, on the Demise of her late Majesty) to Mʳ Farmer Messenger to this Office, but as yet the said Keys are not delivered up, We must therefore desire to remind your Lordship of our former Letter, & that you will be pleased to give directions accordingly."

1715, Jan. 10th. "Copy of my Lords Answer to the Board of Ordnance concerning the key of the Guard house at the End of the Wharfe."

Sirs—I recᵈ yʳ letter of the 7ᵗʰ Instant wherein you desire me to give directions for delivering the Key of the Guardhouse at the East end of the Wharfe. I will speake to the Duke of Marlborough concerning it & am—Sirs—Your humble Servᵗ.

1717, July 5th. The Account of the Pay of the Garrison of the Tower of London [from Janᵛ 20ᵗʰ 17$\frac{1}{4}$ to March 14ᵗʰ 17$\frac{16}{7}$].

This is a True Coppy of the Account of all the Money received and paid on Account of the Garrison of the Tower of London by me—Wᴍ Nicholas."

LETTERS FORMERLY BELONGING TO ELIZABETH (SHIRLEY) COUNTESS
OF NORTHAMPTON.

1713-1737.

1713, Augt. 10th. Dame Ferrets to Elizabeth Shirley. Unaddressed.
" My dear Child.

Tis in this relation i shall ever esteeme you, therefore you may depend upon me, and in wᵗsoever i may [do] most to express my selfe for yʳ servis be free wᵗʰ me and i will readly compose my selfe to yʳ intrest, for as Almightye God hath bin pleased to leave but one of my Famyle, i thinke i am the more obligd to offer upon any consernes of yʳˢ to be redᵈy to inquier wᵗ can be [in] my power to add to yʳ advantage, and recomend it in all times, that you will be very prudent in care off the station you are in, nor do or act in future or present any thing to the preiudise of that inhereitance wᶜʰ God hath given you, i shall now say noe more but trust that you make good use of my advise for yʳ owne binifett and now take my Lave for this present but shall be to you my Deare Child yʳ affectionat Grand Mother

ANNE FERRERS."

[No date.] The Hon. Lawrence Shirley to "Mʳˢ Shirley at the Lady Ann Courtney's in the Pall Mall—London."

" Twickenham Sunday.—Dear Niece I cant by any means prevail with my Lord to look into those Papers, that I brought with me : He says he will neither concern himself with them, nor any thing that belongs to yʷ, as long as yʷ continue under my Lᵈ Abingdon's care. . . . . . He has still a great deal of compassion left for yᵒ, & would willingly be the means of saving yᵘ from the ruin yᵘ must inevitably meet with, from those whose hands yᵘ are now in. Wherefore, if yᵘ will consent to leave my Lᵈ Abingdon, & turn off yʳ french woman (which is another thing he insists upon) yᵘ shall be very welcome to his house ane he will do yᵘ all the servise he can." . . . . . .

1714, July 20th. The Dowager Countess of Arran to the same. Unaddressed.

"I had writt to you sooner Deare Niece, on this sad occasion but
that really I have had so much trouble for it my self, as made me very
unfitt to write on that subiect, but I desire you to believe, I am much
concerned for you, hearing how great a share you take in this inst
affliction you have, in the losse of yr oneley, & kind Brother [Lord
Tamworth], in this change (that hath noe remedy) one must submitt
wth patience to the will of God, who orders all things for the best, &
be thankfull, that it hath pleased God hitherto to preserve you alive, &,
I hope, you will not afflict yr self soe, as to bring any illnesse upon yr
self but that you may be preserved in health, to inioy the fortune that
is now fallen to you, & may be continued, to be an honnour to yr
famyly, & a comfort to yr relations, amongst wch none wishes you more
hapynesse, nor will be readyer to serve you in all I can, than yr Affectionat humble seruant

D[OROTHY] ARRAN."

"[P.S.] Pray present my service to yr Aunts & to Lady Barbery
[Barbara] & Mr Laurance [Shirley] that I am sorry to hear are soe
afflicted."

[1714], July 24. The Countess Ferrers to "The Honrable Mrs Shirley at Staunton in Leicester Shire.—Loughbrough [Post-] Bagg."
Dated in London and franked "Ferrers."

"Dear Madam, we got hear a fryday by six a clock, we had a very
pleasant journey it was not hot nor dusty. That was a bundell went down
by the Mourning Coch, dericked [directed] for me, if you plens to oppen
it yar your shows [shoes], pray send my Slippers the furst opportunyty.
I have sent to Mrs Gilibone, he say he has not bespock you a Saddel. I
desire to do it a Monday & hope to send it the week after. I cannot get
any brown gloves ready Made. Ly Abingdon is in town and Ly
Wenshallcey. The town says Ly B : has 20000llb. left her. I hope it
will do her Servis, and marry her soon. I have seen nobody nor heard
no news. I desire you will let me know how you are yes [this] time,
weather more than useall or les. I desire you will take yr medesons a
week after you are well, I will send you some Spaw Waters a Monday,
that you may recover yr health is the harty prayers of yr obliged humble
Servant.

S[ELINA] F[ERRERS].

[P.S.] My Ld gives his blesing to all I desire mine ware dew [where
due] I cannot write to leua yes post & I for got to charge her not to
speck to Ly Bety let her be never so bad pray tell her this. Sence I
writ I hear [the] Ld T[reasurer] went to the Q : last night & gave her
his Staf Ld Darthmouth & the Dk of Buckingham the say Ld Bishop of
London is to be the furst Ld of Trea : the Bp of Rochister privi Seal. Ld
T : has been here sence I writ with his wite Staf so I believe all I have
writ may not be trew pray send the inclosed to my Mother."

[1714], July 27th. The same to the same. Addressed as the last, and
franked by Lord Ferrers.

Dear Madam—I coud get nothing ready to send you yes [this] week
but hope to send all the next I have bespock yr Saddel the man braut me
one I liked very well but it had two pumels so I have bespock one with
one pumel covered with gray cloth lased with black lase [lace] with
every thing to it for 4l. 10. I hope it will plense you I am to have it a
Satterday sevennight. Ly Angelsey was marry'd last Satterday, Mrs
Pit to Mr Chomley ya [they] ware at St James Church a Sunday very
fine all my Lds Diamonds are come yar is non very large, we have bid
5000lb for Mrs Bouchers house we conclud we shall have it for she says

she will take five thousand Guineas so I believe she wont stand for that.
I desire Jack may take some spaw waters every day and Mr Marthus
desires he may ride a horse back [on horseback] if he wont go before
a Man he [Lord Ferrers] would have Nurs[e] ride behind a man or
one [on] a singel horse & take him [Jack] in her lap y^ar is some drops
for him gon y^es week to take when he wakes before dinner as he uste.
Ld Wamouth [Weymouth] is very ill y^a think he wont livve he hic-
ups so everry night y^a can [hear] him two or three Roomes of[f] L^y
Worsley is with him but non of the famely besides y^ar is a good dele of
company hear b^t y^a will all go as soon as the Q : leves Kinsinton she
has the Gout in her knee a lettel. My L^d has the Gout in his grate towe
of the outher foot but he goes a bout the hovse I give [you] many thanks
Dear Madam for the care you take of my children & hope I shall soon be
with you.

I am y^r Most obliged Humble
Servant
S. Ferrers.

[1714?], July 29th. Dame Ferrers to the same. Addressed : " For
Mrs Shirly."

"Deare Miss,

I have receaved y^r most respectfull kind letter to me wth all the
consolation that i was capable of in the condition i was in, for the reale
sence of y^rs, and my grate Love, hath establishd such an affliction upon
my heart that i could not compose my selfe to write so soounc as i
ought to have dune, besides i have not bin well, but now am better, and
doe assure you as long [as] I have Life will ever express my selfe in my
constant friendship for you therefore watch wth greate prudence to have
a care of y^r present State and be not prevailed wth to pre[j]ud[i]ch y^r
power, you have a fayer fortune be sure you keepe it, and God give you
wisdom and courage to mantaine y^r powers health and life i pray to
Allmighty God give you for this his favour will still be my prayers that
am y^r Affectionate Grand Mother.

A. Ferbers."

[1714], Aug. 12th. The Countess Ferrers to the same. Addressed
"For Madam Shirley at Staunton Leicershire—Loughbrough Bagg"
and franked by Earl Ferrers.

"Dear Madam—

I saw Mrs Ferrers a mounday night she went off the next day out
of Town she is not well I never heard any body so angrey as she is att
his Will she sayd was it love what els coud it be that he shoud leve her
so much she woud have seen him if she had known he had made a Will
& a grate dele more every body says the same she dos. I hope you will
like y^r Saddel he would have had 7. _l_. 10. _s_. if it had been a lose cloth
& y^es way he had 4. _l_. 10. _s_. he can make you a velvet Cover over y^es
or he will change it when you have don with it we are very quiate hear
& y^a think we shall be so, some fear it will not last, y^a believe the
Coronnation will be asson as y^a can get things ready for it, but he is
very stately & everry thing must be very fine he speks nether frinch
nor English he wont be very good Company to these Kings [the Lords
Justices] when he comes (houe ?) are much exalted the lettel D^k of
K[ent ?] has ganed three inches I have seen one of them but he dos not
speak to Subjecks. Pray take no more of the waters sence y^a do not
agree with you I desire if you are not so before five weeks pray take that

purg agane dont ge longer than five weeks I beg. I am very glad to here
you are so well for nothing can be a greater pleasure to
Madam
y^r Most obliged—Humble Servant
S. F.

[P.S.] My L^d gives his blesing to you and all the famely he thought
y^a had been a Buck sent from Chartley everry week he has writ to order
one everry week."

[1714], Augt. 14th. The same to the same. Unsigned and unaddressed.

" Madam,
I have changed y^r saddle for two pumels the maneoly news of Q.
[Anne's] death makes everry body hear very dull I hope you have a
pleasanter time in the Country I was yesterday at Mrs Bondchers My
L^d has baut it he gives 5000^{ll} it is thought very cheap I carryed both
my boys to School I am sory I cannot tell when I shall return to
Staunton for my L^d will stay to see the new K : he cannot be hear in les
than a fourthnight which is grate grief to me for I long to see you I am
in grate hast. My L^d gives his blesing to all mine ware dew My Sister
is y^r Humble Servant."

1714, Sept. 4th. Frances Thynne (afterwards Duchess of Somerset),
to the same. Dated at Leweston, and unaddressed.

" Dear Madam—
I return you many thanks for the favour of your letter & am very
much asham'd you should take any notice of so worthless a thing as the
purse I have a great deal of reason to beg your pardon for sending it
att a time when you was in such affliction for the death of Lord Tamworth, but I knew nothing of his illness till after it was gone, so I am
in hopes you will forgive me,
I am very much obliged to you for the Sence [you] express of our
loss in my Grand Pappa [Lord Weymouth] & join wth you in thinking
that this has indeed been a very Unfortunate summer to us both. My
Sister presents her most humble Ser^{ce} to y^u and the yonng Ladys. I
hope you will do me the favour to accept of the same & believe me to be
Dear Madam
Y^r most affectionate Cousen & obliged humble Servant
F. THYNNE."

1714, Sept. 11th. Dame Ferrers to the same. From London.
Addressed " these for the Honored Mrs Shirley at the Right Honble The
Earl Ferrer's—Staunton Harold in Leicestershire."

" My Deare Child
The letter wherein you intrusted me so freely wth y^r secrett
thoughts came safe to me wch in every part did so much agree wth my
sence of y^r condition that had i bin wth y^r selfe in conference together
could not have bene in any kind more express a prudence then w^t was,
in that my approbation of all you say in that you writ then, i advise you
to keepe firmly to, and looke wth a constant Vigilance to   of oune
interest, this is all i can now say to you being in hopes sonne to see you
in toun, when wee may more at large know one anothers minds,
and pray beleeve now and ever y^t i'm y^r most faythfull affectionate
friend in all your consernes, as y^r oune Mother to the last day of my
Life, in wch you may comunicate y^r thoughts att times when you thinke
ñtt, and nowe farewell till wee meet, but wheare i am y^{rs} as i proffes.
ANNE FERRERS.

¹ [P.S.] My Lady Ferrers did me the honor of a visitt my services to all yᵉ Aunts my serviss to Lady Baberbery [Barbara] the time draws neare for my rent charg remember of it."

[1714 ?] Sep. 12th. The Dowager Countess of Arran to the same. Unaddressed.

" Deare Niece,

I received yʳˢ & I am glad to find you are in good health, I ca'nt blame yʳ inst concern, but in things that ca'nt be helped we must submitt, & look to the present, wᶜʰ is yʳ wellfaire, I received a very oblidging letter from my Lady Ferrers, who professes great kindnesse to you, & how much she will indeavour to serve [you] & make yʳ life pleasant, but I hope in a convenient time, you will be setled well in a house of yʳ own, yʳ fortune being now soe considerable that you may soon have many good opurtunitys of that kind in yʳ choice. I shall always be very glad of any hapynesse that befalls you, & ready to serve you in any thing that lyes in the power of

Yʳ Affectionat
Aunt & bhumle serᵗ
D. ARRAN.

[P.S.] I fancy my Lᵈ Ferrers will hardly goe back into Darbyshire there is soe much to be done in town wᶜʰ will occation yʳ coming the sooner to town I shall be glad to hear from you. I supose my mother hath writt to you since her return from hence. My humble service to yʳ Aunts."

[1714?], Sept. 18th. The Countess Ferrers to the same. Addressed " For The Honᵇˡᵉ Mʳˢ Shirley att Staunton by Loughbrough bag. Lecestershire," and franked " Ferrers."

" Madam,

I am very glad I am now to set a day for yʳ journey Mʳ Kirekland has orders to hire Coches for you one Mickalmas day if you approve of it I believe Fore of my Garls & a Servant may come in the Coch with you if yᵉ do then Martin & the two Children & French women & my Chamber Made & the nursary Made betty Tomson one more that will be most helpfull to them may come in the other. My Lᵈ wont let Jack come if he stays betty Wilkins must. I hope the rodes will be good & that you will have a pleasant journey I sopose you know yʳ Aunts intend to go & live with some of yᵃʳ relations whieh I hope will contribut to yʳ happyness as well as mine & that everry thing may add to yʳˢ is the harty wishes of

Yʳ Most Obliged Humble
Servant
S. FERRERS."

[1714], Sept. 24th. The Countess Ferrers " To the Honᵇˡᵉ Mʳˢ Shirley att Staunton Leicestershire—Loughbrough Bagg." Franked " Ferrers.'

" I forgot to write you a pece of news I heard a bout a fortnight ago. Lᵈ Dunkilen [Dunkellin] is going to be marryed to one Mʳˢ Parker a widdo she has been so but a year & a half she has 7 children & ust to be a cocket with grate spiret, but now I will tell you the good part. She has 800ˡⁱ a year & a house & 25000ˡⁱ in money, her father is very rich & very fond of her he has only one more Daughter he does not care for, he is called Portland Smith. I believe it will make some body very ille agane. I believe the last was owing to yᵉˢ [this] for it has been

P 2

a goode wile about.   I have sent y^r saddel this week I hope you will
like it lor I gave the man y^r note of dericktions y^{ar} is in the case [a]
bundel for my Mother.   I have sent Sewallis a favour I think he
should send it L^y Abney.   I hope Madam it will not be long before I
see you for my L^d has grate maches offered him but he keeps them all till
he sees you.   The wind stands wrong for the K[ing] so my boys go back
to Scool to day y^s [they] both give y^{ar} servis to you so dos my Sister
how [who] is now hear but gos to day hear is a plague amongst the Cows
a grate many peopel have for bid any Milk or butter being used in y^{ar}
houses y^{ar} deyed a 100 Cows in one week at Iselington y^{ar} was severall
Oxen burnt at Smithfeld & tuctel [Tuthill] felds be[c]anse y^s ware
rotten.   The way y^s knew it is y^{ar} brath stinks & y^s shake & dey in
three hours the reason they give for it is y^{ar} has been so littel grase y^s
have feed them with Grans [grains] & that has rooted [rotted] them.   I
can get you no good pens as [you] will givse [guess] by y^{ts} srall [scrawl]
but beg you to excuse it from Madam y^r most Oblidged Humble
Servant,

S. FERRERS."

[1714?] Lady Barbara Shirley to the same.   From Lichfield.
Franked by John Cotes and addressed "For Mrs Shirley att the Earl of
Abingdon's in St. James's Square—London."

"Dear Neece
   I am glad y^u have see[n] my L^y, & get maters as to my sister
Betty; as to my self, I do not care w^t my father thinks; for if it had
been by my advice, I think I had no reason to be a shamed off it, &
n y father has alread[y] showed his ill will to me, as much as he can.
Pray present my humble service to Ly Abingdon; & tell her, I have
sent Mr Harriott the Baily at Astwell to return these arrears to her;
wch I have reason to hope will not be lease than 100^{li}; I am told [that
if] I buy [a] bank bill that bare[s] interest I shall have at the rate of three
per sent if the mony lies in but a quorter of a year, & if it is so I beg
my Ly will lay out my Mony that way.   Pray tell her also that I am very
well assured that their was twenty thousand pound setteled on my fathers
daughters, & that after I was born their was a farder settlement made;
this I had from Cozen Okover who had the writing onc[e] in her hands
to cary to Mr Corben, without my fathers knowledg & she is also a
witness to them.   I hope to get them soon in my owen hands, if they are
in his daughters hands, but she living a great way off it will be at lea[s]t
a week before I shall have them.   I have been this day at Blifield so can
ade no more but that I am y^r affec:

Aunt & Servant,
B. SHIRLEY.

[P.S.] It is reported that my father has given his consent y^u should
have Mr Paget, & has given him his interest to be chose for Staford
shire.   He is in the Country."

[1714?], Oct. 2nd.   The same to the same.   From Lichfield.
Franked by John Cotes and addressed "For Mrs Shirley att the Right
Honble the Earl of Abingdons in St James's Square—London."

"Dear Neece
   I receiu'd y^r Letter but not the acquitence then menshaned.   I
was very much deverted wth the account y^u gave me, & do not questan
but y^u will convince the world, in a Littel time; that y^u are not, w^t my
Lady Ferrers represents, & I think her proseeding on that occasion,
exposes her more than all she has ever done yet: I hope when they find
they can do no good they will be friend[s] again, & hus[h]e all up; for

I think it will be much for their creadit to do so. I think now y^u are in toun y^u would do well, to take advise, as consearning y^r demands from my father; for tho: y^r brothers Will hinders y^r demanding a porshan out of w^t I have, yet I believe, it being due from y^r fathers death, my fathers liabe[l] to pay it y^u out of the arrears, & if not the porshan yet the interest, wch would be considerable; & of great advantage to y^u at this present, for it would help to clear y^r estat against y^u came of age. [My brother] Lory came here to day from Mr Coten's [Cotton's], he has not see[n] Mrs Thacker since, he went their; but she has promes'd to come here; so I hope that matter will succeed, but say nothing off it. Sister Anna came here yesterday. Y^r horse is come well, & I will take great Care off it. I desir y^u will buy me a set of watter Colers, & six littel french cutts, & two or three Ivery plates: by this y^u will see how I entend to employ my self; I have made some efortes at it already; but my Colers are very bad & I want time for practes to emprove my hand, for I make but sad da[u]be of it yet: y^u may give these things to my sister & she will send them with some other things she is to send down. Mr Hill & Chetwen continue to treat still, but have lease hopes than ever, for Mr Bidelf has been here, a making enterest for my brother & the Capten; & he has very good enterest in this town. I shall be glad when the election is over, for we hear of littel else but making enterest now. I shall be glad to hear from y^u often, & hope to hear y^u are very well pleased in the place y^u are in, I will ade no more at present but that I ever am.

Dear Neece—Y^r Affee: Aunt & Servant
B. SHIRLEY.

[P.S.] Pray present all our services to Ly Abingdon. All here are much y^r servants. Pray when y^u see y^r gradmother next give my service to her."

[1714?], Oct. 11th. The same to the same. From Lichfield. Franked and addressed as above.

" Dear Neece

I return y^u thanks for the care y^u have taken of the paint, & believe the Ivory will do well enough for a beginer. I find Mr Millward hase given a very fails account of the Lady days rents in his hands, & he desir'd he might pay the mickelmas taxes out of it, he having no mony of his owen, & they was to be paid as soon as the day was past, & he should not receive any of the rent so soon; so I told him he might, & repay me when he received the mickelmas rents: for I understand those that receive the rents must pay the taxs, but I should tell y^u that Mr Annesley sent me word that if any of the Leases was set to midsummer I had a right to those rents, because my Nephew died after, so I ordered Mr Millward to look into all the tenants Leases, & give me an account to w^t time they was set: but he has not yet: he told me their was one estat that was under set, & that it might be rased 15^{lb} a year, so I bid him send word of it to London; for I had nothing to do w^t that. I believe Ld Abingdon should ask for the Counter parts of the Leases of y^r estate, & if they was looked into it might be of great advanage to y^u. I am going to day to see Mrs Coten & in tend to stay two or three days with her, so can ade no more but that I am

Dear Neece
y^r affec: Aunt & Servant,
B. SHIRLEY.

[P.S.] All here are y^r servants; & wee all desire our humble service to L^y & Ld Abingdon."

Oct. 15th, [1714?]. Lady Anne Courtenay to the same. Unaddressed
" I return Dear M[rs] Shirley many thanks for her oblidging Letters &
should have done it before now but was prevented sometime by my
Concerne for the Death of my poore Sis[r] Bertie who is realy a very great
Loss to her famely & last week I had begun writeing to y[u] but was
seiz[d] wth the Colick before I had finished my letter w[ch] Continued upon
mee for some days & made mee soe weak that this is the first time I
have bin able to take pen in hand since & I can not say my disorder has
perfictly left mee yet, y[r] La[ps] surprized mee by the news y[u] sent mee of
the Dutches of Beaufort & own I can not but think she had much
better have Continued as she was, I hope if my Couzen Catherine
Bertie marys my Lady Norreys will take hir Sis[r] Nany to live with
her.

I am obliged to y[r] La[ps] for y[r] desier of seeing mee but nothing has
yet happend in this Countery to make mee desierous of leaving it but if
I could doe y[u] any service none would bee more ready to take a Jorney
to London than my Self, my Boy is soe delighted wth the present y[u] sent
him that he says he will drink y[r] health for ever & indeed he & his Sis[r]
never doe mis it a day, I think wee are much quieter here than at London w[ch] makes mee wish all my friends wth mee I shall expect in a little
time to hear some news of y[r] La[ps] I am sure none wishes y[r] Happynes
more than I doe who am

Dear Madam
Y[r] La[ps] faithfull Humble Ser[t]
A. COURTENAY.

[P.S.] S[r] W[m] & my litle ones are y[r] La[ps] Humble Ser[ts] & I am the
same to Lady Bab & beg the favour of y[r] La[ps] to get a sight of the bed
as y[u] mention w[ch] I think must be a penyworth & if y[u] think it soe I
shall bee oblidged if y[u] will buy it for me & will returne y[u] the money."

1714, Oct 17th. Lady Anna Eleanor Shirley to the same. From
Lichfield. Franked by John Cotes, and addressed " This for M[rs]
Shirley att the Earl of Abingdon's in S[t] James Square—London." The
seal on this letter represents an amorino springing off the ground to
catch a winged heart.

" Dear nece,
I should not a been so long silant, but that my sister Bar[bara]
writing, I belived y[u] wold loke upon it the same, and I had nothing
more to tell y[u], but what she did, I am extremly well pleas'd y[u] like
being att L[d] Abingdon's, for I dont question but it will be much to y[r]
advantedg, for non more sencerely wishes y[r] happynes, than my silf.
My Brother & Sister, & nece, & my silf, was att the assamble, we
dined at Lady Pies; she inquier'd affter y[u], as did M[rs] Willmot, we
danced, & ther was most of the best company ther, M[rs] Coten says M[r]
Nate Corsen enquiers much affter y[u], & his elder brother drinks y[r]
health to him. I hear M[r] Pagit desires to make great Cort to y[u], so that
he will follo y[r] Brothers maxim, in not taking on[e] deniall. By what
I can hear y[u] will have great store of admi[r]ers; I can give y[u] noe
account of Repton, yett, it is much as it was when y[u] was last hear. M[rs]
frances bagot is just com hear to the Race, in hopes of her loves Company i sepos, to dance, but she will i fear be balked for ther will be tow
ball's, & we shall goe to M[r] Chettings [Chetwynd's?], tho he desines to
envit all upon the race; & has musick com from lester, & has lad out
20 pound in swettmets & hiered the town hall, i am in hast, & wish y[u]
can read this sad [s]croll, i am

Y[r] most Affe : Aunt & Servent,
AN : ELL : SHIRLEY.

[P.S.] My Brother Ler : gives his sarves to y^u, & all the rest of y^r relations hear, & with me wishes y^u much devershon att the Corenation, & hopes y^u will not be uneasy att y^r not being wellcom to the Pellmell, for when they Com to Consider they will soon Chang ther minds ; my sarves to madamasell & Mr Gillbo."

1714, Oct. 31st. The Dowager Countess of Arran to the same. Unaddressed.

" I hope Deare Madam you had my letter I sent you before you came to town, & having not heard from you a good while, I ca'nt forbeare inquiring thus after you since y^r coming to London, where I hope you have been well, I dougt not but of y^r being very easy at my Ld Abington's, where I hear you are, but yet cannot but be sorry at the occasion, of leaving y^r grandfathers house, before a good Husband brought you to one off y^r own, where I hope in due time you will be hapyly placed, having now undougtedly many good offers in y^r choice, & that you will accept of some ⌊one⌋ of them before long, wch is the best setlement y^r friends can wish you. The town now is very intertayning, & I hope you have by this time gott of in some measure y^r malancholy, for the unfortunate losse wch is not to be recalled, I shall extreamely reioyce to hear of y^r well faire, being a very true freind of y^{rs}, & in all things very much

Deare Niece,
Y^r Affectionat humble servant,
D. ARRAN."

1715, Augt. 17th. Revd Walter Horton to the same. Dated in the Cathedral Close of Lichfield and unaddressed.

" Most Honoured Madam

Permit me to address myself to you this day, and even with extasys, & transports of joy to congratulate your having compleated the twenty first year of your age. It was my happiness to dedicate you to the Christian Religion, and it is a mighty satisfaction to me, that you are as much distinguished by your Piety, as by your birth, & quality, & I have with unspeakable pleasure reflected upon that truly noble Idea of Religion, which is so eminently conspicuous in you, which sits as it were in a glorious triumph in your brest, with all the passions in subjection about her, & with all that lustre that a sweet disposition, & excellent sense, & a most graceful amiable Personage, can endear, & recommend. This, Madam, will command esteem, & inhance your Value amongst all that have the honour to know you. This will revive the brightest Images of your Illustrious Ancestors, for the Ferrerses are renownd in our Annals for their generous favours to the Church, as well as for the vigorous Endeavours to maintain the liberty of their Country. May you live many many years. & inherit the Virtues with the fair estates of your Great Predecessors, may you have a most sure, but an exceeding late most blessed Immortality. May you be blest with a noble sweet Companion worthy of you, & may your Children succeed you in your fortunes, may all that prosperity attend you which your own good heart can desire for your self, are the constant & ardent Prayers of

Honoured Madam
Your most devoted & most humble Servant
WALT : HORTON."

1715, Aug. 19th. Mrs Katherine Ward to the same. Unaddressed.

Dear Madam,

This being the Anniversary of your La^{pp's} Birth Day, the same which brings you to the possession of your honourable Estate, & inheritance, I

think it My Duty to congratulate y^r La^p upon the same, with My Most
sincere wishes for your health, & happiness, Long Life, & good Days,
& the best of Husbands, when you think fitt to alter your station, together
with all other enjoyments your own heart can wish, or this world can
afford you. I doubt not Madam but this is a day of great rejoycing
amongst all your La^ps friends, & honourable relations. And we for our
parts, according to the utmost of our poor capacitys have endeavour'd to
perticipate with you as much as it was possible at so remote a distance,
upon the Joyful aecation. Sir Edward Littleton vissits us frequently,
& Mr Ward tells him sometimes that your La^p, & Lady Barbara would
make My Lord Newport, & himselfe the best of Ladys, & if the Heavens
have so great a blessing in store for Staffordshire, how should we
rejoyce ? to have so good Neighbours, & the satisfaction of seeing your
La^p placed so near as within 6 or 7 Miles of each others seat. I have
never had a Letter from your La^p since that I wrote in obedience to your
Commands concerning My Masters Will, & after that I wrote to
Mademoisell to enquire after your La^ps health, hearing you were indisposed, but have never heard from her, which I am very much concern'd at, I hope as soon as this comes to hand Your La^p will honour
me with a Line, for nothing is a greater pleasure to me than to hear
from you often, nor nothing would be a greater trouble than to think I
was forgotten by your La^p. Be pleased to present my Humble Duty
& service to Lady Barbara, & the rest of the Ladys, & I beg of you to
accept of more than be expressed from

Dear Madam

Y^r La^ps Most obedient & most faithful

Humble Servant,

KATH : WARD.

[PS.] Mr Ward is your La^ps Most Humble Servant, & we beg you
will please to give our services to Mademoisell.

"Upon 11th of July last '89 I was at Mr Wrights of Loughborrow
who was a Servant of Mr Ferrers of Walton for some time, & did travel
with him beyond Sea, both in France, & Holland, he told me that Esq.
Ferrers had ·a farme in Holland with a good House upon it, which he
had been wth him at it, & it was called by the Name of Lows Downes,
about seven Miles from the Hague in Holland.—JOHN CODDINGTON."

This I found in an account book of Mr Wards, & believing it might
be of service to your La^p, I have transcrib'd it."

[1716], [Feb.] 22nd. Lady Anna Bertie to the same. Dated as
below and addressed "To Mrs Sherly att a house next Door to the
Dyall in Charles Street near St James Square ; London."

"This is to beg dear Mrs Sherley & Lady babiays pardon for not waiting
on you on mounday morring but my father was att home by himself and
I could not have the face to ask him to give me leave to come to you but
according to my promise will not faile to give you a full and true
account of my journey to Oxford and my proceedings their, my
commpny in the Coach was ane old gontay man and his man and his
maide the old man preteniged great love to me, so you mus think I was
mighty happy, so when I came into Oxford the furist thing I sawe and
heard was K——y how [who] told me that my Lady norrise [Norreys]
was very angrey that I should come to Oxford without and invet[at]ion
from her, but when I saw my Lady shee told me shee was mightly glad
to see me and that I was mighty wellcome to her house, but she sad that
I made her very dull, I put her so much in mind of my sister Nelly
that I doe not much mind what was saide afore; all the Oxford scolrs

aske if I am not a kin to Mrs Elnore Bertie for they nevor saw too so like in·thear lives. This day I was att the Theater to see my lord Aron chose and all the Cry I hear is Aron [Arran] & Ormond for ever & Down with the round heads, and treasion hollied in the streat from morring to night so that you must think I am got into a very vile town. I beg my humble service to Lady bab and I beg her pardon I did not pay her for my head but upon my word I never thought on it till I came to weichem but I shall be in London in less then a forgnight or I will send the mony by the furis[t] opuertunety but pray make a very handsome excuse for me, I have a great Deale to say to you but durst not turst itt in this paper, I did not get out of London till verry late so that I did not come into Oxford till darke night and I was in great Danger of breaking my night, I hope dear Mrs Sherley [you] will be so kind as to send me word when you are my lady, and if you can give favours I hope you will laye one by for me ·and some bride cake for you know what a great lover I am of plumb cake   I had this day the happiness of seeing young Mr Coumton who I ham mightly in love with, I hope you will find out what is meint in this letter but you know what a very good speller I am, so that I will conglude Dear madam your faithfull frind

and humble serveint
to command
A. Bertie.

my sister deisirs her humble service to you I have not time to write to aney body afore twlef a Clock att night, pray derickt for me att my Lady norrise near the Theater in Oxford

Oxford the 22 twelf att night."

[1715], March 5th. ·Lady Dorothy Cotes to the same. Dated at Lichfield and addressed "For the R^t Hon^able the Lady Compton next door to Mr Massy's Wachmaker in Charles Street near St James's Square; London."

Dear Neice,

There is no Change of fortune happens to you wherein I cannot but take a part having allways had so sincere a Concern for you. And therefore must beg leave to congratulate with you on your entering into the happy Estate of Mattrimony ; and as you have all the Prospect of happiness any of your freands can desier so I sincerly wish you all the Injoymente this World can aford.

Your Unkell desires his humble Sarvice to you wishing you all happiness & would have write to you on this subject but, thought it would be less trouble to you to put it in mine ; all mine are your humble Sarvants and

I am Dear Niece
Your Affec. Aunt & Humble Sarvant,
Dorothy Cotes.

[P.S.] I desier my humble Sarvice to your Lord thou[gh] unknown."

[1716], March 6th. Lady Anne Courtenay to the same. Un-addressed.

I have this day heard Dear Madam that y^u are entered into the State of Matrimony & cannot omit taking the first opertunety of wishing y^r La^ps all imaginable Joy & Happynes as I think y^u have reison to propose to y^r self from the good Character wch is soe generaly given of my Lord Compton & I hope he justly deserves it for I am sure none hes a truer

Value for y^r La^{ps} then I have, I believe y^u are at this time much taken
up wth Company. soe will tyer y^u noe longer but to assure y^u I am
        Dear Madam
           y^r La^{ps} Most affec. & Obedient Humble Ser^t,
                           A. COURTENAY.

[P.S.] S^r W^m is y^r La^{ps} Most Humble Sert & wishes y^u much Joy &
we both beg leave to Joyne in the same to my Ld Compton. Nany begs
y^u will accept of her Humble service & good wishes."

[1716], March 10th. Catherine Venables, daughter of Sir Robert
Shirley, to the same. Address torn.

"My waint of heart (Madam) hendered me writing & I had as soon as
I heard, to have wished y^u ioy no boddy dus it more harttyly (for y^r
father and mother sack) I most allwas have a kindnes for y^u and should
be glad if it was in my power to searvie y^u. I am much consearned att
the dispute betwine y^u, and y^r grandfather and his anger, he is your
father['s] father, and for his sack bair it all as well as y^u can and hid[e]
his packen [? passion] as much as you can for his sack and y^r own as it
may as lettel be knon as can be in the famally y^u are now in, he is old,
and so I am I hope y^u will exquise this impertignences, and believe me
to be

        Dear Madam
          Y^r affect : [great] Aunt & humble searvant,
                        C. VENABLES.
[P.S.] My sarvis to Ld Compton."

[1716 ?], April 3rd. Lady Anne Courtenay to the same. Unaddressed.
"I am very much oblidged to Dear Lady Compton for her letter at a
time that I am senceable y^u were so much taken up wth Company the
remembering a friend at soe great a distance at that time was an addition
to the favour but I doe asure y^r La^{ps} y^u could not have bestowed it upon
one who has a truer Value for y^u than my self, I was very glad to hear
by a letter from S^r W^m that y^r La^{ps} inioys y^r health & hope y^u will long
Continue to doe soe, I have bin very ill of my old comyanion the Collick
wch very often returnes upon mee, this place is very dull at present
haveing noe Company & y^r La^{ps} knowing something of my temper may
sopose mee to be a little spleenatick therefore I will tyer y^u noe longer
wth this dull scrall but asure y^u I am,
        Dear Madam
          Y^r La^{ps} Obedient Humble Ser^t
               A. COURTENAY."

[1716], April 8th. Lady Anna Bertie to the same. Addressed "To
the Right Honb^{le} Lady Compton next Door to the Dyall in Charles
Streat near St James Squir—London."

"Madam,
      I received the honour of your L^{dsp} Letter & should have return'd
thanks for it before this time had I not been Confined to my bed
for above this Week by a feaver wich I am now much better of but
I have a great Pain in my head, I wish this Place afor'd[ed] aney
thing to make a Letter aney wayes acceptable but all the talke att
prasint is of a very od Weding wich has lately happned hear, tho you
do not know the Lady I cannot help giveing you an account of, and am
Sure did y^u know her you must be of my Mind that nothing that weres
petticoates need \dispair of a husband, She is a boute three score & has
nether beauty witte nor good humour to recommend her she is of a make
large enough for the Grand Senior. Standing one lucky hour att her

Window thear.past.by a genttellman about the same age who casting
hies eyes upwards beheld this Queen of Beauty & att this time was taken
wth Such a fluttring att his heart that he could not rest till he had
Broke his mind to her and he soon found releif, for theay said Matrimony in a week and hethertoo think themselves they [are the] happyest
Couple in the Kings Dominions, God keep them so say I. My Father
desiens for London next week but 1 am a frad I shall no[t] come w[th]
him tho' my cheafe Beasness is to pay my duty to y[r] Lad[sp] this Place
Grows extreemly plesint, I will not tyer y[u] aney furder att this time
then to assure you I am Madam

wth all respet y[r] L[dsp]
most obliged humble
Servient to Comand
A. BERTIE.

I hope this will find my L[d] & y[r] L[dsp] in good helth my sister desiers
her humble service to y[r] L[dsp] & wishes you all the joy & happines y[u]
can desier.

I should have maid a excuse for the Length of this but that y[r] L[dsp] was
so kind to Desier me to use the same fredome, w[ch] is a Command I very
readly obey."

[1716?], May 8th. Lady Anne Courtenay to the same. Dated at
Powderham and unaddressed.

I am extreamly obliged to Dear Lady Compton for the favour of her
letter & Picture w[ch] I shall sett a very great value on haveing so true a
respect for the originall & S[r] W[m] tells mee he thinks it is very like, I
should not have bin soe long w[th]out returning my thanks for it but have
bin soe very ill w[th] the Colick in my Stomack & Cramp in all my limbs
that for some time I could not hold my pen to write a letter & being soe
well acquainted w[th] y[r] La[ps] good humore makes mee hope y[u] will excuse
it, I am very glad y[u] soe well escaped the robers. I think those who stay
late at the Park have very great Courage, I think my L[d] Torrington
was very charitable in leaving an Estate to one of soe ancient a Famely
& had so little before, my Daughter Nany is very senceable of the Honnor
y[r] La[ps] does her in remembering her in all y[r] Letters & is very often
wishing she could wait on y[u] to thank y[u] for it her self she begs y[r] La[ps]
will accept of her Humble service & I fear I have tyerd y[u] soe will onely
asure y[u] I am very faithfully

Dear Madam,
Y[r] La[ps] Most Obedient Humble Ser[t],
A. COURTENAY.

[P.S.] S[r] W[m] is y[r] La[ps] Most Humble Ser[t] & wee both Joyne in the
same to y[r] Lord."

1716, June 23rd. To Lord and Lady Compton from the Rev[d] Walter
Horton. Dated in the Cathedral Close of Lichfield. The signature
has been cut off.

" My Lord, & Lady,

My sickness hath prevented me from doing my self the honour to
congratulate your thrice happy espousals, but having a little recovered
the use of my hand, permit me to wish you all that lasting joy, that
sweet consolation, that inviolable friendship that can possibly attend so
Hon̄ble, so solemn, so sacred an engagement.

I cannot but with the highest satisfaction reflect upon the promising
Consequences of this blessed union, when I duely consider that both
your familys make the brightest figures in our English Annals.

The Comptons for a long succession of Ages have been celebrated in
other nations as well as in our own, for their gravity & steadiness, for

MARQUESS
TOWNSHEND
MSS.
——
their wisdom, prudénce, & valour, & our late Gracious Sovereign when she summond your Lordp to the House of Peers discernd in your Person the Illustrious Virtues of your Noble Ancestors, & you rarely qualifycd to assist her in perplext & difficult times.

The Ferrers & Shirleys were of old Great Patriots of their Country & your excellent Lady is descended from them both & is as such distinguisd by her Virtues as by her high & truely noble extraction, the humility, & aimable charming Sweetness of her temper will every day appear most lovely in your Lp sight.

That your many many years may glide smoothly on in Peace, that you may be left with a numerous offspring to transmit you illustrious qualifications to Posterity, are the constant dayly Prayers of My Lord & Lady.

Your Honours
Most devoted very humble Servant."

1716, Sept. 25th. Hon. Henry Shirley " To The Right Honble Lady Compton att her Seat att Compton in the Hole Northamptonshire."
" Dear Niece
        I am at a Stand how to begin or what to touch upon, so great a Stranger am I to Divertion as you may judge by the Sequel; when the Compass of 2 Acres confines my greatest Prominade, tho' Boundless my thoughts. Should I tell you I am desperately in Love, 'tis probable tell me it is common, But should I tell you with whom I dare say I may justifie my self, if Phylosophy is no a riddle, & that Beautifull Objects were not made to move the Senses. I have lived since I saw you so much upon Ideas that I am almost Ærial, & could wish not almost but altogether, could I but breath[e] that refresh ment in a Vapour that might be agreeable to Lady Betty Compton. You may think me Romantick, But were you as sensible as my self of what I can (tho' a Paradox) term nothing but insensibility, I am sure your good nature could not but pity me. I have you know the great task to get over, the perswading some to return to their Reason who expect that men without their senses should live by their wits, & whats [more] work without their Liberty. I am so much a Heterodox man in the principles of modern Toryism, that I cannot write of Politicks without thinking that some men are Conjurers to compound others when stated rules in one Reign are reversed in another, all I believe is that I scarce can believe anything that is reported But what I have better grounds for then some imagine. I believe I shall whip up att last to prove my younger Brother not older then myself, which I find to be necessary, & then I will try what Lady Betty will hear from me ; which as it is a thing of the last consequence I think ought to be proved according to law. And then I think to thunder Don Diego a Politicall March who by what I can understand has trim'd his weather cock Conscience to another Point of the Compass. I am very buisy with diverting my self some hours with the Camœnian Muses, & others with my Lord Chief Justice Cook's Crab-stick upon Littleton in the Caracter of Jacobs Modern Justice. I have been so witty since I visited this Mad House that I almost want a new Petticoat my Muses Cloathing is worn so thread bear & so homely that truly its scarce becomes my Modesty to tell the truth were I not a Poet, & much out att the Heels for want of High Church Hereditary Right. I hope you will not be long before you come to Town 'till when Adieu from yn Entirely
H. Shirley.
  Service to my Lord
  And bright Lady Betty &c."

1716, Sept. 30th.· Jane Countess of Northampton to the same.
Addressed " To the Right Honble Lady Compton."

" Since we was to part with my Dear Daughter (wch I do assure you
was with great regreet on my side), I was mighty glad that you had so
fine a day for travaileing ; I hope you found Ld Tamworths family all
well, & that you got away from thence in good time, that you might
perform y^r journey with ease & get into Compton before it was dark.

My L^d sends you his blessing, & we both desire the same to L^d
Compton ; & to both return thanks for y^r kind vissitt. The seeming
satisfaction you showed here, was I do assure you a very real one to me,
& I do promiss Dear Lady Compton, that as long as she dose give me
that encouragement, there is no opertunity I won't improve to give
prooffs, of my real affection to my Dear Son ; wch would be motive enô
for my kindness to you, but the addition of y^r own meritt engages me
dubbly to be

Your most affectionate Mother,
J. NORTHAMPTON.

[P.S.] All y^r B^{rs} & Sis[ters] presents there servises, so doth aunt
Whittle."

[1716 ?] Lady Barbara Shirley to the same. Undated and unaddressed.

" Dear Neece,
I believe y^u will be glad to know, how my brother's affair goes,
theirfore this is to let y^u [know] this last monday he went to Staunton,
to aske my father's consent ; & also to see w^t he would give him in
present. He gave him his consent, he told him if he could get her, but
did not believe he could, & told him he would give him a mentenanze,
but would not name w^t. When he had dun talking with my brother he
went & told my Ly who was very much against it as y^u may easly
emagen ; but to put the better face on it ; she told him he was very
much in the rong to consent to it ; for that he might have 20000l. with
him considering the prospect he had of being Heir, & at last so perswaded my Ld that he was against ; the wch my brother being enform'd
by those that hard the disput, he got a horseback & came a way without
seeing my Ld Least he should for bid him, & yesterday he was to
acquaint Mrs Lister with my Ld answer, the wch she is so well satisfied
with that she has give[n] farder assurances that she will have him, & he
has got a Lazunce ; and the mesanger that brings this to Northampton is
sent for a ring ; so we hope to have it accomplished very soon. Sis[ter]
Catherin is now at Staunton but is to go soon in to Chesshir, one may
easily believe she has no very pleasent time their now. My brother
Cotes is gone to Wood Cote, wch place we have reason to think will soon
be his for his father declines visable every day. I hope if y^u go to
Compton we shall see y^u here in y^r way their, this being a good distance
to make y^r dining place. I believe y^u will not see my brother & sister
Tam :, for they think it not convenant to lie out, & y^u know it is to
fare to com back at night all here are y^r servants, & none more so than
her that is

Y^r affec : Aunt & Servant
B. SHIRLEY.

[P.S.] Pray give our service to Ld and Lady Nor[thampton] & all
the other Lady, & also to Ld Compton."

1734, May 14th.—Lady Penelope Compton to the Countess of Northampton, " att Castle Ashby." Dated at Dover Street.
. . . . " we have been tonight very much alarm'd with a Fire in
Albemarle street . . . . it happen'd to be of the other side of the

way next Bond street, so that our house was not in any danger, but seeing it so near was very terrible, for it burnt very feirce two houses intirely down before they could get any water, it began I think they say in one Mr Cantillions who was quite burnt before it was discovered and they say it was by his reading in Bed but there are so many reports one can't tell what is certain ; it was very near Mrs Shirley which in her condition is very bad but they had no great damage and she sends word she is very well to day ; we were a Sunday to see Ld Compton at Fulham so that I can now have the pleasure of sending your Lady^{sp} word that he is extreamly well ; Sr John Rushout is come to town again we are just going to dine at Bloomsbury and so many of our Friends has been so kind in enquireing after us this morning that I have not time to add any more than to assure dear L^{dy} Northampton that I am

L^{dy} Margaret presents   Your Lady^{sps} Affec : Sister &
her service to you &   Humble Servant
we both beg the same to   PEN : COMPTON.
my B[rothe]r and all Friends."

1734, July 14th.—Lady Anne Compton, "To The R^t Honble the Countess of Northampton at Tamworth." In a child's handwriting.

" Madam

    I hope this will find my Lord & your Ladyship safe and well arrived to Tamworth where I wish with all my heart to be with you. Thank God we are all very well Lady Charlotte desired me to join her humble duty with mine to Dear Pappa & Mamma I humble beg your Ladyship will be so good [as] to give our Services to Lady Betty & Mr Compton & pray remember us kindly to Lady Jane. I am

Madam y^r Ladyships
Most Obedient Servant
& Dutifull Daughter
ANNE COMPTON."

1734, Augt. 17th. Lord Compton to the same "at Castle Ashby in Northampton-Shire — by Ashby [Post-]Bagg." In a child's handwriting.

" Dear Mama

    I wish your Ladyship a great deal of Joy of your Birthday, wishing you may see a great many of them, I hope you will all be very merry. I will be as merry here as possible. There was a Gentleman came from my [Dowager] Lady Northampton's to day, and says she is better than she has been. Pray give my Duty to my Pappa and my Service to Mr Compton, Lady Betty and my sisters.

I am,
Madam
Your most Dutiful son
JAMES COMPTON."

1734, Augt. 19th.—Lady Penelope Compton to the same. Dated at Bracknell and unaddressed.

" If I had not been indebted to Dear Lady Northampton for an obligeing Letter, this Day [being her Birthday] would have claimed a remembrance. . . . . . I did not doubt but you had a good deal of company, betwixt receiving and returning Visits, I fancy it was great pleasure to the old Lady Chester to have an opportunity of meeting y^u for she used to be very hearty and cheerful with her acquaintances ; poor Lady Gore is indeed I doubt in a very bad way for before.I left London Lady Gainsbrough said she expected to .hear of her death every post, it is a great deal of pity, especially since you say he is so much reclaimed that he should be left a Widower again so soon . . . tother day I saw Mrs Vansittart who said that the last time they heard of her she was much better; she is a neighbour to us here about 11 Mile off, and was so obligeing to come to see us, as did also L^d & L^y Arran and L^dy E. Butler who are about the same distance too, Lady Nassau Paulet is within two Miles so that your Lady^sp finds we have some company, but excepting those that we knew before none has come which I am mighty glad of for [we] was not at all desireous of makeing new acquaintances here; nor of having many Visits, for [we] did not think it worth while to keep on our Horses whilst we were out of town not haveing much for'em to do . . . . . I am very sorry for poor Mrs Crofts for she will be a very great loss to the school it was indeed a terrible accident and the most extraordinary too that ever was heard on." . . . . .

1734, Augt. 24th. Lady Anne Rushout to the same. Dated at Northwick.

"Dear Madam,—I should have writ by the return of the Person that brought the Venison to have return'd your Lady^sp and my Lord a great many thanks for it it was extream good, and this day [I] shall treat Sr John Dutton with some of it; the judges dined with us on Wednesday in their way home after finishing their Circuit, Tuesday Sr John is obliged to attend the Chusing of a Mayor at Evesham & Wednesday we go into Buckinghamshire, I shall first go to judge Denton's where after I have stay'd a Week or 10 days shall go to Tring, for about as long a time. Mr Sandys comes here to go along with us. I hope we shall have good weather, for [we] propose going to see Ld Cobham's which I have heard great talk of, I am very sorry to hear of the Misfortune of Dr Croft's Sister, I dont know whether Ld Compton is at Asby this Bartholomew time but whereever [he is] I hope [he is] very well, I beg the favour of my humble service to my B[rothe]r L^y Betty & the young Ladys, Sr John desires his also. This morning he had a Letter from my B[rothe]r Cha[rle]s at Lisbon, he and his Familly were all very well my two Little Girls are mighty well, Betty at this time at my Elbow & begs her respects, indeed she bestows a great deal of her Company upon me which while I am alone is very acceptable, the small pox is a great deal in the town & tho a good sort yet I take all the Care I can it shou'd not come to us, I heartely wish it over as I do with all your family, it would be great Comfort to you and every thing that woud be so is always most sincerely wished by

Dear Lady Northampton
Your most Affectionate
humble Servant
A. RUSHOUT."

1734, Sept. 7th. Nicholas Guillibeau to the same. Dated at Fulham and addressed outside to the Earl of Northampton at Castle Ashby.

"My Lady,—My Lord Compton continues thank God in very good health. . . . . as for Mr Crofts family it is still managed by his Sister in Law. . . . . he intended to have his own Sister Ward but I hear that she has a very bad State of health. . . . . her death is a great loss to him and to the whole School."

No date. The same to the same. Unaddressed.

"My Lord Compton continues thank God in very good health. · · · · Mr Loundes came here Yesterday to see his Lord^sp and found them very well. I have ask^d Mr Leach who is Mr Crofts head Usher if he would

go with his Lord⁹ᵖ to Oxford, he being a Student of that place . . . .
but as it will not be till the 14ᵗʰ of next Month he cant possibly leave
the School." . . . .

1734, Sept. 17th. Elizabeth Rolleston to the same. Dated in London
and unaddressed.

" Madam,

. . . . . . I am overjoyed to hear that your Laᵖᵖ my Lord & the
dear pretty Ladys are in perfect health, I wish you a safe journey to
Compton & a Continuance of that happiness there and in all other
places. I have follow'd Doctor Colis's directions & I have found I
thank God a great benefit by them & (under God) I owe this to your
kind procuring his advice for me, May God reward you for this & all
the other benefits I have been Constantly receiving from yᵘ ever since
I had the honor to be known to you without which (in all humane
appearance) I shou'd have been a Miserable Creature, tis time I repeat
my acknowledgements in every letter so they are still repetitions but
how can a gratefull heart like mine so sensible of my unworthiness &
your great Condescention be able to do otherwise."

1734, Sept. 28th. Nicholas Guillibeau to the same. Dated at Castle
Ashby.

" My Lady,—My Lord Compton continues thank God in very good
health, His Lord⁹ᵖ presents his Duty to my Lord and to your Lady⁹ᵖ
and Services to the Ladies. I had just now a letter from Mʳ Rawlins
in which he tells me that he has taken a place in next Mondays Coach
so proposes to wait upon My Lord on Wednesday Morning for the
Coach has done flying. Mʳ Crofts Sister in Law is this week return⁴ to
London, & She that manages the family now is a Cozen of Mʳ Croft her
name is Turenne. She is pretty elderly but seems to be a good Manager
and very civil to all the Gentlemen, and as for the Table it is kept in
the same Manner as usual."

1734, Oct. 8th. The Same to the Same. Dated and addressed as the
last.

" My Lady,—My Lord Compton continues thank God in very good
health. His Lord⁹ᵖ keeps free from a cold altho they are pretty much
about still. My Lord has drunk but little Malt drink this Summer for it
was but seldom to his liking. I mention this because I have not heard
Mʳ Croft speak of any wine he had receiv⁴ for My Lords use, but often
cals for some of Lord Goring's wine." . . . . .

1734, Oct. 9ᵗʰ. Lady Anne Rushout to the same. Dated at Northwick and unaddressed.

. . . . [I] am sure it woud have been one of the most agreeable
parts of our ramble if I could have waited on my Brother and You, but
our time was much streightned for what we did and besides had the disadvantage of very bad weather great part of the time, it was particularly
unlucky all the time I was in the neighbourhood of Stow, for tho I did
go to L⁴ Cobhams Gardens it was impossible to see any more thɑn that
it appeared very large & great Variety ; but it seems placed in a very deep
dirty Country, when I went to Tring 'twas rather better weather, but
was engaged to dine abroad so many of the few days I stayed there,
that I was in some fear least I shoud not get an oppertunity to see the
new Obeliskt and Temple which Mʳ Gore has built in his Park since I
was last there, which woud have been great pitty they are both so
extreamly nent & hansome, I think he cant find much more to do at
Tring, in my opinion he might quite have finished for it realy is a very
agreeable fine place, the leaving that was great disadvantage to going

directly to poor little Harrow where [the Dowager] Lady Northampton was obliged to send away part of her own familly to make room for Sr John & I for a few days. I found her much better then when I left her, that Air I believe very good & is a place always agreed with her ; at my return Home I found Betty very well but poor Nanny has a terrible cough, which I believe contributes to keeping her weak, for she yet makes very little use of her feet." . . . . .

1734, Oct. 12th. Nicholas Guillibeau to the same. Dated at Fulham, and addressed to the Earl at Castle Ashby.

"My Lady,

My Lord Compton continues thank God in very good health His Lord^{sp} presents his Duty to My Lord and to Your Lady^{sp} and Services to the Ladies. Mr Humes brought My Lords frock and Breeches this Morning and the Hatter has also sent a Hatt. His Lord^{sp} choose[s] to have it it laced, with an open lace."

1734, Oct. 13th. The same to the same. Address torn off. Dated at Fulham.

"My Lord Compton continues thank God in very good health. His Lord^{sp} receiv^d a visit Yesterday from my Lady Cardigan and their two Daughters at my House my Lord being there (for it was Holy Day) : . . . . . My Lords Pocket Money is all spent and his Lord^{sp} desired me to supply him with more so that I have let his Lord^{sp} have ten Shillings" . . . .

1734, Oct. 22nd. Lady Elizabeth Compton to the same. Dated in London.

. . . . . I heard to-day from Fulham that Lord Compton was pure well. Lady Dow[age]r Northampton has had a little of the Gout . . . . . Lady Jane [Compton] was in Town and dined with me to day . . . . . Sir John Dolben's son has had the small pox in the most favourable manner . . . . . . the Princess of Orange went away yesterday. Dr Tessier & the Queen's Nurse is gone over with her, it is generally said that the King of Prussia is dead, but not to be notified till after the Birthday, least it should ccl'pse some of the Finery . . . . . . every body that has been in the Air to-day complains extremely of the sharpness of it, such severe frosts beginning so early is a dismal prospect of a very long Winter, but in the Country you are much less sensible of the badness of it than in town" . . . . . .

1734, Oct. 24th. Nicholas Guillibeau to the same. Addressed to the Earl "at Compton Viniate—Warwick Shire.". Dated at Fulham.

Lord Compton continues in very good health and sends his Duty.

1734, Oct. 26th. The same to the same. Dated and addressed a° the last.

Lord Compton continues in very good health and received his Papa's letter last night. The breaking up [at his school] will be about the 12th of December.

1734, Oct. 27th. Lady Penelope Compton to the same. Dated at Bracknell and unaddressed.

. . . . . "we are still very well satisfied with our little Habitation, for whenever there is a fine day we make shift to get out of doors which agrees mighty well with us both, and L^y Margaret has not had the least cold . . . . . our near neighbours are most of them going soon to town. L^{dy} Preston is already gone and Mrs. Skipworth goes tomorrow & those we used to see pretty often, and Mrs. Prade intends going in a bout a week."

U 24953.

Q

1734, Oct. 22nd.   Nicholas Guillibeau to the same.   Dated and addressed as his last.

The writer reports that Lord Compton continues in very good health and presents his Duty.

1734, Nov. 2nd.   The same to the same.   Unaddressed.   To the same effect.

1734, Nov. 5th.   The same to the same.   Dated at Fulham and addressed to the Earl at Compton Viniate.

. . . . . . "His Lordship continues thank God in very good health, only his hollow Tooth has felt a little uneasy these 4 or 5 days but since I have stopped the' hole with a grain of Mastick it has been eassyer " . . . .

1734, Nov. 7th.   The same to the same.   Dated and addressed a the last.

The writer reports that Lord Compton continues in very good health and presents his Duty.

1734, Nov. 18th.   Lady Anne Rushout to the same.   Unaddressed.

. . . . "Many thanks for the Venison you now send me . . . . I have had no private Letter [that] has mentioned Lady Suffolk's quitting her employ; I read it with surprise last post . . . . Sr John was sent for last Monday in great hast to L^{dn} to poor Mr. Bouverie (a Young Gentleman he is Trustee for) who lay dying "

. . . . . .

1734, Nov. 19th.   Nicholas Guillebeau to the same.   Address torn off.   Dated at Fulham.

. . . . . "I went yesterday to Mr. Wood and bespoke a coach to be here this day Sevnight, the same Coach Man that usd to drive your Lady^{ps} familly will go this journey, he said that they could not do with less than six Horses for the Roads in all likelyeood will be very stiff; and that the Oxford Road will be the safest for to go by, Islip is but indifferent travelling even in Summer.   We are to go to Stokeu-Church the first day and bait at Beaconsfield, and the next day I believe that Wheatley will be the properest place to bait at, and so on to Woodstock "

. . . . .

1734, Nov. 21st.   Lady Elizabeth Compton to the same.   Dated in Golden Square and unaddressed.

. . . . . .   "The number of story's & contradictory reasons given for Lady Suffolk's removing from Court wou'd fill more than ordinary length of one of my Letters (& that generally is een long enough too) my own opinion is that it was her own desire to retreat, her health is bad & the confinement very great, & since her Lord's Death that she was out of danger of falling into his hands, I believe she has been desirous to have Liberty & a little more time at her own command.   Others say that she was at Bath too often in company with Lord B——ke &c. & that it a thing agreed on [at] St James's that before the Norfolk congress was broke up she should be removed from thence. . . . . . Lord Hobbard [Hobart] is to be immediately out, & people conjecture that many more are to follow but I believe nothing is yet done.   Sr John Rushout who is gone out of town will be able to tell your Lady^p much more than I can, as also about Farinelli he having much more judgment in Musick.   All I can say is I think he is charming.   A Scholar of Mr Gates's, Beard, (who left the Chappell last Easter) shines in the Opera of Covent Garden & Mr Hendell [Handel] is so full of his Praises that he says he

·will surprise the Town with his performances before the Winter is
over. . . . . . . I suppose you have heard that upon Mʳˢ Thompson's
(Mʳˢ Dunch's Daughter) being so privately buried Mʳ Thompson has
sent to have her Coffin taken up & open'd, upon which it is found she
was murder'd. Sᵗ George Oxenden owns the having given orders for
her burying, & some people think he must stand a tryal to clear him self
·of the Murder, it at present occasions a great deal of talk, as does also
Lord Falmouth's lying so long unburied. The Widdow refuses to do
it, as does also the Heir, & they are all a going to law, his body is
still at Mʳ Trefusis's where he was gone to make a visit when he died.
Lord Sidney Beauclerk has the small Pox, it is hoped in a good way,
but he will have no Physician, but Dʳ Mead who is they say in great
concern about it—for it seems if he dies without Children the Dʳ is
heir to 1000ˡˡ p añ. Lady Salisbury is come up to her youngest son
who has the small Pox & in a very good way.

Lady Harcourt complains loudly that no one Lord of what is call'd
the Country side has taken any notice of Lord Harcourt since his
coming over, & that all the Court has paid him great Compliments both
Lords & Ladys, & the Beautys of Richmond, Albemarle, Harvey, &c.
—may she says go a great way to biass a young man who has not an
inflexible heart. Lord Carteret is a Relation—Lᵈ Litchfield a neighbour in the Country both in Town but have not been near him. if
Lady Pomfrett sends to me I will do my self the honour to be your
representative & perform your Commissions, as I shall any from dear
Lady Northampton that is in the power of

your most affectionate

I beg my humble   sister and servant
   service to my Brother   E. COMPTON.
   & young Ladys."

1734, Nov. 28th. The same to the same. Dated in London and
unaddressed.

. . . . "On Tuesday Evening I had the honour to represent your
Ladyship at Pomfrets & [I] wish you joy of your God-son Thomas
Fermor, he is like all the rest of her Children a very fine lusty one, &
bawled most lustily at the time of his Christening, which they say is a
good Sign . . . . your Partners were the Duke of Sᵗ Albans & Lord
Lovell, all by Proxy. The Duke in Town but excused his coming upon
aceᵗ of Lord Sidney Beauclair's having the small-Pox & Lord Lempster
[Leominster] stood for him; the other down in Norfolk, his B[rothe]r
the Vice-Chamberlain Coke represented. Mʳ Fermor & Mʳˢ Fermor
were there, no other company, but the other eight Children who were
highly delighted by being all present. Lady Lempster is confined to
her chamber by a hurt she had on her Leg by falling down as she was
getting into her Coach ; (as you desired I left 10 guineas). Lady Harcourt is confined by spraining her foot by falling down as she came out
of the Opera-house ; she is not yet able to perform the Ceremonys at
Assembly but after Christmas designs to have one. The Dutchess of
Dorset is extremely ill again, here in Town ; she looked sadly when
she came up. 'Tis said Lord Scarborough has positively refused to go
into Ireland, & that the Duke of Devonshire who is now named, does
decline it. Lord Godolphin's Gold Key (as Groom of the Stole) is
given to Lord Pembroke, he was offer'd a Pension but that he generously rejected. There is sad to do amongst the Ladys at Court, several
of them not so much as speaking to each other, unless it is (in plain
English) flatly to contradict what each other has said. The Queen
came yesterday morning out for the first time. I was this morning at

St James's She is grown a good deal thinner in the face & paler than she was, but I think she abundantly better for it, & she says she thinks she has got quite rid of all complaints, but the Town says she has got a sore Legg which is very bad, but I dont know whether that is true. Lady Mary Sanderson has been very ill ever since I came to town, & complain'd of great pain in her arm 'tis now feared to be a Cancer. The Dowager (Newport) Lady Torrington is very ill at Bath with a dead Pulsie. Lord & Lady Ranelagh don't come up to Town till Xmas. Lord Malton is made an Earl, they talk of some more as Lord Abergavenny (& one or two besides) which if so I think it very hard as he was the first Baron that the Patent for one of the youngest should be passed before his, & eight new Creations are talked on. I never heard them all & some I have forgott. Sr Wm Strickland, Mr Edgecomb, Sr Rowland Wynne are some of them. Lord Winchelsea desired I wou'd present his humble service to Lord Northampton, & begged he wou'd be so good as to let him know, if whilst you lived in your house in Grosvenor-street, you ever found any inconveniency by smelling of shores or any complaint that cannot be discovered in going to see a house without living in it. Coll Schutz being going to part with it, Lord Winchelsea has some thoughts of buying it, but before he enter'd upon a Bargain desired I would ask my Brother this Question and have his answer. Lady Betty Fielding lives with him, to take care of the little Girl, Mr Buncombe's Brother has written a Play & last night was the Poetts night, I was there & I think he had a prodigious full house, especially considering that the Town is not near so full as it will be after Xmas. a Play comes out now with great disadvantage for 'twas sadly acted, otherwise I think 'tis really a good Play, 'tis a very deep Tragedy, the name Junius-Brutus, & the Story the conspiracy of his two sons Titus & Tiberius & their deaths. I sent the Ducks this day se'n-night down to Ashby . . . . you see I now neither stand upon ceremony nor brevity, but [am] glad of all opportunitys of assuring [you] my Dear Lady Northampton that I am most sincerely

Your Affectionate Sister
& humble Servant
E. Compton."

I beg my most humble service to
both the Lords & 3 Lady's.

1734, Dec. 7th. The same to the same. Dated in Golden Square, and unaddressed.

. . . . . . "Lady Anne Rushout sends me word her eldest Girl has been very ill, but now so much better she proposes being in Town before Ch'istm^s. My Lady Dow[age]r Northampton & Lady Jane came on Munday, the last is extremely well as ever I knew her, but my Lady is quite confined to her Chair, [she has] very little or no pain with the Gout now, but her feet & Aucles [are] so swelled and weak she cannot sett them down to the Ground. Mr Desbourrie is dead, [his family] sent a Messenger for Sr John Rushout last Saturday, but if he had come away post immediately he wou'd not have found him alive, he has left one Brother who is of Eaton School. Lady Masham died yesterday she had been long ill & in Doctor's hands, 'tis said she had great Riches, [she has] left only [an] Only Son & a Gran-Daughter about 7 year old who always lived with her. Poor Lady Salisbury has been in great Pain for her Son who since the small-Pox has had a bad Feavour, & so weak she much feared his recovery, but is now something better & I hope will do well, for she is vastly fond of him, & he has by every body an extraordinary good character ; poor woman she looks mighty thin, but as Mr Cecill recovers so I hope will she too. Ld Oxford they say seemed to decline giving them sisters any trouble or law about the dividend of the D[uche]ss of Montagu's Riches but my Lord Morpeth is resolved to give them all the trouble he can so that they are still in suspence he promised the last Term to make his Plea & have it decided, now it is put off till the next [Term]. Mr Tryon seems to think he goes on successfully with his [Lawsuit], he is now gone down into Northamptonshire to the estate in dispute. Dr Kimberley who was in Town a few days is gone down with him. Coll: Bachwell is come up to Town & laid up hand & foot, [he] has had a most severe fitt of the Gout, but [is] much better in his stomack. I believe I never thought to tell your Ladyship how I was one day surprized at a visitt that was made me, it was before I had been any where out of doors [and so soon] after my coming to Town, that I did not know who was in or out of Town or who was sick or well enough to come abroad, when in comes Lord Ferrars ; I own I was a little surprised not knowing he was so well, he behaved very sedately [and] enquired much after your Ladyship & [your] family. I have seen him since at the Opera & [he] seems mighty well, he does not lie in Town but has his Lodgings still at Kensington. Lord Clarendon is also very well, & every where about; your neighbour still at Mrs French's Sr Jason I remember I heard them speak off when I was at Northwick. I think he is so unhappy in his behaviour no body cares to be much with him, but has Sr Harry Parker been baulked in his Amours & gone down again without a Lady ? The Town has given Lord North one, they name Lady Lewisham, but I don't believe it is true, but London news you must take as I can pick it up. I never pretend to vouch for the veracity of it, but to my latest breath will affirm the truth of my being

Dear Madam,

Your most affection^t

Sister & Servant,

E. COMPTON."

1734, Dec. 12th. George Ballard to ——. Dated at Campden, and unaddressed.

" Revd & Honoured Sir !

Fearing you would think me unmindful of my promise, I have made bold to trouble you with a Note to inform you that I sent a Letter by the next Post to London for the Drawings ; but as yet have received no answer. I fancy the Gentleman who has 'em, hath made a Tour into Scotland in persuit of Curiosities, (for I hear he designed such a journey) which I imagine is the reason I have received no answer. I shall be highly pleased as soon as I receive the Drawings to pleasure my Lady Countess [Lady Northampton] with a sight of 'em : There being no Noble Family to which I owe a greater respect then those of Compton & Shirley. To the former for their great Loyalty & sufferings for K. Charles the first. To the later not only for their steady Loyalty to the same Prince : But for the great affection they have bore to the Study of Antiquities, as Sr Tho: Shirley & Sr Hen: Ferrers, an ancestor of my Lady Northampton's by the Maternal side ; both which are highly Characteriz'd by Sir W. Dugdale in his Antiquities of Warwickshire. And I am infinitely pleased to find this noble & beloved Study of her ancestors to be lodg'd in her Ladyship. I suppose by the many Pedigrees that have been drawn of those worthy Families already, her Ladyships design is in a Historical way : And believing the Inscriptions on the Monuments in Campden Church may be usefull in such a performance, I have copied 'em & sent you ; wch if you judge proper you may please convey to her Ladyship. I have sent no discriptions of the

Monuments believing her Ladyship has seen 'em already wch is all in
great hast, from " etc.

1734, Dec. 19th.   Lady Penelope Compton to the Countess of Northampton. Dated in Dover Street.

. . . . . . " We came hither on Tuesday and had a very good journey
tho' I believe the roads every where this year are as bad as possible. I
dare say you found them but very indifferent going to Northwick, you
sent me word you was there last Moon, I am sorry to find the youngest
Girl continues still so weak in her limbs, for not to be able to go yet I
think is a sad thing, and really great pity for it was a very fine Child,
the eldest I hear is got quite well again, and Sr John and Lady Anne
[Rushout] proposes being in town in a few days, my [Dowager] Lady
Northampton is still confined with the Gout [so] that I have not seen
her yet, but they say she is free from pain and otherwise preety well
only very lame, we saw Lady Betty and Lady Jane [Compton] the
night we came and they are both very well, I hear the town is but
empty but can't tell much of that yet for [I] have seen but few folks
nor have not picked up any news, only I find every body seems charmed
with Faranelli so that the Opera's are constantly crouded. Mr Gore and
Lady Mary [Gore] don't come up till after Xtmas and very soon after
that we may expect the pleasure of seeing your Lady^p, for you gave us
hopes that you shou'd come a little sooner this year then usual ; Lady
Margaret [Compton] desires her humble Service to you and my Brother
to whom I beg to joyn mine as also to Lord Compton and the Young
Ladys and believe me

Dear Lady Northampton
Your Affectionate Sister &
Obedient Humble Servant "
[the Signature is torn off.]

1735, April 13th.   Earl of Northampton to the same. Dated at
Ashby and unaddressed.

"Before this reaches my Dearest Life you will have seen Dr Cotes,
who will tell you how we go on here, & he will tell how our Affairs
stand at Tamworth, which I think are in a much better condition than
ever, at which I most heartily rejoice, & hope by this warning your
Interest there will never be so hazarded again, & I can assure you
our Northamptonshire friends now see, that their Victory here won'd
not have been so compleat had we not succeeded there too. Sir John
Dolben & Dr Kimberley dined here yesterday, they both congratulate
you, & Sir John who had not heard till I told him that you had taken
his Son to a Play, & that he entertained you so well, & was much
delighted himself, was very thankfull to you for your kindness to his
Son, & mightily pleased at the relation, & which he said would be a
better Cordial, than what the D^r had ordered for his Mother, who is in
a bad state of health. I writ by Smith to Ld Middleton on friday, his
horses not coming for him sooner, & at the same time to Kirkland, &
your letters will come to him the same day. The Town Clerk is n
sad fellow : which I suspected. I shall finish all here to be in Town on
Friday or Saturday. I thought Lady Cath. had been satisfied about
the 5^d. I am confident it is right, & 40^ll being paid to Mr. Web,
there is now due to her 10^ll, & 20^ll will be due to Mr. Web in July,
which makes 70^ll. Mr Davys has a brother & Sister with him, I have
not seen him these 3 days. Mr Betty was here yesterday, he looks
poorly. I pray God bless you & our Dear Children I am

My Dearest Life
Your Most Affectionate
NORTHAMPTON."

MARQUESS
TOWNSHEND
MSS.

1736, March 1st. Richard Wycherley to the same. Dated at Walton upon Trent and unaddressed A curious business letter from a bailiff or land agent. It begins and ends as follows :—

" May it please y^r Lady ship

Mr Kirkland not coming to Walton for a considerable time after I came from Compton upon Acc^t of the waters being out (W^{ch} have like to have been the Occasion of several losing their Lives perticularly Abraham Yates & two Gentlemen who were thrown out of the boat into the river the Gentlemen sav^d themselves by Swimming & Abraham by a whip which was thrown to him) for which reason I only had opportunity of inquiring abo^t Dickinsons house who insisted upon forty Shillings a Year . . . . .

My Wife seems to be very easy at present and give a helping hand towards a Livelyhood teaching two or three Girls to sow &^{ca} & I hope & dont doubt but if we have encouragment from all sides we shall do very well but if the reverse my Wife being a timerous Woman and not used to the Frowns of the World will I am afraid run upon some extream for which I should be sincerely sorry having took a good deal of pains hitherto to prevent any such thing.

She has sent for her Sister & so far as I can understand my Mother's story [her Sister] has send word She shall come. I think its a very imprudent Action but being poor and unable to do for her as she might expect I am obliged to yield up the Ghost tho sorely against my Will.

If there sho^d be anything in this Letter not pleasing to Y^r Ladyship I hope y^r Goodness will excuse me for I do assure Y^r Ladyship I have no design in me [to offend].

My humble duty Waits upon My Lord & y^r Ladyships Family."

[1737], April 12th. Lady Anne Rushout to the same.
" Dear Lady Northampton,

The Painter who worked for us at Northwich & Mr Gore at Tring, his Name is Wimpew he lives in Axe Yard Westminster his Price with us was 3 shill^s a day and no Victuals nor lodging but Mr Gore gave him his price & Victuals too, & now he seems to insist upon that. He is a very good workman and painted our House very well."

1737, June 9th. Lady Jane Compton to the same. Dated at Blooms-bury Square and unaddresed.

. . . " Poore Lady Anne [Rushout] fell into her usual misfortune last Tuesday . . . . the little thing was judged to have been a son ; she desires me to present her service to you " . . . .

Same date. John Marshall to the same.

. . . . . " the Damask seete [settee ?] will come by the next returne wth Oriss Lace and other Mettarialls for making a pare of w[indow] Curtains and Vallands."

1737, June 11th. Lady Elizabeth Compton to the same.

. . . . " [I] am not surprized that the Consul [Charles Compton] should be desirous of the next Little-ones being so well answered for, and accord-ing to the old saying I heartily wish it might have all the advantages arising from so accomplished a God-Father's [Lord Compton's] look-ing into the Bason, which would be a great Prospect of all future happiness both to Father and Son.

Poor Lady Anne Rushout is very unfortunate that notwithstanding all her care and Precaution she could not prevent loseing her little one, but she is now thank God as well as can be expected after it, but very weak, last Tuesday was an unlucky day for those mishaps, it happening also to

Lady Carnarvon and Lady Talbot, but those two occasioned by Frights,
one by having her Pocket-Picked at the Play-house & the other by Miss
Talbot's falling down stairs, whereas Lady Anne had nothing of that
nature that she could impute it too.

Lady Francys Nassau has owned her being married to Captain
Elliott to the very great grief of my Lord Grantham, which is much
encreased by his discovering also now that Lady Cowper had a great
share in the carrying on of the affair, it makes many People think that
these disappointments with the many losses in his Family will incline him
to marry again, were the Widdowers as much enclined to do so as the
Widows I think there could be no doubt of it. Lady Erwin is this
morning married to Coll: Douglass, a Lady happening yesterday to dine
in company with Mᵣˢ Nugent, & hearing Lady Erwin was to be married
to day, very unluckily cried out she thought the Devil was in all Widows
this year. She was sadly frighted when she found she had said such
a Paw-word [sic]." . . . .

1737, June 21st. John Marshall to the same.
About furniture and materials the writer has forwarded.

1737, June 23rd. Peter Smaggett to the same at Castle Ashby. Dated
" from the Cabinet in Frith Street Sohoe."
About furniture.

1737, July 2nd. Lady Elizabeth Compton to the same. Dated
Golden-square and unaddressed.

. . . . "Lady Erwins match had long been talked on but my Lord
Carlisle was so much against it & gave so good reasons for being so,
that I believe all her Friends wished it might have been prevented,
(& perhaps when it is too late she may wish so too). I don't know
whether it is the Gentleman you met at the D[uche]ss of Ancaster's,
they say he is a very handsome man, very covetous & very positive
& does already find great fault with her laying out too much money upon
her House, & in her Dress; so that unless she has reserved some money
in her own Power, 'tis thought she will not get much. She has been
presented to the Prince and Princess of Wales & had a favourable
reception, more than Mʳˢ Townshend had of the King when she went
to be so, upon having the place of one of the Dressers to the Princess
of Wales, he positively refused seeing of her. Lady Albermale had a
very narrow escape of her Life, after the Review was over, going to
get into the Queen's Coach (she being in waiting) the mob threw her
down, the Horses being very unruly she very narrowly escaped being
run over " . . . . .

1737, July 5th. Lady Penelope Compton to the same. Dated in
Dover Street. The seal represents a Cupid holding a bow, and its
motto is " TOST-OV-TARD."

. . . . . "Lady Margaret and self are very much obliged by my
Brothers and your Ladysᵖˢ being so kind to desire it and whatever day
next week you please to fix will be ready to obey your summons, and
in order thereto shall send our things by the Carrier this week, as we
have just now settled it with Lady Betty. . . . . . Lady Anne Rushout
is purely recovered Sʳ John and she went yesterday to Harrow, [she is]
ordered to drink some waters that are near her there [at Highwood]
which if they agree with her will determine them what time they shall
stay there." . . . . .

1737, July 7th. Lady Elizabeth Compton to the same. Dated in
Golden-square.

. . . . . . my sisters in Doverstreet as well as my self will with great pleasure set out next Tuesday for Wooburn ; where with your Lady-ships Coach we only beg a chair that holds two and one saddle-horse, we proposing one of the Abigails & one of the Men to go in that, and the other footman on Horseback, & what we bring from London will then return by a Boy that comes along with Mr Woods Coach . . . . . since the small-Pox has been amongst the Boys at Fulham School I am very glad Lord Compton was not gone back . . . . . Lady Francys Bland is very happy in her eldest Sons being just recover'd of the small-Pox. . . . . .

Lady Mary Tryon came last night to Town, & proposes setting out to morrow for Northamptonshire. She is grown pritty big. Mrs Sandys is [glad] I think that she was not catched upon the Road, for [she] has been every day this fortnight in expectation of her Midwives coming up to Town (she was to have in the coach that returned from her son's burying, but a Lady in the Country happening just then to lye-in stopped her) to have gone the journey down with her, and on Monday last she was brought to Bed, the child was born alive but [is] not likely to live." . . . .

Same date. Peter Smaggett to the same. Unaddressed, and dated " From the Cabinet Warehouse in Frith Street Sohoe."
About furniture sent down to Ashby.

1737, July 12. Lady Anne Rushout to the same. Dated at Harrow.
. . . . " I was advised to drink some waters at Highwood-hill which I have constantly done ever since I came here I go out at 7 a clock and am about an Hour and q^r going there every morning they are reckoned of the nature of Tunbridge [water] I was yesterday to make a Visit to Mrs Sandys who was brought [to bed] the Night after I came out of town the child lived 2 days, she is as well as can be expected. . . . . . I hear [the Dowager] Lady Northampton & Lady Jane [Compton] are at Scarborough, Sir John Rushout was obliged to leave me on Sunday to go to Evesham where I am affraid he will meet with much trouble; some whom he thought his friends has deceived him & turned out the Recorder & made alterations in the Chamber. . . . . . Lord Wilmington came to see me from Chiswick on Sunday." . . . . .

1737, July 26th. The same to the same. Dated at Harrow and unaddressed.
. . . . . . " the water I drink every Morning gets me a very good Stomach and agrees with me I am now as well in Health as ever I was in my life, go out very much in my Chair & Coach, but walking these steep hills is a little too much for me. I was yesterday to wait on Ld Wilmington he has engaged me to come again and dine wth him on Saturday, we propose leaving this place the 8 Aug : and going to Tring from thence make a short Visit to L^d & L^y Jersey before we get to Worcestershire. I shall spend great part of this Summer upon the ramble. I hear poor Ld Scarborough is extreamly ill & feared wont recover the Blow he got on his Head from the misfortune of being overturned in his Coach.; L^y Salisbury sent to me to day but I think is not fixed at Bushy. I am very sorry for poor Mrs Robison she certainly will be a great loss to her Daughters. I am glad Mr Stratford has had the good fortune to dispose of his Estate so well, I believe tis easier to find Sellers then Buyers especially where the purchase $_{is}$ large, I know several people that have been long endeavouring to dispose of Estates that can't do it." . . . . .

MARQUESS
TOWNSHEND
MSS.

1737, Augt. 13th. Nicholas Guillibeau to the same, at Castle Ashby. Dated Fulham.

" My Lady We are got to this place thank God very safe & well & in good time & His Lord*p is not at all fatigued, we found all here in good health I am with submission " etc.

1737, Augt. 15th. Mrs M. Tryon to the same. Dated at Bulwick and unaddressed.

Proposing a visit and begging to be met at Wellingborough.

[1737, Augt.—.] Lord Compton to the same. Undated and in a child's handwriting.

" Madam,

I dont doubt the return of your Ladyships Birthday must give great delight to every one that has the Pleasure and Happiness to be acquainted with you, surely then it must give an inexpressible Delight to me and my sisters who are so much obliged to you for your Love and Tenderness towards us ; I assure your Ladyship I most sincerely congratulate you of it, and heartily wish you may see a great many of them iu health and Prosperity. We have had some little Rain since we came to Fulham, but I hope there has not been enough about Ashby to hinder you from riding out. We had a very good journey and found the Roads exceeding, but they were very empty there being but very few Travellers. Mr Lee just called here, he said he was going to the Bishop's, but whether he will dine there or not I cannot tell. Pray present my Duty to my Pappa and my Service to my Uncle, Aunts, and Sisters, together [with] my Congratulations to them on your Ladyship's Birthday. I will now trouble you no longer only beg that you will believe me to be

Madam

Your most Dutyfull Son

JOHN COMPTON."

1737, Augt. 16th. Nicholas Guillibeau to same. Addressed to the Earl at Castle Ashby and dated at Fulham.

" My Lady

My Lord Compton is thank God in very good health and goes on in his Studys with Chearfulness. He found his form advanced in Martial and Horace. Mr. Hume brought some paterns & took measure of His Lord*p last Sunday . . . . . My Wife & I return my Lord and Your Lady*p thanks and are very much obliged for the fine piece of Venison & the Rabets your Lady*p has been pleased to give us. My Lord presents his Duty."

Same date. Hannah Bretland to the same. Unaddressed.

. . . . . I had the Pleasure of seeing dear Lord Compton on Saturday who tould mee all the good family was well, which was a great pleasure to mee at the same time I receved a Side of Venyson and i humbly beg Leve to retourn my good Lord and Lady northampton my most harty thanks ; i was very sorry to heir of Lady mary Gore's death."

1737, Augt. 17th. Lady Anne Rushout to the same. Unaddressed. Dated at the Cross Inn, Oxford.

. . . . " I am convinced you will compassionate the Surprise I have had by Sir John being taken so ill upon his journey & [will be] glad to hear he is better . . . . . the suddenness of our loss of [my sister] poor L^y Mary [Gore] make my fears more than I believe the cause required " . . . . .

Augt. 23rd, 1737. Nicholas Guillibeau to the same. Addressed to the Earl as before and dated at Fulham.

" My Lady,

My Lord Compton continues thank God in very good health and uses what time he can spare from his Books in walking for I take his Lord^{sp} out most Days when the weather permits as soon as School is over til Supper time which is about an Hour."

1737, Augt. 27th. Lady Anne Rushout to the same.

. . . . " I was so uneasy about poor Betty, I could not write one word, her fever was very high & the inflamation in her Throat encreased so fast we were obliged to have her Blooded . . . . . I thank God she is very much recovered Dr Mackenzie from Worcester left her Yesterday Morning . . . . Sir John recovers his Strength and appetite very slow . . . . I believe his uneasiness for the poor child's illness, has been one cause of his not recovering faster " . . .

. .

1737, Sept. 3rd. Nicholas Guillibeau to the same. Addressed to the Earl at Castle Ashby and dated at Fulham.

" My Lady,

My Lord Compton continues thank God in very good health. His Lord^{sp} drinks no Malt Drink the beer here being newer then what He used to have at Home makes him dislike it so I thought to mention this to Your Lady^{sp} because this is about the time your Lady^{sp} used to order some wine for His Lords^{ps} use. My Lord presents his Duty " etc.

1737, Sept. 9th. Thomas Drake to the same, at Castle Ashby. Dated at Whatcot.

After thanks for a present of venison and compliments the writer goes on . . . . " what I wrote was for the sake of my poor wife's health & the benefit of my Dear Children; I own Whatcot to be a most acceptable Gift, and beyond my deserts; & shall ever endeavour to make myself serviceable to the Honble family " . . . . . .

1737, Sept. 13th. Lady Jane Compton to the same. Dated at Studley.

To announce that the Dowager Lady Northampton and herself will start for Ashby on the 19th and expect to reach there on the 23rd.

Same date. Nicholas Guillibeau to the same. Addressed to the Earl at Castle Ashby. Dated at Fulham.

" My Lady,

My Lord Compton has caught a Cold which I hope will prove to · be nothing but the Distemper that goes about . . . . early in the morning I sent for Mr Lounds . . . he ordered his Lord^{sp} some of Gascoin's Powders every 6 hours " . . . .

Same date. Isaac Lowndes to the same. Dated in London. Describing Lord Compton's complaint and his treatment of it.

1737, Sept. 15th. The same to the same. Dated in London. Reporting Lord Compton to be better, but not yet well.

Same date. Nicholas Guillibeau to the same. Addressed to the Earl at Castle Ashby and dated at Fulham.

" My Lady,

My Lord Compton is thank God very well recovered."

1737, Sept. 16th. Lady Jane Compton to the same. Dated at Studley.

To explain that the Dowager Lady Northampton is prevented setting out for Ashby by an attack of gout.

Same date. Lord Compton to the same, in a child's handwriting.

" Madam

I perceive myself now I think quite recovered of my little Indisposition, bleeding at the Nose did me I believe a great deal of good, for it bled a good deal Tuesday night and Wednesday. My Master and I were last Sunday to see my Lady How at Parsons Green who has invited me to dine there some day. Colds are so frequent in London that hardly anybody escapes them, which is occasioned chiefly I believe by the uncertainty of the Weather. I suppose you are now a good deal taken up with Company at Ashby, that came to the Races. I hope you had a good deal of Diversion there. Pray give my duty to my Pappa and my Service to all the rest of the Family.

I am,

Madam,

Your Ladships most Dutyfull Son

JAMES COMPTON."

1737, Sept. 22nd. Nicholas Guillibeau to the same. Addressed as before.

. . . . "I have writ to Mr. Agutter as your Ladysᴾ commanded me for 3 Doz : of Red Port " . . . .

1737, Sept. 26th. Lady Anne Rushout to the same. Dated at Northwick and unaddressed.

. . . . "Lady Jane [Compton] writ to me how much she was concerned at being prevented waiting on you at Ashby . . . . I expect Lord Coventry and his 3 Sons to dinner (& to stay here) in their way to Oxford & these moonlight nights every day [we have] company. Sʳ Robᵗ & Lady Cox dine with us to day. Mⁿ Sheldon I believe is gone to Tesmon to Mⁿ Earmer who is near lying in. Mʳ Skeldon is soon to bring us a new Neighbour the lady's Name is Smith. Mʳ Plowden makes the match, he is employ'd in the same affair for one of his own Daughters to a Mʳ Wright a Gentleman of his own opinion, but Mʳ Plowden is not pleased with it " . . . . . .

Same date. Mrs. Charles Compton to the same. Dated at Cintra and unaddressed.

. . . . . . "Thank God my little Girls have all got mighty well over the small Pox & will none of them be mark'd, as to my little boy he has not had it]but is perfectly well, & seems very strong. I have left him at Lisbon thinking him too young for a journey, his sisters are with me among woods & mountains which this place abounds with & rambles about, from morning to night as for [my husband] Mʳ [Charles] Compton he went to Lisbon two days ago & do not expect him here till the Packet sails for England, but was truly concerned at the melancholy news of poor Lady Mary Gore's Death . . . . .

I cannot help wishing myself with the agreeable company at Castle Ashbey where I have spent my time with great satisfaction, but must have patience & be contented tho' I often think with a mixture of joy & sorrow upon past times, I hope it will be my fate sometime or other to see my friends in England but till that happy hour comes will endeavour to content my self with thoughts that it is for my Childrens good I shou'd remain here.

It was with great regret I left my Quinto & no time can ever make the Town so agreable to me as the Country but Lisbon is very healthy & I believe [has] very good air which makes it supportable.

I am much obliged to Lord Compton for the Honour he has done me [in promising to stand God father to my son] & shall obey his orders punctually. I wish when ever he has the small Pox it may be as favourable to him as it has been to my family, [I] do not wonder at his not returning to School upon that account for it is a distemper with reason dreaded by every body & great joy when well over, I wish his Godson may prove like him in every respect, for by all accounts he is a most charming youth, & I hope he is now convinced I love his uncle Charles & is reconciled to me upon that account, which I beg your Ladyship will tell him with my most humble Service.

As we have nothing but Rocks to talk to [we] can have no news to make a Letter tolerable so [I] will trespass no longer on your Patience than to beg you will believe me with the greatest Respect

Dear Madam

Your Ladyships

Most affec: Sister &

Obedient Humble Servant

MARY COMPTON."

1737, Oct. 1st. Nicholas Guillibeau to the same. The address torn off. Dated at Fulham.

" My Lady,

My Lord Compton continues thank God in very good health as all the boys at our School likewise do, we have had very wet weather for above this week which made me send last Week for a Matt for his Lord^{ps} Chamber to keep it clean so that it may not want washing so often for fear his Lord^{sp} should not take Cold by the rooms not being thoroughly dry. His Lord^{sp} is much more in his Chamber than formerly a writing his Exercises."

1737, Oct. 2nd. Lady Jane Compton to the same. Dated at Studley.

. . . " [I] am directed by [the Dowager] Lady Northampton to present her humble service to you & assure your La^{sp} how very sensible she is of your goodness to her, both in regard of your desire to see her at Ashby, and your obliging concern for her being ill ; she is now pritty well again in every respect but lame, [I] can't say she gets any ground as to that, not being able to bear yet the least upon her feet, that I fear she will still be confined here some time longer ; & the weather being now very bad, I doubt [it] will make the Roads so, for our journey up, which being a very long one gives her a great deal of uneasiness at the thoughts of it ; I am sorry to hear you have had a Cold, & that my Br[other the Earl] has been ill, but by a Letter from Lady Betty today I have the satisfaction of hearing he is well again ; they say it is very sickly in most places, & that few Familys escape either in town or Country, not but that this I am in holds very well. I much wonder Mrs Tate shu'd chuse to come to Northampton at so publick a time as the Horse-races, I hear a great deal of her in this Country not much to her advantage, she was at Scarborough when I was there, I believe she is not greatly pleased with me, for realy I did not care to renew her acquaintance, she seemed inclined to it by sending to enquire after Lady Northampton & me as soon as ever she came there, we took no sort of notice of it, so that she proceeded no farther, nor did I see any body that seemed desirous to keep Company with her she generally came into the Rooms alone, unless [with] Mr Tate, who sometimes came in with her.

Lady Northampton joins with me in humble Service to my Lord & the rest of your Family & I am with great regard

Dear Madam

Your Obedient & Affectionate

humble Servant

J. COMPTON."

1737, Oct. 8th. Nicholas Guillibeau to the same. Addressed to the Earl at Castle Ashby and dated at Fulham.

" My Lady,
        My Lord Compton continues thank God in very good health. His Lord⁑ is making a Latin Epistle in verse to send to the Consul [Charles Compton] by one of his School fellows who is going to Lisbon."

1737, Oct. 11th. The same to the same. Addressed and dated as before.

" My Lady,
        My Lord Compton has got a little running Cold in His Head but is otherwise thank God in very good health. I gave his Lord⁑ some Hysop water last night and if his Cold is no better to night I'll give him the Powder which Mr Lounds sent some time since."

1737, Oct. 13th. The same to the same. Addressed and dated as before.

" My Lady,
        My Lord Compton continues thank God in very good health all but his Cold which hangs upon him still. I have given his Lord⁑ a paper of Powders these 2 last Nights which I hope will do him good. His Lord⁑ presents his Duty etc."

PAPERS RELATING TO THE AMERICAN PLANTATIONS,
ETC.

CAROLINA PAPERS AND LETTERS, 1699-1743.

[No date.]   Doctor Coxe's Memorial in Relation to Carolana. Unsigned.   10½ pp.

1699, Dec. 21st.   Copy of the Report of the Board of Trade, to King William III., on Dr. Cox's Memorial, &c.   [6 pp.]   Together with an Account of the Commodities of the   wth and production of the Province of Carolina, alias Florida.   [4½pp.]
        The Report, which is in favour of Dʳ Cox's claim to the proprietorship of Carolina, is signed by the Earl of Stamford, Lord Lexington, Philip Meadows, William Blathwayte, John Pollexfen, Abraham Hill, and George Stepney.

[Temp. Will. III. or Anne.]   A description of Carolina.   Unsigned and undated.   2½pp.

1719, Jan. 29th.   Copy of the General Assembly's Answer to the [eight] Queries sent by the Honᵇˡᵉ the Lords Commissioners of trade and plantations relating to the State of South Carolina.   10 pp.   Signed by order of the Commons House of Assembly, by T. Hepworth (Speaker), Hovenden Walker, Alexander Parris, B. Schenckingh, George Chicken, Samuel Priolean, and James Moore.   Also by Richard Allein, Rich Beresford, Joseph Morton, Thomas Waring Thomas Smith, and Samuel Eveleigh, [bracketed together as the] Council.

1719, Augt. 10th.   Queries from the Lords of Trade about Carolina, with Answers thereto by John Barnwell.

11th query.—" What is the Number of Inhabitants, Whites and Blacks? "—The Number of white Inhabitants have been lately computed at 9,000 Souls and the Number of Blacks att 12000.

12th query.—Are the Inhabitants increas'd or decreas'd of late & for what reasons ?—Ansʳ : Within these last five years the white Inhabitants have annually decreased by Massacres of the Indians, the Flying off of great numbers to Places of greater Safety, & the Lords Proprietors re-fusing Land to new Comers, & the great taxes that were annually raised prevented others to come in.

Yett the number of blacks in that time have very much increased, for the Pitch & tarr trade prodigiously Encreasing, have made the Inhabitants run into buying of blacks to the great indangering [of] the Province.

13th Query.—What is the Number of the Militia ?—Answer. The Number of [white] men From 16 to 60 Years of Age are computed att about 2000 men [all of whom are bound to serve, and] most of whom being continually employed in the Indian Warrs, Alarms, & Expeditions are very expert able men, little inferior to disciplined troops.

21st (and last) Query.—What are the Establishments, Civil & Military within that Government, and what Officers hold by Patent imme-diately from the Crown ?—Answer : Very uncertain & distracted ; and we know of none besides the Custom-house officers that have any place immediately under the Crown most of whom have Sallarys p^d them in Great Brittain.

The Lords Proprietors had a Govern^r his Sallary 200^{li} p ann.
A Secretary whose Sallary was 40^{li} p ann.
A Chief Justice whose Sallary was 60^{li} p ann.
An Attorney-Generall att 40^{li} p ann.
A Receiver Gen^{ll} } only Perquisites without Sallarys.
A Surveyor Gen^{rall} }

1719-20, Feb. 22nd. " A description of Pansecola in the hands & posses-sion of the French : A Description of Moble, and a Description of Missecippi, in a letter signed by Thomas Smith and addressed to Joseph Boone Esqr, Agent for the Province of Carolina." 2½ pp.

1720, May 25th. Copy of Memorandum setting out that :—
The present proprietors of the provinces of North & South Caro-lina do agree to sell and part with all their Rights Powers & Pro-perties of the s^d Province unto John Falconer, David Barclay, and Thomas Hyam, which were granted to them by a Charter or Charters from King Charles the 2^d . . . . . . for the Consideration of £230,000 etc. . . . . 2 pp. Dated at Bedford Row and signed by John Falconer, David Barclay, and Thomas Hyam [the three Quaker purchasers referred to below], and also by James Bertie (for the Duke of Beaufort), Abraham Ashley, J. Dawson, George Gran-ville (for Lord Carteret), J. Colleton, Lord Craven, and Joseph Boone for Joseph Blake.

1720, Sept. 1st. The Present Establishm^t of the 100 men main-tained by the Assembly of South Carolina in their three Frontier Garrisons reduced to Ster[ling] money. Written and signed by John Barnwell, one of the three Commissioners paid by the Assembly to superintend these garrisons. 1 page.
Note.—The total charge for this Colonial force is £3,214 per ann.

1720 ? Draft of a letter in the handwriting of John Barnwell. Unsigned and unaddressed.
" Where as y^r Lordship directed me to make a Computation of the Lands leying between Carolina Settlements and the French, wch is very difficult to doe wthout an actual Survey.
If I knew y^r Lordship's design in requiring it, [it] is probable I might be able to answer the expectation after another manner, however I will doe the best I can.

MARQUESS
TOWNSHEND
MSS.
———

In the First place Dr Cox pretends a right to all the Land leying to the South and West of Alatamaha River by a prior Charter to the Lords Prop[rieto]rs of Carolina wch is by him called Carolana, & thô he made some faint attempts to begin a settlem^t yet he never yet could aecomplish it, And if he proved to have a better right to those parts then the Prop^{rs} of Carolina he may be prevailed on to part wth it to the Crown for a small Matter, or the same may be forfeited by disuse.

I am informed he is reviving his Pretentions in order to make a bubble of it.

2dly. Now the land leying between Savano River and Alatamaha River was by the Proprietors of Carolina erected into a Margravate by the name of Azilia in the year 1717 & granted to one Sr Robert Montgomery & to his heirs for ever paying yearly a penny per acre quit rent as the land become possessed by him or his Assigns, Provided he did begin his Settlem^t in three yeares; Now the three yeares are expired, & yet he pretends he has an equitable right to it & designs to dispute the same att Law wth the Prop^{rs}. In the main time he had open'd books & took in Subcriptions for 2 millions Ster^g in order to bubble it but the late act of Parlim^t put a stop to it, Yet he is still endeavoring to bring his designs to pass.

This Country of Azilia by Computation may have Fifteen Millions of acres but not above the tenth part fitt for Settlemen^{ts} all the rest being vast pine barrens only fitt for Pasturage for Cattle.

3dly. All the Lands that are good for anything between Savano River & Santee River wthin Sixty mile of the Sea is the present settled part of South Carolina and is already bought of the Prep^{rs} by the people there & contains ab^t twelve hundred thousand acres for wch the Lords has a rent of 500^{li} p. ann there is not above the same quantity between these two rivers & the Mountains good for planting, wch if they sell as they have done the rest of their lands may amount to 24000^{li} Ster^g but it may be an Age before there will be Settlem^{ts} made so far back.

4^{thly}. Between South Carolina & Virginia there lies a vacant Country as large as Great Brittain, wch nobody as yett does much vallue, soe it is impossible to compute it only the Lords Prop^{rs} sold the whole Charter to 3 Quakers att 230,000^{li} a Memorand^m of wch agreem^t I have seen, & find their design was to make a Buble of it, & Mr Boon promissed me to lett y^r Lordship have a Copy of it."

1720. An account of Proper Places for Garrisons in Carolina and the absolute Necessity of doing it speedily. Unsigned. 2 pp.

[No date]. A Memorandum on trade with Carolina. Unsigned. 3 pp.

[No date]. A Memorandum on the Indian Trade of Virginia and Carolina. Unsigned. 2 pp.

[No date.] A proposal for the incorporation of a Trading and Colonising Company by the title of the Merchant Proprietors of Carolina. Unsigned. 2 pp.

[No dale.] Copy of a letter from Governor James Sutherland to Lord *Wilmington?* giving a descriptive account of the Colony of South Carolina. Unaddressed. 6 pp.

1727-8, March 4th. Copy of the Lords Proprietors' Letter to the Earl of Westmorland.

"My Lord—We have now the honour of transmitting to your Lordship as Proposer and Mediator in the affaire the Petition we have signed humbly to be lay'd before His Majesty declaring our Inclination to make an intire Surrender of our Propertys in Carolina to His Majesty and the Conditions upon which we are willing to do it.

Upon this Occasion we think it a peice of Justice due to Coll[ll]
Horsey that he should deliver your Lordship the Instrument which is
a Preliminary to an Agreement. He has under your Lordship been a
Principall Agent in the negotiating and conducting thus far. And as
we hope it will in the Event prove verry agreeable to His Majesty we
take this Opportunity to recomend him to the Minister under whose
Province this affaire may come and also to your Lordship that he may
not be a Sufferer by acting so disinterested a part for the General
Good. And since by Virtue of the Right of our Charter which we are
now proposeing to surrender to His Majesty we did humbly present
him to His Majesty for His Royal approbation to be Governour of
South Carolina, we must now in case this Proposeall takes effect most
humbly recomend him as a Person who will be found in all respects
qualified for that Trust in the present distracted Circumstances of the
Province . . . . We hope your Lordship will take in good
part the mention we make of him desireing your Lordship will lay it
before the Propper Ministers, that we may do him Justice on our
parts and his Service in bringing about this affaire may not turn to his
Prejudice nor pass without its due Reward.

We have one thing more to take notice of to your Lordship which is,
That we never had any propper Notification from M[r] Hutchison of his
being a Proprietor among us (as is customary and necessary upon
those Occasions) and are still ignorant upon what foot that Proprietorship stands, But being informed that he was some time agoe treating
for S[r] John Tyrrell's Proprietorship, notwithstanding he declared
himselfe against the Surrender of the Sovereignty to His Majesty and
never once mett or concerted any Measures for the Settling our offer to
His Majesty, we thought it a propper Step in order to make over our
offer to His Majesty as full and authentic as possible to tender the
Petition to him after we had signed it ourselves without his knowledge
or Concurrance, which we did by our Solicitor and he has signed it.

So that now there remains to compleat our whole Number only Lord
Carteret and M[r] Blake. The latter always resided in Carolina but we
are informed has given powers to his Friends here to join with the
rest of the Proprietors in disposeing to the Crown, whence we conclude
he may be depended upon ; and Lord Carteret being now in Ireland
upon his Majesty's Service [as Lord Lieutenant] we are in no doubt
he will concurr in an affaire which seems to be agreeable to all the
Ministers and tends so much to the publick good. If we can by
any Act of ours forward the concurrance of these two Proprietors
we shall be ready to do it. And as we are most of us frequently
out of Town we have engaged Coll[ll] Horsey, with our Secretary
M[r] Shelton to attend your Lordship's Commands that when your
Lordship finds it necessary we may have notice from them and wait
upon your Lordship to finish this affaire. We are with great Truth
and respect—Your Lordships—Most hum[ble] & Most Obed[t] Servant[s]

Signed. BEAUFORT, CRAVEN, J. BERTIE, H. BERTIE,
J. COLLETON."

To the above letter is appended the following :—

[Copy of] " The Earl of Westmoreland's Certificate in favour of Coll[ll]
Horsey wrote with his owne hand under his Case dated 14th of
June 1729 & delivered into the Duke of Newcastle's Office.

At the request of Coll[ll] Horsey I do hereby Certifie That he was
the first and Principall Person with whom I treated to bring the Lords
Proprietors of Carolina to agree to the Surrender of their Charter to

the Crowne, and I have verry great reason to believe that had it not been for his Assiduity & Address on that Occasion the said Agreement would not have been made, which I hope will prove of great Service & benefit to the Crown. The severall Papers referred to in the Case of Coll¹¹ Horsey, some Originalls others true Coppies at the time of their being delievered wherein I was concerned are in my Custody ready to be produced, as also the truth of other Transactions in this affaire which were not in writing I am ready to give Evidence of when called. Thereunto witness my hand.

June 14ᵗʰ, 1729.   Signed   WESTMORELAND."

1730, July 28th. An undated memorial.

It quotes some of fundamental constitutions of the province of Carolina, states the nature of the Lords Proprietors' grants of lands, and quotes the opinion of the Attorney-General and Solicitor-General, at this date, to the effect that certain grants of land called *Ancient Patents* (of which one had been granted to Sir Nathaniel Johnson) were void for uncertainty."

1730–1732. "An account of the several steps taken by the Privy Council upon granting the Georgia Charter."

This account begins with noting the receipt of the Petition of Lord Percival and others on the 17ᵗʰ Sept. 1730, and concludes with stating that the Charter passed the Great Seal on the 9ᵗʰ June 1732.

1731–1732. Several extracts from letters of Robert Johnson, Governor of North Carolina, with reference to his disputes with Mr. Sᵗ John, Deputy Surveyor General.

1734, Dec. 16th. Governor Gabriel Johnston to Lord Wilmington. Dated at Cape Fear and addressed to "The Right Honᵇˡᵉ Lord President."

" . . . . It is now seven weeks since I arrived here, and found the whole country in the strangest confusion that can well be imagined by the unhappy conduct of my predecessor . . . . I have been upwards of 110 miles by water up the two branches of this river and I really think the Thames itself does not surpass the North East branch for beauty and gentleness. I wished for my Lord Chief Baron here 1000 times last moneth, the climate was so serene, the weather so mild, and and the air so balsamick that I am sure his Lordship would have owned he had passed one Novʳ in his life with pleasure . . . . I do not doubt getting a pretty good estate in this government without doing the least injury to any person or occasioning any complaint especially if I succeed in the petition I design to present to His Majesty after the assembly for a grant of some lands which lye a great way behind the settlements towards the mountains . . . .

1735, Oct. 27th. General Oglethorpe, Governor of Georgia, to the Earl of Wilmington. Dated " From on board the Simond lying in the Downs " and unaddressed.

" My Lord—Before your Lordship went out of town when I had the happiness of discoursing with your Lordship upon the state of affairs in South Carolina your Lordship was so good as to give your sentiments upon the method of strengthening and supporting that important part of his Majesty's dominions in America. I set down in writing, from that conversation the things immediately necessary to be done. His Grace the Duke of Newcastle laid them before his Majesty who was graciously pleased to approve of them (coppys of which I have inclosed to your Lordship).

" As the season of the Year prevented my staying for an instruction from the Council for this purpose I hope your Lordship will excuse my taking this liberty of troubling your Lordship least by the numberless weighty affairs that take up your Lordship's thoughts this might possibly be postponed. I hope from your Lordship's patronage and the importance it is to his Majesty's service that your Lordship will be so good as to forward an instruction to the Lievtenant Governor of South Carolina."

The enclosure is as follows :—

" 1ˢᵗ. That there be an instruction to the Lievtenant Govʳ of South Carolina to recommend to the Assembly to send down two hundred negroes to work for one year upon building a fortress on the Island of Sᵗ Simons in Georgia.

" 2ᵈ. That the Lievᵗ Governor of South Carolina be instructed to publish a Proclamation prohibiting all persons whatsoever from running out any lands to the southward of the River Savannah under pretence of their lying beyond the River Alatamaha under any pretence whatsoever.

" 3ᵈ. That the Lievᵗ Governor of South Carolina be instructed to recommend to the Assembly to pass an Act or Acts for contracting with persons of substance and ability for settling the townships and to give to such person or persons such parcels of lands within the Townships and within six miles round the same and such other encouragements and authoritys as the said Assembly shall find necessary for the better peopling of the townships. And that the Lievtenant Governor do sign grants pursuant to such Acts or contracts provided always that the contractor or contractors shall be obliged to settle six hundred white men women and children in the township for which they contract within six years from the date of the grant and to pay the quit rents within ten Years after the grant. And in case the contractor or contractors shall not within six years settle the whole number of six hundred then to forfeit so much of the lands contracted for as shall be proportionable to the number deficient. And also to forfeit all such parts or parcels of lands as he shall not pay quit rent for when the said quit rent becomes due. And that the deputy Governor be impowered to assent to such Acts when passed the Assembly."

1736, Sept. 21st. Observations on the Spanish Memorial of this date.

1736, ——. " The right of the Crown of Great Brittaine to Carolina, explained." .1¼ pp.

1736, Dec. 24th. Copy of letter from the Trustees of Georgia to the Duke of Newcastle. Dated at the Georgia Office, Westminster, and signed by Benjamin Martyn, Secretary to the Trustees. Enclosing the two following reports.

1736, July —. " The Chicksaws Indian talk. 1st Audience. At Savannah in Georgia. Present James Oglethorpe Esqre [Governor of Georgia] — Andrews and T. Jones Interpreters.

" The Chicksaws first produced their Commissions whereby it appeared they had been declared subjects to the King of Great Britain by the Governors of Carolina and were as such entitled to the help and protection they sought for.

" Postubee Chief of the Chicˢ.—We are come a great way to see you. The sun was very hot and burnt our heads, and we wanted water, yet we would come. We have many enemies; and beg powder and shot.

" Another Chickesaw Chief, Mingobemingo.—My brother, my chief your powder and bullets are warriors, they kill their enemies. We walk about very poor ; we want guns.

" Chick. Postubee.—We are come a long way to see our elder brothers, the beloved men, the Scotch Warriors, and the black kings (so the French teach them to call the Clergy). I have seen Charles Town before ; but I now come to see you and like this place exceedingly.

" Mingobemingo.—We heard you was a red woman's child ; Tonny Craig, Tomee Wright, Billy Greg and — Kilkenny told me so ; but now I have seen you, I believe you have as white a body as any in Charles Town. They told us many talks but you see we did not believe them.

" Mr Oglethorpe.—I am a red man, an Indian, in my heart, that is I love them ; do they love me the worse for that ?

Chick. Postubee.—We believe you are a red man in your heart. We have brought our wives and children to see you too.

Mr Oglethorpe.—Is there anything you want to see or to have ?

Chicksaws.—We are come, and have seen you. Our horses are at Savannah Town, and for ought we know may be lost. Yet we will not go till two or three days hence, we must first have another talk.

Having shown an inclination to see the Light House at Tybee, they were asked whether they chose to go to day ; they doubted whether they should have time, till Mr Oglethorpe proposing it

Chickesaw Mingobemingo said : Why then we will go to see the great house and the great water, Nay, if you bid us we will go over it.

Mr Oglethorpe.—I wish some of your young men would have gone over with me ; for then they might have had help against their enemies.

Chickesaw Mingobemingo.—We are come into our own town, and our own people, and had we not so many enemies, we would stay here till winter. But I have an old woman to my wife, and I believe every man would take care of his wife, and therefore I would go as soon as possible.

The people of Savannah town said I was going to a French town, and a French man. I told them if they were such, I should die quickly ; that I was an old man, and it was time for me to die. The Creeks, the Chickesaws, Obo butchee and the White Men all told us so. That we should be tied, and never return, but we have seen you and are satisfied.

The great talk is given out, and we have a great many smaller talks.

Mr Oglethorpe.—Tomorrow by break of day, I will be with you and hear them.

Chickesaw Mingobemingo.—We heard of Georgia in our own Country. They have a great many talks at Savannah town. They told us you were French ; The Abeencho King said so ; but we were resolved to take your talk, and we have taken it.

My heart is glad as yours. You shall have the rest of our talk to morrow."

1736, July 13th. [At] Savannah in Georgia. A second audience. Andrews and Tom Jones Interpreters.

" Chickesaws.—We are come a great way thro' desarts without water in the hot sun. We are glad to see you, and all the beloved men here together. We received a great letter from the great Mico.

MARQUESS
TOWNSHEND
MSS.
—

We come to you our Mico for assistance. We have had ammunition from the French, but have none now. We want powder and bullets.

'Twas the English first came to our Nation not the French.

We can't tell you the names of all our Enimies, there are so many of them.

The Choctaws, Towassaws, Movilles, and Tomos (these not concerned in the late invasion).

The Yungusses, Tomolohaws (commonly called Ilonois) Nawtowee. and Wrawtonoo: these with the rest that have just now fallen upon us.

Seven hundred men came into our towns twice, but have not killed us all, for some you see are alive yet. The French have forts in all of these Nations, and keep them always in readiness to send against us.

A long time ago we heard from the great Mico. They promised us white men and arms, and to send us white men and writings. The people of Carolina promised them to[o], but never sent them.

We ask nothing besides powder and bullets, but you have a heart.

Mr Oglethorpe.—Have you any friends?

Chickesaws.—None but what are here. But were we to tell you all our enemies, that paper (pointing to him that took down notes) would not hold them all.

The French say your powder makes no noise, your balls drop down as soon as they come out of the guns.

Mr Oglethorpe.—As to that, let some of your young men try, and see whether the powder we give you is good. Take the good and leave the bad.

Chickesaws.—We know it will be good if you give it us. We will not look upon it. The French told us so, but we did not believe them.

Mr Oglethorpe.—But you had better look upon it, lest it should be damaged by coming over the great water.

Chickesaws.—Then we will.

Mr Oglethorpe.—This was needful to talk of. If you have anything else say it.

Chickesaws.—We are but so big (making a small circle with his fingers). You English are so big (making a larger). But the French are quite round us all (stretching out his arms); and kill us like hogs or fowls.

Mr Oglethorpe.—Are the Cherikees your friends?

Chickesaws.—They and they only. The Creeks are almost our Friends, the Albamas Indians are entirely French.

Mr Oglethorpe.—Are the Chocktaws as much your enemies as ever?

Chickesaws.—No, the Chocktaws came not against us in the late invasion except some straglers.

Mr Oglethorpe.—Till I can get you more help can any come to you from the Cherikees?

Chickesaws.—We do not know. They are red people. You know what you can do.

Mr Oglethorpe.—Which of the Cherikee towns were most friendly to you?

Chickesaws.—Tannassee and Great Tilliquo were our beloved towns, till the Creeks killed their chief warrior.

We are told the French will bring great guns to us, but we do no believe they can.

Mr Oglethorpe.—They can't bring them, but they can bring something like them (granados here described). Therefore it is dangerous
to keep within pallisadoes. I was bred to war, and know these things.
I will throw one of them before you. In our wars with them we have
come so near the French as this room is wide, and yet could not come
quite close. Then we threw these things. I have taken them up and
thrown them back again.

Chickesaws.—But the French tell us you have none of them.

Mr Oglethorpe—That you shall see, they are dreadful if a few men
get into a little place. Then if they are thrown, the men can't help
themselves.

Chickesaws.—We say the same.

Mr Oglethorpe.—'Twas thus the French caught the Notches in a
house, and there they could make no resistance. Keep in the open
fields, a good tree these things can't get thro'."

1736-7, Feb. 10th. Governor Gabriel Johnston to Lord Wilmington.
Dated at Brompton on Cape Fear River, and addressed to the Lord
President.

" My Lord—I should have paid my respects to your Lordship much
sooner, if I had not flattered myself from time to time, that I should
be able, along with this to send (in obedience to your Lordship's
commands) some account of the Natural History of this part of the
world. But besides the many unexpected interruptions I alway met
with I have not yet seen the best part of the country, the description
of which would give the most pleasure. I have indeed been in most
of the inhabited parts of the country, and now write from one of the
most pleasantly situated plantations in it, about 100 miles from the
sea, and tho' there are inhabitants 70 miles above me, yet all this is
reckon'd but the fag end of the Province, and the pleasant scenes begin
to open near the mountains, where I design to go next Autumn to view
the land (for which I take this opportunity to return your Lordship
my most sincere thanks) I have lately gott there, and then I hope to
be able to afford your Lordship some entertainment, if you will be
so good as to excuse my [not] putting it in a botanick dress, with
long sounding Greek and Roman names, which have always thrown
me into convulsions.—I am much better qualified, and indeed it is a far
more easy task to describe the genius and temper of the inhabitants ;
it is only to imagine the lowest scum and rabble of Change Alley
transplanted into a a rich and fruitfull country, where with very small
labour they can build themselves sorry hutts, and live in a beastly
sort of plenty and all the rest of their time devoted to calumny, lying,
and the vilest tricking and cheating ; a people into whose heads no
human means can beat the notion of a public interest, or persuade to
live like men, or even to pursue the most commendable and surest.
methods of acquiring riches—who are a standing proof that refined
fraud and dextrous circumvention are not confined to courts, and the
politer societies of men, but may be equally found among the meanest,
most rustick and squalid part of the species. Among them a cheat
of the first magnitude is treated with all the distinction and regard
which is usually paid to men of merit, and conspicuous virtue in other
parts of the world.

" This is truly, and without any exaggeration, the real character of
the generality of people here. There are indeed a few and but a very
few men of integrity and candor, by whose assistance I hope we shall
be able to people the uninhabited parts of the Province with a better
race of men. Before my arrival there was no such thing as recovering

private debts, but for paying the King his rents, it never once enter'd into their thoughts. They fancyed they had taken sufficient precautions against that, and I believe they will scarce ever forgive me for shewing them that they reckon'd without their host. When I look back I am really amazed how we have been able to carry this and several other important points, considering what small countenance we have had from our superiors in England, and that there is no sufficient jail in the whole Province, nor nothing which deserves the name of Militia.

" Upon my first beginning to do business here I imagined like most young beginners, that with a little assistance from home, I should be able to make a mighty change in the face of affairs, but a little experience of the people, and reflection on the situation of things at home has absolutely cur'd me of this mistake. I now confine my care entirely, to do nothing, which upon a fair hearing (for misrepresentations are unavoidable among such a sett of men) can be reasonably blamed, and leave the rest to time, and a new sett of inhabitants, tho I wish our biennial law was repeal'd. It would make the getting of a reasonable Assembly vastly more practicable than it is at pretent.

" It is a great happiness that Her Majesty is so highly delighted with American silk, tho in that affair as well as in every thing relating to Georgia, the people of England seem to me to be strangely deluded. The balls [cocoons] were purchas'd by the bushel in Charlestown and the only person in America who can wind them of[f] is a Piedmontese whom Mr Oglethorpe quarreled with soon after, and I have him now on my plantation, and will not easily part with him. I sent a specimen of his performances to Mr Macculloh which I believe will equal any thing done in Georgia. I made but a small beginning last year, and have now 1400 white mulberry trees, and expect to raise as many thousand against next year. Besides if no cross accident happen I don't dispair of having 20 acres of vineyard and will soon be able to send considerable quantities of wine to England, so that tho I should be debarred from doing much good to this province as Govr, I hope I shall be able to do a great deal as a planter, I thank God I like my present situation extremely well, and shall never forgett how much I owe my happiness to your Lordship. In a little time I shall have all the conveniences and pleasures about me, which can be had in this climate, and tho' the silk and wine should both miscarry (which I reckon from what I have seen to be impossible) I am sure of remitting in a year or two commodities of my own raising to the value of 4 or 500l. yearly home, and to be every year enlarging my remittances.

" Hitherto indeed and even at present it is a little hard, for I had all the ground to clear from trees, and my sallary being paid in bills of currency of this Province, where we cannot as yet purchase any thing that will bear a reasonable price at home, I have not had it in my power to send over much money, yet I have made a shift to make most of my creditors easy except Mr Wright, and it is a most chagreening circumstance to me, that I have not been able to satisfy the only person, who could tierc your Lordship with his complaints, the thought of it have often made me almost distracted.

I am heartily sorry that the several pregnant oppossums I sent last year should have all miscarried, I hope to have better luck this time. The trees I hope came safe.

Against I can gett an opportunity I am laying out for a pair of young buffaloes male and female, they are vastly larger than those of Asia, none of the American quadrupeds approach them in bigness.

The bunch on their back is reckon'd a great delicacy, I wish my Lord Chief Baron [Sir James Reynolds] had one of them dressed by a French cook, I believe it would relish better than his pottage blanc cr the rest of his odious bill of fare. Before I conclude I cannot forbear taking notice to your Lordship of the excessive cold we had here last moneth I never felt any thing so severe in any part of Brittain, the ice was excessively thick in a warm room where there was a good large fire."

1737, April 18th. Daniel Hanmer to Lord Wilmington. Dated in North Carolina, and unaddressed.

The writer complains of Governor Johnston's cruelties to him, and prays his Lordship's interest to procure him the post of Surveyor General of Customs for the Southern District of North America, in the place of George Phenney Esq. who has been dead about four days.

1737, June 2nd. Governor Gabriel Johnston to Lord Wilmington. Dated at Cape Fear, and unaddressed.

"My Lord——As Mr. Phenney Surveyor General of the Customs for the Southern District of America is lately dead, I had some thoughts of endeavouring to succeed him in that post, and to resign what I now have, as it is not possible to hold both, but should be much better pleased if I could by any means obtain it for my brother Samuel Johnston who would serve for one half of the sallary which is in all 500l. per ann. . . . . . . All business is at a stand here untill we hear from the Board of Trade and the Attorney General which I am afraid will not be in haste. These delays are terrible misfortunes to all concerned in distant administrations. Unless there arrives soon some vigorous declaration from home, or an independent company, it will be impossible to keep things long in any tolerable order here. I am exceedingly happy here as a planter, and have only the consolation of being conscious to my self, that it is no fault of mine that I am not equally so as Governor. I beg pardon for detaining your Lordship so long with my affairs. I am with the most profound respect etc. GAB: JOHNSTON."

1739, March 1st. Governor Gabriel Johnston to Lord Wilmington. Dated at Newburn.

"My Lord,—I have just now put an end to another Session of Assembly, and it is with great pleasure I inform your Lordship that they have behaved themselves most dutifully to His Majesty, and with a much greater regard to his governor than I ever expected. Among other good laws past there is one by which a village most conveniently situated at the meeting of the two great branches of Cape Fear River, is erected into a township by the name of Wilmington. The good navigation, and many other natural advantages of this town will very soon make it the capital of this Province.

"I could at present dispose of the 60,000 acres of land your Lordship intended for me exceedingly to my advantage, but I have neither gott a deed for that land from Mr Mucculloh, nor so much as his obligation which he gave, or ought to have given, to Mr Wm Sharp to make it over to me. If your Lordship would be so good as only to mention this affair to Mr Sharp I don't doubt but he would soon bring it to a happy conclusion . . . . .

1740, April 29th. James Glen, Governor of South Carolina, to Lord Wilmington. Dated in London and unaddressed.

"My Lord,—When your Lordship procured for me the Government of Carolina, I made a firm resolution (which nothing shall ever make

me depart from) that I would never again give you any more trouble
. . . . .

"It is near two years since I was appointed, since which time I solemnly declare to your Lordship, that I am above two thousand pounds out of pocket . . . . . . My living here so long (tho' frugally) has been attended with great expence, and the rent of a house, taken for me in Carolina at £100 sterling per annum has been running on, where there is slaves, horses &c. eating me up.

"I have been obliged to mortgage my estate in Scotland for £1500, and I owe several small sums besides, for some of which my rents there are now arrested, so that I shall be ruined past retrieve unless something is speedily done in my favour.

"If £1000 per annum, the usual salary, is thought too much, I should be satisfied with 800, or even with six or five hundred provided I had it from the time of my appointment . . . . Mr. Bing [the Hon. Robert Byng, Governor of Barbadoes] had £1500 for equipage money, besides his salary of £2000 from the time of his appointment, So had Lord How[e, Governor of Barbadoes]. Woodes Rogers [Governor of Bahamas] had £1100, Mr. Popple [Governor of Bermuda] had £500, so had Col. Hope, Mr. Johnson of South Carolina had near £1000, besides the salary of £1000 from the time of his appointment, and Mr. Horsey immediately after his appointment had above £1300. The words of the King's warrant are, " To enable you to proceed in your voyage to America and to settle you in your Government of Sº Carolina."

" But I am sensible that difficultys and delays may attend these proposalls, I therefore earnestly pray your Lordship that you would suffer me to apply to His Majesty for some lands free of quit rents as Mr. Lowndes and Mr. Skelton and others have had. My design is not to sell but to settle them, and I am content that there be a clause in the grant making them revert to the Crown if not duely settled with the usual number of white people within a limited time . . . . . ."

[No date.] A petition addressed by the same writer " To the Right Honoble Sr Robert Walpole Knight of the most noble order of the Garter and the rest of the Lords Commissioners of his Majesty's Treasury," accompanies the above letter; the more interesting clauses of which run as follows :—

" That the sallary annexed by the Crown to the Government of South Carolina was one thousand pounds per ann̄ besides which the Governour had the profitts of an independent company there amounting to about £600 per ann. and also had two beneficiall offices of Navall Officer and Vendue Master which produced £200 per ann. each, and he had also the licensing of all publick houses which brought in communibus annis £100 per ann. which with the countrey sallary (which was £500 per ann.) and the profitts arising from the fees and perquisites which came to about £500 a year more, made the whole of the Governour's income amount together to £3,100 per ann., besides £120 per ann. which the Province used to allow the Governour for his house rent.

" That your Memorialist humbly informs your Lordships there is now a very great alteration made in the profitts arising from the Government, for the sallary of £1000 per ann. which was formerly annexed to it is deverted into a different channell by being taken from the Government of this Province and given to Mr. Oglethorpe [Governor of Georgia] who likewise has the independant company. The two offices of Navall Officer and Vendue Master are given to other persons

by his Majesty's Royall Sign Manuall and the licensing of publick
houses is taken from the Governour and vested in particular persons
appointed for that purpose by Act of Assembly.   And the Province
has likewise discontinued the £120 per ann. usually allowed the Governour for house rent, so that your memoralist unless his Majesty
shall be graciously pleased to extend his royall favour to him, has
nothing left to depend on but the country sallary, which is now reduced to £300 per ann. which the people have declared they will withdraw if his Majesty shall discontinue a sallary to their Governour,
and the profitts ariseing from fees and perquisites which are so greatly
lessened that they do not now at most amount to £250 per ann.   The
truth of which the Secretary of the Province, and severall members
of the Councell and Assembly now in England are ready to attest."

1740, Nov. 21st.   The humble petition of the Council and Assembly
of South Carolina on behalf of the distressed inhabitants of Charles
Town in the said Province—To the King's most Excellent Majesty

" Sheweth—That on the eighteenth day of this instant November a
most dreadfull fire broke out in Charles Town, and in less than four
hours notwithstanding all possible endeavours to extinguish it, utterly
consumed the best, and most valuable part of the said town, and has left
many unhappy families, who by an honest industry applied for many
years past had acquired a comfortable subsistance in the world, exposed
to the severest want and misery.

" That the misfortunes of the unhappy sufferers have been rendred
the more grievous in as much as in that part of the town which was
destroyed stood the largest and most usefull buildings and the much
greater part of the shops stores and warehouses which contained the
goods and merchandize which supplied the whole Province, and which
by this fatal disaster were wholly consumed.

" That the Province at a very considerable expense had lately finished
the fortifications in the front of Charles Town and had mounted the
guns which were bestowed on the Province by your Majesty's great
goodness and bounty but in this dreadfull calamity the carriages of
the guns on the curtain line and some of the bastions which defended the
harbour were also destroyed, the guns dismounted and the place where
they were planted left intirely defenceless.

" That your petitioners have caused a diligent inquiry to be made
into the immediate losses that have been sustained and by the account
already taken according to the nearest estimate that can be made they
cannot amount to less than two hundred and fifty thousand pounds
sterling, but the unhappy consequences which may attend the whole
Province by so considerable a misfortune in a place which was the
general repository of all the goods and merchandize and stores for
warr and defence, and in which the trade and business of the whole
Colony is transacted, time only can discover.

" Your petitioners most humbly beg leave further to represent to your
most sacred Majesty that such is the melancholy and distressed scitua-
tion of this Province that this most severe and terrible event has succeeded the great expence the Province sustain'd in providing for the
publick defence against the impending danger of an invasion from the
Spaniards in the year 1737 which was soon follow'd by the small pox
which raged in Charles Town during the whole year 1738 and swept
off a great number of the inhabitants and by the loss of many more in a
malignant fever in the autumn of the year 1739 and after the great
charge and increase of heavy taxes occasioned by the unfortunate and

unsuccessfull attempt which this Province was prevailed upon to
engage in against St Augustine.

MARQUESS
TOWNSHEND
MSS.

" That after such a continued series of misfortunes to a Province which
has [been] and may be rendred of some use to Great Britain, but who
had not fully recovered, when their late calamities began from the unhappy effects of a bloody Indian warr in the year 1715, we humbly
hope your Majesty in your royal judgment will consider the inhabitants
of this Province as hardly capable at their own expense to defend and
secure this exposed frontier against the attacks or invasion of your
Majesty['s] enemies in the present warr ; or able to give any effectual
relief to the unhappy sufferers in Charles Town who have sustained
so vast a loss, nor can your petitioners flatter themselves with any
hopes of supporting themselves under so many difficulties without
your Majesty's most powerfull and gracious aid.

" Your petitioners therefore most humbly pray your most sacred
Majesty that you would be graciously pleased to take the unhappy
and dangerous circumstances of this Province in general and more
particularly the case of the unhappy sufferers the inhabitants of
Charles Town into your royal consideration and to grant such relief as to your Majesty in your great wisdom and according to
your accustomed goodness shall think fit.

" In the Councill Chamber the 21st day of November 1740.

[Signed by the Clerk of the Council.]

" JAMES KINLOCH."

" In the Commons House of Assembly the 21st day of November
1740.

By order of the House

" WM. BULL Junr., Speaker."

1741. Number of inhabitants in Georgia, by the latest information,
exclusive of the Regiment. 3 pp.

This is a carefully detailed account which concludes as follows :—

" Note, to 9 June 1741, 1527 had been sent on the Charity, and since
then 281 more. In all 1808. Whereof foreign Protestants 839 and
British 969.

" The whole number of inhabitants at one time in Georgia, the most
ever computed were 2000 Souls.

" In 1739 there appeared to have gone at their own expense in all,
from the beginning, 260 besides their wives and children.

" In the 3 first years, persons at their own expense that went were
167, and sent to the Charity 574, making together 741."

[No date.] Petition of Robert Thorpe to the King's Most Excellent Majesty :—

" Shewing—That the late Lords Proprietors of Carolina, by grant
under their common seal bearing date the 25th day of Octr 1726 for
certain considerations therein set forth, did give and convey unto Isaac
Lownes his heirs and assigns one barony or tract of land to contain
12000 acres, subject to one penny sterling per ann. quit rent, which
grant did likewise authorize and require the Surveyor General of the
Province of South Carolina, immediately within 20 days after notice
given him thereof, to allot and set out the said tract or barony of land
in any place within the said Province of South Carolina.

That the said Isaac Lownes, by deed bearing date the 26th day of
Augt 1729, for himself his heirs and assignes, did declare and agree that
his name was made use of in the said grant from the Lords Proprietors
only as trustee to and for the use and behoof of Thomas Lowndes of the

City of Westminster gentleman, his heirs and assignes, and to and for no other purpose whatsoever.

"That the said Isaac Lowndes and Thomas Lowndes in consideration of the sum of 450*l.* lawful money of Great Britain to the said Thomas Lowndes in hand paid by your petitioner, and also in consideration of the sum of 5*s.* of like money to the said Isaac Lowndes well and truely paid by your petitioner, did by deeds indented, bearing date the 10th day of September 1731, grant bargain sell and confirm unto your petitioner his heirs and assignes a tract of land to contain 9000 acres English measure, being part of the said Barony so granted as aforesaid to Isaac Lowndes in trust for the said Thomas Lowndes.

"That your petitioner having thus purchased the aforesaid tract of 9000 acres did apply to James St John Esqr your Majesty's Surveyor general of the province of South Carolina to allot and set out the said Barony so granted as aforesaid who readily performed the same, and that your petitioner did thereupon take possession of his part thereof.

"That your petitioner nevertheless finding doubts arise concerning the legality of such survey, it being made without a warrant had from your Majesty's Governour, impowering the Surveyor General so to do, and finding also the said Governour deny granting warrants to survey lands claimed under patents or grants from the late Lords Proprietors without knowing your majesty's pleasure concerning such grants. Notwithstanding that in an act passed in the 2d year of your Majesty's reign (entituled An act for establishing an agreement with 7 of the Lords Proprietors of Carolina for the surrender of their title and interests to that province to his Majesty) there is an exception in these words "Except all such tracts of land tenements and hereditaments as have been at any time before the 1st day of January 1727 granted or conveyed by or comprized in any grants deeds instruments or conveyances under the common seal of the said Lords Proprietors either in England or in the Province aforesaid.

"He therefore most humbly prays your Majesty
    That as he is seized of the said tract of land by a title derived from the late Lords Proprietors, and long before the time of their surrender of their respective interest[s] to your Majesty, and that for the valuable consideration of 450li lawful money of Great Britain, your Majesty to prevent his being molested in the quiet possession of the same would be graciously pleased to direct the Governour of the province to give him a new grant under the seal of the province subject to the same quit rent, as is specified in his said grant from the said Lords Proprietors.

"And your Petitioner as in duty bonnd shall ever pray.
                                        "ROBERT THORPE."

1742, June 3rd. Copy of a petition from the Council and Assembly of South Carolina addressed to the King. Signed by John Fenwicke, President of the Council, and Alexander Gordon, Clerk of the Council, and countersigned by William Bull, Junior, Speaker of the Assembly. 3 pp.

The petition alleges that the Province is in very great danger from the French troops and prays for speedy reinforcements.

1742, June 15th. William Bull to Lord Wilmington. Dated at Charlestown, South Carolina.

"My Lord—His Majesty's interest being so much concerned in the present application of the Council and Assembly of South Carolina to his Majesty for assistance to prevent the ill consequences that may

MARQUESS
TOWNSHEND
MSS.

attend the designs and proceedings of the French, I apprehend it is my duty, and therefore I beg leave to lay before your Lordship a short view of the present situation of our affairs with regard to our Indian allies, the views of the French, and what is apprehended to be the most effectual means of securing his Majesty's dominions in these parts.

"And first I presume to acquaint your Lordship that notwithstanding our present flourishing condition by the increase of our inhabitants and trade, and the ships of war ordered by his Majesty for the protection of the same, the safety and welfare of this Province depends in a great measure on the friendship of our Indian allies, the most numerous of whom are the Cherokees consisting of about 3,000 men, living to the North-west about 300 miles distance from Charlestown. They are settled at the head of Savana River, and some branches of the Missisippi. The next are the Creek Indians, who live to the South-west about 500 miles distance from hence consisting of about 1,500 men, and are distinguished by the Upper and Lower Creeks. The Upper Creeks are settled on the branches of the River that falls into the Bay of Mexico at the French Settlement called Mobile. When they were at war with us in the year 1715 they permitted the French to build a fort amongst them upon that River near a town called Halbamas. They are now so jealous of the consequences that may attend the Europeans having a possession and forts amongst them, that they have refused us that liberty when proposed for the protection of our traders in case of a war with France. The Lower Creeks live on the branches of the Chattahuchee River, which falls into the Bay Apalachée on the west of Florida. As they lie more in the neighbourhood of St Augustine they have frequently visited and received presents from the Government, but in the present war some of them as well as our other Indian allies have been prevailed with to assist us against the Spaniards. The Creek Indians are esteemed the best warriours except the Chickesaws who live near the Missisippi, and do not now exceed 400 men, who withstood the French and their Indians in several attacks. But they are nevertheless much annoyed, and the trade interrupted by their numerous neighbours, the Chacktaw Indians, who are encouraged therein and rewarded by the French. The Catawba Indians consist of about 300 men living to the northward about 200 miles from Charlestown on the Waterée River which is a branch of Santeé. They as well as the Cherokees have often been molested by the Senecas or Six Nations living near Albany, but Governor Clarke of New York in his last conference with the six Nations, proposed a peace between them and the Southern Indians in friendship with his Majesty's subjects, which the Catawbas and Cherokees, as soon as I had signified the same to them, came down to Charlestown and agreed to. This peace I apprehend to be very necessary to prevent the Indians in the British interest from weakening one another, that they may be the better able to withstand the attempts of the French Indians.

"And I take leave further to acquaint your Lordship that the French by their communication from Quebec through the Lakes and Missisippi River down to New Orleans on the Bay of Mexico have gain'd an interest in and influence over many nations of Indians, who have no friendship or intercourse with any other Europeans, and by that means engage and employ them against the Cherokees and Chickesaws. The French are at peace with and have some influence among the Creeks by their having a fort there. By such frequent enterprizes the French Indians will be improved in the art of war, and the French by their assistance in case of war may greatly annoy if not become masters of this or some other [of] his Majesty's frontier Provinces, (which they have for a long time had in view) if proper measures are not taken to prevent that growing evil before it becomes too formidable to be withstood.

" Such apprehensions has prevailed with the Council and Assembly of this Province [as to cause them] to make an early application to his Majesty for three independent companies, to be garrison'd, under the immediate direction of the Governor, on the frontiers of this Province to protect and secure the inhabitants in the cultivation of their lands as well as the trade with the Indians. But it is apprehended further with great submission that these forces can be of considerable service to this Province if they were to joyn and head our Indian allies when any attempt is designed against us by land. For the greatest service the Indians have done has been when they were headed by white men, several instances of which I beg leave to give your Lordship. The Creek Indians in the year 1702 were under great concern when the Spaniards and Apalachée Indians were on their march towards them; but being animated and headed by the traders then amongst them, they marched out and met those Spaniards and Indians at Flint River, when they fought and got the victory over them. And in the year following they did not march down into the Apalachés settlement where the Spaniards had several forts or attempt a conquest of those Spaniards or Indians till Colonel Moore with fifty horsemen encouraged and led them on in that undertaking, which was attended with so great success that it disabled the Spaniards from giving the least disturbance by land to Carolina during that war. Neither did our Indian allies go to the relief of North Carolina to war against the Tuscarora Indians till they were led on by a number of horsemen sent at the expence of the Government in the year 1711, which they were encouraged to continue till they had subdued those Indians.

" I have thus presumed to be long and particular in representing the state of our affairs which is humbly submitted to your Lordship's consideration, and beg leave to recommend to your Lordship's favour and countenance James Abercromby Esquire his Majesty's Attorney general, who attends your Lordship with this, and is employed jointly with Captain William Livingstone in the application to his Majesty from the Government as assistants to Mr Fury the Agent for the Province, and are fully impowered to proceed in this sollicitation in case of Mr Fury's death or absence. I beg leave to lay before your Lordship by the hands of Mr Abercromby and Captain Livingstone a copy of the petition of the Council and Assembly of this Province to his Majesty."

1742, Oct. 7th. Copy of a letter from William Jefferis to Harman Verelst. Dated at Bristol.

" Here is a vessel arrived from Cape Fear in 7 weeks called the Bumper Sloop by whom I have the Carolina Gazette 26th July last, copy of which herein I send you and a passenger who left Charles Town about the middle of August, says the Spaniards had left Georgia and taken all the cannon at St Simon's with them. This passenger's name is Watson who liv'd in the Indian country."

[The enclosure] from the South Carolina Gazette [of July 26th 1742].

" Last week the several vessels fitted out by this Government to assist Genl Oglethorpe all sailed one after another in order to join the men of war of St Simon's Bar; except the Beauford galley, which did not get out till this morning. Those vessels we hear have on board above 600 Men and one hundred and forty guns carriages and swivels, which with his Majesty's two 20 gun ships the Rye and Flamborough

MARQUESS
TOWNSHEND
MSS.

and the Swift and Hawk snows are deemed a force more than sufficient to deal with the Spaniards on the present occasion.

Those who know the situation of Frederica town upon St Simon's Island (where the General at present stands upon his defence) are under no apprehensions of the Spaniards succeeding before relief comes from hence, for by land, at most, two men only can march up a-breast thither from the place called the Camp at the mouth of the harbour which is about the distance of seven miles and is very convenient for an ambuscade all the way, in which the Indians and Highlanders are of great use and service ; and by water only one vessel at a time can come up to the town, the reach leading to it being very narrow, about a mile in length and is exposed to be raked by an eighteen and two twelve pounders. To which may be added that the number of effective men now with the General (including the Highlanders and Indians) are about 700 as good men as are to be met with any where for their number and they are all in good spirits and have plenty of provision.

On Friday last the pilot boat returned here, which was sent to Virginia by the Governor, with the first news of the Spanish Invasion. She left Virginia the 12th instant and brings an account that Captn Dandridge in his Majesty's ship the South Sea Castle of 40 guns, would sail in two days after to the General's relief. He was just returned from a cruize, and having all his men ready on board, had nothing to do but to take in some more wood and water.

On Saturday last news came thro' private hands that but at sight only of the Flamborough Swift and Hawk men of war, and the Beauford galley, which appeared off the Bar of St Simon's the 13th instant, the Spaniards betook themselves to their vessels with the utmost confusion, and left the General again master of the island.

As these men of war did not make any stay but returned off this Bar the 15th and made a report to Captn Hardy, that they had seen a large Spanish fleet in St Simon's harbour which having been joined by .16 more missing must have been 52 sail.

The whole concern now seems to be that the Spaniards will in the mean time have an opportunity of getting out and escaping before our fleet gets thither which is thought impossible otherwise that they should do, because that they have no vessels of force capable of contending with ours.

Yesterday morning his Honour the Lieutenant Governor, attended by the first troop of Horse Guards, set out for Port Royal and we hear that Colonel Beale has received a Commission from his honour to carry on such works as are further necessary to fortify Charles Town, according to plans approved of in Council."

[1742]. Copy of The Memorial [to King George II.] of the Trustees for establishing the Colony of Georgia in America. Undated and signed by Benjamin Martyn, Secretary to the Trustees. 2½ pp.

This petition is to the following effect :—That the Memorialists were constituted Trustees for establishing the Colony of Georgia by a Royal Charter, dated June 9th 1732. That the King has signified that the Colony should be established for the relief of indigent British people and foreign persecuted Protestants, and for a barrier for the neighbouring provinces, especially South Carolina which had been laid waste with fire and sword by the Indians in 1718. That notwithstanding all difficulties there is now a fair prospect of the Colony being able to subsist itself in a reasonable time. That the supply granted last year in Parliament enabled the Trustees to send over a

considerable number of German and Swiss Protestants and of Highlanders from the North of Scotland who require existence not being
able at first to subsist themselves. That the Colony will be dispersed
unless kept together by a Civil Government at the publick expense.
That the Province, if abandoned may become a prey to the
Spaniards or a nest of pirates. "The French are continually making
new encroachments. They have advanced their frontier towards
Carolina, and have left no means unessayed to gain or destroy the
Indians who are in your Majesty's interest. They have long had in
view a settlement on the Eastern Coast of the Continent. They will
therefore undoubtedly take the first oppertunity of settling themselves
in the Province of Georgia if [it is] deserted. This place besides
other advantages would afford them Ports, by which they would carry
on an intercourse with their settlements in a shorter, safer, and better
manner, than they can at present; As the country between their
settlements and garrisons on the Rivers Mississippi and Moville, and
your Majesty's southern provinces, is plain, flat and open, there is no
other barrier except Georgia for South Carolina, but a few nations
of Indians, far inferiour in number to those in the French interest;
If the French therefore should attempt to settle themselves in the
Province of Georgia, when abandoned, there would be no force to
withstand them; If they should gain a possession of it, they would be
able to supply their sugar Colonies with lumber and provisions: for
which they now almost wholly depend on your Majesty's Provinces;
They might at their pleasure obstruct the trade of your Majesty's
subjects, and most probably in the end make themselves masters of
the neighbouring Provinces."

1742-3, Feb. 1st. Petition to the House of Commons of Alderman
William Baker and others, owners of General Oglethorpe's unsatisfied
Bills of Exchange drawn for his Majesty's service in America. Pre-
sented to the House of Commons at this date.

1743, April 20th. A letter from Harman Verelst to Lord Wilmington, enclosing a copy of his Petition to the Lords of the Treasury
—on behalf of Brigadier General Oglethorpe (General and Commander
in Chief in South Carolina and Georgia)—Praying to be
pleased to grant him assistance wherewith to satisfy the Bills of
Exchange drawn on him by General Oglethorpe for his Majesty's
service.

MASSACHUSETTS PAPERS AND LETTERS.

1730-1742.

[Circ. 1730.] A Privy Council Memorandum on the question of the
Governor's salary. It runs as follows :—

[No date.] A Petition of Governor Shute,—praying to be paid his
salary for the time he attended here to prosecute the complaint
against the Assembly of Massachusetts Bay—And likewise praying that
a certain salary may be fixed on the Governors of that Province for the
future—Having been referred to a Committee of Council—Their l ord-
ships on the

4th March, 1725-6. Refer the same to Lords Commissioners for
Trade and Plantations.

30th March. Lords of Trade reported that they thought the Governor
ought to have a salary allowed him by His Majesty and to be paid at

home untill the people of New England can be induced to make a perpetuall provision for His Majesty's Governors. And that as to his arrears they apprehend the people of New England would never pay them—So submitted to His Majesty.

1726, 21st June. The Lords of the Committee considered the said Report and being of opinion that the Province ought to pay the said Governor's arrears as likewise settle a perpetuall salary on his Majesty's Governors—Referred the same back to the Board of Trade to consider of the most effectuall method to oblige the Couucills and Assemblys to comply therewith.

1726, 28th July. Board of Trade reported that it was just and reasonable that the Province should pay the Governor's arrears, and settle a fixed salary of at least 1,000l. sterling p ann.—And that in order to induce the Assembly to comply therewith it was adviseable for his Majesty to recommend the same in the most strenuous terms under His Royall Sigu Manual to their consideration.

1726, 15th and 18th February. The Committee considered the said Report and ordered the Agents of Massachusetts Bay and New Hampshire to attend on the 22nd of February.

22nd February. The Committee reported a full state of this affair with their opinion that Governor Shute should be instructed to recommend in strong terms to the Assemblys the settling a salary on the Governor of 1,000l. sterling at Massachusetts Bay—and 200l. at New Hampshire—that if they refused to comply therewith it might be worthy the consideration of the Legislature in what manner the honour and dignity of His Majesty's Government ought to be supported in these Provinces for the future.

1727, 28th March. This Report was approved and the Secretary of State ordered to prepare a letter for His Majesty's royall signature agreable thereto. Which was accordingly done and given to Mr. Shute—but he being some time after removed from that Government did not carry the said letter over.

Mr. Burnet succeeding Governor Shute had an article inserted in his instructions containing the substance of the aforesaid letter-to Mr. Shute.

1728, 1st February. An Address of the House of Representatives relating to their not complying with the said instruction was presented to His Majesty—And referred to a Committee.

Same day. The Committee referred it to the Board of Trade.

1729, 27th March. The Board of Trade made Report that they had heard counsell for the Governor as also for the Assembly, and were of opinion that Mr. Burnet should be instructed to insist on a salary of 1,000l. to be by law settled on him during the whole time of his Government.

1729, 22nd April. The Committee considered this Report and heard Mr. Attorney and Sollicitor in support of the instruction and also counsell against the same—and reported as their opinion that this whole matter should be laid before the Parliament.

1729, 22nd May. The said Report was approved by the Queen in Councill—And the Secretary of State was ordered to receive the pleasure of the Crown thereupon.—A complaint of Wilks and Belcher, Agents for New England, against Governor Burnet was referred by the Duke of Newcastle to the Board of Trade the 3rd Octr 1729 who made

Report thereupon the 8ᵗʰ of October.—which being afterwards referred to a Committee of Councill—their Lordships did on

12th Nov. 1729. Examine into the same and make Report thereupon And at the same time proposed that His Majesty would be pleased to suspend his just resentment against the said Province for not having complied with the instructions untill the Board of Trade had transmitted a proposition to the Assembly upon that head and the effect thereof seen.

1729, 2nd Dec. The above Report was approved and the Lords of Trade directed to transmitt their proposall accordingly.—And the order of the 22ᵈ of May last was directed to be suspended till the effect of the said proposall was known.

Mʳ Burnet dying before any thing was done herein, and Mʳ Belcher being appointed Governour, an article was inserted in his instructions agreable to this last-mentioned order—And it was thereby directed that in case the Assembly should not comply therewith, that he should immediately come over to Great Britain to give an exact account of all that had passed—unless he should think it for his Majesty's service to send some other person fully instructed therein.

[1731 ?] An undated Memorial in behalf of the children of William Burnet, Esq., late Governor of the Massachusets Bay. [Signed by T. Burnet].

Sheweth,—That on his Majesty's Accession to the Throne, Mʳ Burnet was the single instance of a Governor displaced : That he was removed from the Government of New York, worth three thousand pounds sterling a year, and nominated to that of the Massachusets Bay, with repeated assurances, that it should be made as good to him, as the other had been.

In his instructions he was ordered to demand of the Province, an annual salary of one thousand pounds sterling, to be settled on him during the time of his Government, and behaved therein so as to deserve the approbation both of the Board of Trade and of the Committee of council, in their several reports to His Majesty, and last of all of Her Most Gracious Majesty, the Guardian of the Realm, in an Order of Council of the 22ᵈ of May 1729.

That the House of Representatives continue firm in their refusal to comply with the royal instruction, for the Governour's salary, yet frequently offered to vote him a larger sum than one thousand pounds sterling for a year, and in August 1729, being the second year of his Government, they voted him six thousand pounds of their money, being near two thousand pounds sterling ; at the same time, offering to make the Act for the provision of the Governour and Government, the first Act that should be past in every Assembly. But Mr. Burnet's instructions not warranting him to accept of such a compromise, he was likewise obliged by them to refuse the several sums thus voted to him.

Being thus engaged in the King's service, without any salary from the Province, and none being assigned him from hence, he was constrained to support the dignity of his post out of his private fortune. So that, what with the charges of his new patents, of his removal and of his necessary expenses, during the two years of his Government, his family are three thousand pounds sterling poorer, than they must have been, had not their father accepted this employment.

Upon Mr. Burnet's death, this matter being fully set forth in a Memorial to His Majesty, an Order of Council was made on the 8ᵗʰ of May 1730, in which Governor Belcher was ordered to demand of the

Assembly of the Massachusets Bay, in His Majesty's name, that they should make good to Mr Burnet's children the sum of six thousand pounds voted to their late father in August 1729, or at least such a sum, as should appear due to him, during the whole time of His Government, at the rate of one thousand pounds sterling [per annum].

Though this would be far short of the loss sustained by Mr. Burnet's family yet the house of Representatives in the Massachusets Bay, have refus'd to give them any further sum, than two thousand pounds sterling, which has therefore been rejected by the Governor and Council, as being so much less, than the sum due to them, upon the foot of the Order in Council last mentioned.

The several matters are humbly submitted, etc. . . . . . .

1732–3, Jan. 5th. Jonathan Belcher, Governor of Massachusetts Bay, to Lord Wilmington. Dated at Boston.

" May it please your Lordship

. . . . This Province, my Lord, is in a miserable condition for want of the necessary supplies of money to the publick Treasury, where there has not been a shilling for nineteen months past, altho' there is upwards of £40,000 due to the officers and soldiers of the King's forts and garrisons, to the Judges, the Secretary of the Province and other people, nor would the Assembly, who have lately sat ten weeks raise any money agreeable to the charter, and His Majesty's royal orders. But they have, my Lord, taken a very extraordinary step upon His Majesty's royal instructions to me (the 16th and 30th) by addressing his Majesty a third time to withdraw them, and in case His Majesty will not hear them, then their Agent is instructed to apply to the House of Commons. . . . .

As to the 16th instruction which limits or restrains the striking of Credit Bills, I believe any man of thought and substance is highly thankful that the Assembly are kept from ruining all the estates in the Province by issuing out floods of those pernicious Bills . . . . . and whereas £125 of the lawfull money of the Province would purchase £100 sterling, yet £350 of the vile Bills that have been issued by the Government will not at this day purchase that sum.

As to the 30th instruction, my Lord, I think nothing can be plainer than that it exactly quadrates with the Charter, and for His Majesty to give it up or condescend to the House of Representatives examining the public accounts of charge of the Government, I shou'd think it as well for them to appoint their own Governour, for, with great submission my Lord, all the struggle in this matter is for power. If every account of the Province must be subjected to a House of Representatives, the King's Governour will be of very little signification. They that have the controul of the money will certainly have the power And I take the single question on this head to be, whether the King shall appoint his own Governour, or whether the House of Representatives shall be Governour of the Province . . . .

The Assembly here has been sitting upwards [of] nine weeks, and would make no supply of money to the Public Treasury, So I dismist them yesterday, at their own request.—And the Government here is in danger of running into all confusion.—The Kings Forts are dropping down, the men ready to desert for want of pay, and every body under great oppression that has money due from the publick. . . . ."

1732–3, Jan. 13th. Governor Belcher to the Board of Trade. Dated at Boston. Endorsed " Copy of a Letter from Govr Belcher to the

Right Honor^ble the Lords Comis^rs for trade and plantations. Sent by Capt. Follers."

"My Lords,—Altho' I have wrote you per this conveyance of the 5th, 8th and 12th instant, yet the ship being detained I think it my duty to say to your Lordships that I have taken all possible care and pains, ever since my arrival to have the long contested boundaries betwixt the Massachusetts and New Hampshire adjusted agreeable to His Majesty's royal orders to me, but I can see no prospect of its being accomplish'd and the poor borderers on the lines (if your Lordships will allow me so vulgar an expression) live like toads under a harrow, being run into goals on the one side and the other, as often as they please to quarrel; such is the sad condition of His Majesty's subjects that live near the lines. They pull down one another's houses, often wound each other, and I fear it will end in bloodshed, unless His Majesty in his great goodness gives some effectual order to have the bounds fixt.

"Altho' my Lords, I am a Massachusetts man, yet I think this Province alone is culpable on this head; New Hampshire has all along been frank and ready to pay exact duty and obedience to the King's order, and have manifested a great inclination to peace and good neighbourhood, but in return the Massachusetts Province have thrown unreasonable obstacles in the way of any settlement, and altho' they have for two or three years past been making offers to settle the boundaries with New York and Rhode Island in an open, easy, amicable way, yet when they come to settle with New Hampshire, they will not do so with them; which seems to me a plain argument that the leading men of the Massachusetts Assembly are conscious of continual encroachments they are making upon their neighbours of New Hampshire, and so dare not come to a settlement. I say, my Lords, in duty to the King, and from a just care of his subjects of New Hampshire, I think myself obliged to set this matter in the light I now do, nor do I ever expect to see it settled but by a peremptory order from His Majesty appointing Commissioners to do it, and those agreed to by both Assemblies.

"1730-1, February. Joseph Talcott Esqre, Govern^r of Connecticutt, Joseph Jenks Esqre, then Govern^r of Rhod[e] Island, and Adolph Phillipse Esqre, Speaker of the Assembly at N. York.—[They] are Gentlemen of good ability and integrity, and altho' the Massachusetts I fear will still decline joyning in] the affair, yet I believe New Hampshire from their desire to peace and good order, would rejoyce to see such a direction from the King, and be glad to be at the whole charge, rather than the dispute should still continue: I therefore humbly pray your Lordships so to represent this affair to His Majesty that there may be an end of strife and contention.

"And if your Lordships approve of the Bill I now send you for emitting bills of credit on a foundation of gold and silver, that I may have His Majesty's leave for doing it in the Massachusetts; I pray I may also have the same liberty of doing it in New Hampshire, where they are in great distress for something to pass in lieu of money, and without speedy help it will be almost impossible for that little Province to support any trade."

1732-3, Feb. 26th. Richard Partridge to Lord Wilmington. Dated in London, Water-Lane, Tower Street.

". . . . The Governor [Belcher] has a hard task of it with the people in maintaining the honour and dignity of the Crown and in pursuing his royal master's instruction, and I really think he has however,

MARQUESS
TOWNSHEND
MSS.

by his conduct manag'd them better than any Govern^r before him has done under such difficult circumstances . . . . I know it will still more envigourate him in the King's service if he could receive a line from some in the Ministry approving his conduct."

1734, June 11th. Governor Belcher to Lord Wilmington. Dated at Boston.

" Much honoured Lord,

Since I had the honour of writing your Lordship last, I have met a new Assembly of the Province of the Massachusetts Bay, and am glad to acquaint your Lordship that they seem at present one of the best Assemblies that this Province has had since my coming into the Government . . . .

I have now the honour to cover to your Lordship a Bill passed by the House of Representatives, and by His Majesty's Council the eight current for £3000 for my support, and am again to pray the favour of your Lordship, that I may obtain the royal leave for giving my assent to this Bill . . . ."

1735. An Act [of the Legislature of Massachusetts] for the more effectual detecting and convicting such as cut, fell, or destroy such trees, as are reserved for the use of the Royal Navy—passed by the Council and rejected by the House of Representatives.

The chief provision of this Act was to make the Surveyor General of Woods (Colonel Dunbar) liable in double costs to those persons whom he might unsuccessfully sue for penalties.

1735-6, Feb. 28. Governor Belcher to Lord Wilmington. Dated at Boston.

" . . . . I adjourned the Assembly here to the 17th of next month, ... they have given some incouragement to the manufacture of potash in the Province, and if it can be brought to perfection, it will be of considerable advantage in the commerce betwixt Great Britain and this place.

" There is a Bill now lying at the House of Representatives, and which has past his Majesty's Council, for the better preservation of the King's woods, and I shall do all in my power, that it may come into a law, although I am very doubtful about it.

" I hope His Majesty's bounty of hemp seed will be here in good season this spring, for incouraging the farmers to go briskly on in raising that Commodity."

1736, May 24th. Governor Belcher to Lord Wilmington. Dated at Boston.

" . . . . I have my Lord, been urging the Assemblies here from time to time to pass some law in favour of the royal woods, and am after all now obliged to say in fidelity to His Majesty, that I have no expectation of anything of this nature to be done here.

I heartily wish the British Parliament would give a bounty on plantation potash, and an additional one to that on hemp.

" There have been, my Lord, within two years past, great discoveries of rock iron ore in a town of this Province call'd Attleborough and some furnaces lately set up; the ore I am told is very rich, and the Iron made from it equal to the best Spanish.

" I think a number of guns of 6 to 8 weight a piece have been lately cast at some of the iron works in this Province, and the metal and workmanship perhaps equal to any that passes the proof at Woolwich.

" So that this Province may in time produce timber, masts, iron, canvas, and rigging sufficient for the whole Royal Navy, and must consequently be more necessary to the Crown of Great Britain, than all

the Sugar Islands, and the whole North America besides, and so
deserve the greater care and incouragement of the Crown . . . . . ."

1736, Jan. 11th. Governor Belcher to Lord Wilmington. Dated at
Boston.

" . . . . . . The Assembly of this Province is now sitting
(and have been for 7 weeks past) and have done very little for His
Majesty's service . . . . . . and I am afraid of having a great deal
of trouble and difficulty with them . . . . ."

1736, May 26th. Governor Belcher to Lord Wilmington. Dated at
Boston.

" . . . . . I have ordered my son [Mr Belcher of the Temple] to
wait on your Lordship with this, which accompanies a small specimen of
candles, the growth of the country from an aromatick shrub we call
bayes ; all the curiosity is, that they are not offensive to handle, nor in
the smell when extinguisht . . . . ."

1736. Abstract of the proceedings [in the Privy Council] upon the
petitions for settling the boundaries between New Hampshire and
Massachusets Bay. 3 pp.

1737, May 13th. Governor Belcher to Lord Wilmington. Dated at
Boston.

"I humbly ask pardon for the trouble of this, which I pray my son
Mr Belcher of the Temple may have the honour to put into your hands,
being to say, that I am told Coll Dunbar (Lieut. Govr of New Hampshire) sails this week for Great-Britain, and that he goes away with
all the ill-nature he can possibly have against the Governour, to whom
he has been but one continual plague, ever since he receiv'd his Lieu^t
Gov^{rs} Commission. Fire and contention being the element he delights
to live in, loving to be restless, and to make every body so he has to deal
with.

" Your Lordship cannot but be sensible of the great trouble and
fatigue I have undergone (since my appointment to this Government)
with one obstinate Assembly after another for my steady adherence to
His Majesty's royal orders ; and I have been often threaten'd by
men of influence, that they would grant me no support, unless I would
go from the King's instructions ; and during the dispute (for about
three years) respecting the supply of the Treasury, I did not receive
one farthing to defray my yearly expence in this Province. And at
New Hampshire, by Col^l Dunbar's little arts and crafts with the
Members of the Assemby there, that Province is at this time considerably in arrears with me, altho' they passed a Law, settling my
salary to be paid half-yearly."

" . . . . . My Lord I can assure you upon my faith and honour that
the Governments of both Provinces have not been worth to me com_
munibus annis £750 Sterling, which is but a poor pittance for the
support of the King's Governour, whom His Majesty in his instructions
to me is pleas'd to call the representative of his royal person in the
Governments, where he has plac'd me, and the support they give me
but barely pay my necessary annual expence ; yet as this is my native
country, where are my family, my friends, and my little fortune, I own
with great and humble gratitude the continance of His Majesty's
royal favour to me.

" I am sensible Col^l Dunbar will do every thing in his power (right or
wrong) to my prejudice, I therefore humbly beg of your Lordship, that his
representations may make no impression, till I am heard in answer.
He wrote me a few months past he did not intend to return hither, but

Marquess
Townshend's
Mss.

to seek some imployment at home: happy will be for this country they may never see him again, where I don't believe he can make out one single service he has done for the Crown, but I am well satisfy'd he has done a great deal to alienate the affections of the King's subjects from his Government; his despotick arbitrary way, as, beating the King's subjects, threatening to burn and destroy their substance &c., will by no means do in civil government.

" The two. Provinces, where I have the honour to command, are in good peace and tranquility at present; but should there be any change of the Governour, I have reason to believe it would throw the provinces into new difficulties, and give the King's Ministers fresh trouble, who have had too much already with this people.

" I am told Coll Dunbar intends to endeavour Mr George Jaffreys may succeed him Lieut. Govr of New Hampshire, who is as opposite to me as Coll Dunbar himself; and with great deference to your Lordship I can't see what advantage it can be to His Majesty's service, or to the ease of his Ministers, to have persons put into post[s] in one and the same Government, who will be continually thwarting and opposing one another. I therefore humbly pray, Col^l Henry Sherburne (who has been for many years of his Majesty's Council in New Hampshire) may succeed Col^l Dunbar in the Lieutenancy in that Province; he is a very worthy gentleman, and would be acceptable to the Province in general and to me in particular . . . . . . ''

1737, Dec. 5th. A letter to Lord Wilmington, in the handwriting of Governor Belcher's secretary, and signed by certain of the clergy of Massachusetts. Dated from Boston in New England, and addressed to the Right Honorable, the Earl of Wilmington, Lord President of His Majesty's most Honorable Privy Council, and Knight of the most Noble Order of the Garter.

" May it please your Lordship,

With all that respect and deference to your name, which the high station wherein his most excellent Majesty, our most gracious Sovereign, has seen meet to place, and so long continue you, together with those accomplishments, which render you illustrious therein; we [Ministers of the Gospel, and Pastors of Churches in his Majesty's Province of the Massachusetts Bay, in and about Boston, crave leave by the hand of the agents for the Province, humbly to address ourselves to your Lordship and to entreat your powerfull favour for the good people of New England, and for the Churches of it, in which the King's person, and family, and Ministers are constantly and ardently pray'd for, with one heart and voice.

" The blessings of his Majesty's reign, which reach us in these distant parts of his dominions, we hope we have a gratefull sense of: in a particular manner we think ourselves bound to bless God, and to thank the King, and his Ministers, for the continuance of Governor Belcher in the chair over us, by whom the King's good subjects of every denomination are equally encouraged in their Duty to God and to the King.

" We look upon ourselves obliged humbly to address your Lordship in this manner, because we have lately seen in some of the publick prints, what we must call a malicious libel, pretended to be written from Boston, declaring to the world—" An universal joy thro'out this Province upon the news of His Majesty's appointing a new Governour over us; more especially among the better sort of people, and Ministers of all sorts "—than which there could not have been published a greater calumny and more injurious falshood: and we beseech your

Lordship to excuse us this zealous vindication of ourselves and our
people from it.

"That those my Lord, who have the high honour to stand about the
King as his Ministers may have wisdom from above for a most
righteous and happy administration is the prayer of my Lord, your
Lordship's, most humble dutifull and obedient servants

Benjamin Colman, Pastor of the Church [in] Brattle Street, Boston.
Thomas Prince, Pastor of the South Church in Boston.
William Cooper, a Pastor of the Church in Brattle Street, Boston.
Nehemiah Waller, Pastor of a Church in Roxbury.
Nathaniel Appleton, Pastor of the Church in Cambridge.
Samuel Checkley, Pastor of the New South Church in Boston.
Charles Chauncy, Pastor of the first Church in Boston.
Samuel Mather, Pastor of the North Church in Boston.
Mather Byles, Pastor of the Church in Holles-street, Boston."

1738, May 23rd. Governor Belcher to Lord Wilmington. Dated at
Boston. 8 pp.

"May it please your Lordship—By one of the last ships from England
my brother Mr Richard Partridge, and my son Mr [Jonathan] Belcher of
the Temple (my stated agents) write me that Mr Rindge of the town
of Portsmouth in New Hampshire had been recommended to the King
to be one of His Majesty's Council for the Province of New Hampshire. . . . . . As to the Massachussetts, the heats and broils
they were in before my arrival and since seem at present to be pretty
well laid ; the opposition and trouble I have and do still struggle with in
New Hampshire has been chiefly owing to the restless temper of Coll
Dunbar (whose natural element seems to be strife and fire) . . . . .
to prevent any Contention or Clashing between the King's Govr and the
Council, which must necessarily be the case, if men personally prejudiced at the Govr, and always opposing the King's authority, must
be members of the Council, and such is Mr Rindge (recommended to
supply the place of Mr Gambling lately deceas'd). . . . .

"I must further beg your Lordship's patience while I acquaint you,
that the latter end of the last month I was serv'd with [a] copy of a
complaint exhibited against me to the King in Council, by a Committee of the House of Representatives of New Hampshire. . . . . .
I am now preparing my answer, and hope to get it ready to go per this
ship. . . . . ."

173⅞, Jan 23rd. Governor Belcher to Lord Wilmington. Dated at
Boston and unaddressed.

"I have at one time and another done myself the great honour of
addressing your Lordship on the affairs of the two Governments,
where His Majesty in his great grace and favour has been pleas'd to
place me; and I am now to beg of your Lordship to lend a listning ear,
while I lay before you the difficult state of this Province with respect
to a medium for the trade, which has been carry'd on for above thirty
years past almost wholly by what are call'd here bills of credit, instead
of silver and gold, of which this country is drain'd by the constant
exportation of it to Great-Britain.

"I would also crave leave to say to your Lordship, that in conformity
to His Majesty's royal orders to me, all the outstanding Bills of
Credit of this Province must be drawn in by the end of the year 1741,
and unless something be substituted in their place, it will make almost
an intire stagnation of trade and a considerable concussion in this little
Commonwealth.

" His Majesty's great goodness and lenity to his subjects has secur'd to him the greatest affection in the hearts of all his subjects, among whom I hope this Province are as truly dutifull and loyal as any part of the King's dominions; and I would now become a humble suitor to your Lordship on account of the difficult circumstances this Province is already in, and will still be more so, for want of something to circulate instead of money from man to man. And I would further pray, that I may lay before your Lordship the inclosed request made to me by the Council and Representatives of this Province respecting a Bill past by them for making an emission of £60,000 in Bills of Credit, which Bill is also herewith transmitted to your Lordship; and according to my understanding of it, is the best calculated for maintaining the value of such Bills as may be emitted in consequence of it, of any Bill that has been projected in this Government, and, as I judge, the passing it into a Law will much advance the honour and justice of the King's Government here, and the safety, peace, and good order of his good subjects.

" I would humbly beg your Lordship's favour in facilitating the obtaining His Majesty's Royal Order of leave for giving my consent to a Bill of this nature; your Lordship's known innate goodness and humanity exercis'd to this people in this article must challenge their highest sense of gratitude."

Two papers were enclosed in the last letter.

(1.) Copy of a Bill of the Legislative Assembly of Massachusetts for the emission of sixty thousand pounds in Bills of Credit, of a new form and tenour to be redeemable by silver and gold.

The Bill provides for the issue of Currency bills of one shilling each, redeemable in silver coin at the rate of 6s. 8d. per ounce Troy, in gold coin at the rate of 4l. 18s. the ounce Troy, and the copy of it is attested as follows :—

" Province of Massa[chuse]t Bay Jany 22nd 1738. The Bill whereof the foregoing is a true copy having been read three several times in the House of Representatives and in Council, pass'd to be enacted by both Houses.

" Att. SIMON FROST, Dep^t Sec^y."

(2.) An address to Governor Belcher from the Council and Assembly of Massachusetts, with the Governor's answer :

" May it please your Excellency,

His Majesty's Council and the House of Representatives in General Court assembled, in consideration of the near approach of the period when all the Bills of Credit now passing will be sunk, have agreed on a Bill for the emission of sixty thousand pounds, redeemable by silver and gold; which Bill your Excellency was pleased, in your speech of yesterday, to inform us you could not consent to consistant[ly] with his Majesty's instruction.

" Wherefore we, His Majesty's loyal and dutifull subjects, crave leave to observe to your Excellency, the great and distressing difficulties His Majesty's good subjects of this Province will be under in supporting the Government and in carrying their common affairs and business, it the aforesaid Bill, or some other of that nature, shall not take effect.

" Your Excellency cannot but be sensible that for many years past the publick taxes for the support of Government have been wholly paid in bills of Credit, by which bills also the trade and commerce have been for near thirty years almost wholly managed, and that the whole of these bills of Credit must be intirely sunk by the end of the year seventeen hundred [and] forty one, and that it will bring great distress if not an

entire stagnation of all trade, if about two hundred and fifty thousand
pounds computed in bills of the old tenour, the sum now extant, should
be, in that short time, intirely taken away, and nothing substituted in
its room, and especially since this Court have in their present Session,
for supporting the credit of their own bills, found it necessary to discountenance those of the neighbouring Governments as being not well
founded.

"We would therefore pray your Excellency's favourable consideration
of this important affair, and how much the safety, interest and quiet, of
His Majesty's good subjects under your Excellency's care depend on
its success, and do entreat your endeavours that your Excellency may
give your consent to this Bill, or a Bill of this nature, the bills to be
emitted thereon being on a different and much better foundation than
those which have occasioned His Majesty's prohibition."

The answer of Governor Belcher, dated 16th Jan. 1739 :—
"Gentlemen of the Council and of the House of Representatives.

"In answer to your Address relating to the Bill for emitting Sixty
Thousand pounds in Bills of Credit, to pass in lieu of the Bills now
extant, which as you observe must be entirely sunk by the end of the
year Seventeen hundred and forty one, and are at present the only
medium of commerce; you may assuredly depend, that I will imploy
my best offices consistent with my duty to the King, that His Majesty's
royal leave may be obtained for giving my consent to a Bill of this
nature."

1738-9, Feb. 5th. David Dunbar to Lord Wilmington. Addressed
to " The Rᵗ Honble My Lord President &c."

"May it please your Lordship—It is more than 7 years since my
Lords Commissioners for trade and plantations were pleased to make a
strong representation to His Majesty in my favour upon the complaints against Govʳ Belcher for setting aside His Majesty's Commission
to me as Lievᵗ Govʳ of New Hampshire, upon which the Govʳ neither
allow'd me any command or share of the sallary, tho' settled on the
Govʳ and Lieuᵗ Govʳ; the said representation was sent to His Grace
the Duke of Newcastle to whom My Lords of Trade have applyed
twice since to obtain His Majesty's pleasure thereupon. Upon which
I have been informed that it was layd by His Grace before My Lords
of the Committee of Council, and it is now in the Office.

"Dureing six years that I was Lievᵗ Govʳ I received no consideration
for the expence which a publick station must subject a man to, and
I have not yet been so happy as to obtain any satisfaction for my
disbursments in endeavouring to add an usefull collony to His
Majesty's dominions, which I should have done ere now if it had not
been defeated by the opposition of Govʳ Belcher, and without any
expence to the Crown, as the quit rents would long ere now have
reimbursed me. Those expences haveing layd me under great incumbrances I was obliged to assign all my sallary as surveyor of His
Majesty's Woods in America to discharge them, and it is yet so
applyed, so that I have not a shilling of it for my own support, and I
have moreover been arrested and imprison'd and am now sued for part of
the said expences, and I must inevitably sink under them, if some relief
or equivalent be not suddainly granted me, which I fear the hurry of
publick affairs will obstruct."

"I have presumed to trespass thus on your Lordship, as a reason why
I really am not able to prosecute the said affair now lyeing before
you in Council, I humbly beg your Lordship will be pleased to see

it and that my Lords of the Committee will give an opinion upon it without hearing council, as I am not able to answer the expence.

" May I further presume to add, that my misfortunes are chiefly owing to a mistake in calling the place I was sent to settle, part of Nova Scotia, which appearing to be part of the Massachusetts Province, I was orderd to remove and quitt possession to that Province, after I had built a fort and barracks for the King's troops sent thither from Nova Scotia; I should be humbly contented with any equivalent in any remote part of the world, no climate or danger would affright me; I have had the honour to be in commission, first from King William in 1697, & rose gradually to be Liev^t Coll° in 1715, and inadvertently parted with my Commission in 1718, piqued, that a younger officer was putt over me by means of my late Lord Cadogan; I was in Parliament in Ireland in Queen Ann's reign, and allways of the side that distinguished themselves in favour of the Hanover Succession, for which I was taken so much notice of that I was threaten'd to be broke. In 1726 I was sent Consul into Spain, and happen'd to do some service there for which I had the approbation of his late Majesty and present Ministry in many letters, and had the honour to be taken notice of by his present Majesty then prince, upon my return from a long imprisonment at Malaga, being taken in the Mediterranean endeavouring to go to Gibraltar on the King's service. I may be so happy as to move your Lordship's compassion upon this narration; my present case my lord is a very uncommon one, I have never been complaind of in any station, and I am ruin'd by endeavouring to do a publique service without any private view to myself, it is a pitty a man should be undone without being charged with a crime.

" I have no claim or pretence to your Lordship's favour but from your universal[ly] known humanity to the distressed, I humbly submit myself to your consideration."

1738–9, March 7th. Governor Beleher to Lord Wilmington. Dated at Boston and unaddressed.

" I humbly beg leave of your Lordship to admit my agents Mr Partridge and Mr Belcher to put this into your Lordship's hands; wherein I first of all give your Lordship my humble and sincerest thanks for the constant course of your Lordship's justice and favour to me in the affairs of my Governments; and in the next place I am to beseech your Lordship's attention for a few minutes, while I say, the last ship from England informs me, that Mr Thomlinson, agent for the House of Representatives of New-Hampshire had, under the name of an appeal from the judgment of His Majesty's Commissioners for settling the boundaries between that Province and this, alleg'd a heap of malicious invectives against me, and by the copy of it, which I have seen, it looks more like a libel upon the Governour, than an appeal in the case mentioned. And I am very particularly to thank your Lordship for not suffering it to be proceeded on with respect to any thing that relates to me, 'till I should be regularly serv'd with a copy, and time allow'd me to answer.

" The affair, my Lord, of the boundaries betwixt this Province and New-Hampshire is certainly necessary to be determin'd for the quiet and safety of His Majesty's subjects of both Provinces, yet I would beg leave to say to your Lordship, that this controversy has been latterly manag'd ou the side of New-Hampshire with great zeal and warmth by those that openly profess themselves the Governour's enemies, and by Mr Thomlinson's bitter invectives, I think it's plain, that they rather wanted an opportunity to vent their ill-nature at the Govr than to do any good to the Province about the line.

" As I know I am speaking in the ears of a wise and impartial judge, I would humbly hope, when your Lordship has consider'd the answer of the Massachusetts Assembly to what Mr Thomlinson calls his appeal, and my answer to the complaints of the New-Hampshire Representatives, that your Lordship will intirely acquit me of any partiality in the part I have acted in this affair.

" And as to Mr Thomlinson's charging me with bribery from the Massachusetts, there never was anything more unjust or unreasonable ; while in obedience to His Majesty's orders I was pressing them to do me justice in making my salary equal to £1,000 Sterling, and they had once and again given me something towards it, to call such a grant a bribe could spring from nothing but the dregs of malice, and an attempt to make something out of nothing. I can, my Lord, challenge the worst of my enemies to charge me (and make it good) with the value of sixpence I have taken directly or indirectly for any thing that has had the least relation to my administration, except the public grants of the Assembly.

" It is, may it please your Lordship, impossible for a gentleman to be at the head of two such Provinces as I am, and not to have enemies, tho' I believe the Provinces, to take the people 19 in 20, were never in greater tranquillity than at this day. And what I am most humbly to beg of your Lordship is, that whenever any thing is laid against me as complaint, I may have the liberty of au Englishman, that is to be serv'd with [a] copy, and time given to make answer, and then, my Lord, I shall not be in much pain, for I am determin'd, while I have the honour to serve the King in the station he has plac'd me, to maintain His Majesty's just right and honour, and at [the] same time to be tender of the liberties of his people ; and these things I think very compatible in an English Governour with an English Government."

1739, Oct. 30th. Governor Belcher to Lord Wilmington. Dated at Boston and unaddressed.

" In March and April last I had the honour of addressing your Lordship in a very particular manner respecting some complaints I heard had been presented to Your Lordship at a Committee of his Majesty's Most Hon^{le} Privy Council against my administration in the Government here and at New Hampshire, and these letters Mr Partridge and Mr Belcher write me they had the honour to deliver to your Lordship which I hope gave your Lordship some satisfaction as to those complaints. By these last ships I have an account from my Agents at Whitehall, that there had been presented at the Privy Council Office a Memorial from one Mr Gulston and Tomlinson and two others respecting the state of the Province of New Hampshire which had been referr'd to the Plantation Board—who had return'd their Report upon it without serving me with a copy and time to answer—but that when it came to your Lordship's Board your Lordship sent it back again that I might have the justice I insisted upon by my Agents but [which] was deny'd by them—vizt a copy and time to answer and this has indeed been the steady course of your Lordship's justice and candour in any thing that has come before your Lordship in the affairs of my Governments for which I give your Lordship my most humble and hearty thanks and shall ever hold myself under the strictest obligations of gratitude. I find the complainants had (in their low art) left out my name that they might say it was not a complaint against me, altho' the whole drift and design of it was to get my Commission for N[ew] Hampshire superseded and the report of the Lords of Trade tally'd with their designs, and had not your Lordship interpos'd and put a stop to the manner of proceeding how severe and extraordinary would it have been to have depriv'd a gentleman of his bread and honour and never to have given him liberty of vindicating himself—I say to have taken his Commission away from him upon the *ipse dixit* of his enemies which upon a fair hearing might appear to be nothing more than a heap of absurdities and falsehoods and the pure product of malice—and when I am serv'd with [a] copy I have no doubt to make this Memorial deserve those epithets—and I do most humbly beg of your Lordship that before any thing be past upon this Memorial I may be serv'd with [a] copy to answer—for it cannot be expected my Agents at a 1000 leagues distance can so fully answer what may nearly affect my interest and honour as I can—There has been my Lord a complaint of this Mr Tomlinson against me and my answer to it lain above twelve months at a Privy Council Office which he seems afraid to bring to a hearing and therefore stirrs up Mr Gulston with the other two to bring on a complaint in this manner—and as it were to shoot me in the dark—But God be prais'd that your Lordship presides at the Council Board with so much justice and honour—I humbly beg your Lordship's patience while I mention an instance of his present Majesty's great justice with respect to one Mr Gledhill Governour of Placentia about ten years agoe upon a complaint that was exhibited against him (I think by Lord Vere). A very great person went to the King to desire that he might be dismist—But the Governour's friends found access to his Majesty and humbly beg'd the Governour might have liberty to answer for himself which the King readily granted. Upon the gentleman's going again to His Majesty to have him put out the King said no sir you told me he was a very good man when I put him in—Yes may it please Your Majesty so he was, but now such and such complaints lye against him—to which the King answer'd they may indeed bear the name of complaints but I shall not dismiss him, let him be serv'd with copies and if he cannot clear himself then let him be dismist—but if he can I shall still continue him as a good servant. He made answer cleard himself and was continu'd—I remember when I was at Court the King's justice and honour on this head were greatly applauded.

" I know myself my Lord, to have made the King's honour and interest with the prosperity of his people so much the rule of my administration at all times that I am under no pain or sollicitude about complaints—if I may but have time to answer—and yet may it please your Lordship there will always be grumbletonians in every Government."

1740, May 14th. Governor Belcher to Lord Wilmington. Dated at Boston.

" May it please Your Lordship—I do in the first place humbly ask pardon for the trouble I am now necessitated to give you upon the late accounts receivd from my friends of the violent pushes of my enemies to get my Commission for this Government and that of New Hampshire superseded, they have not stuck at lying and forgeries to obtain an opportunity of wreaking their boundless malice upon me, of this the Honble Sir Charles Wager can give your Lordship a flagrant instance."

" It is now near 10 years since I arrivd here with His Majesty's Commissions for this and the neighbouring Government in which time I have met with more difficulties than any of my predecessors for my firm adherence to His Majesty's royal instructions and thereby constantly maintaining the honour and prerogative of the Crown and which has made the Assembly of this Province so strait and stingy in their grants for my support that I have been oblig'd every year to spend considerable of my own fortune, to live in some measure equal to the dignity of his Majesty's Commission. I am told that the length of time I have held the Royal Commission has been given for reason why they should now be taken from me; which with great deference I apprehend can be no reason at all. Nor do I believe His Majesty has at any time made that a rule either at home or in his plantations for dismissing his servants. Had I indeed roll'd up a fortune by the favour of the King's Commissions, the length of time might be alleged with some colour of reason for my having a successor. But I must humbly beg leave to lay before your Lordship, the plain and naked truth of the matter in that respect. At the time I received the honour of His Majesty's Commissions I was one of the principal men of trade in this countrey, but at that time I quitted every other way of life and devoted my self to his Majesty's service in the Governments where he had plac'd me and as I observed before have been hitherto a great sufferer in my private fortune, since my coming into the Government, and now to be dismist it without any provision being made for me, would be such a severity as I humbly beg you would let me hope from your goodness may not pass upon me. I have a large family of children and grandchildren and to take away my bread and theirs would indeed be very shocking. And I can assure your Lordship, let my enemies pretend what they please, the people are so easy that I am satisfied 7 in 8 are desirous of my continuance and a change would make great discontents and give the King's Ministers new troubles where they have had too much already. Let me therefore again earnestly intreat for an interest in your Lordship's favour and compassion at this critical juncture.

1740, August 12th. A letter, extracted from a New England newspaper of this date, dated at Boston.

" It is now certainly known that Col. Blakeney brought over more than 30 blank Commissions to be fill'd up by the several Governours of his Majesty's Provinces and Colonies. . . .

" . . . . And in this Province the nomination of ten captains was made, and beating orders issued out the 9th of July ; and in less than three weeks after we had 7 companies compleated, 6 of which made their appearance in Boston by that time, and by this time it is hoped that the ten companies designed to be raised are near all becoming compleated.

" . . . . As these observations afford a convincing proof of a true loyal spirit in the people in the Northern Colonies for the service of his Majesty and their country on this occasion, and of the importance of 'em to the British dominions, even in respect of annoying the enemy in the West Indies, I desire you will give 'em a place in your paper."

1740, Oct. 10th. John Graves to Lord Wilmington. Dated at Nutfield in New Hampshire and addressed " To the Right Honourable Lord Wilmington—Lord President of his Majestie's most Honourable Privy Councel at St James'es Square—London—to the care of the captain by the way of Boston."

" My good Lord.—Amidst the general joy that reigns throughout this Province upon the settlement of the boundarys, and the hopes we have of beeing soon made a seperate Government, and thereby delivered from our cruil oppressors, the great the good Lord Precident's praise is in every mouth, on every tongue, wee at this distance, my Lord, are not unacquainted that it is your Lordship's greatest joy and pleasure

MARQUESS
TOWNSHEND
MSS.

to help them to right that suffer wrong, and to deliver and relieve the
oppressed, of which this Province will bee an eternal monument, and I
hope will transmitt the memory of its deliverer down to the latest
posterity.

But as for me, my Lord, I have not only my share in the general
benefitt, my case is so particular that when your Lordship knows it you
will pardon this liberty. My Lord, my estate in the Province lyes ten
miles within any part of the dividing lines, and seven miles within the
lines the Massechusetts themselves claimed, when they were obliged to
deliver in their claim to the Commissioners at Hampton, yet notwithstanding all this; the Massechusetts Government have for several
years passed distressed me and my neighbours in the most cruil
manner, makeing us pay taxes to that government, or they would seize
on our goods or persons, me they have torn from my family, and
carried to prison as often as I refused paying their unjust demands.
This was my real case, but now I am most happy with my family, in
a peaceable enjoyment of what belonges to us; and in full hopes of
seeing this Province very soon delivered from the oppressive tyranicall
Government it has long ground under, and of becoming a florishing
Province, and usefull to our mother country.

Your Lordship cannot be ignorant of the temper of the Massechusetts
Government, and the Massechusetts Governour, and what scandalous
methods they have taken to procure applications to his Majesty, in
prejudice to this Province of New Hampshire. Suffer me, my Lord,
to acquaint you with what they are now about; my Lord, as soon as
they found that his Majesty had determined the boundarys of that
superbe unruley Provence of the Massechusetts, which had for many
years been making encronchments on his Majesty's Province by granting
away a great many townships thereon; And now those townships
naturally falls within his Majesty's Province of New Hampshire, and
notwithstanding the possessors of those townships were as well satisfied
to fall in his Majesty's Province as to be under the Charter government; it being quite indifferent to them whither they paid taxes
to one Government or the other, as the settlement of the boundarys
only determined jurisdiction, and did not hurt their propertys, yet the
Massechussetts Governor and Parson Wells, and other officers and
servants of the Massechusetts Goverument, have by their threats and
promises, spirited up those poor unthinking people, and have prepared
a great many petitions for them, and have prevaild on a great many
to sign then, therein praying his Majesty to give those townships back
again to the Charter Government of the Massechusetts, and some of
their reasons are, that one part of these great stragling townships will
fall in one Province and the other part in the other Province, as tho
that could be of any ill concequence, more than in great Brittain, where
some towns and parrishes are in two or three countys, and the Government of the Massechusetts are now sending to Great Brittain one of
their Assembley as a private Agent for those townships, butt abbetted
and supported by the publick.

But we trust in God all those petitions will meet the same fate of
another most wicked one which we hear was privately sent home, and
presented to his Majesty, sign'd by six of the Council of this Province,
who have all along signed and done every thing they have been ordered
to do by the Massechussett Government, to defeate the settlement of
the boundarys, and we have great confidence that your Lordship's great
penetration and know[n] love to justice and equity will defeate all
those wicked and crafty devices.

My Lord, I have only to lay my self at your Lordship's feet most
humbly to implore your pardon in presuming (in the fullness of my
heart) thus farr. And I most heartily pray to God, that for the sake
of this his Majesty's Province, and all other his Majesty's American
dominions, that it would please him long, very long, to bless your Lordship with life and health to support your high station, to bee a glory
to the present, and an example to future ages."

1740, Nov. 13th. Governor Belcher to Mr Partridge. Dated at
Boston.

"Sir—I have your kind letters of August the 16th and 18th, September 5th, 13th, 17th and 18th by Laws, Bishop, Perkins and Hall, with
copies of a great number of letters wrote to me from considera[ble] persons, to assist in my establishment. What shall I say, brother? You are
an unwearied good friend. It's impossible for you to do more than
you do for my service and interest. I take a kind notice also of what
you say of my dear Mr. Belcher of the Temple's great diligence and
care in doing every thing in his power that may be of any advantage
to his father.

I see Dunbar has got himself made a bankrupt.—Why don't the
creditors make the rogue sell his Surveyour's place, which may
perhaps fetch 500*l.*, and make the large poundage to them. When he
has got clear of the Statute I suppose I must be plagued with him
again. I am glad to see, by yours of 13th September, you have got clear
of paying J. Sharp's dreadfull bill of 95*l.* ; it would have been a cruel
unjust thing for any body to have expected I should have paid a
farthing of it, when the Province had taken the affair upon themselves for their own vindication.—I thank your care of my letters for
Baron Scroop, Mr. Whitworth, and Sir Charles Wager.—I take a very
particular notice of what past between you and Coll^o Mordaunt,
according to what you write he is capable of doing us great service.

I hope to get time to write him and some others by this ship, which
may be pleasing to them—I now send you Lewis's powers to receive
from Lord Wilmington the money due to the Thetchers, which matter
I hope will be pleasing to his Lordship.—I could not make the thing
move faster than it has. Our worthy friend Coram writes me a particular account of his conversation with his Excellency Mr. [Horatio]
Walpole about Paul the Preacher (as Coram calls him). I find you
had also been with Mr. Walpole when you found Mr. Hyam. I hope
Sir Charles Wager, Captain Coram, Mr. Hyam and you, will be able to
keep H[oratio] W[alpole] in tolerable temper. If Dudley writes him
[that] I hinder his auditing the accounts, he writes him a downright
falsehood, for he has never since I have been in the Government
apply'd to me (according to the best of my remembrance) in any one
thing relating to his office as Deputy Auditor, nor have I ever
obstructed him.—I have a tolerable kind letter from Mr. Walpole
of 10th September per Hall to which I shall make answer in a little
time.

If the Parliament should do nothing this Session about the paper
currency in the Plantations, it will occasion vast ruin and confusion to
the British trade and to all the inhabitants of the Colonies. I say it is
absolutely necessary to be brought under a regulation without delay.
You'll see by my letters and the prints to the Secretary of State, and
Lords of Trade, what I have done about Colman's wicked projection.
Never was there so vile a cheat set on foot, yet what is done about it
will not be sufficient without an Act of Parliament.

Kilby is a sorry fellow, and you must watch his waters, he'll be ready to do any ill office to the Governor he can.—I am glad Wilk's partner would not suffer him to come in with them.—He is generally supposed to be a man of no substance.—If John Merrett is not my friend he must be what I can't believe, for he writes his wife with the greatest respect and friendship to me, and talks bitterly against my enemies, and such paragraphs of his letters she has re'd to me once and again.

I think you dispos'd of the hams very well. Honest worthy Coram is a choice friend, and capable of good service. Mr. Belcher will read to you what I write him about the forg'd letter deliver'd to Sir Charles Wager by Waldo and your reputation is greatly concerned to get Sir Charles answer to what I now write him, in 2 or 3 lines, of Waldo's delivering him or his servant that letter, for it seems he and his friends here absolutely deny that it was he who deliver'd it. So pray clear up the matter and send it to me, because you mention to me, in more letters than one, that Waldo deliver'd it and I have no doubt of it.

I thank you for the Lucern seed by Hall, and pray you to tell Mr. Switzer not to send me any because I wrote him by Waters to send me the quantity now come.

Hall having had the small pox aboard in his passage, the ship rides [in] quarantine below the Castle, so I have not receiv'd the seed, nor the cane you have sent me, for which I see you paid 9l. 9s. 0d. Pray is it so much over the two ounces of gold I sent your nephew to buy the cane, if it be it must be. an extraordina[ry] cane to cost above 7l. sterling. Pray let me know how this is. When I write to my son for anything it is his duty to send it, if he can, or write me he cannot. —He has got into an odd way of treating me lately which makes me justly angry.—I have wrote him largely upon it by this ship, and if he does not for the future strictly observe my orders, he will bitterly repent, when too late, his provoking neglect of me [which] has strecht my patience to its utmost limits. Yet, brother, I love him dearly, and he must not be crampt in his studies, and if he will reform I will still do to the utmost of my power to support him. You must therefore still comfort and supply him. I heartily wish you and Captain Coram could help him to a good wife, or that you could promote him in the way of his profession. He can't now be esteem'd a young lawyer, having been above nine years in the Temple. Good brother, continue te be a father to him. I see all things are tending to a warr with France, which will be a dreadfull thing to all the Plantations, and to this Province in a more particular manner. I have receiv'd the instruction from the Lords Justices for running the line between this Prov[ince] and New Hampshire, which shall be carried into execution as far as lyes in my power—I understand, since the arrival of the last ships, my Enemies have a great dependance upon a revival of the censure past on me last year in the Privy Councill.

I know they would move heaven and hell, if it were in their power, to get me out at the King's return, but considering the vast interest you have made for me, I hope they will be finally defeated and disappointed." —I know I shall stand in need of all the strength you can make, so pray, brother, be still alive and on the sharp look out--I remain--Sir— Your Loving Brother

         J. BELCHER."

1740, Nov. 19th. Governor Belcher to Lord Wilmington. Dated at Boston and unaddressed.

U 24953.   T

"It is some time since I have done myself the great honour of writing Your Lordship, fearing I might be troublesome.

The last spring I received your Lordship's commands, thro' Mr. Partridge, in the matter of two legacies left by Thomas Thetcher to some of his family here, and in which one of your Lordships mannors was concerned. I have taken all the pains I could to comply with your Lordship's orders, and till now we have not been able to do it but by this conveyance I transmit full powers from the legatees of Thetcher to Mr. Partridge, for his receiving their money and for giving the proper discharges. I esteem'd it a great honour to receive your Lordship's commands, as I shall whenever your Lordship can think I may be able to render you any acceptable service in this part of the world.

I humbly beg of Your Lordship to let me hope to be restored to your countenance and protection in all things your Lordship shall judge to be just and reasonable."

1740, Nov. 19th. Governor Belcher to his brother-in-law Mr. Partridge. Dated at Boston.

"Sir—I have your kind favour of 1st of last month, per Comrin, and observe Collo Blakeney's Bill for 150l. sterling sent you by Mr. Oliver was accepted, as I doubt not the others will be which I deliver'd Mr. Gatcomb being for 356l. 2s. sterling, and I think went per Harris about a month agoe. In paying the troops I made a mistake of 10l. sterling to my prejudice, which I must indeavour to rectify with Collo Blakeney and send you his order for it.

I see the merchants had met and sign'd a petition to be delivered the King at his return about *Colman's Land Scheme*, which petition was [drawn up] under the direction of Captain Tomlinson who was wrote to about it while I was in my other Government ; it was certainly an extraordinary step to put any of the affairs of this Province, into the hands of a man who has on all occasions substantially approv'd himself a bitter enemy to the Province. You will find by the prints now sent you, what I have further done for discouraging that wicked scheme, yet I believe nothing less than an Act of Parliament will put an end to it the undertakers are so needy and so violent in the pursuit of it. K[il]by is but an ignorant fellow, and I think will soon overset himself. I see he had been introduced by young Clark to Horace Walpole, for what reason I can't tell, but I take that Clark to be one of my enemies. Before I received your last you'll see what I had wrote Sir Charles Wager and you [on the] 15th currant on the head of the forg'd letter ; whoever may say that I have said Sir Charles wrote me that Mr. Waldo delivered it to him asserts a right down falsehood, for I never said any such thing ; what Sir Charles wrote me about it, I have recited in my letter to him by this conveyance. I see Waldo is trying to take vengeance upon me about it, and had been with Sir Charles, and that Kilby told Allen Sir Charles denies he wrote me that Waldo delivered him the letter, which [he] must say, if he sayes anything about his writing, for he never did write me so. However I am glad honest Coram is positive that Sir Charles told him that Waldo did deliver him the letter, and of which I have not the least doubt, and I verily believe, Dunbar and he wrote the letter between them. I very kindly thank you for being so early with Sir Charles to ward of[f], any impressions they might otherwise have made on him to my prejudice. You seem to think Jer[emiah] Allen is really now my friend, and that being much with Kilby he lets Mr. Belcher into things that are of advantage to me to be known. I have told his brother Mr James

Allen here in part what you write, and that I will serve him at the next election, but it must be kept a secret that the Governor is in his interest, or he may by its being known lose his choice. Mr James Allen has acted very much the Gentleman in the affair I have depending with Lloyd's executors, towards which I paid him the last week two thousand pounds sterling.

I am mightily pleas'd with your prudent suggestions to me about H[oratio] Walpole and Mr. Leheupe, both which things I shall put in practice in the wisest manner I can.

This is the first day of the sitting of the Assembly here, to whom I shall mention the affair of his Excellency the Auditor Generall of Accounts in the Plantations.

I am fully with you that the Assembly can't fail of serving their countrey by doing the two things you mention.

I am oblig'd to you for letting me know what Mr. Hodson said to you respecting Coll° Wendall, and have received that paragraph of your letter to the Coll°, and return'd him my hearty thanks for his sincere respect, for such it is when a man will part with his money to serve his friend, and is what very few will do. Men will make professions, write letters, and make fine speeches, all of which cost nothing, but parting with a man's substance argues real friendship.

I thank your care in sending me the cloathing per Comrin according to my order, as also for the little box done up in blew paper. I have rec'd all in good order.

I have, brother, a chargeable fatiguing time of it, and am obliged to give you and my son a vast deal of trouble, as well as the rest of my friends. What volumes do I write, it must be tiresome for you, and my son, to read and deliver them. Herewith you will receive a great number of my letters; those left open for yours and Mr Belcher's perusall, you'll read seal and deliver, what of them you please. Your friend Dr Lee Dicker is far from a man of the common sort. A most sensible ingenious gentleman. I am told Benning Wintworth intends to push to be made Lieu^t Governor of New Hampshire, but I hope it won't be so, if it should, I pray you to take care that his Comission be drawn onely in the common form, and that he have no power to command in chief when I am in Massachusetts. If he should it would be an actual superseding of my Commission, for he might then call Assemblies, appoint civil and military officers, and do all other acts of Government, and I should be Governor there onely for two months in a year. He might also get an Act past for repealing the Act of setling my salary, and get it fixt upon himself, and continually turn out every officer of my appointment, the minute I get over the line. In short for any Lieu^t Governor to be invested with the chief command, would open a scene of dreadfull confusion in the Government, and among the people, and there can be no colour of reason for transferring the power of the Governor to anyone else while I am in Massachusetts, and the post and carrier pass always twice a week. It might be as reasonable to transferr such a power to some persons in severall counties in this Province that are further from Boston, than Portsmouth is. I have, brother, a hard task in the Government to have such a number of enemies, watching for my halting. and to pick holes, where there are none. I am thankfull to God that I do even so well as I do, and often think it requires a man of greater genius than I can pretend to be, to steer intirely clear, and lick himself whole. However, courage, my brother, and I hope in a little time, we shall weather out these storms, and that things will grow more pacifick. The great Lord Coke took for his motto *prudens qui patiens.* The enemies here say they have letters by Hall that Sb[i]rly's Commission is actually made out and waits only the King's coming for signing it, and I am told the man really believes it tho' I don't, but I do believe they'll all hands join *ultimum facere conatum* at the King's return for my removal. You may depend our N[ew] E[ngland] chaps stay this winter on purpose, yet I am not much concern'd when I consider your unparallel'd vigilance and diligence, and the great interest you have made in my favour. I first of all submit myself to the care of God's providence, and then in the hopes of your further good offices, and success, I shall endeavour to make myself quiet. I cannot conclude this letter without repeating again (altho I have done it times without number) my affection and tender regard to my good and dear son Jona[than] whom I pray you to comfort and incourage in his studies, and to supply him with whatever may be necessary, and at [the] same time tell him I expect he grows a better husband of his money than heretofore, or he must find a way himself to comply with his profuseness. I don't suppose you ever spent near so much annually as he constantly does from your being a married man and with a family, to this day; let that be as it will I grow in years and neither can nor will go on to struggle and straiten myself, as I have done now for near ten years, on his account. He must therefore strive hard to get forward in his practice in the Hall, and as he is turn'd of thirty he is of full age to be married, and I heartily wish he could bring that grand article in life to bear to his comfort and honour. Pray continue to be kind and good and a father to him. Were it not for him I should not so lye in your debt, from year to year, which grieves me, and I am now indeavouring to sell an estate I have about fifty miles from this town to remit you the money, and I will further contrive to remit you some other monies in a little time."

1741, May 23rd. Jonathan Belcher, junior, to Lord Wilmington. Dated in the Middle Temple and unaddressed.

" My Lord, Your great goodness to my father whilst he had the honour of His Majesty's Commissions, and particularly in condescending to interpose for his continuance in the Governments will for ever claim from him and his family the highest possible returns of gratitude and duty.

It will, my Lord, be a secret satisfaction to my father in his retirement, that he has zealously and steadily pursu'd the interests of his royal master, and that his behaviour in the Massachusetts has receiv'd the honour of your Lordship's approbation.

I could not answer it to my father when I see him if I had omitted my humble acknowledgements in his behalf of your Lordship's favour, which I hope will prevail with you to pardon this presumption."

JONATHAN BELCHER.

1742, April 30th. Copy of a letter from Governor Shirley to Lord Wilmington. Dated at Boston.

" My Lord,—It afforded me much pleasure to hear from Mr Tomlinson that your Lordship is pleas'd to permit him to give me and my friends an assurance of your favourable disposition towards me. As this goodness of your Lordship demands my most grateful acknowledgments, so it will excite my constant endeavours to merit your Lordship's favour and protection by the best services I can render to his Majesty and the country, which I am sensible are the only terms of my preserving that most valuable approbation and friendship, which is of itself singly sufficient to recommend me to the esteem of all parties. It gave me also great satisfaction to find by Mᵣ Tomlinson's letter that I was honour'd with the concurrence of your Lordship's sentiments in what I proposed for the supply of the Treasury here, before I knew from my instructions that I was at liberty to give my consent to the issuing of 30,000*l.* Bills of Credit for that purpose ; soon after the arrival of which instruction I made use of that liberty, which his Majesty's service necessarily required I should do, as I had no other possible method of putting the ruinous fortifications of the Province into a defensible condition, and preventing his Majesty's forts and garrisons form being deserted for want of cloaths and pay, or promoting the raising the recruits here for his Majesty's service in the expedition. Upon all which accounts I hope what I have done in the supply of the Treasury will not be disapproved of, especially as I have taken care to put the Province Bills upon a better foot than they were ever emitted on before, by securing all private creditors from being hurt by any future depreciating of those Bills, and putting it out of the Assembly's power to postpone the drawing 'em in beyond their limited periods of payment, which new regulations seem to be the most effectual provision for securing the publick faith and private justice that a paper currency will admit ; and to bid fair for curing the chief mischiefs and inconveniences arising from it to the British merchants as well as creditors within the Province, and in a great measure answer all the ends of his Majesty's instructions for restraining it.

Since my consenting to this supply of the Treasury I have been informd by Mr. Thomlinson that my Lords Commissioners of Trades &c., have declared their opinion against any emission of Bills of Credit in this Province thô the merchants who attended 'em approved of what I proposed; but I may assure your Lordship that whilst the Government of Rhode Island are unrestrain'd in their emissions, all restraints of that sort laid by his Majesty on the Province will be ineffectual to prevent the mischiefs proposed by their Lordships to be thereby cured. For that little Colony will of itself issue Bills enough to supply all New England with a paper medium, and in such case the effect of further restraints laid on this Province will only tend to clogg his Majesty's Government in it with difficulties, and subject the people of it to the necessity of receiving the Rhode Island Bills at any rate, than which (according to their present scheme) there never was a more palpable cheat within any of his Majesty's Colonies, which had the countenance of the Government of the Colony.

"In one of my former I troubled your Lordship with some mention concerning the effects of the late Act of Parliament for suppressing the two money schemes call'd the Silver Scheme and the Land Bank or Manufactory Scheme; since which many persons concern'd in both those schemes have been in great consternation and distress; for the Act has destroy'd the agreements and contracts, which pass'd between the directors and partners of each company, and has subjected every person concern'd in 'em to the demands of all the possessors of the bills, by which means it has happen'd that the honester part of each company, who have comply'd with the directions of the Act by bringing in their quotas of the bills to be consumed, still remain exposed to the demands of the possessors of the outstanding bills and all penalties of the Act, and have at the same time lost all remedy against their knavish partners who obstinately refuse to redeem their respective quotas of 'em, taking advantage of their bonds and other securities for that purpose being annull'd and made void by the Act. To prevent this ruin to many private families and confusion to the publick, the Assembly and Council upon the petition of the worthier part of each of the late companies pass'd one of the enclosed orders No. 1, and most earnest sollicitations have been made to me by the sufferers to give my consent to it; but as the remedy proposed by it is at the bottom founded upon the supposed subsistence of the mutual agreements and contracts made at first between the directors and partners of each of the companies, which are deem'd and declared by the Act of Parliament to be illegal and void *ab initio* I could not possibly come into it. But to retrieve the sufferers and preserve the publick peace and quiet, so far as was in my power, I form'd and promoted the inclosed order of the General Court No. 2, which is consistent with the Act, and I understand has considerably alarm'd the deficient partners, and will I hope, help to make the Act of Parliament have its full effect, and draw in all the outstanding Bills properly. As I troubled your Lordship with a copy of my first Message to the Assembly concerning the settlement of the sallary, I take the liberty to inclose copies of the subsequent Messages between me and the Assembly upon that head, which contain the whole of their pretences for not complying with his Maj^y's instruction and my answer to 'em. How far the Province may be prevailed upon towards complying with the instruction the first Session of the next General Court will determine."

1742, June 8th. Letter of Colonel David Dunbar, Lieut. Governor of New Hampshire and Surveyor General of his Majesty's Woods in North America, to Lord Wilmington, First Lord of the Treasury.

Enclosing a Petition to the Treasury and also his correspondence with the Privy Council, the Board of Trade, and the Navy Board, with reference to his claims for compensation for having built forts at Pemaquid and Fort Frederick and having settled people on some lands which he deemed to be in the western part of Nova Scotia but which had since been found to belong to Massachussetts.

AMERICAN PLANTATIONS, ISLANDS, ETC. (MISCELLANEOUS).

1714–1754.

1714, Oct. 18th. A report on the Plantations of America. In French. Unsigned. 17 pp.

[1715 ?]. A Report prepared by the Board of Trade for the House of Commons, relating to Newfoundland, Nova Scotia, Cape Breton, etc. In book form. 93 pp.

It commences :—

" We have extracted the particulars of what was transacted at the Board relating to the treaties of commerce with France and Spain, and relating to Newfoundland, Nova Scotia, Cape Breton &c. : and have subjoined our reflections thereon together with a state of this kingdom's trade to all parts during the peace after the treaty of Ryswick, and a further state thereof for the three first years of the war in 1702, 1703 and 1704. To which is annex'd an account of the woolen manufactures exported from Michaelmas 1697 to Xmas 1714 with our remarks thereon."

The following paragraphs are still of interest :—

" We say—that formerly the French had no right to fish on the coasts of Newfoundland, or to dry their fish there, but by leave from the

MARQUESS
TOWNSHEND
MSS.

Government here, and for such liberty they paid an acknowledgment. All Newfoundland being always look'd upon as belonging to the English together with the whole right of fishery there.

"Their late Majesties King William and Queen Mary in the Declaration of War against France the 7th of May 1689 asserted their undoubted right to Newfoundland, and assigned the encroachments of the French upon that island, and their subjects trade and fishery, as one of the injuries which occasioned that war."

"In the 10th and 11th years of the reign of that prince there was a law pass'd whereby 'tis enacted that all his Majesty's subjects shall enjoy the trade and fishery to and from Newfoundland &c. And that no alien or stranger whatsoever not residing in England shall at any time hereafter take any bait or use any sort of trade or fishing whatsoever in Newfoundland or any of the islands or places thereunto belonging. . . . .

" . . . . But by the late Treaty [of Utrecht] the French are allow'd to catch fish and to dry them on land in that part of the Island of Newfoundland which stretches from the place called Cape Bonavista to the northern point of the said island from thence running down by the western side as far as Point Riche which is at least one half of the circumference of the coasts of the said Island of Newfoundland.

"The French have indeed delivered up Placentia, and what other settlements they had upon the said Islands, together with the sole right of fishery on the coasts of the other half of the said Island and the propriety of the whole.

"But even this part of the Treaty is defeated by a letter obtained from her late Majesty permitting and allowing the French to keep their possessions in case they stay, or to sell them in case they go away, in consequence whereof they pretend a property in the houses lands and beeches on which the fish is cured, so that if we cannot have them but by purchase very little in effect is yielded to the Crown of Great Britain and our fishing ships are thereby liable to great disturbances, should even the subjects of Great Britain become purchasers of those beeches, which ought to be free to all fishing ships.

"But the greatest discouragements to our whole fishing trade our navigation and our Northern Plantations in America proceeds from that fatal cession of Cape Breton to the French by the late Treaty notwithstanding the early remonstrances and pressing memorials of several traders and others to the contrary."

The letter of Queen Anne to King Louis XIV. above referred to is set out in the earlier part of the same Report, with the following introduction:—

"Before we mention the consequence of Nova Scotia to this Kingdom, with relation to its fishery, and the great quantity of trees fit for the production of naval stores, we shall take leave to make one observation more and that is that when the expedition against Nova Scotia was undertaken Colo Nicholson had instructions from her late Majesty dated 18th of March 1709–10 signifying her pleasure that such persons in the several Governments on the continent of America who should contribute to the reduction of Port Royal &c. belonging to the enemy shou'd have the preference both with regard to the soile and trade of the country when reduc'd to any other of Her Majesty's subjects. This was signify'd to the several Governments by proclamations sign'd by Colo Nicholson, Colo Vetch and by Colo Dudley Governr of the Massachusets Bay. Upon this the people readily and cheerfully came in, undertook the expedition and conquer'd the place. But when Colo Nicholson went over Govern^r of Nova Scotia in 1713 he had a letter from her late Majesty in the words following :—

"'Whereas our good brother the most Christian King, hath at our desire releas'd from imprisonment on board his galleys, such of his subjects as were detained there on account of their professing the Protestant Religion ; we being willing to show by some mark of our favour towards his subjects, how kindly we take his compliance therein, have therefore thought fit hereby to signify our will and pleasure to you that you permit, and allow such of them as have any lands or tenements in the places under your Government in Accadie and Newfoundland that have been or are to be yielded to us by virtue of the late Treaty of Peace, and are willing to continue our subjects, to retain, and enjoy their said lands and tenements without any let or molestation, as fully and freely, as other our subjects do or may possess their lands, and estates, or to sell the same, if they shall rather chuse to remove elsewhere. And for so doing this shall be your warrant. And so we bid you farewell. Given at our Court at Kensington, the 23rd day of June 1713. In the twelfth Year of Our Reign." '

1719, June 4th. Copy of a Report addressed to the Lords of the Committee for hearing appeals, signed by Paul Docminique, Thomas Pelham, Daniel Pultney and Martin Bladen, Commissioners of the Board of Trade who had been required " to consider whether any and what liberty ought to be reserved in the Patent desired by Sir Alexander Cairnes and others to be granted to them of a tract of land on the coast of Nova Scotia for all his Majesty's subjects to fish and cure the fish on the beach there &c." 4½ pp.

1720, July 22nd. William Popple to Lord Townshend.

" My Lord—In obedience to your Lordship's commands I enclose to your Lordship the copy of a representation which I had the honour to acquaint your Lordship was drawn by M^r [John] Lock[e] in 1696. It relates to the defence of the Northern Colonies and proposes that a Captain General shou'd be appointed over them."

The enclosure above referred to is dated at Whitehall Sept. 30th 1696, and signed by Lord Tankerville, Philip Meadows, John Pollexfen, John Locke and Abraham Hills, Commissioners on the Board of Trade. 10 pp.

1720 —. " The present state of the French settlements in Louisiana, with the number and state of the Indians leying between Carolina and Mississipi and of the fatall consequences it will be to Virginia and Carolina to suffer the French to acquire the dominion over all those Indians." Signed by John Barnwell, and addressed to Lord Townshend as President of the Council.

1725, Nov. 8th. Copy of a complaint from four companies of foot, of one hundred men each, posted at New York, against their commander Governor William Burnet, for docking the men of their pay by paying in currency and subjecting them to other hardships. Unaddressed and unsigned. 2 pp.

The third and fourth paragraphs of this complaint run as follows :—

3. " For all Bills of 100 sterling he draws for home he receives here one hundred and sixty-five pounds New York money, with this money he pays the troops and Staff Officers here, all receipts taken from the Officers and sent home to the Agent, Mr Lahoop [Leheup] will justify they are paid in money at eight shillings p^r ounce.

'4· " By paying the troops as above he gits a percusite of above four thousand a year New York money and in his five years has got by paying the troops hear twenty thousand pounds New York money."

1728, Augt. 23rd. Robert Hunter, Governor of Jamaica, to the Duke of Portland [?] Unaddressed. Dated in Jamaica.

" . . . . . . The Spanish privateers continue their insults and depredations of which M^r St. Lo has given your grace a particular acc^t as he informs me. As also of the answer he received from the Spanish Govr on his demanding restitution or satisfaction. He is in a declining state of health, and it is much doubted if he can gett over it but I hope it is otherwise."

1735, Oct. 11th. Lewis Morris, afterwards Governor of New Jersey, to Lord Wilmington. Dated at Westminster and unaddressed.

" My Lord—I have been inform'd that the Right Honble the Board of Trade, barely upon the credit of some letters from Coll° Cosby Governor of New York and part of the Councill there, representing Mr Van Dam President of the Councill of New York, James Alexander and others of that Councill and myself (who have been above fourty yeares President of the Councill of New Jersie) as persons disaffected to his Majesty's person and government and as men who have given Mr Cosby unreasonable opposition in his Administration. . . . . . . I presume so far to depend on your Lordship's justice as to hope that neither of us shall be condemn'd unheard, nor suppos'd guilty of anything we are accus'd of by Coll° Cosby barely upon his saying so. . . . . . ."

1735, Dec. 27th. Henry Cunningham to Lord Wilmington. Dated in Jamaica.

" . . . . . . I have had four gentlemen Wm Nedham, Gershom Ely, Charles Price, and Matthew Concannen Esq^{rs}, recommended to me by the Council and others, as persons of the greatest weight and influence among the people, and fitt to fill up the vacancys. The first was many years Chief Justice and Speaker of the last Assembly, the second has long serv'd his country in Assemblys and is at present Custos of a Precinct and Co^l of a Regiment of Militia, the third serv'd in the last Assembly and is now Custos of the most considerable Precinct of the Island, and the last is Attorney-General. . . . . .

" The rebel slaves since they left the North East part of the Island have been quiet, but I find it is feared by every body of Credit here, that they are settling themselves in some strong fastnesses, and when that is done will attempt to be more mischievous than ever. . . . ."

1736, July 5th. " The representation of Sr Wm Keith, Bar^t, relating to the dividing the Governm^t of New Jersey from that of New-York." [Addressed " To the Right Honble my Lord Wilmington &c."]

" Most humbly sheweth—That next September it will be two years since the King was graciously pleased to receive and approve my humble petition for dividing the Government of New Jersy from New York a copy whereof is hereunto subjoined.

" That my former services in America for the space of twelve years, first as officer of the Revenue over seven Colonies, and then as Governor of Pensylvania above nine years, have been well approved of, without any complaint haveing ever been exhibited against me.

" That my application in many particulars here of late to serve the Province of New Jersey and the great confidence which that people have in my disposition and capacity to promote their interest, as may appear from the annex'd copy of a letter to my self from that Country, sufficiently demonstrat how much easier it would be for me, than for

any stranger amongst them, to propose and perfect what may be thought
necessary for supporting the just authority of His Majesty's Government
in that Province.

"Without derogating therefor from the character of any gentleman
who may apply by his friends for obtaining the same employment at
this juncture, I humbly presume, that the justice of my pretensions,
now of two years standing, to be appointed Governour of New Jersey,
will be considered as preferable to those of any other person who has
not had the experience and opportunity of rendering equal service to
the Crown.

"Those my Lord are the plain facts and circumstances of a case that
humbly claims that protection and countenance which ever flows
from your Lordship's known humanity and tenderness for every thing
which appears to you to be equitable and just."

First Enclosure (in the handwriting of Sir William Keith) :—
"To the King's most Excellent Majesty,
The Representation and Petition of Sir Wm Keith Barrt.

"Most humbly sheweth—That the Province of New Jersey situated
between the Colonies of New York and Pensylvania in North America
is capable of great improvement with respect to its product and trade.
But the said Province haveing of late years been committed to the care
of the Governour of New York, for the time being, render'd it impracticable to obtain such laws and regulations of Government as
were necessary for the country's improvement, because the interests of
the two independent Colonies so frequently interfeir'd with each
other, that the Governour's duty to both became incompatible and
inconsistant.

"That the poor industrious people of Jersey have some time since
petition'd your Majesty for your royal favour by granting a commission to a particular Governour for that Province to reside amongst
them, whom they are both willing and able to support in a decent
manner, and the rather because it can very little if at all diminish the
interest of the Governour of New York, who at this time scarcely
receives from Jersey a sufficiency to defray the yearly and continual
expence of his atttendance on their Assembly, Chancery Court, and
other public affairs.

"That your humble petitioner haveing had the honour to be sent abroad
Governour of Pensylvania in the year 1716 when your Majesty was at
Hampton Court then Regent of the Kingdom, and haveing on that as
well as several other occasions acquitted himself with an unblameable
reputation in the public service, he now humbly implores your
Majesty that in your great goodness you will be pleased to grant him
your Royal Commission to be your Majesty's Governour in and over the
Province of New Jersey, which from his long experience and knowledge
of those countries, he presumes might be so improved, as in a short
time to make that small Government a valuable office without any charge
or expence whatsoever to the Crown."

"N.B.—This Petition was delivered at Kinsington the 5th day of
Sepr 1734 and Recommended by Sir Robert Walpole."

Second inclosure (in the handwriting of Sir William Keith) :—
Copy of a letter dated from Perth Amboy in New Jersey, the 12th
March 1735–6, to Sir Wm Keith Barrt.

"Sir—Our Governour Collo Cosby died the 10th of this instant, and
the Province of New Jersey is determined if possible to have a seperat
Governour and to grant him a support suitable to his character which
they are well able to do. We wish you may have interest to be the

person, that this truely well disposed people may be happy under your administration and equally esteem'd with a neighbouring Colony whose wealth and present reputation is by all hands acknowledg'd to be oweing to your faithfull and discreet conduct. Our people are so sensible of this, that had they a choice, you would certainly be the man, and we are perswaded his Majesty cannot appoint another so capable to raise the revenue of this Province to a sufficient support. Our Council will meet in a few days and per first opportunity you will hear their thoughts, together with their sentiments of the disposition of our Assembly upon this subject, but to gain time, no other opportunity presenting, we have thought fit to send you this via Antegua that you may bestir your self before a promise is made; and that you may find freinds and this oppress'd people relief is the hearty wishes of S^r y^r most humble servants

" WILL. SKINNER.
" AND^w JOHNSTON."

1736, Dec. 10th. Temple Lawes to Sir Thomas ———. Dated at Jamaica and unaddressed. A duplicate copy " per Capt. Poynter."

" Dear Sir Thomas—My last to you was of the 12th Sept^{br} giving you an acc^t of what progress I had made in getting in your friend's debts : and likewise of the deplorable condition of our Island and of the fatall consequences of the Gin Act to the Sugar Colonys in generall. This only serves to enclose you the reasons why some of the Council, who have been abused by the President for not giving their assent to a Bill calculated for no other end but to make him a present of £125, have thought fit to withdraw their attendance from the Board during his administration, and to beg the favour of you to stand by us and to use your utmost interest with the Board of Trade and Secretary of State to support us, in case the President should misrepresent the proceedings of the Board, since we have done nothing more than in support of his Majesty's prerogative and of the King's instructions which he would have broke thro', and for our opposing him in which he taxed us not only with a breach of duty to his Majesty, but a violation of our oaths, in a speech at the close of that Sessions of Assembly.

" If this won't justify us, I don't know any gentleman that has any regard to his honour and reputation [who] would sit at that Board only to be made a tool of, or else to be insulted and abused for not sacrificing his understanding and the interests of his country to the private views of a man who has accidentally got into power. For my part I can swear for myself and can take upon me to answer for the other three gentlemen that we neither have nor can be thought to have any private views, nor any other purposes to serve than the common good of the Island and his Majesty's service. We have no salarys nor posts of profit, on the contrary we are oblig'd to be at an extraordinary expence of 2, or £300, a year in giving our attendance upon the publick service, besides the loss of so much time from our familys and plantations.

" I beg Sir you will represent this matter in such a light to the Board of Trade and the Duke of Newcastle, if we may be justified and supported in the opposition we have made to a President that would have broke thro' a positive* instruction from the King."

The following is the enclosure above referred to. It is endorsed " Reasons why four of the Council withdraw during Mr Gregory's Administration."

---

* Vide the Instruction to Mr. Cunningham not to pass such a Deficiency Law.

" Some reasons why we, the underwritten Members of his Majesty's
Council, do for the present withdraw our attendance from the Board.

" 1st . . . Because the President during his whole Administration
hath taken upon him to act in matters of the greatest importance not
only without but contrary to the advice and consent of the Council.

2d . . . That the Council haveing been oblig'd to a tedious
attendance of fourteen weeks during the last Sessions of Assembly
were greatly harrassed in their persons injur'd in their fortunes and
abused in their stations without any reason that we conceive but to
force their assent to some clauses in the deficiency and Rum Bills,
which they judg'd partial and unreasonable.

3d . . . That the present Session of Assembly was called without the advice of the Council, and without any pressing necessity that
we are informed of unless it were to procure those clauses to be pas'd
in some law before the arrivall of a Governor.

4th . . . That during those Sessions of Assembly the Council
having rejected some Bills that did not seem necessary the President
did in his speech at the close of the last Session insinuate that the
Council were not only wanting in their duty to His Majesty and this
Island but regardless of the oaths they had taken in their stations, an
imputation to which we shall forbear to give the proper epithet, but
which appear'd to us so horrid that nothing should have prevail'd on us
to have given our attendance at this Board, but that the number of
the Council (until this Session) was so small that we could not withdraw ourselves without a manifest obstruction to the publick business.

5th . . . That as we have not yet receiv'd from his Majesty's
Principall Secretary of State and Lords of Trade, any redress for Mr.
Gregory's conduct, pursuant to our most humble Address to His
Majesty and representation to his Grace and their Lordships, we
conceive the Council may be lyable to be insulted on the like occation
by any of their fellow Councillors who may may hereafter assume the
Government.

For these and severall other weighty reasons which we think not
proper at this time to insert we think it inconsistent with our honour
our character or our interest to give our attendance longer at this
Board during the present administration and therefore we take the
liberty to withdraw from the same.

	EDWARD CHARLTON.
	HENRY DAWKINS.
St Jago De la Vega	WILLIAM GORDON.
November 27, 1736.	TEMPLE LAWES.

1737, April 15th. A letter from Richard Fitzwilliam, Governor of
the Bahamas. Dated at New Providence, and endorsed by Lord
Wilmington " Received April 19th 1738." 5 pp.

The writer answers complaints that had been made against him by
Cuthbert Jackson, John White and others, and asks for preferment.

1737, June 30th. Edward Trelawny, Governor of Jamaica, to Lord
Wilmington. Dated in London. 3½ pp.

" My Lord—Our foreign Plantations being under the protection of His
Majesty's Council where your Lordship presides, I beg leave to lay
before you some reasons for not removing any of the eight companies
now established by Parliament in Jamaica.

. . . . . . I am then fully persuaded that your Lordship's
prudence and just regard for the welfare of His Majesty's Plantations,
will not allow you to come into a measure that will weaken and render

MARQUESS
TOWNSHEND
MSS.

insecure so valuable a part of them, and that you will not be of opinion to take a step of such consequence to Jamaica as the withdrawing half the forces from thence, without being moved to it by the Legislature of the Island, who your Lordship may be assured will be glad to save the subsistence money they pay to the soldiers as soon as their safety will allow them to do it."

[1737.] The Case of James Buchanan of London merchant and others concerned and interested in the ship Scipio, Alexander Mackpherson master. Undated.

The case relates to the capture and recapture of this ship in Jamaican waters.

1739, April 22nd. Governor Trelawny to Lord Wilmington. Dated in Jamaica.

· · · · · " I put off the meeting of the Assembly as long as it was possible : they met on the 13th of March ; they persisted in renewing the former clause to tax the Jews. Having received no farther orders from His Majesty and the former Act which provides for the subsistance of His Majesty's Troops being to expire next day, I consulted the Council, who unanimously advised me, for the reasons hereunto annexed, to pass the Bill, in which Bill the country pay of each private soldier is increas'd from six to eight rials per week. I hope your Lordship will be of opinion that I could not avoid doing so without exposing His Majesty's troops to famine, and the country to disorders which might arise from their mutiny, of which they were formerly guilty upon the like occasion."

1739, Nov. 12th. Governor Trelawny to Lord Wilmington. Dated in Jamaica.

" My Lord—Mr. Sharpe acquaints me how much I am obliged to your Lordship for my success in the five Councillors I recommended, a point of great consequence to me in the beginning of Administration ; nor am I a little obliged to your Lordship for the great share you had in the order of Council whereby I had a discretionary power to pass the Bill wherein the Jews were taxed for the current year. Give me leave to return you my most humble and sincere thanks, and to assure your Lordship of my constant endeavour to deserve the continuance of your protection by acting zealously and disinterestedly for his Majesty's service. Since it is his Majesty's determination that I shall not for the future give my consent to a separate tax on the Jews, I will take care not to disobey his commands, tho' I much fear it may embroil me with the Assembly, and hinder them from giving the usual subsistence to his Majesty's independent companies.

On the 6th of this instant Samuel Dicker and Rose Fuller Esqrs and Sir Simon Clarke Baronet were sworn into the Council, pursuant to his Majesty's several orders for that purpose. I delayed swearing in Samuel Whitehorne Esq, upon account of the complaint made against him in the petition and affidavit hereunto annext. I have communicated them to him and had his answer, but wait for the reply of the complainant. As Mr. Whitehorne was recommended by me I think I ought to be the more cautious in admitting him into the Council, before he purges himself more satisfactorily of this charge, being of opinion that if it is proved, it is of such a nature that by my 67th instruction he ought not to be admitted into any publick trust or employment and especially into this, which is the greatest. Edward Garthwaite Esqr the fifth Councillor ordered to be sworn is absent from the Island."

P.S. Vice-Admiral Vernon sailed from this place the fifth inst to attack Porto-hello."

1740, May 3rd. An Extract from the Journal of the Council of Jamaica of this date. Signed by Samuel Williams, Secretary and Clerk to the Council. 2½ pp.

1740, May 14th. The Honorable Robert Byng, Governor of Barbadoes, to Lord Wilmington. Dated at Pilgrim. 1 page.

The writer will transmit to the Board of Trade several Acts which have passed the Legislature and desires his Majesty's leave to appoint Reynold Hooper Esqʳᵉ to fill up the vacant seat of one of the Councillors.

1740, Sept. 10th. Extract from a Letter from Thomas Penn Esqʳᵉ to Mr. Paris, dated at Philadelphia.

"You will find the scheme for raising men in America had had a very good effect, and I believe about 4600 will be carried, from these Colonys; aud though this Province cannot furnish the number my Lord Monson proposed, yet, the eight companys are a considerable number, and are now compleat. Mr. Freame has turned soldier, and has the command of one. We have eight ships ready for their imbarkation, and they are to go on Board in a few days; the behaviour of the Governor, [the Lieut. Governor Theophilus Thomas?], upon this occasion, I cannot help, again, telling you has been such as every man would wish to hear of his best friend, his zeal for the service, and desire to obey his Majesty's commands, has surmounted all the difficultys that have been thrown in his way; but, I believe, there are not many who could have conducted the affairs in the same manner, and brought it to a period. He visits all the companys; sees them perform their exercises, makes speeches to encourage them, and sets before them the great advantages that will attend their serving their country, cautions them against desertions, and gives them mony, out of his own pocket, and, in every branch of the business, acts the most disinterested, and generous part that 'tis possible for any man to do; every gentleman here has endeavoured to do what service they could, and none, but brutes, could avoid it, when they considered the duty they owed their country, and the good example set them by their Governor, who deserves the best Government in the King's gift; great care has been taken to get the best provisions for the men, at the very lowest rates, the Governor scorning to make one penny to himself; and, I hope, when they come to the place of rendevous, our batalion will make as good a figure, as any of our neighbours."

[Circ. 1740.] The humble petition of John Mason and Samuel Mason of Connecticut gentlemen To the Right Honᵇˡᵉ the Lords Commissioners for Trade and Plantations: Sheweth—

That a former petition from your petitioners, in behalf of the Mohegan [or Mohican] Indians, and as trustees for them and their lands, And also another petition proved by two persons' oaths to be signed by no less than 57 of those Indians themselves having been presented to his Majesty and referred to your Lordships, your Lordships were pleased to hear the partys thereon . . . . on the 19ᵗʰ and 20ᵗʰ of Dec. 1739.

. . . . . . in humble hopes that your Lordships will be pleased to advise his Majesty to grant that whole relief your petitioners beg leave to submit the following matters to your Lordships' consideration.

1. That the Indians' clear right to the lands in question, appears incontestably from the solemn judgment unanimously pronounced by Colonel Dudley and the others of Queen Ann's Commissioners in Augᵗ

MARQUESS
TOWNSHEND
MSS.

1705—which judgment, thô execution thereof remains to be done and is suspended, is not avoided.

2. That it was the people of Connecticut who prayed for the Commission of review of that solemn judgment . . . . .

3. That the late Commission which issued, was only in lieu and stead of that which Connecticut themselves had applied for but not taken out.

4. That this late Commission (which was so grossly abused and perverted by the Rhode Island Commissioners) has answered no one end, for which it was issued.

5. That the Indians, nor yet your petitioners, have been guilty of any the least misbehaviour therein, whereby to forfeit their undoubted rights . . . . . .

6. That it has been the boast and glory of this Crown to have founded its Empire in America upon equity and the free consent of the natives, but the grievous wrongs and injustice done those natives by particular men and petty communities, (and of which the late is a most flagrant instance) casts a stain and blemish upon the English nation, and grievously crys for justice and redress. As well also as deserves the same in point of prudence, least the neighbouring tribes to our Settlements should go off to other nations, which it has always been thought good policy to prevent.

7. That no tribe in America ever shewed so much affection or fidelity, or rendered such signal services to this Crown and its subjects as the Mohegans have done ; it appearing by the said former judgment, that they freely gave the first settlers the greatest part of their lands, and that they also constantly supported and defended them therein, with their blood and with their lives, upon every occasion, in all their warrs, and against every enemy.

8. That the royal faith and honour was, in a most solemn manner pledged and given to this faithful tribe, that they should be preserved in their own reserved lands, as appears in the said former judgment, where Colonel Dudley and the rest of the Queen's Commissioners did in her Majesty's behalf return the Mohegans thanks for their zeal and affection to her Majesty's crown and Government and the interest of this nation, and assured them that her Majesty would be *always* ready to take care of them and their people, both in protecting of them & *in preserving of their rights and propertys.*

9. That without a Commission of review, their rights and propertys thus wrongfully invaded must be inevitably lost . . . . .

10. That what the Crown allows on this occasion does not quite defray the expence here . . . . .

11. That it will not be at all necessary that these expences should be again repeated . . . . . but the present desired Commission will be the last, if his Majesty shall be pleased to direct the same to proper Commissioners, and to direct, as was done in the first Commission to Colonel Dudley, and as was also done in the late Commission [for settling the boundaries] between New Hampshire and the Massa[chusetts] Bay, that an appeal should be [allowed to be] made from the Commissioners determination to his Majesty in Co[ounci]ll ; the judgment on which appeal will for ever close and put an end to the matter.

12. That upon the last Commission the Rhode Island Commissioners publickly avow, (upon their own minutes) that in open defyance of the royal Commission and the express comands therein contained, they absolutely and repeatedly refused to look upon the former proceedings, which they were comanded to examine and review—to hear the Indians themselves, whom they had summoned and who were present in court

and desired to be heard, to hear the trustees for the tribe, who were also present and prest to be heard, or to hear their co[unse]ll Mess⁻⁻ Shirley and Bollan two gentlemen of character whom at a large expence they had got to attend the Commissioners, to defend the rights of these poor people. After all which yo⁻ Petitioners humbly hope your Lordships will consider the whole that was done by such Commissioners, as a gross abuse and piece of injustice and utter nullity . . .

13. That it is evident that the pretended release from Ben Uncas would not bear the least opposition or examination, for if it would, the Rhode Island Commissioners would gladly have permitted some one body to have been heard against the same . . . . .

14. That truth is sometimes so very prevalent that it will break out and shew it self notwithstanding the utmost endeavours of artful men to hide and cover the same, and which appears in the present case, for that, of the Rhode Island Commissioners' own shewing, Ben Uncas, if ever he was Sachem, was denyed to be such by the tribe long before the time of his pretended rel[ease]. It was commanded that pending the Commission nothing should be so much as attempted to the prejudice of the Indians, and yet, that pretended release was gained, in point of time long subsequent to that Commission and just when the Commissioners were going to sett—By the Indians repeated deeds of trusts, long since and repeatedly recorded upon the publick records in Connecticut; by the judgm⁻ of Coll. Dudley and the rest of the Queen's Comm⁻⁻ in 1705; by the publick Laws of Connecticut of 13ᵗʰ Oct. 1692 &c., In order to prevent these Indians from being defrauded, the legal trusts of their reserved lands were vested in your petitioners' ancestors, and no deeds from the Indians were to be good without the express consent of their trustees had thereto, which is not pretended to have been had in this case . . . .

" 15. Besides all which, by the last accounts receiv'd from thence your petitioners have undoubted information, that the tribe threaten the said Ben Uncas with death for endeavouring to betray and prejudice their rights, and are full of bitter complaints of the injustice done them, and are restrained by gentle measures used by your petitioners' family, (who have ever been patrons to them for more than a century past) from going off to other nations not in friendship with the English, and even from revenging themselves upon their oppressors, merely from the expectation that upon a representation of their wrongs your petitioners shall obtain justice for them from his Majesty."

1742, May 25th. J. Wimble to Lord Wilmington. Dated at New Providence.

" My Lord,—Pardon me in this, knowing your Lordship's sincerity and value that you have for the British subjects, I take this liberty to acquaint your Lordship of my unhappy misfortune of loosing my ship October last past, on a reef lying three leagues west from Atwood's Keys, latitude 23.10 N. one of the Bahama Islands at nine o'clock in the night by the means of the person that had the command of the watch alter'd his course 3 points Esterly from orders which ran me ashore and by good providence sav'd all our lives and in a few days in my boat I got down to Providence which being upwards of 100 leagues from me, purchasing there a sloop from Capt. [Thomas] Frankland, Commander of His Majesties ship the Rose which he had lately taken from the Spaniards. I mann'd her with 40 men and mounted ten carriage guns and ten sweevels. [I] entered then in concer[t]ship with Capt. Davidson of the Sᵗ Andrew of Rhode Islands mounting 16 carriage guns with 60 men and on the North side of Cuba in the Old Streights of the Bahamas in the latter end of April last we had the good fortune to take 4 small Spanish schooner[s] tho' of little worth, which we sent to Providence in order to be condemn'd and with an account of one of his Majesty's Seventy gun ships being cast away upon the Islands of Tordudas to leeward of Cape Florida a month before. The Spaniards knowing of this they sent 2 or 3 vessels down with about 400 men in order to take them, but the English men having got their guns on shore and their stores, fortifying themselves against any attempt of this nature prevented the Spaniards of their design, killing ¾ of them, and the others return'd to the Havana, upon which the Governor of that place sent down four vessels more with 8 or 900 men to attack them the second time but what success they had I know not, I and my concert would willingly have gone down to their relief by [?but] my pilot and people would not consent to it. This news I had from the Spanish prisoners with an account of 12 sail of Spanish Man of War all lying fitted at the Havana bound to Carthagena. In a day or two afterwards we met with a Spanish ship from Cales to the Havana mounting 30 guns and 250 men and passengers. I lay under her stern for two howers and my concert not coming up and at last having the misfortune to receive a chain shot from the ship's stern chace guns which took my left arm off, about 5 inches from my body, not acquainting my people of this for some time being afraid of discouraging them, loosing a great deal of blood I fell down upon one of the guns and being taken up and carried down to my surgeon and lieutenant dropt off, from the ship's stern & speaking with my concert consulting with him they thought proper to quit the ship—this being unknown to me I was more concern'd for the loss of this valuable Prize (as she might have been if this Accident had not happened to me and my concert had come up) than I was for the loss of my Arm.

If His Majesty would trust me with a 20 gun ship the Spaniards should well pay for it.

I have got further Affidavits of the losses I sustain'd in Govr Rogers time, which I hope will give your Lordship full Satisfaction of the truth of the same, if ever I live to get home to England I shall depend once more upon your Lordship's goodness for payment of the same.

His Majesty's Ship the Rose is lately arriv'd here from S^o Carolina, which will go out in a few Days upon a Cruize—I am affraid (here being but few hands upon the Island) I shall be obliged to go to North America to be mann'd or else to return soon for England.

I have been kindly used here by the Governor in all my misfortunes.

Secretary Rice is also arrived here from North Carolina and gives an Acc^t that Govr Johnson was well when he left that Place, but he has left entirely Cape Fair & settled at Edenton.

The Spaniards have 7 Sail of Privateers fitted out of the N^o Side of Cuba cruizing on the Northern Coast of America and are daily sending in Prizes to Cape Francoi, a French Port in Hispanola.

We have no Command of our men in a Port, they leave us when they please that I am almost tyerd of Privateering. If your Lordship will be so good as to procure me a small Ship in the Nevy station'd here at New Providence, I would not doubt but in a short time to behave as such to give full Content to my King and Country as long as the War should hold, God sparing my Life, a line from Your Lordship of this nature directed to New Providence would be very acceptable.

J. WIMBLE."

U

[1742.] An undated Petition from Sir Thomas Robinson, Bar¹, to the Lords of the Treasury (on his appointment by Letters Patent to be Governor of Barbadoes), for a warrant for the usual allowance or such sum as His Majesty shall think fit.

Enclosed is the following memorandum :—

"26ᵗʰ May 1721. Lord Belhaven receiv'd 1500ˡⁱ for Services performed and to be performed to his Majesty as Governor of Barbadoes.

13ᵗʰ Septʳ. 1722. Mʳ [Henry] Worsley had the same Allowance.

1 July 1731. Mʳ Chetwynd had the same Allowance.

8 July 1732. Lord Howe had the same Allowance.

29 Octʳ 1737. Sir Orlando Bridgeman had the same Allowance.

13 Septʳ 1739. [The Hon.] Mʳ [Robert] Byng had the same Allowance."

[1747 ?] Extracts out of a letter from Mʳ Matthew, Governour of the Leward Islands, to Mʳ Yeamans dated Antigua March 7ᵗʰ. [1½ pp].

The extracts refer to the necessity of putting the Islands into a state of defence.

1754, Sept 9th. A scheme to drive the French out of all the Continent of America. Signed by Thomas Cole. 26½ pp.

LETTERS AND PAPERS RELATING TO THE SIEGE OF QUEBEC.

1758–1759.

1758, Dec. 21st. Lieut.-General Sir Richard Lyttleton, K.B., to Brigadier General the Hon. George Townshend (afterwards 4ᵗʰ Viscount Townshend and 1st Marquis Townshend). Dated in Cavendish Square.

"My dear George,

I beg you will lose no Time, but come to Town directly ; I am not allowed to explain myself by this letter, but you may be sure my Reasons are very cogent. I should not otherwise write in this manner, but it is highly important to you to lose no Time.

Your Faithful Friend,
RICHARD LITTLETON."

[P.S.] Lord Orford's Game is not arrived.

Dec. 28th, 1758. The same to the same. Dated in Cavendish Square.

My dear Brigadier,

Lord Legonier was yesterday in the Closet, your affair was mention'd and very *Graciously* agreed to by His Majesty. I congratulate you most sincerely upon the honour this spirited, and magnanimous acceptance of yours, will do you in the World, as soon as it becomes known ; & upon the Glory you will obtain, and I flatter myself the short Time you will be absent, and the small risque you will probably run, in this Enterprize, will in some degree reconcile good Lady Ferrers to it ; I pity her from my Heart, but her Religion, & Philosophy will I hope, enable her to bear up under it ; & that she will consider how different her Lot is, from the many widow'd wives, who mourn from Year to Year the Absence of their Husbands. I hope you will let her know that in all this matter, I have had nothing more to do than to lend my Hand to the Marshall, & as a Friend zealous for your Glory to applaud with all Mankind a Resolution that you yourself have taken.

I am ever, my Dear George, your most Faithfull & Affectionate,
RICHARD LYTTLETON."

1759, March 14th. Rev[d] Robert Leeke to Lady Ferrers. Dated at Great Snoring. 6¼ pp.

The Postscript is :—

" I am told by those who have been at N. America that tis very probable, as the winds have greatly favor'd, that M[r] Townshend [your husband] by this time is in Sight of the Country, or not unlikely to be landed in it."

1759, April 24th. Brigadier Amherst (afterwards Lord Amherst) to Brigadier Townshend. Dated at New York, and addressed to the " Hon[ble] M[r] Townshend, Brigadier General. '

" Dear Sir,

I had the pleasure on the 13th of this month of receiving your very obliging letter of the 5th of March ; your kind assurances of friendship to me, of which I have so often had proofs, make me very happy and I shall try to prove myself deserving of the continuance of it.

I am in great hopes that this Campaign may be attended with such success as will give me an opportunity of meeting you, but I wont flatter myself you will remain in this part of the world ; I should be sorry you did any longer than you like. Your assistance in the service where I am would be a great help, and very agreeable to me, and you may be assured I would make it as much so to you as I could.

Colonel [the Hon. Roger] Townshend will inform you of every thing that passes here, so that I will trouble you no more at present than that I shall gladly seize every occasion that may offer to convince you of the regard and esteem with which I am,

Dear Sir,
Your most Humble and most Obedient Servant
JEFF. AMHERST."

1759, June 7th. Colonel the Hon. Roger Townshend to Lady Ferrers. From the " Camp at Fort Edward."

" Dear Lady Ferrers,

It is with the greatest pleasure that I can inform you I received a Letter from [my brother] George a few days ago dated at Hallifax May the 1st, the whole Fleet was arrived safe & he was in perfect health ; I have taken care to supply him with fresh Provisions of all kinds, & a large quantity of Vegetables & Roots of all kinds, which are very necessary after a long Sea Voyage, he will want nothing while he is up the River [S[t] Lawrence] that the Continent of America affords & he requires to be sent. Our affairs at present appear very favorable, no accounts as yet of the Enemy having received any Reinforcements, from Old France, & our Fleet under Adm[l] Durel is certainly so very high up the River that it is impossible for them to receive any this Year without a superior Fleet which it is impossible for them to fit out. My opinion of Gen[l] Amherst as an honest good Man, & my attachm[t] to him as a Soldier I thought wou'd never allow me to wish that I might serve under any other person in America, but the tye of Brother & Friend united is too powerful & I confess nothing ever gave me more real concern than not being employed on the same Expedition. I shall write to you by every Pacquet, may our Armys all be successful & Canada reduced this Year, George return home in safety to receive the praises due to him from his K[in]g & Country for his truly noble & spirited behavior in assisting at the Reduction of Canada, the consequence of this conquest can be no less than our giving Peace to France on any terms we please. My love to [my nephew] George & your little folks, & believe me nobody can have a more real regard, affection, & Friendship for you & your Familly than your Affectionate Brother & real Friend,

R. TOWNSHEND.

P.S. Since I wrote this the Lt Governor of New England writes the Army & Fleet were all well at Louisburg, June the 3d, & expected to sail up the River on the 12th. Adml Durrell has been successful and sent in four Prizes. We have no doubts of success. Our Army crosses the Lake in this month or early the next. The Enemy have got up the River a few merch[an]tmen with Provisions & one Frigate before the adml arrived at his Station, they are of no consequence."

1759, July 11th. Revd Robert Leeke to the same. Dated at Great Snoring.

. . . . "When I took my Leave of him, I desired him to accept from me as the best Present I or any one else could make him. wch was a Noble Collection of devotions suited to all Occasions, the Use of this I told him would engage Providence on his Side, & providce would be his only Security. He thanked me, and told me he should make use of it, but must let no other officers know, that he had such a book by him. So prophane is the Army, that they think the help of God is of little or no Mom[en]t " . . . . . .

1759, July 20th. Admiral Sir Charles Saunders to Brigadier Townshend. Dated on board the ' Stirling Castle ' and unaddressed.

" My dear Sir,
    By General Wolfe's desire I have sent you three Long boats for the Hautbitzers great and small, and the Royal mortars, I shall soon send for Cannon as the General designs to make his Attack above the Town. I am with the greatest regard

Dear Sir
Yours
CHAS. SAUNDERS.

[P.S.] I believe it wou'd be best not to let the Enemy see these thing[s] removed."

1759, Sept. 6th. Brigadier Townshend to Lady Ferrers. Dated at " Camp Levi," and unaddressed.

My Dearest Charlotte
    I hope Mr Perceval will arrive safe & bring you these two letters from me. The Happiness of writing to you is beyond all I know. My Concern for your sufferings, my affection for you & your Dear little ones, convince me how unfit I am for this Sceene, which another Month will thank God give a Conclusion to. The Captive Women & Children which I see every Day brought in here, often tell me what I am & who belong to me, but above all, the malencholly News I received the Day before yesterday upon my arrival here from the cursed Camp of Montmorenci of my poor Brother's death has reproved me for not consulting my own nature more, when I ask'd you to [let me] return to the Army. It had then pleaded for you, when you did not plead for yourself & I

had not been now in a Sceene of Ambition, Confusion, & Misery; and
you oppress'd as I know you must be, with Terrours & affliction. I
dare say poor Lady Tounshend too now starts at every knock at the
Door.   Let us look up with hopes my Charlotte to the Disposer of all
things & trust he will in his Mercy & Goodness do all for the best.
I have wrote a line to poor Lady Tounshend to comfort her by con-
vincing her of my own Health & safety.   One month more will put an
End to our Troubles.   I never served so disagreable a Campaign as
this.   Our unequal Force has reduced our Operations to a Sceene of
Skirmishing Cruelty & Devastation.   It is War of the worst Shape.   A
Sceene I ought not to be in, for the future believe me my dear Charlotte
I will seek the reverse of it.

Genl Wolf's Health is but very bad.   His Generalship in my poor
opinion—is not a bit better, this only between us.   He never consulted
any of us till the latter end of August, so that we have nothing to answer
for I hope as to the Success of this Campaign, which from the Disposition
the French have made of their force must chiefly fall to Genl Amherst
& Genl Johnson.

God bless you my most Dear Wife, my blessing to my Children, my
good George in particular, and thank him for his Letters.   I have constantly thanked God for the succes in the Innoculation, a most comfortable circumstance for you.   Mr Barker has been slightly wounded.
Mr Gay quite recover'd & join'd us.   Our Campaign is just over.   I
shall come back in Adl Saunders's Ship & in two months shall again
belong to those I ought never to have left---Adieu---Your most affecte
Husband, & faithfull friend

                                                 GEO. TOWNSHEND.

[1759 ? Sept.] Lady Townshend, to her daughter-in-law Lady
Ferrers.   Undated and unaddressed.

"Dear Lady Ferrers
        I take the benefit of being a little better in my health to day to
thank you for your kind letter some times being very incapable of
writing a single line.

I hope Charles' last letter to you afforded you a relief to your spirits.

I trust in God we shall all soon be in a much happier situation by
receiving the good News we most ardently wish for.

My Compliments to Lady Elizabeth Compton and affectionate Love
to the children.

[1758, Sept. 3rd.] Lieut. Genl John Huske to the same.   Dated
" Fryday noon."
      " My Lady
        I have the infinite satisfaction to acquaint you that Genl Towns-
hend was in fine health & Spirits at the Seige of Quebeck on the 5th of
July, the day it commenced.   This comes by express to Govt this day.
But as Colo R[oger] Townshend is desperately wounded at the seige of
Tyconderogo, under the Command of Genl Amhurst, I take the liberty
to send you this by Express that you may place full faith & entire
Confidence that it is not the Genl but Colonel Townshend that is
wounded.

The express comes from N. York, so your Ladyship cannot possibly
have any Letters from the General.

The news is great,

Tyconderogo & Crown Point are taken by Genl Amhurst, And
Niagara is taken by Genl Johnson (General Prideaux being killed
during the Seige) after a severe Battle with a French Army sent to

raise the seige. I am this **moment going to Oxfordshire post, or** should send your Ladyship all the **particulars, being, with the greatest** deference etc.

J. HUSKE.

1759, Sept. 10th. Revd Robert Leeke to the same, from Great Snoring.

"My very h^d Lady

I had the hon^r of your Ladysps this day, & should have gone immediately to Rainham, & deliver'd y^r Message to my L^d in Person, & deliver'd it with all the tenderness wch the Subject required, & with all the Concern you feel for the loss of Col^l Roger [Townshend] & for my L^d the Parent : But my L^d is not at Rainham, he hath been upon an hired Seat ever since the Middle of July last, at the Edge of Hartfordshire, within 12 Miles of London Nigh the new house Admiral Byng built just before he sufferr'd—but I shall write to my L^d this day & by Letter acquaint him of y^r Kind Concern for his Ldsp & for the great afliction you feel for the loss of his Son.

Y^r Ladysps Letter says, that the Troops with y^r husband landed nigh Quebec the 5th of July last, if so I wonder we have not heard from that part of the world Since, either of the troops being repulsed or the Place taken—if neither Event hath happened then there hath been a long Siege, & I fear many of our Men must have suffer'd, when order'd to march against Stone Walls. . . . . Mrs Leeke presents her duty . . . . we both Pray God to compleat all our happiness in bringing Brigadier Townshend safe into his own Country . . . .

RT. LEEKE."

1759, Sept. 13th. Admiral Saunders to Brigadier Townshend. Dated on board the "Stirling Castle," and unaddressed.

"Dear Sir,

The loss of our friend General Wolfe gives me the greatest concern which in some measure is taken off by the great Victory of today : as I have not heard how you are situated, I have sent all the 24 Pounders, with their Ammunition, that I had Boats for, till those are cleared that are now above. I heartily wish you farther Success, and should be glad to know what I can do to promote it. I have had the dispatches General Wolfe sent me to go with the great Ships. They are not gone, and I shall keep them till I have Yours. I beg my best Compliments of General Murray and that you will believe me most sincerely

Yours—
CHA^s SAUNDERS.

Same date. Lady Townshend to Lady Ferrers.

"My dear Lady Ferrers,

Believe me nothing but the being incapable of writing a single line should have prevented me thanking you for your tender concern for me.

I trust in God that he will preserve the most dear thing to us in life and from that dependance am still able to support myself enough to be in hopes to exist to receive that greatest of blessings.

E. TOWNSHEND.

[P.S.] Charles is with me and writes to you by this post."

1759, Sept. 15th. Hon. Charles Townshend to the same. Dated at Grosvenor Square.

" Dear Madam,
I am very happy to think that any letter from me has given you
any relief: and I shall watch every opportunity of informing your Ladyship of whatever account we receive that can help to alleviate your
fears and support your mind. I would say much more, both of your
situation, Lady Townshend's, my own, our late unhappy common loss,
& many other subjects, but indeed I am not able to bear the reflexions
they bring with them : if it were in my power by any means to assist
you, I should be rejoiced to find myself so useful, but, as that can not
be, I must not add to your grief by dwelling upon the cause of it.

The wind is contrary and no ship could have come up the river this
day : as soon as any news arrives, you will learn it from me. All things
go well, as you know from the last account I sent you.

Lady Townshend continues as she has been : she desires her love.
I beg my Compliments to Lady Elizabeth [Compton].

I am Dr Madam
most affectionately yr's
C. TOWNSHEND.

1759, Sept. 15th. Lord Townshend to the Rev. Robert Leeke ?
Unaddressed.

" Sir—I received the favour of yours by our last Post which informs
me of L^y Ferrers's kind enquiry, through you, after my health under the
great affliction which I now labor under from the severe calamity lately
befallen me ; and I beg that you will be pleased, when you write to her
Ladyship, to return my best thanks to her Ladyship and to assure her
Ladyship that my best wishes do always attend her and all belonging to
her, and that you will believe me to be, Sir, etc.

1759, Sept. 16th. Brigadier-General Monckton to General Townshend. Dated "Camp at Point Levi," and unaddressed.

" Dear Townshend,
I have look'd over such of the Gen^{ls} Papers as related to the
Publick—and can find none that can be of any Service to you—there
is his Commission, the Private Instructions you saw, Copys of Contracts with Mr Baker, and some Reports of Stores &c. As to the Plan
of Quebec, it is not amongst his Papers—But I am told that McKeller
has a Copy.

I should be glad to hear how you go on—Am sorry to hear that you
are out of Order.

I am Most Sincerely yours
ROB^T MONCKTON.

P.S. I shall write to Genl Amherst [and I] should therefore be glad
to know our Kill'd & Wounded & what it is supposed the Enemy
lost &c."

1759, Sept. 17th. Lady Townshend to Lady Ferrers.

" My dear Lady Ferrers,
No situation of my mind or health can ever prevent me from
thinking and being anxious for you and your Dear Children. Charles
writes by this post to you. I trust in the Almighty God that he will
soon bless us with the safe return of our most Dear George.

Your ever Affect.
E. TOWNSHEND.

My best wishes to Lady Elizabeth Compton."

Same date. Charles Townshend to the same. Dated at Grosvenor
Square.

" My dear Lady Ferrers,

I should not forgive myself if I omitted writing one post after knowing you are pleased to hear from us, even when we have nothing new to relate. As yet, the Government have received no further accounts from North America ; but, as I before observed, delay proves caution in the Siege, & caution in that gives us Security. Let me now desire you to conclude whenever you receive an Express that it brings you good news, for otherwise I shall be obliged to defer one day sending you any such account if it should not come to me on a Post day, least the Express should alarm you. I should not chuse to detain you one minute from the news I know your heart beats for, & yet I should not chuse to frighten you by the sudden manner of its arrival, for which reason I desire you will remember to receive whatsoever express I send with confidence & as a Friend.

I beg my affectionate Compliments to Lady El[izabeth] Compton. Nobody loves or honors you, or more earnestly wishes your speedy relief from the unhappy anxiety you live in than

Dear Lady Ferrers
Your affectionate
C. TOWNSHEND."

1759, Sept. 18th. The same to the same.

" Dear Lady Ferrers,

I write again that you may not be alarmed by my Silence, and am happy in the hope of being of the least degree of convenience to you : whose situation claims compassion from every body, and naturally gives me the utmost pain. A ship arrived yesterday from Boston but, having touched at other ports in the voyage, it brings nothing new, yet it is so far agreeable as it confirms the former account I gave you. Yesterday I heard from Lord Townshend, who suffers as we all do, & bears his part in the common calamity. It would be in vain, could I prolong this letter by writing news to you, for to us frivolous things are painful, and, by attempting it, I should only torture myself without relieving you. Lady Townshend desires you will consider her as writing by this letter, and I add, for your consolation, that she is rather better than she has been. My best Compliments attend upon Lady Eliz. Compton."

1759, Sept. 19th. The same to the same. Dated at the Privy Garden.

" My dear Lady Ferrers,

As you may possibly read in the Prints that two Ships are arrived in the River from New York, and might be alarmed for that reason if you did not hear from us, I beg leave to assure you that both the American Ships sailed from New York many days after [before ?] the last Packet Boat came away. Nothing new therefore is come by these Ships.

Upon reasoning with some persons of rank & intelligence in the administration upon the accounts we have, I find it is the general opinion that Quebec will fall without any action, as it is now so invested, no provisions can be carried into it, and the army of the enemy, with the Citadel, will, it is believed, be forced to capitulate or starve. This, I am sure, is a prospect you will be pleased with, and I hope you will every day have fresh reasons to rely upon the speedy and safe return of my Brother.

Lady Townshend desires her love : We beg our compliments to Lady Elizabeth Compton.

I am your most affectionate
CH. TOWNSHEND."

Same date. Lord Northampton to the same. Dated at Castle Ashby.

" Dearest Madam

I cannot deffer one Instant thanking your Ladyship for your most obliging letter ; I wish it had been possible for us to have had your Company as I think you would not have been displeased at a Ceremony I had so long wished for, and that you was in some measure the leading Instrument to the Performance of it, by your very *Seasonable* and *Lucky Drum* ; I beg you will not make any apologies for keeping Betty from us I am vastly glad she can be of Service to you; I hope you will soon have no further occasion for her. I beg you'll present my love to her.

Lady N[orthampton] desires her very best & particular Comp[ts] to y[r] Ladyship . . . . . Dick Bagot . . . . desires you would give his best love to his Niece Lady Elizabeth & that she would provide plenty of Colliflower against the next time she sees him   I will not detain you any longer than to add my love to [your son] George.

[P.S.] Lady Northampton sends her love to her new laughing Sister & hopes that M[r] V[ine]r will soon make her enter into the Matrimonial State " . . . . .

Same date. The Countess of Cornwallis to the same. Dated at Brome.

" My dear Lady Ferrers,

As your Letter was directed to Culford I have but this moment received y[r] comfortable account of the state of things at Quebec . . . . . . I was very sorry for poor Roger, and did apprehend your spirits wou'd at this time be ill suited to receive such a shock . . . . Roger was very amiable & likely to make a figure in his profession. I am glad to hear the Children are well. My L[d], and Molly, desire to joyn with me in assuring you of our best wishes . . . . Believe me

My Dear L[dy] Ferrers
Affectionately y[rs]
E. C.

1759, Sept. 20th. General Townshend to the same. Dated at the " Camp before Quebec," and unaddressed.

" My Dearest Life my Dearest Charlotte—

We have gained a great Day, the particulars you will read in the publick Gazette. Tho I was not in the warmest part of the action ; yet I had more shotts near me than in any other action I've seen. It has pleased God to preserve me for my Charlotte & my George & the rest, and to restore me to you whom alone I have found good & gratefull to me. I have never forgot you in any part of the Campaign. The command of an Army is as disagreable as any other. Men are as mean here as in any other profession.

I fear I have not time to write to any other friend. My love to them all.

I am impatient to see you and am my Dearest Life ever your most affectionate & faithfull Serv[t]

GEO. TOWNSHEND.

[P.S.] My love to Lady Townshend & Charles & to M[r] Vyner & Betty. Desire Mr Vyner to look out for two or three Hunters for me.

Do not think my Dear Life that any Command tempts me to stay. The Troops will soon go into Garrison & then I can sett out with the Admiral.

I'm sure my Dear Little ones are well."

1759, Sept. 22nd.   Rev. Robert Leeke to the same.

" My very Good Lady

. . . . . We are all here under great Concern for poor Roger Townshend. Every Body laments him extremely, as a well dispos'd young Gentleman, a good Soldier, & I really believe a mighty honest, openhearted Gentleman. Such is the Cruelty of War that it destroys Numbers of our fine youth, I trust in God, that all will go well with our great dear friend before Quebec. I begin to presage it will do so, & I begin to think it long to hear the Event of the Siege, it surely must be over by this time.

As I mentioned in my Last, I was vastly pleas'd with Lady Betty's new hon[r]. I do not know any one more deserving of it, & I hope e're long to wish her Joy again of a more Substantial Blessing, I mean a good husband, I think she deserves all that this world can do for her. Now I am congratulating give me Leave, My Lady, to congratulate y[r] Noble family on my L[ds] Marriage into one of the Beaufort family—I think my L[d] hath chosen the very best family in England to be ally'd to & from such an happy Union, of the Northampton with the Beaufort family, I foresee every thing will come that is great & good. There is so much dignity, & worth in each family, that every hon[r], & every dignity of this life will unite in this happy Pair, & I dare say the Blessing of God will go along with the whole " . . . . .

1759, Sept. 29th.   Lady Townshend to the same.

" Dear Lady Ferrers,

I can say nothing at present in the least favourable in respect to my health therefore will avoid dwelling upon so uncomfortable a subject.

Mr Charles Townshend set out on thursday Night for Adderbury ; he entreated Lady D[alkeit]h to be in town herself or to consent to his staying here with me to wait for M[r] Townshend's Arrival; but she would not hear of his proposal persisting still that she should not be in London for an hour or at Sudbrook nor should he remain here from Adderbury even till fryday Morning, by this fatality for I can call it by no other name I am now deprived of the Comfort and support of his Assistance and Company who never left me till twelve o'clock at night.

The North East Wind continues and is directly contrary for having any News from Quebec when it changes I some times think of seting out for Portsmouth ; here I shall not remain.

My best wishes and Compliments attend Lady Elizabeth Compton. My affectionate Love to the children.

E. TOWNSHEND."

1759, Sept. 29th.   George Buckton to the same.   From Tamworth.

A business letter. It is addressed " To the Hon[ble] Genl Townshend —Tunbridge Wells," but it commences with " My Lady " and concludes with " I am your Ladyship's etc."

1759, Sept. —.   Charles Townshend to the same.   Dated at the Privy Garden, "Thursday."

" Dear Lady Ferrers,

I am desired by Lady Dalkeith to inform your Ladyship that she never received any letter from you by M[r] Sykes, and she is very much concerned to think there can, from any cause, have been the least appearance of neglect in her. She has made a very particular enquiry, & is assured neither of our Servants ever received the letter from M[r] Sykes.

I have the satisfaction to assure your Ladyship that a ship has arrived here from Boston with an account from Quebec, dated as far as the 13th

of July ; from which we learn that the navigation of the River was
found very good ; that Mr Wolf[e] had taken a safe Camp on the South
Side of the river St Laurent ; that the landing had been made without
loss, that the Town was open to our artillery & our Camp covered from
the enemy's ; that the French force[s] were behind the Town of Quebec,
that Mr Wolf[e] could wait without annoyance for Mr Amherst ; that
the French force is very small, & that the Seige may possibly be carried
without any action, certainly without any great resistance. This account
is believed in by the Ministry, and I earnestly hope soon to prove the
truth of it by congratulating you upon the safe return of my Brother
Townshend. If you are inclined to be alarmed by the delay recollect that
such delay can only be the effect of caution in the steps of the Seige ;
which caution is our common security for the success of it, &, (for which
I am more sollicitous) a farther argument of my Brother's safety.

Forgive me if I omit the pain of speaking of our late misfortune : my
heart sinks under the blow, and nor time nor any thing can efface the
impression.

Lady Townshend has wrote herself : and Lady Dalkeith has gone to
Adderbury.

You will always hear whatever I have to tell that can relieve your
miserable, affectionate situation.

> I am very affectionately
> yr's
> C. TOWNSHEND."

1759, Oct. 2nd. Lady Townshend to the same. Dated in London.
" Dear Lady Ferrers,

Nothing but the Apprehension that the seeing me would agitate
your spirits too much and consequently be prejudicial to your health,
could prevent me from coming to Tunbridge.

Every body agrees that the first time the Wind changes from the
North East we must hear from Mr Townshend but as yet it is full East.

The poor Norfolk Militia by being pent up so long in the Barracks at
Portsmouth are all a dying of the bloody Flux.

Sr Armand Woodhouse is come to town to see Lord Barrington to
endeavour to get them relieved, but Mr Pitt's being out of town makes it
impossible for their having any immediate redress by being removed
from that duty.

My health is so affected for the last three days that I can with
difficulty write this. . . . . .

> E. TOWNSHEND "

1759, Oct. 5th. · Brigadier General Murray to General Townshend.
Unaddressed.

" Sir,

I this moment had the honour of yours. The shaving Trunk I
think myself obliged to you for, and I enclose an order for the reestablishment of it. I doubt not of its being presented a few weeks after your
arrival in England. As I am sure you are desirous to serve your country
it certainly will avail itself of your inclinations and nobody can wish you
greater success in every thing you undertake than I do. I remember
we did joke about the chairs. I am of your opinion that they are too
heavy for the field. I thank you however for the offer. I send the Map
you mention & wish I had any thing more worth your acceptance. I
have a few embroider'd birch curiosities which lady Ferrers would like
perhaps, and you may not have met with any like them. You will oblige
me if you will accept of them. As I am to stay here you know I can
easily get others for my female friends in England.

I shall look for the letter you mention, take a copy of it, and deposite the original with you. Since so black a lye was propogated I think myself very happy that you will be on the spot to contradict whatever Ignorance, or Faction may suggest.

I have no copy of the paper I sent by you to Gen[ll] Wolfe concerning his Scheme of landing between Point au Tremble and S[t] Augustin, but the publick orders are a sufficient proof of his intention to do it, and likewise of the suddenness of the thought of landing when we did. Indeed his orders throughout the campaign shows little stability, stratagem, or fixt resolution ; I wish his friends had not been so much our Enemys, his Memory would probably have been dearer to his Country than now it can be. We are acting on the defensive, you have the Execution of the plan, and I am well perswaded you will manage it with as much tenderness to the memory of the poor Gen[ll] as the nature of things will admit of.

I find I am not to have the honor of a visit from you so I must take the opportunity of wishing you a good Voyage, & a happy meeting with your friends. I am—Sir

Your most obedient humble Servant
JA. MURRAY."

1759, Oct. 6th. Rev. Robert Leeke to Lady Ferrers.

" My very hon[d] Lady

. . . . Give me Leave to observe to y[r] Lordship, that I a little fear, least y[r] Ladyships Spirits should Sink a little, because Good News is long a Coming from Quebec. My Lady, as y[r] Ladyship believes, that Provid[ce] will Conclude this Great affair & all others for the best upon the whole, under Such a thought of an Entire Confidence in God, there is no room for any discomposure—besides as there is no bad news hitherto, y[r] Ladyship may be sure, that had any Evil happen'd to the General, his friends abt him would have sent a Message—No News therefore is good News— & I must own for myself some time ago my heart was very sad, whenever I thought of him but of late it hath been much otherwise, & therefore my Mind inwardly presages that all is well. That y[r] Ladysp may be ever Easy & well & meet the General soon in Great Safety is the most ferv[t] prayer & most Cordial wish of y[r] Ladyships most Obed[t] & most humble Serv[t]

R[r] LEEKE."

1759, Oct. 14th. Lord Townshend to the same. Dated at Rabley.

L[d] Townshends Complements to L[y] Ferrers and is extremely obliged to her for the account she has been so kind as to send him of M[r] Townshends perfect Health, and is glad to hear that her Ladyship and the Children are all well.

1759, Oct. 23rd. Brigadier Murray to General Townshend. Dated at Quebec and unaddressed. Endorsed "General Murray."

" Sir !—Captain Fraser writes to his correspondent here that you have been pleas'd to speak well of me to some of the great people at home. This is very obliging and deserves my thanks. I never doubted of your doing Justice to all men, & I shall be glad of an opportunity to convince you how truly I am—Sir—Your most obedient & most humble Servant,

JA. MURRAY."

1759, Oct. 30th. Rev[d] Robert Leeke to Lady Ferrers. Dated at Great Snoring.

" My Good Lady

As I had the hon[r] to receive from y[r] Ladyship the pleasing Account first of Mr Townshends safety & imediately after, the hon[r] he had got at Quebec. To both wch I returned my most hearty Congratulations as I do now again & again with the highest Joy I think my Soul ever tasted.

Give me leave now to rehearse with pleasure before y^r Ladysp the many dangers I observe Genl Townshend hath escaped during the Campaign.

If we begin with the long Voyage of nine Weeks passage on the Sea, all wch time, twas a great mercy he Enjoy'd his health, as he never had been Us'd to the Sea much before. When the fleet went up the river St Lawrence there was 3 weeks passage againe—the passage was attended with Infinite danger, to our people at least, who knew little of it. On the way up they met with Six fire Ships Sent down to meet them, with design to have burnt our fleet, W^{ch} they narrowly Escaped, & must have destroy'd them, had the fire Ships met them in a Narrow part of the Channell.

The day after they Landed at St Orleans, a Violent Storm arose, wch dashed many of the Transports to pieces which had it been only one day Sooner, must have destroy'd the whole fleet & perhaps Every Soul perisht.

After they Landed Mr Wolfe says in his Letter They made two Attacks upon the Enemy & was Each time repulsed wth Great loss, & he says further, had be not in one of those Attacks Call'd back the troops imediately, Brigadier Townshends Corps had been Expos'd to Great hazard—a Great escape here, & I think in this instance & some others I see in Genl Wolfe a great tenderness for Mr Townshend.

On the Great Attack when the Victory was got, we had 5 thousand Men only, the Enemy ten, our Army marcht up against a most terrible fire, & held their own till they advanct within 40 or 50 yards of the Enemy, Wolfe on the right, Moncton in the Center, & Townshend on the left,here in these moments was the utmost danger,Wolfe shot in 3 different places of his body, Moncton quite thro his, & Townshend Escapes. If ever I saw a visible protection of Providence over any one on Earth, I see it now over Genl Townshend. God's goodness to him deserves our Utmost wonder, love & thanks.

If there is any one in the world that did not wish Genl Townshend well in this Expedition, Let them look on him *Now* with Confusion of face, when they see him *live*, when many brave men fell ab^t him, when they see him not only *live* but *live* to finish a Victory, wch brave Genl Wolfe began—when they *live* to see him at the head of his Victorious troops Enter the Enemys Great Capital, & see him send word to his Majesty under his own hand, that the Victory was thus Concluded by his own Policy & under his own direction. He hath over come hitherto, winds & storms, a bad Climate all sorts of dangers both by Sea & Land, indeed Every thing, that can make an Expedition terrible, himself untoucht, not a finger aking amids[t] the wounds, death & destruction of many brave men of our own, and many more Experienct Soldiers & marks men of the Enemy.

Let us thank God for this Inexpressible Mercy, & beseech him to preserve him safe from dangerous Storms in his way home. I am a little afraid the Military Glory he hath got this Expedition should encrease his taste for it, & make him fond of the Wars, wch I don't like, for I think still, as I always did, he can serve his Country better at home, but I hope a good peace will be the Consequence of taking Quebec & then there will be an End of all our Wars for the present.

Let me Now observe to y^r Ladysp what I see at home Since the great News Came: a prodigious Joy in all the Villages Nigh me striving who shall out do Each other ; in Market Towns they illuminate &c. Tho it is observed some choose to be in darkness, whilst others set up their lights, but higher up in the Country, I do not hear that they have Exerted themselves like what is done ab^t Fakenham & Walsingham & the villages adjacent.

Tho Great things have been successively done by our Arms all Summer yet Prince Ferdinand's Victory & that at Quebec is the Greatest of all, but Quebec is of the Utmost Importance to the Kingdom & will be of all others most Conducive to an Early & solid peace. The surviving Generals therefore that Commanded at Quebec will ever be seen by the King & Kingdom in the highest pitch of Glory & Esteem.

* I hope y^r Ladysp amidst all this Joy is very well . . . ."

[1759, Oct.] Lord Townshend to the same. Dated at Rahley,— " Wednesday noon."

" Lord Townshend rejoices most heartily upon the happy news Ld Ferrers has been so kind as to send him this morning of the Surrender of Quebec and that Mr Townshend is safe & well; and does most sincerely congratulate her Ladyship upon these happy events, which he hopes will have the further good effect of giving perfect ease and quiet to her Ladyship['s] mind and that her Ladyship['s] health will be restored. He hopes the children are all well."

1759, Dec. 1st. Rev. Robert Leeke to the same.

" Oh Good Lady Ferrers,

I heartily bless God, that I have in my power to wish you Joy of this most Glorious Event—an[d] happy Meeting again with Dear General Townshend wch I do most heartily : I do not remember any Event in life past ever fill'd my heart with a More Substantial & Exalted pleasure. No words can Express w^t I feel. I feel it as it Conduces Equally to y^r Ladysps happiness as well as Mr Townshends.

I need not mention to y^t Ladysp that this good Event Sets every Noble prospect in life before you—oh how great is the goodness of God, you see it now & taste it in great abundance. `Oh ! Lady Ferrers what a firm Relyance upon Providence will it not do ? What is not the Goodness of God willing to do for those that depend upon him. I shall always think that y^r Ladysps Prayers & mine too, have been a great help to Mr Townshend's Security. I shall thank God for this Mercy along with his other blessings to me & beg under this most Joyfull Event, that y^r Ladyship will please to Accept My Congratulations along with Mrs Leekes for there will be None that will Send it more affectionately.

R. LEEKE."

1759, Dec. 2nd. The Countess of Cornwallis to the same. Dated at Culford.

" My dear L^{dy} Ferrers

I am infinitely obliged to You for Your early notice of Mr Townshends safe arrival. . . . . . . My L^d desires to joyn with me in assuring Mr Townshend, that he has no Friends more truly happy than we are with his safe and glorious return . . . . . that you will always be as fortunate, and as happy as You are at present is the most sincere wish of ·

Y^r most Affec :

E : C :

[P.S.] My Ld Molly & Harry desire their kind Comp^{ts} to Mr Townshend & Y^r self."

1759, Dec. 4th. Thomas Beevor to General Townshend. Dated at Hethel.

MARQUESS
TOWNSHEND
MSS.

"My Dear S^r

I coud not without the greatest injury to my inclination, and ingratitude to your friendship, omit paying You my most early respects, on your safe Arrival in this Kingdom: I sincerely congratulate You, on the happy success of an Expedition, which had been by all accounts impracticable, but for the uncommon bravery, and vast superiority of Abilities, in the Commanders of it; in which capacity (Peace to the Manes of poor Wolfe) I cannot help enjoying the happiness of your fortunes in being left the person to compleat it. As Your fate was the chief circumstance of my first enquiry, when I found it so glorious, I cou'd not but reflect with transport, on the situation, in which You were now placed ; respected, and honour'd by your Countrymen, belov'd by all your friends, and bless'd, doubly bless'd in one of the worthiest, and best of Women ; to whose anxious and frequent prayers You may perhaps be indebted for that very life, which is now so great an Ornament to You : this without the least exageration, is now your lot, and 'tis indeed a happy one, your future scene will doubtless be a great one; but pardon my friendship, when I tell You, that I think You merit the one, and will never fail to grace, and dignify the other; Macte Virtute, my Dear George, and believe me when I assure You, that no happiness attending You, will ever give a more real or greater pleasure to any one, than to your Sincere & faithful friend
and humble Servt
THO^s BEEVOR.

[P.S.] Mrs Beevors & my Compliments to Lady Ferrers."

1759, Dec. 7th. Miles Branthwayt to the same. Dated at Gunthorpe.

"Dear Sir—I beg leave to congratulate you & Lady Ferrers on your safe Arrival in England . . . . we are all of us very impatient to kiss your hand at Cranmer & to congratulate you upon your great Success in conquering Quebeck . . . . . Mr Gay has not heard from his son since the taking of Quebeck, which gives him & us great uneasiness . . . . Mrs Branthwayt begs that you will accept & make her best Comp^{ts} to Lady Ferrers, Lady Compton, & your little family & that you will accept the same from Dear Sir" etc.

1759, Dec. 8th. Lord Shaftesbury to the same. Dated at Exeter.

"Lord Shaftesbury presents his most sincere and affectionate Compliments to Mr Townshend, and is extremely thankful to him for the favour of Mr Townshend's inquiring after him in Grosvenor Square. Ld Shaftesbury intended before this to have paid his Compliments by letter, and to have acknowledged the the Honour of the Public regard shewn him by Mr Townshend in the excellent address at the Head of Lien^t Col: Wyndham's book, but business leaves him at present no time for writing. He can not conclude this Note without informing Brig^r Townshend of the perfect Harmony subsisting between the Dorsetshire and Army Corps now doing duty together here I prepose returning into Dorset very soon. Lord Shaftesbury's respects wait on Lady Ferrers."

Same date. Earl Poulett to the same. Dated at Hinton.

"I take the liberty of troubling my honoured friend & kinsman, wth a letter I received from a friend of mine whom I sh^d be very glad to serve, & as I am retired in the country (by being a cripple) I dont know where to apply more properly, wch I hope will excuse the trouble of this letter.

I am glad at the same time of an opportunity of congratulating you on a safe return, & with so much Glory & success, in wch every English-

men takes part, but more particularly those who have the honour of
being related to you.

After being a Cripple for more than two years I begin to feel some
benefit from a Remedy I have tryed for about 5 weeks past, even at
this time of the year, against all the disadvantages of weather.

If I knew who had the managem^t of the new Militia bill, & had the
heads of it sent me, I might perhaps be able to add something to it, who
beg leave to assure my honoured Kinsman that I am wth the highest
regard & greatest respect " etc.

Same date. W. Clarke Woodbine to the same. Dated at Swafham.

" Dear Sir—Mr Chas Brown thinks himself under the highest Obligation for you so kindly looking over the past, in his Affair, says there is
Nothing he so much wishes for as a Comission, and that too by your
means, it will he says, give him a daily opportunity of proving to you
how much he owes to your Favour, & also to the Memory of his & my
much lamented Friend Col^l Roger [Townshend] " etc.

Same date. J. Burslem to the same. Dated at Bosworth.

" Hou^rd Sir.—Please to accept my sincere Congratulations upon the
very great Success abroad " etc.

1759, Dec. 9th. Edward Davy to the same. Addressed.—" For
The Hon : Brigadier General Townshend at his house in Andley
Square, London."

" Worthy Sir.—I sincerely congratulate your safe Arrival, in England
and wish you may live many years, to wear those Laurels in y^r Native
Country, which by faceing so many Foreign, Dangers, you have so
greatly won " etc.

Same date. Alexander Johnson, First Lieut. of Artillery, " to the
Honble Generall Townshend." Dated at Plymouth.

After making suggestions in Tactics and for the improvement of
cartridges this letter concludes as follows :—

" Was is not for fear of incroaching too much on your Patience, [I]
would propose a plan for keeping up, dureing the approaching Peace,
all the Infantry, Saylors, and Marines, at a very little Expence to the
Nation, but must refer that, either to another Opertunity, or my being
honour'd with your Company in Town : [I] must inform you that
Capt Phillips obtain'd a Company in the Artillery from being a First
Lieut.

You'll excuse my courting your Favour, when you consider the
Advantage that may accrue to me from haveing the Interest of a
Military Gentleman, endowed with your generous Publick Character
and Accomplishments ; to deserve the Continuance of which, shall
allways be the Study of he, who has the Honour to be, Sir " etc.

Same date. Benjamin Nuthall, Wine merchant, to the same. Dated
at Lynn.

.   .   .   .   . " Amongst the Multitude of Your Friends permit me to
congratulate You, on your safe Arrival in England, after so many Perils,
& the Acquisition of so much Glory. The great & useful Service
wch You have finisht for Y^r Country, will even Speak of you & for
You wth distinguish'd Honor in this & Future Ages.

I am with the greatest Respect, Sir," etc.

1759, Dec. 10th. John Helder to the same. Dated at Snailwell.

Hon^bl Sir—I beg leave to trouble You with a line to acquaint You,
that I expect receiving about the latter end of Christmas Your half
years Rent, for the three farms   .   .   .   .   .

I wish You Joy, on Your great Success abroad, and sincerely adore the Divine Goodness, which has preserved You, & brought You safe home, to Your Good Lady, & Dear Children and other Hon^bl Relations . . . . . . The Great Mercy shown in sparing & preserving You, has given me another Proof, of the Care of the Divine Providence. You have been carryed thro' the Dangers of the Stormy Ocean, & thro the more dangerous Opposition, of Enemies, in Battle, and return'd in Health & Safety, with Honour, to Your Native Land : I hepe Your Gratefull Acknowledgments to Heaven for Goodness and mercy follow-ing You tho' this voyage, aud that the same distinguishing Goodness towards You will run paralell with your Line of Life ; & fit You for Eternal Glory, hereafter. I rem̃—Hon^bl & Great Sir—Your Dutifull Servt—

JOHN HELDER."

1759, Dec. 11th. Edmond Thomas to the same. Dated at Wenvoe Castle, Glamorganshire.

"Sir.—After begging Leave to join in the Congratulations which every will wisher to his Country pays you, or means it in his own Breast, on your Return after such Interesting Success to every Englishman, I must acknowledge your Goodness to a poor unfortunate Young Man, whom I cannot but feel a concern for, C. Northey, whose Sufferings in a Cause of Glory, will I hope attone for his former Indiscretions. I wish to God you would prevail with his Brother to let them do so with him. I know he entertains a personal regard for you & what you say will have weight with him. Indeed every Motive of Humanity & even Good sense & Decency require it of him, but I must say he has been too hard on this Occasion, for it is impossible the Young Man can subsist with[out] some assistance from his friends till he has a pro-vision made for him. I have wrote to several of them on this Occasion as well as Mr Northey.

I beg pardon for taking this Liberty with you, but your Humanity will I am sure excuse it from one who is with the greatest Regard, Sir," etc.

1759, Dec. 12th. John Jones to the same. Dated at Fàkenham.

[Sir]—It would have been Impertinence for one in my Situation sooner to have offered my Congratulation to my most Worthy Friend Gen^ll Townshend on his safe Arrival and tribute of thanks for his Ser-vices to his Country; but if you'l now permit me to tender the same and to assure you they proceed from a sincere Heart brim full of Joy tis all I have to ask, save that You'l accept the Offer of my most respectful Duty and Services to your Hon^r and Lady on all Occasions for I am, S^r,

Your Hon^rs Obliged and Ever Obed^t Servt
JOHN JONES."

1759, Dec. 13th. Nockold Tompson to the same. Dated at Norwich.

"Sir—After receiving the Congratulations and Compliments of your Country in general and of your many friends in all parts of it, I now presume to trouble you with mine, on your very laudable Conduct, the success of which, sufficiently bespeaks its Praise, especially when com-pared with the unfortunate and uneuccessfull Efforts of the many who live to deplore their own Misconduct, for this you have not only the happy consciousness of your own Mind but also the universal Voice of the Nation ; Among the first the Citizens of Norwich in their publick Address exulted in the relation this County stood in, to him who added Quebec to his Majesty's Dominions. . . . . I will not take up any more of your Attention, than only to assure you with what ardent Esteem I have " etc.

1759, Dec. 15th. Rev⁴ T. O. Young to the same. Dated at Swafham. " Dear Sir,

. . . . Every body here & all over the Country mention you with the most warm & grateful attachment, & pay all 'possible Veneration to your Character—I am confident you will see it in the looks & behaviour of every one you meet with . . . .

T. O. YOUNG.

1759, Dec. 22nd. James Quin to the same. Dated at Bath. " Sir

From a Hart full of Love, Esteem and Gratitude you have the most sincere Congratulations. May your Honours and Happynesses of ev'ry kind be equal to the warmest Wishes of, Sir,

Your ever faith full
and most obedient Servant
JAMES QUIN.

1759, April 30th, to Sept. 18th. A MS. book in cardboard cover endorsed "Orders of General Wolfe." 84 pp.
The phonetic spelling of this manuscript suggests that the orders were written from dictation by a non-commissioned officer.

1759, June 10th. Dispositions generales pour s'opposer à la descente depuis La Riviere Sᵗ Charles jusqu' au Sault de Montmorency, de meme que pour se retirer derierre la rivierre Sᵗ Charles dans le cas que l'on fut forcé à la descente. Projet pour deffendre cette Rivierre et ordre de Bataille pour combattre et pour camper pendant toute La Campagne. 5 pp. foolscap. Subscribed " A Quebec le 10 Juin 1759 " and signed " Le Ch[evali]er de Levis."
This document seems to have fallen into General Townshend's hands on the fall of Quebec.

1759, June 26th to Oct. 10th. General Orders issued to the troops before Quebec between there dates. A stitched MS., in a clerk's hand, without cover or title. 108 pp.

1759, July 28th to Sept. 13th. Rough notes relating to the siege of Quebec between these dates. 5 pp. foolscap.
The account given in these notes of the movements of the British forces on Sept. 13ᵗʰ, when Quebec was captured and Genˡ Wolfe was killed, is as follows :—

Sept. 13th. The Troops landed below the place intended owing to the rapidity of the Tide.

Just before we were ordered to land Capt. Smith, a very active & intelligent Officer of the light Troops, informed the Brigadiers that the naval Officer who was to conduct the first detachment down the River assured him that if he proceeded down by the S[outh] side of the River the Current was so strong that they should be carried beyond the place of attack & probably below the Batteries & the Town & thereupon the Brigadiers (there not being time to report & receive Genˡ Wolfe's directions thereon) authorised him to carry them down the N[orth] side of the River & fortunately it was follow'd, for even there the Boats could only land before daybreak considerably below the place of attack (l'anₑ Guardien) & Col. Howe (now Sir William) found he was below it, & Major Delauney a very active & enterprising Officer who had a command in the light Corps, saying the place was higher up the River, & the Colonel knowing the Consequence of the Enemie's perceiving at day light our situation & being reinforc'd, he order'd that Officer to attack where proposed & very gallantly himself scrambled up the rocky height in his front by which he turning to his left he attack'd & drove the Enemy from their position & most happily facilitated the success of the former up a narrow precipice with an abbatis & a battery just over it which was firing on them.

Just at daybreak another most fortunate circumstance contributed to the success of this critical operation, when the first corps for disembarkation was passing down the N[orth] side of the River & the French Centries on the banks challeng'd our boats, Capt. Fraser who had been in the Dutch Service & spoke French, answered—la France & vive le Roy—on which the French Centinels ran along the Shore in the dark crying—laisser les passer ils sont nos gens avec les provisions—which they had expected for some time.

When Brig[adie]rs Monkton & Townshend arrived to support them Brig. Townshend put his Men in boats behind the Ships which the Enemy was battering, landed them safe, and followd Genl Monkton's [column] to the Ground where the General was forming his line to oppose the Enemy, who was passing with all expedition under their Comander [in] Chief Monsr de Montcalm the River St Charles.

The Troops marchd forwards with the utmost alacrity to possess the rising Ground & were drawn up in a line of battle opposite the Town. Col. Howe with the light Troops was sent to take possession of a 3 Gun battery at St Michel which executed he drove in all the small parties which were posted on the heights & annoyd our Colums going up the Hill.

In forming the line Brigr Monckton commanded the right, Brigr Murray the Center & Brigr Townshend the left, which when forming with Lascells Regiment only was attacked by the Americans & Indians, which he kept in check behind a long roadway assisted by the gallant behaviour of Capt. —— who had quitted a House by mistake which protected the front of the Brigadiers position, but on finding his mistake he dashd back again—attacked them with Bayonets & put all to the Sword within the House. The Brigadier being reinforced by his second Battalion then maintaind his position whilst the Enemy being formed between the Town & our line came down & attacked our front. They were received with the greatest firmness, just before this Genl Wolfe came towards the left & finding all secure on there, he returned to the Center & received a mortal wound in the head & soon after another in the breast & died before they cd carry him to the Water side. Genl Monckton was wounded in the breast. Our Troops had charged the Enemy close & repulsed them & pursued them part into the Town the rest down the River St Charles. Brigadier Townshend was left with one Battalion, when Monsieur de Bougainville was marching from the Woods in the Rear to attack him. He sent his Aid du Camp to collect the Troops as fast as they could & took a position towards the Enemy behind a Ravin & got up 2 pieces of Cannon, & when they were firing he had the mortification to hear that they had brought wrong ammunition, on which as the Enemy was forming in the Edge of the Woods he orderd the Officer to fire with a considerable degree of Elevation, & maintaind his position till reinforced by the return of some of the scatter'd forces, from the pursuit.

1759, Augt. 28th to Sept. 12th. "Copies of Papers that were wrote by General Wolfe and the Brigadiers, before the Operations above the Town of Quebec in 1759." 12 pp.

1759, Sept. 13th. "Return of the Kill'd and Wounded at the Battle of Quebec."

The total is 658 officers and privates killed and wounded, and 3 missing.

The following is the list of the General and Staff Officers killed and wounded :—

Major Gen¹ Wolfe, killed ; Brig' Gen¹ Monckton, wounded ; Major Barré, Adju' Gen¹, wounded ; Colonel Carleton, Q' M' Gen¹, wounded ; Capt. Spital, Major of Brigade, wounded ; Capt. Smyth, Aid de Camp, wounded ; and Lieut. Benzell. Engineer, wounded.

1759, Sept. $\frac{17\text{th.}}{18\text{th.}}$ Copy of the "Capitulation of Quebec as it was proposed yᵉ 17ᵗʰ 7ᵇᵉʳ 1759 & also such as was agreed upon yᵉ 18ᵗʰ." In French and English, eleven Articles. Signed by Admiral Saunders, General Townshend and Mons' de Ramsay, Commandant of Quebec.

The chief clauses to the effect that the garrison is to march out with all the honours of war, and that the property and religion of the inhabitants are guaranteed.

1759, Sept. 20th. General Townshend to William Pitt. Dated at the "Camp before Quebeck Sep' yᵉ 20ᵗʰ 1759—Copy of yᵉ letter sent " to yᵉ Secretary of State, Sep' yᵉ 20ᵗʰ 1759." Endorsed Quebec—Copy of my Relation of the Action to M' Pitt."

Sir, I have yᵉ honour to acquaint you with yᵉ success of his Majesty's arms on yᵉ 13ᵗʰ instant in an action with yᵉ French in yᵉ heights to yᵉ Westward of this town.

It being determined to carry yᵉ operations above yᵉ town, the post at Pointe Levy & Isle d'Orleans being secured, General Wolfe marched with yᵉ remainder of his forces from Pointe Levy yᵉ 5ᵗʰ & 6ᵗʰ & embarkt them in transports which had passed yᵉ town for that purpose. In yᵉ 7ᵗʰ 8ᵗʰ & 9ᵗʰ a movement of yᵉ ships was made up yᵉ river in order to amuse yᵉ enemy now posted along yᶜ North Shore. The transports being extremely crowded & yᵉ weather very bad, yᵉ General thought proper to cantoon half his troops upon yᶜ South Shore, where they were refresht & reimbarkt upon yᵉ 12ᵗʰ at one in yᵉ morning. The light infantry commanded by Col¹ Howe, yᵉ Reg¹ˢ of Bragg's, Kenedy's, Lascelles, & Austruther's, wᵗʰ a detachment of Highlanders & yᵉ Royal American Grenadiers, yᵉ whole being immediately under yᵉ command of Brigadiers Monkton & Murray, were put into yᵉ flat bottom'd Boats & after some movements of yᵉ ships made by Admiral Holmes to draw yᶜ attention of yᶜ enemy up yᵉ river yᵉ boats fell down wᵗʰ yᵉ tide & landed on yᵉ N. Shore within a league of Cape Diamond an hour before daybreak. The rapidity of yᵉ tide of ebb hurried yᵉ boats a little below yᵉ intended place of attack, which obliged yᵉ light Infantry to scramble up a woody precipice in ordᴣr to secure yᶜ landing of yᵉ troops, & to dislodge a Captain's post which defended a small entrenched road where yᵉ troops were to move up. After some firing yᵉ light infantry gained yᵉ top of yᵉ precipice & dispersed yᶜ Captain's post, by which means yᵉ troops wᶦᵇ very little loss from a few Canadians & Indians in yᵉ wood got up & immediately formed. The boats as they emptied were sent back for yᵉ second disembarkation which I immediately made. Brigadier Murray being detached wᵗʰ Anstruther's bataillon to attack a four gun battery on yᵉ left was recalled by yᵉ General who now saw yᵉ French army crossing yᵉ River S' Charles. General Wolfe thereupon began to form his line of Battle, having his right covered with yᵉ Louisbourg Grenadiers on an eminence, behind which was Otway's, on yᵉ left of yᵉ Grenadiers were Bragg's, Lascelles, Kenedy's, Highlanders & Anstruther's. The right of this body was commanded by Brig' Monkton & yᵉ left by Brig' Murray : his rear & left were protected by Col¹ Howe's

MARQUESS
TOWNSHEND
MSS.

light infantry who was returned from yᵉ 4 gun Battery which he had found abandoned & yᵉ Cannon spiked up. Webb's was formed as a Reserve in yᵉ Center with large Intervals between their Subdivisions, & Lawrence's soon after detach'd to preserve our Communication with our Boats. General Montcalm having collected yᵉ whole of his force from yᵉ Beauport side & advancing us shewed his intention to flank our left when I was immediately ordered with Amherst's Battalion which I formed ên Potence. My numbers were soon after encreased by two other Battalions as they arrived. The Ennemies lined the Bushes in their front with 1500 Indians & Canadians & I have reason to think most of their best marksmen, which kept up a brisk tho' irregular fire upon our whole line, who bore it wᵗʰ yᵉ greatest patience & good order, reserving their fire for yᵉ main body now advancing. The right of yᵉ French line was composed of half yᵉ troops de la Colonie, yᵉ Battalions of La Sarre & Languedoc wᵗʰ some Canadians & Indians; their center Column was formed by yᵉ Battalions of Bearn & Guienne, & yᵉ left was composed of yᵉ other half of yᵉ troupes de la Colonie wᵗʰ yᵉ Battalion of Royal Roussillon. Such was as near as I guess their line of Battle. The French brought up two small pieces of Artillery against us & we had been able to bring up but one gun which being extreamly well served galled their Column exceedingly—My attention to yᵉ left will not permit me to be very exact with regard to every circumstance which passed in yᵉ center, much less to yᵉ right. But 'tis most certain that the attack of yᵉ Ennemy was very brisk & animated on that side, our troops nevertheless reserved their fire to within 40 yards which was so well continued, that yᵉ Ennemy everywhere gave way. It was then our General fell at yᵉ head of Bragg's & yᵉ Louisbourg Grenadiers advancing to charge their Bayonets. About yᵉ same time Brigadier General Monkton received his wound at yᵉ head of Lascelles. On their side fell yᵉ French General Monsᵉ De Montcalm & his second in command since dead of his wounds on board our fleet. The ennemy in their confusion flung themselves into a thick copse wood in their rear & seemed preparing to make a stand. It was at this time that each Corps seemed in a manner to exert itself wᵗʰ a view to its own peculiar character. The Grenadiers, Bragg's & Lascelles drove on yᵉ Ennemy with their Bayonets . Brigʳ Murray briskly advancing upon yᵉ ennemy the troops under his command compleated yᵉ rout on this side, when yᵉ Highlanders supported by Anstruther's took to their broad swords & drove part into yᵉ town & part over yᵉ river St. Charles. The action on our left & rear of our left was not so severe. The houses into which yᵉ light infantry were thrown were well defended, being supported by Colˡ Howe who taking Post wᵗʰ two companies behind a small copse, & frequently sallying upon yᵉ ennemy who attackt them . drove them often into heaps. Against yᵉ front of which body I advanced fresh platoons of Amherst's Regᵗ which prevented their right wing from executing their first intention. One of yᵉ Royal American Battalions being detached to a post which secured our rear, & yᵉ other being sent to fill up yᵉ space the battalions advanced wᵗʰ General Murray had vacated, I remained with Amherst's alone to support these posts & keep yᵉ Ennemies right in check. The efforts of yᵉ Ennemy on this side con'd never break in upon this disposition & yʳ hopes of a great body of Indians & Canadians who waited impatiently to have fallen on our rear in case of a defeat were entirely frustrated.

This, Sir, was yᵉ situation of things when I was told in yᵉ action that I commanded. I immediately repaired to yᵉ center & finding that yᵉ pursuit had put part of yᵉ troops in great disorder I formed them as soon as possible. Scarce was that effected when Monsʳ de Boncainville

wth about 2000 men, ye corps from Cap rouge & that neighbourhood,
appeared in our rear. I advanced two pieces of light artillery & two
Battalions towards him but upon two or three shots he retired. You
will, I flatter myself, agree Sir that it was not my business to risk y^e
fruits of so glorious a day & to abandon so commanding a situation to
give a fresh ennemy battle upon his own terms & in ye midst of woods
& swamps where he was posted. I have been employed from ye day
of Action to that of ye Capitulation in redoubting our camp against any
insult, making a road up y^o precipice for our Cannon, getting up y^o
artillery, preparing ye Batteries, & cutting off y^o communications of y^e
Garrison wth ye country. The 17th a flag of truce came out wth proposals
of Capitulation about noon before we had any Battery erected. I sent
ye officer who had come out, back to town allowing them four hours to
capitulate or no further treaty. He returned with terms of Capitulation,
which with ye Admiral were considered, agreed to, & signed on both
sides by 8 o'clock in ye Morning ye 18th instant. The terms you find we
granted, will I flatter myself be approved of by his Majesty considering
ye Ennemy assembling in our rear, ye inclemency of y^o season—which
wou'd scarcely admitt of our bringing a gun up y^o precipice. The critical
situation of our fleet from the Æquinoctial gales calling for our
immediate attention, add to this ye entring ye town in a deffensible state
against any attack which might otherwise be attempted against it in the
winter. This I hope will be deemed sufficient considerations for granting
them ye terms I have ye honour to enclose you—I herewith send you
a list of ye killed & wounded & y^o list of French Prisoners as perfect as
I have yet been able to obtain it. I believe their loss that day might
amount to 1500 they have at least now 500 wounded in their Hospital
General. Another list of y^o artillery & stores in ye town, as well as
those fallen into our hands at Beauport in consequence of ye Victory.
The inhabitants bring in their arms very fast & chearfully take ye oaths
of allegiance to his Majesty. By ye last intelligence from deserters
Monsr De Levy now commands their army. He is returned some say
wth troops from the Montreal side. They are collecting their scattered
forces at Cap Rouge, his left extending by different posts as near us
as old Loretto 6 miles from our camp. Their regular Battallions are
now reduced to 150 men each & are in great want of provisions. I
shou'd be wanting in paying my due respects to ye Admirals & ye Naval
Service if I neglected this occasion to acknowledge how much we are
indebted for our success to ye constant assistance & support we have
received, & to ye perfect harmony & immediate correspondence which
has prevailed throughout our operations in y^o uncommon difficulties
which ye nature of this country in particular presents to military
operations of a great extent, & which no army can in itself solely supply.
The immense labour in ye transportation of artillery stores & provisions
ye long watchings & attendance in boats, ye drawing up our artillery
even in ye heat of y^o action, it is my duty short as my Command has
been to acknowledge for that time how great a share ye Navy has had
in this successful campaign.

I have ye honour &c. &c. &c.

GEO. TOWNSHEND."

1759, Sept. 25th. Copy of a proposal [Signed by General Townshend
and unaddressed] for a military demonstration with 600 or 800 men
on the South Shore [of the River St Lawrence]. Dated 25th September, but endorsed " General Townshend's Proposal—Quebec—Sep^{tr} 23^d
1759."

Same date. General Townshend to ——. Dated at the "Camp befor Quebec" and unaddressed. Copy.

"Dear Sir—The method of sending this will I hope sufficiently excuse yᵉ shortness of the Relation. It being determined to carry [on] the Operations above the Town, the corps at Montmorenci pass'd over to Point Levi. The Posts of Isle Orleans & of Pᵗ Levi being secured, yᵉ General embark'd yᵉ Troops in Transports on yᵉ 5ᵗʰ & 6ᵗʰ; after some movements up yᵉ River to amuse yᵒ Enemy, we landed on yᵉ 13ᵗʰ [and] surprised a French post on yᵉ N[orth] Shore, within 3 miles of yᵒ Town. Our Troops to about 3500 met Mouʳ de Montcalm's Army from yᵉ Beauport side upon yᵉ Heights before yᵉ Town. He began the attack, and was repulsed twice. The firmness with which our Troops bore yᵉ Tirallerie of all their Indians Canadians &c. for a considerable time, preserving their Fire for their Regulars; & the home attack which they made upon the latter with their Bayonets, when they came down to yᵉ Charge, decided yᵉ Day. The Highlanders seconded by Anstruthers pursued them to yᵉ Gates of yᵉ Town with their Broad Swords. We had but 2 Peices of Cannon up & but one played for a considerable time. We took 5 besides a great quantity of Artillery & Stores which fell into our Hands, on yᵉ Beaufort side—as well as in yᵉ Town which surrender'd, before we had a Battery ready, on the 18ᵗʰ Instant in yᵉ morning. We lost poor General Wolfe who fell in the warmest part of yᵉ Engagement. Genˡ Monckton was wounded near the same place & about Yᵉ same time. Monʳ de Montcalm & yᵉ second in Command were also killd. Their Regulars sufferd extreamly—We have a great many of their Officers prisoners. We compute our loss at about 500 killd & wounded; theirs about 2000. The remains of their Army is assembling, & cantoon'd about Sᵗ Augustine. Monʳ de Levi commands. Monʳ de Boncainville had a separate Corps of 1500 men who came upon our Rear just after yᵉ Action was over, attacked one of our Posts & sufferd a good Deal. I write this to you by order of Genˡ Monckton, who tho' wounded in the Breast, is in so fine a way as to be able to do all business but write—I have yᵉ Honour to be with the most gratefull respect—Dear Sir—Your most faithfull & affecᵗᵉ

GEO. TOWNSHEND."

[Quebec].

1759, Sept. 26th. General Townshend to General Amherst. Dated at the "Camp before Quebec." A draft "sent yᵉ 27th."

"Dear Sir—Having General Monckton's Commands to write you a Relation of yᵉ Action of yᵉ 13ᵗʰ, which decided the Fate of this Town & I hope will contribute not a little to yᵉ total reduction of Canada; I have yᵉ Honour to send you a Copy (I believe pretty exact) of my account of that Victory to yᵉ Secretary of State. Were I really to attempt to point out the most striking cause of this successful stroke I must attribute it to the admirable & determined firmness of every Brittish Soldier in yᵉ field that Day; conducted by yᵉ manifest ability of the Officers at this respective Posts. Victory or no Quarter was I may affirm in every Man's Face that Day; the Ground we scrambled up in yᵉ morning, the motions of yᵉ Enemy to surround us, the Time of Tide & yᵉ Heights which command yᵉ Boats taught us this lesson, and thank God the whole army made a proper application.

Genˡ Monckton, who is so well recovered as to command us, will I conclude write to you upon yᵉ Intelligence he has of yᵉ Situation of the remains of yᵉ French Army & how far Things may admit or not of any further movement on our Side. This is not my province. He proposes to leave Genˡ Murray Commander at Quebec. I cannot consequently whenever y⁰ Army becomes a Garrison be of any use here, & may embrace y⁰ leave to return to England you so long ago bestowed upon me. I am sorry y⁰ advancement of y⁰ Season will not allow me to pay my respects to you in America, but shall only say that I shall be one of y⁰ very many who shall think himself happy to serve under y⁰ command. We heard this Day by a Deserter, you had taken Montreal. I hope t'is true. Voila donc Monʳ de Levy investié.

I hear I have got Barrington's Regiment. Alas what a Bouquet this had been a Year or two hence for poor Roger. I assure you I return thoroughly wounded from America. I loved him sincerely.

My respects to all who do me y⁰ Honour to remember me & forgive me Dear Sir for not sending you y⁰ relation of y⁰ Action in my own Handwriting. I had made a thousand Blots. I hope to pay you my respects upon more momentous occasions.

I am with y⁰ most Sincere respect—Yʳ most faithfull & obed Servᵗ
GEO. TOWNSHEND.

[P.S]. There were two field Peices & not only one up in the Action."

LETTERS, ETC. (MISCELLANEOUS).

1700–1791.

[Circ. 1700]. R. H. to Lord Townshend ? Undated and unaddressed.
" My deare Lord

What I had reserved about me wᶜʰ was 500ˡⁱ necessity hath given to Doctors & Apothecaries ; & by what is to be seen by me, to very little purpose, for I am scarce alive. That little flame which is left, if I can get to April may be restored at the Bath. My Brother hath a litter which I did use thither last Summer ; but it is such a torment to ride in it, that I dread the very thoughts of it. Al this is a beggers preamble to you to give him a Coach & horses. That is to say let the Coach be inside & outside as plaine & as meane as may be, not of capacity for more then two to ride in it : only I pray You that it may have two doors, & glasse windows in the doors, that it may be made so long & of such contrivance, as that I may lie on a quilt in it. For the horses, I care not what they be, so they will but draw me twenty mile in a summer's day. This gentleman wil wait upon you, if you have any thing to Command him in this busines, who knows how to convey it to me. The God of heaven & Earth blesse you with al gifts temporal & eternal. Amen saith
Your
R. H."

1701, May 19th. Edward L'Estrange to Lord Townshend (the 2nd Viscount Townshend), Dated at Mileham, and addressed " To the Rᵗ Honᵇˡᵉ The Lᵈ Viscount Townshend at his house in Sᵗ James Street— These present."

" My Lord—My 2 Young Masters were very Well yesterday. Only the youngest was a Little froward wᵗʰ the Cutting of a Tooth."

After giving the replies of the following gentlemen to his Lord‑ ship's offers of Commissions in the Lieutenancy and Militia of Norfolk—Colonel Wodhouse, Sir Ralph Hare, Sir Edward Ward, Major Houghton, Lᵗ Colonel John Harbord, Sir Roger Potts, and Sir Francis Guybon ; All these gentlemen are willing to serve under Lord Towns‑ hend, and rejoice at his Lordship having been appointed Lord Lieutenant of Norfolk.—The letter concludes with the following postscript:—

MARQUESS
TOWNSHEND
MSS.

" My Lord—I just now Rec^d a Let^r from Major Philip Stebbings the present Trea^{er} for the Militia Mony, who desires mee to present his Service to yor Honour, & beggs the Favour to be continued Treasurer, He is counted an honest & substantiall Man, and has bin Mayor of the City of Norwich, he is a Grocer by Trade, and lives in the Market place, & voted for our Kn^t at the last Election."

1701, Augt. 4th.   James Calthorpe to his dear cousin " Mr. Richard Lemon at ye 3 Nuns near Water Lane in Fleet Street London."

" I am most heartily concerned for the loss of our good friende and I must say my good lord and lady are little less . . . . . my servis to y^r sister and cos Cooper."   . . .

1701, Augt. 15th.   The Freedom of the City of Norwich conferred on Lord Townshend at- this date. In Latin, on parchment, with the Corporation Seal attached. Signed by WILLIAM RAYLEY, Chamberlain.

1701, Nov. 20th.   William Cooke to ———. Dated at Ason and unaddressed.

" Since the sodaine & surprizeing dissolution of Parliam^{nt}, & before I received the honour of your letter, I had intimation that those Gentlemen who mett at Norw^{ch} on Saturday last had taken effectuall care to give notice of a generall meeting to be held on Saturday next at the King's head in Norw^{ch} : I did heare alsoe that the Candidates to be proposed to the County would be your selfe & Sr John Holland to whom I cannot imagine there will be any opposition "   . . . .

1701, Nov. 26th.   From the same to the same. Dated at Ason and unaddressed.

" Since my Ld Townshend's servant delivered me your letter I have received one from Sr Jacob Astley telling me he intend[s] to stand againe for the County . . . . soe neare & honrable a Relation as Sr Jacob Astley concerning himselfe at this time I must beg your pardon if I stand neuter "   . . . .

1701, Dec. 12th.   Samuel Fuller to Lord Townshend. Dated at Yarmouth and unaddressed.

. . . . . " the slippery trick the Dissenters acted in the Election here, has so much disgusted those of the Church part as will not vote in conjunction with them & if [it] were not for a particular Obligation to yor Self [I] believe would all be on the contrary part, but as farr as I can guesse there will be few faile you, besides here has been no intimation from S^r J[acob] A[stley] of his resolutions of standing."

1702, April 20th.   Francis Spellman " to Mr Lemon att the Three Nuns near Fleet Bridge in Fleet Street London : " Asking for assistance and begging for a line directed to him at his lodging " att the Golden Cock near East Gate Rochester."

1702, Nov. 2nd.   Edmond Hamond to Lord Townshend. Dated from Southwoolton and addressed " ffor The Right Honble. The Ld Townshend in Soho Square London." An estimate of the value of certain timber in Helvington Wood and Patchy Wood. " The timber is distant from Wells a Sea port but 8 miles and much of it except some great trees may be carryd thither for 8s. p load."

170$\frac{3}{4}$, Feb. 18th.   Dr. Tenison, Archbishop of Canterbury, to Spencer Compton. Unaddressed, and signed, " yor affect^{te} Friend Tho. Cantuar."

" Good S^r.—There is a Bill to preserve Libraries &c. brought into the House of Commons : and if I well remember, You were named together with Sr John Holland & Mr Compton, for the bringing of it in. I have

procured a Copy of it, & I hope it will be much amended before it comes
up to Us; I am not against the Design of it but I think it breaks in
upon the Jurisdiction of the Queen, the Archbishops, divers Deans &
others in their Peculiars, letting in upon them, the B^p of the Diocese &
his officers. . . . I would therefore, gladly speak wth you about this
Bill, that it may be so amended wth You, as to have no Opposition in
our House." . . .

1704, Sept. 6th. W. Wyndham to his "most Dear Brother Ashe
Windham Esqr at Felbrigg," " at the Queens head in Cornhill London."
Dated from Nordlingen . . . " I have wrote to my mother at Felbrigg
twise since my legge is of, and once to Aunt Martha Ashe at Twittnam
. . . . . . Gadford will be a L^t . . . . New commissions will
hardly be given out till his Grace getts to the Hague and then I hope to
have one amongst the rest. Palmes is made a Brigad^r . . . . I cant
imagine what is become of the Spaw waters . . . . I doubt the
waters are spoiled and so the money lost " . . . .

1704, Oct. $\frac{13th}{24th}$. The same "To the Hono^ble Roger Townshend Esqr
in Norfolk.—By Swaffham Bagg." From Nimigue. . . . It was
no small grief to me that I was not in a statu quo to give an account to
you that you might hear of the fate of y^r Friends as well as the Victory
[at Blenheim], but now all that is old, and so is the loss of my legge, but
I can assure you I make no doubt of being in a condition again to serve
her Majesty and my most dear Benefactors at Rainham, as well as ever,
but I pray God to send it more in my power. Coll Palmes who was
the day after the Battle made a Brigad^r gott himself and the Regt the
greatest Honour & Reputation that you can well think, and truly I
believe hardly any one was more instrumental to the Success of that
Day . . . . Your Expression of Concern for me totches me as
sensibly as an Amputation but I must desire that you will have no
further Pity or thought of that Matter for I have not the least Notion
but of being as easy and happy as ever " . . . . . .

1705, May 2nd. Robert Britiffe to Lord Townshend. Unaddressed.
The writer describes the election the day before of a Mayor of the town
he writes from.

1705, May 12th. The Bishop of Norwich to the same. Addressed
" To the right bon^ble my Lord Viscount Townshend at Rhainham in
Norfolk."

The writer has written to the Lord Treasurer about a case he
alludes to.

1705, May 29th. The same to the same. Addressed as the last.
" My Lord,

At length I found my Lord President [the Earl of Pembroke
and Montgomery] who is much your Servt in the affair likely to come
before her Majesty. He adviseth that affidavits should be made of the
crimes set forth in the Petition. . . . . . . I begin my journey to
morrow for Norwich, where I shall be most ready to receive your
Commands.

I am, my Lord,
Your Lord^ps most faithful humble Servt
J. Norwich."

Same date. Thomas Pelham to the same (his son in law). Addressed as the last. . . . . . . " I am much pleased with y^r Success at
Norwich, at the same time I had a letter from my Brother wth the

Sussex Poll wch was thus Trevor 1867, Parker 1416, Peach 1397, Lumnly 895, but the Sheriff in favor of Parker made illegal Adjourn-m^{ts}. So a Petition and Actions will certainly follow. We are in great heart upon the Prospect of a good House of Com'ns." . . . . .

1705, June 28th. Richard Leman to the same. Addressed " To The R^t Hono^{ble} Charles Lord Viscount Townshend att Raynham, Norfolk. These : Humbly : Present."—" When I paid Mr Mason the coal monger the money according to your order I asked what price he would serve your Honour for for what you should have occasion for in the winter he told me he would venter to doe itt att 29s. p chaldron.

I have sent the things Mr. Watts wrote for yesterday by the Waggon this morning.

[P.S.] There is a late report about town that the Lord Keeper will be outt of his place in a very short time : and [that] Mr. William Cowper [is] to succeed him ; Mr Serjeant Weld is of this opinion."

1706, February 17th. Revd Stephen Gardiner to the same. Dated at Norwich and addressed to Lord Townshend in London. The writer entreats his Lordship's interest to procure him some preferment and mentions " My worthy Friend Dr Trimmer has promised me his assist-ance for that purpose."

1707, Jany. 2nd. Marquis of Kent, Lord Chamberlain, to the Hon. Spencer Compton Esqre, Treasurer of the Household of Prince George of Denmark.

" S^r—Having last Year upon Acc^t of some disputes att the Gentⁿ Waiters Table, given directions to the Gentⁿ Ushers not to permit any Page of the Presence to sit at the same Table wth them they having never had that liberty till of late, I am inform'd that Mr Lucas one of the Prince's Pages notwithstanding he had Notice of the Order refus'd to obey it during his waite last Month, wch Contempt of his I desire may be represented to his Royall Highness.

I have now sent the Gentlⁿ Ushers the same Order in writing and hope you will take care that the Prince's Pages of the Presence may be directed to submit to it as well as the Queen's."

1707, March 23rd. N.S. Earl of Gallway to the same. Dated at Valencia.

Recommending to his protection Monsr Jandraut (Gendraut), and mentioning that Lord Godolphin had promised to take care of him.

1707, April 10th. Edward Ashe to Lord Townshend. Dated in London and unaddressed.

" My Lord.

I was in hopes instead of this impertinent letter to have waited on you before this time att Rainham butt buisness, wch I think the more one hates the more itt pursues one, will necessarily deprive mee of that pleasure I fear for three weeks or a month longer. The only chance I have for seeing y^r L^{oshp} sooner is the attendance att the next meeting of the Parl^t on Monday the 14th, when doubtless there is some very extraordinary business to be done, that could occasion so short & so surprising a Prorogation. The reason People talk on here is to prevent frauds that Merch^{ts} may committ by draw-backs & reimporting those goods from Scotland Custome free. I wish a method may be found that may not prejudice the Customs here nor yett be any Infraction of the Union, butt this is thought to be very difficult, & for ought I know may be worth y^r L^{dshp} a journey from Rainam to consult about.

'Tis certain the method our very good Freind the Secretary gott to pass the House of Commons was not approv'd by the Lords, wch has occasion'd the disappointment those had who expected to have heard a speech from the Queen last Tuesday.

Ash Wyndham is come to town & assures mee of your good health as I can y^r L^dshp of all y^r Freinds in town; I wish you much Mirth & Satisfaction att Norwich as to the Politicks I'me out of pain, I make no doubt butt Whiggism will be trimphant. When ever y^r L^dshp appears att the head of itt, that so good a Cause may ever find so powerfull a support is the desire of etc. . . .

[P.S.] My humble service to Sr Cha : Turner and Mr. Walpole.'

1707, April 25th. Edward Nicholas to Spencer Compton.

Recommending the bearer (Mr. Godfrey who was chief clerk to Lord Bellomont whilst the latter was Treasurer to the late Queen) to Mr. Compton's favour.

1707, June 3rd. N.S. Monsr D'Allonne to the same. Dated at the Hague.

The writer notes that in future the acquittances of his pension are to be filled in with the name of Mr. Compton whom he congratulates on his new employment.

1707, Augt. $\frac{3rd}{14th}$. Lord Gallway to the same. Dated at Bellpuig.

" I heartily wish y^u joy of your new employment [as Treasurer of the Queen's Bounties] wch will give me from time to time the occasion of troubling you in the behalf of the poor widows that are now under y^r care. I enclose to you a List of some of the chiefest objects of Charity, wch I hope will come under no exception, in case there be any alteration made in the establisht list, their husbands having been killed in this Service.

I add to this list an old infirm Lady t'would be a charity & great satisfaction to her if her pension was altered in her Grandaughter's name.

The Lord Treasurer [Godolphin] has been often troubled in fav^r of Mr. Genrault, for a pension suitable to his employm^t in the King's service. I thought by Mr. Nicholas's letters that these things had been settled, her Ma^ty doing me the honour to allow of my recommendations in these matters." . . . . .

1727, Augt. $\frac{7th}{18th}$. Horatio Walpole to Robert Walpole. Dated at Paris and unaddressed. Endorsed at a later date " Mr Walpole to Sr Robt Walpole." [*This letter has been misplaced.*]

" Dear Brother—The enclosed is worth notice at this time of day when alterations are making at this Court to show that the Cardinal designs to make none wth regard to measures, of the Union wth England ; as I have hinted in my dispatch to the D[uke] of Newcastle ; but I did not think fitt to send it as part of my dispatch because the person that writes it speakes of you & me in a manner too personall for me to send it directly to the King; thô I thought it necessary to observe that the Jacobites despair entirely of doing anything wth the Cardinal ; His Eminence in my last Conversation wth him took notice of the publick news mentioning my Lord Chesterfeild was to come hither as minister; and enter'd with me a good deal into his L^rdps Character, and seemed to think that a person of his youth witt & vivacity, was not the properest minister to treat wth one of his Eminence's age, meekness, & sedateness, but I assured him that I knew nothing of his coming hither, althô I could not conceal from him my desire of going home ; he replyed he

MARQUESS
TOWNSHEND
MSS.

hoped not, till the generall pacification was finished; I must not omitt
telling you that I do not regard, (after what you hinted to me) what the
publick prints say about his L^{rdps} Embassy hither; but I can tell you
for certain that Mr Arbuthnott the Banker here, has lately received
from his Brother the Doctor advice that L^{rd} Chesterfeild spoke to the
Doctor himselfe to write to him & to tell him that he should want his
assistance in settling his family here, & providing things necessary for
it because it would be very laige; this the Banker has sayd as what the
Doctor had wrote to him more than once; I am y^{rs} most affec^{ly} &c.

H. WALPOLE.

' [P.S. The] Pretender has been at Lorrain & I believe is returned
again to Italy."

1707, Nov. 6th. Lord Godolphin to Lord Townshend. Unaddressed.
My Lord.
The Queen being now fully at Liberty to follow her own inclinations
in disposing of the place of Captn of the Yeoman of the Guard to your
L^p. She has commanded mee to acquaint you, that she is ready to give
it you, as soon as ever you come to town; and as far as it consists with
your own Conveniency, I should think the sooner, the better, in such a
case, as this is; My inclinations have always been very sincere to serve
y^r L^p whenever it was in my Power, & if the success I have had in this
affair bee agreeable to you, it will bee a very great Satisfaction to
My Lord
Y^r L^{ps} most obedient
humble serv^t
GODOLPHIN."

1708, June 12th. N.S. Lord Gallway to Spencer Compton. Dated
at Lisbon.
Thanking the latter for the care he takes of those persons recommended
to his protection by the writer, and asking for a copy of the list of
pensioners that has been signed by the Queen.

[1708 ?] July 21st. Lord Dartmouth to Lord Townshend. Dated
at Queen's Square, Westminster.
" My dear Lord,
I know you will have goodnes enough to pardon my puting your
L^p in mind of an honor (you were so kind to tell me last Winter) you
intended to doe my poor famillie in standing Godfather to my next
Child, which is now come to light, and is so lurg a Boy that I have
some thoughts of making him a Bishop (if the High Church last long
enough). My Lady Halifax has promised to doe me the Honor to be
Godmother and I will lett you know the tother Godfather, as soon as I
know it my self but truely I have troubled so many people upon the
like occation, that for that and another good Reason which you will
easily gess, I am resolved to have no more Children, I thanke God I
have but one Girle, to three Boys, which is some comfort. Pray let me
know who you will appoint to be your proxy and believe me My dear^{st}
Lord with great obligation and Truth your Lordships
Most affectionate Faithfull Humble Servant
DARTMOUTH."

1708, Sept. 28th. John Turner "To His Royall Highness George
Prince of Denmark." Enclosed in an outer cover, addressed "To The
Honble Mr Boyle Secretary off State att his office att the Cockpitt,
Whitehall."

On the outer cover is the following memorandum:—"Putt into the Gen¹ Penny Post office in Broad Streett by Mr Turnor."

The writer offers his services to Prince George in very mysterious language. He would appear to have been either a lunatic or an Alchemist.

1708, Oct. 8th, N.S. Lord Gallway to Spencer Compton. Dated at Lisbon.

"I writ to you some time since to recommend to your favour Capt la Motte Blaguy. . . . I take the liberty to give you the trouble of this to desire you will be pleased to encourage and countenance the said Capt la Motte, in what may relate to the Widows and other Ladies to whom the Queen has granted pensions upon my recommendation, he being a very fit person to manage that affair." . . .

1708, Dec. 13th. Robert Britiffe, M.P., to Lord Townshend. Unaddressed.

. . . . . . "Norfolke att present affords us little news. All things are easy & people satisfyed with the new Parliament. I heare some of our Suffolke Members like their own Country neighbours better then the conversation of the present H. of Commons & are come to keep their Christmas in the Country. Sr J[ame]s Preston was buried the last 'night, Mr F. Neave of Ringland the last week, & Mr Suckling the week before. Our new High Sherriff is not yet sworne nor fined, an Under Sherriff my Friend Mr Churchman is obliged to your Lordship for your kindness to him" . . . . .

1709, March 15th. A. Wyndham to the same. Unaddressed.

"My Lord,

Since yr writing one this day, I hear the Lords without much bustle, & without any Division have passt sentence on the three last Articles; and have agreed on the following Question to be debatd tomorrow the Tories reserving to themselves a liberty of altering it if they think fit.

That the Commons having made good the Articles of Impeachmt agst Dr S[acheverell] he is guilty of a high Crime and Misdemeanr.

Instead of an Act to prevent such Doctrines as Sr's for the future, there will be an injunction to all the Clergy, not to meddle with the Toleracõn, Administracõn & Politicks.

I am

Yr Excellency's

most devotd &c.

A. WINDHAM."

1709, May 27th. Samuel Fuller to Lord Townshend. Unaddressed. Dated at Yarmouth.

Congratulating his Lordship on his appointment as Ambassador Extraordinary at the Hague, asking whom he shall support as a representative of the borough in Parliament in the place of Colonel Townshend recently deceased, and suggesting that Horatio Walpole should stand for Yarmouth.

1709, June 18th, N.S. Draft of a letter from Horatio Walpole to Samuel Fuller in answer to the last.

1709, June 18th, N.S. Draft of a letter from the same to his "Uncle Walpole."

With reference to a Mr Gibbons whom the latter has recommended to Lord Townshend as a clerk. As Lord Townshend's stay at the Hague is uncertain & as on the conclusion of a peace the young gentleman would again be adrift the writer cannot encourage him to come over. The writer has been kindly recommended by M* Fuller to Lord Townshend as proper representative for Yarmouth in the place of Collonel Roger Townshend and has good hopes of success if his relations will join their endeavours to Lord Townshend's.

Same date. Draft of a letter from the same to his Brother Robert.

It concludes :—"I remember [the] L*d Treasurer upon M* Craggs acquainting him that his L*dp's recommendation sec[u]red at the borough where M* Harnage is elected named me, but when M* Craggs fairly made the expence the Objection his L*dp shew'd an inclination to make that easy, but upon notice that none but M* Harnage could carry it, that matter drop'd what may be properly done this way I leave entirely to your discretion however. I am willing to goe as far as 100*l.* or so to serve the Queen in Parliament as Manwaring says."

1709, July 24th. Robert Mann to Horatio Walpole. Dated in London and addressed " To Horatio Walpole Esq*e at the Right Hon*ble the Lord Vis*ct Townshends in the Hague."

Introducing a gentleman (not named) and mentioning that "Lady Townshend comes next week.",

1709, Augt. 4th. The same to the same. Addressed as the last.

" Sir—By your Uncles Command : I am to desire you to petition my Lord Townshend : in behalf of one M* Hackwell : who the Col* hath some*ime since recommended to his Ldsp for a Yeoman of Her Ma*jties Guard : and which his Lordship promis'd to think of, but his Grace the Duke of Leeds interfer'd in the last Vacancy : but now there's an other and which M* Poyntz will give him an Account of : tis y* uncles earnest Request my Lord will be pleased to provide for him and that you'l let me know his Pleasure that I may signifie it to Hackwell. I hope My Lady and her Family gott safe to the Hague." . . . . .

1709, Augt. 7th. D* C. Roderick to the same. Dated at Kings College Cambridge, and addressed " To the worthy Horace Walpole Esq* at His Excellency the L*d Townshend's, Hague."

The writer explains what he has done in the matter of getting Chr. Perin Edwards, who was 11 years old and in the 2*nd Form, on to the Eton Foundation. The postscript is as follows—" When I came home last night from Eton the bearer Mr. Perkins Fellow of S*t John's & y* country man came to offer me this oppertunity being to go Chaplain to the Marquisse of Caermarthen in his new experiment-ship."   .

1709, Augt. 4th. Spencer Compton to the same. Dated in London, and unaddressed.

. . . . . The court Marriage I mentioned in my last Letter is not yet own'd, but I c*d never hear any reason for making it a secret ; The Dean of Windsor is made B*p of Chichester, and D* Robinson succeeds him as Dean of Windsor." . . . . .

1709, Augt. 14th. H. Wither to the same. Dated at Alresford.

. . . . . " We got a Sixteenth place [on the Eton Foundation Election-Bill] which if it happens this year will be soon enough, if not I hope we shall have a forward one the next, for our reputation in the Schoole is very good." . . . . .

1709, Augt. 16th. A. Windham to Lord Townshend.

" My Lord,—M* Payne is dead, and [I] suppose y* Lord*p will have abundance of Sollicitations ab*t it. Mr. Kendall writes me word that he has put in his claim; Major Houghton too has some hopes from his own necessity, & your wonted goodness to him.

There will be no occasion for a clerk till Mic⁵ Sessions, and I believe. No body w⁴ be more generally acceptable than my Unckle." . . . .

1709, Sept. 16th. From J. [or. S.] Houghton in London to Horatio Walpole at the Hague.

" Sir—I ought sooner to have apply'd to you & crav'd your friendship & interest in moving my Lord in my Behalf for the Office of Clerk of the Peace for Norf : void by the death of Mr. Payn." . . . . .

1709, Sept. $\frac{13\text{th}}{24\text{th}}$. Spencer Compton in London to the same at the Hague.

. . . . . . I hope Madame Guirand has before this time been with you, to return you thanks for solliciting in her behalf, the Warr⁴ for her Pension is signed . . . . . . I heartily congratulate with you the great Victory the D. of Marlborough has obtained, though a great deal of pains is taken to lessen it here. I suppose you have heard of L⁴ Gower's death, but I am sure the Dutchess of Beaufort's must be News, for she was brought to Bed yesterday of a Son, and dy'd this Morning.

1709, Oct. 3rd, N.S. Capt John Massey to the same. From the Camp at the Siege of Mons.

. . . . . " The first day I mounted the Trenches Major Mortimer that Superseded me was kill'd, Notwithstanding I dont find that Vacancy will be any advantage to me or any of the Second Officers. Coll. Clayton is dangerously wounded in eye. . Our Regim¹ has already very much Suffered." . . . . .

1709, Oct. 18th. Robert Atwood to Lord Townshend.—" I yesterday received advices from Yarmouth [about a contest at the approaching municipal election.] . . . . . . Mr Fuller & Mr Luson at the same time advised me that Capt. Milleson was just then expiring and desired I would wait on Coll Walpole to know if his place at the Fort was secured for Capt. Spooner." . . . . .

1710, March 3rd, N.S. John Vallance to Horatio Walpole. From London.

The writer this day sent Mr Walpole's Peruque, to the care of Mr Gilbert Black, Merchant at Rotterdam, and has requested the latter to forward it. As he has taken all possible care in choice of hair as well as of fashion he hopes Mr Walpole will like it.

1710, April 5th. Edward Hopkins to Horatio Walpole. Dated in London and addressed " To Horatio Walpole, Esqr, at Mr Secretary Boyle's office at the Cock Pitt."

. . . . . " 'tis in behalf of one Mr Dubois who has some time serv'd the government at Brill."

1710, April 11th. James Barbon to the same. Dated in London and addressed " For Horatio Wallpoole Esqr wth the Right hon^{ble} the Lord Townshend at the Hague."

" Sir,

By my Ld Duke of Boltons Comands You have the trouble of this, who desires the favo^r of You to give the Enclosed the Spediest Conveyance You can to Coll. Crofts."

1710, April 22nd, N.S. James Craggs to the same at the Hague.

. . . " Mr Stanhope & I arrived at Frankfort the 19th inst, he went away the same day by the way of Swisserland, I was obliged to stay for my chaise wch I had left to be mended 6 posts of, & wch came up next morning. I intend to take Venice in my way, & hope to meet my Master at Genoa about the 5th of next month." . . . .

1710, April 26th, O.S. Peter Marescoe at Rotterdam to the same, addressed "For Hieroe Warpoole Esqr at the Right Honorable the Lord Townsend Plenipotentiary from Her Majesty of Great Britain—Inn Hague."

"Sir,

THIS morning the Baron de Weltez sets out for Berne in Switserland ; I am now going, to make the best of my way, for the Brill hopeing to save this Pacquet ; I shall acquaint Robert Pringle, Esqr of the five guinneys rece'ved (from you) so soon as I come to London." . . . . .

1710, May 2nd. James Pelham to the same. Endorsed " Mr Pelham Camp before Douay, May the 2^d. Red : May the 6th."

" Dear Horace,

. . . . I am convinced you intend to keep your promise of making me a great man . . . . . I waited on Mr Cardonell . . . . . by his discourse to me I did not find I was likely to succeed so soon as I think it convenient at this time, he spoke to me of a Company in an old core wch with the Liberty of disposing [of] my own Comission would enable me to buy a Troop of Dragoons." . . . . .

1710, May 20th. James Calthorpe "To Mr Thomas Ward att Raynham in Norfolke—by`Swaffham Bagg."

On business. Dated in London and franked by Horatio Walpole (M.P. for Lostwithiel).

1710, June 15th. Robert Mann to Horatio Walpole. Dated in London, and addressed: " To Horatio Walpole, Esq., Secretary to the Embassy at the Hague."

The writer acknowledges a money draft, and says : " I shall not give any Account of the new Revolutions ; presuming y^r Brother the Treasurer this post writes [to you]."

1710, July 12th. Lord Cornwallis to the same. Dated at Brome.

. . . . " pray send me word whether you come over next winter and if you doe not think this Nation is not run mad. You can not expect any news from hence haveing ben out of town this month my wife gives her Service to you [and I] pray mine to your Master."

1710, July $\frac{7th}{18th}$. Capt. Edward Harrison to the same. Dated at Amsterdam and addressed to " Monsieur Walpole, Secretair de l'Ambassade chez son Excellance My Lord Tounshend ambassadeur de La Grande Brittagne at La Haye."

" At my arrivall here from the East Indies on the 5th Inst,, I came up to this City in hopes to hear of my Brothers but in vain and hearing that you are at the Hague whom I remember to have seen often among them makes me take this freedom desiring you will favour me with a Line or two [to tell me] where they are and how they doe. He to whom the Inclos'd is directed was formerly at sea with me and I heard in India that he had a commission in Coll'l Hils regiment pray S^r doe me the favour to enquire if he is in Flanders and send him this by the first post if we are not soon call'd away I intend to come and thank you at the Hague and desire you will command me anything in my way."

1710 [Augt?]. Colonel John Harbord to Horatio Walpole. Dated at " Hell Voet Sluys Sunday Noon." Addressed "To the Honble Horace Walpole Esqr Secretary to his Excellence the Lord Townshend at the Hague."

U 24953.

" Dr Secretary,

After my humble harty and most affectionate Duty to my ever Honrd Lord & Ma[ste]r Our good Ld Lieuten^t her Maties Great Ambassad^r and Countrys frd wth all the acknowldgm^{ts} I am capable of making, wch I must leave & recomend to Yo^r Friendship &c. &c. I must not forget Yo^r great Kindness to me both in my goeing and returning. And to desire Yow if my good Lord continues his thoughts of sending any Renish to drinck her Maties health & his Lord^{sp} & the Peace and prosperity of these kingdoms together wth Our Allyes &c. I pray let it be sent to Mr Archibald Hoop Merch^t on de Haring Vliet at Rotterdam. I herewith send an Old 20 p. of Gold desiring Youl gratifye Yo^r Clark for my Pass and give the rest to his Lord^{ops} Butler. I have Nothing to ad but that I came of 10 how^{rs} to late for the fleet wherein was a Yorkshire Ma[ste]r [who] w^d ha set me probably but this time neer Gunton where if it shall please We get safe home & Youl be soe kind [as] to call Youl very Much Oblidge,

Yo^r True friend & Servt
J. HARBORD."

1710, Augt. 26. The same to the same. Dated at Grinley, and addressed as the last.

" Dr Bro : Sinner,

This must in ye first place return my very affectionat as well as humble Duty and Service to his Excelencie Our good L^d and Mast^r her Maties Plenæ Potenecary in this Critical Junct^{re}, wch is all I dare say, &c. Nor must I omit my harty thanks for ye hono^r & favour I rec^d from his L^p and to Yo^r Self for yor very friendly care and kindnesse and helping me forward, but ye Days Pleasure I had at the Hague lost me my Passage in ye Fleet wch I came of[f] 10 how^{rs} short of.

And the Packet I came over in (ye Eagle) being the worst Sayler of all ye five was soe Neer being taken by a fr[ench] Privateer] of 14 or 16 guns, as he had his Boat in ye Tackle to com aboard us, and soe small hopes remaind of escaping Dunkerk—as divers Gent. disposed of gold to a sort of Cormor[an]t Damzel who really swall[owe]d it as fast as we have seen Jugl[e]rs play wth balls or. . . . . She swall[owe]d 12 Span[ish] Pistol[e]s of one Gent. & besides w^t she took in of others, a Diamond ring wth div^{rs} Stones of an Ancient Ladys, went ye same way. She offered me much Kindnesse that way but that Little I left being engaged, I left ye Cabbin full of that Sort of buisynesse, and was the only Gent. Passeng^r admitted on ye Deck, to see ye Sport. I must own I had rather chose to ha ben wth my gun in a fur close—tho wthout Brechess, but preferd ye fresh Aire, rather than dying in a hole, soe I had the pleasure of seeing all ye Sport, such as t'was & That it pleased God to give us a longer time. For our Ma[ste]r & Gunner & Doct^r being perfect Mast^{rs} of sayling & all Working like true English Men, wth the Ships Crew, having in a few Mom^{ts} strained all their Canvas & by the help of Oars turnd ye Ships head a differ[en]t course to that ye fr[ench] Man was running vppon us : in that very inst^t, it pleased God to send so fresh a Gale, as before ye fr[ench] could bring their Ship about, he could bring No more Guns to bear on us, then he had bestowed before. We had ye hono^r to give ye first gun, For wch ye ball going Pretty Near, aft^r a Short Pause he gave us 4, and we returned two, being ye rest of our Little broad Side : wch he gave us 3 or 4 for, whereof one brusht Our Main Mast, & so We parted—& soon after the Wind rose very high, and a dismal Night it was, wth Rain alsoe but it blew directly for us, wch was another Signal Evidence of Gods care of us. Having, to Lighten Our Ship for runing whilst ye Privat[ee]r was coming on us,

MARQUESS
TOWNSHEND
MSS.

thrown over Most if not all our Stones [ballast]. And I have I thank God found No ill Effects of lying east 4 Nights, whereof y⁰ last Wett, having given my Cabbin Most of y⁰ time to an Ancient Decayd Gent. woman. And I verily believe a true Religious good Woman, And that her Prayers contributed not a little Towards Our Preservaçon.

As to my Petiçon That if by My Life I might contribute towards y⁰ Peace & Welfare of my Country and continue my care of y⁰ Poor Might be Acceptable to God, I des[ire]d to Live, and I know little else earnestly to Pray for. I suppose our good Lᵈʰ as heard I have yielded to the Importunity of his Lᵖˢ Relations & friends, Tho I dare say No care or Temperance, Can Preserve my old Cotage in London. If You can Excuse this trouble, & what Follows wᶜʰ is to pray Youl make y⁰ best enquiry you conveniently can at Yoʳ Leasure, and send me yʳ answer. Mʳ Gylby y⁰ ownʳ of y⁰ Sunck is my Next Neighbʳ here, and Particulʳ friend, as his Grandfather Cole Gylby was—& Governʳ of New Work [Newark?] in y⁰ Rebellion in Car 1ˢᵗ time & died Dp. Governʳ of Hull, in Car 2ᵈ time and is a very worthy deserving honest Whig.

Our great Du[ke] Enq[uire]d after our good Lᵈ & Mastʳˢ health last Munday & yesterday drunk it very heartily wᵗʰ y⁰ sᵈ Mʳ Gylby; at honest Mʳ Thornhags, & I am Sincerely

Yʳ true Lovʳ & Sert
Jo. HARBORD.'

[Enclosed in a Description of "the Sunk," an Island in the Humber, of about 2,000 acres, situated about ten miles below Hull. It is for sale, and the writer states it is rapidly growing larger through fresh deposits of earth].

1710, Sept. 11th. Samuel Fuller to Lord Townshend. Dated at Yarmouth and addressed "These—To His Excellency The Lᵈ Viscᵗ Townshend Her Majesty of Grᵗ Britains Ambassador At [the] Hague. —Paid 3ᵈ."

About Election matters. The writer is heartily engaged in the interest of Mʳ Windham and Colonel Harbord.

1710, Sept. 22nd. The same to the same. Unsigned.

"My Lord—I writ to your Lordᵖ last post giving you a full acct of our County affairs, and recommending to your Excellency the writing a letter of thanks to John Berney of Westwick Esqʳᵉ who is zealous for us to the last degree; and who is a Gentleman worth the endeavouring to secure in the Whig Interest. . . . . . the Honour of such a letter from your Lordᵖ will be taken most kindly and affix him to our party. Whereas on the other hand, if he should leave us Negus & he wᵈ joyn, fling out Preston and carry a great body of men away that are now with us.

His Brother's [Richard Berney's] standing for Norwich is an unlucky buissness at this time, for it forces him to act for the Torys in the citty. Councellʳ Britiffe rides for us from house to house under Sir Jacob's [Sir Jacob Astley's] own nose; & I hear from good hands that Serjeant Wells will come at the head of 30 men from Bury. We are in daily Expectation of the dissolution but our Election here [Norfolk] cannot be before the 11ᵗʰ of October. I am yʳ Excellencys most obedient "&c."

[P.S.] Young Knight the Flegg Lieutenᵗ to Capⁿ Symonds has flung up his Commission, because wee opposed his being a Commissioner of the Tax at Ferriers instance. Captain Symonds desires it may be given as soon as yʳ Lordᵖ please, to Thomas Cooper Junʳ a good man."

1711, Feb. 13th. Alexander Cunningham to Lord Townshend. Unsigned. Dated at Venice.

. . . . : " yesterday we had the cutting [off] the bull's head and the fireworks performed w^t great solemnitie, and on Sunday we are to have a bull beating in the palace .   . . Our Merch^{ts} tell me the taking of Minorca is fatal to them .   . . . in teen days think to goe for Rome where I shall want for your Ex^{cies} Commands.

. . . . . . My Lord Lonsdale gives his most humble service to your Ex^{clle} and trulie has behaved himself mightie well this Carn[iva]l in all respects. I'm extreamlie pleased w^t him.

1711, Feb. 20th. The same to Horatio Walpole. Dated at Venice and addressed " A Monsieur Monsr Hor^o Walpool Secretair de Sa Maj^{tie} Britanique chez My Lord Townshend à la Hay Holland."

. . . . Mr Molesworth came hither last week and next week is to set out for Florence. . . . . . We think to stay a fortnight longer.

1713, Jan. 2nd. Joshua Beadle to Lord Townshend, from London, addressed to Lord Townshend at Raynham Hall.

The writer has agreed to purchase for his Lordship six chances in the present lottery at three guineas each chance.

1713, July 25th. Edward Ashe to the same, from London. Congratulations on his Lordship's marriage.

1713, Augt. 18th. Charles [Trimnell] Bishop of Norwich to the same. The writer's wife presented him with a son on the 1st inst. " My Lord Sommers and My Lord Cowper did me the honour to stand for him."

17$\frac{14}{15}$, Feb. 23rd. Thomas de Grey to Lord Townshend. Dated at Merton.

. . . " Ar[thur] Branthwayte tells me he acquainted y^r Lordship with his desires to gett into the Parliament House, that you were pleased to encourage him in it & that upon his failing at Castle Rising you told him you thought some double election might be made, when he might be brought in upon the second choice . . . . .

1715, April 30th. John Fleetwood, Consul at Naples, to " The Right Honble the Lord Vicount Townshend his Majesties principal Secretary of State.—Whitehall."

The writer begs his Lordship's acceptance " of a Cask of Lachrimæ " and if the vintage had been better he would have also sent some of Horace's Falernian.

1715, July 28th. Thomas Parker to the same. Unaddressed.

Hopes Mr. Grovenor may have the command of one of the troops of horse of the Staffordshire Militia. . . . . Capt Levinge Sir Richard's son [a relation of the writer's] should certainly be taken care of the first opportunity and have a pension in the mean time . . . . . . he has been 10 years a Capt. always at his Post, stands first in the list of those recommended by Brigadier Gore. . . .

1715, Sept. 11th. Lord Cornwallis to the same. Unaddressed. Enclosing letters.

1715, Sept. 23rd. R. B. to Tobias Jenkins, M.P. for York. Dated at Blyth and directed " To Toby Jenkins Esqre Member of Parliament at Mr Hardings a Book sellors In — St Martins Lane — London — Free."

" I have yours of the 17 Instant, your Frank was struck **out & 4^d** Charg^d Postage . . . . . Davidson's Roguery in delaying

finishing the [Salt-]Pan has broke my measures of coming to London
at Mich[elmas]. S. tells me Burdon is to pay but 28ˢ p tun for his &
my Salt, Burdon has loaded 100 Tun last weeke with you the price I
know not—depend upon it I can settle a Trade to make 40ˢ p Tun all
the yeare round . . . . . tis said Sʳ Jnº Delavall is going to
London by my L[ord] Scarborough's request & will be made Deputy
Governor to Tyn Mouth Castle the truth I· know not . . . . Divers
Reegmᵗˢ gon for Scotland what the Event of that will be God knowes.—
I am yʳ Faithfull Friend & humble Scrt

R. B.

[P.S.] If youl come doune by Sea, I will goe up to London with
you by Sea, when you return, if I can possibly do it.
P.S. Morpeth—Just now Mr Lambert is come to Tom Marrs. I
got him privateley to ask if my Lord design'd for Lincoln sheire this
winter. He sayes my Lord will not stirr this winter from Widder-
ington.

1715, Sept. 24th. Sir Samuel Molyneux to Lord Townshend. Dated
at Sᵗ James's.
Application having been made to His R.H. the Prince for a Grant
of the Office of Chamberlain of Caernaervonshire, Merionethshire and
Anglesey in North Wales to be made during Pleasure to Mʳ Warburton
of Chester, when the said Office should become Grantable by His R.H.
and His Royal Highness being desirous to comply with the said Request
if His Patent for the Principality of Wales were pass'd, Mʳ Warburton
has not thought fitt to make application to his Majesty for the Same
although the affairs of the Country do require the Immediate Constitution of such an Officer without produceing an Assurance to your Lordship that it is agreable to the Prince's desire that he should have the
Employment. Is therefore directed by His Royal Highness to let your
Lordship know that he doth entirely approve of the said Mʳ Warburton's applying to his Majesty for the Grant of the said Office During
His Majesty's Pleasure and hopes your Lordship will give him your
Assistance and Protection therein.

Same date. A letter from the University of Cambridge to the same.
Thanking his Lordship for having procured for the University a grant
from the King of the library of the late Bishop of Ely [Dʳ John
Moore.] Signed by the Vice-Chancellor the Rev. Thomas Sherlock
(afterwards, successively, Bishop of Bangor, Salisbury, and London),
and by Robert Grove, Registrar of University.

1715, Sept. 27th. William Prestland to the same. Unaddressed.
. . . . "Col. Wodehous[e] sent me this morning how poor Mʳ
L'Estrange is dead & with great earnestness begs your favour for Mʳ
Roger L'Estrange his son." . . . . .

1715, Oct. 4th. Copy of Lord Townshend's reply to the University
of Cambridge.
His Lordship acknowledges the above letter, and promises to embrace
every opportunity of testifying his affection for the University.

1715, Nov. 28th. Lord Stawell to the same. Unaddressed, dated at
Aldermaston.
The writer, who is afflicted with the gout, begs his Lordship's permission to write to Lord "Boolingbrooke" on the latter's private affairs,
and to give him an account of the favours that Lord Townshend had
shown to Lady Bolingbroke.

1715, Dec. 26th. Earl of Portland to the same. Dated at St James's Square, and unaddressed.

My Lord—I hope y^r Lord^p will excuse my not having obey'd y^r Commands sooner, in sending this to y^r House. Some familly busines, which now is over has prevented me ; When I had the honour to see you last in the Drawing Roome, I told y^r Lord^p that I desir'd not to change my name, but beeing oblig'd to chuse one by which my son must be call'd, that I had chose that of Titchfield ; I desire y^r Lord^p will give all the dispatch you can to this matter, as you was pleas'd to promise you would, & you'll extreamly oblige him, who is with sincerity & respect,— My Lord — Your Lord^{ps}—Most obed^t & most humble servant

PORTLAND.

Note. The writer was created Duke of Portland and Marquis of Titchfield in the following July.

1716, July 5th. Edward Southwell to Spencer Compton. From Whitehall.

" S^r—I am commanded by my Lord President to desire you would attend at St James's tomorrow at 12 a Clock, in order to your being Sworn of his Ma^{tys} most Honble Privy Council."

171$\frac{7}{8}$, Feb. 27th. Defeazance from Sr Lambert Blackwell to the Lord Carpenter for 2000^{li} in the loan to the Emperor—Coppy.

" KNOW ALL MEN by these Presents that I Sr Lambert Blackwell of St James's Westminster Knt do hereby for me my Executors & Administrators acknowledge and declare that so far as the sum of twenty two thousand Guilders Currant Money of Amsterdam in the Emperor's loan in Holland, in my name and under the Care of Mr George Clifford & Co. of Amsterdam is for the proper account and risque of the hon^{ble} Lieut. Gen^{ll} George Carpenter, & was by his order pay'd for out of the produce of two thousand pounds Bank Annuities."

1718, July 1st. Spencer Compton to ——. Draft. Unaddressed. Dated in St. James's Square.

" S^r—I have received y^r Letter of the 18th of June, with the several Papers inclosed with it ; The Fact is so clearly stated by Mr Jodrell that I can add nothing to it ; & I conceive that I am no proper Judge of the reasonableness of the Demand, the Speaker never having had, that I know of, any Inspection or Controll over the Bills of the Serjeant at Arms. This I beg you to represent to the Lords Commissioners of the Treasury.

I am with the greatest respect *etc.*

S. COMPTON."

Note. Mr Paul Jodrell's Report to the Treasury in favour of the Serjeant-at-Arms' Memorial (claiming payment of certain fees for arresting and keeping in custody Matthew Prior) will be found in the printed Calendar of Treasury Papers under the date 8 May 1718. The above letter was evidently written in obedience to the following Treasury Minute :—" 13 June 1718. Desire Mr Speaker to give my Lords his opinion as to the reasonableness of this demand [of Mr Thomas Wiburg, Serjeant-at-Arms]."

1720, Sept. 28th. William Gordon to ——. Dated at Paris and unaddressed.

To advise that the writer is forwarding, through Mr Arbuthnot at Rouen, a small box addressed to Mr George Ouchterlony containing four wigs made by Monsr Broussin, and that the writer has paid for the wigs 220 francs.

$17\frac{20}{21}$, Jan. 1st.   Lord Conningsby to Lord Townshend.   Unaddressed.
Dated at "hampton Court in herifordsheir."

The writer begs Lord Townshend to prosecute one Edward Wither-
ston, who has been pricked for sheriff of Herefordshire, as he is a
notorious Jacobite; and the writer states that he has forwarded to his
Majesty in Council affidavits " to prove him guilty of an insurrection if
not a Rebellion."

1721, May 21st.   Lord Carpenter to the same.

Begging his Lordship to procure the removal of the attachment that
has been laid on some monies in the hands of Sir Lambert Blackwell, as
the monies really belong to the writer.

1721, June 8th.   Lord Findlater to the same.   Dated at Edinburgh
and unaddressed.

" My Lord—I doubt not bot Your Lop hes ane accompt from the Duke
of Argyl of our proceedings att the election the Earl of Aberdeen hes
caried the return in his favours by a majority of five, bot ther are
several objections made against the titels and qualifications of so manie
of thos [who] voted for him that I believe that matter may yet be retrived in the house of Lords and concerning this a full memorial will
be sent, the Earl of Eglintoun would unquestionablie [have] prevailed
bot that [the] E. of Aberdeen had preingadged mannie befor the E.
Eglintoun sett upp and al the English Lords sent ther Proxies and lists
for Aberdeen ; the torie Lords wer also prevailed upon by the late E. of
Carnwath, Mr Lock of Carnwath and Mr Munk who used al ther interest and influence for Aberdeen bot in a general election I am certain the
Duke of Argyl would have a considerable Majoritie, it is lyke the Squad
may misrepresent my voting for [the] E. of Eglintoun bot I had no
directions from the King or his Ministrie to doe for either and as I told
Your Lop when I had the honour to wait of You the D of Argyl hes
given me full assuranses of his friendship and [the] E of Eglintoun is
my near relation. I am sure I sha ever be most dutiful to His Majestie
and His Government and ther was fullie as manie who have posts in the
Government that voted for [the] E of Eglintoun as ther wer of the
voters for [the] E [of] Aberdeen I relie upon Your Lop['s] protection
to me in my absence and You shall ever command what service is in my
power and wishing Your Lop al success and prosperitie in your administration I am." . . .

1721, Sept. 12th.   Charles Lovell to the same.   From Dover.

After acquainting his Lordship with the intestine Divisions & Com-
motions into which this Corporation is plunged since the Election of Mr
Berkeley & Mr Furnesse, the writer goes on :—

" I Have Endeavoured to behave with all the Prudence that possable
I could in this Affair; but I know, that I have been represented to
the Duke of Dorset, wch am sorry for; altho' can't help it.

On Monday morning my Lord; a Gentleman sailed in the Eagle
Pacq^t Boat with a Fine Gale of wind at S.W. for Ostend. I soon
perceived that he had a Mind to go of In Cogg ; by a Messenger I
sent to him ; So I never waited upon him, nor don't know his name,
nor did I take any notice of his going of, to the Port Master General
in my Daiary.

As I can never think of y^r Lordshipp, without being filled with a due
Sence of y^r Goodness to me ; So I Humbly hope that it will alwaeis
be beleived that Nobody can be more perfectly devoted to yor Lordshipps Service than (My Lord)—yor Most Dutifull & most obedient
Humble Servent,   CHA. LOVELL."

1722, June 7th. Duke of Somerset to Spencer Compton. Unaddressed.

The Duke congratulates Mr Compton on his Election for the County of Sussex, and sends his humble duty to the Prince of Wales. He has given orders to the Keepers in Hampton Court Harte Park to obey Mr Compton's "warrants to kill twelve Brace of Fawnes and six Brace of Fat Bucks this Season for the Prince's Service."

1722, Sept. 22nd. Sir David Bulkeley to ———. Dated at Burgate near Fordingbridge and unaddressed.

Refers to commands lately received from Mʳ Walpole.

1722, Sept. 25th. Edward Nicholas to Spencer Compton. Dated at " Spring Garden " and unaddressed.

" Sir,—I met accidentally with Mʳ Feilding who said Something as if there might be Something like an Opposition wⁿ the house meets on the Choice of a Speaker, this makes me trouble you with this to let you know that tho I set out to morrow for the West I will be back before that day, and if such a thing is suspected I should be glad you would let me know it, that I might use my little interest with some of my Westerne Acquaintance to prevail with them, to doe as I am sure I will who am." . . .

1723, Dec. 23ʳᵈ. N.S. Thomas Crawford " To the Rᵗ Honᵇˡᵉ Robert Walpole Esqʳᵉ Secretary of State &c." Dated at Paris and endorsed " Mr Crawford—Decʳ 23ᵈ N.S. 1723—Recᵈ Dec. 16ᵗʰ O.S."

Private letter—" Sir—Your Brother writes to you and to My Lord Townshend so fully the state of things here that I shall only take the liberty by this occasion to joyn my opinion of 'em in general with his, that in all human probability, this Court will not only att present goe on in concert with us towards the establishing the publick tranquillity of Europe with the same warmth that it did before the D[uke] of Orleans' death, but likewise seek to live in a particular friendship and good understanding with us, at le[a]st for some years, which I hope will be all we shall want of 'em to putt us in a condition of being as indifferent about the continuation of it as they may be.

I beg leave to return you my humble acknowledgements for the goodness you have pleas'd to showe me in ordering the payment of my little arrears att the Treasury, of which Mr [Horatio] Walpole has given me notice, and to assure you that I shall endeavour all my lifetime to merit the continuation of your favour and protection, by acquitting myselfe in the best manner I can as an honest man in the discharge of any trust that may be given me, and by a most sincere and gratefull attachment to you and your family which has engaged me by the strongest motives.

I am with the greatest respect—Sir—Your most humble and most devoted servant

TⱧO. CRAWFORD."

1724, Augt. 20th. Stephen Poyntz to Lord Townshend.

A letter on trust matters. It concludes :—" I have at last gott letters from the Captⁿ of the Portmahone who is at the Nore and (as he says) ready. I hope to wait on your Lᵈᵖ about the middle of next week for my Credentials & Instructions and to embark on Monday sennight if possible."

172$\frac{4}{5}$, Jan. 20th. A memorandum :—
Reced at the Excheq^r this 20th Day of Jan^{ry} 172$\frac{4}{5}$ for the R^t Honble the Ld Visco^t Townshend's one Quarter's secret service due at X^{tmas} last   750 : 0 : 0

p^d at the Treasury	-	1	1
„ Auditors	-	4 16	6
„ Pells -	-	2 16	6
„ Tellers -	-	11	5
Civil List Tax [at 5 per cent]	18 15		

— 38 : 14 : 0

711 : 6 —

172$\frac{4}{5}$, March 12th. A memorandum :
Fees for Passing the R^t Honble the Lord Viscount Townshend's New Privy Seal for 1000^{li} Secret Service.

Signet Office -	- 1 : 18	0
Office Keeper	- 2	6
Privy Seal Office	- 2 : 15	6
Office Keeper	- 5	0
Stamps	- 6 : 0	0
Treasury	- 2 : 2	0
Stamps for the Warrant	7	6

£13 10 6

1725, May 11th. Dr. Samuel Knight to Spencer Compton. Dated at Ely and addressed.
. . . . "I am going forward with the life of Erasmus, intending to make it as perfect as possibly I can especially as to that part of it that he spent in England . . . . I did hope to have had my book out of the presse before August but materials increasing upon me & having several Heads engraven from the paintings of Holben which are lodged in several distant places I fear it will not be ready long before the next meeting of the Parlement " . . . . . .

1725, May 12th. Mrs. S. Ibbot to the same. Dated at Shadwell and unaddressed. Begging Mr. Compton to subscribe for a copy of Mr. Ibbot's sermons.

1725, May 22nd. John Tabor to the same. Dated at Lewes, and addressed " To The Right Honble Spencer Compton Speaker of the House of Commons humbly present these."
Requesting Mr. Compton to recommend the bearer, Mr. Norton to the Duke of Dorset as a tenant for his Grace's farm at Hangleton.

1725, May 29th. The Duke of Montagu to the same. Addressed " To the Right honorable Sr Spencer Compton.*
" Sir, I take it to be a Duty incumbent on me to acquaint you that the ancient Rites in conferring the knighthood of the Bath, whereby each Candidate was obliged to be attended by three Esquires of honor, bearing Coat Arms like is confirmed by the Seventh Article of the Status of the Order of the Bath, & that these Statuts further direct, these Esquirs shall in the Ceremony of this Order, be habited in Surcoats delivered from his Majesties Wardrobe, & also that their Arms shall be affix'd, to the back of the Seats, under the Stalls of their respective Knights, [in King Henry the Seventh's Chapel in Westminster Abbey] in enameled Escutcheons, & during the Term of their several Lives, these Esquirs shall enjoy all Rights, Priviledges, Exemptions & advantages which the Esquirs of the Soveraigns Body, or the Gentlemen of

---

* Mr. Spencer Compton was created a Knight of the Bath, on the revival of the Order, on the 18th of May 1725.

the Privy Chamber do lawfully enjoy, or are entituled unto by virtue of any Grant Prescription or Custom whatsoever & their eldest Sons shall have & use the addition and Title of Esquirs in all Acts Proceedings & Pleadings &c⁵. You are fully appris'd that the Dignity of any regular Military Order, will be maintain'd by an exact observance of the Statuts I must therefore request you to transmit as soon as possible the names of those Esquirs with the respective places of their residence & what Coat Arms they are severally entituled unto, that his Majesties Royal Intentions, in this respect may be fully answered."

July 7th, 1725. William Inge to the same. Dated at Thorp Constantine and unaddressed.

After high encomiums on the Speaker's address to the Managers for the House of Commons against "The Great Offender" (the Earl of Macclesfield) the writer goes on to say that he has shown his zeal for religion by his endeavours to encourage the building of a new church and the providing a Churchyard in Birmingham.

1725, Sept. 14th. William Munday to the same. Unaddressed.

With the greatest Submission I do presume to write this to your Honor to acquaint you of the State of Mr. Travers health. When I returned from Coventry he had been delirious some daies, but was grown sensible again, since wᶜʰ he has seemed to continue so, but is so very weak, & likewise bedrid, and able to take only a little Sack Whey downe, that Mr Holditch his Nephew & the Apothecary &c think he can't last long. . . . . Mr Cary has ordered me to give your Honor the earliest Notice of his Death, and I will do it if possible. I hope whoever has the Succession [to Mʳ Travers office in the Prince's household], your Honor will vouchsafe me the Favor of your Recommendation . . . .

[P.S.] A letter will come soonest to me at William's coffee house in Dover Street."

1725, Sept. 16th. The same to the same.

"Rᵗ Honᵇˡᵉ Sir, My Dear Master departed this life 25 Minutes past twelve the bearer my Brother brings this Notice from Sir," etc.

Same date. Henry Powell to the same. Dated at Richmond old Park and unaddressed.

The Prince's wines on new racking are grown better beyond Expectation. The writer is told that Mr Clayton is to be Mr Travers's successor.

1725, Oct. 7th. J. Butler to the same. Dated at Warminghurst Park and unaddressed.

" Sir, Mr Eyre wrote me word last night his son Thomas Eyre, who is yᵉ young person yᵉ Princesses were inoculated from, was Yesterday to deliver his Petition to yᵉ East India Company to go this Year in their Service as Factor to Bengule ; He says his son has already served them gratis upwards of 4 Years, that he has recᵈ pretty good assurances from some of yᵉ leading Directors that he shall go ? if in yᵉ Station of a Factor as he petitions, he shall then be favoured, as Mr Eyre is told some others have been, wᵗʰ almost a Year of yᵉ Usual Time, but if he must go [as] a Writer only, & begin his 5 Years of Service abroad, & loose his 4 Years of Service here, in which he has spent a great part of his Fortune, Mr Eyre thinks it will be something hard, therefore has desired me to mention this to You, since one word from You Sʳ to Govʳ Harrison, or Sʳ Mathew Decker can't fail of Success, if you would honour him so far." . . . . . .

1725, Oct. 15th. Sir Matthew Decker to the same. Dated from St James'[s] Square and unsigned. Addressed at foot to " The Honb^{le} Sir Spencer Compton " and endorsed " Sr Mat^{hw} Decker."

. . . . " as to Mr Eyre's affair, he is a young Gentleman, between 19 and 20 year, and under 21. The Comp^y never sends out any body for factor, of wch I gave a hint to ye Gentleman yesterday when he brought me your Letter. I don't mention this to insinuate that he shall or can not go, this year in ye said post, for I am in great hopes that I shall obtain this for him, and if others shoud know his age, that we may even at your Consideration, break thro' this rule, but onley if I shoud miscarry in this Design, and that he goes out as a writer, that it will not be ye worse for him, in point of advancement hereafter, for in this Case, I'll procure him a year or Two in his Time, so that by our way he may come as soon to be a Junior Merchant (wch is ye Channel of advancem^t) as if he went out a factor this Season, but as I say here before I flatter myself I shall be able to compass this." . . . . . .

1726, Augt. 13th. Robert Corker to the same. Dated at the " Hotwell Bristoll " and unaddressed.

" Honble S^r

The Death of my Dear wiffe in Jan^{ry} last prevented my Journey to Londⁿ wch I was determined to begin in that month, & my Reumatick disord^{rs} Encreasing I was advised to drinke these waters wch I have been useing Ever since ye beginning of June last & I praise God wth very good Success. Upon ye News (wch I rec^d here) of Mr Vincent's death after ye Coynage was begun, thinking it both for the Princes & the Countrys Service & for ye Security of the Tyn Manufacture that the Assaying thereof should be perform'd by a Sworne Officer I recommended to ye Dept^y Assaym[aste]r as he had begun to goe through ye Coynages & discharge ye duty of Assaying ye Tyn wth ye utmost Skill & Care untill his Royall Highness signified his further pleasure wth respect to ye Assaym^{rs} Office, and as I have been always watchfull for ye preservation of this branch of his Royall Highness's Revenue & likewise to keepe up the reputation of this Noble Commodety wth Success hitherto & haveing heard some complaints of ye badd quallety of Tyn lately sent abroad, I thought this was my Duty & hope S^r it will meet yor Approbation.

Assoon as I heard of this Demise I likewise judged it proper to write a Letter to Mr John Johns (ye present Acting Mayor of Lostwithyell) who wth his Brother lately Deceased have kept ye Mayors Office of that Borrough betwixt them (sometimes alternately) for at least 20 y^{rs} putting him in minde of some discourse wee had formerly in wch They both promised me to devote them Selves to ye Princes Service for one Member at least. They haveing then promised one to M^r V[incen]t but he assureing them ye interest he made was alsoe for ye Pr[ince of Wales] & useing Some further prevayling Arguments it was to little purpose to proceed any farther at that time wth those people of wch I tooke ye liberty then to give y^r Hon^r an Acc^t and as I judged this a proper Juncture to renew our correspondence I wrote him two lett^{rs} on ye Subject from hence and presume to send you both his lett^{rs} enclosed in answere to mine I dont perfectly know upon what foot ye Borrough of Lostwithyell stands at present whether theres any dispute at Law about ye Mayoralty nor whether any Measures are taken to engage this Borrough, but my zeale for his Royall Highnesses Service prompted me to goe thus farr wch I hope will excuse my freedome & if herein I have yor Approbation I shall esteeme myself happy as I shall at all times in executeing any of yor Commands.

S^r, I lately received a letter from Mr Nicholson Master of the Pew-
terr^n Company full of Complaints of ye badd quallety of ye Tyn in
generall of Ladiday [Lady-day] Coynage wch is very surprizeing since I
never before heard of a whole Coynages Tyn complained of, & wth his
letter he sent me the Ma^r & Wardens Essays [assays] of 5^{ps} [*sic*] and
9^{ps} Tyn taken by them, which letter & accounts I have sent to Mr Cary
fearing I have already given You too much troble & if it be thought
convenient noe doubt Mr Nicholson will Attend any time & Explain
himself further on this Complaint.

I shall only crave leave to add my humble Opinion that the Deputy
Assayma^r (at least) should be a persone of Judgm^t in Mettals to be able
to take a true Essay in Tyn especially & to be a man alsoe of Probity y^e
honour of the Comodity & Security of the Tyn trade depending very much
on a faith.full & skilfull discharge of the Duty of his Office.

All wch is most humbly Submitted to yor great Wisdome by " *etc.*

1727, June 18th. Horatio Walpole to George Tilson. Dated at
Paris and unaddressed. Endorsed, in George Tilson's handwriting,
under this date, " Mr Walpole—&r[eceive]d ½¾ p Walton near Delder."

" Dear Sir—I hope this will find you safe over [the] water, & overtake
you at the Hague, thô by what Mr Robinson tells me who arrived
here last night, I am afraid his L^{dp} will have been gone farther not
intending to stay above two or three days there, whereas I had heard
he would continue at least a week in Holland; especially at this
juncture when the Pensionary is given over, and great intrigues are on
foot for his successour, the accounts we have had here speak very
favourable of Mr Slingerlandt, thô his frequent & violent indisposition
by the gout may be a great objection to him; by the first safe conveyance lett me know how this great affair is like to goe.

The inclosed pacquet for Lrd Townshend is a sample of Cambrick,
sent me privately from St Quintin being made of Scotch thread, this is
an affair that should be managed wth great caution & secrecy at present
for fear of giving jealousy to our freinds here; and perhaps nothing
should be hastily done in it at this juncture, the envy against our
Commerce is butt too great already, I am y^{rs} most affec^{ly} &c.

                                        H. WALPOLE."

1728, Feb. 12th. Robert Britiffe " To The Right Honble the Lord
Lynn att his house in Whitehall."

The writer is sending Court rolls and Surveys of the Manor of
Shipdham.

1728, June 29th. Thomas Consett to Lord Wilmington. Dated in
London and unaddessed.

" My Lord—A Year is not a Day to the happy but the unfortunate
think every Minute a Day & every Day a Year. The Application of
the latter Part of this Maxim approaches too near myself, & my Heart
[is] so full of it, that I am not able to add more than that I am—My
Lord—Your Lordship's most obedient humble serv^t.

                                    THOMAS CONSETT."

1728, Augt. 30th. Edward Harrison to Lord Townshend. Dated
in London and unaddressed.

.... " Grayham y^r Apothecary has been dangerously ill but I am
told he is upon the recovery. We have no manner of news from
abroad but they begin to talk at Paris, of returning all hands to the
Congress in order to do business, and the French are terribly disappointed by the Queen's bringing another girl after such mighty
preparations to celebrate the birth of a Dauphin " ....

1729, Jan. 14th. Robert Mann to the same. Unaddressed.
The writer has searched the books of Chelsea College and cannot find that Mr Gibbons has been on any pension list since 1717.

17$\frac{29}{30}$, Jan. 11th. Robert Daniel to the same. Dated at Brussels.
" My Lord—I intreat Your Lordship will have acceptable my most hearty wishes, that all manner of Blessings may attend Y^r Lords^p during the Course of the New-year we are entring upon, & that Yr. Lords^p may long enjoy the Fruits of that great Work the establishing a general Peace, in the transacting of which Y^r Lords^p has had so great a Share.

I beg leave to improve this opportunity to remind Y^r L^p of my humble Request, to be considered for the 7 or 8 hundred Pounds I am the worse, since I am at the Pension & lost the Freedom of Postage. I have the greater hopes of Y^r L^p's countenancing my Request, by that Your Lordship approved of it to the Earl of Chesterfield."

1730, April 20th. Robert Britiffe to the same. Unaddressed.
. . . . " I hope I shall be excused putting your Lordship in minde of a promise of giveing the place of Clerk of the Peace to my nephew Mr Britiffe upon the death of Mr Berney. I hear he was very ill the last week " . . . .

1730, Augt. 1st. A. Cracherode to the same ?
About his Lordship's trusteeship under the Earl of Bradford's Will.

1730, Nov. 15th. Lord Hobart to the same ? Dated at Blickling and unaddressed.
. . . . " I think myself very much obliged to you for so readily accepting of me I am not certain whether your Lordship intends to let the Furniture remain in the House if so I very readily agree to the Proposal of giving two hundred Pounds for it 'till Michaelmas next " . . . .

1731, April 24th. Edward Harrison to Lord Townshend. Unaddressed.
My Lord, I should not have been so long without enquiring after your Lords^{ps} health if I had not mett with a new sort of work, that I little expected. No sooner had I finished my India labours for the season, and begun to promise my self some recess from business, but the rupture of the Woodwards where I have kept my Cash many years, came upon us like a thunder clap without any manner of warning and to the great surprize of all mankind. It was my particular misfortune to have paid in a great deal of mony in March most of which should have been paid away the 25th, and on the 24th they stoppt payment & shutt up shop.

Being the greatest Creditor in this unhappy affair, I could not think it prudent to refuse being one of the Assignees, to have an eye to my own concern and endeavour to save as much as possible out of the wreck. By what I have allready experienced, I flatter my self, that it will be well for me and all the concernd, that I did accept it, but it is a great addition to the other business I had upon my hands, and will cost me a great deal of time, and close application, the credit of the shop having been very extensive, in so much that I can already see we shall have the accounts of above six hundred people to settle, before any dividend can be made of the effects ; and the best part of them are in English houses at Lisbon & Cadiz, but in secure hands for as farr as I can see at present, and upon the whole I believe there will be no great loss at last, tho it will require much time and patience to bring matters to a conclusion.

We are the more surprizd at this bankruptcy because the men have allways livd close, aud at no manner of expence more than absolutely necessary. They have had more business than all the Bankers in the Citty putt together. All the gold and silver imported and exported ever since the year 1720, has passed thro their hands, and thereby they must have been gainers of £4000 p^r anu^m, besides the proffit of a very great and constant circulation of Cash. It does not appear that they have ever drawn any sums of money out of the shop for their own particular account and benefit, nor that they have ever dealt for one thousand pounds 'n Stock of any kind. But tis plain they have been grossly abused & cheated by extravagant and knavish Servants, & have given a large credi to some of the Jews who have overtraded themselves, & cannot pay otherwise than by giving us their assignments of their goods at Lisbon and elsewhere, which we choose to take rather than pull them to pieces, and among them is the famous Pinhero in for £57000. He is the person that was negotiating a Loan with Kinski for the Emper^{rs} service some time before your Lord^p left us.

There is also one Paz a famous Jew gone off for a great sum of money, and thereby four or five considerable houses in France and Holland are undone, more will soon follow in France Spain & Italy if the Flota money is not deliver'd, and on reasonable terms, which I see little or no likelyhood off at present. As to our new Treaty, the Dutch are debating the Accessions, the French are mute, and we have no answer yett from Spain that I can learn. I have advice from Mr Tinker, by whom Mr Gore sent the diamonds, that he is well arrived at Porto Bello and hopes to find a good market for them at the approaching fair. From the E^t Indies we have no ship yett arrivd but two are daily expected. I thank God we are all in pretty good health at present, tho' the N.E^t winds have been very severe for six weeks, and done much mischief both to the fruit and corn; there begins to be a great demand from France for corn, and some ships Ladings are allready bought up for that market. I am afraid your old Servant Capt Cooper of the Townshend packet is lost, between Falmouth and the Corunna; Sam. Buckly and I shall be the greatest sufferers. However amidst these losses and disappointments (which I cant say sett quite so easy upon me as they would have done in my younger days) it will be great comfort to me to hear that your Lord^p enjoys good health in your retirement."

1731, June 9th. N.S., Hon. Charles Compton, British Consul-General in Portugal, to Lord Wilmington. Dated at Lisbon and unaddressed.

" My Lord,—It was no small satisfaction to me . . . . to find that you approved of my Actions in the Affair of the Mediterranean Passes . . . . . . we hear the Bill is past, that was depending in Parliament to make the forging such Passes felony which I hope will put a stop to the Counterfeiting any more. Your Lordship so kindly desires to hear as soon as Mrs Compton is delivered that I am under an indispensable obligation to acquaint you by this first oppertunity that she was brought to bed of a Girl the fourth Instant, and also to return my sincere thanks for the Honour you do us in standing God-Father to this new born Child . . . . . I am with the greatest Respect My Lord, Your Lordships most Dutyfull Nephew & most Obed^t humble Servant   CHA: COMPTON."

1731, July 3rd. Edward Harrison to Lord Townshend.

" My Lord,—I coud not bring my self to trouble you upon the loss of my grandson Dear Neddy [Townshend] having ever since been under a terrible suspence with respect to [his brother] George's safety, till yesterday when to the great comfort of us all the Doctors agreed to pronounce him out of danger. I make no doubt but Ld Lynn has constantly advisd your Lords^p of what has passed, I have not dared to venture into the house, during this calamity, for fear of my daughter [Lady Lynn] . . . . I have not been wanting in making your compliments to Mr Gore. Our last letters from Portobello gave hopes of a good market [for your diamonds] and I wish may go well with Spain till we get clear of them and if they catch me again in their corn I will give them leave to pound me. Till we give them up our annuall ship, and some other useless things we shall never be well with them for a year together " . . . .

1732, Jan. 12th N.S. Hon. Charles Compton to Lord Wilmington. Dated at Lisbon and unaddressed.

. . . . . . " Our chief talk here, is upon the gold and great Quantity of Diamonds the last Rio Fleet hath brought ; on the arrival of which, the King of Portugal under pretence of discovering who had brought Gold in a clandestine manner, seized all the letters that came by it, & ordered them to be opened, which put the People of Business in great fear ; those who had run any gold were ordered to deliver it up or to say to whom it was sold, or go to Prison ; A Method likewise was taken in Relation to Diamonds, all that came in Letters, of which tis said there was a vast quantity, were seized, & the letters after some time sent to the several Persons to whom they belonged. But as there is no Law against importing of Diamonds less severity was used for the discovery of them. By this method the King has got into his own Coffers almost all the Gold that was run, no less than 2880 Pounds Weight & a great part of the Diamonds that came in the Fleet, & it is not yet determined how the Proprietors of either are to be treated. The Penalty of running Gold is very great, Confiscation with Banishment or the Gallies, & the temptation to it is also great, the King's Quinta & Duty of Coinage was before last year upwards of 26 p. Cent., but now by a New Law it is reduced to about 20 p^r Cent. I have by this Post wrote to the Duke of Newcastle more particularly on the affair of Diamonds, & I beg you will give me leave to lay the same thoughts before your Lordship, which are as follows—as the Increase of Diamonds from the Braziles is a growing Trade I conceive the Duty in England upon rough Diamonds may prove in time a disadvantage to the Nation. If a duty was paid only on cut Diamonds imported, it might not be amiss ; but to lay a Duty upon rough stones, the greatest part of which are sent abroad after they are cut seems to be discouraging a trade which leaves a great deal of Profit behind it. The Price of Cutting of Diamonds I am well informed is one with another twenty shillings a Carrat ; a hundred thousand Carrats therefore cut in England, will leave in England a hundred thousand Pounds, & this Quantity from our best advices may at least be reckoned will come yearly from the Brazile Mines. I include not in this Computation Freight & Commission, which are no inconsiderable Articles. While Diamonds came only from India & the Trade were solely or chiefly in our own Hands, there could be no ill Effect in laying a duty upon them, but since the Discovery of other Mines, the Case is quite altered, & it is easy to foresee that People will prefer those Places in Europe, where no Duty is paid, & where there is no Risque of Seizures. England has at present the Reputation of Cutting Diamonds better than any other Nation perhaps it might be right to preserve the Advantage it has gained ; for doubtless in a little time the Number of Diamond Cutters will encrease ;

& if greater Encouragement be given in France, Holland & other Places, it is reasonable to believe that Workmen who follow Encouragement, will soon appear, & who may arrive in time to as great a Perfection as those in England. Besides the Duty on Diamonds is small, and as they are easily run, I am apt to conclude his Majesty reaps very little Benefit from it, nothing I imagine in proportion to the Disadvantage the Continuance of this Duty may prove to the Nation. I have submitted this to his Grace's better Judgement as I do now to your Lordship's, whether the Affair is worth the Consideration of a British Parliament. I cannot conclude without offering Mrs Comptons most humble Duty to your Lordship."

1733, Jan. 21st. John Waple to Lord Townshend. Dated at Symmonds Inn and unaddressed.

. . . . "Mrs. Harrison writes me word that her Broker acquaints her that some small matter might be made of York Stock if so yor Lordship will please to consider whether it may not be advisable to part with it." . . . . .

1733, Sept. 29th. Charles Bridgeman to Lord *Townshend?* Dated in London and unaddressed.

"My Lord,—Just after Your Lordp spoke to me at Hamp[ton] Court on Sunday last, my good Friend & Patron orderd me to desire my Cosin Bridgeman not to engage his Vote, & this was the whole of his order at that time: I was since down with my Cosin at Hartford, & he very kindly promis'd me he would not; While I was with him, he told me that Sr Thos Clark & Your Lordp were in the same intention of nominating a second Candidate [for the borough of Hertford], which I was glad to hear, hoping it was what my Patron meant, but as it was not then certain to me, I could request my Cousin no farther. Yesterday I attended my Patron at Hamp[ton] Cot and acquainted him with what I had done, and likewise that I found Your Lordp & Sr Thomas joyn'd in nominating Mr Braccy [Nathaniel Brassey], he was pleased to say that whatever Your Lordp & Sr Thomas Clark did, he should approve; this I was glad to hear, & it occasions this Letter to Your Lordp, not doubting but the great regard my Cosin has for him & You will induce him to declare his other vote, for the Person You recommend . . .

P.S. I have acquainted him I have wrote to Your Lordp. If there is occasion for a Letter to me please to direct it to my house in Broadstreet near Poland Street S. James's, London."

1733, Nov. 27th. Earl of Gainsborough to Lord Townshend. Dated at Exton and unaddressed.

Asking that "Walgrave, or Symons the late Deputy" to Spencer the Post master at Stamford may be appointed to succeed the latter who has been dismissed for negligence and insolence. "There is a report that one Bletsoe, a Bonesetter, is designed by Lord Lovell [the Post Master General] at ye intercession of Mr Cust, for ye office in case Spencer is remov'd: But if he is put in ye whole Town of Stamford will be in an Uproar, & I shall take it extreamly ill that Cust shd be indulg'd in his Request for a noisy, bullying Fellow, hated by all ye Town, & I be deny'd in mine for one out of 2 Men who have good Characters . .
. . . Mr Goodhall, a Friend of mine, is one prick'd [for sheriff] for this next Year. He realy has not 6 pounds a year in the County, & has begg'd of me to get him excus'd " . . . .

1733, Dec. 24th. Robert Britiffe to the same. Unaddressed.

"My Lord,—I was favoured with your Lordship's & tooke an opportunity to write to Mr Lucass who is concerned for Mr Beagham in his affaires, that he w^d pay the Rents due or else w^d lett Mr Beagham who lives in London know that if the money is not paid within a Month he must expect to meet with trouble upon that omission.

I am a stranger to the Gentelmen in this County or City of Norwich who have a Right to vote for Members of Parliament for the University. I spoke to Capt. Scottowe, who hath a Son ('tho removed from Cambridge) [who] hath a Vote, to send to him & engage him for Mr Townshend & not to engage his second Vote att present, Dr Fowle who is Brother to Commissioner [John] Fowle of the Excise Office, hath a Vote. I spoke to him yesterday—he said he knew six more who he hoped to engage. Mr Townshend had sent to him he told me he had sent two Letters to him & never rec^d any Answer of either, which I find gave him some uneassiness. I shall take care to use my Interest as farr as I can upon this occassion. If L^d W[inchilse]y will not allow his Brother [Mr Edward Finch-Hatton] to declare to joyne or not M^r [Thomas] Townshend sh^d come to some resolution in what manner to act, for I apprehend itt may be difficult to prevaile upon persons to suspend their second Vote.

Itt seemeth to be the opinion of our Freinds that wee stand well in this County 'tho I beleive there never was soe much paines taken upon an Election, or Arts & Insinuations made use of to prevaile upon the Freeholders of all denominations, as hath been used by S^r E[dmand] B[acon] & his Freinds they are indefatigable & no Costs spared, our Freinds are also industriouse, I had Mr Lucass of Shipdham with me yesterday who I have att last brought to declare for us & to give me leave to make use of his name & declare he is soe. I have been several times attempting itt, but c^d not prevaile upon him to declare before. He was with S^r R[obert] W[alpole] when in Norfolke, but I am told gave some hopes that [he] w^d not directly promise. He hath now assured me of his Vote & interest which I hope may bring us att least twenty Votes, wch w^d have been against us. He himself was always in a different Interest. He is an Attorny, but I am satisfyed he hath more than 1000l. per Ann. I begg [you] will excuse the length of this.

Ro: BRITIFFE."

173$\frac{3}{4}$, Jan. 6th. The Hon. Augustus Townshend to "Lord Lynn at his house in Duke Street near St James square London." Dated at Madras.

. . "I have made a very bad Voyage but I hope I have improv'd myself so much as to make it up to me for you no they are both to my own advantage I hope my dear sister is well & all nephews as is

Your most affectionate
Brother
A. TOWNSHEND.'

1734, July 6th. Robert Britiffe to Lord Townshend.

The writer does not approve the deed sent by Mr Amyas for Lord Townshend's purchase from Mr Cotton of an estate at Honingham, but has prepared an Article to answer his Lordship's design.

1734, Oct. 6th. Thomas Minors "To the Right Honble The Lord Lynne at Denham." Dated in London, at the sign of the Vine in Lombard Street.

"My Lord—I think it my Duty humbly to acquaint your Lordship of the Death of Mr [Charles] Shales, who was principally concerned in the Execution of the Office of his Maj^{ties} Goldsmith, to which Office I was admitted & sworn in by Your Lordp^s Appointment : Mr Shales dyed the 5th inst of a Dropsy, and was 73 Years Old. And as by Mr.

Shales Death the Execution of my said Office is devolved wholly upon me in joint partnership with Miss Mary Shales (Mr Shales Daughter) I take this Opportunity till I can have the honour of waiting upon Your Lordship in Person, to beg the Continuance of your Lord^{ps} Protection."

173¾, Jan. 19th.   Thomas Eyre, of the East India Company's Service, to Lord Wilmington. Dated at Fort St David.
. . . . " the General Notion of the former flourishing Condition of Business in the Indies is still so strongly retain'd in England and with so little reason, that the sending a Writer out is reckond a mighty Boon, thô in fact (pardon Sir the freedom of Expression) it is but an Errant Phantasma and he would go barefoot for what he could do for himself without the help of some Patron or Friend to assist him for the few first years of his time here, and it is much the same in proportion to the Degree of the higher Stations " . . . .

1735, Sept. 8th.   Charles Townshend to Lord Lynn. In a child's handwriting.
Dear Papa,
            I hope you are well and my mamma and I hope that Suffolk as agreed with my mamma and you and M^{rs} dinely. I hope we shall have the pleasure of seeing you all down here if you have any time to spare we received a couple of cakes a sunday last pray send us down a suit of cloes for we want some sadly.   I left my grandmamma and my sister and mis wastel in very good health ; pray give my duty to my mamma and thank her and m^{rs} dinely for their kind letters.
                    I am your most
                        obedient son C : Tow :"

1736, April 13th. Sir William Billers to Mrs Harrison "att her house in Cavendish Square." Dated in Cheapside.

To ask, on behalf of Capt. Tolson and himself, that Mrs Harrison will weigh off the next day the Rattans she had sold to them at 45 shillings for two hundred and a half weight wch is computed at 1000 rattans.

173⁶⁄₇, Feb. 24th. Thomas Lowndes to Lord Townshend. Dated at Whitehall.
" My Lord
            Your Lordship may remember when You was Sec^{ry} of State that I carryed through the Carolina contract by your Lord^{ps} Countenance without giving your Lord^p any trouble. For I never once waited upon You.
It is now in my power to shew your Lord^p and the rest of the Noblemen and Gentlemen of Norfolk how to keep your Tenants from being imposed upon by the Butter Factors without laying any restraint upon Trade. What I have to offer is of the greatest Consequence to your own and your Neighbouring Counties ; I mean this as a small return of Gratitude. For I am with the greatest respect " *etc.*

1737, June 9th.   John Amyell to Lord *Townshend* ? Unaddressed.
The writer expects Mr. Branthwayt will perfect certain conveyances when he is in town.

1737, Aug. 2nd.   Edward Weston to Lord Townshend. Dated at Whitehall and unaddressed.
The writer encloses a copy of his letter to Mr. Scottowe and will forward the latter's answer.

MARQUESS
TOWNSHEND
MSS

1737, Nov. 17th. Robert Parker " To The Worshipfull Alderman
Harvey of Norwich." Dated at Comenda Fort on the coast of Guinea.

" S^r—I sende you a sample of Cotton the grouth of this Cuntry, spun
by the Natives on long Powles, as they walke up and down the Fields,
it may be had I believe in considerable quantiteys, I desire the Favour
of you to advise if it may not be useful in some part of your Manufactur
and the just Value of it. An other thing is worth your notice, the large
quantity of Says, Persetts, Long Ells, &c. that comes upon this coast
to severall Thousand pound p Ann, are most of them caried up into
the Cuntry some Thousand some Fifteen Hundred Miles, th'are take a
Peices and unwove, and again made into Cloath of thier own devising,
I purpose if possible to sende you a Sample of the Negroes Ingenuity, if
an Opertunity offers before the Ship sailes, Youll be surprised at an other
thing, that out of a Hundred or a Hundred and Fifty thousand Pounds
worth of Cloaths of all soarts that anually comes upon this Coast, how,
they should be consumed amongst a People that never wears either Cap
Coat or Breches, nor make use of any in their Household Furniture,
all that prodigious Stock of Goods is consumed, except what they take
a peices, as I observed before, in having fine Cloaths of all the different
soarts, about two Ells long wch they weare about their Wasts, and lye in a
Nights, their riches seames to concist in that, some has Ten to Fifteen
apeice of such Cloathes and then the Capushears, as they are called or
properly our Cuntry Justices, they have from Ten to Twenty and some
Fifty to a Hundred and Fifty Wives & Concubines, these must all have
Dashees or Presents of Cloaths, and then their Kings exceeds Solomon, I
wont say in Wisdom, but in Wives & Concubines, and they must be all
supplyed wth Store of fine Cloaths, the demand some time is so great
that if a Ship of a Hundred Tun was loaded, wth what pleases them,
wch I really beleiv might all be furnisht out of your Citty, such a
considerable Loading might, I say at some times be sold off in three or
four Days, and pay'd for in the finest of Gould, or that wch is as good
Eliphants Teeth, without being conserned in Slaves. You would do
well to wright to some Friende in London to get an abstract of Ten or
Twenty Guinea Voyages from the Debentures then youll se what
Species of Goods are usually sent upon this Coast. There is a Vast
Number I know of Chiloas Gingams Cuttances Bombay Stuff Teer-
suckers Cherryderreys Chints Aligars Celampees &c. ; of all East Indey
goods I am verey well assured that most of all these might be either
imitated or some thing in lew [lieu] sent from you to supply the place
wch would set to worke a vast number of Hands, better that our own
Cuntry People should earne moneys that give such incouirgment to the
Chines [Chinese] & Indians.

As I remember when Sr Robert Walpole was at Norwich in 1738 by
an Invitation from your worthy Bodey he made a Speach which was after
printed wherein among other things at the conclusion he assures your
worthy Bodey he will make it his Studey to promote the Trade and
Manufacture of Your Great Citty, I know him to be a Gentlmⁿ of so
much Honour that he onely wanted an Opertunity and now one will
be flung into his Hands, he was so good to me at my first asking
wch was but three days after I landed from Georgia & Carolina in
September was Twelve Munth, to recomende me to be pricipall Agent
at Gambia, the African Directors paid me a great deale of respect upon
that Acc^t and offered me to my Choice either that or Widaw, another
place upon this Coast, but upon inquiry boath them places being
unholsom, and the Comp^y as usuell incisting upon [my] buying up so
much of their Stock wch at that time did not concist wth my Pocket

having layed out severall hundred Pounds in Georgia in erecting Saw
Mills and brought them to great Perfection, wch was as fine Cut as ever
any Wainscott sawn in Holland, samples of wch I sent to Parisburg,
Savana, and Charles Towne and some to the Trustees in London, after
I had brought my Works to that Perfection that the Mills wth a little
addition would have earnt me a Thousand Pound or Twelve Hundred
Pound Sterling p Ann, I was by the Violence of that Government,
drove from my Workes, by three armed boats sent up purposely to
destroy them. I came to England hoping redress from the Trustees,
but to their great Honour and Justice they paid me never a
Farthing, tho Truth of it is I promised the poore deluded People there
to set their Oppressions in a faire Light, as I did, and tould S^r
Robert Walpole at my first interview I would do it at the Hazard
of my Life, these were the reasons why I had not money to purchase
the Comp^y Stock.

If my Thoughts should be approved off then I am perswaded if you
ask Sr Robert Walpole to recomende me to be one of the Principalls
of this place in the roome of Mr Esson deceiced, it may easiley be
dun, it will then put it into my Power effectually to serve you and
take all Opertuniteys of advising you from time to time what may
advantage the true Interest & Trade of the Citty of Norwich, please
to let me have your thoughts, in duplicates for feare of miscariage
directed to me to the Care of my Wife Mrs Eliz. Parker in Lynn."

1738, June 22nd. A. Windham to *Charles* 3rd *Viscount Townshend?*
Dated in " Lester Street" and unaddressed.
. . . . "Madam Woolmoden [Valmoden] is in Pall Mall wth her
Husband, but is at Kensington several hours in the day : She has fine
black eyes, & brown hair, and very well shap'd; not tall, nor low, has
no fine features, but very agreeable in the main. She appears at the
drawing-room like one that has been used to the courts of Princes. It is
not doubted but that she will soon have an Apartm^t at Kensington.

It is not known where Admiral Haddock is gone, whether to the
Straits, or to the W. Indies.

Lord Hardwick has lent Mr Erle of Heydon 16,000^li at 3 & ½ per
cent : and I heard yesterday of a Gentlemen who has borrowed money
on the S[outh] S[ea] Annuity at 2 & ½.

I was on Monday at Ld Bolingbrook's Country House. They ex-
pect^d him there every day : and the News of this day speak of his
coming : tho' I could see no preparation in the Kitchen for it : the
House & Estate is now upon sale : for wch reason I suppose the
Gardens are quite neglected.

Your Lord^ps is scheming so for the good of the Country, that all Norfolk men are full of your praise."

1740, March 26th. Rev. Edward Francklin to Lord Townshend.
Dated at Rainham and unaddressed.
"My Lord—I had answered your Lordship's most kind Letter before
this, but did not return from Wisbech till last Saturday, having been
desired to preach the Assize Sermon at Bedford. And it being
so near Lady Day I was willing to defer writing two posts longer that I
might send your Lordship a Receit in part of a year's Composition,
which I do with the utmost gratitude and thankfulness. Mr Case has
not been yet at leisure to examin with me the Writings relating to
Rainham Livings, but as soon as he can spare a Day I shall be ready.
Your Lordship's Commands with regard to the present Representatives
I shall most diligently and zealously perform, and I hope your Lordship

will not fail of the desired success. I have nothing material to write about the present Opposition being so lately return'd into Norffolk, but only that at Wisbech enquiry has been made for saleable Estates of small value in this County and one is already bought at the price of Fourscore Guineas by a person who is known not to be able of himself to purchase. Whatever I shall be assured of with respect to this Affair that may deserve your Lordship's knowledge I shall take care faithfully to transmitt, and what may lye in my Power in this or any other Way to serve your Lordship I shall take the highest Pleasure in thereby testifying how much I am etc.

Edwd FranckLin.

[P.S.] I hear that Young Mr Horace Walpole is to be joyned with Mr Thomas Townshend for the University of Cambridge next Election."

1740, Nov. 2nd. George Harrison to Lord Townshend. Dated at Balls and unaddressed.

". . . . I am to see Mr Glinister here on Wensday which will enable me to give a more perfect account of his success in obeying your Lordships Comands."

1741, March 27th. Hon. Horatio Townshend to Lord Wilmington. Dated at New Ormond Street and unaddressed.

About the heavy discount on French bills.

1741, May 9th. Sir John Hynde Cotton to *the same?* Dated at Madingley and unaddressed.

Thanking his Lordship for espousing the cause of the writer's son in the Cambridgeshire election.

[P.S.]. . . . . " my Marlbro' Election kept me a few days too long."

1742, April 1st. Lord Lymington *to the same?*

A letter of compliments.

1742, May 22nd. Hon. George Hervey, afterwards Earl of Bristol, to Lady Townshend. Dated at Ickworth and unaddressed.

"Madam,—I am very sorry to find by a letter from Lord Lincoln, that after your Lordship had done me the honor to write to me, the post had done me the favor to loose it together with his, what a disagreeable *miscarriage,* how unkind an *abortion!* I should have thought that these things only cou'd have happened to M^{rs} B——l. Are you not surprized, Madam, how I came to learn these technical words? I heard them but today. Your Ladyship's friend Mrs Eldred has taken no notice of us since we came into the country, yet have we had the honor of two or three Aldermen with their *Ladys & Misses.* I beg if you hear of any Camp there is to be in England, or of any new regiments that are to go abroad, you wou'd be so good as to let me know, for else these are my quarters, & you will find my calculation about my staying in the country too true; for tho' I was told when fir.d I came down, I was only to be here ten days or a fortnight, yet now that time is expired there is no probability of my going to town. Has your Ladyship got your house in the country? I shall grow so rich during my retreat, that if the widow insists on ten additional Guineas, you may draw for it from my Banquers at Bury. May I enquire how Lord John does? It is relatively to you that I am sollicitous about his health, since I remember some very gloomy days in Grosvenor-street on his account. Lord Bristol often drinks your health to me, which is seconded with infinite pleasure by me, my poor *flirtation* is' never included; you accused me Madam, of having a *violent passion,* the fact I own tho' not the person to whom it was

apply'd, it was they who did apply who cou'd lay the chief claim to
that, & to the entire esteem, of Madam
Your Ladyship's
Most obedient humble Servant,
G. HERVEY."

1742, Aug. 12th. Hon. George Compton to the Earl of Northampton. Dated in London and unaddressed.
A business letter.

1742, Augt. 19th. Lord Hervey to Lady Townshend. Dated at
Ickworth Park, and unaddressed.

"Madam—The last Post (the most welcome Messenger that ever
arriv'd at Ickworth) brought me the Honor of your Lady᷎ᵖ Letter; &
tho it is impossible for any Body to be more obliged & pleased than I
was with the Favor of so agreable a Distinction, yet it was no small
Allay to that Pleasure, to feel the Severity, as well as Politeness of
your Reproach, in condescending to thank me for giving, what I ought
to have pay'd my humblest & warmest Acknowledgments to You for
your Indulgence in receiving: since I am very sensible when you allow
the Copy a Place in your House, you confer an Honor upon it, equal to
the Pleasure you give the Original, when you admit him there.   .

If there was a Dearth of Talk (too often mistaken for Conversation)
in the Party you mention, I think a more proper Addition could not
have been made to it, than that you tell me of, since as far as the bare
Evacuation of Words can contribute to make such Partys what they
call *go off well*, I will stand Godfather to all their Lungs, & would as
soon answer for Articulation flowing constantly through the Channels
of those Mouths as I would for Water in the Channel of the Thames.

I am very sorry to hear poor Winnington has in reality been downright ill, & am sure the Symptoms must have been very strong when
your Infidelity on that Chapter could be converted into Faith : but if
I was in his Place I could never forgive your drawing any Parallel between him & the Man with whom you coupled him on this Occasion,
since I think Nature has made as full as great a Difference in the Furniture of the Insides of their Heads, as I dare say the Faces of their
Wives will do in the Ornament of the Outsides.

I had some thoughts once of sending this Letter to my Servants in
London, with Orders to have it smoak'd like a Westphalia-Ham, in a
London Chimney, before it was presented to Your Lady᷎ᵖ, knowing
how little Chance it must have to be well received when you reflect it
is the uncorrected Produce of the intolerable Rusticity that must reign
threescore miles from London ; but upon second Thoughts fearing no
Quarentine would be deemed by Your Lady᷎ᵖ sufficient to purge it of
such a Plague, I laid this Project aside, resolving to lose no time in
assuring you with how much gratitude warmth & Truth I am—
Madam
Your Lady᷎ᵖ's
Most obliged & most obedient
humble Servant
HERVEY."

[No date.] From the same to the same. Dated "Tuesday morning"
and unaddressed.

"Your Lady᷎ᵖ does my Taste great Honor to think it worth consulting in any thing, & a very undeserv'd one if you let it be any
Guide to your's with regard to what I now send back to you. As far
as my Plate-Skill goes I think them very pretty, but as uselessly pretty

as the Face of a virtuous Beauty or the Head of an injudicious Wit. I
call'd at your Door on Sunday Morning but had not the good Fortune
to find you, & by the Equipage I saw at the Door should have fear'd
you were in danger of the Ill·Fortune of going somewhere into the
Country farther than half-Way to Knightsbridge, had I not luckyly
recollected that *One Flesh* may sometimes resemble the double Man
Odmar talks of in the Indian Emperor, when he says *one half lay upon
the Ground, the other ran away :* which half I would have you resemble
I dare not suggest, but firmly believe you will guess right. I am—
Madam   Your Lady⁸ᴾ⁸

Most obedient humble Servant,
HERVEY."

1742, Dec. 14th. A letter addressed to "Hugh Cholmley Esq., at
the Dial House, St. James's Place, London," from certain inhabitants
of Whitby, Yorks. Signed by Joseph Holt, Peter Barker, Miles
Breckon, Alderman Boulby, Thomas Milner, John Yeoman, Robert
Robson, William Coverdale, and John Rymer :—

"Sir—Finding ourselves under a necessity to apply to Parliament for
redress in the unhappy affair of the Bonds entered into by us and many
others with the Crimps to his Majesty for the Duties on Coals at the
Port of London.

Wee take the Freedom to give you the trouble of a Copy of our Petition
on the other side drawn in London and to inform you it has been signed
by Persons concern'd at Yarmouth and Scarbro and by all here and that
it is sent to Sunderland and Newcastle from whence we expect it will
soon be sent up to be presented to the House.

And therefore wee begg leave Sᴿ to desire yⁿˡˡ be pleased to favour
us with your Interest therein, and to excuse this trouble."

1743, Augt. 8th. Lord Townshend to ——. A Draft, unaddressed·
. . . . . . "I find by Mᴿ De Grey's letter that he is in an infirm state
of health." . . . . .

1743, Sept. 3rd. Lord Hobart to Lord *Townshend?* Unaddressed.
The writer will be glad to rent his Lordship's house for a year.

1745, Sept. 1st. Hon. Charles Townshend to Lord Townshend. Dated
at Scarborough and unaddressed.

. . . . "my want of health arises I believe more from natural infirm·
ities than any uneasiness of mind . . . . . but I am convinced I often
suffer illnesses which have no other source, than a constitutional weakness of body."

1746, May 15th. Lord Godolphin to the same. Dated at St. James's.
Giving his Lordship notice to pay in future 4 per cent., instead of
3½ per cent. upon the £7000 he has borrowed for the writer on mortgage, or else to repay the loan on Novᴿ 18ᵗʰ.

"The money above mentioned . . . . vested in me in trust for my Lᵈʸ
Sunderland " . . . . .

1746, July 2nd. O.S. Henry Nisbet to ——. Dated at Terhuyden
Camp and unaddressed.

"Hurry & Confusion which is the Prologue to a Camp hindered me
for informing you sooner of my safe Arrivall in Holland which is of all
countries the most·inhospitable & affords the greater Scope for Sentiment when I consider the species of the people we are to fight for.

Yesterday we were reviewed by our grey headed Marshall [Prince
Charles of Lorraine] who it seems only waited for us to strike his Blow
for we expect to march in a day or two having this day received bread

& forrage for six days. The French have abandon'd Antwerp leaving
four thousand men in the Citadell which some People imagine we shall
besiege, but if I may be allowed to anticipate the Maneuvre of a great
Generall I shou'd think we wou'd goe upon the Maese for two reasons,
first the defleiency of forrage we shou'd find in the Pais reconquis, second
the facility of joining the Austrian reinforcement that has been at Venlo
for some time past.

On the other side you will find an accurate account of our strength
having rode round the whole Army this morning and taken down the
number of Squadrons & Battalions it consists of.

I intend tomorrow to goe to Hogstraten there to see the Pandours &
Hussars. As soon as we join the Imperialists we shall have a Line of
Battle which I will send you of my own Drawing.

My Compliments to all sentimental People. You know how few
they are.—I am.—Y^r aff^{te} Friend &c. &c. &c. &c. &c. &c. &c. &c. &c.
　　　　　　　　　　　　　　　　　　　HEN. NISBET.

	Batts^s 70.			Squad^s 154.	
Austrians -	-	- 30	Austrians -	-	- 70
English -	-	- 04	English -	-	- 09
Han[overian]s	-	- 16	Han^{rs} -	-	- 26
Hessians -	-	- 06	Hessians -	-	- 08
Dutch -	-	- 14	Dutch	-	- 41
	Totall	- 70		Totall	- 154

exclusive of the 20,000 Imperialists."

* 1746, Sept. 30.　General John Campbell (afterwards Duke of Argyll,
to Lady Townshend. Dated at Inverary.

My dear Lady Townshend. It is high time that I should in private
life follow the example of some of His Majesty's rebellious subjects
who have come in and surrender'd to the Royal Mercey hoping forgiveness.

You know that some time after the loss of my late Mistress I put
myself under your wing as my Queen ; as to you my Princess I own but
one crime, that of Omission, yet, to so good, so kind a friend, even that
calls alowd and demands asking pardon and forgiveness, I ask it, I
expect it, and considering (as I think I wrote your Fatt friend and
Neighbour [? Sir Robert Walpole.]--) the Crime carried with it its own
punishment by being so long deprived of a most agreeable Correspondence, I hope for the best.

When I told your Ladyship that I have wrote more for these last ten
Months by-past than any Clerk in Office you'll tell me it is condemning
my self, I deny it, I was not pleasing my self which would not have been
the Case had I been writing to you ; In short since I left London and
arrived in this Country I can not say that I have had one agreeable or
pleasant Moment, Nothing but hurry and anxiety of minde; excessive
fatigue, together with a great deal of bad health. And since I return'd
here from my Island expedition most'ly coufined to the House and so
worn' out that I begin to think of another world, I wish it was Whitehall. But before I leav this, Christian like, I desire once more to be
forgiven by my friends, and doe most frankly forgive my Enemys, I
have t'is true had some revenge off them, and may say that in my Turn
I gave them (as they did me) no small trouble and I think did some
good to the cause I was engag'd in, But I must, I will have done with
my self, but never with you; for in truth I am with the utmost

Sincerity, affection and esteem Dear Lady Townshend's most obedient &c. &c.

JOHN CAMPBELL.

P.S.--I rejoyce with you, pray tell me if Miss Townshend is as handsome as ever after that dangerous but natural operation the small-pox? Is Mr. Townshend as much in love with you as when I left him? and lastly is his father jealous of him? I can't say but I am.

I condole with you for the loss of a friend, make my Complements to those you chuse to see in private at White-Hall particularly Lady Sophia T: and our Missie; tell her I must and will kiss her when meet,—but very gently.

Put Lord Baltimore in mind of me, I love him as I hope he does me, ask him who knows it, If at my first setting out I had not a very pretty Jaunt from Portsmouth by Sea to this Country.

The Expedition I undertook in Quest of the Younger Adventurer. Round and through what is cali'd the long Island (for I visitted, landed, and marcht through most of them as well as the Isle of Skie, to wich place I traced him) is some what curious, You will further tell his Lordship that I look't inn at St Kilda which in the Map is lay'd down to be 20 Leagues to the Westward of the Harris and North Uist, but I think it is not so much. From all which if he is not nervous he can give your Ladyship some notiou of the Navigation. Pray tell him likewise that I was so happy as to meet with a most agreeable Complaisant Commodore who not only enter'd heartily into my Schemes but gave me full powers so as that I was in effect a kind of Lord Admiral.

After communicating to Commodore Smith my Intelligence; what I intended, and that I desired only the Furnace Sloop and a Folkstone Cutter (he had with him) together with the arm'd Wherries I had fitted out before his Arrival. He consented and approved of my Plan, But like himself (a most Judicious Sensible Humane Man) told me·that it was not much out of his way and that he must attend me with two 40 Gun Ships to take care I was not pick't up by a French Privateer, In short he was Zealous and like a father to me, ply'd off and on St Kilda till the Search was made. And gave Orders that any of the 20 Gun Ships I mett at Sea should be at my disposal, and sent me such Provisions as by the Returns from the Sloop and Cutter be found necessary. I mention all these particulars only to shew Lord Baltimore that Sea, and Land Officers who have nothing but the Service at Heart may be brought to agree; And I must further observe that there was not a Captain or Commander upon this Station that made the least Difficulty in taking their Orders from me.

Having forgott myself, fancying I was talking to you this P^t S^t has swel'd beyond the Bounds of a letter, so that I must have done—and leav it to another opportunity off giving you and his Lordship some further Account of this last forementioned Expedition in which I had very near succeeded. As a proof of which I hereto add what Captain O'Niel who was taken prisoner by one of my Parties and sent to the Earl of Abermarle setts forth in His Declaration or rather Examination, I have it under his own hand and you shall see it. "The Prince [Charles Edward] and O'Neil went to the Hills and stay'd there all night, after which we heard that General Campbell was at Bernera so that wee were then surrounded with Forcess and was at a loss what to do, Wee mett a Younge Lady one Miss [Flora] McDonald. Captn O'Neil advised the Younge Lady to assist the P. in making his Escape to the Isle of Skie, which she at first refused, but by Force of Argu-

ments and telling her that the Prince should be in Women's Dress she
at last consented; she parted with us and desired we should stay at
Corrodale till we should hear from her, which we did for two Days
without hearing from our Younge Ladye; this made the P. very uneasy
thinking she could not performe her promise, so that at last he
determin'd to send O'Neil to General Campbell to let him know he
would surrender himself Prisoner, But while in this thought a Message
came from the Younge Lady desiring us to come to the Point of
Rusnith [Roseneath] where she would wait [for] us."

The Younge Lady, the Lady Clanronald and all concern'd in the
escape are sent Prisoners to London. I can not but say I have a great
deal of Compassion for the Younge Lady, she told me that she would
have in like manner assisted me or any one in Distress. Adieu Adieu
Dear Lady Townshend.

My Comp⁸ to the lively Mʳ Townshend.

If your Ladyship has any Commands for me to direct to Edinburgh.

You have spoild [my son] Frederick he gives himself airs and won't
write to me, I have some thoughts of forbidding him White-Hall as a
punishment."

1747, June 5th. Jasper Bull to Lord Townshend. Dated at the
New River Office and unaddressed.

Mentions Lord Townshend's dividends on a half share : Xmas 1745,
£50. 11ˢ.; Midsʳ 1746, £52. 11ˢ.; Xmas 1746, £47. 11ˢ.; and Midsʳ
1747, £65. 3ˢ. 7ᵈ.

1747, June 16th. Horatio Walpole to the same. Dated at the
Cockpitt and unaddressed.

. . . " I learn by other good accounts that the compromise in choosing
Mʳ Armine [Woodhouse] & your son [George—to represent Norfolk in
Parliament] will certainly take place . . . . . I sett out for Woolterton
on Fryday early, & purpose if my infirmity will permitt, to be there on
Sunday.

The Parliament certainly breaks up tomorrow, will be dissolved by
Proclamation, and the Writs will bear teste on Monday next."   ·

1748, June 2nd. Hon. Charles Townshend to Lord Townshend
Dated in Jermyn Street.

. . . . " The illness of which I complained in my last, is entirely removed . . . . . I congratulate you upon the revolution in the corporation
of the Fens & upon the change of measures which the Duke of
Bedford has declared shall follow from it. Lord Duplin tells me has
not only turned out the old officers, but that he has openly professt a
design of amicably & resolutely carrying into execution that plan for
the interest of all partys which you and others have been so long
contending for . . . . Roger is in great health and desires me to
present his duty to you. My love waits upon my sister."

This letter bears an endorsement " This Letter is dated the 2 July
1748 it ought to have been dated June the 2ᵈ 1748.—My son Charles'
letter to me."

1748, [June] 19th. The same to the same. Dated " Sunday the 19th
1748 " and endorsed " This letter was wrote in the summer 1748."

" I am sorry I can not begin this letter with a report of the Bishop of
Salisbury's answer to your Solicitation [on my behalf] . . . .

Since I wrote last I saw Mʳ Bacon who heard the same account from
Lᵈ Dupplin that I gave you of the late changes of administration in the
Fens . . . . .

I have hitherto been kept in London or rather from my journey to Scarboro' by Solicitations from Yarmo[uth] for Mr Morton & others, which are material on account of the persons desiring them . . . . in the next week I shall set forth . . . . . I have been to see Sr W. Calvert, my Uncle Tho : Townshend, Mr Cornwallis, Mr Pointz & my Aunt Molly at their several houses in the country . . . . .

I have lodged in Craven Street since I left your house because I was not willing to hire new lodgings for so short a time " . . . .

1748, July 15th, N.S. Hon. George Townshend to the same. Dated at Endhoven.

. . . . . " however dissadvantageously my presence has stolen by under the shade of Silence & the Cloud of Awe, yet that I am known enough to you to bid myself assert, & to persuade myself I shall be behind when I do myself the Justice to assure your Lordship that no Son whose Interest whose success in every View, & whose opportunity of gratifying every Desire depended entirely on the Duration of his Fathers days, ever felt a deeper concern, or a more fearful alarm at an incertitude of what was so worldly essential to him, than I did from the contents of your Lordships letter . . . . . Such my Lord is my just concern at your illness. . . . .

[P.S.] Our Army is now in Cantonment & the Duke is to set out for England in a few days it is not determined who is to attend him as yet."

1748, [July] 17th. Hon. Charles Townshend to the same.. Dated at Scarborough " Sunday the 17th 1748."

. . . . . . " though it is a great while since I set out it is but a few days since I came here. Upon trial I found myself unable to bear the fatigue of a long stage & a journey of three hundred miles by short stages is a work of time . . . . . . there is another reason why I should be willing in particular to accept at this time a seat at the Board of Trade. Your present allowance to me is a very large one, larger not only than what I as your younger son could have asked, but than perhaps you can out of your encumbered estate conveniently pay & therefore I could wish to give you relief by receiving a creditable post as a Lord of Trade from the Government. . . . . . I do not know how this would suit with the interest to be kept up at Yarmo' which certainly a seat at the Admiralty would strengthen & establish immoveably. . . . . . . Mr Pelham is just returned from his tour & if you approve it I will write to him." . . . . .

1748, July 17th. Rev. William Samuel Powell to the same. Dated at " St John's College " and unaddressed.

Endorsed by Lord Townshend " Mr Powell's letter to me about the Election of a Chancellor at Cambridge."

The writer promises to promote the Duke of Newcastle's election to the Chancellorship in succession to the Duke of Somerset who is thought to be dying.

1748, July 26th, N.S. Hon. George Townshend to the same. Unaddressed. Dated at Eindhoven and endorsed by Lord Townshend My Son George's letter to me.—Recd on the 20th July 1748 O.S."

. . . . . . " It is certain here that H.R.H. the Duke will soon set out for England but what day or who he will take with him remains still a most profound & impenetrable Secret . . . . . . Our Army is here in the most perfect State of Inaction, the Beauty, Address, Discipline & Spirit of our Troops is really a most maloncholy object when such are unsuccessfull and are so unfortunate as to be oblig'd to give up such a

Cause. The other day we used to inly ruminate the Enemy's irresistable Superiority, an[d] now the greatest Part inly rumirate the reduction
the Nation will soon be oblig'd to make, and in one day discharge a
number of Men from her Service that no other Nation in Europe would
be glad to engage & entertain in a time of the most settled Tranquillity"

[P.S.] I hope my Sister [Audrey] is well & [my brother] the Captain
[Roger Townshend] when you heard from him, my love to them both."

1748, July 31st. Hon. Charles Townshend to the same. Unaddressed.
. . . . . "I hear Ld Anson succeeds to Ld Monson's office & his removal makes a vacancy at another board . . . . . my love waits upon
my sister."

1748, Augt. 16th, N.S. Hon. George Townshend to the same. Unaddressed, dated at Eindhoven.
The writer hopes to have the honour of attending H.R.H. [the Duke
of Cumberland] to England & begs leave to draw on Messrs Child by
next post for his " Quateridge " [or his allowance].
[P.S.] " I have received from Norfolk theCompliments & Invitation of
the Gentlemen of the Constitution [club] Feast for the 1st of August. I
hope they have given you the same Notice on this occasion that the
Feast may have been attended with Rainham Venison." . . . . .

1748, [August] 19th. Hon. Charles Townshend to the same. Dated
" Friday the 19th 1748," and endorsed by Lord Townshend :—" Mem.
This letter wrote about the latter end of the summer."

1748, Sept. 2nd. Sir Thomas Hare to the same. Dated at Stow near
Downham. Endorsed by Lord Townshend :—" Sir Thos Hares letter
to me about Denver-Sluice and our Sute depending thereon."

1748, Sept. 13th, N.S. Hon. George Townshend to the same. Dated
at Eindhoven.
. . . . . . " not being one of those who had the honour of being named
to attend his Royal Highness & being assured on the contrary that his
Royal Highness would not stay above a fortnight : I thought it better
not to apply for Leave of Absence. . . . . . In case the Duke should
stay in England longer than expected or his Return be defer'd
for any time I shall not fail of waiting on you as I shall upon such
Information imediately apply for Leave. . . . . . .
I am sorry I cannot enliven my letter with some sort of News, so
supinely is every thing abroad 'involved either in dull Inaction or
impenetrable secrecy."

1748, Sept. 17th. Hon. Charles Townshend to the same. Dated in
Carey Street.
The writer has been staying in the town to press the claims on the
Treasury of some of his Yarmouth constituents.
. . . . . . " Dr Dyom will be with you in some part of this month, but
at present he is in Derbyshire. Dr Hardinge thinks me the better for
Scarbro' but as my appetite is less than ever it was, I doubt whether I
have made any advance towards general health . . . . . . [my brother]
Roger is at Hampton Court, & when I have said this I have said all I
know of him for he has never been here since I came, and writing letters
is not his custom." . . . . . .

1748, Sept. 26th. Copy of a long letter from Lord Townshend to his
son George explaining how Child and Co. had come to return his
Draft for Quarterage.

1748, Sept. 28th. Draft in Lord Townshend's handwriting of a letter asking Colonel Dusy [Ducie?] to give his son Roger (who is Ensign in the first Regiment of Guards) a month or six weeks leave. He has been with his regiment eight or nine months and his age is between 17 and 18 years.

1748, Oct. 1st, N.S. Hon. George Townshend to Lord Townshend. Dated at Eindhoven.

The writer is astonished at Mr Child protesting his Draft for £200. It concludes: " I find myself too much concern'd to say anything that can entertain your Lordship at present & therefore will take my leave with my usual declaration & which no Circumstances can ever alter that I am with the greatest respect

Your Lordships most Dutifull Son."

1748, Oct. 10th. Copy of a letter from Lord Townshend to his son George. Dated at Rainham.

About the returned Draft.

1748, Oct. 15th, N.S. Hon. George Townshend to Lord Townshend. Dated at Eindhoven.

. . . . " I shall only thank you for the candid & paternal manner in which you have review'd the whole affair & for the immediate redress you have given it. I propose waiting on you in Norfolk within a few days after I arrive in England. I am afraid the Service of Parliament will be such as will afford but little pretence for my absence being call'd a neglect of my Duty to my Country. His Royal Highness [the Duke of Cumberland] likes the Greyhounds I gave him so much that he has desired me to secure him another brace not very nearly allied to the former that he may be able to secure the breed for Windsor." . . . . .

1748, Oct. 15th, O.S. Draft of Letter from Lord Townshend to his son George, urging him most strongly to visit his constituents as soon as he arrives in England " as he ought to do if he desires to be ever chosen again by the County."

1748, Nov. 2nd. Hon. Charles Townshend to the same. Dated in Craven Street.

" Dear my Lord,
. . . When I came here I found many letters of notice from my friends whom Mr Pellham had desired to advise me of his intention to give me the seconding [of] our address, but I came too late & lost the opportunity in despite of his endeavors who delayed naming any other person until Sunday night when Mr Cha: Yorke was appointed. Mr Pellham told me on Tuesday how sorry he was this had happened & added he was the more sorry as my appearance on this occasion would have given him an opportunity of honourably mentioning me to the King, who would have been by this means prepared to grant readily what Mr Pellham said he every day thought of asking for me . . . . . Mr Stanhope is now dying & I am confident I should have succeeded him if I had been concerned on Tuesday last. Mr Pelham hinted this to me, & I am sure he is impatient to serve me " . . . . .

1748, Nov. 5th. Hon. George Townshend to the same. Unaddressed. Dated at Eindhoven. Minuted by Lord Townshend. " My son George to me Rec^d on the 31st Oct. 1748, O.S."

Assuring his father that he will proceed to Rainham immediately he arrives in England, and begging him to dismiss one of the grooms he has sent with three horses to Rainham.

1748, Nov. 9th. Sir Edmund Bacon to the same. Dated at Garboldisham and unaddressed. Endorsed " Sr Edmund Bacon's Letter concerning Stibbard & Guist Comons."

The writer, who claims to possess a right of Freewarren at Ryburgh and Guist granted by Edward the Second and confirmed by Henry the Eighth and Queen Elizabeth, complains that trespassers have sheltered themselves by giving out that Lord Townshend will protect them.

1748, Nov. 14th. Copy of Lord Townshend's answer to the last.

1748, Nov. 19th. Sir Edmund Bacon to Lord Townshend. Dated at Garboldesham, and unaddressed.

The writer offers to dine with his Lordship on Friday next, and will have great satisfaction if matters may then be accommodated.

1748, Nov. 29th. Hon. George Townshend to the same, at Rainham. Dated in Craven Street.

As I have now gone through the Ceremony of waiting on the Royal Family & kissing hands, attended this day the Opening of Parliament & voted his Majesty an address of Thanks for his Speech . . . . I shall wait on you in the Country immediately . . . . . my brother Charles was this Evening taken very ill . . . . Doctor Harding . . . . . hopes he will soon be better . . . . . my Brother was in such Pain that when I arrived he could utter but very little " . . . . .

1748, Dec. 2nd. Copy of Lord Townshend's answer to the last. From Rainham.

1748, Dec. 3rd. Copy of a letter from Lord Townshend to his son Charles, from Rainham. A letter giving advice, and expressing regrets that Mr Pelham had been so unfortunately disappointed in his kind intentions.

1748, Dec. 5th. Copy of a letter from Lord Townshend to his brother Horatio acquainting him that he is sending him the horse called White Stocking.

1748, Dec. 6th. Horatio Walpole to Lord Townshend. Dated at the Cockpitt and unaddressed.

About the interest on a £3000 Mortgage (due to the writer's daughter Mary) with reference to the bankruptcy of Lord Townshend's agent Mr Sutton.

1748, Dec. 8th. George Townshend to the same, at Rainham. Dated in Craven Street.

. . . . " We have no News in Town worth sending you, the attention of the Political Part is chiefly engaged on the Northumberland Election which is to be heard at the Bar of the House. Mr Allgood opposes much personal Merit & behaviour in the late perilous times with as it is said a good Cause against Lord Ossulstone the Court Member & a great reluctance is expected on some part of the Court Members to support him " . . . . .

1748, Dec. 8th. Hon. Charles Townshend to the same. Dated in Leicester Street and unaddressed.

" Dear my Lord.

. . . . I have asked Mr Pelham for the vacant seat in the Admiralty but he tells me he can not promise it to me, that he will mention me among the Candidates to the King & say that it is **your request** that I may have it. S^r P[eter] Warren insists upon it & I believe will be complied with. As I am not only not advantageously known, but not even personaly to his Majesty it is little likely I shall have his preference " . . . . .

1748, Dec. 9th.   The same to the same, at Rainham.   Dated in Leicester Street.

The writer has seen Mr Pelham who, holds out no hope of his obtaining the desired preferment and was not much pleased with his Lordship's letter.

1748, Dec. 10th.   Copy of Lord Townshend's answer to Horatio Walpole's letter of Decr 6th about Mr Sutton's becoming a Bankrupt.

Dec. 14th, 1748.   Copy of a letter from Lord Townshend to the Duke of Newcastle.

Congratulating his Grace on his return to England and begging him to use his influence on behalf of the writer's son Charles that the latter may be appointed to the vacancy at the Board of Admiralty caused by the death of Mr Stanhope.

1748, Dec. 14th.   Robert Masters to Lord Townshend.   Unaddressed, dated at Benet College.   [Corpus Christi College, Cambridge].

" I am just now return'd from the election of the Duke of Newcastle our Chancellor, whereupon I beg leave to congratulate y^r Lordship as bearing so near a relation to him . . . . . The Master of Peter house died here the night before last, & 'tis confidently said will be succeeded in that preferment by Dr Keene . . . Mr Greene of St Johns, & Mr Younge of Trinity our Publick Orator, are talkt of as Candidates for the Regius Professorship but which or whether either will succeed in his application [I] cannot speak with any degree of certainty " . . . . .

1748, Dec. 15th.   Horatio Walpole to the same.   Dated at the Cockpitt and unaddressed.

Endorsed by Lord Townshend " Horatio Walpole's Letter to me acquainting me of his being satisfyed of my paying the Interest due on his Daughter['s] Mortgage to Mr Sutton his Agent."

1748, Dec. 16th.   Copy of Lord Townshend's answer to his son George's letter of Decr 8th.

The writer urges his son to do little favours for Norfolk people in order to increase his popularity with the small freeholders.

1748, Dec. 17th.   " Copy of Lord Townshend's letter to John Sharpe Esq. about Mr Sutton's being a Bankrupt and his Desire to have his Deeds placed in other hands."

1748, Dec. 21st.   The Duke of Newcastle to the same.   Dated at Newcastle House.

" My dear Lord

    I had the honor of Your Lordships letter, relating to the late Vacancy in the Admiralty, & had before acquainted Mr Townshend, as my Brother had done also, that it would not be possible to serve him upon that Occasion, & indeed the King was then resolved to give it to Mr Villiers, which he has since done.   Your Lordship may be assured that my Brother & I shall be extreamly glad to shew our Regard, to One so very deserving in himself, & so very nearly related to us, as Your Lordships Son ; I am very sensible of Your Goodness & Inclination towards us, & shall do every thing on my Part to deserve the Continuance of it, being with great Truth, my Dear Lord, Your most affect humble.

                                                    Servant
                                            HOLLES NEWCASTLE.

1748, Dec. 22nd. John Sharpe to the same at Rainham. Endorsed "Mr Sharpe's letter in answer to mine about my Title Deeds which are in Sutton's Hands."

1748, Dec. 27th. Hon. George Townshend to the same. Dated in Craven Street and unaddressed.

"I should have been with your Lordship before in the Country if my Brother Charles had not had a very severe relapse just when he proposed to set out . . . . Mr George Selwyn I hear intends to wait on you with us in consequence of your Invitation . . . .

We have no News in Town except that one of our Transports with a great Number of Invalids & thirty four Officers is gone to the Bottom but I hope we shall hear it still contradicted.

The Northumberland Election is at last given up by the Ministry, the Iniquity of the Sheriff in Lord Ossulston's behalf having been too flagrant to admit of his Conduct appearing before y^r House."

1748, Dec. 29th. Draft of a letter from Lord Townshend to his son Charles, begging the latter not to come down to Rainham.

1749, May 3rd. John Noyes to Lord Townshend, in Albemarle Street. Dated at Gray's Inn.

The writer is informed that the half of a King's Share in the New River Company will be extremely well sold at £3000, and that it is thought £2750 is more likely to be offered for it.

1749, May 30th. Thomas Nuthall to the same. Dated at Crosby Square and unaddressed.

"I wrote to your Lordship by the Penny Post last night, that I had agreed for the sale of your [half] Share of the New River Cop^y. £2801 was the price " . . . .

1749, Oct. 7th. D. Rushworth to the same. Dated at the County Hospital Northampton and unaddressed.

An application for a contribution towards the support of the Charity.

1749, Nov. 10th. Charles Hardinge to the same. Dated at Buxton and unaddressed.

"My honoured Lord

. . . . The D[uke] of Devonshire's memory is not exact as to the pedigree of Miss Belvoir, & the Confederate Filly, but he says they are both as famous & as high-bred, as any Mares in England. The D[uke] of Rutland has promis'd me the pedigree of Miss Belvoir, & I shall see him soon. Fleece'em is the finest Horse I ever saw. Black-Legs is dead : As to your Lordships desire not to be stinted in the Number of Mares, I will answer for it you shall find no difficulty . . . As for Sir F[rancis] Drake's Mare, I find he has been ofer'd 150 for her & therefor I have said nothing to him upon that head " . . . .

1750, July 4th. Invitation from the Constitution Club at Norwich to Lord Townshend, begging him to accept the enclosed ticket for their Feast. Signed by the Stewards, T. Hardingham, C. Newman and Ja. Scott.

An engraved ticket for a Constitution Feast at the Kings Arms on a later date, viz. August 1st, 1755, filled in for " The R^t Hon. Lord Viscount Townshend " now accompanies this letter.

1750, July 5th. Michael Houghton to Lord Townshend. Dated at Dalham.

With reference to the letting of a farm.

1750, July 8th. Samuel Arnull to the same. Dated at Newmarket.
. . . . "young Ebony is not ariv'd hear yet. Mr Pitt desird me to give his Duty to your Lordship & to let your Lordship know that young Ebony shoul go 3 or 4 days in a close of his which has very good Rowin in it . . . . Mr Pitts close is 4 acers & better & has a house to put the mare & foal in if requird " . . . .

1750, July 13th. The same to the same. Dated at Newmarket.
"Last night I Rec'd your Lordships of the 9th which I should a had sooner but was then at Peterborough to ride a Mare of my Lords which was 2nd out of 6. Mr Crofts mare woon. She was out of a Childers mare & got by my Lords Arabian. Ebony is this day arivd with hur filly at her foot safe at this Place & are both well " . . . . .

1750, Dec. 12th. John Sharpe to the same.
Informing his Lordship Mr Hood the clerk to Mr Sutton's Commission of Bankruptcy has found all his deeds and is ready to deliver them to Mr Child or his Lordship and the mortgagees.

1748, May 8th. Augustus Hervey, afterwards Earl of Bristol, to Lady Townshend. Dated on board the "Phœnix in Vado-Bay," and unaddressed.
" Tho' I have never receiv'd one line from D[ea]r Lady Townshend since I left England, yet I cannot help writing one now by Capⁿ Foulks who has the Adm^l's Leave for three Months, & who has been abroad with me the whole time of my being out : he will tell you how well Jemmie is that I have taken him into this ship with me, & shall take all the Care of him in my power. The Sea has given him an opportunity to practise his wild Spirit, & tho' a little endanger'd by the Heat of our warm Climate, yet all is well again ; he is forgiv'n on promises of future reserve ; The young Dog got ashore when I was up at Turin, & *went astray.*

Pray now let me ask you (for I know you are sincere) what has prevented your writing to me after promising—was it that you had promis'd or was it that you heard of my Success and at once imagin'd I became Worldly ? If either, permitt me to say you are to blame, I'm sure Mr Selwyn will agree with me, & Mr Hume will condemn you. I have wrote three or four letters to you, and am heartily sorry if you have never had them ; I'm sure you'll repent of not having wrote to me, when I tell you that except [from] my Mother, I have receiv'd no letter from any Relation ; I have [had] only one from my Uncle Aston ever since I have been out of England.

I shall referr to Capt Foulks all Particulars concerning myself & be content with telling you, that if 'tis Peace, I hope not to see England [for] some time, as I'm in a Ship that I flatter myself will be station'd here.

You cannot expect to hear any News from me ; and to tell your Ladyship the Truth I'm at a loss for a Style at present, least if I write in my usual one to you I shou'd offend, because I have not had the Satisfaction since I have been out to hear your approbation ; for which reason I had better be quick in assuring you that this is only for an opportunity of convincing you that Nothing can prevent my ever remaining—Your Ladyships—Most faithfull & Obed^t humble serv^t.
A. HERVEY."

[No date]. The same to same. Written at " Portsmouth Tuesday Morning," and unaddressed.
" Tis probable D[ea]r Lady Townshend that you may have flatter'd yourself my being out of Town wou'd prevent your being troubled with

me longer, but you see I'm as incapable of refraining from this kind of proxy Visit when absent, as I am solicitous of ever being with you in person when possible. I own this miserable Situation I'm now in, better qualifies me for a correspondent of yours than was I induced to be one of the World from the imaginarry pleasures of a gayer place: The People here I think are rather more fit to converse with than any where else, for they railly appear too ignorant to be knaves: yet with all this *Temptation*, I'm inclined to wish myself among the *Wise Great* again. The D[uke] of Hambleton is here, very ill; on my Arrival I went to see him, as I was in a *Sea Port Town*, I thought myself nearer my *home* than he c^d [be], & therefore was in hopes to be of service to him, in getting his People and things on b[oar]d for him; but I found he had alter'd his Intentions of going by sea to Lisbon; he so is weak, he can't undertake the Voyage for fear of his Stomach, having been twice taken with very severe Vomitting of Blood—they say he can't (poor Man) live many days longer; No Wonder! for the Instant he recovers a little, he drinks 'till four, five, & six in the Morning. I'm going to live aboard for the Time I am here, how long it will be before I can ask [for leave] I know not. for my Ship is not yet quite ready for the Dock; tho' I hope I shall be able to meet Mr Townshend, & methinks I w^d not desire to be happy while he is otherwise; had I a probability of ever being so. No, I have learn't to love him from Character, & my soul shall sympathize with his; It has been charm'd, when perhaps his was in raptures; why should it not mourn, now his is in Sorrow. Yes, believe me if I cou'd alleviate the Pains he now feels, by taking a share to myself, I wou'd support my additional Burthen without a groan. Adieu I imagine I must have tir'd you; I wish you'd endeavour if 'twere possible you cou'd me, by reading your sentiments. God bless you, here are impertinent people coming in on Bussiness & I can only beg you to be assur'd that I am not capable of saying I was, if I was not most sincerely.—Y^r faithfull affectionate & Obed^t Sert

A: HERVEY.

[P.S. Please direct]. To *me* Command^r of the Princessa at Ports-mouth."

1751, Oct. 9th. Lord Townshend to Henry Pelham. Draft in the handwriting of Lord Townshend. Dated at Rainham. Unsigned and unaddressed. Endorsed "Copy of My Letter to Mr Pelham."

"Sir—It gave me no small concern when I had the honor of waiting on you last, to find that the request I then took the liberty of offering to you surprized you in the manner you were pleased to say it did. It is now 30 years since I first came into Parliament, and the request I made to you that I might be allowed to have a share in the subscription for Ann[uitie]s and Lottery, in case there should be one granted for next year, is the first of this kind I ever made to you or to any Minister since I have been in Parliament. You know, Sir, for how very small a part of the 30 years I have held any place from the Court and if, under these circumstances, I did ask for a larger share in the subscription than may be usually given to every particular person who has the good fortune to be favoured by you, I really do not see why you should be so much astonish'd at my request, as you seem'd to be.

If many Persons who have raised large fortunes by the indulgence they have mett with in being permitted to advance their money to the Public on all occasions have been admitted into such subscriptions upon all occasions of this kind to such a degree as has entitled them to a quantity of Tickets from every subscription little inferior to what I have desired at this time, can it be thought any presumption in me who have never in the course of 30 years, troubled any Ministry with any sollicitations of this kind, to express my hopes that I might be favor'd for only one year with a number of Tickets perhaps a little larger than what has been allow'd to them or to some of them, as often as they have subscribed ?

I have been credibly inform'd by Persons speaking upon authority which cannot be doubtfull in this case that a Merchant in the City was allow'd to subscribe in his own name 100,000*l.* in this last subscription for Ann[uitie]s and Lottery, this sum entitled him to 3333 Lottery tickets.

If the near relation which I have the honor to bear to you, the desire I have (for reasons perhaps not entirely unknown to you) of being able to do something for my family, the obligations which you are so kind as to profess you have to my Father, incline you to show to me any degree of favor beyond the instance I have given, I shall be obliged to you for it ; if not I beg leave to remind you of the promise you lately made me that I should have leave to make such a subscription as shall produce a quantity of Tickets equal to the highest number which shall be allow'd to any other particular person whatsoever.

I trouble you with this letter as I have found from experience that when I wait upon you I can never have an opportunity of speaking my whole mind to you without interruption.

I am with great Respect and Regard—Sir—Your most Dutifull and affectionate humble servant."

1752, March 12th. Josiah Tucker (afterwards Dean of Gloucester) to Lord Townshend. Dated at Bristol and unaddressed. It was probably sent under a cover addressed to the Author of 'National Thoughts.'

"S^r—I was in London when You did me the Honor to send your *National Thoughts*, wch came in two Covers, neither of them *Franked ;* W^{ch} Omission I very readily impute to ye Carelessness of yor Bookseller. Your Sentiments as to ye Connection between Morals & Commerce are entirely the same with my own ; And I have always looked upon ye Notion, that *Commerce is founded in Luxury*, to be a very fatal Mistake. The true Foundation of *National, Extensive,* & *lasting* Commerce are such *Artificial* Wants as are either *virtuous* in themselves, or at least not inconsistent with Virtue ; And every Deviation from this Rule promotes Commerce in the Body Politic no otherwise than as a Fever may be said to promote the Circulation of ye Blood in the Body Natural.

I find ye present deplorable State of our Poor, in the Consequences of wch all Ranks & Degrees must necessarily be involved, is come to such an height as to put several eminent & worthy Persons to think seriously of a Remedy :—But without pretending to ye Spirit of Prophecy, or depreciating any Scheme that has been offered, I will venture to foretell, That no effectual Cure can be had for ye Evil, till ye Common People are excluded from their present Influence in the Business of Elections. And let us suppose ye best Schemes imaginable & ye best guarded, they will immediately degenerate in our present Circumstances into *Electioneering Jobbs*. Indeed all Parties will exclaim agst each other for doing such bad things, but all will do ye very same in their Turns. And ye only Cure of ye Evil, is ye Removing of ye Temptation.

You have considered ye Case of ye Bounty upon Corn with great Exactness. But . . . . . ye Exportation of Corn is not so encouraging a Trade as is commonly imagin'd; And there is scarce a Merchant who hath followed it for ten years together, but complains that he has lost money. And indeed there is some Reason; for it is a kind of Lottery, in wch there are a few Prizes & many Blanks

. . . . .

As to ye Manufacture of Spirituous Liquors, We all see ye Inconveniences arising from ye excessive Use of them in these Kingdoms, but we seem to think, that no Harm ensues from ye Exportation of them to our Customers abroad. Whereas in my humble Opinion, whatever is pernicious to our Customers, will in ye end be detrimental to Ourselves. And ye Havock, wch Rum hath made among ye Indians on ye Continent of America, is a melancholly Proof of this Observation. But, indeed we do export considerable Quantities of home made Spirituous Liquors to Africa, & other Places; And cheap enough;—An eminent Merch^t of this Place assuring me, that he can get any Quantity from Worcester to be delivered at Bristol from 14^d to 15^d p Gall : the Duty being drawn back.

Thus, S^r, I have ventured to give my Thoughts with that Openness & Freedom, wch yor Goodness will excuse, as considering it to proceed from an upright Intention. If I have not been sufficiently reserved in my Stile & Application to You, the Ignorance of yor Quality must be my Excuse. And I remain," etc.

1752, April 2nd. Lord Townshend to Rev. Josiah Tucker. Copy. Dated at Grosvenor Street, and endorsed "Copy of my Answer to Mr Tucker's letter Dated April 2^d 1752." 5 pp.

" Sir—Not long since a letter from you was left at my house by a Porter inclosed under Cover directed to me by another hand. I had great pleasure in reading it and was still more pleased when I considered that it gave me some pretensions to trouble you with one, and to express my hopes that I may have the satisfaction of seeing you when you shall be up in Town again. Your Remarks on *National Thoughts* are made with great Candor. That Pamphlet was, I believe, wrote & printed in a very great hurry to answer a particular view just at the time when it was published; and I have good reason to believe that the Appendix was drawn up in great haste after the Pamphlet was sent to the Press. If this be the case, it is not a matter of surprise that what is offer'd in that short appendix, upon a Point of so extensive a nature as that of the Bounty on Corn is, should not carry that clearness in Proof which every one might expect and has a right to demand before he does give up a general receiv'd opinion which he has embraced, and more especially upon a point where as a Landowner he is greatly interested. Tho' I cannot within the compass of a letter pretend to demonstrate to you how great the Damages are which do arise to the Nation and to the Farmer in particular from the Bounty which is allowed on Corn, yet I do beg leave to say that I think that the truth of this Proposition may be demonstrated as clearly as any Proposition in Euclid . . . .

I know from the reason of things and from information that there is no Nation in Europe which has or can grow Corn so cheap as England has done for some years past. But I must deny the consequence drawn from hence that therefore you should allow a Bounty for exportation. For it is an absurd piece of extravagance, pardon the expression, to allow a Bounty to export what will find a Vent without it and the Bounty in this and all cases (if the exporter does sell the Corn abroad proportionally cheaper on that account, which perhaps is but seldom the case) must have this bad effect of enabling foreign Countries to feed their Manufacturers and Labourers of all kinds at a cheaper rate with our own produce than we can feed our own. A great deal more may be said on this subject which I must now omitt . . . . . . But give me leave before I conclude to say in answer to yours that if I could be satisfy'd that the abolishing the manufacture of Spirituous Liquors in England would put a stop to the manufacture of those Liquors in all Countries, I should readily agree to have the manufacture of them totally stopt here. But as I think our Debauchery of this kind would in such case be supported by foreign liquors intirely, we should under such a Regulation not only loose our people['s] but give great encouragement to a foreign manufacture, and consequently be the sooner ruin'd . . . . . One word more to another Point. It is my Opinion that if we could be so happy as to break through the Custom of Annual S[essio]ns of P[arliamen]t we should soon find that *Electioneering Jobbs* ond *Jobbs of all kinds* would be less frequent. My meaning is that there should always be a P[arliamen]t existing in the Kingdom but that it should not meet in time of Peace oftener than once in 3 years. I would not have a law to fix this but the Commons in time of peace should grant supplies for 3 years. Excuse the trouble I give you here and favour me when you come to London with an Opportunity of explaining my self more clearly and fully than I can do in a letter, which I have wrote in some hurry, my time being now and having been for some time past pretty much taken up with business.—I am—Y^r most Obedient Servt."

1752, April 5th. Rev. Josiah Tucker to Lord Townsend. Dated at Bristol.

"My Lord—This Morning I had ye Honour to receive a L^r from your Lordship; for wch I think myself obliged to make a speedy Acknowledgment in ye most humble Manner. Your Lordship's Goodness is very great, & deserves my particular Thanks for overlooking some expressions in my Letter, not sufficiently respectful to a Person of yor Rank & Station. I really did not know, Who was concerned in *National Thoughts*, & therefore wrote to Mr Doddesley the Publisher, to request him to direct my Letter to ye Author, & send it to him: And your Lordship has been pleased not only to accept ye Sincerity of my Intention, but to honour me with a most obliging & instructive Letter.

Tho', my Lord, I cannot yet see all things precisely in the same light that you do, I begin to make some Approaches towards it; & find, that as to ye general Plan & fundamental Principles of Commerce I am so happy as to have my Sentim^{ts} approved of by yor Lordship in every particular. And I wish every Land Owner in G. Britain thought of Commerce, ye Increase of People, & of their Industry and Morals in ye Manner Your Lordship hath so justly recommended to them, & joyned in vigorous Resolutions of destroying Monopolies, exclusive Privileges, Companies, & Preemptions of every kind: For most undoubtedly all these are prejudicial to ye time, National, Landed Interest. If we had greater Numbers of People, ye Question about ye Expediency of a Bounty upon Corn wo^d cease of course, because there wo^d be a sufficient Price in our own Markets. But as ye Case stands at present, I wo^d not, for my own Part, take away the Bounty from ye Exporter all at once, but lessen it by Degrees, & at ye same time encourage the Encrease of our People by proper Laws, & a well founded Police.

In *National Thoughts* I observe all ye Schemes offered, are of y^e *preventive kind;* that is, they are rather calculated to remove ye Temptation, than to punish ye Crime. This is beyond Dispute, ye best Method upon every Acct, & ye thing ye most wanted of all others in these Kingdoms. In short I cannot help declaring my Opinion to your

Lordship, That tho I believe our Laws in general are as good as most
of our Neighbours, our *Police* is ye most defective, & ye worst calculated
to prevent ye Subject from transgressing ye Laws, of any in Europe :
Indeed we are multiplying Temptations, & laying new Baits of Pleasure
every Day, & then make a Wonder, that our People are grown so
abandoned & debauched.

Your Lordship is pleased to observe, that Farming is a Species of
Manufacture ;—I think so too ; And am so pleased with ye Idea, that I
beg leave to make ye following Remark :—Farming is not only a Manufacture, but ye most important, & requires as much *Skill & Application*
to make a Figure in it, as any Trade whatever. And yet ye Art of
Farming has been surprisingly improved within these last few Years :
tho no Persons were obliged to serve a regular Apprenticeship to this
Business ; why therefore sho^d there be any Apprenticeships served to
other Trade, wch are confessedly more easily attainable & of less Consequence to ye Publick ? . . . . .

I most humbly thank your Lordship for your kind Invitation wch I
shall embrace with Pleasure when I come up to Town. This will
probably be ye next Winter, if I can finish a Task wch is now set me ;
viz. To write a Treatise upon ye Principles of Commerce for ye Use
of ye Prince of Wales, & to be entitled, *The Elements of Commerce &
Theory of Taxes.* If your Lordship has minuted down any Thoughts
having a Tendency to these Subjects, I hope your Lordship will pardon
the Presumption, if I desire to be honoured with a Sight of them.
And I remain, with very great Esteem and due Respects. . . . .
                                     JOSIAH TUCKER."

1752, April 13th. Lord Townshend to the Rev. Mr Tucker. Copy.
5¾ pp.
     This letter is a closely reasoned argument against Corn Bounties ; it
concludes :—
     " One would think from the general cry of people that Corn is a drug,
and that therefore it is impossible to find a foreign Markett for it, and
that it cannot all be consumed at home. We must lower our Rents,
Tennants cannot pay their Rents, they will be undone and such like
exclamations from all Landlords as well as Tenants ; I say that when I
hear all this I conclude that the general sentiments of people are, that
the poverty of a Nation is created by plenty, and vice versâ that the
Wealth of a Nation consists in its having a scarcity of every thing, that
when Corn is in plenty here there is less profitt gott by sending it
abroad than when it is scarce at home . . . . . For my part I
think that the Wealth of a Nation consists in being provided with plenty
of every thing. I think that England is at present in a very unnatural
State, Money is cheap and every thing else is dear. This situation she
is brought into by the many absurd Laws we have, and it is the most
dangerous situation that any trading Nation can be in. And I fear
that unless some of these Laws be repealed that we shall soon see a
decline of Trade. This observation on our present state added to that
of the melancholly state of the lower class of People was the occasion of
the attempt I made this last winter to draw up a Bill for opening the
course of Industry, a Copy of which I herewith have taken the freedom
of sending to you inclosed under two other different Covers ; and I hope
you will excuse its not being a fair one. If you shall find it worth your
notice I should be glad to hear your thoughts upon it. I am satisfyed
I have tired you as well as myself with this letter. I must therefore
take my leave of you and will with your approbation trouble you on

some other occasion with what I did intend now to have offered to you relating to our Poor Laws and upon the subject of our Taxes."

1752, April 22nd. Rev. Josiah Tucker to Lord Townshend. Dated at Bristol and unaddressed.

. . . . . . "Your Lordship has been extremely obliging & condescending, I sincerely thank You for it: But I beg leave to express my Obligations more particularly for having my Prejudices removed by y^r Lordship's kind Instruction. You have sufficiently convinced me that Bounties cannot be of any *National* Service to a Manufacture wch is passed its Infancy. . . . . . . If ye Nation was eased of this Expence, the Savings might be applied to making up the Deficiencies in certain Branches of ye Revenue, wch I hope will be occasioned one Day or other, by a Repeal of these absurd Laws, wch pay a Tax upon Raw Materials, & other Articles necessary for carrying on a Manufacture. . . . . . . It seems a Land Carrier may carry Coals to what Distances he pleases, without paying any Tax ; But a Carrier by Sea must pay a Duty from one Port to another ; And this too in a Country whose Glory it is to be a Maritime Power. And to complete ye Absurdity, this Coal wch is taxed if used in ye carrying on any of our own Manufacturers, shall be sent to all our Rivals to be used by them Duty free. . . . . . .

I am mightily pleased with yor Lordship's general Remarks, & manner of accounting for People's frequent & gross Mistakes in ye Affairs of Commerce : It certainly is as yor Lordship observes, by arguing from Particulars to Generals ; whereas in this Case a Man sho^d form to himself a General Plan drawn from ye Properties of Commerce, & then descend to particulars & Individuals, & observe whether they are co-operating with ye general Interest : Unless he doth this, he studies Trade only as a Monopolist, & doth more Hurt than Good to the Community.

When Your Lordship is at Leisure I shall be very glad to be favoured with yor Thoughts on Taxes ; And from what I have seen already, I promise to myself much Advantage & Instruction. It seems to me, that ye Affair of Taxes may be compared to the Pruning of a Tree ; wch if done with Judgm^t, will make ye Tree grow ye better . . . . . certain it is that a judicious Application of Taxes to check ye Follies & prune away the Excressences of High Life, & prevent ye Idleness, Dissoluteness, & Intemperance of the Poor, is so beneficial to Commerce that it may be much questioned whether ye whole of Trade doth not derive all its Motions from it. If Ale & Strong Beer were at 1^d a Quart, all our Manufactures would be ruined.

I rejoyce greatly to find that yor Lordship has taken in hand ye Repeal of ye 5th of Q. Elizabeth, [cap.   ]   May you prosper in it.

Our Manufacturers in this Part of ye World are all ready to petition for ye Opening of ye Turky & Hudsons Bay Trade ; And wo^d soon appear with proper Representations, if they had any Person of Weight & Spirit to head them in Parliam^t. I beg pardon, my Lord for this very long & tedious Letter."

1752, May 5th. Horatio Walpole to Lord Townshend. Dated at the Cockpit.

"My dear Lord,—If this finds your L^{rdp} in the Country, & you have leisure enough to look into your late father's Political papers, I should be glad to have a sight of those letters that he wrote & received while he was Ambassador in Holland in the late Queen Ann's reign, because I have under my Consideration, some Posthumous Works of the late Lord Bolingbroke, & the sight of your father's papers might be of Service to sett in a true light, the false & scandalous misrepresentations of the transactions in wch Lord Townshend had been greatly concerned. You will excuse this Liberty & believe me ever to be with the greatest respect."

1752, May 6th. Lord Townshend to the Rev. Josiah Tucker. Rough Draft, dated at Rainham.

Sir—I came to this place on Friday last when I rec^d your most obliging letter of the 22^d last Inst.

The Bill I sent to you was drawn out pritty early in the last Session, but not before the House of Commons were actually enter'd upon the consideration of various Schemes for forming new Regulations in the poor Laws ; and as I then found that the Ministry endeavour'd all in their power to prevent any matters being offer'd to Parliament which might protract the Sessions and disappoint His Maj^{ty} in his intentions of setting out for Hanover in this Spring, I chose rather to lay the Bill aside for the next Sessions, when the hurry which appear'd in this would not exist and people might, as I thought, possibly be better inclined to give it some degree of consideration when offer'd at a time of more leisure.

The earnest desire I have to see this point brought before Parliament may move me to present this Bill, thô I do not think my selfe in any degree well qualifyed for such a task and I wish I may be so fortunate before the time comes as to prevail on a more able Person to present this or some other Bill of the like purport. You need not give your self the trouble to send back the copy I sent you, but let me have the additional clauses you propose. And when you come to Town we may consider the whole together.

I happen'd one morning long before I troubled you with National Thoughts, to shew the Bill to an acquaintance of mine, who is a Member of the House of Commons and our Conversation turning afterwards on Trade, he recommended to me your *Reflections on the Expediency of a Law for the Naturalization of Foreign Protestants* which I soon afterwards sent for. I thought it the best Pamphlet I ever read and I sent several copies to Norwich, Lynn and to different parts of Norfolk and Suffolk.

In my enquiries for this Pamphlet I mett with your Essay on Trade published in the year 1750 which I must confess was likewise new to me. From this work I found that your general maxims *of Trade* are good and pure, & that your knowledge in all the Branches of Trade is very extensive & far beyond mine . . . . .

I agree with you entirely in your general plan of Trade, that all Companies, and exclusive Priviledges ought to be abolish'd. All Monopolies in every shape are destructive to the Trade and good order of the Community. I think as far as I have been able to consider it that your Essay on Trade is a most masterly performance . . . . . . But I do not agree with you in what you propose for regulating the Poor or in your Courts of Guardians, nor can I be of opinion that a Militia can under any supposed circuumstances be tolerable in a *trading* and *free* Nation.

You will wonder, but it is very true, that I had not seen or even heard of S^r M[athew D[ecker']s Essay on the causes and Decline of the Foreign Trade till I found it quoted in your Essay. I have since got it and have dipp'd into it, though I have not had time to read it through regularly. I like it much. The general maxims are good but he sometimes mistrusts their guidance in the application to particular cases . . . . He desires very truely that where Trade and Industry are left open and free to their natural courses labor will be cheap and that the price of manufactures are determined cheifly by the price of labor. That in the woollen manufactory the price of the manufacture to that of the material, wool, is as 3 to 1. That a Bounty on exported wool thô absurd and destructive hurts that manufactury only, but that a Bounty on Corn, as it supplys the Foreigner with our Corn at a cheaper rate than an Englishman can have it, makes his labor cheaper than the Englishman's and consequently enables him to underwork is in *every manufacture*. Notwithstanding all this sound Doctrine he proposes to form Companies and to erect Magazines of Corn in every County for the management of our Corn. A most surprizing absurdity and inconsistency !

If Trade and Industry and all our Ports were thrown open, and all Duties, Prohibitions, Bounties, and Monopolies of every kind whatsoever were taken of[f] and destroy'd as you have very judiciously proposed, you would, I am perswaded, soon find that private Traders here would erect Warehouses for Corn as they have done for other manufactures and we should then have them on a reg[ular] and natural footing and this Island would then be, as Holland has been, the great market of Europe for Corn. But as long as the Bounty remains this cannot be . . . . . if Trade and all matters relative to it were put on your Plan money and every thing would be in great plenty and very cheap and the nation would be rich and powerfull. And could I be [so] happy as to see your Plan establish'd I should not be alarm'd if I heard that the King of France was chosen King of the Romans. All Europe must bow to England when in such a Situation.

Your Remark on the Regulation of the Duty on Coals give me new information . . . . I did not know that this Tax was so absurdly circumstanced as you inform me in your letter, and your observations upon it are very just.

I agree with you in every observation you have made in your letter upon our Laws of Trade but I cannot agree to what your neighbour the Merchant asserts that we do export great quantities of spirituous liquors to Africa and diverse other Countries. He is mistaken, we do not export any Spirituous Liquors to any part of the Globe but to the Coast of Africa and no great quantities go thither . . . .

You seem to think that if the Bounty on Corn was taken of[f] and Trade in general put on the Plan you have recommended that Ale & strong Beer would be sold at 1d. a Quart. I really cannot see how it is possible to suppose that Ale and strong Beer should fall to that price or to any price near that.

Your general plan would promote a general spirit of Industry and must in consequence in its operation reform the morals of the poor; when the poor are allow'd the priviledge of making use of their senses they will not be so inclinable to drown'd them as they now are in the lazy idle way of Life in which our Laws oblige them to live. Lay aside the custom of annual Sessions of Parliament and the general disposition of the rich will be reform'd. But no further on this Head . . . . . .

P.S. I am glad to hear that the manufacturers in the West begin to see their own interest and I wish them encouragement and success in their present desire. If you approve of it I will try if I can find out one of the House of Commons who may disposed to head them."

1752, June 1st. Rev. Josiah Tucker to Lord Townshend. Dated at Bristol and unaddressed.

. . . . . . " I find you fix upon that Method of raising Taxes, wch is mentioned in ye Essay on Trade p. 148, 149. And indeed I do give my opinion now, as I have done it there, that it is so much ye best, & very

practicable ; And now were once our **Taxes** put upon that Footing, I do
agree with yor Lordship, we need not care, who is Emperor of Germany or K. of France. Our Finances wo^d then be upon a right Foundation, all Trade free, & Ports open : And ye whole Édifice of
Governm^t might be compared to a stately Structure where ye nicest
Proportion was observed, & where all ye Parts mutually strengthen each
other . . . . . .

The Plan of ye Treatise I am now upon is as follows :

1. I consider in a Preliminary Dissertation y^e *Commercial* nature of
Man as arising from two distinct Principles, & different kind of Wants,
viz. *Self Love & Social Love ; Animal Wants & Social Wants*. And
as ye Entranc in o Society multiplies all our Wants, & Self Love is
much the strongest Principle in Human Nature ; hence I infer ; that
every Man is naturally a Monopolist . . . . . .

If I do not tire Yo^r Lordship I wo^d add one subject more : M^r
Addison in his Travels speaking of the Rep[ublick] of Lucca, has the
following remarkable Observations :—

" It is very pleasant to see how the small Territories of this little
Republick are cultivated to the best Advantage ; so that one cannot find
the least Spot of Ground, that is not made to contribute to the Owner.—
This Republick is shut up in the Great Duke's Dominions &c." Here
My Lord, You see all ye Disadvantages of Situation ; not one Sea-Port,
or Navigable River : And yet all the Proofs & Symptoms of a flourishing
Commerce. Is it possible therefore to get some Insight into the Police
& Regulations in this Republick for an Encrease of People—Preserva-
of Good Morals—Free Trade—Sufficiency of Current Coin—and judi-
tious Taxes ? If a proper Information co^d be procured of the Particulars
perhaps some Use might be made of it in an Application to ourselves ; And we might learn what the Size of Hercules wo^d be, by
Measuring his Foot.—I am, *etc.*

JOSIAH TUCKER."

1752, July 2nd. "To the Honorabill Lord Townshend att His House
in Grovner square—London—this "

Honrabil my Lord—I hombely beag your Lordships pardon for tro-
billing your Lordship with any thing of this kind but I have bin Lame
this 2 years of ye Roumits as thay call it & have had all most all
the Doctars in London & have bin in hige parke Hosptel but got
no Good & thay all say as nothing will do me any Good but y^e
Bath & there I can not goo for I have nothing to go with. God
hellp me for it hase cost me above 3 scouer pounds all wrady .
. . . . but as my Housband was an olld sarvant to
your Lordship & I had ye Honer to sarve your Lordship some time till
wee mariyed & both sarved your Lordship soberly & honistly but I had
ye misforting in maring your man Bing[a]men Higgins that is all y^e
offence I hope wee ever did as I no of & I hope & dont dout that your
Honer will be so charatibell & good as to besto something of a poor
lame cripill for if I can not git to go to Bath I will to ye Dockter Ward
. . . . I must gitt to goo som whear or to ye parish if I dont
git my Lims—My Good & Hornabill Lord I shall for ever pray for
your Lordship & am your Dutifull & obedent & Houmbill sarvant

GRACE HIGGINS.

I log att Mr Brook's in Lankister Courte next Door to ye French
Horne in new Bond Street Grovner Squear. I must gitt out of town
for cheapnes."

1752, July 13th. Rev. Josiah Tucker to Lord Townshend. Dated at Bristol and unaddressed.

My Lord—Yesterday's Post brought me a most obliging Letter from yor Lordship. . . .

I am to set out ye 20 for Wales, in order to take Possession of a small inconsiderable Prebend in the Church of St Davids; but shall hasten back with all possible Expedition, & hope to be in Bristol again by the beginning of August, to throw myself at your Lordship's feet. If you come here by ye 3^d or 4th; I flatter myself that nothing but inevitable Accidents will prevent me from writing to you. And I have ye greater Desire of doing it, as I hope to improve by ye Honour of your Conversation in many particulars, of wch at present I very much doubt my own Judgment :—Only as to ye Bounty on Corn I make no scruple to declare that I am entirely convinced by yor Lordship's Arguments ; And if ever my Pamphlet on Naturalization sho^d have a second Edition, I shall be very glad to let ye World know, to whom I am obliged for that Emendation. If Your Lordship will please to admit me as yor Disciple, I hope to make up in Docility what I may want in Judgment.

I find by ye daily Papers, that there is a subscription of Noblemen & Gentlemen all over England for the *Preservation of ye Game.*—I have no Objection agst such a Design : But, my Lord, you are ye only Nobleman I can find, who expresses any Concern for the *Preservation of Trade ;* An Object certainly as well worthy ye Attention of Persons of Birth, Rank, & Fortune, as Hares and Partridges.

I send a duplicate of this Letter to yor Lordship's House in Town, least ye present sho^d miscarry.

JOSIAH TUCKER."

1752, Augt. 17th. William Gale to the same. From Chippenham. Returning thanks for a book, and sending compliments.

1752, Sept. 18th. Earl of Orford to the same. Unaddressed. Dated "Tuesday Sep. 18th," and endorsed in Lord Townshend's handwriting "1752—Sepr the 18th Ld Orford's letter to me."

" My Lord—As there has been a Subscription set on foot for yearly Races at Swaffham, and it seems to be the Sence of the Gentlemen of the County in general that such a Meeting is wanting, I should be much obliged to your Lordship if you would show your Approbation of it, by giving me leave to set you down as a Subscriber. As your Lordship has formerly been a Friend to the Turf elsewhere, I flatter myself you will not be unwilling to encourage it in your own County, and that you will excuse the liberty of this Application from—My Lord—Your Lordships—Most Obedient humble Servantt

ORFORD."

1752, Nov. 27th. Augustus Hervey to Lady Townshend. Dated at Genoa and unaddressed.

" This is the third letter I have wrote to your Lady^{sp} since I have been abroad; & I must repeat my usual complaint of never hearing from you—tho' I must own it has been y^r former kind Indulgence that has only intitled me to expect it now—As to George [Townshend] I look upon him as a Man burried in the Matrimonial Sepulchar & till he is wak'd out of his Tomb by the Squalling of half a dozen Bratts expect to know no more of him : But I confess (let me vent myself by chideing) I did not imagine Lady Townshend wou'd so shortly forget one of her Chimney Corner party. Your Lady^{sp} has a thousand subjects to write of that you know are interresting to me — your own Well fare, George's (toute ingrate qu'il est), in short write of *Die Junké*

any thing that relates to you & recals the many hours you have permitted me to pass away at Whitehall. For my Part unless I could
send you a Month's Sun or a Basket of Fruit, I know of nothing in
this Country that would give you a moment's pleasure or amusement.
For unlike our Lady *Caroline's*, our Lady this, our Lady that, our
Miss this, our Miss that, the Women are all so poor that their outsides are no better adorn'd than the Insides of the Men; they are as
dirty & as Frippery as their Gallants are vain & ignorant, & the
Commerce of the one as little desirable for want of a right Pride; as
that of the other is from a wrong one. There is nothing more common
in Italy than to see a great Princess who will return a Visit to no Lady
of an inferior Title, stroling round the Streets for amusement & in a
continued Conversation wth her own Footmen who to facilitate this
entertainment walk on each side of her Coach, holding by the Doors.
They play for Half-pence wth the utmost Avidity; & he that will be
cheated of three & six pence never fails of going away wth the Reputation
of being the most gallant man of the Company. I was delighted wth
a thing say'd the other day by one of their own Countrymen w^{ch}
putt their understandings in a light equally true & ridiculous. The
Italian Women (say's he) are such Fools that if three of them
are gott together; tis possible that one may say 2 & 2 makes 4,
another that 2 & 2 make 5, & whilst the dispute grows warm, the
third shall be embarrass'd wch to decide for. The Men are not in
a Form, one Degree higher : they are too proud to seek or suffer
the Company of their inferiors; too jealous to be pleased with that
of their equals; & too ignorant to be able to bear their own. However
I have had the good Fortune to meet wth two or three here who both
know 'tis possible to communicate one's Ideas in other Languages besides
Italian, & have a notion of there being inhabited Country's beyond the
Alps; two Branches of knowledge that few Gentlemen or Ladies on
this Side of them arrive at. I pass a good deal of my time wth them &
wth more pleasure than I have done any part of it since I left Lisbon.
Indeed I have been ill with a Pleurisie, & therefore bad Health, or bad
Objects, I dont know w^{ch}, or perhaps both, have quite cured me of
flirting; 'tis so long (tell Lady Caroline) since I have seen so spruce a
Toylet as hers, that I have hardly the Idea of one; and if I venture
ever again to accost a fine Lady, I believe it will be blushing, stuttering,
twisting my Thumbs, & so much in the style of Sr Willfull Witwood,
that if the Lady refused *to fetch a Walk* I should be extreamly puzzled
for a second Question to putt to her; & in much greater Confusion to
ask her the last Favour, than any Woman in France or Italy I believe
ever felt in granting it. Your Lady^{sp} wont credit this change perhaps;
& I wish I did not feel it, but I am absolutely an old Fellow. I rejoice
in basking in the sun; every Limb is a Barometre, & foretells Rains,
Winds, Snows &c.—I begin to tell storys of what I was; pretend to
despise Pleasures I am past taking; rail at Wine because I drink none
(nor have not since I left England) condemn gaming because I have no
spare Money to play; & like the Dog in the Manger stare at every
charitable Gentlewoman, that throws her oats to these Animals who
are glad to eat them; tho' perhaps like most other reformers my only
quarrel to the Banquet, is not being bidden or not having an Appetite.
Now Dear Madam after what I have acknowledged myself dwindled
into; 'twill be impudence to expect y^r Lady^{sp} will allow such a
Creature much of y^r time; but 'till I come to a pair of Spectacles, a
news-paper, and a Pipe, & confining my whole Conversation to Virtue &
Vice wthout having a view to either in my Conduct I flatter myself now
& then you'll hear me relate extraordinary things over a Cup of M^r

MARQUESS
TOWNSHEND
MSS.

Johnson's good Chocolate in a Morning; & when Mrs French or Lord Waldegrave's ingaged sometimes allow me to make a fourth in an Evening at Whist: & whatever changes you may discover in my *Person*, *Parts*, or *Conversation* there is one wch I'll venture to assure y^r Lady^{sp} you will never find, wch is my being otherwise than—Madam—Your most faithfull Oblig'd & Obed^t Servt

A. HERVEY.

Forgive my having made as many Blotts as lines but I have not time to write it over again. I am going to a very great Ball & Feast, & the Post will be gone too early in the Morning for me. I beg a thousand kind things to George & respectfull ones to Lady Ferrers—for *all the rest* speak of me (as Othello says) as I am—nothing extenuate."

1753, Jan. 20th. Lord Townshend to his son Charles Townshend. Rough draft ; unsigned.

" Dear Charles—I was most extremely concerned and surprised upon reading the contents of the letter your servant brought to me on Wednesday last. I am thoroughly sensible from what I have experienced from your constant and uniform conduct towards me that nothing I can offer on this occasion to dissuade you from your present scheme will or can have any effect. But give me leave to remind you that if your income in your present situation is so strait and severe as you represent what a melancholy situation must you and your Lady be in if you marry with the additional income of only £700 per ar^{um} at the most. The reversionary expectations which as you say attend the Lady's fortune are not as you truely observe objects to a person in your situation. Advice from me is never agreeable to you nor would you ever throughout the whole course of your life hitherto attend to it so that I shall not detain you long even on this occasion.

I am indeed very sorry to hear that you have enter'd upon such a scheme and project as this is, but it is your own and I will have nothing to do with it.

I am equally surprised to find that you call on me to make up the fortune of this match. It is not in my power to advance anything on any such like occasion; nor were it in my power would it be in my disposition to make any advance upon a match which cannot be made suitable to your present circumstances. I desire therefore that I may hear no more of this, and am determined to give no further answer about it.

I am with best wishes for your prosperity

Yours most affec^{tly}.

1753, March 12th. W. Bowyer to Lord Townshend.

" My Lord—That you may not think I have been remiss in executing your Commands, I beg leave to inform your Lordship that I proposed to the Public Advertiser to insert an Advertisement of the Letter on Industry as published in the Gazetteer. But I was rejected as one that offered at an Absurdity. We could sooner lay open all Privileges of the City than break through such a Punctilio.

I take the Freedom underneath to draw up the Clause of the Act in the Sense I understood your Lordship. I have forgot the very words otherwise I would have adhered more closely to them.—I am, my Lord —y^r Lordship's most dutiful & obed^t humble Servt

W. BOWYER."

-[At foot] " AND be it enacted by the Authority aforesaid that all Persons whatever shall be at Liberty to use, exercise & follow any mannal Labour, Art, Mistery or Occupation now used & exercised, or which shall be hereafter used and exercised in any Parish, Precinct, Hamlet, Borough, Town or City Corporate throughout England and Wales and Berwick upon Tweed, any Law or Custom to the contrary notwithstanding. SAVING nevertheless to all Bodies Corporate all such other Rights, Privileges, & Immunities as they now respectively enjoy.

Or if a PROVISO is more approved of,

PROVIDED always that this Act shall not extend to prejudice or infringe any other Rights, Privileges or Immunities which the several Bodies Corporate throughout England, Wales, and Berwick upon Tweed do now respectively enjoy."

[1753, March.] Rev. Josiah Tucker to the same. Undated and unaddressed. Endorsed by Lord Townshend "Answd on the 17ᵗʰ March 1753."

"My Lord—I am just returned from a Set of honest Merchants, true Friends to Trade. They have some intentions of printing off a 1,000 Letters of last Tuesday's Gazetteer, to disperse about, but have a Scruple whether they can justify it, without yᵉ Leave of yᵉ Author. Now as I imagine the Author may be known to Your Lordship, I hope you will pardon this Application for Consent. It is a pity, so excellent a Peice was not put into every Man's hand in yᵉ Kingdom. The Post is just setting out; I am, my Lord, with due Thanks for all Favours—Yoʳ Lordships ever obliged—and most humble—Servant

JOSIAH TUCKER.

P.S. [My] Humble Respects wait on Mʳ Townshend."

1753, May 5th. John Watkin to Lord Townshend. From Yelvertoft. Asking for his Lordship's influence to procure him the appointment of Steward to Sir Jacob Astley at Hillmorton.

1753, Dec. 6th. Hambleton Custance (Sheriff of Norfolk) to George Townshend, M.P. for the County of Norfolk. Dated at Norwich and addressed "To the Honᵇˡᵉ George Townshend, Esqʳᵉ—Member of Parliament—in South Audley Street—Westminster."

"Sir—It is with great Concern that I am obliged to give you any Trouble on this or any other Occasion, but I find myself necessitated to request your good offices with Mʳ Pelham and the other Lords of the Treasury in my Behalf, on account of another unlucky Escape of the Smuglers &c. from the Castle: The manner by which it was effected you will find by the enclosed wᶜʰ is an Abstract of a Letter to me from the Deputy Sheriff, & in wᶜʰ you will observe that two of the five Smuglers are retaken. I beg leave to assure you that nothing shall be wanting on my part for the Recovery of the rest, having sent out proper Persons to every part of the Coasts of this and the neighbouring County. I am with the utmost Respect—Dʳ Sir—Your most faithfull & obedᵗ humble Servᵗ   HAMBLETON CUSTANCE.

1753, Dec. 26th. Rev. Robert Potter to ———, From Reymerston.
. . . When first I married [my stepfather] Mʳ Colman persuaded me to entrust him with £340 (my wife's money) promising to give me security for it " etc.

1754, Oct. 5th. Copy of a letter from Lord Townshend to the Rev. Philip Yonge, D.D., Master of Jesus College, Cambridge. Dated at Rainham, and endorsed by Lord Townshend " Copy of my letter to the Vice-Chancellor of the University of Cambridge."

" Sir—Having observed that several public Exercises have been lately instituted in your University with premiums annexed to them for the improvement of Education by the advancement of Knowledge, and that among these provisions no incouragement is given for the Study of the Theory of Trade, I take the liberty of desiring to know from you, Sir, whether it will be agreeable to the University if rewards of the same nature with those lately granted in the other branches of learning should be given for the promotion of this.

It is unnecessary for me to point out the infinite advantage which would result to the Public if young men could be led early in Life to a diligent Study and correct knowledge of a Science so very important in it self and so intimately connected with the affairs and Interests of this Kingdom as the subject of Trade is ; nor have I any view in making this Proposal but to express in part the gratefull sense I have of the many obligations which my Family have received from the University of Cambridge by an Institution which I should hope they would approve of, as it is but one step more in the System lately began, and as I am confident that, if it be accepted and strictly pursued, it will contribute to the honour of the University and the solid advantage of the Country. I am—Sir—Your most obedient humble servant   [TOWNSHEND.]

1754, Oct. 6th. Rev. Dr. Yonge to Lord Townshend. Dated at Cambridge, and endorsed "The Vice Chancellor's letter to me dated Oct. 6, 1754 in answer to mine of the fifth Instant."

"My Lord—I have just now rec^d the honour of your Lordship's letter, & will take an early opportunity of communicating it to the Heads of Colleges. Your Lordship's great attention to the publick good is as conspicuous in your generous offer as your regard to this University, which can never do enough to repay the obligations it owes to your Lordship's Family.—I am, my Lord—Your Lordship's—most obed^t humble sert   P. YONGE."

1754, Oct. 12th. Duke of Newcastle, Chancellor of the University of Cambridge, to the same. Dated at Claremont.

"My Lord—I am very much obliged to your Lordship for your very kind letter, and for your proposal to encourage in our University the Study of Trade, & Commerce, which is certainly of such infinite Advantage to this Country. I expect to see the Vice Chancellor soon, and will then consider with him, how to proceed, and in what manner your Lordship's views for promoting that scheme, may be best answer'd, & your kind Intentions take Effect. In the meantime, allow me to assure you, that Nothing shall be wanting on my part, which may contribute to the Success of such an useful Design, & I beg leave in the Name of the University also to return you my Thanks. I am with the greatest Truth & Respect—my Dear Lord—your Lordship's—most obed. Humble Servant   HOLLES NEWCASTLE.

1754, Oct. 14th. Horatio Walpole to Lord Townshend. Dated at Wolterton, and unaddressed.

"My Lord—I took the liberty some time since to ask the favour of Your Lrdp to communicate to me your late father's letters & papers as ambassador & Secretary of State, being employed in spending my Leisure hours to vindicate the administration in wch his Lrdp was concerned from the false & injurious calumny of the late Lrd Bolingbroke's posthumous works. I have gone so far as [to] what relates to the negotiations in 1709 & 1710, in wch Your father was Ambassador & Plenip^{ry} signing with the D. of Marlborough ; and his papers relative to that transaction in wch he had so great a share would be of great use to me in making my work more perfect & correct ; the communication of them for wch I will give

you a receipt, & faithfully return them to Your L^{rd}p again, will extreamly
oblige him who is with the greatest respect—My Lord—Your L^{rd}ps—
Most obed^t & most humble Servant.   H. WALPOLE.

The Rough Draft of Lord Townshend's reply to this letter is dated
at Rainham Octr the 19th 1754, and runs as follows :—

" Sir—My Father did during his retirement here in the Country in the
latter part of his Life determine to write a History of his own times ;
which he had entered upon, and thô he died soon after, yet as he had
resolved rather to take the trouble on himself of drawing up this Historical account than to leave it to any other hand, I think that he has
by such his resolution plainly signifyed to me his inclination and desire
that these papers which he has left in my custody should not be perused
or made use of by any other hand. I should otherwise have been glad
to have complyed with your request and am with the greatest Regard—
Sir—Your most obed^t humble Servant "

1754, Oct. 17th. Rev. Dr. Yonge to Lord Townshend. Dated at
Cambridge and unaddressed. Endorsed " The Vice Chancellors letter
to me dated Oct. 17 1754. Rec^d on Saturday the 19th of Octr 1754."

" My Lord—At a meeting of the Heads [of Colleges] on tuesday last
I communicated to them your Lordship's letter to me, and I have their
commands to return your Lordship their thanks, and to assure your
Lordship of their desire to promote all kinds of knowledge in the
University. That of the Theory of Trade, how beneficial soever it may
and must be to the Publick, is so entirely foreign to the present System
of our Education that the introduction of it will most probably be
attended with some difficulties. But as those difficulties do not lead us
to decline the acceptance of your Lordship's Offer, which we for our
parts are ready to receive with great gratitude, so we hope that they will
be soon overcome when your Lordship's Design shall be more fully
explain'd. Before I communicate this affair to the rest of the Univer^y
it is my Duty to make his Grace our Chancellor acquainted with it, who is
so good to us as to condescend to take into his consideration every thing
that concerns the honour and Interest of the University.—I am, my
Lord—Your Lordship's—most obed^t humble sert

                          P. YONGE."

1754, Oct. 26th. Lord Townshend to the Vice Chancellor of Cambridge (Dr. Yonge). In duplicate. The original draft in Lord Townshend's hand, and a corrected copy. Each 5 pp.

" Sir, I am much obliged to you for having communicated to the Heads
[of Colleges] the Proposals I took the liberty of making through you
to the University, and it gives me great satisfaction to hear from you
that they have so entirely approved of my Motives & design in making
it . . . .

The premiums I would propose to give are twenty Guineas each to
the Authors of thé two best Dissertations which shall be made by
gentlemen of the University of any Rank or Degree upon Subjects
included within the Theory of Trade, and appointed by those who shall
be the Judges at the time under this Institution. The Prizes to be
given according to the opinion of the Judges, and either to be delivered
in money or vested in any other shape as shall be determined, previous
to the execution of the design itself, at a meeting of the Heads. The
Persons I should desire to name for Judges are the Vice Chancellor
for the time being, the present Master of Trinity [Dr Robert Smith],
the present Master of Christ's College [Dr Hugh Thomas] and two
other Persons from the Body of the University to be named by me ;

MARQUESS
TOWNSHEND
MSS.

& the three first of these Judges to continue such as long as they are Heads of the University, and the two last as long as they are resident in it; reserving to myself a power, which I perceive has lately been reserved in like cases, of filling up the vacancies which shall happen . . . . . I could wish the Dissertations might be wrote in the English Language and that those which carry the Prizes might be read by the Authors of them in public on a Day to be appointed near to Commencement " . . . .

1754, Nov. 3rd. Dr. Philip Yonge to Lord Townshend. Dated at Cambridge, and unaddressed.

" My Lord, I have communicated your Lordship's last favour to the Masters of Trinity and Christ's in particular, and this day in the customary speech at the expiration of the V[ice] Chanc$^{r's}$ office I made the senate acquainted with your Lordship's kind design. The two masters desire me to pay their compliments to your Lordship, and there seems to be no doubt of the senate's giving your Lordship a testimony of their gratitude to your Lordship as soon as my Successor shall be establish'd in his office. Doc^r Thomas will be elected, and will probably take his seat tomorrow.—I am, etc.

P. YONGE."

1754, Nov. 5th. Lord Townshend to Dr Philip Yonge. From Rainham. In duplicate. An undated rough draft in Lord Townshend's hand, and a fair copy headed " Copy of my letter to Dr Yonge." Both unsigned.

" Sir—I return you many thanks for the candor you shewed to me by [the] reception you gave to the Proposal I offered to you when Vice-Chancellor, and for the countenance you have given to it by your recommendation of it to the Senate in the customary Speech at the expiration of that Office. I likewise beg that you will be pleased to present my compliments to the two Masters, with my thanks to them for their kind acquiescence to that part of my scheme which relates more particularly to them, and am most heartily glad to find it is your opinion that the Senate will approve of what I have taken the liberty to offer as a method for introducing the Science of Trade into your University."

1755, Jan. 18th. Lord Townshend to Dr Hugh Thomas, Vice-Chancellor of the University of Cambridge. Draft in Lord Townshend's hand.

" Sir—Dr Yonge your late Vice-Chan^r having informed me, in his letter on the 3^d of Novr last, that he had acquainted the Senate with my late Proposal to the University in his customary Speech at the expiration of the Vice-Chan^{rs} Office, and that there seemed to be no doubt of the Senate's approving of it, I have some hopes that my Proposal may be received thô I have not yet heard anything further relative to it.

There was one point left unsettled in my letters to Dr Yonge which was the nomination of the two Judges from the Body of the University : and it may not be improper I should name them now in case the University should admitt of the introduction of the Theory of Trade in the manner which has been proposed. The Persons I should desire to appoint, under the conditions which have been mentioned in my former letter to your late Vice-Chancellor, are the Reverend Mr Courtail of Clare Hall and the Reverend Mr Balguy of St John's College. I am—Sir—Your most obed^t humble Servant "

MARQUESS
TOWNSHEND
MSS.
—

1755, Oct. 29th.   The same to the same.   A draft in Lord Townshend's handwriting.   Dated at Rainham.

"Sir—Mr Greaves having intimated to me that you expressed to him,
when I had the honor of meeting you and several of the Heads at
Fulburne, some desire that I would draw up some questions on the
Theory of Trade, I have taken the liberty of sending to you the inclosed
paper containing such questions on that Subject as have occurred to me.

I am very doubtfull whether these questions are so perfect as they
ought to be; and do hope therefore that you will be pleased to give
them no further regard than you shall find they do deserve; and I have
with greater chearfulness complyed with your request being satisfyed
from your candor that you will not think that by offering these
questions to you and to the Gentlemen who have the direction of this
Institution, I am presuming to dictate to those who have more knowledge
and better judgement than myself.   If there be any among them which
can be made proper questions, such will receive your corrections, if
there be not any such you will reject them all.   I am with Truth—Sir
Your most obedt humble servt."

[The Questions enclosed].
"What influence has Trade on the Morals of a Nation?
On what circumstances does the populousness of a country principally
depend?
Has a free trade or a free Government the greater effect in promoting
the wealth and strength of a Nation?
Can any restraints be laid on trade or industry without lessening
the advantages of them?   And if there can, what are they?
Is there any method of raising taxes without prejudice to Trade?
And if there is, what is it?
What are the uses of money in trade?
Is it more for the advantage of a trading nation to have regular troops
or a Militia."

1755, Nov. 15th.   Capt. the Hon. Roger Townshend to his father
Lord Townshend.   Dated at Mitcham.

"My Lord—I did not receive your Lordship's Letter till yesterday
on my return to this place after a Weeks absence & attendance on Sr
John Ligonier who has acted a very sincere & friendly part towards
me; I acquainted your Lordship with Sr John Ligonier's having
appointed me one of his Aid[es] de Camp a favor I had no right to
expect from him as I was scarcely honor'd with his Acquaintance; the
many advantages that must of course arise to me in my Profession from
the Friendship & Opinion of that Great Man made it of all other the
most desirable Post in our present situation of Affairs.   It has always
been customary for General Officers to name and chuse there own
Aid[e] de Camps & I don't believe there is an Instance of its ever
having been refused before; to make the refusal the more cruel and
severe the Duke [of Cumberland] has consented to Lord Loudon's
appointing Capt Campbell who is in the same Regiment with me & of
the same Rank & did not apply till many days after me; thus my Lord
am I deprived of the same means of recommending me in my Profession
which every other Capt in my Profession enjoys.   What is the real
Cause of the Duke's hatred to me I am not in the least able to guess,
Sr John Ligonier asked him if my behaviour either in my profession
or towards him had been disagreeable to his Royal Highness; he said
he had no kind of objection to any part of my behaviour since I had
been in the Army but that I positively should not be his Aid[e] de

Camp; S[r] John has been extreamly hurt at the Usage he has been treated with & has several times endeavoured to dissuade him from such barbarous behaviour but without success. The General is determined he will name no other person & the Duke is determined not to consent. It is very hard that my Brother's Quarrell with the Duke shou'd be continued to me. I was in no ways concern'd in it nor did I ever say a Word in the least tending to reflect or call in question any part of the Duke's conduct, but yet he is determined I shall not rise in my Profession. It does not become me to treat a person in his Station with that Freedom which I really think his hard Usage of me deserves; I can conclude nothing less from his Cruelty towards me but an absolute Scheme of driving me out of the Army. How much more noble wou'd it have been in a Great Man to have waited till he had caught me erring in me [sic] Profession ; he might then have employed all his hatred against me without drawing upon him[self] the odious Names of Cruelty & Tyrrany. Every independent Person has condemned the Duke extreamly & several of his Friends have declared they endeavor'd to persuade him from it. It is a melancoly Subject for me to think off, let me behave with ever so much Bravery & Conduct & deserve Preferment, as long as he commands I shall remain in my present Post. I honor & love the Army & the only Ambition I have in this World is to do my Duty in my Profession & [I] desire to be made an Example off if I am guilty & neglect[ful], but to be punish'd when I am conscious I am innocent is treatment every Man of spirit & honor must feel & complain off. I have troubled your Lordship with a real state of my Case S[r] John Ligonier will do me the Justice to confirm it; I suffer so much at present from the Duke's treatment & my disappointment that I am afraid my Letter may be confused which I hope you will excuse ; our Regiment is ordred to march on Wednesday to East Grinstead where my Company will be quartered it is in Sussex.

The House of Commons satt till Six OClock on Friday Morning M[r] Pitt & many other members spoke ag[t] the Address ; I am much obliged to you for the 50£ Note you was so kind as to send me & am youre Dutiful Son.

Roger Townshend."

1755, Nov. 28th. Rev. Edmund Law, D.D., Master of Peterhouse, to Lord Townshend. Dated at Peter House and unaddressed. Endorsed, under the same date, in the hand of an amanuensis, "Dr Law (ViceChancellor of Cambridge) his letter to me approving those questions I sent."

My Lord—I received the favour of your Lordship's Letter to my Predecessor, with the Questions inclined, w[ch] appear to be all very proper, & I hope be properly treated of in their Season ; I shall not fail to lay them before the persons appointed to determine finally on this Subject at the usual time, & do myself the honour of acquainting your. Ldsbip with their determination, w[ch] I don't doubt but will prove agreeable to y[r] Ldships good & generous intention, & thereby be the highest satisfaction to—my Lord—your Lordships most obedient humble Serv[t]

Edm. Law."

1756, Jan. 21st. The same to the same. Dated at Peter House and unaddressed. Endorsed, under the same date, by Lord Townshend, "D[r] Law (Vice Chancellor of Cambridge) his letter to me inclosing 2 printed Copys of the Question on the Theory of Trade for the year 1756—Answered on the 26th Jan[ry] 1756."

" My Lord—I rec[d] y[r] Lordships Commands by M[r] Powel[l] & immediately call'd a meeting of the Commissioners to settle the Question for this year, as y' Lordship will perceive by the inclosed, w°h if it prove agreeable to y' Lordship's intention it will be the greatest satisfaction to all the persons concern'd & in particular to—My Lord—Your Lordship's most obedient humble servant

EDM. LAW."

1756, Jan. 26th. Lord Townshend to Rev. D' Law. Copy. Dated at Rainham, and endorsed in Lord Townshend's hand, " Copy of my letter to D' Law Vice Chancellor of the University of Cambridge in answer to his dated Jan'y the 21st 1756 in which he sent me the printed Copy of the Question on the Theory of Trade for the [year] 1756."

" Sir—I receiv'd the favor of yours by last Post, with Two printed Copies of the Question which the judges have order'd for this year.

The ingenuousness of my temper obliges me to confess to you that I did not imagine I should be so unfortunate as to find that every one of the Questions, which I took the liberty of offering to the consideration of the Judges would be rejected by them ; and that I am much disappointed to find that the question, which was placed first on the paper, was not approved of.

The Question I mean is this, *what influence has Trade on the Morals of a Nation.*

This is in my opinion the best Question that can be put on the subject of the Theory of Trade. I should take up too much of your time if I was now to enlarge on this Question : I shall therefore only beg leave to mention, one remark or two which occur to me upon the Question which the Gentlemen have thought proper to publish for this Year.

The first part of their Question to wit, *What causes principally contribute to render a Nation populous ?* would, I allow, be a very proper question, if the words which follow had not been made part of the question, *& what Effect has the populousness of a Nation on its Trade ?* and the Question without this addition would have been of the same purport with one of the Questions I sent to you, thô expressed in different words.

The question I allude to is this. *On what circumstances does the populousness of a Nation principally depend ?*

The Theory of Trade like all other subjects of Science must be allow'd a free and unprejudic'd inquiry.

But the Freedom of the first part of your question is destroy'd by the latter part of it. For this addition must be understood in some respects as explanatory of the former part of the question, and it likewise indicates that those, who form'd the question, are of opinion that they [sic] are more causes than one which do principally contribute to render a Nation populous, and that they apprehend that the candidates for prizes on the Theory of Trade might neglect to enlarge on that of Trade.

But suppose it be allow'd that Trade if the only cause, or one of the principal causes which contribute to render a Nation populous ; does it follow that the populousness of a Nation must necessarily increase the trade of it. If Trade be the cause of the increase of people, it cannot surely properly be said that the populousness of a Nation is the Cause of Trade, for the effect can never produce its cause.

Suppose a Nation become very populous from the greater freedom it enjoys in Trade than its Neighbours are possess'd of ; and let us suppose that on a Sudden these freedoms are taken away by impolitick laws which restrain their Trade, such as lay heavy burthens upon it by

` taxation on necessaries of Life,·by duties on imports and ·by bounties on exports, and throwing every branch of Trade into some, kind of monopoly, will any one think that in such a Case the number of its people can support the Trade, or rather must not the consequence of the loss of its Freedom in Trade be a loss of its people?. Is it not evident that numbers of its people must fly into other countries for imployment where Trade is less incumbered and more free..

The answer therefore to the latter part of the Question viz. *and what Effect has the populousness of a Nation on its Trade,* seems to me to be, that it cannot necessarily have any effect at all upon its Trade.

I have here from the good wishes I have for the success of this new institution taken the Liberty to express my Thoughts to you on this question proposed for this year. You will I hope excuse this freedom and believe me to be—Sir—Your most obedᵗ & humble Servᵗ"

                                             [TOWNSHEND].

1756, Jan. 28th.   Rev. Dʳ Edmund Law to Lord Townshend. Dated at Cambridge, und endorsed in Lord Townshend's hand, "Dʳ Law (Vice-Chancellor of Cambridge) his letter to me in answer to mine of the 26th Insᵗ."

" My Lord—I receiv'd yʳ Lordship's favour of last Post with concern as it gave the parties in the Trust committed to them by your Lordship the severe mortification of perceiving how far they had faild' in their endeavours to discharge it acceptably. As I had the honour to bear some share in this Trust, I think myself obliged to lay before yʳ Lordship as plain & particular an account of our Conduct as I am able to recollect After reading over all yʳ Lordship's Propositions & the very obliging Letter wᶜʰ accompany'd them, a previous Question was put whether any variation in them might be agreeable : When it was the opinion of those who appear'd to have the best means of being acquainted with yʳ Ldship's real Sentiments, that such alteration wᵈ not give offence. We had then a long consultation on the Subject, & the first Question relating to the influence of Trade on Morals I apprehend[ed] might be postponed on accᵗ of the great corruption for some time visible among the trading parts of our Nation ; witness the late uproar rais'd about the general Naturalization & Jew Bills. The second Question seem'd to be pitchd' upon chiefly for its seasonableness in our present Situation, & the addition made to it in order to bring the general Design of yʳ Lordship's Institution more directly & immediately in view, as well as give the greater scope to writers on this Subject, by not only explaining how far Trade shᵈ be consider'd among the principal causes of well peopling a Country, but likewise shewing in what respect the number of Inhabitants must put a People on employing many of their hands that way, & thereby reciprocally of encreasing & improving the materials, & promoting the several branches of Trade by repeated Trials.—But I am not presuming to dispute these points with yʳ Lordship. The Question ought undoubtedly to have been sent to your Lordship before it was published, wᶜᵇ omission, with any other impropriety, I hope yʳ Lordship will be so good as to excuse from persons so little conversant in subjects of this kind.

I beg leave to congratulate yʳ Lordship on your late recovery & am in all duty—Your Lordships—most obedient humble servᵗ. ·..· ·’ ..· ·."

                                             EDM. LAW."

1756, Feb. 16th.   Lord Townshend to Rev. Mr. Powell. Draft. Unsigned and unaddressed. Dated at Rainham.

"Dear Powell—I was indebted to you for one letter, before yours of
the 15th came to my hands this morning, which I should have acknowledged if I had not been unwilling to give you too frequent interruptions; and it was once my intention to send you the Vice-Chancellor's
answer to my letter (which I now here enclose for your perusal) but I
was afterwards of opinion that there was no necessity for giving you
the trouble of a letter upon the late absurd conduct of your Vice-Chancellor, since what was done could not be prevented. I have indeed had
a good deal of difficulty with my self to avoid sending the Vice-Chancellor an answer to his letter. It concerned me very much to find that
the Vice-Chancellor has been pleased to insinuate in his letter that my
dislike to the *very absurd* question which has been advertized and which
contains no more than that the cause produces the effect and the effect
the cause, arises from my being displeased that the questions I sent
were rejected; thô I had expressed in my letter which accompanied
them, my assent that they should be corrected or rejected as the judges
should think most proper.

What I said in my last letter to the Vice-Chan[cello]r was that I
thought myself unfortunate that all my questions should be rejected;
and I cannot see, with great submission to his sentiments, why the
circumstance of my having expressed myself in this manner, as I did
in the letter which accompanyed the questions, should make it improper
in me to give any opinion on the question they have fixed on? or that
there is any inconsistency in my conduct under any construction. I
say'd correct any of the questions or reject them all as you shall judge
most proper; will the Vice-Chancellor suppose that, when I wrote this,
I could imagine that any one of my questions would have been so
altered as to be made nonsense or that they would all be rejected for to
give place for a more improper question than any of them?" etc. etc.

1756, May 22nd. Rev. R. Browne to Lord Townshend. Dated at
Walton. Asking to be appointed to the living of Hanbury which will
shortly be vacant by Dr Horberry's acceptance of a college living.

1756, June 2nd. Lord Middleton to Lieut.-Colonel the Hon. George
Townshend. Dated at Wollatton.

"Sr—I am concerned for the occasion of your letter, having been in
hopes peace would have subsisted in the neighbourhood of Tamworth
this whole parliament, and as your's and Lord Weymouth's interest
seem'd, for I was much a stranger to the transaction, to unite in the
last election the change of the Unckle for the Nephew [Viscount
Villiers in the seat of Thomas Villiers] I should have conjectur'd would
have made no alteration in the agreement. I have no property in the
town, nor ever cultivated any interest by purchase near it having no
other view than being a promoter of unanimity among my acquaintance,
and by having now resided so many years at Wollaton my influence in
the place is not worth requesting; but small as it is in case of opposition
it must go in conjunction with my old friends who I suspect will not be
forgetfull of Mr Floyer's hard fate [at the Tamworth election in 1741].
I am with great regard" etc.

1756, June 11th. "A copy of a Letter to Lord Jersey upon the
affairs of Tamworth." Dated at Audley Square.

"My Lord
        When I had the Honour to see you at my House you seemed to
desire I would give your Lordship no vexatious Opposition at Tamworth, to which I very readily assented & further declared I would
inform your Lordship as early as possible with my Determination with

MARQUES
TOWNSHEND
MSS.

respect to the ensuing Election—I came to Town last night and can assure your Lordship that notwithstanding the appearance of an Agreement made at the last Election at Tamworth with respect to future Vacancies—totally without my Knowledge and tending to prevent my Family Interest from having the least Weight there, yet my Lord, as I do not now intend to oppose Lord Villars [Villiers], I have avoided any Measures which may put him or his Friends to any Trouble or Expence.

I hope your Lordship will do me the Justice to believe me when I assure you that altho' I cannot concur in the measure as settled, yet that I rejoice in any Circumstance which gives so much Satisfaction to one from whom I have received so many Civilities, & for whom I have so much regard & respect, & am My Lord—y^r Lords^{ps}—Most obed^t Humble Servt GEO: TOWNSHEND."

1756, June 11th. Lord Jersey to Lieut.-Colonel the Hon. George Townshend. Dated at Grosvenor Square—"6 o'clock Afternoon."

"My dear Sir—I no sooner received your most obliging letter of this morning than I endeavoured to pay my Acknowledgements in Person. They are so warm, & so sincere as I can't forbear conveying them by this the most likely Opportunity first to reach you ; I know nothing that may have passed on former Elections, but I have many reasons to rejoice that there is to be no Opposition on this ; They are not altogether selfish, but regard families that I must ever esteem, and not only families, but Persons ; particularly Lord Weymouth and your self ; It may be improper for me to say more at present than that I have the highest Value for you both, & to assure you which I do with the greatest truth that I am with the most friendly regard—Your obliged & faithfull humble Servt—   JERSEY."

1756, June 24th. Rev. Dr Law to Lord Townshend. Dated at Peter House and endorsed by Lord Townshend "Dr Law Vice-Chancellor of Cambridge his letter to me—Received and Answ^d on the 26th June 1756."

"My Lord—I have the pleasure to acquaint your Lordship that your Lordship's prizes for this year are adjudged to [the Rev.] M^r [William] Bell of Magdalen College, & Sr Lobb of St Peter's College, whose Dissertations shall be transmitted to your Lordship as soon as they have been read before the University. There were nine in all & several very good ones, wch your Lordship may at any time command from—My Lord—Your Lordship's most obedient humble Servt

EDMUND LAW."

1756, June 26th. Lord Townshend to Rev. Dr Law. Endorsed "Copy of my Answer to Dr Law Vice-Chancellor of Cambridge letter to me dated the 24th Inst."

Sir—I received your Letter of the 24th Inst this morning, and shall in answer only mention in a few words that when you, the Vice Chancellour of Cambridge, did in your letter of the 28th of Jany last seem to charge me with inconsistency of conduct and did mention in that letter, *that the first question relating to the influence of Trade on Morals might as you apprehend be postpon'd on account of the great corruption for some time visible among the trading ports of our Nation ; witness the late uproar raised about the general Naturalization & Jew Bills,* I did resolve to let the Institution drop so far as I have been concern'd in it and to give my self no further trouble about it, you need not therefore give yourself the trouble of transmitting to me the two Prize Dissertations.

There is not any moral Duty which is not of a Commercial nature. Freedom of Trade is nothing more than a freedom to be moral Agents. And since a free moral Inquiry into this most interesting Theory, on the Observance of which the happiness of this Life and of the next do entirely depend, cannot be allow'd at your University I have done, and have nothing more to add than that I am—S^r—Your obdt humble Servt."

1756, Oct. 22nd. Richard Dacres to Lord Townshend. Dated at Gibraltar and endorsed "Richd Dacres Letter to me from Gibraltar acqua[intin]g me that he had embarked my barb Horse on board the Rising Sun for England, and likewise inclos'd a Bill for Charges [of] keeping at Gibraltar from April 1756 to [the] time the Horse was embarked."

"My Lord—I have the honour to acquaint your Lordship that I have embarked on board a Transport Ship called the Rising Sun, Daniel Peak Master, an Iron Grey Barb Horse for your Lordship, being the same which was purchased long since by Mr Petticrew, & left in my charge by [Lieut.] Genl [Thomas] Fowke [Governor of Gibraltar] at his departure from hence. I used all possible efforts to get him a passage on board a Man of War, but found it impracticable, and indeed I think he is safer where he is, by being in a large commodious Ship, under Convoy, and were he in a Man of War he must run the Risque of being thrown overboard in case of meeting an Enemy. He is embarked in extreme good order, & has excellent Accomodations aboard, & I much hope that he will arrive safe & prove entirely to your Lordship's satisfaction . . . . . .

In the same Ship with your Lordship's Horse I have embarked a Mare for H.R.H. the Prince of Wales, & a horse for Mr Thistlewayte of Hampshire, and the Man who has the care of them home, & who is named Thomas Bicknell is to return to Gibraltar immediately after he has delivered them. I have made no Bargain with him for his Time & Trouble, but have left that matter entirely to the Owners of the Horses.

It will give me great Satisfaction to hear that the Horse is safely delivered into your Lordships hands, & meets your Approbation, after the great Sums and frequent disappointm^ts which I am sensible he has cost; and if your Lordship will be pleased at any time to honor me with your Commands I shall be proud of the opportunity of shewing with how much Respect & Attention I have *etc.*

RICHD. DACRES."

Same date. A copy of the above letter, endorsed "1757—March the 25th—A copy of Richard Dacres letter the original of which was sent this day to Messrs James & Thos Tierney Merch^{ts} in Mark Lane."

1757, March 8th. William Fitz-herbert to the Hon. George Townshend. Dated at Boyle Street, Dublin.
Enclosing the writer's views on the Militia.

1757, March 19th. Thomas Bicknell to Lord Townshend.
"My Lord.—I am the Person orderd over from Gibralter to take under my care a Barbary Mare belonging to the Prince of Wales and a horse of the same Country for your Lordship . . . . . having from the 18th October to the 31st of January continually had the Inspection and care of your Lordships Horse. The necessary expenses as to Feeding &c. I have been paid for being so much out of my own Pocket, but my Care Trouble and attendance I humbly beg leave to refer to

your Lordships Goodness and Generosity. Any Commands of your Lordship my be directed for me at Lt General Fowkes in South Audley Street wich will be most gratfully remembered by my Lord your Most Humbly Obedieut Servant,

THOS. BICKNELL."

June 18th, 1757. William Pitt, afterwards Earl of Chatham, to the Hon. George Townshend.

" Dear Sir,
Tho I can have nothing to inform you of relating to the Duke of Newcastle's transactions, in order to a junction, which you are not acquainted with from his Grace, I should be extremely happy of an opportunity to have some conversation with You, on a Subject, which but just now has taken its final and conclusive turn, and must receive a Negative or Affirmative Answer. The D. of Newcastle and Lord Hardwicke have repeatedly declared to Lord Bute and myself that They coud add nothing to the efforts already made with regard to the Points of difficulty, now immoveable and in their express Opinions, necessary to be comply'd with, as neither They nor their Friends are disposed to resist any further. I am obliged to be at home on business to morrow morning, which, I hope, will be my Apology for taking the liberty to propose to you so great a trouble, as that of calling at my House to morrow between ten and eleven, if it be not inconvenient to you to do me that honour. I am ever with the truest esteem and respect.

Dear Sir
Your most obedient
and most humble Servant
W. PITT."

Friday 7 o'clock.

This letter is endorsed with the following memorandum in the handwriting of the Honble George Townshend :—

" N.B : This was the first time for about a fortnight I had heard any thing from Mr Pitt, during which time the Negotiation for a Ministry went on in his & Ld Bute's the D[uke of] Newcastle's & Lord Hardwicke's Hands.—On the Friday night June the 18th 1757, I received this Letter & the next morning waited on him with my Brother, & to our Astonishment heard him avow the ridiculous & dishonest Arrangement of Men which is now to take place—not the least adoption of any Publick System of Measures being declared or even hinted at by him.

Upon this occasion I without hesitation declared my resolution to be no part of it—my Brother did the same.

GEO : TOWNSHEND."

London, June 20th 1757.

1757, Nov. 6th. Capt. the Hon. Roger Townshend to his father. Dated at Winchester and unaddressed.

My Lord—I received your Lordship's kind Letter with the inclosed Bill of 50£. on Mr Child for which I beg you to accept of my most sincere thanks. The Letter you was so kind as to write to me before I went on our late unfortunate & disgraceful Expedition [to Westphalia], with the enclosed Note I did not receive 'til I was on board the Man of War & had no opportunity of acknowledging the receipt of it. I appropriated it to the use it was intended for & discharged my Servt, & I give your Lordship my word of honor that I will in in every respect adhere & keep to that Scheme of Oeconomy which I know is absolutely necessary for my own happiness & will I hope recommend me to your Lordship's favor and opinion.

I beg leave to declare myself intirely ignorant of my late servant's conduct concerning the Old Chesnut horse, your kindness to me on every occasion if I have a spark of gratitude in my composition, must make it impossible for me to act so low & base a part; I hope extravagance has been my greatest Crime, & as I have suffer'd & know that it was you alone that freed me from my misfortunes, it would be unpardonable conduct in me towards your Lordship, if the business of my life was not to follow that Plan lay'd down by you & do everything in my power that was most agreeable to you.

I've parted with the 2 Mares & the Brown Gelding, I did not recolect when I sent my Servant your mentioning the Cbestn^t horse was disposed off. I can easily furnish myself with a strong horse & that with the Black Colt will be all I shall keep.

An Inquiry is much talked off into the Conduct of our General [the Duke of Cumberland] that commanded our late Expedition [in Westphalia], it was well named the secret Expedition, for without a real & honest Inquiry takes place it will ever remain a secret to me.

Our going to America early in the spring seems at present to be believed. I cou'd wish for a better. A commission eight years a Captain is being very much out of luck, but however if they will not prefer me I can^t help it, and must be contented to go upon another Expedition with the Buffs.—Your Dutiful Son.

RO : TOWNSHEND."

1758, Feb. 12th. The same to the same. Dated on board the Namure and unaddressed.

"My Lord—The ships are ready and Admiral Boscawen came on board last night, we wait only for a fair Wind; the Ships orderd to sail with us are, Namure, Adm^l Boscawen; Royal William 90 Guns, Princess Amelia 80, Invincible 74, Lancaster 74, Vanguard 74 to join us at Plymouth, Prince of Orange 64, Centurion 60, Burford 74, Eight winterd at Hallifax [in Nova Scotia], several are already gone with convoys; when the whole Fleet is collected together it will amount to 24, Sail of the Line besides Frigates; a Fleet superior to anything the French can fit out.

I have been apply'd too by a friend of mine to sollicit your Lordship in his favour, for a Scarfe, when you have a vacancy; his name is Derby he lives at Winchester, if you are not under Engagements to any other person Mr Derby will think himself highly honor'd & infinitely obliged to your Lordship for the Scarfe. I know him to be a worthy good Man & I should be happy in obtaining him this favor of your Lordship

Your Dutiful Son
RO : TOWNSHEND."

1758, Sept. 26th. Hon. Charles Townshend to his mother.

"My dear Lady Townshend,—Your Ladyship has heard from my Brother Townshend that he has been so kind to us as to call at Adderbury in his journey from Bristol to London; and, tho' his visit was short, it was long enough to manifest, what I was very happy to find, that he never was in better health or spirits. The success of the Militia in every County in which it has been at all countenanced, & the notorious opposition or contempt of the Ld Lieutenant in every County in which it has been ill received or forgotten, fully proves how indifferent at least, if not favorable, the general opinion of the kingdom is to the measure; which I should hardly have mentioned to your Ladyship, if the measure itself were not the Child of your Son ; which I know from most pleasing experience, is a consideration of great & irresistable weight in your judgment. George seems more intent upon his command in the army than ever I saw him : The retreat of his formidable & abdicated Enemy [the Duke of Cumberland] ; the disreputation of almost all the senior officers hitherto employed, & the infinite Honor naturally bestowed upon commanders successful in this perilous time all unite in indulging & inflaming his original Genius & uncommon Talents for the army.

He seems also to be not a little urged & accelerated by the quick rise & very promising prospect of preferment & command now opening to Roger ; whose situation must improve every day, as his ability grows from experience ; opportunitys occurr from his situation ; and advancement follows from his service. General Amhurst speaks of his diligence, attention, & capacity in the most favorable language, & I should do him injustice if I did not acknowledge, how much he is likely hereafter to make a very considerable figure in a profession, whose importance & necessity grows too fast upon us in this Country.

I learn from Lady Essex's letters to Lady Dalkeith that she lives entirely with Lady Ferrers at Bristol : Lady Ferrers gives the same account of their intimacy in her letters ; which I only mention without comment ; entreating you not to construe my words, til I see you, & from a desire of obviating prejudice, not affecting disguise.

Last week we sent you some venison & two Pineapples ; did they arrive safe, or where (*sic*) they good ?

Lady Jane Scott left us on Sunday ; as she came, she went, oppresst, unintelligible, wretched, healthy & whimsical, a monstrous appetite : good nights : occasional unguarded chearfulness, & premeditated spleen & despondency are certainly no proofs of real illness & yet these are all the symptoms of it she has. I wish she is not in danger of a complaint still worse than ill health.

A thousand thanks to you for the many Gazetts you have sent us : They are infinitely agreeable to us, and most so, as they are testimonies of your affection : which is, in the estimation of us both, the most valuable possession we have or can enjoy in life.

If I have in any thing a real satisfaction it is in acknowledging the happyness I have in your affection & in saying in return how sincerely & invariably I am—Your most affectionate & faithful

C. T.

[P.S.] Lady Dalkeith bids me say for her whatever words can say in declaring her love & Honor for you."

1759, July 23rd. Charles Burney to Philip Case. Dated at Lynn and endorsed, " Mr Burney to Mr Case about Musick."

" Sir,
I fear I shall not be able to propose any useful hints as to the Furniture of the Barrel Organ you mentioned to me, unless I was informed what Stops it contained, what is its Compass, together with the Size & Number of its Barrels. However I will suppose it capable of performing the following Pieces, wch in the serious Way w^d if well adapted to the Instrument afford great pleasure to the admirers of such Compositions.

1. Corelli's 8th Concerto (or the favourite movem^t in it).
2. He was despised & rejected—in Handel's Messiah.
3. Powerful Guardian—set by D^o.
4. Return O God of Hosts—in Samson.
5. Tis Liberty alone—in Judas Maccabeus.

6. Handel's Second Organ Concerto, or Part of it.
7. Geminiani's 1ˢᵗ Concerto op. 2ᵈᵃ, or Do.
8. King of Prussia's March.
9. March of the 3ᵈ Regiment of Guards.
10. Hasse's 1ˢᵗ Concerto.
11. Rende mi il Figlio mio, del Sigʳ Cocchi, nel Ciro riconosciuto.
12. The Simphony & last Movemᵗ of Handel's Coronation Anthem.

If these Compositions or any Part of them should be approved & practicable, it will be necessary to have them judiciously suited & adjusted to the Genius of the Organ & filled up with such Simphonies & accompanymᵗˢ as will best compensate for the Want of a Voice in the Songs or a Number of Instruments in the other Pieces.—I am, Sir,—Your Most Obedᵗ & Most Humble Servant,

                                        CHAS. BURNEY."

1759, Nov. 27th. Judith Irving to Lord *Townshend?* Unaddressed.
A letter asking his Lordship for his interest in procuring promotion for the writer's husband Major Irving.

17⁵⁹⁄₆₀, Feb. 15th. Robert Johnson to the Hon. George Townshend. Dated at Sandy, Bedfordshire.

" Sir,—When I purchas'd Mʳ Long's Estate at Cavenham in Suffolk, he told me you had given your consent to inclose a small piece of ground that lay between two of my Closes near the house; but as I am now become the proprietor and have some thoughts of putting that Scheme in Execution, [I] don't think myself sufficiently justify'd to take out a writ to do it, without acquainting you therewith and haveing your farther permission for that purpose. If there is any thing I can do for you in that Country or elsewhere, please to command, your very assured

                        Humble Sert RT. JOHNSON."

1760, Dec. 2nd. Edward Weston to Lord Townshend. Dated at Scotland Yard, and unaddressed.

" My Lord—Having long been sollicited by Mʳ Case my deputy in the Office of Clerk of the Peace [for Norfolk], who I understand is honoured with Yʳ Lᵖˢ particular Regard, to surrender that Place to him ; As the Value of it to me is of late years so greatly lessened, (partly by the Decay of Business, & partly by the Claim of my said Deputy to Fourscore Pounds ꝑ ann. out of the Profits, in lieu of 50 or 60, for which he long executed the Office) that it has brought-me-in this last year no more than 19 ᵖᵈ ; I have at last determined to comply with those sollicitations. And, as I am obliged to yʳ Lᵈᵖ for the long Enjoyment, which I have had of it, I think it incumbent on me to acquaint you with my Resignation, hoping it will not be disagreeable to you, & taking the same Opportunity to return my sincerest Thanks to Your Lᵈᵖ for so great a Mark of your Favour, & to assure you that I am with the greatest Gratitude, as well as Respect, & shall be always—My Lord— Your Lᵈᵖˢ—Most obliged, and most obedient humble Servant

                                        E. WESTON."

1761, May 15th. A receipt for a " Moiety of the Expences of the [Norfolk] County Election 1st April 1761."

It begins :—" To 63 Staffmen and Chairmen at 10ˢ each; " and ends :—" Paul Ald[erman] Rogers your Subscription to the Norwich roads 10.10.0, and ends " Total 102.5.6 " with the following receipt at foot.

. "1761. May 15th. , Rec^d of the right bon^{ble} Geo: Townshend by the hands of Mr Chas Townshend One hundred and two Pounds five Shillings and Sixpence in full of the Contents by me

NOCKOLD TOMPSON."

176¼, Feb. 12th. Lieut. William Brograve, R.N. (commanding the Albany Sloop in Portsmouth Harbour) to the Hon. George Townshend.

The writer begs General Townshend to use his influence so that he may sail in the Albany, or in a larger ship, under the orders of Admiral [Sir George] Pocock [K.B.], on the Expedition then on foot [for the capture of the Havanna].

- March 2nd, 1763. Lord Townshend to his son Charles. Draft, dated at Rainham.

" Dear Charles—You may remember that about the beginning of last Decr upon reading the paragraph in the General Evening Post, which informed the Public of your Resignation of your former Place, I immediately wrote you a letter from Balls expressing my joy and congratulations to you on that wise guiding of your self, as you did by this act put your self into that state of indepen[den]cy which was necessary to enable you to act that truely patriotic part which your country seemed more immediately to call for at that time. If I contradicted the general forms of behavior which prevail at this time in troubling you with a letter on that accasion and it be not the mode now for a Parent to shew any concern for the wellfare and happiness of his Son, you acted like a man of fashion in taking no notice to me of that letter and in preserving that silence towards me, which had been observed by you towards me for a considerable time before I wrote that letter and which you have not broke through.

As I am too old to alter and cannot easily extirpate that Parental concern and affection, which, by a long indulgence of them, are deeply rooted in my heart, you will I hope forgive me that I do now trouble you again, thô not with that joy which attended my other letter, with a transcript of a paragraph out of the North Briton of Saturday last which is as follows, viz.

That great reformer of abuses, the new Whig head of the board of Trade, has just condescended to stipulate for an additional Salary without Power, as the price of his support of this Tory government. I am— Dear Charles—Yours most affec^{ly} "

1763, May 24th. Rev. T. O. Young to the Hon. George Townshend. Dated at Caius College Cambridge.

" Dear Sir—I have not been able to purchase one of the Caricatura's of Wilk[e]s—They are only at the Coffee houses—A Printseller has promis'd me two by to morrow night. If he does not disappoint me, you shall receive them on Saturday. . . . .

I am, Dear Sir, your most affectionate and faithful servant

T. O. YOUNG."

1763, June 2nd. Hon. George Townshend "To Mr Otley at the Angel, St Edmunds Bury, Suffolk." Dated at Newmarket.

The writer begs Mr Otley to hand the enclosed letter to a Serjeant or Corporal of the Norfolk Militia who would call for it.

1764, March 17th. Colby Bullock to George fourth Viscount Townshend (afterwards first Marquis Townshend). Dated at Shipdam and unaddressed. Endorsed " Mr Bullock on his appointment of Executor to the late Lord's Will."

" My Lord—The sense of the obligation and Duty I owed to Your Lordship's Father when living, will I hope excuse the liberty I now take of expressing my very sincere and deep concern to you at his Death. . . . . Mr Case informs me of your having seen the Will, which I have not yet done, nor shall do, 'till I am assured from Your Lordship of your consenting to my acting in it. If my Name and Agency therein receive your approbation, it will be my constant endeavour to cooperate with the other Gentlemen in the best manner I can of performing the Trust reposed in us ; but if your Lordship shall on any account judge me to be improper, I shall without reluctance decline all concern in a Business, to which Obedience to the deceased Lord's commands is the sole motive I can have of proceeding to take my share in it." . . . .

1764, April 30th. Hon. Charles Townshend to the Duke of Newcastle. Dated at Grosvenor Square. [Copy.]

My dear Lord—I have this Evening the Honour of Your Grace's Letter, which is writ upon so many very interesting Subjects that I am not able to resist the desire it has raised in me of speaking my Sentiments fully to Your Grace, tho' with the utmost defference.

Your Grace's knowledge of the World and great experience in public business necessarily make me distrust any opinion of mine from which you differ ; yet, upon further Reflection, I have not found reason to change the Idea I lately expressed to you of the temper, character and deadness of the Time we live in. Recollect, My Lord, the ingratitude you have yourself met with : the desertion of the Majority of the Whiggs ; the many great names and Familys who have abandoned all Union from obligation and consanguinity, upon the frivolous distinction of supporting the Person of the King : the successful attack made upon the freedom of the Press : the quiet reception of every Act of Violence offered to Persons and to Things, and the perfect state of tranquility in the City and in the Counties which now seemingly takes place under a Ministry, lately so odious, and still so rash :—Are not these proofs that the national Temper is subdued ? That Opposition, by so often deceiving, has lost the power of raising Confidence ? And that indifference and distrust are became habitual and general ? I wish any degree of Spirit, Care or Attention were able to reform this Error, or to awaken Men to a Sense of Danger, but I expect it not, and, I should disguise, if I did not frankly confess to you that I despair of any such Revolution.

Your Grace seems to regret that a stand was not made upon the unjustifiable treatment of our Friend the Duke of Devonshire ; I had not, at that time, the Honour of being in His Grace's Confidence, and therefore I know not what he himself wished ; but, certainly the gradual overthrow of the Whiggs at Court was too quietly submitted to in the several preliminary steps, and could never, in my opinion, have been completed, if it had been at first resisted. Each separate personal injury was, I fear, too far considered as an individual case, whereas, if the very first Attempt had been made a common Cause, the defence of the whole would probably have been not difficult. I agree with your Grace, that the Minority, in defiance of all Disadvantages, made the Ministry and the Crown look pale upon their Numbers in one part of the last Session, and it is now said perseverance and activity would have given Success. Perhaps this may be true ; but, if it be, what was the sudden and secret Cause which slackned their Activity ? Some impute it to jealousy ; but to jealousy in whom, and of whom ? others to inattention ; these to disunion, and those to want of suitable and interesting Questions of Business. As to the Visit to Cambridge, I know how loudly I have been condemned for that absence; but, My Lord! such loose Censure does not even dwell upon me ; especially when it comes from Men with whom I have acted *voluntarily*, not by compact ; from Opinion, not Obligation, and who have no right to circumscribe any one Sentiment or direct any one Action of my political conduct : in whose Plans I had originally no participation, whose Systems I am not bound to adopt, and to whom I stand, in no Sense, nor any degree accountable. Let them distribute their wild Panegyric and Censure over their Glass as Wine warms and Prejudice dictates ; I shall still, unmortified by their harmless dissapprobation, be ever pleased with having obeyed your Commands, and endeavoured at least to assist my Friend Lord Hardwick and his Family at Cambridge. I say this as often as I hear it, which is almost every Day, from some of our most zealous Friends. who continually speak of this Event, either in direct Terms of blame, or by insinuations which are more offensive.

- The Duke of Devonshire and Lord Rockingham have done me the Honour of dining with me this Day, but we were not alone, and our Conversation was at large. Your Grace hoped something would have been settled, and you see the necessity of a Summer Plan preparatory to the Winter. I have said this : but my Idea goes farther, and you will forgive me if in this critical Minute, perhaps the last of deliberation I should open my Mind freely ; in the language of a Man who would bring things to a decision; and who, being at liberty to act as his judgement advises, waits for the communication of such a systematical and probable Plan as may induce and justifie those who shall again embark.

For myself, I am of Opinion, My Lord, that the Minority should be strengthened, if it can *be done upon proper Terms*, by a connexion with Lord Bute, or with Lord Holland, or by the reconciling Lord Temple and Mr Pitt with Mr Grenville. Because I think the Party in the House of Lords is weak, in the Court, odious, and in itself not sufficient to success ; at least with this Parliament, when there is only one Court, so young a King ; at the close of an unpopular War, and in an Age of extravagance, indigence, immorality, and indifference.

I presume not to enter into the reciprocal aversions and late resentments which may be to be considered under this Head ; too new in the Confidence of Your Grace and the Duke of Devonshire, and too much a stranger to the Voice of the Duke of Cumberland, to venture upon so private a Subject; I only express my wish, and presume to suggest what I think expedient and necessary to give opposition, force.

Could both of the former of these be done, or (which I still more wish) could the Family reconciliation be accomplished, the next Thing would be to review the Minority and to allot to particular Men their separate Departments in speaking to individuals ; from which revisal and explanation it would be learnt how far late inactivity has lessened Numbers, what may be hoped upon another Trial, and what Assistance is requisite.

To gain upon the Minds of the People a Daily Paper, upon the Plan of one of the present Prints, should be set up, and circulated, diligently, but quietly ; and two good Pens should be employed to write from Materials, suggested by Men of Knowledge, and subject to their inspection. Some leading Men in each Town through the several Counties should be admitted to Confidence, and be persuaded to give their Clubs and Districts the Tone of Conversation, recommended from hence.

A Committee should be appointed to consider and prepare Heads of Business for the next Winter, and in one Word the Kingdom should be kept warm, and the Chiefs attentive and laborious during the recess.

Sr William Baker should be desired to put the City in motion, both as an Example to other Counties, and as an attack nearest home.

Your Grace will perhaps say, this is mighty well : but reconciliations with Lord Bute or Lord Holland, and the restoring of Harmony between warm and alienated Relations are all impossible, and I shall believe it upon your Testimony; presuming only to add, that if that be the case, I should apprehend the Minority, unable, as it now stands, to break the Ministry, unwilling to accept the only Allies useful or necessary, and composed of parts not perfectly united, may possibly not much advance in another Session ; weakened by the conclusion of the last, perhaps lessened in Numbers, certainly in public opinion : No general Warrants to arraign : no extraordinary Measures, and no ground of Debate but the Army, the Navy and the several disputable Speculations which may occur about the State of the Debt and the Condition of Public Credit.

I must again beg Pardon for taking up so much of your Time, but my mind is full both of matter and anxiety. I could not resist the Impression, and it is perhaps right I should take an Opportunity of saying not only what, but all I think to Your Grace. My View in doing it is honest, for I profess I wish to see decision, and have long tried to enforce that Doctrine. As things now stand, the Ministry are strong, the Minority not in strength or reputation : Lord Bute forced to keep neutrality at least, and the public grown familiarized to an Administration they see so little opposed : Mr Legge I fear will not recover : Mr Pitt seems withdrawn into himself, and retired to his Family and Amusements : other Men act as they did, seldom seen and inexplicit, while the Ministry diligently pick up Individuals every day who see no other prospect, nor hear of any other Union. For my own part, I prefer, it is evident, the Characters, Claims and Interests of those I have voluntarily supported to those of all other Men, and, if any hope should remain of Success, there is no situation or advantage I would not again risque or sacrifice ; but, My Lord, it must be [with] a reasonable hope of success, resulting from Union, Plan, Activity and Strength. I am far from being in a Condition to make even this prudent, after my Family disappointments and the little favour I have ever met with from former Administrations, but there is nothing I would not do to support those I prefer upon a System which has in it any Evidence of real concert, consistent Plan, and solid grounds of Strength. I have now suggested the Means which have occurr'd to me, but I am as open to consider any other, and only dread the loss of more time in more broken Consultations, imperfect Plans, and indecisive Seasons. Let me add, that the generous manner in which Mr Pitt behaved to the whole Party last Year, his Name, his Weight, his Talents all make his concurrence a necessary part of any Union ; and I should very much fear any Plan would be found ineffectual, which had not both the lustre of Mr Pitt's accession to it, and the declared and active support of Lord Hardwick's Family, few Men in' this Country being equal to Mr Yorke in that Importance, which I thank God still results from Abilities, Integrity, and Independence.

I will certainly wait upon Your Grace at Clermont, and the Duke of Devonshire says he will bring me.

The Bishop of London [Dr Sheldon] is expected to die every Minute, and Warburton is declared to be his Successor. Lord Sandys has accepted a Pension of £1,500 a Year which he consented to take on Condition he was permitted to draw up the Reasons of the Grant, which Privilege of drawing his Nightcap over his Eyes was, I believe, never refused to any Deserter at his Execution.

I beg my Compliments to the Duchess of Newcastle : I have just
seen Conway who will dine with your Grace at Claremont on Friday,
if we should learn from the Duke of Devonshire that Your Grace
approves of that Day."

1765, June —. A receipted bill for wine.
Lady Townshend is debtor to John Cole and paid 7s. for four bottles
of Port wine and 3s. 6d. for two bottles of Lisbon.

1765, Aug. 2nd. George Shirley to Lord Townshend. Dated at
Lower Eatington.
" My Dr Lord—By a Messenger from Tamworth who arrived here last
night at 11 o'clock, I recd the enclosed, & an other from Ld Aylesford
expressing his great inclination that Mr Smith shou'd be in your Lordship's interest. His Lordship's letter to me I have sent to Mr Willington by the return of the Messenger, & shall follow it this evening . .
. . . I have seen Mr Meacham of Stratford whose brother is with
us, & he tells me his father in law, who is concern'd for Lord Weymouth, thinks his Lordship's interest much lessen'd by the present
Contest, & has no hopes of success " . . . . . .

1765, Oct. 29th. An Agreement between Lord Townshend and
Lord Weymouth concerning the Burgh of Tamworth. [Dated at
Grendon Hall.]
In Consideration of the present Contest against Mr [Edward] Thur-
low the Candidate upon the Mannour Interest being dropt, and of Lord
Townshend's concurring in his Election ; Lord Weymouth agrees that
upon Lord Townshend and Mr Luttrell contributing each Five Hun-
dred Pounds towards it, Lord Weymouth will provide a Seat in and
during the next Parliament for a Person to be named by Lord Towns-
hend ; that such Seat shall be found for [sic] Weobly, unless Lord
Weymouth can purchase another certain Seat, in which Case Lord
Townshend and Lord Weymouth are to pay in equal Proportions so
much of the Price of it, as shall be given on the Score of securing Re-
Elections :
But if the Seat shall be found at Weobley, in case of the Death of
Lord Townshend's member at Tamworth, the Member he shall have
named for Weobly shall vacate his Seat.
It is further agreed that Lord Weymouth will use his Interest to
fill up one half of the Corporation with Lord Townshend's friends, as
soon as can be done with Security and Convenience to the United
Interest.
[Signed] TOWNSHEND [and] WEYMOUTH. Witness[es] ROB. BERTIE
[and] S. STANTON.

Same date. An election agreement, dated at Grendon Hall.
" An agreement between Lord Townshend, Mr Luttrell, and the
Under-written, relative to the Borough of Tamworth ;
Mr Luttrell and his Friends who now support the Castle Interest
engage in Consideration of Lord Townshend naming Mr Luttrell in
that Interest at the next General Election to support henceforth the
Nomination of the two Members which shall be recommended by the
Manour and the Castle thereby to promote the future Tranquility of
the Town by resisting any third Interest.
But it is understood and agreed that in Case Mr Luttrell shoud
happen to die during the next Parliament the Nomination of a Member
to succeed him shall fall intirely to Lord Townshend.
[Signed] TOWNSHEND ; J. LUTTRELL ; S. PIPE; J. OLDERSHAW;
JNo WILLINGTON. Witness[es] ROB. BERTIE [and] S. STANTON.

1766, Jan. 8th.   Draft letter of Lord Townshend to Mr Whiston
Dated at Rainham.

" Mr Whiston

Your Sincerity & Integrity makes me desirous of preserving
your Acquaintance, and the promise you made me of communicating
your Observations upon the Necessities of the Poor, & the means of
releiving them, affords me an occasion of giving you these Assurances.

By a friend of Tamworth, I have this opportunity of repeating my
good Wishes to you ; It is the more agreeable to me because no Election depending, it cannot be so directly interpreted as an interested
Compliment, an Influence I know your honest Heart disdains; but
when I confess my Desire to consult you for the Sake of Thousands &
to derive assistance from you in many Instances which perhaps my
Rank cannot so easily procure, I am sure you will readily contribute,
& you may be assured that I will not only most earnestly consider the
Lights which you may afford me upon this Subject; but that I will
either apply them myself, or recommend them to others of more Ability
in such a Manner, as may contribute to the Success of that Measure
which every honest & humane Man ought most devoutly to wish.

The Distress of the Poor in this Country is certainly a Circumstance
which reflects the greatest disgrace to [the] Honour of this Great
Country, and occasions the most radical National Imbecillity. Both
as Christians & Legislators it crys out against us ; whoever can adjust
& establish this great Point will deserve more Honour than Twenty
Modern Cato['s] with as many admiring Senates at his Heels. If I am
not mistaken the American Colonies have in 25 Years doubled the Number of their Inhabitants from Gt Brittain (I exclude Foreigners entirely
in the Computation) How many more have starved here that might
have work'd there ! or at home ? Luxury among one part & Misery with
the Other is daily expelling our Inhabitants by Thousands & then we are
surprised that our Empire should be moving.

Adieu my worthy friend I heartily wish you & yr Family, all health
& shall allways be happy to be of use to you & to them.

Yr friend & Wellwisher
TOWNSHEND."

1766, June 5. Hunt Walsh to Lord Townshend. Dated at Dublin, and
unaddressed.

. . . . . As to the state of our Politicks, we have had a variety of
Disputes during the course of this Sessions, which have probably made
a greater noise on your side of the water, than they have upon the
Spot. The Patriots began the Sessions with a Minority of about ten,
but on the Address to His Majesty for limiting the time of our Parliaments sitting, they mustered above ninety, and upon several other
motions had between fifty and sixty, a great matter of Debate among
us rises from a power our privy Council assumes of stopping our Bills,
and not letting them go to England after they passed our House ; the
Parliament do not allow there is any Law for this. Sir William
Osborne, and Mr Flood, are the chief in the Opposition and are
certainly very able Men, we are fond of imitating our Neighbours, and
set up for great asserters of liberty. By the last Packet there is a
report that you are to succeed Lord Rochford at Madrid, if so we can
not expect to have the Pleasure of seeing you here for some years. I
am, my Lord " etc.

1766, June 21st.   Castell ? Bacon to the same. Dated at Elcham.

" My dear Lord,

I beg'd yr Ldship in my last Letter that You would be so good as
to give me a Hurdle of old Hounds to hunt the Otter. . . . . . The

MARQUESS
TOWNSHEND
MSS.

Bearer is the Person, who is to look after the Hounds & therefore if
You can supply me with a Hurdle, please to order them to be delivered
to him.

I am very much obliged to You for the Intelligence You sent me,
& I dare say, that You will very soon be sent for to the Queen's
House.

I see by the Gazette that Ld Granby is no longer Ld Lieut. of Derbyshire, for I thought he woud have been continued in it at least, 'till
the Duke of Devonshire was of Age. . . . . .

C. BACON.

1766, June 24th. Dingley Ashham to the same. Dated at Coning-
ton, and unaddressed.

. . . . . "I am sorry you've lost so many of yor young [grey]
hounds. I have some of the same litter I sent you as clever as any
w^{t}ever, and enter as well—there was one sent by mistake wch if too
little for you I shall be glad of again—the best respects of all here wait
on you and Lady Townshend."

1766, June 25th. C. BACON to the same. Dated at Elcham.
My Dear Lord

I am much obliged to You, for the trouble You have given yourself in endeavouring to furnish me with Hounds for Otter Hunting,
But from the present State of your Kennel, I beg You woud not think
any more about it, for I shall continue to wage War against the Otters
insidiously, with Traps Steelfalls &c. instead of open force I
was well informed that Newfoundland Dogs are the best in the World
for Otter hunting, & therefore last year Commodore Palliser was
desired to bring some over with him, & accordingly did so, ... He
ordered a man to lead them up from Portsmo[uth]. Whether the man
was an American or not, I dont know, but that he was a villain is most
certain, for not liking his errand, & out of revenge as is supposed to the
Boatswain, from whom he rec^d his immediate Orders, in coming to
Town, he made the Dogs swallow pieces of Spunge & thereby killd
them all—The Commodore is to bring some more over, when he returns,
& I hope they will arrive safe—Our intercourse last Year with the
Plantations in every respect, was very shocking & bad " . . . . .

1766, Oct. 24th. Charles Townshend to Lady Townshend. Unaddressed, but indorsed " Cha. T. to his Mother."

Dear Madam.—Your Ladyship will forgive my not having sooner informed you of the calamity which we have suffered in our Family by
the death of M^r [Campbell] Scott, but, in the affliction of Lady
Dalkeith under so very severe a misfortune, I have realy been incapable
of any attention beyond herself. I had the good fortune of being able
to break the sad news gradually to her, and time to bring Sr W. Duncan
& Mr Hawkins within reach before she suspected any thing. By
these means the immediate shock was in some degree alleviated, and the
blow itself the better resisted. Soon after bleeding, she sunk into a
calm habit of melancholy, and I led her into a discourse upon her only
remaining son. His character, his settlement in life, & his return to
comfort & support her. This turn of discourse had the effect I wished,
for it induced her to communicate what she felt & served to divert her
mind to fresh objects. I took the moment & sent for the Duke [of
Buccleugh] by express. . . . .

Yr's most affectly,
C. T."

G[rosvenor] S[quare] Oc[tober] 24, 1766.

1767, May 30th. William Wilkin to the Dowager Lady Townshend. Dated at Fordham.

. . . . . . " We should have been much better than any could have expected, but we have every day constant heavy or great rains, and the wether over and above cold, which hurts the Stocks of all Sorts of Cattle, and nothing grows, what will be the end of these unnatural times, I cant judge as yet, I have been very wet two Days, and that have given me a great Cold, which I hope will not last long. My Doctor advises me to bleed which I purpose to doe this morning. It is a very sickly time in the low Countrys, and in the Isle of Ely "
. . . . .

1768, Augt. 12th. Lieut.-Colonel George Williamson to " His Excellency Lord Viscount Townshend." Dated at Woolwich.

" My Lord,
I have had the honor of a letter from your Lordship and am very unhappy to find I have given you some offence in too anxiously soliciting for my Son's Promotion . . . . [I] had no other meaning by speaking to Lord Granby than hopeing that his Lordship's recommendation of my Son would render the Young Man more worthy of Your Lordship's Patronage " . . . .

1768, Augt. 14th. Dr Richard Chenevix, Bishop of Waterford, to the same. Dated at Waterford.

" My Lor[d],
I take the first opportunity, when I think your Excellency may be returned to Dublin, to express my most dutiful acknowledgements for the great honour you did me in coming to the Episcopal House. I wish I had been more in readiness to receive your Excellency in such a manner as your own high rank, as well as your Station entitles you to, but I arrived but the day before your Excellency, and when I was in Dublin I did'nt think your Excellency woud honour me so soon with your Presence. I must make you my Excuses for not having sent you some cold Provisions to Dungannon Fort, but I was absolutely ignorant that it was a Place destitute of Accomodation, and did'nt know it till after your Excellency was gone from Waterford. Thó I am unwilling to trespass upon your time, yet I must beg leave, before I conclude, to express my gratitude for the many marks of affability and kindness with which your Excellency has been pleased to honour me and which I shall always remember with due sentiments. I am with the utmost regard respect & submission . . . .

R. WATERFORD."

1768, Sept. 27th. John Powdick to the same. Dated at the General Post Office.

The writer solicits his Lordship's interest to procure him the appointment of Post Master at Thetford.

1768, Nov. 13th. Revd Francis Wollaston to the same. Dated at East Dereham.

The writer begs Lord Townshend to forward his views as to an exchange of his living for another.

1768, Nov. 22nd. Richard Woodward to Lady Townshend. Dated in New Street and unaddressed.

The writer begs her Ladyship's influence with the Lord Lieutenant in favour of his son-in-law Capt George Robinson, who sold out of the 65th Regiment in Augt 1767, and who would willingly again purchase.

MARQUESS
TOWNSHEND
MSS.

1768, Dec. 8th. Rev. Francis Wollaston to Lord Townshend. Dated at Charterhouse Square.

. . . . "As to Mr de Grey, his illness was a tedious fever which ended in abcesses formed in his throat, that were very painful and dangerous, as they sometimes prevented his swallowing. We hope however he is now out of danger" . . . . .

1768, Dec. 20th. Robert Wilmot to John Lees. Dated at St James's.

. . . . . "Lord Frederick Campbell arrived in Town last Saturday. I have called twice but had not the good Fortune to find his Lordship. I am told that Lord Percy and Sir George Macartney will set out some day this week for Dublin."

1768, Dec. 23rd. Rev. Francis Wollaston to Lord Townshend. Dated in Charterhouse Square.

My Lord—I am afraid Your Excellency will think me impertinent in again troubling you with a repetition of my application . . . . I understand the Rectory of Bow in Cheapside is shortly to be resigned, & is in the gift of the Arch-bishop of Canterbury ; whether Your Excellency would chuse to procure that for me from him (in the manner you proposed with my Lord Duke of Grafton ; or in any other method you see proper) which being better than my vicarage is more than I could get by exchange . . . . . or Your Excellency may perhaps not chuse to ask for it . . . . .

PS.— . . . . I have since heard that the Arch-bishop intends to compliment the Duke of Grafton with it, so that if from either of them Your Excellency could procure it for me, it would lay me under the highest Obligation.

1769, Jan. 1st. O. Wynne to the same. Dated at Haslewood.

"My Lord,—I have just heard that You intend to pay a Visit at Elphin, & Boyle, in a few days, and to shoot at Rockingham, if so, I flatter myself that I shall have the honor of seeing Your Excellency, & Your friends, at this Place.

I am just twenty Miles from Boyle, and the Road is very fine, I think I can promise You some pleasant Shooting, & You will see a Romantick Country ; if I find that I am to expect the honour of Your Company here, I shall be ready to assist you with horses or Carriages, I am with the greatest Respect, Your Excellency's much obliged, etc."

1769, Jan. 21st. Rev. Francis Wollaston to the same. Dated in Charterhouse Square.

. . . . . . "I am sorry to find by him [Mr Lees] that Your Excellency seems to have misunderstood my intentions concerning the resignation of Dereham ; the Rectory of which, being a Sinecure of £300 ₽ an. & compatible with anything, is by itself, in general estimation, equal to any other living of £600 ; & therefore was not in my thoughts to part with. But the Vicarage of about £200 ₽ an., if Your Excellency could obtain for me a living in or near London, would thereby be vacated. . . . . . If, in exchange for that part of my living which is of £200, I wish by Your Excellency's interest to obtain one not less than £300, I hope you will not think me unreasonable" . . . . .

1769, Feb. 17th. Capt. William Wolseley—"at Mrs. Berner's, grocer, Panton Street Leaster Fields, London"—to Lord Townshend.

The writer, who has been 14 years in the army and served three years in Germany, gave £3,500 for his Troop in the 8th Dragoons and now is unable to sell in the regiment above the Regulation price. The value of his commission, and £17,00 his wife's fortune, is all that he has to subsist on after selling out. Cornet [William] Clive of Lord Pembroke's Regiment, [the 1ˢᵗ Dragoons] brother to Lord Clive, and Capt. Falkner of the Guards, are desirous of purchasing the writer's Troop.

1769, May 6th. Lieut. John Crosse, Commander of the Hornet Sloop of War, to Sackville Hamilton. Dated at Dublin, and addressed to Sackville Hamilton Esqʳ at the Custom house.

The writer, having been desired to assist in apprehending John Connor a proclaimed smuggler, explains that he is under orders to sail for Liverpool, where he expects to find orders to deliver up his command; but that he will call at the Isle of Man on his way to Liverpool and will acquaint the commanding officer of the King's ships, who he doubts not will repair to Dublin without delay.

1769, May 9th. Sackville Hamilton, Principal clerk to the Commissioners of the Customs and Revenue in Ireland, to Mʳ Waite of Dublin Castle.

Enclosing the last, by direction of the Commissioners, to be laid before the Lord Lieutenant.

1769, Aug. 9th.—H. William Wilson to Lord Townshend. Dated at Kirby.

"My Lord—I was honoured wᵗʰ your two Letters the same post, and take the first opportunity of returning your Lordship thanks for your very obliging Offer of your house at Rainham which I should wᵗʰ great pleasure [have] accept'd of, but since my last I have buried my Uncle of Didlington who has left me Sole Executor so [I] shall spend [a] great part of the Sporting Season there, but shall always be happy to pay my Respects at Rainham on your return " . . . . .

1769, Aug. 10th. Rev. Francis Woolaston to the same. Dated at East Dereham.

My Lord—The sollicitude of all my friends to have me once more settled in their neighbourhood, together with my own inclinations urged me last summer to make application for a removal from hence : & I would apply no where but to Your Excellency . . . . . though I could have wished to have received some advancement at Your Excellency's hands, & therefore did decline one opening by way of Exchange last winter ; I could not refuse an offer that has since been made by the Bishop of Rochester [Dʳ Zachariah Pearce] at the request of my brother Heberden ; nor with so aged a Bishop could I delay passing through all the forms at once : & therefore, being summoned last week to London from whence I returned yesterday, [I] was a few days since collated to the Rectory of Chislehurst in Kent ; a situation most agreeable & on all accounts most desirable. I hope your Excellency will excuse me in this. It is my maxim to keep always steady to my principles, & [to be] gratefull to benefactors ; among whom I have hoped and shall hope always to reckon Your Excellency."

1769, Oct. 28th. Mrs. Robert Orme to her sister-in-law Lady Townshend.

Dear Madam,

"I have long wished for an Occasion of writing to you but the Resentment of all my Family except that of my poor Brother Charles was so great that it deterr'd me from making any other Application but Sir William Draper who was so feeling and humain as to have at heart a Family Reconciliation filled me with joy at his Account of your great Benevolence Compassion and good Will. It is therefore Madam in Consequence of what I think my Duty that I trouble you with this

-Letter to return you my most gratefull thanks for your kind and affectionate Behaviour, and also to beg of you dear Madam to use all your Influence upon my Brother to forgive me and my Children, and be assured that I shall ever retain the most most grateful Remembrance of it.

Clyst, October 28ᵗʰ. AUDERY ORME."

1769, Dec. 28th. Rev. K. Percival to ——. Dated at Dublin, and unaddressed.

. . . . . " Lord Townshend has not had a satisfactory sessions, the conclusion of which you see in the Votes of the Commons . . . . . the Opposition he met with laid him under a Necessity of giving whatever he had to dispose of to such Members as supported him in the House. This has in a great measure put it out of his Excellency's Power to do anything for my brother William . . . . My Brothers Health is declining, & the Expenses of his Family encreasing, his eldest Son has been above a year in the College, his Second is Apprentice to a very respectable Merchant, & his third still at School; they are all very well disposed, & behave intirely to the Satisfaction of their Friends " . . . . . .

1770, Feb. 13th. Simon Fraser to Lord Townshend. Dated at Percy Street.

" My dear Lord—I have been very much concerned these two weeks, that no information reached me upon material Matters, which deserved your Lordship's Attention. I called at Lord Weymouth's Office the morning after The Duke of Grafton's resignation, and I was told that an official Letter had been sent to acquaint your Excellency of it, and as the most experienced Politicians could not guess what effect that Event would have upon the present Administration, it was necessary to wait the fate of two or three questions in the house of Commons, before a Conjecture could be formed about Lord North's Situation ; and by the division yesterday in both houses, it is evident, that the Ministry has got additional Strength. I have desired that the Minutes should be sent to your Lordship, and by them, you will see the Motions which were made Yesterday in the house of Commons, by Mʳ Dowdswell, and in the house of Peers by Lord Chatham seconded by Lord Cambden, and it was an exceeding good debate. The Duke of Grafton Lord Gower, and Lord Mansfield distinguished themselves upon the Side of [the] Administration. To day the Countenances of the friends of Government is cleared up, and all partys agree, that we shall have no Change this Winter. I have taken some trouble to enquire about your Excellency's Situation, and I sincerely believe that it is seriously intended to continue your Lordship in the Government of Ireland, and to support you firmly in it. The many unforseen events which have happened here, rendered it impossible to give the Dispatch transmitted by Mʳ Swan a final and decisive Consideration, Mʳ Wood told me yesterday that he carried it by Lord Weymouth's desire last Sunday to Lord North, and that it would, in all probability be answered in the Course of the week. I hope it will be entirely satisfactory to your Excellency and that you will be enabled to govern Ireland upon true Constitutional Principles, and to bring forward some independent gentlemen who have supported your Lordship's Administration at the risk of their own political existence.

Lord Legonier cannot live many days. The Duke of Gloucester will certainly have the first Regiment of Guards, and I have heard it surmised every where that Your Lordship has very good pretensions to the third ; I humbly submit it, if your Excellency may not apply to His

Majesty, by a Letter addressed to Lord Weymouth, there cannot be
any impropriety in this Application, as there is no Commander in Chief
at present, if Your Lordship shall think proper to inclose the letter to
me, I will take Care to deliver it, and perhaps an opportunity may offer
of having some Conversation with the Secretary of State [Lord Wey-
mouth] upon the Subject.

General Cornwallis desires to be very affectionately remembered to
Your Lordship and he wishes to have his Regiment quartered this year
at Waterford, & if it makes no alteration in the arangement of Quarters
it would be very agreeable to me. The General, in the most delicate,
& tender manner desired me to mention his wish, to have an Ensigncy
in his own or some other Regiment for a very near relation of his.
He is well aware of the difficult Situation in which your Excellency
must be frequently placed with respect to political Connections, and he
is far from desiring this instance of your Excÿs kindness to him, if it
lays you under any inconvenience."

1770, April 10th. The same to the same. Dated in Percy Street.

"My dear Lord—I had the honor to see Lord Weymouth this Morning, and was happy to find that he had an Opportunity to receive His
Majesty's Pleasure so soon, upon the most material part of your
Excÿ's Dispatch; 'it will be transmitted to Your Lordship by this
night's Post, and as the Parliament is not to meet it will not be
necessary for me to apply to any of the Members to repair to Ireland.
Mr Conolly left town last Sunday ; and he will give you an Account of
what passed in the house of Common here about Irish affairs; Deyson's
Pension is much talked of; and I find that it is disclaimed by some of
the Ministry ; if it is considered as good ground for opposition here,
Your Excÿ may imagine how much may be made of it in Ireland " . . . .

1770, May 1st. Lord Barrington, Secretary of War, to the same.

The writer informs the Lord Lieutenant that the latter had been
appointed a Lieut.-General.

Same date. Viscount Clare, M.P. for Bristol and ex-President of
the Board of Trade, to the same. Dated in London.

"My dear Lord—I feel in common with my late Brothers, Messrs Ellis
and Grenville, your Excellency's very kind attention to our Interest,
altho I do not mean to avail my Self of it, as I hope to qualifye in
Ireland. But my Obligation to your Excellency is the very same. I
know how well you understand and have at heart the Importance of
the Linen-manufacture to Ireland. I wish that others Natives of that
Country, who are indebted to it not only for their Existence but for the
means of preserving it, members of both Houses here, were half so
zealous in their Endeavours for its Service : but many of them forsooth,
are too great to bend their Attention to such low Concerns, and we
were left, as usual, in the House of Commons with very few indeed
belonging to Ireland either by Birth or Fortune, to determine upon the
Continuance of the Bounty now given in common to certain Species of
British and Irish Linens exported from Great Britain. The Friends of
Manchester took advantage of this thin Attendance to come to a Compromise with the Scotch, by which a Part of the Bounty was to be taken
off from those Linens and apply'd to chequed and striped *British* Linens.
I soon perceived and exposed the Injustice of this Proposition. The
Scotch adhered to the Compact with us, and the Friends to this Expedient
did not venture to propose it in a formal Question to the House. The
Bounties upon Linens will be continued. But as it proposed to give also
a small Bounty upon British chequed and striped Linens, I shall try
whether we can not obtain the same for those of the manufacture of

Ireland, which are *now* prohibited to be imported here by an excessive Duty. I shall also endeavour to have the Bounty upon white and brown Linens of Great Britain and Ireland, which is now absurdly confined, extended to printed Linens of the same Species. But in neither of these Propositions have I much hopes of succeeding.

I wish when there is a Vacancy at the Linen-Board, to be appointed a Trustee ; and, without much Vanity, my Country-men ought to wish it at least as much as I do ; for I mean, when I return into Ireland to make myself as much as I can master of that important subject.

I hope I said nothing in my last Letter to convey an Idea to you as if you had been reflected upon by your Country-man, or any other person, in the Debate upon the Irish Pensions. · Not a Glance of that Tendency was thrown out : and when Justice was done to your Love for Ireland manifested upon that and every other Subject, it was Praise, not Vindication. I do not believe we shall rise quite so soon as was believed. I think we shall sit three weeks longer, even if no extraordinary Event shoud happen. Wilkes is my near Neighbour, and passes every Day before my Door as unnoticed and unattended as any other Passenger.
CRAGGS-CLARE."

1770, May 26th. Rev. T. O. Young to Lady Townshend. Dated at Northchurch.
. . . . . "Now our Parliament is up, the News Papers seem to turn their patriotic attention to Irish *grievances,* & the Guild of Merchants begins to share the Paragraphs with our Common Councell." . . . . .

1770, June 2nd. Lady Mary Compton to the same. Dated at Bruton Street.
. . . . . . "for the last three Weeks, they [*i.e.* fires] have been more wanted than in the Depth of Winter. The [King's] Birthday [June 4th] being so near, I imagine as soon as that is over, the Town will empty very fast ; a few people will be obliged to attend, till her Majesty's Month is up."

1770, June 5th. Mrs. Elizabeth Drummond to the same. Dated at Wimbledon.
. . . . . . " I think you managed very cleverly about my Lady Arden [the Countess of Egmont]. I wish it had been an English Peerage, but as she wisht to have it, I own I am very happy it is done, I realy was much surprised for I had never heard a word of it till she came & told me it was done. . . . . I suppose you have heard of all the Weddings & of the *New Club.* I fancy it will not last long. Some friends of yours is of it, & I have been told is sorry for it but have not resolution to scratch their Names out. . . . .

1770, June 8th. Hon. John Townshend to the same (his mother). Dated at Eton.

1770, June 10th. Mrs. Manby to the same. Dated at Denver Cottage.
. . . " I suppose your Ladyship has heard that Lord Buckinghamshire is going to be married to Miss Conolly a young Lady of blooming Fifteen. . . . . . Mr Henry Dashwood is going to be married to a Daughter of Sir John Rous's, she is very young. It is thought they won't marry till Sr Thos Peyton is dead. . . . . .
J. MANBY."

1770, June 10th. Hon. George Townshend to the same (his mother). Dated at Eton.

1770, June 11th. Mrs. Turner to the same. Dated at Warham.

. . . . " This corner of the county is at present quite gay [I] assure
your Ladyship that both Concert's & Play's are with in our reach. The
Former we owe to a few Gentlemen, who in the Spring agreed to meet
once a Month at Fakenham, eat together there, & have a little Musick
before & after their repast—as they were most of them performers on
some instrument, a little addition to their Band was deem'd sufficient,
& to procure that a Guinea each was to be subscribed, out of which
their Dinner was likewise to be furnished. . . . . Ladies can gain
admittance only with Tickets, but of them every subscriber has the
disposal of two. . . . .

The plays are at Walsingham—the Lynn Company arrived there about
Ten Days ago—open'd the Theatre (commonly called a Barn) on
Wednesday last, & propose acting constantly three times a week during
their stay which [I] fancy will be at least a Month longer. . . . .

Private Letters, as well as the Publick Papers, say Lord Buckingham
is very soon to be married to Miss Connolly [I] cant say I am at all
surprized at the shortness of the time he allots to Mourning: tho' own I
am exceedingly so to find that Cupid, & not Plutus, influences him in
his present Choice. . . . .

A. TURNER."

1771, Jan. 22nd. Sir George Savile, M.P. for Yorkshire, to Lord
Townshend. Dated at Rufford.

The writer begs that his Lordship will appoint Ensign Nicholls
(Senior Ensign of the 54th Reg^t, and formerly in the writer's Regiment
of Militia) to a Lieutenancy as it is understood that a Company is to be
added to each Corps on the Irish Establishment.

1771, Augt. 30th. Lord Sandwich, First Lord of the Admiralty, to
Lord Townshend. Dated at the Admiralty.

" My Lord

I am honoured with your Excellencies letter recommending
Captain Schomberg to succeed to the vacancy in the Dorsett Yatcht,
and tho' by a letter I have from him at the same time he seems inclined
to accept that Command if it should be offered to him, yet I am persuaded
when he comes to reconsider the matter, he will not persevere in that
pursuit, as I have informed him by letter that the person who retires to
that Command cannot have any claim to be employed in active Service
in his Majesties Navy in case of war, or future desire to go to Sea, in a
Line of battle Ship.

What I have hitherto said relates however only to Captain Schomberg,
but I am coming to a more disagreeable part of this business, namely,
that there is another person strongly recommended by Lord Rochford
for this Command, & recommended many months ago, who is disposed
to take it on the usual conditions & as a retirement out of the active
Service of the Navy, what am I to do between your Lordship's & L^d
Rochford's desire ? You are both my friends, & friends from whom I
have received the most essential proofs of kindness. . . . .

SANDWICH.

[P.S.] I mention nothing about Captain Shirley for whether it is
him or Captain Schomberg, it is exactly the same thing to me, upon the
conditions above mentioned."

1771, Sept. 4th. Captain Alexander Schomberg to the same. Dated
at Windsor.

. . . " I would not again venture to be so importunate in my
Correspondence, were it not that I find myself under the disagreeable
Necessity of explaining to you the impropriety (I will not call it by a

MARQUESS
TOWNSHEND
MSS.

harsher name) of Lord Sandwich's interposition & misinterpretation when he writes to you of the *determined incompatibility of my acceptance of the Dorset Yatcht with my future employment in any active Service.* His Lordship may have determined this in his own Mind, but the fact is incontrovertibly otherwise : & when I had the Honor of waiting on his Lordship, I gave him a Case in Point. I mentioned Capt Weller who commanded a 74 Gun Ship in the last War after having been for some time Commander of the Dorset Yatcht, & who is now, on account of his bad Health on the list of retired Admirals, to which his Lordship replied that he *was not then at the [Admiralty] Board."* . . . .

1771, Sept. 9th. The same to the same. Dated in London.

"Impatient at the Earl of Sandwich's conduct I hurried to Town, but it will be a Week before I can see him & I fear unless your Lordship is pleased to move again I shall be defeated. The Time presses & I wish to save [the] post. Your Lordship will forgive my writing to you as it were on one Leg but delays are dangerous & I have made up my Mind for having again the Charge of your Person across the Sea.

My Noble Lords at Whitehall think me weak enough to *leave* my Cake and gnaw the *Streamer* but they are mistaken.

Your Lordship is the best ju[d]ge of their power ; they may tear the Yatcht from me, but they shall not gain, what they labour at, my Consent.

Excuse this Hint & this hurry my Lord I have thought it right to give you this intelligence, & I hope I have not misjudged."

1771, Sept. 11th. Solomon Schomberg to the same. Dated in Whalebone Court, Lothbury.

. . . "Allowing for human Infirmities, my Conduct in a Period of upwards of three very expensive Years in your Excellency's Service, has, (unless, Indigence is criminal) been strictly irreproachable ; What Debts I have contracted, were created by Necessity, unavoidably incurr'd by my Situation, by Illness & other adventitious Circumstances, & not through Choice or Extravagance." . . . .

1771, Oct. 2nd. Lord Sandwich to the same. Dated at the Admiralty.

"My dear Lord,—It gives me great pleasure to be able to inform Your Excellency, that I have contrived to accommodate the person recommended by Lord Rochford, otherwise than with the Command of the Dorset Yatcht ; & that I am therefore ready to obey Your Commands upon that Subject.

I must beg however before the Commission is made out, to receive your final & explicit determination between the Captains Shirley and Schomberg ; your last letter went on a supposition that Captain Shomberg would not accept it ; but whither he is extremely indigent, or extremely infatuated, or whither he may think my situation here not permanent I know not, but he persists in his acceptance of the Yatcht if it is offered to him ; contrary to the opinion of his best friends, and of every Officer in the Sea Service with whom I have conversed upon the occasion. I am sure, my Dear Lord, you who are a Military Man, & have the most proper notions of the sort of delicacies due to the preservation of a military character, will not think the carrying passengers for emolument is a proper school for a person that is to command a fleet ; if lucre is a person's object let him have it, but then do not let him aspire to honours that for the good of the Service must be pursued thro' a different channel. I own I wish you had never mentioned his name upon this occasion, as it will probably lose an Officer to the Navy who might hereafter have made a considerable figure in his profession : & will postpone a very good man who you wish to serve [Captain Shirley], who is related to your family, and who I think much the properer man for the employment in question." . . . .

1771, Dec. 19th. Hugh Massy to the same. Dated at Suire Castle, near Cashell.

The writer begs Lord Townshend to appoint Simon Durdon Esqre, of the city of Limerick, High Sheriff of that county for the ensuing year.

1772, Feb. 19th. Capt. Alexander Schomberg to the same. Dated at Dublin.

The writer suggests a plan for attacking Copenhagen should we ever break with the Danes.

1775, March 8th. John Hely Hutchinson, Provost of Trinity College Dublin, to the same. Dated at Trinity Coll.

This letter refers to an appointment which the writer has recently received from the Government.

1785, July 24th. Lord Orford to the same. Dated at Norwich.
My Dr Lord

I am sorry to inform you that Master Money ascended alone under the British Balloon at four o'clock yesterday afternoon. The Balloon rose to a great Hight & took a direction towards the Sea. . It was seen entering over the Ocean about a League south of Lowestoff at a very great Hight at Six of Clock. By which Circumstance I am greatly apprehensive for his Safety. Nor can I account for his thus continuing in the Air but that by some accident perhaps the String which connects the Valve was broken or by the Collapsion of the lower Part of [the] Balloon (for twas not half full) the String w^ld not act upon it. It gave me great Concern to hear that Your Lordship had received a Wound from your own Sword. I hope you are now perfectly recovered & that we shall soon see you in the Country.

ORFORD."

1786, Jan. 30th. Arthur Young to the same. Dated at Bradfield Hall.

" My Lord

The more I reflect on your Lordship's discovery in feeding cattle and sheep with the trimmings of plantations the more important it appears to me ; & I am confirmed in the opinion by that of every person I have mentioned it to. This makes me anxious to have y^r Lordship's account of it, wch I hope you will favour me wth. It will convince the world that y^r retirement when in the country is no less dedicated to the service of mankind than y^r more active exertions have been, to promote that of the State.

I was lately in High Suffolk to view their cows, & met with a good farmer who wanted a farm ; his name Kent ; I told him of y^r Lordship's & believe he will go to see it."

My most respectful Compt^s to Lady Townshend—I hope she will by & by let a Cow rival a greyhound.

1791, Feb. 21st. The Chevalier D'Eon to the same. Addressed to " My Lord Marquis of Townshend—No. 14 Weymouth Street."

Mlle D'Eon est bien fachée de ne s'etre point trouvée chez elle quand Milord Marquis de Townshend lui a fait l'honneur d'y passer. Depuis ce tems elle a été incommodée, Sans cela elle auroit été lui presenter ses respects & à Milady.

Si Milord a la bonté de lui faire dire le jour & l'heure qu'elle peut le voir elle si [sic] rendra avec empressement ; l'homme qui garde la porte de Milord dit à toutes le personnes qu'il ne connoit pas que Milord n'y est pas.

1791, March 4th. Lord Orford to the Marquis Townshend. Dated at Eriswell.

" My Dr Lord

May I beg of your Lordship to send the Inclosure to Ld Frederick. I am now to return your Lordship Thanks for Ld Sheffield's Pamphlet in which as in all his Lordship's there is much to be approved of, tho' not the whole work. I cannot for instance agree with his Lordship & the Yarmouth merchants that t'wod be right to take off the Penalties to which ships are liable for smugling Corn. The Argument that the Owner shou'd not suffer for the Fault committed by his Captain is not consistant to the Laws of this Country which in every Instance make the Master responsible for the offences of his Servants. Your Lordship's Coachman for Instance driving your empty Carriage against an other you tho absent cou'd be obliged to pay all Damage incurr'd, & I am persuaded that if the Penalty was to be changed from Confiscation to one Hundred Pounds agreable to Ld Sheffield's Proposal that the whole Corn Bill wou'd be reduced to a Piece of Waste Paper, for the Merchant wou'd run so small a risque whenever t he Markets either at Home or Abroad were so high as wou'd indemnify him for speculating on the Chance of Detection.

Farming & Farmers go on well this Winter. Corn continues increasing in Price and I am certain from my own returns that they have not had so good a Year among many Past as the Last.

If you chuse to breed by a very fine Indian Wild Boar sent from Madrass to Lt C^o Hughes, now at Houghton you will be welcome to serve as many Sows as you please."

INDEX.

I.

P.

F F

Quarantine, observations on ; 107.
Quebec ; 269.
  siege of, papers relating to ; 306 *et seq.*
Queensberry :
  Duke of (1711), letters of ; 79, 81.
  —— (1704), papers by ; 153.
  Duchess of, mem. by ; 41, 42.
Quesne, Mons. de, letter of ; 64.
Quiddenham, Sir T. Holland at ; 19.
  letters dated at ; 28.
Quin, James, letter of ; 322.

R.

Rabley, letters dated at ; 316, 318.
Raby, Lord (1709) ; 58.
  at Hanover ; 77.
  letters of ; 80–85.
  his regiment in Spain ; 80.
  his departure from Berlin ; 81, 85.
Radburne, John, letter of ; 129.
Radford, John, sent to the Tower ; 44.
Radnor, Earl of (1714) ; 221.
Ragotzy, Prince, and the Emperor ; 80.
Rainsford, Mr. Justice, opinion by ; 27.
Ramos, Diego, declaration by ; 116.
Ramsay, M. de, commandant of Quebec ; 324.
Ramsey, Mr., his mission to James I. ; 22.
Ranelagh :
  the ship ; 77, 85.
  Earl of, Paymaster-General ; 217.
  Lord and Lady ; 244.
Rantzau, document signed ; 96.
Ratisbon ; 80.
  document dated at ; 119.
  diet at, Protestant ministers at ; 57, 59.
  Evangelical conference at ; 108.
Ravanel, Captain, wounded ; 71.
Rawcliffe ; 164.
Rawlins, Mr. ; 240.
Rayley, William, chamberlain of Norwich ; 329.
Raymond, Sir Robert ; 211.
  paper signed by ; 144.
Raynham or Rainham Hall, Norfolk ; 27, 58, 87, 330, 331, 340, 356, 364–370, 376, 397, 402, 406.
  East, Ludgreves in ; 37.
  Martin, townsmen of ; 25.
Re, Claudio Francesco, letter of ; 121.
Rea, Lord, his clan ; 195.
Reade :
  Robert, letter of ; 25.
  William, consul at Tripoli, his pay ; 126.

Reading ; 212.
Redall, Peter, a prisoner ; 11.
Redburn ; 5.
Redgrave ; 6.
Reed, Sir Thomas ; 137.
Reede, Baron L. de ; 51.
  de Renswoode, Baron F. de ; *ib.*
Reeve, Richard, merchant, petition of ; 134.
Rehbinder, General :
  sent to Briançon ; 53.
  his advance towards Briançon ; 56.
  reinforced ; 58.
Renard, Mr., his letter on South Sea affairs ; 107.
Renfrew, minister of ; 178.
Retford, East, election for ; 137.
Revel, ships under Sir J. Norris at ; 91, 93.
Reymerston, letter dated at ; 382.
Reynold, Sir James, Chief Baron ; 264.
Rhine, the, operations on ; 19.
Rhode Island :
  governor of ; 276.
  government of ; 293.
  commissioners of ; 303, 304.
Rhone, the :
  French troops on ; 56.
  overflow of ; 83.
Rice, Secretary ; 305.
Richards, Gen. Michael, of the Ordnance ; 223.
Richardson, Lord (1661), letter of ; 25.
Richelieu :
  Lady ; 69.
  Duke de, letter of ; 113.
Richmond :
  Surrey, court at ; 8, 12.
  —— House ; 205.
  —— old park ; 346.
  Duke of (1734), grant to ; 122.
  Alex., letters of ; 190, 191.
  the ship, captured by the Spaniards ; 149.
Riga :
  siege of ; 65, 70.
  protection of trade at ; 91, 92.
  the ship ; 138, 140.
Rindge, Mr., recommended for Council of New Hampshire ; 280.
Ripperda, Duke of, project laid before ; 196.
Riva, Mons., letter to ; 109.
Rivers, Earl :
  (1712), governor of the Tower ; 210.
  (1712), master of the Ordnance ; 211.
Robartes, Jhon, a prisoner ; 11.
Roberts :
  Mr., consul at Elsinore ; 87.
  Francis, commission to ; 200.
Robinson :
  Dr., dean of Windsor ; 335.
  or Robertson, Alex., of Strowan ; 198.
  Capt. George ; 401.
  Dr. John, Bishop of Bristol, letters of ; 127, 129.
  Sir John, deputy constable of the Tower ; 46.

Y.

Z.

LONDON : Printed by EYRE and SPOTTISWOODE,
Printers to the Queen's most Excellent Majesty.
For Her Majesty's Stationery Office.

HISTORICAL MANUSCRIPTS COMMISSION.

[32]

THIRTEENTH REPORT, APPENDIX, PART VI.

THE

MANUSCRIPTS

OF

SIR WILLIAM FITZHERBERT, BART.,

AND OTHERS.

Presented to both Houses of Parliament by Command of Her Majesty.

LONDON:
PRINTED FOR HER MAJESTY'S STATIONERY OFFICE,
BY EYRE AND SPOTTISWOODE,
PRINTERS TO THE QUEEN'S MOST EXCELLENT MAJESTY.

And to be purchased, either directly or through any Bookseller, from
EYRE AND SPOTTISWOODE, EAST HARDING STREET, FLEET STREET, E.C., and
32, ABINGDON STREET, WESTMINSTER, S.W.; or
JOHN MENZIES & Co., 12, HANOVER STREET, EDINBURGH, and
90, WEST NILE STREET, GLASGOW; or
HODGES, FIGGIS, & Co., LIMITED, 104, GRAFTON STREET, DUBLIN.

1893.

[C.—7166.]   Price 1s. 4d.

CONTENTS.

E 64159. Wt. 5262. n 2

THE MANUSCRIPTS OF SIR WILLIAM FITZHERBERT, BART., OF TISSINGTON, CO. DERBY.

WITH the exception of the contemporary accounts of the Pretender's march through Derbyshire, &c., in 1745, which are printed at the end of this report, the documents noticed in it were found at Tissington Hall as a separate collection in three portfolios, among a great quantity of correspondence of much later date.

From the fact that the letters contained in these portfolios are all addressed to G. Treby, afterwards Chief Justice, and that the bulk of the other papers in them are connected with the Popish Plot, with which he was also connected as chairman of the Committee of Secrecy and in various official positions, it seems clear that these papers once belonged to him. It is not clear, however, how they came to Tissington. The only hint to be found upon the subject is a note (without name or date, but in the handwriting of Sir W. FitzHerbert who died in 1791) in one of the portfolios that the Mr. Marsh, whose letters and papers were found together with Treby's Manuscripts, was an attorney of eminence, and of an exceedingly fair character in London, who died about 1765–1770 near 80 years of age; though he could not have been Justice Treby's clerk on account of the lapse of time, he may have been the clerk's son. This would bring down the date of the discovery of the papers to about the time when Sir W. FitzHerbert, grandfather of the present owner, was a barrister in London, and suggests the conclusion that we owe the preservation of this small portion of a once large and valuable collection of historical documents to him.

It will be noticed that the papers deal with four distinct subjects. 1. Letters from General Monck; 2. Private correspondence addressed to Mr. Treby; 3. The Popish Plot documents; 4. The Rebellion in 1745. It has seemed therefore that it is better in this report to depart from the usual strict chronological order, and to take the papers according to the subject rather than according to their dates.

In the first 20 letters of the third division we have an unusually curious and interesting set of documents, for they are evidently the original letters of the secret correspondence between the Courts of France and England in the latter part of the reign of Charles II.

The only cyphers (as a rule) made use of in these letters were certain numbers in the place of names. The body of each letter seems to have been written in an ordinary hand, only with sympathetic ink, probably with lemon juice as is suggested by Coleman himself in a letter of his printed in the State Trials, which having once been brought to light is still legible, though oftentimes faint. Sometimes the whole of a letter has been written in this light brown ink; sometimes the secret writing occurs as a part only of a letter, of which the rest is written in common black ink, upon ordinary harmless topics; sometimes it appears as interlineations throughout a letter written with common black ink.

In order to bring out these characteristics as far as possible, these 20 letters have been copied line by line, as in the originals, italics being used to represent the common writing in common black ink, the usual type being used to represent those portions which are written with the sympathetic ink. The interpretations of cypher numbers (sometimes in

MSS. OF SIR W. FITZHERBERT. brackets, sometimes as interlineations) are given here as they are in the originals. These are all written in black ink, and are the work, it would seem, of those who were employed to decipher and prepare the letters as evidence. In the same way, the underscoring of certain passages seems to be the work of these interpreters, and to be intended to mark passages of specially incriminating weight. None of these letters are signed, but it seems probable that some of them were written by Sir W. Throckmorton, and others by Mr. St. Germaine.

The rest of the letters belonging to the correspondence of this conspiracy are copies of other letters of the same nature as those noticed above. The words found upon many of them "translated by &c." evidently mean, in many cases at least, translated out of cypher or sympathetic ink, as in several instances both the originals and the transcripts are preserved. A careful comparison of these copies with the originals shows that the copies are quite accurate.

In order still further to represent the nature of these papers a few notes have been added, and all editorial additions are in italics, enclosed within square brackets.

Upon the whole, there would seem to be little doubt that all these papers are either a part of the actual letters, or formal copies of original letters, which were seized in the house of Mr. Coleman, secretary to the Duchess of York, and made use of for his prosecution.

In the earlier portion of these notes mention has been made of the existence at Tissington Hall of a large quantity of other correspondence. The bulk of them are Lord St. Helen's correspondence between the years 1795–1835; it is not reported on because so much of it is of such recent date, though there is very much in it of great interest. Among his correspondents are King George IV., the Princess Elizabeth, the Princess of Orange, Mr. Canning, Lord Chesterfield, Lord Exeter, Sir Thomas Lawrence, Mr. Wilberforce, the Duke of Wellington, the Prince of Sweden, Madame de Stael, Lord Malmesbury, Mr. Gally Knight. There are also many letters between Gally Knight and George Ellis when abroad in 1788, official correspondence with foreign ministers and with the ambassador at St. Petersburg in 1802, and correspondence with the British Museum, &c., &c., &c.

SPEECH of the LORD KEEPER COVENTRY at the Star Chamber.

1626, June 7.—Four closely written sides of foolscap of instructions to the Judges about to go on circuit.

Besides the ordinary duties in court they are to see to the carrying out of the laws against Popish Recusants, and especially watch those in authority who are suspected of misleading others. The increase of Popery and backsliding in religion must be counteracted. The law of confinement at home of Recusants should be enforced. They flock in companies to their public meetings, especially in the northern parts, as to St. Winnifred's Well. Such things should be prevented.

Mischief also arises from the non-attendance of Justices of the Peace at Assizes. It is disrespectful to the Judges; and it deprives the Justices of the lessons they might learn as to their duties. This neglect tends to produce neglect at Quarter Sessions, and again in their several localities.

The number of Justices of the Peace has been diminished. The best men in the counties are to be chosen. This will make more efficiency.

Disorders in ale houses is the greatest source of evil in the commonwealth. They ought to be few in number, and only in open streets, for the reception of poor travellers which are not able to lodge in inns. The Judges should agree upon some common course in this matter, and proceed against the alehouse keepers, and those of the Justices who wink at their proceedings. In this county there are 1000 ale houses in one Hundred. How many thousands of wicked men must there be who spend their time and estates to support all these !

Workhouses should be built, and stock provided for the poor.

Bridges and Highways should be attended to.

Lastly. It is now a time of war and his Majesty hears that there are many deserters. If any such are found and their offences do not merit death, they must be punished publickly and sent back to their regiments.

Endorsed. " MSS. in Shorthand."

A Copy of a Letter from an Officer of the Army in Ireland to his Highness the Lord Protector concerning his changing of the Government. [*Signed*,] R. G.

1654, June 24. Waterford.—A long letter of 25 closely written pages protesting against the present government which is nothing better than a monarchy bottomed by the sword' and 30000 men. As things are now enormous sacrifices and sufferings have been incurred in pulling down a legal monarchy somewhat too tenacious of power, with the result that the present government is yet more autocratic and arbitrary.

The writer is in favour of a free and equal commonwealth.

General G. MONCK to Major RALPH KNIGHT.

1659, August 13.—" In pursuance of an order of the Councell of State dated the seaventh instant these are to authorize and require you to give orders to the officers comanding the severall troopes of my ownc Regiment of Horse to recruit to eighty in each troope (officers included) and to take care that such as you entertaine bee well affected persons, well mounted and arm'd, and (as neare as you can) old soldiers, and this to bee done with as much speed as may bee. And the Deputy Commissaries of Musters are hereby required to passe such men as you shall entertaine by vertue of this order upon the musters as they shall appeare."

The SAME to Colonel KNIGHT.

1659-60, January 3. Whittingham.—" 1 have received your letter and am glad you are gott safe into Newcastle, wee shall be at Morpeth to morrow night and the next night att Newcastle. I shall desire you if you heare of my Lord Lambert's advancing towards Newcastle againe to give mee notice of itt, and send out some men for that purpose to discover, which is all att present.

Let me know whether the Lord Lambert's forces bee broken or not, or what other intelligence you have."

The SAME to the SAME.

1659-60, January 4. Morpeth.—" I have received your letter, and am glad that Tinmouth Castle hath declared for the Parliament butt I would have you deale with them, before I come, to march out of the Castle, and I shall appoint quarters for them in the country, and to that purpose I would have you write to them. For the officers that were going for Scotland I would have stay there till I come tomorrow."

The SAME to the SAME.

1660, April 17. St. James'.—" I desire you forthwith to give orders to the officers of the respective troopes of your regiment to call together

MSS. OF SIR W. FITZHERBERT. the non-comission officers and soldiers under their respective commands, and then to tender them the address lately subscribed by the officers of the army for their subscriptions, and to discharge out of their troopes respectively any non-commission officer or soldier who shall refuse to joine in those subscriptions, and you are to direct the officers not to lett them knowe the end for which they are to come together untill their meeting, and the tendring of the said address unto them."

The Same to the Same.

1660, May 3. St. James's.—" Haveing received a letter and declaration from his Majesty whereof the inclosed are copies, and the officers at the head-quarters haveing subscribed an address, of which the copie is alsoe inclosed, declareing their satisfaction in the said letter, and declaration, and their expectation of the enioyement of much tranquility and happiness under his Majestie's Governement, I desire you will communicat them to the officers of your regiment and tender the address to bee signed by all the commission officers under your command, and when subscribed to returne it."

The Same to the Same.

1660, May 23. At the Cockpitt.—" You are to march (uppon notice given) with my owne regiment, your regiment, and Col. Cloberye's regiment of horse, to Blackheath, where you are to drawe them upp and make a stand uppon the said heath whilst his Majestie is passing by. And I shall send you notice of the time by the officer whom you send with me."

The Same to the Same.

1660, May 26. Canterbury.—" I desire you will not faile, with your owne, Colonell Cloberie's, and my regiment of horse, to bee att Blackheath uppon Tuesday morning next to bee drawne upp against his Majestie comes by according to your former orders. Whereof I desire you nott to faile: and to order them nott to fire till the Kinge bee passed by."

The Same to the Same.

1660, May 26. Canterbury.—" Having appointed the Lord Fauconberge's and Lord Howard's regiment to meet att Blackheath on Tuesday morning next by seaven of the clock, I desire you will drawe them uppe according to former orders, in five divisions, leaving a convenient distance betweene each regiment."

" My Lord Howard and Lord Fauconberge are content that the Scotch regiments and theirs shall take place according to the date of their Commissions."

The Duke of Albemarle to Sir R. Knight.

1661, June 8. The Cockpitt.—" I received yours of the 5th instant, and soe soone as monies come in you will receive your pension out of the Exchequer, butt att present there is none to bee had, and soe itt will nott bee fitt to move his Majestie in itt till there bee money, butt when itt is seasonable I shall assist you what I can."

The Same to the Same.

1661-2, January 18. The Cockpitt.—" Permit the bearer hereof Sir Ralph Knight with his servant, horses, swords, and necessaries, to passe about his occasions in Yorkshire and other parts and to repasse without molestation."

The Same to the Same.

MSS. OF SIR W. FITZHERBERT.

1662, March 29. The Cockpitt.—"I received yours of the 24th of March instant and thanke you for your care in promoting his Majestie's service heere in speaking to Captain Parke to raise a troope for Portugall, butt there was an intention (when I wrote to you) to raise seaven troopes heere and now there is but two to bee raised, and the officers have already received their leavy, but seing Capt. Parke is soo willing to goe I shall bee mindefull of him uppon the next occasion."

The Same, with others, to the Same.

1662, June 25.—"Whereas his Majestie by his Proclamation dated the 22th day of June 1662 requires all officers and soldiers that have served in the armyes of the late usurped powers to depart out of the cittyes of London and Westminster on or before the 26th day of this instant June. And whereas the bearer hereof Colonell Sir Ralph Knight was lately disbanded out of the late army in pursuance of an act of Parliament and thereby conceives himselfe concerned to take notice thereof and yield obedience thereunto. And whereas it appeares by a certificat of his Grace the Duke of Albemarle that the said Colonell Sir Ralph Knight hath faithfully served his Majestie and did correspond and joine with the said Duke of Albemarle in his Majestie's most happy restoration. These are according to the power given us by the said Proclamation to will and require all his Majestie's officers and others whom it shall or may concerne to permitt the said Collonell Sir Ralph Knight quietly to remaine and bee within the said Cittyes of London and Westminster and the parts thereabouts without their lett or molestation for the space of twenty daies next after the date hereof as they will answer the contrary. Given under our hands the 25th day of June 1662 and in the fourteenth yeare of his Majesties Reigne."

[*Signed*]　　ALBEMARLE.
　　　　　　　LINDSEY.
　　　　　　　WM. MORICE.

The Same to the Same.

1667, July 31. The Cockpitt.—"I received your letter dated the 29th of July. Sir Stephen Fox has money in a readiness to paye your troope. But as to your pension, money is soe scarce that I would not have you come upp about it, because I would bee loath you should loose your labour."

The Same to the Same at Yarmouth.

1667, August 13.—"It is his Majestie's pleasure that on Fryday the sixteenth of August instant you disband your troope of horse att the towne of Yarmouth, and that upon their disbanding you cause them to deliver in to the Mayor of Yarmouth all such armes as you received for them out of his Majestie's stores, to witt pistolls with holsters, hacks, breasts, and potts, the said Mayor of Yarmouth being appointed by the Commissioners and by the Lieutenant Generall of his Majestie's ordnance to receive the same for his Majestie's use.

"Sir Stephen Fox will furnish you with monies to pay them upp to the said sixteenth of August inclusive, and also with fourteen dayes pay more for the officers and soldiers (beyond that time) which his Majestie is pleased to allow them to defray their charges in returning to their homes. And you are to take a receipt under the hand of the said Mayor of Yarmouth for the armes you soe deliver unto him and to send the said receipt unto mee."

MARTYN RYDER to his kinsman GEORGE TREBY at Plymton.

1671, September 9.—I do not think we shall have much news the rest of this vacation.

You know how far the new farmers have gone with the King for the Customs. One patent was sealed for the best part of it, and that for wines was drawn. But they upon confidence of the money they had already paid, and the interest they had, thought they might make better conditions and add some other clauses for defalcations. The King did not like this, but being more than ordinarily moved told them that he should never have an end with them at this rate, nor any certainty in his revenue, and that if they would not accept the terms already agreed upon, they might leave it. "My Lord St. John forthwith, with the consent of the rest, delivers their patent into the King's hand, who accepts it and lays it by. This has made much adoe and stir in the town." The farmers complain that Bucknal has been beforehand with them. The Court complains of St. John that he is dirty, and some say he is forbid the Court. Negociations followed, but Michaelmas was so near that farmers could not be found in the mean time, and Lords Ashley and Clifford, propose to have it done by commission. "But wno should be the men? Ashley nominates Mr. Upton and Mr. Millington, merchants. The King, Sir William Tompson—the Duke of York, Mr. Buckworth, and Capt. Cock. Sir Thomas Clifford, Mr. Garraway. All were accepted but the Duke's two, and the four are to manage the whole. It is further said that Lindsey, the goldsmith, is to be treasurer, and Man their secretary. The merchants are very well pleased with this alteration, upon the presumption that they should meet with nothing but hardship from farmers, some of which were needy enough and design nothing but their own advantage. But they hope better from such men as these who are put in to do justice between the King and his people, without the least respect to their own advantage, for they are to have very considerable salaries, the least says 1600 . . . 2000 per annum each. What will be the effect of this sudden change time will show, but 'tis believed that the farmers doe very much repent of that d[emand] . . . for they have paid in £60000 advance but are to be reimbursed when the King has money. The King told Sir W. Tompson [he] did pitch [upon him] because he thought he would do his [duty] and that without the least recommendation from any person."

The King has not yet gone to the race. Lord Henry Howard is gone to prepare Norwich Castle for his reception, and Lady Arlington is to provide her house.

Some think that Ashley will be now made Treasurer that he may superintend these Commissioners.

It is said the farmers will not sit down quietly, but will try what law and equity will do for them. The money for bribes &c. is certainly lost.

M. RYDER to G. TREBY, M.P.

1677, March 30, Exeter.—The chief case at the Assizes was that of the town of Plymouth v. Strode. The verdict was against the Lambhay, upon sufficient evidence.

The little man is very much affected and is determined to prosecute you, and has already set out for London.

He is principal agent too in the presentment against the Mayor of Plympton for not taking the Sacrament and Oath according to the new Act. You will be as much surprised as I am at this. The Grand Jury have found a bill. Some of our friends would have contrived to baffle this if it had not come on while they were engaged at the bar. This may affect you, for the Act makes void all acts done by those who have not complied with the law. I submit that you prevail upon some of the eminent men in the House to bring in a Bill to explain the Act. Many will have cause to lay hold of a general clause of this kind. Pray advise the Mayor.

Sir Francis Drake will now be with you and will tell you of the discontent of your friends because you did not appear at the election at Ashburton. They attribute the loss there to you, and charge you flatly with breach of promise, and desertion of the good cause. Mr. Coplestone goes further than Sir Francis and says that you promised to send Mr. Edmund Pollexfen of Plymouth in your stead if you could not attend. Pray justify yourself for neither coming nor sending to your friends both here and in London, for I assure you there is a very loud clamour here.

JOHN HUNGERFORD to the SAME.

1677, May 13.—I am not enough of an astronomer to know whether the comet's tail points to England or France, nor if the eclipse shall have its effect here or in Madagascar, but I am apt to think an honest House of Commons may make fools of French comets, and English eclipses too.

I dare say people will very unwillingly part with money, unless they are assured it is to build ships to make war with France, and not to buy rich Georges and Garters.

DR. EDMOND HAL to the SAME.

1677, Jane 7. Plymouth.—If it is true that the Duke of Ormond intends to visit Oxford on his way to Ireland, I pray you to use your interest with Lord Ossory, that I may be presented. This will save me the trouble of exercise and the charge of fees, and I shall not be so much as obliged to keep an Act. I desire you to cease your endeavours to obtain a Mandamus. If I cannot proceed in my business when the Duke comes to Oxford, I will wait till I go to London.

COLONEL E. GROSVENOR to the SAME.

1677, August 21.—" The king is expected to day at Whitehall which I desire to see in order to Butler, who yet lives, how long I know not."

The SAME to the SAME.

1677, September 15.—" Dear Sonn Treby. Your passionate memory of the dear deceased still adds to that great kindness I have had for you since my first knowledge of you."

The SAME to the SAME.

1677, September 25.—" Poore Butler he is hanged at last, and I believe dyed as much a Christian as any that ever was turned off a lather, and as innocent, foe says his enemies."

JOHN ELWILL to the SAME.

1677, December 8. Exeter.—Begs for information as to the disposition of the Court, and likelihood of a French war, because this is of importance to himself and others who have property abroad and floating on the waves.

The swiftness of the French victories in Flanders, and the readiness of the English make him think a rupture may occur shortly.

WILLIAM COURTENAY to the SAME.

1677, December 10. Fowey.—Pity the miseries of the wretched people here. " Here is no claret within our rates."
[*Twenty-six lines of shorthand follow.*]

JOHN ELWILL to the SAME.

1677–8, March 11. [Exeter].—The time allowed is so short that many, and especially in this city, will lose heavily. Had the date been the 31st of this month few would have complained.

" Forreigners, especially the Germans, write me despairingly of any succours from England, and will not entertaine the belief of England's hearty conjunction with the Confederates against France. If more than ordinary probability of such a war appears, a timely notice from the prospect of it would import much.

" I shall use double diligence to help Mr. Horsman in getting an indifferent jury, or to instruct some that are common and usual jurors. My uncle Rodd and I intend, God willing, to accost a ruling man in that employment, whom I hope to bend to our favour. Mr. Tremain shall be consulted with, and whatever is within the sphere of my power is assured in this service. My service to my uncle T. B."

ARTHUR PERRYMAN to the SAME.

1678, April 12 and 26. Hardwicke.—Two letters about a law suit.

P. VENTRIS to the SAME.

1678, May 21. Ipswich.—Let me desire the favour of you to give me some account of next Tuesday's proceedings.

JAMES TREBY to his brother the SAME.

1678, May 27. The Golden Fleece.—Has just arrived in the Downs. Hopes to see his friends very soon, if he is not pressed away. Understands that it is very hard to escape. If pressed I shall have no hope of ever seeing you more. Last Friday night, about about 9 or 10 o'clock, the Woolledge frigate and the Lark came up with us and pressed several of our men, and said they had orders to press every man except the Commander himself, and that we should not have a man left when we came to the Downs. Our men are now packing up their goods, ready to be gone.

1678, June 5.—The Sum of the Arguments on both sides of the Bar of the House of Lords upon the petition for the honour of Viscount Purbeck.
[*Sixteen foolscap pages of small MS.*]

COLONEL GROSVENOR to the SAME.

1678, August 17.—You will receive better accounts than mine; so I will only say that men are shipping over, both horse and foot, but whom we are to affright with it I know not. Much provision has gone over and a large artillery. It is persistently affirmed that Hide is gone over (and that is true) with a project of peace signed, offensive and defensive, with the Dutch and Spaniards, and room for the Germans if they please. Andrew Marvell died yesterday of apoplexy. I rejoice in your pleasant victory at Exeter.

W. HARINGTON to the SAME.

1678, August 17.—Things are in such a chaotic state that what I write as fact one day is untrue the next. I will only speak now of two facts. The peace of Nimeguen, and the fighting at Mons between the same parties a few days later.

The first alone was no little surprise to us as you will easily collect from the first proclamation which summoned you to meet upon the 29th instant. The Dutch were induced to make a separate peace by their great losses and poverty, and by a foolish jealousy that the Prince meant to use their forces to set himself up over them.

English troops were within 12 hours march on the day of the fight. The Duke of Monmouth posted to the Dutch army from Brussells and reached it before the fight, and appeared very active in person, to the no small regret of the French.

[*A very long letter dealing with the various aspects of affairs*] " which are very mysterious."

HENRY HATSELL to the SAME.

1678, August 27.—Great quantities of hay have been shipped for our horse and dragoons.

I have talked with some of the Scotch who came out of France. They say that their regiment of 3000 men, and the English and Irish, were sent into Dauphine (which you know is the farthest part of France) and there the Duke of Monmouth's regiment of foot, and some of his regiment of horse, and all this Scotch regiment were disbanded, one or two companies at a time, and obliged to travel through France, receiving about a crown a-piece, some more, some less, for their expenses. All who desire it are taken into pay here. The Irish regiment chose to continue in the French service. The greatest part of the Duke of Monmouth's regiment is kept there, being dispersed among the other troops.

"The Duke of Buckingham has not been seen abroad these three weeks, which gives occasion of discourse, some saying that he is sent by the King on a private message into France, others that he keeps concealed with a miss. The Duke of Monmouth came hither on Tuesday last, and went forthwith to the King at Windsor. The Duke of Lauderdale came two days before."

At the Berkshire election where Lord Sterling had a majority of 60 over Mr. Barker, a gentleman of good estate in that county but who lives at Clerkenwell, but there will be a double return because of some dispute about votes, Mich. Mallet spoke some mad, extravagant words, viz. that the King was a rogue, which confirm the idea that he is mad. He is committed to the custody of the Black Rod.

Our soldiers in Flanders die apace, it is supposed from their intemperate eating of fruit.

COLONEL GROSVENOR to the SAME.

1678, August 29.—Our only news is that today 49 of your members met and by commission were prorogued to the 1st of October.

W. HARRINGTON to the SAME.

1678, September 3.—I have little of fact to communicate beyond what is told in the Gazette. But all Christendome is in expectation what will come of the negociations abroad, and I will give you my conjectures. The great question is, will the peace of Nimeguen be ratified ?

I believe on the whole that it will be.

[*A very long letter discussing the above question.*]

MSS. OF SIR W.
FITZHERBERT.
—

H. HATSELL to the SAME.

1678, September 7.—The question of peace or war still hangs in the balance. Our troops only await a fair wind to sail into Flanders. Our soldiers there are very sickly. Lord O'Brien has died of the distemper he brought thence. Mr. Offley the lawyer has been ill a long time. The Bill of Mortality was 530 the last week. The country towns for many miles about are as sickly as London, which is imputed to the unusual heat of the weather, as well as to eating fruit. Yesterday week the King dined with Sir George Jefferies at his house near Windsor, where he was treated magnificently. The Duchess of Portsmouth was there.

"Three of the four men that were tried for robbing Sir Robert Viner's daughter were found guilty, but they were reprieved. All the evidence was that they were of the company that forced her away from Sir Robert, but Mr. Wroth took her handkerchief, and when she cryed stopped her mouth with it, and that he took it out of her mouth again, and what became of it afterwards she knew not, and that she lost an amber necklace, and somewhat else of small value. And yet they were found guilty. The story of the Libber was cited. It is supposed they will not be hanged."

The SAME to the SAME.

1678, September 14.—It is expected that Parliament will meet on October 1st, and so continue.

The King and Court will be here the week after next. Lord Sunderland is sent for. It is supposed because his Majesty is displeased with him for some affair in France, or that the French King complained of bold expressions used by him to himself.

Several gentlemen lately come from France say they saw the Duke of Buckingham there, but incognito, in a dark periwig, without a star, and this is now believed.

Michael Mallet has been to beg the King's pardon, but the King said he would leave it to the law.

Endeavours are being used to get Sir William Temple chosen burgess for Southampton, in the room of Sir R. Ford, and Capt. Shales for Hull.

The soldiers quartered in the towns on the river below bridge are to be removed inland forthwith, and those or board ship are disembarked. The hay that was shipped is also landed again.

W. HARRINGTON to the SAME.

1678, September 17.—I rejoice that while so many of your House, and others, are dying in this great mortality, you are well. I think you will consult your own security by hastening to London rather than stay where you are [at Plympton]. Serjeant Hardy and Mr. Crouch, two members of your House, and Robin Offley are dead. The last is to be buried today at St. Pancras in the fields.

Reports from abroad.

" I had almost forgotten to tell you that our Turkey fleet in the return home about the straits mouth met with 20 sail of great French men of war, having only two small English frigates for their convoy. But by some strange inward suspicion Sir John Narborough thought so small a convoy would not pass them safe through the straits, and therefore came up with 7 great ships, where he found the French cruising and viewing the fleet, which was putting itself in a posture of defence. Upon his coming in several boats, passed between the commanders upon pretence only to know of what nation each were. But after some com- plaints the French veered off, and the fleet passed on their voyage, though it was looked on to prove like that of the Dutch Smyrne fleet, and may likewise prove the fore-runner of a war.

"Here is news I am sure will look strange to you, that Chiefe Baron Montague is like to goe off, and George Jefferies succeed in his roome. The fault objected is said to be the judgment given in the case of Cooke and Mountague. The story is too long for a letter, and my paper too much spent, and my time and strength too . . .

"My pen hasting I slipped a material passage, that the French Ambassadour by a memorial delivered in lately desires the King to withdraw his forces, for that they have noe occasion for them."

RICHARD MITCHAEL to R . . MITCHAELL at his house in Moone Lane, neare the great tree. From a poore Plymouth captive in Argeir.

1678-9, January 14.—"My dear. With my unspeakable love to thee and our poore children, and my kinde love to our parents, and to all the rest of our friends and acquaintance in generall, haveing now an oppertunity to write I would not neglect it, hopeing of your good healths, as blessed be God I am in at the present writeing. My deare to heare of your healths and welfares would administer a great deale of comfort to me in this my comfortless and destitute condition it hath pleased the Lord to cast us into, I being with many hundreds more taken by the Turkess, and brought into this place, being sold. To relate the sadness of our condition is beyond the tongue of man to express, and little or noe hopes of redemption. Oh how it would make a heart of stone to weep to see the barbarous and inhumane usage of Cristians in this place, some drawing carts like horses with irons of great weight upon their leggs, with many a blow, and some a hundred at a time upon the bare soles of their feet, with a thick rope; others carrying of durt; others digging in the vineyards, with very small allowance of bread and water. And many others more barbarous usage than I am able to sett down. The Lord bear upp our spirits if it be His blessed will, and in His due time redeem us out of the hands of those unreasonable men. There is a hundred and five English ships taken, sunk, and burnt, this war, and what will be the event of all God in his infinite wisdom knows best. If it would please the Lord to put into the king's heart, or the hearts of the country, to contrive some way for our redemption, it would be a happy thing, before the pestilence begin, which is every summer. It swept away last summer above eighteen hundred Cristians. If it were the will of God I could heartily desire to see my native country once againe, but if He have otherwise ordained it, the Lord satisfy all our spirits, and help us to live soe in this world as we may meet together with joy and comfort in the world to come is the prayer of thy faithfull and ever loving husband till death in captivity.

RICHARD MITCHAELL."

H. HATSELL to G. TREBY, at Salisbury.

1678-9, February 1.—The discourse about the invalidity of the dissolution is laid aside. It arose from a scruple of Mr. Browne, Clerk of the Parliament.

It is now taken for granted that the Parliament is well dissolved. The Speaker was not sent for, as reported.

The election for London is to be on Thursday next. Mr. F. of Spridlestone wishes to be your partner at Plympton.

JOHN POLLEXFEN to his cousin G. TREBY.

1678–9, February 4.—About the election at Plympton.

Lord Russel stands for Bedfordshire, Mr. Montague for Northampton-shire, and Mr. Seechivrell for the town, not for the shire; Sir Nicholas Cary at Gatton; Sir Robert Paiton for Middlesex.

There is no choice yet for the City.

Yesterday a man was committed about firing the Temple, now when burnt two of the Duchess of P. servants are fled upon Netterfield's information.

Godfrey's murder will be tried on Thursday. Sir Thomas Meres meets with much opposition at Lincoln.

Sir John Narborough has returned from Algiers without making any peace, but will return thither.

Powell will be chosen at Cirencester, but Sir William Coventry endeavours much to be excused.

Lord Latimore was on his way to Yorkshire to stand for the shire, but was brought back by some intelligence which met him on the road.

Mr. Savil is to go as envoy to France.

Sir Francis Winnington has gone down to attend to his election.

The Lord Chancellor has orders to inquire what Justices of the Peace do not do their duty against Papists, that they may be put out.

There will be a Common Council to-morrow, and the election next week.

COLONEL GROSVENOR to the SAME.

1678–9, February 4.—I hear Mr. Strode will contest your seat. Pray attend to your own interests, and not labour for others.

My service to all our good claret friends.

HENRY POLLEXFEN to the SAME.

1678–9, February 7. The Temple.—My cousin Edmund Pollexfen is going down by coach to join you. I heartily hope you and he may succeed, and that this will lead to his settling in his own country.

Another informer named Needham has come in and was examined yesterday before some of the Lords, Lords Essex and Bridgwater, and taken into protection by the Duke of Monmouth.

Barry, Green, and Hill, were arraigned yesterday, and will be tried on Monday.

H. HATSELL to the SAME.

1678–9, February 8.—Mr. R. Strode, whom I met two days since, hardly denies that he means to stand for Plympton. Simon Hele avoids speaking to me.

Most of the elections so far are good.

Lords Russel and Bruce are in for Bedfordshire.

The trial of Berry, Green, and Hill, is put off until Monday.

Bedlow was accused yesterday before the King and Council of speak-ing scandalous words against the Duke of York. The case is put off until Wednesday. It seems that he was drunk; and his accusers, some of his guard, were not very sober.

[*It seems from the language used in this letter that Hatsell and Treby had married sisters, the daughters of Colonel Grosvenor.*]

JOHN POLLEXFEN to the SAME.

1678–9, February 11. London.—There is much discourse about the elections, which are in general good.

Sir J. Williamson has surrendered his office to Lord Sunderland, and MSS. OF SIR W.
FITZHERBERT. Sir J. Coventry will surrender his it is said to Sir Lyonel Jenkins. Berry, Green, and Hills, were tried and condemned yesterday.

H. HATSELL to the SAME.

1678-9, February 15.—Lord Cavendish and Mr. Sacheverel have been elected for Derbyshire without spending a penny. Mr. Powle is in for Cirencester, and Mr. Garway for Arundel. Mr. May and Major Breman (reputed to be a great fanatick) for Chichester. The two Berties finding themselves too weak at Stamford came thence on Tuesday last, and the next day Sir Christopher Cust and Capt. Hide (two friends of Lord Exeter) were chosen.

The elections generally are good. Sir R. Peyton and Sir W. Roberts are. chosen at Buckingham, which Sir R. Temple has lost. The Duke of Buckingham went himself to that town and made it his business to persuade the people not to choose Lord Latimer or Sir R. Temple.

It is not true that Berry, the porter of Somerset House, has made a confession since his condemnation, but he has sent for a Protestant clergyman, and Dr. Lloyd has been to him. But I can have no certain account of it.

Mr. Montague is chosen for Huntingdonshire. He had intended to stand also for Northamptonshire but was chosen here. Yesterday he was before the King and Council upon summons. The King told him that he understood that he was chosen a member of Parliament. That they were shortly to sit, and therefore he would say nothing to him now; hoping that they would do him right, and so discharged him of attendance.

W. HARRINGTON to the SAME.

1678–9, February 20.—We can talk of nothing but the elections. Much trouble has been taken to baffle Sir Thomas Player, but the current in his favour was too strong to be withstood, and in truth they were all chosen very clearly and without any poll demanded, save only between Sir Robert Clayton and Sir Joseph Sheldon, but the latter was prudent enough to retire. In truth the City judge they have been very kind to choose any of our aldermen, considering how the Commons have been dealt with by that court, and I am assured they have chosen the best of them.

The Westminster election began yesterday.

On our side Sir Stephen Fox and Sir W. Poulteney. On the other Sir William Waller and Sir Philip Matthews. The latter set up so late, and treated so little that most thought it imprudent. "But though at first Sir W. Waller's number seemed a cloud no bigger than a man's hand, before night it covered the whole heavens. So great is the merit of priest catching, and so little the credit of a courtier amongst the mobile. The poll began to-day and may last three days more, the electors being 25000 in number.

"The cry and number of suffrages on Sir W. Waller's side this day day was much the greatest, not without great reproaches cast upon Fox, according to the humour of the rabble, although it is thought it hath not cost him less than 1000l. to purchase their goodwill."

Will. Ashe and his brother are in for Heytesbury. Will. Trenchard has beaten Harry Bertie at Westbury, and both Charles and Peregrine Bertie are cast out at Stamford. Prideaux and Jack Trenchard have carried Taunton, where the contest lay between Jack and Sir William Portman. He won but by one vote.

I only mention those who are our common acquaintances. The elections on the whole go well except as I hear among your heathen neighbours in Cornwall. I heartily congratulate you on your success at Plympton.

"Mr. Montague (I mean Ralph) being said to be gone into Northamptonshire to manage his election as was thought, was pursued with a message to appear at the Council Board. Which was accordingly sent to his father's house. But being invited into Huntingdonshire by the gentlemen there to avoid the opposition that was raised against him in Northamptonshire, and to gain time, embraced the invitation, and was chosen without trouble with one night's stay, and had this advantage thereby, to be absent when the summons came. Howbeit he had it afterwards, but being now under priviledge the stile in which it was directed was very modest, viz. to appear when he conveniently could. Which he did forthwith, and was asked why he left Paris before his orders came for his return. To which he sayed he had advice that his return was ordered, and being indebted upon the king's account 8000*l*., and fearing an arrest, he went to meet his orders at Callis, which he did accordingly. Then he was questioned about his correspondence with the Pope's Nuncio, which he denied. And last of all was demanded the keyes of his cabinet (which it seems they had not opened, though seized you know when); but he said he remembered not then where he had hid them, and so he was dismissed with this only that he should send them when he could find them."

Several letters from Portugal say that a Spanish and French fleet were to have landed men at Milford Haven, if the Plot had taken effect, but they were dispersed in a storm. This is agreeable to Oates' information.

The sad story has just come that St. John's College Cambridge is nearly burned down, and three priests taken with fire balls.

P. Ventry to the Same.

1678–9, March 11. Ipswich.—I very desirous to receive a letter from you, being much at a loss for an account of the state of things in this conjuncture, and especially to interpret the Duke's departure.

Sir Robert Southwell to [the Same].

1679, March 28. "Spring Gardens.—I have now in obedience to the orders of the Lords of the [Committee] of Examinations about the Plott dated the 15th or 25th instant reviewed all those bundles that were sent from the Councill of matter arising since the first of January last. The 24 papers found at Tixal I gave you in their order Tuesday night with a general list of their contents, and last night I did extract out of certain papers sett apart and given unto you the remarks which hereafter follow. In three letters writt from one William Southall of Staffordshire of December 31st, January 25th, and February 20th, he says that Mr. Higgins who [went] by the name of Robert Palmer was taken at Highone, that he proves [a] priest and is sent to goale. That Thomas Mauloe proves a priest and sent to goale. That Francis Levison (who I suppose is brother at least to that Lewsen or Levisen who mett with Miles Prance at Bow to write the narrative of Sir Edmondsbury Godfrey's merther) was taken by Justice La . . . and sent to gaole. One Peters a Jesuit (often accused by Dugdale for the conspiracy) is there also in gaole. George Hobson (formerly a tenant to the Lord Stafford, and lately tenant to the Lord Aston and knowing of the conspiracy as is testified by Mr. Dugdale's first evidence of the 24th or 29th December and 21st of Feb.) is in the same goale. One Nor[th] (servant to the Lord Aston, and nephew to Pickering) is in the same MSS. of Sir W. Fitzherbert gaole for infamous words against his Majestie testified by Mr. Dugdale in his deposition either of the 24th or 29th of Decr. last past. There is also one Cotton, Priest to Mr. Heveningham whom Dugdale often. mentions to be engaged in the conspiracy, but being 86 years of age and infirme hee remaines with a mittimus in the hands of a constable . there.

"In Mr. Southall's said letter of the 20th of Feb. notice is taken of · Mr. Howard of Hore-Cross, who when Southall came to his house with a warrant to search he kocked a pistol at him. That in his house there : were Popish books and vestments whereof he had informed the Justices . that Mr. Gerard had acknowledged and now deliver'd up according to . order the deed lodged with him, by which Dugdale gave £100 towards the Plott, which is a high instance for giving credit to . . ales evidence. That in the same letter it is said that Mr. Lewson Gowre being at the sessions did observe Sir Symen Deg to give the charge more favorable concerning Papists then others, and did thereupon tell him he spoke more like a Jesuite then a Justice.

." In a deposition taken by Mr. Anchitel Grey in Derbyshire on the 22th of January, it appears, that one George Godfrey, who sometimes was called Golding and sometimes Wilford, was a Franciscan Fryar, and resorted sometimes to Howbec, is now taken and in Derby goale.

" Memorandum. That on the 24th December being the day that Miles Prance brought all his evidence to the Councill board, one Abraham Gory Granger, who then lay in Newgate for being a notorious counterfeiter of hands, he desiring to bee heard was then also brought and did informe of certain commissions unto which he had counterfeited the King's hand, and named the Lord Bellassise, one Brattle the Essay Master of the Mynt, and Mr. Fox who lived at Arundell house, to bee the promoters of this work, as will appeare by his information then taken, but what between the hurry about Prance, and the informer's ill life, there was not much notice taken of the matter, more then to remand him to Newgate, where I suppose he now lyes.

" That a letter was given in by the Bishop of London on the 7th of February, is dated the 15th January, writt in French and directed to the Lord of Bellassise. It seemes to bee writt from a Nunnery where he hath a daughter. It encourages him to persevere unto the end, and to think upon the glorys of martyrdome.

" Memorandum. That on the 15th of March Edward Lloyd swears that on the 30th of Sept. the Lord Powis with his Lady going towards London, did call at their house, and asked him, whether hee heard of the discovery of the Popish Plott. Now the Lord Powis being examined on another occasion did declare that he came not into London untill Saturday the 4th of October, and sett out from Powis Castle on Tuesday the first of October, but whether it were on Monday the 30th of Sept. or even this Tuesday tis improbable hee should know of the discovery of the Plott from the information given at the Councill Board, which came not there till Saturday the 28th September. so that [if] Lloyd deposeth true his Lordship must have heard of it by some other way [before].

" Memorandum. That among the Tixall Papers No. 9, there is a letter of the 28th December 1676 writt from the present Lord Aston to his father, which shows how great kindness the Lord Stafford professed towards them, and that they were procuring some letter of favor from his Majestic which it seems cost this Lord much hammering perhaps if such letter were seen [it would] give light to other things.

"Also in the Tixall bundle No. 3 there is a letter signed Thomas
Whitgreve without date or place, by which it appears the Lord Aston
had been twice at his house, and if that letter were writt since Mr. Otes'
discovery it would import very much, especially if this be the same
Whitgreve who is a Justice of the Peace of whom Mr. Dugdale can give
 .   .   .   t evidence of his correspondency with the Papists.

"There was found by Sir William Waller in the Savoy two letters
which have in them much variety of matter about Popish buisseness.
One of them is of the 28th of July 1676 from Douay wherein .   .   .   .
is mentioned. The other has no date, but was writt from Ro[me] to
Stapleton President of the Benedictines and from an agent sent thither
to sollicite their affaires.

"There is another letter dated the $\frac{18}{19}$th of January last from Brussells
writ from an English Priest but in Italien. It is directed to Monsr.
Trevars a domestic of the Spanish Ambassador's, and in that there is
another letter in Italian to the General of the Carmelites Missionarys in
England. Whether this Generall be Trevars or no, or some other
person, is matter of enquiry, and the rather from an account given lately
by Sir William .   .   .   .   to the Duke of Ormonde, and sent over by
his Grace, wherein are some things very remarkable.

"There was found in the house of Mr. Daniel Arthur but the papers
left there by one Sarsfield and belonging unto him. The original
commission granted on the 20th of May 1668 by the Cardinal of Dando
.   . then Legat a Latere in France, whereby power is granted to the
Augustine Fryars (among other things) to dispense with all vows
(except those of chastity and religion), and also with oathes, where there
is just cause, and also in other cases and irregularitys even as the Pope
could dispense with the same.

" As for the manifestations that Popery was taking growth and shaping
itself into forme, and distributing into several precincts the care and
management of the cause, and particular persons to preside in such
precincts and to bee accountable for the same in their ecclesiastical
matters, not only the blew book found in Ireland's bag, containing the
names of 300 Jesuits will manifest the same, but other papers now lying
in Fenwick's bag, as also the papers found at Comb in Herefordshire;
and how farr they thought their matters advanced even in May 1666
will appear by the commission I gave you where Austin Hungate
President of the Benedictines, impowers one Stapleton, another
Benedictine, as if they were even then in hopes of all. This commission
was brought in by the Earl of Essex, together with a note for £1,500
which is given to Mr. Attorney General to try if that money bee not
recoverable and forfeited to his Majestie.

"If the Lords please that I should proceed to reduce the matters
contained in those 20 papers of informatiou given by Mr. Dugdale,
Prance, and Needham, which I formerly put into your [hands] that is to
fix things upon persons, it will not onely require a long [time] .   . but
it were fitt that I had all those papers at my own house, or by parcells
at least, that I may with more attention consider and digest the matters
contained therein, tho in truth this work would best bee performed by
such as are knowing in the law."

Endorsed Letter read March 29, 1679.

SIR JOHN TREVOR to the SAME.

1679, March 31. Inner Temple.—I have been ill and out of Town.
If the Committee have any commands for me upon the examinations or
papers delivered to you, I am now ready to obey them.

JOHN REEPE to the SAME.

1679, April 18. Plymouth.—I write because of the deep misery of many of mine, and many others' friends, and relations, which they suffer, since the memory of living man, in Turkish slavery. I wish with all my heart you may be able to find some way to assist them.

SIR ROBERT SOUTHWELL to the SAME, in the chair of the Committee of Secresy.

1679, May 10. Spring Gardens.—In answer to your enquiry I have sought everywhere for the cover of those Tixall papers, that you might see how the seal appeared, but in vain. It was only a wrapper, without any writing within, and I threw it aside, together with the post-label sealed on to it. The seal (or to the best of my remembrance the two seals) on it did not appear to have been abused. I could not suspect that any paper was missing, because no schedule was sent me with them, or any intimation (that I remember) that there was so considerable a paper within. This I presume you will see in the letter from Mr. Lane, and Mr. Congreve, which was also in the same wrapper, and dated about the 24th of January last, which you have in your hands.

"The packet was brought me by a post boy at 10 o'clock at night on the 25th of January, as I was among my papers about the Plott. And it being directed to myself, and Mr. Lane's name on the outside, I presently concluded the wallet had been found. But when I opened the packett, which presently I did (as in duty bound, knowing that speed might have been required in things of that nature) I run over all the papers, so as to see there was nothing that answered my expectation. And as soon as the Lords of the Commission of the Council met, I laid all before them truly and faithfully. And I do upon my salvation declare that I never had or saw any other letter of my Lord Stafford's, than that which is now in your hands, and therefore it hath laid a great weight on my spirits now for these five weeks past, that no report has yet been admitted from me, pursuant to the vote which is upon the books, viz. that I should seek and enquire for some other letter of my Lord Stafford's, which God Almighty knows, I never saw in my life."

I beseech you let me have justice, and let the Committee report to the House that I have faithfully delivered up all the papers I received from Tixal.

HENRY TREBY to his brother the SAME.

1679, May 26. Wrington.—If Lord Peters is found guilty and his estate forfeited, and it be given to any person you know, or can make interest with, I desire you will endeavour to get me the office of collecting the rents of the manor of Brent, it being near me.

J. HORSEMAN to the SAME.

1679, May 27. Plympton.—I have acquainted Mr. Reepe with your answer to his letter about the captives in Algiers, and Merrifield, and others also. They are very thankful to you for your readiness to assist them if opportunity offers. Old Richard Clarke's youngest son Thomas is a captive, and his widowed mother is too poor to help to redeem him.

We all in the country are in great expectation to hear of the Lords' trials, the more that they have been so often put off.

A great part of Honiton was burnt last week, on both sides of the street.

SIR ROBERT SOUTHWELL to the SAME.

1679, May 31. Council Chamber.—"The Lords of the Committee of Examinations are now sitting, and would be glad presently to speak with you."

JOHN RUSHWORTH to the SAME.

1679, July 11.—"I am loath to send to you for the Earle of Strafford's trial before you have done with it, but that at the present I must take something out of it, to corroborate some passages in my second part, which I intend shortly for the presse. Be pleased to send it by the bearer."

J. RICHARDSON to the SAME.

1679, August 9.—The Council has adjourned to the first Wednesday in October.

Mr. Jennyson was examined the day they adjourned, which was the day you left town, and has made a fuller discovery of the Plot it is said.

Some of the elections are over. At Amersham, Algernon Sydney is chosen and Sir Roger Hill; at Wendover, Mr. Hampden and Backwell; at Queenborough, Lord Dunblaine and Mr. Herbert. In Essex they elect on Tuesday next, and in Surrey Lord Longford desists for this time.

Mr. Starkey has accidentally blown his thumb off.

——— to his cousin THOMAS LITTLETON.

1679, August 14. Worcester.—This being the last place on the circuit I will tell you about it. The number of causes have been few, but of signal importance. At Gloucester one Hanslip was arraigned as a Popish priest. At his trial (which I saw) great numbers of vestments, crucifixes, B . . . ., altar-stones, mass books, pictures, and such like trumpery, were brought into court, and upon these and other very strong evidence he was convicted, but is reprieved by some private order. But the thing chiefly remarkable in his trial was the notorious equivocation, or rather perjury, of some Popish witnesses that were often present at Mass with him, and had been seen so, and had confessed it to some Protestant witnesses present in court, yet they did utterly deny everything, having first equivocated as long as they could. Three others were indicted for seditious words spoken a little before the discovery of the Plot. One for saying that before Christmas there would be another King. Another that there would suddenly be such a blow in England as it had not felt for a long time. The third that the Papists will be uppermost once again, and will suddenly have their chapels, and other churches, and church lands again. And other words concerning Popery. The two first were found guilty, but the third escaped, there being only one witness against him.

A Mr. Arnold and a Mr. Price have been very active in those parts, and found when Lewis was arrested a vast quantity of Popish trinkets. Under an Order in Council they had all been burnt, and could not therefore be produced at the trial. He was convicted upon the evidence of many witnesses, but reprieved. "He wears a great periwig, and I am confident I have seen him often in Farr's Coffee-House, and elsewhere."

A woman swore against him that she had paid him about 10l. to get her father's soul out of purgatory. "To which he said that he called God to witness that he never had a grant of her. No, said she, for I paid you in good shillings and halfcrowns. To which I observed he did

not answer a word . .. . But the thing most observable was the
return of the Grand Jury, out of which Mr. Arnold did challenge 8 or 10,
and did prove them to be suspected Papists, or that their wives, or near
kindred, were Papists. And the Petty Jury, though returned over by
accident, yet had many challenged out of it upon the like account, that
you may see how this pest hath spread itself in Monmouthshire." At
Hereford one Kemble was convicted of being a priest, but reprieved.
Father Harcourt would have been convicted upon the examinations of
3 Popish witnesses, taken before Justice Manwaring, had they not
impudently denied at the trial all that they had before sworn and
subscribed to.

The trial of several priests at Stafford was put off on account of the
absence of Dugdale in London.

A zealous Papist there was convicted and sentenced to the pillory for
saying that Parliament never did good to King or kingdom, and that it
will never be well in England until the King rule without a Parliament,
as the King of France does.

It is much to be noted that all these things appear in the first circuit
after the discovery of the Plot.

A law ought to be made to disable Papists from being witnesses, at
least in any case between a Papist and a Protestant.

JOHN POLLEXFEN to the SAME.

1679, August 19. London.—Opposition to you at Plympton does
not seem very probable. I have written to Cousin Hum. to keep
possession of the meaner sort of electors by some expenditure in good
ale.

Most of the elections within 60 miles are over. Most C, though at
Windsor such are not like to get in.

" The Duke's daughter, Lady Anne, will go to-morrow for Brussels,
and the deep politicians of the Coffee House would suppose she would be
married to the Dolphin of France, and that Cleveland hath been the
marriage maker. The Lord Chief Justice is much censured by all.

" Sir Nathaniel Herne is dead, so cousin Ryder may have a fair berth
at Dartmouth."

WILLIAM HARRINGTON to the SAME.

1679, August 19.—The most remarkable thing about the elections is
the success of Colonel Sydney at Amersham where he was brought in by
the activity of two or three persons, though he was wholly unknown
there, and he defeated Sir William Drake, an inhabitant and lord of
the place. Sir Roger Hill is returned with him.

The next most observeable thing is the Essex election. Here Sir
Elias Hervey was persuaded to decline joining Colonel Mildmay, his
former associate, and take in Sir Thomas Middleton.

They appeared in the field on Tuesday, supported by the Duke of
Albemarle and most of the principle gentry. They were opposed by
Colonel Mildmay who, upon the refusal of Sir E. Mildmay the night
before to join with him, had taken in a young Mr. Honeywood (candidate at the last election for Malden). Lord Gray of Warke managed the
country very briskly for them, and the two parties nearly came to
blows. Sir E. Mildmay's party, though not a tenth in number when
drawn up in the field of their opponents, called for a poll. But after
dragging it on until noon on Friday they then retired on finding that
they were in a hopeless minority.

Sir E. Mildmay must now go to little Old Sarum. He will hardly
recover the good reputation he formerly had in that country. Sir

MSS. OF SIR W. FITZHERBERT. Richard Temple and Lord Latimer are returned for Buckingham. Sir Richard had the majority clear, but Lord Latimer had but six voices, and Sir Peter Tyrell as many, so as they say that Sir Peter had this reason to contest it, for that in the judgment of Parliament, Lord Latimer being returned by one of the six, the vote of him that returned him will be cast out, and his number reduced to five. Howbeit there is apparent reason for a new choice.

Hertfordshire has been at a loss, being resolved against Titus one of their late members for his ill behaviour in the matter of the D[uke]. Titus means to try for Huntingdonshire, where Price retires. Kit Vane had rather stay with his wife in Kent than travel to Durham.

I must not omit an answer of a countryman to a great man, during the Essex election, who told him he had better be at home looking after his harvest. He retorted he had rather trust God with his crop, than the devil with the choice of Parliament men. Others saying they would venture their corn to save their land. That county too which set so good an example in their choice of knights, did not put them to the expense of a penny. Several declaring at the time of the poll that they would sell their horses, or their corn, rather than be wearied out by their adversaries. But the two competitors did bear the charge of their men. Other counties are likely to follow the example of these who should no longer be called Essex calves, but worthies.

Now I have given you a hopeful account of a resolved people and a good Parliament "Good Mr. Speaker." They threw a dead dog into Chief Justice Scroggs' coach at Gloucester where Bedlow had been holding forth.

[*A long letter full of election reports.*]

GEORGE BRADBURY to the SAME.

1679, August 22.—I was at the Election at East Grinstead. Mr. Goodwin Wharton and Mr. Jephson are chosen. Mr. Powle who also stood is chosen at Cirencester. It is thought he meant to keep Grinstead for Sir Thomas Littleton, who it is now likely will not get into this Parliament. To make him some amends Lady Lyttleton has £6000 as next of kin, though very remote, to a Mr. Lewis of Sussex.

The greatest election tumults were those in Essex where the Duke of Albemarle received many affronts. The poll there lasted five days. "At Windsor, where the election is not yet passed, they cuff and cudgel one another every day, and there is so much hollowing that they disturb the King's fishing, with Winwood and Starkey against Cary and Powney."

Lord Barkley of Barkley is to be an earl.

I tell you little private stories for want of public ones.

THE SAME to the SAME.

1679, August 26.—Congratulations on his election.

Details of an attack of illness the King had been suffering from. It came on on his return from hawking at Lady Portsmouth's.

The doctors call it an intermitting tertian.

Bulletins are sent twice a day to the Lord Mayor.

Beds are being prepared at Whitehall, as if the King and Queen would come there to-morrow.

JOHN RICHARDSON to the SAME.

1679, September 2.—The King is well again. He now talks of coming from Windsor to-morrow fortnight.

- The Duke of York went to see him this morning, from St. James'.

W. Harrington to the Same.

1678, September 2.—The Duke came in haste to London last night, where few knew of his arrival, being Monday about 11 o'clock, and went in haste to Windsor this morning. This, added to the King's illness, caused much surmising.

These two great accidents may give you vigour in seeking for those great things which were the subject of your debates when you were last assembled.

Hampshire, following the example and zeal of some others, has thought fit to put up Lord Russel, though at a great distance and knowing nothing of the matter, against Mr. Noell, their Lord Lieutenant. Accordingly he and Sir Francis Rolls were chosen by a great majority. The countrymen also declared that the election should not cost their knights a penny, though the poll should be kept open a month.

Honest Tom Haselrige is dead, and is to be carried to-day into Leicestershire for burial.

The Portsmouth voyage has been the death of several of those who accompanied the King, and it is believed had some part in the King's illness, which was serious.

H. Hatsell to the Same, at Plympton.

1679, September 6.—The Duke of York posted from Harwich attended by Colonel Churchill. It is said that he was sent for by the advice of some of the Privy Councellors, but the Gazette says he came unexpectedly. Most of the great persons about the Court have waited on him, and kissed his hand. But he refused that honour to Sir Thomas Armstrong, being offended (as it is supposed) at some words he spoke a few weeks since in favour of the Duke of Monmouth's legitimacy.

The King is weak but can take walks in the park.

The Town swarms with pamphlets. Two or three appear every day.

It is uncertain if the Duke will return to Flanders at all.

Titus Oates to The Same.

1679, October 25.—"I pray you to take notice that Thomas Knox hath petitioned the King to order him those papers, which the King hath not granted, but ordered his Councell to have them of you, which if you deliver them I suppose it may tend to help their memories, they haveing as I understand forgotten what they did contrive against mee. Sir I hope you will not deliver them if by any meanes you can keep them by law, for you received them not of the Counceil but of the Committee of Lords."

Tit Otes."

J. Ellwell to the Same.

1679, October 27. Exeter.—The late prorogation is the cause of much talk. It is thought another may spring from the same root. It is thought that the same motive will operate in January as well as in October.

Many of your friends are in despair, expecting nothing short of ruin for the nation if destitute of Parliament.

Many would wish a petition to be presented first from London, and then from all the counties, that Parliament may sit in January and continue sitting until some terms are made about the King's person, and the Protestant religion. All agree that London should lead the dance.

MSS. OF SIR W.
FITZHERBERT. None however will put this in practice unless it is approved of by you and Mr. Pollexfen.

"Let all alone awhile saith this person, till the two Dukes jangle, &c. I find only one thus thinking, which I thought fit to communicate to you."

On a blank side there is a great seal of shorthand.

DR. N. CARY to SIR G. TREBY, at his house in Fleet Street.

1679-80, January 22.—I congratulate your honour, and do not agree with some that you are to be the less esteemed.

H. HATSELL to the SAME, at Launceston.

1679-80, March 13.—Our only news is that Sir George Jefferies is to be Chief Justice of Chester, and to continue Recorder. Sir Job Charlton is to be a Judge in Westminster Hall, if he will accept it.

JOHN TRENCHARD to the SAME.

1680, August 2. Taunton.—Desiring him to defend Mr. John Freine, an acquaintance of his at Taunton, in a suit brought against him by Sir John Cutler for words spoken at the late election here.

He will wait upon you as you pass through this town on your way to Wells.

The greater part of the counsel are engaged on the other side.

H. HATSELL to the SAME.

1680, September 4.—The contents of Bedloe's affidavit are not yet publicly know. Bedloe's wife was present in the Chamber when the affidavit was made, and desired a copy, but it was refused her.

On his return from Bristol he waited on the King at Windsor, and on Wednesday the 25th following. A copy of the affidavit or a part of it was read before the Council at Whitehall. On Sunday following the Council sat at Windsor, were was a great debate.

It is generally believed the Parliament will sit a very little while, however it will be convenient that the members attend.

Giles has a long time well recovered of the bruises he received when he stood in the pillory. He was to have stood again last week, but it was countermanded from Windsor. On Wednesday last another order was made at the Sessions for his standing to-day at Gray's Inn Gate, which he did accordingly.

Mrs. Cellier was committed about a month since for printing her narrative, and one sheet of it was taken in the press. But she was bailed, and the whole is since printed, consisting of about twelve sheets, which she openly sells at her own house. The chief design of it is to justify herself and blacken Dangerfield. That the Popish Plot is a fraud. She abuses Oates and Bedlow, and says that the papers were laid at Colonel Mansell's lodgings by contrivance between him and Dangerfield. There are reflections upon Lord Shaftesbury and the Duke of Buckingham. And the King is abused for she says the St. Omer youths came over here by his command.

There are many impudent lies in it, and it seems to be written to defy justice.

J. POLLEXFEN to the SAME, at Plympton.

1680, September 7. London.—There is nothing worth reporting.

It is said the Duke has made an offer to the King of retiring from Court and from all business.

Mrs. Cellier's narrative, which most think is a great libel on the Government, is openly sold in the streets. It is probably the work of a cabal of Papists, but the news of the Duke of Monmouth's reception in your parts balances it.

The SAME to the SAME.

1680, September 7. London.—The King is expected at Whitehall to-night on his way to Newmarket on Thursday, where he will stay about three weeks or a month.

An express from Tangier says that an attack is preparing.

The SAME to the SAME.

1680, September 14. London.—Mrs. Cellier is at last arrested, and is to lie in prison until she pays 1000*l.*, then to give surety for good behaviour, and to stand in the pillory.

There is no appearance that the scheme of things will be changed.

Essex and Radnor have thoughts of desiring to be excused from attendance in the C.

The Chancery gentlemen are still very dilatory about the captives money.

H. HATSELL to the SAME.

1680, September 18.—There is little news.*

Mrs. Cellier stood on the pillory at the Maypole today. She was much pelted but not hurt. There was a guard of above 400 men. It is said she had an headpiece and armour as Giles had.

The Duke of Monmouth went five days since to Lord Lovelace's. Lord Shaftesbury who came to town a week since has a tertian ague.

J. POLLEXFEN to the SAME.

1680, September 18.—Marshal Bellesfond has arrived from France and has gone to Newmarket. He is the man who was here to concert affairs in 1671.

It is computed the above two millions have been already spent about Tangiers, and that it will require 900,000*l.* more to finish the fortifications.

PHILO TREBY to the SAME.

1680, November 2.—I humbly tender my advice in the present conjuncture viz. Tacking the revenue of the Crown to the Laws established for Religion.

The plan seems very simple and easy.

HEADS of a PAPER of ADVICE from Friends in the Country to G. TREBY, M.P. [*No names.*]

1680, November 2.—

1. If the House is dissolved or prorogued this month send forth a remonstrance to the whole nation.
2. Pass no bill sent down by the House of Lords which the Court desires, until the Succession and the Protestant religion are secured.
3. Pass a bill to exclude the Bishops' votes, as they show themselves enemies to the Commons.
4. Let the House of Commons hold a strict correspondency with the City.
5. Endeavour to secure good Protestant officers for the Militia.

JAMES CARTER to the SAME, at Mr. Starkey's, bookseller, within
Temple Bar.

1680, December 13. Penrhyn.—"The last post brought the news of
your being sworn Recorder. It was generally satisfactory here, but
especially to me who have ever prophecied for you great eminency, and
bid you prepare for the highest offices. Nor am I more pleased with
your advancement, than with the manner of it, which was not by dull
climax in Common Law road, but at once, per saltum."

Compares him to Elijah. Begs for a letter before he becomes too big
a man for " poore Jim's " acquaintance.

1680, December 20. Warrant for the apprehension of John Marshall,
ate servant to Thomas Bowyer of Luntlow in Hereford.

[*Signed.*]   W. WILLIAMS, Speaker.

H. TREBY to the SAME.

1680–1, January 9.—Some merchant law questions.

It is reported here that the King is afraid any longer to trust the
rebellious city of London, and that he has removed all his soldiers from
quartering in it, and also from the factious town of Plymouth. We are
told that 500 soldiers and a troop of horse are to be sent to subdue it.

[LORD CHIEF JUSTICE]. FRANCIS NORTH to SIR GEORGE TREBY, Recorder of London.

1681, April 8.—" I had intimation from my Lord Mayor and yourself
that you desired the assistance of me and my Brethren the Judges that
are in town to-morrow, the afternoon, at the Old Bayly, concerning the
removing an Indictment of Recusancy preferred against the Duke of
Yorke. I shall attend you at 3 o'clock being the time appointed. This
is to let you know I think it will be convenient to have Mr. Attorney
Generall present, if he will be there, or Mr. Sollicitor Generall, if you
concurre with me, I suppose you or my Lord Mayor will send to desire
them to be present."

There are about 14 *lines of shorthand at the foot of the page.*

SIR ROBERT SAWYER to the SAME.

1681, May 21.—I thank you for your remarks. It was done in haste,
and ought to have been for high treason for compassing the death and
deposing of the King but uttering and publishing &c.

Pray let Sir W. Turner amend the commitment.

The SAME to the SAME.

1681, May 21.—I have answered to the Old Bailey that I find cause
to charge Samuel Harris with high treason, and have given direction to
Sir W. Turner accordingly.

SIR JOHN BERRY to the SAME.

1681, October 19. Mile End Green.—The unexpected verdict of the
jury in the case of Mr. Wynell and King surprises me very much, as I
hear it did most that were on the bench. And I believe you, with all
your experience of proof of so much provocation, have hardly met with
so severe a verdict. No man could forbear drawing his sword having been
cudgelled as he was, much less in the disorder he was in at that time.

I doubt that unhappy circumstance of his drinking the Duke of
York's health irritated the jury.

I pray you make such a representation to the King on Wynell's behalf as may facilitate an appliction for his transportation, or at least reprieve.

Many shorthand notes.

SAMUEL CARTER to the SAME.

1682-3, January 1.—There is an action against me. I will tell you the truth. About a year ago an attorney of this place gave me ill language in a tavern and I boxed his ears. The quarrel was made up. But again about a month since the very same man in the very same place gave me much the same vile language, and to the best of my remembrance I gave him much such another box on the ear, to which he answered with a bottle which he threw at me. I replied with candlesticks, which slightly bruised his head. Pray advise me.

WILLIAM LEWIS to the SAME.

1682, December 20 and 30. The Gatehouse.—Has been nine weeks in prison, and cannot get his trial or be allowed bail. Begs for aid and advice.

JAMES CARDROW to the SAME.

1684, December 22.—An ingot of gold had been more proper for me to present you with, though to a new married man a gad of steel may for the present be more serviceable.

TITUS OATES to the SAME.

1684-5, January 30.—"I must pray you to consider of what letters you have of Mr. Coleman's, to the end that I may make use of them att my tryall. I must interest you to show mee what favour you can. It is my right to be preserved by all and every of those whom I have faithfully served. I have no more but assure you I am your affectionate ff. and servant

TITUS OTES."

The SAME to the SAME.

1684-5, February 3.—"I humbly beseech you to appear for me, Mr. Tempest will attend you with a breviat of my cause, which I beseech you to accept; if there bee any of Mr. Coleman's letters I must begg the favour to lett us have the use of them. I am certain noe man hath a better cause then I, but I expect to bee run.downe.

TITUS OTES."

There are sixteen lines of shorthand at the foot of the page amongst which are the names "Tempest, Feb. 4; Wallop;" and one or two dates; and a few lines more in the margin where the words occur :— " May 5, 1685, o. Subpœnad. Polln. Wm. Williams and Mr. Tonson."

JOHN POLLEXFEN to the SAME.

1685, June 6.—Croydon. I thank you for your letter, but I could not go up to put in a petition in so short a time. The Mayor of P. was returned by his deputy and not by himself as the Mayor of Thetford. In some cases there may be as much difference between a Mayor and his deputy, as between a Lord Mayor's horse and a Lord Mayor.

I shall not be in town until after the holidays.

RALPH GRAINGE to the Same.

1685, June 7.—Your petition to the House of Commons was read on Thursday morning and referred to the Committee of Privileges.

As I was going about it to Westminster I met Mr. Ash, who undertook it, but he put it upon his brother, who did it so well that Mr. Curoway recommends him. I first as you desired informed Mr. Henry Pollexfen. He would not give any advice but sent me to his brother, and he sent me the enclosed.

CHARLES FORTESCUE to the Same.

1686, August 3. Plymouth.—A business letter describing a property worth more than 400*l.* a year on sale in that neighbourhood.

GEORGE SPRY to the Same.

1688, December 24. Place.—I hear that the Prince has been as well received in the city as he was by the county gentlemen where he first landed.

"Our country, though it did not express. theyre zeale soe farr as it might by attending his person, yett it hath soe much favoured his designe that it was the first in England that unanimously associated and addressed, which I suppose will be generally followed, soe that we need not feare the coming in of popery to this kingdome for the future."

Some shorthand notes.

ANONYMOUS to the Same.

1688-9, March 18.—If steps are not taken to stop some of the preaching in the country, and compel the ministers to pray for the King and Queen, and take the oath of allegiance, people may very possibly be led into a rebellion. This comes out of Somersetshire. No longer since than this day week there was at Broomfield near Bridgwater at Mr. Hellyer the minister's house a meeting of twelve of the neighbouring ministers. Of those twelve only one had publickly prayed for the King and Queen. The business of nine of these gentlemen was to play upon and bait the honestest amongst them. Mr. Hellyar and Mr. Anthony Clarke of Enmore and Charlinch, and others, declared that they would never obey the Bishop's orders to pray for the King and Queen, and only yesterday many of them prayed in the churches for the Prince of Wales. Mr. Thomas Jenkins who serves Durston and North Newton, says he will die before he takes the oath. At the said meeting those present did also declare that the present Parliament is no Parliament. Mr. Hart of Taunton is the chief promoter of this faction, and the ministers take their line from him.

WILLIAM PAWLETT, Recorder of Bristol, to SIR G. TREBY, Attorney General.

1689, September 5.—The goal delivery at Bristol is finished and three are condemned to die. One for sheep stealing, the second for felony without benefit of clergy, for personating a landed man, and the third for procuring the second to do so. The two first are notorious rogues and cattle stealers, and the Mayor and Aldermen tell me that the whole country will cry out if they be not hanged. But the third is only 24 years of age and it might be best to transport him.

"That which occasions you this trouble is to know whether it is best to hang the two first or not, because here is a discourse that the judges have hanged very few in their circuits but murders and for rape.

"What power have judges to transport those who are convict of small felonies though not clergyable. Here are two boys, the eldest not twelve, convicted for taking a purse clam et secrete with 40*d*. in it, whom I reprieved before judgment, because so young, upon their friends' petition to transport them."

JONATHAN, BISHOP OF EXETER to the SAME.

1689–90, January 14. Trelawney.—I thank you for your letter in which you communicate to me the opinion of the Lords Commissioners of the Treasury of my right to a moiety of the treasure taken out of the sea by Mr. Ford. When I waited on Lord Godolphin he did not seem to think there was so much hast, but believed it would keep cold till I came again. I have sent my patent, under which I claim, to the Treasury. I am not well enough to come to town.

Signed J. EXON.

JAMES VERNON to the SAME.

1689–90, February 14.—"My Lord Shrewsbury going out of town, gave me directions to send to you to know what is done in the non prosequi against the Jews which his Lordship the Earl of Monmouth and Mr. Hampden had his Majesty's orders to speak to you about . . . . The reason of this enquiry is in order to give notice to my Lord Mayor, for without satisfying the Jews in this particular, what my Lord Mayor has been negociating with them will have no effect."

A few words in shorthand, and " £30000."

— COURTENAY to the SAME.

1690, June. L . . ham.—Certain Jacobites hereabouts swagger and cluster against our present happy settlement, vaunting that they hope shortly to see some of their neighbouring Williamites, whom they name, safe enough. They defied a good Protestant parson who was in their company to inform against them if he dared ; and they and a neighbouring Justice of the Peace can be proved to have drunk to King James's health.

[*Endorsed*,] "Cousin Croker."

DR. JOHN TILLOTSON to the SAME.

1690, July 3, Edmonton.—I beg to introduce the bearer Mr. Hook, son of a worthy man Dr. Hook, who was vicar of Halifax where I was born. He is not personally known to me, but I recommend him on the credit of his testimonials.

J. E. to the SAME.

1690, July 21.—I am but one and know not how to get any joined with me to do zealously what is fit to be done.

Things are very loose in the country, only the Hand that works miracles saves us.

The Test is the bulwark of the three kingdoms. Money is the sinew of war. Can they be well affected who tell people that the late poll was never intended to raise more than half what the former did ?

"If the pulpits uttered nothing of state matters the people, who notwithstanding are pretty hearty to the Government, would amend and reform. All good men desire good Sheriffs the year ensuing.

"I gave the Under Sheriff a guinea on Saturday last, who returnes thanks. It is 21 shillings more than he deserved. Though by this his foul mouth will be stopt, who thought Mr. Tozer promised and was bound, which may contribute to it. Risdon Esq., a Papist near Totness, L. Gatfick an attorney, and five or six more notorious Jacobites, are secured by the Deputy Lieutenant's warrant. Others may be seized in a few days, as John Bere, &c.

"I intend to visit the maritime parishes on our river, and persuade seamen to list themselves in the fleet. Some one captain of the neighbourhood would draw many."

J. Ev . . to the SAME.

1690, July 23. Exeter.—"On Sunday evening the F[rench] F[leet]. consisting of 115 sail of great and small ships, appeared before this port, and doe still remain there, except 14 galleys, who are gone into Torbay. These drew the last night very close to the shoar, but retired on seeing some beacons on fire. All the militia of the county of Devon is raised, and warrants issued out this day for the posse, all directing their course to Torbay. Never was there known more unanimity and resolution than appears in the people to hasten to hinder their landing, which hitherto hath not been attempted, neither doth it seem very probable they they will.

"If a landing were designed, a far greater number of ships would appear, fit for the transport of horses, artillery, &c.

"The reason why the fleet stays here may be the strong west wind, which is in their face, if they intend for Brest or Ireland, and noe place more favourable than Torbay, and the bay from thence to Portland, where their ships may safely ride at anchor. The only danger that might touch them is from fire-ships, of which I think they have not the least apprehension.

"Here is a report that Col. Godfrey's regiment of horse, with two Dutch, are coming westward. It were to be wished they appeared here as soon as may be, to animate and range in order vast numbers of volunteers that would join them. If any passages of moment occur they shall be transmitted you."

[The SAME] to the SAME.

1690, July 28. Exeter.—"On Saturday last the French gallys approached Tingmouth, and fired many great shot towards the shoar, which frighted all people in and about the place, and made them fly into the country. Their small boats then landed about 300 men without any opposition, who burnt two small fishing towns, East and West Teignmouth, and all the ships and boats in the harbour, one or two only excepted, which they could not well reach. They rifled the houses before they set them on fire. They broke down all the seats of the Church, tore in parts the Bible and Book of Common Prayer, carrying away the Chalice. They found one man, whom they killed, saying to him, What you English dog, you will have a new King, as he told the person that took him up before he died.

"This done they retired to their small boats which carryed them off to their galleys, and they to the fleet lying before Torbay, where they abide, to the unspeakable shame of this nation.

"Our militia is in arms, and the posse raised. Great cheerfulness appears in the country to do their utmost to hinder the descent of the enemy. Sir Wy, Sir J. D., with many volunteers, are in the places of danger to signalize their zeal for their Majesties, and publick safety of the country.

"We want extreamely a number of good officers to discipline the raw countrymen, of whose faithfulness to the Government we have full assurance. You may doe great service to the kingdome by setting

forward some brave horse commander to visit these parts as soon as MSS. OF SIR W. FITZHERBERT.
may be. It's not very safe to give the reasons of this suggestion."
Six lines of shorthand follow.

GILBERT [BURNET] BISHOP OF SALISBURY to [the SAME].

1691, April 6. Salisbury.—One Dr. Beach who has a living within six miles of Salisbury, not only has not taken the oaths, but did with a high hand ride about the country and dispute against the taking of them. He obeyed his suspension, but when the six months were out he returned to his pulpit. He names no King nor Queen in his prayers, and reads the collect for the King, without a name. He observes no fast days, and in some visits to the sick, he denounces damnation to all that are for this government. When one of his parish pressed him to pray for the King and Queen, and to consider that God had raised them to the throne, he answered No, he that raised them to the throne was he that carried Christ to the pinnacle of the Temple.

He has used me rudely and boisterously. He is set on by some in London who found him a man of a rugged and fierce temper.

"The Bishop of Bath and Wells came and lay at his house a few days before he began to preach again, but how farre he wrought on him is that which I cannot affirm. I gave Institution to one who was presented to his living six months ago, but he has not been able to procure himselfe to be inducted, the church door having been always kept shut against him."

There is reason to think that the Under Sheriff has an understanding with him.

"The Dr. was in the church in his formalities, but no resistance being made no induction could be had, for the Dr. would not goe out of the Church, and the Sheriffe pretended, and had under the hand of counsell from London, that he could not force him to goe out."

Would it not be well that the Dr. should be brought before the Council as one who is notoriously disaffected? The Chancellor of the diocese, Dr. Woodward, is now in London, and I have desired him to wait upon you.

As to this man he is a pest in the country, and is likely to wear out the clerk who is presented to his Living.

JOHN PULTENEY to the SAME.

1691, April 10. Whitehall.—Lord Sydney has repeated his commands to me to send to you for the two warrants for Mr. Parson's pardon, which I spoke to you about yesterday in the lobby of the Council Chamber.

JOHN FORSTER, Clerk of the Peace for Staffordshire, to the SAME.

1691, April 29. Stafford.—In the name of the gentlemen of the county to ask for directions as to the method of proceeding against the Roman Catholics.

LORD SYDNEY to the SAME.

1691, April 29. Whitehall.—The King's pleasure is that Major Robert Parsons, who is accused of killing —— Wade, Esq., be tried at the King's Bench Bar.

LORD NOTTINGHAM to the SAME.

1691, "J. 11." Whitehall.—Mr. Justice Ayre has admitted to bail Abel Dennys of Newcastle though he is charged with high treason, in corresponding with and aiding the King's enemies, and especially by aiding them with such things as they need for their fleet.

"I do not know that he' has that authority out of the King's Bench, or how he comes to use it in showing any favour that may be denied to such enemies of the Government. I pray you let me know the state of this matter, for I believe the utmost severity of the law will be expected against such offenders, which are very numerous and hitherto, I know not how, have escaped."

RALPH GRAINGE to the SAME, at Tunbridge Wells.

1691, July 31.—"This afternoon Mr. Sollicitor sent to me about the examinations of Lord Preston and Crewe (?) being wanted, and desired to know if wee could come to your study for them. I took the keys of your chamber study, and mett Mr. Sollicitor at your chamber, who told me that the Lord Preston refused to be a witness, and hee being now in London it is resolved to have him bound over by some Judges, to appear and give evidence the next sessions, and in order hereunto they want his examination to produce to the Judge, and my Lord Nottingham spoke to Mr. Sollicitor this day at a Cabinet Counsell (which was as I understand about this) to enquire if any related to you could come at it, which was the reason of his sending to me, and we both went into your study together, and there found them upon a shelf. But we considered that it might not be prudent to produce them until you were acquainted with it, and gave directions, not knowing what ill use they might make of it that such things of secrecy might be come at by others in your absence; and therefore we laid them in the same place we found them, and hee hath given notice to Lord Nottingham that they cannot be come at, soe that you will have a letter this post from the Secretary. And I thinke if you write to him to order some to come to me, with directions to look for the key of your study at your chamber in your study at home, and to goe along with the messenger and open your study at your chamber, and to deliver the papers concerning Preston and Crewe (?) bound up and lying on a shelf over against your deske, this will bee (as seemes to me) without suspicion. But I beg your pardon for taking upon me to advise you . . . .

"This morning a waggon was seized at Southwark, that came from Dover, upon information that it contained French goods, and the goods being unloaded, at the bottom of the waggon, in an old coat, was found a great pacquett of letters, which Aaron Smith tells me was carried to the Custom house, and one of the letters being there opened, they say it contained the carrying on Preston's plott still, and directions for a rising, and the manner, and time. They at the Custom house were surprised at it, and sealed up the letter, and immediately sent up the whole pacquett to the Secretary. Mr. Sollicitor says that there was abundance of letters, and that half of them were not looked into when he came from Whitehall, nor knowes not what was in those that had been perused."

1691, August 12.—A certificate signed Anthony Bowyer that Nathaniel Lane of Croydon, mercer, constable, had been very diligent in apprehending and prosecuting disaffected persons, with danger to his life.

Followed by another signed by C. Whitelocke certifying that Fane is maliciously prosecuted in return for his good conduct in then King's service.

LORD SOMERS to the ATTORNEY-GENERAL at Tunbridge Wells.

1691, August 22.—There is nothing of any importance to communicate. You could never have been out of Town when you would be less called upon on business.

You at Tunbridge Wells are engaged I know in making us news for the winter.

MSS. of SIR W
FITZHERBERT.

SIR JOHN MOORE to the SAME·

1. 1691, October 28.—Understanding from the Sword Bearer that you intend to honour the Lord Mayor with your company if you could be accommodated with furniture for your horse, I send you the best I have, desiring your acceptance of it.

JOHN COMBES to the SAME.

1691, November 26.—Thanking him for his favourable introduction to the late Lord Chief Justice Pollexfen, and his encouragement to come out more into the world.

The wind has hitherto sat in my face and I believe will ever do so unless you are pleased to change the point.

The EARL OF MARLBOROUGH to [the SAME].

1691, November.—A request that he would order a *nolle prosequi* to be entered in the case of one Edwin Broxup who having served in the Guards for 26 years, and nothing to subsist upon but an allowance from the writer, was now prosecuted by the beadle of his parish of St. James' for not finding a watchman.

LORD NOTTINGHAM to the SAME.

1691-2, February 15. Whitehall.—Enclosed are the papers I mentioned to you this morning which I desire you to consider and return to me with your remarks and amendments of the clause in such manner as will answer objections, as soon as you conveniently can. "I am likewise to desire you to consider the clause in the East India Company's charter, whereby the King has power to determine it in three years, because the Committee of Council will ask you some questions about it, and does desire you and Mr. Sollicitor to be at my office a Wednesday at 6 o'clock in the evening."

The SAME to the SAME.

1691-2, February 25. Whitehall.—"I desire you and Mr. Sollicitor will at the end of the Council be at my office at 7 o'clock on Monday, and meanwhile to consider whether the King can incorporate a *new East India Company*, with liberty to trade, during the three years that the old company must subsist, concurrently with the old one.

"I desire you will send me to-morrow before noon the heads of *those Bills which Sir Richard Reynell*, and you, have agreed upon."

The SAME to the SAME.

1691-2, February 27. Whitehall.—"I send you by the King's command a copy of the charter of *Dublin Hospital*, that you may consider of the validity of it, . . . and report as soon as possible.

"His Majesty would likewise have you prepare the draught of a *Proclamation* for declaring the war of Ireland to be at an end."

SAMUEL EYRE to the SAME.

1692, March 30. Newhouse.—The favour you have been good enough to seek for me from the King is the thing I have hitherto vigorously declined, for it would check my freedom and not be profitable to me who use not a bar practice. Your letter is a surprise to me, but you have great influence with me, and therefore I pray allow me a little time to consider of it.

The Same to the Same.

1692, April 5. Salisbury.—I have received your second letter and
hope to wait upon you soon.

J. COMBES to SIR G. TREBY, Lord Chief Justice.

1692 (received), May 11.—I can no longer attend to my duties. Pure
necessity makes me take a resolution which all the world will consider
ill timed and imprudently executed. It wounds me also to lose all my
worthy friends. I beg your Lordship will so counter-work my folly
that the City may not suffer in their choice for want of time. I believe
if I should stay a week longer in Town I should never go out of it alive.

JOHN POLLEXFEN to the SAME.

1692, May 17. Wenbury.—I cannot come up until the election is
over "nor then if I can be excused, for I cannot leave my family behind,
this corner being soe haunted with French privateers, and the country
near the sea so depopulated by the militia when drawn off, and the
severity used in pressing, that it lies at mercy. The easterly winds have
disappointed the French. Happily the Parliament may [soon] adjourn
till winter.

"A French fleet came up the Channel soe far off land as probably
might have surprised part of ours without notice of their approach, if
the strong easterly winds had not prevented them, which forced them to
come in sight of the shore, and cast anchor at the Start. There they
stayed about four days, but the wind continuing against them, I believe
they looked on their design as spoilt, and that are returned, being seen
off Falmouth last Thursday."

SIR THOMAS TAYLOR to the SAME, at his house in Hatton Garden.

1692, June 5. Maidstone.—Your Lordship goes the home circuit.
I beg that you will hold the Assize at Maidstone, (of which I have been
chosen burgess). It is the most convenient place and has good accommodation. Assizes have been generally held there, at least 50 times to
once elsewhere.

LORD NOTTINGHAM to the SAME.

1692, July 16. Whitehall.—The Queen desires to know if Daniel
Scole a soldier in Brigadier Leveson's regiment who has been condemned at Kingston for murder, is a fit object of her mercy.

Another object in the reprieve is to avoid any disorder which might
arise if the soldier were executed whilst his regiment is at Kingston,
whence it will remove in a few days.

RALPH GRAINGE to the SAME.

1692, August 2.—Mr. Attorney General has asked for but cannot
get leave.

"This morning the Lords of the Cabinet early went for Portsmouth.
All were designed to goe, but I learn that my Lord Pembroke (by
reason of Sir R. Sawyer's death, as conceived) and Lord Godolphin
did not goe. Of the Admiralty the Lord Cornwallis is onely [gone].
The secret is that the instructions being opened when the transport
ships came into the fleet, and that being for the descent either at St.
Malo, Brest, or Isle of Ree, the admiral called a councell of the flag
officers, when it was resolved that it was impossible to make it at St.
Malo or Brest, the French having soe fortified both places, and drawn

down thither great forces. And for the Isle of Ree, in regard of the distance and danger of those seas, and the season soe far spent, it was altogether useless to attempt anything there. These resolves being sent up to London, is the occasion of the Lords' journey, our fleet being come to the Isle of Wight. I also perceive that there is a misunderstanding between the land and sea officers about the instructions, which seem to give more authority to the general at sea, than the sea officers think he ought to have, and some attribute to this the spring of the former resolves, and non-prosecution of the descent. The Cabinet before they went discoursed with divers experienced persons in sea affairs, and that knows the coast, and as I understand, goes with a persuasion that the descent is possible in any of the places.

" About 11 o'clock this day one Withers, Adjutant General of the Army in Flanders, who came from thence, got here, and the Queen not being at Whitehall, went to the Queen at Kensington, and was immediately dispatched after the Lords were gone to Portsmouth. We have noe particulars of the news he brings, but is in general that the loss was not so great in the late actions as was believed."

The SAME to the SAME.

1692, August 20.—Various items of foreign news.

LAWRENCE HATSELL to the SAME.

1692, August 22. London.—The news in the Gazette is good, and people are in good spirits. The Jacobites wager £100 to eight guineas against Dunkirk being in our possession by December 25, which shows that they believe it will be besieged.

RALPH GRAINGE to the SAME at Tunbridge Wells.

1692, August 23.—I have no news. A Holland post has come in to day, but I could not learn what it brings. I dined last Sunday with the Lord C[hief] J[ustice] Holt, where we drank your health. He tells me that some of the officers at Portsmouth were indicted before him at Winchester for embezzling the King's stores, and that the Council designs a special commission to some of the Judges to go into Hampshire to try them. I perceive that it is left to him to name the Judges, and he was mentioning you for one. If you would have me say anything to him I shall do as you direct.

The Town is very empty. Almost all our acquaintances have left it.

EDWARD COOKE to the SAME.

1693, August 18. Plough Yard.—Anderton's paper is printed at last, and we are here credibly informed that above 10,000 of them have been sent all over the kingdom before one of them was heard of publickly in this great town. I was lately with Mr. Secretary Trenchard who discoursed with me of it, and would be very glad that an answer should be made, provided it were done by a good hand. I proposed Dr. Wellwood, who I hear has promised it, and he said there could be no better person to do it with smartness. He desires me to ask you to let the Dr. know all the real matters of fact about yourself and the jury, and the trial. This may prove a good service to the Government.

SIR FRANCIS DRAKE to the SAME.

[1693], August 31. Buckland.—I pray for your advice as to a fit person in my place in case of a new election at Tavistock.

E 64159.

It is mightily inconvenient to me to serve again, and the air of the Town is very prejudicial to me.

For the present the H[igh] T[ories] and J[acobi]tes of this town are mostly at Mr. Mannington's devotion. But I am told his party is not so considerable as it was. That he. lives in the neighbourhood is an advantage to him, and I doubt it will be somewhat difficult to carry the seat when I lay it down, unless some pretty considerable person is brought forward.

My Lord of Bedford's interest will be needful. I have not yet mentioned my intentions to that family. Meanwhile I will sound the family at Ford.

The SAME to the SAME.

1693, September 29.—We'll give some account of the Assizes. Mr. Abraham Trout who has been added to the Commission of the Peace is zealous for the Government, and has always been an opponent of the Tories.

His estate is some £500 a year, but for want of quality, or other reasons, his appointment is grievously stomached by many of the gentry, and they have complained to Lord Rooksby. "Their chief dependence for redress is upon Sir E. S., who is very obliging to all, and looks so extremely brisk and prosperous, as if none of our misfortunes could in the least ever affect him." Probably the attack will prevail, for while his enemies are bitter his friends are lukewarm.

I write thus early that you and the Lord Keeper may know what is designed, and something about the man.

SIR EDWARD BALSH to the SAME.

1694, March 26.—Begging very earnestly for 10 or 20 shillings [? pounds] of his bounty.

LORD HERBERT OF CHERBURY to the SAME.

1694, May 25. Leicester-fields.—"This comes in behalfe of one William Carrol who stands indicted for feloniously takeing a gelding, valued 12 (?) with Humphrey Woodman. This Carrol is not of age. This is his first offence, and he has very good relations. Therefore my request is, if he be found guilty, he may be transported, and you will oblige &c."

SIR MILES COOKE to the SAME.

1694, July 28. London.—Complimentary. "I will give you a true state of the affairs of Christendome. My Lord Barkley doth sport it upon the coast of France, and when he comes neere enough to any town that deserves it, he complements them with his . . . and hath fixed soe many houses . . are like to put all Normandy into a flame."

Many remarks about the use of our fleet in the Mediterranean.

G. BRADBURY to the SAME at Appleby.

1694, August 14. The Middle Temple.—Little business was expected this summer circuit, and those who attend your Lordship may likely feel some ill effects of the Paper Act, but I who stay at home find the benefit of it from your Lordship having afforded me so long a letter.

Complimentary. "The Doctor who crossed the Alps to find the New Testament MS. in which the text 'There are Three that bear record &c,' was not, did not make so lucky a discovery (it being in favour of the Unitarian heresy) as the other did who met with that convocation book, which helped to make him an orthodox Dean. Sir Thomas Stanley against whom there was a warrant for High Treason, and who had been searched for in the country, was apprehended on Friday last, going by a wrong name, in Holborne ; but Colonel Parker is escaped out of the Tower. He was first missed on Sunday morning, his door being bolted on the inside. The matter was examined yesterday by the Privy Council, and referred to be examined by my Lord Chief Justice, who this afternoon has committed one Still to Newgate for High Treason, (the warder at whose house Parker was a prisoner).

"Sir Cloudesley Shovel on Friday last coming from Spithead with the English fleet into the Downes, found there a Sweede and a Dane men-of-war. The Sweede struck sayle, but the Dane refused till after two single shots, each exchanged upon the other a broadside, by which several men on both sides were killed and wounded, and the Dane struck."

Letters came yesterday from Admiral Russell dated July 25 in Altea Bay near Alicant.

He reports that the French fleet has gone out of Toulon.

SIR JOHN LOWTHER [of Lowther] to the SAME.

1694, August 16.—Excusing himself from waiting upon him in person, and inviting him to pay him a visit as he leaves Carlisle.

LORD SALISBURY to the SAME.

1694, August 18.—Under the late Act he is obliged to obtain his consent to any lease of Salisbury House and garden and tenements &c. Is now making such a lease to one John Hodge and sends it herewith for his consent.

S. TRAVERS to the SAME.

1694, September 12. Tunbridge Wells.—"While your Lordship was on circuit a friend of mine recommended to my acquaintance a very honest and learned gentleman, Dr. St. Clair, who for many years, till Mr. Boyle's death, had assisted that great man, not only in all his Philosophical and Mathematical experiments, but in preparing what he published on those subjects. Whereupon I resolved to set aside an hour a day for two months to rub up my old notions, and see them reduced into practice by a course of chymistry. If your Lordship had been in Town I would have consulted your Lordship before I prepared my cellar for that purpose, but I was so far from doubting your approbation, that I promised myself the honour of having your Lordship to see some of the more curious experiments, since it lay so conveniently for you, when the dispensation of justice and State affairs would allow you leisure for such a diversion. But to my great surprise my servant, coming this day from London, tells me he hears your Lordship is not willing I should proceed. If at my coming to Town, which will be in two or three days, there remain any scruples with your Lordship which I cannot remove I will desist. But if, as I am apt to believe, your Lordship's name is only made use of by peevish humorists to divert me from my purpose, I shall not only insist upon my right of making what use I please of my lodgings, and of giving whom I please free access to them, but I will protect the Doctor from any impertinent trouble that they shall give him. Tis hard that the Temple, which allows free egress and regress to all the dregs of mankind, where perriwig makers, shoemakers, brandy sellers, and fruiterers, keep open shops, should make difficulty of suffering a Member of the Society to receive visits from one of the most learned and ingenious mathematicians and philosophers in England; especially since among the known rules of the Society, the very staircase where the dispute lies, has for many years harboured wives, misses, and costermongers. But I am transported beyond the bounds that health prescribes to a water drinker, and that decency requires from one that writes to a person of your Lordship's character, and therefore I defer troubling you until I have the honour of waiting on you."

WILLIAM PAINTER to the SAME.

1694, October 13.—On the determination of the Exeter College case three of the Judges were for Dr. D. Bury, but Lord Chief Justice Holt concluded positively for the Visitor. He was of opinion that the Visitor has power to deprive a Rector, as you argued when you were counsel for the Visitor. The Visitor has brought a writ of error which will be before the Lords at the opening of the next Session. The Bishop of Exeter has directed me to inform you of this fact.

THE DUKE OF BOLTON to the SAME.

1694, December 22. London.—Having been summoned to be with his Majesty on Monday I shall not go into the country at all, and wish to know when you can let me have the paper I gave you to-day.

LORD KEEPER SOMERS to the SAME.

1694-5, March 1.—I mentioned Mr. Lechmere to the King last night, but find there is little hope as so many other applications have been made already.

I also mentioned to him your notion how seasonable it would be to get an Act to dissolve the County Palatine of Lancaster.

He is altogether of your opinion, and desires you to draw a short Act for that purpose. He hopes it will be quickly done, because the session being so far advanced, there is no time to be lost.

LORD LUCAS to the SAME, at Kingston.

1694-5, March 13. The House of Lords.—I would not write if I did not think it for the King's service.

" I suppose there may be several men fitt for the service in goale now at Kingston. If your Lordship will be so kind as to let the bearer have them, I will give my word that they shall be sent abroad, and you will very much oblige &c."

G. BRADBURY to the SAME.

1694-5, March 14.—"The mollifying words which your Lordship sees in the vote which passed on Tuesday last in the House of Commons against the Speaker, they connived at, and suffered him to slip in as he was putting the question. The next day he sent a letter (in cover to Mr. Goddrell) directed to the Honourable the House of Commons, that as he was dressing himself to go and attend his service there, he was taken with a violent fitt of the cholick, and he hoped he should be well to attend next day. Upon which they adjourned till the morrow. And this day he sent another letter that his indisposition continued. Thereupon the House proceeded to choose a Speaker, and there being a division, it was carried in a very full house for Mr. Paul Foley against Sir Thomas Littleton, by thirty voices. The new Speaker is to be presented to the King to-morrow morning in the Lords' House; after which it is generally said they will proceed further against the late Speaker to commit him to the Tower, and many say to impeach him. There is a great eagerness among them to know where the secret service money of the East India Company has been disposed, and I hear it is intended to put a clause into the Bill now depending for taking the public accounts, to subject this new matter to the enquiry of those commissioners."

FRANCIS WYATT to the SAME.

1695, June 8.—I beg you will not hold the Assizes at Horsham for the small pox is now there, and as I have never had it I am afraid to wait upon you there.

ANONYMOUS to the SAME.

1695, June 24.—Self interest is the motive which sways our great men. The writer disapproves of hospitality to French fugitives when our own people are suffering.

W. TRUMBULL to the SAME.

1695, July 2. Whitehall.—Being informed that at a meeting of the Jacobites last Saturday night, they determined to try to have the trial of the late rioters put off, and boasted that they had stopped the mouths of three witnesses already, and hoped, if this delay could be obtained, to silence others, by showing them how former witnesses had suffered by ill usage from the Government, thinks it his duty to send the information.

LORD KEEPER SOMERS to the SAME.

1695, November 13.—"The King having commanded me to be at Kensington this morning, I am apt to think he will speak to me upon that subject which my Lord Shrewsbury, by his direction, recommended to your Lordship's and my consideration.

"That makes me very desirous to see your Lordship before I went, and therefore if it be not inconvenient, I would hope your Lordship might take Powys House on your way, when you go abroad this morning."

DR. SHERLOCK to the SAME.

1695, November 14.—Yesterday Mr. Gale came to acquaint me that your Lordship would excuse me from preaching for you next Sunday and had appointed him supposing it might be inconvenient to me to preach this term. I told him it was no inconvenience to me, and it was the same thing to me whether I preach or not having provided a preacher for the Temple. But if you wish to hear him I am well pleased it should be so.

LORD KEEPER SOMERS to the SAME.

1695-6, January 25. Saturday.—"The King at the earnest desire of the Bishops, has determined to publish something of the nature of the enclosed paper. He has directed me to desire your Lordship to alter it so as it ought to be, and if it be possible to return it to me before 5 o'clock tomorrow in the evening. It seems to me that the latter part of it is not as it ought to be."

There are some 25 lines of shorthand on the blank side containing a few plain words " dissenter " " Trinity " " worship " &c.

BARON POWYS to the SAME.

1696, April 5. Exeter.—We have been so full of business on this
circuit I have hardly had time to eat or sleep. But this your county of
Devon does vastly surpass the rest in business, and I do not think it
possible to go hence before next Friday though I came here yesterday
week.

Great numbers of clippers and coiners are for trial. But I shall be
very careful not to charge the King with more rewards than needs
must.

In all my charges I have asserted the present Government with much
boldness, and with I think good results, as I gather from their looks,
and the numbers who signed the Association, and the loyal party in
every county have thanked me.

I wrote to the Lord Keeper about Cornwall, how untoward I found
it, but I brought them to a somewhat better pass before I had done
with them. I also find the county of Devon, as you said, just not one
jot better than it should be.

" I have here also promoted the House of Commons Address, and the
High Sheriff, most of the Grand Jury, and many of the Justices of
Peace, have signed it. But Sir George Chidley, Sir Peter Prideaux,
Sir John Pool, and some others are forming a different thing, a kind of
an empty Address without an Association. They shewed it to Sir Francis
Drake, (who has signed the other) and he unhappily shewed them the
great absurdities and defects of theirs, whereupon they have somewhat
amendid it. I chid him, and he is sorry for it, for the worse the better.
Yet it continues but a very indifferent business, and I having declared
that I would not meddle with any but what was the same as the House
of Commons, I hear they intend to have it presented by my Lord of
Bath.

. " I got Sir Francis Drake, and Colonel Waldron, to sit with me
for an hour this evening, and I discoursed them fully about this
county.

" They tell me I have done a great deal of good both in this county
and city, and have put spirit into the King William's friends, by my zeal
and resolution."

I have ordered two indictments to be drawn against one Henry
Legasick, a known Jacobite, and an attorney of great business, especially
among the Jacobites, for threatening those who would not drink King
James' health. The Grand Jury found against him, and I sent for
him into Court, and committed him, though he had four counsel and
some others that spake in his behalf. I persisted and declared that I
would certainly commit the greatest man in the county of whom I
should have a like suspicion of being concerned in the late plot. This
has startled the Jacobites hereabouts, and made much noise. But the
more noise the better, and therefore I did it the more publickly. I have
also had indicted some strangers who have spoken disrespectfully of the
King, and intend when I sit again in the city on Tuesday next, to
sentence them both to stand two market days in the pillory in this city,
and be fined, and imprisoned. When I pronounce the sentence I will
discant upon the necessity of the words " Rightful and Lawful" in
the Association.

I have some matters of weight to be imparted to his Majesty, but not
fit for a letter, relating to some things much amiss in the counties of
Devon and Cornwall. I will tell them to you and to the Lord Keeper.
I have taken great care in all my charges to point out how careful the
King and Parliament have been to establish a good coinage, which has

been destroyed to such a degree by clippers and coiners, as to be more injurious to us than the French war. That quantities of milled money are coined every week, and that the worst is passed. None of this money is here yet, but it will be dispersed gradually, and they must have patience, and stretch their credits for a short time.

"Yet really after all God grant there be not some mischief with the common people, especially in these remote parts soon after the 4th of May ; and pray speak that some courses be speedily taken it' possible to disperse the new money, for I doubt the old milled money, and clipped sixpences, and punched money, will not be sufficient to furnish for common necessaries, and people will not starve. Though I may say the Commonalty will venture it as far for this government as for any that ever was. I hear the Jacobites are in notable hopes that a sort of confusion will happen about the 4th of May for want of money, especially so near the King's going, and therefore the greater care must be taken. I am very glad the guineas are thus fallen &c."

Sir Francis Drake to the Same.

1696, April 6. Exeter.—When I first came here I supposed we should have made more of the Association, there seemed to be an almost universal inclination for it. But one night we lost many having "notions put into them that Harrow on the Hill stood in a bottom, for that the word ' Rightful ' was to break the Act of Settlement." Moreover they could not consent to the word ' revenge.' " So nice are some of us grown since we hunted the poor fellows that followed the Duke of Monmouth, after the whole of the design was entirely defeated."

This defection is owing to some of our leading churchmen. But we owe a million of thanks to those who recommended our Judge to this station. By his brave resolution he has done much to save our credit. The life of what we have done is mostly owing to him.

There was a most abominable Grand Jury provided. In it many Non-Jurors, which the Judge having notice of discouraged that panel, and we had a new one.

Sir William Courteney has subscribed. But really the zeal and arguments of the Judge have had the greatest effect, and I guess the disaffected party will rule their tongues a little better for the future.

We have among our refusing Deputy Lieutenants honest gentlemen. It is absolutely necessary there should be a new Commission.

I shall not be sorry if the report that we are to have a new Lord Lieutenant is confirmed. This is a conjuncture such as cannot be hoped for again, and I hope it will be duly improved.

I am almost ashamed to speak of the condition of our militia. The commissions to the Colonels came last week, and they, under apprehension of what may happen upon their not subscribing the Association, are not likely to be very active in settling their regiments.

We are in but an indifferent condition to withstand any attempt if one should be made. " The Sheriff too being such a contemptible old woofe, and the Under Sheriff no better affected than he ought. I hate, my Lord, so much as to complain and now to be an accuser, but really we are too much out of order to be altogether silent."

Loyal men ought to be supported, but the majority of the commissions go to those who hesitate to sign the Association.

" Some, I must do them the right to think, wish well to the Government, but they are commencing to break off from some that have heretofore governed them."

1696, April 12. Whitehall.—" I think it a great misfortune to me that I cannot enjoy your good company this day at Lambeth, by reason of the long debate we are like to have in the House of Lords. The Thanksgiving day may be I presume a free day on all hands, and then if it be convenient for your Lordship I shall be very glad to see you."

JEREMIAH WHITE to the SAME.

1696, April 17.—Submitting a print from Sir B. Showers' brother for perusal.
On the other side a quantity of shorthand.

LORD CHIEF JUSTICE HOLT to the SAME.

1696, April or May.—" I entreat your favour in perusing the inclosed and to reforme the errors in it. I designed to have put it into the hands of my Brother Powall, to have communicated it you, but I heare he is with your Lordship."
Some shorthand follows.

JAMES VERNON to the SAME.

1696, May 16. Whitehall.—By command of the Lords Justices I write to ask your opinion upon the clause in the late Act for the better security of the King's person relating to the security to be given by those who have come over from France since September last, for their departure out of the kingdom.

The SAME to the SAME.

1696, July 21. Whitehall.—The Lords Justices, being in daily expectation of letters from the King in relation to Sir J. Fenwick, wish to know if it would be very inconvenient to defer the trial till Monday, though Mr. Justico Rokeby should then be obliged to go out of Town.

SIR J. ELWILL to the SAME.

1696, July 22. Exeter.—Private business : " A great deal of sourness was shown by some of our neighbours the last sessions week, on the occasion of leaving out of the Lieutenancy some of their friends. Sir P. P.; Sir J. Ple ; Sir W. Dke ; and Sir H. Ackl.; were the murmurers, and concluded with a motion to Sir F. D. ; Sir William Davie ; myself, and others, to join in a letter to our Lord Lieutenant setting forth the work of the gentlemen left out, and desiring his Lordship to put them into the Commission. The managers were Sir William D[ra]ke and Sir H. A[cland], the rest supplyed fuel to maintain the flame. The persons left out were named Sir T. pmt (?), Sir Archi. Chester ; John Gifford ; Francis Turfd ; and Thomas Drew ; with Mr. Coffin. Unless these be put into the Commission it was said there would be feuds and animosities abounding amongst us, and they would be transmitted to posterity. It was added that these gentlemen had associated, or would do so. Sir F. D., to whom the motions were directed, replyed that if any were left out, it was their own fault, in omitting *voluntarily* to associate at the Assizes, and that he could not but wonder at the pretended ill consequences of leaving out such men. Whereas not a thought could be entertained formerly of any inconvenience by neglecting Sir William Davie; Mr. Calmady;

Mr. Harris ; Mr. Ar(siot ?), gentlemen of £2000 or £3000 a year. Sir
H. A. in a heat replyed that it was a neglect . . then to passe by these
gentlemen. Shall we do the like now? This was not satisfactory to
Sir F. D. who told Sir J. Ple, that should never write in favour of
such as dissuaded him and Sir P. P. from signing the Association at the
Assizes. Whereupon Sir J. P. said, I see we cannot agree, let us have
a couple of bottles to reconcile all. Which diverted the discourse and
opened a way for us to separate."

Afterwards there were some hot words between Sir F. D. on the
Bench at the Castle, and Sir W. D[ra]ke. In the end each held their
ground. Some men I find will go *driven*, who cannot be *led*.

" The Lord Lieutenant has a handle offered him to manage all the
Tantivy men, by impowering some, and neglecting others who have
most scandalously refused to give a necessary security to the Government in the day of distress. They may fret and foam until they see
the little good they do thereby. In a short time they will compound,
and be as flexible as any, in the opinion of your faithful servant."

The SAME to the SAME.

1696, July 29. Exeter.—Private business. Some disaffected persons
cannot conceal their joy arising from the separation made by Savoy.

" The fleet lies in Torbay. The sight thereof doth not terrify the
French capers who lye lurking on our coast, and take small vessels at
the entrance of our harbours. It were to be wisht some very
particular care were had to scour these seas of that destructive vermin."

ADMIRAL RUSSELL to the SAME.

1696, August 3. Chippenham.—Is anxious to wait upon him at
Cambridge Assizes. Supposes that Friday will be the first convenient
day.

[SIR J. ELWILL] to the SAME.

1696, August 3. L . . ok.—Had had a very satisfactory conversation of some hours with Sir William Courteney, who is zealous for the
government.

We expect good success in settling the militia both in the city and
county.

Our enemies offer a composition, viz. that those who are left out of
the Lieutenancy and have now signed be put in.

The Lord Lieutenant has not thought fit to give any answer. It is
affirmed that the Earl of Bath has given those gentlemen directions to
get into their hands as much power as possible.

Sir G. Ch. is insufferably insolent. If he is not dismissed the Bench
many will abstain from attendance for the sake of peace.

SIR MILES COOK to the SAME at Cambridge.

1696, August 4. London.—News from abroad.

" I heard Sir Stephen Fox tell the Archbishop of Canterbury, that the
army in Flanders could get no money in Flanders (no not for subsistance
money) but upon a rebate of nine shillings in the pound, which must
needs disgust the army, and was cause enough for the hasty coming
over of my Lord Portland to remedy so fatal a defect. He brought
over with him one of the chiefe directours of the Bank of Amsterdam,
who (upon the moral assurance I hope we have given him before he

went back again) will procure £200,000 from that bank, upon very valuable consideration you may be sure. My Lord Portland meets every day with some of the Lords Justices Commissioners of the Treasury, and several of the rich money-minded men of the city, and they are laying their wise heads together to contribute something like the philosopher's stone, but with what success I cannot yet perfectly learne, though the lying posts seem very sanguine in the matter."

The French are so posted that it is not likely there will be much fighting this summer. We shall do no more by land than we have done by sea, the burning of so many poor villages being but a small equivalent for the charges of a royal navy.

The SAME to the SAME at Norwich.

1696, August 13. London.—You will like to have some news.

This is likely to be the civilest campaign ever known; 400,000 fighting men, and not one bloody nose, nor as much blood likely to be spent as was shed by Lord Jefferies in his summer campaign in the west.

There is nothing but marching and counter-marching like a game at chess.

I am sorry my Lord Portland has not been more successful. "He finds that one thing more is needful besides the hearts of the people, and that is the philosopher's stone. Our bullion is almost melted down already, and the golden citizens padlock their guineas as they do their wives, so that men will as soon part with their teeth as their guineas. And this upon a foolish opinion that hath got into the heartes of the wisest of them, that the first thing the Parliament will doe when they meet, will be the heightning of guineas at least to 25s. the peece. But be that as it may, I cannot learne by my best enquiry that my Lord Portland hath as yet got together above £50,000, and that too of the Jews who have dealt like Jews in the matter, almost to the tune of 20 per cent."

Thinking men believe this difficulty about money will produce a peace. "The royal fleet rides safe in Torbay being no wayes terrified with the vast number of French privateers that almost surround them."

BARON LITTLETON POWYS to the SAME.

1696, August 25. Henley near Ludlow.—There has been a great deal of business this circuit, which seems to show that money is not so scarce as is pretended. Throughout the circuit [Hereford, Shrewsbury &c.] guineas and milled moneys, but chiefly good broad hammered money, appeared in sufficient quantity to do the business, and the Welsh money was remarkably broad. "So that I am fully convinced of the truth of the sentiments of my truly ingenious friends Mr. Clerk, and Mr. Lock, that there was left not only a good stock of passable money in the nation, but also that it would come out as soon as the hopes of the going againe of clipt money was over. For that end I have in all my charges &c. endeavoured to convince the people of that false imagination got amongst them (partly by malice, and partly by ignorance) that next Parliament will make clipt money to pass againe ; as also of another pernicious opinion got amongst them that guineas will also be raised as being of greater value than 22s., and (as they say) going for more in Ireland and Holland. But I believe I have convinced them that the par between gold and silver, now that we have milled money, can never permit guineas to be higher, and that what happens in Ireland and Holland is merely from the fallacy of the return thither.

"I have most industriously cheered up the people with the hopes of money in plenty suddenly, not only in my charges, but also in my common discourse, and I am told with very good success. And I found by the countenances of my auditories that they were very much refreshed by the reasons I gave them, and letting them know how exceeding diligent the Lords Justices were about the matter.

. "Yet after all it must be confessed there is a great want of money, and this new coin does disperse very slowly, and it is a perfect novelty (especially in these remote parts) to the common people to get a little in their hands. I purposely took a good quantity of it out of London with me, and chiefly of shillings and sixpences, and did take care that all my middling and lesser sums should be paid in it. And I doe the like here at home, and the country people seem mightily pleased to receive forty or fifty shillings together, all in new money, and I mix them some of all sorts that they may show about that it is coming.

"I hear there is a great arrear of Excise in Ludlow and other places for want of good money, and I know not how the taxes and other publick payments will be paid, unless the remains of the clipt money shall be taken. And yet that would have a fatal consequence, for it cannot be taken in so suddainly but that all broad money that is now come out will be in danger of clipping. The mischief of the coin is greater upon us than that of the French war, but I hope the worst is past.

"I did lately look into Oates' first narrative, and there he says that the adulterating of our coin was one of the Popish contrivances against us.

THOMAS BLOFELD, Alderman, to the SAME.

1696, August 25. Norwich.—An apology, with reasons, for his absence from the Court at Norwich.
Fourteen lines of shorthand follow.

LORD SOMERS to the SAME.

1696, September 2.—"I perceive we were all in a mistake yesterday, for in expectation of your Lordship we did not send for the Sheriff to come in to us, so far were we persuaded, we should have spoken with your Lordship. I must acquaint you that the Lords Justices have a farther design of discourse with you about Sir John Fenwick's trial, so that they will be very desirous of seeing you at their next meeting. But if it be so that you determine to go for Tunbridge, I will acquaint them on Thursday with the contents of your letter, and will make the best excuse I can."

SIR MILES COOKE to the SAME.

1696, September 8. London.—It has been reported that the King of France is dead. But I have pointed out to people that that is impossible for that persons of that magnitude are always complimented with a comet before their exit, or they are carried away in a whirlwind as Oliver Cromwell and Elijah were. The negociations for peace go on, very much forwarded by the King of France's illness. The mercers and ladies are much displeased that the Court will go into mourning this winter for the Queen of Spain.
News from abroad.

BARON LITTLETON POWYS to the SAME at Tunbridge.

1696, September 16. Henley.—Suggesting his own transfer to the Common Pleas in the place of Judge Powell deceased, and asking for his recommendation.

MSS. OF SIR W. FITZHERBERT.

P. Holt to the Same.

1696, September 16.—Sends an enclosure from his brother and begs for a continuance of his interest for an office which the King has written to say he will not dispose of until his return.

J. Vernon to the Same.

1696, September 18.—The Lords are unwilling to interrupt his use of the waters but must summon him to attend the arraignment of Sir John Fenwick on Wednesday next.
Within the letter there are 10 *or* 11 *lines of shorthand.*

Sir J. Combe to the Same.

1696, October 6, Daventry.—Has benefitted by the waters at Astrop. Recommends Mr. Wright of Oxford to be the successor of the Recorder of Chester if he is promoted to Westminster.
Mr. Hooke has in his own right a higher station.

Secretary Trumball to the Same.

1696, November 2. Whitehall.—Your attendance is required by his Majesty at Kensington at six o'clock this evening precisely.
Endorsed, Sir J. Fenwick.
1696, November 2.—*Three sides of shorthand.*
Endorsed, Sir J. Fenwick.

Lord Keeper Somers to the Same.

1696, December 5.—" I return Mr. Petit's collection. I did also persuade Mr. Attorney to send to him for his assistance, that he might have some advantage for his pains. Mr. Attorney has as I understand pitched upon Mr. Pratt for one who is to be of council at the Lords' bar. I know your Lordship has a favour for him, and therefore I hope you will send for him and advise him what he is to say, and how he is to manage himself in that place. It may be a very happy opportunity for him if he recovers as much credit to the King's Council in the House of Lords as they lost in the House of Commons. I do not know who else is to attend as council."

Baron Powys to the Same.

1696–7, January 10.—Will attend him at the House on Tuesday, for I suppose that business will be put off till then.
Mr. Harcourt may be back from Oxford by tomorrow evening, if summoned last evening.

John Sharp, Archbishop of York, to the Same.

1696–7, February 20. Bishopsthorp.—Lady Abdy widow of Sir John Abdy of Essex is prosecuting a maid of hers for setting fire to some outhouses. She then thought that if convicted the girl would be executed, and she was for letting the prosecution fall though she should pay the forfeiture.

I advised her to let the law take its course and then apply to the Judge for the favour of transportation, if he found the woman an object of compassion.

As you were the Judge I am obliged in accordance with my promise to trouble you with a request that you will see the lady.

MARTYN RYDER to the SAME.

1696–7, March 16. The Middle Temple.—"The trouble of this is occasioned by the proceedings of the House of Commons this day upon the Bill against selling of offices. My information says when the debate came on Mr. Attorney General offered the like proviso for the offices of the Court of Chancery as was for my Lords the Judges which was · att . . . . received. Then another like proviso was offered on behalf of the City of London. And then (jocularly) for all the Cities and Corporations, which their representatives said they thought they were obliged to offer for such as chose them. Then the debate growing more warm, it was by another sort of men thought the Bill was over-charged, and then the question being putt, whether all the provisos should be allowed, it was carried without a division that none at all should be passed, not even that which the Lords' House had added as a salvo to your Lordships. Mr. Attorney (as Mr. Petitt tells me who spake with . . . this evening) says that Mr. Attur (?) thought it would occasion the losse of the whole Bill. But your Lordship knows that depends on the resolution of the Lords whether they will adhere to the proviso for the Judges, and therefore I thought it my duty to inform your Lordship what I could learn, to the intent that you might (if thought expedient) write to some Lords on the subject, or take what other course you think proper." *Some pencil shorthand notes.*

The DUKE OF NORFOLK to the SAME.

1696–7, March 21.—To draw his attention to a case of jury packing in the case of Lord Walden, which is to be tried at the Sussex Assizes.

The case was adjourned by Judge Eyres for this reason, and now the very same jury has been chosen.

LORD CHANCELLOR SOMERS to the SAME.

1697, April 23.—"I wish I might know by a line from your Lordship whether you think it most for the King's service that the vacancy should be filled (of which mind the King seems to be but not with any positiveness), and if so my next request is that you would send mee the name of the person. I am to acquaint you that, if at all this time, it must be done this night, because the King proposes to be going early tomorrow.

"I could not learn my Lord Chief Justice Holt's mind clearly in this busines the first day of term."

VISCOUNT LONSDALE to the SAME.

1697, May 3.—To represent the hardships inflicted upon ignorant country people by grasping attornies. A poor tenant had been sued in the county court for £4 by splitting it into two or three actions. The defendant was willing to appear and had one of these men for his counsel. The plaintiff recovers. The process is executed. Then comes Mounsey the Attorney offers to manage this suit at his own cost, and prosecute the bailiff for executing a process in a case wherein the court had no jurisdiction, and thus they make a prey of ignorant country men.

JOHN WILLIAMS, BISHOP OF CHICHESTER, to the SAME.

1697, June 11. Chichester.—Would be as lenient as possible in the pitiable case of Mr. Rothurl against whom a bill of non-residence was found.

**MSS. OF SIR W.
FITZHERBERT.**

BARON POWYS to the SAME.

1697, October 1. Henley.—Pressing for his promotion in Chief Justice Treby's Court.

SAMUEL ROLLE to the SAME.

1697, October 9. Pittletoune.—Enclosing a request from the Justices of Salisbury for his opinion whether Mr. Clark, having been found guilty of manslaughter, may be bailed.

FRANCIS CATER, Mayor of Coventry to the SAME

1697, November 8. Coventry.—At the last Assizes you were pleased to take notice of the alterations in the Town Hall which is now one of the best in England, and to encourage us to expect a levy on the county to pay for it. A discontented set of disloyal men, who were ousted from power in a trial at the King's Bench last Easter, now oppose the levy. Pray advise the bearer Mr. Fulwood, our steward, how we should proceed.

SIR F. DRAKE to the SAME.

1697, November 11.—To consult him about Mr. Berry's candidature for the office of Town Clerk for Plymouth.

"Our high blades of the clergy are very wroth and uneasy, and will be sure to do all the mischief they can. The Church is in utmost danger they say, not only from the dissenters but from some great men which are not Christians. The name of one of them (he is now going a great embassy) I have learnt. They are very hot indeed, but I have broke pretty much their measures hereabouts, and am apt to believe it is no difficult thing to make them a little cooler."

W. PENN to [the SAME].

1697, November 22. Worminghurst.—"Worthy friend. The time drawing on to recommend the gentleman in whose favour I solicited thy kindness and interest, I presume to remember thee in his behalfe, and most earnestly to begg that it would please thee to make it thy positive request, being first noe great thing, nor without example ; next that it is giveing a young gentleman birth into the world, and that will sincerely and virtuously use the favour. I know very well to whom I write, one that knows the use and abuse of forms ; mercy is better than sacrifice ; and the Sabbath was made for man, and not man for the Sabbath ; much better may I say that forms are made for men, not men for forms ; and certainly they should not be put in the scale against ingenuity and industry for bread. I will add that Sir F. Winnington assured me at parting he would give his assistance, tho' he said thy request was enough, if made heartily for him. I begg this freedom may not lessen thy good opinion of him that is with a long acquaintance, and reall esteem, thy obliged and faithfull friend.

R. GRAINGE to the SAME at Maidstone.

1697–8, March 22.—The Dean of York's judgment has been reversed by the Lords, "without any debate in the House after counsel heard, but immediateiy a general cry reverse, reverse."

LORD HATTON to the SAME.

1698, April 26. Kirby.—Desiring him to stay proceedings in the case of Mrs. Ann Jeffreyes, a prisoner for debt until he can give full information about her.

MSS. OF SIR W.
FITZHERBERT.

J. LOCKE to the SAME.

1698, May 17. Oates.—You pour favours upon me without my asking. I had thought of stopping you on the high way, according to the privilege you allow me, when you passed this way the last Assizes, and to make a petition to you for my cousin King, a student of the Middle Temple, but my health has prevented it.

My cousin has informed me how good you have been to him, and I am not less obliged to you than he is.

LORD CHANCELLOR SOMERS to the SAME.

1698, July 13.—" I told the King of the ques[tion] your Lordship had a mind to have answered, and he commands me to say he thanks you, and if he may have the determination of that matter he would rather the person should not be chosen."

JOHN POLLEXFEN to the SAME.

1698-9, January 13.—Recommending Mr. John Davy, a rich merchant of Bideford, for the office of Sheriff in the place of Mr. Luttrell who cannot afford it.

W. PENN to the SAME.

1699, February 20. Worminghurst.—"Worthy and old friend. I must venture to recommend Sir R. Cullen's brother in law to thy favour, who has I hope outlived the objection against his being accepted as I requested two years ago, haveing been of the house ever since, as thou wert pleased to advise, in order to facilitate and give a better pretence for the favour of comeing to the barr. I must add that a new Judge is very warm upon us, I know not why, and upon me very reflecting, which is I think below his place. I hear he is very much thy servant and has reason for it, I beg he may be softened by thy larger mind, and better conversation. Pardon this freedom from an old and true and respectful friend."

R. YARD to the SAME.

1699, August 18. Whitehall.—By the command of the Lords Justices I am to desire you to be present to perform the office of Speaker of the House of Lords, at the prorogation on Thursday the 29th inst.

In another letter of August 21, it is said that Lord Chief Justice Holt will undertake this duty.

The DUKE OF NORFOLK to the SAME.

1699, November 14.—My uncle, Mr. Esmé Howard, now a prisoner in the Fleet by some mistake has not obtained the benefit of the Act to which he is entitled. I have a great deal of reason to believe he intends to be just to his creditors, and I recommend him to your goodness so far as the law will allow.

LORD CHANCELLOR SOMERS to the SAME.

1699-1700, February 5.—" The life of the Recorder is despaired of. I take the liberty to put your Lordship in mind that it is of great consequence he should have a good successor, and that nobody can contribute so much to effect it as your Lordship."

MSS. OF SIR W.
PITZHERBERT.

The SAME to the SAME.

1699-1700, February 22.—"Mr. Lacy has applied to me to stop the Writ of Error as not lying in the case, and his and the Bishop's counsel are to be heard this afternoon. I doubt I cannot so properly have your assistance in Court because you are now acting as a delegate in the cause, but I beg your advice and opinion what is proper for mee to do in this matter. . . . .

If you do not come to the House I hope you will write me a line before the afternoon.

I am to desire you to consider the point which my Lord Jersey mentioned to you, that so you may be ready to speak to it tomorrow if there be occasion."

CHIEF JUSTICE HOLT to the SAME.

1699-1700, February 23.—"The Lord Chancellor desires your Lordship to be at the House of Lords this day, and if your Lordship can I may have a little conference beforehand. Therefore if your Lordship will be pleased to step up to my chamber as you go to your own you will oblige &c."

LORD CHANCELLOR SOMERS to the SAME.

1699-1700, March 10. Sunday night.—"If it were possible for mee to speak a few words with your Lordship tomorrow morning about a thing which will come on in the House of Lords about the Bishop of St. David's I should be very glad. I do not know how practicable this is because of your going out of Town, and therefore I submit it wholly to you."

MARTYN RYDER to the SAME.

1700, August 23. Exeter. "I came hither last night and found the Judge trying our Dartmouth cause. It lasted from 2 to 9 o'clock, and then the Jury was sent out, but with harsh directions as Sir W. Y., and Sir John E., and Mr. D., told me. And being willing to know more, and that from the lawyers, I went this morning, while the Jury was at the Crown Bar, to Mr. Pratt in the same, and other like company, and he told me in general that he never heard such law in his lifetime."

The case is about the Corporation and its constitution.

The SAME to the SAME.

1700, September 6. Tavistock.—I was at Plymouth last Tuesday, and invited my brethren the Aldermen to dine with me. They were very well pleased with my company and my treat which cost me five guineas.

They unanimously agreed, being well satisfied with them, and in accordance with your recommendation, to choose the same burgesses again. They would not choose the Mayor this year, they said, for that might be a rub to my election.

Mr. Alden is to be the new Alderman.

[*A long letter full of details of his dealings with the Aldermen so as to preserve his Lordship's interest.*]

THOMAS GIBBON to the SAME.

1700, September 25.—Renews his application in spite of the advice in answer to his former letter.

MARTYN RYDER to the SAME.

1700, September 27. Goodmeavy.—*A long letter chiefly upon private business.*

I cannot but smile at Thomas Gibbon's wish to be a serjeant.

It is something unusual too that R. Tracy should come from Ireland as a qualification for a Judge in England.

The Recorder of Grantham would fain have a coif. He is a gentleman of £1000 a year, and keeps his coach, and would grace the coif.

HUMPHREY PERYE to LADY TREBY, Hatton Garden.

1715, July 13. Stafford.—Advice upon private business. .

We have had great tumults in this county. The Wolverhampton Meeting House was pulled down by the mob on June 29, on the fair day there. The cause of the rising was this. Mr. Gros: and some other gentlemen in a publick house there heard some men in another room singing some old seditious song, and sent to desire them to stop. They refused, upon which Mr. Gr: committed one of them to a constable who put him in the crib or stone-house. Whereupon the mob rescued him, knocked down Mr. Gr :, though he ran one or two of them through the body, and then went to the Meeting House. There has been a similar riot at Stafford, in which the country people joined, and also at Stone and Walsall.

The Sheriff has been called upon to raise the posse.

POPISH PLOT.

[LETTERS, &c. SEIZED IN COLEMAN'S HOUSE, AND DEPOSITIONS, &c.
USED AGAINST HIM AND THE LORDS, &C.]

[*Twenty original letters 1674, Oct. 19, to 1675, May 1, some altogether and some partially written with sympathetic ink.*]

[? SIR W. THROCKMORTON to E. COLEMAN.]

1674, October 19.—"I agree with you that the only meanes to win the Kinge to the Duke's interest, and to take him off interely from the friendshipp of the Parliament, would be money, for the reasons you alleage in your last letter of the 2d instant, which I have just now received. But the meanes necessary to continue it are so excessive that, even according to your own opinion, and the discourse we had when you was here, what the Pope could contribute would be nothing in comparison of what is needed, and in the obligation he hath also to assist other friends who are in greater straites. I likewise doubt whether the Pope would resolve upon what you propound, considering the little stress can be laid upon the King's will, it being to be feared that all imployed that way would soone be lost, without any advantage to the Duke or his associates, which we have reason to feare from his ordinary manner of proceeding. It would therefore be necessary in my opinion to have at least some probable assurances that we might imploy for the advantage of the Catholiques and 140 ——— what otherwise we are obliged frugally to manage for them in other partes, before the proposition be made to the Pope, which is not to be undertaken in soe general and obscure termes as you propound it. For what remaines

the Nuncio is on the point of going to Rome, having already leave to
retorne. The negociation of the businesse you propound will belong to
his successor, but he will retain the same passion which he had for the
Duke's service, as well at the Emperour's Court as at the Pope's. If
he shall have any part in the affaires of England he will not faile to
informe you more particularly of his departure. I pray you assure the
Duke of what I have told you."

"Translated by Sir Humphry (Winch ?)."

[SIR W. THROCKMORTON to . . . . .]

[1674], November 28. Paris. "*I did at last deare Governour after
many traverses get well to this place on Sunday morning about 8 a clock.
I had my old torture at sea again 2 dayes and nights. I embarqued
at Rye the same night I came thither and could not get a ship under
£8 there being indeed but that one in harbor which was to carry me
to Diepe, but the winds weare, and I think ever since have been, so
contrary that I beleeve shee could not have performed her voyage by
this time. I put myselfe in at last into a fisher boat and so by force of
oares landed on Friday in the afternoon where I beleeve never noe
gentleman before landed, and so on foot and on asses and animals
they called horses we got to St. Valery, and so to Abbeville, and thence
poste to Paris with onely three halfe crownes in my pocket. They
weare very strickt in searching at St. Valery, my wife's smoks have
gon to wrack, the little bundles of your other frinds I hid and so saved,
but the great box there was no such dealing with. I told them it was
sent me by the Lady of the Duchesse her bedchamber, and that perhaps
it was sumthing sent by her Highness to her Mother, but all would not
serve. So at last I prevailed with them not to open it and that I would
leave it there till we got an order from hence for it. This I thought
was the best for if they had opened it it had certainly been lost. I have
been twice to see the Resident but he was at St. Germans, as soon as
we can meet we will contrive what can be done. I found my gentlewoman heer almost as bare of money as myselfe, I have therefore been
forced to draw a bill of £100 upon Mr. Mawson at halfe usance,
another time you shall have longer warning for the payment, but now
coming just out of England I was ashamed to doe it. You doe not
expect any newse yet from a man or that one has seen anybody. Mr.
de Rohan and Mr. de Villars weare yesterday beheaded, their crimes
are not said to be so heinous heer as we were tould in England. My
Lady is so peart that I can not beleeve she was ill. She is very much
your and your Lady's humble servant. I hope I need not say so for
myselfe, for I'm sure you must either beleeve me so or the ungratefullest
wretch alive.*

[*See Note in the middle of the next letter.*]

" I went on Munday to visit 6 (Mons. Pompone) at his master's house
and had sum discourse with him with which he seemed much sattisfyed,
but being interrupted there by busines he tould me he would cum next
morning hither by eight a clock and so did and we weare locked up
2 howers togeather, where I made him such a discourse, and gave him
so exact an account of the state of all things that I think truly I never
seed man better sattisfyed in my life, and hee tould mee that he would
rather in anything have me speake with 8 (the Fr. King) myselfe, for
that it was impossible to carry all the perticulars so exactly in his head
as I did, but that it would be difficult to contrive it as it ought to be
with privacy. I had a paper in my pocket which had all the heads of
my discourse in it, which I had wrot in French to facilitate my dis-

course a little, for you can not imagine it is alltogeather so familiar to me as my owne language, which I pulled out and shewed him, he was extremely pleased with it, and tould me if I durst trust him him with it hee gave me his honour, noe man living should see it but 8 (the K. of France), and that he would on Thursday return it mee. I tould him with all my heart, but as they weare only my perticular thoughts and observations, and such as I considered (*indistinct*) he should give (*indistinct*) to them or me as I was. He replyed such things as I spoke must all wayes be cre[di]ted, for that though I tould them things they knew not before and went farther to the bottum, yet by all other circumstances they krew it was true, and that besides I must not count myselfe unknown to 8 (the Fr. King) or him, and so complimented mee. In fine hee tould mee he see the danger as well as I, mais quelle remede, I tould him to that as you may gues and that then I durst answer it with my head to secure them, but that there was noe mincing but they must absolutely trust A (the Duke), hee said there was noe difficulty in that but that I knew hee could say noething positive of himselfe, but that when he returned me my paper he made noe question but he should give me an other with it such as I could wish. He was very inquisitive how A (the Duke) was disposed about his daughter. I think they are sufficiently informed of and incensed against S (Lord Arlington) and for the discourse of underhand intelligence with R (the Hollanders) he swore it was false, hee asshured mee too that hee was now fully sattisfyed that it was A (the Duke) and onely hee and not S (Lord Arlington) had lately donn F (the Parliament) busines as much of it as was donn ; in short I hope we are where we could wish."
Endorsed November 28, 74. *and a few signs.*

[Sir W. Throckmorton to . . . .]

[1674], December 1. Paris.—"*I gave you last post an accompt of my jorny and what this post to say to you I know not, and yet I'm sure you expect I should write to you. I have been at Courte and fancy that all men's minds there are much bent for peace, of which they conceave great hopes by the acceptation of our mediation, and weare it not for my Lord Arlington's jorny into Holl[and] and the match between the P[rince] and our young lady, which generally is talked of as an affaire fait, I thinke they could shew gaye countenances enough. This is my observation of the Courte in generall, of their statesmen and ministers you will not desire, knowing how little I am able to pry into them, to give you my thoughts, though I must tell you I have been to visit Mr. Le Pompone and most of the others, but I suppose you will gues right that that was more out of vanity to shew the world that I was knowne to such persons, than out of hopes to make any advantage by my visits. I have been to visit my Lady Shrewsbury, to whom Mr. Serjant is now Confessor, all I can say of that busines is that shee makes strong resolutions, and he has great faith. Pray ashure your Lady that my wife and I am her humble servants, and salute all the rest for me who you thinke should be pleased with a brotherly kis.*"

[*The above is the first page of the letter in dark distinct ink. The next three pages are in the same hand and the same light brown ink as the interlineations of other letters.*]

. . [*an illegible figure*] " (Mr. Pompone) returned me my paper againe yesterday and told me 8 (French King) had been and was

extremely sattisfied with it, that noething pleased him more than the
assurance I thereby gave him of my confidence, that A : [the Duke]
was resolved to continue his kind purposes to him, that he desired me
that I would [as]hure A : (the Duke) that noething should turne
him from his towar[dness] him, and that he should not rejoyce in
anything more than to be able to help him to bee or to se . . . him
by any meanes chiefe tutor for our company for that he very well knew
that noething but that could secure [*so far all is underlined in
black ink*] his owne stake there what therefore his sentiments of S
(Lord Arlington) weare we might gues and how gladly ~~we should~~ (sic)
he should see him disposed of as we desire, but that he thought his
medling in it would rather hinder than advance [the de]signe.
However that he was willing to receave directions from A : (the Duke)
in it, and that he should allwayes be reddy to joyne and work with him
in any designe he should judge for the good of the comon trade that as
for the G (?) to be he judged it ad . . . . [*4 or 5 words
illegible*] wrecke (?) but that the feare being yet pretty far of and the
P . .—R (Spaine, the Emperor, Holland) haveing chosen X (the
King) for the umpire of the [dif]ference between them and him, he
thinks he may stay a little in that part (?) till he hears from X (the
King) upon his umpirage and see what course he intends to take for it,
but that he absolutely relyed upon A : (the Duke) for the chusing of
proper sides]men] in that busines, for that he put his only confidence
in him for it. He tould me moreover that 8 (French King) would
gladly have write to A : (the Duke) but for [fear] of accidents which
might turne it to bothe their disadvantages, but that as he absolutely
beleeved the accompt I gave him of the company and trade, and A :
(the Duke) his great affection to him, though I had no order from A :
(the Duke) for it because he very well knew how I was concerned for
him, so he hop I . . . . . . put y . . . . . confidence
in this that I tould him from his part I tould him that all this was very
true . . . . . . but for all that to . . . . working for
G (?) might be dangerous and that therefore I desired him to have
8 (the French King) to consider . . . . againe, that for my parte
bee see I was an unemployed person in it and had noe other desire
but their good as they weare comon traders, but that by what an right
I had in the trade I thought they aught to loose noe time and to hazzard
little accidents for soe great a good, for that at this rate of 3rd hand
talking they would never [under]stand one another or effect anything,
and though they . . . . me great honour to offer [me] soe much
trust upon my private credit that . . . by that meanes and general
talke they . . . . [ne]ver be able to carry on trade roundly;
w . . parted then with this after . . discourse and many
arguments that he would again propose [*2 or 3 words illegible*] and
that he thought my reasons weare soe convincing and kynd . . . .
that he doupted not but 8 (the French King) would eyther [*4 or 5
words illegible*] to write and that in 4 or 5 dayes I should heare from
him . . . . . . Pray direct your letter A . . . M[ercier]
au coine de la rue St. Benoit Fauxbourg St. Ge[rmaine] [*a line
illegible*] the sum for you [*a line illegible*] I could of my . . nd
heer and . . . others make halfe an O (50 m . .) try you what
you [can] [*3 or 4 words illegible*] in case 8 should be backward
in that part and that that ingredient should be requisite to carry on
the work."

Endorsed " December 1674 " *and some shorthand notes.*

MSS. of Sir W.
Fitzherbert.

[Sir W. Throckmorton to E. Coleman.]

[1674,] December 8. Paris.—"*Your Thursday's packet came yesterday, though I have noe letters perhaps they are not delivered all out
yet and so I may have them anon. Your Munday's is not arrived,
yet indeed we have had such boisterous* . . . .
*expect any certainty in them. The Ambassador whoe had his last
night tells me there is not one word of newse from your side, and truly
I think we can be quits with you, for though I was at St. Jermains
yesterday I know not what in the world to tell you except you can be
delighted to heare brave storys of the galantry that is to be there at
Christmas, a new opera, maske,* [pa]*rades, and God knows what not.
The Germans repassing the Rhine which I tould you in my last we
had a hot story of, but yet I saw noe great reason for it proved indeed
but a story, though it be true too sum regiments of hors and dragoons
did pass it, but it is not to retire but to inco:node if not block up Brisack
on the side of the river. Brother Joseph is goeing back to-morrow to
Antwerp. I must beg you to present my humble service to your Lady,
and to whom else you think would care to receave it and I care to give
it to. As to yourself I hope there remains nothing now to be said upon
that score.*

[See note in the middle of the last letter.]

" I spoke with 6 (Pompone) again of whom I had almost the same
story I gave you in my förmer, but that . . . ly had not had
opportunity to speake to 8 (French King) yet about his writing . . .
. . . but that hee . . . . and much . . that, they seem to
wonder much they heer noething from X (the King) yet upon this late
busines . . . . heer has had yet noe manner of orders
but it concerns them as themselves say to have A : (the Duke) their
frend in this busines, but yet I begin to doupt they would willingly
engage him to be so through the reason of his own interest and as many
fair words and what else you please but pens, and that that is the
reason . . . . wave writing yet for feare of comeing to close
dealing, that is F (the Parliament) is yet far off and they think can not
possibly com to joyne till the spring, if in the meane time by A : (the
Duke) his hearties for them which as I said they think his owne
enterest and their great expressions of kindnes will engage him too,
they can get a good accomodation and regulation among all the
desenting . . . . rs they have their ayme if not they think the
same price will doe 4 months hence as well to stop them as now though
they are infinitely mistaken [as I tell you ?] all I can for to keep that
interest on foot against against them will certainly be the great .
. . . . perhaps the only meanes . . . . them of compassing what they so much desire . . . .
. . . reddy money you know . . a heard thing especially to merchands, if you can think of anything more for me to say upon this score
pray write it a freash that I may shew it them, that is what you think
that they should see, for 6 (Pompone) desired me that I would let him
know when I heard anything, but if I heer noething from you . [T] .
think it is the best way to lett him alone a little, perhaps it may make
the forwarder, especially if < (Swead) and R (Holland) courte X (the
King) so much to draw him the won way and the other the contrary as
I heer they doe, and if A : will but play that game cunningly he may
certainly bring 8 (French King) to what he pleases, then (?) I must
confes I would rather have him have 00 (£200,000) of K : (the catholiques) than 000 (£300,000) of 8 (the F King) that is to get G (Parliament dissolved) for that would shew 8 (French King) what A : (the D)

was and would make him much more helpful and complai[sant] to him.
But heer is the werck you'll say and I must confes it is such a one too
as takes up my thoughts night and day, and I would have L (Coleman)
think of it too for it would bee a great work as it is a difficult one and
perhaps it is an absolute necessary one. I shall in a little time let you
know somewhat certain from . . . . . but I believe I may
venture to promise halfe a 0 (hundred thousand pounds) from hence sure
a 0 (£100,000) on your side might be compased. The man I see often
spoke to you of in their busines is the best man in the world hee
swearing it shall not stick at all his stake but A : (the Duke) shall be
accomodated."

[*The passages from*
  "F is yet far off" to "stop them as now" ;
  "if A : will best play " to "complaisant to him" ;
  "I may venture to promise " to the end,
are underlined in black ink]:
[*Endorsed*] "December 8, 1674," *and a few shorthand marks.*

[SIR W. THROCKMORTON to E. COLEMAN].

[1674], December 15. Paris.—
"6 Came to town last night but I am of opinion still
We have have had 3 pacquets com in within these 2 dayes,
which have brought the three of your letters for all
which I am very thankfull to you. I wonder much
you should not have receaved my first, I put it under
cover of one from my wife to your nurse it is there
that I ought not to [sp]eak to him again till I hear . . .
you must be pleased to enquire for it. I never . .
from L (Coleman) and that for many reasons drawne both [fr]om
mist you poste yet since I came but last, and then
L : his owne letter from observation of things heer
I had so little to say, especially Mr. Bernard being
and from discourse which I had lately on the Exchange
very importunate to have his seat, that I thought my wife
with X (the King of England) his factor heer; he is certainly one of the
might serve for covert as well as mine having a little
shrewdest dealing men that I know, and that makes me
busines too that called me owt, I could make you the same
extremely close with him, pretending great ignorance
excuse now for want of matter but that I feare you
in all sort of comerce, but for all that his good . . [*torn off*]
should suspect it weare rather lazines if I . . . . ,,
me, as he would have me believe it, th . . . [*torn off*]
you twice togeather, you shall therefore in . . . ,,
turally from him, that we are never . . . . . [*torn off*]
be pleased to know that I know noething at . . . . ,,
is as after as he can contrive it, he . . . . [*torn off*]
sober earnest wee have heard noething . . . . ,,
. . ite of himselfe to dine with me which is a freedom
of at least, from Mr. Turenne since wee have been tould
you know not usually taken by Merchands, and
that he is marched with near 15000 foot and 12000 horse with
upon all little occasions . . . ting me, but he enters with
a full-purpose to beat the Germans back over the Rhine
with great seeming confidence and freedom into a dis-
this is a pretty brisque enterprise, and the newes will be of

MSS. OF SIR W.
FITZHERBERT.

course of the moste misterious points of our trade
great consequence eyther for peace or war, perhaps
now what his desire in this may be God knows
this is an observation you might make in Eng[land] as
but I'm sure if it be to pump me he shall lose it
well as I heer; I will therefore say noe more but
for I never discover more knowledge of anything than
that I am your Ladys most humble servant
a man of my converse in the world and general (?)
which he is well acquainted with must have . . . tainly be thought
to have ; or perhaps it may be that by that ould frendship I have had
with L (Coleman) he may thinke to secure him by mee and so if trade
goes naught on the other side, for you remember how C and D (Lord
Berkeley and Sir E. Layton) have allwayes spoke of his behaviour
between Z and S (D. Lauderdale and Lord Arliugton) and how he
they say have attached himself to the later, ingratiate himself at last
with A: or perhaps he may have a reall intention of serving A: this
if you please, in charity and generosity we will believe but in prudence we will not trust too, and therefore [I] continue the same
ignoramus, and the more full he is in his prayses of A: and in
discourses of . . . X. and Z and U (the King, D. Lauderdale,
Lord Trevor) [the less] I eyther know [of their] concerns or anything else. Often we talke of 8 and 1 (French King, Mons. Louvoy)
and 2 or 3 (warr, peace) and in this discourse he told me the day
before yesterday that he found that 8 (French King) and his had great
expéctation of what S (Lord Arlington) should doe for them, nay that
he beleeved they might have such [?] confidence in him or it, he
wondered how they came by it for hee would have me to understand it
was not by him now whether this be a wheedle of theirs upon him, or
that hee intended it as one upon me I know not, but their backwardnes
heer makes me suspect H (Mons. Ruvigny) has sum underhand
dealing, and that hee may keep them heer in expectation of it, and that
he . . . . hand that it is time enough to think of
G (Parliament dissolved) if that failes, and that A will let everything
slip to secure G however for his own sake, and at last if all does faile
that which we ask, they think is a sure card to make X and us doe
what they list which noething else will : Now me Now me thinks
indeed in my humble judgment I would not have A: faile [or taile]
 . . [*torn off*] . . . I would have him push with all the . .
[*torn off*] . . . . may inable for G (Parl. dissolved) and I would
have [*half a line torn and illegible*] . . for ou my consciemce [*one
or two words torn off*] much in his power with 00 or 000 (£2 or
300000) . . doe it as with them, and then if he would give me
leave methinks I could turn it infinitely more to his advantage by
showing them how little hee wauted 00 or 000 to help him in that or
anything . . . and that now if they would come upon terms to
settle things equally and faire between us . . ., without which
certainly noething can laste, ... wee will, being thereto led
a little by interest but much more by inclination, geve them the preference and refusal in all bargains, but if not truly we may then truly
tell them we must endeavour to make our best market. They know
the advantage fortune has now more than ever put into our hands by
giveing us the seales to bould wherein all European commodities must
be erayed (?), and I hope then G (the dissolving the Parlt.) being
compased A (the Duke) will never suffer X (the King) againe to quit,
that if this doe not bring them to anything you can call reason I will

give you my head, for I must tell you 8 [or S] is mightily devided at
this very lower in his thoughts and perhaps more agitated than ever
he was in making any resolution haveing (?) or I am much mistaken
one boote on and . . . . . ., a (fancyed ?) sum thing . . . .
in him making him a little weary of what is on allreddy, and another
thundering sumthing enclining him to boote and spur them both try
your lady's letter and you will . . . ."

[*The letter is endorsed*) " Paris, December 1674–5," (*and at
the head of the letter in the same hand as the endorsement*]
" Mons. Pompone."

[SIR W. THROCKMORTON] to MRS. COLEMAN.

1674, December 15. Paris.
" *Thousand thanks deare madam for yours by Sir H. Fitz James*
and with all this his chiefe frinds as 6 (Pompone) and 7 (Albert)
I ashure you the longer I am at Paris the more I shall
and 1 (Louvoy) as much devided about 2 (war) or 3 (peace) as is poss-
esteeme my owne country, not butt that I like Paris extream
ible. Now I say with all this if A: could strike
well, but cannot find itt soe farr exceed London as is said
that stroke without them you should see what an opera-
Yett one a good score. However I should be glad to settle in it.
tion it would have, now I say with all this
Mayn [?] you mention related cheefly to Mons. Barnard who
if A: could strike that stroke without them you should
I supose more a courtyer than a friend, pray letts know how je
see what an operation it would have, and on my
dans doth, I am sorry hee's relapsed, newes I have non and I
[*torn*] I believe a quarter of 0 (£10C000) or les in the glistering
have got a scre eye soe dare say noe more but that
mettal to K (the King) himself in his owne pocket may
I am hartyly deare Madame yours . . faithful humble sarvant
I wish you a hapy mery Christmas
sway as much upon an occasion with him as ten times as much to put
into the comon stock or buy land with, and if such a busines [*3 or 4
words illegible*] for A : (the Duke) he may make his accompt on it when
he please he shall not want it long for that purpose. I then resolve
not to see 6 (Pompone) for these reasons [*one word illegible*] you say
you had not spoke with A : (the Duke) but that he had had a long
discourse with H (Ruvigny) which you know not what it was, nor
what A : (the Duke) knew of (Lord Arlington) his busines nor
what perhaps he now would have one doe. H. (Ruvigny) doupt
. . [*one or two words illegible*] failed to write what he knew and
what A: tould . . . I will not therefore com to them with my
fingers in my mouth or to be caught [*one word torn*] that I resolve not
[*one word torn*] them till I heer from you againe. You say not a word
how the acceptation of X (the King) for umpire relishes with you, nor
what X intends, whoe shall goe, and so forth, pray be plaine in all
these points. Your derection is a Mr. Mercier au coine de la rue
St. Benoist, Faubourg St. Germ[aine] . . . I have asked you [*one
word illegible*] too but you forget it.
    I wrote to you in my first letter to Mrs. Bradshaw about the £100, I
doupt I must have more ere long, but you shall have six weeks time for
it. What you wrote heer about my helping myself to money, that way
which you mention is a ticklish point the man is of a jelous humor and
if I should [do anything] should look like selfe interest I should spoile

all, you may be sure I say all too him [what you can] imagine, but I must not seem to aime at that but let it com of itself. Adieu, I am sure I am tired."

[*From*] "If A: could strike that stroke " [*to*] "for that purpose " [*is underlined in black ink*].

Endorsed with the date and some signs.

[SIR W. THROCKMORTON] to E. COLEMAN.

[1674,] December 29. [Paris.]—" Your letters are not yet com so I have noething to say upon that subject, and to the busines of our kinsman you know I can say noething neyther till I heer from you. Newse we have little. Mr. de Turenne his march has severed Monbeliard, and his letters of the 23rd say that hee having stayed sum time to make a great provision of bread, that hee might not for want of it be forced to anything hee had not a mind to, was resolved to march that day [with] the whole army towards the enemy who are now gathering together about Colmar in Alsace, and that if they did not think fitt to repas the Rhine but that they would stay him there, hee would fight them. The French counsels depend much upon the succes thereof for I doe not find that notwithstanding they have taken a resolution for the raising of a great number of French horse 6 weekes agoe and that money is reddy for it, that yet they [goe] on with it, and I believe the stop may proceed from thence to see the event, how well weighed their counsel is I know not. Brede I was tould yesterday was at last resolved on for the place of treaty, but whether this be absolute true I know not, though it was tould me by a good man whoe said to have it from Mr. de Tellier's owne mouth, but I can scarce beleeve the Prince of Orange will expose his juggle to the vewe of his owne people soe much as he will by having the treaty in the midst of them. You will heer of a defeat of some of the French troopes with Mr. de Turenne, and perhaps it may gather before it comes to you like a snow ball. The truth is this as Mr. de *Lorges* himselfe relates, that 300 foote and 50 horse being sent out under the comand of Mr. de Barlement, a co[lonel, were] cut of, the colonel and the captain of the hors both made prisoners, but that they defended themselves very exterordinarly well for many howers, killing above 80 of the enimy upon the place. To give you a more exact detalle is I thinke not necessary but may prove troublesome. I am your's and your silent lady's most humble servant."

Endorsed "Nothing in hit. No. 11 [or 41]."

—— to ——.

N.D.—" I am heartily glad to hear by your lady by your lady (*sic*) you will be returned to *London* to receave this which I pray loose no time to show his H. I wrote you word before you went that I thought I should soone bee in England, for I am confident they would have sent mee but your going into Flanders, of which they had notice before you could have been cros the sea, how I cannot emagine, but sure I am they tould me of it as soone as I came to the army, I suppose may have hindred that and retarded the propositions which I have order to make his H. till now, for they have been much disquieted about it, and I have had much adoe to ashure them that I was confident there was noething designed by it to their prejudice, for that I was sure the D. was as much by inclination as interest disposed to prefer their alliance and friendship to all others, and that they should take it for a certain rule that if they weare not wanting to themselves, we should never be wanting to them.

The K. is . . heer is certainly disposed as much as can bee for the interests of his H :, but is wise and very cautious, however by these propositions which I have order to make to his H :, and which are word for word as I took them from Pere Ferrier's mouth, for I wrot them downe presently and shewed it him afterwards [to] keep it for my justification, that I wrote noe more than I was ordered, you will see that it onely now depends upon his H : to consider of a way that will best secure his interests, and withall a good correspondence with them heer, for that wee must allwayes perswade our selves is the thing they propose to themselves by it, I say let but his H : consider of that, and then what hee would aske of them heer in order to it, and I doupt not God willing if hee will honour me with with his instructions and comands but I shall procure him anything which in reason hee can expect eyther of money or anything else, if therefore his H : shall bee pleased to think well of this and proceed in it, I will meet you anywhere privately to receave his H : comands and instructions by you, or if hee will I doupt not but I can put myselfe in a private way to com for a night to receave his orders myselfe. I pray bee very cautious that there be noe suspetion given of any thing [of] this with you, for the K. is very scrupulous heer, even of some of his chiefest ministers, whome perhaps hee may apprehend people have been or at least have endeavoured to bee dealing with, and P : Ferrier possitively charged mee to communicate it to noe one living but the B : of Dublin, of whome they have a good opinion, for hee said they would have to doe in it with none but us, but I prevailed at last that I might doe it by you or Col : Talbot in England, for that being they would not yet let me goe myselfe it was impossible but I must employ sumbody therefor I could not else write to the D, and if I answered for you as myselfe, to which at last they consented, I intended to have taken the liberty to have wrot to his H : but this to you will I thinke doe better. I pray you therefore present my most humble duty to him, and if I have don anything amis in this it is for want of judgment not affection and duty, and I am shure of one thing that if perchance our councels should goe [an]other way I have don noething that can prejudice him, if they bee not, but that this alliance shall be judged advantageous, I have had the good fortune to worck myselfe into such an esteem and opinion heer with sum of the ablest to serve his H : that I am an honest man that I dare promis myselfe they will put confidence in mee, and I shall bee able to serve him, for to doe which I pray ashure his H : with all humility that I shall always be reddy to venture my life and fortune."

[*The whole of this letter is written in the light brown ink. The passage from "for that I was shure the D." to "wanting to them," is underlined in black ink.*]

To Mrs. COLLMAN in her *Lodgings* in the pell mell near St. James.

N.D.—I thinke I must state the case in writing aguine and give
Had it not . . . to have charges deare madame you had received
it 6 (Pompone) to shew 8 (Fr. King). I doupt 9 (Bp. Dublin) sending
to 1 (Louvoy) his father for you
my thanks for your last long before this which now was designed
must know that 9 (Bp. Dublin) is the lyeingest rogue in the world has
son
you by Mr. Oglethorpe . . this is to my sister Aymondsold but your
don our busines noe good, for he speakes with confidence and

newes [?] *last night changed it telling us the dismall news of Putney*
makes them beleeve he is the Mr. in the world with A : (thé Duke) and
which I am extream sorry for, but very well pleased she has soe good
tells them whatever he pleases, which must make them have
a comforter as your ladyship. *Deare madame ashure her of my most*
harty
a meane opinion of A : (the Duke), or if they doe or doe not absolutely
sarvice, and all imaginable care to serve her both as to the
beleeve him must make them the more diffident of R (Sir Will. Thr.)
telling itt and and putting Mis in morning, the first I will not be to,.
the truth is I wonder 6 (Pompone) does soe well with R (Sir W. Throg.)
as he does
hasty in becase I desire a little your advice about the last . . .
considering that [*torn*] (B[ŗ Dublin) speaks the contrary with as much
I could gladly stay for and ·nay if luck serve have it in 10 dayes
authority as appears to them as R (Sir W. T.) does what he sayes
time, and I'll get stays &c. ready, cloth I think is not·soe good heare
 . . tould you all that was between him an 1 (Louvoy) his father
or soe·cheap and thé sumer will now draw on apace for I thinke
 . . weekes agoe, for I trace him everywhere, and
crape or such a sort of thing will doe best in all respects, butt · ·. ·¹
sure never man made . . . . hood lyeing and knavery. . . :¹
. . [*torn*] ·. · . . . *in England, and my sisters ,and I will* ·. ·.
. . . . · his business as·he·does. I·had yours of the 4th and·
. . . ·*to be informed exactly what the mode is heare for most great*
folks
if I think it as proper after a night's consideration
the warr· has made morners. *Mrs. Jane I think should have a gound*
and petycoat
as I've yet I may break it to 6 (Pompone) next time I see him ·
for I like it very well.

Why should you not get H (Ruvigny) write to 6 (Pompone) ‘the
discourse L (Coleman) had with him and his likeing of it, it would
help R (Sir W. Throg.) mightily at least it would give him sum more
credit I am overjoyed to heer what you say about G (dissolving Parliament), though 000 (£300000) should not be compassed, not that it
shall make me a jot the less active or solicitous for it, for I am I ashure
you of your opinion as much as is possible that noething will settle
businesses lastingly like joyning [*torn*] (Fr. King) and A :'s (the Duke)
interests togeather, and when I tould you there might be an advantage
made by gaining G (Parlt. dissolved) without 000 (£300000) I did not
meane . . . [7 or 8 *words illegible*] . . 8 (Fr. King) but only
that that would make those about 8 (Fr. King), seeing the power A :
(the Duke) has, a little more reasonable, and that then they will [come]
with A : (the Duke) to terms [and] accomodation more equall than
now they will, and let us think or propose what we please it is certaine
that noething but a [part ?] balance of things cau keep their interests
long linked, and therefore I judged it for A : (the Duke)
of some kind of crape or other for there is cheaper heare I beleive than
in England
advantage by such an action to gaine that reputation
and according as it is bye it heare, or else leave it till she comes over
with·them as shall shew them their benefit of coming
ˋ*But my sister must lett me know whether she'll pay for the makeing*
[to] such an accomodation with him . . . which then
or noe, let·mee know her mind with the first and accordingly I'll

lives, I never was blinder nor wearier in
Madame and beleeve mee ever your faithfull humble sarvant. **Cloth**
surge
my life so adieu. I could not help the £100 bill
or such things will be both dearer for Mrs. Jane eyther heere or in

. . . .

for my soule. Pray tell Maurin I have don   .   .   .
[*Two lines illegible.*] "

[SIR W. THROCKMORTON to E. COLEMAN.]

1674–5, January 9. [Paris.]
I tould you where I was yesterday but 6 said noething to me
I have had . . . . my last to you both yours of the 21st and 24th
indeed I did not see him at his owne howse nor did not
last past and the enclosed to Mr. Bernard in the later which after have-
think it fit till I heer from you what you said in yours of
ing shewed D. G. I have sent him but heare not how he relishes
the [31st ?] in French which I tould you I could not reade if
it not haveing seen him since, but I am a little of your Lady's mind
hee had accoasted me in . . . . I would have
that you have not made your courte over well by it. Your Lady has
. . . . best I could with what I did . . . out but to goe
at last opened her mouth as you call it for my wife has had
. . . . without certaine knowledge of what
the honour of a letter from her, which shee this morning before
you meant I thought was not prudent. I am glad [M's ?]
her eyes were open called for a fire in her chamber that she
supper took soe well but I . . . . you doe you
might rise to answer, but I undertooke that you would asshure
will be laughed at as well as ruined . . . . my
your Lady of the receipt of it and make her compliments too
temper soe well as you doe. I beleeve they are not
which upon my accompt pray doe for I think I deserve
easy heer with G. his long stay for though 8 his brother
it haveing saved you 10d., though not to exact too much
know not much of the trade, nor is one that one can take meaning
from you neyther there was sum selfe consideration
by, yet I perceived by him that they were alarumed.
in it too, for perhaps I saved myselfe noe lesse in fier
I long hugely for a letter from you that I may see 6, pr
I went yesterday to St. Jermain on purpose to heer what
be careful in writing, for that paper is naught and yon
was said there concerning Mr. de Turenne. In the first place
blot mightely. I know not what to make of this busines
the King and his ministers say they have had noe courier
of Turenne, it is strange to me they should know noething
nor direct newes from Mr. Turenne these 12 dayes which is what
in 12 dayes, it is certain much depends on it, you
[*hear if it goes on*] . . . the busines I tould you in my last **and**
the accompt of that
must make the best of it though I write you cleerly how
for aught I heer they pretend to have noe other way neyther

MSS. OF SIR W.
FITZHERBERT.

I take it to be, and the truth is I doe not thinke there
but by a servant of the Count of Broglins whoe came to fetch a
has been a battle, or that they are retreated neyther, but
chirurgeon for his master, by whome was given such an accompt
that is it undoes the 8 his busines. Be sure if you can that
as you have seen by the foregoing poste, a 2d. accompt which
A : never pardons the insolence you mention. Grotian is
was published yesterday morning is a letter from a comissary
about to buy Abselys place, I know not if the Duke be
of the munition at Langres to Mr. de Louvoy in which he tells him
yet made acquainted with it for I have it as a great
by the by after haveing spoke to his busines that he had received a letter
secret, but be sure you doe what you can to hinder it for
from another comissary in the army who tould him that Mons.
he is the malitiousest rogue alive, I can not tell you
de Turenne had forced a pas over a little river, that they dis-
all I know of him heare, how he takes when he thinks
puted it hard, that wee lost a good number of hors in the action
himself safe J (D. of Monmouth) his parte against A : (the Duke) his
interest

but that in time they possest themselves of it with great
the Duke may have his choise from my knowledge of 2
losse to the enemy takeing several colours and much baggage
or 3 . . . . . gentlemen that have double his estate and
and that now they had the passage open to Brisack, that hee would
I daresay will venture it all to obey and execute
say noe more of it beleeving they had the detalle of all at courte
his just comands, and will stick to him and have interest
long before now, in this the man was mistaken for we owne
in their countreys too. I have done all my endeavour
noe such thing at Courte but conclude our couriers must be
to informe myself of 8 his stock for the next yeers
taken or killed, however I finde that they all conclude that this action and
trade, and truly all people concerned in it affirm it is
that Count Broglins man speaks of, this last being not dated, is the same
great, yet I can not imagine what makes them soe backward
The Comissary tells you farther that the army weare near one the other
and that

in equipping for the summers voyage as they are if it be
infallibly if the enemy retreated not Mr. Turenne would fight in a day
or two, which was
not want of monny reddy. What meane you by A :'s not knowing of
your writing
likely enough he having orders for it and now a passage open to him,
but that the
I beleevo my [Lunt : ?] voyage was none of A :'s . . diate imprudence
but it
communication is soe free between him and Brisack for all that, truly
I can not well com-
was to satisfy her vanity which he ought by no meanes to have
prehend for I'm sure they are much stronger in hors than hee and
therefore methinks
consented too, for such synes of her power with him still makes even
till they are beaten visits should not be very safe. This relation of the
letter bends
those whoe love him well feare the truth of the strong report that she

severall other people of quality, I had as I give it you from Monsieur
Crene . . . . .

is with childe againe. As to the thing itselfe it is to his own con-
an other story they had that the Germans had laid a bridge over the
Rhine and that infallibly
[sic] quences, but I am sure in prudence it ought to be very covertly for
part of their army would retreat over there, and the others at Strausburg,
but how

for certainly ncething will doe him soe much good in X his family
they came by this infallibility of knowledge truly I could not learne
neyther, all I
and with all his tennants in the country especially, let them be of what
can therefore tell you of certainty is that K. Lewis has still the same,
brave manlike
religion they will, as a persuasion of his virtue and truth
looks that ever he had. I could wish N's frend hanged as she intended.

< will certainly [declare news?] if he had don it six weeks agoe
relation shee has to me, which will not, suffer me to say so at least, but
what a devill shall I
it had certainly been a considerable service for 8 for it had eased the
doe with her, I can not imagine I vow. It seems I must taste of all,
sorts of afflictions,
gentleman in I. much by the diversion whoe now must beare the whole
brunt of it alone. Adieu.

(P.S.) Just now the Marquis de St. Prery comes in from St. Germans
. . . . there was noe other newes this morning
. . . there from the army but what I have writ to you."

[*Endorsed*] " Jan. 9. 1675–6. *Some signs and*
1 D 7 Monm. M I D."

[*All the writing in this letter is smaller and less distinct than
that in the former letters*].

—— to [E. COLEMAN].

1674–5, January 12.—I have not yet received Monday's letters.
Turenne has gained a great advantage over the confederates. The
news had been delayed by the capture of a courier. They had been
very uneasy at not receiving news, and few believed that they had not
received any.

A short account of the battle or battles.

[*There are faint traces of writing in light brown ink between
the lines, but only a single word here and there is legible.*]

[—— to ——.]

[1675], January 19. [Paris.]—I tould you in my last that I had
mist of 6 (Pompone) but would goe againe
I am very sorry to heer how it is at last ended with our frend
on Wendesday which I did and discoursed your letter to him as
I am afraid poor man he was not prepared for such a jorny, you
fully as I could for thovgh I was twice with him that day yet
may be sure all shall be done for his daughter imaginable, truly
we weare interrupted both times, I thinke I tould him
she deserves it for she behaves herselfe soe well that all the world
however as much as you could desire and he had noething
loves her, your freend Mr. le Brune's landlord is hugely taken with her
to contradict the great advantage I maintained it would

MSS. OF SIR W.
FITZHERBERT.

I could wish for more than one reason it were a match £9000
be for him to gaine G (the Parlt. dissolved) nay he granted me it
· would beé
a yéer is a brave estate especially in so worthy a man's hands, and
of greater advantage for him than anything < (Sweade) could doe
for that which sum people perhaps would make an objection is·one
doe for him, but yet he said plainly in the circumstances'
of the cheefe reasons makes me desirous of it, you gues what I mean
8 (Fr. King) was in it was impossible for him to part with 000
and I beleeve the mother would heare reason enough upon it too
though for never soe great a benefit. I asshured him A
but pray say not a word of this however to anybody, for I am
was noe more positive for 000 (£300000) nor did noe more value
for I am sure if he should intend it, he would scorne to doe it without
it than he did durt, and that he very well knew X (the King) might doe
. *3, mother, for he is the orderlyst man in the world. I pray*
. *'. well without him too as with. him, but that if X (the King) was*
'' .. '.. .. . .. that noebody is more her humble servant·
. . . '.'· such a humour that noething but that could prevaile with
than I am; God comfort her about her landlady though I doe
him what was there to be said to·it, yet I was·sure if A (the Duke) un-
not beleeve you had any hand in it.·
dertooke it; he would doe for 8 (the French King) as for his own soule
and that therefore if 8 (the Fr. King) durst but play an open game
with A (the Duke) as A doeth with 8 had with confidence put the
busines· in his hands, I was sure if it weare· in his power he would persuade X (the King) to take the meanest of 000 (£300000) relations in
000 (£300000) his roome, for as I said before he knows it is more to
sattisfy X (the King) his humour than for any real want of 000
(£300000) and therefore to be sure if he could persuade X (the King)
to take the meanest of 000 (£300000) relations, in the stead of 000
though hee weare not of O (£100000) his force hee would, or if A (the
Duke) could by any meanes raise any of his owne relations to neer the
degree of 000 (£300000), he would never have entertained a thought
of accepting 000 (£300000) from 8 (the French King) for·I ashured him
A (the Duke) scorned to have any private designe upon 000 (£300000)
for himselfe and so did A's friends too L (Coleman) and R (Throckmorton) whoe wished but for all their good, that the thing must be
donn, but cared not one farthing which way. 6 (Pompone) tould me
that A (the Duke) and H (Ruvigny) . very great, and that A
opened himselfe with . . . . . -fidence to him, and 6 (Pompone)
seemed to hint that yet A had never urged for 000 (£300000) to him
and therefore civily seemed to infer as if it were more L (Coleman) and
R's (Throckmorton) pressing than A's (the Duke) I tould him that I
beleeved A (the Duke) had never mentioned it to"
   [*A loose sheet, written in the same ink and hand as the above, which
seems to be the continuation of this letter.*]
   " H. (Ruvigny) for that I was sure he would never ask it by him [or]
anybody else. I ashured him L (Coleman) or R (Throckmorton) cared
so little for the thing that I durst in their names ask him to employ
anybody else in it, and to shew him that they had noe designe in it but
X (the King) and A.:'s (the Duke) service and the comon good, which
will make them [as] much concerned for 8 (Fr. King) as for the other
two, he should find that they would continue to doe the same good
offices though they weare not trusted by him, that ever they had don.
That it was possible enough they might have been misrepresented by

such people as wished 8 (Fr. King) as little good as them, and that
perhaps A : (the Duke) himself [had not] escaped them, but that a
little time would shew which was which. I asked him with a little
scorn what great service G. (Lord Arlington) had done him with R
(Holland), he smiled and sbooke his head ; I asked them then how
they would beare it if he should [be . . . .] for that I did not doupt
but H (Ruvigny) had tould him of the designe, he seemed to be
surprised at it and tould me truly he had not heard of it ; in fine being
interrupted againe hee desired me me that we might have sum dis
course an other time and so we parted. What you will make of this
I know not, but I will sum time hence, when I heer from you more,
see him againe, for the present I can not I have such a swelled face
with goeing to him the other day when I was ill allreddy, that it is not
possible for me to goe out. The truth of it is I beleevo they doe not
know how to parte with 000 (£300000) as times are with them now,
beside perhaps they rely upon A :'s (the Duke) doeing it without the
help of 000 (£300000) and perhaps beleeve, and not without sum
reason, that all that . . (Coleman) . . (Throckmorton) tell them
is without hook aud for private ends, and farther perhaps they knowing
the natural kyndness X (the King) has ,for 000 (£300000) conclude, let
me say what I can, that [at] the last push 00 (£200000) will prevaile
with X (the King) to doe what 8 (Fr. King) desires, and so resolve to
let A : try what he can doe alone first. I must, to be just, not forget to
tell you that there weare all the fine and kind things imaginable said of
8 (Fr. King) his [aide] to A: (the Duke), but you know what are words
and what are deeds. Try your lady's letter that's . . . .!" [A
note] "See your Lady's letter."

[———] to COLLEMAN Esq., Secretary to her R. Highnes at his Lodgings
in the pell mell neare St. Jameses, London. Anjleterre.

1674–5, February 6. Paris.
I count myself most exterordinarly unhappy that
I received yours on Munday night of the 21st last past [torn]
illness has hindred my seeing 6 (Pompone) since businesses
I was soe ill I could not read it being twice let blood
goe with G (Lord Arlington) as they doe, I asbure you if it had been
with
that day, I have now at this time a glister in my belly
but that hassard of my life had laine at stake   I should
so that I make as wry faces as lines though all appre-
have ventured it to have given you an answer this
hensions of ill I thanke God are past.   I would not
poste but it would have alarumed all the world to
however mis you a post whilst I can write though
see one goe out in such a condition, by the next poste
I am not able to tell you anything more but that
however I promise you an answer for I [torn]
I am your's and your lady's most obedient servant.
speake or write to him, if H (Ruvigny) has but in any menire
Pray give this enclosed to the person mentioned in my
don his parte I promis you I will doe mine, and if
last post, for it is the same should have gone   .
8 (the Fr. King) will doe noething I know not how to help it, but
then, and if there be any answer to it as is ex-
the truth is he has so meane an opinion of X (the King) and
pected, be pleased to let it be conveyed as

all his partners that I doupt he thinks scarce anything they
you had this. Adieu.
can doe worth 000 (£300000), it must be therefore I beleeve sumthing
imediately from A : (the Duke) that I must tell him that will perswade
him to hope for better things when he shall govern. Adieu I can say
noe more."

[—— to E. COLEMAN.]

[1675,] March 23.
" It is I whoe ought to dispaire of being understood
for I find I am not at all, [the mis]tery was not about the concurring
I had deare Ned since I wrot last to you both yours of
or not concurring, but that is past now and it is vaine to spend
the 2d and the 8th, but that of the 22d past I have hithertoo
time and paper paper to canvase it, I doe belceve that if I had
heard noething of. I am glad my Lord Berkley goes ple-
halle in my head that you have I should not doe the quarter part soe well
nipotentiary, I hope he is pleased now and Sir Ell. Layton
and I am very sensible how you are put to it for monny and how
too, I hope you say compliments now and then from me to
much I encrease your troble in it, but pray doe not beleeve that that
them, though I give you not the troble of desiring you.
lessens mine at all, but on the contrary it has made me almost
I doe not know the gentleman you meane as you name him to
distracted, and so peevish now and then that I have scarce known
me that you would have me goe to visit, but that I may [not]
what I have writ or said for the devil take me if I doe . . . . .
faile till you write to me againe I will visit all comers
that I would rather at any time have given a finger than draw
that I can any wayes judge to be likely to be the man.
a bil upon you, knowing your circumstances, I have not seen
My Lord Marshall I heer came last night, or at least was
6 yet, I have not been very well, that is not so well to waight
expected. Mr. de Thuly came the night before. We have
for him to have as it weare an accidental oportunity for
noe newse at all, at least I know none, the truth is I have
unles you bid me absolutely I still think it not proper
not been very well with . . eat this week and goe not much
for me to goe on purpose to him. R (Throckmorton) has tould
                                                    L (Coleman) all [he]
abroad, I shall therefore troble you with noething more
could about his frinds, and the truth of it is I doe not see
at present but the ashurance of my being yours most faithfully.
how it is possible for him considering the circumstances [*one or two
words illegible*] to them that L (Coleman) seems to expect, and he
should be as glad as L (Coleman) to compas. R (Throckmorton) is
much trobled about A. for he feares he has been misunderstood, it is not
but whatever he has writ of these frinds he is still ashured they will
make good, that is whence once they have made an acquaintance with
A : (the Duke) they will serve him with all that they have in the world,
he does not meane by the acquaintance that A : (the Duke) shall ta . . .
upon them, or that they are so vaine to expect he should unbusum himselfe to them save a faire reception such as becomes him [and] them
will please them much, and then that they see him put in a practice a
little what you say he so much resolves, it is not what they suspect
himself perhaps [*a line illegible*] . . of his personal vertues, but I

E 64159.

know they are much startled to see all sorts of rogues countenanced about him as much as ever; they and I know [*2 or 3 words illegible*] 9 (Bp. of Dublin) has said that his brother has secured himselfe. for that he had made his peace with F's (Parliament) frinds and particularly with him and his caball [*2 words illegible*] turned out of the same place to him that L (Coleman) is [to an]other, he brags publiquely of the power [his bro]ther has still with A: (the Duke) R (Throckmorton) knows that in great part this last is a lye, but R (Throckmorton) cannot deny that A: (the Duke) uses him . . . . so, which these frinds of his whoe see things a little at a greater distance than he has don have reason enough to suspect that he may discover [enough] of A: to betray A: and them too should they doe anything whilest hee and sum such which I cannot so safely describe continue about A: sum of these men entend to be about Easter in your toune, you shall see them, and you shall take a safe opertunity to carry them to A:, and I am confident it is not onely this that you speake of but their skins that A: may have of them. But if I should propose any such thing to you now, with all these circumstances of A:'s not joyning with L absolutely in his resolution concerning such a thing, and then they with all these feares and suspetions, which their seeing A: and discoursing with you will dissipate, I say if I should pres such a thing to them [*one word illegible*] it would perhaps [make] them suspect R (Throckmorton) and L (Coleman) too to be of the same mind as 9 (Bp. of Dublin) brother onely for to get for themselves, and so put them wholly of of the busines of serving A: (the Duke) being thereby perswaded that it is A:'s fortune or folly always to be encompased and advised by knaves. The sobrest men whoe cum over from you say that X (the King) and A: (the Duke) weare never kinder in their lives, pray God they be so heartily, and then I have sum little fancy that serves me instead of the secret which you said you weare not yet permitted to discover to mee. I can with this lay [pre]sume that A: (the Duke) may be in a pretty good condition, but without that I ashure you it seems very desperate to mee, for I ashure you I have of late apprehended X (the King) more than F (the Parliament) for him, pray cheer us a little if you can, and tell us as much as you can with safety how things stand between them, and in all other circumstances, for unles G (Lord Arlington) been able to drawe of X (the King) who[ll]y from A: (the Duke) and that X (the King) is party to it, I feare noething for A: (the Duke), but on the contrary all this may worek to good [it or A] against the other ⌒ (heretiques) as well as K (Catholiques). Adieu, pardon all frailtys and beleeve me yours constantly."

———— to MONS. JEROME BOTEMAN chez Madame Helstop vis a vis L'Ambassadeur de Portugal dans le Pelmel a Londre.

[1674-5,] February 20.—"I am not at all [surprised] at what I heer of U (Lord Treasurer) [*another name illegible*] it would have been much had thi[ngs b]in otherwyse than they have [*one word torn off*] let us remember Dr. Crytons cat and wee never will confide' in them or rely so much .

Monsieur

on them as that anything they doe shall be able to dismay us, and I hope A: (the Duke) is not at all by what has hapned yet. R (Throckmorton) has done what has been in his power with 6 (Pompone), the whole busines, as he has tould you in his 2 former, is put into H (Ruvigny) his hands, and truly as much as appeared to R (Sir W. Throckmorton) with auspicious circumstances enough, it is

MSS. of SIR W. FITZHERBERT.

J'ay mis Madamoiselle Cortnay entre les mains d'une forte honeste

therefore now between A (the Duke) and H(Ruvigny) for it seems

to R (Throckmorton) that the thing must

femme, dans le même chariot il y avoit un merchant

be done by R (Throckmorton) or that they have not a designe of doeing

it at all, and

Anglois, et de bonne compaignie pour elle, je luy ay donné

if it should happen to be the later for Jesus sake be not dejected at it,

20 skelins outre les 20 que vous luy avez donné a Londre

but on the contrary encourage and comfort A : (the Duke) all you can,

for on my

je n'ay oser luy donner la reste de £5 puis que vous ne m'en

soule and conscience without affecting the preacher, I dare confidently

avez pas donner ordre, nous nous somme donc separer le

utter my opinion that God intends it for his good and that if he please

vendredy . . . [illegible] . . . . samedy ou soir la ou

but now to make use of those rare vertues of courage and constancy

j'ay trouver tous le monde en parfaite santé, mais mon mal

[with] which heaven has endued him, all this will turn to his glory and

ad-

heur est que je ne puisse pas passer avant le 24 . . .

vantage. My humble opinion in his case then if I might give it

que la carosse ne passe que tous les dimanche, tout le monde

. . [illegible] . . . . that if 8 (Fr. King) shall still continue to

dodge and

icy vous salue, j'ay delivré toutes les lettres de Madame

[give] A : (the Duke) noe vigorous assistance for G (dissolving Parlt.)

that the A : shall not continue

Mons. le Docteur est à Roan, si je vous puisse rendre

to shuffle betweene G (Parlt. dissolved) and F (the Parlt.) as I have

given you my reasons in my former

quelque autre service lorsque je seray au Mans je vous

letters, but in God's name let F (Parlt.) proceed and prosecute his sute.

prie de commander.

It is true this is not the way one would have chosen if 8 (Fr. King)
would have been perswaded *Monsieur* to understand his owne interest
but if that can not bee, what great prejudice can accrue to A: by F
(the Parlt.). None in the world say I *Votre tres humble et tres*

if he pleases but with magnaminity
and scorn to shake of those little wretches and their counsels whom he
has with so

obeissant servitens Brebion.

much patience [hither]too suffered to baite him, continually
to stoope and sneake to F (the Parliament) [*a word torn off*] resolve
never to receave them [ag]aine that have once betrayed him. [*One or
two words torn off*] the other side put on . . . [cou]ntenance but
[. with . all] a mind full of noble and vertuous resolution and courage
which will make him look bouldly upon his worst, and make good use
of his best fortune. I say if he pleases but to doe things and besides
[*3 or 4 words illegible*] by the regulation of his family [*1 or 2 words
illegible*] as the vertuous conduct of his owne person, how much he abhors
and detests the debauchery of X (the King) his howse, which has made
it so odious to all the nation and the world, hee will find that hee will
have all the wise, sober, good, people, and such as are worth having,
as well **1** (Protestants) as K (Catholiques) on his side, and he shall
have [the fortune ?] to see U (Lord Treasurer) and Z (D. Lauderdale)

E 2

and G (L. Arlington) and all the rest of that cruc knock themselves to peeces with F (the Parliament), and his resolution, and courage, and vertuous behaviour will not only keep F (the Parliament) at a bay ⌈3 *or* 4 *words illegible*⌉ but will keep him also in his [owne] bounds [*two words illegible*], for it is by X (the King) his stooping to F (the Parliament) that prejudice and disreputation will in great measure redound upon A: (the Duke) that A: is to apprehend damage from, now this A: his resolution will in great mesure prevent by keeping F (the Parliament) in sum sorte within his limits, and it will over and above, when G (L. Arlington) and U (L. Treasurer) and Z (D. Lauderdale) shall have brused one another and be at last all crushed by F (the Parliament) necessitate X (the King) to throw himselfe into A:'s (the Duke) armes, whoe by that time shall not onely be strong in reputation, but in reallity too by the conjunction with him of all [good and vertuous] and generous men of whatsoever party, with which then he shall usefully be able to serve X (the King) and himselfe, for bee not persuaded that ⎩ (the Protestants) and K (Catholiques) make a difference in this point, but between such as are rogues and denye a faction. And to shew you that this opinion is not onely speculative but that I can give you a prove that A:'s (the Duke) cause by what is hapned yet is not at all lost or deemed desperate in the opinion of [*two words illegible*] . . en [*one word torn*] you find that A. is disposed to take this way and this way defend his birthright, his honour, and his conscience all together, I will then make you a proposition of a number of persons whoe you will not doupt have honour, and courage by this their resolution, and I ashure you are reckoned among the sobrest and wisest part of the nation most L (Protestants) [and ?] have at least in shew and £4000 or £5000 a yeer a peece, whoe ask [in this re]spect noe reward or offices, but only ask that A. (the Duke) will give them ashurance that hee will no[t be per]suaded heerafter to abandon his owne intrest and them, and they will give him all the ashurance [on oth]er sides [*one or two words illegible*] desire, that themselves and their fortunes shall sink and swim with him, and these are such as I dare answer shall perform their promis, and not doe as U (L. Treasurer) and Z (D. Lauderdale), and sum of them perhaps have good intrest with F (the Parliament) too, that is are of the same family, but [*one or two words illegible*] weare of his cabal, but I am engaged upon my honour not to discover them till I know A. (the Duke) will take that course that they may be useful to him, for they are unwilling, as you will belcevo they have reason, to expose themselves and fortunes, and doe A. noe service neyther. For to deal plainly with you they are soe afraid of sum that A. (the Duke) has about him, whoe they say betray him and would doe them so too, that they by no meanes dare discover themselves [though] their hearts they [say are] for A.'s cause and his dis[po]sition which keeps multitudes of others in the same suspense say they. For they all avow that it is not his being for K (the Catholiques) startles them, they ask but A. to be resolved to continue governing himselfe with vertue and moderation to throw of such people · as they say are about him and betray him, and then give them his word and they will stick by him against G (L. Arlington) his party and sum of F.'s (the Parliament) too, but if ever he receaves any that have betrayed hee will goe nigh to ruin X (the King) his fortune, that is allwayes abused by knaves when they see it for their purpose and never trusted nor relyed on by honest [men]. I had your's of the 4th just now. Mr. Boteman sets out on Sunday."

Endorsed with 3 or 4 lines of signs.

—— to E. COLEMAN.

[1675,] April 10. [Paris.]—" The post is of late very slow for we have not your Thursday's letters yet. I have therefore but very little to say to you, for heere is noe newse at all, that I heere of at least."

The business of Bordeaux is ended. It seems likely to be an ill precedent.

I will be civil to the gentleman introduced in your last letter. I will communicate all news to you as I do to Mr. Tuly. I have given my opinion on his affair two posts ago, and my judgment on the proposed union.

" I doe not doubt but you will be very cautious and circumspect, I can not however but feare knaves have great advantage over an honest man. I long to have an answer of mine by Capt. Bourgh. I sometimes fancy I could be servisable to my cousin A (the Duke) in the terme, if it weare but to goe ofer roads and help a little to instruct his counsel, but that is as you shall judge . . &c. . . . . P.S.—I have had this enclosed by me a fortnight in hopes of an oportunity of sending it another way, but I dare not venture the young lady's indignation any longer. I hope it will cost you noething. I will put it up to the best advantage."

[*Endorsed*] " Nothing. No. 42."

[—— to E. COLEMAN.]

[1675,] April 17. [Paris.]—" Dear Ned, heering noething from you this post nor you saying not a word in your 2 former

Having been to visit my wife I have seen noebody since
that you had any of my leters or tooke any notice of what
I came back and therefore have not one word of newse
I said in them, I know not whether you may have
to tell you, I must onely owne the receipt of your 2 letters which
receav'd them, which puts me in sum paine I
I told you in my last I had not for they both came an
tould you in sum of them of 9 (B. Dublin) I spoke my opinion
honer after I had sent mine, vid: that of Thursday was sca-
of his brother, and the . . . preposed, and I wrote
vennight last with one in it to D : S: which I delivered, and
twice also about Mr. de Tuly, I wrote you also a
the newse letter of Monday following, but by this last post
long letter by Capt. Bourgh, and of all this you take
which came in yesterday, which should have been of thurs-
noe notice which makes me doupt they are mis-
day last the 1st of April I had none from you though I had ·
carryed, what I have said at any time concerning my-
several others and therefore if you writ I conclude
selfe is not out of any uneasines of my own skin
it is miscarryed. Pray doe me the favour to tell my friend
or consideration of myselfe but of others where-
Mr. Boteman that I had his cheese and that it was very good
of you are the chief, my zeale to serve my country
and that I thanke him kindly, but that my wife's thing hee
is I ashure you as great as ever it was and if
speaks of there is noe newes of it. My wife is pretty
for promoting or endeavoring that now I beg all my live
well and much your humble servant. Betty is mightily improved
. . . . . after I shall not repine at it but all that

MSS. of SIR W.
FITZHERBERT.

. . . *girle fancys herself a princes too, being companion*
I say and meane is that if I cannot be **serviaable to**
to 2 or 3 there where she is of her owne age, whoe are
him as I am sure I am not now to him heer it
all very fond of her. I pray be pleased to present my
vexes me to the heart that I put you to all these . .
humble service to your Lady and allow me the favour to
. . . without doeing him any good, and therefore
subscribe your most faithful humble servant
I would have you consider if I can not sum way serve him, or if to ease
you he could not put me in the wars where I might have livelyhood, or
else if you think not best that I return, and I call God to witnes I
consider you more than myself in all this for I know how you are put
to it, and that I cannot ease you in one shill[ing] and this before God
is all that trobles me, for as to an estate or fortune I thanke God it shall
never breake my heart, I mean the want of it, but as long as I have a
foot of land, eyther present or reversion, you may account yourselfe
master of it, for you know our friendship has been such a great while
that you might command me and what I had, but in especially upon
this occasion you shall have power to dispose of it tomorrow and I will
trust Providence for the future, and this upon my salvation is true.
Therefore after all I have said I can only ad consider it and yourselfe,
and dispose of me as you please. Pray be careful of yourselfe for I am
assured there are people who are resolved to ruin you I mean even in
A's (the Duke's) good opinion. 9 (Bp. of Dublin) and his brother are
desparate villaines and care not what they doe, the first is the greatest
rogue alive. It is not possible for you to imagine how great a villaine
hee is, noe I believe there was never such another born. Adieu, God
keep you. I am reddy to goe or doe anything when you will."
Endorsed "Warns him about his enemys about the Duke, calls Bp.
of Dublin and his brother villaines &c. "

[——] to E. Coleman.

[1675,] April 27.—[Paris.] "When I tell you I have not yet been
able to read any of your three letters you will not wonder I mist you
last post, nor would I write now to any[one] . . . in the world but
yourself to tell you [that] . . . within a fewe howers after my last to
you an unlucky accident was like for ever to have saved you all trobles from
me in short I was run through the thigh into the groyne which cutting all
those great vessels there caused me to loose more blood than ordinary
men have in their bodys. My life the best chirurgeons of Paris tell me
is secured, how it may be for the use of my leg because of the nerves I
can not yet tell. I tell you noething of the busines because if I can
conceal it none in world shall know it, fewe in Paris yet know that I
am hurt, nor shall they if I can help it, wherefore dear Ned if you
should heer talke of it that I am very ill or so say that weare strange
for I never mist you but one post these six moneths. My landlord is
very kind to me and will be a great helpe to me in this business. Adieu
I have don to much alreddy."
Endorsed "No. 45. Nothing. [*and*] ii. "
[*The handwriting is the same as the secret writing of other letters.*]

[—— to E. Coleman.]

1675, May 1. [Paris.]—" I have received all your letters since my
last and have also communicated the last to all your frinds as you desired. I find you have not understood me formerly, but that is past

and if it please God to spare my life bread and water in any corner is
too good for me, so it is not much matter as to me how anything goes.
As for my [cousin] A pray God he was well advised in his last generous
speech you mention in yours, silence in my poor judgment would better
have suited his affaires. As for myselfe heer is the 12th day that I lye
upon my back not able to turn me in my bed. Feavor God be thanked I
have little now, and perhaps you would wonder I should have any,
being almost every day let blood besides 3 or 4 quarts of blood I lost at
first, and taking noething in the world but barly water, not so much as
one crumb of bread since I was hurt. I have 3 the ablest chirurgeons in Paris who exercise their talents upon me frequently in making
incisions &c., one you will perhaps say is more than the care of my
carcase deserves, and truly so say I too for how to pay them at last I
know not but by giving them the skin they have made sporte with so
long, but it was the kindnes of those whoe vallew my life more than I
doe whoe brought them when I was not in a condition to resist. The
trunck with linnen you mention is at the Lady Wymondesly, Jenny
Pary knows where, it is not worth the charge to send you the key, but
pray take and open it at your howse, and use what you please of it, which
sure you might have done without your formal asking leave. Adieu
dear Ned, I am almoste tired to death though this be a 2 dayes work.
Sinews and arterys being cut cause me convulsions which much distemper
me."

Endorsed " Mentions a speech of the Duke's, prays God it may not
have hurt him, he thinks silence had been better. No. 43."

———— to ————

[*Only the latter portion of a letter, all written in the light coloured
ink.*]

" vous son nailterey. These are my instructions word for word. I
have sent you this by an expres whom I have tould that it is of great
concern to my private fortune &c. which he beleeves. He is an h[onest]
fellow and a good Catholique, but I pray keepe him in this opinion as
well as you can. I could not tell whoe to send better for he is a fellow
I'm sure loves me very well. I wonder my coming over should be talked
of soe much in England. I wrote . [*torn*] . . . . but agon,
indeed I spoke of it heer pretty publiquely, by direction, that I feared I
should have sum busines might call me into England. I must begg you
to make sum shift to send me sum money for I have but 14 pistols left
in the world and have made use of D. Arthur's credit too. This has
cost me . . . They offered mee heere what monay I would but I
would not take a farthing though they would very faine have had
me, but I was resolved they neyther should have that seeming hank
upon mee of being obliged by them in that nature, nor the worst of my
enemies should have to object against me that I was led by my own
interest, so that I pray if wee can let . . . make sum shift for the
present, and if God bless our endeavours I doupt not we serve a master
will doe sumthing for us, and if wee be unfortunate enough to miscarry
I am content to sell my little to pay my depts, and eat bred with the
remainder. You may cut (?) of this from the instructions I have sent
you also the letter from P. Ferr[ier] to his H : by which I am to have
credit."

MSS. OF SIR W.
FITZHERBERT.

[TRANSLATIONS of a Number of LETTERS from PARIS, 1676, January 5 —1678, October 5, most of them probably from ST. GERMAINE to E. COLEMAN.]

SUBSTANCE of ST. GERMAINE'S LETTERS to COLEMAN.

No. 5.

1675–6, January 12.—" Saith that nothing be done in France except the Duke doth show that he either wisheth it or thinketh it fit. St. Germain desires Coleman to send him a memorial of what is fitt to communicate to Ruvigny's successor. St. Germain hath writ Coleman by [Mr. Warner] of the $\frac{8}{18}$ January about a matter. . ."

No. 10.

1675–6, January $\frac{11}{21}$.—" I have writ to knowe the conduct which St. Germain ought to use towards the French King's confessor, and the new ambassador, for St. Germain cannot do anything till he knows Coleman's thoughts. Ruvigny's secretary and the English ambassador's secretary gone for England. Ruvigny's brother the Abbot came to St. Germain about the prorogation, but could do nothing till he knew Coleman's thoughts. St. Germain observed to the French King's confessor the Duke's great power by the disgrace of law persons, and the vigorous counsells necessary to succeed in the trafficke of the Catholicks which came to the Duke by Coleman's inspiration who is linked to the comerce of the King, the Duke, and Catholicks. If the ambassador be preposest he may act in a way which may not be for the affayres of the Duke and the Catholicks."

No. 11.

1675–6, January . . .—" St. Germain is glad that the Duke and Catholicks have reaped the profit of his actings, they act differently with him in giving him no share in the comerce of the Duke and English Catholicks with the French King's confessor and the new ambassador. If he be not authorised by the Duke and Catholicks to carry on their desires to the confessor, what can he doe. Let St. Germain be instructed how he ought to carry himself to the new ambassador."

No. 12.
No. 13.

1675–6, January 26, February 5.—" Hath nothing in it."

1675–6, January 29.—" If the Duke's letters to the King of France hath noe successe St. Germain cannot enter into the comerce till Coleman get him money from the Duke."

No. 14.
No. 15.

1675–6, February 15.—" Signifies little."

1675–6, February 9.—" The Duke and Catholicks highly convinced of St. Germain's actings. St. Germain have strongly urged to the French King's confessor that he should not suffer any to transact with the King but the Duke of Yorke, and that Coleman was the fittest to bring things about. They say Coleman is for violent counsels, and being come but newly in the comerce would be the cheife of the trade and is not authorised. The confessor would have the Dutchesse write the French King."

No. 17.

1675–6, February 26.—" Speakes that the confessor would speake to the French King about 100000 crownes. It will be almost impossible to get it."

No. 18.
No. 19.

1675–6, February 23.—" Is not of any importance."

1675–6, March 1.—" I expect the Duchesses letter to desire St. Germain's letter to treat with the King of France. St. Germain is of Coleman's opinion concerning the Lord Treasurer which is necessary to be known in the French King's shop or it will hurt the comerce."

No. 20.

1675–6, March 8–18.—The Catholicks have desired me to write to Coleman to knowe the condition of their affaires. If he could obtain

the papers from the Duke [soe?] Louy wanted he might have ended
the busines with the French King, he wants money to be serviceable
to the Duke and Dutchesse having noe order to act. I am glad with
what the Duke hath done, for the grand Treasurer hath great hopes
about discourse the Duke have had with the Treasurer, but if the Duke (*sic.*)
anything with the French King but through the confessor they will
prefer the good of France before the Catholick religion, and of the
Duke and others about (?) England for the advantage of France,
counsells of war have here an absolute power which is not for the
[busines] of England and the Catholicks. Montecuculi and the Duke
of Yorke are the two first that put it in the Dutchesse head to thinke
closer of the trafficke than she had done."

Endorsed "Tenn letters of Germain to Coleman. Abstracted by
Sir John Knight, Sir Thomas Lee, Sir Robert Sawyer."

[*Another double sheet in continuation.*]

" Substance of some of St. Germain's letters to Coleman."

1675–6, March $\frac{18}{28}$.—I "delivered yesterday the Dutchesse letter to No. 21.
the confessor for the King of France, he carryes a memoriall to speake
efectually to the King to her satisfaction. The confessor hath Coleman's letter, he may answer it when he hath seen the successe. The
King of France is melancholy and the Emperor armes powerfully, *the
Duke's Treasurer is well disposed* to the good successe of this busines,
as they tell St. Germain. Coleman must be better known to the
confessor and French King by the negociating the trafficke, and wishes
the Duke had some occasion to send Coleman to France to treat of some
point of the comerce. St. Germain gave the confessor a memoriall of
the affayres of Antwerp, the confessor is to act so that the French
King may write back to the Dutchesse. *If Coleman would come
impowered to France with the Duke's commission he may* obtaine
something of the promises. Send me newes of Dutchesse Mazarin and
the Dutchesse of Portsmouth.

1676, March 29.— The confessor have done his duty in the Dutchesse's No. 22.
busines and followed the memoriall. I hoped to have satisfaction for
the merchants of Antwerp who would settell a new factory in some
other citty of that country, as Lisle, but the King of France had
said that sort usually promise to ask nothing for their manufactures
but when they get their desires then they are burdensome to the
publicke. The English Embassador's secretary is not Coleman's
friend, concerning the Duke and that Coleman had made a proposal to
the Duke that had displeased him, and his secretary insinuates into the
Confessor's afectiun that he may make what impressions in him he pleaseth,
so the affayres of England, and the Duke and Catholicks be prejudiced if
he designes contrary to Mr. Coleman's designes.

1676, April $\frac{5}{15}$.—The French King will write to the Duchesse No. 23.
concerning the busines on foote to give her satisfaction. The new
ambassador's secretary is Darvest [?] with a German to befriend him
to the Confessor and seemes zealous for the Duke. I desire to know if
the Duke have trusted him with the secret of his affayres, St. Germain
entertaynes him to understand things that may be usefull to Coleman."

1676, April 12.—" Courtin will not appeare publickly at London No. 25.
that he may take measures."

1676, April 19.—" Sayth St Germain hath writ to the Confessor *all* No. 26.
that Coleman desires as to the Archbishop of Dublin's designes and

[Father Shelden] . . . . the temptations offered to Montecuculi, his conduct was surprising for the assistance St. Germain sought for was that he might serve the Duke."

No. 27.

1676, April 22.—" The Confessor shall understand the Dutchesse opinion of the French King's letter which mentioned [not her first omission, nor the busines under consideration. Madam de la Tremblaye's busines is every day more and more disordered betwixt Cardinal Altieri and the French King, it is hard to obtayne anything from Rome, I did not beleeve the Duke and Dutchesse ought therefore to listen to Spayne for it cannot be done without breaking with France, the consequences of which ought to be weighed, things in Rome may be changed, the Pope cannot be alwayes the same, who cannot hold out long, and it cannot be done without an open declaration against France."

No. 28.

1676, April 30.—" Courtin left Paris yesterday and will be at London before this letter. The Ambassador of England's secretary in France visited St. Germain . . . showed him what Coleman had written and the complaynt of the Ambassador, who denied strongly he had spoken it but said it was his master, and the secretary said all went very well in Coleman's shop."

No. 29.

1676, May 3.—" The secretary of the English Ambassador in France hath desired St. Germain that his name might be put on the letters that should be sent to his Secretary that they may not be opened at his house. I know not what he meanes by it."

No. 30.

1676, May 6.—" St. Germain have a . . . inclination to follow his traffick, which makes him desire letters from the Duke and Dutchesse that he may make it apear he is desired in England to be left in the shop. If St. Germain could obtain the Duke, Dutchesse, or Coleman's letter to the Confessor, and to St. Germain's master who is employed here as Strange is in England, he may continue here and be usefull to the Catholicks. The Confessor is a little bould man and rash in many things, but by no means trust him. You mention not any affaires of England nor of the money the King will make use to satisfy his creditors, nor of the dissolution of Parliament, nor of the man that is to succeed St. Germain. Can it be possible that the Duke and Dutchesse should permit Mazarine to succeed the Dutchesse of Portsmouth ; nay will the King do this discurtesy to the Duke and Dutchesse. Madame la Tremblay have writt to me to treat of her busines but I do not relish it."

No. 31.

1676, May 10.—" Hath nothing at all materiall in it."

No. 32.

1676, May 13.—" Hath nothing in it."

No. 33.

1676, June 15.—" Mr. Grey came to see me to let Coleman know the English Ambassador's Secretary visited him and spoke of Coleman in an angry manner as if the Duke was offended with Coleman for bragging that he made the Duke doe what he did."

No. 34.

1676, June 21.—" Mr. de Grey doe not write Coleman this post but wisht me to write you that Shelden told the English Ambassador's Secretary that the Duke had chid Coleman ; St. Germain expects the Duke of Yorke's papers, in his favour the Secretary is St. Germain's friend."

No. 35.

1676, June 24.—"I received from Coleman the money he sent. I will be carefull that money will efect all that Coleman intends. Lord Berkly as Monsr. Leighton tells me is preparing for Nimeguen, and Monsr. Montagu is to be here in his place. *The King's Confessor would know if the new Ambassador that is to come from England be* Coleman's friend, and if £100000 [or Crowns] may be usefull to Coleman and his other friends, and if it be it's necessary Coleman should speake to Ruvigny

of it that he may be well received by him. *In short* 100000 *crownes*
lyes ready expecting the orders of Coleman. Is Coleman one of the
new Ambassador's friends in England, the English Secretary came to
me yesterday half drunke and said Coleman is out of favour with the
Duke. All this puts Mr. Grey in pain."

1676, June 28.—"I shall not speake of the busines of Antwerp till
the man you write of is come back. The Dutchesse desire of having
Patouillet in her house they say the Duke concernes himself in. It is
discovered she hath moved for it at Rome. It is fitt her desire should
be satisfied because it will [help] St. Germain here to serve his friends.
Mr. Coleman must perswade the Dutchesse to write to Monsr. de
Champis, who is the same person here as Mr. Strange is among you, to
give her that person. It is needful to know what the Duke's confessor
saith of it to the Duke and Dutchesse."

1676, July $\frac{1}{11}$.—"The difficulties that occur touching the sending
Patouillet in the place of St. Germain occurs to me. If the Duke would
cause one to write to the King of France to write the King of England
to give St. Germain leave to come to England to cleare himselfe it might
be obtained.

*I have received the great packet which Boatman sent me from the
Lord Bellases, I desire you to keep me as much as you can in his good
opinion,* because he is a man hath much obliged me to be his servant."

1676, July $\frac{5}{15}$.—. . ". came to see me and desires his letters may
be addressed to himselfe. If you take care that the Duke and Dutchesse
persist in their desires to have the person proposed in St. Germain's
place he will be able to serve his friends."

1676, July $\frac{8}{18}$.—"Hath in it nothing of moment."

1676, July $\frac{12}{22}$.—"Hath nothing of moment."

1676, July $\frac{15}{25}$.—"St. Germain is obliged to Coleman for his paynes
[or papers] he wanted. Ruvigny is bent against the Jesuits and the
Duke and Coleman. Ruvigny told me the King of England had taken
from the Portugall Ambassador the use of his Chappell, and finds the
storme will fall on France and the Catholicks, and it will ruin the
Catholick religion and prove fatall to the Duke, for which he blames the
Jesuits and Coleman who are in greatest aversion to the Protestants and
to one part of the Catholicks and the Ministers of State those that are
of the condition of the French King's Confessor and the Duke's doe act
imprudently in that they are intangled betwixt the King and the
Catholicks and would produce an unlimited authority, and such steps as
Coleman makes must destroy them, and they will atribute all this to
France, and the persecution will be against the Duke and the Catholicks
and all the Jesuits, and above all against France."

1676, November $\frac{4}{14}$.—"The King's Confessor have answered the
Duke of Yorke as you knowe the King of France doth not seem eager
in your busines, and its said such letters from foraigne parts are not to
him acceptable."

1676, November $\frac{8}{18}$.—"Speakes about perfecting that of the
merchants of Antwerp, and satisfying the desire of the Dutchesse,

knoweth somewhat about the King of France his sonne but must first knowe the truth if the Prince of Orange's designe that soe nearly concernes the Duke, for there is no pleasure in taking false measures."

1676, November 11.—" I gave a memoriall about the merchants of Antwerp, he hath heard Ruvigny's confessor sent word that the Duke of York was a lost man, and that some of his friends gave him pernitious counsells, and he gave too great credit to them. You see by it Ruvigny is noe friend to the Duke, aud governes all the comerce. Coleman must look into it."

1676, November 18.—" That Coleman might have a pension, for though the state he be in may hinder it, yet the life he will put into busines and the service he renders to the Catholicks will incline the Pope to it, to whome he must ——"

1676, April 18.—St. Germain hath somewhat to say about the English Ambassador's Secretary, but by Coleman's letter I see he desires that nothing should be writt to him of the Secretary's actions. Knows nothing of Coleman's proposition to the Duke, but hears it was refused. What you write about the Parliament's dissolution is held to be certayne. The French King is on [too] . . ill termes with the Pope and Catholicks to ingage on that side in anybody's favor. It is wisdome to expect a better conjuncture."

Endorsed " No. 21. From Sir J. Trevor."

[ST. GERMAINE to E. COLEMAN.]

1675-6, January $\frac{5}{15}$. Paris.—" I have sent you back the answer of two letters of Madamoiselle de la Tremblay. St. Germain a year ago told you of his departure as a secret. I know that the Spanish Ambassador took part with St. Germaine only in order that there might not be any French about the Duke or Dutchesse. I think his successor ought not to be taken from the country of the King's Confessor, or of the Duchesse. St. Germaine thinks that a justification of his conduct is absolutely necessary, more for his companions' and the Catholics' sake than for his own. Mr. Courtin is named as Ambassador to England. St. Germaine does not find the opinion of Coleman concerning his voyage into England in the company of the French Ambassador, De Ruvigny's successor, convenient. Having been with the Dutchesse he would not for anything in the world be with de Ruvigny's successor, for his own credit and for that of the Duke and Dutchesse. Moreover it could not be done unless the Duke obtains it from the King of France.

He may however come in this manner for a short stay, and then return, or else enter into the Duke and Dutchesse' service again.

It is not likely the Duke will give notice that he desires this.

St. Germain will speak today to the King's Confessor for a pension for Coleman.

St. Germain owes the Duke's treasurer 20 guineas. It is all he has left of that which he received from the Dutchesse and for his furniture, and he has great need of it, were it only to pay for the postage of English letters."

[*Much more about schemes for St. Germaine's future employment and advantage.*]

Endorsed No. 6.

—— to MR. COLEMAN.

1675-6, January $\frac{8}{18}$. Paris.—" I did not think to have writt to you this day but that Monsieur the Duke of Mazerin having charged me with two letters and praying me to engage some of our friends to serve MSS. OF SIR W. FITZHERBERT. him with their Royall Highnesses in his designe which he hath to reduce his wife to her duty by all the wayes of sweetness which they can employ. I did believe you would be willing to contribute all your cares to soe good a worke, you may assure their Highnesses that Monsr. the D. of Mazarin is altogether disposed to receive his wife with all the sincerity and kindness possible, and to forgett all that's past and to live with her in a manner that shall intirely satisfie her and does pray their Highnesses to give themselves the trouble to be his arbitors as to this agreement. . 3° to obtain the same consent of his wife. 4° that besides a separation which she demands and one or two other articles of the like importance, to which he cannot nor ought not to condescend without loosing himselfe to the world, he is ready to agree to any thing their Highnesses shall ordaine, and that he most humbly prayes their Royall Highnesses to determine this difference as soon as may be to prevent the evil consequences that may happen in your Court; and prays in fine their Royall Highnesses not to acquaint any one, but those whome he employes in it, with the great desire he hath expressed for accommodation, for feare the Duchesse his wife will become more difficult and draw some advantages from it against him. I adde further that the stay and sight of this Duchess in England is not advantageous to Madam Duchess of York and that this vagabond life is not very honourable, that she hath a spirrit that is jocund and perhapps dangerous that may inspire ill councells into soe sweet a Princess as her Royall Highness and that in the end it is to be feared that your great Master who is not an enemy to faire ladies espouse not the interest of this faire lady in such a manner as will not be honourable to you or us, that this accomodation is her strict duty before God; that this Duchesse is obliged to say many things against her husband to justifie her selfe all which are false, and in the end I pray you to returne me an answer as soon as you can for to intrust me of all that is to be done to make this negotiation succeed; the Duke hath writt to my Lord Bellises to serve him with their Royall Highnesses; see then that you give that Lord this lettre of the Duke's and take together such measures as are necessary to determine this

488

difference. I was at the K. of France his Confessour but could not find him. I will use my endeavour in that I told you of, speake not to the D. of York of the twenty guinnies unless to good purpose I had

39 93

rather you would think of the letters of the Duke & Duchess for the King of France for they would be more advantageous to me. I pray

34

you make my compliments to my Lord Peterborough & Count

35

Montecuculi. I have sent to Monsr. Benifeild and desire you to communicate to him what I have writt to you concerning this affaire of the D. of Mazarine, doe not show him my letter but tell him what is contained in it to this point."

" Translated by
Richard Temple.   Superscribed to
                                                        Mr. Coleman,
                                                            London."

Endorsed " No. 7. Nothing in it." •

[The SAME to the SAME.]

1675-6, January $\frac{12}{22}$. Paris.—" St. Germaine will not accept Coleman's suggestions that he come over with the Ambassador except upon the

MSS. OF SIR W.
FITZHERBERT. understanding that it is to be only for a time until his affairs are settled, and that he may have the employment he had in the commerce. St. Germaine much wishes for information from Coleman as to what things should be communicated to de Ruvigny's successor."

"Translated by Sir George Downing."

Endorsed " No. 8."

———— to MR. COLEMAN the Duchesse of York's Secretary.

1675-6, January $\frac{15}{25}$. Paris.—" I am not satisfied with your letter of Twelfth day even Sir—it hath given mee imperfect newes, and doth neither tell mee all that I am to say, nor what I am to doe, as to what it saith to me, I hope that after you shall have well cryed the King's drinkes you will let me know all concerning this matter; you yet owe me answers to three of my letters at least that is to say to that of the $\frac{5}{15}$ of January to that of the $\frac{8}{18}$ and that of the $\frac{12}{22}$ without reckoning this which mentions the others. Think of paying mee all these debts. The last which I received from you is of $\frac{6}{16}$ of January, Mons. Ruvigny is said to have complained of . . . [*torn*] of the King of France, Mons. St. Germain, and their friends. They have no hand in his conserne, but why doth he suffer his wife to doe all things according to her fancy it is written hither that the enemy of Monsieur St. Germain is there always that 14 of the domesticks are turned away because they are of the number of the Catholiques and the French Catholiques have made a complaint about the business of the Cooke. all this having been written out of England just after the business of St. Germain hath done him noe good : but undoubtedly St. Germain hath behaved himself in this business like an honest and a worthy man. The brother of the wife of Monsieur Ruvigny hath yesterday gone on a visit to Mons. St. Germain about this matter and desires him to go and see the confessor of the King of France and give a good character to him of Mons. Ruvigny and his wife. I should be very glad that Coleman would lett Mons. St. Germain know what he ought to doe upon the request of this lady, and whether he should speak to the Confessor of the King of France concerning this matter not that they think that they can both together doe anything therein, but that Coleman may see that wee will doe all that he thinkes fit, here is not any newes at all. There is a discourse of the manifest of Don Juan. I have not as yet seen it. The Secretary of Mons. Ruvigny is yet here and is to goe see [*torn*] Mons. St. Germain which runs concerning M. St. Germain and the Confessor of the King of France makes the former more considerable than ever, but he dare not bragg of anything."

" These translated by
Sir George Downing."

Endorsed No. 9.

[ST. GERMAINE to E. COLEMAN.]

1675-6, $\frac{\text{January 22}}{\text{February 1}}$.—" In fine Sir they have spoke plainly to you about the affaire of St. German, he has told me that when he left England, he bid it adieu for ever in his own thought, and when he he writt to Coleman twas only to show what was to bee done, supposing they desired to see him again. Although ·by other letters he was well informed, there was some in England that neyther loved him nor wish't MSS. OF SIR W. his company below. What the Duke has said to Coleman is very FITZHERBERT. oblidging ; St. German is glad that the Duke and the Catholicks have reaped the profitt of what he only receives the comendations; whilst in truth hee is punisht for having deserved that prayse; or to say better used as if hee had not merited it, there are 2 things that make it plainly appeare that they act very differently with him from what they tell him ; the one that in the country where he is, they give him noe share in the comerce of the Duke, and the English Catholicks, with the King of France the Confessor and the new Ambassador, which, would bee the only true sign of the pretended satisfaction they make show to have of him, and in truth was the only thing he expected, when hee quitted England, as that which would have lett the King and his Confessor see that the Duke was effectively satisfied with his conduct, for tell mee in truth Sir you that understand the world, how can a man appeare in theyr presence, or addresse to them having nothing to say. The other thing is that the Duke is contented with a generall answer in the bysinesse of St. Germaines friend without sending the answers to him himselfe ; which they will be sure to make onely to his friend ; all this letts St. German see clearely, they are content to draw all the advantages they can from his affaire and not at all concerned whether hee profitt in the least by it or noe. Mr. Monticuculi has made word bee sent mee that he had perform'd what hee promis'd St. German and that he should have letters of it by the 19th instant ; hee has not yett received them ; tis the onely thing he has pretended to, because twill bee a full proofe they are satisfied with him in case the Duke would helpe in earnest, and not after a superficiall manner, which St. German apprehends much, they had promist alsoe the King of England's letters, and even those of the Queen besides all this, this kindnesse would putt him in a condition to continue his comerce, for his misfortune having left him without money or pension which he formerly disposd of at his pleasure, hee is reduced soe low that he canot enter into the trafick, not having wherewithall to pay for the letters; France has not heard of the Swedes successe, soe St. German doubts it, hee expects Coleman's answer to all that is in this letter which hee desires you to comunicate to him for if he is not authorised by the Duke and the Catholicks to carry theyr desires to the Confessor what can hee doe in the favour of Coleman, who wants not enemyes who write hither against him, as St. Germain has allready sent Coleman word, weigh well these things, and cause St. German to bee instructed how he ought to behave himselfe hereafter, advise Coleman to take care to prevent the new Ambassador, for assuredly the Secretary of the old one will endeavour to pursuade this, to act like the other to gain creditt by that means to whatever hee has done good or bad. I am told a pleasant story that Luzancy has here held forth most edifyingly to the wife of one waiting man to Mr. Ruvigni as shee has been Madam de Ruvigni's woman ; if shee prove it and will make the drole better understood, The D. possibly will not bee displeas'd to know and publish it. "Richard Corbett" [*is written at the head of the letter*].

Endorsed No. 11.

The SAME to the SAME.

1675-6, $\frac{\text{January 26}}{\text{February 5}}$.—Application for payment of a pension granted by the Duchess of York to an English widow who is with the Nuns of the Visitation of St. Mary, at Dieppe. Mr. Bedingfield knows how to send the money.

MSS. OF SIR W.
FITZHERBERT.

If the Duke's letter had come a week since, as Montecuculi promised, St. Germaine might have received something of the King of France.

Pray tell M. du Puy's I am in great want of my trunk, without it I cannot live long here where people never tarry when they are unprofitable.

"Hen Capell" [*at the head of the letter*].

Endorsed No. 12.

[The SAME to the SAME.]

1675–6, February $\frac{9}{19}$.—I know not why my letters are so long on the way unless it be the fault of the keys of the boxes where post letters are put, and so may be carried too late to the English post. I will send a person today on purpose to the post house with this, and not to the boxes. I have twice requested you to present my respects to my Lord Peterborough, and to the Marquis Montecuculi, whose cyphers are 10 and 2d respectively.

[Complains of irregularity in correspondence.] Montecuculi to St. Germaine gives him but little hope, and 41 or Mr. Ruvigny begins to fear that Montecuculi has not managed the business with Lord Peterborough, as he promised.

This delay is enough to do away with all the feelings of kindness which the King of France and his Confessor have now for St. Germain, who desires no more than a letter of recommendation in general to the King of France in favour of his nephew (St. Germaine).

"I have no great converse with the man of St. Louis, for reasons I'll tell you in time, and who will call himself Warner when I shall speak to you off it. Tis Mr. Sheldon's humour to love war wherever there is, and I am sure he is not Coleman's friend, no more than those are who love soft and cowardly counsells which Mr. St. Germaine did not dare name having no cypher to describe it to Coleman in."

St. Germaine has spoken highly of Coleman [*as in the epitome*] but he does not carry weight as he would if he were made a confidant in the whole affair. It is said that Coleman is for violent council &c. [*as in the epitome*].

St. Germaine is anxious to be useful to Ruvigny.

"Translated by Mr. Neale."

Endorsed No. 15.

[The SAME to E. COLEMAN.]

1675–6, February $\frac{16}{26}$.—"I received yours of the $\frac{10}{20}$ instant. Mr. St. Germain was this morning to see the King's Confessor and the new Embassador Mons. du Ruvigny, they both of them have a great kindness for you. And Mons. Ruvigny told Mons. St. Germain that he would see you as soon as he gott to his house in England. If you would communicate any thing to him you may write it to Mons. St. Germain. But for the King of France's money he is so alarmed on all sides that it will be almost impossible to gett the 100,000 crowns. The Confessor has promised to speak earnestly to the King about it. I writ you a letter for his Royal Highnesse, but you say nothing of it, no more than of the two friends. I have 3 times mentioned to you the King goes into Flanders and the Duke of Orleans will be generall under him. I have not time to say more. Madam la Tremblay desires you'd assist her in the design she has and that you'd offer her your MSS. of Sir W. Fitzherbert. services, doe what you can for her. She had another project which sheel tell you of herself. If I had time I'd desire you more att large to serve her."

Endorsed No. 15.

Enchitell Gray to Mr. Coleman.

1675-6, $\frac{\text{February 23}}{\text{March 4}}$.—Your last letter by which you acquaint mee to have received mine of the 15th 19th and 22 of Feb. is without date. I thank you for the pains you have taken to see (34) the Earle of Peterburrow and (35) the Count Monticuculi and for the offer you make mee from (62) Mr. Coleman upon whom I will rest my selfe intirely concerning the affaire of (49) Monsr. St. Germain. This (44) Monsr. Colbert attends with impatience the letter of (93) the Duchess to work strongly with (488) the King's Confessor neare (163) the King of France. (49) Monsr. St. Germain will indeavour to see (451) the Secretary and will thank him for what hee has said of him unto (62) Mr. Coleman. Hee will see him to-day and will comunicate that answer, to write again on Saturday to (62) Mr. Coleman. That which (488) the King's Confessor shall have said to him. (163) the King of France appears of late very sadd. They say 'tis because Easter approaches. I'le tell you for news the Prince of Conde excuses himself from going to the warr. Hee is retired to Chantilly twelve leagues from Paris. The Chevallier D'Humieres brother to the Marshall of that name is sent to the Bastile for having demanded leave that he may not goe to the warr and to give his regiment to his nephew, who comanded in Alsatia and was taken prisoner by a party of the enimy when hee went out upon a party. But Floranzen hath killed too or three hundred of those men and if our comander had not binne taken the affair had binne very well for us. I know itt by a letter from the sonne of Monsr. Vantelett who was in the action. Monsr. de Vantelett salutes you. Visit sometimes Monsr. Tartereau, bee so kind to mee to salute him on my part, in earnest ; and madam your wife to whom I am a most humble servant. Send mee word if you have received a letter which I wrote to his Royall Hinesse the Duchess of Yorke 26 January 5 February of which you have not spoke.

Endorsed No. 18. [*A Copy.*]

[St. Germaine to the Same.]

1676, $\frac{\text{March}}{\text{April}}\frac{29}{8}$.—"*Add to the Epitome*" that the memorial contained an expression of the Duchess' displeasure at not receiving an answer to her letter of last year. Desire Coleman to write speedily to St. Germain to assure him that the merchants of Antwerp have wherewithal to establish themselves without being chargeable to the public.

News from the seat of war.

I am extremely obliged for your kindness to those good people who have passed into France. Pray thank the captain of the yacht who took care of them.

What is the truth about the Duchesse of Mazarine ? The Duchesse of Cleveland is visited by all the English. I have not yet seen her. What do you advise me to do? It is said she intends to retire to an Abbey of the Cordeliers at Longchamps in the Bois de Boulogne, two leagues from Paris.

1675–6, February 15.—I received your letters and the same day saw the person you desired me to speak with. He was a little surprised that there was no letter from the Duchess to the King of France. He promised to speak to the King. "I told him Mr. St. Germaine would be glad of the businesse, that it might make it appear to England and the Duke that they had some kindness for him in 112. He fell a laughing upon it and told me that the King of France was hard to be pleased in those kind of matters, so I think it were necessary that the Dutchesse should write a short letter to the King of France, and that Mr. St. Germaine should deliver it to the Confessor."

[About the Fleet at Messina.]

You are liberal of your news to Mr. Warner, who ought to repay you. I have little to give but I am willing to serve you.

I am in the greatest trouble because I hear nothing of my trunk and box which are in the hands of Mr. du Puis and which he had promised to send me with Mr. Bedingfield. I see that having driven me out of England nobody cares what may become of me in France.

You are now the only man I can trust in.

You owe me an answer to four letters.

"Translated by Mr. Neale."

Endorsed No. 14.

[The SAME to the SAME.]

1676, April $\frac{8}{18}$.—"Translated by Sir E. Dennys."

I believed that the King of France had himself remembered his omission to answer the Duchess's letter, but now understand that it may be due to Ruvigny's letter upon the subject. It will be necessary for Coleman to write to St. Germain and let him know if the King has written the letter, and if she is satisfied, before St. Germain writes anything to the King's Confessor.

St. Germaine had something to say to Coleman about the Secretary of the English Ambassador, but as what he had already said gave displeasure he will say no more now. Perhaps it will be necessary to hinder the French Ambassador who is going into England from discovering his mind to the Secretary as St. Germain was informed yesterday by the Confessor he intends to do. St. Germain cannot understand how the King of England could dispose of 12, 84 [*note*] (not in the key) nor in whose favour. It is a riddle which both of us would like to understand, for it seems that he is in a better condition to receive than to give.

What you write about the dissolution of Parliament is held as a thing most certain.

"What Coleman writes about Madame de Tremblay and the little inclination 35 [*note*] (not in the key) now hath for 88 (Madame de la Tremblay) and for the people of 120 (France) because he is not satisfied with the conduct of 163 (the King of France) towards his master, makes him fear least he should serve 49 (St. Germain) as he doth 88 (Madame de la Tremblay) about which matter he desires a frank and sincere enlightening from 62 (Coleman). But to speak the truth I take that to be a meer pretence of 35 who will meddle no more with those things, for he very well knows that 103 (the French King) is upon too ill termes MSS. OF SIR W. FITZHERBERT. with 25 (the Pope) 47 [*note*] (not in the key) and 45 (Catholick religion) to engage himself to make any step on that side, in anybody's favour, and you see the reason of it. It is therefore wisdome to expect a more favourable conjuncture, and in the meanwhile not to neglect one's old friends."

For my part I have no concern in that business and care only for the interests and that passionately of the Duke, Duchesse, Coleman, and St. Germaine.

St. Germaine has sent two books to the Duchesse, and would have been glad to send presents to the Duke, Coleman, and the Confessor, but had no opportunity, and might also have displeased others . .
"Poor 49 (St. Germaine) knows not which way to go to work to do what he hath a mind to, yet in a little time he hopes to send as many to 62 (Coleman) by another opportunity."

You do not take enough care of your health.

I have taken the liberty of writing to the Duchesse of York but do not deliver the letter till the present comes.

[*Copy.*] *Endorsed* No. 24.

[The SAME to the SAME.]

1676, April$\frac{12}{22}$.—I enclosed a letter which I beg you will present to his Royal Highness with two books you will receive from Madame de Glascock. I hear here several matters relating to the Duke of York, but do not take the least notice. St. Germaine has had a conference with the Secretary of the new Ambassador and has engaged him in a firm friendship with Coleman. Mr. Courtin hopes to get dispatched the beginning of next month, and is to abide in London for some time without appearing in quality as ambassador that he may better take measures as to lodgings and all the rest.

[*Copy.*] *Endorsed* No. 25.

[The SAME to the SAME.]

1676, April$\frac{19}{29}$.—St. Germain understands perfectly all that you have written and believes that he comprehends more than you would have him know. [*Next follows the epitome.*]

Montecuculi's conduct is suprising to St. Germaine who finds, since he has heard from Coleman, that he is concerned therein as well as others, and suspects that they are but pretences to evade serving him for the future. The matter however is of small consequence, only it is a wonder they refuse poor St. Germaine so small a comfort for the injustice done to him.

[*Copy.*] *Endorsed* No. 26.

[ST. GERMAINE to the SAME.]

1676, $\frac{\text{April } 22}{\text{May } 2}$.—[*In addition to the Epitome*], I beg pardon for my last letter. I was in an ill humour for my affairs are in a very ill condition. I fear St. Germaine will be removed from the place where he now is. I shall run out of my wits if poor Madame de la Tremblay's affairs do not go well.

St. Germaine will write on indifferent topics to Montecuculi. Had not written before because he was a little disturbed.

News from the seat of war.

Copy. Endorsed No. 27.

F 2

—— to MR. COLEMAN.

1676, $\frac{\text{April 30}}{\text{May 9}}$.—" I have not received any of your letters these two posts. I do not doubt but your great business hindered you. Yet I am not without great concern for it upon many reasons that you understand well enough without my telling you. I have given to Mr. Doleith who goes with Monsr. Courtin into England the first volume of the Croisade to present to Her Royal Highness the Duchess. I desire the favor of you to present this Mr. Dolbeith and my book to Her Royal Highness and to make my most humble excuses for not having sent the first volume of the Croisades before the second supposing she had already read it. I do not know if the history of the government of Venice be come to your hands. I desired long ago that you might see the manifesto which Mr. de St. Germain made in his defence, you have not written me word that you have seen it, or like it and what you think fit to be added or taken away. Mr. Bedingfield may have it or Mr. Strange. The trenches of Bouchain would not be opened before the fifth of May, our stile. The Canon was not to arrive before two days past, being thursday the —— May. The King is about Quesnoy and secures Monsieur's army that lyes before Bouchain and all our frontiers from the ennemys that are about St. Ghilain and Mons. The fight of Messina is false. Mr. de Navailles has defeated three or four hundred men of the garrison of Feguieres. Upon the King of England's declaring that the qualities given or omitted should not any way prejudice the rights of those that should give them or not receive them, the King after two protestations made in the hands of the King of England for his rights and pretentions consents to treate the Prince of Lorraine with Brother and Duke of Lorraine, so that 'tis believed your King will send by his Ambassador in Holland the passeports to the Plenipotentiaries.

" Monsieur Courtin left Paris yesterday and will likely be at London before this letter. Mr. Guery his Secretary went away a day before and will come to London with him, he desires your friendship.

The 451 (Secretary) of 41 (the Ambassador) of 110 (England) in 120 (France) visited yesterday 49 (St. Germain) and shewed him a letter which acquainted him with all that 62 (Coleman) had written to 49 (St. Germain) concerning the dissatisfaction and complaint of 400 (the Ambr.) of 170 (the King) in 120 (France) and denyed strongly that he had spoken, but said it was his Master, 49 (St. Germain) confessed to him that amongst three or four persons that writ to him sometimes one had sent him word that the 41 (Ambadr.) was dissatisfyed with him and resolved to speak to 39 (the Duke of York) with some sharpness but the 45 (Secretary) said that he feared nothing of all this. He added that all went very well in your shop. 'Tis written from 110 (England) to 49 (St. Germain) that 91 (Sheldon) is gone for 120 (France) pray tell me if it be true? If things do not change in 110 (England) in favour of 49 (St. Germain) it will shortly cause a change in his concerns and they talk of giving him a little shop to govern that shall be altogether conformable to his trade and will carry him fifty leagues from the place where he is at present. As he has always forseen this and thought himself not at all fit for that trade he had desirred that something might be done for him that 62 (Coleman) knows of to secure him from it and become more usefull to his friends in his first trade ; if things happen not according to his desire he is resolved to do what pleases God ; it will be well to acquaint 62 (Coleman) of all this if you think fitting."

Endorsed " No. 28."

[St. Germaine] to Mr. Coleman.

1676, May $\frac{3}{13}$.—I am somewhat grieved not to have received any letters from you these four posts. I do not know if it is that they are miscarryed or that you have not written any to me and supposing that you have not written if it be by reason of your businesse or dislike and if it be by reason of any dislike, if your dislike proceed from that I am unusefull to you or that I have disobliged you. All this puts me to a non plus that you might clear me of by declaring my sentence in for me that I may take my resolutions after my condemnation. In the meanwhile I will tell you that if this last cause be the occasion of my disgrace, which I can hardly believe from so true a friend as yourself, I cannot find after a long scrutiny that I have committed any sin that deserves such punishment whatever suspition may have been conceived by my friends who ought never to condemn theirs without hearing them. And I shall therefore bear my condemnation with much tranquility of mind, provided I may understand it, for in truth t'is something hard that on a suddain nothing is said to me without any charitable information in what manner I am to be treated, but perhaps I am troubled without reason ; that may very well be, t'is your part to inform me of my good or evill destiny : in the meanwhile I will act according to my custome giving you notice of the depart of Mr. Courtin and his son and Mr. Dolbeith who you will see shortly. They are well informed with your merit. Last Tuesday at ten o'clock the armies of the King and the Prince of Orange were very near each other. The King had sent for Monsieur the Marchal de Crequy to the camp before Bochain with 20 squadrons that may make 2,400 horse; t'is not known for what. Mr. de Vivone has given some discontent to our fleet for having not permitted them to find out de Ruiter, which he did for feare that during the battle he might loose Messina and as that town was to chuse their magistrates on St. George's day 24 April he would keep all the French men near him. We have made a logement on the counterscarp of Bonchain free from the canon. St. Germain has told me that he hath written all things to the 488 (King's Confessor). Pray tell 62 (Coleman) Sir. This is all I have to say at present only that the 451 (Secretary) of the 400 (Ambr.) of 110 (England) in 112 (France) has had a fansey to pray 49 (St. Germain) that his name might be put upon the letters that should be sent to this 451 (Secretary) of 110 (England) that as he says they may not be opened at his house. I know not what he means by it nor 49 (St. Germain;) but so it is. The armies are drawn of from each other as they say."

Endorsed No. 29.

The Same to the Same.

1676, May $\frac{6}{16}$.—I am troubled about the affairs of St. Germaine.

There is a great difference between St. Germaine and Mr. Coleman. The latter has far more business on his hands and runs far greater dangers, yet after all he is a merchant set up for himself and may cease his trade when he will, whereas St. Germaine is only a journey-man and may be sent anywhere and thus be prevented from carrying on his traffic to which he has an incredible inclination. This it is which makes him desire letters from the Duke of York, and a pension from the Duchesse, so that it may appear to those in England that it is desired to keep him in the shop. Coleman ought seriously to consider this, for

things cannot possibly remain much longer as they are now. I promise
you I will henceforth say no more about it. Your reprimand is
infinitely dear to me, and I would rather receive such than that you
should be silent for 3 or 4 posts.

"Mr. St. Germaine has told me that being naturally very punctual he
has already writt those thoughts which he conceived the Dutchesse had
in her head concerning the King of France's letter to the King's Confessor, with reflexions upon the consequences that may happen thereupon,
but after I have acquainted him with what accounts you have given me
from Mr. Coleman, I doubt not he will write to the King's Confessor,
and send him word that Mr. Coleman hath discoursed with the Dutchesse
after the manner which was fitting and has left her in the opinion she
ought to have of France and the King of France. The King's Confessor or the new Mr. Rouvigny is charged with a second hooke which
you know of for the Dutchesse, as I sent you word. This Confessor of
the King, to describe him to you, is outwardly well enough, and does
not discourse amiss, but is a little soul, vaine, and rash in many things,
and one that many times talks too much. Take your measures accordingly. One may make use of these qualities to fetch things out of him,
but by no means trust him with them."

You do not mention the affairs of England &c. [*as in the epitome*].

What has become of Mr. Sheldon. He promised to come and used to
be a man of his word, but now it is said he does not mean to come.

[*Describes the taking of Bouchaine.*]

[*About the Duchesse Mazarine as in the epitome.*]

All I have said to Madame de la Tremblay is only to comfort her as
best I could.

Will Mr. Sheldon go to Rome? Address your letter for me to
Mr. de Clairambant at the Silver Master in St. Anthony's Street, as I
live such a long way from the post.

Endorsed. "No. 30."

"*Cypher numbers are used for the proper names as usual.*"

[ST. GERMAINE] to E. COLEMAN.

1676, May $\frac{10}{20}$.—Mentions the death of Mr. Cranmer's son aged 16.
The boy died a good Catholic.

[*Endorsed*] "31. Nothing."

The SAME to the SAME.

1676, May $\frac{13}{23}$.—I have read your letter of $\frac{8}{18}$ to Mr. St. Germaine
and he desires you to informe Mr. Coleman that he is extremely obliged
for it. St. Germain has quite lost his supply of money without which
it is impossible for him to continue his negociation with Mr. Coleman.
He feels that he has wholly broke word with Mr. Coleman because of
this wicked money, and that he cannot be of any use in the future.

[*The letter is addressed to Mr. Coleman, and endorsed No. 32. The
usual numbers are used in the letter for the proper names.*]

[The SAME] to the SAME.

1676, May $\frac{13}{23}$.—"I have received yours of the 8/18 instant, and answer

49

it instantly to lett you know that I have read it to Mr. St. Germain,

MSS. of Sir W.
FITZHERBERT.
—

62

who desires you to assure Mr. Coleman that he is extreemely obliged to
him for all the good will he has had for him, and will remember it for

$\quad\quad\quad\quad\quad\quad\quad\quad\quad$ 62 $\quad\quad\quad\quad\quad\quad\quad$ 100

ever : that for labouring in what concernes him, Mr. Coleman may make
use of all conjunctures which he thinks favourable, and wait as long as he

$\quad\quad\quad\quad\quad\quad\quad\quad\quad\quad\quad\quad$ 49

pleaseth, but as to the rest the true reason that has made Mr. St. Germain appear somewhat pressing that he has quite lost his supply of

$\quad\quad$ 80

money, without which it is impossible for him to continue his negotia-

$\quad\quad\quad\quad\quad\quad\quad\quad\quad$ 62

tion with Mr. Coleman. This is the reason why he desires him to
write to him no more, not being in condition to receive his letters because

$\quad\quad\quad\quad\quad\quad\quad\quad$ 80

of this wicked money, which has wholly broake word with him and which
being gone without hopes of returne, deprives him of the meanes of
finding such a friend elsewhere and it was certainly the feare of this

$\quad\quad\quad\quad\quad\quad\quad\quad$ 49

desertion which Mr. St. Germain infallibly foresaw that forced him to
make steps which have seemed too urgent in the meane while it is necessary that he carrie himselfe as I have now said. It is likely also that

$\quad\quad\quad\quad\quad\quad\quad\quad\quad\quad\quad\quad$ 39 $\quad\quad\quad\quad$ 93

he will heereafter bee useless to the service of the Duke and Duchess and

$\quad\quad\quad\quad$ 300

.of the Catholiques. However it falls out his good will will never be
wanting. Pray lett me know of your receiving this letter, and believe mee
more your servant Sir than any person in the world. The Prince of
Orange keeps constantly close in his quarters, and it being impossible to
force him there, and he having more provision than was thought men
belcevo the King will remove his station, and they talke of his returne to
Paris, after his having sent away a great detatchment for Germany
where it is supposed that the enemies army is very strong. No other
news at present."

Endorsed. " No. 32."

[*At the head of the letter*] " Sir Cyril Wyche."

[The SAME] to the SAME.

1676, June $\frac{15}{25}$. Paris.—"I must begin with telling you that 48.—
prays you to return thanks to Coleman for the news he learnt of Mr.
Morpary whereof he expects the execution as soon as may be, he
assures me he has been above 3 months with his friends in order to
maintain the corrispondence which he has with Coleman and that
pure necessity obliged him to speak and act as he did, hereafter his
affairs will change and for ever as he hopes because his friends in France
will soon be in condition to render him no longer troublesome unto any.
They say that Mr. Patouillet will have the vacant place, pray what is
there of it ? Mr. Gray came to see me and desired 48.— to let Coleman
know that the Secretary of the English Ambassador here gave him a
visit and spoake to him of Coleman in an angry manner, as if the Duke
was offended with Coleman for bragging that it was he that made the
Duke do what he did, in a word that he spoak and bragged too much.
48.— has desired me to write thus much unto you to the end you may
have the goodness to tell it to Coleman. I hope to write to you duly
once or twice a week. We have no news but what is old and what

MSS. OF SIR W.
FITZHERBERT. you know, I only write unto you now to acquaint you with the sentiments of acknowledgement which 48.— has for the favours of Coleman he would be very glad to know if he ought not to write to the Duchesse and how he ought to do it."

Endorsed " Translated by Sr. Robert Markham."

[The SAME to the SAME.]

1676, $\frac{\text{June 21}}{\text{July 1}}$. [Paris.]—" Endorsed Cler. July 1st 1676.

" I have received your letter of the $\frac{12}{22}$ of June which came to my hands a little too late. By the first post I will send you a certaine addresse whereby I may receive your letters betimes. I do not now repeat my thanks for your favours because I have done it already in my two former. As yet I have not received that I expect from Mr. Morpain who hath satisfied himselfe with giving me the information that he hoped I should have it in a little time. Mr. de Gray whom from this time forward we will call 87 came to see me this morning. He desired me to tell you that he would not write to you this post because I do. He also entreated me to send you word that you might tell 62 (Coleman) that what the 45 (Secretary) of 41 (the Ambassadour) ——— from 110 (England) in 120 (France) had told him of 62 (Coleman) came from 91 (Mr. Sheldon) who had told him where he now is, and that 39 (the Duke of York) had chid 62 (Coleman) in publick. Sheldon knowing of it 49 (Mr. St. Germain) wrote about the businesse of Antwerp and is much amazed there hath bin no answer to it after three letters which he hath written to 488 (the King's Confessor). You may see that 49 (Mr. St. Germain) broake off his correspondence only out of pure necessity, but since a doore hath bin opened for his entrance into it againe to be sure he will not give it over of his own accord. Moreover this 45 (Secretary of the Embassy) from the 150 (the King of England) pretends very much to be 49 (Mr. St. Germain's) friend, and to desire to live in a perfect good understanding with him if 62 (Coleman) by that meanes can make use of him to get something done for 62 (Coleman's) advantage. 49 (St. Germain) doth impatiently expect the 39 (Duke of York's) papers, there being one or two persons actually dead whose imployments might be obtained if one had good recommendations. Those papers cannot come too soone, and the affaires already had bin done if they had come; but it is necessary they should be as perswasive as the quality of him that writes and of him to whom they are written to be writ. For news 1. The King sends out to forrage all about Mons, Cambray, and Valenclennes, that he may destroy that country, and cutts down all the wood he can to lay the country open. 2. Condé is wonderfully fortified, and the designe is to make it a kind of impregnable island. &c "

[*General foreign news and reports.*]

"Send me word whether Mr. Patouillet shall have Mr. St. Germain's place, and in what condition that affaire is. I must needs know it . . . . . . What say you of 488 (the King's Confessor) and of the 451 (the Secretary) of 41 (Mr. Ruvigny) that is new come, what becomes of the old one."

[*At the head of the letter*] " Charles Cottrell."

Endorsed No. 31.

[The SAME to the SAME.]

1676, $\frac{\text{June 24}}{\text{July 4.}}$ [Paris.]—" I wrott to you by the last post and write
again today to give you notice that the little 80 (money) came to me
last Thursday. I received it with all the demonstration of friendship
which I owe to him from whom it came. I pray you let 62 (Coleman)
know this and assure him that I will have all possible care about it, and
will order it so by my cares that that little 80 (money) may affect all
things according to the intention of 62 (Coleman). I expect a word from
62 (Coleman) to know if I should write to 93 (the Dutchesse) to pay
my respects concerning that you know of, and in what termes I ought
to do it. As for those papers which you believe you can help me to,
they would be of great use to me at this very moment for a very fair
occasion does now present itself, and if I had them I doubt not but I
should succeed in my designe. You have need of all your goodness
not to be tired with my importunities My Lord Bartley as Monsr.
Leighton tells me prepares himself to be gone for Nimeguen within five
or six weekes: and that Monsr. Montague is to come hither in his
place "

[*General foreign news.*]

" 48 (the King's Confessor) prayeth 62 (Coleman) to let him know
whether the new *Ambassador that is to come from England into
France be a friend to 62 (Coleman), and whether 48 (100000* crownes)
may be useful to 62 (Coleman) and to his other friends near 41 (Mr.
Ruvigny) and if it be it would be requisite that 62 (Coleman) *should
speak of 48 (100000) crownes to 41 (Mr. Ruvigny) to the end that he
may be well received by him, in short 48 (100000 crownes) lye ready
expecting the orders of 62 (Coleman).* Are they pleased with the new
Ambassador in England, and is 62 (Coleman) one of his friends ? His
Secretary and 488 (the King's Confessor) are they friends to 62 (Coleman)? What does 98 (Mazarine) and 89 (Portsmouth) ; they said the
other day that 89 (Portsmouth) was dead. 48 (St. Germain) hath
written to 488 (the King's Confessor) for the merchants of Antwerp.
87 (Monsr. Grey) is newly gone from me and prayed me to put his letter
into mine. He sends you no newes because I have given you that
little there is. He desires you to direct your letters alwayes to him for
the reasons he gives you, and he assures me that he goes —— for to send
you some that are better. Yesterday the 451 (Secretary) of 110 (England) 400 (Ambassador) in 120 (France) came hither to me being halfe
drunk and told me many things concerning the new 41 (Ruvigny) of 110
(England) in 120 (France), he pretends that 62 (Coleman) is much out
of favour with 39 (the Duke of York) and that he knew nothing of the
change, and that the union which 62 (Coleman) hath had with 41
(Ambassador) of 120 (France) in 110 (England) is the cause that the
new 41 (Ambassador) [*note*] (Courtin) of 120 (France) in 110 (England) does not look upon him. All this puts 87 (Mr. Grey) in paine,
and much more 48 (St. Germain), endeavour to know the truth of it
from 62 (Coleman) and send us word. When you write to me hence ·
forward use this addresse without anything else; For Monsr. Corbett
Advocate in the Counsell, in the street of Guinquampois att Paris.
Your letters come to me so late that I cannot answer them till next post,
but by this way I shall have them in a moment."

[*At the head of the letter*] " Charles Cottrell."

Endorsed " No. 35. Cler. July 4, 1676. Satterday."

MSS. OF SIR W.
FITZHERBERT.

[The Same to the Same.]

1676, $\frac{\text{June } 28}{\text{July } 8.}$ "[Paris]."

"I have written four letters and had no answer. I wished my letters to be directed to Mr. Corbett because he dwells just against the Post house, and is careful to get and send on my letters quickly. I will not write about the Antwerp business until the King comes today or tomorrow.

"Here is a business whereof I think myself obliged to give you notice, 93 (the Dutchesse) desires to have Monsr. Patouillet in her house, and they say that 39 (the Duke) concernes himself about it; in the meane time those persons with whom 49 (St. Germain) dwells have already retained him for them, and this desire of 93 (the Dutchesse) who hath moved for that at 43 (Rome) is discovered, especially since that 488 (the King's Confessor) had desired that that should be done for the former person. Two things oblige me to write to you to pray you to tell 62 (Coleman) that 49 (St. Germain) would be very glad that 93 (the Dutchesse) should continue in her first resolution because it is fitt her desire should be satisfied, and moreover because by that meanes 49 (St. Germain) will find an imployment in the towne where he now is, which will fix him there for a long while, and will free him from the fear he is in of being sent somewhere else, and by that meanes he will be in a condition to serve his friends according to their desire. Let 62 (Coleman) think well of what I write in favour of 49 (St. Germain) who if that person go to 93 (the Dutchesse) shall have that which was destined for him here; therefore 62 (Coleman) must needs tell 93 (the Dutchesse) that the friends of 49 (St. Germain) had engaged that person for themselves, and that it would be needful for 93 (the Dutchesse) to write or cause a little letter to be written to Monsr. de Champs (who is the same person here as Mr. Strange is amongst you) for to pray him to give her that person, and not to oppose her satisfaction in that point, for by that meanes the thing will infallibly be done. If one could obtaine one little word by letter from 93 (the Dutchesse) for that person the thing would go so much the better. But there is no time to be lost for there are those which will strive to prevent 62 (Coleman) with 93 (the Dutchesse) by getting her to retard her request by a yeare longer, that is to say, for ever, for if that busines be not done now it will not be done at all. I have convincing proofes of it. If 62 (Coleman) would write alsoe himselfe to 488 (the King's Confessor) to signify to him that oue can by no meanes refuse 39 and 93 (the Duke and Dutchesse) without disobliging and vexing them it would not be amisse, but it is necessary first to know what the 488 (the Confessor) of 39 (the Duke) has said concerning this matter to 39, and 93 (to the Duke and Dutchesse) for I doubt not but he has bin writt to about it. I beg one word of answer concerning this affaire as soone as may be by the addresse of Monsr. Corbett . . . . The nephew and neece of Mr. Gray arrived here yesterday. The uncle salutes you, and the nephew will be shortly at London."

[*At the head of the letter*] "Charles Cottrell."
Endorsed "No. 36. Cler. 8 July."

[*In these three letters the names are inserted after the numbers in a blacker ink than the rest of the letter.*]

[The Same] to the Same.

1676, July $\frac{1}{11}$. Paris.—"I have already writt thrice unto you to give you thanks for the last obligations I have unto you, which enables me to continue my thanks, as I doe by this letter with all my heart and as I shall doe till I hear of your receipt of them. 87— is come to see Mr. St. Germain this morning and desires that Coleman would send him his news directly to himself. Mr. St. Germain and 87— will join together to communicate to Coleman what shall happen, remember to direct my letters to Mr. Corbet Advocate of the Councill to the end I may receive them in good time. I writt to you about the difficulties that occurre· touching the sending of Mr. Patouillier in the place of Mr. St. Germain· and what is to be done thereupon. But there is come a thought into my head about this Mr. St. Germain which you may communicate to Coleman if you think fitt, which is if the Duke and Duchesse of Yorke would cause one to write to the K. of France's Confessor to engage him to speak to the K. of France to write to the K. of England to desire him to consider of the justification of Mr. St. Germain and that he would give him leave to come over and clear himself and that he might be under the protection of Mr. Ruvigny, the said Confessor will assuredly most efficatiously do it, and obtain it of the K. of France for reasons which I will acquaint you with in due time, but if you doe not judge this fitt pray at least get the Duchesse to write or cause a letter to be written as soon as may be to the person who holds the same place now as Mr. Strange dos with you (whose name I have acquainted you formerly with) that he may grant the request of the Duchesse for this is of the most utmost consequence to St. Germain. I am much concerned that I have no news from you, I know not why you are so silent. I am affraid that what I writt to you concerning your Ambassador's secretary is the cause, pray free both me and 87— from our fears. Maastricht is invested they say by the Prince of Orange, and that the King who came hither but on Wednesday night last is about to returne again. Others say the peace is made with Holland and that Brabent is given to the Prince of Orange and that they will let him take Maestricht whilst the King will take Valanciennes and Cambray, I referre my selfe to the issue. The process of Madam Brinvilliers is much advanced, but is a great secret yet. Pray think on Mr. St. Germain and on me. I am just now told that one belonging to the house of Conde is come to advertise the F. Confessor of the Duke d'Enguien to be in readiness to depart on Munday and that the King goes too. St. Germain has not· yet seen the King's Confessor who came hither but on Thursday and is most extremely full of visitors, but he will see him and speak to him ere, long."

Endorsed " Translated by Sr. Robt. Markham. No. 37."

[The SAME] to the SAME.

1676, July $\frac{5}{15.}$ Paris.—" Your letter of the $\frac{29 \text{ June}}{9 \text{ July}}$ could not come with more expedition. I am much pleased with this way and desire you alwais to use it. I have spoaken to the K.'s Confessor concerning the Antwerpe merchants, he told me the K. of France having given it in commission to one of his most trusty ministers of State to inform in that matter what was to be done the said Confessor thought that affair had been answered, but seeing that Minister of State is not here he could give me no farther account thereof, as soon as I understand that that Minister is here I will see him. 87 came to see me this morning as he used to doe every post day, he presents his service to you, having nothing more than I have to acquaint you with, only he desires that the news he was wont to receive by Mr. Botteman may be addressed

MSS. OF SIR W.
FITZHERBERT. directly to himself, seeing that will be most usefull to him, for that this post in he has not yet received those letters which were directed to the little banker. The affairs of St. Germain will goe well here if Coleman take cair the Duke and Duchess of Yorke persist in their desires to have the person they have proposed to be put in the place of Coleman's friend (for if they press it never so little more they will assurelly have him) and then St. Germain will be sure to be with Mr. Warner, to doe then what he did when with the Duchess, and thereby be able to continue to serve his friends as shall be judged convenient. But if Coleman judges the Duke has any remains of kindness for St. Germain the occasion is fair, for (since the K.'s Confessor had a designe to have that person near himself whom the Duchess desires) if the Duke would cause one to write to the said Confessor signifying that if he cannot have that person he desired they should send him at least St. Germain, I am sure the Confessor would then propose it to the King of France to write to the King of England, to the Duke, and to Ruvigny, to testifye he would be very glad leave might be given to St. Germain to make known to the King and Parliament the truth of his case after which one might act with the Parliament and the House of Commons by Coleman's and St. Germain's friends to obtain of the Parliament a favourable audience. These are visions that come into my head it is for you to chouse which will be best and propose it to Coleman as you shall think fitt. The French Ambassador's Confessor has written to St. Germain and acquainted him with the sentiments Coleman has of him, and he has desired me to tell you that he is very much obliged to Coleman for them, the Duke and Duchesse have also spoaken very kindly of him to that Confessor as he wished, and I desire you on his behalf when you have a fitt opportunity to testifye all the acknowledgements that this deserves. If the papers come they will be of great use. Maestricht is entirely free, there was a correspondance in the town held with the enimie for getting the magazine on fire but it being discovered the enimies are retired, Mr. De Monbron has surprised a 1000 of the garison of Cambray 400 are taken 600 defeated. The affair of Madam Brinvilliers goes on apace, yesterday the Commissaries confronted her with a certain advocate named Briament who had been tutor to her children they made not an end till six aclock at night, the advocate spoak much in the matter and there are all ready erected scaffolds *a la grava* where she is to be executed. Things are kept very secret and there are some in great fear who seem to put a good face on the matter. I have received the letters of my Lady the Countesse I shall expect her orders, but am afraid the thing can not be done on the conditions she desires."

Endorsed "Translated by Sir Robert Markham. No. 38."

[The SAME] to the SAME.

1676, July $\frac{8}{18}$.—"For newes I have but two things to acquaint you, one is that the siege of Maestricht is formally laid, there are fourscore pieces of ordinance brought from Holland to batter the place which is beseiged by an army of twenty seaven thousand men and there is likewise an other army in the places round about to prevent its being surrounded consisting of thirty thousand more. The garrison is well accomodated in all respects, hath six thousand foote, twelve hundred horse and three hundred dragoons; Letters are expected from Monsr. Louvoy on his return to resolve the time of the King's departure; the other part of news is that Madame Brinvilliers was yesternight

about halfe an hour after seaven of the clock executed ; her sentence
was to make amend honorable, that is, to stand in her shift about
her other habits, a rope about her neck, bare footed, which was done
before the Church of Notre Dame, from thence shee was carried
in a tumbrill to the place called the Gréve, there to have her head
cut off, the body burnt and the ashes throwne into the fire ; before
all which I should have told you shee was put to the rack ordinary and
extraordinary, shee had spoken the night before with the Father
Chevigny, father of that oratoire, and the morning after they had read
her sentence shee thanked the judges for having used her so favorably.
Shee confest herselfe to Monsr. Pivot Doctor of the Sorbon saying that
there needed no rack shee would tell all, and indeed shee was three
hours with two Comissioners of Parliament, but shee confessed only
what concerned herself that shee had poysoned her father three times
in two years and her two brothers, shee hath chardged no confederate
wnich was the cause that shee was put to the rack ordinary and extraordinary, but shee would discover nothing. She hath showed in all a
great deal of resolution and prescence of mind and all Paris was I think
at her execution. I know not yet all the particulars. I attended last
night to have heard some news from you but I received none yet—think
of what I writ and I pray instruct mee in every thing.

The trenches before Philipsburgh were opened $\frac{2}{12}$ instant at night
the governor made a sally and having repulsed the enemy, he att the
same time caused a man to slip out to give the K. advise.

I have seen a letter from the camp of Monsr. Luxenburgh that sayes
he hath got sixty pelces of canon and is going to attaque the lines of the
enemy, he hath made a detatchment to joyne Monsr. Crique to fall on
the enemy on an other side."
Endorsed " No. 39. Translated by Mr. Cheyne.'

[The Same] to the Same.

1676, July 11, Paris.—"I am much obliged to you for the cair you
take of my little affairs, I have recived the great packet which
Botteman sent me from Lord Bellasis. I advise you to keep me as
much as possible you can in his good opinion, because he is a man has
much obliged me to be his servant I have already told you that your
letters will be very serviceable to me but they will doe me no good if
they come not directly to my self for they arrived yesterday in the
afternoon and I have not received them yet, besides when we shall have
them at the first hand, with one stone you will kill two birds for I
will show them to Mr. Julij and your banker shall not faile to see them
time enough for him. My nephew will depart please God on Monday
sennight. This is all I have to tell you at the present, when Mr. Julij
writes to you I need not put you to double charges because there is no
post but I see him an hour before the currier goes."
Endorsed " Translated by Sir Robert Markham."

[The Same] to the Same.

1676, July $\frac{12}{22}$.—" I have received yours of the $\frac{8}{18}$ July and I believe
you should answer article by article, St. Germain hath desired mee to
tell you that you will oblige him to renew his acknowledgements to
Coleman which yett are not without much regrett for that Coleman
advises him that 'tis not necessary that he should write to the Duchess

touching the affaire of mony which infallibly shewed him that 'tis
Coleman alone that hath chardged himself with the mony for St. Germain,
which St. Germain would never have suffered, had he had the least
suspition of it, and most assuredly being of the humour I knew him,
and how he understands things, he will doe his business sooner or latter.
Thursday's post is come but I have no notice of the papers wee must
expect, and is it not troublesome, St. Germain as he told mee was
againe yesterday to speake with the Confessor, touching the merchants
of Antwerp, but he was shut up about affaires and not to be spoken
with, but St. Germain intreated a domestick of the Confessor's to put
him in minde and I believe the Confessor desires that he who is to
succeede St. Germain in his place of England should live with the
Confessor, and be one of his; if the Duchess and Coleman will make use
of this conjunction and write to the Confessor to put him in minde of
the affaire of the merchants of Antwerp the business would succeed, my
thoughts are, that Coleman should write to the Confessor as from the
Dutchess to give him the severall notices or to send St. Germain where
he was before, that is to say that the King of France should write to
yong Ruvigny that he should take care of the affaire of St. Germain
with the King of England and the parliament till it were well understood,
or if that cannot bee, that they should send to the Dutchess him who
pretends to the place of St. Germain, for by this meanes the Confessor
could not but send the person whom the Dutchess desired, and at the
same time something should be said touching the merchant of Antwerp
—·—that if the Dutchess would cause it to be positively signified to the
Confessor that he think no more of him whom he desired and also to
sound the . . . affaire of Antwerp . . I believe this would be the
shortest way, it's true St. Germain would suffer by it, but what matters
that? I am affraid for Coleman if once they come to declare
against the Catholique religion, the Catholiques and consequintly
the Duke of Yorke: In the name of God instruct mee well of every
thing that passes heerin. I have not yet heard any thing said of Madame
de la Tremblay, which I expect with some impatience, and for the
notice you give mee to her advantage and by my solicitations I will
ingage her all I can to induce old Ruvigny to performe his duty to the
King of France and the Ministers of State. I protest before God that
'tis now the only thing I aime att, I believe you see well enough why,
and I pray you to give me exact account of all that I shall entrust you
with to Coleman, because I cannot write to him but by you. Lett me
understand what is done with you in the affaire of the successor of
St. Germain, for I shall not name him hereafter but by the name of
Successor. The Confessor doth his business and will see to it . . .
. . . The Embassador is writ to to speake of·it to the King of
England as of a traffiquer who might be prejudiciall to the Dutchess
and Duke; is that true? if the Dutchess bee stedfast most assuredly
St. Germain will have his place, if not, he knows not what will become
of his trade, but if the Dutchess give way handsomely to the Confessor,
there is nothing which the Confessor will not likewise agree to, wherefore Coleman must manadge this conjuncture and that he ask in
requital the affaire of Antwerp . . . . . . and the fixing of
St. Germain in the same place to carry on his traffick; this is all that
can be said on this matter, Ruvigny is mightily prevented in whatsoever
may be objected against the Catholiques and against those of England
which are the friends and kindred of St. Germain. St. Germain knows
he speaks very ill of them I pray say nothing of it. The Trenches are
opened before Philipsburgh, says one letter that I have seen, they are

MSS. OF SIR W, FITZHERBERT.

not distant about one hundred and fifty paces from the ditch on one side and on the other three hundred. This letter construes that Mons. de Luxumburgh is going to fall into the retrenchments of the enemy and Mons. de Crequi likewise in severall places. Maestricht is also beseiged; 'tis thought the defiles will hinder Mons. Schomberg of releiving it but the towne is well fortified and the garrison neere eight thousand of the best men of France, 'tis said our army will besiege Yprés, Aires or St. Chilian. Some letters say Palermo hath civilly sent back the Spaniards, Naples hath given five hundred thousand crownes to repair the Spanish fleet. The Swedes are in their portes as 'tis said. It appears that Madame Brinvillieres hath bin too favorably treated by the parliament and 'tis believed the depositions shee has made are kept secret ; this is all I know."

Endorsed " No. 41. Translated by Mr. Cheyne."

[The SAME] to the SAME.

, ·1676, November $\frac{4}{14}$.—" I thought to have sent you some news of Monsieur de Ruvigny, of his secretary, of Madam de la Tremblay, and of the King's Confessor. But I am not further instructed than I was, seeing that I could not speak with some nor meet with others. I saw Mr. Gray and his nephew, which last shewed himself very civill to me upon Mr. Coleman's account and promised to tell me news from England. Tis only by publick report that I learnt what is said of Mons. de Ruvigny his Secretary, and of the Embassador at Nimmeguen. Truly I am sorry for it and sometimes I fancy that Monsieur St. Germain might have been instrumental in it by shewing the letters to (Mr. Gray) I told him my mind as to that and found him much of the same mind insomuch that he told me he would for his part write about it to Mr. Coleman by way of complaint. I know him to be a person most ready to serve friends and no less sensible of other people's misfortunes. Madam de la Tremblay is resolved to write to him who writ to her. But it was impossible to transact any businesse the last time he was here, because Monsieur de Ruvigny's wife was present all the while, and never out of sight. He will return an answer as soon as possible, and you may assure of it him that you know, here is no news stirring. You know what Mons. de Ruvigny's Secretary told him concerning his friend, and now Monsieur de Ruvigny protested that he had shewed himself very much concerned about it to the King of France and Monsieur de Pompone which Monsieur de Ruvigny's Secretary has given sufficient testimony of. It happens very often that you omit several articles of my letters and leave them unanswered which is some trouble to me. So you slighted that passage concerning the good office I intended for our friend by endeavouring to procure him a pension out of an estate of Catholicks in France and to have it confirmed by the Pope, being he is a Catholick. I know not whether or no you have proposed the matter to our friend, nor how he likes of it. Therefore I desire the favour of you to acquaint me with it. Neither do you tell me any thing about the merchants of Antwerpe. The King's Confessor has answered to the Duke of York as you know. But when all is done the King of France doth not seem to me very eager in the business. And it is said that letters of this nature which come to him from forrein countrys are not acceptable to him. We must have patience. You send me not a word of your Monsieur de Ruvigny or of his Secretary, nor of the King's Confessor. Doth Mr. Coleman see them? Is he a friend of their's? At last what do you say of the successor? I know him not; but he

MSS. OF SIR W. FITZHERBERT, was highly commended. Is it true that the Duchess of York's Confessor is threatened to be brought before the Parliament? I thank you for your care in the concern of the money in the King of England's behalf and those he owed money to. I assure you that I am as well pleased with you as if it were my own concern. We may chance upon that propound to you a small business which might be of some use, if Mr. Coleman doth but think it feasable."

Endorsed " No. 53."

[*At the head of the letter*] " Sir Gilbert Gerard."

[The Same] to the Same.

1676, November $\frac{8}{18}$.—" You have sealed your letter just upon the date of it, so that I cannot tell what day it was when you writ. On Wednesday last not hearing from you I wrote another letter to give you such information as I had ready for you and this day I write one only to give you notice, that I received your last, wherein you mention two things. The one about the merchants of Antwerp. Monsieur St. Germain told me to that point, that he dwells in the same shop of the King's Confessor, that he may come more freely to speak to him, and that he was gone for that purpose to his storehouse two several times, but found him so taken up that he was fain to put off the business to this day. However Monsieur St. Germain is of opinion that he must see Monsieur de Louvoy his father who gave the advice to the King of France about giving satisfaction to the Duchess of York. When all is done he is the person that must bring the business to perfection and whose hands it must needs go through. The other business concerns your Embassador the King's Confessor and Monsieur de Ruvigny. Wonderfull things are said here of Monsieur de Ruvigny and of his complacency for the King of England's inclinations. Nay he used this very word that he obeys him in all things, and intends to represent it as a very meritorious thing to the King and his Confessor. Monsieur St. Germain himself fears that if he should say what he heard of Mr. Coleman about that business, he should not be welcome, because Monsieur de Ruvigny and the King of France's Confessor not being of Mr. Coleman's opinion have undoubtedly disproved his conduct in France. Can no ways be found to get the Duke of York to acquaint the King's Confessor, or the King of France himself, with the opinion he has of Mr. Coleman? I know something about the King of France's son. But I dare not tell it you before you have acquainted me first with what you know of the Prince of Orange, whether it is true or no that he is to go for England about the design so much noised abroad, and which nearly concerns the Duke of York? You can not but know by this time the design Monsieur St. Germain had formed in Mr. Coleman's behalf. 'Tis for you to let me know, whether it is convenient that he should go on with it. For there is no pleasure in taking false measures. The King's Confessor has writ to the Duke of York to thank him for the letter he had received from him in Monsieur St. Germain's behalf, but Monsieur St. Germain is not the better for it, and in all likelyhood shall get nothing by it. However he is as thankfull as he ought to be. Send me some news of the Duchess of York's Confessor, and of his successor."

[*Endorsed*] " No. 54."

[*At the head of the letter*] " Sir Gilbert Gerard."

MSS. of Sir W
Fitzherbert.

[The Same] to the Same.

1676, November $\frac{11}{21}$.—" Yesternight the King of France his Confessour
came back from the visite hee had made to the King. But it was
impossible for mee to speake with him either then or this morning when
hee had shutt himself upp to write. I had given him a memorial concerning the merchants of Antwerp agreeable to Mr. Coleman's letter for
treating with the King of France on that affaire, and hee it was that
ask'd mee earnestly for it. I will write you word on Wednesday what hath
been done in it. I have thought it fitt notwithstanding by this post to
informe you of a thing worth your knowledge, which is that St. Germain
told me that in discourse held th' other day with the King's Confesseur,
he learnt from him that the Ambassadour's (Ruvigni's) Confesseur had
sent him notice that the Duke of York was a lost man, and that he had
it from the Ambassadour's (Ruvigni his) owne mouth. Thus you see
the representations the Ambassadour gives of the D. of Y. to our friend
the King of France. You may judge by this what to expect of this
Ambassadour (Ruvigni) in favour of the Duke of Y. St. Germain
added that the same Confessour had written in the same letter that the
friends of St. Germain of England who drive on the same trade with
him did give pernicious councils to the D. of Y. and that hee gave too
great a credit to them. You may see by this whether this man is
mistaken in his imaginations, and meantime 'tis hee that governs all
that commerce. At least I feare it so. I write thus much to you, to the
end that you may advertise Coleman of it, and that hee according to his
wisdome may look into it. I have thrice been to visite the Ambassadour (Rouvigni) without finding him at home. It's some time since
I saw the Secretary. I think that Coleman would doe well to write a
word or two to the King's Confessour, but it should be something worth
its paines, and should require an answer. For this Confessour is a man
to bee press'd, and who of himself is too closse. And at the same time
St. Germain would be obliged to Coleman, if in the same letter hee
enquired of the Confessour what newes of the successe of that affaire
the D. of Y. did recommend to him a favour of St. Germain. There
is no other newes, but of the peace with Poland, and of the Confederates
retreat from before Deuxponts. Some say Mons. de Crequi pursues
Mons. de Zell, and others on the contrary that Mons. de Zell will block
up Mons. de Crequi, who hastens all hee can to gaine an advantageous
post, without which hee is lost. Wee must wayte for the successe.

" Since my letter was written, I have mett with St. Germain, mighty
froward at what was said to him by a friend who was just come from the
Confessour, being there when hee made answer to the Confessour of the
Ambassadour (Rouvigni). This friend told him that the Ambassadour
(Rouvigni) would spoyle all, and that hee had not the right apprehensions
of things, to which the Confessour answered him that twas St. Germain
must say this of the Ambassadour (Rouvigni) but that St. Germain was
not well informed. St. Germain's friend replyed to the Confessour that
what hee spoke hee tooke it from his owne self, and not from St. Germain.
By which you may perceive how strongly the Confessour is prepossessed
with the abilities of the Ambassadour (Rouvigni), and how necessary it
will bee by some lucky hitt to gaine the Confessour's beliefe that St.
Germain is not so ill informed and that Coleman hath greater power
than the Ambassadour would have it believed."

Endorsed " No. 55."

[*At the head of the letter*] " by Puckering."

E 64159.

MSS. of Sir W.
FITZHERBERT.

[The SAME] to the SAME.

1676, November $\frac{18}{28}$.—" I am much obliged to you for your letter of the $\frac{9}{19}$ instant. My writing now is but to thanke you for it, having nothing new to send you. No not so much as of the merchants of Antwerp because the Confessor can doe nothing as yett. The Secretarie is gone for six weekes into the country as he sent St. Germain word. The Ambassadour (Rouvigni) is never to bee found. I have not seen Madame de Tremblay this twelve dayes. I have read your letter to St. Germain who was a little surprised at what you tell mee, that Coleman is incognito in the place from whence you writt to mee, and the rather for that the D and Duchess had hidd him goe into the countrey. St. Germain hath paraphrased much thereupon and is a little troubled at it. Putt us out of paine about it, if you can. My lodging being now in the rue St. Antoine at Mr. Warner's, it is but seldome I can see (87) Mr. Gray and his friend, because tis so far off. I am going into the country till newyeares day, but that shall neither hinder you having mine or my receiving of your letters, or doing whatever you desire of mee, as well as if I stayed in Paris, of which I shall not bee very farr off. *The affaire of the pension* concernes Coleman only, and St. Germain wishes that the King of Fraunce would doe something in favour of some of his nephews, according to the letter from the D. of Y. to the King's Confessour. And this something, for example, might bee a good benefice encouraged with a pension in favour of Mr. Coleman, for though the state hee is in may be a hinderance of it, neverthelesse the life hee'd put to it, and the service hee renders to the Catholiques is more than a sufficient *cause to incline the Pope unto it to whom it must* . . .
This is what in my last lettre I thought by your meanes Mr. Coleman should knowe. My last acquainted you with such conceptions as your Ambassador (Rouvigni) and his Confessor had of Mr. Coleman. After that hee may see what kind of people they bee."
Endorsed "No. 56."
(" The Rest of St. Germain's letters abstracted by Sir John Knight.")

[The SAME to the SAME.]

1676, $\frac{\text{December 22}}{\text{January 1}}$.—I have received two letters from Madame de Framlay by your means, and direct the answers to you.
I grow jealous of Mr. Warner who receives letters from you weekly while I live in expectation. The plenipotentiaries parted on Monday.
Three pieces of news are reported from England. Do you know that Father Shelden goes to trade with your incognito ? Do not mention this. He told Ruvigny that he feared Coleman was not his friend on account of the businesse of the Archbishop of Dublin. I presume that what I say to you is the same as if I said nothing.
" Translated by John Reresby."
Endorsed "No. 5."
Two pages of MS. Q. 23, 24, missing.

[*A portion of a letter.*]

"Confessor that the King ought not to do business with Denmark except through 39 (the Duke of York). That friend shall be called hereafter 41 (De Ruvigny) for I have not any name for him in the cypher."

MSS. OF SIR W. FITZHERBERT.

"Translated by Rich. Temple."
Endorsed "No. 3. These first six were perused by Sir Thomas Lee. Altered (?) by Sir John Knight."
"St. Germaine's letters to Coleman."

[ST. GERMAIN to E. COLEMAN.]

1678, October $\frac{5}{15}$. "Pour avoir voulu defendre le Duc de York pendant six mois on me siffle maintenant quand j'avois parlé ; Pour me restablir il faut que Colman m'en donne les moiens en me donnant des avis justes. Vous me dites que le Duc de Bouquinquam [Buckingham] a fait de sa teste dessein ce qu'il a fait, et cependant on me dit hier qu'il va Ambassadeur en Espagne ; comment cela s'accorde il ? Laiton partit de France depuis deux jours pour Angleterre ou qu'il sera Secre. du Duc de Bouquinquam en Espagne si ce l'est Roy d'Angleterre est l'intelligence de tous."
Endorsed "St. Germain's last letter to Coleman. Not to be decyphred."

INSTRUCTIONS.

"A French paper intituled Instruction."

. . Sa M^{tie} tres Xtian avoit grand envie de m'envoyer eu Angleterre mais quel n'osoit pas de peur de donner quelque ombrage et qué pas la mesme raison il ne m'osoit pas encore parler de sa propre bouche, mais quil me prioit de vouloir assurer son Altesse par quelque secret moyén que sa Matie pran[ds] part en tout ses interests et quil luy servira en toút ce que luy tenu . . . . fort p[er]suade que my Lord Ar : nest ny dans les entiro . . . de sa Ma^{te}, ny dans cettes de son Alt. quoy que quelques uns travaillient a luy persuader ny que le reassemble de cette Parli^{mt} peut estre utile pour le R : Britanique ny pour son Alt : quoyque my Lord Ar : par ces ag[en]cey veut soustenir &c. si doney son Altesse le droit a propos d'avoir une l'arl . . . quil luy assistera de sa bource pour en faire une telle comme il souhaitte, et quil luy prie de luy vouloir faire des propositions la decrés oú súr aucune chose quil jugerait apropos et utile estans resolú de faire tout son possible pour son service. Le Pere me dit encorre le friponery de Mons. de Sesaite et la follie des quelques autres des nostres mais que non obstant tout cela, et ausi quoy quil que sa Ma^{te} scient fort bien qúe son Alt avoit envoyé en Flandres, le quelle en verite donnoit en peu d'ombragé non obstant tout cela sa Ma^{te} estoit resolu de confier entierement en son Alt : et luy donner toute l'assistance imaginable, mais qúe súr toút il prioit son Alt : qué par ces soins et ses complaisances l'tacheroit de confirmer une perfaite intelligence avecq son frere. Il me disoit de[p]lus qué si Mr. de Ruevigny nestoit pas un home a votre gré, ne en la quelle on poúvoit avoir toute la conféance, que S : A : n'avoit que me donner les moindres ordres pour le fair scavoir a sa Mt. . . '. un tacheroit y envoyer une personne comme . . . . "
[*This is the end of the sheet.*]
Endorsed "Num. 41. Instructions."

LETTERS. 1675 and 1676.

W. LEYBOURN from Rome to E. COLEMAN.

AN EPITOME OF THE SAME. [*Original.*]

MISCELLANEOUS LETTERS.

[*The following portion of an Epitome of many letters, apparently
from W. Leybourn to E. Coleman, is the only part extant.*]

" particularly to Lord Arundell. I long for your next because it
promiseth much which straitnes of time made you omit in your last.

" July 10.—My last which was by the last post acquainted you that
the letter of the Duke of York to the Pope was received. The good
man in reading it could not abstain from teares. Cardinal Norfolk doth
[*illegible*] answer, will shortly be sent, though upon the matter it
hath been done anticipatedly. Greater tenderness with expression of
kindnes and esteem could not be expected as you are desired to signify.

" July 16.—What hath come to your mind concerning a match with
the Prince of Florence and our Lady Ann deserves better reflexions
than I am able for the present to make of it. Setting aside the interest
which might move the Duke of Florence to desire it, I am verily
perswaded that the greate respect he hath for the Duke of Yorke would
set a great weight upon his inclination to carry him towards it. I had
yesterday a letter from the Duke of Florence who continues his pressing
earnestnes for compassing the busines which hath been so often mentioned. I doubt it may linger a great while if such a reason be expected
as may satisfy the enemies of religion. I thinke it might suffice to
alledge that Mr. Plat is very unwelcome to the Duke of Florence.

" July 30.—The court here will not be well pleased till the new
difficulties which obstruct the peace of Nimeguen be removed.

" July 24.—Mr. Gr[ane] is your servant this day he bath a brief of
the Pope in answer to the letter of the Duke.

" August 6.—These must acknowledge the receipt of yours dated
June 28 and July . . . . The postscript in one of them was very
welcome for the satisfactory matter it gave me for a letter to the Duke
of Florence after two weekes silence to the point he is so much
concerned for. The same post did also bring me a letter from Lord
Arundell to the same effect, which I shall thank him for shortly.
Cardinal Norfolk hath writ to the King . . . sent a letter from the
Queen of Sweden desiring him to take her . . . . protection in the
treaty in Nimeguen. Reasons to prove the J . . . . . [*End of page.*]

[*The beginning of another page.*]

" pretences are sent to Mr. Cook. Cardinal Norfolk would be well
pleased if Mr. Coleman would promote this interest with the Duke.

August 13.—I have had thanks this week from the Duke of Florence
for the account I gave him the last of what was contained in letters
from Lord Arundell and Mr. Coleman about Mr. Platt.

August 20.—We have had this week three from you, one of them
gave hopes of a letter from the Lord Arundell. I am indebted to our
friends in Fleet Street for two letters.

September 11.—A brief was sent last year dated about the moneth of
May, and carried from hence by an Irish Bishop. Cardinal Norfolk
would know if it were delivered to the Queen, the answer was late
expected. Cardinal Barbarin is in pain to know whether a picture
which he sent to her R[oyal] H[ighness] hath been received.

November 20.—Yours of October 5 and 8 found me in the country
with Mr. Gra[ne], tomorrow we return to Rome. I am sorry that my

letter of September 11 as to that part which was in cypher, after the
trouble it had given you, proved at length not intelligible. That which
Cardinal Norfolk would know if delivered to the Queen was a brief sent
to her from the Pope last yeare about the moneth of May and given by
Cardinal Norfolk to an Irish Bishop who not passing by England
delivered it to the Lady.

November 28.—The confidence with which Mr. Coleman ends his
letter to the Prin . . . doth much please, but that delivered by
Mr. Cann in naming . . . to Dutches Lauderdale the correspondent of Cardinal Norfolk is · . . . . wondered at. I hope Mr.
Coleman will on this accident judge . . . necessarry to proceed
with more caution and send a false name to write to him. Cardinal
Norfolk hath had some answer from Portugal but no resolution, England's
competitor is not Ca. Destrè but Rospi[gliosi] to whose unkle the
Prince and Princess of Portugal owe their . . .. [one word torn
off] December." [End of page.]

" December 18.—We are told the Duke of Modena intends a journey to
London. Cardinal Norfolk will to his power second the demand which
Barberine is to make in behalf of Prince Renaldo, he saith that concerne was never touched by the Duke or Dutchess in any letter to him,
nor did the Dutchess of Modena when she was here seem to relish it
much.

"January 1, 1678.—The letter of the Duke to the Pope about the
marriage of his daughter to the Prince of Orange hath been delivered.
I confess the Pope remains satisfied that the Duke was in no fault, but
in his intended answer will not touch the poynt. The busines of the
Prince Rinaldo I fear is not yet ripe.

"October 1, 1678.—Intercepted. This week's post brought but one
from you under date of August 23. It was almost overtaken by an
express dispatched from Nimeguen by the Pope's Nuncio who yesterday
morning brought the welcome news of a peace made between France
and Spayn. His Holiness went the afternoon to St. Marie Major to
thank God for that publick benefit, and Te Deum like to be sung."

[W. LEYBOURN to E. COLEMAN.]

[1676], April 17. Rome.—There is little to write of. Mr. Gr[ane]
sends thanks for your weekly favours, and desires me to let you know
that the Duke's letter to the Pope, given to Mr. Cou, has miscarried.
The nuncio at Paris acknowledges the receipt of the packet in which
it was and says he sent it on. The Cardinal of Norfolk has informed
the Pope and Cardinal Cibo who says the only remedy now is a
duplicate.

Things go on slowly as usual in the palace. It is reported that the
Pope will shortly call to town some of his kindred and confer honours
upon them without salaries. Your wise men much mistake foreign
occurrences. There is no truth in the story that his Highness was
expected in a few days in Florence, and Sir Bern. Gascoyn had been
sent by the Duke to meet him at the frontier. Other reports concerning England are equally untrue though affirmed confidently. The
Pope has lately given small pensions to the Cardinals. It is said the
Cardinal of Norfolk has for his share 1600 crowns, part whereof will
expire at the end of 6 years, according to the style of pensions given
upon benefices in Spain and Portugal. This help it is thought bears
but small proportion to his necessities. " But in this interested country
and thrifty pontificate any little provision of this kind is thought considerable."

W. LEYBOURN to E. COLEMAN.

[1676,] May 2. [Rome.]—I have received your letters of March 17 and 20. The two preceding letters were lost, having been taken a few leagues from Brussels.

the Duke's
" What you wrote of   115   being advanced one step towards the
Card. Norfolk
R. C. religion was a most welcome news to   990   who pre-
Pope   Card. Altieri
sently rejoiced 150 and   330   with it, and now your's of the
Card. Norfolk our Pope   Card. Altieri's
27 hath fully compleated,   990   150   and   330
the Duchess's
joy with it, as also   70   mother and grandmother who are in
Rome   Card. Norfolk
55 and   990   presently acquainted, noe wonder if fooles
take like fooles and knaves like themselves. Your correspondent I
assigned you is your humble servant, but wee will not aiwaics too often
trouble you with superfluous expensive letters, specially myself who am
the Duke
mightily streightned for want of time. My humble duty to   115
the Dutchesse
who I will serve unto death the best I can as also   70   who I
Catholique
hope will bring forth a happy   200.   Some are anxious to know
who will be Godfathers and Godmothers."

The SAME to the SAME.

1676, May 16. [Rome.]—" I receive together your two of Friday
the Duke
the 7th and Munday the 10th Aprill, being much rejoyced   115
the Duke
doth soe well not doubting of God's blessing, but if   115   or
Duchess   the Archbp. of Dublin   Rome
70   employ   28   or his adherents in   55
Catholique
it will but confound them and the   200   affaires with chymericall
Rome
visions, which at   55   are not esteemed more then to spoyle
Rome   Benedictine
reall affaires. Neither will   55   esteeme a   831   comeing
on such things as belong not properly to his trade, but suppose
his businesse is to gett a little money for himselfe, which is not soe
Prince Rinaldi's   Card. Norfolk
easily parted withall. And as to   634   affair   990
hath twice (although nobody ever spoke to him of it) spoken earnestly
about, but as affaires stand nothing can at present be done for many
Card. Fr. Barberine
reasons, and you may be sure that   31   who hath soe long
the Dutchesse Mother   Rome   Card. Norfolk
endeavoured it, and   78   now at 55 and   990
will doe their best when a fitting time and occasion will bee, without
Archbp. of Dublin
others foolish impertinent busy bodies; and as to   28   pre-
Duke
vailing with 115 in his late resolution, few or none will beleive it here,

he being so used to write falsehoods and forgeries, that his saying it MSS. OF SIR W. FITZHERBERT.
maketh it not beleived, but if it were soe de bono opere non lapidamus
te. He did his duty for which God recompense him. And as to what
Mr. Sheldon   the Archbp. of Dublin
37   pretends to say in the other point betwixt   28
                              Rome
and his [*one or two words torn off*] 55 needeth not such learned
witts to teach those who know·bet[ter] [*one or ·two words torn off*]
have already as foolishly been fidling, but neither fidler nor fidlestick
is regua[rded]. They may teach fooles to dance if they can, for that
tune soundeth not . . right where a better is used. The best
            Mr. Sheldon   Duke   Dutchesse
employment   37   can for 115 and   70   is to become
a Benedictine
        83   and pray for them quietly whilest haveing nothing else
to trouble you withal at present I am yours as you know."

                    [The· SAME to the SAME.] ·

[1676,] June 20. [Rome].—No news.
                        the Pope   Pr. Rinaldi   a Cardinall
" Whatsoever I can with   150   for   634   being   346
                                    .   the Dutchesse
I shall doe my best in, and I am glad   70   will write to
the Pope   .   .
        150, ·which if·ever before done it's a wonder it was not delivered
        Card. Altieri   .
as   330   (who should know) tels me, but when this cometh I will
        .   the Duchesse .   .   . ...
deliver it, and tell both. how   70   supposed hitherto a former
                                        the Duke's . .   . | ·
was. Your correspondent will be ready to obey   115   .commands
when he shall be honoured with them, and certainly hath good abilities
                            a Bishop   England
for it. The new invented reports of   436   for   251   are chymeras,
                                        the Benedictine
that baveing long since been disposed of, although   . 831 ·· . and
                                            England
others played the fooles to stop the execution of it in: 251,   when it
was not intended to be made use of ·but in due time, which others (at
            the Benedictines
least as good as   . 831 : ' ·.and the Caballers) ought to judge, and
when due time will be the same party, per ·so vel per alium, vel alios,
                                    the Benedictines
may doe what will be to be done, for since   831 ·   could not
        a Bishop   Bishops
gett to be   436   they would have two   436   in hopes to be the one,
                                Ireland   Armagh
which would be altare contra altare, as in   10   betwixt 90 69 79·(?)
    Dublin
and · 28, but would be ever pejor priore, soe that they may set their
minds and tongues at rest, and look well to what is committed to them.
The French fired the Spanish and Holland shippes and galleys · at
Palermo most shamefully as I suppose you·will·heare·more particularly
from others. They say many of English ·marriners· were with the
French & . . · Yours as you know.".
· [*The figures given as* l· *in these·letters· may be* 4'*s*.]

: original letter, of which this is an exact copy, is also in this
on. The interpretations of the cypher numbers are in a different

A Note.

ie letters next following were written from the same place (Rome)
. Leybourn to Mr. Coleman. Mr. Leybourn is said to have been
ine of a Secretary to the Cardinal of Norfolk."

[On the same page and in the same hand.]

W. L[EYBOURN] to E. COLEMAN.

76,] September 5. [Rome.]—" Sir, I found in one of your last
, to Mr. Grane a desire of more punctuall correspondence from
ien ordinary whilst the conclave sitteth. This desire shall be
yed with so farr as it is possible for me, but I feare your
ity will not thereby remaine fully satisfied :
*he following upon a loose sheet seems to be the continuation
iis letter.]*—Satisfied. Those within the conclave, who look
religiously upon their obligation, keeping their secrets to them-
; and amongst the great variety of reports which fly abroad it is
easy to distinguish truth from falsehood. I shall therefore be
ng in delivery of such particulars, leaving you to the publick fame,
h in the case may upon the matter be relyed upon as well as the
igence of those who pretend to have the best information. You
ind here the list of the Cardinalls, which you desire, ranged under
severall parties or heads, but the order of their promotions is not
tly observed, especially in the creatures of Altieri and Urbini (?)
before the other of the same name dyed was called S. Sisto)
ld bee in the fourth place, and Batadonne in the 9th. There may
ber pretenders to the Papacy besides these which are mentioned,
marke those which are most remarkeable.

inal Norfolk	hath	received	letters	from	the	King & Duke
990	89π8	0774ω2	ϙ4π49φ	09λϵ	500 9y2	115

yning	his	adherence	with	France which	he
δyxys	8xφ	9284⊙4y74	Lxπ8	152⌐8x78	84

eereth	by	this	post	that	to	the Duke	the Secre
⌐404π8	38	π8xφ	μλφπ	π89π	πΛ	115	21λ6⌐xⱮxφϟ

| he Duchess will see. |

π89παπλ113   I refer you to other particulars to
                my Lord Arrundell and   Cardinal Norfolk
. I have writ unto   ϵδⱮx02 9θιωy241 9y2   990

Mr. Hayd. Car. Norfolk will not accept the offer from
  ϵθ ϧ984φ   990   ⌐xⱮ yλπ 9774μδπ π84 λ649 69λϵ
ce of Albi, dreading the dependence which would follow
2 λ6 9⌐3x 2θϟ92xyϛ π84 z4μ4yzϟy74 ⌐8x78 ⌐λⱳⱮz 6λⱮⱮλ⌐
ke offer from Spaine hath been refused
tL 4 λ664φ 69λϵ   125   89π8 344y θ46ϟφϟ2. Many are of
on the conclave will last long, especially if the Freneh persist in
animosity against Altieri, who will be able in spite of them to
er the election of any whom they would endeavour to have chosen
out his concurrence. It would be a great service to the
ch if this quarrell (which seemes to have no deep bottome)
taken up. The present conjuncture seems most proper for it
Car. Norfolk might be a proper instrument
     990   ϵxϟ8π 349   μθλϟθ xyφπθxϟ4yπ I hear our

countryman the Cardinall of Norfolk hath his health well in the MSS. OF SIR W
FITZHERBERT. Conclave, and gaines much in the opinion of his brethren. As matter occurres to feed your curiosity you shall hear further from your most humble servant W. L."

The SAME to the SAME.

1676, September 21. Rome.—"Sir. The letters which came from you the last week had been acknowledged and answered by the ordinary way, had not the expectation of the great businesse perfected this morning made mee willing to deferre writing two days longer. Cardinal Odeschelechi is the person on whom the great lott is fallen by an unanimous consent of the electors, and who was designed before by a general desire of the people: the two great Catholick Monarchs concurring likewise in the election by their approbation of it, we have reason to promise ourselves that great matters will be done in his pontificate for the advancement of Catholick religion. Wee want here noe more at present to render our joys compleat then to bee assured that your Mistresse is happily delivered of a young Prince. This wee hope will be the subject of your next letter which therefore is expected with great impatience. My Lord hath by the currier who carries these writt both to your Mistresse and the Duke. You neede not be put in mind how requisite it is that the Dutchesse lose noe time in this occasion, but write with what convenient speed she can to his Holinesse, from whom she may promise herselfe all expressions that ought to be expected of a most tender and fatherly affection. The time I have for writeing of this is stolne from other businesses, which now calling for it againe oblige me to subscribe &c. &c.

Card. Norfolk judgeth it necessary that the Duke write also to
    990   xω234π8 xπ γ474φ908 π89π   415   Lθxθ4 94φλ. θλ
the Pope and that the Dutchesse Southampton
    450   and that 21 λ670   may doe well to propose.
What was writt in the last letters concerning Prin. Rinaldi will be taken into serious consideration. Greater difficulties are to be overcome then you there, without a long discourse, will easily be perswaded of. However the person to whom the businesse is recommended will not be wanting on his part."

[*In the margin.*]

(This last P.S. is writt with the Cardinall's hand.) "Just now I understand of the Dutchesse delivery of a Princesse, which I told the Pope and all the Cardinalls of, who are all very glad. · The Pope's name is Innocentius XI."

[*Copies.*]

[*A line has been run through all the cyphers in these letters which makes some of them difficult to determine.*]

ALBANY to ———

1674, June 5. Brussels.—"Jay receu ce mesme jour nosne lune du 22 de passe, qui est la seule que j'ay recen depuis nosne depart. Je suis marry d'entendre que Mrs. Clement agree mon service et attend avec beaucoup d'impatience les occasions de luy faire paraitre le zele que j'ay pour cela. Obligez moy de le . . . . des nouvelles de ce qui se passe par de la dont je vous auray une obligation tres sensible."

Endorsed "de Monsr. Gabriel. 9C0."

ALBANY to ————.

1674, September 4.—" Je suis fort marry d'apprendre par votre lettre du 14 du passé que les affaires de M. Clement continuent dans le mauvais penchant qu'elles ont fuis et qu'on doutoit si fort du mauvais succés de son procés. Je suis tousjours dans la curiosité de scavoir si le rapport s'en fera au mois de Novembre et vous prie de m'en mander les particularites le plus distinctement que vous pouvez. Je n'oublie pas l'advertissement que vous m'avez laissé touchant vos lettres lorsque vous fustes icy mais il no m'a pas esté d'ancun usage jusques à cett heure. Obligès moi de la communication de vos nouvelles le plus souvent que vous pouvez et croyez que je suis plus que personne du monde."

Endorsed " No. 7. "

ALBANY to ————

1674, September 28. Brussels.—I have received this weeke two of your letters, dated the 4th and the 7th of this month by which I understand in what condition the Duke's process is. I was ravished to find by the last that the tryal will be put off to another tyme, against the generall opinion. Without doubt this will extreamly rejoice the Pope and the Emperor whereof the first imployeth all his power, to accomodate the differences betweene Spaine and France, and I doubt not but the consideration of contributing by this meanes to the advantage, of the Duke and of the Catholiques, will further incite him to solicite this affaire upon the relation which the Nuncio, will make to the Pope of the importance of its successe for the Catholiques of England.

As for the Emperor he is soe zealous for the Duke's service, that I am assured he will omitt nothing on his side to facilitate whatever he shall find tend to the good issue of this affaire, whereof I will write to him particularily. Continue only to impart to me all the light that may serve to direct what it is to be treated on, I hope the next winter will give opportunity for more happy negotiations even to the mediation of the Pope, whoo hitherto hath not beene able to act att all as you have knowne from other partes.

Endorsed " No. 9."

[*At the head of the letter* (17), *and*]. " Translated by Humphrey Murch."

———— to ————

1674–5, March 16.—" Truly I am soe great a blockhead that what you think needed not have [been a] mistery to me would have continued, soe I am confident till Doomsday without this eclarsisement for I must confesse it should have been the last thing I should have guest you should make a secritt of for I should never have imagined it should have been a hazard to have said I could not read that letter. I am sorry you had not my two letters, I sent them you in the Abbot's packett, you must not lett them bee lost, for besides that I write very freely in them there is a letter from the old Gentleman to the Duke inclosed in one of them. What you understand not about allowing my cause the Duke time for the payment, those two mislayd letters will have eclarsised which I will not doubt but you have before this; I am sure I meant it not for any money to bee paid to mee or for mee but onely to pursue that way of writinge and to tell you that I gratiously allowed him his own time and way to doe his own buisnes *after I had don what* I could and what I thought. You are in the right the *Bishop of Dublin* and Lord Arrundell are not without the French King, *as they are then* with the French King and have all that I can do for them to boot [*two words torn*] Duke himself in the posture of his cause to bee sure may MSS. OF SIR W. FITZHERBERT. have employed himselfe all the faire sober honest or wise men of the Parliament his friends on his side who really may stand aloof [from] the French King be joyned with him for the French King's pract[ices] you know whether deservedly or noe ; it is no matter but they are suspected by a great many good men of the parliament family who wish the Duke well and loosing them may be a loss indeed to the Duke. On the other side let us see what advantage the Duke may have being joyned with the French King supposing it heartily and really on the French King's side and that he would employ all his interest in his buisenesse. Money indeed is a cuning sophister and has interest upon a great many of Parliamt. friends, but then they aro such as when they have promised £1000 all you can desire are not to be relyed on, you know those whome money have a power with are the scum of the family who will promise one thing to day and act quite contrary tomorrow, as Ruvigny his predecessor was formerly found to the French King coste, and the one of the other, nor could you believe it unlesse you thought mee such a one too as wee know him to bee, our outward secret is well and hee seeth it very often for hee is not so [great] a foole not to know that I have discovered them, Thrugmorton knows not what to say to Coleman and Ruvigny's discourse nor what judgment to make of Pompone and Ruvigny their proceedinges, to deal freely with you Thruckmorton is nettled at it and thinks the Duke has a great deal of reason to resent it, for what is this discourse between Coleman and Ruvigny to the performing what Pompone promised Thrukmorton, Ruvigny comes now to enquire of Coleman how hee shall place sum trust not to proceed to a tryall and their decisun of all but to stave of the brunt till the French King have made an end with Holland, the Emperor and Governors of the Spanish Neatherlands and then sayes hee to the King and Duke and all of you, now gentlemen do what you please. Ruvigny should be hanged in my poore judgment, durst I . . . . the Duke or Coleman before I would say a word to him or help him in the least but after all that has been said send to Pompone . . . [*a different hand*] Pompone promised Throckmorton not to dare trust the Duke with £100000 or half £100000 his interest but comforting to Coleman whom to lay out abroad pec . . to an attorney. I say againe mee thinks I would show them I could drive on my interest without them and leave the heretick's whelp to follow his, and if the Duke and Coleman doe not find their account by these and if it should happen soe againe the Duke were in a worse condition than ever, besides hee shall have the . . . to have trusted to people who have used him ill and would trust him noe more than a common solicitor of that cause ; that is my sentiment I must confesse, if there be hazard in all sides I would choose that way that I might perish the more honorably. I shall submit however and shall if I can take some handsome opportunity of speaking to Pompone ; as to my friends you speak of I have told you in mine last post how it was with me.

" They are not people who I must pretend to governe or propose things abruptly to I loose my credit with them then, but as I have already told you if once they were handsomely introduced and received by the Duke I am sure they and what they had would lye at his feete."

Endorsed " No. 36." [*And a few signs.*]
[*A copy.*]

[St. Germaine to E Coleman.]

1675, April 13.—" I hear that Capt Bourgh, by whome I wrot fell sicke by the way, I know not therefore if you have received it yet or noe. The

summ of it was to desire you a little to consider what I were best to
doe, you are the properest to judge how I may serve my [cousin] A the
Duke or whether I may be serviceable att all or noe, for that way, a pro-
hability of it, soe I have but bread to keep me alive, I prefer before all
other things in the world. But supposing I could not be usefull in that I
have I thinke but two things to propose to myself, and those I mentioned to you and desired your direction for my choise, it is either to
retire or to endeavour to push my fortunes in the wars abroad. For the
first I told you (though I hope I should bear it well enough to Germany)
it is not to be done out of gaietie de ceur, and for the second I have
onely Spaine, France, and Holland, to thinke of. For the latter truly I
have noe great minde to it, I hate the people and their cause. For the
second I like them very well but as I told you att large theire troopes
consists of two sorts, eyther natives or foreigners. For the first theire
pay is soe small, that there is never a Collonel who spends not 1500
pistols a peece att least more than the proffitt of the regiment, and that
you know is not for my purpose. For the second they are either
Sweeces, Italians, or our King's subjects. Of these latter there are
foure regiments of which Doughlas and Hamilton are first for Lieu-
tent Collonel to Monmouth which is equall to any other Regiment; and
Churchill I have wrot to you any times these three mouthes about being
assured that neyther Churchill nor Clarke would come over any more,
but heareing nothing from you of it makes me conclude that eyther you
have seen not those letters, or that there is nothing to be done in it, and
consequently noe thoughts of any thing for me in France. Wherefore
then my last hope must be for Spain in which I told you my cousin A.
the Duke's recommendation and help would be verie necessary, and
therefore desired you if things went soe that you thought there could be
noe use of me another way to sollicite my cousin A . the Dukes cause
this turn etc. that you would speak to my cousin A. the Duke about it,
for if I loose this campayne too I must never thinke of souldiering
more, for the lost of two yeares in an active war is never to be recom-
penced in my age, and if war must be my trade I had better lost a limb
then last campayne; but you know I have not wherewithall to volunteere
it any more, wherefore if you judge I am not likely to be usefull to A
the Duke pray try what might by A the Duke's interest be in Flanders,
for it is an idle unacomptable thing for me to be thuse, you will know
my meaning I hope especially if you have my letters, I would not
willingly be such a burthen to you as necessaryly I am without some
hopes of serveing A. the Duke yourselfe as [my] owne self att least by
it, and that I cannot express . . . what I now doe for I cannot soe
much as convince my cousin A. the Duke by this life that I would serve
him, that, I am a little capable of it and that I might share of his good
opinion, at leaste, it hath nothing else to give the same is being ruined
and if I am to begg it shall not trouble me, if I can but serve him, or att
least convince him that I would, and if I cannot doe that I would then
desire you to advise me which of the other two propositions you are
for.

I have been forced to draw the bill uppon Mr. Arthur this post, you
will be pleased to acquaint him with it that it surprise him not.

It is this makes me presse you to advise me, not any other impatience,
for I know if it be likely that I can eyther serve A. the Duke or
my selfe by my stay here you will not grudge any paine uppon that
accompts, but if there be not that I would not presse you for money att
present, and ruine us more if it be possible att last without any
prospect of good to some of us.

I have noe letter these two last posts from you so₂ I have little to say to you, and the trueth is D. S. has kept me three honres this morning, I will see your friends as soone as these great holy days are over. We have here a report that Mr . . . . in the neighbouring of Gent I was told last night that Madam de Montespan has retired herself without the King's knowledge into a nunnery, and thence has writt to desire him never to see her more. There are discants made upon it some that it is zeal and that she intends to change, others that it is only to whet love, what there is of that I know not but the matter of fact I believe is true though I have not been att court, however pray name me not for the author. Pray persuade yourself and Lady that noe body loves you more nor is more your humble servant than I am."

MSS. OF SIR W. FITZMERBERT.

ALBANY to ——

1675, June 3.—" Vous avez deja . . sans doute appris par les nouvelles publiques l'affaire de 220 qui vous servira d'une exposure . . . . de l'affection de 250 aux affaires de 289 dont vous pouvez ainsy . . . une consequence tres assurée de ce que vous desirez esperer quand les affaires de Mr. Clement aurez besoin de l'assistance de 900. Je suis bien aise d'apprendre que ses affaires ne recoivent jusquis a cette heure aucun preiudice dans le proccs [*2 words torn off*] et si servis [*torn off*] . . . . le detail de vos affaires comme vous m'aniez faier esperer par . . . derniere lune de 7 Avril, apres laquelle ie n'en ay pas receu d'aucunes j'en attend avec impatience de recevoir plus que [*torn off*] . . . se depense [*torn off*] ce que ie crois de m'envoyer de nouvelles de Mr. Clement . . . ceque nous luy aurez faier esperer de m'informer tres particulierement de ce que se passe en un moment."
Endorsed " 900."

E. COLEMAN to the INTERNUNCIO.

1675, August 30. Windsor.—" It is true sir that (250) the Pope hath given us a dear and evident mark of his affection toward the (260 of 289) Catholics of England. But (Mousr. Gabriel) the Internuncio hath testified noe lesse in doing justice to the merits of (220) Cardinal Norfolk, which he mentioned in his letter of the 6th of July, since wee have reason to attribute his success to the just (or favourable) character that Monsr. Gabriel (the Internuncio) hath given of him. I doe not at all apprehend that (Monsr. Gabriel) repenteth himself of the good offices that hee hath done him, but that hee will find them recompensed by the satisfaction which hee will receive in his friendship.

" As for (Monsr. Clement) the Duke, I beleeve that hee hath already found the effect of your prayers, and that hee hath almost surmounted all the difficulties which have opposed his establishment. The face of his affairs is well changed, for wee now passionately wish to see the coming on of (125) the Parliament, which wee soe much feared before, and while it was held doubtfull whether we ought to meet or noe, wee employed all our power to bring it on, which point we have gained but within these few days. And for my part I noe ways doubt that wee shall receive as much good by it as wee apprehended of ill, provided that (Monsr. Clement) the Duke, faile not in the execution of the good resolutions which hee hath taken. There is but one thing to bee feared where I have a very great apprehension that can hinder the success o our designes, which is a division amongst the (260) Catholics themselves, which hath already broke out at Paris amongst some (260) Catholics of (289) England touching some difference of opinion in their debates.

" I find that some of them have sent their complaints to (900) Rome to have their antagonists condemned. I have no intimate acquaintance with the person complained of, and I dare affirm that hee hath made . . . ice as many (260) Catholics in (289) England, of those which were [*one word torn off*] before as any other person of his quality, and that hee is as well inclined toward (250) the Pope, and his whole family as the best [of the] accusers, and I assure you hee hath many friends here of the first rank of (260) Catholics, who would not engage in his affaires if they did not believe that hee marched steadily toward the common end, although hee affecteth sometimes to express himselfe somewhat different from some of his brothers. As for mee I beleeve there is too much passion on both sides, and if it shall soe fall out that his enemys prevail against him, and procure his condemnation at (900) Rome, I [am] afraid that divers others will take occasion from thence to fall [upon] many (260) English Papists before (125) the Parliament, desir[ing] its friendship about some extravagant propositions concerning the authority of (250) the Pope, to which the other (260) Catholics ca[nnot] submit; which will give occasion to (125) the Parliament to . . . their conjunction to those who require it upon the conditions before mentioned, that is conditions prejudicial to the authority of (250) the Pope by the hatred which they bear to all the (114) Religion of the (260) Catholics, because they may persecute the rest of them with m[ore] appearance of justice, and ruine the one halfe of them more easily than the whole body at once. Soe that it seemeth to mee that all the (114) Religion should bee much more severely dealt with by reason of their complaint than now it is. It would be very improper in the present conjuncture of our affaires to make any division betwixt the (260) Roman Catholicks of (289) England upon any occasion whatsoever.

" But for my part I doe not perecive any prejudice that can befall (114) the Religion from any of those things against which some persons [seem to] bee soe furiously enraged, because to my apprehension there is n[othing] contained in them, but what hath heretofore been maintained [seem to] of worth and honesty, with the general approbation of the w[hole] world, ard particularly by D. Elizade a Spaniard in his [work] entitled *De forma veræ religionis et invent* . . . .

If you doe not understand the subject of this letter our friend from whose hand you shall receive it will informe you, and let you know the persons and all the matters which have passed betwixt them, and when you shall bee fully possessed of them, and shall possibly come to bee of my opinion that it is necessary to prevent all differences betwixt the Romanists of England at this present conjuncture I hope you will contribute your utmost endeavour to prevent the condemnation of (900) Rome in anything that may occasion a breach among the Catholicks of England. I very well know that Monsr. Clement (the Duke) will hold himselfe much obliged by those who shall concerne themselves in the pacification of this disorder, from whence wee dread soe much mischief, and that (700) the Emperor and (Monsr. Gabriel) the Internuncio cannot performe an office more gratefull to him than to prevent (250) the Pope, or any of his family, to embark themselves in this affair which would raise some dispute among us, &c."

"Translated out of French according to the key received from the Committee of Lords for examining Coleman's papers."

—— to MR. COLEMAN.

1675, December $\frac{11}{21}$. Paris.—" I found your letter at my arrivall at Paris which gave me a most sensible joy to see myself yet in your

MSS. OF SIR W. FITZHERBERT.

remembrance, and more in your favour for which I thank you with all my heart as for a present the most precious I could receive on your parte and I conjure you to treate me as the most pasionate of your friends and the most faithful of your servants. I have spoken con-
62   488
cerning Mr. Coleman to the King of France's Confessor and I found
300
him well disposed to enter into the commerce of the Catholiques, but to
91
tell you the truth I have cause to believe that father Sheldon hath
62   136
made some ill impressions of Mr. Coleman to the King of France as of a person whose advice is too violent to succeed in the traffick wherein
39
the Duke of York is ingaged. I will endeavour to discover the truth in a little time, they have expressed to me a great desire to help the
300   . 39
Roman Catholiques and the Duke of York in their business but it's feared that some merchants that are come to thwart them should not
163
alter the King of France as to the point of money for they say they see noo fruite of it, and moreover there are some that doe much decry the
39   163
Duke of York in the mind of the King of France as if he had no creditt at home little feared and less capable to execute anything; you may believe me, if I am deceived send me word exactly what there is to be said in it for they will heare me, and I hope to speak with the
163
King of France in a few daies; you know who I am. I salute Madam your wife, my respects to all my friends, I am come hither the day before yesterday which was Thursday and I write to you to-day being Saturday, my letter ought to be with you on Wednesday or Thursday, Sir 'tis your humble servant Dr. Ponthieu for it is soe that you ought to write the adress of your letters for me, I am at the College of Dermont in St. James Street. I think you had best address your letters to me myselfe without passing them through the hands of Mr. Warner. The letter that was given you was not from Madam
88
Ruvigny but from Madam de la Tremblay who writt to me from
163
Paris. I tell you again that the King of France is not resolved to
41.
recall Mr. de Ruvigny from the traffick he hath engaged him in; he knows he hath done more hurt than good, but other considerations retard that affaire. One of your friends says that he will see if he can
62
make him understand things; but Coleman must unfold to me very well what he aimes at and the meanes to arrive to it; the same friend says
163
alsoe that he hath made the King of France his Confessor conceive that
163   160
the King of France ought not to doe any business with Denmarke but
39
by the meanes of the Duke of York and he promised & hath engaged
488
himself upon his life to the Confessor to make all things succeed soe

MSS. OF SIR W.
FITZHERBERT.

they go by that way. Hath he done well, and doe you know that friend?
41.

He shall be called hereafter Monsr. de Ruvigny for I know not any name for him among your cyphers."

"Translated by Richd. Temple."

Superscribed for Mr. Coleman, Secretary to Her Royal Highness."

[*Endorsed*] " No. 3. These first **six** were perused by Sir T. Lee. St. Germain's letters."

———— to ————

1675, December $\frac{15}{25}$. Paris.—" I cant help writing to you againe this weeke, having two things to communicate to you, one is that I've seen Father Sheldon, who dessignes to goe and transact concealed in your country. He thinks to begin his journey in 8 or 10 days, but take no notice of this for feare it be known who told it you. He would by all means that I should carry him to wait upon the King's Confessor where he uses his own uttmost endeavours as also the interest of every body besides to ingratiate himselfe he will not be thought a marchant and therefore weares a sword and lodges with the Archbishop of Dublin. They both of them as I am told presse forward that businesse whereof he writ to you, and which you communicated to me. The other thing is that the King's Confessor told us that the King of France did think in good earnest to recall Mr. de Ruvigny from the management of his affairs in England. But Father Sheldon does not like him that is to be sent in his roome, because he says he is not of those men hero which are most fitt for our designs, altho he be very dextrous, and I am of his mind as well for that reason as for others which I know which I cant tell you as yet. Therefore if you'l tell the Duke if there be any man for the purpose here which he approves of, he needs but signifie it to Mr. Ruvigny and heo'l work so with the King's Confessor that it shall be effectually proposed to the King. This would be a great advantage to the designs of the Catholicks. I expect to hear from you. I saw my Lady Throckmorton yesterday, who came to Paris to ly in, and goes back to Pontoise within few days, she has gott a paine in her leg, which has continued since her lying in. My most humble service to Mrs. Coleman be known ike to nobody else because I dont think it necessary it should be known I write to you so often.

[*In another hand at the beginning*] " Duncombe."

[*An original letter.*]

DE PONTHIEU to ·————.

1675, December $\frac{3}{13}$. Calais.—" It is impossible for mee to abstaine from writing to you any longer; I do not know how I stand with you, but I assure you that I ought to be extremely well thought of having never done anything in relation to you that could render mee unworthy of the friendship which you have allways had for me; and I dare even say that I have always done things so as to merito still more. For all this will you not take it ill if I speak freely to you, me thought I saw all your kindnesse towards me grow somewhat cold the very last moments of my stay in England; and I was fully resolved to clear this point before my departure, had it not been so precipitated. God did not permitt it, and our will must yield to his; yet remember that I am unsatisfied in the matter; and nothing is able to cure me, if you have not the goodnesse to show me some real marques of the same confidence with which you were heretofore pleased to honour me; and which made MSS. OF SIR W. FITZHERBERT. mee passe soe many happy houres in your company. I carry your cyfers with me, and I tell you of it that this may serve you whether you intend to make use of me, or that you think it fitt to doe otherwise; However in what place soever God puts mee you shall always have a most obliged, most faithful, and most diligent servant. My leaving London without being justified troubles mee much, and would vex me infinitely more if I had not done on my part all that a man of honesty and honour could doe. Think of me as of the person in the world who is most, &c."

Endorsed "No. 2. Nothing."

EDWARD PETERS to MR. TUNSTALL at BURTON.

1677–8, February 23.—"I have but tyme to conveigh these following particulars to you; first I am to give you notice, that it hathe seemed fitting to our Master Consult' provincial to fix the 21st day of April next, styl. vet., for the meeting att London of our congregation on which day all those that have right off suffrage are to bee present there, that they be ready to give a beginning to the same on the 24th day which is the next day after St. George his day, you are warned to have jus suffragii, and therefore in case your occasions should not permitt you to be present you are to signify as much to the end others in their ranckes bee ordered to supply your absence; everyone is minded also not to [hast] into London long before the tyme appointed nor to appear much about the Towne till the meeting bee over, least occasion should bee given to suspect the dessigne. Finally secresy as to the tyme, and place is much recommended, to all those that receive summons, as it will appear of its own nature necessary. 3° pro Domino Solono debito Benefact. prov. Linensis.

I am so straitened for tyme that I can only assure you I shall bee truly glad of obliging you any ways.

Sn yor Servant E. D. P.

Postscript.—Pray my services where due."

[*A copy.*]

"SOME NOTES OF EVIDENCE."

1678, October 29.— (fol. 101) "Coleman acknowledged that Lord Lords' journal. [*Three lines of shorthand.*] A[rundel] of W[ardour] knew of Coleman's going over to the Internuncio at Brussels.

1678, November 8.—"Lord Arundel does not deny it." [*This entry is crossed out.*]

"Lived with Mr. Coleman as his footman for about a year and half John Tewdor. before his imprisonment, in which time his Master did frequently visit my Lord Ar[undel] of Wa[rdour], sometimes once or twice in a day, and in the afternoon of the day before his apprehending his master was twice at my Lord's, and he was that afternoon allso with Mr. Wright.

"The 8 following receipts and papers, among others, were found in Tis said Bradley seized them. my Lord Ar[undel] of Wa[rdour's] possession.

"Three several receipts given by J. Fenwick, dated 15 February, 1675, Boatman and 12 January, 1676, and 23 January, 1677, for three several sums of £25 · · away can prove these hands tis thought. paid by his Lordship for three several years pensions for his grand child Hen: Arundell (or Spenser as he is sometimes called) presumed to be for his maintenance at St. Omer.

"Another paper, which appears to be the same handwriting with [*Six lines of shorthand, struck out.*] the other three, that is Fenwick's, which states the first account

E 64159.   H

MSS. OF SIR W
FITZHERBERT.
———

saying Henry Spenser arrived at ~~Flamsteed~~ St. Omers July 26, 1673, and said he was there at £25 per annum.

Can prove.
(sic.)

"A receipt given July 23, 1678, by William Ireland for £10 paid by my Lord Ar[undel] for my Lord Tenham.

"A receipt given his Lordshipp November 20, 1675 by ~~William Ireland~~ James Corker for £30 being consideration [*one or two words torn off*] due to William Brent Esqr. to whose use and by whose appointment 'twas received.

(sic.)

[*A Shorthand Note.*]

"A like receipt given July 18, 1669 by Henry Latham for £30 due to Brent April 28 before.

"A like receipt given December 1, 1674 by the same for £30, due to him for 6 months allowance for £1000.

"Upon which writings these observations may be made

"1. It hereby manifestly appears that my Lord had such a grandson at St. Omer, which hugely confirms Mr. Otes' testimony.

"2. It shews his Lordshipp had correspondence with Ir : Fe : &c. (tho 'tis mentioned in the Lords journal that he denyed any such correspondence).

"3. In the paper which states the first account about H. Spenser, the word Flamsteed is plainly legible, though there be, as here, a line drawn through it; and then follows the word St. Omer. Now Otes sais Flamsteed was a word of cabal or cypher, to signify St. Omer, and it seems it ran so much in the Jesuits head that he had writt it before he recollected himself, and this too confirms Mr. Otes.

"4. As to the money paid to Mr. Brent's use I know not any observation to be made. I suppose upon the score of the phrase-divinity they would not call it interest or usury, though it was no other.

"5. I adde this observation that upon the 6 receipts dated February 15, January 12, July 23, November 20, July 18, and December 1, there are indorsements titleing or noting the contents of the several receipts, and those indorsements are writ in the same hand that the indorsement on the drawn-bill above mentioned is viz The Act of Parliament drawn by Mr. Attorney &c., supposed my Lord Arundell's owne [hand].

"Give in evidence the convictions in the Oxford circuit, and that of Redding.

JAMES SALGADO to ———.

[*A document of ten pages in Latin purporting to be a letter from Salgado a Spaniard to his spiritual father with a report of a confession made to him as a priest, by one Netterville, a prisoner in the Marshalsea.*]

Netterville had received a message from the Lords in the Tower desiring him to find some man to swear that the Plot originated with the Duke of Buckingham and Lord Shaftesbury. He therefore bribed the man who stole the King's crown (Salgado does not remember the name) to swear to this effect for £500, and the man revealed the whole matter to the King's Secretary. (*Homo taliter conductus totum negotium Regio Secretario revelavit*). Upon this Oates and Bedlow were sent to see Netterville in the prison, and he then expected to be called before the Parliament. In which case he said he would say nothing but that he had heard this story from Father Kelly. While we were talking a woman, a friend of his came into his cell (*cubiculum*) and he spontaneously said this woman has come to me from the Lords in the Tower, because it might excite suspicion if they sent a man.

I then asked him if he would hold to this statement of his intercourse with the Lords, and he in a timid voice cried out Anglice 'O Lord,' I only speak of it to you as a priest.

Then he said that he had procured his freedom from Father Kelly by giving ten shillings security for him and five to the Justice's clerk. That Kelly had been ungrateful, and that his name in prison had been Samuel Mons, or Ormond. I do not remember which it was.

Then he said he was not ready for confession at that time but asked me to come to him again the next morning. He then confessed nothing but that Oates and Bedlow had asked him whence he got the money, and he had answered from Ireland. "Quod satis impertinans ad confessionem existimabam"

Then he said Oates was a villain. That he was always wanting money from the Superior when he was a Jesuit, and had taken up this course of obtaining money when it was refused him by the Superior.

Then he asked me, extra confessionem, when the Lords would be brought before Parliament and said he feared they were in great danger. I asked him how he lived. He answered coldly of his own means or by help of his friends.

This is all. It seems to me that he is supported by the Lords in the Tower. I do not think he is altogether innocent, but I leave him to God.

"In Vine Street at the sign of the Vine near Hatton Garden. Jacobus Salgado, Hispanus."

"PRESBYTER CONVERSUS."

The SAME to the SAME.

By your orders I visited Netterville again on May 3.

He repeated the former statement that he thought the Lords were in the greatest danger, especially because the Earl of Shaftesbury, their sworn enemy, was to be their judge.

He also said that he had obtained the freedom of a certain Russell and Kelly, and that the name of the man who stole the crown was Berry. I pointed out to him that he was not bound to keep faith with heretics, and pressed him to tell me what he had written to the Lords. He answered that he would willingly do so, and that I could safely correspond with Talbot his relative, who is now under arrest in Ireland. He told the woman of his dealings with me, and when I remonstrated he said she was most zealous in the Roman Catholic faith and could be trusted.

"I strongly advise that the jailers should be instructed to watch and apprehend this woman."

[*Copy.*] *Endorsed* "From Sir Thomas Meres."

"MR. JOHN FENWICK'S PAPERS, opened the 5th of October 1678.

1678, October 5 :—

1. A general Alphabet, or list of names and addresses.

2. Another folio for addressing of letters.

3. A general account of receipts and payments of money for the use of young men admitted to the seminaries &c. A thick folio.

4. Another thick folio of accounts of money received and paid in generall, in which Mr. Busby is very often mentioned, where among other particulars there is an entry in August last that £400 was left with R. Hinton, goldsmith, at 5 per cent. to be called in at 20 days notice.

5. Another thin folio, being a list of names and some small money mentioned, marked C.

Two bundles looked through, which contain letters from all parts generally relating to money for the supply of novices at St. Omer's &c.

Also catalogues of their names, and the several forms and classes they
learn in.

Also of their true names and false names, and several addresses to find
out people up and down here in England.

-Reliques with a little book.

Some letters of Mr. Ireland, laid by on purpose to compare his hand.

Some notes of Mr. Fenwick's laid by for the same end.

Also some notes of a letter signed by Titus Oates, laid by for the
same end.

Lists for sixteen counties that show the false names, the true names,
the country's condition, arrival, departure, some of debts due, some of
payments, and the party taking care of each district.

Lists of sums due at St. Omers for the particular parties therein
named.

Bills of exchange (the duplicates) from 1676 to 1678 for £6703 10s. 6d.

· "A minute of several letters found in the papers of Mr. Fenwick,
searched the 5th and 6th of October 1678.

1678, August 18.—Hen. Tas. to Mr. Fenwick.—Chides him for
saying and unsaying the certain price of maintaining lads at St. Omers.

That hereafter he should himself come into the country and agree for
them.

That if Mr. Ireland were then out of towne his letters ought to have
been opened by Fenwick and answered.

A Bill of £106 sent to Mr. Ireland last month.

1678, August 20.—James Butler observes that Mr. Ireland was not
in towne, but it does not appear where his letter was writ.

1678, July 31.—W. Dickfield *Smith* adviseth that they are busy
among their countrymen in the hospitals, snatch some out of the enemy's
claws at the last gasp.

April 24.—Father Penington tells . . . how zealous he is, and
hopeful the work, if assisted.

1677-8, February 13.—A letter from Ignatius Pippard. Mem. under
this name go letters to Peter Talbot.

1677, May 9.—From Alanson at St. Omer to Fenwick, that he
should disperse some papers on the recess of the Parliament.

1668, July 25.—From Charles Stanner to Richard Bannister, how
£1500 was given to them by one Roger Manners.

1667, June.—Extract of Mr. —— letter to Fenwick about £6000
given by the Lady Mordant to be laid out at Holywell. And another
paper by Fenwick.

1677.—Copy of the Will of William Peters, son of Sir Francis Peters,
Bart. Gives all his estate, real and personal, to Peirce Butler, Edward
Coleman, and William Gawers. Revoking all other wills.

1678, May 22.—Mr. Thimbleby, alias Ashby, from St. Omer, talks
of April's assignations, then he complains that Mr. Coleman fails to
send his news letter which was expected so long, as his nephew was
there on free cost.

1678, September 6.—Mr. Lewis tells Mr. Fenwick of a mission newly
sent, one Henry Powell.

The lad now in custody.

1678, September 13.—From . . Clare at St. Omer to Richard
Thimbleby, by which it appears this man was returned from the Bath.

An account of the rents of some marsh lands near Feversham.

1678, August 25.—From Stapleton, rector of St. Omer to Fenwick. Touching a mission to Sevill (which may be Crump now in Newgate). That Mr. White was hard at work, and making all haste over; Carey was preparing to go on to Rome.

That if from this hemisphere he could discover a storm threatening, though afar off, make what haste you can over that we may at least reap some fruits of our labours and expenses, by a good use of that which they have produced.

Nil mihi rescribas attamen ipse veni.

Mons is not relieved, which is a sign the Confederates fall short of their aim.

1678, September 29. Stapleton to Fenwick.—If you please to inform Mr. Blundell of —— you would oblige me. Be sure your next brings us good news of our master.

From MARYLAND.

1678, June [or January] 12.—Mr. Forster writes to Mr. Fenwick a large account of 24 reconciled &c. and then a full state of their temporal —— what land, what cattle, what tobacco, what debts, and where.

1678, April 19.—A letter from Samuel Terrill to Fenwick. He appears to have some office in the custom house.

1678, August 7.—A letter from Edward Preswick to John Groves about a "box of oyles," and some marked C.

Assigning Counsels' parts for the Lords trial.

Mr. Powle - -	To open the evidence.
Mr. Serjeant Maynard - Sir Fr. Winnington -	To peruse the evidence.
Sacheverell - Trencher - -	Lord Arundell.
Col. Titus - Sir H. Capell -	Lord Peters.
Vaughan - Seymour -	Lord P.
Sir T. Stringer Sir T. Player - - Sir T. Meeres -	Lord Bellasis.
Sir T. Lee - Mr. Treby -	Lord Stafford.
Mr. Serjeant Maynard - Sir Fr. Winnington -	To sum up the evidence.

AN ORDER IN COUNCIL.

1679, October 15.—Upon the petition of Thomas Knox that he, being summoned before the Committee of the House of Lords upon information that he had scandalised Mr. Oates, may have certain of his papers which were delivered to the Secret Committee of the House of Commons, and are now in the hands of Mr. Treby, Chairman of the said Committee; it is ordered that the papers be deposited in the hands of the clerk of the Council who shall act upon their Lordships' directions.

The papers were delivered to the Committee on April 29, 1679, and consisted of four letters directed to Mr. Knox, subscribed, W. Osborne, John Lane, dated April 2, 4, 6, 20th.

An Information by Thomas Knox.

One of W. Osborne and J. Lane's relating to his Majesty.

INFORMATIONS, DEPOSITIONS, &c.

1678.   Dec. 24.   *S. Dugdale.*
  „   Dec. 29   „   „
1678-9. Jany. 8, 11, 17, 11–22, 23, 24, 31.
  „   February 12, 21, 21, 24.
  „   March 21, 24, 25, 26, 27.
  „   April 14.
1679.   March 26.   *Bedloe.*

1678, December 24.—" The INFORMATION of Stephen Dugdale gentleman late servant to the Lord Aston of Tixall concerning the Plott
against our Soveraigne Lord the Kinge as followeth.

1. That Informant saith that presently after one Howard, Almoner to
the Queene, went beyond the seas hee was told by George Hopson,
servant to the said Lord Aston, that there was a designe then intended
for the reformation of the government to the Romish religion.

2. Hee informeth that in the beginning of September 1678 hee mett
in Tixall nigh the Lord's gates the Lord Stafford, who said to this
informant it was sadd that they were troubled for that they could not
say their prayers but in a hidd manner; but suddenly there would be a
reformacon to the Romish religion, and if there .was but a good
successe they should enjoy their religion. And upon the 20th day of
Sept. last, the said Lord Stafford told the informant that there was a
designe in hand, and if hee this informant would undertake the designe
hee should have a good reward and make himselfe famous.

3. Upon the aforesaid day immediately after this informant went into
the chamber of Mr. Francis Wrie, *alias* Evers, a Jesuite in Tixall, and
asked him what the Lord Stafford meant by those words and after hee
had made him to sweare secrecy upon his knees hee told him hee might
be a person employed in the worke and make a good reward, that would
make him famous, and hee then told him hee must be instrumentall in
taking away the King's life, and that it should be done by shootinge or
otherwise and that this informant need not to feare for the Pope had
excommunicated the Kinge, and that all that were excommunicated by
him were hereticks, and they might kill them and be cannonised for
saints in soe doing.

4. This informant saith that the said Evers and Hopson both said
that the designe was as well to kill the Duke of Monmouth as the
King.

5. That George North (nephew to Pickering and servant to the Lord
Aston) lately told this informant that they had taken his uncle (meaning Pickering) and putt him into Newgate and thought the King
deserved such an execrable death as was intended him, because of his
whoreing and debauchery.

6. That Mr. Evers said Mr. Bennifield had a packquett of letters
delivered to him from the Post house which he fear'd the Lord Treasurer
had notice of and therefore had delivered them to the Duke of Yorke
and the Duke delivered them to the King and that the King gave them
to the Treasurer after hee had read them, but that the King did not
believe them, and therefore it was happye or else the plott had been
discovered.

7. That he had received many packquetts of letters for Evers some
of which this informant broake up and found them to be and tend to
the establishing of the Romish religion.

8. That he had received severall sumes of money himselfe and knew
of diverse others that were employed to putt forth money which was
and is for the Jesuitts use."

MSS. OF SIR W. FITZHERBERT.

[*Endorsed*] "Received at the Committee from the Earle of Essex and there read 24 January 1678-9."

1678, December 29.—"Mr. Stephen Dugdale further saith that since the 20th day of Sept. last the Lord Stafford did promise him £500 as to the carrying on the Plott &c. And that Mr. Evers should give him instructions about the same, and that the Lord Stafford told him he did not doubt of his fidelity, for Mr. Evers had given him a good character to be trusty, and the Lord Stafford further told him that there was a designe to take away the life of the King and the life of the Duke of Monmouth, and that severall other persons were to be imployed in the designe besides this informant. And that this had been throughly considered of, to bee the fittest way for the establishing the Romish religion. And at the same time the Lord Stafford laid his hand upon his head and prayed God to keep him in his right mind and to be faithfull to what he was intrusted in, and forthwith the said Lord went out of the hall in Tixall into the parlour, and further saith that shortly after Mr. Evers imposed the same matters on him this informant and he doubting of the Lord Stafford's payment Mr. Evers promised him the makeing good my Lord Stafford's promise, and told him that Mr. Harcott and Mr. Ireland, Jesuitts, should pay him, who had sufficient in their hands to defray it and other charges whatsoever. And further that Mr. Evers told him this informant that severall gentlemen in the county had moneys in their hands for the carrying on the worke, but were shie to it here but had entred into covenant for it at St. Omers and that hee received a letter from Mr. Warner a Jesuite which did confirme the same and that the said money should be speedily returned into the hands of Mr. Harcott the Jesuitt. And further saith he saw a letter directed to Mr. Evers which he broke upp and read and knowed it to be the Lord Stafford's writing and that therein was written that things went on well beyond seas for the carrying on the designe and soe he hoped it did soe here in England.

And further Mr. Evers told this informant that there were severall Indulgencies for the pardoning those that were concerned in the designe, and these he believes came from Mr. Ireland."

[*Copy. Endorsed*,] "Delivered to the Committee by the Earl of Essex and their read January 4, 1678-9."

1678-9, January 8.—"Mr. Stephen Dugdale aged about 40 years being sworne saith that having been soe lately on his journey he wants a little time and rest to put in writinge the things he hath to informe concerninge the plott, but that he had already written one particular concerninge the Lords Stafford which he presented and thereupon his first deposicon of the 24th December and his seconde deposicon of the 29th followinge was both read and he did in virtue of his oath acknowledge that all the substance thereof was true. Then the paper which he delivered in concerning the Lord Stafford was alsoe read. Hee further saith that he was bred up a Protestant till he was about 20 years old and then beinge persuaded by one Knight a priest to turne Papist he hath ever since remained in that religion. Onely that upon New Yeares day last he once went to the Protestant church, that when the said Knight dyed he delivered him up to the tuition of Evers a Jesuite that lived with the Lord Aston for about 15 years and that by the meanes of the said Evers who had sworne him to secrecy and given him the sacrament for severall times he was brought into great trust amongst the Jesuits and usually called by them honest Stephen and was often in their secret counsells at Boscobell and at Tixall, sometimes in the chamber of Mr. Evers and sometimes in his owne chamber there. And he believes there are some here in towne that can testify how much he was intrusted by them.

That he hath no malice or quarrell to any person and that he was a true loyall subject to his Majestie as any could be till within two yeares last past that he was persuaded by the Jesuit to evill designes against his Majestie, which designes had been on foote for about these six yeares but at last beinge prevailed upon he had willingly engaged and undertaken in the designe of killing the Kinge and was to have come up by order of the Lord Stafford in the beginning of October last upon the promise already mentioned in other papers; unto which he further adds that Mr. Evers told him and he thinkes the Lord Stafford did soe too that if he effected the matter he should have his pardon and be alsoe canonized for soe doinge. That Mr. Evers and Mr. Ireland told him he should be here in London provided for by him the said Ireland and Mr. Harcoat and be sometimes with Mr. Parsons at Standon who knowes all the matter, and sometimes here in London, and that here being come up, he should know more of his company and receive his instructions how to proceed. He saith that Ireland had been with him this summer at Tixall and thereabouts and went so far as Holywell being in all about a month or six weekes in the country, and that he came up before them about the middle of September last and the reason why the examinent followed not in the beginning of October as was intended was because newes came of the discovery of the plot made by Mr. Oates. He further saith that in sometime after the said discovery, when orders and proclamations began to come forth, his feares increased soe much that he complained to Mr. Evers concerninge the danger he might be in and did fear that his name might be put into some of the proclamations. Whereupon Mr. Evers persuaded him first to make his escape into Ireland, he having then mony of his owne and of the Lord Aston's to supply him, but hearing that the ports were shut he did not take that course but being by Mr. Evers advised to run away and hide him where best he could he did the night before he went take severall letters and papers which he stuft in his breeches and going to the house of one Eld that hidd at Tixall he did burne them there in the house of his two daughters Ann and Eliza Eld, this latter being a fellow servant with him at the Lord Aston's, but they knew nothing of their contents but have reported as he heard since the burning of those papers telling one Perrcy the gaoler's wife and others thereof. These papers would he said have revealed much of the business but the next day which was about the 19th of November last he fled, Mr. Evers first telling him that he would excuse it to my Lord and give out, which he himselfe alsoe did, that he was gone to see for money to pay what he had lost to Sir John Crew and others, that hee owed mony unto, being for the most part what he had lost upon wagers of a foote race on the 21st of October; and Evers further said that he would alsoe give out that the examinent was gone about some particular business which he had imployed him in that being gone he went among other places to the house of one John Bond whose neice was his friend and who had five yeares before persuaded him to be a Protestant. That he was in a great fright and did to her begin to impart some little thing of the plot, but she appeeringe much startled thereat he presently denied all againe. This place was about 12 miles from Tixall and here he went and hid in a hay mow from about a houre before day till some part of the night followinge having something brought to him by Robert the servant to eat; that here he sent for two friends to come to him but before they came while he lay in the hay

mow John Bond went forth to enquire what he would hear concerninge
him, and not hearinge of much harme he let him come in and lodge the
rest of the night in his house where he was private in a chamber all the
day following. Then when his two friends came to him they conveyed
him to the widow Walker by a common side near Newton and there
he continued close from Friday to Monday being now nearer home than
before and as then he was drawing towards Tixall in the night he was
about the 3rd December last taken by the watch that were abroad and
carried before a Justice of the Peace, and from thence to Stafford where
they who were his creditors hearing of the trouble he was in and that
if he got free, which he was like to doe, they would hardly get their
mony or see him againe (so much was he noted to be intimate with the
Jesuits who were now spoke of about the plott) that he had actions laid
upon him by all to whome he owed but a groate. That while he did
absent himselfe and before he was taken he did endeavour to get out of
the hands of Richard Gerard Esqre. a certain deed by which he had
made over to the value of £500 of his estate to the Jesuits in case he
dyed without children, they having promised him to say severall masses
for the good of his soule. That his lands were worth about £700 in all
and his debts not halfe soe much, besides he had severall debts owing
to him, but having found difficulty to get this deed backe into his hands,
he did in meeting Arthur Fox, a servant to the Lord Aston, desire him
to go to his Lord to begge his assistance about the recovery of his
deed, for he understood that his Lordship had noe minde to see him
considering the great rumour about the plott. That he did rather
desire when he was taken to draw homewards because he heard his
name was not in any of the proclamations and soe he thought himselfe
safe. That though he had been longe troubled in minde yet he had
noe intention to discover any thinge, untill at last observing by the
proclamation which gave pardon to those that discovered before the
25th December, and alsoe a reward the time was almost out, he thought it
high time to discover, which he did to Justice Lanse and Justice Vernon,
but did it not untill the 24th December, and then did it not for any
profit that was mentioned ; that besides his examination that having
being taken in the country he did informe Mr. Lane of some letters
which he thinkes may yet be found in a place where they were by him
layd at Tixall house and not burnt by him when the rest of the papers
were, and believes they are such as will give some light to this business,
and that Mr. Lane did imploy Mr. William Touthall of Pancarth
according to his directions to finde the said papers out. He further saith
that he hath seen and had severall treasonable letters from Ireland,
Harcoat, and Grote, relating to this business, and seen other letters from
St. Omers and particularly from one Warner, and hath particularly seen
letters from one at Paris whose name he could not recollect. That he
did not know Otes or Bedlow though he had been at the house of
Bedlow's mother who lives at a common near Bristoll, but that he hath
often heard both their names in letters as persons imployed, and
particularly that Bedlow was employed upon severall messages about
letters by William Harcoat the Jesuit ; he further saith that Mr. Evers
did formerly acquaint him that there was here in London the last
summer was 12 months a great meeting of the Jesuits in relation to this
designe and that upon recollection he remembers well the Jesuits had a
meetinge here in London the last springe for that Mr. Evers and other
Jesuits of Staffordshire went up unto it about Aprile. That he knowes
Pickering having lived in the towne where Pickering was borne, and
knowes alsoe his nephew George North that lived with the Lord Aston,
but knowes not that Pickering was employed to kill the Kinge. He saith

that Mr. Evers told him how that Mr. Fowler of St. Thomas was either excommunicate or to be excommunicated for not consenting to this designe being one that was sollicited thereunto. That Mr. Heveringham did consent as Mr. Evers told him to give money thereunto somewhat more that his name might not be put in writing as one who was listed in the designe. Alsoe that one Howard Esqre., son of Sir Robert Howard of Wales, would be instrumentall in giving of mony. Alsoe that one Broadstreet a Priest had actually contributed his mony thereunto and was to be an actor in the conspiracy That Mr. Evers did press him earnestly at the time he went to escape to be secret and keep councell of all and that he should if he were ever brought to examination deny his knowledge in every particular, which he then and when he burnt his papers was resolved to doe. He saith that he was told that Mr. Evers had made his escape out of a window a little from Boscobell on or about Christmas last, he saying that when the Lord Stafford offered him the £500 it was in a roome at Tixall in the Lord Aston's house in the roome where his Lordship lay. That he is not certain whether the Lord Aston be engaged therein, onely he once attending at the doore (to say somewhat to the Lord Stafford about a footmatch, which was a sport his Lordship loved) while the Lord Stafford and the Lord Aston walked together in a longe parlour and the Lord Stafford havinge spoken he heard the Lord Aston reply that there would be much difficulty in the trusting of persons in the thinge; to which the Lord Stafford answered that the Lord Aroundell of Wardour might be trusted and that he was a man with whome he would trust his life. But the examinant doth thinke that the Lord Aston did not consent to the designe, that the greatest debt for which he was clapt up in Stafford is 100 guineas, which he lost to Sir John Crew at the said foote race, and that the other debts are smaller sums which he hath a great deale more than will satisfie having lands and debts due to him, and he presumes that he can here in towne procure baile for all that he owes"

[Copy. Endorsed.] "Stephen Dugdale's examination about the Lord Stafford."

DEPOSITION of STEPHEN DUGDALE.

1678-9, January 11.—" Besides what I have formerly given in of Mr. Evers, I have this more.

That hee at severall tymes, told me that the Pope out of his revenue had graunted summes of money towards the putting the Irish into a condition of opposing the now established government for it was his gracious pleasure to consider what a tyranicall government they lived under ; and I opened a letter to the same purpose which came from Paris, which was directed to Mr. Evers but the person's name I have forgotten, but it was that he had lately received a letter from Rome to confirme that the Pope did still hold his good purpose for the speedy releiving the poore Irish, and that they were considering how to procure them men as well as money, but about that and other things, there would shortly be an expresse from thence to England which would be about the latter end of March and the said Mr. Evers' company was required in London together with Mr. Cottons, Mr. Gavens, Mr. Peters, and Vavasors.

This letter above said was dated to my best knowledge the latter end of February 1677-8, and accordingly Mr. Evers did come to London and Mr. Peters, but whether the other two were there I know not, but I think they were, and when Mr. Evers came home he told me Mr.

Ireland and Mr. Simmons would be in the country the latter end of June for considering the best way and means for the carrying on this great worke as it was soe called.

I doe acknowledge I have severall tymes been with Mr. Evers, Mr. Vasasor, Mr. Peters, Mr. Levison and sometimes Mr. Ireland, at Tixhall and at Boscobell upon adviseing with them which way might be the fittest way for the reformation, and it was alwayes supposed that to endeavour to disturbe the peace in Ireland and Scotland which would be a means to weaken England soe much that their attempt might the easier be managed, which could not be done without good assistance from beyond seas, which as Mr. Gaven said we need not feare, for although they had great troubles of them both in Flanders and France and those countryes there would not be men and money wanting to carry on the designe for the glory of Almighty God which wee need not feare but he had a great blessing in store for us, and with his assistance it will, if we have but patience to waite for his mercyes, bee accomplished. And then our endeavours must be for doeing our parts here which is not only to kill the King and the Duke of Monmouth but as much as we could to lessen the power of the rest. Mr. Peters answered are you sure the gentlemen all be true to us in assisting with money for if that should faile our owne stock would quickly faile. With that I told them I would give an hundred pounds more then that I had made over to Mr. Gerrard which was taken very thankfully with promises that I need not feare to have a free pardon procured for my sinns past and be placed a saint in heaven for all eternity insomuch that I had been instrumentale in soe good and pious a worke. Mr. Vavasor said that those moneys which were neer upp in tyme should be called in. Mr. Jackson being the person chosen out for that purpose and Mr. Evers for the rest near him. And Mr. Evers was appointed to goe to Mr. Draycott, Sir James Simmons, Mr. Hevenhingham, Mr. Peters, was to have received of Gerrard but because he was the priest of the house he desired Mr. Evers he might doe it, who said he would. Mr. Gaven undertook for severall private gentlemen about Woolverhampton some of them asked who must speake to Mr. Howard it was said Mr. Broadstreete. Mr. Evers said he would doe it himselfe, but for Mr. Herbert Aston he was in debt, and therefore he must not be looked on as the rest, but Mr. Vavasor said it was for a good charitable use, God would blesse his increase, and as the money came in it was to be returned into the hands of Mr. Harcott and Mr. Ireland, and hereafter order would be given how it must be disposed of and if any doubt did arise they should repay to Mr. Bennifeild and he would give satisfaction. And at another tyme Mr. Ireland told mee when I came to London he would give me instructions and give me order how I should proceed, to all which I did seem to be very well content, and did protest I would be faithfull while I had life. Mr. Ireland told me that when he came to London he would speake to Grobes that I might have notice how things went on, for as yett he could not tell while he had spoke with my Lord Bellasis and my Lord Arundell of Wardour who proved the loyalest men of trust and counsell of any persons in this world; but before I had my letter from Mr. Ireland he was taken to Newgate. I saw a letter from Mr. Harcott who told Mr. Evers that he had lately received a letter from Mr. Warner I think his name was, wherein was that Mr. Warner had used all diligent care that could bee for helping forward the worke in hand. And there was four hundred pounds in mony in Mr. Ireland's hands which came into his hands lately for teaching the young gentlemen, who wisht that they might putt it into Shirley's hands with the rest till we should have need of it. And that I heard Mr. Peters tell Mr. Evers that

MSS. of Sir W.
Fitzherbert.
—

hee was very gladd that it fell out soe well that Mr. Whitebread was
come in Superior of the Jesuits for he would be very carefull in
carrying the businesse on ; and that he was a close man in all his
businesse, to which I made answer that I was very glad to hear it fell
out soe well too. And at that tyme both Mr. Evers and Mr. Peters
said, that my Lord Arundell of Wardour was the only man we had to
trust too for he was a very wise man and much in favour with the
Duke of Yorke ; and not long after I had three letters inclosed in a
letter of mine, from Mr. Bennifeild one and one from Paris and one
from Mr. Harecott ; that from Mr. Bennifeild was to lett Mr. Evers
know that he had spoke with my Lord Arundell of Wardour and my
Lord was very willing to assist in what was requested by Mr. Evers
and Mr. Vavasor, but these letters never came to his hands besides
a great many more which I intercepted and burned. And not long
after I was in discourse with Mr. Evers in his chambers, and was
askeing him wether some others of note did not countenance the
worke besides what he had spoke of, and he told me yes, but they
were in other places where the businesse went on as well as here.
Mr. Evers told mee at this tyme, that he had writt to Mr. Bennifeild, and to request my Lord Arundell of Wardour to be assisting in
the matter which now is in hands. And I asked him what whether
he was to doe anything of it or noe ; and he told me he was to
undertake the most part of the designe and with my Lord Bellasis
to give order, both as to that of takeing the King's life away and the
Duke of Monmouth's, and for establishing the Romish government.
And about the middle of September last, a letter came to my hands of
Mr. Evers, for his letters were directed to mee, which I opened and
the words were to this purpose, that he had been with my Lord
Arundell, and my Lord Arundell had told him that he had spoke to the
person that he was requested to speake to, and it was both their
opinions that it was the best way to make as much speed in their
designes as might bee, the person's names which sent the letters I know
not, for their was but two letters for his name which was J. W. And
at first when this businesse began, it was not for takeing the life of the
Kinge away, but to provide themselves with money and armes against
the King died, for it was thought the Duke of Monmouth would stand
for it, and their hopes would be frustrated for ever haveing the Romish
religion established. But they seeing it was the endeavour of the
King to establish the Protestant religion soe firme as it should not be
moved for the future, it was by degrees thought that this way that is
now discovered was the fittest way. I chanced to come into Mr. Evers
chambers and hee being gone to masse I found a letter on his table
whose subscription was Bazill FitsHerbert, which was directed to Mr.
Evers, wherein was written that he gave Mr. Evers many thanks for his
great care and diligence in the great worke, which was soemuch for the
setting forth the glory of Almighty God, and further told him that hee
had spoke with his brother Gifford of Chillington, who promised
together with himselfe to venture both lives and estates in that good
cause, and that Mr. Evers would be sure to sweare all those within his
preciucts to secrecy whom he did intrust, that they should not so much
as tell one another till just the tyme, and that very speedily he would
goe to St. Omers and see what forwardnesse things were in there, and
if he had goue on prosperously he should have speedy notice for putting
the rest of the things in order there, and that he would be pleased to
speake with Mr. Broadstreete or send Mr. Dugdale with a letter to him
that he would meete him in London, as I think it was in July last, and
that I myselfe was to have an equall share with Captaine Adderley, who

was a man intrusted to keepe things in order after the most of the businesse should be over, but what parte it should be could not be known till after this was over, for it must be cheefeley determined by my Lord Arundell and some other persons, but it should be such a share as should make me happy and my posterity after mee. All which I excepted of with abundance of thankfullnesse. When this was promised there was in company Mr. Evers, Mr. Gaven, Mr. Peters, and Mr. Levison, which all promised to see it fullfilled."

[*Copy.*]

FURTHER DEPOSITIONS by MR. DUGDALE.

1678–9, January 17.—" 1. That in summer at a race which was to be run at Iching hill I mett with one Mr. Humphrey Elliotts, I think his name is, I am sure his name is Elliotts, and meeting at Rudgely at the house of one Mr. John Polletts which keepes a publiqe house, he and I after some discourse of the race did fall into discourse of Mr. Ireland, told me there had been some discourse of mee when his cousin Ireland was at Wolverhampton, and I pressed of him that I might know what it was and he told me it was not unknown to mee for his cousin Ireland said you was to goe very speedily to London upon an occasion hat would cause him upp very speedily, but before he the said Elliotc went he had some businesse to doe in the country, which he himselfe could not well do without Mr. Perrey the lawyer, but I was something startled to heare he should know any of it, and denyed I knew anything of it, and upon that he comended me for my care, and further told me I need not feare him, for if I suffered he was like to suffer as well as I.

2. Hee further told me that his cousin Ireland should have been at London a great while since but for waiting to see the foot race over, for there was some gentlemen which he was to speake would be there, but before that foot match was over he came from Wolverhampton to Tixall and told me he could not stay the race, for he had received 3 letters which chidd him that he had made so long a stay, who the letters came from he did not tell mee, but only his sister for one and she he told me was very angry, but told me that my Lord Stafford would stay and that he would leave his mind with him, and to take care for my coming upp, and begged of me whatsoever I did not to impart my mind to any person except my Lord Stafford or Mr. Evers or whom they should appoint me to speake to of it, and I should see in a short tyme the darke clouds would be over, and the cleare light would appeare, and bid me not to be afraid for my Lord Stafford, and Mr. Evers would take care of me till he saw me into towne.

3. Besides for the carrying on the worke in other countryes there was for a parte of Worster there appointed one Mr. Turner, and three more whose names I have forgott, and for a parte of Derbyshire and a parte of Nottinghamshire was appointed one other Mr. Turner, Mr. Bennett, and Mr. Poole of Spinkhill, which was to take care of their liberties as well for engaging persons as for raising money of the gentlemen, and to give accompt to their Provincials which was appointed already for that purpose. Mr. Evers and Mr. Peters told me this but beside that Mr. Poole told me himselfe of it at Sutton in Scarsdale, but he told me then that he did believe that Mr. Turner was not a fitt man to be imployed in that worke for although he was a priest he was very much given to drink, and when drink is in the head the witt is out as he said, so it was thought more fitt in his stead to take in Mr. Ayreps priest of Hassop, and wished I would acquaint Mr. Evers with it, presently Mr. Evers went over thither but what he did conclude I know not, for I did not aske.

MSS. OF SIR W. FITZHERBERT. Further there was oft mentioned one Mr. Richard Needham, a Dr. of Physick, which lives at West Hallum, 4 miles from Derby, who was to receive orders from Mr. Poole and Mr. Bennett, and be at their command, and his sonne, and once I was sent to Mr. Needham with a letter, the contents of which was to desire he would be at West Hallum on a day which I have forgott, and that both Mr. Powderhill might be acquainted likewise and the priest which was there. I saw him then and have severall tymes heard his name, but at present have forgott it, and when I came there Mr. Needham and I discoursed very freely of it, and he as well as my selfe was very forward for the promoting the work on, and further told me, that he had been out about that businesse since he rested above 200 miles, for although his sonne was a good Christian enough, yet that was not a thing to be trusted to every one, and at that time I told him he might assuredly expect a good reward, and he told me, he did not know, he putt it to the gentlemen whether they would give anything or nothing, he thought his paines well bestowed in soe good a work, that it should fall out in his dayes, that it might be spoke of in after ages, that honest Dick Needham was a promoter and one intrusted for the establishing of the Romish religion, and the subvervision of the heretical government, to which I answered with a plausible assent, and I further added that I did believe Mr. Evers to be a saint upon earth he answered me he did believe he was a very good man and one that made it his businesse for promotion of God's holy church.

4. That I have severall times been told by Mr. Evers and Mr. Gavon about providing armes, but never heard that any was provided in England, nor any gentlemen that had any in keeping, but severall tymes that there was provision made beyond seas and that Mr. Evers and Mr. Cotten went beyond sea for that purpose, and that Mr. Evers told me severall tymes what good provision was made, and I intercepted severall letters that came to Mr. Evers from St. Omers and Paris, that they were in good forwardness and that they had disbursed sometymes £500, and some accompts, and the particulars named was £700, in some of which letters was pressed to Mr. Evers about returne of moneys, for the discharging those accounts, upon which I have seene letters of Groves, and letters to Mr. Ireland, Mr. Bennifield, and Harecott, for the sending moneys over to those persons, and further that the said Mr. Ireland and Vavasor differed in accompts about the same last time Ireland was in the country, and the said Mr. Evers sided with Mr. Ireland about those accompts, so that Mr. Ireland received the full summe of his accompts, and about July last a packquett came directed to me from Mr. Evers which came to 2s. 6d. which I opened, and they were accompts how that all things was ready which was bespoke, and all payd off, and there wanted nothing but orders how they must be disposed of, but how it was ordered I never knew, and that when I have been in businesse with them, it hath oft been given out that the King of France did know of this and would be aiding and assisting in this designe, which I was ever against, for I told them I was afraid he would rather worke for his own advantage then any good for us, and they would have told me that we need not feare we was able of ourselves with good care to putt those fears out of doors, and answer was made, there was in England above 200 thousand men which would prove true if occasion were with some supplyes which we were sure of from other parts."

[*Copy. Endorsed.*]—"Given in to the Lords of the Committee and then read before him, and they were also read before his Majesty in Council in the afternoon."

INFORMATION of STEPHEN DUGDALE.   MSS. of SIR W. FITZHERBERT.

1678–9, January 11—22.—" He sayth that upon notice of the murder of Sir Edmondbury Godfrey he much blamed to Mr. Evers the indiscretion of that businesse, as a thing that might help to discover their designe, but Mr. Evers told him it could not doe much hurt, for he being a man much given to punish debauchery, it would easily be thought that some of them had done it.

1678[9], January 13.—" Mr. Dugdale being called in they knew each other, and when Mr. Dugdale put Parsons in mind that he and Mr. Fox had taken their leaves of him att the stable door at Tixhall, he sayd it was very true though he had forgott before, but would have acknowledged it if it had come into his mind.   Parsons being withdrawne says he knew not whether he be a Jesuite, but that he is a priest for att Tixhall he heard him 'say masse and was att Tixhall according to the tyme he himselfe declares.   Dugdale adds that when Ireland came to Tixall in August he told him of his haveing been att Standon, and spoke of his acquaintance with Mr. Parsons, and how the examinant att his coming up should sometimes be with Parsons at Standon, and to take instructions from him while there, and sometymes Mr. Harcoat and Ireland here in towne, and then to take his instruction from these about his designe of killing the knight; is ordered that Parsons be sent to the Gatehouse as by the following warrant :—"

1678[9], January 20.—" Dugdale is sent for and examined. He speakes particularly of the hideing certain letters in a wallett with money.   He knowes that Mr. Forster was acquainted with Ireland, and that one Father Arthur an Irish priest being sent for over by Benningfeild and Harcoate came downe to Tixall and had been att Mr. Fowler's.   And this Arthur spoke much of the French King.   He alsoe remembered that one Rider a joyner came to Tixall, and commending of the murder of Sir Edmondsbury Godfrey sayd that he and one Tunks a shoemaker in the Strand should have been concerned, and that one Conniers was concerned in it.   He alsoe spake of a letter writt, as he thinks, by one Roper in the Tower which came to Sir James Symonds in Staffordshire that gave them much content."

1678–[9], January 20.

Notice being given to his Majestie that the Lord Aston did attend according to his summons Dugdale was first called for, who gave an accompt of a clossett where he hid the wallett in which was money and some dangerous papers, whereupon there is read to his Majesty the accompt sent by Mr. Lane and Mr. Vernon to the Duke of Monmouth how that the clossett was rifeld, the wallett, papers, bookes, and all things there taken away.   And upon reading alsoe the examination sent up of the two maids what they sayd gave extraordinary credit to Dugdale's evidence, not only affirming all he sayd, but somewhat more touching two books of accounts which Dugdale then sayd had noe reason in them, and should not be burnt as the letters were, and they agreed just in the tyme with Dugdale viz. the 19th of November. Upon this his Majesty gives order for a new inquiry to be made about the rifling this clossett, and Dugdale being asked by his Majesty what he was to doe, and by whom councelled in this designe he answered directly that he was to be instrumentall to kill the King and was councelled and animated therein by Mr. Ireland, Mr. Evers, and the Lord Stafford.

" He made mention of somebody in whose bookes here in towne it would appear that he was a man trusted by the Jesuits, of which and what he sayd about Mr. Whitby of Great Hoywood and John Taylour, he is to put it downe in writing and he was interrogated in severall points which he had spoken to before. And that part was read againe in his examination of the 8th instant about discourse in the Long Parlour att Tixall between the Lord Stafford and the Lord Aston about the difficulty of trusting persons and the good opinion the Lord Stafford had of the Lord Arundell. After which he withdraws and the Lord Aston is called in and upon his examination which shall hereafter follow, he is sent to the Tower."

1678–9, January 22.

"Mr. Dugdale is called in and a paper by him this day presented is read, and he further says that he carryed a letter from Evers to Sir James Symonds desiring him to pay the money he had promised, Mr. Evers being then called upon by Ireland, Harcot, and Beningfeild for the collections to be carryed abroad by Sir John Warner for the purchaseing of armes.

That Mr. Evers was to receive somebody and the rest to goe by returne, that Sir James is younger brother to Symonds an active Jesuit. That Carrington and Tarbox were two messengers employed in carrying of letters. That Francis Titter is priest to Mr. Fowler and cannot be ignorant of this plott. Mr. Dugdale is ordered to give an account in writing about a great meeting at Boscobell in August last.

He says that Arthur the Irish priest dined with the Lord Stafford at Tixall, and that Arthur told him and Evers of Whisle Bourn and severall others engaged in the businesse of Ireland, about which the Lords appoint Sir Robert Southwell to take a particular accompt and to send it to the Duke of Ormond in Ireland."

INFORMATION of S. DUGDALE.

1678–9, January 23.—"About August or the beginning of September last there there was a greate meeteing of the Jesuites and Secular Priests at Boscobell, besides other private gentlemen that was to be there, and I myselfe promised to be there alsoe. At that meeting there was accounts to be sett right betwixt Mr. Ireland and Mr. Vavasor about money which he had laid downe for carrying on this greate worke, and other things which was betwixt them, but the chiefe cause of our meeting was to consult and consider wayes and meaines for the carrying on the worke which both Mr. Peter and Mr. Vavasor tould me, and against this meeting promised a fat buck, but was deceived and soe was forced to send to Mr. Chetwind of Angestry to borrow a peece in Mr. Francis Aston's name and there was none but halfe a haunch, and it was just laid to the fire, but Mr. Chetwinde caused it to be taken up and sent it, and that venison was eaten at that meeting and I haveing promised to be there had much ado to keepe myselfe from goeing, but I told them that I had appointed busines amongst the tennants, and could not goe if they would give me 1000l. and soe I came off, but they were very angry.

There was another contrivance which I was guilty on myselfe as much as any, but it was with their advice, that packet to Bennefeild was one thing to keep the King from beleeving anything, that there was any plott but a forgery, which was very much rejoyced at when wee saw what effect it wrought with the King, for presently upon it the King as I thinke went to Newmarket and said wee if the King beleeved anything of it he would not have gon.

Another thing that as I said before I was guilty of to write letters and scale them which contents was for fireing of townes and meeting at certaine places, which might be a meanes to keepe the people from beleeving anything of a plott, for we thought the wiser sort would thinke if there was anything of a plott those men which were the inventors would not have lost soe many letters of such concerne, which did partly keepe the people from beleeving as it was intended, but this was after Mr. Otes confession.

And that Mr. Evers did sometimes ask the gentlemen till he was imployed in this worke of the plott, and then Mr. Towers taught them for Mr. Evers had worke enough besides.

This is the truth
STEPHEN DUGDALE."

MSS. OF SIR W. FITZHERBERT.

[*Some shorthand in the margin.*]

EVIDENCE given in by STEPHEN DUGDALE against SIR JAMES SIMONS &c.

1678-9, January 24.—" I have seen in a list amongst Mr. Evers' papers of gentlemen's names which did pay towards this wished designe, amongst which was Sir James Symons £1000, Mr. Hovenhingam £2000, Mr. Dracot £3000, Mr. Gerard £500, Mr. Howard £2000, of all which sumes was received in part and returned towards the discharging the accounts of armes which were provided beyond the seas. And every of the aforesaid gentlemen was to have a share and offices appointed. But in all our meetings it was never agreed what their parts should bee, and the notedst gentleman of all these was ever Sir James Simons, being as they said a very active person and one that would be found a well qualifyed person, but as far as I ever understood their places was to bee appointed here in London by some of those great ones whom I have formerly mentioned. But there are several persons' names besides those I have named in that same list. And there are other persons which entered their names beyond seas, for this note was but only for Mr. Evers' private use. And to that end Mr. Evers and Mr. Coten were sent to St. Omers about 2 or 3 years agoe, for the sake of other persons which were very fearfull. And some others paid their money to Mr. Bennifield, Mr. Ireland, and Mr. Harcott, and Mr. Evers hath been appointed to receive acquittances for them which acquittances I have seen come in Mr. Evers' letters. One to Sir James Simons at one time was for £300 which was noted in the acquittance for a charitable use, but it was for the carrying on this wicked designe, or Mr. Evers told me not true. Most of the persons about Woolverhampton Mr. Gaven took care to receive of and discharge them. I asked Mr. Peters how the rest must bee had, for these gentlemen when they were altogether would bee but a few ; he answered mee, I need not fear, there was care taken for that, and such care that at one hour's warning they would bee ready, but as he said they had formerly been told that none except the gentlemen were soe much as to tell one another till the very time, of which I never inquired after that time, but I perceived that a great number was knowing by their fear, when I was taken, and several desiring mee, when I was at Stafford privately that if I knew anything of them not to mention their names which I faithfully promised I would not. And I must ever bee of this mind, that never anything could be better managed than this was by the priests, and soe it would have bin found if Mr. Otes had not declared it, which God forbid but he had. For I am sure but thinking of the sad effects hath almost made me distracted. As alsoe to hear their wicked designes and doctrines dayley. And to prevent melancholy I did several times either run myselfe into company to drink or some manner of lewd idle discourse, of which there are many to witness, and that I never was addicted to it before ·this wofull engagement in this most horrid and wicked designe. And from ever having or consenting to such again, God of his mercy protect mee, as I hope he will, and all Christians from the very name of it."

[*Copy.*]

1678-9, January 31.—" The Information of Stephen Dugdale late of Tixall in the County of Stafford taken upon oath before the Right Honble. the Lords of the Committee of Examinations this 31st day of January 1678-9.

" The Informant saith that about Michelmas last an Irish priest whose name was Arthur came to the house of the Lord Aston at Tixall and dined there. That after dinner Mr. Evers, the Jesuit of the house, Mr. Arthur and himselfe went into Mr. Evers' chamber where Mr. Arthur declared that by command which hee had from Mr. Bennifeild and Mr. Harcote, hee came from Ireland to London, and he said hee found things in a pretty good condition but not soe well as hee could have wished ; his reason this informant heard not, because hee was then gone down for a bottle of wine, but when he came up again Mr. Arthur being in discourse with Mr. Evers did make a sudden stop, but Mr. Evers told him hee need not fear for Stephen was a very honest man, and after a while Mr. Evers told him this informant that the gentleman was one intrusted for carrying on the business in Ireland, as well as wee did it here in England. To which bee the said Arthur answered that hee hoped it would appear in a short time which of the two nations would be found the best Christians, meaning Ireland would bee found truest in that designe, for the English would be false. But hee farther said they in Ireland had a good assurance from France of a reasonable supply both of men and money, which hee said hee hoped Almighty God would assist them with all in regard they lived like poor slaves under a merciless government. That in discourse concerning the good hopes of success in Ireland the said Arthur mentioned at least twenty names of Priests and Jesuits that were active and imployed in the carrying on of the business, among which the informant remembers one Mr. White because hee had been two or three times at Tixal some years agoe, and when the informant asked if it were the same Mr. White they spoke of that had been there both Evers and Arthur told him it was, and the informant being asked what other names hee doth remember of those that were mentioned, hee saith that to the best of his remembrance, French and Byrne were two. And that this Arthur was toward fifty years of age, indifferent tall and slender, of a long visage, and brown complexion."

[*Copy.*]

1678-9, February 12.—" The Information of Stephen Dugdale late of Tixhall in the County of Stafford taken upon oath before the Lords of the Committee of Examinations the 12th day of February 1678-9.

" The Informant saith that about the month of July or August 1677, soon after he was by Mr. Evers admitted into the secret of the designe for the Romish government, there came to Tixall one Carrington, whom the Jesuits thereabouts employed as a messenger of trust in their businesse ; he brought a letter to Mr. Evers from Mr. Vavasor who was then at Woolverhampton or Boscobell. And meeting the informant in the hall desired him to give it to Mr. Evers. The letter from Mr. Vavasor did inclose in it severall others, as one from John Grove in London who in a part of the sheet of pay writ some news in short but . . . . his signeing Mr. William Harcot began a long accompt how he lately had received the two inclosed letters one of them from St. Omers which was signed by Monfort, Warner, and Peters, as the informant thinkes, and four whose names he remembers not all, and this letter did referre to another letter from Paris to the three parties first named. And the same was signed from Paris by two names whereof he thinkes Clifford was one, but he cannot swear that this letter did contain the opinion and advice of those att Paris upon a letter which it seemes had been first writ from England to St. Omers and from St. Omers transmitted to them. The scope of which advise was this, that by all meanes care should be taken not to let armes appear or any appear in armes till after the death of the King, because they had fully considered that when any sudden death should befall the King it might be easily be layd to the Presbiterians who had killed the late King and were still enemys to the King and government. Therefore they advised that all ways should be taken to give out and possesse the people before-hand, that the Presbyterians were the only enemys, soe that when the King should be killed those of the Church of England would presently be incensed and take up armes to revenge it, and rather crave the aide of the Catholiques then be afraid of them, and therefore it was fit they should be in readinesse to make the first allarm, and give out that all was done by the Presbyterians. And then by a little assistance from abrode the worke would easily be compassed. This was the substance of the letter from Paris, and they did further desire to have the same sent into England with the opinion of those of St. Omers upon it, and those of St. Omers did in their letter much praise the advise from Paris, adding nothing else of their owne to it besides comendations, but passed unto other of smaller concernes, as that Mr. Evers should call to one Gerard of Lancashire and Gerard of Hilderson for 50*l*. due for teaching of their children or relations then and such like things.

Mr. Harcourt further added that his letters from St. Omers being directed unto him he had communicated it as alsoe that from Paris unto Mr. Bedingfeild, and Mr. Ireland, and likewise to the Lord Arundell, Lord Bellasis, Lord Stafford, and six or seven more, whom the informant hath forgott, by all whom it was highly comended as good advise and that all should endeavour upon any differences in Parliament or any other disorder still to give out that it was those blood sucking King selling Presbyterians that were the authors of it.

" The Informant further sayth that Mr. Evers did show him the sayd three letters sent from Mr. Harcott and then soon after the same day sent them by the same messenger to Carington under a cover to Mrs. Here-ningham at Aston to be shown to her husband, and to Sir Jeames Simons their son in law, and to come back at night with the same letters, as he did. For that the informant did see Evers show them to the present Lord Aston in the parlour after supper his Lordship having been abroad before, and he beleiving them to be the same letters he had seen in the morning, for the messenger was then come back and two of the letters lay by on the table, and the third they were reading by the fire, and he does verily believe they were the same hands and the same letters, and the messenger was there detained all night, and made much of by the informant according to order, and in the morning Mr. Evers sent him back with an answer to Mr. Vavasor, but Mr. Evers kept still the letters from Mr. Harcot. And the informant did afterwards hear Mr. Evers and Mr. Gaven discourse together touching the said letters and in comendation of the good advice. And they named severall friends in their discourse that were engaged at Paris whom he remembers not.

" And the informant further saith, that coming once into the chamber of Mr. Evers when he was gone up to masse he found one of those letters namely that from Paris, and had curiosity to read it againe, and son he took it with him, and hearing how angry Mr. Evers was upob missing of it with the woman who cleaned the room, as if she had swept it into the fire on the like, he forbore to returne it back. But that this was one of the letters which were sealed up in his wallett that was hid in the closett of Mr. Evers when he ran away from Tixall about the 19th of November.

"And he further sayth, that Mr. Evers did tell him the letters from St. Omers were brought by a particular gentleman into England, and from London to Mr. Vavasor by some freind, which the informant does the rather beleive for that he tooke notice there was noe postmark upon the said letters to Mr. Vavasor.

This is the truth
STEPHEN DUGDALE."

1678-9, February 21.—" The Information of Stephen Dugdale late of Tixall in the county of Stafford takeu before his Majestic in Councill this 21 day of February 1678-9.

" The informant saith he is acquainted with one George Hobson now in the goale of Stafford as being accused by the informant. That the said George Hobson came the last summer, to live with the Lord Aston as his gentleman to waite on him, having in the same quality served the Lord Stafford, by whom he was recommended and with whom or some of his sonns or near relations he had (as Hobson told him) lived for about fifteene yeares.

" He further told the informant that he had been at Rome waiting on some of the said Lord's sons and with the present Cardinall of Norfolke. That he had at his leisure studied some parte of the mathematicks and particularly that of astrologie and that Lilly had instructed him. And the informant alsoe having been taught by a mathematician to survey land did likewise endeavour to learne something in astrologie, soe that the said Hobson and the informant did sometimes discourse and comunicate concerning such things, and they grew soe intimate that when the said Hobson did perceive how much confidence Mr. Evers placed in the informant, and that he was alsoe called into private discourse by the Lord Stafford; or whether it were that the Lord Stafford or Mr. Evers had told Hobson that the informant was ingaged, but he the said Hobson did enter into free comunication with him concerning the plott. telling him that he had for seaven yeares past knowne of the designe for reformation of the government to the Romish religion, and that he ever thought and said, that disturbance in Scotland and Ireland would best helpe to bring this matter about, and that it would not availe to take off the King, unlesse the Duke of Monmouth were alsoe disposed of. And among the severall discourses which the informant can call to mind, he does remember the said Hobson told him, that from a certain old booke of prophecies which was at the Lord Stafford's house, they had greate hopes and encouragement for their proceeding, and it points out this reformation of the government though it were very hard to be understood. But he plainly said that if this undertaking did not succeed they must never expect the like opportunity again for the establishment of the Catholick Religion but still be governed by hereticks, which might plainly appeare by the King's doeing every thing for them to make that sure.

" Hee further saith that when once he did in discourse tell the said Hobson it would cost the Pope no small summe to bring this designe about, and how would the Pope spare so much, as having warrs and businesse of his owne like other Princes, Hobson replyed that he had taken a good accompt of things when he was at Rome, and that the Pope's revenue was £24,000 a day; of which the Informant afterwards makeing som mention to Mr. John Sandbich a cousin to the Lord Aston, and to Mr. Phillipp the minister as they were drinking a bottle of ale in the house of Walter Eld, Hobson came to heare of it and chid the informant for speakeing of the said revenue.

MSS. OF SIR W. FITZHERBERT.

" Hee further saith that, as he was one tyme sitting by the kitchen fire, the said Hobson came and whispered to him that he and another person had calculated the King's nativity, and that severall things fell out right, in fact according to their calculations, but before he ended the discourse or came to say what was the upshott of that calculation, they were interrupted by other company.

" Hee further saith that upon notice received that Otes had discovered the plott, the said Hobson fell into a deep melancholy, soe as to keepe his chamber for two or three dayes, and sending for the informant he did among other discourses lamenting this misfortune propose that they might erect a scheme for tryall wether Otes had really discovered or noe, accordingly he drew the scheme and by both our judgements thereupon, it did appear to us that Otes had made discovery. Whereupon he fell to blame and condemne the heads engaged in the designe that they should ever trust such a fellow as Otes was, and that if something were not done to prevent it this discovery of Otes would make all their future expectation impossible.

" The informant further saith that upon his examination on the 24th of December last the said Hobson was apprehended and examined before the Justices, and ordered to be sent the gaole at Stafford; but the Constable being the Lord Aston's tennant, did first permitt him for one night to lye at Tixall, where being in the kitchen and speakeing of what the informant had confest, he said aloud in the hearing of many and fetching a sigh, I'll warrant that my Lord Stafford's businesse is done. This informant hath been told by Elizabeth Eld who said she herselfe and Mr. Phillipps the minister of the parish, and the cook were then present."

[*Copy.*]

1678-9. February 21.—" The information of Stephen Dugdale late of Tixall in the county of Stafford taken before his Majestie in councell the 21st of February 1678-9.

The Informant saith in addition to what he hath already spoke concerning the Lord Stafford that about the same tyme (viz.) in September last the said Lord did in the great parlour at Tixall discourse to Mr. Evers and the informant the reason of his dissatisfaction against his Majestie, towards whom hee had long carried himselfe with all sorte of loyalty as he had towards his father, but that he and others had thereby had their families ruined. And in particular, that the old Lord Aston had been a great sufferer, and his father the Ambassador had spent thirty thousand pounds out of their owne estate, but that there was noe hopes of any recompence for he saw plainly as any thing fell to bee given it was rather disposed of to rebells and traitors and those who had served against the King, rather then to those that had been loyall. And therefore those things had wrought with him, and were sufficient to change his mind towards the King, if there were not the matter of religion in question which was a consideration above all others.

" His Lordship further took notice how that, at any sessions of Parliament when there fell out anything to the prejudice of the Catholicks the King was alwayes willing to expose them to the Parliament's mercy both in estates and anything else that might befall them.

[*Copy.*]

MSS. OF SIR W.
FITZHERBERT. 1678-9, February 21.—" The Information of Stephen Dugdale late of
Tixall in the county of Stafford, taken before his Majestic in Councell,
on the 24th of February 1678-9.

" The informant saith that he hath before in discourse acquainted the
Lords of the Committee that while he was in prison at Stafford and
before hee came to make his confession, there was much discourse spread
abroade about that hee confesse and discover, upon which report Elizabeth Elde was sent over by the Lord Aston to Mr. Fitter, the priest of
Mr. Fowler at St Thomas, desireing him to have a meeting with his
Lordship in a certaine field called Brancote nere the River side, which
was done accordingly, and when Fitter came home bee told one of Mr.
Fowler's daughters what had past, namely, that they discoursing of the
informant and the danger of his discovering all, the Lord Aston did
even weepe, and that Fitter did tell his Lordshipp hee even suspected
the informant would prove untrue, and that his Lordship had done ill
that hee did not dispatch him before ever hee went out of his house.
This discourse the said daughter of Mr. Fowler told the said Elizabeth
Elde as being a messenger of trust imployed to bespeake the said
meeting. And the said Elde did come to the informant while hee was
in prison at Stafford, which is but two miles from Tixall and from whence
he had some messenger or other every day, and did relate this whole
matter unto him.

" Hee further saith that after hee hath made his discovery, and that
thereupon the Justices issued their warrants for the seizure of George
Hobson and George North (which North is nephew to Pickering) both
of them servants in the house of the Lord Aston and that the warrants
were served by Edward Preston the Constable of the place and servant
to the said Lord. It was reported that the said Lord Aston should
thereupon say in great passion, that hee was sorry hee had not run the
informant thorow with his sword before hee went out of his house, the
report of which words comeing to Mary and Elizabeth Stevenson or to
one of them, daughters to the then mayor of Stafford, and by one of
them to the wife of . . erry the informant's gaoler and then telling the
informant thereof, hee did presently report this story to Joseph Tarboy
a servant of the said Lord's who came to see him in the prison, bidding
him to tell his Lord that hee the informant was sorry his Lordship
should have had any thoughts to doe him such injury. Whereupon the
next day after the said Tarboy returned to the informant and in his
company Preston the Constable who had apprehended Hobson and
North to testify (as accordingly he was sent by his Lordship) that he
never heard his Lordship say soe, and that his Lordship did send him
word and declare that hee never wisht the informant's finger to ake, but
wish'd him all the happiness hee could imagine, and hoped all would
doe well and that the informant might come backe to his Lordship's
service. This past in the presence of the gaoler's wife, who did
confirme to them what shee had heard as aforesaid.

" The informant further saytn about the beginning of September last
Mr. Evers did tell him in great secret that the Lord Aston was to goe
in October next to St. Omers and probably from thence to Paris. And
the informart did conclude, from the manner and hints of Mr. Evers'
discourse, that it was to doe somethinge in relation to the designe for
Evers, and hee were then speaking of the designe, and how some out of
caution would only agree to have their names entered at St. Omers, as
it had beene before when, about two yeares since, hee and Mr. Cotton
went over to enter names, and had continued to be done by others since.
And upon the . . . . of this discourse Mr. Evers added that when
my Lord was gott over, they should here more of the businesse.

" About the middle of September the Lord Aston himselfe told the MSS of Sir W. Fitzherbert. informant in great secrecy, and whereof nobody was to know, that hee was intending to goe beyond sea and should want money, and therefore that presently all the tennants should know that they must bring in their rents by a foitnight after Michaelmas, which was the [time] to be fixed unto them, and that if they failed thereof they should be warned to leave his land the Ladyday next following, for although formerly hee had borne with them, yet that now hee would not. And the informant gave the same warning accordingly. But the informant says that after the news came that the plott was discovered, hee never heard my Lord to speake to him more of his goeing over."

[*Copy.*]

1678-9, March 21.—" The Deposition of Steven Dugdale gent. taken upon cath the 21st day of March 1678 before the Earle of Clarendon one of Her Majtys. Justices of Peace for the County and Liberty.

" This deponent saith that for these two years past, all or most letters that were sent to Mr. Evers were directed to the deponent and that about the 13th or 14th of October last (but of the time he is not very certain) there came two letters from Harcoate and Bennyfield to the said Mr. Evers. In one or both of which letters was expressed that this night Sr. Edmundberry Godfrey is dispatched, which when the said Evers read to the deponent, the deponent tould the said Evers he would be hanged if that did not overthrow the whole buisnesse, which made Evers answer noe, it will not be taken to be us, for he used to punish lewd persons, and such as used to go to debauched houses, and it will be supposed to be some of those that have killed him. And the deponent being hereupon further interrogated whether he had not formerly tould the Committee of the Councill as well concerning the tyme, and of the person or persons who writ the letters, as of the discourse which passed between him, and the said Evers therupon, or whether any member of the said Committee, or the clerk of the Councill who then attended them did tell him that it was not materiall to make mention of the said time or persons? The deponent saith that he did never mention anything either of the said tyme, or of the said persons unto that Committee or to the Clerk of the Councill attending them, nor was he ever tould by any of them, that to mention the said tyme or persons was not materiall. And he does upon his oath declare that although he did mention that circumstance to one Mr. Charles Chetwin when they discoursed about the murther, yet when he came before the said Committee, it being at a tyme when he brought much other evidence in writing with him, it did not occur to him .o mention more then what is set downe in the entry booke of that C ummittee. He being then asked as it were by chance, what was said amongst them upon the said murther. . . . . And further he thinks himself bound to testifie that it was scarce possible to have more care taken, than was taken to set downe all things he said with exactnes, and without adding or diminishing, for so it was ordered by the Comittee, and so put in practice by Sir Robert Southwell that attended them.

[*Signed*] Stephen Dugdale."

1678-9, March 21.—Another copy of S. Dugdale's deposition and but only extending as far as the words " those that killed him."

[*Apparently in Dugdale's own hand.*]

[*Signed*]. Clarendon.

Information of Stephen Dugdale.

1678-9,March 24.—" I saw a Letter from Mr. Whitebread directed to Mr. Evers but inclosed in Groves's letter to myselfe wherein was that

MSS. OF SIR W.
FITZHERBERT. there was great hopes now that things will goe on well if there be diligent care taken in the management of it, which can never be if it be communicated to every idle fellow therefore be sure you doe not trust any but whome you have made tryall of, for if it should be discovered we both ruine our designe and all concerned in it, for those persons which are for the purpose, noe matter whether gentlemen or not, so they be cunning, desperate, and trusty, which choice made here I feare not, for there hath beene spetiall care taken that noe opportunity might be lost, and what persons you think fitt, lett me have your answere next weeke ; sende to Boscobell and there will be a messenger to bring them to me. I neede not say much more to you in reguard, you are fully acquainted with the business and how it is to be caryed on by Mr. Ireland. It hope you put the gentlemen in minde for the getting what mony you can.

" Pray sende me worde by your next how my Lady is. I thinke to be for St. Omers next weeke.

[Signed]   STEPHEN DUGDALE."

S. DUGDALE'S INFORMATION.

1679, March 25.—" Some tyme before Michaelmas last, my Lord Stafford and my Lord Aston, went to Mr. Heningham's of Aston, where there was to be severall other gents, as namely Mr. Garrard of Hinderston, Mr. Peters a priest, Mr. Evers a Jesuite, Mr. Draycott of Peeneslow, Mr. Cotton a Jesuite, and Mr. Gaven a Jesuite. The cause of which meeting was to confer about my Lords Aston's goeing into France, Sir James Symyns being solicited to have gone with him, and Mr. Draycott alsoe. My Lord Stafford was to have gon, but by reason of his age, and other inabilityes desired that his son might goe in his steade which was granted, and by the circumstances which I have formerly mentioned, they were to goe to take order about the disposing of the armes provided beyond sea. And about the tyme before mentioned Mr. Howard of Hoare Cross came to Tixall to consult with Mr. Evers and my Lord Stafford and my Lord Aston about the same business, and for his going over with my Lord. And as I understood severall other gents besides those mentioned was to have gon over whose names I cannot remember by reason I had only the account from Mr. Peters and Mr. Evers and Mr. Gavin. But it is certain they did intend to goe and for that purpose. They had provided horses in the cuntry and would gett better att Pancridge faire, to take over along with them. And that Mr. Gavin att most meetings alwayes with greate courage told them that were there actually concerned that the designe now in hand was good and well pleasing with God, which he proved by Scripture, by Councells and by Examples, as namely one particularly how meritorious the work was, experienced by one that was in the Gunpowder Plott whose name was Gardiner that there had by his reliques severall miracles beene wrought. Whose names would ever be famous, for that his name was to be entered into the Kalender, and soe should all those who were concerned in soe important a business, for the distroying of heritiques, and esstablishing the Roman Catholique religion in England, and that not only Gardnett but alsoe all the rest of his coadjutors and had any hand in the concerne and for a certainty of this I have beene often told as well by Mr. Peters as Mr. Gavin that it was for noe other ende they went over then for the disposing of the armes and the ratifying of orders. My Lord Aston being allways very cautious did not openly appeare but held conferences only with priests and some certaine gents.

[Signed]   STEPHEN DUGDALE."

MSS. OF SIR W.
FITZHERBERT.

INFORMATION of S. DUGDALE.

1679, March 26.—" Mr. Evers tould me [it was] about July '78 the Duke of York had promised that he would accept the crown and that he would establish the Romish religion and I saw it writne in a letter from Mr. Bedinfield the same, and I ever understood he would accept it as under the Pope. The letter writ by Mr. Evers to Mr. [T]orner last somer was that hee might speak to Mr. Perpoint that he might be mindfull of his promiss which he maid last year when Mr. Evers was in towne, his letter I was by when it was writ, and sent away by Mr. Herbert Aston's man which was going to Mr. [T]hundlebigg.

STEPHEN DUGDALE."

S. DUGDALE'S DEPOSITIONS.

1679, March 27.—" A Circumstance relating to the letter which came from Mr. Harcott directed to me Stephen Dugdale att Tixall but intended for Mr. Evers concerning the murder of Sir Edmondbury Godfrey which confirms the tyme it came to my hands.

" It was about a week before a foot match was run in Cheshire betweene Sir John Crew and me, for I remember that a weeke before the match was run there came to me the footman that was to run the race with Sir John Crew's man, urging me to goe along with him to see him run. But I having just before received that letter was soe much troubled in my mind about that and other things which discovered the plott and followed Sir Edmondbury's death, that I would not goe, Mr. Evers telling me further at that time that if the plott should be discovered there would be a great persecution. And the said Stephen Dugdale says that the sayd match was run 21 Oct. 1678.

[Signed]   STEPHEN DUGDALE.

And the said Stephen Dugdale on the next morning following the receipt of the said letter goeing with one Mr. John Sawbridge and Mr. Phillipps to one Wattrells to drinke a bottle of ale, I told them that I heard there was a knight killed in London. This was a post day or two before I heard he was found, which I suppose they will remember.

[Signed]   STEPHEN DUGDALE."

DUGDALE'S PAPER.

1679, April 14.—" Ever since May '78 it hath been our constant hopes that by May '79 all things would bee over and every thing settled in a good condition, for it was ever intended that November, December and January, '78, would see all the sharpest of the work, and that a Protestant should not be alive but what had given very good assurance of there zeall to the Church of Rome, this was comonly spoake of all last summer mongst those which were conserned in the plot, and by others too whisperingly, for allthough he knew of something extraordinary was in hand I never found he knew anything how it must be affected, but there was care takne by the priests that you should all have notis at the very time he were reddy, and armes and everithing fit for the purpose. I have sometimes tould Mr. Evers I wonderd what the multitude must do for armes for it was imposible to affect anything without good store of them ; hee would usually tell me I need not truble myself, for their was care takne in all places that nothing should be wanting, which I was allways desiring to know, which caused my opening so many letters, but could receve not any further sattisfaction but what I have formerly spoak of being provided beyound sayes, and I am certain those

MSS. OF SIR W.
FITZHERBERT. gentlemen I have formerly named must needs know where these armes is, if their be any in England, for there ware constant meeting of them for contriving ways how the work would be best affected, for woue part was always intended a massacray in all places where it might be best affected, and it was belleived it would put such a teror of the rest that they would rather run then stay, but those was to be served so as presbiter, then those that flead there was an armey to cutt them of as they went, this was as well to be don in Ireland and Scotland as in England, besides Mr. Evers, Mr. Gavan, Mr. Peter, Mr. Gifford, Mr. Luson hath very oft tould me thus, and I pretending my zeall in, they would very oft speak cheerfully to me and say, fear not Mr. Dugdale you shall in a short time see good times, and that I should be a happy man, boath in this world and the world to come. I do remember once my Lord Stafford was by and used the like words."

DUGDALE'S EXAMINATION.

1679, March 27.—"In the letter from Harcourt wherein was the intelligence of Sir Edmundsbury Godfrey being despatched it was added they were fearfull that things would come out more and more, whereupon Mr. Evers said if it did there would be very sore persecution."
Endorsed " Dugdale's Examination at the Committee of Secrecy."

BEDLOW'S INFORMATION.

1679, March 26.—"Upon Tuesday the 26th of January Mr. Na. Reding told me that my Lord of Powis, my Lord Stafford, and my Lord Petters, Sir Henry Tichburn, Mr. Rooper, Mr. John Cassell, and Mr. Ratcliffe, and Mr. Daniell Arthur, would make an acknowledgment to me worthy of so grate a kindnes and the saveing of theire lifes if I would shorten my evidence upon thaire tryalls and bring them of thaire charge of high treson, and likewise he told me he knew it was not fitting or anyway to my advantage to run at the whole head of men, but I should gaine my poynt if 2 or 3 did suffer for the plott, and by this meens I might secure the same reward from the Parliment, and another from those gentlemen besides, and said he would go to the Lords in the Tower who had imployed him, to know more from them how to proceed.

"Afterwards upon the 14th of February I did meet Mr. Reding at the Palsgrave's Head tavern where he told me these Lords and gentlemen did not thinke it safe for them to go on farther till they did find what and how far the next Parliament would proceed, and if they should be brought on their tryalls thay would give him severall writings for setlements of estates from them to him, in ten days after thair tryalls, if he could bring them of from theeir charge, which writings was to be immediately drawne, and he to keep them and would be bound to me for them that they should signe and seale them after thaire tryalls, besides a good reward in redy monye.

"Munday March the 24th I being in the Spaker's roome with Mr. Reding he told me the Lord Treasurer was sent for by the Blake Rod, and now my lord Stafford and the rest did believe I could do him and them a grate kindnes, and bid him tell me that he had one estate in Glostershere that my mother was with him about 18 yeare since to take a lese of him, and that there was but 2 yeare to come but the present tenant's lease would be out, and that my Lord Staford would give me that estate for 21 years without paying any rent to him so I would shorten my evidence against him .and bring him of; and that he had orders from my Lord to draw the writeings in order to it.

" This with many other pasages I have from time to time informed the prince and my Lord Essex of and other frends."

EXAMINATIONS, DEPOSITIONS, &c.

1678, Oct. 11.—J. Curzon
  „   „   —J. Boatman (bis) } Coleman's servants.
  „ Dec. 9.—Gratiano.
  „ Dec. 21.—E. Everard.
1679–80, Feb. 7.
   „ Feb. 12.
   „ March 24. } E. Needham.
   „ April 30.
   „ March 15.—M. Ball and a letter to Lord Herbert of 19th.
1680, April 2.—Th. Marshall.
  „ April 28.—J. Sanders, C. Sands, and Colster.
  „   „   —J. Sanders.
  „   „   —D. Colster.
  „   „   —Ch Towneley.
  „   „   —Jo. Byford.

The EXAMINATION of JOHN CURZSON, Coachman to Mr. Coleman.

1678, October 30.—" This examinant saith that he hath lived with Mr. Coleman as his coachman neare six years and all that time ordinarily hath every week carryed his Mr. to my Lord Arundel of Wardour's house in Lincoln Inne fields some times more and sometimes less and some times twice in a day when my Lord was in town. And also carryed him often to my Lord Powys' house in Queen Street and Vere Street. And several times to my Lord Peter's when he was in town.

" And often to my Lord Bellasse's, and to my Lord Baltamor's and to my Lord Castlemayne, and the day before his Master was committed he carryed him to my Lord Arundle of Wardour's twice or thrice and this examinant saith on the Sunday after dynner the day before his Master was committed he carryed his Master to Doctor Short's lodgings in the Strand and there took up Doctor Short and they went into Chancery Lane to one Mr. Wright a lawyer, and carryed them to Mr. Wright's lodgings where they stayed two or three hours, and then he carryed his Master to my Lord Arundell of Wardour's where he had carryed him in the morning, and then from thence he carrying his master homewards in the Strand, one Mr. Cotton a kinsman to his Master mett him and stayed the coach and whispered to his master and as this examinant believeth acquainted his Mr. that his house was searching, and thereupon his master commanded this examinant to turn the coach and to drive to my Lord Arudell of Wardour's, which the examinant did doe accordingly, and after some stay there the examinant carried his master into Lombar Streét where this examinant sot his Master downe, but where his Master lodged that night this examinant knows not, and there was one John Tother who there wayted upon his master as a footman and this examinant saith he often carryed his master to St. James and sometimes to or three times in a week . . . . and believes he went to Mr. Langhorne's house and sometimes to the Myle house to . . . house which may be Mr. Saunder's, and more he saith not. The mark of John Curson ✕.

Taken before us upon oath this 30th day of October 1678.
    Edmund W. Wyndham.
    Thos. Stringer.   Will. Glascock."
    P. Howard.

MSS. OF SIR W.
FITZHERBERT.

The EXAMINATION of JEROMEY BOATEMAN, servant to Mr. Coleman.

" This examinant saith he hath served Mr. Coleman above five years last past in the quality of a cleark and servant in his chamber and is by his birth a Wallowne neare Mons in Hennort [Hainaut]. That this examinant did transcribe his master's letters by his order and did communicate such of them as his Mr. gave him leave to his particular friends for this examinant's private advantage.

" The copy of the original of which letters were all entered into a book by his Mr. own hand or by this examinantt, which books were taken by those that apprehended his Mr. as he beleeves, but there was a book that was filled up with letters which was not taken as this examinant beleeveth but what his master hath done with the said book this examinant knows not. This examinant further saith that his Mr. to the time of his commitment and two posts afterwards did instantly and severall pacquetts of letters from foreigu parts.

" This examinant saith that the night before his master was taken his master did lye at his mother's house or lodgings Aldermonbury, who lives with Mr. Mitten her son in law as he beleeves.

" That he heard nothing of his master being questioned till the Sunday night before he was apprehended. This examinant saith he doth not remember that his master lay abroad any one night but the night before he was taken all the time he lived with his master, and this examinant hath served my Lord Arundell of Wardour, my Lord Powys, my Lord Bellassis, and my Lord Peters and the Lord Castlemayne, at dynner with Mr. Coleman severall times.

JEROME BOTEMAN.

Taken before us the 30th day of October 1678.
Tho. Stringer.

P. Howard.
Will. Glascock.   C. Harbor.
Edward W. Wyndham."

[*The two papers endorsed*] " from Sir Thomas Stringer."]
[*These three examinations are upon one sheet of paper.*]

The FURTHER EXAMINATION of JEREMY BOATEMAN taken this—of November 1678.

" This examinaut saith that the copy of the originall letters that were sent to this examinant's master were entered into a hook . . . of his master's handwriting and some with this examinant's and the letters themselves this examinant beleeves his master bound up in bundles, that one great book was full of copies of letters and the other was about half full, that which was half full this examinant beleeves was taken away by those that searched the house. The other beok full of copies of letters this examinant is informed since this last examination that the same was burned by this examinant's master or his command. This examinant positively saith that there were two books in which copies of letters were entered, and this examinant believeth there was three, and this examinant further saith that two or three posts after this examinant's master was taken into custody letters came from beyond seas directed to his master, some of them this examinant opened and left upon a table in his master's house, which this examinant beleeves were burned by his master, and another this examinant delivered to his master being in custody with Mr. Rutter the messenger, and this examinant saith that he hath been beyond sea four times since he came to his master, once he went into Britany to carry a letter from the Duchesse of Yorke to Duke Muzerin, and once with his master, and another time with his mistress, and then to fetch her home. This MSS. of Sir W. Fitzherbert. examinant further saith that he beleeves all his master's letters were taken by the messenger.

Taken upon oath

JEROME BOTEMAN.

Thomas Stringer."

1678, December 9. Bristoll.—" The further information of . . Gratiano, taken the ninth day of December 1678.

" Who sayth upon his oath that upon the third day of August last past Josephus Georgenie a Græcian Bishopp as hee styles himselfe being then in this citty did in his discourse say unto this deponent that hee did not question but that the Duke of Yorke would be King of England in a short tyme and that then he the said Georgernie should be preferred to a Bishoppricke under him in [th]is Kingdom.

DOMINICO [GRA]TIANE.

John Lloyd, Mayor,
John Lawford, Ralph Olliffe.
Tho. Stevens."

E. EVERARD'S INFORMATION.

1678, December 21.—" The information of the plott was five yeares since made by me, but was supprest, and was again given into the Committee of the Lords sitting in Parliament at Westminster on the 21th of December 1678 by me Edmond Everrard.

" Whilst I was employed as agent at the French Court for the English Militia's concernes, one of the officers (now Sir John Fenwick) brought me first to the acquaintance of my Lady Anne Gordon (sister to the now Marques of Huntley in Scotland); she after about a yeares frequentation communicated unto me certaine important secretts concerning a Popish plott against England.

" Shee is a lady of a vast correspondency amongst the Clergy and Nobility almost through all Europe, liveing ordinarily as a free person in nuneries, and was then in a Convent in Paris. Att a time I surprised her with two of the cheife Scotch Seminarists at Paris in a deep darke discourse of the English affaires, and as soon as my Lady made them understand I was one of her privatest freinds and catholiquely affected, (it being fitt shee should so imagin for that time) they then began to speak plaine enough to lett me perceive that the discourse tended to some sudden design for the subversion of the English governement and Governour and the setting up Popery here in England.

" But on some day of the month of Nov: 1673 I enquired of my Lady what those misterious discourses meaned shee had with the Scotch Preists; shee after long importunities and protestations revealed unto me that which followes.

(The charge against the Lady Huntley.)

1st. That there was now a grand designe on foote in England for the settleing of the Catholique faith there publiquely.

2dly. That there was also a project against the Parliament that made such a stir (as shee spoke) and was their main obstacle, either totally to dissolve it or to sow some division betwixt the King and it, where his majestie also should find potent adversaries of the Remish nobility who would cut out work for him.

3rdly. That there was a very considerable party in England who laboured to make the Duke of Yorke King. But that the Scotts indeed were more for the Duke of Monmouth's being such if meanes

MSS. OF SIR W.
FITZHERBERT.

could be made to bring him over to it, wherein shee conceived I
might be an usfull instrument haveing beene imployed under
him. But said I, what do they meane to do with the King
himselfe ; shee answered :—

4dly. That the King of England would be made away and dispatcht
after his father, so that he would not be in a case to anoy any
body.

"Then I enquired by what meanes they thought to bring such matters
about, and who were the leading men in the contrivance and who the
under agents to carry it on, she said that all that was to much for me
to knowe at the first time, besides that it was then to late at night, but
that at my returne, withen 3 dayes (for avoyding of suspition) I should
be fully satisfied, but I insisted that those were grand affaires whereof
she spoke, for which consequently shee needed to have more then
common grounds, shee replied that I ought not to doubt but that she
had the best corresponding in England, Scotland, and France, as having
on the one part Madam de Gordon her Aunt (one of the cheile Ladyes
of the Duchesse of Orleans) who was taken to be of the fittest for
intelligence and intrigues at the French Court, and on the other side
that shee received letters almost every weeke from the eminentest
churchmen on this side and that side of the seas, as also from some of
the greatest noblemen in England and Scotland, as from her brother
the Marquess of Huntley, my Lord Oxenford of Scotland, Mr. Maitland
(somewhat concerned in the secretariship of Scotland) and from the
Earle of Rothes Chancellor of Scotland ; But shee run out into some of
his love rommance with her, so that I leave to others to inferr from
the premisses to which, either to love or to the plott, part or all of this
his letter, correspondency must be referred ; and to confirme farther the
credit I must give to her words she drew forth a bag full of letters (a
matter of a bushell) and showed some more in a cabinet saying, are these
all about trifles thinke you ? Shee let me see farther a picture in migna-
ture of the said Chancellor, and went about to read one of his letters
(of a large and illshaped caracter me thought) but withheld referring
me to the forementioned three dayes forme. But I at last askt her
how she could avoyd suspition if so many letters were directed to her
in her owne name, she told me she had taken a good course for that
because her correspondents had severall names for her, and part of her
letters were directed to Mr. Conne a Scotchman liveing at Paris as
agent for the Pope, others were adressed to Mr. Dallison her Scotch
phisitian there, some to Father Joseph Prior of the English Benedictines
at Paris who was her Confessor.

The charge
against the
Talbots.

"Now in the interval, haveing beene before recommended by Dr.
O'brien, Dr. Molony, priests, and others to Coll: Richard Talbot and to
his brother Peter (the pretended Archbishop of Dublin) for a person
that carried on business after the formallities of the French Court, and
the Coll: haveing made some tryalls of me, he on a time desired me to
be assistant to his brother the Bishop (not long since come out of
England). The Bishop desired I should go complement on his behalfe
the Marshall Belfount (grand Steward to the French King) and knowe
when he might be introduct by him to the French King's audience
about the business whereof he treated with the Marshall himselfe,
while he was in England in or about the yeare 1670, the Marshall
being then at court (kept at Versailles). The Bishop would have Mr.
Moore a philosophy professor in Graslin Colledge to accompany us
theither next day. Haveing layne that night at Versailles and the
Bishop striveing to make us all merry on the good Catholiques' account,
I took the opportunity to enquire whether he thought it not fitt to com-

municate to me the heads and grounds of this affaire, **wherein he was**
pleased to make me his speaker and introductor at court. Least, said
he, any occasion might happen for you to second it, the business that I
am about to represent is this :

1. It is a business (said he) which mightily concernes the welfare of
   the Catholiques in England and especially in Ireland.
2. That he was to propose wayes to the King of France whereby to
   releive them in their present extremities and persecutions and
   to undertake their protection, and some of his wayes was to
   arme some Irish and to secure a seaport town in Ireland for the
   French.
3. He said that he had a speciall good warrant and commission for
   this his negotiation from some of the greatest persons in
   England.
4. That he was to solicit his Christian Majestie for a pension or
   arrears payable to himselfe. The next morning I went to the
   King's riseing to acquaint the Marshall Belffond that the Archbishopp Talbot was in towne to waite on his Majestie and him.
   Hee wisht me to introduce him. The Marshall knew him at first
   sight and embrac'd him, and told the King of it, his Majestie
   receiving him with great civility lead him into a private roome
   where Mr. Moore and I following them he beckoned to Mr.
   Moore who had the papers to advance. But I from the doore
   saw the Bishop present a letter to the King with other papers
   which I think were sealed. I overheard him speak to the King
   in Italien, their conference lasted about halfe an houre, and
   though his Majestie be of a morose temper yet he often smiled
   as at propositions that pleased him.

" But at our coming off from court I enquired of the Bishop of the
good success of his negotiation, which I told him seemed to be of other
or more matters then he acquainted me with. No, said he, 'tis but of the
same matters I spoake to you off last night, whereof he said I should
knowe more seeing he must come to court againe and againe about it,
though the King promised all satisfaction possible and hopes of a good
issue, so not to increase suspition I urged him no farther, but parted
from him for that time to Paris.

" Yett observe that one Mr. Coome a Scotchman who was formerly the
Pope's Nuntio and there his Agent at Paris had almost every day private
conferences with both the Talbotts, and waited betwixt them and the
Nuncio then being in Paris, and the Talbots and this Coome came also
often to my Lady Huntley though my Lady had also another pretext to
see Coome.

" The very same night I did communicate all that past in this Peter
Talbott's negotiation to Sir Robert Welsh, as I had don before that
other treason of the Lady Huntley's, both fearing least this grand secrett
might dy with mee, and having many enemies dayly threatening me
then at Paris, and for that this Sir Robert was a man that still made
much verball professions of his sufferings, actings and loyalty for the
King of England, our naturall prince, in such former discoveries. But
Sir Robert's true caracter I found out too late. However he most
unfaithfully forthwith discovered all to Collonell Talbot, both that of my
Lady Huntleye's and the Talbot's business, and that I intended speedily
to go for England to accuse both him and his brother Peter. The
Coll : faining to keepe his bed desired to speck with me at his owne
lodging. The circumstance of the message with the premisses weighed,
I took one or two along with me to his very antichamber on some pretext
or other ; he presently frouningly desired to knowe when I intended

for England and when I had seen Sir Robert Welsh. By this I presently perceiving I was betrayed pretended another occasion of that
voyage, for which besides I seemed not to be very earnest, if either in
Paris or with the now Duchess of Yorke (then at Paris) he could
procure me some fitt employment so as to be her secretary, &c. Att
first he went about to dissuade me from coming over into England at
all, then began to threaten me manfully, and that if he heard I did otherwise then I said in stealing away for London on such accusations against
them, and the Catholiques, he would infallably procure that I should
forthwith be committed to the Tower or to the Gate-house at my
arrivall in England, which accordingly happened according to his spite-
full prophecy after or about seven dayes I arrived here at London.

"So seeing the effect of his threatenings fall out so punctually and not
doubting but that he with Sir Robert and other their correspondents
there were the under contrivers of my 4 yeares close imprisonment at
the Tower, though a very remote surmise was put in by them against
me for a pretext, therefore I say I was afraid to charge them much and
but warily whilst I was in prison fearing worse from any friend of
theirs."

Evidences.

1st. The aforesaid Sir Robert Welche's evidence may first confirme
the truth of this my information, for he being now in London can
witness that I disclosed to him all the said treason about 5 yeares
since in No. 73. so that it cannot be imagined that this information
is any new matter fitted for the times against Papists, and if he
denys it, it may be made out against him by the following and other
evidences I can bring.

2. It appears that Sir Robert after my confinement acquainted
Mr. Secretary Coventry of the said informations for I have seen
some of Sir Robert's letters, which I could not but knowe, in the
secretarie's hands, out of which he examined mee upon the said
treasonable points in the presence of my Lord of Bathe, Newport,
and Bellasis . . . . whence I inferr that the secretary
must needs have knowne the said matter from Sir Robert and
consequently that the secretary himselfe may witness that he then,
now 5 yeares since, was informed of such things to have beene
past and discovered in France.

3. And whilst I was in the Tower I began to discover some of these
matters to Sir John Robinson, but whether it was that he took
such Popish plottings to be unlikely, or that he took such
discoveries from me to be a devised starting from the onely point he
would have mee confess concerning the Duke of Monmouth
(against whom I neither had nor thinke any can have the least
occasion of conceiving any mischife), but however it was, Sir John
made very slight of my information concerning the Huntleyes and
Talbots, of which I am sure I began to relate unto him att the
least. But how farr he suffered me to proceede I cannot now tell,
both for that it is 5 yeares since, and haveing extreame hard usage
wherewith Sir John did usually alarme and trouble my thoughts,
of which neither his Majestic nor the Duke of Monmouth knowe,
as my Lord Northampton told me since.

4. And since my releasement of late from the Tower, I yet went
thither at the beginning of this last sessions of the last Parliament
to desire Sir John to second me in the receiving of the said
discoveries, but he at my first speaking rejected my proposalls
referring me to the Secretary of State; but I had severall reasons

to think that he especially or some Parliament man would be more MSS. OF SIR W.
FITZHERBERT. fit introducer for one that was in my circumstances.

5. Coll : Justin Macarty now in London and then in Paris can I beleive testify the same, that either by Sir Robert Welsh's report, or the generall fame he hath then heard, that I did accuse the Talbots and Huntely in the said year 1673.

6. Nay and one Captain Barret now also in town told me a matter of 3 weeks before this information was given in on the said 21 of December to the Lords, that it was generally given out amongst the Irish Catholicks in Dublin and here that the Talbotts were above a month before committed in Ireland upon my accusing of them of these points, wheras since I came into England I never spoke of these matters but about three years agoe to the said Sir John Robinson. and now of late to the Committee of Lords ; whence it may be inferred that the Talbotts or other of their friends privy to the matters thus accusing themselves before hand, before I had accused them, is an argument that long before these present times there were such matters spoken of by me in France, and that it came to the knowledge of many Irish ; and the Talbotts themselves foreaccuse themselves in a manuer ; and doubtless where confronted to me they cannot deny it, as my request is they might be sent for and brought from Dublin Castle to London ; there being other wittnesses of the King's evidence that can accuse them as I came to know but a week before I gave this information to the Commons now sitting, not knoweing of it att all when I had given my charge against them to the Lords on the 21 December. And then the Lords promised the Talbotts should be sent for, yet they are not yet come though it be 3 months after."

" This information was given in writing in the Honble. House of Commons sitting in Parliament at Westminster on the four and twentieth of March 1679 by

EDMOND EVE[RARD]."

R. NEEDHAM'S CONFESSION.

1678-9, February 7.—" I doe confesse that I have been in company severall and many times in the company of many Priests particularly Mr. Poole, Mr. Turner, Mr. Heaton, Mr. Evers, Mr. Vavasor, Mr. Peeters, Mr. Busby, all which are priests, and one lay man one Mr. Sherbourne, which persons at times I have been in company of when these words have been spoake. That before long they hoped for better times, that if things went on right it was expected the King might not live long, and then the Duke of Yorke would be King, who had given good assurance for the establishing of the Romish religion, but some of the company supposing the Duke of Monmouth would stand up for the government, and soe it was thought fit that necessaryes might not be wanting for carrying on the designe. And I doe confess I have been imployed, and uppon this occasion, by the aforenamed gentlemen for the carrying and receiving of letters for any thing I know to that purpose, and I doe confesse I have been severall times att meetings where the discourse hath been tending to the aforesaid, and alsoe about Michaelmas last I was with Mr. Busbie the priest lately mentioned, and being in discourse of State affaires I told the said Mr. Busbie I was doubtfull that the expectation of our hoped for designe would not prevaile as regard our adversaryes were so powerfull, he answered that the King shortly would be disposed of and then the Duke of Yorke would be set up as King, and doe confesse I have been with Mr. Evers

K

severall times and had severall discourses as tending to the good and propagation of our religion, as also I doe remember that sodaynly after that discourse which Mr. Busby and I had, the plot being then discovered Mr. Busbie, one Mr. Sherbourne aforenamed, and one Mr. Shippie a priest, fled and they were never seen nor heard of since by me, and furthermore if any thing hereafter I should remember I shall be willing to give you account off, for my memory being ill and many troublee upon me I do not know whether I may be mindfull of all at present."

(*Signed*)   RICHARD NEEDHAM.

Sworne before the
  Lords of the Committee
    7th Feby. '78·
      PHILLIP LLOYD."

DR. RICHARD NEEDHAM'S PAPER.

1678–9, February 12.—"Since I was last before your Lordships it hath beene my sole meditation (together with the craving pardon of God and with the desire to illuminate mee in this so high a worke, and withall to doe no person wrong) to give my most gracious Soveraigne and your Lordships the best satisfaction which lay in my power, my memory decaying, and my senses being tosticated with worldly affaires how to maintaine my family, and pay the world its due, and the businesse being some tyme since perhaps hath taken me off somethings I have heard, the tymes and places, to which if I had a thousand lives to save by it, and as many souls, I cannot give your Lordships a relation, but to wrong both my soul and the parties, only this, which I hereafter mention ; being a company of us together at a meeting, wee were all enjoyned to say so many prayers for the Pope's good intention, and carrying on the great work, which was commended by the persons in my last deposition, the injunction being made in my presence, Mr. John and Mr. William Pontrill's, together with others whose names I doe not know, and what part they might have in the designe I doe not know, in regard the instructions was to be received from theire priest Mr. Bushie ; those things have happened within this two moneths or thereabout and the business was discovered before my full instructions was given me, therefore I humbly beg your favourable opinion of the truth, which ever during life, shall procede from his Majestie's most loyall poore subject and your humble petitioner.
I accept this to be true."

(*Signed*)   RICHARD NEEDHAM.

R. NEEDHAM.

[1679], March 24.—"I humbly beg your pardon for my grosse absurditie for offendinge your Lordships (through my mistake) soe highly when I was before you last but one, it was onely my wronge supposition who thought your Lordships had only intended to have examined me and not for that I did remember any thing more at that time. My Lords I have meditated upon every particular worde by worde in my deposition, how to pitch upon the parties, times, and places, where and by whome, as if I were before the great tribunall seate of God to give your Lordships better satisfaction, but beinge two or three yeares since at the least, I cannot with these confused idle braines of myne doe it, though I suffer death for it, not to say punctually, but to my best knowledge, it was with Mr. Evers at Tixall, about three yeares, since or upward, who sayd before longe, he hoped for better times, that MSS. of Sir Wm Fitzherbert. if things went on right, it was expected the Kinge might not live longe, and then the Duke of Yorke would be Kinge, who had given good assurance for the establishinge of the Romish religion ; a man, I suppose of the family, beinge by (for I was but a stranger there), sayd he did not, qnestion but the Duke of Monmouth would stand up for the government, and therefore they thought that necessaryes should not be wantinge for carryinge on the designe ; and as to whome the letters were transported by me, hath been from Mr. Evers to Mr. Turner, and from Mr. Busbie to Mr. Turner, and returned from him to them agnine ; and as to those who used to be with us at times, at our meetinges were one Mr. Sherbourne, Thomas Richardson, Joseph Spar, and his sonne in law I knowe not his name, and some woomen whome I knowe not, onely Mrs. Smauley, and Mrs. Brontnay, and as to my wive's speeches that she should never see mee againe, I doe beleive she had heard me say somethinge before concerninge the plot, wherein she conceived danger, as alsoe I am confident she was at the injunction, and to the Pontrills, in respect of theere beinge at the injunction, I have cause to thinke thay knew somethinge, otherwise they were alwayes very strange to me, as I was a stranger indeed.

"" My Lords this is all I can say, which I hope your Lordships will have a favorable construction of and be pleased to intercead for me to my most gratious soveraigne for my pardon and the freedome of your most humble petitioner."

Richard Needham.

1679, April 30.—[*Another copy of the last Information with the following additional passages*] :—" I likewise remember that beinge some halfe a score of us at a meetinge we were all enjoyned to say soe many prayers for the Pope's good, and carryinge on the greate worke, which was commanded by the piiest Mr. Bushie, the minutes being made in my presence, Mr. John and Mr. William Pontrills, together with others whom I doe not know, and what part they might have in the designe, I doe not know, in . . the instructions was to be received from the priest Mr. Busbie ; these things have happened within this twelve months or there abouts, and the business was discovered before my full instructions was given me, I owne Mr. Busbie and Mr. Poole, two Jesuits, were the persons who brought me in as both givinge charge of the injunction, I owne my goods I sould in parte to pay my debts, and rent, and in parte to buy some corne to make me bred, though it would not extend to it, thinkinge if they should be seised, I should not be able with . . . . . nd to pay my debts, and soe be cast into prison, and for the worde which my wife sayd that she would never see me againe, I am very confident it was through some words which she spoake before concerninge the plot."

Richard Needham.

1678-9, March 15.--Shrewsbury, County of Salop, Michael Ball, examined before Edward Phillips Esqre. mayor of the said towne, this 15th day of March 1678, deposeth as followeth.

. " Who upon oath saith that he this deponent standing att his house doore being in Mardell in the said towne of Shrewsbury about May, June, or August, next comeing will be two years, he saw two carriages viz.: a waggon and cart standing in the said streete, hee this deponent goeing to the said carters asked them what those carriages were loaded with, who answered they were loaded with muskett and pistoll barrells, and puting his hand in the said cart and **waggon** did as he this deponent beleive **feall both** muskett and pistoll **barrells,** for that he this deponent put his fingers into the muszles of **some of** them, and he this deponent doth further say that he pulled out a pair of horse pistoll barrells askeing the carters whether they would sell them, who replyed they were given them by account or tale, and if they did not deliver them **soe** theire wages would be stopped, and **said** that they were to carry them to my Lord of Powis, and asked of this deponent which was the best and nearest way to Red Castle, and further saith that the cause of his this deponent talking with them was because there were very good horses in the said carriages and that one of the said carters did pull out of his pockett a note of directions of the way to this place aforesaid and said he, this deponent, did give him a true account of the way according to his noate."

MICHAEL BALL.

T. BROWNE to the LORD HERBERT OF CHERBURY.

1678–9, March 19. Salop.—" In obedience to your Lordship's command I addressed myselfe to the mayor of this place, who I found most ready to sattisfie your Lordship's request, and immediately sent for Ball, who upon oath as you may find by the inclosed hath fully declared what he knowes which at present is all your Lordship requires.

[Enclosure.]

My Lord,

If another witnes be necessary there is one in Oswestry by name Katherin Jones a chimney sweepe's daughter who then drew drinke att the Green Dragon in this towne to the waggoner and carter, when Mr. Ball made the discovery, one Hugh kept then the Green Dragon who now absconds but may be found upon occasion by

Your Lordship's obedient servant
G. B.

Pardon haste good my Lord."

1679, April 2.—" The Examination of Thomas Marshall gentleman taken upon oath the 2nd of Aprill 1679, before the right bonble. the Earl of Clarendon, one of his Majesties Justices of the Peace for the said County and Liberty.

" This deponent saith that he hath bin four yeares in November last in the English colledge of Secular Priests in Lisbone in Portugall, and that he came from thence on or about the 6th of February last, new stile, and that Mr. John Betts being one of his masters for Philosophy, the deponent in the latter end of January or beginning of February last waiting at the said Mr. Betts his chamber doore in order to do some exercise, heard Mr. Roger Hesqueth (who with Mr. Howard the Lord Viscount Stafford's sonne was there in the said Mr. Betts his chamber) say wee have brought our pigs to a faire market, we have used all meanes possible by sending missionary priests to convert England, and probably might have done it if Oates had not putt a remora to our designe, and I thinke the best way may be to contrive the death of Oates, whereupon the said Betts replyed, that's impossible, for Catholicks being soe severely persecuted there can be noe uportunity for it, whereupon the said Mr. Hesqueath replyed, Mr. Booth is an ingenious man and we will send him by land to England, and I question not but he will effect our designe in killing of Oates. The deponent further saith that at his comeing from Portugall he demanding of

Mr. Booth when he was for England, Mr. Booth told him that he had some earnest business that would not suffer him to begin his journey this month, soe sent a letter by this deponent to Dr. Parkot which he desired the deponent to deliver with his owne hand, but the deponent not meeting with the said Parkot at his lodgeing he hath since received a letter from John Brett porter to the said Colledge (which was sent to him to the harbour in Lisbone but not received by the deponent till after he had bin sometime in England) to desire him to secure the letters he brought for England by wraping them in a foule shirt or trusting some of the seamen with them. That the deponent suspecting some dangerous matter in the said letter to Parkot opened it, which was to deplore the tyranny which the Roman Catholicks groane under in England, and that now since he had so faire an oportunity of conveying his letter he would speake in more cleare termes then formerly which was that they must contrive the death of Oates. This deponent further saith that he hath unfortunately lost the said letter but very well remembers the contents of it to be as above."

[*Endorsed*] "Received from Sir Thomas Lee who received from Mr. Relf."

1679, April 28.—"The examination of John Sanders, Christopher Sands, and Daniell Colster, taken before Sir W. Waller.

"This examinant saith, that about a fortnight past hee came from St. Omers out of the Colledg of English Jesuits in company of Mr. Christopher Sands, and that about a month before he left St. Omers he was desired to take a journey into England by one Mr. Roger Copley, from Mr. John Carryll now a prisoner in the Tower, in case he could say anything in behalf of the Lords or anything relating to Mr. Oates."

[*Signed*]   JOHN SAUNDERS.

" The examination of Mr. Christopher Sands taken before mee this 28 April 1679.

" This examinant saith that about a fortnight past hee came from St. Omers out of the Colledg of the English Jesuits in company of Mr. Sanders, but on no other account then in obedience to the King's command and to save his estate.

CHRISTOPHER SANDS."

" The examination of Mr. Danniell Coulster taken by mee this 28 April 1679.

" This examinant saith that on Sunday was sevenight he came from St. Omers out of the English Colledg of Jesuits in company with another young English student at the instigation of the Superiour of the Colledg as likewise the desire of severall Roman Catholicks in England for the justification of the Roman Catholick caus, and in relation to Mr. Otes.

DA. COULSTER."

" Memorandum.—That the said Gifford said that his Superior of the Colledg at St. Omers had sent him over to swear in behalf of the Lords and that he must obey and would right or wrong. This he said in the presence of us here under written.

ROBERT CHAMBERLAYNE living in Arundell Street.
MARK GOUDDALL over against Sr. Thos. Clarges.
WILLIAM WALLER."

1679, April 28.—" The further examination of John Saunders, *alias* Fall, *alias* Palmer, the son of Stephen Fall barber in Falcon Court in Flecte Streete now deceased, taken this 28th of Aprill 1679 before us Sir William Waller Bart. and Edmond Warcupp Esqre. two of his Majestie's Justices of the Peace in the said County and Citty.

"This examinant saith, that hee hath been a student at St. Omers for two yeares and halfe last past, and came thither in grammar, and is mainteined by the Carrylls and particularly Mr. John Carryll the elder, and he saith that Mr. Thimbleby and Mr. Peters were ministers there, and Mr. Ashby, Rector, and Mr. Thomas Stapylton is now Rector, and Father Nevyll is now minister there. And hee further saith that Mr. Copley coming over into England went to Mr. Carrell and returning to St. Omers where bee asked this examinant wether hee knew any thing of Mr. Oates, who went by the name of Sampson Lucy; who answered that from the first time the said Mr. Oates came to St. Omers hee never went away, till hee went for good and all, and he remembers that Mr. Oates was there in Lent time last yeare, but was not absent from the colledge five daies in the said time, when he was att Watton as hee heard; and one Edward Evers as this examinant remembers went with Mr. Oates thither, and he remembers that Mr. Oates was standing as the procession which passed in Corpus Christy day, which this examinant saies was after the time Mr. Oates saies hee was at the consult of the Jesuites in London, about May precedeinge as this examinant heard, and this Examinant saith that bee knoweth the premises to be true because he saw Mr. Oates sit at the refectory table in the colledge: and hee saith that Mr. Oates would not be absent at any time from the colledge 3, 4, or 5 daies at any time, but this examinant must know it, this examinant constantly observinge who were at the refectory table, this examinant sitting at the Syntaxin table which was just over against the said table where Mr. Oates sate; and hee saw Mr. Oates in the infirmary, but he knowes not how often Mr. Oates was sick, but there are other witnesses can prove how long Mr. Oates was in the Infirmary, and hee saith that hee never knew or heard Mr. Oates did any ill thing, or was thought an ill man, but was kind and familar among the students, and this examinant saith that there are about 15 or 16 persons that are come over from St. Omers, on the same errand this examinant cometh for, some being lay brothers, some students, and some servants, and that they and hee are sent over to testify for the Lords in the Tower, what they know of Mr. Oates, and hee saith that hee came very much against his will, but was commanded by Mr. Carryll to come, and can testify noe more against Mr. Oates, then is conteyned before herein: and this examinant came over with Christopher Townley, who also went by the name of Sands, and this examinant receaved three pounds partly of Brother Harry and partly of the Procurator Bushby, for his journey into England, and this examinant was recommended to my Lord Castlemaine by a letter which Christopher Towneley had at St. Omers: and they were bid to goe to Mr. Robinson's at Charing Crosse where my Lord Castlemaine lyes, and the Lord Castlemaine's footeman went with this examinant to Mr. Schard's house where this examinant was taken; and this examinant saw Townley deliver the letter of recommendation to Mr. Robinson; and hee further saith that about the time the noyse and rumour of the plott in England was spread abroad, there was likewise a report at St. Omers that the King was killed, but how or by whome he heard not; and this examinant saith he doth not believe there is any plott of the Jesuites or Papists against the King or government, although he hath heard many reports to that effect. And this examinant saith, that his

'Superior told him that hee could not bee saved if hee took the Oathes of Allegiance and Supremacy when he came into England : And further saveth not."

[*Endorsed*] " from Sir W. Waller."

1679, April 28.—" The examination of Mr. Danniell Coulster *alias* Gifford, taken this 28th day of April 1679 before us Sir William Waller, and Edmond Warcupp Esq. two of his Majestie's Justices of the Peace in the said Citty and County.

" This examinant saith that his father was Sir Joseph Coulster sometimes a Protestant but as this examinant verily beleives at his death a Papist, since the death of his ,father for the space of 7 years within 3 months hath been educated at the · English colledg of Jesuifs at St. Omers, and maintayned at the charge of Collonell Charles Gifford of Chillington in the County of Staffordshire his father in law, and all such sums of money as for his mayntenance used to be remitted, were payd to Thomas Staplefor, Rector of the said. colledg, and his predecessor Richard Ashby at Thimbleby. This examinant saith that about last Christmas was twelve months he saw Mr. Otes in the forementioned colledg and that from that time he was continualy residing there untill the middle of June following, unless for two or three dayes at one time he was absent, and that during such time as he was in health there, he saw him once in two nights. On Sunday was sevenight this examinant at the instigation of the Superiour came away from St. Omers and arrived at London on Thyrsday night last, having received of his Superiour three pounds towards the bearing of his charges, and by his Superiour was recomended by letter to my Lord Castlemain. Being arrived in London this examinant in company of Joseph Dallison a student in the said Colledg went to waite on the sayd Lord Castlemaine, and by the said Lord were recomended to a Lady in Arundell Street at the hous of Mrs. Seilliard, the Lord's footman going along with them ; at his coming away the two Jacksons, Mr. Parey, two of the Palmers, and one Mr. Stapleton, and Mr. Townley, all young students were absent out of the colledg. He likewise declares that the end of his being sent into England was to proove Mr. Otes his being at St. Omers from Christmas was twelve month to the middle of June next following. Some of the forementioned absent persons this examinant believes might be come over for the same designe and end with himself. Being examined whither he heard anything of the King's being dead, he declares that about three years agoe he heard such a rumour, but never since. And further this Examinant saith not."

[*Endorsed*] " from Sir W. Waller."

1679, April, 28.—" The examination of Christopher Towneley truely called Christopher Madgworth, *alias* Sands, son of Hughe Madgworth of Preston in Lancashire, taken this 28th day of Aprill 1679 before us Sir William Waller, Barronett, and Edmond Warrupp Esqr., two of his Majestie's Justices of the Peace in the said County and City.

" This examinant saith that he hath knowne Doctor Oates ever since the month of December stylo novo ,1677, and hee then sawe him at St. Omers in Flanders where this examinant was a student, and that Mr. Oates then stayed till June 1678 following as hee believes, but hee cannot say but that the said Mr. Oates might bee absent from St. Omers in that time for severall daies, and at severall times, but not absent above one week at a time, this examinant being lodged in the colledge where Mr. Oates was, but did not see him daily : and he further saith that hee changed his name 'soe often becaus he would not bring his friends into trouble. And he further saith that he was comanded by Thomas Stapylton, Superiour of the colledge, to come over to England on purpose to be a witnesse for the Lords in the Tower, being allowed three pounds by his Superiour for his charges as is usuall, and since his arrivall which was on Sunday was a fortnight he hath been maintained by the Lords in the Tower. And he saith that hee hath about 30 pound per annum settled by his father upon him upon an estate in Preston, which his brother who is turned Protestant now keepes from him, he confesseth he hath been sixe yeares at St. Omers but is not yet in Orders, and there studyeth humanity; hee further saith Mr. Parry, Mr. Palmer, Mr. Stapylton, the two Jacksons, and Henry Palmer, and Charles Gifford, now prisoners with him, were all absent from the colledge and believeth that all those come to bee evidence for the Lords in the Tower, and he saith that his instructions from the Superiour was to come over and sweare that Mr. Oates was but once from the colledge at St. Omers from December 1677 to June following, and that it was in the month of June only, and he further saith that hee is to bee a witnes for the Lords, and for all others in the Tower, as he believes, and that by being a student only hee could not know what plott was carrying on by the Jesuits here in England, but there might be a plott and hee not know it; and hee saith that the rumour of the country was that the King was killed but how hee was killed he did not know, and was usually reported once a year since this examinant hath been there that the King of England was killed: and he further saith that hee was directed by the Lord Castlemaine to lodge at Mrs. Seliere's house a midwife in Arundell Streete, and hee saith that the Lord Castlemaine defrayes all their charges; and hee saith that the Lords in the Tower have the Superiour's order to this examinant to come into England upon this occasion: and he further saith that Mr. Oates went by the name of Samson Lucy when he was at St. Omers. And further sayeth not."

CHRIS. TOWNELEY *alias* Wadworth *alias* Sands."

[*Endorsed*] " from Sir W. Waller."

1679, May 6. Suffolk.—" The information of John Byford of Stoke next Clare iu the said county, laborer, taken upon oath befcre Sir Gervas Elwes Bart. and Thomas Golding Esqre. twoe of his Majestie's justices of the peace for the said County the sixth day cf May in the one and thirtieth yeare of his Majesties raigne A.D. 1679.

" This informant saith that being at the house of William Lord Petree, at Thornton near Hearn Gate in the County of Essex aboute a fortnight or three weekes after Midsummer last was twelve month, upon the account of killing and destroying the ratts in the house and out houses of the said Lord Petree, being the imployment of him the said informant, the park keeper goeing into the park of the said Lord Petree about eleaven of the clock in the night, asked this informant to goe with him which this informant consented to and being in the said parke he this informant perceived at some distance from him flashing of fire like lightning whereupon this informant bid the keeper take notice of it. But the keeper not minding what he saide the informant told the keeper that hee would goe nearer to see what it might be, for he could not think it to be lightning there being then noe clouds in the skie it being a very starr light night. But the keeper seemed very unwilling he should goe that way. However he this informant went through a thickett of trees within tenn or eleaven rood of a valey or bottom from whence he had perceived the said flashing of fire and there he sawe perfectly a number of men on horse back

about three or four score as neare as he could guesse wheeling and
tacking aboute and often fireing at each other, which he perceived
by flashing in the pan without shooting but whether with pistolls or
carabines he knowes not. Soone after he this informant returned to
the keeper whoe asked him what he had seen, whereupon the informant
told him all the particulars above mentioned to which the said keeper
made noe answer, soe the keeper and he this informant returned to the
house of the said Lord Petree and went to bed, and the next morneing
he this informant came away and callinge at a house in Chelmsford
that sold beere told some persons whoe were drinking in the said house
what he had scene they the said persons whoe were all unknowne to
this informant made a pish at it and told him this informant that such
musterings had beene often scene there and that it was noe newes, and
this informant further saith that meeting one Cox whoe had beene
faulconer to the said Lord Petree about five or six weekes agoe, he
this informant speakeing of this matter to the said Cox he the said Cox
drew out his knife and threatened to stab him and called him lyeing
knave and roage for speaking such words.

Sworne before us the day
and year aforesaid.   JOHN BYFORD.
  Ger : Elwes.
    T : Golding."
[*Endorsed*] "from Mr. Titus."

1679, May 7.—"The information of Matthew Claye of Desborrowe
in the County of Northampton taken this 7th of May 1679 before mee
Edmund Warcupp Esq. one of his Majesties Justices of the Peace in the
said County and Citty.

"This informant saith, that he lodged in Mr. Blaesdon's house an
Apothecary in Arundell Streete, and hath known him for about two
years, and the last spring the said Mr. Blaesdon coming to Mr. Charles
Howard's in Ducken Streete in Arundell buildings, Mr. Howard
. . . . the informant to him . . . dg there. And this informant . . . that he never knewe Mr. Jolly a . . lour in Drury
Lane or his wife or to his knowledge ever was in the said Jolly's house,
or left any trunks or goods, but saith that possibly a brother of this
informant by name Danyell Clay might know the said Jolly, because
hee belonged to the Spanish house, which brother went beyond sea about
foure months since, and is at Paris as this informant beleives ; and
this informant further saith, that the trunks and clothes therein, and a
hatt and hatrase and some small lynnen and twenty pounds in mony
sealed up in a bagge, which were found in Mr. Blasedon's house when
this informant was taken, are his owne proper goods ; and that the plate
and loose monyes and the books and other things in the clossett, belong
to Mr. Blaesdon, to whom this Informant desires they may bee restored.
And this informant further saith that hee knew the Jesuits to bee of
corrupt principles and that he therefore cared not for them. And that
hee kuewe Mr. Oates at the said Mr. Charles Howard's house, and hath
heard Mr. Howard often to dissuade Mr. Oates from becomeing a Jesuite,
however this informant beleives that Mr. Oates went to St Omers a
little before the last spring, and stayed some time among the Jesuits
there, and returned again, and was here in the months of April and May
1678, and this informant sawe him in both those months in the said
house of Mr. Charles Howard in Ducken Streete, and this informant
further saith that Mr. Charles Howard in the month of June last past
turned the said Mr. Oates from the Jesuits, and put him upon some

other employment. And this informant further saith that Mr. Oates then told this informant that hee lodged in Cockpitt Alley ; and further sayeth not."

MATTH: CLAY.

[*Endorsed*] "from Sir J. Trevor."

MATTHEW CLAY'S EXAMINATION.

1679, May 8.—"Knew Mr. Otes the last spring and not before. Saw him at Mr. Howard's in travailler's cloaths. Then Mr. Charles Howard said there is a gentleman would be a Jesuite, but I have turned him off from that.

"He saw him there 2 or 3 times, but he said he was sure he saw him the first time in April."

Two INFORMATIONS of W. OSBORNE, relating to the EARL OF DANBY.

One paper containing several Memorials of W. Osborne and J. Lane's relating to the Queen.

One information of J. Lane's concerning an attempt to commit an unnatural offence made on him by Mr. Oates.

MILES PRANCE.

1679, January 11.—W. Lloyd's report.
,,   January 13.—Examination.
,,   March 19.—Examination, pp.1–10, printed, *State Trials*, VII. p. 1231 ; pp. 11–13 not printed.
,,   March 22 —Information, printed, *State Trials*, VII, p. 1233.
And Informations against Thomas Sutton and Richard Tesborow.

W. LLOYD'S REPORT.

1678–9, January 11.—"This evening I was at Newgate to visit Miles Prance as I had done twice before by order of the Lords in Counsell. I found him in one of his melancholy fits. He was near half an houre coming out of it before he knew me and after that he grew very sensible and spoke everything with good coherence. When he was well come to himself Capt. Richardson askt him concerning the names and habitations of those 4 persons that spoke of killing the Earl of Shaftsbury. He gave him the account that was desired, and said they spoke of killing 2 or 3 other Lords, but he remembered none of them but the Earl of Shaftsbury. When Captain Richardson was gone he told me he had something to impart which he desired that I would make knowne to his Majesty as soon as . . . and it was, that since the 5 Lords were sent to the Tower, as he was standing at the shop of one Mr. Boys near Ludgate there came to him one whom he familiarly knows tho he could not now hit on his name. It is one that was formerly servant to Mr. Sheldon the Almoner, and is now butler to the Lord Arundel of Wardour. This man fell into discours with him and hearing him complain how ill the times were for poor Catholics told him it would shortly be otherwise, and when he enquired how ? told him that Mr. Messenger (a servant of my Lord Arundel's) had undertaken to kill the King. I desired Mr. Prance to tell me all that the butler had said of that matter, he told me it was to this effect, That the butler being in the room with that Messenger and another, heard them speak of delivering the . . . . . . of prison, and that Messenger said the only way to do it was by putting all in distraction. (This Prance repeted severall times) and to do that he said I will kill the King as soon as I can get opportunity to do it.

" Prance also told me that the butler told him that Messenger was to have a great reward for it if he lived and it would turn to his if he died in the action.

" I askt Prance whether he beleeved this of Messenger. He told me he did for he heard Messenger say some while since at Bradley's house at the 5 Cans neer the Turnstile in Holborn that the Catholic religion would be set up shortly all over England, and when one said that it would never be done by this King for he is of a contrary religion, Messenger said he will make him turn.

" Among them that were to kill the Earl of Shaftsbury he had named one Benedict Prosser a silversmith. Now he told me that Prosser was intimate with Messenger, and that Prosser had told the said Prance that if there should be an army he hoped to have an ensign's . . . under my Lord Arundell."

" Of all these things he offered to make . . . . "

Examination of Miles France.

1678–9, January 13.—" Examination of Mr. Prance before Secretary Coventry upon oath January 13, 1678.

This examinant saythe

" Kelly and Greeme Fitzgerald and others had before designed the death of Sir Edmundbury Godfrey. That night they did it they sent to call him to them.

" Being asked who were the designers hee seyd Vernatt, and Fitzgerald, and another, whose name hee knoweth not.

" Being asked why they chose such a place hee seyd they were resolved to have done it in any reasonable place, nay in the lane going downe to his owne house.

" The seyd examinant avereth that hee and Maddison and Staley were at the Crosse Keys in Covent Garden, and Maddison seyd to Staley that the Earle of Shasbury was a greate persecutor of the Papists and hee deserved to dye as soone as any man, and that hee and 2 or 3 more Lords, whose names he knoweth not, should die as soone as they could find convenience to dispose of them.

" The seyd examinant seyth that Adamson seyd (Messenger and others being in the company) at the seyd tavern that my Lord Shasbury having beene fierce in prosecuting the Papists he thought it was no crime to kill him, and another time Mr. Bradshaw at this examinant's shopp seyd they thought it no more sinne to kill a Protestant then to kill a dogg, nor did he thinke it a sinne to kill any man that hinders the Papists in theyre religion.

" The seyd examinant seyth that Bradshaw and Maddison always carryed pistolls in theyre pocketts.

" The seyd examinant scyth that Mr. Prosser seyd that hee hoped the Catholique religion would soone reigne, and that whosoever was against it did not deserve to live, and named the Earle of Shasbury, Duke of Buckingham, and others.

" This examinant sayeth that one Gascoyne, a Frenchman and a taylor in Russell Streete, seyd hee wondered his Majestie would suffer the Catholiques to bee . . . . for it was no more to do the King an iniury then another man, and if it were in France he would have been kild long since and this hee heard him say twice.

" Taken upon oath before me   Miles Prance."
    Henry Coventry."

1678-9, March 19.--" The examination of Miles Prance, Silversmith, taken upon oath the 19th day of March 1678-9, before the Marquesse of Winchester one of his Majestie's Justices of Peace for the said County and Liberty.

"This examinant saith that he and Mr. Maddison, a barber in Holbourne, and Mr. Staley, were drinking at the Crosse Keys Taverne over against Staley's house about a fortbnight before the said Staley was taken, where complaining of the great persecution that the Papists lay under, and that if they did not take some speedy course to destroy their enemies they should be ruined, the said Staley and Maddison resolved to kill the Earl of Shaftesbury as the ringleader of the mischeife that they feared would fall upon them, Mattison saying that he would engage three, viz. Adamson a watchmaker, Prosser a silversmith, and Bradshaw an upholsterer, and the said Mattison comeing afterwards to the deponent's shop showed the deponent a pistoll he had prepared for that purpose. This deponent further saith that meeting with Adamson at Patties at the White Post in Vere Streete, and discoursing of newes. Adamson said that they should all be undone if they did not looke about them, therefore they were resolved to kill the Lord Shaftesbury, he alsoe speaking the same thing to the deponent at the Gridiron in Holbourne. This deponent likewise saith that Prosser told him that he was undone and he intended to kill the Lord Shaftesbury, for he with others of the Lords intended to undoe the Lord Arundell who was his very good customer, the said Prosser telling the deponent at another time that he was to be an ensigne under the Lord of Arundell. This deponent alsoe saith that Bradshaw in discourse with him said that he would make noe more to kill a Protestant than to kill a dog or a catt, and that he was resolved to kill some of the busy Lords, but the first should be the Lord Shaftesbury and the said Prosser showed the deponent a pistoll at the same time.

"This deponent further saith that he the deponent, Mr. Messinger, and Prosser, and Mattison, were at Bradley's in Holbourne about five weekes before Staley was taken, and the said Messinger much complaining of the severity of the lawes that were against the Papists, and much fearing that they would be putt in execution against them by some that were noe lovers of them, and particularly the Lord Shaftesbury, who did most buisy himselfe about them, said that there must bee a speedy course taken to prevent it ; and this deponent saith that some time after this the said Presser told him that the said Messinger was the person that promoted the killing of the Lord Shaftesbury.

"The deponent further saith that Mr. Goscene told him both in Covent Garden and in the deponent's shop that the King and Parliament would undoe them, and if he were to kill a man he would kill the King as soon as any man, and if he had him in France he would have killed him before this. This deponent further saith that about 6 months since he heard Mr. Mathews, the Lord Petre's priest, say that his Lord and the Lord Bellasis with some other Lords, would have a good army, and that he hoped the Catholicks' religion would be settled in England. This deponent further saith that about a year since he heard Mr. Singleton a priest say in the presence of Mr. Hall that he hoped he should be settled in a Parish Church before a twelvemonth, and that he did not feare but that the Catholick religion would raigne in England, and that he would not make any more matter in stabing 40 Parliament men than to eate his dinner. The deponent saith that he hath alsoe heard Mr. Byfleet and Dr. Guilding say severall times that they have turned diverse people from the Protestant religion to the Catholicke religion, and they hoped they should have many more.

The deponent alsoe beleives that the said Hall knows where the said Singleton, Byfleet, and Guilding are, for that they used to be alwayes at Hall's house, and the said Hall alwayes received the money for the said Singleton which was to be distributed for masses for the dead. This deponent further saith that Mr. Groves told him that this was no plott but a plott of the Protestants owne making, and when his uncle was condemned, he said that they were all rogues that swore against him, the deponent then asking him what he thought of the 50,000 men which he knew were to be raised, the said Groves replyed that might be in jest. The deponent further saith that Mr. Ridley, a chirurgion at the Lord Baltimore's house in Wilde Streete, told him severall times that he hoped to be chirurgion to the Catholicke army in England, and that the Lord Bellasis would much stand his friend in the concerne. This deponent further saith that the Lord Arundell of Wardour's butler told him that Mr. Messenger was to kill the King, and that he was to have a good reward if he saved his life, and if he were killed the said reward should be distributed amongst such friends as he should appoint, by the Lord Arundell, the Earl Powis, and the rest of the Lords that were in the same plott. The deponent further saith that meeting with Mr Messenger after that he asked the said Messenger why he would kill the King, the said Messenger answered who told you of it ? The deponent [said the] butler told me, the said Messenger replyed, we are off that thing now, therefore desired me not to speake of it to any body. Afterwards the said butler came to the deponent's shop and told the deponent that he had received great anger in that he had told the deponent of what Messenger was to attempt. This deponent further saith that somewhat above halfe a yeare since he heard Mr. Wolston Paston say that young Sir Henry Bedingfeild, of Oxburrough Hall in Norfolke, was to have a commission from my Lord Arundell for a troupe of horse in the army to be raised by the Papists.

[*Signed*]   MILES PRANCE."

[Another copy of Prance's information continues—]

butler came to my shopp and told me that hee received greate anger in telling me what Messenger was to attempt.

Mr. Lafeare a priest came to my shopp to buy a second hand silver hilt for a sword. I asked him what hee would doe with it for hee had a sword already ; hee then said that hee knew not what tymes wee should have therefore hee would gett him a good sword with such a hilt to it.

" I mett Mr. Moore that belongs to the Duke of Norfolke rideing in the streete on a very fine horse, a little while afterwards I mett him in the lower courte at Somersett howse and speaking of that brave horse Moore wished that he had tenne thousand of them, and hoped that in a short tyme they might have them and men well armed for the Catholick cause.

" I came to the chamber of Mr. Ireland in Russell Streete some tyme before Michaelmas last, Mr. Fenwicke and Mr. Grove being there present, the said Ireland did declare that there would bee fifty thousand men in armes, I asked where they would bee had, and what to doe, Ireland said wee must have them in a short tyme to settle religion or else all would be ruined, I asked who should command them, Fenwicke made answer that they should be commanded by the Lord Arundell, Lord Bellasis, and Lord Powis, I asked him what poore tradesmen should then doe. Fenwicke replyed you need not feare trade, you would have church work enough. Soone after Mr. Groves came to my shopp to buy two silver spoones for a christening, where he was to bee godfather. I asked him what office hee should have in the army, hee answered hee did not know. I asked him who was to governe this army, Groves said Lord Powis, Lord Bellasis, Lord Petres, and Lord Arundell, who had commissions."

INFORMATION of MILES FRANCE.

[1679], March 22.—"In the month of August 1678 I having occasion to write to a friend in the country, but not knowing how to send I went to Mr. Paston who lodged at one Bamber's a taylor in Duke Streete, who gave me an account where to send to him, and wee immediately fell into discourse concerning the present posture of affaires, and hee bid me not feare for wee should suddainly have better times, for in the first place hee said that the King was a greate heretick, and that the Lord Bellasis and Lord Arundell and Lord Powis and Lord Petres would have a very good army for the disposing of the King and the suppression of all the hereticks, and then the Catholick religion should bee established and flourish in this nation, hee alsoe said that the above named Lords had given out commissions allready to some gentlemen in the country whome hee named to me, that was, to one Mr. Talbott of Longford, and to Sir Henry Bennifeild of Oxborough hall in Norfolke, and one Mr. Stoner, who lives within foure or five miles of Kingston upon Thames.

"Also about two yeares agoe one Towneley of Towneley in Lancashire came up to London with his two sonnes, which he was carrying over to Doway, hee alsoe brought along with him his two brothers to keepe him company, and they tooke lodgings at one Ayry's howse in Drury Lane, where Fenwick lodged, and in a short tyme two of them went over to Doway with the two ladds, and left the other here, who in the absence of his brothers declared very often to my wive's brothers and to Adamson, that when his brothers came backe again from Doway, they expected commissions from the above named Lords for the raising of men to carry on the Catholick cause. This my brother and Adamson often told me at Pedley's in Vere Streete where wee had a clubb very often of none but Papisst.

MILES PRANCE."

"Alsoe about the same tyme that the fowre Lords were in the Tower, that is the Duke of Buckingham, the Lord Shaftesbury, and the Lord Wharton, and the Lord Salisbury, that one Mr. Kightly came to me, and greatly rejoycing at their imprisonment said that now is the tyme for the promoting of the Catholick religion, because of the difference that was amongst the Lords, and that if the Duke of Yorke did but follow the business closely, which the Catholicks had grounds to believe hee would, then they did not doubt but that it would bee settled at that present juncture of time."

(Signed) MILES PRANCE.

INFORMATION against THOMAS SUTTON.

N.D.—"Joel Monkesley deposes that the said T. Sutton brought to him a week before last Whitsun week two papers, one entitled "A Short History of the Convention or new christened Parliament;" the other "A Letter to a member of the Committee of Grievances." The last he left and it was carried first to the Lord Mayor, and then to Mr. Wynn, Secretary of State. The other paper he carried away with him, but he told the said J. Monkesley that he saw the author of it that same night, and that he was not a Papist.

" He also deposes that the said T. Sutton had said to him on May 31st last that King James would soon be upon the throne. He also at the same time showed him a written paper relating to the actions of Dundee in Scotland. Thomas Pultey deposes that on Friday, May 31, the said T. Sutton brought him two papers, one written, the other printed. The former came from the Duke of Gordon's secretary, the latter he believes was the same as the " *Letter to a Member of the Committee of Grievances.*"

The said Sutton a little after his arrest told the said J. Monkesley that he had found the paper entitled " *A Short History &c.*" in the street, though before the Lord Mayor he denied that he had ever shown it to the said J. Monkesley. Since then he has confessed to the said J. Monkesley and to one James Cheney, that he had received the said paper in a letter from an unknown hand."

The EXAMINATION of RANDAL JONES of Shrewsbury, blacksmith, living in Smadale.

1679, May 28.—" He remembers that about a year and a half since he saw a laden waggon standing by his door, and on looking into it he saw musketts, and other shorter arms, and some trunks and baskets. The waggoner told him that he was taking these things to Lord Powis at Red Castle.

" He did not take notice of the exact quantity but remembers that there were several bundles with about twelve muskets in each."

The INFORMATION of THOMAS RICHES of Theergaton, Norfolk, husbandman, taken before WILLIAM WINDHAM, Esq. of Felbrigg.

·1679, May 14.—" Deposes that he was in the service of Richard Tesborow of Flixton for a year from Michaelmas 1674, during which he contracted a great intimacy with W. Hownsam the park keeper.

" One night in May, 1675, they went abroad a drinking, and on their way home he asked W. Hownsam if the story that his master had arms underground was true. He said yes, and one day when the master and mistress were walking in the park, and the coast was clear, they went together into the small beer cellar. There they took up two or three pavements and found an iron grating, and some steps into a vault, about 16 feet square, where there were arms and armour enough to furnish 80 men.

" T. Riches further saith that about the month of June, in 1675, he one day saw Mr. Peregrine, brother to Mr. Richard, Tesborow kneeling upon the grass at the back of the house. The said T. Riches, being curious, went afterwards to the place and there found a stick in the ground standing up about one inch, and near at hand the flags were loose. He took up some of them and found a board and under it a brick vault, but it was so dark he could not see what there was within.

" He also saith that about the same time he overheard Mrs. Tesborow say to her maid servants that she hoped ere long to wash her hands in Protestant blood.

[*Signed*] W. WINDHAM.
     THOMAS RICHES, his mark.
     DENNIS HUNTON, his mark."

ROYAL WARRANTS.

Twenty five royal warrants all signed William R. addressed to the Attorney General ordering him to prepare Bills, Patents, and for Inventions, Pardons, &c. Amongst these there is the appointment of

Sir William Phipps to be Captain General and Governor in Chief of the Province of Massachusetts Bay in New England, with definition of his authority and powers. The appointment of Sir Edmund Andros to be Lieutenant and Governor General of Virginia. The appointment of Dr. Sherlock to the Temple. A warrant for Commission for the Convocation, November 26, 1689. One for the ratification of the Articles of Limerick, and one for ratifying the capitulation of Galway. And an order dated January 9, 1689, for a general Pardon to persons convicted of High Treason in 1685, and ordered to be transported to the West Indies. The list contains 867 names.

THE REBELLION IN 1745.

H. CHALLONER to ———

1745, September 22. Morpeth.—"By certain advices this morning (by Mr Lodington who we sent to Berwick for intelligence & by an express to Sr Harry Liddel) our army commanded by Sr Jno Cope was quite routed yesterday morning near Preston panns, where Sr Jno Cope & some more fled & got off in a boat, & Brigadier ffawke & Lascells got to Berwick; they engag'd about six yesterday morning, & the Highlanders fired in platoons a few fires, then rush'd upon our people sword in hand, which struck 'em with such a pannick that they all fled in less than half an hour. Some of the Dragoons 'tis suppos'd would fly to Berwick. This moment an express is arriv'd & the Boy says they hear they are pursuing our remains to Berwick. The Highlanders were suppos'd about six thousand, & Sr Jno about four thousand with the irregulars. No account certain of the Dutch, this is all we can hear att present, we are all in the utmost consternation here as the rebels may be with us in a short time."

——— to ———

1745, October 14. Morpeth.—"The rebels are yet in their camp near Edinburg, they have ordered a number of horses to be in readiness for them at Dalkeith (the Duke of Buccleugh's) at an hour's warning. There seems to be a great bustle in their camp as if they intended a march very soon, but which way their rout is intended they are cunning enough to keep a secret. They have gutted the Earl of Stair's house and plundered all his tenants, not leaving them either cow, sheep, or horse; they have ordered all their out parties in, who were collecting contributions and committing outrages for 20 miles round their camp and upwards, some say parties of them have been as far as Kelsoe and Jedburgh. We now are not so much afraid of a visit from them in this part as heretofore, as we are now certain that a camp of considerable force is formed or forming at Doncaster, which we hope will soon march this way to our protection, we likewise expect a body of forces to land at Sheilds daily, a flyboat came in last Fryday with baggage, &c. convoyed by a man of war, and the saylors judge the transports can't be far off. By the best calculation we can get the rebels are about 11000 strong, and by robbing the gentlemen farmers round the country they have got together about 2400 horses, and if you'll believe the Caledonian Mercury they are encreasing very fast numbers being added to 'em daily.

"According to Brigadier Fowke's letter, the rebels were expected to begin their march as last Tuesday."

———— to ————

1745, November 4. Morpeth.—"This day 7 night came in here the Royal Yorkshire hunters, commanded by General Oglethorpe, with Captain Gowland at the head of them, on their march against the rebels, who made a fine appearance and do an honour to their King and country. Yesterday in the afternoon Marshal Wade and General Huske arrived here from Newcastle with a party of troopers, several carriages of baggage, and about 100 foot belonging to the royal regiment of Yorkshire hunters, headed by Mr. Thornton who raised 'em at his own expence, and are to join the army. The above generals, etc. returned to the camp at Newcastle to-day upon account of the following express, the whole army was expected here to-day, and we are to encamp on Cottingwood. This morning we received an express from Kelsoe that on Fryday last at 8 o'clock in the evening, the rebels' army to the number of 5000 marched from Lesswade nigh to Dalkeith. On Saturday another body marched from Dalkeith at 9 in the morning with the Pretender at their head, and yesterday at 9 o'clock (says the writer) I being near Gingle Kirk, saw another body of the rebels consisting of about 1000, march to Lawder 10 miles from Kelsoe, this last body are said to be for Kelsoe last night or this morning, so for Jedburgh, and then to join the main body who are said to march by Howgate, Mantly, Peebles, Drumalier, Real, Locharby, Greeta Green, Carlisle etc. Wee fear they will harrass our forces most desperately, unless we had another army in the west to drive them to a hold—nothing material since my last till now.

"The 7 regiments of foot from Williamstadt landed in the river last Monday night."

———— to ————

1745, November 10, 12 att noon. Carlisle.—"The rebels are gott through Esk, and crossed Eden att a place called Peathwash, and have taken up their quarters att Greendale, two miles from hence, where they are encamped, and we expect every hour they will attack us. We are in great spirits and resolved to give them a warm reception, we have taken a spy since the above was wrote. The messenger says that when he came away the cannon began to play and continued to do so till he got to Penrith.

"Carlisle, Novr. 10th, 10 att night.—The rebells finding they could not carry our towne are moving up the river and its expect'd they will pass over four miles east of us.

"Newcastle, Novr. 12th.—The artillery marched southward today and the army receiv'd orders to march tomorrow. When the artillery had march'd four miles southward they receiv'd orders to stop and the orders to the army are countermanded.

"Copy of a letter from Marshall Wade to the Mayor and Gentlemen of Lancaster, dated Newcastle, Nov. the 6th 1745.

"I have just now receiv'd the favour of your letter of Novr. 5th with the enclosed intelligence from Dumfries for which am very much obliged to you all, tho' I had receiv'd the same word for word from Carlisle. I never doubted your showing the commendable zeal, which you have done on this occasion. I think you have acted very prudently in the resolution you have taken to ship off the guns and other warlike stores should the rebells approach you, for if their main body should venture to march into Lancashire it will be impossible in your present situation to repell their force, but if they by quick marches should enter your county I propose to march to your relief, by the first way that is

E 64159.

L

possible for the artillery to pass, which they tell me is from some part of Yorkshire. All the advice I can give, is, if you have any forces, as most of the counties have, to make use of them by dividing into small parties, who may fire from every hedge, to keep the rebells from separating from their main body to pillage and plunder, which I think will embarrass them more than any other method that can be expected from the county regiments, and it is my humble opinion that the further the rebells penetrate into England the more certain will be their distraction, tho' particulars may suffer by their bold attempt."

Copy of the Pretender's Summons to the Mayor of Carlisle.

" C. P. of W. R. of the Kingdom of England, Scotland, France, and Ireland, and of the dominions thereunto belonging.

Being come from our father to recover just right with full authority we are sorry to find you should prepare to obstruct our passage. We therefore to avoid the effusion of English blood doe hereby require you to open your gates, and let us enter as we desire in a peaceable manner, which if you do we shall take care to preserve you from any insult and sett an example to all England of the exactness with which we intend to fulfil the King our father's declaration and our own. But if you shall refuse us entrance, we are fully resolved to force it by such measures as Providence has put into our hands and then perhaps it will not be in our power to prevent the dreadfull consequences which usually attend places taken by assault. You may consider seriously of this and return an answer in two hours for your delay we shall take for a peremptory refusal and shall take those methods that are likely to succeed."

J. LISTER to RALPH KNIGHT.

" The following is copy of a letter I have just received from Sir J. Ramsden.
                              Byram November 22, 1745.
" Lord Lonsdale has this morning received an express with the following account of the rebels.
                              Penrith November 20, 1745.
" Copy of a letter from Mr. Cooper to the Postmaster of Brough.
" The Highlanders have been coming in here ever since 4 in the afternoon to nine, some houses have 100 a piece. The whole body we have good reason to believe is moving southwards, we have about 3,000 in town, what in the neighbourhood we cannot yet judge. Tomorrow is to bring us several thousands more. I have been twice called upon before the Commissaries &c. for the Post Office accounts here. They talk high but I have agreed to wait upon their Principal or even their Prince himself before I can settle. Express to Mr. Wade went at seven this morning. Mr. Wade was at Hexam yesterday. The advanced guard at Hayton Bridge; the Chevalier's van guard gone to Ld. Lonsdale's and adjacent places at two this afternoon. Rout Lancashire. Penrith 12 at night.
                                               J. R.

You'll see by this account that there has been no foundation for the report which was current all here-abouts yesterday of the rebels being expected at York tonight which I congratulate you upon.
                                               J. LISTER."

. Blyth 5 o'clock.

MSS. OF SIR W
FITZHERBERT.

ROBERT WILMOT to ————

Mansfield. Fryday 2 o'clock.

" Our advice from Darby just arrived is that the highland army artillero
had set out 9 this morning with great presipiation for Ashburn having
received advice of an opposition by the Duke's army at Swarston Bridg
in their way to Loughborough."

JOHN PAGE to ————

" The rebels are setting out of Darby at two o'clock but which way we
know not but have just now sent out men to know, we are afraid now
they will pay us a visit one hour more will make us [easy] either one
way or other by putting us out of our state of uncertainty.

4 o'clock.

" They are gone from Swarsonbridge where they took a horse from a
carrier, his shoes and a shilling. The officer gave the man his money
again and paid for his shoes but kept his horse."

ROBERT BATES to DICKENSON KNIGHT.

" Mansfield Woodhouse. Friday morning, 6 o'clock.—I hope all is
easy here. The Highland army did not stir out of Darby yesterday. I
had two expresses from Mr. Wilmot importing the same. The Duke of
Cumberland is within 3 or 4 hours march of it, and is determined to
fight, if possible, upon their first motion. ' · · ·'

" Worksop. Friday, past 10 morning.—Yester night I had a line from
Doctor Hickman which say Mr. Coomp's brother-in-law see an expres
from Dover that Admiral Rowley had destroyed the Toulon fleet. I
shewed his Grace of Devonshire that part of my letter which he did not
seem to credit."

JOHN WHITAKER to the SAME.

1745, December 2. " Monday night.—My business last Sunday was
to watch the motion of the rebels. Stockport Bridge being broke down
obliged them to cross a ford near Cheedle, which took them near to the
middle in water, with as much eagerness as a dog after a duck but with
less concern ; when come out again they walked at a prodigious rate,
they came by about 9 o'clock in the morning and continued till four in
the afternoon. I could not find out by any means where they intended
to lodge that night. I this morning went out at four for Macclesfield
where I found most of them if not all. Severall marched all night, they
are got very close together and keep so which looks as if they expected
an engagement, which is thought will be in 48 hours. They are in very
high spirits and want to meet Ligonier. I left Macclesfield at 2 this
afternoon, they have been marching all night, the Pretender I left in
town where I left all the artillery which consisted of 14 pieces of cannon
and a very few mortar pieces. There were severall Manchester gentlemen that joined the rebels, who informed me that 20,000 French were
actually landed in England, which account came to the Pretender this
morning (not to be credited) they are full of money, they give out they
are 20,000 and one fifth more which follows them. I dare say all their
army was in Macclesfield today. I could not learn whether the Pretender was to move this day, those that went march'd for Congleton.
They are determined to make the best of their way to London. I
imagine they will be stopt very soon.

" From Sheffield. Tuesday morning. Came into Worksopp about
8 o'clock at night.

"Warslaw 5 miles from Leek. 12 o'clock Tuesday.

The whole body of the Highland army lay last night at Macclesfield and all entered Leek this morning at nine, how much farther they go don't yet know, they were yesterday pushing for Wales, but took this sudden turn, as I guess to avoid the Duke of Cumberland's army. I expect they will march for Ashbourn and Darby, but hope the army will be able to give 'em battle soon. I can't know how the army lies because they are between the army and me. I wait here for return of spies sent to Leek. I don't think they will come our way but advise that people be sent towards Derby for intelligence. Keep things pack't up but don't move till you hear from me again.

W. Cartwright."

"P.S.—Advice from Leek. The Duke of Cumberland sent 16 men to Leek, to order the people to get their effects and send him an express on their approach and he would attack him there. People now who are in this house who have seen them at Macclesfield say they seem lame with their march and cramble much. Fresh advice from Leek. They are marching full drive for Ashborn ; no baggage comes up. This looks well. Now for £30000. Blue Bonnet.

"Wednesday morning 9 o'clock. Mansfield.—Just now advice came that the rebels entered Ashbourn yesterday at 3 o'clock.

"The above are the freshest advices we have."

The SAME to the SAME.

Thursday. Past Noon.

"The rebells were the last night at Derby, Ashborne, and Wirksworth. It's thought their route is southward by Nottingham or Loughborough. I don't hear where the Duke of Cumberland is. The Duke of Devonshire and 800 men are at Mansfield, got thither last night about 6 o'clock, they lay at Derby but had orders to march from thence yesterday morning one o'clock to Nottingham, and as soon as they had well reach't it they had farther orders to march to Mansfield. It's said the rebels have surprised and taken prisoners 11 Light horse belonging his Grace of Kingston, one of which is an officer and seven Light horse belonging his Grace of Cumberland, that the men have their hands tied behind them and are obliged to march with the rebels. No certain news of Marshall Wade, an express went to him yesterday and one returned this morning, but where he is is a secret.

R. KNIGHT to ———

Chesterfield. Wednesday eleven o'clock.

"By express from the Duke of Devonshire from Derby the van guard of the Rebels came into Ashbourne about 2 yesterday and was expected at Derby last night when the messenger came away my Lord's horses were ready for him to move and all the men drawn out ready to march.

"They gave out a day or two since they were for London. Their getting betwixt us here and the King's army has prevented me in my intention of going to it from hence.

"It's supposed the King's army was'nt above eight or ten miles from em."

The SAME to ———

Mansfield, eleven o'clock Fryday Decb.

"We were much alarmed here last night with a report of the rebels being within a few miles of this place. The Derbyshire forces left us in no small hurry and confusion which contributed a good deal to encrease the allarm. We sent our horses to Warsop that they might be out of danger at all events and were resolved ourselves to wait the event. The rebels sending out of Derby to press for horses in some places there abouts was all the foundation there was for the report. By a person from Derby going to the Duke of Devonshire we hear the rebels were at Derby at two o'clock this morning but seem'd preparing in order to march, it was supposed towards Leicester. They were in possession of Swarson bridge on the Trent and that part of the Duke's army was not far off them. Other reports say that the greatest part were supposed to be at or near Lichfield."

—— —— to —— ——

"1745, December 4. Blith.—A spy left Macclesfield at 2 of clock in the afternone yesterday, says that part of the rebels marched for Congelton on Munday night, the. main body followed yesterday morning, going to meet Ligoneur army near Newcastel-under-line. He saith that there was not above 3000 well-armed, the others with rusty guns and a brace of pistell each man, the boys pitchforks, while a great many rode horses; the battell will probably be fought tomorrow."

JOHN HOLLAND to RALPH KNIGHT.

Chesterfield, Saturday 2 o'clock.—" We have been alarmed here from the Duke of Devonshire's servant reporting as he passed here about seven in the morning from Chatsworth to the Duke, that the Highlanders were marching at one this morning, part Chesterfield road, the other Bakewell. Sent out immediately four persons different roads. Two of them are arrived and brings us certain accounts that they marched at one o'clock this morning from Ashburn towards Leek and continued marching till seven, when the artillery moved and were seen three miles on Leek road. So this proves a false alarm. By accounts I received from Derby this afternoon a small party of Highlanders returned to Derby last night and were there at 8 this morning when the messenger came away. We are advised here as a certainty, that Marshal Wade and 8000 forces were at Doncaster last night, and the Royal Hunters at Blyth. Do not hear where Ligonier is."

—— —— to —— ——

Sunday night.—" By an express to-day to the Dutchess of Devonshire the rebels left Leek at 3 o'clock yesterday morning, on their way to Macclesfeild, one that has been with 'em six days says they are not above 4000 fighting men, & those much dispirited & tir'd with marching—the Duke of Cumberland lies at Derby to-night with 5000 men—the Duke of Devonshire set out to-day from Retford with his men, to join the Duke's army."

JOHN BILLAM to ——.

1745, December 7. Sandbeck.—" I have been this day at Doncaster to waite upon Marshal Wade with my Lord's complements etc. who come there last night, together with Generall Wentworth, Generall Oglethorp etc., the Marshall had two expresses last night giveing him an account that the rebels was returned back into Lancastershire upon which he sent to the foot, who are at Ferry Bridge to halt, until further orders; all the horse are at Doncaster, except what went to Bautry yesterday; it's expected the whole army returns into the north againe for they were contracting with carriages to goe with them. I hope you continue to favour me with what news you hear, which will further oblige."

MSS. OF SIR W.
FITZHERBERT.

————— to —————

1745, December 8. Chesterfield.—"I have had no news in my private
letters since I saw you ; but what all or most of it is in the Gazette or
publick papers, or would have sent it to amuse you a little. 36 persons
joined the rebells at Manchester, all whom except two are taken in
Carlisle ; these two went with the Pretender. Doctr. Douglass, Doctr.
Salkeld, Davison a grocer, John Graham an apothecary. John Clayton
a smith, Francis Hewit a linnen draper, joined the rebels at Carlisle, are
inhabitants of the place. The Mayor and Town Clerk of Carlile are
sent to London to take their tryals there.

" N.B.—My friend writes I suppose it be those appointed by the
Pretender. I imagine it will appear the surrender of Carlile to the
rebels deserves inquiry.

" On Fryday last they had rejoycings at Manchester for the taking
Carlile, all windows in towne were illuminated; the loyal gentlemen
met and drunk several loyal healths. The Pretender was carry'd about
the streets in effigy (dressed in plad and armed with sword and target)
by the populace. A person on horseback went before him beating a
warming pan, and crying out, King George for ever ; no warming-pan
brood ; no warming pan Pretender; and at proper places the mob made
a stand and cryed aloud, No Jacobite parson, No Jacobite doctors, No
Jacobite constables, Hanover for ever, the Duke of Cumberland for
ever &c. No one insulted, no mischief done. In the conclusion they
burnt the effigy in great form.

N.B.—One Coppock, a clergyman in Manchester, joined the rebels
and Dr. Deacon, a conjuring physician, sent his three eldest sons, who
are now prisoners. The constables of Manchester ordered 50,000 bullets
to be made for the rebels, and sent southward after them. This one
constable owns, but the poor fellow was pistoled into it. The same
Mr. constable attended the rebels, hunting for arms and horses with
a Bible in his hand, in order to swear the persons they went to."

————— to —————

1745, December 8. Barwick.—"General Handyside arrived here
yesterday from whom we learn that the rebels in Scotland are 4050
strong including 800 French, and that he had ordered the bridge at
Stirling to be undermined and put powder under it that in case the
rebels come that way to blow it up to prevent their passing with their
artillery, which consists of 18 fine pieces that they have got from
France."

Manchester, December 10.—" I go there this evening when the rear
of the rebels had just left the town on their way to Wigan. I left our
army coming into Macclesfield this afternoon, which is as follows
Sir J. Legonier's horse, Bland's, Lord Mac Kerr's, Lord Cobham's
dragoons, the Duke of Kingston's and Montague's light horse, with
about 300 foot, who are determined to march day and night till they
come up with them, horses being prest for the foot ; the rest of
Ligonier's army and artillery encamped near Coventry."

Doncaster, December 12.—" General Oglethorpe with Sir George's
dragoons and ten men out of every troup in Wade's and Montague's
horse, and the Royal Hunters went from Wakefield to Huthersfield on
Wednesday morning in pursuit of the rebels. Wade's army went from
Wakefield to Leeds on Wednesday morning, and 'tis said was to proceed
from thence to Newcastle."

Bawtry, December 14.—" General Huske at his own earnest request MSS. of Sir W Fitzherbert. was gone from Ferry bridge with five regiments of foot and four pieces of cannon, not doubting but he will have it in his power either to harass the enemy or stop them at a pass near Penrith.

" I wish this be true but doubt it. I think he might have got to Penrith before the rebels, it being exceeding good turnpike road to Greta Bridge and from thence to Penrith."

——— to ———

Saturday Evening six o'clock.

1745, December 9. Chesterfield.—" At one o'clock yesterday morning the rebells began to march from Ashburn, Leek road. Parties continued marching till seven when the artillery moved. The Pretender went about seven. They plundered very much, were more abusive then in their first visit, and lived altogether on free quarter. A party of horse continued till twelve in town.

Sunday Evening seven o'clock.

" By an express just arrived from Leek I have the following particulars. A thousand rebells marched last night from thence for Macclesfield, att six this morning the remaining body began to march the same way. At eight the artillery marched. A coach and six with about 40 horse left Mr. Mills' house about eleven. Twelve horsemen returned presently into town demanding horses at three or four places and threatening to shoot people if not produced. After an hour's search left the town. Mr. Mills', Mr. Lockett's, and the houses of the principali inhabitants in . . . have been totally stript and plundered taking their linnen . . . . apparell and every thing valuable and ransacked and disfigured . . . houses entirely, Mr. Lockett senr. was detained prisoner a . . . time and ordered to be shot if he did not produce his son. It . . . apprehended these outrages arise from the town apprehending two rebells who stayed after the rest in their first visit to steal horse and were sent to Stafford jail. Mr. Mills, Mr. Statham, Mr. Lockett junr., the constables, and principall inhabitants, left the town on the approach of the rebells. I have 4 more spies amongst them or will be amongst them tomorrow evening. I have sent William our huntsman to hunt them to Manchester or see if they take Chester road.'

———— to ————

1745, December 10th.—" The rebels marched from Manchester and took the rout of Wigan, part of them were seen two miles beyond Wigan two miles wide of the road to Preston as if their intentions were to go to Liverpoole. The Duke who is in pursuit of them was expected at Manchester tomorrow. The country people and militia are breaking up the roads and laying trees across to impede their march, and it is not doubted but care will be taken to break down Ribble bridge near Preston. The day they left Manchester they demanded £4000 which the inhabitants refused to pay. The rebels destroyed at Manchester all their provisions, liquors etc. This account came from Sheffield yesterday the 11th. It came thither by one of their spies who was at Mansfield on Thursday and saw some of the Duke of C[umberland]'s officers come in there to demand billets."

JOHN HOLLAND to DICKENSON KNIGHT.

1745, December 12. Chesterfield.—" The van guard of the rebells entered Macclesfield on Saturday evening, on Sunday came their main body, then artillery arrived there about five that evening.

MSS. OF SIR W.
FITZHERBERT.

"Lord Elco with the van guard got to Stockport Sunday evening at six; on Munday about noon came their whole body much in confusion and hurry, and marched to Manchester that night without halting in town. Their horses were tired, and their foot so foot-sore as could scarce march. Four persons riding through Stockport Saturday in the night refused to be stopt by the watch, on this the watch fired amongst them, and killed a rebell, which so exasperated the rebells that the town in their councells was ordered to be burnt, but for their other officers who opposed it. They have taken Mr. Allcock, Senr., an attorney, Mr. Robinson a grocer, Mr. Bore, Mr. Osborn, with them prisoners for going only to speak in behalf of the said watch and company. As also led away James Lucas the constable with a halter about his neck, and Peter Lewach, and Ralph Kemp are prisoners amongst them for striking a Highlander. They burnt Joseph Stockport's cow-house and barn and destroyed his cattle, for shooting the rebell on Saturday, and have taken the father, an old man of 90, prisoner.

"The van guard of the rebells marched from Manchester on Tuesday morning, about nine towards Wiggan. The artillery betwixt eleven and twelve, the rearmost of them about four. The contributions (which it's said was £2,500) was ordered to be paid in by five, for which they have taken hostages, and seemed in great hurry. If they had stayed another night, the town was determined to give them battle, and for that purpose had got about 4000 ready to rise.

"The Duke of Cumberland with his army lay att Macclesfield on Tuesday night, and sent his orders to Manchester for to make ready for his army the next day. Most of the foot are mounted by the country in order to make double marches, the people are very diligent in repairing the roads for his army, and bringing in horses to draw his artillery, which is drawn night and day. As the Duke marches about 20 miles a day, it is expected he may overtake the rebells in 2 or 3 days.

"By an express since from Manchester, the mob rose upon 4 or 500, that were left there on Tuesday evening betwixt four and five o'clock, and fired a gun at them; upon which the rebells shot a man and boy dead, and wounded another in the shoulder, and then marched off.

"The messenger met the Duke of Cumberland with about 2000 horse and dragoons coming into Stockport betwixt ten and eleven on Wednesday morning.

"All the Stockport gentlemen are returned home except one Watchman, and one man that knocked a Highlander down and took his plunder from him.

"A gentleman in the Peak advises me this evening, that one part of the Duke's forces marcht by Stockport the other towards the Witches; and it was expected, that the two bodies might reach Wiggan, and join on Wednesday night, and hope all our forces may be att Preston to night. The Ribble and Lancaster bridges he hears are pulled down. The Duke declares he will not sleep, till he has seen them.

"All my accounts agree that the rebells and their horses are much fatigued, and their chiefs very much dejected."

Ten o'clock Even.
1745, December 12. Chesterfield.—"I have sent you our accounts and hope the next will bring account of the utter destruction of the rebels. I have sent Mr. Knight's pistols.

"I have sent two spies after the rebels at 5 this morning."

The SAME to the SAME. MSS. OF SIR W. FITZHERBERT.

Saturday Even 5 o'clock.

1745, December 17. Chesterfield.—"The King's forces are in eager pursuit of the rebells, a considerable number of horse and foot have passed through this place, we have a large body here this night; we were in great expectation of seeing the Duke here two days ago, but he halted three or four days about Macclesfield and went this morning through Weemslow and Holling ferry for Wiggan which place he designed to reach to night. It is generally supposed the van guard of the Duke's army which lay at Wiggan last night will come up with the rear guard of the rebells to morrow or Sabbath day, they did not march from Preston till this morning. A party of Marshall Wade's light horse went through Bury at seven o'clock this morning to join the Duke. Marshall Wade has detatched five regiments to march with all speed to interrupt the rebells betwixt Kendall and Carlisle. Thirteen rebells prisoners in Manchester house of correction, and we hear severall more taken att Wiggan, being stragglers tired with marching, which is apprehended to be the reason of their stay at Preston.

Sunday Even 6 o'clock.

"The rebells left Preston on Fryday morning in great distress, att which time the van of the Duke's army was but six miles from them, and part of Marshall Wade's light horse had joined those of the Duke's, so it's expected they would be up with them on Saturday and barrass them in the rear till the rest can get up.

"The Duke and the rear were to be at Wiggan on Fryday night. It's said that Marshall Wade has detatched a party to give them the meeting betwixt Kendall and Carlisle. It's not doubted but they will be in time, we are informed that the party which composes the van of the Duke's army are volunteers and choose to take the part of harrassing the rebells, and we imagine the Duke's staying 2 days att Macclesfield was to draw up the rear and give them refreshment. It is said the van that is near the rebells is about 4,000 horse old and new.

Manchester, Tuesday evening 6 o'clock.

"Yesterday we had the following accounts from Preston. The main body of the rebels left Preston on Fryday morning Decr. 13. The same day there came in there 120 of the Duke of Kingstone's light horse, the Duke of Cumberland's hussars, and the Royall Hunters.

"The same evening came in St. George's Dragoons, a detatchment of Wade's horse, another of Montague's old horse, and Oglethorp's.

"About 2 this afternoon, we had an account that the hussars and light horse came up with the rear of the rebels on a moor, about midway betwixt Garstang and Lancaster yesterday; when a slight skirmish ensued and it's said one or two of the light horse were killed, but we have no certain accounts what the rebels lost. However as there was no lodging there for our horse their commander thought it best to return to Garstang and the rebels proceeded to Lancaster that evening, when they arrived there we are told they hanged three of the King's friends.

"It's said the rebels hearing a party of Wade's foot were att Kendall intended to halt at Lancaster.

"The Duke with part of his forces went through Warrington and would be at Lancaster to night if the rebels had quitted that town, the detachment of foot that went through our town, would be att Preston to night.

"Manchester paid 2,500 by way of contribution.

"General Oglethorp drew up the van of the King's forces composed of Duke of Kingstone's and the rest of the light horse and hussars, and

MSS. OF SIR W. FITZHERBERT. Lord Elco the rear of the rebels on Hilmoor, 5 miles short of Lancaster, and Lord Elco has possession of Lancaster. The rebels were at Lancaster on Sunday morning and did not seem to move, having notice General Husk was got to Kendall with five regiments of foot detached from General Wade's army.

"The Duke of Cumberland was att Preston on Saturday, he expected to be att Garstang Sunday evening.

"The rebels' artillery is now in the van, the horse in the rear. Their are 17 right-Hungarian hussars with our army."

"The two first accounts are the reports of the spies, the last the contents of three letters I received from Manchester."

The Same to the Same.

Wednesday morning, Kendall.

"The Duke's horse and one regiment of granadiers march'd from hence till they came to Clifton-Moor, about 2 miles from Penrith, 14 miles from Kendall, where they arriv'd about 4 afternoon, when our hussars and rebels had severall fires at one another for about an hour. Our horse and dragoons were immediately form'd into a line of battle, the foot being behind, and a draught out of three regiments of dragoons was detached and marched on foot towards the enemy, commanded by Coll. Honeywood, being about 150. They marched to the bottom of the moor, where our hussars informed them they were, but it being near 5 and dark, our men could not see them till they were upon them, nor even till they gave fire, for they were intrenched in a deep watry ditch beyond a hedge; as soon as our men had receiv'd the fire they returned it with the fire of platoons, and immediately after with a whole volley, which was performed with admiration. Then the rebels ran away, and our men gave a hussa and followed; they run the length of one field, and then gave us another fire, and we returned it, then they attacked us sword in hand, but it being very dark, and our men having great heavy boots, and it being among ditches and hedges and soft watry ground, made it worse for our men. We had 11 men killed and 18 wounded, amongst which was Col. Honeywood, and a Captain, but none mortall. Our men all stood under arms all night (which was a very cold rainy one) expecting a battle next morning, for the rebels' artillery march'd over this moor about 2 this afternoon. Five rebels found dead in the field next morning, and thirty-nine taken prisoner by the country people, most of them wounded, and seventeen found dead next day in the river and ditches thereabouts, and I dare say a great many more were killed. The rebels march'd with their artillery from Penrith about 6 this night, and took about 100 inhabitants with them, with lanthorns and were made to lead their horses all the way to Carlisle, where the dogs got about nine next morning.

"The Duke and his horse got into Penrith Thursday morning about nine, and his foot that night and Friday. All Thursday and Friday the country people, hussars, and Hunters, were continually bringing in rebels into Penrith so that there is now kill'd and taken upwards of 200. Lord Elco is taken, he got a cutt in his throat by our hussars which was sew'd up, but doubtfull whether he will recover. Capt. Hamilton is taken, and one who came from Manchester, who after taken requir'd quarter, which was granted, after which the rogue fired a pistol at one of our hussars. Friday about 150 of the better sort of the rebels advanced from Carlisle towards the river Aske, but Gen. Huske being there with 3000 men, part of Marshall Wade's army and 2000 Whitehaven men, joined them, which obliged the rebels to retreat to Carlisle. There will be 12 pieces of cannon and 2 large battering MSS. OF SIR W. FITZHERBERT. pieces immediately brought from Whitehaven to the Duke's assistance. His whole army will march from Penrith towards Carlisle this morning being Saturday. Gen. Wade with his army was att Newcastle on Wednesday night last, so I hope a few days will make an end of all the rogues."

Chesterfield, 23 Decr. 1745. 12 o'clock at night.

" The above I received by express from a particular friend, which I hope may be depended upon. The accounts from Brother you'll see are premature. I have enclosed the contents of all accounts I have received as they vary so much. Sir Charles Molyneux, gentlemen, and others wait for accounts therefore please excuse hurry."

SAMUEL HOLLAND to JOHN HOLLAND.

"Dear Brother,—Having just now received the following accounts, I thought proper to send it you, by a special messenger. Mr. Simns brought them both from Norton. The one is the express sent from Chattsworth to Mr. Offley, which is pretty much the same we received, only more particular, the other is an express sent to Sheffield, which Mr. Wadsworth brought to Mr. Offley's.

"My Lord,—Brough, December the 18th, in the morning.—I have just now received a letter from Mr. Burn of Orton, that General Oglethorp is in his house, and that the town is full of our forces. Our messenger was amongst them; and the Duke of Cumberland has taken the rear-guard of the rebells at Shap; and sent an express to Appleby to summon all the country to join them att Brougham, as soon as possible this day, with such arms as they can get, to persue and take the rest. The above is from Sheffield by an express come in there.

" Wednesday 10 o'clock night.—Lord Lonsdale has had an express within this hour from Mr. Armitage, dated this morning, and he says last night the Duke was att Shap, within six miles of Penrith, where he had taken all the rear guard of the rebells, and was within 4 miles of the main body.

" The day before the advanced guard of the rebells was beat back from Emmont Bridge, and chaised to Kendall, by the country rising upon them ; that the Duke of Perth, and the two ladys, were taken by the way ; but the Duke is so ill it's thought he is dead by this time.

" The advanced guard of the rebells were, their Prince, the Duke of Perth, and all the Lords as before.

" P.S.—Pray excuse all faults for am so overjoyed I scarce can contain myself."

JOHN HOLLAND to DICKENSON KNIGHT.

1745, December 19. Penrith.—" My last was from Kendal on Tuesday. Yesterday morning wee passed over the dreadfull fields of Westmoreland and came to Shap about 2 in the afternoon, where we heard that the rear of the rebels was about 6 miles before us, whereupon we martched forward to this place, but were stopt 2 miles short of it by about 800 of the rascals at a village called Clifton, which they had taken possession of, and had lined all the hedges about the place ; we drew up in order on a common about a quarter of a mile from the village, by this time it was almost dark, hit our hussars and a party of Cobham's and Bland's dragoons dismounted, got into the fields and after a sharp fire of a quarter of an hour we cleared the fields and hill of them, and then took possession of the place and continued in it all night, our army

MSS. OF SIR W.
FITZHERBERT. remaining on the common, where they were drawn up, we lost about 12 dragoons, and it is unknown what number of the rebels was slain, for they carried many away and threw them into a river hard by, we found only 5 this morning on the field, we have taken 50 prisoners this morning. My Lord Duke is very well after this fatigue of lying under arms all last dreadfull wet night, and I hope this night's expected rest will refresh him and all of us, tho' beads are almost out of fashion with us. The rebels made this stand to secure the retreat of the remain body, who went from hence during the scirmish, and I suppose are before now at Carlisle, but I hope we shall demolish them all before they reach Scotland, we are now but 16 miles from Carlisle, and I suppose shall be before it tomorrow; the Duke of Perth was very active last night, we hear of one of their great officers being wounded but cannot say who, poor Colonell Huneywood received wounds, and we fear he is in danger; we were on an eminence and saw the action thro'out, but encountred with nothing but the long night and comfortless weather, for it began to rain at 3 in the morning and continued till this day noon. My best wishes attend all at Thoersby, this is no time for compliment, but I am hartily, tho' not a little fatigued."

JOHN LAUD to ———— MASSON.

1745, December 28. Sheffield.—"The following account came from the surgeon to General Wade's horse to his brother here, and I doubt not may be depended on."

" Bishopp Aukland, December 24, 1745.
" I imagine you received a verball account of our arrival at Barnsley, here I found the two regiments when all march'd for Pontefract, except a detachment of 60 men from each regiment, which together with 300 Dragoons, the Royall Hunters and Georgier Rangers, where I intended by forc'd marches to join the Duke at Preston. I would gladly have gone and offered myself to the Collonell (as they had no surgeon with them) but it could not be admitted of. We march'd from Pontefract to Knaresborough from thence to Rippon. As our Generals had resolv'd to cantoon the infantry from Burrowbridge to Newcastle the army did not move together but in divisions of 2000 each. So we halted at Rippon that we might not fall in with the foot upon the march, from Rippon to Richmond, from thence to Bishop Aukland, which prov'd too long fatiguing marches, thro' exceeding deep dirty roads, here we have halted, but expect to march tomorrow or next day. You have heard no doubt of the precepitate retreat of the rebels out of England. The first place the horse could overtake them at was near Penrith, their rear guard finding themselves too closely pursued, drew up in Clifton field behind the hedge, the afternoon was very hazy, and it was near 4 o'clock before the people came up. The Duke ordered Bland's dragoons to dismount, they formed and march'd up to the enemy. A brisk fire began from behind the hedge which was return'd by our dragoons and continued pretty smart for a few minutes, but they quickly turn'd taile, and the whole 400 dispers'd, they found about 18 killed and wounded upon the spott, and in the adjacent lanes and hedges, 30 were taken prisoners, and the country people brought in 30 or 40 the next day.

" Poor Philip Honeywood was shott in the neck, two more officers wounded, and about ten dragoons killed and wounded. We heard no more of our brave Duke till today, when we had an account, the rebels not being able to pursue their retreat any longer, where obliged to take shelter in Carlisle, where the Duke has pinned them up, and perhaps before you receive this has destroyed their whole power, at least you may be very sure, you'l hear no more of their marching either into England or Scotland. We have made another detachment of 80 men from two regiments, and they have mounted 1000 foot at Newcastle. This reinforcement has joined the Duke before Carlisle, 6000 Hessians are actually landed in Scotland. So that if it was possible for the rebels to escape the Duke, they are very certain to be cut off before they can reach the Highlands. The Lord be thanked our good friends the Dutch are order'd home, these gentry have given us more trouble than it may be proper to speak of, but while we wanted their assistance it was not proper to complain. The next news I hear from Carlisle. . . . .

Jervase Wright."

" Yesterday we had a confirmation of this from a person in Carlisle, to his brother here, but I have not time to go and see it now."

—— —— RAVEN to —— —

1745, December 10. Manchester.—" I came from Litchfield yesterday when I saw the Duke of Cumberland and the regiments following, Ligonier's Horse, Bland's, Lord Mac Ker's, and Cobham's Dragoons, the Duke of Kingston's and Montague's Light Horse, with about 1500 foot, who are determined to march almost day and night till they come up with the rebels. The rest of the army is encamped on Meridan Heath near Coventry, where the artillery is left, that they may march the more expeditiously after them, they press horses for the foot that they get forward with the horse. The town of Macclesfield is almost ruined by the rebels. At the approach of the King's forces into the town I never saw such a chearfulness, and rejoicing in my life. Yesterday a small party of rebels was plundering near this town ; one of the inhabitants fired a gun and killed one of 'em on which his comrades burnt his house and forced two of his neighbours along with 'em with halters about their necks, and made 'em walk barefoot with their boots upon their shoulders. On their leaving this town they obliged 'em to pay £2500 contribution, and when they went off they fired some guns and wounded several people in a terrible manner. The rebels left Manchester about 2 hours before Mr. Abraham Cave and I got in.

" Mr. Burdon's account is almost exactly the same with the above, he says the rear of the rebels marched out of Manchester towards Wiggan on Tuesday in the afternoon, and so northward as fast as possible, and that our army entered Macclesfield about 3 o'clock in the afternoon the same day—he farther adds they are informed by a letter from Newcastle by last night's post, there is a body of 5000 rebels, Scotch and French in arms in Scotland with a train of battering cannon, and they give out they will besiege Stirling and Edinburgh. Epworth, 12 December."

—— —— to —— —

1745, December 15. Evening. Manchester.—" By an express from Lancaster dated this morning at 9 o'clock, we hear that the body of the rebels was then there, but what they designed to do was not known, being they heard a detachment of Wade's army was at Kendall, and t'was reported they hanged 3 men (but does not say who they were) at that place, and says yesterday a detachment of the Duke of Kingston's light horse, and a party of hussars and Royal Hunters, commanded by General Oglethorpe, came up with the rear guard of the rebells about

MSS. OF SIR W.
FITZHERBERT. 3 or 4 miles beyond Garstang under the command of Lord Elcho, upon which they turned about, and a pritty warm skirmish ensued, in which General Oglethorpe has one man killed and one took prisoner, owing to a fall from his horse, but what numbers of the rebels was killed is not known, upon which they retired and agreed in a councill of warr to return to Garstang and wait for the remainder of the army to come up, which is expected will be there to night."

———— to ————

Durham. December 17.—"General Wade's army is divided and marches in eight columns, the first of which will be at Newcastle tomorrow.—It is reported the Duke of Perth is taken prisoner on account of his falling sick, and Lady Ogilvie also taken prisoner, and that the Duke's army has harassed and broke the rebel army, and that 500 of them are within five miles of this place, if so as the passes are most of them stopt into Scotland I hope that our different columns will pick up a share of them. General Wade's army now lies under cover of night. This comes from an officer of Wade's army.

1745, December 19. Doncaster.—"A messenger going from Lord Malton's to London gives an account that the Duke of Cumberland haith taken the artillery and baggage of the rebels and cut off the rear of them."

———— to ————

1745, December 19. Chesterfield, Thursday Noon.—"On Thursday December the 12. A large body of dragoons with four troops of the Duke of Kingston's horse, and 1500 Foot, entered Manchester in the evening.

"On Friday 200 of the Duke of Montague's Old Horse, and 200 of St. George's Dragoons reached Preston that evening from Rachdale.

"Twelve of the Duke of Kingston's light horse, sent from Manchester to reconnoitre the rebels, returned from near Garstang to Preston on Friday night, with intelligence that the rebels were about Garstang.

"Saturday at noon 12 Yorkshire Rangers, who were advanced within a mile or two of Lancaster to reconnoitre, were pursued by a large body of rebels. They came up with their horses being wearied; one was shot refusing quarter, the other two surrendered, and taken prisoners to Lancaster.

"There were no persons hanged at Lancaster as before reported, the rebels plundered extreamly there, breaking open chests, cuppords, and everything in their way, and taking away everything that was valuable. The same was done in Preston, and all other towns they passed through, the same in all country places where they came.

"On Sunday before day most of the rebels left Lancaster, their rear got to Kendall about six that evening; the country people about Kendall opposed their van guard, killed two rebels, and took one prisoner, and the rebels killed three country people.

"Their hussars marched out of Kendall Sunday evening for Penrith, within a mile of Penrith the country assembled to oppose them with scythes, pitchforks, guns, swords, &c. These hussars took one countryman prisoner, and returned about five on Monday morning to Kendall. On Monday before it was light, till nine, they continued marching from Kendall for Penrith in order to be in Carlisle on Tuesday, and from thence proceeded to Scotland.

"The rebels give out 10,000 French were to have landed in Wales, but received an express in Derby, that they proposed to land in Scotland, whom they are returning to join.

"The hussars, rangers, part of the light horse, and part of St. George's and Montague's, got to Kendall on Monday evening. The Duke with the rest of the horse were at Lancaster that evening.

"About three that afternoon was met the Duke of Kingstone in his coach with Lord Byron a mile south of Lancaster, two troops of his horse attending, with 200 foot mounted on country horses.

"Our foot and some Yorkshire Blews imagined may make 3000, were in Preston on Tuesday and halted.

"It is confidently reported at Preston that the Duke has received an express on Saturday there, part of our horse marching for Lancaster returned to Garstang, and the other part from Garstang towards Preston, and the foot return'd to Wiggau on Sunday and billets came to Manchester for 7000 men on Monday night.

"On Sunday our forces were ordered to march again after the rebels as fast as possible ; had it not been for this they were so near the rebels that they must have come up with them before this time.

"The rebels artillery march'd night and day before them with a proper Guard, who take horses from the country people, and when those can march no further, take more.

"Att Manchester, Preston, and where our forces came, there are great rejoicings by ringing of bells, bonefires and illuminations in every window.

"14 rebels are prisoners att Garstang, and 16 at Manchester.

"The Duke declares he will follow them to their very doors in the Highlands.

"The above received from 2 spies just arrived, who were taken prisoners by the rebels Saturday afternoon, and releas'd att Kendal on Munday. The rebels have taken their horses.

"Ten of clock Thursday even. We have just received accounts from Chatsworth that the rebels were at Shap on Wednesday morning and that General Oglethorpe was got before them, and had join'd a detachment from Marshall Wade's army.

"The Duke of Cumberland set out from Kendal at 6 o'clock on Wednesday morning and declar'd he wou'd not sleep till he came up with them."

H. RUSSELL to ———

1745, December 23.—"From Penrith without date an express to Manchester.

"The Duke has had a slight skirmish with the rebels, has lost ten men and the rebels 100 ; it was believed if his foot had been with them he had done their business.

"Our foot got to Lancaster on Wednesday afternoon, and 1500 horses were waiting there ready to mount them as soon as they had dined.

"2000 more of the Duke of Cumberland's foot were to be in Manchester on Saturday. The 6000 that remained of his army are gone to London from the country and the places adjacent.

"Marshall Wade's army was at Burrough Bridge on Sunday the 15th, from thence were detached a 1000 picked men to march directly for Hexham to prevent the rebels returning into Scotland. The rest in severall columns marched directly for Newcastle. The last division would be there last Saturday.

"From Bolton.—Sir, I was in Preston on Sunday the 15, the town was in the utmost hurry from an express that came that day to the Duke, the purport was a great number of French were landed in Kent. Upon this the soldiers att Lancaster and Garstang returned to Walton

MSS. OF SIR W.
FITZHERBERT.
on this side Preston that night late. The foot which were advanced within two or three miles of Preston were ordered to return that night to Wiggan, and all the soldiers had orders to be in readiness to march early in the morning for London.

"About four or five on Munday morning, another express came with an account that it was a false alarm. A gentleman of fortune who was in the room when the Duke received it, and heard it read, told me the contents were that Vernon had taken and destroyed 17 transports and 4 men of war and that the Duke might follow the rebels, whereupon he jumped about the room for joy and declared he would follow them to the furthest part of Scotland, but he would see an end of them, others told me Vernon had only taken one French East Indiaman and a Privateer full of men, a little time will convince us how it is.

"About 8 on Munday morning the Duke with about 3000 horse and dragoons set out for Lancaster, on Tuesday morning at 9 o'clock marched from Lancaster for Kendall, on Wednesday upwards of 2000 foot marched from Preston to Lancaster. I was told by an officer on the road they had received orders to goe forwards to Burton without halting in Lancaster. All the horses within 15 miles of Lancaster were pressed to forward them.

"About 11 o'clock that day an express brought account by word of mouth to Lancaster where I then was the rebels were stopt att Penrith by a detatchment from Wade's army and had retreated to Shap and that the Duke set out of Kendall att 6 in the morning with his men to visit them."

"The rebells held out the white flag and wanted to capitulate but the Duke sent them word he could not capitulat with rebells upon which they surrendered upon the Duke's mercy. The Duke will be in town Sunday or Monday, but I have great reason to believe he will very soon after go into Scotland, which I and everybody else heartily wishes he may, and if he does, don't doubt but he will soon put an end to this ugly rebellion, there was but one of our people killed at Carlile."

——— - to ———

1745-6, February 3. Edinburgh—."After the uncommon fatigue, which his royal Highness the Duke underwent in his expeditious journey to this city, none expected a speedy march of the troops; yet to every one's surprize he dispatched the business of the army and marched it in less than 24 hours after his arrivall. The whole troops were in motion on Friday at 5 o'clock in the morning, and expressed the greatest eagerness to attack the rebels. General Huske led the van, his Royal Highness set out soon after the artillery, and passed through this city in the Earl of Hoptone's coach, amidst a prodigious crowd, who expressed their satisfaction by repeated acclamations of joy, and prayers for his success. Att a quarter of a mile's distance, his Royall Highness mounted his horse, and was soon up with the army, which lay that night att Linlithgow. The rebels called in their stragling parties, and seemed to prepare for a general engagement, which was expected on Saturday. No time was lost, for early that morning the artillery moved, together with Lord Cobham's, and 4 troops of Lord Mark Kerr's dragoons, which were all the horse that had joined, Legonier's, and Hamilton's, being left to patrol near this city. The quickness of this motion, and the alertness of the army, equally surprised and terrifyd the rebells, who, that morning having blown up their powder magazine in the church of St. Ninian's, fled with the greatest precipitation without the least regularity, and made such haste, that they got to the north side MSS. OF SIR W FITZHERBERT. of the Forth by the ford of the Trew that night.

"The Argyleshire Highlanders, and dragoons under Brigadier Mordaunt pursued, and took possession of Stirling; where they found the rebels cannon etc, on Sunday his Royal Highness entered that town, and was saluted by a triple discharge of the great guns from the castle, which he had so seasonable releived.

" Several prisoners are come to town already and we hear of a great many more. General Blakeney fired hotly on such as were within reach of his guns. Such a speedy deliverance to the south part of Scotland was beyond the warmest expectation, and the inimitable bravery of his Royal Highness, who has freed the better half of North Brittain from oppression, slavery, rapin, and blood, in the short space of three days, will be ever gratefully acknowledged by all the friends of liberty.

" The army under his Royal Highness consists of 14 battalions and 2 regiments of dragoons; it marched in 2 columns by way of Barrowstonners and Lithgow ; the Argyleshire men under Lieut. Col. Campbell led the van, and on Friday night were cantoned towards the river Avon in the front.

" Yesterday the most devout thanksgivings were put up to Almighty God for this begun deliverance from this wicked and unnaturall rebellion.

" Severall gentlemen, volunteers, made prisoners in the action near Falkirk and confined in the Castle of Down by the rebels, have made their escape, and are come to this city, as has likewise Major Lockhart, and Mr. Gordon of Ardock, who having happily convinced the officer on guard of his folly, engaged him to come along with them, and he is admitted to bail.

" A letter from Stirling says that the Earl of Kilmarnock, and several other officers of distinction amongst the rebels are made prisoners.

" The rebels published a proclamation at Stirling offering a reward to any who would discover the author of that *damnable lye* that the person commonly called the Duke of Cumberland was arrived in Scotland, so apprehensive were they that their army would fly on the approach of that illustrious young hero.

" February 4.—It is this day reported that the Highlanders are dispersing, and forcing the country people to exchange cloaths with them. The Duke has ordered the Argyleshirmen and dragoons to pass the Forth in pursuit of the rebels.

" The *Hazard* sloop of war has sailed from Montross for France with the French ambassador, and some chiefs of the rebels on board.

" The Pretender and rebels are marched up to the Highlands having abandoned Perth yesterday.

Newcastle, February 7.

" An express this day brings advice that the rebels still fly before the Duke who was to be at Perth yesterday.

" Cameron of Lochiell's brother is taken prisoner.

" The Prince of Hesse onboard the *Gibraltar*, man of war, and three other men of war, and 30 transports of the Hessian troops, passed our barr yesterday, and as the wind is fair, they will, 'tis hoped, be landed at Leith this day.

" The Duke of Kingston's light horse went through here yesterday for Scotland."

MSS. OF SIR W.
FITZHERBERT.

——— to ———

"1745–6, February 4. Newcastle.—"One of the King's messengers went through here this morning with an express from the Duke of Cumberland whom he left at Stirling yesterday morning at 5 o'clock. The Duke gave him a strict charge not to stop or sleep till he had his dispatches.

"The brave Duke on Sunday forenoon advanced within a small distance of the town with his army drawn up expecting the rebels coming, but on the contrary they run off as fast as they could in the utmost confusion, crossing the river upon floats, which they had made before, severall were drowned, vast numbers killed by the cannon of the castle, and by a seasonable salley made by the garrison, besides prodigious numbers surrendered themselves prisoners of war, particularly Lord John Drummond's regiment, after himself was killed near one of their own batteries. He says scarce 40 of the whole regiment went off with the rebels, we have taken all their tents, cannon, ammunition, baggage, and most of their arms, and to compleat their ruin all their provisions, all this without the loss of a man or the least hazard of the Duke's person. All this he declares he saw with his own eyes, and further that as he came from Edenburgh he met on the rods nigh 100 waggons ladened with all sorts of provisions for the army.

"Our acccunts by express both to Berwick and this town are as follows:

"Upon Friday morning last the army marched from Edenburgh westward, and at nine the Duke of Cumberland followed, but on Friday evening at six o'clock the rebels began a most precipitate retreat from Falkirk and Stirling by blowing up this magazine of powder in St. Ninians's Church near Stirling, nailed up all their cannon, leaving all their baggage behind 'em, and passing the ford att the Trew about 5 miles above Stirling. As soon as the rebels had passed the Forth they divided themselves into eight different bodies and were making up to the north. Lord Loudon will be an over match for any of these parties, and its not doubted but be the Argyleshire men and a few troopers will ferret 'm out and bring them to justice.

"Some say the rebels fled so precipitately, that they had not time to nail up their cannon.

"It's said the rebels attempted to bribe the principall gunner of Stirling castle but, he having tho honour to communicate the affair to the general, he made a very good use of it by suffering them in an intended general assault on the Castle to come as near it as they pleased, and they not doubting but they had the gunner on their side came just under the guns in great numbers, which the general perceiving ordered the guns to fire and killed some hundreds of the rebels."

———

——— to DICKENSON KNIGHT.

"A copy of a letter sent us by Dr. Herring."

1746, April 26.—"By an express this day at noon from the Duke at Inverness there was 2,500 of the Rebels killed & most of the general officers either killd or taken prisoners. This express left the Duke in pursuit of the Rebells.

Taken 5,000 stand of arms & 30 pieces of Cannon.

Ld Strachallan killd.

MSS. OF SIR W.
FITZHERBERT.

    Mackintosh ditto.
    Ogilvie ditto.
    Appin ditto.
    & many more taken.

Totally dispersed, not 200 hundred to be found in any place together.
Earl Cromarty taken with 100 of his men."

A TRUE AND PERFECT RETURN OF ALL PAPISTS CONVICTED IN THE
NORTH RIDING OF THE COUNTY OF YORK [1716].

Birdforth Allertoushire Weaptakes.

William Pinkney of Thirsk, Gen.
William Dale of the same, Grocer.
John Dale of Thornbrough, Yeom.
Richard Briggs of Upsall, Yeom.
Cuthbert Tunstall of Nether Silton, Gen.
John Pinkney of the same, Gen.
Henry Dinmore of Sowerby, Gen.
Thomas Moor of Angram, Gen.
William Dale of Coxwold, Yeom.
Thomas Dale of Newbrough, Yeom.
William Mitchell of the same, Gen.
John Smith of Oulston, Yeom.
Francis Kirke of Kilbourne, Yeom.
John Dale of Keswick, Yeom.
Edward Danby of Barroby, Yeom.
Thomas Danby senr. of the same, Yeom.
Thomas Danby junr. of the same, Yeom.
Christopher Danby of the same, Yeom.
Richard Burgess of the same, Yeom.
Henry Webster of Knagton, Yeom.
Peter Barker of the same, Yeom.
John Parvin of the same Yeom.
Thomas Parvin of the same Yeom.
John Bussey of the same, Yeom.
Christopher Pibus of the same, Yeom
Robert Wood of the same, Yeom.
Roger Meynell of Kilvington, Esqre.
Adam Dale of the same, Yeom.
Thomas Sampson of the same, Yeom.
Richard Gowland of the same, Yeom.
Anthony Whitfield of the same, Yeom.
Thomas Dale of Thornton le Street, Yeom.
William Jackson of the same, Yeom.
William Rowtless of the same Yeom.
Richard Coward of the same, Yeom.
John Mayes of Yarme, Esqre.
Francis Welfitt of High Worsall, Yeom.
Richard Dalton of the same, Yeom.
Richard Bell of the same, Yeom.
William Bell of Girsby, Yeom.
William Nesham of Upper Dinsdale, Yeom.
Marmaduke Palmer of Hutton Bonvill, Yeom.
Laurence Dalton of High Worsall, Yeom.

Hang West Weapentake.

Mr. George Reynoldson of Bainbridge.
John Todd of the same.
Dorothy Blaids of the same.

Margaret Walker of Askridge.
George Kirkley of Downholme.
James Alcock of the same.
Mr. John Coates senr. of East Witton.
John Coates junr. of the same.
William Staveley of the same.
William Staveley junr. of the same.
John Staveley of the same.
William Petch of the same.
George Pearson of the same.
William Aller of the same.
Henry Petch of the same.
Edward Staveley of the same.
Marmaduke Grainger of Grinton.
John Petch of Burton Constable.
Mr. John Reynoldson of Leybourne.
James Allen of the same.
Edward Holmes of the same.
Francis Dent of the same.
Peter Blenkinson of the same.
Thomas Edmondson of the same.
George Allen of the same.
George Brown of Midleham.
Matthew Straker of the same.
Richard Holmes of the same.
Christopher Stracher of the same.
Simon Scroope, Esqr. of Thornton Steward.
Mr. Christopher Scroope of the same.
Mr. James Aller of the same.
Henry Homer of the same.
William Cooper of the same.
John Milborne of the same.
Robert Marwood of the same.
John Cooper of the same.
William Wetherall of Belerby.
Robert Weatherell of the same.
Christopher Dane of Wensley.
Christopher Dane junr. of the same.
Matthew Bell of the same.
Edward Harrison of the same.
Charles Robinson of the same.
John Robinson of the same.
Mr. Michael Errington of the same.
Mr. Thomas Errington of the same.
Mr. Anthony Metcalfe of the same.
Simon Collyer of the same.
Jeremiah Day of the same.

Gilling West [Wapentake.] George Meynell senr. of Aldbrough, Esqre.
George Meynell junr. of the same, Esqre.
Robert Walker senr. of the same.
Robert Walker junr. of the same.
Joseph Griffin of the same.
Robert Shaw of Newsham.
Henry Thompson of the same.
Robert Smithson of the same.
John Thompson of the same.
William Appleton of the same.

Chr. Hamon of the same.

Thomas Wiseman of Kirkeby Ravensworth.

Anthony Richardson of the same.

Thomas Wilson of Kirkby Hill.

Mr. Robert Collingwood of Barningham.

Marke Berry of Forcett.

Robert Berwick of the same.

Bryan Moor of Hartforth.

George Kearton of Muker.

John Kearton senr. of the same.

John Kearton junr. of the same.

James Miller of the same.

Simon Miller of the same.

Ralph Lomas of Reeth.

John Kearton of the same.

William Robinson of the same.

Daniel Close of the same.

James Barningham senr. of Arkengarthdale.

James Barningham junr. of the same.

Luke Barningham of the same.

Joseph Barningham of the same.

John Barningham of the same.

Anthony Barningham of the same.

Joseph Hamond of the same.

Michael Hamond of the same.

Christopher Barningham of the same.

John Barningham junr. of the same.

Christopher Barningham junr. of the same.

Ralph Milner of the same.

William Hutchinson of Melsonby.

Thomas Mayor of Lartington, Esqr.

Laurence Hodgson of the same.

Henry Boldron of Latons.

John Allen of the same.

William Loftus of the same.

William Pearson of the same.

Thomas Clayton of the same.

John Witham senr. of Cliff Esqre.

John Witham junr. of the same.

William Witham of the same Esqre.

Ralph Perkin of the same.

John Musgrave of the same.

Robert Dale of Hutton.

Robert Atkinson of the same.

John Kipling of the same.

Thomas Wilson of Ovington.

Marke Apleby of the same.

Mr. William Lidell of Thorpe.

Marmaduke Tunstill of the same, Esqre.

Marmaduke Wilson of the same.

James Dobson of Epleby.

James Foster of the same.

Thomas Fowler of the same.

William Fowler of the same.

Thomas Maltus of Marrick.

John Maltus of the same.

Gabriel Appleby of Dalton.

MSS. OF SIR W.
FITZHERBERT.

Paul Maltus of the same.
Matthew Pattison of the same.

Langborugh. William Chappelow of the same.
Weapentake. William Knaggs senr. of Skelton.
William Knaggs junr. of the same.
John Knaggs of the same.
Zachary Moor of Colthouse, Esqre.
Martin Adamson of the same.
George Adamson of the same.
Thomas Taylor senr. of Moorsholme.
Thomas Taylor junr. of the same.
John Taylor of the same.
George Easton of Gisbrough.
Francis Snawdon of Commondale.
John Snawdon of Westerdale.
Christopher Duck of the same.
John Duck of Danby.
George Hollest senr. of the same.
George Hollest junr. of the same.
Robert Suggitt of the same.
John Ward of the same.
Henry Harrison of Glaisdale.
Thomas Garbutt of the same.
John Knaggs of Ugthorpe.
William Hodgson of the same.
John Dale of the same.
Gabriel Dale of the same.
Christopher Knaggs of the same.
Robert Atkinson of the same.
William Stangbow of the same.
Thomas Hodgson of the same.
John Hodgson of the same.
Andrew Towsey of the same.
Zachary Garbutt of the same.
Paul Snawdon of the same.
John Mercer of the same.
Peter Garbutt of the same.
Michael Snawdon of the same.
John Wilks of Egton.
George Wilks of the same.
William Wilks of the same.
Richard Harland of the same.
John Harrison of the same.
Thomas White of the same.
William Harrison of the same.
John White of the same.
George White of the same.
William Barton of the same.
William Beane senr. of the same.
William Beane junr. of the same.
Israel Raw of the same.
William Lowson of the same.
John Lowson of the same.
George White junr. of the same.
Francis Peirson senr. of Egton.
Francis Peirson junr. of the same.
John Lyth of the same.

William Lavecock of the same.
William Snawdon of the same.
William White scur. of the same.
Christopher White of the same.
Ralph White of the same.
Francis White of the same.
Matthew Raw of the same.
Henry Lawson of the same.
Michael Raw of the same.
Thomas Harland of the same.
George Barker of the same.
William Smith of the same.
Richard Harland senr. of the same.
Richard Harland junr. of the same.
Thomas White of the same.
Thomas Lavecock of the same.
William Constant of the same.
Francis Harland of the same.
John Constant senr. of the same.
John Constant junr. of the same.
Matthew Beane of the same.
John Robinson of the same.
John Hutchinson of the same.
Francis Thorpe of the same.
Thomas Shaw of the same.
Richard Smith of the same.
Robert Hill of the same.
Stephen Wilson of the same.
William White junr. of the same.
William Stephenson of Barnby.
William Dale of Mickleby.
John Unthank of Ellerby.
John Coale of Staythes.
John Garnett of Easington.
James Hall of Low Worsall.
Anthony Hoggard of the same.
Thomas Hoggard of the same.
Cornelius Coale of Staythes.
William Pearson of Stokesley, Esqre.
Christopher Peart of the same, Gen.
William Burne of the same.
Jame Kirby of the same.
Robert Mason of the same.
John Fisher of Yarme.
John Grayson of the same.
John Mayes Esqre. of the Fryeridge neare Yarme.
William Grayson of Yarme.
William Simpson of the same.
Lionel Slator of the same.
William Allyson of the same.
William Wattson of the same.
Joshua Smith of the same.
Mrs. Mary Taylor of Busby.
William Passman of Crathorne.
John Comeforth of the same.
Ralph Wellfitt of the same.
Robert Mennill senr. of the same.

MSS. OF SIR W.
FITZHERBERT.

Robert Mennill junr. of the same.
John Wellfitt of the same.
John Passman of the same.
Hugh Sayer of Rudby.
John Sayer of the same.
Alban Sayer of the same.
Thomas Sayer of the same.
Thomas Midleton of Midleton.
John Sayer of Castle Leavington.
Thomas Bell of Pickton.
Thomas Bell of Appleton.
Stephen Tiplady senr. of Hilton.
Stephen Tiplady junr. of the same.
John Calvert of the same.
Thomas Darnell of the same.
Ralph Grainger of Ormesby.

Bulmer
Weapentake.

Ralph Reynold of St. Mary Gate.
John Bell of the same.
John Robinson of Wigginton.
William Salvin of Easingwould, Gen.
John Hardcastle of the same.
William Hall of Linton.
John Hall of the same.
Anthony Hunt of the same.
Andrew Chambers of the same.
Thomas Chambers of the same.
Ralph Hall of the same.
Henry Hunt of the same.
Thomas Hunt senr. of the same.
John Nelson of the same.
Thomas Hunt junr. of the same.
Edward Munday of Cornebrough.
Thomas Clarke of Whenby.
Thomas Sturdy of the same.
William Leach of the same.
Francis Hornsey of the same.
Thomas White of the same.
John Scott of the same.
William Craggs of the same.
Thomas Cholmley of Bransby, Esqre.
George Wilson of the same.
Francis Cholmley of Bransby in Stearsby, Gent
James Atkinson of the same.
George Jackson of the same.
William Hardwick of the same.
John Ward of the same.
George Speed of the same.
Thomas Wilkinson of the same.
George Wilkinson of the same.
Edward Belwood of the same.
Matthew Crosby of the same.
Timothy Taylor of the same.
William Hornsey of Skewsby.
Thomas Corneforth of the same.
Francis Turner of the same.
George Turner of the same.
Nicholas Turner of the same.

Michael Rouckless of the same.

William Rouckless of the same.

Thomas Smith of Tirrington.

William Thwing of Heworth, Gen.

Richard Frankland of Farlington.

Joseph Frankland of the same.

Jurdon Sturdy of the same.

Phillip Kendell of Welburno.

MSS. OF SIR W.
FITZHERBERT.

Rydale
Weapentke.
Pickering,
Lyth and
Whitby
Strand
Weapentakes.

Charles Lord Fairfax of Gilling, Papist.

Christopher Simpson of Grathland, Yeom.

John Nessfield of Eskdaleside, Tanner.

Henry Pearson of Whitby, Yeom.

These persons before named were convicted as Popish recusants att the generall Quarter Sessions of the Peace holden at Thirske the tenth day of April in the second year of the reigne of his Soveraigne Lord King George in pursuance of an Act of Parliament passed in the first year of his Majestie's reigne intitled an Act for the further security of his Majestie's Person and Government and the Succession of the Crown in the heirs of the late Princess Sophia being Protestants and for extinguishing the hopes of the pretended Prince of Wales and his open and secrett abettors.

Llang East
Weapentake.

William Thwaites of Cattherick.

Mr. Heddon of Bedale.

Anthony Metcalfe of the same.

William Grainge of the same.

John Robinson of the same.

Richard Metcalfe of the same.

William Grainge of the same.

Miles Lodge of Brompton.

John Adamson of Swinton.

Henry Jackson of the same.

William Pickersgill of the same.

Christopher Tideman of Moulton.

William Smithson of Newsham.

Robert Shaw of the same.

These persons last named were convicted as Popish recusants att the generall Quarter Sessions of the Peace holden att Thirske the fourth day of Aprill in the seventh yeare of her late Majesty Queen Ann.

This is a true coppy of all the Popish recusant convict wittness my hand and seal this 17th day of December 1717.

FRANKLAND."

J. A. BENNETT.

THE MANUSCRIPTS OF THE DELAVAL FAMILY, OF SEATON DELAVAL, NORTHUMBERLAND.

These papers relating to the Delaval family who were the former owners of Seaton Delaval in Northumberland, are now in the possession of Mr. John Robinson of Newcastle-on-Tyne.

Some of the most interesting of the letters calendared, were written by and to Captain George Delaval, about the beginning of the 18th century. They refer principally to naval matters, particularly with reference to the Moors and their Christian captives. The detailed instructions given to Captain Delaval by Sir George Aylmer in November 1698 (p. 3) may especially be noted. There are some amusing letters from Foote, the actor, to John Delaval, giving the theatrical gossip of the day ; and a letter from Mrs. Astley to her sister Mrs. Delaval (p. 15) shews the interest taken by the public in the Duchess of Hamilton, one of the beautiful Miss Gunnings, and the excitement which her appearance created everywhere.

DELAVAL MSS. FRANCIS, EARL OF CUMBERLAND to SIR WILLIAM FENWICK, SIR GEORGE SELBY, and SIR RALPH DELAVAL, Deputy Lieutenants for Northumberland and Newcastle-on-Tyne.

1611, November 6. Londesborough.—Sending them letters of deputation for the lieutenancy of the county. *Signed.*

NORTHUMBERLAND.

1611, December 20.—A list of the names of gentlemen of Northumberland to whom privy seals were directed for the loan of money to the King.

FRANCIS, EARL OF CUMBERLAND to SIR JOHN FENWICK, SIR RALPH DELAVAL, and the rest of the Deputy Lieutenants for Northumberland.

1627, April 15. Londesborough.—Concerning the exercise and training of the Northern Counties according to the model appointed for the rest of the Kingdom. *Copy.*

R. DELAVAL to his father, SIR RALPH DELAVAL, at Seaton Delaval.

[16]74, June 13. Paris.—I have written to you almost every post but have not had the least line from you, which makes me fear that you have forgot me, as well as the rest of my friends. In my last I gave you an account of my ill condition which is every day worse by my own folly and my wife's great unkindness ; but I may find a way to be even with her yet. If I could come home without money I would, but that is impossible, for I may as well starve here as anywhere.

There is no news here but of the great action at Besançon, which the King has taken. The French confess the loss of 3000 men. Since then he has taken Dole in eight days, where he lost, as they confess, 2000 men. He is now going for Flanders, and intends to sit down before Brussels.

.L G—— to SIR RALPH DELAVAL, in Northumberland.

1681, September 9. The Hague.—Lady Elizabeth Delaval has turned me away from her service. She has gone to Scotland and before she went, she made her will, and made it so that your family shall have no benefit. Sir Harry Bellairs is her chief adviser and was witness to her will and said "Your Ladyship does nothing but what is just. Sir Ralph is fool and knave, governed by his sot wife."

EMANUEL BLAKE to his uncle [FRANCIS BLAKE].

1682, August 29. London.—The Duchess of York is brought to bed of a daughter, which is a baulk to expectation.

The SAME to the SAME, at Ford Castle near Berwick-on-Tweed.

1682, September 12. London.—Concerning an apprentice. *Signet.*

H. DUKE OF NEWCASTLE to [SIR RALPH DELAVAL ?].

[16]82, November 2. Welbeck.—I do wonder the Romanists will appear in public places. I am a friend to many of them, but I shall never be of their religion. Since you mention Mr. Howard, I acquaint you, upon Lord Carlisle's wish, that I have written to Lord Halifax to desire that he may be this year sheriff.

" My daughter Albemarle haveing violent fitts of the mother, trebles me exceedingly."

EMANUEL BLAKE to his uncle, FRANCIS BLAKE, at Ford Castle.

1682, November 25. London.—Congratulating him upon the approaching marriage of his daughter Eleanor. *Signet.*

HOLLAND.

[c. 1683.]—Essays on the History of the House of Nassau, Princes of Orange, and Founders of the Commonwealth of the United Provinces. *Probably translated from Sir Aubrey du Maurier's Memoires pour servir à l'histoire de Holland. See " Notes and Queries." November 9, 1889.*

SIR F. BLAKE to his son, FRANCIS BLAKE, at Ford Castle.

[16]84, April 10.—A letter of condolence upon a death in his family. *Postscript.*—" Your brother is well. Wee ordered your sister to invite severall praying friends to meet togeather to give thancks to our good God for hearing our prayers for his wife's restoration to health, and to give 5l. to the poore, which was done last weeke."

BRISTOL.

1696[-7], January 24.—A list of fee-farm rents in Northumberland given to the Merchant Adventurers of Bristol, incorporated by Edward Colston for the maintenance of twenty-four poor people in an almshouse built there by him. The yearly total is 237l. 3s. 4d.

[BERWICK-ON-TWEED.]

[1698, August 1.]--A list of the persons who voted at the election for Blake, Ogle, and Hutchinson.

NORTHUMBERLAND.

1698, August 4.—A list of the persons who voted at Alnwick at the election of the knights of the shire, for Sir John Delaval, Sir Edward Blackett, and William Forster.

ADMIRAL MATTHEW AYLMER, Commander-in-chief of the ships in the Mediterranean to CAPTAIN DELAVAL, in command of the *Coventry*.

1698, November 20. Aboard the *Boyne* in Cadiz Bay.—Whereas I have appointed you with Captain Watkins to treat with the Alcaid at Tangier. You are hereby directed and required together with the said Captain to go on board the *Medway* in order to proceed and go ashore at Tangier. Upon your arrival and communication with the Alcaid you are to talk with him equally, both of a peace and the redemption of our captives, but not to conclude anything.

You are to know the chief end for which you are sent is the redemption, that of a peace being only a pretence, supposing they will not talk of one without the other; but if they will enter into a negotiation about the redemption without treating about a peace you are to proceed that way.

If the Alcaid should press for a peace before the redemption, you are to seem to put it off, giving him reasons to this purpose, as, how can a peace be sincere at the same time our people remain in slavery, and that there is no possibility of an agreement without the redemption.

If it should be desired of you to go to Mahoni, you must tell him your orders go no further, and if he seems earnest for it you must write to me for leave.

You must press him with as much gentleness as you can, continuing still to your points, but not in a heat, to come to a speedy conclusion, and the lowest that they will take for each man. For other points, as the letting him know the strength we shall have constantly in these parts, with that we shall have in England at sea and land, with the great power and riches of our country, that is left to you; only I will give you the following caution, that the Moors will have a great opinion of you the closer you keep to your point, but not so as to give them distaste, as I said before.

It will not be amiss that you tell the Alcaid the great opinion I have of him, chiefly for his kindness to our nation, or anything that may make him more earnest in our service. You may also say that notwithstanding other nations had gone by other hands to treat, yet I was resolved to do it only by his, or anything to this effect.

If he happens to ask about the siege of Ceuta, or whether we were to send any troops there, you are to say in general terms that all things of that kind are lawful in war, but that you were not well informed in that affair, telling it in such a manner as may leave it in doubt.

If it happens in discourse so as it may properly be brought in, you may say that the last news brought me an account of seventeen men-of-war more, coming here, and that all ships have soldiers. Let this rather be drawn from you.

I shall send a ship every four or five days to Tangier for letters. You are to let the Alcaid know that he will be gratified if our captives are redeemed, and you are to tell the same to Hodge Lucas his secretary.

You are to get all the information you can from the English and French merchants at Tetuan and Tangier.

In your discourse with the Alcaid you are to bring in that I have cleared ten sail of ships, of which three are gone cruising in the Straits, the rest you do not know where.

If you send me any letters you must take care of writing what is not proper for them to know.

You must take all the care imaginable to find if they trifle with you, in which case you must ask for leave to return; and you must propose this whenever you think he has no more to say, observing as near as DELAVAL MSS. you can how far his power extends, which you may by your delay, for then doubtless he sends to Mahoni.

You are to let me know when you are ready to return, that I may send the *Medway* for you. *Signed.*

The FRENCH PROTESTANTS at Miquemes to [CAPTAIN GEORGE DELAVAL] Ambassador from England.

1699, October 7-17. Miquemes.—Petitioning him to obtain their freedom from slavery by allowing them to pass as British subjects.

TERTIUS SPENCER to GEORGE DELAVAL.

1700, July 5. Cadiz.—Concerning the redemption of captives from the Moors. *Five pages.*

The SAME to the SAME, in Gerrard Street, London.

1700, July 19. Cadiz.—Condoling with him on the death of his brother James, and concerning negotiations for raising the siege of Ceuta.

The SAME to the SAME.

1700, October 1. Tetuan.—Concerning the raising of the siege of Ceuta, and the redemption of the captives.

CAPTAIN DELAVAL to his brother, EDWARD DELAVAL, of South Dissington.

1700, October 13. London. — Concerning their brother James's money.

FRANCIS BLAKE to his son [in-law], EDWARD DELAVAL, at South Dissington, near Newcastle.

1701, March 25. London.—My wife and I have been several times to see a "fly a bed" and they make nothing of asking 60*l.* to 80*l.* for a bed at the first rate, which I think very unreasonable. The Act of Parliament causes the high rate upon silks. In order therefore not to disappoint you, my wife is willing to give you damask bed at Ford.

THOMAS, ARCHBISHOP OF CANTERBURY, SIR NATHAN WRIGHT, the EARL OF PEMBROKE, the DUKES OF DEVONSHIRE and SOMERSET, the EARL OF JERSEY, and LORD GODOLPHIN to CAPTAIN GEORGE DELAVAL, commanding the *Tilbury.*

1701, August 14. Whitehall.—You are with all convenient expedition to repair with the ship under your command to Tangier; and whereas there is a provision made of gunlocks, powder and other things for the redemption of his Majesty's subjects in Barbary, you are, with all expedition, to redeem those now in captivity in Fez and Morocco, or as many of them as you can. You shall deliver the present for the King of Fez and Morocco and you shall let the King know of his Majesty's intention to continue in friendship and good correspondence with him, and accordingly you are to endeavour to renew the truce now subsisting, for one year at least. *Signed. Seal. Countersigned by James Vernon.*

DELAVAL MSS. The FRENCH PROTESTANTS and others, at Miquemes, to [CAPTAIN GEORGE DELAVAL] Ambassador from England.

1701, December 18. Miquemes.—Petitioning him to obtain their freedom from slavery.

TERTIUS SPENCER to GEORGE DELAVAL, Ambassador from his Majesty of Great Britain, on board the *Tilbury*, in the bay of Tangier.

1701, December 19. Tetnan.—Sending a letter for Mr. Packer and hoping that his chest of plate and other things would be sent on board by the next day. *Signed.*

TERTIUS SPENCER to ANTHONY PACKER, in Cadiz.

1701, December 19. Tetuan. — Giving details concerning the negotiations being carried on between the Alcaid and the English ambassador.

CAPTAIN GEORGE DELAVAL.

[1702.]—An account of his negotiations as ambassador from the Queen of Great Britain to the Emperor of Morocco.

MORPETH.

1702, August 27.—A list of the persons who voted at Morpeth at the election, for Emanuel How, Sir John Delaval, and Richard Bellasis.

TERTIUS SPENCER to GEORGE DELAVAL, in Cadiz.

1702[-3], February 28. Tetuan.—Concerning the negotiations for the redemption of the captives, which had been suspended.

SIR FRANCIS BLAKE to his daughter, MADAM DELAVAL, at South Dissington.

1705, September 13. Coggs.—On private affairs. Mentions his daughters Dalston, and Kennedy.

[CAPTAIN GEORGE DELAVAL.]

1705-6, March 3.—At a council of war held on board the flag ship *Ranelagh*, at sea. Present Sir John Leake, Admiral Wasenaer and seven captains, English and Dutch.

Whereas it was resolved at a council of war of the 19th of February to detach as many ships as could be spared, to endeavour to meet with and convoy the Brazil fleets, after the expedition to Cadiz was over, which being unsuccessfully attempted by the galleons getting to sea before we could get to that place, and having followed them without success, and it likewise being considered that the *Pembroke, Leopard, Garland,* and *Roebuck,* which were intended with four of the States General ships to go upon the aforesaid service, were not ready to sail when we left Lisbon and were ordered to join us off Cape Spartel or at Gibraltar, to which place in all possibility they are gone; it is resolved that we cannot come to any resolution therein till these four ships have joined us.

JAMES WELWOOD to SIR FRANCIS BLAKE, at Coggs near Witney in Oxfordshire. DELAVAL MSS.

1707, April 17.—Informing him that his son-in-law Trevanion was very angry at not being paid the 500*l.* which had been promised, and that he must expect the worst if he did not pay. *Signed.*

JAMES ROBERTSON to SIR FRANCIS BLAKE.

1707, May 28. Ford.—I am come to acquaint you that Her Majesty's interest is much neglected because the Roman Catholics meet in several places within my parish of Kyloe (Keylo) with coaches and horses of a considerable value. Wherefore I pray and beseech you to grant me a warrant to seize upon their horses and arms, or otherwise give you reason to the contrary.

J. CHETWYND to [GEORGE ?] DELAVAL.

1709, November 23, *s.n.* Turin.—On private affairs.

ITALY.

1709. — An account of a tour in Italy. *Forty-one pages. Damaged.*

ROBERT BLAKE to his father, SIR FRANCIS BLAKE, at Coggs.

1710, November 13. London.—If you will send my sister Trevanion any of your country rarities I shall partake of them. A villainous popish priest contrived my brother Nugent's will, and he was persuaded by a scandalous, broken captain to execute it. My service to my sister Mitford.

The EARL OF DARTMOUTH to [CAPTAIN GEORGE] DELAVAL.

1711, July 10. Whitehall.—I send you a copy of a memorial presented to the Queen by Don Luis, wherein he desires a powerful squadron may be immediately ordered to Brazil to make head against the enemy who he supposed were gone that way; but you will represent to the King of Portugal, how impracticable it is for her Majesty to comply with this request before she is informed what force the King himself is providing for this service, and by what time the ships of the States will be ready to join them, their High and Mightinesses being equally obliged by treaty to protect the Portuguese dominions in America; and that no time be lost, her Majesty has already directed her ministers at the Hague to concert proper measures for the defence of Brazil or the recovery of any place there that may happen to be taken.

· The Queen is further pleased to order that you acquaint his Portuguese Majesty in the strongest terms that are consistent with decency, the just reasons her Majesty has to be uneasy at the present management of the war on that side, that after so vast an expense to her Majesty and her people, and when we have so great a superiority over the enemy both by the goodness and number of our troops, no use should be made of it, nor any design formed for the advantage of the common cause upon which the security of Portugal seems so much to depend. You will urge this as far as possibly you can, and let his Majesty know it is still hoped the season is not so far spent but something may be yet undertaken for the interest of the alliance and that

DELAVAL MSS. such fine troops will not be suffered to waste without being employed. *Signed.*

SIR J. LEAKE, SIR G. BYNG, and SIR GEORGE CLARKE to the EARL OF DARTMOUTH.

1711–12, March 7. Admiralty Office.—We will send orders to Rear Admiral Baker when he proceeds to the King of Portugal's Brazil fleet, to see the ships bound for the East Indies into the latitude of the Western Isles, and that if the Brazil fleet arrives at Lisbon before he sails, that then he is to consult with the Queen's envoy there, and see the aforesaid East India fleet into the sea. *Signed.*

The EARL OF DARTMOUTH to [CAPTAIN GEORGE] DELAVAL.

1711–12, March 11. Whitehall.—The enclosed letter from the Lords of the Admiralty will show you the directions that have been given here for the security of the Portuguese East India fleet and for bringing their Bahia trade safe home. When much care is taken by the Queen to protect their ships, it would be very hard for them to be at the same time inventing new methods for interrupting the commerce of her subjects, and I hope you will be able to press this argument so as to divert them from these unjust projects. No strangers pay here to the militia, and I believe it would be very hard to find a precedent in any country for the duties they would now extort from British merchants at Oporto. *Signed.*

The EARL OF DARTMOUTH to [CAPTAIN GEORGE] DELAVAL.

1712, June 24. Whitehall.—The Queen having given direction that the London News, published by authority, should hereafter be written with as great care as possible, I am to desire you to transmit to my office by every post an account of such occurrences together with all printed papers, as you judge may afford proper matter for the Gazette.

The QUEEN to JOHN, KING OF PORTUGAL.

1712, November 6. Windsor.—Congratulating him on the birth of his son. *Sign Manual. Latin.*

J. BURCHETT to CAPTAIN GEORGE DELAVAL.

1712, November 20. Admiralty Office.—I send you herewith orders to the captain of the *Royal Ann,* galley, at Port Mahon to cruize against the rovers of Scilly. If you shall find the people of Scilly have committed acts of hostility, or that there is any obstruction to the renewing the truce on the part of the Emperor of Morocco, so that you shall judge it necessary to send the said order forward to the captain of *Royal Ann,* you will do so, otherwise you will return the same to me. *Signed.*

J. BURCHETT to CAPTAIN GEORGE DELAVAL, Envoy Extraordinary to the King of Portugal, at Lisbon.

1712–13, January 9. Admiralty Office.—Enclosing a packet to be forwarded to Captain Trevor, commander of the *Royal Ann,* at Gibraltar. *Signed.*

The COMMISSIONERS OF THE NAVY to [CAPTAIN GEORGE DELAVAL].   DELAVAL MSS.

1712–3, January 30.—Enclosing an extract from a letter of the officers of Lisbon complaining that they could not get their stores from the *Samuel*, merchantman, without paying the customs duty on them. *Copy. Extract.*

J. BURCHETT to CAPTAIN GEORGE DELAVAL, at Lisbon.

1713, July 27. Admiralty Office.—Enclosing important despatches for Captain Padden of the *Ruby*, at Gibraltar, and Captain O'Brien of the *Success*, storeship, at Lisbon.

J. FOWLER to CAPTAIN GEORGE DELAVAL, Envoy at Lisbon.

1713, August 27. Admiralty Office.—Sending instructions to Captain Padden of the *Ruby*, about the supply of the ships under his command with wine and oil. *Signed.*

LORD GUILFORD, PHILIP MEADOWS, and THOMAS VERNON to [CAPTAIN GEORGE DELAVAL].

1713, September 18. Whitehall.—Her Majesty having appointed us her Commissioners of Trade, we find it necessary to have the Portugal book of rates, the *Pragmaticas*, and other orders relating to trade. *Signed.*

J. BURCHETT to LIEUTENANT FRANCIS DELAVAL, at Wills's Coffee House, at Scotland Yard Gate.

1714[–5], March 7. Admiralty Office.—Conveying to him permission to retire from the Navy on half pay. *Signed.*

The EARL OF CARLISLE to CAPTAIN GEORGE DELAVAL.

[1715,] November 27. Castle How.—Promising his support to the candidature of Francis Delaval, as against Mr. Douglas, for the seat vacated by Mr. Forster in the county of Northumberland.

FRANCIS DELAVAL to his father, EDWARD DELAVAL, at Newcastle-on-Tyne.

1717, December 17. London.—They talk here of a reconciliation between the King and Prince and I hope it is true.

SIR GEORGE BYNG to ———.

1718, August.—Giving an account of the engagement between the English and Spanish fleets off Cape Passero on July 31, 1718, and enclosing a copy of Captain Walton's letter from Syracuse dated August 6, 1718. *Copy.*

FRANCIS BLAKE DELAVAL to his father, EDWARD DELAVAL, at Newcastle-on-Tyne.

1719, March 26. London.—The Admiralty have this day given me a commission to command the *Gosport* a new forty gun ship. She is at Deptford and I shall go down on Saturday to put her in commission.

We are expecting every day to hear of the Spanish fleet on our coast, and there is a report to-day of their being seen off the western coast, but I hope Sir John Norris will meet with them.

The COMMISSIONERS of the ADMIRALTY to CAPTAIN DELAVAL, Commander of the *Gosport*.

1719, April 14.—Directing him to repair with his ship to Longreach and thence, having taken on board ammunition and stores, to make his way to the Nore and there to press as many men as he could to complete his complement. *Four signatures.*

The SAME to the SAME, at Longreach.

1719, April 22.—Directing him to join the *Bideford* at her cruising station off Inverness and to act under her commander's instructions, to prevent the enemy from landing any troops thereabouts. *Four signatures.*

The SAME to the SAME, at the Nore.

1719, April 23.—Directing him to search all ships he shall meet with on his way to North Britain ; and in case he shall find that the enemy have seized Inverness, he is to assist the King's land forces towards recovering it. *Five signatures.*

J. BURCHETT to CAPTAIN DELAVAL, at Inverness.

1719, April 27. Admiralty Office.—Sending him the proclamation for the apprehension of James Butler, late Duke of Ormond, and other attainted persons, and directing him to search all ships he got sight of, for the late Earl of Mar. *Signed.*

CAPTAIN FRANCIS BLAKE DELAVAL to his father, EDWARD DELAVAL.

1719, May 15. Cromartie Harbour.—I am but just come to anchor here. The rebels with the Spaniards that are landed are but twelve hundred in all, as they tell us here, and our forces at Inverness will be as many as they in three or four days. The rebels were by the last accounts about forty miles from Inverness, so that I hope there is not much to be apprehended from them.

Pray my love to Nanny and my compliments to my aunt, and to cousin Hebdon, and Mamma.

The COMMISSIONERS of the ADMIRALTY to CAPTAIN DELAVAL, Commander of the *Gosport*, at Inverness.

1719, May 22.—Directing him to repair to Sunderland and to take on board as many " keel men " as the magistrates there and at Newcastle could supply him with, and then to report himself at the Nore. *Three signatures.*

The SAME to the SAME, at Sunderland.

1719, June 3.—Directing him not to impress any " keel men " who had submitted and were willing to return to their work. *Three signatures.*

The SAME to the SAME, in Sunderland Road.

1719, June 10.—Directing him, in consequence of the disturbances among the " keel men " on the rivers Wear and Tyne being appeased, to return and report himself at the Nore. *Three signatures.*

J. BURCHETT to CAPTAIN DELAVAL, at the Nore.

1719, June 26. Admiralty Office.—Application having been made to the Lords Commissioners of the Admiralty by the Muscovia Company for a convoy to see their ships, bound to Revel, Narva, Viborg, and Petersburg, in safety, in regard that it will be otherwise impracticable for them to proceed on their voyage, they having received advice of an English ship bound to Petersburg being taken, carried up to Stockholm and actually condemned, aud that the English merchants residing there apprehend the free trade to the parts conquered from Sweden is granted only to the Hollanders; I am commanded to signify to you their Lordships directions that you take under your care when you proceed to Riga with the trade bound thither, all such merchant ships as shall then be joined to you, bound to the said ports of Revel, Narva, Viborg, and Petersburg, but before you proceed as high as Riga you are to apply to Sir John Norris to let him know these instructions, so that he may take such measures as he may think proper. *Signed.*

The COMMISSIONERS of the ADMIRALTY to CAPTAIN DELAVAL, Commander of the *Gosport*, at the Nore.

1719, June 26.—Informing him that his ship had been appointed to be convoy to the merchant ships bound for Riga for stores for the navy, and directing him to take under his charge all merchant ships at the Nore or in Yarmouth Roads bound for the Baltic. He was to remain at Riga thirty days, and then to return with such ships as might be ready to sail. *Three signatures.*

J. BURCHETT to CAPTAIN DELAVAL, Commander of the *Gosport*, at LONG REACH.

1719, December 2. Admiralty Ofhee.—Giving him leave from the Commissioners of the Admiralty to come to town on private affairs. *Signed.*

J. BURCHETT to CAPTAIN BLAKE DELAVAL, Commander of the *Gosport*, at Deptford.

1719-20, January 18. Admiralty Office.—Directing him, on behalf of the Commissioners of the Admiralty, to use his best endeavours to enter volunteers to make his ship's complement. *Signed.*

The COMMISSIONERS of the ADMIRALTY to CAPTAIN BLAKE DELAVAL, Commander of the *Gosport*.

1719[-20], January 26.—Directing him to repair as soon as possible to Galleons Reach and having taken in there guns and powder, to proceed to the Nore. *Three signatures.*

SIR JOHN NORRIS, Admiral of the Blue, to CAPTAIN DELAVAL.

1719-20, February 20.—Directing him to use his utmost diligence to get his ship in readiness for sea so that not a moment be lost, and

N 2

when she should be ready, to proceed to the Downs and put in execution his former orders, taking care to send an account of his proceedings to the Admiralty and himself. *Signed and altered.*

THOMAS SWANTON and six others to CAPTAIN FRANCIS BLAKE DELAVAL.

1719[-20], February 27. Navy Office.—Informing him that orders had been given to supply the *Gosport* with surgeon's necessaries and a copper kettle. *Signed.*

SIR JOHN NORRIS, Commander in chief in the Baltic, to CAPTAIN DELAVAL, in Galleons Reach.

1719-20, February 28.—Informing him that a suspension of arms had been agreed upon between the King and the King of Spain, and had been signed on the 18th instant, whereby it was agreed that all ships and goods should be restored which might be taken in the Baltic and Northern seas to Cape St. Vincent after twelve days from the day of signing, after six weeks from Cape St. Vincent to the equinoctial line, and in all the seas in the world after six months from the date of the convention. *Signed.*

The COMMISSIONERS of the ADMIRALTY to CAPTAIN BLAKE DELAVAL, Commander of the *Gosport*.

1720, April 7.—Directing him to repair to the Nore, with his ship, without loss of time. *Three Signatures.*

The SAME to the SAME, Commander of the *Worcester*, at Long Reach.

1720, December 6.—Directing him to discharge his guns and powder at Deptford and then to give such of his ship's company as shall desire it, leave of absence for six weeks. *Signed by Sir G. Byng and two others.*

THOMAS SWANTON and six others to CAPTAIN FRANCIS BLAKE DELAVAL, Commander of the *Worcester*, in Long Reach.

1720[-1], March 22. Navy Office.—We have ordered your being supplied with a copper pot. *Signed.*

[The KING OF GREAT BRITAIN] to the KING OF SPAIN.

1721, June 1. St. James's.—Expressing his willingness to give up Gibraltar, and promising to obtain the consent of Parliament on the first favourable opportunity. *Copy.*

SIR JOHN NORRIS, Commander in chief of the ships in the Baltic to CAPTAIN BLAKE DELAVAL, Commander of the *Worcester*.

1721[-2], February 3. London.—Directing him to put his ship in commission as speedily as possible, and when she was ready to proceed to the Nore and await further orders. *Signed.*

THOMAS CLUTTERBUCK to the LORDS JUSTICES [of IRELAND].

1724, May 21, London.—Informing them that the King had appointed the Bishop of Meath, Lord Kilmaine, the Honourable St. John Brodrick and himself, Privy Councillors of Ireland.

HENRY WILLIAMSON to [ARCHDEACON KING].

1726, November 28.—Urging him to go as chaplain to the embassy to Vienna for which he was specially fitted on account of an old prophecy, which had been found during the siege of Vienna by the Turks, that "a" Protestant King should be archbishop of Vienna. The prophecy had been examined by Monsieur Jablonski, chaplain to the King of Prussia, who wrote that it was meant "of one King, an archdeacon in England," and that it would be accomplished in 1727. *Copy.*

The SAME to [the SAME].

1726, December 5.—Acknowledging the receipt of his answer to the preceding letter and sending a copy of Monsieur Jablouski's letter.

DANIEL JABLOUSKI to HENRY WILLIAMSON.

No date.—A long religious letter concerning the prophecy. *Copy. Enclosed in the preceding letter.*

HUGH, BISHOP OF ARMAGH, and THOMAS WYNDHAM to the LORD LIEUTENANT of Ireland.

1727, September 23. Dublin Castle.—Enclosing a petition from Andrew Killinghusen, minister of the German protestant church in Dublin, for payment of his salary of 50*l*. a year. *Signed Petition enclosed.*

H. PELHAM, Secretary at War to LORD CARTERET.

1729, April 15. Whitehall.—Sending an order from the King empowering him to appoint Courts Martial in Ireland.

The LORDS JUSTICES [of IRELAND] to the LORD LIEUTENANT.

1732, May 10. Dublin Castle —Enclosing a scheme laid before them by Sir Edward Pearce, the King's Engineer and Surveyor General, for employing part of the foot forces in making a navigable canal between Lough Neagh and Newry. *Three signatures.*

GEORGE DODINGTON to [F.] TOWNSHEND.

1739, September 10. Eastbury.—On behalf of his deputy, Mr. Bayly, who wanted a place.

The LORDS JUSTICES of IRELAND to JOHN POTTER.

1740, September 19.—Granting him a suite of apartments in Dublin Castle. *Three signatures.*

EXPORTS.

1740-1, January 28.—An account of the woollen manufactures exported to Turkey between Christmas 1720 and Christmas 1740; the total value being 3,582,931*l.* 16*s.* 8*d.*

IMPORTS.

1740[-1], February.—An account of the cotton imported from Turkey between Christmas 1720 and Christmas 1740; the total amount being 6,550,694 pounds of cotton wool and 1,187,323 pounds of cotton yarns.

The SAME.

1740[-1], February.—An account of the mohair imported from Turkey between Christmas 1720 and Christmas 1740; the total omitting the years 1735 and 1740, being 4,106,105 pounds.

T. TOWNSHEND to [GEORGE DODINGTON ?].

1740[-1], February 17. Cleveland Court.—Concerning an appointment in the gift of the Duke of Newcastle.

F. BLAKE DELAVAL to MATTHEW RIDLEY, at Newcastle-on-Tyne.

1742, December 1. London.—Declining to purchase the estate of Newsham, which would require too much money, but wishing him a purchaser to his satisfaction.

The EARL OF CHESTERFIELD to ———.

1745, July 23. London.—*See English Historical Review, Vol. IV. p.* 752-3.

[The EARL OF CHESTERFIELD] to ———.

1745-6, March 6.— *See English Historical Review, Vol. IV. p.* 750.

NORTH CAROLINA.

1746.—A series of complaints brought against Gabriel Johnston Governor of North Carolina for having violated the constitution of that province in different ways. *Copy.*

VISCOUNT STRANGFORD to ———.

1746[-7], February 24. Dublin.—Concerning a lawsuit which concerned him greatly and in which he had suffered a great loss by Lord Chesterfield's departure, who had conferred the deanery (of Derry) on him.

VISCOUNT STRANGFORD to ———.

1747. March 26. Dublin.—On the same subject. *Copy.*

THOMAS LINDSEY TO COLONEL OWEN WYNN, in Abbey Street, Dublin.

1747[-8], January 29   Milford.—Concerning an attempt made upon the Protestants, and the murder of Robeit Miller by Mr. Brown.

DON JAIME MAZONES DE LIMA to —— WALL.

1748, October 1. Aix la Chapelle.—Concerning the progress of the negotiations for the peace, and the difficulties caused by the Duke of Newcastle's covetousness and unreasonableness. *Copy.*

—— WALL to DON JAIME MAZONES DE LIMA.

1748, October 12.—An answer to the above. *Copy.*

The PALATINES in NORTH CAROLINA to KING GEORGE II.

[1748.]—Petition to have the land on which they had been settled by Queen Anne, reserved to them; their title having been disputed by Colonel Francis Pollock, who had threatened to dispossess them and settle certain Scotch rebels in their place. *Copy.*

JOSEPH TUCKER to ————.

1749, April 5. Bristcl.—Concerning a pamphlet to which he had written a dedication and had it printed. It was then sent up to town to Mr. Trye the bookseller in Holborn, with instructions to send a quantity to the pamphlet shops in Westminster Hall.

THOMAS DELAVAL to his brother, JOHN DELAVAL, in Albemarle Street, London.

1751, July 27. Hamburg.—Asking for a loan of 120*l.* to pay debts incurred through his inexperience and the sharp practice of those amongst whom he was living.

THOMAS DELAVAL to his sister[in-law] MRS. DELAVAL, in Albemarle Street.

1751, October 11. Dresden.—I will skip over everything until my arrival at Meissen, about twelve miles distant from this place, where the manufactory is, where all the ware known by the name of Dresden china, is made. They shew you everything from the mixing of the clay till it comes out to its last perfection. There is not anything which is not represented in this European china, which in my opinion is every bit as curious as that of China. The only fault I find is that it costs something more.

The Court being at Leipsic, where I was some days ago about business, I was obliged to make a metamorphosis from the apprentice to the cavalier and was presented with half a dozen of my countrymen to his Polish Majesty. As to the Court I must be silent. You have no doubt heard of Count Bruhl, who is the Duke of Newcastle of Saxony. His expenses are only much greater. I leave you to judge of the others by those of his wardrobe, which are 15,000*l.* sterling yearly, after my calculation, which I assure you is a moderate one. I saw upwards of four hundred suits in it, mostly of rich embroidery.

Picture galleries and curiosity chambers there are no end of; one of which is of seven separate apartments, to fill which one would think the

DELAVAL MSS. whole East had been robbed. There is such a profusion of rubies, emeralds, onyxes ; in short, all the jewels one can imagine.

R. ASTLEY to her sister, MRS. DELAVAL, at Doddington, near Lincoln.

[1752 ?] April 14.—It is almost incredible what a crowd of people was at Newcastle waiting to see the Duchess of Hamilton.

She, according to her usual goodness to the public, contrived to stand a few minutes on the steps at the "Iron" ; but when the Duke came out he was much offended that the people should dare to lift their eyes to so divine a beauty, and protested if he had had a pistol, he would have fired among them. When he was in his chaise he bade the postilion drive on, and the more he drove over the better.

SAMUEL FOOTE to JOHN DELAVAL, at Doddington.

[1752,] September 30.—After a day spent with Lord George Manners at Ancaster and another with your uncle at Wasingby, we have this evening reached the metropolis.

Lord George purposes to send Mrs. Delaval and you a letter of invitation to his house. Though this step may not be strictly consistent to the usual forms of provincial politeness, yet, as they are people of quality and on the whole a good acquaintance, I would advise you to relax a little in ceremonials.

This town is as empty as your Aunt Price's head.

[JOHN DELAVAL ?] to ——.

No date.—You seem to think we could have prevented Foote's coming here, which was impossible as we did not know of it till he was in the room. Remonstrances had no effect. My brother had been here two months and we believe would have stayed till the meeting of Parliament, had we not been uneasy at Foote's being here, which we believe was the occasion of his leaving Doddington. The day after he arrived, my brother and he went to Lincoln and stayed there all the race week and the day after set out for London.

SAMUEL FOOTE to JOHN DELAVAL, at Seaton Delaval.

[1753,] January 17. Pall Mall. The theatres have each produced a pantomime. That of Covent Garden is the *Sorcerer*, revived, with a new piece of machinery that is elegantly designed and happily executed. The subject is a fountain.

The *Genii* of Drury Lane has some pretty contrivances, but the inspector complains of its being barren of incidents, defective in the plan, and improbable in the *dénouement*. We have had no new comedies but one given by Mr. Weymondsell and his lady. John Child is gone to France ; the fair frail one turned out of doors, and a suit for a divorce commenced.

Francis's tragedy called *Constantine* is to be acted at Covent Garden. The *Gamester* is soon to be played at Drury Lane. I am writing the *Englishman at Paris* for Macklin's benefit.

G. DELAVAL to his brother, THOMAS DELAVAL, at Seaton Delaval.

1753, February 12. Mortlake.—It was in the *Daily Advertiser* that upwards of four thousand ladies and gentlemen had been assembled at Seaton Delaval to see the rope dancers.

SAMUEL FOOTE to [JOHN] DELAVAL.   DELAVAL MSS.

[1753,] March 13. London.—" In the North ! What do you do in
the North, when you are wanted in the West."

I suppose the post will bring you the *Brothers*. You will find some
good writing but as a play, it is a heavy, uninteresting, bad-conducted,
ill-judged, story. The recorder of your town of Newcastle has lately
occasioned a small inflammation at Court. About four months since he
dined with Lord Ravensworth, and taking up a newspaper which
mentioned the Bishop of Gloucester as the Bishop of Chichester's
successor in the Prince of Wales's family, declared that was the second
great officer about the Prince, whom he had formerly known to drink
treasonable healths, Andrew Stone being the other. Lord Ravensworth made a report of this to the Cabinet Council, which the two
delinquents, with the Solicitor-General, he being equally culpable, were
ordered to attend. Sundry examinations were had, and the result of
all is that the subsequent loyal attachment of these gentlemen should
obliterate the stain of their former principles, and the prosecution be
branded with the ignominious titles of groundless, trifling, and vexatious.

G. GUADAGNI to ——.

1753, March 20. London.—I have the misfortune to be about 500*l.*
in debt, which is owing to my going to Ireland last year and losing all my
winter employment, but I hope soon to be able to pay 300*l.* out of the
" oritorys " and concerts I am engaged in.

FRANCIS DELAVAL to his brother [JOHN DELAVAL].

1753, March 23.—I am just come from Mr. Foote's farce, which
went off with applause. Miss Macklin danced a minuet, played on a
" pandola," and accompanied it with an Italian song, all which she
performed with much elegance. There were some silver cockades at
the play-house for Lord Carnarvon's marriage with the rich Miss
Nicholls.

THOMAS DELAVAL to his brother, JOHN DELAVAL, at Seaton Delaval.

1753, March 27. Hamburg.—My brothers set out yesterday for
Berlin and propose making a tour through Germany.

I have been inquring about our small coals, and propose trying a
cargo or two soon. I should be glad to know what price you could
afford them for if a third part of the better coals were mixed with them.
If the cargo sent by Captain Read cost no more than six shillings the
chaldron, there must have been near a hundred per cent. got by them.
Signed.

The SAME to the SAME.

1753, March 30. Hamburg.—Coals are worth about ten shillings a
chaldron. If you send any, take care to have some of the better coals
mixed with the small ones. It will help to bring them into better
repute.

SAMUEL FOOTE to [JOHN] DELAVAL.

[1753,] April 5. Pall Mall.—The *Englishman at Paris* has been
better received than I expected.

Garrick and all the *deliciæ* of the theatre say kinder things of it than
modesty will permit me to repeat. Upon the whole it was damnably acted.

DELAVAL MSS. Macklin miserably imperfect in the words and in the character. You might have seen what I meant. An English buck by the powers of dullness, instantaneously transformed into an Irish chairman.

Miss Roach accompanied by some frippery French woman, occupied, to the no small scandal of the whole house, the Prince's box, whilst the Duchess of Bedford and others were obliged to take up with seats upon the stage.

I set out for foreign parts the first of May. I do not know whether I shall arrive time enough in France to put up a few Masses for the propitious delivery of Mrs. Delaval; but let me be where I will, I shall not fail to pronounce for her a *Juno Lucina fer opem,* and I do not know but that may do as well as an *Ave Maria.*

— DE REVERSEAUX to — CHAMPSEAUX.

[1753?]—An account of the family, life, and misfortunes of Miss Roach. *French.*

SEATON DELAVAL.

1792, February 1.—An estimate of the expenses for refreshments, attending the play at Seaton Delaval. The total amounts to 33*l.* 14*s.* 10*d.*

[The SAME.]

No date.—An epilogue to the *Fair Penitent* written by Lord Delaval and spoken by the Earl of Strathmore. *Thirty-nine lines.*

The SAME.

No date.—A return of the persons within the township of Seaton Delaval and parish of Earsdon, who from age, infirmity, or any other cause, were to be removed in case of invasion, with the number of ticket and cart in which they were to be removed, and with the number and station of each cart.

HARTLEY COLLIERY.

1797, May.—Estimate of the expense of erecting an engine at Hartley Colliery for drawing the water from the Main to the Yard coal seams, being about thirty fathoms, with a twelve-inch bore. The total amount is 1369*l.* 2*s.* 6*d.*

All the MSS. described above are now in the possession of Mr. John Robinson, of Newcastle-on-Tyre.

RICHARD WARD.

THE MANUSCRIPTS OF THE EARL OF ANCASTER,
AT GRIMSTHORPE, CO. LINCOLN.

It is to be regretted that there is not more matter amongst these papers
relating to Catherine, Duchess of Suffolk, and her husband, Richard
Bertie. The history of their flight from England and of their wander-
ings on the continent is well known, but any addition would have been
welcome which would have helped to fill in the blanks of that romantic
story, or which would have given us further details of the childhood of
their celebrated son—afterwards Lord Willoughby in right of his
mother—who was christened Peregrine, the wanderer, from the circumstances of his birth. We have however an exceedingly complete
account-book kept at Grimsthorpe and at the Barbican in London
during the years 1560 to 1562, when the Duchess and her husband had
returned to England and were reinstated in all their possessions. This
book gives a large number of details concerning their private and public
life, their charities, amusements, journeys, personal and household
expenses and allowances, presents to the Queen and others, the attend-
ances of the Duchess at Court, and the number and expense of their
domestic servants.

The bulk of the earlier papers relate to Peregrine, after he had
become Lord Willoughby. They consist for the most part of his
official correspondence for the years 1585 to 1588, when he was in
command of the English forces in the Low Countries, and are chiefly
written in Dutch or French, and some few in German. From their
nature they are mostly formal, but attention should be called to the
letter written by Lord Willoughby in March 1587, shortly after the
execution of Mary Stuart, to Dauzay, the French Ambassador in
Denmark, which gives the official, if not the true, version of Queen
Elizabeth's motives and feelings on that vexed question.

To go to a later date there are copies of several letters which passed
between Charles I. and Montagu, Lord Lindsey, in March 1646, with
regard to the holding of Woodstock against the Cromwellian troops.
The King seems not to have thought the post sufficiently important for
Lord Lindsey, and he accordingly summons him to Oxford in the most
complimentary manner.

At page 252 is a letter, unsigned, but probably from Charles Bertie
to his brother, the Marquis of Lindsey, in which he gives us an account
of how Harley endeavoured to conquer the opposition of some of the
representatives of the Vere family, who had a natural dislike to his
being created Earl of Oxford, and how he — Harley — warned them
that another would have the title within a month, if he did not.
The writer winds up by suggesting that "we should tell Harley
" what steps have been made to procuring you another title, and try to
" engage him to assist in it, upon giving him noe trouble in this point."
This proposal if carried into effect was doubtless listened to readily by
Harley.

ANCIENT DEEDS.

There are in the muniment room at Grimsthorpe a great number of mediæval deeds and court-rolls. The following appear to be the most interesting of the deeds, the first three being remarkable as stating a villein was "brother" to a man of wealth and high position:—

[*Circa* 1160.]—Radulfus filius Gilleberti omnibus amicis et hominibus suis Francis et Anglicis salutem. Sciatis me dedisse Radulfo villano, fratri meo, totam terram de Steping, in pratis et pasturis, in moris et mariscis et omnibus asiamentis que ad eandem terram pertinent, preter iij bovatas terre quas Tainca tenuit. Totum quod superest terre quam habui in Spepinga dedi predicto Radulfo et heredibus suis, tenendum de me et heredibus meis in feodum et hereditatem pro servicio dimidii militis pro omni servicio quod ad me pertinet. Hoc autem tenementum volo ut bene, libere et honorifice teneat. Et hoc concessi ei quod non mutabo eum hoc servicium suum de manu mea et heredum meorum. Ego et cepi homagium predicti Radulfi quando hanc donationem ei feci coram his testibus, Waltero abbate de Kirkested et Waltero priore, Ricardo incluso, Radulfo cell[erario], Willelmo filio Aet', Ricardo de Hornecastr', Waltero capellano de Barden', fratre Thori et fratre Gosce, et Radulfo filio Radulfi, Willelmo Gri', Simone filio Hacon', Johanne de Edlintun'et Ancheti de Edlintun', Pagano mac°, Willelmo de Puleberge, Reinerio coco, Ada Grim, Thoma de Belesterue, et Edwardo Multon.

[*Circa* 1160.]—Radulfus filius Gileberti omnibus amicis suis et hominibus Gallicis et Anglicis salutem. Sciatis me concessisse et c[arta con]firmasse Radulfo rustico, fratri meo, terram de Stepingia, tenendam et heredibus suis de me et heredibus meis [pro servicio di]midie partis militis. Et sciatis ipsum Radulfum facere iiij°r partes et Robertum Travers quintam hujus medietatis militis. His testibus, Willelmo filio Cunen, Alvredo de . . . dford, Bodin de Fenne, Ernisio de Lam'tunia, Willelmo filio Alvredi de Tedford et Radulfo fratre suo. Valete. *Fragment of equestrian seal.*

[*Circa* 1200.]—Radulfus filius Radulfi filii Gilleberti omnibus hominibus presentibus et futuris salutem. Sciatis me concessisse et hac mea carta confirmasse Radulfo villano, avunculo meo, et heredibus suis totam terram quam Radulfus pater meus dedit illi in Steping', habendam et tenendam de me et heredibus meis cum omnibus rebus et pertinenciis et frangisiis que ad eandem terram pertinent, sicut carta patris mei testatur, scilicet faciendo quatuor partes servicii dimidii militis. Testibus, Ricardo abbate Kirkestedie, Simone de Crevecur', Petro de Screinbi, Johanne de Horrebi, Willelmo de H'eeford, Radulfo de Stavenesbi, Alano de Aistrebi, Simone de Frisebi, Alano de Keles, et Waltero fratre ejus. *Equestrian seal.*

[*Circa* 1200.]—Grant by Philip de Kima to the church of St. Mary, Kirkesteda, and the monks thereof in frank almoin, of common pasture in Wildemora for the good estate of himself and his heirs and the souls of his ancestors. Witnesses:—Lambert, prior of Kime, Thomas, son of William de Heint', Ralph son of Ralph son of Gillebert, Humphrey de Welle, Geoffrey de Clincamp, Walter de Alford, William son of Thomas, William son of the grantor, Elias de Helpringham, Nicholas de Ros, William Bacun, William de Wdetorp, Elias de Brunna, Spiri the chamberlain. *Equestrian seal.*

[1147–1162.]—Grant by Robert de Gant, with the consent of his wife Adeliza Paganell, to the abbey of Vaudey of ten acres and a rod and a half of wood on the north side of the road which is called ' Leuigatha ' in exchange for ten acres on the south side which he had previously given, but which Robert de Langhatuna claimed. Witnesses :—Angerius and Michael, monks, Jordan, Remigius, Ralph de Brunna, Roger the Smith (*Faber*), Ailsi and Syward, lay brethren (*conversi*) of Vaudey, Hugh de Gant, Robert de Langathuna, Ralph Scroph, Arebernus, Alan Ke, Ailbrict and Robert his son, Robert le Franceis, Ovuti and Geoffrey his son, Lambert son of Godwin de Swinsteda, Geoffrey Costard Ralph Cem[en]tarius de Scotelthorp, William son of Payn, Nicholas son of Godric de Anacastro. *Equestrian seal.*

1334, June 16.—Renewal and confirmation to Robert de Scardeburgh, prior of Bridlington and the convent of that place by Henry de Beaumont, Earl of Boghane and Murref and Constable of Scotland, and Isabella late the wife of John de Vescy, of a charter by Sir Gilbert de Gaunt granting to them certain rights of pasture at Edenham, which charter had been maliciously destroyed by John Cadinot, servant of the said Henry and Isabella. Dated at Newcastle-on-Tyne. *Equestrian seal and seal of arms.*

1384.—Ordinance of John, Bishop of Lincoln, concerning the chantry of the Holy Trinity, Spilsby, founded by Sir John Wylughby and the Lady Joan his wife, for a master and twelve chaplains. August 3 *Episcopal and capitular seals.*

1400.—Agreement between the Abbot and Convent of Kirkstead and William de Wylughby, knight, Lord of Eresby, concerning the advowson and endowments of the church of Wyspyngton. October 15, 2 Henry IV. *Ecclesiastical seal.*

1410.—Demise by Joan, Duchess of York, late the wife of William de Wylughby, Lord of Eresby, to Robert de Wylughby, Lord of Eresby, of lands, etc., in Friskenay, Ingoldmels, Tateshale, Hundylby, Menyngesby, Biscopthorp, Kirkeby by Bolyngbrok, Thurleby, and Spilsby. 2 September, 11 Henry IV. *Fine heraldic seal of the Duchess.*

1401.—Demise by William Roos, Lord of Helmesley, Simon Felbrygg, knights, Master Peter de Dalton, John de Tenelby, clerks, William Michell of Friskeney and Albin de Enderby, to William de Wylughby knight, of the manor of Oyreby. Dated at Eresby, 16th February, 2 Henry IV. *Two heraldic seals and four others.*

1407.—Grant by William de Wylughby, knight, Lord of Eresby, John son of Robert de Wylughby, knight, John de Teuelby, clerk, William Michell of Friskenay, Albin de Enderby and Robert de Kirkby, parson of the church of Bolyngbroke to William Hardegray, master of the Chantry of the Holy Trinity, Spilsby, and his successors, of messuages and land in Askeby. 3 February, 8 Henry IV. *Two heraldic seals and four others.*

1547.—Grant by Thomas maltby, clerk, master of the Chantry, or College, of Holy Trinity in the church of Spilsby and the chaplains of the said chantry, or college, to Katherine, Duchess of Suffolk of all their lands and rights within the realm of England, together with the advow-

sons of the churches of Overtoynton, Kirkeby, and Eresby, with the
chapel of Spilsby. 14 September, 1 Edward VI. *Ecclesiastical seal
and four signatures.*

LETTERS AND PAPERS.

THOMAS BERTIE.

1550, July 10. London.—The arms of Thomas Bertie, of Berested,
drawn out by Thomas Hawley, Clarencieux King at arms. *Copy in
the handwriting of William Dugdale. See Glover's heraldic collections, British Museum.*

KIRKSTEAD ABBEY.

[15—.]—An account of Kirkstead Abbey from its foundation in the
year 1139. *Imperfect.*

CHRISTOPHER LANDSCHADE to CATHERINE, DUCHESS OF SUFFOLK.

1569, August 8. Tavernes.—Informing her that at her request he
had gone to Heidelberg and had done his best to get as speedy an
audience as possible with his master the Palsgrave Frederick, for the
English ambassadors. Also informing her that to allay the anxiety of
the wife and children of his master the Palsgrave Wolfgang he was
sending the bearer of this letter, Robert Weidencop, into France to
make personal inquiries after him; and as the usual ways from Germany
to France were closed, he begged her to assist him in getting conveyed
by sea to La Rochelle or elsewhere in France, and also, if he required it,
to advance him money, which should be repaid at the next fair of St.
Bartholomew. Also sending her messages from his sons Jean Dieter
and Jean Lanschade de Steinach. *French.*

SIR HENRY NORREYS to LORD CLINTON, Lord High Admiral
of England.

[1569,] December 10. Niort.—"If after large silence I shoulde
write large letters, it were the next waies to fall from one extreme into
another. But because your Honor shall sufficiently understand such
thinges as hath already passed, touching the dealing of peace, the other
occurrances shall not be verie tedious.

The town of St. Jean d'Angeli having valiantlie susteyned the King's
armie the space of six weeks and more, in the end wanting municon,
and being out of hoope of succor, the second of this instant Piles the
capptaine there, yeldinge the place, departed with armes, bagge, and
baggage, was conducted by Monsieur de Biron to Tailbourg, going from
thence to Coniac. Thre daies before the rendering therof, Monsieur
Martigues in vewing the breach was stricken with a harguebusade in the
head, whereof he incontinent died.

The Prince's armie is near Montauban, and we understand here the
Admiral presentlie beseigeth Aagen upon Garonne. Here is likewise
come news that Nismes in Languedoc is surprised by the relig[ion in]
those parties.

The Cowntie Ringrave being dead, the King hath directed his
regiment to returne into Germanie. There is likewise divers broken
companies of fotemen casstd, and manie of men at armes placed in
gernizon.

It is thought that the Kinge will next attempte Coniac, and afterwards
advance forward to the river of Dordoigne." *Signed.*

MSS. OF THE
EARL OF
ANCASTER.

NEWS LETTER.

[1572, August.]—An account of the massacre of Saint Bartholomew.

"JOYS, the froylicke pointre" to ——

1572, August 17.—A humble request to be paid for the painting of a
carriage. *French.*

RICHARD BERTIE.

[c. 1572.]—The title of Richard Bertie to the style of Lord
Willoughby of Willoughby and Eresby, in the right of the Lady Catherine,
Duchess of Suffolk, his wife, debated before Lord Burghley, Thomas,
Earl of Sussex, and Robert, Earl of Leicester, Commissioners appointed
for the purpose. *Imperfect.*

HANS LANDSCHADEN VON STEINACH to his son, HANS CHRISTOFFEL.

[15]78[-9], March 20. Lunœ (Luneburg).—A rule of life for the
guidance of his conduct in youth and age, towards God and man.
German. Fifteen pages.

DON FELIPE PRENESTAIN, Ambassador from the Emperor, to ——.

1579, May 27. "Di Comitio di Polonia."—Giving an account of
his embassy to the Prince of Muscovy, who was anxious to make an
alliance with the Emperor, the Pope, the King of Spain, and the
other Christian Princes, against the Turk; and describing the reverence
expressed by the Muscovites for Rome and all the holy places, and
especially for the shrine of Our Lady of Loretto, and expressing his
opinion that the people might be easily brought back into the bosom of
the Church. *Italian. Copy.*

PEREGRINE BERTIE to his "good lady" [LADY MARY BERTIE].

[c. 1580.] Willoughby House.—" I am not little greved that I have
not on this time resolved the doubte I lefte you in, and so much more as
I feare it hath caused your unquietnes, in whom I make more account
of than of my selfe or life, and therefore resolve yourselfe that if I had
had fit time I would not so slightly overpasst it. But the truth is, by
other trobles, have yet hard nothinge of that matter worthy the sendinge,
yet did I thinke not to lose so muche occasyon, since I know not whan
to recover it agayne, as to let understand how uncurteously I am dilte
with by my Lord, your brother, who, as I heard, bandeth with parsons
against me and sweareth my death, which I fear nor force not smallie,
but lest his displeasure should withdraw your affection towardes me,
otherwise I thinke no way to be so offended as I can not deffend. And
thus good Lady parsuade your selfe no lesse than you shall find I will
give cause or perfourme above all thinges which you wishe me well to
let nothing greve you whatsoever you shall heare do happen. For my
owne parte my good or ill fortune consisteth onely in you, whom I must
request to accept as well this scribbled well meaning as better eloquence,
excusing my imparfactions with my trobled mind, which are locked upp
so fast as I could skace try get pen and paper to be the present messengers
of my pore good wishes."

PEREGRINE, LORD WILLOUGHBY to SIR FRANCIS WALSINGHAM, the
Queen's Principal Secretary, at the Court.

1582, July 12. Kingston-upon-Hull.—" If misfortune of tempest
had not spoyled my second shippe, wherin my stuffe and necessaries
was, breaking har topmast, and driving har to sutch a leake as she
and har company was in danger, besides coutynuall winds against
us, your letters received the 11 of July had found me nerer Coppen-
haven than Hull. Beinge no lesse willing—tho somewhat discouraged
to have lost my labor and chardge—to have obeyed the counter com-
maud of my stay, than most redy and desirous to imploy my selfe
and all miue whatsoever to accomplishe any service acceptable to har
Maiestie and hars. And therefore, Sir, your last instructions shall be
with no lease care and diligence delivered than the first was with all
duty received, assuring you as I will be sylent in concealing my
advertisment of this cause, so shall I as constantly as though I tooke
knowledge of none but my selfe—tho flying with sutch plumes as I
borow of you—declare what is commanded me, and do all the officis I
may to prevent the evill, persuade the good, and maintaine so effectuall
an amitie as may be answerable to both their honnors, safetie of their
countries, and your good desire ; being right glad you have recommended me and the cause to so virtuous a man as upon your intelligence
I assure myselfe the Frenche embassadour to be, and more I thinke
myselfe beholdinge unto you that it hath pleased you to assist me with
so sufficient a gentleman as Mr. Wade, hoping in God my service shall
take lyke effect to your wise and grave directions. And so cutting
shorte the rest of my letter because we have no occurrences of importance, save only of pirates mutchlie daly complain'd on, worthy your
advertisement, I cease from troblinge you."

RUY LOPEZ to LORD WILLOUGHBY.

1585, January 22. At Court.—The Queen and the Lords of the
Council are all in good health. As you have already heard, one of the
principal members of the Council has been sent by the Queen to the
Low Countries as her Lieutenant General, and was received there very
royally by the States, who have given him ample authority for government. The Earl of Leicester conducts himself very prudently, to the
satisfaction of the Queen and the States.

The Prince of Parma is in want of provisions, and the people are
beginning to die of hunger in Bruges, Antwerp, and the other places of
which he is governor. Don Antonio has come here, a fugitive from
France where he would have been killed by Duke Mercoeur if he had
not had warning. He was compelled to fly La Rochelle, and his
suite were seized and sent with his baggage into Spain to King
Philip. Our patroness, the Queen, favours him and hopes to assist him
to recover his throne which has been so tyrannically usurped.

The Secretary of State has been very ill with a dropsy but is
better now.

Sir Philip Sydney remains in Zealand in a very strong position. The
Earl and he are preparing for action in the coming season. We have
no news from Captain Frobisher (Furbiger) nor from Sir Francis
Drake (Drag). From Spain we hear that they are preparing a maritime
force of importance. We are waiting to see what they will do.
Italian. Signet.

Monsieur dell' Atrech, Secretary to the Duke of Savoy, to the Grand Chancellor of Savoy.

MSS. of the EARL OF ANCASTER.

[15]85, March 14. Sarragossa.—Giving an account of the cordial reception given him by the King of Spain on his arrival at that city. *Italian. Copy.*

G. Gilpin to Lord Willoughby, Governor of Bergen-op-Zoom.

1586, April 5. Utrecht.—Sending him a packet which had come from Denmark. *French.*

Charles de Coucy (?), Sieur de Famars to Lord Willoughby, Governor of Bergen-op-Zoom.

1586, May 1, old style. Utrecht.—Sending him some arms by order of his Excellency. *French. Signed.*

The Deputies from the States of Brabant to Lord Willoughby.

1586, May 2. Gertrudenburg.—Enclosing a request from the inhabitants of the village of Brecht for the release of certain prisoners. *French. Three signatures. Seal of arms. Request enclosed.*

Jacob Muys van Holy to Lord Willoughby.

1586, May 19, new style. Dordrecht.—Concerning the release of Baptist Moy, merchant, and Bellerus, bibliopole, of Antwerp, who were prisoners in his hands, and whom he proposed to exchange for his son Hugues Muys van Holy, a soldier in the company of Monsieur de Famars, Governor of Malines, who had been taken prisoner by the Spaniards. *French. Signed.*

The Same to [the Same].

No date.—On the same subject. *French. Copy.*

The States of Zealand to Lord Willoughby.

1586, May 20. Middelburg.—Urging him to be upon the watch. *French.*

The States General to Lord Willoughby.

1586, May 24. Utrecht.—Begging him to put a stop to the "insolences, petulancies," and "immodesties" which were daily committed at Bergen op Zoom by ill bred young people who disturbed divine service with shouts and the blowing of horns, and by throwing stones through the windows. *French. Signed* Chr. Huygens.

John Bellerus to Lord Willoughby.

1586, June. Antwerp.—On behalf of his son Luke Bellerus, a prisoner at Bergen-op-Zoom. *Latin.*

Le Norman de Laurueter to Lord Willoughby.

1586, June 2. Copenhagen.—Informing him that he was about to start on a mission to Lapland to settle a boundary question with Russia; and that the King of Denmark his master was very favourable to the interests of the King of Navarre. *French. Signed.*

COUNT MAURICE OF NASSAU to LORD WILLOUGHBY.

1586, June 4. Middelburg.—Asking that no one might be lodged
in the room in which the charters and other documents relating to the
marquisate and house of Bergen-op-Zoom were kept. *French. Signed.
Seal of arms.*

The DEPUTIES from the STATES OF BRABANT to [LORD WILLOUGHBY,] Governor of Bergen-op-Zoom.

1586, June 4. Gertrudenburg.—Presenting him with a petition
from three inhabitants of the village of Brecht, for the release of certain
prisoners. *French. Petition enclosed.*

The SAME to the SAME.

1586, June 6. Gertrudenburg.—On the same subject. *French.*

The SAME to the SAME.

1586, June 9. Gertrudenburg.—On the same subject. *French.
Seal of arms.*

The SAME to the SAME.

Same date and place.—On the same subject. *French.*

Pierre DE VUYTENRECHT to LORD WILLOUGHBY, Governor of the Marquisate, Town, and Ports, of Bergen-op-Zoom.

1586, June 11. Tholen.—A letter of apology. *French.*

The DEPUTIES from the STATES OF BRABANT to [LORD WILLOUGHBY].

1586, June 13. Gertrudenburg.—Requesting him to release the
burgomaster of Moll, Bales, and Dessel, called Jacob Sneyers, who had
been taken prisoner when bringing in his contributions to Bergen-op-
Zoom. *French.*

[LORD WILLOUGHBY?] to the KING OF DENMARK.

1586, July 4, new style. Bergen-op-Zoom.—Giving an account of
the progress of the campaign in Holland and Germany. *Latin. Copy.*

SIR PHILIP SIDNEY to LORD WILLOUGHBY.

1586, July 14, new style. Flushing.—His Excellency thinks it is
high time that the companies which are lying between Ramekins and
Middelburg should make sail to Flushing. I beg therefore that you
will give orders to all the boats to sail to Flushing and anchor there.
French. Signed.

R. EARL OF LEICESTER to [LORD WILLOUGHBY] Governor of Bergen-op-Zoom.

1586, July 11. The Hague.—Ordering him to send a hundred and
fifty pioneers to Terneuse and Spele in Flanders, there to be employed
as Mr. Rowland Yorke should appoint.

COUNT HOHENLO to LORD WILLOUGHBY.

1586, August 8.—Sending a gentleman of his household to him.
French. Seal of arms.

The SAME to the SAME.

1586, August 12. Gertrudenburg.—Concerning the movements of
cavalry. *French. Seal of arms.*

CARLO LANFRANCUI to LORD WILLOUGHBY.

1586, August 19. Antwerp.—Madame de Beauvois has written to
me from Brussels that a priest of her household, called Alessandro le
Grande, and her son's tutor, Ubreto Belar, are prisoners at Bergen op
Zoom, and that they are to be ransomed for 700 florins. She begs you
will send them to her with a trumpeter, and she will give orders for the
payment of the ransom and of all other expences. *Italian. Signed.*

ANTONIO, KING OF PORTUGAL to LORD WILLOUGHBY.

1586, October 19. Umzee.—"J'ay scu le bon tractement et faveur
vous aves faict a mon fils Don Manoel, estant pardella, de quoy je vos
suis grandement tesnu, et vos en remercie bien fort, vos asseurant que je
le recognoestray en tous les endroits qu'il plaira a Dieu m'en donner le
moyen. J'envoye pardella Edoart l'arm, gentilhomme de ma maison a
aulcunque * * affaires, et luy ay comande de vos voir. Je vos prie de
le croire en ce qu'il vos dira de m part, et de tesnir la main vere monsieur
le conte de Lest [Leicester] et les Estats d'Olande, affin que je
puisse par votre moyen receyvoir quelque avancement en mes affaires,
qui se doivent traicte avec heurs." *Signed. Seal of arms.*

BERNARDUS CONDERS AB HELPEN to GERHARDUS ERBANUS GELDENHAURIUS, at Embden.

1586, November 28. Herborn.—News from Sarragossa of the 22nd
October 1586.
The Queen of England's famous pirate "Draco" has struck a blow
at India and taken several islands. He has also stolen and taken to
England three and a quarter millions of dollars besides other valuables.
Twelve ships sailed fifteen days ago from Biscaya with 1500 soldiers
and 1500 sailors on board; they were laden with arms, and ammunition for 2000 men. It was not known when they started who was to
be the general, but instructions were to be sent to sea after them. God
knows where they are going. My impression is that England had better
look to herself on the Scotch coast. *Latin.*

COUNT MAURICE OF NASSAU to LORD WILLOUGHBY.

1586, December 13. Middelburg.—Concerning Abraham Fischmeester who was a prisoner at Bergen-op-Zoom. *French. Signed.
Seal of arms.*

MICHAEL AULLIER to LORD WILLOUGHBY.

1586, December 14. Lillo.—Concerning the Secretary of Woest-
wesel who was a prisoner. *French. Signed. Signet.*

Robert, Earl of Leicester to the Sergeant Major of
Bergen-op-Zoom.

1586, December 30. The Hague.—Requiring his attendance at the
Hague in order to give his opinion of the best way of quieting the dis-
content among the soldiers at the castle of Wouw. *Signed by* John
Wilkes *and* G. Gilpin. *Seal of arms.*

A Plan.

[c. 1586.]—A plan of a Dutch port; perhaps one of the ports about
Bergen-op-Zoom.

Lord [Willoughby] to [the Earl of Essex].

[c. 1586.]—Concerning supplies for Bergen-op-Zoom. *Copy.*

The Same to [the Same].

[Same date.]—On the same subject. *Copy.*

The States General to Lord Willoughby.

1587, January 6. The Hague.—Thanking him for postponing his
proposed journey to England and for his services in the matter of the
castle of Wouw. *French.* *Signed by* Maurice of Nassau, John Wilkes,
and G. Gilpin.

The Magistrates of Bergen-op-Zoom to Lord Willoughby.

1587, January 10.—Asking him to obtain the confirmation from
the Queen of their rights. *French.*

The Same to the Same.

1587, January 17. Bergen-op-Zoom.—Informing him that they had
heard that the enemy were advancing upon them, and begging him to
give timely warning to the garrison of the castle of Wouw.

P. Lord Willoughby to --— Dauzay, French Ambassador
in Denmark.

prattiques nouvelles contre sa personne discouvertes—esquelles Monsieur de Chasteauneuf s'est trouve bien avant jouant su rolie, voire sans la sceu du Roi votre maistre—l'ont entierement forcée ; et croy fermement que sans l'importuniti des uns et l'evident danger menace des aultres, elle ne s'y fust jamais consentie. Ce que tesmoigne le grand dueil de sa Majestie seule, parmy les feux de joye et rejouissement general de son peuple." *Copy.*

MSS. OF THE EARL OF ANCASTER.

LORD [WILLOUGHBY] to [the EARL OF LEICESTER.]

1587, June. B[ergen-op-Zoom].—Asking for the payment of some money to Captain Carsey. *Copy.*

[The SAME] to [the SAME].

No date.—On the same subject. *Copy.*

The STATES GENERAL to LORD WILLOUGHBY, Governor of Bergen-op-Zoom.

1587, July 4. The Hague.—Requesting him to give all the assistance in his power to Martini, the Auditor General, who had been sent to Bergen-op-Zoom for the service of his Excellency and the country. *French. Signed by* Gilpin.

COUNT MAURICE OF NASSAU to SIR JOHN WINGFIELD, Governor of Bergen-op-Zoom.

1587, July 7. Middelburg.—Asking for the two companies of his . Zealand regiment. *French. Signed. Seal of arms.*

AMBROSE MARTINI to LORD WILLOUGHBY.

[1587, July ?]—Directing him on behalf of the Auditor General to send a peasant, who had been taken prisoner, to Middelburg. *French.*

PHILIP, COUNT HOHENLO to LORD WILLOUGHBY, Governor of Bergen-op-Zoom.

1587, July 7. Gertrudenburg.—Informing him that General Norris had asked to have the English infantry who were in his camp sent to him, and begging him to send some troops in their place. *Seal of arms.*

The SAME to the SAME.

1587, July 8. Gertrudenburg.—Thanking him for his letter. *French. Seal of arms.*

COLONEL J. BAX to LORD WILLOUGHBY, Colonel of the English Infantry at Bergen-op-Zoom.

1587, July 13. Middelburg. --Agreeing, with the consent of the Earl of Leicester, to bring his company to Bergen. *French. Signed. Signet.*

JEAN REYNHOUTS DANCKAERTS to LORD WILLOUGHBY, General of the English Infantry, and Governor of Bergen-op-Zoom.

1587, August 11, new style. Middelburg.—Announcing that he had left Utrecht and come to Middleburg. *French. Signed. Signet.*

MSS. OF THE
EARL OF
ANCASTER.

1587, August. Bergen-op-Zoom.—Since your departure we have not failed of our endeavours to take any good occasion that might happen. "Wee sent out many espyalls but none be retorned, by reason whereof we dout least they miscarry. My owne trumpet is now come home, who was but hardly entertayned, and not suffered to passe any further than Antwerp, but blindfold. Yet he advertiseth for certaine that at Burgamhoult the enemy lyeth, to his weening, 2000 strong, and at Dambrugh 1000 strong. The first place being strongly fortified, with only one advenue unto yt, and the other so diched about, as that they are strongly entrenched."

The letters "which should have bene found here by Count Hollock's (Hohento) secretaryes information, are not yet receyved, by reason that they who should have delivered them, mist their way. And touching our fortifications here, ymediatly upon your Excellencie's departure, they all retired, by reason that they of Zelland doe not pay anything, and besides finding the bad humour of our Burghmasters disposed rather to leave all things in so weake estate as they be then to have them amended."

LORD [WILLOUGHBY] to [the EARL OF LEICESTER].

1517, August 2.—"I have indeavoured all I may, not only to prepare for th' enemies coming, but to cut off by intelligencies some of his purposes. But for what appertaines to the towne, unless your Excellencie succours us we are sure of nothing. They procede like crabbs backward, advantagous to the ennemy and extreame daungerous to us. They have promised to imploy the 16000 florins of theire owne inventions and fortifications in the new haven, and now they would consume even that title we have, to the contynuance of their follies and abuse of youre treasure. I beseach your Excellencie by open audience, discover these paltry proceedinges. For my owne parte I will with sutch soundnes as becomes an honest man, averre and justify all things; and if it were once brought to sutch a triall it would increase my trust. Riswick the cheife plotter of these unessary change, chalenges mutch from Mr. Gelligre.

For matters abroade th'ennemy is very strong in horse and foote on this syd about Turnhout and that way, where they have cut downe your corne and are ruining it. I could have wishd your horse had comme soner and we had ben renforc'd, as I wrote in my last letters, with some companies of foote. It had ben to be hoped we mought have donne some good. I have yesterday sent letters to the contribu. torie townes to bring in a hundred wagons for the fortifications, and sent out some espies to th'enuemies camp, whereof your Excellencie shall be advertisd." *Copy*.

The SAME to the SAME.

1587, August 4.—"There is retorned yesternight an espyall of myne owne company who hath ben abroad, and reporteth that th'enemy marched yesterday from Turnhout to Hogstrate with eighteen cornets of horse and fourteen ensiegnes of foot; and there is intelligences from Antwerp that they are to be seconded by all the forces there, and the rumour is that they intend to sett downe before this towne, or Huysden."

JACQUES TUTELERT to LORD WILLOUGHBY.

1587, August 16 [new style]. Lillo.—I have received your letter informing me of the designs of the enemy upon this fort. As however they can for the present do nothing on account of the full moon, I must decline your offer of assistance, especially as I have just received a strong reinforcement of infantry from my friends in Antwerp. The artilleryman (*canonier*) whom you mention, has been sent to Walcheren. My friends in Antwerp tell me that the enemy intend to attack Bergen·op-Zoom; in any case their infantry are moving towards Maestricht. *French. Signed.*

COUNT MAURICE OF NASSAU to LORD WILLOUGHBY.

1587, August 18 [new style]. Antwerp.—Asking him to set at liberty a gentleman of Brabant named Van der Meeren, who was an old servant of his house and who was a prisoner at Bergen-op-Zoom. *French. Signed. Seal of arms.*

LIEUTENANT GUILLIAME DE VISSCHER to LORD WILLOUGHBY.

1687, August 23 [new style]. Lillo.—Concerning runaway soldiers. *Dutch.*

The ELECTOR OF COLOGNE to LORD WILLOUGHBY.

1587, August 24 [new style.]. Dordrecht.—A complimentary letter. *French.*

PIETRO DI VUYTENRECHT to LORD WILLOUGHBY, Governor of Bergen-op-Zoom.

1587, August 27 [new style]. Thoyen.—Sending him a peasant with news from Antwerp. *Italian. Seal of arms.*

EMMERY DE LEW to LORD WILLOUGHBY.

1587, August 29 [new style].. Willemstadt.—Asking him to send the Irish hound (*levrier d'Irlande*) which he had promised to give him. *French. Signed. Signet.*

HENRY HERST to LORD [WILLOUGHBY].

1587, August 29 [new style]. Dordrecht.—Informing him that he had written to the Marshall General begging him to ask his Excellency to write to all gentlemen out of the country who were in harmony with their views, to work for the cause; and asking Lord Willoughby to do the same. *French. Signed.*

JAQUES TUTELERT to LORD WILLOUGHBY.

1587, September 1 [new style]. Lillo.—Informing him that a sergeant of Bergen-op-Zoom who had just been liberated from the fort of Dordam had had some conversation during his imprisonment, with Mondragon, and that he had shared the lodging of the Governor of Dordam. He might therefore have some information to give *French. Signet.*

GUILLAUME DE POUDRE, Bailiff, to LORD WILLOUGHBY.

1587, September 1 [new style]. Zierickzee.—Informing him that the new fortifications at Bergen-op-Zoom would be no use if the island of Tertole were not strengthened and the town of "Reymersveale" enclosed. *French. Signed.*

MSS. of the
EARL of
ANCASTER.

P. Lord Willoughby to the Lord Marshal.

1587, August 23. Bergen-op-Zoom.—"I hartely thank your Lord-ship for your honnorable remembrance to his Excellencie for the necessities of this garrison, for which your Lordship writeth that his Excellencie will geve present order. Yt is more then t me yt were done, but yf anie inconvenience or extremitie shall happenythrough the want of yt, the fault wilbe held others and not myne, having discharged my ducty with importunate solliciting of the same these six weekes at the least.

When your Lordship writeth that his Excellencie is displeased and discontented with me for runnsoming awaie some prisoners without acquainting him first therwith. I well hoped that my labours, hazard of my lief, and spoile of my hving, adventured for his sake—wherin his honde to me is farre greater then myne to him—might have letted him from light suspicion, bad conveyning, and hard and straite laeing to them that neither crave, nor have tasted, any liberalitie but from the highest.

I can not but think yt straunge that myselff being a follower of his Excellencie, and who have alwaies endevoured to awnswer his Excel-lencies expectation with all correspondencie of duetiefull affection, should onely be made a president, when not any other is impeached, or so much as onece called in question in like case; drawing th'example eyther from Count Hollock his opposite, Schenk at Nays, or from commaundors of other places.

If yt may be indifferently determined by th'auncient presidentes and customes of this garrison, I will not challenge that my person and qualitie hath deserved as much—spoken without disparagement to any —as those before remembred, or the cautionarie townes, with whom his Excellencie doth not deale in like sorte.

For your selff, as I offered yow of curtesie what your selff would so yf there be due to yow, I hope your Lordship will draw the president from other garrisons rather then from so neare a frend as I think your Lordship holdes me: but when all is done the matter is not worth so much as the paltrie drosse worketh. I respect more the priveledg of the place then proffit. I love to speake plaine. A Provost Marshall of Berghen councells not me, whom yf I had knowen to have offended, I could not have slacked to have punished; and if he have misdone let him have his desertes.

Judge better of me—my Lord—then that any petie companion minister or officer should overrule me, or a storme of any trouble disgrace me, having not done any thing which I would not have tryed before th' indifferent face of all men.

Yt is true. I am and wilbe duetiefull where I am called to obedience; yet right is due from the greatest to the meanest.

I wish—though I have bene alwayes sett at the cartes tayle of all men in any meanes that might countervaile my charge—yet that I might be esteemed as I am and according to the place I bould. I would geve more then the raunsomes of all those that were brought to Berghes to resigne yt with the same good opinion I came to yt.

To be short: what yow maie challenge off frendship is as large as your self will sett downe, and I professe yt simply without shadow: what of duety, must be referred to presidentes and martiall courtes determinable by a councell table.

For his Excellencies displeasure I am right sorry for yt. I wish he had any could please him better. I nourish not my selff with any humour of honnour or proffit of this journey. I would I had paid the best raunsome to depart with his favour, and purchase myne owne quiet at my howse : and let others plaie their partes and sett forth their greatnes. I am glad I know the world, and the very thing yt self of these prisonners, which is now caryed like a huge mountaine in a miste, will prove but a skorne of ill intelligencers, when the world shall know my proceedinges. I need not send you any newes of our new Governours in the Iland of Tertelle, the practise on foot between Sevenbergh and Huysden, how many shippes are launced into Andwerp river, whither th'enemy marcheth : for I am sure eyther they be but fables, or before this knowen unto you."

Postscript.—" The particularities of your secrets be more particulerly published at Antwerp, then—I think—the most of your selves know them there." *Copy.*

The Lord Marshal to Lord [Willoughby].

1587, August.—" The circomstances of my letter are for want of apt construction taxed. Peruse them well and you shall find it matter answering what was prononc'd by you in his Excellencie behalfe, and no part thereof touching your selfe."

" For Georgio Cressiere his ransom, it is not yet all out received, neither did I therein stand with you to render you your due. Knowing it by many presydents in that place your right, and I my selfe sutch a debtor, I hope as you dare trust for so mutcbe."

The prisoners " are all straightly kept save Torrise. I wish he were in the Secretarie's hand to exchaung for Teligin, or to work some other feate in England withall, and on that condition " I wish his Excellency and you had them all.

The Duke's army remains at Turnhout. It is affirmed constantly they come hither. Howsoever we are furnished, and attend their coming with earnest devotion.

Lord Willoughby to [the Earl of Leicester].

1587, August 28. Bergen-op-Zoom.—Excusing himself and giving his reasons for having ransomed the prisoners. *Copy.*

The Same to the Same.

1587, August.—Sending Dr. Masset to solicit the States General for money. *Copy.*

[Lord Willoughby to the Earl of Leicester.]

1587, September 2.—Having surprised two letters of the enemy's, I send them to your Excellency. " The contents I leave to your judgment, and I do .bt not but some part of them may move you to laugh.

For our state at Berghen, it is as your Excellencie left it, but much porer. Great inconvenience is like to happen, for that we shall misse our weakly lendinges, if by your Excellencie's care and providence it be not prevented. The daunger of a malcontentment your Excellencie is the best judge of in sutch a frontier place.

The statesmen are redy to dy and mutin. My credit is determined with the towne who makes difficulties that no necessities or fortifications can be advanced because no restitution is mad of money alowed (?) by your Excellencie's owne order and mine, under them disbursed ; so that all thinges remaines full of doubts and hazards. I cam hether this day with Sir Rychard Brugham to geve what helpe I could ; but I find all things here so backward as I prevaile nothing of my labour and hope."

Postscript.—" I hope your Excellencie will give me leave in this hard time, and priviledge, as well as others, to make my best of my owne prisoner, Martin de la Faile, wherein I shall nothing hold myselfe deceived of your honorable favour ever protested to me."

The REPRESENTATIVES of the States of Brabant to LORD WILLOUGHBY.

1587, September 12 [new style]. Dordrecht.—Sending him a copy of a petition addressed by Brabant to the States General. *French. Two signatures. Signet.*

J. LEGROS to LORD WILLOUGHBY.

1587, September 15, new style. Axel.—Giving reports which had reached him concerning the proposed movements of the enemy. *French. Copy.*

COLONEL COSMO DE PESARENGIS to LORD WILLOUGHBY.

1587, September 20 [new style]. The Hague.—Asking for the release of one of his soldiers who had been taken prisoner with Martin de la Faille. *French. Signet.*

ADMIRAL JUSTINUS OF NASSAU to LORD WILLOUGHBY.

1587, September 23 [new style]. The Fleet.—Sending him some arms which were on board the Brussels fleet. *French. Signet.*

[LORD WILLOUGHBY to the EARL of LEICESTER.]

1587, September 15.—" Having employed all my credit, labour, and travayle, for the sustenance of the poor and miserable souldiours here, who now at last being driven to a marvailous great extremitie, I am told in the most humblest and earnest manner that I may recommend their distressed estate unto yow. I know your Excellencie's continuall and most honnorable care for your poore souldiours, but I am very well assured that yf your Excellencie had eyther seen or heard their case, yt would not a little have moved your compassion to their remedy. And although it be a great want unto them to lacke victualles and provision, yet is the same so much the greater by reason of the absence of divers of their captains and officers, by whose presence and orderly care they might have been much eased, and inconveniencies the better prevented, whereunto they are dayly subiect.

I doubt not but your Excellencie will take order to send both thence and thether where the necessitie is so great. And as for provision of victuall for these poore companyes in the States pay, yf yt shall stand with your Excellencie's pleasure to authorise me to receyve the contributions of the countree, I doe not doubt but to relieve them, much to your honour, and the advancement of the service. And that it may be cleered to your Excellencie that I seeke yt not for any benefit to my selff, I desire that yt might like yow to joyne with me therin, Sir Richard Brugham and the Sergeant Maior Generall, or whom other you shall think meet, for I am daily so ymportuned with their continuall necessityes, as having already stretched my credyt to the uttermost, I know not how any longer to relieve them."

The only news is that " Counts Hollocks and Maurice came downe yesterday to the flett, for whose arrivall ther was much triumph as that ther was whole tries of cannon shott pealing, and volleys of small shott continued for the space of three or four hours, insomuch that all in Bergen " supposed the enemye's fleet had assailed them and that they had been wonderfully hotly engaged. The 'poor souldiers wished they had had but the third part of the value of' that that was so vaynly shott away, to have filled their hongry bellyes.

They of Lillo have taken very rich prisoners, Italians and merchants. The Italians being men of very great qualitie and very well apparelled." *Copy.*

The SAME to the SAME.

Same date.—It is said the enemy's camp is appointed to rise presently. They remain yet at Turnhout.

Colonel Bax and his brethren under cover of requiring money due for their entertainment, send out soldiers into Guelderland who commit many outrages with horrible murders, unto such as have your Excellency's safeguard and protection, whereby the country is much spoiled. If you would give order that they might be paid out of the contributions of the country it would satisfy them.

Touching Monsieur de " Thorise," I will do my endeavour to compound with the soldiers for him for as reasonable a ransom as I can. *Copy.*

On the same sheet is a copy of another letter from Lord Willoughby to the Earl of Leicester, dated September 11, from Bergen-op-Zoom.

[The SAME] to the SAME.

1587, September 18.—" Upon Saturday last at night my selff with some nombre both of horse and foot went out in hope to have done some enterprise upon [   ], but by misfortune two of our wagons, wherin were our chieffest engines and fireworkes, broke by the way and unluckey fell into the water; by meanes whereof our staie being the longer before we came there, and the latter parte of the night proving somewhat light, we were discovered and th'alarme geven before we could come to doe any thing, so that we retorned ymmediately.

At my goyng forth I had geven order to some horsmen of my companie to goe toward the Prince's camp to learne some tongue of their intention, or to see yf they could take any prisoners by whom we might receyve any certan intelligence.

By the way beyond Callempthowt they met yesterday marching hitherward the Marques of Grasta accompanyed with 2500 horse; and thinking me to be abroad, supposed yt had bene my company, and so without dowbt or suspition aproched to them and were overthrowen, some sore hurt and other some taken prisoners; onely of seventeen there escaped but two.

In th'afternoone the alarme came hither to us to Berghen, but with some twenty or thirty horse; wherupon we sallyed, but they staied not our comming, and the Marques himselff came not much neerer then Calempthout; we went within two English miles of them, and so finding some of our men lying there hurt, returned and brought them with us.

Before our men were overthrowen they had taken one that came from Coradin who told them that he heard yt reported from his master that Count Hollack had promised the delivery of Lillo, Huysden, and Gertrudenberghen, to th'enemy, and that for certaine their camp is apoyncted to rise this week; and how like yt is that their disseigne is for this place, the manner of the Marques his presenting in such sort may geve great presumption.

And besides this bearer, a sergeant of Captain Vredalls, can advertise your Excellencie of certain reportes of Mounsieur la Roche, for which purpose I send him unto yow."

The Same to [the Same].

1587, September 22.—*See " Five Generations of a Loyal House,"* p. 134. *Copy.*

The Same to the Same.

1587, September.—*See " Five Generations of a Loyal House,"* p. 137. *Copy.*

The Bailiff, Burgomasters, and Sheriffs of Tertolle, to Lord Willoughby.

1587, October 7 [new style]. Tertolle.—Sending him a present of faggots for the use of the soldiers. *French.*

The Same to the Same.

Same date and place.—On the same subject. *French.*

The Representatives of the Estate of Brabant to Lord Willoughby.

1587, October 10 [new style]. Delft.—On behalf of the Estates of Brabant. *French. Two signatures. Signet.*

Louise de Coligny, Princess of Orange to Lord Willoughby.

[1587,] October 23 [new style]. Flushing.—Concerning the release of the Secretary Grimaldi and the Sieur de "Thoures." *French.*

Lord [Willoughby] to [the Earl of Leicester].

1587, October 14.—Informing him of the capture of a gentleman whose ransom was estimated to be four or five thousand florins.

The Same to the Same.

1587, October 16.—The reports of the gentlemen who were brought in prisoners here, touching the great levy of men, preparation of munition, and tools, and instruments for pioneers, is confirmed for certain.

Captain Barnard, a Frenchman who went forth hence, is returned, and advertises for certain that the Governor of West Friesland has marched to the Duke's camp with thirty companies of foot, and four companies of horse. I have also ascertained by some peasants who are come hither that the company from Sluys are already arrived at Turnhout. How far all these occasions may tend to gather the enemies intentions your Excellency can best conceive ; wherefore I most humbly beseech you to assist us with the companies that I remembered before unto your Excellency. *Copy.*

[The Same to the Same].

1587, October 25. Bergen-op-Zoom.—The enemy's intention for this place is diversely confirmed. There is returned from their camp at Turnhout a drum of mine who ascertaineth me that Sir William Stanley with all his regiment is come thither and that he saw them come marching in. There were looked for at the camp last night 3,000 new Italians who were marching within a little of them. The Marquis still holds my trumpet, but it is reported by a trumpet of theirs who has come hither that it is for no other occasion but while they have sent to the Prince to know his pleasure touching the former challenge. And it may well be that if they mean to attempt this place, they will the rather enter into the action to draw forth so many brave men into it. Therefore I beseech you to ascertain me of your pleasure therein, and that if we shall proceed in it, that you will lend me a horse and assist us with some new supply of gentlemen for the accomplishment of the same.

I would also ask for some money, which I am utterly without, neither is there any to be borrowed in all the land. I have bestowed much in reinforcing my company and new apparelling them, and cannot have my account for them, but above all other men am least respected by the Treasurer. *Copy.*

[The SAME to the SAME.]

[1587, October.]—Informing him that he had heard from a spy that Mondragon had obtained a footing in the fort of Lillo and intended to make an attempt on it that night. *Copy.*

The SAME to the SAME.

1587, October. Bergen-op-Zoom.—Last night came home my spy. His advertisements were that the Prince is very retired at Brussels, so that none may speak with him. An Abbot from West Friesland arrived lately, making great complaints of our people. There are great rumours of reinforcements, and it is privily whispered that Bergen will be attempted. *Copy.*

[The SAME to the SAME.]

1587, October.—A memorial concerning the pay of the soldiers. *Sent by Captain Salisbury. Copy.*

[The SAME to the SAME.]

1587, October.—A memorial concerning prisoners and the pay of the soldiers. *Sent by Captain Martin. Copy.*

[The SAME to the SAME.]

1587, October.—Defending himself from accusations which had been brought against him, and begging for assistance. *Copy.*

MATTHIAS DE L'OBEL to LORD WILLOUGHBY, Governor of Bergen-op-Zoom.

1587, November 10 [new style]. Middelburg.—Sending him pills and an ointment for a friend; also sending messages to Sir John and the Countess. *French.*

[The SAME to the SAME.]

No date.—Sending pastilles and ointment.

LOUISE DE COLIGNY, PRINCESS OF ORANGE to LORD WILLOUGHBY.

1587, November 11 [new style]. Leyden.—Concerning the exchange of the prisoners "de Torreze and Grimaldy" for Monsieur de Teligny. *French. Signed.*

MSS. OF THE
EARL OF
ANCASTER.

The STATES GENERAL to LORD WILLOUGHBY, Governor of Bergen-op-Zoom.

1587, November 17 [new style]. The Hague.—Requesting him to receive George Matruyt as their commissioner. *French. Signed.*

LORD [WILLOUGHBY] to ——

[1587, November.]—Relating the ill treatment he had received concerning the prisoners. *Copy.*

LORD [WILLOUGHBY] to [the EARL OF LEICESTER].

1587, November 8 [old style]. Bergen-op-Zoom.—As the States make no great haste to send any reinforcement of men, I would require your Excellency that Colonel Fremyn's company might rise from Axell and come hither. The States will succour them more than us "for Pifron depends upon them, and Counte Solmes hathe speciall interest and commaundment in the man. Your Excellencie can judge howe uncertaine yt is is to knowe the enemies resolucon, and how necessarie is to prevente the wurste. I doubt not but my Lord Marshall and Jenibell have informed you of our wants."

Postscript.—"Moudragon hath begune at Bruxells to conferre about theis matters in hande, being a man well acquainted by his owne practise with the state of theis parts. There is launchett at Antwerpt five hundred flatt bottom boates. They of Lillo looke every foote to be assailed by them and the reste.

All the Italian companies are marched from Turneboulte to Antwerpe. The Marques of Guasta with his troupes remaine still at Turneholte. It is likelie that shower will fall here with some darke mone, yf you mak us not stronger. They knowe our weakenes and mortalitie.

The Duke of Parma marched yesterdaie to Malines with the newe Italian companies. All the saddles and launces provided are shipped this daie. The Duke is looked for att Antwerpe." *Copy.*

MAILLART MAERTIUS to LORD WILLOUGHBY, Governor of Bergen-op-Zoom.

1587, November 28 [new style]. Bergen-op-Zoom.—Sending him a letter from Colonel Mondragon. *French. Seal of arms.*

P. LORD WILLOUGHBY to the LORD MARSHAL of the forces in Flanders.

1587, November 19. Bergen-op Zoom.—"I thanke your Lordship for your carefulnes. I know we shall have all things supplied in good will, and attend laizure. I am inforsed to be somewhatt sharp. I know not whence it riseth, but men grow most careles of their duties. When the time most requireth, my officers go hence without leave, and suffers their gardes to be unkepte, so that they ennemy sends and receaves intelligences by corruptions of the gards. And our men runne away daly notwithstanding their hath been proclamed straight penal lawes to sutch gardes, and as good order as may be set downe. There is now absent Captain Vavasour's lieutenant without my leave. Himselfe hath been long sick and his auncient also. For want of loking to there hath ben som fault on his gardes. If you would call his lieutenant, sharply reprove him, and cause his Excellencie as of his owne care to have discipline observed, your Lordship shall do good to the service." *Copy.*

[LORD WILLOUGHBY to the EARL OF LEICESTER.]

[1587, November.]—A memorial of matters to be considered on his behalf before his Excellency's departure. *Copy.*

CAPTAIN PAUL BAX to LORD WILLOUGHBY, General.

[15]87, December 3 [new style].—A letter of congratulation upon receipt of the news of Lord Willoughby's appointment [as general of the forces], and regret at his departure from Bergen-op-Zoom. *French. Signed.*

COUNT MAURICE OF NASSAU to CAPTAINS JOHN, PAUL, and MARSILIUS, BAX, at Bergen-op-Zoom.

1587, December 12 [new style] On board the *Biervliet.*—Directing them to proceed with their companies to Stanesand and await his orders there. *French. Signed. Seal of arms.*

CAPTAIN PAUL BAX to LORD WILLOUGHBY, General.

1587, December 16.—Asking him whether they were to obey the orders of Count Maurice. *French. Signet.*

M. MAERTIUS to LORD WILLOUGHBY, General of the Infantry.

[15]87, December 16. Bergen-op-Zoom.—Concerning the provision of horses for the cavalry, and enclosing a letter from [Sir William] Read, Governor of Bergen. *French.*

The ESTATES OF BRABANT to [LORD WILLOUGHBY].

[c. 1587].—Concerning the questions in dispute between them and the States General. *French. Copy.* •

COUNT DE MEURS to [LORD WILLOUGHBY].

1588, January 22, old style. The Hague.—Informing him that the city of Utrecht was unable any longer to maintain the troop of horse quartered there, and requesting him to remove them to some other quarters. *French. Copy.*

ADOLF, COUNT OF NEUWENAR to LORD WILLOUGHBY, General of the English forces.

1588, January 22, old style. Utrecht.—Informing him that he had heard that Count Hohenlo intended to make an expedition against some of the hostile cities in his government of Guelderland, and promising to give all the assistance in his power. *French. Signed.*

[LORD WILLOUGHBY] to —— DEVENTER, Burgomaster [of Utrecht].

1588, January 24, old style.—Sending the Sergeant Major to confer with him, being unable to come himself on account of indisposition *French. Copy.*

The BURGOMASTER of ZERVOL to LORD WILLOUGHBY.

1588, February 7, new style.—Enclosing copy of their letters to the Count de Neuwenar and the States General. *German. Copy.*

GERBHARD [TRUCHSESS], Elector of Cologne to LORD WILLOUGHBY.

[15]88, February 10, old style. Houstadyck.—Asking for a convoy for his servant. *French.*

[LORD WILLOUGHBY] to the STATES of UTRECHT.

1588, February 12, new style. The Hague.—Promising to pay the charges for the English troops at Utrecht out of the first moneys received from England. *French. Copy.*

The QUEEN to the STATES GENERAL of Holland.

1587[-8], February 12 [old style]. Greenwich.—Concerning their hostility to persons well disposed to herself. *French. Copy. See State Papers, Holland, Vol. 50.*

The QUEEN to her " cousin," COUNT MAURICE OF NASSAU.

1587[-8], February 13, old style.—On the same subject as the preceding letter. *French. Copy. See State Papers, Holland, Vol. 50.*

The QUEEN to her " cousin," COUNT HOHENLO.

1587[-8], February 13 [old style].—On the same subject. *French. Copy. See State Papers, Holland, Vol. 50.*

The QUEEN to [LORD WILLOUGHBY].

[1588], February [13], old style.—Extracts from a letter to be shewn to the States General. *French. See State Papers, Holland, Vol. 50, for an entire copy of the letter in English.*

[The SAME] to the SAME.

1588, February [12 ?, old style.]—Instructions to settle the disputes between the States General and the city of Utrecht, and also to interfere on behalf of Colonel Sonoy and the captains of Naerden, who were unwilling to alter the terms of their oath. *French. Copy.*

The COUNCIL OF STATE to LORD WILLOUGHBY, General of the Queen's forces.

1588, February 23, new style. The Hague.—Requesting him to send orders to the Lieutenant Governor of Bergen op Zoom to permit the company under Colonel Frewin to leave that town and go to Rotterdam. *Signed by* Chr. Huygens. *French. Seal of arms.*

[LORD WILLOUGHBY] to SIR WILLIAM READ.

[15]88, February 23, new style. Utrecht.—Concerning the payment of troops out of the contributions received from Brabant. *French. Copy.*

COUNT MAURICE OF NASSAU.

1588, February 24 [new style]. Horn.—His Excellency having seen an extract of a resolution of the Council of Naerden by which it appears that Captain Rancy having been asked by the said Council if he would obey the patent of his Excellency of Nassau, replied, that according to the charge given him by the Earl of Leicester, he could not quit the place unless his Excellency and their Lordships, the States of Holland, should by deed declare to him that he was no longer obliged to obey the orders of the Earl of Leicester. Wherefore his Excellency, by advice of the deputies of the States of Holland, declares by these presents that the above mentioned captain and all other persons under the government of Holland, Zealand, and Westfriesland, are not bound to obey the orders and commands which the Earl of Leicester laid upon them before his departure. *French. Copy.*

The Council of State to Lord Willoughby.

MSS. OF THE
EARL OF
ANCASTER.

[15]88, February 26. new style. The Hague.—Recommending him to keep an eye upon Captain Salisbury who was suspected of being in communication with the enemy. *French. Signed by* G. Gilpin.

[Lord Willoughby] to Count Hohenlo.

1588, February 17, old style. Utrecht.—Expostulating with him in the name of the Queen for attacking the house of Councillor Brakel. *French. Copy.*

William Bardesius to the Council of State.

1588, February 27 [new style]. Verwaertshone near Medenblick.— Concerning the disputes about the pay of the soldiers at Medenblick. *French. Copy. See State Papers, Holland, Vol.* 50.

Lord Willoughby to the Council of State.

1588, February 18, old style. Utrecht.—Informing them that Count Brakel had come to him to expostulate at the action of Count Hohenlo who was besieging his castle of Brakel in North Holland. *French. Copy.*

The Council of State to Lord Willoughby.

1588, February 29, new style. The Hague.—Regretting to hear of the attack made by Count Hohenlo on the house of Brakel, and enclosing a copy of the preceding letter. *Signed by* Chr. Huygens. *French. See State Papers, Holland, Vol.* 50.

Lord Willoughby.

1588, February.—A list of the correspondence of Lord Willoughby concerning his charge, during the month of February.

Paul Buys to [Lord Willoughby].

[1588], March 7, new style. Amsterdam.—Concerning the disbanding of the company of Captain James de Rancy. *French. Copy.*

Captain James de Rancy to Colonel Colthagh (?) at Utrecht.

1588, March 8, new style. Naerden.—On the same subject. *French. Signed.*

Gerard Proninck, called Deventer, to Lord Willoughby.

1588, February 29, old style. Utrecht.—On the same subject. *French. Signed.*

The Queen to the States General.

1587[-8], March 12, old style. Greenwich.—Exhorting them to union, and appointing Lord Willoughby and Mr. Killigrew mediators between them. *French. Copy. See State Papers, Holland, Vol.* 51.

The Queen to Count Maurice [of Nassau].

1587[-8], March 18, old style. Greenwich.—Urging him to purge himself from the imputations made upon him in respect to Colonel Sonoy, and informing him of the appointment of Lord Willoughby and Mr. Killigrew to settle the matter. *French. Copy. See State Papers, Holland, Vol.* 51.

LORD WILLOUGHBY to [the STATES GENERAL].

1588, March 25, The Hague.—" Aprez avoir nagueres delivré lettres
de sa Majeste et faict certaines propositions de la part dicelle à
l'endroict du Collonnel Sonoy, surquoy ont ensuiviz diverses communications de ulterieures procedures, sans touttes fois avoir receu finalle
resolutions de V.S., n'ay sceu obmectre pour la discharge de mon devuoir
d'advertir sa Majeste sincerement de tout qu'estoit passé. A laquelle il
a pleu respondre qu'aiant veu mes lettres addresses taut a sa dite
Majeste que aultres, et entendant que la principale cause qu'a esmeu le
Collonnel Sonoy a refuser de se conformer à la demande de V. S. estoit
en respect du serment pruis à son Excellence, Monsieur le Comte de
Leycester comme lieutenant de sa dité Majeste. Et comme depuis le
dit Sieur Comte a resigne son gouvernement general qu'il tint pardeca, ce
qu'estoit par acte de resignation envoie au Sieur Herbert, estant a cause
du quel partement dicelluy n'a esté delivree, sinon puis nagueres quand
l'aultre acte estoit renvoie au Sieur Killegrew pour la presenter a V. S.
Ce que sa dite Majeste aussi espere estre faict. Je vous ay a declarer
qu'icelle entend maintenant que les deux poincts differentiaux touchant
la reformation de la commission du dit Sonoy en l'amoindrissement de
son garnison en la dite ville soient pas luy cedez et accordez,
moyennant qu'il y soit continue en sa charge comme du passe, sur
assurance que sa dite Majeste veult que vous soyt faict, qu'il se comportera
dorsenavant avecq obeissance a la deue execution de tels commande-
ments que luy seront faicts de la part de V. S.

Et afin que le dit Collonnel aie cognoissance, tant de la dite asignation,
comme aussy que cecy est le plaisir de sa dite Majeste, icelle m'a com-
mande que j'envoiasse quelque gentilhomme de ma part pour d'aultant
plus tost adjurer le dit Collonnel a se conformer en ce que dessus, estant
en effect aultant que par c'y devant par V. S. n'est presente et requis du
dit Sonoy, vous pouvant assurer qu'accordant au plaisir de sa dite
Majeste à l'endroict que dessus sera donne singulier contentement a
icelle. M'aiant aussi dechargé qu'aprez l'establissement d'ung couseil
d'estat selon le contenu du traicte, je m'emploieroy d'assister par touts
mouers possibles a viuder et mettre fin a touttes jalousies, diversions,
differences, et questions, generalles et particulieres, et que tout ordre
souvenable soit mis pour le bien conservation et service du pais."
*Three copies, two of which are in Dutch, and one signed by Lord
Willoughby.*

The STATES GENERAL to LORD WILLOUGHBY.

1588, April 3, new style.—Replying to the proposals made by the
Queen on the 12th of February, old style, concerning Colonel Sonoy.
Dutch. Signed: J. Aerseus. *See State Papers, Holland, Vol.* 51.

The SAME to the SAME.

Same date.—Another copy of the above. *At the end it is stated that
this reply was presented to Lord Willoughby by the deputies of the
States at his hotel at the Hague on the 4th of April 1588, new style.*

SIR JOHN WINGFIELD to the STATES GENERAL.

1588, April 4, new style. Bergen op Zoom.—Warning them against
putting too much reliance on the proposals for peace. *French. Copy.*

MSS. OF THE
EARL OF
ANCASTER.

. LORD WILLOUGHBY to the STATES GENERAL.

1588, April 5, new style. - The Hague.—Concerning the fitting out of twenty ships by the States. *French. Two copies. Enclosed is a copy of part of a letter from Sir Francis Walsingham on the same subject.*

- LORD WILLOUGHBY to his agent, ETIENNE LE SIEUR at Aruheim.

1588, April 6, new style. The Hague.—Concerning the President of the Provincial Council of Friesland who had been confined to his house ; and giving orders that no mention was to be made of the President's affairs at the assembly of the States, as the matter was to be settled by the Council of State. *French. Copy.*

LORD WILLOUGHBY to MONSIEUR DE AYSINA, President of [the Council of Friesland].

1588, April 6, new style. The Hague.—To the same effect as the preceding letter. *French. Copy.*

HESSEL AYSINA to LORD WILLOUGHBY.

1588, April 6, new style. Leuwarden.—Informing him of the arrival in that town of Monsieur Poelgeest, Secretary Zuylen and Pensionary Copper, who had been sent there by the States General at the request of the deputies. *French.*

COUNT WILLIAM LOUIS OF NASSAU to LORD WILLOUGHBY.

1588, March 27, old style. Leuwarden.—" J'ay receu vos lettres et complains avec vous le miserable estat de ce pouvre pais, tant plus qu'il semble que quelques uns que le desiroient soulager et ' cercher remedes vont augmentans les miseres et accelerans sa mine. Dieu face qu'ils se recognoissent quelque jour, et que toutes les dissensions et dissidences osteés, nous puissions unanimement travailler a l'augmentation de sa gloire et conservation de son eglise, laquelle n'est environné que de trop d'ennemiz mortels, ayant jure son extirpation, sans que par discorde domestique nous la nuisions nous mesmes. Quant a moy je m'esforcerai pour demour toujours le mesme en continuant de plus en plus la sainte querelle pour laquelle beaucoup de mes proches parens ont laissé leur vies, y ayant aussi dedié la mienne quand il plaira à Dieu ; et ne laisserai en ce petit gouvernement mien de faire mon possible, a fin que les discordes puissent estre assopies et deracineés.

Les estats de Frize ne sont pas assembleés pour le present, mais je communiquerai vos lettres avec leur deputez ordinaires, pour adviser ensemble en diligence de tout ce qui sera necessaire en ung affaire di si grande importance, voire, dont depend tout ce qui nous doit estre le plus recommandé en ce monde." *Signed. Seal of arms.*

LORD WILLOUGHBY to CAPTAIN RANCY.

1588, April 6, new style. The Hague.—Concerning the movement of troops. *French. Copy.*

ADOLF, COUNT OF NEUWENAR to LORD WILLOUGHBY.

· ' 1588, March 27, old style. Arnheim.—Concerning the movements of troops. *French. Signed.*

[LORD WILLOUGHBY] to the STATES GENERAL.

1588, April 7, new style. The Hague.—Concerning the movements of troops. *French. Copy.*

COLONEL SONOY to LORD WILLOUGHBY.

The Castle and house of Medenblick.—
nderstanding which subsisted in that town between the well disposed inhabitants and the soldiery. *French translation from the Flemish. Copy.*

CAPTAIN DE SOISSONS and another to LORD WILLOUGHBY.

1588, April 9 [new style]. Naerden.—Informing him of an attempt by the enemy on the town of Amersfoort. *French. Signed.*

CAPTAIN RANCY.

1588, March 30, old style. Utrecht.—An account of the examination of Captain Rancy made by G. de Proninck, concerning the condition of the town of Naerden. *French. Signed.*

The MAGISTRATES OF UTRECHT to LORD WILLOUGHBY.

1588, March 30 [old style].—On business. *Dutch. Seal of arms.*

LORD WILLOUGHBY to the MAGISTRATES OF UTRECHT.

1588, March 31, old style. The Hague.—An answer to the preceding letter. *Dutch. Copy.*

The STATES GENERAL to the MAGISTRATES OF UTRECHT.

1588, April 11, new style.—Concerning the affairs of Captain Rancy. *Dutch. Copy.*

The STATES OF HOLLAND to the MAGISTRATES OF UTRECHT.

1588, April 11, new style. The Hague.—On the same subject. *Dutch. Copy.*

LORD WILLOUGHBY to COUNT MAURICE OF NASSAU.

1588, April 11, new style. The Hague.—Concerning the affairs of Sir William Drury. *French. Copy.*

LOUISE DE COLIGNY, PRINCESS OF ORANGE to LORD WILLOUGHBY.

1588, April 11, new style. Middelburg.—On behalf of a soldier named Saint Laurent, a native of the town of Orange, who had been imprisoned. *French. Signed.*

COUNT MAURICE OF NASSAU to LORD WILLOUGHBY.

1588, April 2, old style. The Hague.—Concerning Colonel Sonoy. *Dutch. Signed. Eleven pages.*

COUNT MAURICE OF NASSAU to the STATES GENERAL.

1588, April 12, new style. The Hague.—Begging that Sir William Drury might be relieved from the governorship of the town of Bergen-op-Zoom. *French. Copy.*

LORD WILLOUGHBY to the CAPTAINS, OFFICERS, and SOLDIERS, OF NAERDEN.

·1588, April 13, new style.—Concerning Colonel Dorp. *Dutch. Copy.*

LORD WILLOUGHBY to CAPTAIN SOISSONS and another.

1588, April 13 [new style]. The Hague.—An answer to their letter of the 9th of April new style. *French. Copy.*

LORD WILLOUGHBY to the MAGISTRATES OF UTRECHT.

1588, April 3, old style.—Concerning the movement of troops. *Dutch. Copy.*

LORD WILLOUGHBY to H. KILLIGREW, SIR WILLIAM REED, SIR JOHN MILFORD, and GEORGE GILPIN.

1588, April 3, old style. The Hague.— Authorising them to proceed to Medenblick, in his place, to confer with Colonel Sonoy. *Dutch. Two Copies.*

The STATES OF UTRECHT to LORD WILLOUGHBY.

1588, April 5, old style. Utrecht.—Stating their inability to continue their payment of the troops. *Dutch.*

The MAGISTRATES OF UTRECHT to LORD WILLOUGHBY.

1588, April 5 [old style].—On the same subject. *Dutch.*

LORD WILLOUGHBY to COUNT MAURICE OF NASSAU.

1588, April 6, old style. Utrecht.—Concerning Captain Rancy. *Copy.*

G. DE PRONINCK to LORD WILLOUGHBY.

1588, April 6, old style. Utrecht—Concerning Captain Rancy. *French. Signed.*

The SAME to the SAME.

1588, April 7 [old style]. Utrecht.—Sending Captain Blunt to him. *French. Signed.*

[LORD WILLOUGHBY] to the MAGISTRATES OF UTRECHT.

1588, April 7, old style.—An answer to their letter of the 5th April. *Dutch. Copy.*

[LORD WILLOUGHBY] to the STATES OF UTRECHT.

1588, April 8, old style. The Hague.—In answer to their letter of the 5th of April old style. *French. Copy.*

The STATES OF OVERYSSEL to LORD WILLOUGHBY.

1588, April 8, old style. Kampen.—Thanking him for propositions brought to them by Monsieur le Sieur. *Dutch. Seal of arms.*

The STATES OF UTRECHT to LORD WILLOUGHBY.

1588, April 11. Utrecht.—Concerning the advances of money required for the support of the English garrison. *Dutch.*

The STATES GENERAL to LORD WILLOUGHBY.

1588, April 21, new style. The Hague.—Informing him that they were sending the Sieur de Vanderbek, pensionary of Flushing, to Bergen-op-Zoom. *French. Seal of arms.*

The SAME to the SAME.

Same date and place.—Requesting him to send reinforcements to Bergen-op-Zoom. *French. Seal of arms.*

G. DE PRONINCK to LORD WILLOUGHBY.

1588, April 12, old style. Utrecht.—Concerning the supply of horses for the army. *French. Signed.*

The STATES OF ZEALAND to LORD WILLOUGHBY.

1588, April 22, new style. Middelburg.—Hoping that all the differences which had arisen in that island might be settled. *French. Seal of arms.*

[LORD WILLOUGHBY] to COUNT DE MEURS.

1588, April 13, old style. Medenblick—Concerning the movements of troops, and the unwillingness of the city of Utrecht to receive his company for a few days. *French. Copy.*

The MINISTERS OF MEDENBLICK to LORD WILLOUGHBY.

1588, April 24, new style. Medenblick.—Petition on behalf of the oppressed citizens of Medenblick, and particularly those of the reformed religion. *Latin. Copy.*

CAPTAIN JAMES CRISTAL to LORD WILLOUGHBY.

1588, April 25, new style. Medenblick.—Asking for his arrears of pay. *Latin. Signed.*

P. LORD WILLOUGHBY to COLONEL SONOY, and the officers and soldiers of Medenblick.

1588, April 25, new style. Medenblick.—Declaration promising payment of the arrears due to them. *Three copies ; two in Dutch, one of which is signed by Lord Willoughby, and one in French.*

The SOLDIERS of MEDENBLICK to LORD WILLOUGHBY.

1588, April 25, new style. The Castle of Medenblick.—In answer to the preceding declaration, and asking that the payments might be made with as little delay as possible. *Two copies, one in Dutch, one in French.*

[LORD WILLOUGHBY] to the MAGISTRATES of Bergen-op-Zoom.

[15]88, April 25, new style. Medenblick.—Notifying them of the appointment of Sir William Drury as governor of their town, and requesting their good offices on his behalf. *French. Copy.*

[LORD WILLOUGHBY] to the MAGISTRATES of UTRECHT.

1588, April 15, old style. Medenblick.—Regretting that he had not been able to come to Utrecht and settle matters there, in consequence of the troubles at Medenblick. *French. Copy.*

MSS. OF THE
EARL OF
ANCASTER.

[LORD WILLOUGHBY] to COUNT HOHENLO.

1588; April 16, old style. Medenblick.—Sending him a copy of a letter he had received from Gertrudenburg, and promising to come to meet him at Dordrecht. *French. Copy.*

ADOLF, COUNT OF NEUWENAR to LORD WILLOUGHBY.

1588, April 17, old style. Utrecht.—Promising to send him fifty horses to Arnheim. *French. Signed.*

LORD WILLOUGHBY to the STATES OF FRIESLAND.

1588, April 27, new style. Medenblick—Expostulating with them for the ill-treatment received by President Hessel Aysina and other persons who were well disposed to the Queen. *French. Copy.*

The STATES GENERAL to LORD WILLOUGHBY.

1588, April 27, new style. The Hague.—Asking him to be at the Hague by the following Monday in order to be present at the installation of the Council of State. *French. Seal of arms.*

[LORD WILLOUGHBY] to the STATES GENERAL.

1588, April 19, old style. Medenblick.—Promising to come to the Hague as soon as possible. *French. Copy.*

COUNT MAURICE OF NASSAU to the MAGISTRATES OF ENKHUIZEN.

1588, April 30, new style. Medenblick.—Concerning the punishment of certain soldiers who had spoken ill of the Queen of England, on board ship before Medenblick. *Dutch. Copy.*

[LORD WILLOUGHBY] to the INHABITANTS of MEDENBLICK.

1588, April 30, new style—Proclamation for the pacification and settlement of all the disputes and differences which had arisen in Medenblick. *French. Copy.*

The STATES GENERAL to the MAGISTRATES of NUARDEN.

1588, May 6 [old style]. The Hague.—Concerning Colonel Dorp. *Dutch. Copy.*

The QUEEN to the STATES GENERAL.

[15]88, May 30, new style.—Concerning the ill treatment which Colonel Schenck complained of having received at their hands. *French. Copy. See State Papers, Foreign, Holland, Vol. 53, same date.*

COLONEL SCHENCK.

[15]88, May 30, new style.—Questions addressed to the Council of State on behalf of Colonel Schenck, with their answers thereto. *French. Copy. Enclosed in the preceding letter. See State Papers, Foreign, Holland, Vol. 53, same date.*

LORD WILLOUGHBY to the GARRISON of VERE.

1588, June 20, new style. Middelburg.—A proclamation. *Dutch. Copy.*

LORD WILLOUGHBY.

1588, July.—A list of the papers concerning the charge of Lord Willoughby in the Low Countries, during the month of July 1588. *French. This list corresponds with the papers calendared.*

COLONEL FREMIN to LORD WILLOUGHBY.

1588, July 1, new style. Bergen[-op-Zoom].—Concerning the loss of the castle of Wouw. *Seal of arms.*

LEONARDO — to his "brother" MONSIEUR D'AMANT, Chancellor of Brabant and President of Flanders, at Madrid.

1588, July 3, new style Brussels.—"Nous sommes icy attendant d'heure a aultre l'arivee de l'armee navale dont la Capitaine Morosino nous en at grandement augmente l'espoir par ces nouvelles de l'avoir laissee en mer, dont il en arriva nagueres a Dunkerche, et vous asseure qu'elle nous fait icy grand besoing pour descouvrir l'intention de ces deputez d'Angleterre quy semblent n'altendre pour se resouldre par tant de longueurs, que a quelle fin qu'elle demandrat, pour en ce cas se determiner. Mais l'opinion de plusieurs est que n'aurons repos que de la veoir victorieuse, dont son Altese se tient tout prest a la recorder au poinct de son arrivee avecq bon nombre de batteaux bien esquippes, esperant que Dieu nous armerat de vigueur, donnant la crainte aux ennemis, puisque c'est pour l'augmentation de sa gloire et l'advancement de notre liberte. Nous en verrons en peu de jours quelque effect." *Two copies. Endorsed "Littre intercepte."*

[LORD WILLOUGHBY] to the STATES of OVERYSSEL.

1588, July 4, new style. The Hague.—Urging them to keep on good terms with the Council of State and the United Provinces. *Dutch. Copy.*

[LORD WILLOUGHBY] to the GOVERNORS and other officers of the towns of Friesland.

1588, July 4, new style. The Hague.—A safe conduct for the bearer, Aysina, who was a messenger from the Queen. *French. Copy.*

LORD WILLOUGHBY to the COUNCIL OF STATE.

1588, July 4. The Hague.—Stating that as the Queen had refused to allow a cessation of arms to the Prince of Parma, it was very important that the towns of Bergen-op-Zoom and Ostend should be well supplied with ammunition and provisions. *French. Copy.*

LORD WILLOUGHBY to the MAGISTRATES of DORDRECHT.

1588, July 7, new style. The Hague.—Thanking them for supplying his company with oats. *French. Copy.*

LORD WILLOUGHBY to MONSIEUR DU FAY, ambassador from the King of Navarre.

1588, July 7, new style. The Hague.—Concerning three French soldiers who had deserted. *French. Copy.*

ELIAS LE LEON "Drossart" (Judge) of Bergen-op-Zoom to LORD WILLOUGHBY, at the Hague.

MSS. OF THE EARL OF ANCASTER.

1888, July 8, new style. Bergen-op-Zoom.—Asking that Sir William Drury might not be removed from the governorship of the town. *French.*

LORD WILLOUGHBY to MONSIEUR DANSICK, French Ambassador to Denmark.

1588, July 8, new style. The Hague.—" De l'estat des Provinces Unies des Pays Bas, a la defense et protection desquelles je tiens presentement la bonne main, suivant la charge a moy donnee par sa Majeste d'Angleterre, ma maistresse, je ne vous escry rien en particulier, car j'estime qu'aves entendu que les affaires, gloire au Seigneur, y sont presentement en estat fort raisonnable, veu que depuis la perte de la ville de L'Ecluze en Flandre, l'ennemi n'a riens execute a son advaintaige. Bien est vray que du passe. plusieurs occurrences ont ente icy a la main, lesquelles on en peu juger n'estre advantaigeuses au bien publique. Mais comme de present ces incidens sont redresse, j'espere que les affaires de pardecha, par la grace du Seigneur, s'achemineront dorsenavant de jour a autre de bien en mieux, comme plus particulierement pourres entendre par Messieurs les Embassadeurs de ces Provinces qui s'acheminent pardela. Touchant les affaires d'Angleterre j'entens qu'on y ratent l'ennemy en bonne devotion." *Copy.*

GEBHARD [TRUCHSESS] ELECTOR OF COLOGNE to LORD WILLOUGHBY.

1588, July 1, old style. Houstardyck.—Sending M. de Dort, Heinrich Carven, Secretary of the Court Palatine, and the Licentiate Lodingius, to confer with him. *French. Signed. Seal of Arms.*

[LORD WILLOUGHBY] to the ELECTOR OF COLOGNE.

1588, July 11, new style. The Hague.—Regretting that he would be unable to come to visit him for two days. *French. Copy.*

[LORD WILLOUGHBY] to [ELIAS DE LEON], "Drossart" of Bergen-op-Zoom.

1588, July 13, new style. The Hague.—Asking for the release of a prisoner. *French. Copy.*

LORD WILLOUGHBY to the STATES OF OVERYSSELL.

1588, July 16, new style. The Hague.—On the same subject as the preceding letter to them of the 4th of July new style. *Dutch. Copy.*

[LORD WILLOUGHBY] to the STATES OF FRIESLAND.

1588, July 8, old style. The Hague.—Concerning the treaty of peace with the Spaniards. *French. Copy.*

LORD WILLOUGHBY to the STATES GENERAL.

1588, July 18, new style The Hague.—Proposition concerning the two thousand soldiers which the Queen wished to withdraw from Holland on condition that they should supply properly the towns of Bergen-op-Zoom and Ostend. *Dutch. Copy.*

The STATES GENERAL.

1588, July 18, new style. The Hague.—Resolutions of the States General on the same subject. *Two copies, one in Dutch, one in French.*

The COUNCIL OF STATE.

1588, July 19, new style. The Hague.—The opinion of the Council of State on the preceding resolutions. *Two copies, one in Dutch, one in French.*

The STATES GENERAL.

1588, July 20, new style. The Hague.—The resolution of the States General based on the opinion of the Council of State. *Two copies, one in Dutch, one in French.*

SIR WILLIAM DRURY to LORD [WILLOUGHBY].

1588, July 20, new style. Bergen-op-Zoom.—Informing him that the commissary of supplies at Bergen-op-Zoom refused to provide for the company of Colonel Fremin. *French. Copy.*

[LORD WILLOUGHBY,] to [ELIAS DE LEON,] " Drossart " of Bergen-op-Zoom.

1588, July 10, old style. Dordrecht.—Asking him to see to the better accommodation of his troop of cavalry. *French. Copy.*

[LORD WILLOUGHBY] to ARNOULT NICOLAY, President of the Council of Holland.

1588, July 20, new style.—Asking that prompt justice might be done in the suit of Robert Streat. *Dutch. Copy.*

LORD WILLOUGHBY to the " ESCOUTELLE " of DORDRECHT.

1588, June (July) 22, new style. Middelburg.—Sending him a sum of four hundred flemish florins. *French. Copy.*

The STATES GENERAL and the COUNCIL OF STATE.

1588, July 22 new style—" *Solution des difficultes trouvees en l'instruction de Conseil d'État par les Etats Generaux.*" *Translation from the Dutch into French.*   1

The PENSIONARY ROELS, Secretary to the States of Zealand to LORD WILLOUGHBY.

1588, July 23, new style. Middelburg.—A complimentary letter. *French. Signet.*

ADOLF, COUNT OF NEUWENAR to LORD WILLOUGHBY.

1588, July 13, old style. Utrecht.—Sending William de Boerkholt, *Drossart* for his Countship of Meurs, and another, to confer with him on behalf of the inhabitants of his said countship. *French. Signed.*

MSS. OF THE
EARL OF
ANCASTER.

[LORD WILLOUGHBY] to the COUNT DE MEURS.

1588, July 30, new style. The Hague.—Asking him to give free passage to forty arquebusiers of the company of Colonel Morgan, and the same number of the company of Captain Champernowne, who were on their way to England. *French. Copy.*

[The SAME] to the SAME.

1588, July 31, new style. The Hague.—Asking him to assist Captain (sic) Morgan in recruiting his company. *French. Copy.*

[ADOLPH, COUNT OF NEUWENAR] to the QUEEN.

1588, August 5, old style. Utrecht.—Declaring his readiness for union and to settle the dissensions lately arisen. *French. Copy. The original is among the State Papers, Holland, Vol. 56.*

[ADOLF, COUNT OF NEUWENAR] to SIR FRANCIS WALSINGHAM.

1588, August 5, old style. Utrecht.—To the same effect as the preceding. *French. Copy. The original is among the State Papers, Holland, Vol. 56.*

[ADOLF, COUNT OF NEUWENAR] to the EARL OF LEICESTER.

1588, August 5, old style. Utrecht.—To the same effect as the preceding. *French. Copy.*

LORD WILLOUGHBY to [THOMAS] KILLIGREW.

1588, August 25, new style. Middelburg.—Concerning the movements of troops. *French. Copy.*

The QUEEN to the STATES GENERAL.

1588, August 27 [old style]. St. James'.—Appointing Colonel Morgan to be governor of Bergen-op-Zoom in the place of Sir William Drury. *French. Copy.*

SIR WILLIAM DRURY to LORD WILLOUGHBY, at Middelburg.

1588, September 6, new style. Bergen-op-Zoom.—Informing him that the enemy were marching in great numbers towards Brabant, and had already come to Wilbrouck and Nil, and that they were expected to lay siege to Bergen-op-Zoom, and asking for assistance. *French. Signed. Seal of arms. Enclosed in a list of supplies required.*

G. DE PRONINCK or DEVENTER to LORD WILLOUGHBY.

1588, September 8, new style. Dordrecht.—Informing him that the states and magistrates of that city and provinces were sending, upon the advice of the Count of Neuwenar, a hundred soldiers to his assistance. *French. Signed.*

ADOLF, COUNT OF NEUWENAR to LORD WILLOUGHBY.

1588, August 31, old style. Utrecht.—Informing him that he had been obliged to move the cavalry of Captain Morgan from Rhenen to Amersfoort, and to move the troop of Monsieur Boris from Amersfoort, and garrison them at Wageningen and Rhenen. *French. Signed. Signet.*

MSS. OF THE
EARL OF
ANCASTER.

[LORD WILLOUGHBY] to RICHARD ALIN.

1588, August 31, old style.—Instructions to proceed to Count [Maurice] of Nassau and inform him that the Duke of Parma had arrived at Antwerp and that he was expected to attack Bergen-op-Zoom. He was to ask the Count to beg the States to send supplies of ammunition, provisions, and men, to that town, and he was to address himself to Messieurs Killigrew and Gilpin for their advice in everything. *French. Copy.*

[LORD WILLOUGHBY] to COMMISSARY DIERTYTS.

[15]88, September 12, new style. Bergen-op-Zoom.—Giving orders for the supply of provisions and ammunition for the use of the five companies of infantry sent by the States General for the defence of the town. *French. Copy.*

LORD WILLOUGHBY to COUNT [MAURICE] OF NASSAU.

1588, September 12, new style. Bergen-op-Zoom.—-Asking for reinforcements and especially for a supply of provisions. *French. Copy.*

[LORD WILLOUGHBY] to the QUEEN.

1588, September 4 [old style]. Middleburg.—"There hath not wanted in my unworthie selfe any earnest desire to have long ere this presented that duetie to your most Excellent Majestie which I desire above all thinges in the world 'to accomplish, but onely some good occasions, knowing it most unfit for Princes—whose cares are infinite, though their perfections be excellent—to be incombred with impertinent causes. But now the bazarde of your Majesty's bravest troopes on the side, trayned up with your Majesty's great charge, together with the reputation of the nation and your speciall service, yf th'enemy should be incouraged by the defeate of your subjects, having turned his forces from his sea journey hither, seemed unto me matters worthie your Majestie's consideracon, concurring in this accident of th'enemies presenting before Berghes, which place, when we were not divided, exceeded not above 1200 men, and the place not tenable with as many more in all martiall men's opinion. In these great occasions I have presumed to breake silence, which might ells have become me better—and with the unfained offerings of my life and fortune, from the first time thereof to the last end vowed to your sacred self—to know your Majesty's pleasure how I shall employ my self, holding this place I unworthely doe for your Majestie. And having no meanes of men, money, or provision, to succour them from the States of this side, I can conceive no certain way to incourage or relieve them, but with communitie of the perill to spend my life together with them—in the place —for your Majesty's service." *Copy.*

[LORD WILLOUGHBY] to G. GILPIN.

1588, September 14, new style. Middleburg.—Sending him a letter to be delivered to the Council of State. *French. Copy.*

LORD WILLOUGHBY to the COUNCIL OF STATE.

1588, September 14, new style. Middelburg.—Concerning the persons by whom despatches to the Council of State should be signed, and also concerning the oath to be administered to the soldiers in Holland. *French. Copy.*

MSS. OF THE
EARL OF
ANCASTER.

The COUNCIL OF STATE to LORD WILLOUGHBY.

1588, September 14, new style. The Hague.—Concerning supplies of provisions and reinforcements of men. *French. Seal of arms.*

LORD WILLOUGHBY to JOHN HOUSTIN.

[15]88, September 15, new style.—Instructions as to the demands to be made by him to the Council of State on behalf of Lord Willoughby with regard to the supplies required. *French. Copy.*

The STATES OF UTRECHT to LORD WILLOUGHBY.

1588, September 6, old style. Utrecht.—On the same subject. *Dutch.*

ADOLF, COUNT OF NEUWENAR to LORD WILLOUGHBY.

1588, September 6, old style. Utrecht.—Regretting that it was impossible for him to send the companies of Colonel Morgan and Captain Champernowne to Bergen-op-Zoom until the soldiers when he had sent to the assistance of Colonel Schenck at " Bon," by order of the Council of State, should return. *French. Signed. Signet.*

The MAGISTRATES OF UTRECHT to LORD WILLOUGHBY.

1588, September 7, old style.—Concerning the removal of the companies of soldiers under Captain Morgan and Captain Champernowne. *Dutch. Seal of arms.*

SIR WILLIAM DRURY to LORD WILLOUGHBY.

1588, September 17, new style. Bergen-op-Zoom.—Giving an account of a skirmish with the enemy, and reputing the capture of a soldier with letters, coming from Breda. *French. Signed.*

The COUNCIL OF STATE to LORD WILLOUGHBY.

1588, September 19, new style. The Hague.—Requesting him to act in concert with Count Solms who was then at Teitholz. *French. Signed* Chr. Huygens.

COLONEL FREMIN to LORD WILLOUGHBY.

1588, September 10, old style. Bergen-op-Zoom.—Asking for a passport written in Latin, on parchment, and signed and sealed. *French. Signed.*

LORD WILLOUGHBY to the COUNCIL OF STATE.

1588, September 12, new style.—Proposals on behalf of the Queen for changing certain troops of cavalry into foot soldiers. *French. Copy.*

ODOARDO LANSANAJA to LORD WILLOUGHBY.

1588, September 20, new style. Breda.—Asking for the release of his son. *French. Signed.*

LORD WILLOUGHBY.

1588, September 22, new style. The Hague.—Regulations as to the issue of soldier's passes. *French. Copy.*

[LORD WILLOUGHBY] to CAPTAIN CHARLES DANZGILES (?).

1588, September 13, old style. The Hague.—Ordering him to proceed with his company to Bergen-op-Zoom. *French. Copy.*

The COUNCIL OF STATE to LORD WILLOUGHBY.

, 1588, September 24, new style. The Hague.—Informing him that they had sent Colonel Morgan to Bergen-op-Zoom to take command there in the place of Sir William Drury, to whom they had announced their intention by Commissary Parasis. *French. Signed* Chr. Huygens. *Seal of arms.*

The MAGISTRATES OF ZERICKZEE to LORD WILLOUGHBY.

1588, September 25, new style. Zerickzee.—Sending him a supply of provisions. *Dutch.*

The STATES OF ZEALAND to LORD WILLOUGHBY.

1588, September 26, new style. Middelburg.—Informing him that they had sent assistance to Bergen-op-Zoom. *French. Seal of arms.*

The SAME to the SAME.

Same date and place.—On the same subject as the preceding. *French.*

J. VAN HOULT to LORD WILLOUGHBY.

1588, September 16, old style. Middelburg.—Giving an account of his journey and of his negotiations with the Council of State, and also informing him that the Duke of Parma was said to be gone to Breda and to be very ill. *I. enci.*

The COUNCIL OF STATE to LORD WILLOUGHBY.

1588, September 26, new style. The Hague.—Sending a list of the supplies which they had sent to Bergen-op-Zoom. *Signed* " Chr. Huygens." *French. Seal of arms.*

COUNT MAURICE OF NASSAU to LORD [WILLOUGHBY].

1588, September 27, new style. Huypen.—Informing him that he had good reason to believe that the enemy had relations with the town of Bergen-op-Zoom, and that they were only pretending to lay siege to it until their accomplices could carry out their wicked designs. *French. Copy.*

ADOLF, COUNT OF NEUWENAR to LORD WILLOUGHBY.

1588, September 17, old style. Utrecht.—Asking him to send him a patent by virtue of which he could exact obedience from the English soldiers in that city. *French. Signed. Signet.* ·

The COUNCIL OF STATE to LORD WILLOUGHBY.

1588, September 27, new style. The Hague.—Sending him back the prisoner, D'Ayala, for the purpose of discovering who were the persons who were in communication with the enemy. *French. Signed* G. Gilpin. *Seal of arms.*

JACQUES TUTELERT to LORD WILLOUGHBY.

1588, September 27. Lillo.—Sending him six gunners for the service of Bergen-op-Zoom, by order of the States of Zealand. *French. Signed.*

HANS VAN LOO to LORD WILLOUGHBY.

1588, September 18, old style. Doesburg.—Asking for arrears of pay. *French. Signed.*

[LORD WILLOUGHBY] to the COUNCIL OF STATE.

1588, September 28, new style. Bergen-op-Zoom.—Asking them to send the reinforcements which were promised to him before he left the Hague. *French. Copy.*

The COUNCIL OF STATE to LORD WILLOUGHBY.

1588, September 28, new style. The Hague.—Directing him to husband all the provisions and ammunition which had been sent [to Bergen-op-Zoom], and not to touch the magazine except in case of necessity ; also to see that the *"vivandiers"* and other persons accus-tomed to supply armies with provisions, were on the spot ; and to send a list of all the stores which had been received. *French. Seal of arms.*

The SAME to the SAME.

1588, September 29, new style. The Hague.—Asking him to give all assistance to the commissary who was being sent to Bergen-op-Zoom with money for the payment of the Dutch troops there. *French. Signed* Chr. Huygens.

LORD WILLOUGHBY.

1588, September [20, old style]. Bergen-op-Zoom.—Proclamation appointing Sir William Drury to the command of all the English com-panies in the forts adjoining the town of Bergen-op-Zoom. *Copy.*

THOMAS SUIGO and PEDRO DE LUGO to the DUKE OF PARMA.

[1588], October 15 [new style ?]. Bergen-op-Zoom.—Concerning the proposed betrayal of the North Fort. *Spanish. Copy.*

THOMAS SUIGO and PEDRO DE LUGO to SIR WILLIAM STANLEY.

[1588], October 15 [new style ?]. Bergen-op-Zoom.—On the same subject. *Spanish. Copy. On the same sheet as the preceding.*

The QUEEN to LORD WILLOUGHBY, Lieutenant Governor in the Low Countries.

1588, October 9. The Manor of St. James's.—*See Five Generations of a Loyal House, p.* 225. *Sign Manual.*

JOHN OWEN to THOMAS SUIGO.

1588, October 9 [old style ?]. The Camp.—I doubt not that your readiness to serve will "fynd fould recompens and satisfacon att the Duke's hands if it plese God it be performed and go forward ; if nott, your good will is alwayes to be respected and considred as occasion shalbe presented. Whatt was reqyred in your leters in your behalf is granted by the Duke, assuredly, and whatt more as shall apere by the same.

I am very glad for your own frends and others that it was your hope to enter into this matter, and shall be gladest of all if it be brought to end, which we desire, assuringe you thatt when I may staud you in sted, you shall be assured of me in all I can." *Copy.*

The DUKE OF PARMA to WILLIAM GRIMSTON.

1588, October 8 [old style?].—Articles for rendering the fort called the New Sconce, at the head of Bergen-op-Zoom. *See State Papers, Holland, Vol. 58, same date.*

BERGEN-OP-ZOOM.

1588, October 10 [old style].—A list of soldiers taken prisoner at the North Fort. *Spanish.*

The SAME.

[1588, October.]—An account of the attempt to betray the North Fort into the hands of the Duke of Parma by Suigo and Lugo. *Three narratives, all imperfect.*

LORD WILLOUGHBY.

[1588, October.]—A list of his correspondence and papers for the month of October. *Nearly illegible.*

JOHN CEPORINUS, Minister of Medenblick to LORD WILLOUGHBY.

[c. 1588.]—A complimentary poem. *Latin.*

LORD [WILLOUGHBY] to the STATES GENERAL.

1589, January 25, old style. The Hague.—Stating that he had done nothing concerning the expedition to Portugal except what he had been commanded by the Queen. *See State Papers, Holland, Vol. 61, same date. French. Copy. Attached to this copy is a draft of another letter from Lord Willoughby to the States General, which was not sent.*

The STATES GENERAL to the MAGISTRATES of Bergen-op-Zoom.

1589, March 8, old style. The Hague.—Concerning musters. *Dutch. Copy. See a French translation in the States Papers, Holland, Vol. 62, same date.*

CAPTAIN WOLFUNCKLE to LORD [WILLOUGHBY].

1589, April 18, new style. Ostend.—Asking for an appointment. *Dutch.*

GERTRUDENBURG.

[1589, after April.]—A statement of facts concerning the siege of Gertrudenburg, written by Lord Willoughby for the purpose of explaining a *placeat* published by the States General of Holland on the 17th April 1589. *French. Copy signed by Lord Willoughby.*

The SAME.

[Same date.]—A list of papers relating to the preceding pamphlet. *French.*

The Same.

Same date.—A printed copy of the last two documents. *French.*
On the first page it is stated to be a translation from the English.

LORD [WILLOUGHBY] to the LORDS of the COUNCIL.
Same date.—On the same subject. *Copy.*

The QUEEN to LORD WILLOUGHBY and ERESBY, Captain General
of the forces sent in France.

1589, November 9. The Manor of Richmond.—*See Five Generations
of a Loyal House, p.* 274. *Sign Manual.*

NEWS from FRANCE.

1589, November 15, old style.—An account by Lord Willoughby of
the doings of the French King from October 31 to November 8th.
Copy. See State Papers, France, Vol. 94. *November* 14.

MONSIEUR DE GUITRY to LORD WILLOUGHBY.

1589, December 6.—" J'ay faict entendre au Roy ce que m'avez escrit.
Vous verres sa vollonte par sa letre. Je vous puis asseurer qu'il n'a
donne ny ne donnera congez a aucun Anglois que par vostre adviys, et
qu'il ne veult que les trouppes se desbendent et separent, mais au
contraire, il veullt que marchies ensemble, et dans quelque temps il
vous permetera vous retirer ainsi comme il vous a promis. J'ay faict
donner des logis dans la ville du Mans pour les Anglois mallades et
blesses." *Also a copy of the above in a later hand.*

LORD WILLOUGHBY.

1589, December.—Notes of his answer to the letter from the Lords
of the Council received the 15th December 1589.

LORD WILLOUGHBY to SIR FRANCIS WALSINGHAM.

1589[-90], January 8. Dives.—" Having so convenient a messenger
as this bearer, Monsieur Farrat, who is sent over by the King, I could
not let him passe without some remembrance of my love and affection
unto yow. Our troopes are already all come downe hither to Dives,
some of the sick men are already sent over, other some now ready to be
shipped." *Signed.*

The SAME to the SAME.

1589[-90], January 9.—" The ill newes of the unhappy incounter
betwixt Sir William Drury and Sir Jhon Burgh, cannot but as it fell
to sone, be reported sone inough, notwithstandinge the mischance
being, as it is, not remediable. I would not let passe the good that
may by your good favour happen thereby to this honest, valiaunt
gentleman, the sergant major of my regiment, for that company in
Flushing which of late appertained to the said Sir William Drury
while he lived." *Signed.*

[FRANCIS] PANIGAROLA to the DUKE OF SAVOY.

[c. 1590.]—An account of the state of France, divided into five
heads, under the first of which he gives an account of things past and
present ; under the second he prophecies of the future ; under the third

E 64159.

Q

he treats of the remedies so far as concerns the choice of a new king; under the fourth he points out the disposition and intentions of France in the choice of a King; and under the fifth he shews the Duke what he can do for his own service. Finally he gives him a short sketch of the characters of the principal persons, male and female, who were interested in the affairs of France. *French. Copy.*

The LORDS of the COUNCIL to LORD WILLOUGHBY of Eresby.

1594, August 11. Greenwich.—Directing him to call together Sir George St. Pole, and Philip Tyrwhitt, Anthony Ersby, William Pelham, William Watson, William Rigdon, and Gregory Wolmer, Esquires, or such of them as he should think meet, to enquire into certain charges brought against the Earl of Lincoln. *Nine signatures.*

LORD WILLOUGHBY to the EARL OF ESSEX, Master of the Horse.

1595, June 14. Emden.—"Since my arrivall at Huosden (Huisduinen) by contrary whether in a bad hoy, I passed by land to Meddenblick, to Staveren, to Lewarden, to Groningen, and the Ems, to Emden, having had no convenient meanes in all my passage to send unto your Lordship till I came hether; and sutch accidents as either from the Earle's Chancelour or the towne's relation, I could busily collect I send your Lordship."
Postscript.—"Her Majesty askinge me of my retorn, I told har if I could I would be at hoame at Michelmas. But having pas'd this spring alredy, if I shall find good of the next fall, I hope har Majesty will by your Lordship's good meanes excuse me for the benefit of the spring to come also, especyally my licence being so large."
This and the subsequent letters from Lord Willoughby to the Earl of Essex were given to the Earl of Lindsey by John Castle, clerk to the Lord Privy Seal.

The SAME to the SAME.

1595, June 16. Emden.—Recommending to his favour certain merchants of Emden whose ship, homeward bound from "Fernandobuck" in Brazil had been seized by an English man-of-war off Lisbon. *Signed. Seal of arms.*

The SAME to the SAME.

1596, August 28.—Asking for his interest with the Queen that he might obtain the Governorship of Berwick. *Signed. Signet. See Five Generations of a Loyal House, p.* 317.

The SAME to the SAME.

1596, September 12. Knatsall.—On the same subject. *Signed. See Five Generations of a Loyal House, p.* 319.

The SAME to the SAME.

1596, November.—Enclosing a paper for his perusal.

The SAME to [the SAME ?].

[1596, November ?]—Concerning the draining of the fens. *Signed.*

The SAME to the SAME.

1596, November.—Informing him that he had sent a copy of his paper, by Sir John Buck, to the Lord Treasurer. *Signet.*

The Same to [the Same].

[1596, November.]—Asking for his interest with the Queen that he might be appointed guardian to the child of Sir John Buck who had died the previous night. *See Five Generations of a Loyal House, p. 320.*

The Same to the Same.

1596, November 22.—Asking for his interest with the lieutenant and the other commissioners for soldiers in Lincolnshire that the bearer might have the place of muster master in that county in the room of Sir John Buck. *Signed. See Five Generations of a Loyal House, p. 534.*

Lord Willoughby to [the Earl of Essex].

[15]96[-7], January 7.—Sending him letters from Nuremberg.

The Same to the Same.

[15]96[-7], March 16.—A complimentary letter. *See Five Generations of a Loyal House, p. 531.*

The Same to [the Same].

1597, April 12.—A complimentary letter. *See Five Generations of a Loyal House, p. 329.*

The Same to the Same.

[15]97, April 27. Grimsthorpe.—A letter of compliments and thanks. *Signet.*

The Same to the Same.

1597, May 22. Grimsthorpe.—On behalf of his kinsman, Thomas Willoughby. *See Five Generations of a Loyal House, p. 533.*

The Same to the Same, Lord General of all the Queen's forces.

1597, October.—A complimentary letter. *See Five Generations of a Loyal House, p. 533.*

The Same to the Same.

[1597, London.]—Regretting that he had missed seeing him.

The Same to [the Same].

[c. 1597.]—" By chaunce I pased their, though I beinge not of the elect commannded to shoote my bolte. My loving dutie to you and my country makes mee thus bolde, though some would extenuate my sence, and have not spared it, as I heere saye. - They shall not except agayuste my syncerite, wherout only I confesse I have comitted this folly, to myngle my dropps 'with suche excellent ryvers. And I seeke neither prayse nor place shall appeare, for after I have kyssed Her Majesty's hands and your Lordship's, I will leave my fortification of castells in the ayer, and fall to the plough and carte for my children, least I dye unfortunate in a spitle, and they begg miserable for my mistakinge humors that liked the world better than an hermitage." *Signed.*

The Same to [the Same], Earl Marshall of England.

1597[-8], March.—Recommending John Carew. *See Five Generations of a Loyal House, p. 325.*

MSS. OF THE
EARL OF
ANCASTER.

The SAME to the SAME.

Same date.—A complimentary letter. *See Five Generations of a Loyal House, p.* 326.

The SAME to the SAME.

1597[-8], March 23. Grimsthorpe.—Concerning the governorship of Berwick. *See Five Generations of a Loyal House, p.* 327.

The SAME to the SAME.

1598, April.—Concerning the difficulties of his task. *See Five Generations of a Loyal House, pp.* 327–8.

—— to ——.

[After 1598.]—*Endorsed* "A French minister's discourse touching the peace" between France and England. *French. Copy.*

NEWSLETTER.

1622, September 10. London.—Giving an account of the progress of the campaigns in Germany, Holland, and France. *French.*

The EARL of BRISTOL.

[c. 1623.]—Interrogatories administered to the Earl of Bristol and his answers thereto concerning his embassy to Germany. *Copy. Imperfect.*

CHARLES I. to [the COUNTESS OF HOLDERNESS.]

1626, March 2.—Promising to continue the grants made to her by the late King. *Signed.*

CHARLES I. to the COMMISSIONERS OF SEWERS on the North-east side of the river of Witham, co. Lincoln.

1634, July 20. Apethorpe . . . .
" Sir Anthony Thomas knight together with our loving subject John Worsopp Esquire, having many years attempted the general work of draining the Fens and surrounded grounds in our county of Lincoln and elsewhere. And lately undertaken that particular level on the north and north-east side of the river of Witham, called (as we are informed) the east and west fens, north fen, Earls fen, Armtree fen and Wildmore fen commons, and the adjacent several drowned grounds, have by God's blessing, and by and through their own extraordinary labour and sedulity, and their and their friends disbursements and adventures of great sums of money expended, now lately accomplished the draining of the said grounds, and making of them dry and fit for arable, or meadow, or pasture, to the improvement (as is alleged) of forty-five thousand acres of land, and the bettering of many thousands more: The which we well understand to be no small enrichment of those countries; And being thereof certainly advertised by sight of an Act or Ordinance of Sewers, expressing a declaration under some of your hands and seals, that the said undertaken work is now done by the said Sir Anthony Thomas and John Worsopp, within the time limited ; We therefore in our gracious respect towards our said well deserving subjects, that have approved themselves therein real performers of so great a work, both for their remuneration and for example and encouragement to others, do will and require you, that you fail not to

do to them speedy justice in and by an equal and most indifferent partition and setting forth by metes and bonds of such parts, portions and allotments of these drained lands, as your former Acts, Orders and Decrees of Sewers did grant, promise and appoint to them for recompense of their said undertaken work of draining; And that you forthwith decree the same unto the said Sir Anthony Thomas and John Worsopp their heirs and assigns for ever to be holden of us, our heirs and successors, as of our honor of Bullingbrooke in our said county of Lincoln, with such privileges liberties and immunities as you shall think fit. And you are also to require all those, which pretend interest to any of the said lands, that they give ready obedience to your order, and quietly permit the said Anthony Thomas and John Worsopp to enjoy their allotments peaceably and without interruption, according to their agreement, As they tender our displeasure and will answer the contrary at their perils. Given under our Signet. At our court at Apthorp the twentieth day of July in the tenth year of our reign."

MSS. OF THE
EARL OF
ANCASTER.

SIR PEREGRINE BERTIE to his father, the EARL OF LINDSEY, Lord Chamberlain of England, at his house in Chanel Row, Westminster.

1639[-40], March 5. Berwick.—I have been with the Mayor and some of the chief burgesses of the town, and have used the best means I could for advertising your desires for making Mr. Cooke a burgess, but I find no " cheerefullnesse in them of pleasuring of your Lordship." All the news here is that some of the works of Edinburgh Castle on Monday last did slip down.

CAPTAIN JOHN BALLE to [the EARL OF LINDSEY].

1639[-40], March 3. Berwick.—Informing him that Sir Robert Jackson had that day mustered the garrison. *Signed.*

GEORGE MOORE to the EARL OF LINDSEY, in Channon Row, Westminster.

1639[-40], March 10. Berwick.—Informing him that by the malice of Sir Robert Jackson and others, he had been detained as a clipper of the King's coin, and asking for his assistance. *Signed. Signet.*

GEORGE ROUS to [the EARL OF LINDSEY].

1639[-40], March 24. Berwick.—A letter of compliments and thanks.

CAPTAIN JOHN BALLE to [the EARL OF LINDSEY].

1639[-40], March 24. Berwick.—On private affairs. *Signed.*

SIR MICHAEL ERNLE to the EARL OF LINDSEY.

1640, March 25. Berwick.—All those parts upon the borders are commanded to be in readiness when there shall be occasion. There is strict watch kept at Dunse and Kelso, but only in the night, and officers are appointed for these places. *Signet.*

CHARLES I. to [MONTAGU,] EARL OF LINDSEY.

1642, October 27. Aynho.—Condoling with him on the death of his father. *See Collins' Peerage, Vol. II., p. 16. tit., Duke of Ancaster. Also a copy of the same.*

MSS. OF THE
EARL OF
ANCASTER.

The Same to the Same.

1645[-6], March 19. Oxford.—" I thanke you for putting yourselfe into Woodstoke, it shewing that you reeke all occasions to shew that affection which I have alwayes knowne you to have to my service. But I do not judge that place fitt for you to stay in, others being good anufe for it, and you fitter for a better imployment. Wherefore I command you to returne to your waiting here."

Postscript.—" The longer you stay you will the more displease two faire ladies." *Copy.*

The Earl of Lindsey to King Charles.

1645[-6], March 19. Woodstock.—" When I received your command I acquainted Captain Fawcett with it, whereupon he represented the condition of the garrison, if I left it, to be this; that divers since the horse lay upon this place and wanting their pay were gentlemen, others for want of the same discontented. A great part of these have been of your guards, and good words from some of their old acquaintance will satisfy them. Divers gentlemen that are reformadoes, which are comed in, he believes are easier commanded by me than they will be by him, and all are reddier to performe their duties; I being an eye witness may present their service performed to you Majestie."

Our provisions have been much spent " by reason of Camfield's horse being so neare this place. This month the souldiers have beene fedd with the store bread, and hath much exhausted the provision, and for all it hath beene often demanded and desired but not so granted, but lately theire hath beene a little recruite to add to the store ; yet the house shall not be lost, but kept till the last minute as a person of honour is bound to do." *Copy.*

Charles I. to the Earl of Lindsey.

1645[-6], March 20. Oxford.—" There is no more reall testimony of true service than this kinde of disobedience, to which my answer is that if upon further tryall of the disposition of the officers and souldiers you finde that you may come to your waiting here without eminent hazard of loosing the place, then I shall immediately exspect you. Otherwise I leave you to do what you shall finde most necessary for my service." *Copy. This copy is on the same sheet as the preceding letter from the King of the 19th March.*

Sir Thomas Fairfax to the Speaker of the House of Peers.

1646, May 4. Heddington.—" Having received a letter from the Duke of Richmond and the Earl of Lindsey of which this enclosed is a copy, I thought fit to present the same to the House ; with this desire, that if it may not be of prejudice to the public affairs, their desires may be answered they being already secured at Woodstock. They are persons of honour and have engaged themselves neither directly nor indirectly to act anything against the Parliament. But what shall be commanded concerning them shall be observed.

[Enclosure.]
The Duke of Richmond and Lennox and the Earl of Lindsey to Sir Thomas Fairfax.

1646, May 2.—" His Majesty having thought fit (as he expressed to us) in person to draw nearer to his Parliament, which hath always been our humble opinion and advice we who have followed him in the relation of domestic servants, would not remain in any place after him, to expose ourselves to a doubtful construction with the Parliament, of having other business ; nor have we other design in coming then to pursue our obligation to the King and the Parliament, without meddling or disturbing affairs therefore desire in order to that, we may have leave as others not better hearted to the peace of this kingdom have had to come to London, go to our own homes, or continue here if the time yet be not unfree of jealousy, or that it may give any offence, which we have ever desired as much as in us lay to prevent, the procuring this favour of the Parliament by your means will oblige us."

[P.S.]—Here are with us Sir Edward Sidenham, Sir William Fleetwood, Mr. J. Cary, servants to the King, who are of the same mind with us, and desire to be presented to your favour in the like manner.

PHILIP SWALE to WILLIAM MABB, servant to the Earl of Lindsey, at Lindsey House near the Parliament Stairs.

1667-8, March 3 (3rd of first month).—On business. *Signet.*

PHILIP SWALE to ROBERT, EARL OF LINDSEY, at Lindsey House.

1667-8, March 9.—On business.

PHILIP SWALE to WILLIAM MABB, at Lindsey House.

1667-8, March 24.—On business. *Also six other letters from Swale to Mabb on business.*

RULES FOR COURSING THE HARE.

[*Temp.* Charles II. ?].—Orders Laws and Rules for coursing of the hare agreed upon (ever to remain) for such as delight in the same sport set down by the Right Honourable Thomas Duke of Norfolk William Lord Marquess of Northampton Henry Earl of Huntingdon Edward Lord Clinton Lord Admiral Lord Barkley Lord Scroope Lord Burrow Lord Sheffield Lord Willoughby Sir John Syllyard Sir Robert Terwhit Sir Francis Leake Sir Jarvis Clifton and divers others at Sleaford as followeth.

Imprimis no wager to be won or lost unless the course stand half a mile, but if the hare be killed within the half mile or otherwise the course be ended then the worst dog shall pay for the hare finding.

Item if it happen a hare to go to the covert being above half a mile unturned the dog that leadeth to the covert winneth the course.

Item if a brace of dogs running together the one giveth a turn the other serveth and giveth another and so they continue to give many turns no coat happening that dog that giveth the first turn winneth the course because he first commandeth the hare and so all the other dogs turns were but services to his.

Item if a brace of dogs run and before the hare be turned the other goeth by him that going by, is to be accounted but a turn because the other perhaps had no perfect sight and did not strain himself, but after one turn every coat is accounted two turns.

Item if a brace of dogs do run and the one doth give many turns and coats more then the other and before he comes to the covert he stand still in the field the other doth but run with her to the covert though he never turn the hare yet he shall save the course because the standing in the field is the greatest foil a dog can take.

Item it is to be noted that every bearing or taking of the hare is accounted for a turn.

Item that no wrench or wease slip or go by shall be accounted or spoken of more then is before in the fourth article.

These laws and orders were set down and subscribed at Sleaford by the noblemen and gentlemen before mentioned and by John Cupledike Robert Markham and many other gentlemen.

PEREGRINE BERTIE to his brother, [ROBERT] EARL OF LINDSEY, at Grimsthorpe.

1691, May 2.—Giving an account of the sudden death of Lady Abingdon and of the grief of his brother [the Earl of Abingdon], and her family.

The SAME to the SAME, at Willoughby in Lindsey Coast.

1692, June 25.—There is likely to be a match between Lady Katherine Manners and Sir John "Luson Goore," whose estate is given out to be 7000*l.* a year, but Lord Rutland cannot be persuaded to give more than 15000*l.* They demand 20000*l.* Lord Fanshawe has bought an estate near Hungerford in Wiltshire. My Lord Huntingdon's crime is that upon receiving King James's letter of invitation to come and see the Queen delivered he sent it up to Lord Nottingham with his duty to the Queen, and desired he might have leave to go over for such time as the Queen thought fit, to see her Majesty delivered, and then would return. The Queen struck out of the Council, Lord Halifax, Lord Shrewsbury, Lord Marlborough, and Lord Torrington, the first for not coming to the Council, the latter because she is displeased with them.

PEREGRINE BERTIE to his sister[in-law], the COUNTESS OF LINDSEY, at Great Thorpe near Stamford.

1693, April 22.—Count d'Estrées is coming to Brest with his squadron, which makes us believe there may be a near engagement. Sir John Cutler has left his daughter the Yorkshire estate which he bought of Sir Thomas Chichely, which is worth 5000*l.* a year.

The friar and Italian captain who had agreed with the French to set the Spanish Armada on fire when the French appeared before Naples, are both executed.

PEREGRINE BERTIE to his brother, the EARL OF LINDSEY, at Grimsthorpe.

1693, May 25.—Regretting to hear of his wife's illness and giving foreign news. *Signet.*

The SAME to the SAME.

1693, May 27.—On business concerning the felling of timber at Grimsthorpe by Lord Willoughby. *Signet.*

The SAME to the SAME.

1693, June 3.—On the same subject.

The SAME to the SAME.

1693, [June] May 6.—On the same subject.

The SAME to the SAME.

1693, June 10.—On the same subject.

The SAME to the SAME.

1693, June 15.—On the same subject, and giving some news from abroad.

The EARL OF LINDSEY to his brother, PEREGRINE BERTIE.

1693, June 15.—On the same subject.

PEREGRINE BERTIE to his brother, the EARL OF LINDSEY.

1693, July 4.—On business concerning an advance of money.

The SAME to the SAME.

1693, July 6.—On the same business, and giving foreign war news.

The SAME to the SAME.

1693, July 11.—To the same effect as the preceding.

The SAME to the SAME.

1693, July 23.—To the same effect as the preceding.

The SAME to the SAME.

1693, July 27.—Giving an account of the action before Luxembourg.

M——— to the COUNTESS OF LINDSEY.

[16]93, August 24.—On business. *Fragment of signet.*

PEREGRINE BERTIE to his brother, the EARL OF LINDSEY.

1693, October 7.—On business.

PEREGRINE BERTIE to his brother, the EARL OF LINDSEY.

1694, November 10.—His Majesty arrived yesterday at Margate The Queen is gone to-day to meet him at Dartford or Gravesend. We discourse of nothing but a peace, yet prepare greatly for a war, and we think to lower the land to one shilling in the pound and so to give it for twenty years, which is Paul Foley's invention, but not liked by many.

You see by the *Monthly Mercury* the conditions of peace that are offered, by which we are to get nothing but to be owned, and the French King not to assist King James or his heirs, but to allow a stipend from hence and to live where he shall not give offence to King William.

The SAME to the SAME.

1694, November 26.—Concerning the intention of his nephew Philip [Bertie] to stand for Stamford in the place of Captain Hyde deceased.

The SAME to the SAME.

1694, November 27.—On the same subject.

The SAME to the SAME.

1694, November 29.—I am glad to hear that Stainford is so inclined to choose my nephew Philip. I was afraid my Lord of Exeter would have set up his son, but he declines it, and I believe Sir Purey Cust will not be very willing to enter into battle with so great a family, for I told him he must expect, if he stood, to spend 500*l.* or 600*l.* in the election. He would have fain made a bargain with my nephew to spend nothing and then I suppose would have treated them privately at his own house. I suppose you have interest enough with Sir Richard Cust to make his son lay it down, and then my nephew will come in easily. But courtiers must venture their fortune, and they can have no better lottery than our House to push their fortunes in.

The SAME to the SAME.

1694[-5], March 10.—Yesterday was Mr. Wilson killed in Southampton Square by a Scotch officer who, it seems, thought himself better able to satisfy an unknown lady than the other, and it is thought that the lady who kept Mr. Wilson, was willing to have a change, and that she set them together by the ears. The town is in great expectation to know who this lady is, and it is believed it will come out, though Mr. Wilson gave the key of his " scritore " to a friend of his to give to his mother, and desiring him to see his papers burned, and gave them sixty guineas and a broad piece, to see it completed.

Your son Philip is made a manager of the " Million Act " which will be worth 100*l.* a year to him. I think your family has a great deal of reason to be satisfied with this Government.

JOHN WALPOLE to the COUNTESS OF LINDSEY, at Chelsea.

1704, July 7.—On legal business.

—— to [the COUNTESS OF LINDSEY].

1709, December 6.—We have had several reports here about my Lord Chancellor being laid aside, but I cannot find that there is any great ground for them. It is also talked about this evening that the Treasurer also is to lay down, and Lord Halifax to come into his place; and some, I find, think that he and the Chancellor are so linked together as that if the one goes out, the other will do so also. Lord Wharton it seems is a declared enemy to both.

[The SAME to the SAME.]

1709[-10], January 26.—Concerning proposals for settling the differences between herself and Lord Lindsey.

[The SAME to the SAME.]

1709 [-10], February 7.—Dr. Sacheverell is to be tried in Westminster Hall, and scaffolds will be set up there as soon as the term is over. This may perhaps bring Lord Lindsey up. Mr. Dolben, the chairman of the committee against Sacheverell, is Archbishop Dolben's son, but has not by a good deal his father's character. I hear of no other Mr. Dolben in the House.

[The SAME to the SAME.]

1709 [-10], February 21.—I waited yesterday on Mr. Charles Bertie. We discoursed about your Ladyship's concerns, but I found he was wholly ignorant of what was intended. He only said that Sir Thomas Powis told him that matters were likely to be agreed between you. Lord Willoughby was with him when I went in to him, and General Farrington. I perceive by them that the Lords have mightily intrenched upon the Lord Great Chamberlain, and not only appointed themselves such a number of tickets by their own authority, but attempt to contract my Lord's own box.

[The SAME to the SAME.]

1709 [-10], February 23.—This town is in so great a ferment at present upon the trial of Dr. Sacheverell as I believe never was known. The mob are of his side and attend him with loud huzzas at going to Westminster and coming back, every day ; and their cry is "No presbyterians, no meetings, for the Queen and the Church." And with this cry they attended the Queen's chair through the Park yesterday. In short men's eyes and minds are wholly turned upon this affair, so that there is a stop to all business.

[The SAME to the SAME.]

1709[-10], March 4.—We have no mob since Wednesday night when they did great execution upon the Meeting Houses. The militia are up through the whole town. Sacheverell's counsel were heard yesterday and to-day, and I do not hear that they are advanced further than the first article. " Your Ladyship has the humble thanks of our whole house for your puddings and griskins."

[The SAME] to the SAME.

1709[-10], March 6.—This affair of Dr. Sacheverell stops all sorts of other business. The pleadings of the managers and of this counsel are all over, and now the matter is before the Lords. Lord Nottingham put this question to the judges, whether any indictment wherein the express words of the criminal were not inserted, was good in law. The judges had time till to-day to give their answer, which was that in their Courts it was not good, but they were no judges of parliamentary proceedings, so that now the Houses are looking after precedents, and some hope the Doctor may come off by this means, for I am told that in the parallel cases of Mainwaring and Sibthorp the words upon which their impeachment was grounded are expressly set down in the indictment. To divert your Ladyship I will set down a short epigram that goes about the town concerning the burning the Presbyterian pulpits It is this—

Most moderate Whigs, since you do boast
That you a Church of England priest will roast,
Blame not the mob if they desire
With Presbyterian tubs to make the fire.

[The SAME] to the SAME.

1701[-10], March 16.—It is now past eight and the Lords as I hear, are all still sitting. There has been hot debate about the first article of Dr. Sacheverell's impeachment relating to non-resistance, and we are impatient to hear the event. I saw this morning the funeral of Lord Chief Justice Holt pass by, in order to carry him to Redgrave in Suffolk. It is looked upon as something strange that a new Lord Chief Justice should be created before the other was in his grave. *Signet.*

[The SAME to the SAME.]

1710, April 8.—On legal business.

[The SAME] to the SAME.

1710, May 16.—"As for your boarding, I cannot think it fitt your Ladyship should expose yourself to the fatigues and hazards of the seas and journeys, and be changing of your climate at this time of day, nor can I imagine where you could board in England with so numerous an attendance as of ten persons with you, especially if a person must be with you whom few familyes will care to receive, unlesse one of your own way. It may be it would be more practicable to hire a small house in some cheap and wholesome country for a yeare or two, then to board in any family, but this matter requires a further consideration."

[CHARLES BERTIE?] to his brother [the MARQUIS OF LINDSEY].

[1711, May] 12.—"I saw Mr. Harley yesterday at the House, when when we talk'd over the affair of the title of Oxford which he thinks is in the crown to dispose of, when they please, and the Queen's Council are of the same opinion. I told him I differ with them, but the result of all our discourse was that he hoped I would take care that your Lordship nor none of your family—for whom he protested great service—should take it ill of him, since it was not his seeking, and he assured me he would not take it amiss from your self and family that you enter'd a *caveat*, being seen that would not stop the patent, and would preserve a show and colour of right for the heir general. I told him I would enter the *caveat*, to be entered in the Chancery, beliefing it would give you a little more time to think before it got to the Greate Seale Mr. Cross went thither last night and brought me word this morning that Lord Keeper sent for him in and told him he should not stop the patent an hour for the *caveat*, and desired to know if his Lord had council ready to defend the entering of the *caveat*, which he said he should hear. There is yet noe *caveat* entered, for Mr. Cross went to Hackerley to draw one, but he could not tell how to doe it, uppon which he went to the Keeper's thinking the Secretary there would have shewed him how they were drawne, but he did not and told his Lord your servant was there, who sent for him in presently. Mr. Cross told me alsoe that Mr. Hackerley said you had noe right, soe I fancy you will not employ him in it. I should think you cannot have a better man than Sir Peter King, if you designe to have it argued. I believe you will consider the matter with your friends."

"One thing more I should tell you, which is that Harley told me yesterday that he was sure that some body else would have the title in a month if he had it not, which is a sign there will be more honours granted. I sent you here inclosed the letter I received from Mr. Harley, which I desire you will return me. If you think it best to be quiet in this affair I should think we should tell Harley what steps have been made to procuring you another title, and try to engage him to assist in it, uppon giving him noe trouble in this point."

Postscript.—"I have shew'd your warrant for the rooms to Lord Abingdon, and told the Speaker yesterday you would accommodate the House of Commons. I have not delivered the warrant yet, for I fancy there should be some words in it to signifie her Majesty's pleasure, and also a warrant to the Wardrobe to furnish them. Let me know in your next if I am under a mistake."

LINCOLN RACES.

1723.—Articles to be observed for the Ladies Plate at Lincoln. *Draft.*

THE REBELLION OF 1745.

MSS. OF THE
EARL OF
ANCASTER.

1745, October 1.—A voluntary subscription for the security of his Majesty's person and Government and for the payment of such forces as shall be raised within the county of Lincoln began at the Castle of Lincoln.

	l.		
Tyrconnel -	- 300		
Ric. Hardwick	- 50		
Fr. Whichcote	- 100		
E. Pelham -	- 100		
Thos. Trollope	- 100		
Ger. Scrope -	- 100		
Luke Williamson for Ld. Fitzwilliam - } 500			
Thos. Scrope	· 100		
John Cust -	- 100		
Rob. Vyner -	- 100		
Wm. Noel -	- 100		
Hen. Bradley	- 10		
Fra. Vane -	- 30		
Tho. Vivian -	- 40		
Evd. Buckworth	- 40		
Savile Cust -	- 50		
Ancaster -	- 500		
Scarbrough -	- 500		
Mouson -	- 500		
Vere Bertie -	- 100		
T. Whichcot	- 100		
Thos. Chaplin	- 100		
William Irby	- 100		
G. Storm for himself and the Freeholdrs. Crowle Althorpe &c. - } 150			
Hen. Pennant	- 50		
John Healey	- 60		
C. Reynolds -	- 40		
J. Tyrwhitt -	- 100		
John Buisliere	- 100		
M. Boucherett	- 100		
Robt. Cracroft	- 60		
Jno. Michell	- 100		
Clemt. Tudway	- 50		
Willm. Welby	- 50		
Edmd. Turnor	- 50		
Jas. Pennyman	- 50		
G. Gregory Junr.	- 50		
J. Seaford -	- 05		
Samuel Salter *Cl.*	- 15		
Wm. Johnston	- 30		
Jno. Arnold -	- 10		
Jno. Harvey	- 20		
Jno. Hooton	- 5		
John Peck -	- 15		
John Robinson	- 15		

	l.		
Samuel Rolt	- 5		
Josh. Pearl -	- 10		
Thomas Jesson	- 03		
Saml. Hunter	- 10		
Geo. Denshire	- 10 10		
Tho. Brown -	- 20		
Lawee. Monck	- 10		
Gilbt. Benet *Clk.*	- 05		
Edwd. Hales	- 10 10		
Thos. Adam	- 20		
Wm. Bassett	- 20		
Jno. Whitelamb	- 5		
Benjn. Bromhead	- 20		
Thos. Wallis	- 40		
Thos. Wallis M.D.	- 25		
Griffth. Nelthorpe	- 40		
J. Whichcot	- 20		
George Brown Mayor of the City of Lincoln - } 100 for the City.			
F. Flower -	- 50		
John Maddison	- 40		
John Pindar	- 30		
Robt. Woodhouse	- 30		
Thos. Becke	- 30		
Geo. Tolland	- 5	0	0
John Hodgson	- 4	4	0
William Johnson	- 5	0	0
Wm. Seller -	- 7	4	0
Wm. Cheales	- 5	0	0
Jno. Bland ·	- 5	0	0
Ebenezer Cawdron	- 6	6	0
Wm. Anderson *Clk.*	- 20	0	0
J. Maw -	- 20	0	0
J. Wilberfoss	- 30		
J. Crompton	- 25		
Cranwell Coats	- 25		
J. Marshall -	- 20		
J. Maddison	- 10 10		
Henry Revell	- 15		
Nathl. Robinson	- 10 10		
J. V. Tapsford	- 10 10		
Benjn. Collyer	- 10		
Matts. Hawton	- 10		
Jonan. Rudsdell	- 10		
John Every -	- 10		
William Oates	- 4	4	0
George Clarke	- 4	4	0
Joseph Brackenbury	5	5	0

	l.				l.		
John Baxter -	4	4		Fra. Bernard -	20	0	0
Simon Every -	5	4	0	R. Butterwood -	10	0	0
Carr Brackenbury -	20	0	0	W. Holgate - -	3	3	0
Weston John Smith	20	0	0	Jno. Jenkinson -	42	0	0
John Smith - -	10	0	0	John Green - -	15	0	0
Willm. Hasledene -	2	10	0	James Bolton -	5	5	0
Fitz. White - -	21	0	0	J. Pahams - -	2	12	6
Adlard Sq. Stukeley	20	0	0	John Coltman -	10	0	0
Anthony Taylor -	10	10	0	Shelley Pennell -	10	0	0
Edward Saul -	10	10	0	Jno. Disney - -	80	0	0
Wm. Scortreth -	5	5	0	John Harrison -	20	0	0
J. Walls - -	21	0	0	Sir Henry Nelthorpe subscribed in another paper -	100	0	0
John Ferrand -	5	0	0				
Robt. Pindar -	3	3	0				
Hen. Browne -	21	0	0	Tho. Shaw for Edwd.			
John Curtois Jr. -	4	4	0	Greathed - -	21	0	0
Tho. Shaw *Clerk* -	10	0	0	Benj. Walker -	10	0	0
J. Linton *Clerk* -	10			Geo. Boulton -	5	5	0
Lang Bankes -	10			Adrian Hardy -	5	5	0
Jos. Dixon - -	10			T. Pownall - -	10	0	0
Richd. Gilbert -	15	15		Chris. Nevile -	100	0	0
James Ward -	10			Jno. Middlemore -	50	0	0
J. Curtois - -	4	4		Wm. Kirke - -	3	3	0
Edwd. Beresford -	5	5		Charles Beridge -	15	0	0
John Turner -	5	0	0	Bas. Beridge -	20	0	0
Geo. Stow - -	5	0	0	Thos. Trollope -	20	0	0

Sir Joshua Reynolds.

1759, June 10.—Receipt signed "J. Reynolds" for thirty guineas from the Duke of Ancaster "being the half payment for the pictures of the Marquess of Lindsey and Lady Mary Bertie."

INVENTORIES.

Tattenhall.

c. 1522.—An inventory of beds, bedding, and hangings brought from Tattenhall. Among the hanging are, a piece of roses and leaves, a piece of "Our Lady," a piece of the story of Moses with the tables, and pieces called the "Ragged staffe," and the "Vyneyard." At the other end of the book are receipts for the year 1522.

Plate.

1535, December 18.—An inventory of plate for family and church use, taken at Southwark.

Amongst the articles of church plate are, crosses, chalices, cruets, paxes, "holy water pots," images of saints, remonstrances, and censers, all of which except the two last are gilt.

The Duke of Suffolk.

1546, May 22.—A list of all the horses, mares, and geldings belonging to the Duke [of Suffolk] in his stables and pastures at Grimsthorpe.

The totals are—Ninety horses and geldings of all ages and both ambling and trotting, and thirty-five mares both ambling and trotting, "as well of the stood as for the careage."

The DUCHESS OF SUFFOLK.

1551.—An inventory of apparel and other things and lent by the Duchess to her sons, the Duke of Suffolk and Lord Charles Brandon; and bought by her.

In the list of articles lent to the Duke of Suffolk are—A black velvet gown furred with sables and guarded with "passamane" lace, which came in his chest from Cambridge ; a velvet cap with fourteen diamonds; another velvet cap with fourteen rubies ; a diamond set in gold ; a "sallet" with four emeralds ; pearl buttons ; and a dial of bone.

Amongst Lord Charles Brandon's things are—" The wardshipe and mariadge of Mistress Anne Waddell " ; a suit of crimson satin embroidered with silver, given to the Duchess by the King, with buttons of gold ; a night gown of grogram furred with jennet ; and a cape with seventeen pair of "agletts" and sixteen buttons ; and a broach. *Two Copies.*

[GRIMSTHORPE.]

[After 1601.]—An inventory of furniture and other articles. *Mentions* Sir Montagne's chamber, Sir Thomas Willoughby's chamber, the Queen's chamber, the Presence chamber in which was a picture of " my old Lord Peregrine " and " my old Lady Mary " ; the " gazing " chamber, and the Earl of Rutland's chamber.

[SIR OWEN WYNN.]

1676, December 1.—" A note of all my plates at Caetmehor."

Includes—A great frame with five plates on it for sweetmeats ; a silver box with three dozen counters in it, with the arms of England and France ; another silver box with three dozen new groats in it ; six silver spoons " with the crucifix upon the end of them that were my great grandfather William Gwith (Griffith) ap Robin, of Cotswilliah" ; a naked boy in silver with an inkhorn in one hand and a candlestick in the other ; a big silver bowl that " my mother Powell gave my sonn Sir Richard Wynn " ; twelve trencher dishes with the Gwydyr arms ; a " little pott close cover'd to put a wax candle in to read by." *Endorsed* " a note of all my silver plate except those at Weeg which are considerable."

ERESBY.

1723, September 13.—A list of articles belonging to the late Duke of Ancaster and bought for 557*l.* 2*s.* 3*d.* by his son. *Signed.* " Ancaster Albemarle Bertie, Thomas Farrington."

DIAMONDS.

1725, March 27.—Statement by Jacob Duhamel of the weight and value of the diamonds in the necklace and buckle belonging to the Duchess of Ancaster. The necklace contained forty diamonds weighing a little more than thirty-eight carats, valued at 651*l.* 4*s.* The buckle contained thirty diamonds weighing a little over seven carats, valued at 71*l.* 3*s.* The largest brilliants were valued at 20*l.* a carat.

SWINSTEAD HOUSE.

1725[-6], January 22.—An inventory of goods belonging to the late Duke of Ancaster. *Amongst the pictures are*—Mary, Queen of Scots, King George, The Princess of Wales, Lord Lindsey, Lord and

Lady Tyrconnell, the Duke of Ancaster, Lady Eleanora Bertie, Albemarle Bertie, the Duke af Buckingham, Lady Betty Cecil, and others. *At the end is a list of articles taken from Grimsthorpe to Swinstead.*

GWYDYR UPPER HOUSE.

1728, April 1.—A list of articles in Gwydyr Upper House delivered to Thomas Wynne by order of the Duke of Ancaster.

RAINBY.

1730, August 25.—An inventory of goods belonging to the Duke of Ancaster at his hunting seat at Rainby.

SWINSTEAD.

[c. 1735.]—An inventory of household furniture belonging to the Marquis of Lindsey, the Honble. Albemarle Bertie, and the two Miss Nichols.

GWYDYR UPPER HOUSE.

1737, June 8.—An inventory of the goods of the Duke of Ancaster at Gwydyr Upper House.

HUNDRED OF BABERGH.

1514-23.—Certificate of Sir William Waldeyn, Sir William Clopton, George Mannok, Robert Crane, and Robert Ford the Elder, commissioners concerning the mustors and for valuing men's substance in that hundred.

Among the proprietors were the Queen, the College of St. Gregory in Sudbury, Sir Edward Nevyll, the Duke of Norfolk, Sir William Waldegrave, Lady Peyton, the Guilds of St. Peter, St. John, the Trinity, and St. Christopher in Boxford, the Provost of Cambridge, the Abbess of Dartford, Sir Richard Fitzlawes, Lady Salisbury, the Abbess of Malling, the Earl of Oxford, and many others.

POETRY.

A volume of poems, chiefly political and satirical, of the seventeenth century. *Some of them printed in the " State Poems."*

HOUSEHOLD ACCOUNTS.

1560-2.—An account book of the household expenses of Richard Bertie, Esq., and the Lady Katherine, Duchess of Suffolk, his wife. Among other items are the following :—

" Wardrobe of Robes."

1560. " Five yards and a halfe of hamphere kersey at 2s. the yard to make hose for Thomas Hallydaye, Dicke with the croked backe and others."

1561, April. " Paid at London for ten onzes of granado silke for my masters shirtes, at 2s. 8d. the onze."

Same date. To Mistress Knowles and eight others, 13s. 4d. each " for velvet to garde theire lyverye gownes."

1562, February. " A payer of Valencian gloves for my master, 10d.," and " a hatt of thrimmed silke, garnished, and a bando of gold, for my master at his coming to Grimsthorpe, 18s."

1562, May. " Geven to suche gentlemen as attended uppon herr Grace at the Corte, which they shuld have bestowed upon their lyveries save for the Statute of apparell," *3l. 6s. 8d.*

" Children of honowre."

1561, December. " Two dozen of points for the two Polish Georges."

1562, May. " Paid for bowes and arrowes for " George Sebastian, *6s.*

1562, June. " Paid for a cawle of gold " for Mistress Susan, *45s.*
" Paid for two grammar bookes for the children, *2s.*"

" Wardrobe of beddes."

1560, October. To Richard Thomson " for dryinge of two fether bedds, *2s. 8d.*

1562, February. " For three dozen of rushes for Barbican and my Ladie's lodging at the Corte," *6s. 8d.*

1562, March. " For clensing the house at Grimsthorpe in February, *2s.*"

1562, April. " For a candlesticke for a watche light, *3s. 10d.*"

May. " For a dussine of bromes for her Grace to burne, *6d.*"

June. " For making cleane of herr Grace's chamber at Grenewich, *12d.*"

" Gyftes and rewardes."

1560, December. " To a man of my Lorde Clinton's which broûght a feasant and two partriges," *3s. 3d.*
" To George, Mr. Pellam's man, to funishe himselfe lord of Christmas and his men in a lyvery, *40s.*"

1561, January. " To Sir Fraunces Foskewe's players which came to offer them selves to playe before my Lady's Grace, *3s. 4d.*"

February. " To Mistress Brodbank in reward for kytchinge ·forty-four ratts at Valdey, *3s. 4d.*"
" To one which played the hobby-horse before my master and my Ladie's Grace, *6s. 8d.*"
" To the servants of thouse at Upton," *11s. 4d.*
" To certen men which opined gappes for my master and my Lady's Grace as they came from Upton," *3d.*

March. " To my Lord Ambrose Dudley's man which brought letters the twenty-first," *2s.*
" In rewarde to the servants in Mistress Sissell's house," *6s. 4d.*

1561, August. " To two men which played upon the puppetts, *6s. 8d.*
" Given by my master's commandment to the kepers of the lions at the towre at London in May last, *6s.*"
To Cockrell " to bye him a payer hervest gloves," *3d.*
" To Mistress Ashelye's man at the Cort " who " lett my master into the privy garden, the Queue being theare, *3s. 4d.*"

September. " To Mr. Peregrine, Mistress Susan and the rest by her Grace to by their fayrings of a pedler at the gate," *2s.*
" To a wyfe of Lowth which made wagers agaynst the Lorde Admirall's coming to Belleaw," *2s. 4d.*

October. "To my Lord Robart Dudleye's players at Grimsthorpe, which ofered themselves to play but dyd
not, 10*s*."

"To Pretie's wife to by achates for herself and herr
children in herr Grace's absence," 40*s*.

1561, November. "To Monsieur Le Forge which presented a lock,
20*s*."

"To a bonesetter dwelling in Walbroke for setting
in of two joynthes which weare out in younge
Gerves' ancley," 3*s*. 4*d*.

1561, December. "To Mr. Rose and his daughters which played
before her Grace in her sycknes," 13*s*. 4*d*.

"For the poore of St. Giles' in Barbican, 5*s*."

"To two of my Lord Robert Dudley's men which
came to play before them upon the drume and
the phiph," 6*s*.

"To my Lord of Arrundall's players," 6*s*. 8*d*.

"To the waights of London," 5*s*.

"To David Suls in gold for a new yers gifte for the
Quene,' being five onzes and three peny waight,
14*l*. 10*s*."

"To him for the workemanship," because "the
peece was not well wrought, he had but
4*l*. 14*s*. 8*d*."

1562, January. "To divers noblemen's trumpiters to the number of
ten, 20*s*."

"To the Queen's trumpiters," 20*s*.

"To Handforde of the Black Swanne in Chepe a
goldsmith, for a chesse borde and a set of men
given to the Queue, 7*l*."

"Given to Ladie Knowles in a payer of sleves for a
New Years gifte," 6*l*.

"To the Quene's violens," 20*s*.

"To the Erle of Warwyck's players," 7*s*. 6*d*.

1562, February. "To an Etalion which shuld have menestered
medicine to herr Grace for the small poxe, 5*s*."

"To Mr. Catlyne, Lord Chief Judge in a standing
cuppe of sylver," 11*l*. 13*s*. 8*d*.

"To Judge Browne in a standinge cuppe of sylver,"
11*l*. 5*s*. 4*d*.

"To Dr. Keyns in a cuppe of sylver all gilt, for his
paynes taken in the sycknes of her Grace and
Mistress Susan," 5*l*. 14*s*.

"To Chaterton for his paynes with her Grace in my
Lady Marle Graye's chambre, 6*s*."

1562, March. To "a shipman which brought her Grace a carnary
byrde, 20*s*."

"To the collectors for Powle's steple, 6*s*. 8*d*."

May. "To one of the gromes of the Quene's stable which
brought my mistress a horse to ryde with my Lord
R[obert], 3*s*. 4*d*."

"To my Lord of Burgayme's man," 6*s*. 8*d*.

"To Mistress Asheley's man that brought her Grace
to Barbican with a lytle wagon, 12*d*."

1562, July. "To the Quene's players which played at Grims-
thorp," 20*s*.

"Wurkes and Buyldings."

1562, January. " To a paynter which drewe the picter of two children," 2s.

" To a man which laded water owte of the cellor at
Barbican," 6d.

1562, March. " To a paynter which went to the Corte and drew
herr Grace's armes for herr sadle, 20d."

" Husbandry."

1560, October. " For a pound of longe peper for medicines for sicke
cattell," 7s. 6d.

" Necessaryes."

1560, December. " My master lost at blancke dise," 1d.

1561, January. " To Sandon's wife for birche for rodds," 3d.

„ July. " For my masters losses at the buttes," and " paicing
for all the contrey men which toke his part," 2s.

1562, January. " To my master at tables with herr Grace," 12d.

" For a payer of syssers to poll the boyes of the
kychen," 6d.

" For meat for the turky cockes at Barbican," 2s.

March. " To the companie of the Goldesmithes for warning
of my Ladie's sylver dust boxe when it was stolen
owte of herr chambre at the corte," 6s. 8d.

June. " To a 'portingall by her Grace for two ouzos of
muske," 3l.

July. " Paid for plantan water and rosemary water," 4d.

October. " Paid for a boote for the mote at Beleaw," 17s.

" Bakhowse and Pantire."

1561, November. " Paid for a basone and ewre with a nest of bolls
which weare gevin to Mistress Carrowe of sylver
fashion," 12s.

1562, May. " Paid by her Grace for one dozen of sylver plate
trenchers, 26l."

" Bruhowse and Buttry."

1562, February. " To Gomport brewer for three barrells of strong
beere at 7s. the barrell, and for thirty five of doble
beere at 4s. 4d. the barrell," 8l. 12s. 8d.

" Cellor."

1561, July. " For six gellons and a pottell of wormwood wyne,"
10s. 10d.

November. " For amending the vice of one of the cuppes beinge
the Quene's new yere's gift the last year " and
other items, 17s.

" Paid to Mr. Atkinson the Quene's purvior of
wynes, for one hogshed of claret wyne, 50s."

December. " For a pynt of claret wyne in herr Grace's sycknes,
Father Frier not being within, 2d."

" For five quarts of claret wyne " to make jelly, 20d.

1562, January. " For one gallon of Ipocras," 4s. 8d.

March. " For one pynt of Jubilatie, 3d."

June. " For two gallons of Renish wyne to fill the grett
vessell at Barbican," 3s. 4d.

" Spicery, Chaundry, and Lawndry."

1560, Octobre. " For a pounde of anne's seed," 14d.

" For one pound of rosin provided for staffe torches,"
3d.

R 2

November. "For a stone of candlewicke," 3s. 8d.
     "For eight pound of waxe," 8s.
1561, July. "For six pound of peper bought at London, 19s.
    For one pound of ginger, 3s. 8d.
    For one pound of synamond, 10s. 6d.
    For one pound of cloves, 11s.
    For one pound of mace, 14s."
    "For one pound of iseinglasse, 2s. 6d."
September. "For four pound of graye sope, 12d."
October. "For one pound of bisketts, 16d."
December. "For six white printed lights," 2s. 6d.
1562, February. "For wafers when my master and her Grace dyned
    with Dr. Keyns," 20d.
    "For elecompaine rotes," 1d.
1562, March. "Due to Modie grocer of London," 21l. 19s. 6d.
    Among the items of this bill, the bulk of which
    items were sent to Grimsthorpe, are a "topnet" of
    figs, great and small raisins, "lycorns," fennel
    seeds, marmalade, "cakes of castle soope," green
    ginger, "sokett," and sweet soap.
1562, September. "For three dozen pounde of cotton wycke," 3l. 6s.
    "For six dozen of harde wycke," 18s.
    "For a barrell of swete sope at Sturbridge," 50s.
1562, October. "Redd waxe for my master," 4d.

       "Kychen."

1560. October. "For eight hundred salt fishe," 26l. 13s. 4d.
    "For a hundred lynges," 7l.
1561, February. "For paintinge of George of the kichen's coote,"
    10d.
1562, September. Paid for wafers to make marchepaines," 1d.

       "Jurnying."

1561, October. Her Grace's charges in coming from Grimsthorpe to
    London with her train. At Huntingdon supper
    and breakfast, 46s. 4d. Drinking at Stilton, 15d.
    Dinner at Royston with other things, 39s. 11d.
    Supper and breakfast at Puckeridge, 54s. 1d.
    Dinner at Waltham, 17s. 1d. and 2s. 9d. for drink
    at Walsworth, Ware, and Hoddesdon. Total
    8l. and 6d.
1561, November. "For the suppers of twenty four persones at the
    Swanne at Charing Crosse which attended upon
    her Grace to the Corte, 11s. 4d."
    "For a carre to bring a bedde from my Lady
    Katherine Capell's to Barbican when herr Grace
    was sick," 4d.
1562, June. Paid for boat hire, and carriage of "stuff" for her
    Grace and three servants to Greenwich, 3l. 7s. 4d.
    Paid for the hiring of "fifteen persons at the Corte
    at Greenwich by the space of twenty daies,
    3l. 10s. 4d."

       "Stable."

1561, December. "For a payer of silke raines for my Ladie," 26s. 8d.

GRIMSTHORPE.

1561, March ——— "The booke of records for the Kycbyn," being
a list of the bills of fare for all the different tables. *Mr. Bertie and the*

Duchess do not appear to have observed Lent, which however was strictly observed by every one else in the house.

MSS. OF THE
EARL OF
ANCASTER.

ACCOUNTS.

1580 ——. A list of expenses at Barbican from June to December 1580, chiefly for law and household matters.

The SAME.

1583, November ——. A list of expenses at Grimsthorpe or London.

LORD WILLOUGHBY.

1587-9, ——. Particulars of moneys paid to Lord Willoughby's company of horse, and other soldiers. *Two books.*

RICHARD WARD.

A MANUSCRIPT BELONGING TO LIEUTENANT-GENERAL LYTTELTON ANNESLEY.

General Lyttelton Annesley kindly sent for the inspection of the Commissioners the original diary kept by his ancestor the Earl of Anglesey, who held various high offices of State during the reign of Charles II. The historical interest of the extracts from it which are here printed is not great, but the diary as a whole is remarkable as showing how a man of the strictest puritanical training could live in almost daily intercourse with some of the most profligate characters of his time, without his own character and habits being in any way affected. Burnet describes the Earl as " A man of a grave deportment." The diary extends over a period of about four years and a half, there being an entry of the writer's doings on nearly every day in that time ; but the passages from it which follow contain all the matter therein which seems to have any value at the present day.

May 8, 1671. I went with my wife to see Bulstrode and lay this night at Kensington house. I went every day after but the Lord's day to London about business and returned at night.

The Lord's days went to Kensington church in the morning, and in our own chapel Mr Agas preached afternoons.

She died Friday May 19. May 21. I had first notice of Lady Rutland's death.

May. 26. I went early to London on many businesses. Begun the Bible again. This morning considering the great decay of piety and increase of profaneness and atheism, and particularly my own standing at a stay if not declining in grace, I fixed a resolution to renew the course I had in former times held of watching over my ways and recording the actions and passages of my life, both to quicken me in good ways and to leave a memorial thereof to my posterity for imitation, and to give God the glory of his guidance and mercy towards me and mine : purposing also to review the time past of my life and for the same ends to reduce all the passages thereof to writing that I could find memorials of or recollect : so to redeem the time because the days are evil.

May 27. Went to London to speak with the King before he went to Windsor, and did so.

This went not on.

    Contracted for Newport Pagnell manor fee farm rent in reversion at 8 years' purchase. And for the mills in possession by entering it in the minute book.

    Wrote letters to Ireland; and went to Kensington to dinner. Spent the afternoon in reading, contemplation and conference, Dr Owen and his wife coming to us in the evening.

28. Went to church in the morning and heard Dr Hodges, Dean of Hereford. Several friends came to dinner and we had good discourse. Heard Mr Agas in the chapel afternoon. I had much relenting consideration this day of the intemperance the society of a great man had surprised me into 3 or 4 times since the King's restoration: perhaps God permitted me to fall, because I was too apt to pride myself that in the whole course of my life I was never before overtaken with drink; and I bless God I have the more abhorred it since, as I do myself for it: and bless God he never suffered me to be polluted with strange women, the sin of the times. As I was in the proper work of the day several persons of quality came and interrupted me successively; when gone, I returned to my closet work. Lord, pardon the diversions and drowsiness of this day!

    Thoughts possessed me this day of building a library at Bletchington for the advancement of learning and religion in my family.

May 29. I went to London in the morning and returned to dinner with Sr Char. Wolseley and Lord Power, &c. with me. I spent the afternoon comfortably with my Christian friends, went to London to supper and came back safe to bed.

30. Spent the morning in devotion, reading and some business. Afternoon went to London about the subsidies of Westminster; made my report to the Committee of the Irish affairs; wrote for Ireland, &c.

31. Went to London to the African company and other business: came back to dinner. Afternoon conversed with friends and visited Aldn Erasmus Smith, Mr Nye, &c. and spent some time in reading, &c.

June 1. Went to London in the morning; did divers business and the usual duties. Returned at night.

June 2. Went to London in the morning to the Gambia Company's meeting. Afternoon was at Mrs More's hearing against Lady Morgan, at Council. Contracted with the Trustees for the manor of Newport Pagnell fee farm rent, &c.

3. Spent the morning at home in reading, writing & divers business. The afternoon the Bishop of Durham and many other friends from London took up the whole time almost.

MS. OF :
LIEUT.-GEN.
LYTTELTON
ANNESLEY.

4. The morning was at church at Kensington : at noon found the Duke of Buckingham and Lord Ashley come to dinner, and others : after noon heard Mr Agas in the chapel. After sermon came Lady Tyrill, &c., Lady Marquess of Worcester the younger, Lady Seymour and several others; by which the duties of the day were interrupted, which I endeavoured in the evening to redeem.

6. Went to London to meet a Com^ttee of Council ; did several business and returned by noon. Lord Keeper and his Lady, his son and daughters and many other dined with us, and stayed much of the afternoon ; and others came in.

June 7. Went to London about business of the navy chest and subsidies.

8. Went to London to the Gambia Company and Com^ttee of Council for Ireland, and returned to dinner. After dinner young Lady Ranelagh and her mother and several others came. I spent the rest of the day in study and the usual duties.

9. Went to meet the King at Council at Hampton Court according to summons and dined there : read over the book called the Unreasonableness of the Romanists ; a very good discourse, especially the preface.

10. This day I spent at Kensington in reading and business and the usual duties. I read through Glanville's book against Dogmatizing ; the scope of it is good, and 'twill not be amiss to read it again : he is much for De Carte's philosophy and against Aristotle's.

11. In the morning went to Kensington church ; in the afternoon heard Mr Agas in the chapel. Read through the Triumphs of Rome over dispersed Protestancy : a notable book, being a true character of the corruptions of that church out of their own authors, and to be further perused as I go on in my book against Popery.

1671. June 17. Went to Hampton Court in the morning ; met the King there and dined with him : went in the evening to Windsor. Lay at Mr Baker's.

18. Was at the King's chapel in the morning carrying the sword, there being no Knight of the Garter attending, though a collar day. Dined at Lord Chamberlain's who invited me. Was at the parish church afternoon.

19. [Cipher :—the King ?] gave me little comfort, for though he confessed upon my putting him to it that he had nothing against me, and that I had served him well ; yet 'twould be very inconvenient, he said, for his affairs, to take off my suspension and restore me, and said he thought he had offered me fair to settle 3000^ll a year on me for my life without putting me to any trouble. I told him 'twas my honour, and to be in his service I prized most ; and after I should be in the execution of my place a while, I would surrender it upon such

terms as should satisfy him, and expect some other
employment. I discoursed further at large with
him, but found him hardened, yet told him I
hoped he would at length do me justice which
was all I asked. I told all to Lord St Albans
in whose lodgings this discourse was, who vowed
to second it with all his might, and would see
me at London.

20. Spent till 3 of the clock at home, then went on
business to London. I did the usual duties.
Carried Arthur to a school.

21. Went to London on business in the morning: returned
to dinner with Dr Owen and his wife. Spent the
afternoon in visiting and reading and the usual
duties.

22. Went to London in the morning to Council, the
King coming thither; and by his direction signified
by my Lord Ashley, who delivered me from His
Ma^{ty} the Report concerning the state of Ireland:
for that end I made the said Report at Council,
His Ma^{ty} himself also directing me in person so
to do. Lord Duke of Ormond and Mr Attorney
and Lord Arlington shewed anger at it, but in
vain. I spent the rest of the day in business.

23. Went to London in the morning: saw Ld Lieut^t L^d
Ashley (who had command from the King to me
about a warrant to be drawn to proceed in the
business of the Report) and Ld St Albans, &c.;
and prepared the said warrant and did several
business.

24. Spent all day at Kensington in reading and other
business. Ld Ashley, Lord Ranlugh, my two
brother Ashfields, &c. dined here, and much company after noon. Sent the warrant I drew yesterday by Lord Ashley to the King, and had much
discourse with him, &c.

25. The morning I went to Kensington church; the
afternoon heard Mr Agas in the chapel. Ld Dover
and several others dined with us, and much company, Lady (? Chaworth) Mr Attorney Montague
and his wife, &c., came after noon; which was some
interruption to duties, but I spent what time I
could in them.

26. I went in the morning to London on business and
returned to dinner; afternoon spent most with
friends; son Power and daughter &c., came in the
evening and supped with us; and went after that
night to Colebrook in their journey for Ireland,
leaving my grandson John Power and his maid
with us: God preserve him and them!

July 2. In the morning was at the King's Chapel. Got not
an opportunity to speak with the King for justice
about my office till the evening, when I could do
no better; by Lord St Alban's advice I accepted
what appears in the warrant I drew next morning.

5. Spent all day at London: set Charles to school at
Newington.

MS. OF
LIEUT.-GEN.
LYTTLETON
AN NESLEY.

8. The morning I went to London on business, and returned to dinner. The afternoon I went to Court, and did prepare the warrant for the Duke of York's conveyance of land to me, and the usual duties. My Lord Arlington told me the King had seen the warrant about my office of Treasurer of the Navy, and agreed to it all but the words ' to my satisfaction ' ; and six of the Council signing warrants for my 3000ᴸⁱ a year, he wished me to speak to the King of it.

9. Went to church with the King in the morning ; spoke with him of my business, who said he was resolved to be very kind to me, and would speak with Lord Arlington to dispatch my warrant. I dined with Dʳ Bridiock, Dean of Salisbury, who invited me yesterday. Gave my warrant for the Duke of York to Mʳ Wren to get signed.

10. This day I stayed at Windsor, and spent most at Court, the King having upon my further address yesterday required my stay till tomorrow, that the business of the navy should be heard ; and I was summoned then to be at Council by nine in the morning. I did the usual duties ; and in a special manner sought God's protection for next day, this being my birthday and I now 57 years of age ; the Lord sanctify the rest of my days more to his glory ! Duke of York agreed my warrant.

11. At Council in the morning the business of the navy was heard between the two Sir Thomas's, and it appeared I had kept to rules in the Treasury better than those before or after me, yet no justice done me. I went after noon to Stoke, where the King dined.

12. Went the morning to Court about my business ; but the King being gone very early to Hampton Court, I went thither, and returned with the King, whom I spoke with about my office : he told me he could not now, but when he came back from Portsmouth he would settle all to my satisfaction. Then I moved him about the reducement of the quit-rent of Beare and Bantry, which he granted, and signed the warrant at night.

15. Spent the morning in business at London, writing letters to Lord Orrery, son Power and brother John ; Lord Chief Justice Vaughan and several friends visiting me. Spent the afternoon at Kensington in business and taking the air, and did the usual duties.

16. Went to church at Kensington in the morning, and to our own chapel after noon : the Lord pardon slight performance at both I Several friends dined with us. I did spend the rest of the day in reading and other duties.

19. Went to London in the morning, and Lord Ashley, &c. calling me, we went to Lord Lieuᵗ Barkley's to dinner at Twickenham, where we met also the

Duke of Bucks and Secretary Trevor, but did
little business. The Duke in great kindness expressed his confidence in my friendship, and his
design to have me Chancellor; being, as he was
pleased to say, the fittest man in England, and
the present Keeper a poor weak man not filling
so great a place: when he pressed to know my
opinion, I said I was not ambitious of it, and it
was an envious and troublesome employment.
He told me somebody must have it, and he believed
he could get it me, and he thought they might
live easily with me as a friend: I said, what the
King pleased, so I was not excluded all employment, should satisfy me. He enjoined me secrecy,
for the Lord Arlington, if it were known, would
tell it as news to the King to disappoint it: to
induce me he said he thought he could get the
Keeper to be willing to give off, and be satisfied
some other way; and so left things. I came
home at night and did the usual duties.

21. After noon begun my journey with my family to
Bletchington, and went that night to Wickham to
bed, the Lord Wharton overtaking us, and making
us see his buildings at Woburn by the way.

22. Went to dinner at Bletchington. After noon did
several business, set the house in order, and did
the usual duties.

23. Heard Mr Hooke at church in the morning, and Mr
Agas at home after noon, and did other duties of
the day, only friends gave some interruption.

31. Sr Tho. Spencer, Mr Horwood, Mr Jervis, Mr
Underhill, Lady Jenkinson, Cousin Borlase, &c.

Son Thomson came to dinner; my wife being gone for my
came with daughter Anne, I made them very welcome, and
my wife. spent most of the day with them till my wife came
home.

Aug. 1. Spent most of the day at home, the Bishop of Oxford
and Sir Wm Fleetwood dining here. I went to
Mr Dormer in the evening, and had the sad news
of my son Annesley's dangerous sickness; the
Lord be merciful to him!

2. Went in the morning to Grayes; stayed there all
night, and viewed the house and grounds.

3. Came back to dinner to Bletchington, seeing Sr
Timothy Terill, &c., by the way. Spent afternoon in business and usual duties.

4. Dined at Woodstock with Lord Lovelace, but
suffered no excess in drinking, using caution
against it.

6. Heard Mr Hooke in the morning, and Mr Agas after
noon, when sad letters came again from Belvoir of
my son's dangerous sickness: I dispatched the
messenger Rowland back at night with letters to
them all, and sent Dr Forrest also with cordial
waters.

7. Spent all day at home, Lord Lovelace and much
other company dining here.

MS. OF
LIEUT.-GEN.
LYTTELTON
ANNESLEY.

9. Spent this day at home, Sr Tim. Terill, his lady and daughters coming also to dinner. I did the usual duties, & heard well of my son at night: God be praised !

10. Spent at home, the Bishop of Oxford and divers others coming to dinner.

14. Spent the morning at home in business; the afternoon went a visiting, and sent my coach to Oxford to fetch my son and daughter Annesley come from London.

15. Spent the whole day at home, blessing God for their safe coming home, my grandchild Frank Annesley arriving also from Belvoir.

18. Went with most of our friends to dinner to Sr Timothy Terill's, being invited yesterday ; daughter Thomson was come before we came back. I did some business and the usual duties : sent my coach to Stokenchurch.

19. Went out in my son's chariot at 6, and was at Stokenchurch by 10, and thence in my own coach by 4 after noon.

25. Was at London about business, and writing letters all day, and did the accustomed duties. The Duke of Bucks was with me and spoke of the presidentship.

26. This morning at 5 o'clock Sr Richard Astley went in the flying coach towards Bletchington. I spent all day at London in business. Dined with Ld Barkley, who assured me all were for my being Keeper, but Sr Tho. Osborne opposed ; that the Keeper himself was infirm, and willing to give off : he said he spake not this by rote, but on good grounds. He told me also Lady —— had refused to see him. I was also by divers told the news was I was to be Privy Seal and Lord Ashley Treasurer ; but sure I am fit for no place if unworthy my own, nor desire I any unless better courses be steered. I did the usual duties. This day's discourse calls to mind how Lord Ashley yesterday complimented me about the Lord Keeper's place, being pleased to tell me none would fill it better, and that if he had any power he would endeavor it.

Sept. 1. Spent at London, being at Council in the morning.

2. Sent for by Lady Peterborough : found her sad by her evil usage, and comforted her what I could : she told me all his unkindness, but wished me to forbear speaking to him till she saw me again.

3. Went to London in the morning and saw the Duke of York early, taking the liberty to discourse with him of what people talked of him and the Countess of Falmouth, commending the Countess of Northumberland to him for a wife, giving her her due praises, as I know none deserves more, having known her from her childhood. He thanked me, and said there was no ground for the reports of him, which he had heard from others, and told me all which had passed between him and the King,

which was presently after his wife's death, viz.
that he left him free to himself, and that when he

Countess of Northumberland for a very fine lady,
and said if the King would have him marry
abroad he should choose for him, if at home he
would chose a wife for himself; and I observed
he was from this time very merry and pleasant
whilst I stayed.

I went then to my Lady Peterborough, whom
I found in the old manner very sad and weeping,
my Lord not having been at home that night,
and using her very ill and with threatenings when
he last saw her; having for above a year and a
half forsaken her bed and taking his pleasures
elsewhere : he also encouraged child and servants
against her, and bid the servants not answer her
when she spoke to them, and said they should not
value her a ' chif ', but spit in her face if he bid them.
She said she had no friend, and her heart was even
broken with discontent ; she had borne long, but
now had no hopes and could not rest ; and she
was ' hared ' and her memory gone, and could be a
housekeeper no longer, which was all he used her
for ; and that with harshness and rigour, never
giving her a good word, but pawning all she had :
and begged of me with tears, being his friend, to
see what I could do, for else she would leave off
all business, and go to her prayers for him. I
comforted her what I could, and promised my
assistance, though a tender business.

I was the morning at Whitehall chapel, and spent
the afternoon at Kensington in duties.

4. Went to London with six horses in the morning,
Ld Lieu^t of Ireland being to go his journey; we
parted very kindly. I did several business; got
Sir James Shaen made Secretary to the Commission for the lands in Ireland, with the King's consent. Spoke with Lord Peterborough, who took it
kindly, denying much his lady said, but taxing her
of great unquiet; but offering me to make me judge
of all differences, and promising kindness if she
would not disquiet him. I spoke with her also in
the evening, who denied all, and said he cared not
what he said, and that she had not seen him these
four days. I moderated both what I could, and did
the usual duties. Lyndon came to me in the
evening, having been three days in town.

6. Was all day at London. Perfected my counterpart
to the Duke of York of the lands granted to me by
him, viz., Ballysax, &c. Was at the Commission
for Ireland, and at Council : did several other
business, and the usual duties.

8. Went to London early; was at Council : did several
business and the usual duties. This day S^r ——
—— told me Lord Ashley had asked him yesterday

before we met what lands I had' gotten more than
I should by the settlement. He answered, I had
got 1700ll a year less than I should.

Captain —— told me he had the same day asked
him what I meant that I and Sr James Shaen had
abused them in the Report concerning Ireland,
and kept him in the dark; but he would not be so
used. God forgive this false man and pretended
friend! Lord St John got me to go with him to
the Comrs of the Treasury this afternoon, endeavours being used to get the King to break his
contract for the Customs' farm; I did my part
as his trustee, yet persuaded them to fair things
towards the King.

13. This day spent at London at Council, and several
business. Lord Arlington showed me a base
trick, speaking to the King (when he was giving
him direction to pass my warrant for 3000ll a year)
to have me surrender my office first, which was
never so much as mentioned before, but left as the
security for my due payment, as appears by the
draught of the warrant. I refused it, and told the
King this was not Lord Arlington's first ill office
to me; neither can I do it for many reasons. I
told several friends of this, who all justified me in
it. I did the usual duties.

14. Spent all day at London. Got Lord St John and the
rest of the farmers to submit to the King, so they
might be secured savers. Did several other
business, and the usual duties.

15. Spent at London at Council in the morning, at the
Commission of Ireland after noon, and did other
business; particularly brought the late farmers to
agree for a security for their money very moderately, and carried it to the King; and did the
usual duties.

Oct. 10. Spent this day at home. Lady Pesly and five or
six other ladies, Mr Lenthall, two Mr Dunces &c.
dining, and divers of them supping here, and
spending most of the day in jollity. I did the
usual duties: the Lord pardon all amiss!

12. Spent the morning at home. The afternoon went to
Oxford and found the waters very [high?];
therefore came home by Hedington and Islip. I
did the usual duties.

13. Wrote to son Thomson and his father by my daughter
returning, but after she stayed till next day, and I
went with her to see Arthur, sending her coach
before.

14. Went at 8 in the morning with my daughter Thomson
in my coach to Buckingham; was there by eleven,
where my grandchild Arthur Thomson met us
after two. Having dined, I came back with my
other daughters and Mr Forbes in my coach, and
they went to Haversham; we were at Bletchington
by five. Some of the usual duties I was forced to
put off till next day.

17. Spent this day at home: Mr Holoway dined with
me; we had much discourse of the country, &c.
He told me I was generally beloved, but by the
clergy, who reported I carried Dr Owen to
Windsor to the King in my coach; a loud lie,
though I know no hurt in it. I did several
business, and the usual duties.

21. Went to London and spent all day there, being at the
Irish Commission after noon; and did the usual
duties.

22. Went to the chapel at Whitehall in the morning,
Dr Tully preaching. I heard Mr Agas after noon
at Kensington, and did the usual duties.

23. Was at London in the morning about business at
the Irish Commission, &c. Spent the afternoon in
sorting papers, &c. at Kensington.

[1671-2.]

Jan. 2. An extraordinary Council being summoned to I went
out of my bed to it, and gave the King faithful
counsel against his seizing men's moneys, &c.;
and so did most of the Council, but 'twas not
followed. God amend these [beginnings] of evil !
I came home ill, and continued to keep my bed
till Jan. 9th the day before my son Arthur going to
Mr Hoblon's.

21. In the morning heard Dr Stillingfleet at St Andrew's
and Mr Agas after noon, and did other duties of
the day.

22. The morning was at the Commission for Ireland and
other business; the afternoon visiting and business
and the usual duties.

23. Was with the King in the morning in private ong,
who was very kind and free, telling me al his
designs against the Dutch and for liberty. I did
several business, and some duties.

24. Spent the morning at the Irish Commission: the
afternoon at Council; and did some duties, and
endeavoured to make peace in my family.

25. The morning kept my son Annesley and Thomson
from a quarrel, and was at the Court of Appeals.
The afternoon at the Treasury about the Irish
establishment; and in the evening at Mrs Banke's
funeral, where I heard Dr Stillingfleet. At eight of
the clock the King's playhouse took fire, and most
of that side of Russell Street and many other houses
thereabout were burnt down, and we in Drury
Lane and all about in great danger ; but the Lord
had mercy, and by great industry and blowing up
houses the fire was overcome: I had no rest, but
sat up almost all night, even till six in the morning.
The Lord pardon sin, which brings judgements !

March 2.
Saturday.
Continued very ill of the gout from Febr. 22 to
this day, though I went sometimes out; and particularly Tuesday and Thursday last to the Reader,
Sir Francis Goodrick, of Lincoln's Inns' feast,
where the King, Duke of York, &c., were on

Thursday; and did duties as I could, being still very lame.

17. The gout still continuing; yet I went to Council yesterday, and to the Irish Commission the day before, and abroad every day, and did duties as I could.

8, 9, 10, 11. } All this time ill in bed of the gout.

12, 13, 14. } All these days ill in bed of the gout.

15. I was at Council, where I spoke my mind freely to the Declaration offered by the King for indulgence; observing the Papists are put thereby into a better and less jealoused state than the dissenting Protestants : see my notes.

16. Ill in bed of the gout.

17. Was at Council: spoke my mind to the Declaration against the Dutch, and proposed the last treaty might be observed in not seizing of merchants' goods, but giving time to withdraw if war were judged necessary, &c.

18, and to April 6. } Ill in bed of the gout.

April 6, 7, 8, 9, 10, 11. } Ill still of the gout, but got up some days, though I could not get abroad.

12. I wrote to Lord St Alban's and Lord Arlington, though still ill of the gout.

13. Lord Chamberlain came to me, and told me he and Lord Arlington had a good time with the King yesterday for me : that his Maty would give me the mastership of the Rolls, instead of my office of the Navy, if I would accept it, and clear all for time past. I said I was willing to serve and please the King his own way, and liked better to be among lawyers, as I was bred, than in any other course.

21. In the morning heard Dr Tillotson's excellent sermon at Whitehall against the Papists on 1 Cor. 3. 15.; After noon Mr Agas at home, and did other duties of the day.

22. Moved the King in the morning to have Dr Tillotson's sermon printed which he said he liked; but I had long dispute with the King which I will not mention, he giving no direction for the printing. The afternoon I was at the Irish Commission and Council Committees.

May 29. Was the morning at church at Court. Afternoon spent most with the King, the news coming in the morning of the fleets engaging yesterday.

30. More news came. I spent the morning in reading and at Court. Dined with Lady Peterborough; was after noon at Court, and did some business and duties at home.

31. The morning was at Council, and about my own business at Court : the afternoon also at Whitehall ; Sir John Trevor's funeral being in the evening.

June 22. This day I spent most at home in business, and sadness for my grandchild Franck's illness of the flock pox, this being about the 11th day ; and did duties.

23. After commending the sweet babe to God, I went to Lincoln's Inn to church about nine of the clock ; after I was gone she sweetly slept in the Lord. The Lord gave, and the Lord hath taken away, blessed be the name of the Lord, who hath taken her from the evil to come ! The 28th of this month she would have been 17 months old, being born Jan. 28. 1670, about five in the evening.

I heard Mr Agas after noon.

The child was buried at 10 of the clock at night in St Martin's chancel.

I did other duties ; wrote to my son, and comforted my daughter.

July 3. Spent the morning at Council ; the afternoon at the Earl of Sandwich his funeral, in gown and hood,

Sandwich. as one of the assistant eight Earls to the chief mourner the Earl of Manchester, and did duties. He was buried in Queen Elizabeth's aisle in Henry the Seventh's chapel.

18. Went after business done at home to Lady Cranborne's to Twickenham to dinner, and visited several friends coming home ; and did duties.

19. Spent the morning at Council ; the afternoon at the Council of Plantations about the Duke of York's business : the rest at Marybone, and did duties.

20. This morning I spent at home and at Court. The afternoon I went to see Mr Lewis his school at Tottenham High Cross, and after wrote letters and did duties.

21. Was at Court in the morning and heard Dr Cartwright preach ; the afternoon Mr Agas at home, and did the usual duties.

22. This day went with the Earl of Essex to St Alban's,

Essex, Earl. and stayed there, sitting up with him and the ladies all night.

23. Took leave of him in the morning : came home about 9 o'clock, and went to bed till about noon, sleeping, and then rose to dinner. After noon I did several business at home and abroad, and wrote to Lord Lieutenant of Ireland Lord Berkley in answer to his, and did duties.

29. Spent the morning at Whitehall and at home, dining at Lord Devonshire's ; Lord Burleigh's daughter being baptized by the name of Christian. I played part of the afternoon ; did business the

Dick rest, and duties ; and had letters of my son Richard's

chosen fellow. election at Magdalen College to a fellowship, the 26th.

30. This being a stormy wet day, I spent most at home, and wrote letters and did duties.

MS. OF LIEUT.-GEN. LYTTELTON ANNESLEY.

Aug. 4. Was the morning at Whitehall; carried the sword, and heard Dr Barrow or Barwick; the afternoon heard Mr Agas and did other duties. And in my great perplexity for want of 1200^{li} S^r St. Fox came himself to me, hearing I had sought for him, and freely lent it; God's providence be magnified!

5. Spent the morning in receiving and paying this money to the chest, and directing Altham's journey to France with my daughter Thomson: the afternoon in other business for money, and did duties; my son is bound with me for it.

21. Went to dinner to Lord Berkley's at Durdans, and returned at night, 13 miles; and did duties.

Sept. 17. The morning spent with my sister and at Council; the afternoon at home till about 5 o'clock, went to meet friends at Captn Rosse's and stayed till ten: Lord pardon neglect of duties!

28. Spent the morning in business, and sitting for my picture: the afternoon writing letters, and did duties.

29. Heard Mr Lee of Hatfield the morning at Court; no such great preacher as famed. Mr Agas afternoon, and spent the rest of the day in duties.

1672, Oct. 1. Spent the morning at Council. After Council the King told me he had directed my grant to pass, and expressed much kindness to me and confidence in me. I thanked him for his justice, and said I hoped I should deserve new favours: I held the bason after at healing. This day Duke of Ormond being applied to for signing Captn Rosse his Report for 1000^{li} a year quit rents, seeing my hand to it and Lord St Albans', asked Captn Rosse what share we two had for signing. I have deserved better of him, but it seems his Lordship used to take bribes, that suspects me who never did, but have refused great ones. I corrected also this day his Grace's Beagle Vernon for reporting, which the Duke also spread even to the King's ear, that I would have bought Ruthorne's 3000 acres for myself, and because I was denied opposed his and Vernon's pretences. The King, who knew the falsehood as well as himself, called him lying knave, and ordered him to correct his order.

King's justice to me.

D. Ormond's enmity.

24. Spent the morning at Whitehall; then dined at Draper's Hall at the military company's feast, with the Duke of York and many of the nobility, &c. The evening spent at home, and did duties.

Nov. 17. This morning the great seal, which was sent for last night from the Lord Keeper, was delivered to Lord Shaftsbury as Chancellor. I heard Dr Alestree preach; the afternoon I heard Mr Agas, went to visit the sick Bishop of Chester, and the late Lord Keeper, and did duties.

Earl Shaftsbury Chancellor.

18. This morning I spent at Whitehall and visits. After

I saw the Bishop
of Chester, and
took my last leave
of him.
dinner went to congratulate Lord Shaftsbury, and after mutual expostulations of what was past, we concluded in promises of friendship. I supped with Lord Poor [Power] and officers.

21. Spent this morning at home in business; dined at Lady [Dow.] Devonshire's; the rest of the day in visits and duties. This day also Lord Duke of Ormond made great professions of friendship to me, and told me if any expressions or actions had proceeded from him which seemed contrary, he asked my pardon : this being at Lady Devonshire's, where Lord Chancellor and much company dined, he said he would take another time to open himself more fully to me. I was delivered from a continued slander.

April 10. Spent the morning at home : the afternoon at the caveat against Lord Power's grant, and at home till eight of the clock that we went to Lord Astley's funeral, who was buried in St Martin's church under the communion table. After return home, Lord Mohun moved me with great civility and expression of kindness for a match with my

Phil.
daughter Philips, wherein I gave him fair reception. I did duties after.

11. The morning I spent with the King and at Council. His Ma^{ty} was very kind to me ; and told me in the room within his bed-chamber, being in private with him, that he had resolved to make me Privy Seal ; and I assured him I would make use of his favour to do him the better service. My Lord Mohun continued his addresses with more civility, desiring only my daughter, and leaving all things else to my self, whether I gave anything or nothing. I did the usual duties.

21. Found that some had been undermining me with the King, and shaken him so far as that he told my Lord Arlington that it was not reasonable I should have my 3000^{li} pension and the privy seal both : which being acquainted with, I went to his Ma^{ty} before supper, and upon reasoning matters with him set all right and disappointed my enemies, and his Ma^{ty} bid me come next morning, and I should have the privy seal. I did duties, and secured the assistance of friends.

22. This morning I attended the King, who before he

Privy Seal.
went to Sheerness delivered me the privy seal in the purse, with great expression of his value of my services and trust in me, and that he was resolved of further instances thereof. I kissed his hands, and after congratulations by his Royal Highness and the generality of the Lords and others, returned home with it, store of company dining with me. The afternoon sat in Chancery, and did duties.

23. Spent this day at home in business, and receiving the congratulations of the Lord Treasurer, the Marquis of Worcester, Lord Halifax, Chancellor of the Exchequer, Lord Devonshire, Lord Salisbury and multitude of others; and did duties.

MS. OF LIEUT.-GEN. LYTTELTON ANNESLEY.

Lord Marshal and Sons; Sᵣ Cha. Cotrel: the Clerks also of the Privy Seal.

24. This day many more of all sorts came to congratulate me. I went at noon to my Lord Chancellor's in my gown with the seal and took the oaths of allegiance and supremacy and the oath of Privy Seal; the Earls of Craven and Carbery, Lord Mohun, Lord le Power, Sᵣ Edward Sydenham, the Clerk of the Crown, Mᵣ Agar and several of my own servants and others being present; and dined there, though it was my wedding day and much company at home, to whom I returned as soon as I could; and made Devereux Browne my steward, and did several business and duties. The Swedish resident visited, as that of Genoa did yesterday.

Earl of Berkshire, &c.

26. This morning Sᵣ Franc. Goodrick, Mᵣ Day, Sᵣ Nic. Pedley and Mᵣ Thomas Manly, Benchers of Lincoln's Inn, came, being sent by the Society to congratulate my being Lord Privy Seal, and desiring leave to put up my arms in their hall window by the Lord Chief Justice Fortescue. Lord and Countess Dowager of Kent, Lady Prat and many others came to congratulate also, and Sᵣ Lioliu (Leoline) Jenkins, Lord Burlington, Mᵣ Waler, Mʳˢ Middleton, Lady Harvy, &c. This morning I first sealed seven privy seals; see the dockets. I made visits, did several business and duties.

29. Spent the morning most abroad. The rest of the time the Master of the Rolls, Duchess of Somerset, Col. Fitzpatrick, Sᵣ Andr. Henly, Danish Resident and many others came to congratulate me, and I did several business and duties.

May 20. This morning about ten of the clock at Lambeth, the Archbishop of Canterbury married my grandson John Power, not eight year old, to Mʳˢ Katherine Fitzgerald, his cousin german, about 13 year of age. I gave her in the chapel there, and they answered as well as those of greater age. The wedding dinner and supper I gave them, and the rest of the day and till 12 at night was spent in dancing, &c. and they lay in my house. I did duties, and commended them to God's blessing.

June 16. Spent the morning with Lord Treasurer and in visits and business. The afternoon at home, sealing and other business, and Lord Ranelagh came to me, and told me he and Duke of Bucks, &c. having dined together, they had discourse of me, and that the Duke expressed great kindness to me, and said he would make Sᵣ Tho. Osborne and me good friends. Lord Treasurer Clifford had said

s 2

before to me he would appoint a time to do the
same before he gave up the white staff, it being for
the King's service we should agree well. I did
duties also.

21. Went this day to Rislip to see Lord Chandos his
house and Lord! it is a pitiful place. Came home
at night, and did duties.

Sept. 20, 1673. The morning was at the Admiralty Commission, and
thence at our desire met with the King at Lord
Arlington's, finding that our cables and anchors
were like to be to our disfurnishment lent to the
French to supply their great loss by the late storms;
yet we did all we could for them out of the Dutch
prizes, &c. The afternoon did business at home,

Richmond Duke. and at six went to Duke of Richmond's funeral
in Henry the Seventh's chapel, having mourning
for gown, hood and clothes sent to me. I did usual
duties.

Oct. 27. The morning spent in Parliament. After dinner my
wife fell into such a Bedlam railing humour because
Mr Heather came to tell me (when I had forbid
pantaloons for Dick) that she had ordered him to
make them, that I was never so abused in my life,
and this Mr Gache and others by, and all my
daughters; which put me in a resolution to bring
her to better terms, than to be counted a [cipher].
I spent the afternoon at Tangier and Admiralty
Commission, and at home sealing, and did duties;
referring my cause to God, who changes hearts.

Nov. 10, 1673. This morning I spent at St James', and at the
Admiralty Commission: the afternoon at Court
and at home, and did business and duties.

26 This morning I spent at home in business and sealed.

Duchess of York. The afternoon I went to see the Duchess of York,
but could not. The rest till nine spent at the Admiralty, where the words of a cheat upon the King
by the new grant of victualling passed from the

Lord Treasurer Lord Treasurer, which Sr Tho. Littleton resented
and it with the words "no more cheat than he that
Sr Tho. Littleton. said it"; the Treasurer replied he would deal with
him elsewhere, that he was a cheat or knave, and
he would prove it: some of us went and acquainted the King, and with the proposal of the
victuallers for continuing a while longer. I did
the usual duties.

27. This morning I spent at home; the afternoon went

Mrs Thomson to good Mrs Ellena Thomson my sister-in-law's
funeral, and saw her laid in the vault at Cree
church in London. I did other duties.

March 27, 1674. The morning heard the sermon at Court: the afternoon was at Council, and did other business and
duties; sealed in the morning also, and was at
Tangier Commission. After Council Lord Arling-

ton, upon my passing Lord Rochester's grant by the King's command, said, before Lord Keeper and many more, that I understood not the duty of my place ; that he never looked for better from me, that by God I served everybody so, and would do so to the end of the chapter.

29. The morning heard the Bishop of Chester at White-hall, after I had been with the King telling him of Lord Arlington's usage on the 27th, not as complaining, which I told his Maty I had never done in 14 years' service of any my fellow servants, but as a business his Maty was most concerned in : his Maty said he had done insolently, and should hear of it. The afternoon heard Mr Squib at home, and did other duties.

July 13. Spent this day at London in several business, and in the afternoon Dr Tillotson, Dean of Canterbury, baptized my son Annesley's boy James; my wife godmother, Lord Roos and Lord Montague godfathers, by deputy. I did duties also.

Grandson.

Aug. 4. This day I spent at home, Dr Drope, Mr Browne, Mr Smith and Mr Bayly of Magdalen College coming all to me before dinner, and other friends : they four stayed all night. I did duties.

Sept. 10. Spent much of this day in examining the robbery committed on Captn Robert Thornbill last night, and sent Hugh Parry to Newgate. The afternoon went to London to find out the rest of the thieves, and wrote to Sr Wm Turner about them. Stayed all night at my house in Drury Lane, and did duties.

11. At my lodgings in Whitehall examined John Griffith another of the robbers, and Andrew Daber the butcher; was at Council, and did several business and duties. Lord Arlington was made Lord Chamberlain ; Sr Joseph Williamson Secretary and sworn Councillor. I stayed in town and did duties.

13. After night shut I went to my daughter Mohun, she and her husband being desperately out again. I cannot but blame both, but her most being my ungracious daughter and breaking all my advices and carrying herself irreligiously. Among other expressions she said she would be a common whore before she would submit to her husband's will in what I thought fit; if she had not been married I had beat her, I did call her "impudent baggage," and said she carried herself like a whore, and left her with resolution to see her no more. This was after her husband had sworn never to strike her nor give her ill words.

Dec. 2. Spent most of the day in reconciling my daughter Mohun and her husband, and supt with them and left them in bed.

J. J. Cartwright.

INDEX.

Errington :
  Michael, of Wensley, 180.
  Thomas, of Wensley, 180.
Ersby, Anthony, 242.
Esk, the river, 161.
Essex, 18, 19, 20.
Essex :
  (Robert Devereux, 2nd) Earl of,
    letters to, 212, 242, 243, 244.
  (Arthur Capel), Earl of, 12, 16, 23,
    119, 139, 272.
Estrées, Count d', 248.
European commodities, 55.
Ev., J., letters from, 28.
Everard, Edmund, his information,
  (Popish plot), 141.
Evers :
  Mr. See Wrie.
  Edward, 150.
Every :
  John, 253.
  Simon, 254.
Examinations, Lords of the Committee
  of. See under Lords.
Excellency, his, (? Leicester, Robert,
  Earl of), 213, 215, 216.
Exchange, the, 54.
Exchequer, 4.
Excise, 43.
Exeter, 8.
  letters dated at, 6, 7, 8, 21, 28, 38,
    39, 40, 41, 48.
  assizes at, 40, 41.
  Jonathan, Bishop of, letter from,
    27.
  Bishop of, (1694), 36.
  Lord, 13, 250.
  College. See under Oxford.
Exports, English, to Turkey. See under
  Turkey.
Eyre, Samuel, letters from, 31, 32.
Eyres, Judge, 45.

F.

F., Mr., of Spridlestone, 11.
Faille, Martin de la, 218.
Fairfax :
  Charles, Lord, of Gilling, 185.
  Sir Thomas, letter from, 246.
  —— letter to, 246.
Falkirk, 177, 178.
Fall :
  John. See Saunders, John.
  Stephen, 149.
Falmouth, 32.
Falmouth, Countess of, (1671), 267.
Famars, Charles de Coucy, Sieur de,
  Governor of Malines, 209.
  —— letter from, 209.
Fane, —, 30.
Fanshawe, Lord, (1692), 248.
Farmers, 6.
Farrington :
  General, 251.
  Thomas, 255.

Farr's Coffee House. See under London.
Fauconberge :
  Lord, (1660), 4.
  —— his regiment, 4.
Fawcett, Captain, 246.
Fawke, Brigadier, 160.
Fay, Monsieur du, Ambassador from the
  King of Navarre, letter to, 232.
Feguieres, garrison at, 84.
Felbrygg, Simon, knight, 205.
Fenne, Bodin de, 204.
Fenwick :
  Sir John, letter to, (1611), 186.
  —— (d. 1697), 16, 40, 43, 44, 113,
    116, 117, 141.
  —— papers of, 115, 116, 117.
  Mr., 157, 158.
  Sir William, letter to, 186.
Fernandobuck in Brazil, 242.
Ferrand, John, 254.
Ferrier, Père, 58, 71.
Ferrybridge, co. York, 165, 167.
Feversham, 117.
Fez, 189.
  and Morocco, King of. See
    Morocco, Emperor of.
Fischmeester, Abraham, 211.
Fisher, John, of Yarm, 183.
Fitter, Mr., a priest, 134.
Fitzgerald :
  Greeme, 155.
  Katherine, 275.
Fitzherbert, Bazill, 124.
Fitz James, Sir H., 56.
Fitzlawes, Sir Richard, 256.
Fitzpatrick, Colonel, 275.
Fitzwilliam, Lord, (1745), 253.
Flamsteed, (a cypher to signify St.
  Omer, q.v.), 114.
Flanders, 21, 57, 80, 99, 108, 123, 151,
  186, 208, 210, 232, 233.
  English troops in. See under
    Army.
  French victories in, 7.
  the Lord Marshal of the forces in,
    215, 222.
  —— letter from, 217.
  —— letters to, 216, 222.
  President of. See Amant,
    Monsieur d'.
Fleet, the. See under London.
Fleetwood, Sir William, 247, 266.
Floranzen, —, 81.
Florence, 101.
  Duke of, 100.
Flower, F., 253.
Flushing, 210, 241.
  letters dated at, 210, 220.
  pensionary of, 230.
Foley, Paul, Speaker of House of
  Commons, 36, 249.
Foot forces, the, 197.
Foote, Samuel, 200, 201.
  letters from, 200, 201.
Forbes, Mr., 269.
Ford, 34.
  co. Northumberland, letter dated at,
    191.

HISTORICAL MANUSCRIPTS COMMISSION.

Date.	—	Size.	Sessional Paper.	Price.
				s. d.
1870 (Reprinted 1874.)	FIRST REPORT, WITH APPENDIX - Contents :— ENGLAND. House of Lords; Cambridge Colleges; Abingdon, and other Corporations, &c. SCOTLAND. Advocates' Library, Glasgow Corporation, &c. IRELAND. Dublin, Cork, and other Corporations, &c.	f'cap	[C. 55]	1 6
1871	SECOND REPORT, WITH APPENDIX, AND INDEX TO THE FIRST AND SECOND REPORTS - - - - - Contents :— ENGLAND. House of Lords; Cambridge Colleges; Oxford Colleges; Monastery of Dominican Friars at Woodchester, Duke of Bedford, Earl Spencer, &c. SCOTLAND. Aberdeen and St. Andrew's Universities, &c. IRELAND. Marquis of Ormonde; Dr. Lyons, &c.	,,	[C. 441]	3 10
1872	THIRD REPORT, WITH APPENDIX AND INDEX - - - - - Contents :— ENGLAND. House of Lords; Cambridge Colleges; Stonyhurst College; Bridgewater and other Corporations; Duke of Northumberland, Marquis of Lansdowne, Marquis of Bath, &c. SCOTLAND. University of Glasgow; Duke of Montrose, &c. IRELAND. Marquis of Ormonde; Black Book of Limerick, &c.	,,	[C. 673]	[*Out of print.*]
1873	FOURTH REPORT, WITH APPENDIX. PART I. - - - - - Contents :— ENGLAND. House of Lords; Westminster Abbey; Cambridge and Oxford Colleges; Cinque Ports, Hythe, and other Corporations, Marquis of Bath. Earl of Denbigh, &c. SCOTLAND. Duke of Argyll, &c. IRELAND. Trinity College, Dublin; Marquis of Ormonde.	,,	[C. 857]	6 8
1873	DITTO. PART II. INDEX - - -	,,	[C.857i.]	2 6
1876	FIFTH REPORT, WITH APPENDIX. PART I. - Contents :— ENGLAND. House of Lords; Oxford and Cambridge Colleges; Dean and Chapter of Canterbury; Rye, Lydd, and other Corporations, Duke of Sutherland, Marquis of Lansdowne, Reginald Cholmondeley, Esq., &c. SCOTLAND. Earl of Aberdeen, &c.	,,	[C.1432]	7 0
,,	DITTO. PART II. INDEX - - -	,,	[C.1432 i.]	3 6

Date.	---	Size.	Sessional Paper.	Price.
				s. d.
1877	SIXTH REPORT, WITH APPENDIX. PART I. - Contents : – ENGLAND. House of Lords; Oxford and Cambridge Colleges; Lambeth Palace; Black Book of the Archdeacon of Canterbury; Bridport, Wallingford, and other Corporations; Lord Leconfield, Sir Reginald Graham, Sir Henry Ingilby, &c. SCOTLAND. Duke of Argyll, Earl of Moray, &c. IRELAND. Marquis of Ormonde.	f'cap	[C.1745]	8 6
	DITTO. PART II. INDEX - - -	,,	[C.2102]	[Out of print.]
1879	SEVENTH REPORT, WITH APPENDIX. PART I. - - - - - Contents : — House of Lords; County of Somerset; Earl of Egmont, Sir Frederick Graham, Sir Harry Verney, &c.	,,	[C.2340]	[Out of print.]
	DITTO. PART II. APPENDIX AND INDEX - Contents : — Duke of Athole, Marquis of Ormonde, S. F. Livingstone, Esq., &c.	,,	[C. 2340 i.]	[Out of print.]
1881	EIGHTH REPORT, WITH APPENDIX AND INDEX. PART I. - - - Contents : — List of collections examined, 1869–1880. ENGLAND. House of Lords; Duke of Marlborough; Magdalen College, Oxford; Royal College of Physicians; Queen Anne's Bounty Office; Corporations of Chester, Leicester, &c. IRELAND. Marquis of Ormonde, Lord Emly, The O'Conor Don, Trinity College, Dublin, &c.	,,	[C.3040]	8 6
1881	DITTO. PART II. APPENDIX AND INDEX - Contents : — Duke of Manchester.	,,	[C.3040 i.]	1 9
1881	EIGHTH REPORT. PART III. APPENDIX AND INDEX - - - - Contents :— Earl of Ashburnham.	,,	[C.3040 ii.]	1 4
1883	NINTH REPORT, WITH APPENDIX AND INDEX. PART I. - - - Contents : — St. Paul's and Canterbury Cathedrals; Eton College; Carlisle, Yarmouth, Canterbury, and Barnstaple Corporations, &c.	,,	[C.3773]	[Out of print.]
1884	DITTO. PART II. APPENDIX AND INDEX - Contents :— ENGLAND. House of Lords, Earl of Leicester; C. Pole Gell, Alfred Morrison, Esqs., &c. SCOTLAND. Lord Elphinstone, H. C. Maxwell Stuart, Esq., &c. IRELAND. Duke of Leinster, Marquis of Drogheda, &c.	,,	[C.3773 i.]	6 3
1884	DITTO. PART III. APPENDIX AND INDEX - - - - Contents :— Mrs. Stopford Sackville.	,,	[C.3773 ii.]	1 7

Date.	—	Size.	Sessional Paper.	Price.
				s. d.
1883	CALENDAR OF THE MANUSCRIPTS OF THE MARQUIS OF SALISBURY, K.G. (or CECIL MSS.). PART I. - - - -	8vo.	[C.3777]	[*Out of print.*]
1888	DITTO. PART II. - - -	”	[C.5463]	3 5
1889	DITTO. PART III. - - -	”	[C. 5889 v.]	2 1
1892	DITTO. PART IV. - - -	,,	[C.6823]	2 11
1885	TENTH REPORT - - - - This is introductory to the following :—	,,	[C.4548]	0 3½
1885	(1.) APPENDIX AND INDEX - - - Earl of Eglinton, Sir J. S. Maxwell, Bart., and C. S. H. D. Moray, C. F. Weston Underwood, G. W. Digby, Esqs.	”	[C.4575]	[*Out of print.*]
1885	(2.) APPENDIX AND INDEX - - The Family of Gawdy.	”	[C.4576 iii.]	1 4
1885	(3.) APPENDIX AND INDEX - - Wells Cathedral.	”	[C.4576 ii.]	2 0
1885	(4.) APPENDIX AND INDEX - - Earl of Westmorland ; Capt. Stewart ; Lord Stafford ; Sir N. W. Throckmorton, Stonyhurst College ; Sir P. T. Mainwaring, Misses Boycott, Lord Muncaster, M.P., Capt. J. F. Bagot, Earl of Kilmorey, Earl of Powis, Rev. T. S. Hill and others, the Corporations of Kendal, Wenlock, Bridgnorth, Eye, Plymouth, and the County of Essex.	,,	[C.4576]	3 6
1885	(5.) APPENDIX AND INDEX - - - The Marquis of Ormonde, Earl of Fingall, Corporations of Galway, Waterford, the Sees of Dublin and Ossory, the Jesuits in Ireland.	,,	[4576 i.]	[*Out of print.*]
1887	(6.) APPENDIX AND INDEX - - - Marquis of Abergavenny, Lord Braye, G. F. Luttrell, P. P. Bouverie, W. B. Davenport, M.P., R. T. Balfour, Esquires.	,,	[C.5242]	1 7
1887	ELEVENTH REPORT - - - - This is introductory to the following :—	,,	[C. 5060 vi.]	0 3
1887	(1.) APPENDIX AND INDEX - - - H. D. Skrine, Esq., Salvetti Correspondence.	,,	[C.5060]	1 1
1887	(2.) APPENDIX AND INDEX - - House of Lords. 1678-1688.	,,	[C. 5060 i.]	2 0
1887	(3.) APPENDIX AND INDEX - - - Corporations of Southampton and Lynn.	,,	[C. 5060 ii.]	1 8
1887	(4.) APPENDIX AND INDEX - - - Marquess Townshend.	,,	[C. 5060 iii.]	2 6
1887	(5.) APPENDIX AND INDEX - - - Earl of Dartmouth.	”	[C. 5060 iv.]	2 8

Date.	—	Size.	Sessional Paper.	Price.
				s. d.
1887	(6.) APPENDIX AND INDEX - Duke of Hamilton.	8vo.	[C. 5060 v.]	1 6
1888	(7.) APPENDIX AND INDEX - Duke of Leeds, Marchioness of Waterford, Lord Hothfield, &c.; Bridgwater Trust Office, Reading Corporation, Inner Temple Library.	,,	[C.5612]	2 0
1890	TWELFTH REPORT - This is introductory to the following:—	,,	[C.5889]	0 3
1888	(1.) APPENDIX - Earl Cowper, K.G. (Coke MSS., at Melbourne Hall, Derby) Vol. I.	,,	[C.5472]	2 7
1888	(2.) APPENDIX - Ditto. Vol. II.	,,	[C.5613]	2 5
1889	(3.) APPENDIX AND INDEX - Ditto. Vol. III.	,,	[C. 5889 i.]	1 4
1888	(4.) APPENDIX - The Duke of Rutland, G.C.B. Vol. I.	,,	[C.5614]	3 2
1891	(5.) APPENDIX AND INDEX - Ditto. Vol. II.	,,	[C. 5889 ii.]	2 0
1889	(6.) APPENDIX AND INDEX - House of Lords, 1689-1690.	,,	[C. 5889 iii.]	2 1½
1890	(7.) APPENDIX AND INDEX - S. H. le Fleming, Esq., of Rydal.	,,	[C. 5889 iv.]	1 11
1891	(8.) APPENDIX AND INDEX - The Duke of Athole, K.T., and the Earl of Home.	,,	[C.6338]	1 0
1891	(9.) APPENDIX AND INDEX - The Duke of Beaufort, K.G., the Earl of Donoughmore, J. H. Gurney, W. W. B. Hulton, R. W. Ketton, G. A. Aitken, P. V. Smith, Esqs.; Bishop of Ely; Cathedrals of Ely, Gloucester, Lincoln, and Peterborough; Corporations of Gloucester, Higham Ferrers, and Newark; Southwell Minster; Lincoln District Registry.	,,	[C. 6338 i.]	2 6
1891	(10.) APPENDIX - The First Earl of Charlemont. Vol. I. 1745-1783.	,,	[C. 6338 ii.]	1 11
1892	THIRTEENTH REPORT - This is introductory to the following:—	,,	[C.6827]	0 3
1891	(1.) APPENDIX - The Duke of Portland. Vol. I.	,,	[C.6474]	3 0
	(2.) APPENDIX AND INDEX. Ditto. Vol. II.	*In the Press.*		
1892	(3.) APPENDIX. J. B. Fortescue, Esq. Vol. I.	,,	[C.6660]	2 7

Date.		Size.	Sessional Paper.	Price.
				d.
1892	(4.) APPENDIX AND INDEX - - - Corporations of Rye, Hastings, and Hereford. Capt. F. C. Loder-Symonds, E. R. Wodehouse, M.P., J. Dovaston, Esqs., Sir T. B. Lennard, Bart., Rev. W. D. Macray, and Earl of Dartmouth (Supplementary Report).	8vo.	[C.6810]	*s.* 4
1892	(5.) APPENDIX AND INDEX - - - House of Lords, 1690–1691.	,,	[C.6822]	2 4
1893	(6.) APPENDIX AND INDEX - - Sir William FitzHerbert, Earl of Ancaster, &c.	,,	[C.7166]	1 4
	(7.) APPENDIX AND INDEX - - - The Earl of Lonsdale.	*In the Press.*		
	(8.) APPENDIX AND INDEX - - The Duke of Rutland, Vol. III.	*In the Press.*		
	(9.) THE FIRST EARL OF CHARLEMONT - Vol. II. 1784–1799.	*In the Press.*		

[33]

THE

MANUSCRIPTS

OF THE

EARL OF LONSDALE.

𝔓𝔯𝔢𝔰𝔢𝔫𝔱𝔢𝔡 𝔱𝔬 𝔟𝔬𝔱𝔥 𝔥𝔬𝔲𝔰𝔢𝔰 𝔬𝔣 𝔓𝔞𝔯𝔩𝔦𝔞𝔪𝔢𝔫𝔱 𝔟𝔶 ℭ𝔬𝔪𝔪𝔞𝔫𝔡 𝔬𝔣 𝔥𝔢𝔯 𝔐𝔞𝔧𝔢𝔰𝔱𝔶.

LONDON:
PRINTED FOR HER MAJESTY'S STATIONERY OFFICE,
BY EYRE AND SPOTTISWOODE,
PRINTERS TO THE QUEEN'S MOST EXCELLENT MAJESTY.

And to be purchased, either directly or through any Bookseller, from
EYRE AND SPOTTISWOODE, EAST HARDING STREET. FLEET STREET, E.C., and
32, ABINGDON STREET, WESTMINSTER, S.W.; or
JOHN MENZIES & Co., 12, HANOVER STREET. EDINBURGH, and
90, WEST NILE STREET, GLASGOW ; or
HODGES, FIGGIS, & Co., LIMITED, 104, GRAFTON STREET, DUBLIN.

1893.

[C.—7241.]   *Price* 1s, 3d.

INTRODUCTION.

Two collections of historical letters and papers belonging to the Earl of Lonsdale are calendared in the following pages. The larger and more important is that preserved in Lowther Castle, in the neighbourhood of which the possessions of the Lowther family have lain from a very early period of English history. In the reign of Edward I. " Hugo de Louthre, miles," was sitting in Parliament for the county of Westmorland ; and from that date down to the present the family name appears constantly in the returns of members from that county or from Cumberland. The other collection is in the Castle at White-haven, with which town a branch of the family became connected in the seventeenth century.

At Lowther Castle are two manuscript note-books of proceedings in two of the parliaments of Charles I. The first of these extends from 24th April to 12th June 1626, when Charles's second parliament was hastily dissolved, on its determination not to proceed with the question of subsidy until the charges against the Duke of Buckingham, and other grievances, had been properly considered. The greater portion of the notes appear to have been made during the time the debates were going on—the handwriting is therefore some-what cramped, and the meaning of the entries at times rather vague, but a careful transcript of the whole has been made, which will be found a very important addition to the printed Journals of the House of Commons and to the other known sources of our information about parliament at that period. The subjects mainly under discussion during the six or seven weeks that this record was kept were the proceedings of the select committee on the charge against the Duke of Buckingham and the doctors' evidence before that committee touching the alleged poisoning of King James ; the terms of the remonstrance to Charles on his imprisonment of two of the members, and of the re-presentation to be made to him of the abuses which had crept into the government. A comparison of one entry under June 1, 1626, with an entry of the same date in the printed Commons' Journal, shows that "Mr. Lowther" was the compiler of these notes. There were, however, two members of that name then sitting in the house, John, member for Westmorland, who was knighted a few days after the above date, namely, on June 6th, and Richard, probably a younger brother of John, who was member for Berwick. The second note-book is written with greater neatness and regularity, and is probably compiled from memory or from rougher notes made during the debates. It reports some of the proceedings of the parliament succeeding that dissolved in 1626, between 4th June 1628 and its adjournment on 26th June; and again between its meeting on 20th January 1629 and the 20th February, when it was adjourned and subsequently dissolved. The petition of right and the bill of tonnage and poundage were among the chief matters debated; and among the speakers it is interesting to note the names of many members who have not hitherto been chronicled as taking any active or prominent part in establishing the principles of parliamentary government which were then being mooted almost for the first time.

The third manuscript volume described in the following Calendar is an account of a little tour through the lowlands of Scotland to Edinburgh made in 1629 by C. Lowther (probably Christopher, afterwards rector of Lowther) and two others, which is not only of much topographical interest, but also gives amusing pictures of the social habits of the people with whom, sometimes by necessity and sometimes by choice, they were brought into contact. Among the districts most fully described is that of Selkirk, the remarks upon the natives of which are not flattering; in the town the travellers had for their lodging "a choking, " smoky chamber, and drunken, unruly company thrust in upon " us called for wine and ale, and left it on our score." At Galashiels they stayed with Sir James Pringle, and narrate many curious customs observed at his hospitable table. Under Edinburgh they describe the law courts, and give a plan of the interior of the building, which is reproduced on p. 80 of this volume, and endeavour, perhaps not successfully, to show the manner in which the sittings were conducted and justice administered. Here and there in the journal are notes on the method of bleaching linen, the measures of corn and liquids, and the **coinage and dialect of the country.**

Among the miscellaneous seventeenth-century papers are some relating to the proceedings taken against the Quakers in Westmorland, and giving the names and abodes of those imprisoned in the gaols of Appleby and Kendal in 1665 ; some letters from Queen's College, Oxford, showing the classes of students and the nature of the education in vogue there about 1670 ; and letters of Sir Thomas Osborne, afterwards Earl of Danby and Duke of Leeds. To the time of the Revolution belong some curious letters to Sir John Lowther from Carlisle, detailing the manœuvres by which Sir Christopher Musgrave secured possession of that garrison in December 1688 ; and among the many correspondents of the first Viscount Lonsdale, temp. Will. III., are the king himself, Lords Nottingham, Shrewsbury, and Godolphin, and Sir George Rooke, whose letters, though not of great historical importance, are interesting for their references to the events of much moment then passing. The letters of Bentinck, the first Earl of Portland, which belong to the same period, are more remarkable for the quaint French in which they are written than for any light which they throw on public affairs. Of the reign of Queen Anne are letters to and from Thomas, Lord Wharton, two of which give brief but graphic accounts of debates in November, 1705, on the Union with Scotland ; others were written at the time of his being Lord Lieutenant of Ireland. In September, 1723, Lord Lonsdale writes a curious narrative to his cousin, James Lowther, of the conduct of the Duke of Wharton and Sir Christopher Musgrave. These personages paid a visit to the Duke's estate in Swaledale near Richmond, in Yorkshire, and there compelled the country people to drink the Pretender's health, themselves pulling off their coats and waistcoats and falling upon their knees to do due honour to the toast. The matter was quickly brought to the notice of a neighbouring justice of the peace, but he, whether from sympathy with the sentiments expressed or from fear of such great men, did not care to meddle with the matter. Under the year 1733 will be found a long letter of the Duke of Newcastle upon the state of Europe generally, and in 1745 is a curious minute by the same Duke about George II.'s treatment of his brother Pelham. Three or four letters about the rebellion in the latter year will also be read with interest, as well as some from Henry Fox,

when holding office in 1755, 1756, and 1760. In 1757 the
active politician John Robinson was at work in Whitehaven
and Appleby settling election matters there, and his letters to
Sir James Lowther from those places give an amusing picture
of the methods adopted to conciliate both the electors and the
mob. Illustrating the history of the early years of the reign of
George III., we have letters of the Earl and Countess of Bute,
Lord North, and George Grenville, one from the Duke of Rutland in July 1779 requesting Sir James Lowther's interest on
behalf of "Lord Chatham's son, Mr. Pitt, a particular friend of
mine," who has declared himself a candidate for Cambridge
University, and one very long letter and two short ones from
Lord Rockingham in 1780 on the proposed measures of parliamentary reform. In March 1781, the Duke of Rutland writes
to congratulate Sir James Lowther on the success of Mr. Pitt's
first appearance in the House of Commons, and Sir Michael le
Fleming in an undated letter appears to refer to the same occasion when he writes that "Mr. Pitt, your member," was beyond
anything he could have had an idea of, and that the whole
House was astonished and pleased. There are many interesting
though not historically important letters of Pitt to Sir James
Lowther, afterwards Earl of Lonsdale, and to his kinsman and
successor in the title, Sir William, between 1783 and 1805.
The correspondence in December 1788 and January 1789 is
much concerned with the severe illness of the King, and includes
letters and a memorandum by the Prince of Wales on his proposed regency. A letter from Robert Thoroton, in Dublin, gives
a glimpse of the state of Ireland in 1796. A long letter from
Sir John Beckett, from Leeds, touching the supplies of corn and
the cost of living in 1800, compared with previous years, is
worthy of special notice. Among Sir William Lowther's correspondents was his old tutor and connexion by marriage, Dr.
Thomas Zouch, of Sandal, near Wakefield, a learned divine
and author of repute in his day. The Rev. Henry Zouch, an
elder brother of Thomas, was a correspondent of Horace
Walpole, and Walpole's letters to him are in Lord Lonsdale's
possession; they are, however, all printed in Cunningham's
edition, with the exception of two of slight importance.
Henry, too, was a very active magistrate, and carried on a good

deal of correspondence on public affairs with persons of more or less prominence. Among the letters written to him were one or two from Wilberforce; David Barclay, of Red Lion Square; Samuel Glasse, of Greenford, Middlesex; W. Weddell, member for Malton; Sir Richard Hill, who writes from Harley Street in 1789; and Archbishop Markham. These letters, however, have little interest at the present time, and are therefore unnoticed in the following Calendar.

To students of the personal and political history of the opening years of this century two bundles of correspondence, entitled "Correspondence relating to Mr. Pitt's death" and "Negociations with the Grenville party" respectively, will be of surpassing interest. In dealing with letters of such comparatively recent date and touching upon topics not without their bearing upon controversies of the present day, it has been thought best to print the large majority of the letters at full length, and to leave each reader to draw his own conclusions from them. The names of Lord Lowther's correspondents at this time will suffice to show the great value of the views expressed by them on the political crisis of 1806; among them are :—the Earl of Essex, Lord Mulgrave, Lord Camden, the Earl of Westmorland, W. Spencer Stanhope, George Canning, George Rose, Charles Long, afterwards Lord Farnborough, Lord Melville (Dundas), and Lord Grenville. Contemporary with this correspondence, but found in another bundle, is a remarkable letter of William Wilberforce to Lord Lowther, with which a note from Henry Brougham, then comparatively unknown, is enclosed. In this note Wilberforce is asked whether Lord Lowther would be likely to lend his support to bring Brougham in for Westmorland, where a vacancy had just occurred. Wilberforce is not at all enthusiastic in the matter, rather the reverse, but the account which he gives of Brougham's career up to that date is noteworthy. Lord Lowther's reply is very brief and emphatic. This little episode in the life of a remarkable man appears to have been unknown to his biographers. The selections from the correspondence at Lowther Castle conclude with letters of the Hon. Henry Lowther to his father, chiefly when engaged in the Peninsular War. It should not be omitted to mention that there are also a large number of letters of the poet Wordsworth, which have been recently examined by Prof. W. Knight for the purposes of his new Life of Wordsworth; no extracts, therefore, are given from them in the Calendar. Among other letters of the present century at Lowther Castle, which, for various reasons, have also been omitted from the present report, are some from Dr. Burney, dated at Chelsea College, between 1806 and 1812; from Lady Hester Stanhope, 1805–1808; from Watson, Bishop of Llandaff, written between 1803–1811; and from the Duke of Wellington, 1827 and later.

At Whitehaven Castle are preserved a few letters of Roger Kirkby, who sat in the Long Parliament for Lancaster, to Christopher Lowther in July and August 1641, narrating some of the proceedings in the House; a remarkable letter of William Penn, from "Pennsberry," in 1701, to Sir John Lowther, showing the difficulties with which he had to contend in the colony named after him; a few London news-letters, temp. Queen Anne; and letters of Bishop Nicolson of Carlisle in 1714 and 1715. Sir John Lowther, of Whitehaven, was a Commissioner of the Admiralty from 1689 to 1696, and there is a large collection of Admiralty books and papers relating chiefly to those years. The interest of these is purely official, and hardly any original letters of any kind were found among them.

J. J. CARTWRIGHT.

THE MANUSCRIPTS OF THE EARL OF LONSDALE.

I.—AT LOWTHER CASTLE.

" The Justice Diet.

1567. 6° die Maij.

An Estimat of a proportyon for the Assises.

A howse	First prepar a howse And sume stuffe Carlell with a Barne and horse gresse and fyre	-	v^{li}
beiff	*yt* two fat oxen from Blaikston -	-	vij^{li}
mutton	*yt* xxiiij^{li} fat wethers from Louther	-	vj^{li}
veale	*yt* xij veale Calues in the markett	-	iij^{li}
malt	*yt* xxiiij^{li} bushell malt from Louther	-	iiij^{li}
wheat	*yt* xxiiij^{li} bushel of wheat from Louther	-	vj^{li}
whyn	*yt* A Tonne of wyne at Newcastell	-	x^{li}
kydds	*yt* xij kydds at Carlell market -	-	xx^{s}
lam	*yt* xij lames in the Countre	-	xx^{s}
wilde ffoule	*yt* wylffoule in the Countre	-	xl^{s}
conyes	*yt* x dosin Conyes at Wyrkinton	-	v^{li}
capons	*yt* Capons fat -	-	v^{li}
chekyns	*yt* xx dosin Chekyns in helton -	-	xx^{s}
spice	*yt* Spices from london -	-	v^{li}
rewards	*yt* in Rewards for Venison bringing	-	xl^{s}
gaulv	*yt* house room to Skepp (Shap ?)	-	v^{li}
	yt pegs -	-	xii."

[*Endorsed*]

" Rychard lowther being Sherif Anno 9 Elizabeth."

[1626. Notes in Parliament:—*a small 4to Volume.*]

24 April 1626.

" Select Committee examining divers privately and hearing the house or some disliked Glanville in the chair desired the opinion of the house how to proceed, signifies also new matter not fit to be published to all lest discovery of persons and matter might prejudice the cause.

Sir Clement Thockmorton shewed the dislike of the proceeding, privately estranging the members unparalleled.

Sir Walter Earle doth defend it by precedent of Merchant Adventurers but it was by order. Gave reason enforced against him.

Ordered 3 of the Select Committees to take examination of any if sick and to return it in writing and any to be present at Select Committee, to reduce the old matter into form, but they have said it is new matter.

Upon the question whether Select Committee may bring in new matter propounded to them concerning the Duke, though neither house directed heads, house divided 60 odd that they may, yet maintained most and better reasons to the contrary for the prejudice that may follow, for so may a Select Committee take what they will, refuse what they will,

A

which only the house should do, and so shall we be guided by a few who prepared may blind our reason, we strangers which debated first and considered at Committee could not be but should be parliamentarily a dangerous plot for a favourite Parliament, now the contrary.

Ordered at Select Committee none to interpose in the ordering of the matter, or penning, but all be present at examination at will.

Mr. Jefford reports the leave given and notice to the Duke by notes, and said he might send for copies. The Duke took it well; said after Lords sat he would give answer, which he did and gave all thanks for this favour, since he desired nothing more then to satisfy us. That he gave thanks for the notice, and though it might prevent perhaps our transmission to the Lords, which he considered how grievous it was, the Lords would not give leave, but he pressed it not though necessary, because the King's business and the occasions did so press him, that it might spend time to his prejudice which he himself had rather endure. Knows his hazard to be reported to the Lords, yet will not he while he hath any favour forbear to do the best offices that he can for this house nor he will not hinder the King's business. Shews his zeal to his country declared upon the dissolution of the treaties, and how hazarded King's favour in that for to [do] good to his country, and to satisfy this house, howsoever now thought.

1. Duke no author of Recusancy as yet unresolved.

2. Resolved at Committee the Duke cause of loss of Rochelle in not well guarding since treaty dissolved, and not in the house resolved.

3. Plurality of offices in one hand to be affixed on him.

Resolved on him as before in the house.

4. That Duke is affixed to the sale of honours to Lord Roberts.

5. King's revenue to maintain honours instanced in his mother, two brothers, brother in law and niece.

Resolved the Duke a cause of bestowing honours of those for whose maintenance King's revenue exhausted.

6. That Duke cause of ships delivered to French employed against Rochell.

Resolved in the house the 10ᵐ*l.* of India Company an undue extortion by Duke.

7. Sale of Judicature, Cinque Ports, Treasurer-ship affixed on him by the question.

8. Intercepting, exhausting, and misemploying of King's revenue. Chelsea house agreed a cause, and all the other lands put upon Duke also.

Doctor Ramsay.

There was neither eating, drinking &c. but by consultation; this they know not, every consultation was set down under their hands; he knows not who made it, but the general voice was, it was made in the Duke's Chamber, divers physicians by when it was applied by Hayes, none contradicting, but about an hour after he died; laid on at 4 of clock to worst side eight, continued till midnight and after he declared his dislike to Gibb and Dishington. It was taken off because King swooned, the next night he asked Chambers and him what made him so evil last night, they gave natural causes as cold, as height of disease, but he said no, it was that he had from the Duke of Buckingham, but whether he meant the plaster or potion he knew not, but the Duke brought him a potion twice and gave it, at the beginning of his fit, but the third time King refused.

An hour or half betwixt the potions and so the third time, then he put it away with his hand.

Doctor Moore shewed a bill of the recipe, the symptoms that followed was panting, raving, sounding, uncertain beating of pulse; he saith the ingredients of the bill were by them subscribed to be good, upon question loco et tempore. Doctor Moore brought the bill after to be subscribed from the Duke, but whether they were in or not we know not, he thinks it was intended they should subscribe it was the same drink, but he knows nothing to induce his intendment, *all physicians did subscribe alike*, the effects were all one of drink or plaster; subscription required Sunday or Monday, but what the reason he was required to subscribe he knows not. Sir William Paddie made the bill of it, he doth not know that the Duke ever caused other physic to be ministered.

Doctor Atkins. Few of them acquainted with it before, but they were told after, but they did not know what was in it, drink nor plaster, before applied; he was told it was treacle done by Duke's mother. They did nothing but by general conference entered and written, they directed a plaster but to King's apothecary. If it was treacle would do no hurt, his fever did grow upon him worse and worse until he died, but he was better before, and they conceived the disease to be declining until that this was offered in the prohibited time, they rather disliked but would say nothing lest might offend Duke and the King. Doth not know that Duke did know the prohibited hours. Chambers and Ramsay and Cragthen. The bill of the ingredients was shewed after by Doctor Moore from Duke and justified in due time and place to be successful, but whether made of those particulars he knows not, the subscription was only of the Duke, they think this drink not good in this time. Doctor Moore not sworn physician to his knowledge nor told him that he made it, he knows not the effects, he was dry at his , his humours in good temper.

[April 25.] Sir Benjamin Rudyard moves subsidies lessened in the gentry not in nobility nor clergy, yet brought to half, whereas other men's lands are higher rented than of old; therefore desires to improve the old wages, for a gentleman at 20*l.* ennobled 300*l.* therefore desires by Exchequer rolls to be augmented, and to maintain ports at country charge, and ships, therefore desires we so proceed as to make the Parliament his favourite to exceed 4*s.* the pound.

Sir George Moore agrees, dislikes adding above 4*s.*; compares kingdom to a common pasture, care it be not overcharged, sellers makes fall buyers will not rise.

Wandesford desires a great committee as parliamentarily to proceed upon.

Littleton in the chair.

Vice Chamberlain, none to move unnecessaries nor long orations, wherein interlocution must avoid contention, accounts his message. When we proposed supply all our debate truly reported, King satisfied, expected we think of necessities in time, and preparation of aid, now how to amend it first in number, then in weight.

Stroude junior. The King's necessity though put on us, we did not agree to the 50*m l.* a month abroad, wherefore we did not bring it.

Clark speaks for dejected subjects, grievances sowed only in the ear, not redressed. Habeas Corpus stoppeth execution. precedency, extortion in Courts, crime, fees extraordinary in probate, citation for fees. Exchequer fees advanced 1*l.* in 2*s.* from 6*s.* 8*d.* to 18*l.* 6*s.* 8*d.* prescribe in 30 years so may it therefore.

Offices in all Courts Westminster alike; sheriffs sell their offices, now applies as in a field to long for the day, those drones he would cast out the Commonwealth the home he cites the hedgehog.

May not subsidies and grievances go on as well as subsidies and privy seals; now to give no more, but engage at next sessions, and so from sessions to sessions while war continues.

Sir Nicholas Saunders would not have subsidy, lest it be an annual revenue, besides cannot be maintained in this Court; therefore proposeth a help not new, honourable and profitable to King and pleasure to subject: wards and purveyance to be taken at contract, which King James gave way to, this provides for future—agreed to be 200^ml. by year.

Browne. No more Subsidies, but to augment them; those under 5l. to stand; above doubled; wards &c. good if feasible, so resumption.

Martius. Maturity of counsels, and means good, but both spend time, which lost they will not redeem, and though country's wants opposed to King's he thinks now [countable]; looks upon building porticoes apparell &c. tells the tale of the geese roasted by sticks—proposeth 2 s[ubsidies] 2 fifteenths.

Crew agreed supply, move a Committee of 12.

Sir Richard [Grovenor]. Give: not endanger Commissioners as 12 H. 7. and H. 4., times when the gift so great.

Diggs. Country poor; who otherwise say fit to be cast out of Court, if add more subsidies they will spare themselves: desires to advance the higher sort.

Kirton would not pay the dishonoured money: the rest to be considered of.

Chancellor Exchequer. If King not satisfied in 5 days must go to new counsels, now time to resolve actions though after council in power before—if time would suffer, to increase proportion of subsidies were good; though no success; no cause to deny payment. He recites particular charge fleet will take, all this [granted]. Presseth resolves of right understanding; King and people cannot be unless his holy anchor be taken hold of, therefore desires first to resolve to give, next how, and what presently.

Wandesford. To resolve to give, tomorrow what to give. Glanvile dare not blame counsels; desires to know from us how to ground them. If burden be greater than that the kingdom can bear will be amiss, therefore would not have us talk of poverty to encourage enemy. Desires to resolve to give, after consider what.

Sir E. Spencer hath a motion, but desires all to be brought in, to take the best.

Resolved to augment and enlarge the gift already intended to the King.

Doctor Betwin a sworn physician attended much. There was as he heard plasters and potions ministered, without assent as King told him, a julep given and a plaster to his stomach; order given for their medicines by one consent for most part, not for this. He heard it acknowledged that Duke told King he had used such plaster and it had done him good. He had a note given after of the ingredients, and he saw it, but knows not what was in it. Before the plaster given the disease somewhat declined: he came to him three or four days ere he died. The note was sent to them after King's death that day or next to know whether the plaster or julep did hurt; it was sent in a note Doctor Atkins hath, but Sir William Paddie or Doctor Moore hath it, they conjectured by smell of plaster it was like the note. Doctor Moore joined in advice before the plaster, and was most part there, they saw the King talk with him, and wished them to advise with him, and approved their opinions to agree often. Woolfe hath the note to which the hands are, who made them he knows not, he found his fever more, and yet no symptoms but before a stopping of his breath by other causes; the fever increased, he smelt it, it was of treacle as the note shewed, he saw no inconvenience in the plaster.

Doctor Chambers a sworn physician said there was a plaster when they were to purge, which they desired to be taken away when they purged about the fifth fit; it was above a fortnight ere he died. He heard no effect of it, but murmured because they consented not, but he was little worse, we directed a plaster before. They heard this plaster given divers; Warwick, Carie, Duke, and had done good before; that Hayes the King's surgeon applied it, as thinks, but he took it away. He was well the Saturday when he left, and on Monday ready to go abroad; to have fit that night, not well on Tuesday when he returned nor ever after: and Harvey, that night with King, told him the King worse that night, and if had like could not scape; the plaster he had was applied in cold fit, taken away in hot. The night after Ramsey and he watched in the violence of it; King said he was far worse. He comforted him, and said he abhorred hot drink, yea a toast in it, though they prescribed it: they gave me warm drink that makes me burn and roast so, and would have given more: but he was cold. The drink prescribed was but a posset, but he said that whatever was said was written down and brought to the Council in the morning.'

The drink the Duke gave was a posset with gillyflower he drank off, resolved, a hot drink after cold, and to refrain, but not burned. ' He would say, Will you murder me and slay me? What advised was underhand. Asked of the paper to certify, he was uncertain.

[Dr. Harvey.] A plaster applied to his side, thinks twice, first his fit worse, secondly done in the afternoon at the beginning his fit, the King desired it; commended by Duke as good for him, and Earl of Warwick his opinion asked before done; he gave no opinion because ingredients not known. He gave way to it, thinking it easy, and could do no harm; he thought it not against his opinion nor consultation, and King desired it, it being external, to work while he by; and it was hot, and at his hot fit they took it off. Lister present at the laying it on. The posset drink the Duke prepared; the King called for it, drank once or twice; because it was commended King desired it; because the medicine Duke and Warwick had used it, King determined to take it. He knows no advice of doctors to take it. Sunday; King heavy, he got him to rise; said better, but found heaviness at his heart on Monday, as in other fits, and he feared that fit would be worse because had less fit before, which he told physicians, his disease not mending when that done. He first that spoke of King's demise before that fit twice, and he was in fit before next consultation. Lister, Moore came; he thinks Atkins. Lister opposed the posset thinking King called for drink; the night before the ague in his opinion still increased: on Saturday at conference the physicians thought not the King was mending. The day the King died upon, knows Sir William Paddie brought the note: and it was approved and might be used: generally they disliked a plaster, but not this. They said the plaster was a secret of a man of Essex; Hayes laid it on, King liked it as approved and experimented it, and King took divers things whether they would [or] not, undervaluing physicians. He commended the posset.

Doctor Lister heard and saw a plaster applied; thinks it was of Limithridate (?) as said he smelt it and it seemed so; he was on Sunday with the King. Contrary to Harvie he was not present when applied, nor advised not in it: for the diet they advised [?moncorn]. King was loth to have plaster off; though at hot they disliked it, at cold good. He present at posset giving; who gave it he knows not, and he tasted of it after. Came with plaster, resolution was but restraint, if could do it well, but he wished him forbear, yet took it, and thought it could do no harm, for he observed the gilly-flowers in the taste of another pot, part of it wherein it came. Harvie there ; Moore joined in consultation subscribed it, let blood in known vein, and the fit more moderate but no declination ; he did wait till he died. Subscribed Doctor Paddie's note ; said he came from King or Lord Duke or both ; he never heard King dislike it.

Levestone heard of it, but not present at plaster; never heard King speak of it nor the drink, one fit better after the plaster.

Hayes, sworn surgeon. Plaster applied twice or thrice last Monday; he at doing of it, Lord Duke's folks brought it in.

Second time he put it on by King's command to make the plaster out of the box. Baker brought it up and tasted it when he gave it me, he put it on leather one to stomach twice. He told physicians of it some stood by 4 the clock afternoon and one always there : that night he went to bed till almost day, but he thinks he was at taking of it off, he heard the Duke not persuade him but told it had done such good, no physician disliked, it was left to the room keepers to dispose of, he knew it laid on before, some doctors not content with it, yet he did it by King's direction.

Arundel heard it called for and all present; Duke went to London and physicians directed ; he examined posset he saw made in Duke's Chamber. Baker one as he thinks perhaps he errs in that, Baker a barber, many about it, who brought it up he knew not ; he saw the King drink of it he helped to mix it with gillyflower, he thinks not one in the Chamber but did taste of it, he a great deal often. Syrup came with the box whether in bowl or tankard the posset was he knows not, trorgill or mithridate predominate in plaster, he neither said nor thought that doranis was in it.

Sir Edward Payton of toad's flesh, he said of frogs.

Doctor Moore no sworn physician came Thursday seven night to King before he died, he was there every day, he was at all consultations after he came save one ; he set his hand to them, agreed or parted. Apothecary Woolfe hath resolutions, no plaster directed by the physicians. A plaster applied not spoke of by the physicians that he knew. Warwick commended us Duke he saw it taken off. Harvie saw it applied but not knowing the contents he said he to blame. Crag and Harvie all day there taken off about 8 o'clock when cold fit left, lest with sweat fell off, whether Warwick and Duke commended it or not he knows not, a letter was written to the maker who writ it was London treacle and juice of citrons ; all joined to have the letter written. Hayes said it was plain posset drink with hartshorn in it, because Crag and Gib had spoke it did hurt, a note was made at Sir William Paddies instance what it was, not hurtful resolved ; after bleeding fit left but no declination of disease and ever after had a fever.

Buying offices Monday Exchequer Chamber.
Lord Morley's Bill Saturday first in turn.
To account upon oath on Monday.

[April 26.]   Wednesday how to augment supply.
Wilde cites the manner of tastes 8, 9th 10th habit seised his land H. 3 merchant noble.

Desires knight's service into socage.
Sir G. Moore : multitude of Commissioners, tenders subsidy.
Justice of Peace 20l. desires to add subsidy.

Sir John Savile at breach of treaties engaged all to do it and thinketh breach with Spain best peace being to this Kingdom. Other relief than subsidy. King must hold if we go on else we cannot undertake war, sell King's revenue he will go on, else lack endanger us; 3,000^l. men no sent to bear subsidy but a million from 4^s. to 8 he dislikes, remembers 2 subsidies first protested never to be precedented, yet precedented next Parliament, by him said no, if offer for words been accepted better to crown by 3 millions or this Baronet's arrears to pay to King to be 66^l. 13^s. 4^d. [   ] 100l. knight father dead not in field 30l., justice 20l., he being 30^l offers 15^l at first subsidy.

Sir William Bulstrode confident England send fleet to make Spain smite; dislike Spanish hearts in English bodies.

Recusants forfeits King's own and one subsidy more.

Hobie : Act of Parliament of subsidy powerful enough in fining [protesters] and choosing them; would take away certificates. Landlord pay highest subsidy laid of any land since Queen Elizabeth's time. Compares to Fleet Street Conduit if stopped to go to spring head and so come down not make a new well; this done adds a subsidy.

Carvell : to give out of usury practised by King, King extorted fees, sold office and Church livings, if a part of lawful penalty, acquitting the payers and punishing receivers only to produce it.

Carrington rejects this as too long, indeed impossible.

Smyth moves enhancement, double recusants.

Sir Edward Sands : necessary and difficult. King to others we to him engaged moves order we fly at all; first to amplify this—2, addition; 3, all projects; desires to sell on first for order, statute mentioneth utmost value, to increase it adds not to King for we cannot exceed utmost, not to enhance it to Queen Elizabeth's time, not now so alter. Building apparel furniture and signs of wealth. Causes of poverty, impositions add to poverty, we could do more for 5 than now for 7 by that means when Queen Elizabeth's subsidies number increased diminished in value fifteen and subsidy were 150^m, last under 70^m; he concurs with Sir John Savile titles of honour to pay [increment].

Wilson shews how Carleton taken at Lancaster had instruction to gather 70^m for Doway, expressed in a petition, and he cites Chancellor of Duchy to have it in his hands.

Chancellor Duchy had on examination sent off a contribution by hearsay from a man to no purpose so take heed of hearsay.

Wandesford approves Sir E. Sands but not to idolize supposeth the best way to increase, desires every county to bring in their subsidies and present their opinions.

Sir Dudley Diggs : the utmost value beyond charge and maintenance is intended in subsidy.

Sir P. Hamond : to make mean commissioners and move to meet together to assess by voices.

Vice Chamberlain : no orator nor actor, no loss of time against Elliott we must be *pro lege pro grege pro rege;* he had here we move conquest, not if we lose not opportunity D. Wymy [Weimar?] General of Denmark's force he gone back in despair for our confusion here Denmark hath 55^m men embrace opportunity shall have advantage ; Eliott's distinction, likes not of Eliott, likes not of augment and addition, desires one subsidy.

Chancellor Exchequer : the new proposition of difficulty requires new Parliament far beyond 5 days desired and the increase in those given. The conquering speech he doth dislike.

Secretary : certo this enlargment by us is but that which is given as before for King by Commissioners, may expect advancement we can do no more.

Resolved to add another subsidy to the 3 subsidies intended for supply.

Mr. J. Delbridge Factor had privilege being heard.

[April 28.] Thursday: agreed continuance of statutes to be on Saturday.

Spencer: to aid King move for tonnage and poundage to be brought to a book of rates and a remonstrance because of the last stay and then the Kings profit and our right to be remonstrated by a sub-committee.

D. D. moved farmers who take customs by Privy Seal to be sent for.

Ordered a sub-committee June to make rates, and a remonstrance desired: avoided, meet two Star Chamber.

Though customs taken before Parliament at change of King yet never after Parliament's as now, therefore the customs that received if contrary may be questioned, the question avoided lest send and not punish prejudice.

Glanvile commanded by 12 to report the plaster and the posset drink to King James before his death: he reports substance of process attended by sworn physicians, general direction nothing but by advice, particular moment a drink before fits, affirmatively none contrarying applied at prohibited times plaster and posset upon declination, it was done by direction of Duke continued most part of the night then took off grew worse, the raving &c. mentioned by one Hart and Draght. The note brought after to have subscription served to be good loco tempore, some directly denied it; that Paddie and Moore came from Duke upon some muttering, the posset likewise drunk, one saith King had it of Duke; 2, 3 refused another drink, once plaster taken off because made him worse he asked why worse. Ramsey &c. answered for cold: King said, It was that I had of the Duke.

They think it to be added to Duke's charge as a transcendent presumption of dangerous consequence.

Primrose his testimony urged by Sir Walter Earle in his confession; he saith he eat of it, that the Countess said now was the time to lay it on.

[April 28.] Umpton Crooke by privilege of Parliament had examinations taken against him in Chancery, by letter from Speaker suppressed, yet commissioners sent for though knew not but by his allegation that he was Parliament man, the party plaintiff also sent for because he said Crooke came in by bribery and corruption.

Bill of apparel reported by Norris.

We added proviso for war; on election if Lords dislike they offer conference, not we.

Waudesford reports the great Committee's resolution of the Select Committee, if the fact merit.

Consulted no physician but by common assent, they sent after medicine given to us, to Duke, and to King, to advise to give, to take no more.

Resolved that posset drink given contrary to direction, without advice, disliked after if madman excuse against common person excuse not against King.

Plaster given before King worse after, declining before he in King's Bench refused to lay it on so King's physicians dissuaded second time as he saith.

Doctor Moore recusant to practice.

The application and drink transcendent presumption, dangerous consequence.

· Regular potions receipt from Duke by Baker his recovery, his joy to be experimented for King given col Core. He contrary physician, being treacle only. Physicians say King compounded of inverting quality.

Hayes : King commanded to fetch Duke's plaster, how that he had from Duke made him sick.

Resolved Duke gave drink plaster applied by his direction.

Resolved as Select Committee this to be annexed to the Duke's charge.

They observed no contradiction but Duke's direction and contrary direction.

Maule not called because upon hearsay desired direct for another business which he found foul, never intended upon first two for life yet conceive somewhat material.

Chancellor Exchequer : these seem presumptions to us which to Kings and their near ones are but liberty, the word presumption seems to induce a crime, therefore thinks this to be no cause for a charge.

Sir John Eliot without knowledge or consent applied 2 they refused proceeding until taken off.

Sir F. Steward : King could not endure hot drinks as Chambers said, therefore how King could desire it judge.

Sir Thomas Gurnie : sorrow to speak here against opinion, once more after that conference, heard it at Court first and since that great rashness and indiscretion, if wise men always wise fools might beg.

· Newbery : Southampton had no evil intention when he would have ₁surprised Queen Elizabeth for an hour or two to have removed some from the Queen, yet was it adjudged treason.

. .Sir .Walter Tirrell shot at stag, killed King, no treason, no evil intention.

Duke received it 30, killed him 60. The boldness.

Resolved, an act of transcendent presumption of dangerous consequence.

Vice Chamberlain Diggs remembered so well of old that he cannot forget him late this not fit to be added if taken by most senses not to be added but as this, or if freer, wider, higher matter.

Marriott : why rested so great a while was a parliament before then, if no evil intent, no danger to him, why to be charged ; if this added silence the rest, thinks the Committee intended well to preserve blood royal rather than impeach him so dear to the King and same. Cites Ambassador [Crive] from Venice a letter writ from him so opposite to Pope or Spain as he hold a patriot of that Commonwealth.

Muscano his Secretary gathered matter of infamy to disgrace his master's merit ; he therefore sent for, imprisoned 3 years, the master came home, after the inquisitions upon fame enquired witnesses could not justify, cost lives ; the man brought such particulars as seemed to accuse, and condemned to higher court where to death he hung out.

His name razed out, confiscation.

They out of office as 6 monthly now found first false, the second just witnesses ; executed ; restitution by Court ; all that could be but could not give life.

We concluded fair cause to enquire, we have proceeded to accuse. Concluded as before, we remit it to other courts. What they will do we know not who may not be accused by fame, have a commission of enquiry, therefore desires this charge not to be added.

Long justifies his argument fire and ashes, he spoke of the ashes in free conscience he judge equal to and not in indite, he had rather to have this set on Duke than this house having so far condemned the fact, we but inquisitors they to judge.

That Committee resolved this to be annexed to Duke's charge.

[April 29.] Vice Chamberlain shows how the plague in Paris and Venice, and other great cities through Government doth little hurt, in other places such excess; desires a bill, offers his knowledge to help.

Can the King make no profit by the ordering.

Chancellor Exchequer: King having given way against Duke, and hearing of new matter to be brought against Duke, wherein desiring his honour should not be in suspense, desires not hinder the business of commonwealth; it may be presented cares not whether to King or Lords.

Montagu resolved to be transmitted with the charge and aggravation 1. Publishing doctrine contrary English church established by the articles and homilies. 2. Seditious passage to disturbance of church and state. 3. To draw English to Romish, disgrace of Protestant divines.

Profaneness and scurrility at preaching and other divine exercises.

Required by Sir Nathaniel Rich to be transmitted by message to be delivered at Lords' bar by Mr. Pim, as formerly done by Sir Edward Hobie against Bishop of Durham.

Resolved accordingly, and the exceptions to be left in writing with the Lords, first to be approved by the Committee.

Monday 9 of clock French porter stayed to be put to question upon Duke.

Mr. Selden: in Sir Robert Howards' case, the High Commissioners under Lords to be questioned and questions prepared by Committee.

Sir H. Martin heard before proceeded to censure; acknowledgeth if true the offence great. Recites the resolution of the house of his claim that ought to be allowed, denied.

He a Commissioner, but denieth breach of privilege. Mentioneth 2 answers both good, one for the men, another for the matter, the matter is resolved and now must believe for the man.

He maketh 4 heads. 1. He knoweth not that he ought to have privilege. 2. Not bound by reason to know it. 3. He overruled and passive as he. 4. It becomed not his degree.

To the first. Parliament begun February continued till May divers prorogations by proclamation last from 3 of March till 20 of April. King died 27 March; his first wrong was 5 of March, if he did ever the first day he Parliament man notorious honourable etc., then claimed no Parliament, [March] 17 he argued it shewed how Keeper gave privilege for that. Keeper denied for that all reasons avoided as no good challenge so to have privilege he knew not.

2. Judge though must know things proper to his Court yet not things *dehors* as physic, Parliament, he not experienced, not read, so not bound by law or reason to know it, he understood not difference 'twixt prorogation and adjournment, but if Parliament had sat reason might prove it but not now upon adjournment; where he sits alone he will allow it and *peccare tutiore*.

3. He overruled he gave no opinion it came not so low as control, but overruled as he was.

4. When all Lords there he had no power, and discretion would not be should speak but when it is not in his element.

Should he say to Lord President, you have been judge of law have no knowledge; and contradict, he a judge at his cost, attends not of his will nor of purpose, confesseth an error in knowledge.

29 Elizabeth, Martin's case time of privilege uncertain, now students say 16 days allowed, clerk of Parliament saith no, therefore not to be intended to have so great knowledge as to know it, desires now upon occasion to think well of it for 25 to 8 it came in upon head of Church. 1 Elizabeth settled, it checketh Popery until Gondomar took out recusants from it; prayeth since they have no profit to have good opinion.

Speaker to speak with his hat off that is a member, so put off to Sir H. Martin when he questioned him upon interrogatories.

Ordinary Commissioners do not imprison closely nor excommunicate and imprison simul et semel.

[May 1.] The young Lord Digby under 16 years petitions the Commons and desires to be inherited of his honour unspotted more than any other thing, and his petition saith aspersions were cast upon his father by L.D. both before the King and both Houses in Parliament, and his father petitioned Lords in Parliament shewing how the Duke had abused in his relation both the King and both the houses and desired that we to be pleased to hear him to avoid the aspersions else to clear his honour of those imputations laid upon him upon record, and he annexed the copy of the articles his father did present in the Lords' house against the Duke ut sequitur.

1. That Duke conspired with Gondomar to carry the Prince now King into Spain to be perverted in religion and instructed in their religion.

Porter acquainted with it and messages delivered by Porter for a ground of that matter, and upon Porter his return leave gotten for the Prince to come yet plotted and purposed by Duke before.

3. That Duke possessed Spain with his intention of their religion yea so far concurred as to adore their sacrament and came not to our prayers there and caused Spanish to propose worse conditions than before for matter of religion.

4th. That Duke often moved King James to write to the Pope and a letter drawn which he so opposed that the Duke obtained it not while Bristoe here. Duke after procured letter to Pope writing therein *Sanctissime Pater.* Pope sent a Bull to him Duke to procure him to proceed to convert the Prince.

6. He discontented Spain so in his course that Spain broke off the match in dislike of him for his aims not obtained was the cause of breach.

7. He made use of Prince's letters to his own ends and by counsel.

8. That King abused both houses in every particular of his narration which he will prove.

6. In procuring favours from Spain bestowed by Duke on base persons for his lusts' satisfaction.

10. He being solely sent Ambassador did leave such scandal behind him ; he cause of palatinate not restored.

11. He wronged Bristoe in these aspersions.

12. That he Earl Bristoe revealed all this to the King James who assured to hear him and said he would hear him, he sent a little before his death when he being perplexed by the Duke died, being much pressed with the Duke his miscarriage towards him.

[May 2.] Sir D. Diggs reports the evils, two, diminution of honour and strength, stoppage of trade.

Causes next resolved.

1. Seas not guarded since treaty.
2. Plurality of offices.
3. Honours sold.
4. Honours of men not deserving.
5. Exhausting and intercepting King's Revenue.
6. Selling Judicature places.
7. Ships to Rochell sent [against] our religion.
8. East Indies merchant oppressed 10ᵐ*l.* extorted.

9. *St. Peter* of Newhaven stayed whereby a general embargo.

10. Consideration of the King's sickness, physic and plaisters Duke applied without physicians assent.

Find body 4 parts.

1. Offices consist of many parts in him and others, buying Admiral. Wardenry neglect abuses 5 blemishes first extorting Indies, delivering ships, practising against Rochell.

2. Honours sale. King's loss by it.

3. Intercepting and exhausting with particulars.

4. The King's death.

Drawn into articles by the lawyers of the 12 offices proof or to look it by calendar as every particular is suited with his proof.

1. Duke's offices having been exercised by several persons, and every one requiring an able man he young ambitiously got them, excluded deservers of hope.

Admiralty bought against statutes for justice, castles or fortresses, he adjudged disabled to hold it. Duke gave for the office and surrender 3000*l*. to Admiral, and an annuity of 1000*l*. per annum for his life, whereupon Duke got them for life 28 January, 16 James. These do concern justice, and he useth them against the law.

Wardenry of Cinque Ports and constable of Dover.

Duke paid 1000*l*. to Lord Zouch and 500*l*. per annum, he surrendered to King, and Duke obtained them, 6 December, 22 James. These concern justice and fortresses.

Treasurership, December, 18 James, procured by him to Lord Manderville, for which he received 20000*l*.

Master of Wards to Cranfield, for which he is since by him appointed, had 6000*l*.

East Indies ships warlike to be nourished. Duke by colour of Parliament abusing the house hearing of [Ormous?] good success, moved Lords whether he might stay, agreed, he might, when petitioned, he denied stay by him, but offered to move for them, yet gave leave after preserved in Admiralty to bring in 15^m*l*. after petitioned Duke, protest no release till he agreed. 23 of March they considering their loss agreed to give him the 10^n. for his false pretence of rights.

Narrow seas not guarded, Duke ought to endeavour to supply wants from Lords and King. Duke for 2 years last hath neglected his duty and broken trust whereby the strength decayed, seas infested by pirate and the dominion like to be lost.

Peter of Newhaven laden with 40^m*l*. in amity with King taken by his extraordinary commission upon pretence of Spain; and cochineal, gold jewels worth 20^m*l*. taken out delivered by Duke to Marsh though ship and goods ordered to be delivered and so decreed except hides ginger &c. yet Duke did detained the things to his use, and after unjustly caused the ship to be detained.

Ships as fortresses to be kept no man to be dispossessed of his property in his goods. Duke as Admiral did procure the Vanguard with all furniture to be sent into France, and with menaces caused 6 merchants with her to be delivered to the French King contrary to his office.

Against Rochell he contrary to King's zeal knowing them to be employed against Rochell our religion, and so used since, contrary to King's purpose yet intimated they were not nor should be so employed at Oxford contrary to King's purpose and abuse of both houses.

2. Compulsion to buy honour whereas honours due to virtue he perverted it and enforced Robert Rich to buy honour against his will.

Procuring honours to kindred mother brothers and allies by him whereby noble barons prejudiced and King disabled by their grants and pensions.

3. Intercepting and exhausting King's revenue; he not content what had got 14 James procured 700^l old rent, 16 James 120^1 old rent to have reprisal of bailiffs fees &c. evil precedent; after he surrendered 700^1 per annum and got other lands in lieu, and tallies struck for money paid never received but by him.

Disbursed King's monies besides all his rewards got, Privy Seals for allowance of payments and releases. Got like monies for Navy contrary to Exchequer Order, and his estate so mixed with King's as not discernable. Got releases of his receipts for his honour's maintenance.

14 June 14 James Beckelsone 700l. And then the Schedule was read reciting the particulars; his endeavour to get the prizes to Marsh's hands.

To Sir Anth. Ashley for marrying his cousin a blank.

4. The King's physic: where physicians to be sworn, King's person so sacred as none to minister otherwise. His physicians upon consultation nothing to be done but by general advice and commanded a restraint before fit. Duke contrary his duty and these, caused certain plasters to be prepared and drink to be ministered, notwithstanding it had evil effects and that physicians refused until removed, he when King in declination made them be applied and given, whereupon great distempers and evil symptoms appeared, and physicians did after advise Duke to do so no more, which is by us resolved a transcendent presumption of dangerous consequence.

Cary of countess of Middlesex and [Hertford].

The officer of conference said that the 6000^l was disbursed.

Sir Robert Howard heard and believed that Berkshire was to have 5000^l or 15^m. out of Brayden for Master of the Horse.

Sir Robert Pie saith 3000^l of Duke's monies paid to Lord Admiral about the time.

Sir William Russell: that 5000l. for navy was reimbursed by Treasurers to Duke, employed upon navy 3^m. paid about villany.

He had a commission to take prizes adjudged to dispose by Duke's command now a new commission in purpose at King's dispose.

Sir John Epsley: a commission to how St. Peter (?) have to sell the prizes and bring to Exchequer before upon necessity sold 800^l. to pay labour.

Sir William Howard.

Sir William Munson: that upon resignation of the Admiralty he was offered privy seal had Mowbray annexed, received the 3000^l.

Sir Robert Pie had the 6000^l. again and 120$^{m\ 1}$. more when he made Treasurer.

Lord Cary said that Middlesex told him when he Master of Requests agreed this in effect by Falkland.

Chancellor Exchequer moves after orders of transmission to have the subsidy proceed to passing for until passed as law cannot have credit, ordered to-morrow morning to be done.

[May 3.] 8 of the 12 each assisted with two to deliver the Duke's charge; 2 to prologue and epilogue; six to the parts.

The eight, Diggs Eliott Earle Pim Selden Whitby Wandesford Herbert; each one two assistants. The assistants to enable them with reasons, precedents to speak, but not to speak; the 24 to agree how to distribute the business amongst them.

Litleton reports resolves; the increase by a subsidy to be paid the last of July 1527.

So resolved *nullo contradicente* in house.

Sir Diggs desires from committee 12 to know whether they shall proceed with more, to enquire of new, and proceed with what hath some proof of.

Speaker accords.

Chancellor Exchequer from King expects an end of inquisition and that Commonwealth be no more hindered nor his honour in suspense, but to be presented.

Eliott: to preserve our liberty not lay them by, but to have liberty still to present more.

Diggs presents preamble and conclusion last read we by protestation saving liberty to add, and reply, and to offer proof; pray Duke to be put to answer and such proceeding examination may be had of every of them as to law and justice.

The preamble shows how the Commons by their Bill declares against the Duke of Buckingham with all his titles misdemeanours misprisions offences and [crimes] hereafter following and him do thereof accuse.

Sir Ed. Sands thinks not necessary both to plead it verbally and deliver it in articles too, for so was done in Middlesex case.

Diggs intended both, and to enforce them with proofs and precedents.

In Sir Robert Howard's case resolved that the proceedings in the High Commission against him within the sixteen days of the day of prorogation, notwithstanding the proclamation for further prorogation shall be all annihilated and all that ensued thereupon void.

But after long debate resolved not to write to the High Commissioners, because most Lords, to annihilate them, both because it is against our dignity to entreat and not prevail, so likewise not to command because we cannot enforce.

And though moved that there being a sufficient number of commoners Commissioners to keep a court and to annihilate the proceedings, yet they being opposed by the Lords the greater; therefore that way also shunned.

But the commoners Commissioners being brought in and reprehended were admonished to see it done and at expectation; if not then to join to Lords since but one body and the wrong to our privilege equal.

In this case was cited the case of two knights Sir William Pope and Sir   Marshall in chancery, where a decree being given for money promised upon sale of honours was by order of this house sent to Lord Keeper by Sir Edward Sackville now Lord of Dorset to be taken off the file, but our order neglected and nothing done upon it.

For if any Court of Westminster break our privilege because they are members of the Lords' house it seems we have no remedy but to complain to the Lords.

[May 4.] Sir Thomas Hartop Sheriff of Leicestershire for offering an arrest upon a commission of rebellion to Sir H. Hasting being in election for Knight of Shire, though he elected yet brought to bend on his knees and upon submission ordered to pay charges, and discharged.

Moved by Drake, Sir James Parrett to retract pensions, disafforest, to take recusants' lands to supply King.

Sir George More: a commission was 7 years since for this, where these and many more are inquired of; it was a summer's work.

Bish moves the words in and a message to the King to ask.

Ordered a Committee to draw a remonstrance to King for rectifying his revenue upon these grounds to-morrow Exchequer Chamber.

Sir John How then moves to consider since in suspense whether Duke cause of evils in religion.

Corrington to note it if he adored in Spain as in articles alleged ; to hear witnesses.

Sir L. Dives names Everard as a witness.

Sir Robert Pie notes how he hated by Papists ; infers that this a practice of Papists, he observes the current of those that 18 James went one away now go another way. Dislikes this ; supplemental proof is with Lords, let them there try it for their lives.

Vice Chamberlain : unless this zeal turns into fire, motion turns sometimes into commotion, he doth desire preventive care ; who may not put off his hat when sacrament came by, as he did, Lord Admiral of old did, he hated because that this match affects not papacy, so Spain hates because he served not them, Olivares hates because he suffered not Prince to be converted ; he joined in articles against Armenian most freely under his hand.

Kirton thinks he hath so carried that he may be hated of both Protestant and Papist ; desires the notice taken of young Digby's petition in it, never had one so charged stood before King and to tarry in Parliament, desires to go to Lords to have him removed.

Wandesford enforceth if it be but complaint less matter, yet he Ambassador representing King to adore mass, in such matter of treason to be sent for.

Sir John Epsley shows how King of Spain played tricks and kneeled never before to draw in our King, he did not nor Duke but Sir John did, Duke knocked him on head to rise, and did call him great ass.

Speaker enforceth it as a charge directly in the petition, not upon fame, but direct, and desireth direction.

Eliott mentioneth the treason charged on Duke by Bristoe in Lords' house fit to be committed as in felony not allowed ; hears this not prosecuted, wonders at his power, England Ireland Scotland elsewhere this affrights, he to stand uncommitted, moves if Lords have not done their duties we to desire it of the Lords.

Petition to King considering his charge our greatest supply, conceive best to maintain it to strengthen his revenue to the ease of the Commons as he desires, wherein offers our service which we hope to shew to his honour and profit.

[May 5.] The Wire Drawers counsel heard in the house urged against Bill of Apparel that it was profitable to King's Commonwealth, to have the trade, for they give $3d.$ the ounce for bullion where the Tower for Mint gives but $\frac{1}{2}d.$ which occasioneth much custom, and bullion to come in ; they also shew how of $1l.$ they make $3l.$ how our money is now unprofitable to convert, that all that is worn leaves still a third part after the wearing.

A committee to be to pen a preamble to subsidy because increased from 32 Elizabeth first two unto 4 and 8 fifteens 43 Elizabeth, more King James time, now in more haste than ever.

Hoby urged out of King's message nothing to be done until Duke transmitted.

Sir Benjamin Rudyard not to suspect King to take money and refuse justice, some think King cannot govern humour when needs press, he thinks freeness better th'other humour for Italy.

Salt Salt (sic) agreed for the patent.

The order read not to come in until grievance be answered 27 March then the other order read for the last subsidy. ·

Chancellor Exchequer desires good reason why bill subsidy not to be brought in, none so near as we to King, speaks with passion, before he speak what King commanded, and until find them faulty desires to think they speak with equal affection.

King desired if out of jealousy we delay the subsidy he take it as neglect of his affairs and his person.

His former message mistaken, bill of subsidy to come in last.

Wilde moves after grievances by Whitby to be presented after Duke thinks toucheth on liberty.

Chancellor Duchy privileges gained by King's request.

Chancellor desires committee for preamble as suiting King's ends; have not we our own ends in it.

Carnell : we come only to give subsidies; wisheth his treasure may be as Queen Elizabeth not to be on suddens but out of providence before need. So 18 James subsidies granted ; hope to sit, but all dissolved ; so shows all failure of promises on states part, therefore first purge corruptions, then give, therefore prays no bill in till order be performed and grievance answered.

Waudesford : to hold our power, agree to committee but not to cross any way first order, no jealousies to be talked of when we delay but proceed parliamentarily, hopes all so cleared no putting off again give King a committee ourselves the time.

Vice Chamberlain : this motion begun in March now May, question not whether give but to set pen : *qui egrotant animo dolorem non sentiunt*, grievance sick of, see not the sword upon us, prejudice to report, soldiers mutineers, time passed friends despair because intend only, the fear of Carnell hinderance, grievances redressed by justice and grace from King's good heart but great hurt, will give both, sell neither, if we proceed thus committee may do what will but when this published is it not abuse.

Desires to accommodate and proceed to both glad upon petition of estate will be sufficient; shall we be talking of grievance until enemy come upon us, desires committee presently to consider our first occasion.

Eliott : interruption cause of delay not want of sense, we sick in mind feel not body, he said *animus sequitur corpus* the body grieved.

He answers King great hurt we contract not the other great hurt they intend, desires King know we confident on him, desires him so of us ; moves Tuesday Committee.

Savile Exchequer Chamber Tuesday there.

18 James Sir Robert Flood Sir H. Britton cast out as a projector so moved for Mr. Moore for his monopoly of the Salt patent.

[May 6.] Order from King James to take off the file proceedings in High Commission against Bishop of Bangor.

D. Diggs : introduction and preamble.

Herbert : plurality, buying of offices.

Selden : narrow seas, *Peter* stayed.

Glanvile : Rochell ships, East Indies, extortion.

Honour judicature Whitby.

Honours ; maintenance of King's revenue portions and consumption of physic ; Wandesford.

Conclusion, recapitulating, Eliott.

Speaker none to except but poundage.

Commons declare and accuse Duke of misdemeanours misprisions offences and crimes.

Chancellor Duchy asketh upon what ground we go by bill in this form unprecedented of late.

Selden : of late we accused by word St. Albans and Middlesex ancient words and writing ; 50 E. 3, 28 H. 6. 10 R. 2. examples of both. 50 E. 3. Adam de Burie accused by Long ; bill hereunto annexed so 28 H. 6.

Allowed by question the bill of preamble to go.

2. Plurality of offices procured by him by exorbitant ambition to discouragement of others ; allowed.

3. Who buy offices direct or indirect &c. he disabled. The Duke bought Admiralty and surrender of it to intent to obtain it and got amity of King, and he occupied them ever since contrary statutes ; allowed.

4. Cinque Ports in like sort allowed.

5. Where Duke ought to have kept seas and endeavoured to get supply from King and Lords he neglected trust, whereby trade decayed, infested with pirates.

Sir Robert Maunsell saith narrow seas is fro Calis to Beachy Head, and therein no haven, meant off sea coasts.

6. *Peter* of Newhaven, Mellein Master, Duke retained gold pearl to his use and stayed ship to public violation of justice.

Vice Chamberlain's letter sent into the house that they wonder we so follow private quarrels that a Brussel's recital in *St. Peter* transcends the house his sense, for meant only the illegal stay.

1. Makes *Peter* seised first by pretence of Spanish.

2. We give scandal to Governor of Newhaven, *scandalum datum et acceptum*, desires to proceed, this to be recommitted.

Eliot wonders that any private man should say that it is against sense of the house, which is the act formerly, thinks the exception unnecessary and recommitment necessary.

Chancellor Exchequer desires forbearance humbly of sharp reprehension.

Pim affirms they [objected] parliamentarily and desires his motion may be effected.

7. East India Company : Duke abused Lords in Parliament, extorted 10^m*l*. which he by his minister from February agitated, in March twelvemonth moved Lords, 5 March said he no occasion of stay, desired their reasons yet gave leave to fall down to Tilbury, he procured suit lor 15^m*l*. not released until he satisfied in his false pretence.

Glanvile conceives we abused in our desire of stay by answer Duke had stayed it before.

Recommitted as *St. Peter* was.

8. Rochell ships delivered and law of property of the merchants' ships taken : allowed.

9. The employment of them against religion contrary to King's intention and abused both houses by intimation and violating the treaty.

10. Perverted old way ; made Roberts purchase his Lordship of Truro by threatening.

Glanvile moves that Lord Roberts may have a cause not to be dishonoured because compulsion.

Sir Robert Pie and Sir William Strowde ; that he did offer 20,000*l*. for it before and was denied by Duke.

11. Lord Treasurer and Master of Wards, sold, Duke procured.

12. Honouring his kindred who on King's revenues maintain to prejudice Barons by their [victuals ?] ; allowed.

13. Intercepting and exhausting King's revenue, not satisfied with what King gave, procured a grant of mandamus 32^m*l*; got monies for

victualling navy whereof King can expect no account being out of
Exchequer way, addeth a schedule of other particulars 14 Jan. 14 James
700*l.* rent.

1623—Whaddun -	- 51 3^s	Exchange with		
Hartington	- 700^l	York House	-	- 140^l
14 James—Combe, &c.	- 114^l	1622 -	-	- 160^l
Bisley Gloucester	- 53			⎧ 800^l
Timber wood -	- 80	Earl Norris	-	⎨ 1636
Slate -	- 500^l	1200^l -	-	- 4000^l
One Rent	- 56	995^l -	-	- 1860^l
Leystone	- 114	9850^l -	-	- 1000
	11981 4	600000^l -	-	- 1906^l
		for navy -	-	- 476
		20^{ml} -	-	- 3284
Pensions paid by King 2000^l.		pensions 2^{ml}	-	- 30000^l
for him, his endeavour for prizes		Ireland 7^{ml}	-	—
60^m Middlesex fine 20^m.		per annum -	-	- 2500

Middlesex got by kindred marriage 120^m*l.* To Sir E. Villars 3,000*l.*
Pertock a pension of 1,000*l.* by year.

14. King James his physic ministered presumptuously and the particular supposition of the 2 witnesses recited.

Epilogue; Duke to be put to answer and according to law and justice
to proceed.

To meet afternoon at the committee and to vote all as well committed
as these alluded.

Monday 7 [*sic* 8?] May.
Vice Chamberlain reports King's answer.

That King content that we consider his revenue; desires committee
not great lest his weakness be discovered, his officers shall attend.
Desires we to set down heads and acquaint him with, and King will
assent both to rectify and to augment King's revenue as we desire.

For license of ordinance transporting King his father granted it, that
Lords of Council did think it no error to transport by license thinking
it a popular error.

King desires us to have reasons that moved Lords; to do then what we
will.

Desires Committee to send for proofs to give information.

Desires Committee for estate to be limited.

For the speedy redress of the evils the kingdom suffereth and for the
King's honour the commons prefer this bill of titles and accuse the
Duke.

By protest saving reply, further proof, new accusation, desires law
and justice.

2 H. 6. Sir John Mortimer.

17 E. 4. Accusation before Lords against Duke of Clarence, Lords did
not commit but Commons came up and requested it and he was committed
to Tower.

Vice Chamberlain: they have used precipitation and we shall spend
more time about it, then we have to go to conference, where we want
example, must care what we leave to posterity, his saying after [learned?]
in precedents.

He speaks lest Republic consisting of King, Peers, Commons be
disturbed.

King gave liberty with regret, we to proceed but on what before us.

Shall we oppose him whom King hath thus declared his affection, if not forborne at King's request yet go not too far.

If Lords will not, how can we mend it, consider lest offends Lords.

Temps E. 3. Baron [Graystock] Captain of Berwick left it to Lieutenant; he adjudged to death because taken though Lieutenant died in place.

11. R. 2. R. Weston not dying in the castle hanged and drawn.

St. Peter stayed against common Law and the marine law.

Diggs in his preamble compared commons to earth the centre, judges to air that counsel them in their labours, Lords to planets, King to sun, Duke to a prodigious comet drawn out of the dross of the earth even above the planets as one said to be into the chair of Cassiopœia which prognosticates the ruin of commonwealth ; said the many evils we suffered in the large circumference by many signs drawn from one point, the Duke.

Resolved Wednesday 8 o'clock to proceed with the other half of Duke's charge to committee of Lords.

Mr. Noy to the question of Duke's commitment to be desired at Lords upon notice of the commitment with the Lords, ours charging him but as misdemeanours.

2. H. 6. Sir John Mortimer committed for treason to H. 5. broke prison, made it high treason by commission indicted at York Castle, sent into Chancery, delivered in Parliament by Chancellor by King's command brought to Lords' bar by lieutenant of Tower. Indictment read before all Lords and Commons, he confessed, Commons prayed judgement, he hanged drawn and quartered set up, not committed at Commons request for there before.

Hear Digby as we hear articles.

Now whether Commons thrust in or called in office.

Informed Digby gives articles ; another saith, it is treason ; this is no ground for us.

Upon once reading we not fit to pray commitment for treason for we forejudge Lords.

If we pray Lords to be acquainted with it then if they give leave we may examine and proceed as the cause requireth.

Browne thinks on his carriage slighting therefore "dicere causam in vinculis," but not until his charge be given.

Wandesford : we came with jealousy that things would prove as now, gathered at Oxford where Parliament was rent in pieces he being named, though we offered to supply.

All causes meet like a centre upon him ; he wonders at his confidence not his innocence, therefore we to require commitment, slight Noy's precedent, thinks the things we charged fit be in other names. King committed Somerset for felony.

If want a precedent to make this a precedent.

Treason alleged, one part proved, thinks we may justify it to the Lords, and then to leave it to God.

Chancellor Duchy fears new precedents lest end not in ourselves, if we do new, King new, Lords new, a sharp spirit hurts his cause desires moderation ; we cannot require it but by taxing Lords, God [grant] our posterity curse not us as ancestors did passionately ; suppose treason put against 12 of us should we presently commit our members.

Fulgoone : we sit here to make precedents, his yesterday carriage fit for commitment.

Corriton takes hold of 12 of us, this the cry **of the whole land, thinks** words to be added to the charge to require.

Sir G. Moore fears not new precedents for **reason did guide the first,** thinks justice will not allow us **to commit before we examine the cause** as in all cases, therefore moves stay.

5. R. 2. Complaint not treason, confessor sequestered from Court, but at 4 feasts.

11. R. 2. M. De la Porte got crown lands without consideration; he answered, Commons replied, committed before judgment to constable, after bailed.

21. R. 2. Canterbury accused of treason for executing articles, commitment desired, Lords advised.

1. R. 2. Sir John Farrar for giving ports and forts to French, though committed cleared, yet re-committed

To propose reasons to Lords whether commit or no.

Chancellor Exchequer : this request of commitment is a prejudice which ought not to be but upon certain knowledge with full authority, doubts if do.

We cannot believe him guilty yet which is the first judgment, for he hath yet a right to his fame, therefore no certain punishment upon uncertain crime, late no such precedents, last if authority either of the cause or person.

Digby's copy is but a relation, if we proceed offered the cause, therefore to leave it to Lords.

Long heard Speaker say it was felony if one give physic and the other die being no physician.

Littleton : nothing with us to commit for but misdemeanours, so all judges opinion 28 H. 6. Duke Suffolk. For things depending before Lords we may move the Lords parliamentarily.

Upon accusation of treason we may pray commitment howsoever it be, so here.

This sticks with him ; here is no [appeal ?] therefore cannot but go conditionally.

Fanshaw 1 Hen. 4. no appeal for treason, shall be preferred in Parliament, in time to King.

Selden : for our own accusations we may, for the other charge we ought. 29 Hen. 6. in like presentment as we.

Duke accused for conspiring with Gondomar to carry Duke [sic : ? Prince] to Spain to be converted in religion ; this a persuading King's Subject to treason, this is treason, by 23 Elizabeth, 30 less to bring from Rome excommunication so 12 Rich. 2. adjudged in Parliament, because one procured King to write to Pope to make Ireland a kingdom, as derogatory from King.

Notice sufficient if hear but of it, but now it is a record there we may take notice of it.

They perhaps have reason not to do it on proof, we none.

2 Hen. 6., 17 Ed. 4. we desired judgment upon their record, because we affirmed indictment true supposed then we may and did then examine it.

We have sent to call for their Lords absent. 11 Rich. 2., 17 Ed. 4. whole house prayed judge upon Duke of Clarence.

For 1 Hen. 4. whether accusation there properly by appeal in Parliament.

How appeals expanded knows not, but 7 Hen. 4. many rolls of accusation there : so 17 Ed. 4. but that an Act of Parliament, all present.

Vice Chamberlain sees neither precedent nor reason to guide him, precedents on both sides, to do what just and equity; no accusation in Lords' House, this against Duke but a recrimination be it either if he committed evil consequence.

Lord Conway desired to be committed by Bristoe, refused by Lords, the times noted, precedents full of faction and destruction. Philip Commines said when God left English and fell upon themselves lost all in France.

Duke's carriage aggravates instead of compassion, let us not be carried into an evil course.

1 James. Sir H. Neville, no gallery then but as good reverence, presented 10 points, 1 of treason, for as it stood no man knew when he was safe, desired it to be no longer. Committed *ad poenam* we cannot do unheard and custodian needs not, he will not fly.

Fortescue remembers thing 1 James. Sir Francis Goodwin returned knight, a competition all business stayed till that King desired to let them both alone, Goodwin   and so done.

Diggs: if these might not trouble us he wished he in the upper world.

He thinks commitment necessary; appeals of Committee outed for parting; not so in accusation, we not so but on our own grounds we may go on.

Dudley Diggs thinks him dishonoured by his confession of Cinque Ports and casting first stone he wondered, therefore cause, thought men would make him see his fault; he was struck at his presence, too much countenancing to see and hear his accusation but Middlesex, St. Albans, Norwich, all not like him though he not discouraged; he thinks it fit to be done, it is upon record not answered, therefore desires to decline; this no recrimination attorney accuseth Bristoe, no precedent prejudicial he remembers Chancellor Duchy neglect precedent now to use precedent of power when never like precedent of power.

Then not to fear confronting.

Resolved on Tuesday we sitting until three of clock that we go with a request to Lords for Duke his commitment and a committee to prepare the manner.

The house divided upon the question, 226 for commitment, 125 no, when ayes gone out noes would yield they to have honour in it, would not take it, the house within would also go out; the greater number opposed and did make a terrible contestation offering &c. and fearful to see what a great number opposed will not do, the lesser number glad to yield to what desired though Privy Council there said the greater number might fine and imprison less.

[May 11.] Thursday.

Gyles the person sent for at Balan's suit for his scandalous life, and his doctrine and notes in the margin of the Book of the Synod of Dort scaring our writers, esteeming most fables and lies.

The Commons taking into their serious consideration the manifold and apparent mischiefs and inconveniences under which this renowned kingdom suffereth, threatening danger to it, have by search of causes found that they do principally flow by the abusive carriage of the Duke of Buckingham, whereof he hath been now impeached by us before you, besides an accusation by a Peer before you of treason as we hear; therefore they with one voice declare, holding it dangerous for present and future that a man of his eminence so accused should hold such strength and sit as Peer to know the counsels; wherefore thought it duty as by law and reason to commend their unanimous consent, as to desire that they will commit the Duke his person to safe keeping.

Lords returned answer **by Nathaniel Rich who carried up the message**
that they would return answer **by their own messengers and consider** of
it in due time.

Then were Sir Dudley Diggs who made the prelogue or preamble, and
Sir John Eliott who made the epilogue, sent for by two messengers; the
servant told them that two messengers were come for them privately,
and they did go out and were carried to the Tower, supposed for their
presumptuous carriage or aggravation and amplification of things &c.

All at silence till restored safe, they cleared by protestation.

[May 12.] Vice Chamberlain when we in silence desires to continue
it till done, notes Pim to have moved well to proceed wisely to stay the
cry of rising, he riseth to speak to waken the silence, he thinks it time
to get off the rock we fallen upon.

Tells his story; he at sea out of way fell on divers sands; at length
stuck; all amaze, one 'stood up to see which way we came on, by the
compass went same way back.

He now a passenger not the pilot desires to look how we came on,
and so to go off we had like [tortoises?] before, never stuck until now;
desires some to think how we came on, in missing our course, former
Parliaments have done it and rectified themselves, if he fell on
particulars desires the house not to apply it to the house.

Found in former Parliaments the silencer parrot the wisest so it be
not in opinionality as now : we came on to the rock by an order to give
them leave to enforce their matter at the conference, proved a meeting,
but what did enforce matter we bound to maintain by six; the matter
went within compass except a slip but for preface and conclusion against
a man; he saying he yet *rectus in curia* cried no; by many offered to
stay if we weary; if not *rectus* not condemned: they called him still
" this man, this man " prologue and epilogue still touched on him " this
man, this man." Sir F. Bacon used to introduce his matter by poetry and
history a man most elegant though likened to a meteor, yet was . . over
King, every one bound to find causes of evils and remedies, evil they
taken away he hears for scandal in words taken by King touching the
point of King's death as though it were hastened prologue said by [means
used]; he would therein forbear to speak further, in regard of the King's
honour that is now living. King's reason to be sensible, for strangers
in Court believe it was said; this depends of true or false information.

Epilogue; he heard never the like in Parliament but when a criminal
at law for treason, speaks not out of offence given him by his sharp
speech, for he had patience.

He grieved to hear him dishonour himself; dishonour himself and the
cause as he protested, this not in his charge, but he went against the
sense of the house, a point he studied much, made it his child. As the
ship *St. Peter* went to Rochell they say restored but I know it not, he
said it by obedience; he was informed in house and private, what needed
he such voluntary ignorance to enforce in the plaster as though *aliquid
latet quod non patet*, left evil, believe this not directed, but the house
declared that there was no evil intent. Observes many other points but
will not be an advocate against him; his own pleading too much doth
reflect upon him.

The evil and the cause; now to remedy. All lives fortunes and honours
here embarked, if any do to endanger ship though a cockboat call him
off, we danger of tempest from abroad, need therefore to care to save it,

without alteration, he hath heard new counsels (meaning from King) brought hither.

Knows not whither it may reach, but while we do worthily *will not; all other monarchies changed by new counsels, the medium betwixt prerogative and tumultuary licence, this way to preserve it. We here in happiness look like men, in other nations like ghosts in canvas and wood. Showed what he said, how sent out in their language*, given to Ambassador.

This speech exceedingly disliked though I see not the cause somebody much to blame for it.

We began in this business in a great committee, now in great extremity; therefore desires a great committee to consider and to reason pro and con.

Sir Benjamin Rudyard conscious we doubtful King he heard one word spoken, would no more.

Kirton thinks Vice Chamberlain's word subject to as great interpretation : they imprisoned with them ; desires he may set down their charge, that we at committee to consider whether the house did authorize them.

Committee commends their learning and knowledge and beliefs.

N. Rich thinks we should shew no opinion ; glad to hear it is no worse from him ; far from us to justify what not in charge. No man here but grieves to see our liberty suffer as now in high measure as ever in men's memory.

First therefore to desire solely to procure for our liberty, then to have a grand committee to do it.

Sir Edward Spencer : such words aid no plots; if those words were said by Vice Chamberlain that the King if he should not be sensible of something he were not worthy of his crown he desired to explain.

He explaineth he delivered nothing by command ; he told what he conceived cause, because he did name no man, the King said if he should not be sensible of his father's death he were not worthy of his crown, for so the King said.

Rouse approveth the interpretation.

Resolved by question to proceed in no other business until righted in our liberties.

Resolved by question to have great committee to consider how to do it.

Moved to have key up at committee.

Chancellor Exchequer moves against that, as a fundamental law of house, though once done at this Parliament,

Ordered to have the key, because when it is disliked many great persons draw with their money (?).

Wandesford ; glad too to see how advisedly we proceed; bath heard a member taken out of Parliament ; two, for they know not what, never heard.

Root of all misinformation if we look back : easy to see cause, desires remonstrance; desires to move King to write that Duke the misinformer and to have our liberties home.

Sir John Saville served in 3 Princes times; he committed out of the house 3 weeks, heard nothing ; he asked of Lords why served not for the delay. He asked the cause ; sent back to go to Queen.

Lord Knevet moved for him as now to have a petition to Queen to know cause ; house answered would not conclude privilege broken, house petitioned to know the cause; delivered, no cause assigned.

Wisheth a mannerly remonstrance to ground nothing of Vice Chamberlain.

Sir Thomas Hoby ; hear that said he was committed by council before Parliament sat, but he will in modesty conceal the cause.

Finds the whole sense of the house grieved ; if for offence at conference we or Lords should have taken it and called answer, but sent for without cause known unprecedented but to find no cause.

Long : 2 Hen. 4. Commons shewed no person committed but for treason and felony, and [assented] and that in King's presence, he thinks Duke always cause. Hears they their papers and lodgings ransacked : he in his opinion condemned, hopes none so impudent as to testify otherwise than here : desires all to be restored.

Sir John Savile was taken upon the door of the house 10 days after Parliament began.

Noy if committed for things foreign we satisfied if by our command to justify, if exceed to condemn.

If we charge Duke if untrue dishonour to us.

Likes no precedents until cause known ; reason the best precedent.

Sir Richard Hutton.

Newberie : King to give account to God, not to us, and cause, if prerogative and laws clash ruin of kingdom : laws here violated ; desires to have restitution and to punish them, else we all to go by them, since they by our command.

Remonstrance ordered to be made by question for the imprisonment of 2 members, and to show how good purposes and proceeding we had and how interrupted, and how we intend to proceed to his honour.

[May 13.] Saturday.

Sir B. Rudyard : King's honour to be most dear to us we therefore shunned aspersion of King's Government, much less his honour, fame will by growing spread such reports all over. *Quod recipitur est secundum modum recipientis.* We to bring to punishment him that spake it or him that poisoned it, now we all engaged in it.

Vice Chamberlain desires to engage ourselves with judgment and discretion ; he finds *modum recipientis* spoken here carried with contrary instruction ; not one man informed King of this but four or five, which King yesterday informed him of again, if they were mistaken he thinks more might be, he doth think they were mistaken. Desires to fall on the information, because a tickle point ; lets know for loss of time now spent, that as yesterday broke silence, and yesterday satisfied what was spoken ; asked his authority for speech had but truth at supper he asked King cause of offence at D. Diggs in particular, he desired to put it in writing ; King said no, it was the sense of divers, he said to King how tender we, that he not worthy to live that spoke them or commended : King said house did take it right, thinks house commended not, he took like course therefore as his predecessor did in like case. Thought D. D[igges] used it as a paraphrase of the text far from the text and so this he said by explanation.

Kirton : he hath well acquitted himself before we took him for the author ; if they did it by our command, we guilty, to desire King to have agents punished, for thinks it treason in highest degree to set this division 'twixt King and people.

Sir Nathaniel Rich thinks him as a traitor that doth not endeavour to vindicate honour of King and kingdom which this prodigious traitor hath raised : shall neither Commons nor Lords take notice, and yet it came to King, therefore to . . . . he spoke not to say this nor to this effect, nor so commanded by us, nor we had it not.

Littleton stood by and on his life said no such thing, and spoke to King's honour, said my Lords the Commons commended that in all they have not found anything that reflected on King's honour that dead is, or is now.

Sir F. Steward, who ever informed are traitors in heart, which he will prove.

Resolved by question that every one shall protest before God that he never counselled that D. Diggs should.

2. That he heard him not speak these words.

3. That he believeth not that he spoke them.

4. That he did not affirm he spoke the words or to that effect.

This was done and who sick gone unto, and so the house having cleared itself and the members of those speeches by Sir D. Diggs, notice was taken of it at Court by the King and Council and Sir D. Diggs sent out of the Tower without any petition, and came into the house the next day being Tuesday; there gave thanks to the house, shewed the King's grace to him, and his content; desired to proceed and petition for Eliot which he thought would do, and then the Chancellor of Exchequer delivered a message from King how King satisfied was cleared, loth to infringe privileges, yet Eliot detained for matters extrajudicial also. That word after desired to be explained, but nothing done nor agreed to be done until privileges righted.

15. May. Heads for Conference.

How head of impeachment of Duke's speeches delivered.

2. How D. Diggs committed for words supposed spoke there by command.

3. How informed by D. Carleton by leave from the King that the words were proved.

4. That King informed by 4 or 5 concerned a malicious and wilful misinformation.

Reasons.

1. For that he had contrary order.

2. For that the words were contrary.

3. If spoken should be observed by Lords and us; if it should; so this misinformation reflected on King as aspersion; the which we grieve to hear, abhor to think.

To show how breaks privilege by commitment; discouragement makes division 'twixt King, noble and commons. If this not discovered, occasioneth the like colour of truth also: show how we cleared, that if the Lords would have apprehended and controlled to remember West, or 2 Rich. 2. 303. 2. Rich. 2. *vel* 2. Philip and Mary of those that raise sedition 'twixt Lords and Commons and the punishment.

To have punishment inflicted according to justice and their demerits.

How course may be taken by both houses for the discovery and punishment.

D. Diggs dare not speak against, where goes further then him; imprisoned was disgrace, now grace new, desires all to be left out concerning him.

Recommitted to comprehend Eliot.

Vice Chancellor expoundeth the extrajudicial to be high crimes committed against the King out of this house, so commanded to declare; desires to proceed with the business of the house which was the King's message.

Kirton: if we not satisfied in what, who can speak safe.

Sir Robert Harley: question whether we may proceed, a member thus taken.

Corrington: question also whether fit.

Sir Peter Heyman: to be informed if felony treason or peace, else we judges and to hear it.

Sir William Spencer : to take liberties in consideration else by such a colour may every man be taken and this made no house.

[Streignish, Strangeways ?] moveth we to clear him of things done in the house and for the house.

Nathaniel Rich ; not to clear him until accused, for he is not charged as Diggs, for he may [be] committed in Parliament time but such cause should be made known, else may concern all, to desire to know the cause.

Wandesford ; just to be cleared of what he did by the command of the house, then petition for cause.

Vice Chamberlain : the evil construction abroad of what he said to break silence made him silent since. Rather judge than subject him to reprehension ; concurs to clear him in all he did by command ; but if he did exceed, the last day he did say somewhat not with sense but against it, and so he thinks he did ; and when desired he will do it, there were points he present when King took exception, and fit to remonstrate, to crave cause, wherein King denieth him no absolutely. Times such now as a man may offend tender ears, thinks this business fit but not all the business, else we may be irremediable, desires to leave land as liberty to posterity. Temps Queen Elizabeth members taken yet privileges continue, Sir Antonie Cope, Sir H. Bromley, Sir John Savile yet house proceeded. 35 Elizabeth Attorney Woods, Morris, Sir Edward Hoby, Beal Clerk of Parliament all committed yet proceeded, and all ended happily, not petitioned ; he desires to petition and also to proceed.

4 Hen. 8. Richard Strode occasion of law against all proceeding against Parliament men.

Therefore to prevent precedents now and avoid past.

Sir Hoby : not time to clear before accused, answers precedents, not for public speech in house, so as house would not petition for them ; not so now. Parry was hanged drawn and quartered sitting horse, so desires remonstrance.

Sir G. Moore ; happy for subjects to be free in England, honour King so preserved, differs from last, thinks we should clear him before charged notwithstanding this *nescio quid vult ista purgatio mali*, yet like speech offensively taken. To precedents ; he present when all committed, cause known, no breach of liberty, motion made for change in church government, Queen prohibited by message, Cope delivered a bill after to make alteration, Mildmay said stand by a short Bill to cut off the heads of all : the laws past for which he taken.

Morris did like after commanded ; so the rest, but Bromley charged for meddling in succession, so Beall, all which slipped away without notice.

Chancellor Duchy : King can do no wrong, say no wrong. He saith high crimes not to be supposed, but it is so to answer to God, if do wrong perhaps who go to him will tell no reason for state, which if we suppose then lose we our labour of conference, therefore he indifferent if rest upon this or go with remonstrance, for this entered so is no breach of privilege, therefore desires to go on with business.. King might have said so an D. Diggs would nothing but truth, so not so said.

Browne : 34 Elizabeth resolved by all judges King nor Council cannot commit above 24 hours, but must assign cause if habeas corpus come.

Mason : not to commit but for felony or treason.

Sir D. D. that he used words perhaps beyond command, but if matter considerable then papers.

Vice Chamberlain: this not time to clear him, he hath no accuser, he aimed, but knew not hit off.

Sir D. Diggs cause so is cleared, his a mixed cause, partly that at conference, partly else perhaps by his papers as Sir D. Diggs, perhaps by other matter before, precedents he cited as accidents not justified.

Beall committed only for bringing subsidy roll that belonged to us not Lords to confer. Desires to on with religion; war, sickness, &c., now depending before us to go on.

[May 19.] Friday after Ascension.

Vice Chamberlain signifieth after long silence how the King sent a warrant to deliver Sir John Eliot, and he is coming.

Yet no business proceeded in until heads of conference read reciting as before the heads.

Further shows our protestation to contrary, but all as before.

Vice Chamberlain saith he expressed not himself well when he said he had had it of 4 or five, for he said it arose out of notes which King sent for four or 5, now common report coming to King he sent for notes.

For business it seems none but remonstrance and conference, he at liberty, takes away the remonstrance, if proceed desires recommitment.

Objection that upon answer can have no reply, best to be spared.

Bish charged him that he said King told by 4 or 5 as Chancellor Exchequer.

Chancellor Exchequer said King was so informed not told by 4 or 5 which makes difference; King called for notes upon evil sound, which taken with no evil sense, might be mistaken, desires to proceed.

Diggs thought unfortunate committed, now more if prosecuted, hath had such fair carriage; desires to proceed or re-committed.

[May 20.] Saturday 'a letter agreed to be sent by Speaker, to stay judgment against Mr. Moore until privilege examined, notwithstanding supposition of his consent.

Chancellor Exchequer showed how Sir John Eliot made a negative answer to things done without the house and extrajudicial and the King hath accepted it, note not satisfied so he was sent for to his chamber, and King gone; liberty to come hither and he came in.

Then moved some to charge him because said all from top to toe to give occasion.

Vice Chamberlain chargeth not, expecteth thanks, commands what house directed, what more disliked; conference first divided concerning an impeachment of a great Peer of the realm, the words they used of respect wounded the person, disrespect the cause; commission was to amplify and to aggravate his part, his was to contain him within the compass of his chapter and recapitulation, but if anything new without his charge.

1. Began with a character of Duke his mind only bad; compared to a beast "stellio stellionatus"; so changeable as none could tell what to make of it.

2. Contrary to sense of the house in doubting the restitution of ships went to Rochell, which he was certained of by letters, a needless un-acknowledgment proceeding out of obedience as he conceived he related.

3. This word of, "this man," this man offended many as a great indignity to any man in all countries.

4. Historical comparisons as parallels 2: the one of Sejanus, the other Bishop of Ely, *audax superbus adulator;* of *venena venefica* would not speak. That of Sejanus was further applied to top of Government per-haps than he meant.

5. The greatest sharpness that above all injuries further meaning King's physic and would not speak; doubted to think out it off with words of Cicero as though had not words enough to express it. Speaking of the last charge as though somewhat more therein covered that were not discovered. So desires he may clear himself for he accuseth not.

Sir John Eliot excuseth his not coming by ignorance of the favour bestowed on [him] till near eleven, or heard of discharge yesterday. He confesseth the obligation to Vice Chamberlain to give him occasion to discharge himself. The charge; many particulars concern his fitness or unfitness; to serve here dearer than life; asketh time to answer them particularly. Speaker proposeth them particularly.

He answereth and showed his method that he did not exceed; to avoid tautology he changed the names, as ambition for offices. This part was in English, collusion *dolus malus* and he found this short but expressed it by a metaphor of *stellionatus* from a beast of divers colours, thereby he did express the art to merchants entrapping at Dieppe.

2. His colouring to the King the ships to go another way.

3. The abuse of Parliament by disguise possessing us after he knew ships were delivered otherwise.

2. His profession of obedience, he will therein be neither short nor over, desires no favour not to of &c. that he said he did not know the ships delivered though he heard it for so he said in the house, and so yet.

3. "This man, this man" he speaks not as some by book, he confesseth by contraction, if of Alexander *ille ipse;* to call him a man thinks no offence, thinks him no good man.

4. For Sejanus and the intimation that there was something for the Lords to go further.

Tells what he meant by Ely, who was only named 4 Rich. where are many charges: he took what fit, luxurious, misemploying of King's revenue, conferring honours of obscure men, boldness paralleling it now to this time when King's order contradicted *per totam insulam publice proclamat · percat quum omnes opprimatur quem omnes opponunt* Sejanus in effect *Stellionatus* that he did *clientes honoribus et provinciis adornare* how he was *laborum imperatorum socius* there used *venenas* and *veneficas*, for there comes in his lust to Livia his poisoning of Drusus; those he excluded as impertinent; if he apply it not, he meant it not; let not their interpretation be his fault. Now many of those books bought since, more than within a twelvemonth before.

5. Last; for intimation of *aliquid latet,*—

Interrupted by Wandesford and required to show how he meant these examples; nothing further than this person not to any greater which he did accordingly and said for he sacrifice himself for King so soon as any.

Gives words of 5th charge so near as upon having used corruption, extortion, oppression, &c. and after wonder how could subsist being so proved, being dangerous in state so many faults, not without art, honours of kindred to support him and alliance, then set on King's revenue, then this later as a boldness more comparing it to fire; and not content with injuries of justice, honour, state, but attempts person of King in such a sort as fears to speak, doubts to think, least as Cicero use *gravere quem res exiget vel leviare quem causa postulat;* and left it to the Lords' consideration.

Two things more he observed unanswered, his manner and matter. 1. Too much vigour; what his nature not his fault, seldom felt passion, though his love may covet it. 2. Though he was to be contained in his rude epilogue, if any particulars be without he will answer, but he knows none but passages, as his exclusion.

Resolved by question he exceeded not his commission given by the house at conference.

So for Sir D. Diggs for all, being before but one point.

Sir Robert Harlow desires hereafter no aggravation to be admitted hereafter, but first to give in heads in the house.

This denied, lest might seem to disallow what was done.

[May 22.] Mr. Pim moved for a bill, not remonstrance, but the committee both. He ; this will do no good, for that liberty of speech we have, and the example of deliverance better then that of imprisonment, but the sufferance was in King James time said Rich and Queen Elizabeth's time when we made remonstrance, and answer and reply, letters, protestation and dissolution, freedom of speech, person, information, therefore to avoid dispute desires a Bill. Temps. H. 8 produced Act of Parliament lost not got by debate.

Wandesford for Bill and to proceed to business.

Glanville : resolved 18 James we no power but to fine and imprison. Lords to judge, then was a bill proposed and agreed upon.

Ordered a committee to consider whether a remonstrance or Bill, protestation or all, and to prepare it.

Afternoon Star Chamber.

Sir F. Foljambe brings in a letter out of Yorkshire, read because brought by member of house before the speaker read it. Sir John Savile's letter copied to John Harrison, D. Foxcroft, Sir Thomas Medcalfe, &c. He gives account of Parliament concerning their [charter ?] ; he after moved the inconveniences in setting down the trade being many and the mischief if merchants debarred of free trade.

They so resolutely bent and eager in pursuit of a great man that they will hazard the state of Commonwealth as he fears rather than St......

He spoke of 30m. men meant not short; desires to use care and expedition to maintain his credit.

Sir John desires who offers copy to prove it, if this be a true copy desires to have his hand and head struck off for he deserves no less.

Foljambe hath order for witnesses to prove it.

Pim moved that he should clear if he spoke to that effect.

Sir John denieth that any can be showed, and he denieth his writing; he subscribing or directing any such clause.

He in the end denied to answer by order of house and it was allowed.

Glanvile : his judgment of himself is like to be true by his consent if it be true.

Ordered to withdraw and to come in upon suit of the wronged gentlemen and to acknowledge an error in his place which he did.

Mr. Whitby to-morrow to report the grievances.

Wandesford reporteth the humour that Sir W. S. [?]

Chancellor Exchequer moves to proceed on King's revenue and to bring in preamble of subsidy.

Wednesday morn for revenue.

Thursday the naval war.

All general committees to proceed.

Tonnage and poundage Wednesday afternoon.

[May 24.] Wednesday—Whitby reports grievances formerly not answered or not well, and new ones.

1. Impositions : presented 7 James that by law none can be imposed but by Parliament, show impositions and desired to lie all down, not answered but now added.

Resolved by question to be presented as great grievance.

3. James—the license of wines enhancing price by dispensation of antiquated laws by subject. King did answer after that patent ended no more granted, patent now ended, yet the license kept on foot by this general dispensation: desires to have the law repealed. Resolved to be presented as grievance.

Ferdinando Gorges' patent, 21 James, to restrain the free fishing in America, his answer short; because they were to give satisfaction for wood desire liberty for wood at pleasure, not within a quarter of a mile of the planters' habitation or fishing.

4. That the begging briefs, 21 James, presented to be totally prohibited: answered none to be but upon certificate in sessions and that county one: this is not observed as by precedent for a bridge at Westminster. Resolved to be represented.

5. Sir John Meldrum's patent at Winterton Ness exacting above proportion fit for a light house at Winterton Ness, from 6d. to 3s. 4d. extorted and enforced. Answered to refer it to committee of both houses to proportion it, first thought to pray a conference yet resolved to represent it because it is judged by us properly.

6. New surveyorship of coals erected; 7s. 6d. a chaldron paid for transport, 12d. for import within kingdom and to bring contents to discharge; bonds entered for so doing, yet cockets denied to discharge their bonds until 4d. a chaldron paid to Surveyor, prays to have the bonds discharged which were extended for the projectors benefit, being 1200 bonds.

Resolved to petition to have the 1200 bonds discharged.

Sir Andrew Boyle and Collum the projectors and prosecutor sent for to the house.

7. Merchant Adventurers' patent answered; they satisfied and dyed and dressed at liberty, yet the imprest of 7s. 6d. a cloth continueth; abated to half and to cease in August 1627.

To petition to lay down the imposition totally.

8. Where States imposed 32s. of English cloth as consumption money to our hindrance, and the [weighing?] to be brought to one place drawn now to 28.

To desire King to now move for help while they need.

9. Fees of Customers, exacting in some case equal to custom: desires now to be reformed, for worse than before, by allowance to take fees.

10. Merchants having dispensation for 30m. cloths desired to have 20m. more: this not answered. Cumberland his patent expires this May—now to repetition.

11. Pretermitted custom misgrounded upon Statute of tonnage and poundage by Nicholson's projection, by colour of equity, upon wool, to be laid down.

Answered at next meeting to do what is fit for a good king.

Desires now to provide for it in the new Bill of Tonnage and Poundage, upon which grounded, and now not to repetition upon it not singly lest we admit others, but to mention tonnage and poundage exacted illegally so, thereof.

12. Tonnage and poundage taken without act to be presented as a grievance; and to consider under whether this or impositions pretermitted, custom to be.

13. The impositions of currants to be presented.

14. The Deputy Alneager exacting 1d. for ½d. and upon shop keeper, King answered should mended; to desire a Bill to regulate it.

[May 25.] Thursday before Whitsuntide we adjourned without any intimation from the Lords or King until that day sevennight, as we may upon such festivals, but upon other occasions some thought we might not, and the Lords did not adjourn until Friday, and then until Friday after us.

[June 1.] Thursday we met; read some bills; I reported Mathew Hutton's bill; committees ordered, and no more.

On Friday we called the house according to our order at recess and 25 only made default, on whom by former order 10*l.*.apiece was set for a fine and further as the house should think fit, but no order for levying it and reasonable excuses were admitted after to divers.

Saturday after bills read and the order then to read engrossed bills read; some perceiving that the Lords not having the Earl of Arundel restored them confined nor the Bishop of Lincoln as I remember some mentioned.

Moved to have the house turned to a committee and so was to consider of heads for a conference with the Lords, because of our privileges, and reasons to be showed why we proceeded no slower.

1. How the Duke standing impeached before them of treason, and by us &c., in contempt was made Chancellor at Cambridge: the actors and instruments to be considered, he now accumulating offices, it being before one of the charges.

2. How some employed that &c. and Montagu that inclines to arminianism, like to bring in half popery or arminianism.

3. The interruption at Oxford, he being means to call us thither and dissolve us there when he touched.

4. The making Lord Embercourt that was a presenter a Baron, who had no estate in lands, who was declared with us for him as it were to make a party at this time, what justice could be expected.

5. The words he spoke of new counsels and the commoners' coats and clouted shoes: other countries grown upon new counsels when parliamentary liberty was turned to tumultuary licence, or to that effect.

Upon which subject Mr. Moore speaking; how impossible that was to [be] effected in England, how our Yeomanry here one would beat 10 of the slaves of France, and the King if he would keep his [*blank*] must preserve their liberty; and that if a tyrant were here is no forts no cities &c. to enthral us, therefore impossible.

Therefore he being interrupted, because he did bring such high points into supposition or doubt, was committed to the Tower, and after to be considered of if to be put out of house, but at first no more because all men did take he ment no evil, and he even in his speech commended the King his pious and gracious Government and showed these were but fanatic fears, yet this slip of words thus censured, as if a man besides intention kill &c. and though madman King is sacred and so tongues to be wisely moderated.

Saturday the King sent answer to the Lords how by many his great occasions he could not so ripen the matter for the Earl of Arundel as yet, but considering his great occasions he would haste as much as he could, and if before Wednesday sevennight he could he would, but then upon the word of a King he would restore him or else show his causes to satisfy, that they might more cheerfully proceed in business.

They notwithstanding as I heard adjourned until Wednesday or Thursday as [*blank*].

[June 5.] Monday the house resolve to send to the Vice Chancellor, Doctors, Proctors, Regents [?] to certify of the election of the Lord Duke as an affront offered to the house and for the miscarriage and contempt to the house.

The King sent a message to stay the letter, holding it **derogatory** to his prerogative to intermeddle with the Universities or **the election, which** if any error was in it belonged to him to correct.

We by message answered him that it was done in a contempt to us as **we** conceived. We sent not for them as delinquents, we desired not to encroach upon his prerogative, but he that so stood accused and their burgesses being amongst us, and for them so accusing him he ought not to have been chosen; whereof his majesty being rightly informed, how this was an accumulation of the things complained of, would give leave to proceed.

The King sent back answer by the same messengers the Chancellor of the Exchequer and others how all corporations were derived from him, he bound to maintain them especially the Universities, that he would and was resolved so to do against whomsoever that did purposedly or by accident impeach them. He did think the election good, and would not have it questioned; but if any particular persons did miscarry themselves he was content we should examine them, but he said a man accused was not condemned nor lost not his fame, therefore, &c.

Yet Sir John Hotham thought we might proceed with the letter, which was read, reciting the affront that the Duke accused in Parliament of treason should be chosen.

The Chancellor of Exchequer protested against the knowledge of the accusation of treason, so did Noy.

Note.—For they meant in the Lords' house, but in our house they admitted there was none, and because the letter was so directly, it was then put over unto a new day Friday for debate.

[June 9.] Friday the house having intimation of a letter from the King, sent a message to have a copy of the Duke his answer to which they might reply it being put in yesterday.

The Lords sent word we should have answer by messengers of their own with all possible speed but sent none that day.

But proceeded against Earl Bristow, being all the forenoon in examining as I heard 2 witnesses for the King against him, the afternoon for him.

Then the same day the King's letter to the Speaker, by the intimation in it to be publicly read, was read, showing how we could not be ignorant how time was delayed, how he had called us, represented the danger of the state by enemies &c. and required advice and help in the things undertaken by our counsel, called God and men to witness [he] had done his part whatsoever happened hereafter; therefore required us to perfect our own promise to send up subsidy bill by the end of the next week without any condition, else he would take all delays and excuse for denials and take other resolutions.

After long debate the consideration of it was deferred until Monday.

Divers propositions then made to go on with the business of the commonwealth, tonnage and poundage in book of rates continuance of statutes; grievances first to be presented, and the most materials as the naval war &c. to be ordered by a committee which to proceed in first, but this denied.

Then the reasons for a fast to be desired were read, and we to desire the Lords to join but because they comprehended not *causa causarum* as seemed they were recommitted.

[June 10.] Saturday some bills reported, new heads for declaration to be proposed. The new counsels executed in taking tonnage and poundage without Parliament.

1. His abuse of the Parliament in his relation false from Spain 21 James made a record, being but a conference and entered as a Parliament

roll now produced against Bristoe as on accusation and laboured to prejudicate it.

That the King shall not give nor make contract for his crown revenue, under danger.

The Duke his casting all his excuses upon the King that was and is as in evil odour of his Government.

To protest God and the world we used no delay, but proceeded parliamentarily for relief.

Sir Edward Coke who was made Sheriff of Buckingham and came not to the house nor no new writ went out being served with a subpœna by the Lady Clare was allowed his privilege 9 June.

ᴸ [June 12.] Monday a declaration read of all hindrances in parliamentary proceeding begun at Oxford and so till now, and all put on the Duke, the making of Sheriffs sending Glanville to Calais, denied by him so the dissolution at Oxford by the Council.

Then the King's letter taken into consideration, and after dispute until four at clock resolved by question not to proceed with subsidy, but to make a declaration as before, with this, that we may have justice of the Duke and then to proceed to read the bill, with show to pass it within the time (query the event).

The Parliament then by message from the King under great seal ended.

[1628, Notes in Parliament :—*a small 4to Volume.*]

" 4th June, 1628.

A bill for the reversal of a decree in the Court of Wards which was had after fine and recovery, and upon pretence it was had by fraud which was said ought not to be admitted : this the first reading of this bill.

A petition concerning the Adventurers and Planters of the Somers Islands called the Bermudas, which shows that the sole commodities transported from thence is tobacco, of which the imposition was but of late 3d. a pound, and now it is increased to be 9d. which doth now lie so heavy upon them that they cannot subsist by it being now a full value of the third part of the value though. A Select Committee to take consideration of this business.

Sir E. Coke : I am to make a report of a great and weighty cause, wherein the King's Council had time to come and answer but they did not. There is required upon all the brewers in London and within four miles of it 4d. a quarter of malt that they shall brew, and it was grounded upon agreement betwixt them and the Green Cloth, but it was also agreed by both parties this imposition to be against the law. But the brewers said that it was not voluntary, for the King being indebted to them 1,500l. they refused to serve the King, and thereupon they were imprisoned and so they made this composition which indeed was rather an imposition. But though it were voluntary, yet it was not good as it was adjudged in 17 Edward III., the merchants agreed to give the King so much for all things both imported and exported, and this was not good, for that it was a grievance to the subject. And in the Exchequer they were compelled upon their oath *perdere se ipsos* upon their oath, and no man is bound *perdere se ipsum* and the King gains nothing, for the gentle projector he hath purchased 500l. per annum and built houses, and the King loseth, for it offered to serve the King for 24l. a ton, and he payeth 32l. a ton, and in 5 Edward III. the city hath a charter confirmed by Act of Parliament that no purveyance shall be taken in London, but this extends not to the four miles, and so they insisted not much upon that because it extends not to it.

It is said that there is a great defect in powder for the defence of the kingdom, and that it is sold out of the Tower to whom we know not, it may be to our enemies; it lies us open to our enemies at sea, and being reduced into one hand, it had advanced it 3 a pound of late, and it is said that the ships that are furnished for great voyages do not deliver back the powder, which is a great neglect.

Alderman Clitherow :—If the matter and materials of which it is made grow so scarce, if this be neglected, and the carriage of it away be permitted, for we had much of our saltpetre from Poland and that now we cannot have it, nor from Germany; and desired a Committee may be chosen to consider of it. And whereas it is said that 1,000 tons of ordnance hath been of late transported into Dunkirk and other places and Mr. Waller said that he hath heard that every year this three or four years license to carry out 400 tons of ordnance; and that is Burlemacke, for which he hath a warrant, and that is or will be 400 pieces of ordnance; and license given to the Committee to examine all those things and send for witnesses &c.

And said that the materials of which the ordnance is made of lieth in Sussex and Kent, and the mines be almost spent so that require good consideration : this referred to the former Committee.

A message from the King by the Speaker of this House,—That his majesty upon the petition of both Houses having given you a full, royal and just answer, for that you and your posterity may hereafter have cause to bless God for it and his Majesty, it is now time to conclude this sessions and to fall on that which may be of most importance, and that he will abide to that answer which he hath given us, and that he will really and royally perform it, and that this session shall continue no longer than the 11th of this month : therefore he willeth us to fall in hand with that which may soonest conduce to that end, and that we should not entertain any new matter, and if there be any new matter of complaint we may be sooner called together again to have redress for what shall be amiss.

Doctor Mannering's charge engrossed, and sent up to the Lords, being of the Convocation house, wherein he showeth that the slow proceedings of parliament is not sufficient to supply the King in his wants, and by preaching of two sermons touching and tending to division.

A bill touching apparel sent down from the Lords,—That none but the King and his mother, brother, sister &c. shall wear any gold or silver lace or tissue or any embroidery thereof or anything made thereof about their apparel, coaches &c., and to forfeit 20l. half to the poor and half to the informer, this to begin after the 1st of March next, and to continue unto the first session of the next parliament.

Sir E. Coke takes exception to this bill at the first reading, being agreeable to the orders of the House, though not usual.

1stly. That this as in all other former penal bills and acts, the informer ought to inform in the county where the offence is committed for the peace of the subject ;

2ndly. That the soldior whose bravery is his honour may be excepted;

3rdly. Whereas it is said that it is enacted by the assent of the King, it was never heard of before, but that it was enacted by the King with the assent of the Lords and Commons et non e converso.

An act for the restitution of the blood of Carew Raleigh, his father being attainted of high treason; and to be so restored as if his father had not been attainted. (Committed.)

Sir Dudley Digges reports from the Committee of Trade and tells what the Captain say to the King at the battle of Agincourt, when the King asked him what he thought of the French army.

But let me sweeten my report with the comfort that we have by the work of [*blank.*]

I will observe now to you the dangers and in that two particulars general :—

1st. The complaint of the decay of navigation, and their disturbance when they come home by imposts for our merchants ; they meet with many enemies, with storms, with Jews and all nations and are hone [?] enough from them all : but when they come home they are much discouraged by the neglect of the settling the bill of tonnage and poundage.

But for the particulars which ariseth from a petition made by Trinity House :—there hath been lost 148 betwixt Dover and Berwick, at Harwich 8. Ipswich 38. Newcastle 23.

The cause of it : 1. Disorders and errors before they come to employment. They are stayed by commands when they are ready for going out, and when they are released, yet the mariners are taken away and they put to seek new men to their great loss and disadvantage, and put upon winter voyages and so many lost ; and mariners discouraged by pressing ; so that whereas in the western coast there was 3,000 mariners, now there are not 500, and the ships that are pressed have not pay sufficient, for they have but 2s. a ton, whereas they might have much more of others.

2nd. Mischiefs when they are abroad, by the command of ignorant captains ; and the soldiers have not clothes, for they are kept from them that they run not away.

3rdly. Inconvenience and mischief ; after employment being not paid : and the merchants endeavour to build them unserviceable lest they should be taken up.

The consideration of the Committee upon this is, 1st That formerly to encourage men to build ships there was 5s. a ton paid to the builder to encourage him. For further encouragement, that the 2s. which is given for a ton, it may be advanced to 3s. and this to be known before the ships go out. Also that the mariners and others which are behind for their pay may have it out of those subsidies ; and some things which he hath thought fit himself, he will take time to move to this house, that may be for the increase of navigation and for the weakening of the enemy.

Sir John Eliot : You see what the limitation of our time now is, which is fit to be employed for the good of the King and the country.

At the conference touching Doctor Mannering in the Painted chamber the charge being delivered and enforced by Mr. Pym which he first read, which tended to divert the King from calling of parliaments :—' I shall the more confidently speak in this because there is nothing to discourage me, if you look upon your honours, the honour of the King.'

At the committee of grievances, Sir Edward Coke in chair, touching the patent granted to the Exchangers, that the sole and all monies shall be paid to Exchangers and to pay to them 1d. in 6s. 8d. which takes away the profit ; for the inconvenience, it was declared vivâ voce by many merchants, that by reason of this office whereas they before bought money in specie, now it being advanced 10d. in the ounce by this the loss is now ; whereas there was gain before when they might sell it to the goldsmith.

Another exception is that there [is] another patent of the same office yet in being and not surrendered before the grant of this to the Lord of Holland, to Sir Edward Villiers, and besides there is no mention in the latter patent to the Lord of Holland of the former patent to Sir Edward Villiers.

Responded: there is a difference betwixt *Custos Cambii;* that which is the keeping of exchange that is the profit of the exchange.

6 Hen. III., m. 5. This is also an office of trust, and being granted to the Lord of Holland for 31 years is void, because it may come to his executors or assigns not skilful; but for life it may be, as in Sir George Reynolds case, 9th Report.

Responded: that that hath been divers times before granted for years as in 6 Hen. III., m. 5, and others, and the difference betwixt a ministerial or a judicial office as it in Reynolds' case, and in this case, which stands of his proper feet. [4. Exception: it is an office of skill, and the patentee hath no skill, for it not enough that his deputies have skill, but that the patentee have, otherwise void as it is in Darcy's case in the 11th Report.]

Mr. William, one skilful in gold and silver mines, said that there is no mine of gold, but gold is found in little round pieces, being washed by the water: and there is great diversity betwixt gold, some is mixed with silver, and so much less, and it is not possible if he be not skilful to know the worth, which my Lord of Holland is not.

Calthrop: When it is granted to one of such dignity as a Lord whether he not have a deputy for his dignity, vide 9th Report, Earl of Shrewsbury's case 8 Edw. III., p. 3, m. 21. '

Resolved when he dieth the exception is taken away, for it may be otherwise with his executors.

5th Exception is that the commonwealth hath entrusted the King with this power, and when he grants it for 31 years he puts the power out of himself, and by the same reason he may grant it in fee simple and grant all officers under him.

An ounce in the Mint makes 7s. 1d.

Vide 9 Edw. III. which concerns the exchange of money and bullion.

5th June, 1628.

A message from his Majesty by [*blank*].

To let us know that he will not alter the prefixed time before set down, without alteration; and because that cannot be if you enter into any new matter which may exceed the time, therefore his Majesty requireth you that you enter not into anything which may lay scandal or aspersion of the estate or the ministers thereof.

Sir Robert Phillips: We came hither covered let me say with injuries, and we have forgotten them as much as may be. If it be a crime to love his Majesty too much we must be guilty of it, since our intention was only to show his Majesty in a humble manner what might have been good for him and the kingdom. But since our sins be such that we cannot be permitted to do the good which we all desired, let us show his Majesty by a humble declaration of our true intention, and then since we cannot serve him here, let us desire that we may return home and pray for him.

Sir John Eliot: Touching our miseries and misgovernments.

The Speaker told him how unwilling he was to interrupt him, yet the King when he delivered this message commanded him that if the House did not observe this that then he should put them in mind of it.

Sir Nathaniel Rich: We fear the safety of the King's person, the altering of religion, and subversion of the state and kingdom, and let us go to the Lords and declare this, and the violation of our liberty of the parliament, and make a protestation of it there; for this tieth us up against all our liberties which is not to be endured; but if we may not let us sit still.

Resolved upon question; that every member of this house hath spoken nothing but dutifully from the beginning of the parliament to this time.

The House resolved into a committee to consider of the message delivered by the Speaker from the King, Mr. Whitby in the chair, and to consider what was to be done for the good of the King and kingdom.

Sir Edward Coke: This is the greatest violation that ever was, for in former times the parliament complained of the King's son, great Dukes, &c. and it was parliamentary, as 7 Hen. IV. n. 32, 34, and that there was no head that Sir John Eliot spoke of but there was redress for it in former times.

And I think the Duke of Buckingham is the cause of all this, and so long as those courses are God will not go with us neither by land nor sea, and personal matters are the grievance of grievances, and if all our miseries be looked into I think they will all reflect upon him, and let us go to the King and show him this, for that person is grievance of grievances.

Sir Robert Mansell: I stand up to speak in discharge of my duty though the weakest, and we were all at first transported with passions by the message, and now we have recollected ourselves and shown us to be men and not the sons of women: my motion is that we go all of us to the King and prostrate ourselves before him and show.

Kirton: That honourable gentleman that spoke so well and shown us so good a way, that I think we will all follow him, though with loss of our lives, and it is this great Duke that breeds all this danger: he hath gotten the strength of the kingdom into his hands of General by land and sea.

Shirland: We are so near the marriage of misery that if I do not now speak I must for ever hold my peace. Though the conception of the journey I will not say was not Spanish, yet the event I am sure was Spanish. We have betrayed Denmark, the French protestants, the Netherlanders. Are not the prime men in Court papists, and are and have not eminent men and captains been papists? Are not the papists at home connived at and compounded with a low rate? The Arminian faction encouraged and fostered, which was that which hath overthrown the Low Countries, and though religion cannot be altered at one time yet it works much.

Mr. Valentine: He which is called the General of soldiers minded to cut our throats: he is the common enemy of the kingdom, and is and must and shall be and can be no other.

Sir John Scidmore: We must do that which is good and likely to be so; it is agreed that necessity is the cause, and take that away and take away the effect: and though particulars have suffered some pressure, yet that hath been done for saving a general deluge and a swallowing up.

Sir Edward Coke: Somewhat in justification in our proceedings 18 Jac., the Commons' protestation, that the privileges of parliament are the ancient birthright of the subjects; and that every member hath free liberty to speak and bring to question anything, and to be free from imprisonment, and all this confirmed by Act of parliament.

Sir William Becher: I shall speak that which I know. I have been with this person now in question at the Island of Rhe and I speak it upon hope of salvation that I have ever observed [him] so votion and affection to his country as that he hath further than any man else, and hath ever so expressed himself.

Mr. Selden moves that the declaration or remonstrance to the King may be framed of these four heads;

1. Our dutiful carriage that we have used hitherto.
2. Of our privileges now infringed, and the protestation in 18 Ja.
3. That the Duke may be represented to be the occasion for avoiding his own censure of this unhappiness.
4. That which shall be for the good of the King and kingdom.

This resolved of by question to be represented to the King in our remonstrance.

Sir Thomas Germie [Jermyn] moves that we may put the question for our liberties, but for the great person now named not without good proof he may be so represented him to be the two, not only common enemy of this kingdom but also of all Christendom, without hearing what answer he can make for himself.

His Majesty wisheth that you remember the message last sent unto you whereby he hath set a day for the end of a sessions, and his Majesty lets us know that he will certainly hold the day prefixed without alteration.

And because that cannot be if the House should fall upon new business :—

His Majesty therefore requireth that you do not enter into or proceed with any business which may spend greater time than his majesty hath prefixed, or which may cast scandal or aspersion upon the state, government or ministers thereof. This is the message verbatim.

Resolved that we should go to the King ourselves by way of remonstrance, touching the infringing of our liberties, the clearness of our intentions, that we were doing that which were both for the good of the King and kingdom. The heads of this to be :—

1. The hazard of innovation of religion.
2. The hazard of innovation of government.
3. To take into consideration all our misfortunes and the occasion thereof, and the causes.
4. The hazard of the King's person; since all the forces are drawn into one hand.

This resolved to be one declaration with the four resolutions of the other side.

6th June.

Sir Francis Arland saith that he will not give his voice to accuse him before we hear him or any thing proved against him.

Answered that the parliament hath a double capacity, one a Court, so it hath another as a council, and as a council we may do this without proof.

A message by the Speaker from the King.

His Majesty's pleasure is for the present to adjourn the House to to-morrow.

A message for His Majesty by our Speaker.

6th June.

His Majesty hath understood that [by] the message lately received you have been restrained of your just liberty : he is pleased to declare his intention not to be to restrain the just liberties of the subject, but only his desire in the manner not to touch him by accusing his ministers which have given him counsel for things past, so that this may be.

Sir Benjamin Rudyard : This day is appointed for the taking into consideration the answer of the petition ; and I desire we may not dispute this too much, because it may be thought to have various constructions ; but let us humbly desire that his Majesty would fully declare himself shortly in the usual manner, such as may stand with his heart.

Sir Robert Phillips : Though this day was appointed for the consideration of the message, yet this interposition hath diverted it, and I think it is not King Charles advising himself, but it is King Charles advised by disordered counsel that hath occasioned this, and let us go on with that which we were in hand with, that the sub-committee may take that into consideration the heads resolved on yesterday, only excepting the breach of our liberties which his Majesty by his own goodness hath prevented ; and also to show'his Majesty the state of things at home with the things abroad with a mutual relation one to the other.

Sir John Eliot : I shall 'speak this day with as great joy as I did yesterday with sorrow. Two propositions now in consideration ; one touching the answer to our petition, and that I think there be so many so well affected to his Majesty's service, that they will move so much with his Majesty that he will of his own goodness give us an answer without our suit, for if we should desire it we should go to the Lords, and that might cast us upon new rocks, dangers, and difficulties, which is neither fit for the hazard nor time. I desire we make a humble representation or remonstrance of our loyalness and of our intentions both for the good of his person, his state and kingdom.

Mr. Coriton : The answer may receive various constructions and so it may receive a good one and so I take it, but howsoever the Lords and Commons have agreed this to be our rights, and I think no minister of justice dare do to the contrary, and I think this may well satisfy; and not to desire a further answer, especially since the King hath declared he will stand to this answer.

Mr. Pym : The answer is defective, first it hath no relation by any words to the petition, neither by words of according nor no other, and for that I am of opinion that that rest unto whether we hear the King will of himself make an explanation.

Sir John Eliot : In difference of opinions there are difference of expressions, and there hath been some strained constructions made of some words which he spoke, by way of expression of the duty to the King and country. He spake thus that he hopes that we had hearts, hands, and swords to cut the throats of the enemies of the King and Kingdom (and state, as some say).

And resolved upon question, that in those words he did not exceed his duty and allegiance ; and that therein we all agree.

The House resolved into a Committee, Mr Whitby in the chair, and to take into consideration the danger of the King and Kingdom, and , the causes thereof.

Sir R. Harlow ; The way of our proceeding, that those collections which were yesterday voted, to be read.

Additions to the heads for the remonstrance to the King : 1. The decay of Shipping and trade, and the materials thereof, that is oaken timber.

Pym : Two things to be enquired of ; a negotiation for the toleration of religion in Ireland, which I hear is nearly effected ; 2. What is become of the merchants' goods foreigners that hath been stayed in recompense of ours taken, and no recompense returned for the loss of them.

Sir Nathaniel Rich : The fear of innovation of religion ;

1. By tolerating papists, and not execution of the laws. Which Mr. Whittiker : That in Drury Lane there are three houses for one [sic].

2 The doctrine of Arminianism fostered and favoured in court and
by proclamation, by hindering the printing of orthodoxal books,
and giving free countenance to the other.

3. The neglect of preaching God's word.

4. That an army averse to religion to us is now amongst us, which
breeds much suspicion.

Mr. Jordan: In Holborn there is 1500 papists and 100 priests and
100 baptized in the Queen's House, which ought not to be.

Sir Edward Coke : The commonwealth doth flourish when religion
doth flourish, and they do live and die together.

In 1 Hen. V. rot. parl. the Commons pray that the King may
promise nothing which may not be performed. When the King of
Spain came with his invincible navy in Queen Elizabeth's time and was
overthrown, the Catholics of England sent John and Christopher Wright
to tender their service to the King of Spain, and he answered them that
the English Papists were dearer to him than his Castilians. But for
all this the Papists be in a wise case ; for what said the Spanish Captain,
what said he :—We will send the papists souls to heaven, but for their
lands and goods we will take them, for they are our prey.

And in Queen Elizabeth's time an express clause that the recusants
shall not have the two parts, which now they have, and this is certainly
an express toleration by this commission directed into the north.

2. The second head is the fear of the subversion of government and
innovation thereof :

1. Cause of this fear is this,—1. The levying of 1100 horse to come
out of the Low Countries, for what end not known, and riders for them
which Sir John Strangwish said was as great an encouragement as can
be to the enemy to see our weakness.

Kirton : There is a commission of excise, a copy of which may be
seen in the Crown Office.

Sir Walter Earle : The foot forces and especially the Irish which are
not well affected, they are here made garrisons ; not needful, and tending
to danger.

3. A third head : What is the causes of our disasters abroad.

1. That there is either insufficient or unfaithful generals or both, who
are not qualified for this. And this instanced by a book printed with
the authority of my Lord of Wimbledon, and the plot which was employed upon Calais was intended for St. Lucar when they were ignorant
of the place, as appears by the book.

Sir Robert Mansel : Since I have been thrust out of the Council of
war I have been at the school of obedience, and will rather expose
myself to your censure than to neglect my duty. With what success
could England undertake that business and not know the fort of St.
Lucar. Why were they not called that knew it as well as the right hand
from the left, and doth he that speaks to you ; but for that there was
nothing but error in the undertaking and composition of it, it was not
undertaken in a seasonable time ; the ships, their victuals, their men
were not proportioned for this design.

Worthy men neglected and mean men and pages preferred, and such
like.

Sir Francis Annesley : I pray you let us not accuse generals without
particulars, and for the unworthiness of any let them be named and
know what it is, and then we may proceed. And for those who are so
worthy which are not preferred, it were good they were named, and the
pages if any be made captains it were good we knew them, and not to
accuse men in general.

7th June 1628.

Sir Peter Midleton produceth a note that there are 58 ton of ordnance now ready to be transported into Holland to Rotterdam, which is desired ; that Mr. Chancellor is desired to move the King that they may be stayed. Mr. Burlemacke called in and asked whether he have a Commission for the transporting of ordnance, and he confessed it. Mr. Chancellor : It hath been deliberately argued at the Council table, and there by plain demonstrations shown that if they were not had from hence they might be had from other parts, and then it would be a hindrance to ourselves.

At the Grand Committee Mr. Whitby in the chair ; Mr. Burlemacke answers; touching the horse to be brought into England :—1. That he had a warrant from the King for to pay 1300*l.* for the levying of arms, and 1500*l.* for arms, and he heareth that 1000 horse was levied, but whither they are to go he knew not, and he thinketh that there are men likewise to come with them.

John Dalbers, Sir William Balbord King [*sic*].

The privy seal ; for to buy 1000 horse 15000*l.*, 5000 muskets cost 5000*l.* the rest of the 30000*l.* for pike, costles, and other furniture.

The ships was to be provided for 6 months, so that it is not likely to be for England.

9th June 1628.

A message from the Lords to desire a present conference with us touching the answer to our petition of Right.

The Conference. My Lord Keeper said that because the good of this kingdom consisted in the good intelligence of this people which doth much consist of the King's answer, and therefore for the good correspondence which hath ever been betwixt both Houses they thought fit to acquaint us, that they resolved to petition the King for a clearer and a more satisfactory answer, which they desired us to join with them, if we so pleased.

Mr. Coriton : There is no such haste (and not liked of).

Agreed and so resolved upon question, that we should join with them in the petition for a clear and satisfactory answer, in full Parliament ; *quod acta.*

Littleton : reasons for the not passing of the Lord of Devonshire's bills being, to enable him to sell land being but tenant for life, his son an infant and the inheritance with him.

1. He is an infant, and we are his guardians, and we must do as he would : and peradventure he would not have agreed to it.

2. It is an example and a precedent to future time to take away all certainty in conveyances.

3. It takes away a fundamental point of justice to take away land so settled, and we are a Court of Justice.

Rowles his reasons : Though land be given him in value, yet that reason will not remain to posterity, but the example will.

2. If it be for the advantage of an infant, it need not be so much desired.

If an action ancestral be brought against an infant, he must have his full age and not admitted by his friends; and if in a personal action he must plead by his guardian ; and if he misplead, he must answer for it ; and if the infant be prejudiced I think those that have ventured collateral security would be loth to pay what the infant shall be prejudiced.

Jones : There is 20000*l.* in statutes and there may be judgments, and then all this land shall be liable to it. and there is no justice for the son to be punished for the iniquity of his father, when he receives no benefit by him, for all this comes by his grandfather.

Shirland: The old Earl of Devonshire having land by descent and purchase to the value of 16000*l.* per annum, settles this land to the Earl that now is, for life, without impeachment of waste, the remainder to the infant the Lord Cavendish that now is in tail with remainders over.

Whereas it is said we break a rule of justice, I say we do not.

For if the infant have a recompense, then it is a legal answer.

For though it be agreed that tenant in tail cannot do anything to the prejudice of his issue, yet if tenant in tail grant a rentcharge for the extinguishing a dormant right it is good and bindeth. So if an infant make a lease without reservation of rent, it is void, yet if it be without a rent reserved it is not void but only voidable. And for the statutes and recognizances they are all cancelled and vacated.

Mr. Bish: I was inconstant and unresolved in opinion what way to give my opinion before he spoke, and now I am of a contrary opinion, for you take away 2600*l.* per annum to his wife for jointure, and rob Peter to pay Paul; this is no justice. And the case of the granting a rentcharge is far different from this.

Mr. Noy: Touching the value in recompense, which is matter in fact, we must believe information, and he doth bind himself for all manner of waste which is a great recompense.

Whereas it is said we go against the will of the owner, in that we must consider the will of giver is to be observed, and in that when land is settled by a public act, and when by private, where by this it is fraud if he so convey that it is not liable to his debts; therefore the parliament ought to enable this land to pay this debt.

11th of June [1628].

A message from the King that he understandeth that the House desires to have the Petition of Right with the answer to it to be enrolled in the Parliament Roll and in the three Courts of Record in Westminster, and that it may be printed; which His Majesty doth agree to all, both for his own honour and our safety, which did much please, and humble thanks returned.

Mr. Solicitor reports the alterations and agreements at the Grand Committee for the Subsidy bill, wherein the baronets of England are discharged of being 50*l.* men in lands in the subsidy.

A bill to settle divers lands and honours and divers goods and chatteis to be to the Earl of Arundel and the heirs male of his body, the remainder to the Lord William Howard and the heirs male of his body, the remainder to the Earl's right heirs, with a saving to the rights to all men. Two read at one time, and approved, being to make perpetuities by act of parliament, for the good of the earldom, and Sir Edward Coke wished every nobleman would do so that there might be convenient maintenance for the supporting the earldoms and dignities.

An act for to enable Dutton Lord Gerrard, to make a jointure to any wife which he shall marry, and to provide portions for his daughters and his other children.

A report by Mr. Pym, for the Grand Committee of religion, touching Doctor Montague.

The first motive to move them to take this into consideration is out of the writ of summons to consider both of spiritual and temporal matters, and they know that if it were a matter of religion not settled there were another place fitter, but being settled this court of parliament was to punish and to regulate such offenders.

Second motive was for the unity of religion.

3rd. That they should take example to precedent in former parliaments, who have likewise taken this into consideration, the three last parliaments.

They have found that this doctrine tends to popery, and his tenets ; and now dispersed and maintained by Doctors and Bishops, and in many conferences.

Articles exhibited against Richard Montague, Clerk.

1. For printing divers books as " Answer to the Gag to the Protestants," another an " Invocation of Saints," etc., wherein he maintaineth divers points against our religion now settled.

As men justified may rise and fall from grace.

2. That the Church of England doth differ from the Reformed Church,

3. That doth scandalize those that are conformable by the name of Puritans, whereby he hath laboured to bring them into the King's high displeasure, that was.

4. That he doth nourish and hold many opinions of the Arminians.

5. That there is no difference of faith betwixt the Church of Rome and ours; and that their Church is builded upon the prophets and Apostles, and there is no danger in their tenets.

6. He doth falsify the articles in reciting them.

7. He doth falsify the book of Homilies.

8. He doth falsify the book of the Common Prayer book, 36 p.

9. He doth seek to breed sedition in the kingdom by making a separation by the name of puritans, for the first occasion of this name was from those that differ in some opinions and ceremonies from the Church of England, but he hath extended it to those that are pure in heart, and make an outward show of conformity.

And he saith that those are a strong and potent faction averse to the state, addicted to anarchy, and to shake off monarchy, and so brings them into the displeasure with the King, knowing that kings are jealous of power and faction, and shows that they are as far from piety as those that are addicted to popery.

Then he seeks to make them odious with the people by saying that they were brought in by the devil.

Appeal page 64] No difference betwixt Papist and us in free will. Gag „ 186] and our conclusions are all one. And for Real Presence, we do jar and jangle infinitely without cause : and so takes away all importance in matters of religion.

And whereas the papist says we make God the author of sin by necessitating all our actions, and those tenets are to avert men from the truth; now he seeks to convert men, by extolling the pope to be the great bishop and the ancient, and doth defend him not to be Antichrist.

225 page Gag. He saith that pictures are and may be used for helps in devotion, and the cross.

9. He seeks to compose our religions, whereby he would take away our religion.

10. He shows how and what difference there is betwixt the divines of our own nation, and so doth scandalize our religions by our own men.

Campanella, 25 Cap : shows how the only way to disturb and conquer a state is to breed division in the nation.

10. By falsifying King James his book by express contradiction to the King.

Quicksilver spirits, child ravished spirits, thieves, liars, and so he calls men of his own profession.

. Ordered that the articles prepared should be presented to the Lords as a charge against him, and Mr. Pym to make it good.

The Commission for Imposition to the Lord Keeper, the Lord President, Lord Chamberlain, the Lord Duke, and all or most of the Privy Council, for giving supply to our friends and allies, and for maintaining of our kingdom, and for that money being the principal sinew of war, we willing to take into consideration what way to raise moneys by way of imposition or otherwise, for the inevitable and pressing occasions of the state, and for your doing of this, this shall be your sufficient warrant, and that you make return hereof presently after you have brought this to any maturity.

Sir Nathaniel Rich : A good physician doth look into the state and region of the body before he doth administer cure, and we find that the whole body of the state is sick and diseased in every part, except only the head, which we with one voice agree to be right.

The numbers of the disease is 10.

1. Fear of innovation of religion, by a countenancing of popery against the King's answer.

2. Favour that they find in the court as the Countess of Buckingham.

3. Conferring places and honours upon them.

4. A kind of toleration by commission, which hath much multiplied that religion.

5. The growing number of the Arminian faction by the countenance [of] them in court, by preferment.

6. The discountenancing of books against those Arminians.

7. The want and decay of preaching by the much discommendation of it.

8. A dangerous revolt from the true religion in Ireland.

9. The circumstance of time is to be observed when there is a powerful hand abroad to extirpate our religion and likely that there is a co-operation at home.

10. Letters procured to stay proceedings at Sessions against recusants : as that Lord.

2ndly. The fear of innovation of government.

1. By the breach of the fundamental points of our liberties ; and in that the misinformation of the King of the willingness of the loans when it was not so.

2. By billeting of soldiers not removed, and the Irish not well affected in religion.

3. The taking of customs without the bill of tonnage and poundage, which is dangerous.

4. The project to bring in the German horse and 40,000*l.* employed for them.

5. The commission for raising money by way of imposition, which they conceive to be in a manner of an excise.

7. By removing worthy men from deserving their places.

8. The drawing of all the forces both by sea and land into one hand.

Sir John Eliot would not have this added, because it makes not for his end, and it was done in King James his time and so reflects not upon the Duke, so left out.

9. added. The proclamations being against the law, as for buildings for eating flesh in Lent, and going down into the country in Christmas.

3rdly. The causes of all our disasters in our attempt.

1. The insufficiency and unfaithfulness of our generals, in the three late voyages, the want of valour, the expense of a million of money, dishonour, and the loss of 1600 men of late; transported ordnance from

1623 to 1628, 1721 tons; the loss of 1600 common soldiers by taking unseasonable times.

4. The decay of the forts in the Kingdom by not maintaining them, the want of provision in them.

A 5 general head [*sic*]. The want of powder in the Tower, for there is but now 60 last of powder when there should be 300 last always, and the King buying powder there was sold the last year 864 barrels, and the King paid 8*l.* for powder, whereas he might have it for 3*l.* 3*s.* 8*d.*

6 and 7 heads. The decay of trade, and the loss of ships and mariners, and therein represent a catalogue of the names and number of our losses, to be had by instruction of the Trinity House.

Note.—Mr. Nicholas said that the King's ships were never so strong by 20 sail.

6. The want of the guarding the narrow seas, for there is but 6 ships, and they lie in the harbour and do no service, but hurt.

2. They are not paid and so discouraged.

3. They are not allowed to take free prizes, but must have letters of marque to their great charge of 8*l.* when they would do it at their own charge, and a tenth part being to the King, and a fifteenth part to the Lord Admiral.

4. The ships are taken from the merchants when they are provided to go out, to the great discouragement of them.

Now to provide remedies for these things, and to add if any thing be to be added, you may do it in your wisdom.

Sir Miles Hubert: There is one part of the order not yet performed and that is the cause of these, and that is I think as every man's heart can witness, the Duke of Buckingham.

But advised, that these heads be voted before we proceed to the causes and the remedies, and then that will be seasonable.

The Chancellor of the Duchy reports from the King that his heart is as firm to religion as any, and that he will take all occasion to suppress all Popery and Arminianism.

The six heads before mentioned resolved upon question to be heads of our declarations.

Mr. Long: Now it is seasonable to show the cause, and not balk the truth, and that is the Duke of Buckingham. I do not say he is the cause that is the only cause, but I may well say he is a cause of all these.

And first: His mother is there by his favour there fed and discountenancing religion, and York House the place of consultation for Arminianism before the Duke: and that for the first.

For the second. [*Blank.*]

For the third—He is the general of all and the causes of all.

For the fourth, the decay of trade: He hath made journeys to take away their voyages.

For the fifth, for the decay of shipping: Though I cannot I suppose others can.

For the sixth: The want of guarding the narrow seas is apparent. And I have cleared my conscience in this, and what I leave others may glean.

Sir John Maynard: For the first, in Spain I heard him so argue and maintained it as I wondered. And for Arminianism I have heard him protest against it.

Chancellor of the Duchy: We have lost much good which might be cause we had not that we desired. And the King desires you to leave all personal things, and that his Majesty would take it as a great favour of us and esteem it great moderation and temper: and you will if you go this way remember that I have given you good counsel.

Coriton: For our disasters at the Island of Rhe, he gave the French and now comes to take it from them. For the entry of the island I will not speak for it was done with honour though with loss, and he did not as he was advised to come away and take the fruits of the island, and employed Dalbeares for [blank].

For victualling of Rochelle, in place of that they victual Dunkirk, and it seems we rather take counsel with Spain to deliver that we have up to the enemies. And he is the occasion of all these.

That Dalbeares is made a man so contemptible and those accused for entertaining him. You may know an action of his of trust to the Count Palatine, when he might have betrayed him, if he had not been trusty, to the enemy, and have had 100,000*l.* for it.

Sir Benjamin Rudyard: I would not have us to take that course which may not hurt him, and do ourselves no good. Every thing must have time to seek and prepare things, but when we tell the King of these faults, no doubt but the King will reflect upon those who are faulty.

Sir Henry Martin: Natural motions are swiftest in the beginning and slowest in the end, violent motions the contrary; and I desire we may follow the natural motion. Let us look to the end, and endeavour to make that more possible which we desire, and let us endeavour to breed in the King rather an apprehension of our general care than any private passion. And this I humbly desire.

Sir Edward Coke: For his two motions they are clear contrary, but let that lie aside. I do clear my gracious sovereign, for he seeth with other men's eyes, and works with other men's hands: so if there be a fault in the judges it is not the King's; if the Treasurer offend, the King is not to blame. You see the King of Spain aims at a general monarchy, and for that I will say no more of that, but all goes wrong, and we must set the saddle of the right horse, and that is the Duke of Buckingham; and this clears the King.

Captain Price: Why we should heap up all these things and grievances, and then leap upon him presently without any other preparation or proof, when we have protested by the mouth of Sir Henry Martin, that we will avoid all personal things, and I will not say fall upon him expressly against the Kings command: and I cannot with my conscience and by an implicit faith condemn a man I know not guilty, and I shall clear him to I see the contrary.

Mr. Spencer as much, that [blank] 2 Hen IV, n. 11.

Sir John Scidmore: To go upon general opinion I count it no justice, but he is likely to be a great good to the Kingdom, for there is many that will testify he was the cause of the calling this parliament, and that it is like to be a good to the whole Kingdom, and I am persuaded he hath done many good offices, and why we should so fall upon him I know not, and I think we are all persuaded the King would take it well if we should leave persons.

Resolved upon question, That the excessive power of the Duke of Buckingham and the abuse of that power is the chief cause of these evils to the king and kingdom.

Nota.—1. No proofs, but disproved.
      2. No reasons answered of the contrary part.
      3. The particulars under every general head refused to be put to the question, but to involve many particulars which had no relation to the party under general heads.

4. No man heard with patience that spoke of the contrary part, but derided against reason.

Sir Nathaniel Rich presents the remonstrance of the evils of this Kingdom, and the Duke the cause of them all.

' Most dread sovereign, we knowing your Majesty's royal and true intention for to be for the good of your Kingdom, and knowing our duties to be called to present and advise your Majesty of the state of this Kingdom, which now stands much distressed.

' And we protest that in this we do not, and it is far from us, to cast the least aspersion of your sacred Majesty. And we do humbly thank your Majesty for your gracious answer to our petition of right. And we knowing that your Majesty cannot be so well and truly informed as by us, and we therefore humbly present the fear of some secret working tending to the innovation of religion.' And then goes on with the particulars, which see before.

[14 June?]

Doctor Mannering impeached by the House of Commons for his seditious doctrine, and Judgment decreed by the speaker of our house, in the name of the House of Commons, against him, for it.

. And the Lord Keeper called him twice to hear his judgment, which was that the Lords upon the impeachment of the Commons, have adjudged, 1. That he shall be imprisoned during the pleasure of that House. 2. He shall be fined 1000*l.* 1. 3. He shall be suspended from his living for three years, and disabled for ever to preach at Court and to receive any dignity, and that an able preaching minister shall serve that cure out of the profits of his benefice. 4. That his book shall be burnt, and a proclamation to call in all the books, and all to be burnt.

Selden : As we have shown, the excessive power of the Duke of Buckingham is a.great cause of the evils and dangers of this kingdom, :for that cannot be in any man but it is dangerous or inconvenient.

. Yet the abuse of that power or his power is not desired to be rem[ed]ied, nor no desire represented to the King for the remedy.

Therefore resolved *sur* question that a clause shall be added concern- ing the abuse of that power, and to be this, to desire his Majesty, since the Duke of Buckingham hath such power and that he hath abused this power to refer to his Majesty's consideration whether it may be safe for the kingdom to continue him in such trust, or for the King to have him so near his person.

17th June, 1628.

Sir Walter Earle : Of the loss of ships within the 3 years 50, and odd ports, of which 24 no certificate.

The number of the ships taken by the enemy 100 ; cast away 133 ; 100,000*l.* value, more.

Lesser ships 125 taken.

In all 260 ships taken and lost of the value of 197,000*l.* 130 lesser ships under 100 ton, the value not yet known. The French merchants loss esteemed to be 70,000*l.*

The pardon : Desired that the heads may be seen of it in this House before the subsidy bill passeth, for it is desired that those that be crimi- nally accused may be excepted ; for though it be of grace, yet it may be so as it may strike at the whole bottom of our judicature. Not granted by the King.

The subsidy bill sent up the 17th of June.

Exception taken by the Lords at a conference, that in the preamble of the bill the Lords were left out, and to continue the good correspondence betwixt both Houses, they thought fit to move us, if we thought fit to give warrant by the House, that at a conference betwixt both Houses, the word Commons may be put out, " We your humble and loyal subjects," as it hath bee includeth both.

9 Hen. IV., *idemnite nominis* [*sic*]; no conference to be touching the bill of subsidy.

Selden : I wonder that they should think that we have done them injuries, for unto 1 Eliz. the Lords were not named, and the last parliament the Commons were only named, and so no necessity of alteration, for before Henry VIII. time they were never named for their assent supplies the naming of them. And the bill of tonnage and poundage is plainly the grant of subsidies, and we name only the Commons and not the Lords.

Sir Nathaniel Rich : The subsidies have ever been propounded here by the Commons and never by the Lords, and so in the preamble the proposition comes only from the Commons. But when it comes to the enacting they are joined with us, that is in the giving. And at the end of the sessions, the speaker delivers this bill as a gift from the Commons and not naming the Lords as it is no bill else, and it hath a special answer. In 39 Eliz., the Bishopric of Norwich, a proviso then was added at a conference, they being loth to send down the bill, which doth fit this case. (The ordinary way is if any alteration be made of any bill it must be sent down, and agreed to by us and then sent up again.)

Glanville : As the bill of subsidy moves from us, so must the amendment.

19th June, 1628.

Taken for a rule that a bill voted and sent up to the Lords, cannot be sent down to be amended without they make their alterations and then we may agree to it ; but the subsidy bill though it be mended and sent down, yet conceived we cannot agree to the alteration. *Sed quaere de hoc.*

The King's answer to the Remonstrance read by our speaker ; which was :—

That after his answer to our Petition of Right, he did not expect any remonstrance, and this consisted of matters of religion and matters of state, which did more properly belong to his knowledge than ours ; and he thought before this that we had understood the state of the kingdom, but now he understands that we do not understand it so well as he thought we had done.

And [as] we had taken time to draw this he would take time to consider of it and to answer it as he thought fit, or as it deserved.

My Lord of Cork, by name Boyle, his counsel heard in the full House, for that saving of all the right of my Lord of Cork in the province of Munster, which he bought of Sir Walter Raleigh for 1500*l*. which then worth 200*l*., per annum, and Mr. Carew Raleigh seeking now to restore his blood, and to enable him to take by descent what his father had ; and though peradventure some things be not observed, as matters of attornments, liveries of seisin, enrollments, whereby he may pick some quarrel, yet having paid the full value as appears that none would have given more, he thinks : and his humble suit is that there may be a proviso in this bill to the Earl of Cork that he may not be troubled or sued for it ; and my Lord of Cork hath bestowed 20,000*l*. for the plantation.

The answer for Mr. Carew Raleigh :—That for the payment of the money that it is matter of fact, and will trouble this House, and they may trouble this House so long that he shall not get his bill to pass this sessions. But we say it is worth 60,000*l.* per annum, and there be many defects which we now peradventure know not. But if my Lord of Cork have such right, he need not fear ; for be it by law or equity as it must be, he may defend it, for neither of these be taken from him. For he desires only to be enabled to sue for that which is his right. And if my Lord of Cork have no right why should he desire that he may not sue him. And in the bill there is a proviso that Mr. Raleigh may be sued, and it were hard if he may not sue for his right. And if there be any defect in the conveyance, it falls to the King by the attainder of Sir Walter Raleigh, and [*blank*].

Sir Edward Coke : This proviso is prejudicial to the King, for it confirms all letters patents which were made of such lands, manors, &c., which we know not how and what defects there be in them, and there be granted concealed titles which we condemn, and therefore I would have no proviso added.

Mr. Browne : Whereas it is said it must come to the King if there be any defect, and not to the heir ;—it may be otherwise ; for if Sir Walter Raleigh had an estate in tail, and then he makes a feoffment in fee, and covenants to make further assurance, and is attainted before further assurance, the King cannot have anything but the heir may, by this restoring of his blood, as if he had never been attained. And the planters under him being many and protestants, it were hard for them to be put out.

And Masons said, This being a bill of grace it were hard to prejudice them who were not faulty. For the purchasers might be well advised by the counsel to proceed with their purchase ; for when Sir Walter Raleigh is attainted if there were any defect his heir cannot take advantage of it : and the King having confirmed it by act of parliament he cannot take any advantage ; and so there is no fault in them for they could not know of this restitution. And by this the son should take advantage of his father's attainder, for his father's covenants for better assurance being avoid by his attainder whereby my Lord of Cork was disabled to have it, now Mr. Raleigh shall take advantage of his father's attainder.

Selden : Restitution is for enabling him to be in the same manner that he should be if no attainder had not been, and if there were no saving in this bill the land forfeited he should be restored too. But that he is not by the saving to the King and those that claim under him, and if this proviso were added, then it were against the nature of all the bills of this nature as if one were naturalized to all intents and purposes excepting only to one A.B. this were such a thing as hath not been seen.

A message : That the Lords had sent to the King for the cancelling of the commission and warrant for raising money by way of imposition or otherwise ; which were cancelled before the King and sent down to the Lords to see it so, and they sent it down to us to see it also.

And Coke said, that we have had a judgement for our liberties by our petition of right, and now in *præsenti parliamento* we have had execution of it. This to be entered in the book.

Mr. Ball : In all particular bills there are general savings of all others' rights, for that it cannot be that all others' rights can be examined. I conceive we do him an apparent injustice if we do not admit such a proviso.

The King having but a right of action, if there were a defect in the conveyance, [it] is not given to him by the attainder.

Mr. Glanvill: The very attainder is and works a release in law, and doth confirm his title, as it was the opinion of the whole committee; and if he never be restored then the Earl of Cork is well, and if he be not restored he hath no wrong, and so I think the proviso may well pass and the bill also.

Sir John Eliot: For matter in fact it is doubtful for the payment of 100*l.* which was in difference for the 500*l.* was confessed to be paid, and it is more suspicious, because they offered proof here where we could not hear it, and did in the Lords' house where they do hear witnesses.

Resolved upon question, the proviso shall be added that the son shall not take advantage of the attainder of the father, and if Sir Walter Raleigh had been living it had been justice, and the law would have compelled him upon his covenant to have a farther and good assurance, and his son shall not be in better case.

June 20th 1628.

Voted upon question that the imposition of 4*d.* upon a quarter of malt in London and within four miles was a grievance as well in the creation as in the execution, especially being of a native commodity, which King James was willing to have made a law against all impositions being native.

A petition for the privileges granted to planters in the Somers Islands, and for easing them of impositions set upon the tobacco.

With other petitions presented to his Majesty in the name of the Commons in the behalf of them.

And moved that all new matters may be forborne being this sessions growing towards an end, and the things now in hand may be perfected.

Moved that a petition may be prepared to his Majesty to show the inconvenience of calling men of 40*l.* land to be knighted, and to desire that they may not be troubled for their appearance.

Sir Thomas Wentworth reports that a commission or patent was granted to one Levett for taking toll of every 20 cattle 6*d.* every pack horse ½*d.*, &c., for sheep at Willa bridge and Firre bridge, and they found that the bridges were in good repair at the time of the patent granted, and other towns were bound to their repair, and so they adjudged a grievance both in the creation and execution, and a petition ordered to be drawn to present to the King.

Title to the petition exhibited by the Lords spiritual and temporal and the Commons in this present Parliament assembled, concerning divers rights and liberties, with the King's royal assent in full parliament.

Wherein Sir Edward Coke observed at the conference that writs are to be sent to the Common Pleas and Exchequer, but to the Chancery and King's Bench there are no writs directed. For the Chancery is *coram domino rege in cancellaria,* and the King's Bench is *coram domino rege ubicunque fuerit*; and the chancellor ought to deliver it to the chief Justice *propriis manibus,* and then that makes it a record as well as if it were removed by *certiorari mittimus,* or any other way, and the Chancellor is to receive it *propriis manibus.*

Mr. Banks in the chair for the bill of tonnage and poundage; and Mr. Dawes' information.

The subsidy upon the book of rates comes to about 150,000*l.* per annum. The imposition is about 45,000*l.* per annum, which is upon lead, tin, and baize, and to be deducted out of this last 25,000*l.* per annum for defalcations.

Sir Dudley Digges moves that we should all join to desire his Majesty for a recess, that we may upon our next meeting consider of some things for the settling of the King's revenue, and to go on with a proposition made and approved touching the settling of some plantation and trade in the West Indies.

Sir Edward Coke: I will undertake if superfluous expenses in the household, wardrobes, the Court of the Duchy to be united, the Court of York taken away, which I hope the Yorkshiremen will have wit enough to desire, the Courts in Wales and such like; and it appears by 6 Edw. III. n. 4, 50 Edw. III. n. 5 et n. 26, that this hath been done in former parliaments, to look into the King's revenues, the Court of Wards, and Forests. But I would not have a message sent to know of the King how long.

Sir Miles Fleetwood: I will make it appear and undertake to raise a constant revenue to the King out of the Court of Wards, the Forests, and Recusants, which yield not to the King now 60,000*l.*; and I dare say and undertake to raise at least 250,000*l.* per annum.

Sir Robert Pye: I desire that no man may go out of the House with that opinion that any such sum may be raised, and let us not propose much and fall to little or nothing; and I think they are projectors who are to make great show and perform little.

21st June 1628.

Mr. Banks' report of Sir Edward Sayer, and shows the examination of Mr. Dawes, and Sir Edward Sayer's answers, which was that Sir Edward Sayer came to Mr. Dawes to move him to join with him to make a new book of rates, which Dawes denying and saying it was a difficult thing, the other replying said it was easy to be done by making 1*s.* 2*s.* throughout the book.

He answers that he said that in some things the book of rates might be made double, but not in all; and that he doth not remember he said that 1*s.* might be made 2*s.*, and he said that what he had done in this he did it by the King's command, which the Committee conceived to be no warrant for him to do anything against the law, but that he might have answered his Majesty so.

The King's message by Mr. Solicitor, that he understanding that Sir Edward Sayer was questioned, that his Majesty did out of his desire to be informed of the Customs and the book of rates and so commanded them two to inform him of it, and how it stood.

Doctor Mannering's submission, he acknowledging it at the Bar his high offence to God, the King and Commonwealth.

Dawes said further that Sir Edward Sayer came to him and asked him if he were not sent for by the House, and he said no. Then Sir Edward Sayer said that if he were he answered not upon oath, and therefore he needed not to say anything of this business which passed betwixt them. (He denies the last part of this.) And he said further that Sir Edward Sayer said to the King before him that he might make one shilling 2 through the book of rates, and he was the projector if any were. (He appeals to the King for this.)

This reported to the House.

Sir Edward Coke: He being a member of this House, and dissuading men from true and plain dealing with this House, it is against the liberty of this House, and to disparage this which is the general inquisitor for the whole kingdom, which if it be neglected all is nothing.

(8 Eliz., Long's case, turned out of the House.) And therefore moves that he may be cast out of the House, and sent to the Tower, to remain there during the pleasure of this House.

This resolved upon question.

Selden : The jurisdiction of our House is properly of the members of our House, and upon those that offend against the House; and therefore though he be put out of the House, yet being an offence against the House, he may be kept in the Tower during the pleasure of the House.

And resolved : That Sir Edward Sayer is unworthy to sit ever again in this House.

23rd June 1628.

A letter sealed and put under the door, with directions to this House, and superscribed with this, " Cursed be he that doth not deliver this letter "; and disputed whether this letter should be first viewed by the Speaker, or by a certain number of the House ; and resolved that a Select Committee to withdraw into the Committee Chamber to consider whether it be fit to be read in the House, and if it be not, to give some general reason why it should not.

Sir Edward Coke reports it not fit to be read, for it is a Jesuitical and devilish plot, and something which is not fit touching his Majesty's person, which upon the reading but of one line we thought it not fit for the eye of any subject to look upon it, and therefore we read no further of it, and thought it fit to send it to the King to deliver it to His Majesty's own hand : and so ordered.

Sir William Fleetwood reports the opinion of the Committee touching the petition of the goldsmiths against the exchangers of money.

The points were two : First, if the commission were legally granted and if there be any such granted. Secondly, of the inconvenience, which was proved by many merchants, by prohibiting them to sell to the goldsmith, for if they carry it to the Mint the goldsmith must first make it fit for the standard in the Tower, and there they lose.

Secondly, If we carry it to the Exchanger we cannot have so much by 6d. an ounce as of goldsmiths, and there being 30 ounces in a £100, they lose 15s. in £100; and so they bring no bullion over now as they used to do, and if they do, but very little.

Thirdly. They cannot get money of the changers for it, and upon this for the inconvenience of it the Committee resolved that it was a grievance in the execution, and for the legal part they left it to the House to judge, there being then no lawyers, (but they found that the Mint was lessened the last year by it £150,000).

For matter of law, there was no opinion in it, nor voted.

Mr. Speaker said the King's care was only that no inconvenience should be, and he granted only *officium cambii*

Mr. Banks touching the legality of it : I think it illegal as it is granted; for when there is negative words in it as that none shall buy any bullion, that is not good.

Mr. Noy reports the Act for continuance, repeal and making perpetual divers acts and statutes. Only 4 Hen : VIII. proposed to be revived, for making bulwarks by the sheriff or Justices of Peace.

p. 1 Eliz., fry of fish ; 13 Eliz., touching ecclesiastical livings; 3 Jac., for avoiding delays in executions; 21 Jac., usury; these made perpetual.

Omitting 24 Hen. VIII. breeding of cattle ; 3 Ed. VI. 5 Eliz., for cattle : by question resolved these to be omitted from continuance.

43 Eliz. additions, for the taking of prentices (7 Jac. for repairing the sea banks in Norfolk) not resolved, but respited. This continued to the next sessions, and not to the next sessions of parliament.

Repeal 16 Hen. VIII. and all but 1 Hen. VII. touching liveries.

Revive 4 Hen. VIII. for making of bulwarks. Upon question not revived.

The bill engrossed.

A message from the King that upon Thursday next he meaneth to make a sessious, and then to prorogue it to October next, when if please God we shall meet again. This delivered by the Chancellor of the Duchy.

Banks his reasons for his former opinion of the grievances of the exchangers, both in creation *et* execution.

9 Hen. V. 2, 9 Ed. III. cap. 2. These statutes no power for the merchants to make a trade of it, and they do not prohibit him.

18 Edw. III. cap. 6.

3rdly. It is matter of trust, and this granted for years; if he die, the trust shall be in nobody to administration, and then peradventure committed to a woman, or a child.

4. It requires skill, and he hath license to execute it by deputy, and they may have no skill.

Selden : This consists of a patent, indentures and proclamation, upon the patent and indenture, the patent recites that it belongs to the King to have the power.

In the body it is to have the said power and office of the exchangers, according to the indentures, and in the indentures the King covenants with the Lord of Holland and his deputies that he shall have the sole exchange of money and bullion. For the first part, for the exchange of money, there was and is such an office, and it is lawful, and it is called *officium cambii*, and this appears by the Charter 20 Hen. I. 35 ; and this was in King John's time, and Fleta said that that belongs only to the King.

25 Edw. III. printed est dit none shall exchange money but the King's exchanger.

3 Hen. VII. cap. 6, and so much as only toucheth matter of money it is not against the law, but yet I think it is void because it is in another. But for the exchange of bullion, which he hath by growth or imported, by the common law this might be sold in any other place as other merchandize might, if it have not the King's coin of it, for that *vide* Domesday, *tyle homme tyent* by such service, and white money ; and in Hen. II *temps* in rents, that the sheriff brought them in either in mass or bullion, which shows that bullion was not (f. 82 Dyer) then appropriated, but it went as other commodities did, &c.

9 Hen. VII. f. 16, *in det sur ob.* to pay *aurum purum, quod monster q. c. fuit bullion.*

This appears by the common law, and how it is any way altered by the statute that is to be seen for that which concerns this is 9 Edw. III. differ in the French from the English, which sets men at liberty for gold to sell it where they will.

4 Hen. VII. a restraint from the goldsmith not to buy gold ; which needed not if the King's exchanger had had the sole power. This toucheth only gold, so silver seems to belong to them, though 9 Edw. III. says that all bullion brought in shall be brought to the exchanger, yet this doth not exclude him from selling to others in the negative.

If there be a penal law it is true the King may pardon it, but he may not dispense with it by the statute of 21 Jac : of dispensation ; therefore so much as concerns the restraint of bullion to the exchanger, it being or amounting to a penal law, the Kings patent and indentures is a dispensation, and so void by 21 Jac.

The confirmation of the pardon brought in by Mr. Attorney as a message from the Lords.

Sir Robert Pye. The mint hath raised to the King sometime 7000*l.* per nunum, and upon such occasion it hath come down to 1500*l.*

Am[brose ?] Browne : It is a monopoly, and not excepted out of that statute.

Resolved upon question, that the patent accompanied with the indentures and proclamations were a grievance both in the creation and execution.

Ordered that the bill of tonnage and poundage and a bill for arms to be first set in some forwardness.

New stamps for gold made ready for new coining, and the meaning is the pound weight to be made into more pieces.

Tuesday [afternoon] the 23rd of June.

The House resolved into a committee, Mr. Banks in the chair, touching a way for the bill of tonnage and poundage, and impositions.

Sir Robert Phillips : Since 12 Jac. : we have scarce made our claim to our right for the grievance of our impositions, for before there was no sound complaint but presently there was redress.

The [blank].

Sir Edward Coke : This case is of more weight than difficulty. There is *custuma magna et parva et antiqua et nova ;* and the custom consists of wool, wool fells, leather.

Rotuli parliamentorum 3 Edw. I. rotuli patentium 3 Edw. I. m. 1. 25 Edw. III. returna brevium ; 25 Edw. I, confirmationes cartarum printed. All these ancient customs and new are proved to be granted by act of parliament by the Commons as appears by those statutes before ; and it is not said to be granted by the Lords. So that the King hath nothing of right without the grant by act of parliament.

25 Edw. III. because wool was turned into cloth therefore the King can have no subsidy upon them.

13 Hen. IV. n. 18, for maintaining of Calais etc., the King could lay no impositions.

Every king of England hath taken our grant of the subsidy for tonnage or poundage : if could lay impositions what needed he take it by act of parliament. Since we have no time to settle it we have no way but to set down our birthright, and in a humble petition to desire his Majesty not to take it without an act of parliament

Sir Nathaniel Rich : In 13 of Henry IV, it was but granted for years, as for one, two, three or more ; and with this condition, that the King should not take it as a right, nor to make a precedent. And therefore I would not have the King to conceive it to be his right, but the love of his subjects.

Carew : If we go by way of petition or remonstrance of our right, and to desire our right may not be infringed, and then to have it infringed, whether it will not be more prejudice to us than [if] we never had made it ; for to have a violation of that which we claim to be our right is a negation and a denial of it.

Selden : I shall less doubt this infringing than anything ; and whereas it is said that in 1 Eliz. : in the preamble, that the Kings of England have ever had this bill of subsidy of *tonnagium et pundagium* for life, for this it is not well applied if it be looked upon.

Sir John Finch : I delivered a message to the King which might peradventure be mis-conceived, for that the end was to know when we should have a recess, and though it would be here conceived that word to be properly intended that to be an adjournment, yet by many wise men it is conceived and so taken to be a prorogation.

Resolved upon question, that a committee shall draw up a remonstrance of our right and the undue taking of the subsidy of tonnage and poundage without act of parliament, and the reasons why we cannot now grant it.

Bowdler's case.

Mr. Selden reports the matter touching Bowdler a bastard, wherein he showeth that Mr. Bowdler being a bastard died intestate. The judge of the Prerogative Court Sir Henry Martin, hath got almost all the personal estate ; and it consists of these three parts :

1st. The proceeding in the Exchequer Court. He thus dying Sir Edward Warden and Ford being the next of kin came and obtained letters of administration, this to be *pendente lite*. After this the Attorney General sues in the Exchequer for the King. setting out that those goods which no man else hath property in, the King ought to have them, and to dispose of them. After this a subpœna awarded, and the same day an injunction to the ordinary not to grant administration, and to the administrators enjoined not to meddle as administrators, and then a commission and commissioners appointed by Mr. Attorney to collect up the debts of the intestate, and they to keep this personal estate for the King's use.

The defendants appear upon the subpœna and demur upon the bill, showing he was no bastard, and meant to make that the point of the issue ; but before publication, upon a motion it was ordered that a case upon the general matter should be made, whether a bastard dying intestate should not have his goods to the King and this was a project to bring all dying intestate to be subject to the judgment of this case. After this a petition was made to the King to refer it to all the judges in England : and so it resteth.

2ndly. How the personal estate now stands, that is being to the value of 3000*l.* and all in bonds except only the value of 20*l.*

3rdly. For the projector (one Bland as it was thought), who being a principal prosecutor of this matter is a principal witness.

Mr. Wilde : For matter of law in this case, I think it clear the King hath no property in the personal estate of a bastard dying intestate. For admit he were no bastard, and so dying, the ordinary hath the sole power for committing administration, and that is given either by the common law or by the statutes of 31 Hen : III. 31 Edw : III. and these statutes give it to those who are lawfully akin, not tainted with any blot or crime. And if it cannot be committed to them, then we must resort to the common law, and then the ordinary hath disposing to pious uses.

Sir Edward Coke : The question is admitting him to be a bastard and dies intestate, if that King shall have the goods or no.

1. The King claims it as supreme ordinary to dispose of it. And if he cannot have it so, then he claims by pretence of property, *quia est nullius filius*, having no hereditary blood. (I never heard the like.)

There is no book of the law that speaks of bastards dying intestate, but of dying intestate generally..

In rot. clausarum, 7 Hen : III. m. 16, the goods of the intestate were wont to be taken into the hands of the King, and it is true, for his debts &c. And this did not belong to the King but to the lords of manors, as appears by many books, and in these 2 Ric : III. p. 11, Hen : VII. f. 12 b. These belonged to the lords and not to the ordinary, nor the King ; and they had only the disposing by way of administration, and not any property in it. So the supreme ordinary is gone, for it is gone to the ordinary as appears by Grisewell's case in (Common Pleas ?) : The ordinary hath the property, as the statute of Westminster the second, saith in express words, and he must pay the debts. For hereditary blood (31 Edw : III.) in Croft's case in 21 Eliz : they adjudged the King shall not meddle with the goods of an alien, *à fortiori*, not in the case of a bastard ; it concerns all the sons of Adam.

21 Hen. VIII

This commodity hath a common lawyer that he doth not commonly die without children and intestate.

Mr. Noy : The names of projectors are now turned to proposers. The inconvenience is great, for if the ordinary say he made a will the Exchequer may say he died intestate. The goods should be subject to two jurisdictions, and if they go to the ordinary he is subject to an action of debt, while if it come into the Exchequer I know not what remedy he hath against the Court.

2ndly. It is not needful that they be akin, for his friends shall administer ; nay he hath natural kindred, though he have neither wife nor children, yet his mother and her kindred are sure akin, and natural kindred is sufficient.

For 7 Hen. III., that the King shall take the goods of the intestant into his hands, that is if the party be indebted, and he shall only hold them till he know who shall pay them. The statute of Westminster, the second, gives debt, but if the King shall have them, who shall have debt against him ?

Resolved upon question that of bastards dying intestate the ordinary ought to commit administration as in the cases of other persons.

Resolved upon question, upon the report of Mr. Ratcliffe, that the prohibiting of the King's subjects from fishing at Greenland by the Muscovia Company is a grievance to the subjects ; and this to be drawn up in a petition to be presented to the King.

The 25th of June 1628.

The bill for Brumfield and Yare to make the tenants of those manors freeholders which before had an estate from 40 years to 40 years for ever descendable as land in fee simple, and the King by covenant was bound to make them such estates, and they having given a valuable consideration, it was resolved upon question that this should pass for a law, and this to be a confirmation of their estates, though it was said this was a very dangerous precedent for selling the King's lands.

Hackwell said that he had looked to two bills of resumptions, and there was ever exceptions of those lands for which there was paid valuable consideration, and here was such a consideration, ergo.

But Dudley Digges said that there was a protestation the last parliament that there should be a resumption, and no lands should be confirmed, and but that this was covenanted for an Act of parliament before that time, otherwise if it were for my father I should not agree to it.

A bill for prohibiting children to be sent over the sea with an intent to be popishly bred up in any religious house. This bill passed both Houses.

The bill of continuance, repeal, and making perpetual of divers statutes. Three times read, and passed for a law, and sent to the Lords.

2. 9 Hen. V., cap.: 2, touching the alloy of money.

Mr. Selden moves that since the administrators of Bowdler are bound by bond not to meddle with the goods, and the Prerogative Court bound by the Exchequer not to meddle with them but as they should order, and therefore that it may be intimated to the Lord Treasurer the opinion of this House that the Ordinary may have the ordinary power as n other cases. But this void.

Ordered all members of the House that have any bills to bring them in to the clerk against the next meeting.

The remonstrance touching the causes of not granting the subsidy of tonnage and poundage, sets forth the greatness of our business, the many interruptions, and now the shortness of the time for an end of this sessions doth prevent, and lest your Majesty might be misinformed that it is a thing due and not of the mere love of your subjects, we are forced out of the duty we owe to you and those whom we represent to make this our humble declaration, that it is the undoubted right of the subject and that agreed to by your Majesty in our petition of right, that no tallage nor tax shall be levied without assent in parliament, therefore we desire your Majesty that nothing may be taken otherwise, and we hope your Majesty will observe it, now knowing it.

And shows how that it will be more prejudicial than if there had been only an adjournment, for then our intended grant would have related to the beginning of the parliament, but now that cannot be. And that is voluntary they show how it hath been sequestered into the hand of your subjects, and upon occasions of war granted and afterwards omitted, to the intent that no claim may be made of right, and that it hath been manifested by divers answers of your progenitors, that it is and hath been accepted as other subsidies of the good will and benevolence of your subjects, which answer is " *Le Roy accept le benevolence de ses subjects*," and it hath but lately granted for life ; yet they hope upon their next meeting to settle it in as large and ample manner as may stand with the convenience of trade. And they desire your Majesty not to take it ill of those that refuse to pay without warrant of law.

Resolved upon question that a remonstrance to this purpose shall be presented to the King.

Mr. Noy : All that is taken above the great custom and petty custom is impost that is illegal, and that is the bill of tonnage and poundage &c. or other impost. And I would not have it desired that he should absolutely forbear it, but that he would not have him to take it of right.

Coriton : The end of this is contrary.

Noy : I see the sense of the House is to have this request to his Majesty not to take it. I would have something added, for this three year it hath been taken, and seizure for not payment hath been, but there hath been no judgement given by them knowing it against law. Yet by 14 Edw. III, if any land goods without agreement for them they may be seized for the great custom and little custom, and under that pretence they will keep them for the tonnage and poundage and impositions, therefore if we do not desire that there may be no seizure for any such things but that they may lawfully land their goods paying the customs ; but this not added.

Mr. Selden reports the difference betwixt this pardon and 21 Jac., and the differences are of three sorts.

1. Some are pardoned here which are not there.
2. Some things contrary.
3. Some things are pardoned which are also excepted.

In the body here is added for licence of alienation, this relates to 31 of January last.

Except all books against the King.

2. Except all alienations which is as large as the pardon.

4. In larging for liveries and oustertraynes, from 10 Jac.

5. Except more pardon than before, all persons except they be in five prisons (or otherwise restrained of liberty is left out).

6. That all collectors of subsidies &c., are pardoned without time.

7. An exception for not taking of knighthood, never before excepted.

8. Extends to the last King and this, for subsidies.

9. Except all such causes as were appointed to be heard in the Star Chamber during this session of parliament ; and so larger.

10. Except all offences already adjudged in the High Commission or before any other ecclesiastical Court for any deprivation, degradation &c.

11. Except all extortion of clerks &c. added.

12. Except all offences done for buildings inmates in London, being done contrary to the law, and the King's proclamations. This agrees with 21 (but only not thought fit). An omission in the end that this shall be in force to pardon all claiming under the king's letters patents, and this is omitted, and this only refers to the king which belongs to him.

Ordered the House being resolved into a Committee the House shall debate this to-morrow.

The 26th of June.

Upon the reading of the remonstrance for the bill of tonnage and poundage, Mr. Maxwell came with a message from the King that the House should go up to him, which they did, and being come, the King said ;—That he had called us to tell us the occasion of the prorogation, and for that he understood we were in making a second remonstrance, and therein we made a false interpretation of his answer to our petition of right, and that it was never his intention to debar himself of the tonnage and poundage which his progenitors had enjoyed and which was his right, and which he would not depart with, and therefore he thought good to let us know his meaning and commanded the judges to take notice of it. Yet to show the true intention to perform his word he will ever preserve it, and that hereafter we shall have no cause to complain ; and this he thought fit to let us know, that no man may go away with a misconception. After this the Speaker presented the bill of subsidy in the name of the Commons as their free gift, and then desired pardon for all errors that hath been committed this parliament, if any there were, and particularly for himself, with a desire that those bills which had passed in both Houses his Majesty would be pleased to give his royal assent. Then was read the titles of the bill for divers abuses committed on the Sabbath ; 2ndly. A bill for prohibiting the sending over any to be popishly bred beyond the seas ; 3rdly. An act touching alehouses ; 4thly. The bill for the continuance and repeal of statutes ; the subsidy for the clergy, with divers particular bills for private men. The public bills had this answer, " Le Roy le voyt "; the private, this, " Soyt faite come est desire." These bills thus passed, the Lord Keeper did prorogue this parliament to the 20th of October next. And this was the end of this Sessions ; with no great content, for they desired an adjournment or recess.

Nota : The pardon not accepted, though the largest, except 21 Jac.

The parliament holden by [blank] the 20th of January 1628-9.

The first thing done after prayers, the Clerk read a bill for prevention of corruption in Courts of justice by laying great penalties of those that buy any judicial places ; and also upon them that take or give any reward for effecting anything in question, with a strict oath to be administered to them which shall receive' or have any place of judicature.

Then the Speaker did remember the House of their usual order first to settle all the standing Committees, and the appointing a Committee for priviledges or elections, wherein the House confirmed all those which were before; where note that all things which was before must be again confirmed, or otherwise it is not good.

Mr. Jordan moved to know the pleasure of the House, whether inasmuch as his fellow Burgess was chosen Mayor of [*blank*] whether he might serve here or was tied to attendance there.

Resolved that he should attend here, and all particular service to cease for the general.

21st January.

Mr. Selden moves that a Committee may be named to see whether the petition and answer made by the King be recorded in the parliament Roll and in the Courts of Westminster, as was promised by his Majesty, and also to see what hath been entered in the journal book of the parliament since the ending of the former session. Which upon view was found that the King's speech, which was a comment upon his answer, was added by his command, the consideration of which is referred to Tuesday next, how much herein the privilege of the kingdom and the subjects are infringed. And he reports how all our liberties have been since infringed, by the order in the Exchequer that after a replevin under the great seal, the execution thereof hath been stayed by their order, and in other things, and desires that a Committee may be chosen to seek out wherein the liberties have been infringed, and represent it to the House.

Secretary Coke moves that we should not seek occasions, but rather that they should seek us: for is there not a Committee of the whole House for grievances, and why should we make a particular Committee since there is a general? And I think there is no man here but desires a fair correspondence betwixt the King and his subjects, which if we proceed moderately I doubt not but we shall sooner effect our desires.

Sir John Elliot moves that the printer may be sent for that printed that addition, besides the petition, and answer to know by what authority it was done, since those two were to go alone: which was agreed to.

Much disputed whether to have a standing Committee for to inquire and present the grievances to the House, and wherein the liberties have been invaded.

Sir Dudley Digges: I am jealous that the manner may by sinister constructions mar the matter, which if we be cautious and be not too hasty to seek new ways, which may be thought to be, if we pursue this way to have particulars where the general may do as good service and not be so subject to misinterpretation. And we must not only respect our own intentions, but what constructions others may make of it.

Mr. Price of the same opinion, and tells how that it hath been taken notice of in other places to the great dishonour of the House, to subtract a parliament out of parliament.

Sir William Herbert: This comes near the Spanish Inquisition to make particular inquisitors.

Sir John Elliot excepts against the words, and moves that the gentleman will be more cautious, that he let not such words fall.

Littleton: This is no new way but necessary, for if we should stay to particulars occasioned the consideration, we might lose the matter, and suffer prejudice in the meantime.

Sir Thomas Hoby: I will not say that this is a new way, but this is the course; that if any member of the House prefer a petition to the committee of grievances, he need not set his name to it, but it may come in so by petition. But if a stranger prefer a petition he must have his name to it, and defend it; but since the members have that liberty, it may be better done that way.

Sir Nathaniel Rich: This is no unusual way, and it is not proper for the committee of grievances, for that is proper for the well-being of the subjects; but this doth touch the very being of them, and therefore proper for a proper committee.

And upon his motion:—

Resolved upon question, that the whole House shall be resolved into a committee, to consider all those things wherein the privileges of the subjects have been infringed against the petition of right; and to begin on Tuesday next at 9 o'clock in the morning.

Mr. Norton the printer, being asked by what authority the addition was added to the petition of right and the answer, doth say that he had a warrant, but doth not remember from whom. To prevent any misdealing Mr. Selden, Littleton, &c. appointed to go with him to see the warrant immediately.

23rd [January].

A bill for reversing of a decree in Chancery made against Laurence Lownes, sheweth:—Whereas Peter Bland did for divers considerations convey by bargain and sale, fine and other conveyance, settle to the said Laurence Lownes two manors worth only 200*l.* per annum, and for which he hath paid and secured to be paid above 3000*l.*; and the same estates by a decree in Chancery upon a pretence that the same was got by fraud, and when the said Peter was of sick and weak estate and not of a disposing memory, which as in the bill is alleged was not so as is pretended, and that this is a dangerous precedent to subvert the common conveyance of the land by a decree in equity, which heretofore hath not been: and since the said decree is only reversible by the high House of Parliament it is desired the same decree may be reversed and made void, against the parties for whom it was given; saving to all others their rights, &c.

A question whether a writ for election may be granted by the Lord Keeper in the vacation upon a prorogation, or by the Speaker, or may by both; this referred to the committee of priveleges.

Mr. Rowles reports how his goods were taken for not payment of custom as was usual, though he offered security to pay what was due by law or adjudged by parliament, but his proffer was refused, and [*blank*] said if Mr. Rowles had all the House of Commons in him he would [do] what he did. Where upon he brought a replevin, which [was] got with much ado and delivered it to the sheriff, but the execution was stayed by an order of the Exchequer. Afterward he brought another replevin in London returnable in the hustings, and the officers taking them to deliver them to the party; but they were rescued and so he could not have them. And he had divers other goods which was seized, amounting to the value of 5000*l.* and their own demands was 200*l.*; which in King James's time, when any denial was made they did but seize so much goods as amounted to their own demands, but now they do it with that violence that they take all.

Officers: Worsenam, Dawes, Carmerden, John Baupage, Mease, Rodgers.

Mr. Littleton: Two things are considerable in this; first whether tonnage and poundage be due without act of parliament, and it is clear it is not, and in Edw.: III.'s time it was taken from the King and given to the merchants for the guarding of the seas, and it hath been given for years.

The second thing is whether a parliament man shall not have the privileges for his goods, as well as for his person. For [*blank*]. 18 Edw. I. 12 Edw. IV.

Secretary Coke: I would that we proceed as judges, and not to prejudicate the matter nor to aggravate it; for in weighty matters we ought to be moderate and move slowly, for it may be, though I will not say, that all the things may not be true.

Sir Benjamin Rudyard to the same purpose. Parliament party not to be in love with monarchy.

Moved by Phillips, Coriton. &c. That a special committee may be named to take a particular disquisition and examination touching Mr. Rowles's information.

Mr. Selden: His information consists of two parts; first that which toucheth him as a parliament man, his privilege ought not to be referred to a committee, but for the House to take it upon the relation of the member: and whereas it was said that it may be untrue, that is not parliamentary. And for the other I think it fit to be referred to the committee, as it is a wrong to the subject.

Secretary Coke: That which I said, that it may be, I might be untrue, I might have said it affirmatively, and I pray you that you will have as much credit to one member as to another. But note that he spoke to the question in this speech, otherwise it had been against order.

Resolved that a committee to be named to consider of the information of Mr. Rowles, which toucheth the infringing of the liberty of the subject in general.

Resolved that those officers (*page devant*) to be sent for to answer their contempt to the House touching Mr. Rowles; and also to attend the committee to be examined touching the other matter before, in the Court of Wards this afternoon.

Mr. Selden reports that upon examination of the printers for the first impression without those additions, there were 1500 printed, sitting the parliament and before they were dispersed. The next day after the parliament Mr. Attorney sent for him to his chamber and told him that this impression was not to go out so, and afterward Mr. Attorney sent for him to Whitehall and gave him a warrant for the imprinting of those papers which were pinded together. And the Lord Privy Seal also sent for him to his house, and told him that the first impression was not to be printed alone.

Secretary Coke reports from the King that he avoweth that it was by his warrant and direction, and his Majesty doth avow it.

24th [January].

A message from the King by Secretary Coke.

That the King hath taken notice of a debate amongst us touching the seizure of the Merchant's goods, and willeth, that we should forbear any further dispute till to-morrow at 2 of clock, when the King will speak with both Houses himself in the Banqueting House, of which we are to take notice. To which agreed.

Sir Robert Phillips appointed to sit in the chair for the courts of justice on Tuesday.

25th [January].

An Act for the explanation of a branch of the statute of 3 Jac. for suppressing Popish recusants, and the discovery thereof.

An Act preferred for the confirmation of a decree made in Chancery by the Lord Keeper Lord Coventry betwixt Laurence Lownes and Peter Bland, for which a cross-bill is preferred; which see before.

Serjeant Digges complains of a breach of a liberty of parliament, for that he two days after the last sessions of parliament, the party knowing he was a parliament man, was served by a subpoena in to the Star Chamber, for which he was ordered to be sent for, and also his master which commanded him. *Quod nota*, being upon a prorogation.

An Act sent down by the Lords for the better maintenance of the ministry by disappropriation without license, notwithstanding the statute of mortmain. And those who shall disappropriate any such impropriation shall have the presentation; but if the impropriation be in one hand and the vicarage in another, he which gives the impropriation shall have the first presentation, and he which hath the vicarage the next, and so *vicissim*.

An act for free marriage at any time of the year.

An act for avoiding adultery or fornication, and [*blank*].

26th [January].

Mr. Waller reports how there are divers ships provided with corn and ordnance for Spain our enemies, and considering how advantageous it may be to our enemies and prejudicial to ourselves, which being now raised from 20s. to 30s., and the ports from which corn comes in time of dearth as Dantzic &c. are shut up, which if we give this power or allow of this we shall be put to a great deal of misery. The consideration whereof is referred to a Committee, and all that will come to voice. Alderman Pace, Ricard are men employed in this service, and are to be sent for to attend the Committee.

Secretary Coke: This business hath been well settled. We know his Majesty hath come a great pace unto us, it is necessary that we go with some paces unto him, to which end I present this bill, which I desire we may give a reading unto it which may give a good satisfaction to other Kingdoms how willing we are to supply and defend him and the kingdom. We know how potent the kings of Spain and France are, there is one danger more added, which is the loss of every sound; nay, the House of Austria hath made themselves masters of all the principal ports of the Baltic sea, and there is now a fleet of 50 ships provided with men and ordnance, for what service it is to be feared. Our gracious King is preparing a fleet, which if this be forward it will much advance the service of the King and the Kingdom.

Sir John Elliot: I do not stand up to retard this business but rather to forward it, which will not be by a present reading but rather by a preparation of other things to give this a freer passage to it, which might otherwise receive some stand. And whereas it is said that this is one of the ordinary means for enabling the King, it is not so, for Fortescue the learned justice says that it was one of the extraordinary means.

Mr. Selden: I think it is against the fundamental liberty of the House to have it read, for since it is truly a bill of subsidy, whether it be fit to be so offered to be read before it hath received any debate in the House, which is not usual to prefer any such bill before debate.

Sir Dudley Digges: It is impossible that this bill should in all things square with the bill of subsidy, for that we see the wisdom of our ancestors to grant it in former [times] for life; and for that principal objection, that it is against the fundamental liberty. I have known that such bills, nay the bill of subsidy, hath been brought in by the King's council.

This being long disputed the bill was not read.

Mr. Rous: This being so well settled, let us consider our right in our religion, which hath been confirmed by the King of Heaven and earth, which hath been so violated and Arminianism so much increased. For if you look upon him, he gives his hand to the papist, he to the pope, who takes the King of Spain by the one hand and the King of Spain [*sic ;* France?] by the other hand.

Sir Francis Seymour: I know that what is done in the country is undone in the city touching religion, and the King's name used in it, which is a great scandal to the King's profession and his answer to our petition of religion. And if you will know who is the man that doth this you may ; if you do but consider this point you will easily know, nay I think every man that sitteth here doth know it. Herein I have cleared my conscience.

Mr. Coriton: We must look at the route. There are some persons near the King, I mean bishops, that we know not how affected, and it is not Montague or Cosins alone but some others that are actors in it.

Sir R. Phillips : Two things that are to be feared, the one open and public, and that ancient, the other novel and subtle, which is the ready way to subvert religion and to bring alteration. While religion flourished, how prosperous and fortunate hath [been] our enterprises, how well have we agreed in parliament in those times ; but since what success have we had in our wars, have our returns been with victory, have we so agreed, have we not had the loss of the hopeful prince, of his most miserable death ? and this is God's justice upon us. That we may divert those punishments which God hath justly inflicted upon us, let us humble ourselves before God by fasting and prayer, and to that end let us join to move the King.

Secretary Coke : I have been bold to give sometimes cautions that we should not do anything in religion except that which concerns matter in fact, for other things we know belongs to another place, and not proper for us to be disputed.

Shirland : Though the greatest part of the kingdom be sound, but there be divers particular persons who have the ears of majesty to subvert the settled government ; for they put the King on things not lawful, and they weaken him by opposition and make their quarrel the king's, and so set difference betwixt the King and the people, and so to work their own ends.

This resolved to be taken into consideration by the Committee for religion, and all other incidents belonging to religion.

Resolved that a petition shall be drawn to move the King for a fast, and to move the Lords to join with us.

His Majesty's speech in parliament the 24th of January 1628–9.

My Lords and Gentlemen. The care that I have to remove all those rubs that may cause misunderstanding betwixt me and this parliament made me call you hither at this time. The occasion was a particular complaint lately moved in the Lower House. And as for you my Lords of the Higher House I am glad to take this and all other occasions I may, to declare that as you are the nearest in degree so you may be furthest from misunderstanding.

The complaint I speak of is for staying of some men's goods that denied tonnage and poundage. This I am sure may have an easy and speedy conclusion, if my actions and words were rightly understood : for if men did not imagine that I have taken these duties all this while as pertaining to my prerogative, certainly I think they would never have made any question to have passed them by bill, by which it will both clear my future proceedings and make good my by-past actions; as likewise in my speech, in that part of it the last day of the session that concerned this point, I did not mind to challenge tonnage and poundage as a right, but to show you the necessity and not the right by which I was to claim it; for my intent ever was and yet is by the gift of my people to enjoy it, assuring myself according to your open profession, you want but time, not will to give it me.

Therefore since now there is occasion, I do expect that you do make good your former promises; and by passing of a bill to take away the question that riseth in this matter, whereby the only rub that most troubleth this question will be taken away.

Lastly I do wish that we may not be jealous one of another's actions. For, for my part, if I were given easily to take exceptions, an order made in the Lower House on Wednesday last might have given me some scruple; for by the too large end of that order it might have been understood that you took upon you liberty to be enquirers of men's actions; but when I look to your actions I find you only hear complaints and not seek offences. This I speak to show you how loth I am to make any ill interpretation of your actions. I hope you will likewise give the deaf ear to those that may make any ill rumours of me, that so, we beginning this session with a mutual confidence one of another, we may end it in a perfect good correspondence.

27th [January].

The petition to his Majesty for a public fast and prayer.

A conference desired with the Lords touching this petition which [blank].

A message from his Majesty:—Having understood that their remonstrance was called for to take away all doubts, hath sent it, but he hopes that you will go on upon better grounds than before, and he also commanded me to let you know that he expected that you give the bill of tonnage and poundage the precedence before any other business, to take away all difference which may arise betwixt him and his subjects: which if you do not, he shall think that his speech on Saturday, which seemed to be so much applauded, did not take that effect which he expected.

This was occasioned by a report from the committee of religion, that the remonstrance being required there, the clerk made answer that his Majesty sent for him and commanded him to deliver the remonstrance to him.

Sir Walter Earle moves that religion is to be preferred before all things, without which life, liberties, and laws are nothing.

Mr. Waller: I had rather ask the way to any strange place of a plain country carrier who travels that way daily than of any cunning geographer who only discourseth of it, and setteth not a foot that way. And I would have these foxes, these little foxes who cunningly seek to divert the King, and are so dangerous: therefore let us look them out.

Mr. Pym: For popery which is one disease.

1st. How the laws are neglected against recusants.

2ndly. How and by whom the laws are dispensed with, and by whom favoured.

3rdly. How ceremonies are crept in, as at Durham.

For Arminianism which is more subtle and so much more dangerous, and for that if we look to the Articles in Edw. VI., Ridley, 39 Articles in Queen Elizabeth, the Articles agreed at Lambeth, these I call witness for our religion in the affirmative.

Two things upon his Majesty's speeches, which is his profession of it in general ; secondly, his desire of union, which if predestination, free will, and general grace, were preached with tenderness. And also to enquire who those be that profess it, and also the countenancers of it, and those that have preached, nay being silenced, in the King's presence, which I think will be proved. And also that it be looked what parliaments have done in former times, and also by whose means and licences books touching that have been printed, and others refused. We know that the Convocation is but a provincial synod, and cannot as now it is bind any man in matter of religion or state. And the High Commission Court we know is derived out of the Houses of Parliament, and therefore can be no hindrance for us to proceed in this matter.

Granting of pardons. ·

28th [January].

A message from the King :—That he hath taken notice of the debate in this House touching tonnage and poundage, of which he hath given us a sufficient answer, and he expects as before that the bill of tonnage and poundage should have the precedence. And he hath taken notice of the debate of religion, and expects no remonstrance touching that, and moves that we will not fall upon things which concerns us not, and if we do offer anything which is new or not known before, he will take it into due consideration.

Elliot : This often iteration of messages doth hinder us more than anything, and [blank].

An extract out of a little book of records of the parliament, 1612, [sic] 17 Jac.

1st. A particular of the good laws intended by the Parliament, touching swearing, non-residents and plurality of benefices, that ecclesiastical persons should only use the spiritual sword of exhortation and not the temporal. 18 particulars to be contracted for, for 200,000l. per annum to be paid to his Majesty.

Things complained upon and redress required :—

1st. New impositions ; not to be taxed without assent of Parliament.

2ndly. That the Commission ecclesiastical enabled by 1 Eliz. cap. 1, may be abridged, that they may not have such large liberty to fine and imprison, not properly belonging to the spiritual jurisdiction.

3rdly. That proclamations be not made to alter or make laws.

4th. That writs of prohibition and other writs be not denied in stay of justice or the common law.

4th. That ancient laws for selling of wine being become impossible there may no license with *non obstantes* for them, but that they may be repealed.

5th. That impositions and letters of licensing alehouses, &c. be suppressed and hereafter avoided.

6th. That the imposition of 12 in a chaldron of coals, being challenged by prerogative, may be forborne, and not to make such dangerous precedents.

29th [January].

The Committee makes a report that they have found upon examination that three ships are freighted with corn and other provision for Spain, by which the enemy will be much strengthened, we much weakened ; for [blank] hath given 100,000 ducats to the King of Spain, for the bringing of victuals or other manufacture.

Sir Francis Cottington shows how that it is true that such a license was also granted by the King of England for carrying out of manufactures, which hath been and will be to his advantage 100,000*l.*, which how much it will advance the King in these times of necessity I leave it to this House to consider.

The House turned into a Committee, Mr. Pym being in the chair and matter of religion being the matter to be treated of.

Sir Benjamin Rudyerd.

Sir Robert Harlow : I shall be glad to divide the matter into :—

1. What our religion is : the Articles made in 1562 in Queen Elizabeth's time, the Articles made at Lambeth, the Articles in Ireland ; King James also by his wisdom and pen in the synod of Dort being solely guided by our example.

2. The danger of our religion is the bringing in of popery and Arminianism ; first, by a book written by Mr. Richard Montague, then by one of Doctor Jackson, another by Doctor Cosens, chaplain to the Right Reverend Father the Bishop of Winchester.

The remedies which I shall present are two : first, that we make an unanimous profession of our religion ; secondly, that we desire a conference with the Lords to join with us in a remonstrance to represent these persons to the King, that they may have condign punishment. The motives are that the people are drawn for the King's subjection.

Mr. Spencer : I desire and think it fit when any man is accused to name particulars in what part of his book he doth not conform himself to our reformed religion, for I think there be some that oppose that seek to bring in novel opinions.

Sir John Elliot : We are not here to dispute of our religion, for that God be thanked is already settled, and it might bring us into a labyrinth. Whereas it is said by some that it is a parliamentary religion, it is not the true religion because that parliament confirmed it, but the parliament confirmed it because it was true. But one thing I fear in the declaration of his Majesty above all other, for in that we may have our religion at one instant overwhelmed.

From the Convocation, if we consider how it is made, will bring another great fear. King Edward the VI., what he said of the Bishops, that some for sloth, others for luxury, &c. are not fit to sit in those places. We know that at the reading of the Creed in the primitive church men did stand not only bare headed but with their swords drawn to defend their faith, and now we will scarce do one. But for the first let us set down our religion, and then we may know what to take exception at.

Sir Nathaniel Rich : It is an easy thing to see the difference betwixt two opinions, but difficult to know the reasons of the diversity, for the matter of the difference we may take it into consideration, but not the latter.

We do claim, profess and avow for truth the sense of the Articles framed 1562, which were confirmed by Act of parliament, 13 Eliz., 1571, which by the public acts of the Church of England and by general and current exposition of the writers ; and we do reject the sense of the Jesuits and Arminians and all others wherein they do differ from us.

Mr. Spencer questioned, for that he said that the Articles of Lambeth were recalled or suppressed by an act of state ; and the same questioned by the Queen that the Bishop might incur a premunire ; but this with much ado was quieted and proceeded no farther.

That we the Commons assembled in parliament do claim, profess and avow for truth that sense of the Articles of religion which were established by parliament in the 13th Elizabeth, which by public acts of the Church of England and the general and current exposition of the writers of our Church hath been delivered unto us, and we do reject the sense of the Jesuits, Arminians, and all others wherein they differ from us.

This resolved upon question.

This declaration to be made.

An answer to the King that we cannot yet entertain the reading of the bill of tonnage and poundage.

30th [January].

A petition of John Predian, gentleman, against Henry Alein having preferred a scandalous petition to the King, together with 13 articles containing the most of the Arminian opinions, and accusing the Bishop of Lincoln.

1. Puritan faction to agree *in tertiis* with the Jesuits.

That he defends the rigid opinions of predestination.

That he calleth the petitions of parliament, the petition of puritans.·

That he defendeth the opinions of Doctor Mannering, and all the Arminian opinions.

That those sectaries and maligners do especially oppose royal prerogative.

That Justice is no measure betwixt the King and his people.

That he averreth that the writing of his book to be a service to his Majesty, which is Doctor Mannering's opinions.

That the Bishop of Lincoln charged the King with mutability, for giving two diverse answers to the puritans at Oxford.

The House.

The petition of William Jones against the Bishop of Winchester. Whereas divers opinions maintained by Mr. Montague against the tenets of our church, upon proclamation for the confirming of him Bishop of Winchester if any would prefer any Articles against him to show why he should not be confirmed, the said William Jones preferred divers Articles against him for the writing of divers books against the religion professed, yet notwithstanding he was confirmed ; which illegal confirmation and his new broached opinions he desire you will be pleased to take into your pious consideration, and so to do as you shall think fit .

Sir Henry Martin : The form of election of bishops is after a *congé d'élire*, which is license to the Dean and chapter to choose, yet they must choose who the King shall name, and who shall speak against this election or confirmation shall incur a *præmunire.* And it is likewise true that proclamation is made if any will speak against his election he may, but yet he shall not ; when they go to choose the bishop they pray that the Holy Ghost should direct them, yet shall choose such a one as is named. And I wish this ceremony might be left, for the form is as if they were free, but yet they are bound.

Selden : The form of choosing of bishops being altered by the statute of 25 Hen. VIII, cap. 20, by which first letters missive by the King 25 Hen. VIII. were sent to the Dean and Chapter to signify who he will have chosen, Cap. 20. and then a *congé d'élire* to choose such a one, and then for the Archbishop to confirm him. But he taketh the meaning of this Act not to exclude exceptions which are legal, but make that a *præmunire* when refusal is made without such due exception.

Doctor Eaton saith that before this statute the King did nominate as now, as this statute was properly made for confirmation.

But he saith that the reason as he hath heard for which the articles were not accepted of against him was, because there was no advocate's hand unto them, therefore they were illegal.

Ordered that this dispute shall be referred to another time, for to be argued by both lawyers of the House.

E 2

Mr. Speaker in the Chair.

The petition read which Predian preferred to the King and the articles which were preferred against the Bishop of Lincoln.

He is called in and examined touching the petition, and the articles which he confesseth, and that it was his own handwriting, but denieth any encouragement that he had from any, and also that he intended puritans to be only Nonconformist.

January 31st.

Mr. Pym in the chair;

Resolved that matter of Arminianis.n shall be first taken into consideration and debated.

Sir Nathaniel Rich: The better to find out those of that sect, we must know what the public acts of the Church are, and then we shall know those that dissent from them. And for the first I think these to be public acts of the Church.

1st. Catechisms made and confirmed by Act of Parliament. Selden accord.

2nd. The Articles of 13 Eliz., and the Common Prayer book are public Acts of the Church.

3rd. The Articles of Lambeth.

Selden said that that could not be a public act of the Church, for that cannot be a public act which is not done by a public authority, for such an assembly cannot be any such act of the Church. Nor can I call as hath been said the Synod of Dort, nor the Articles of Ireland, nor the doctrine of the Church of Scotland, nor the readings in the Universities, which be things without authority; for if they be not true and not agreeable then they should bind us, which we would not then agree to, therefore we must be cautious what we make to be the public acts of the Church.

Bills sent down by the Lords.

1. An Act for the better preserving his Majesty's revenues.
2. An Act for the advancement of trade.
3. An Act for the taking into execution those which shall be delivered · by privilege of parliament.

The Articles of Lambeth, 1595.

1. That God hath predestinated certain men unto life, certain reprobated unto death.

2. The moving or effectual grace of predestination unto life is not the foresight of faith, or of perseverance, or of good works, or of anything in the persons predestinated, but only in the will of the well pleased God.

3. There is a definitive and certain number of the predestinated, which can neither be augmented nor diminished.

4. Those who are not predestinated to salvation shall be necessarily damned for their sins.

5. A true living and a justifying faith and the Spirit of God justifying is not extinguished, it faileth not, it vanisheth not away in the elect either finally or totally.

6. A man truly faithful, that is such a one as is endued with a justifying faith, is certain with the full assurance of faith of the remission of his sins, and of his everlasting salvation by Christ.

7. Saving grace is not given, is not communicated, is not granted to all men, by which they may be saved if they will.

· 8. No man can come unto Christ unless it shall be given unto him, and unless the Father shall draw him; and all men are not drawn by the Father, that they may come to the Son.

9. It is not in the will of every one to be saved.

These were the conclusions of the Reverend prelates and learned Doctors heretofore, then cursed be all turbulent Arminian innovators, who dare impugn them now.

Put forth by Mr. William [Prince?] of Lincolns Inn.

February 3rd.

An Act for advancing of trade, that all merchants or traders may sell or transfer over bonds, bills or other specialties, without penalty, by a deed sealed and signed, and the assignee to have as full property and as good remedy as though the bill or specialty had been made to him.

An Act for the naturalizing of the Lady Strange, who was a French-woman, and daughter to a peer of France, now a professor of this religion.

The King's reply to our answer touching the bill of tonnage and poundage.

Mr. Pym in the chair.

Sir John Elliot moves that for the manner of our proceedings we may not seem to make or give any jealousy to that cause we have in hand being without question, but that first we seek and fall upon them, and make our charge on them which have erred from our profession, and then the Articles of Lambeth will come in as evidences against them, for a constant profession of the same.

[February 9.]

Sir John Elliot reports the proceedings touching the petition of the merchants for tonnage and poundage, and that Sheriff Acton being examined answered so as was thought fit the Committee should desire this House that he may be sent for to the House to answer his contempt.

Doctor Steward's argument touching the confirmation of the Bishop of Winchester.

Two questions whether the exceptions exhibited were legal or not.

Secondly, whether exceptions legally put in do make the confirmation good, yea or no, and if they be to be ready to be proved, I think then they do disable him.

Third, what should ensue if it should be void, yet should not lose his bishopric, but he should be in the same state as he was before the confirmation.

Doctor Tawbott's argument.

Two kinds of exceptions against persons to be elected bishops. 1st in respect of the person elected; and 2ndly the manner of election.

1st for the person. There be crimes which are called *delicta graviora*, and if those things which touch matters of religion be such, which I will not dispute but must leave, then the exceptions be legal, and so his confirmation not good.

For the second question propounded :—because confirmations were had repentively [*sic*], it was ordained that proclamation should be made, that if the confirmation were not litigious they should be confirmed after such citation or proclamation. A Constitution of Justinius that exceptions propounded and not allowed do make ordinations void, and by the same reason it doth make confirmations.

And though there be no nullity ordained in the law, yet when the law appoints a form which is not observed, that makes a nullity in itself.

Sir Henry Martin's answer:—that if the exceptions be proved that these do as well extend to the election itself as to the confirmation.

Sir Henry Martin: Since 25 Hen. VIII. we proceed in a strict form of which he hath a copy, from which he doth not swerve, and this doth differ from the Canon Law, for after a bishopric become void, and the king sends letters missive to the dean and chapter, and if they choose within 12 days then a confirmation is necessary; if they do not, then the king may present by his letters patents without confirmation.

And not that what privilege the pope had before 24 Hen. VIII. the king had given by act of parliament, and upon the presentation by the pope, there was no exception to be taken, and so continued to Queen Elizabeth's time, which in 1 and 8 Eliz. was thought fit to be altered.

And that it was convenient thus to be, the parliament in 25 Hen. VIII. found what difference there was in cathedral churches by such exceptions; and therefore to put an end to such differences the king had this conferred upon him.

Now for the first exception, without relation to the statute, for it is true that such citation is not to be set but on the church where the bishop is to go to, for betwixt the bishop and those persons of that church they are of that fold, and so a privy betwixt them, but those that are not of that fold they have nothing to do in it.

And a nullity doth not go further than the express words, and not by implication. And a refusal of exceptions though they be legal cannot make a nullity. But things that have been so long used, it is not good in my opinion to dispute it further.

Doctor Steward prefers a petition that proceedings in law may be stayed against him.

12th [February].

Mr. Sherfield in the chair. Wherein is taken into dispute, touching the bill of tonnage and poundage, with all the incidents unto it: and therein as an incident the judgment to stay the execution of a replevin for the delivery of the goods, and also the information in the Star Chamber against the merchants sitting the parliament. For the first the Judges have two capacities, one judicial, another extra-judicial. We know the common case: the Judge seeth one man kill another and the jury findeth another; the judge being asked what he would do in this case, who answered he might give judgment according as the jury found, but he would move the king to pardon him; who much commended the uprightness of the law. And this case in the Exchequer: here was an affidavit true in one respect but false in another, but they gave their judgment according to the matter before them. The words were, that the customers took it for duties due to the king, which might be true and false. But when we send to them to inform them truly it may be reversed, and then the replevin may have its proceedings, for they have now declared that those duties were intended for tonnage and poundage, which cannot be any duty due, but there might be some old customs which might be said duties.

13th [February].

Resolved that those who have petitions or bills depending shall have privilege for their persons during their prosecution.

And the consideration whether such persons that have a cause depending and process served on him [sic] shall be void.

Ordered upon question that signification should be given' to the Lord Keeper, that inasmuch as Mr. Foulkes, Mr. Phillips, Mr. Gillman are to have privilege of their person, that no attachment shall issue out whereby their persons may be in danger of arrest.

Doctor Moore's relation of the Bishop of Winchester's speech.

That he going to him after some conference had said that he had. heard him preach some pretty things against papists in King James his time, but he must not do so now.

That you have a brother that preacheth against bowing at the name of Jesus and the altar.

For changing the communion table, which he commanded, for he said that the table before stood like a table in an alehouse.

In private houses crosses used by napkins and profaning it by setting cups of wine, beer, ale, at every corner.

14th [February].

A Committee to consider whether the Lords may receive a complaint and give judgment against any Commoner, unless he be first questioned and transferred from the House of Commons.

Mr. Pym in the Chair.

Sir Thomas Hoby reports that the prisoners taken at Clerkenwell suspected to be popish priests, one of them was condemned for treason; and a warrant from the Lord Chief Justice to reprieve him. And for the other nine who refused the oath of allegiance [they] were discharged and released by a warrant from the Lord of Dorset.

Secretary Coke's Report.

Upon January last Humphrey Crosse gave intelligence to me how that great provision was carried into a house where nobody dwelt.

And upon warrant to search the house they found one Laythome who pretended to be the keeper of the house for the Earl of Shrewsbury, and they found therein vaults and cellars in lurking places.

That they are Jesuits and priests as appears by their books, reliques, copes, their founders, their provision of [blank].

Domus probationis sancti Ignatii societatis Jesus.

The order for government.

2. A special direction from the provincial congregation and Father Blunt, for the government.

A note how to answer any questions touching religion.

And a note of all the papists in the province, and how they are summoned.

The Bishop of Chalcedon made governor.

16th [February].

Mr. Hilton of Westmoreland his petition against Sir John Savill for his goods taken away, being a man conformable, and desires redress. A committee appointed for the examination of it, in which the knights and burgesses for Westmoreland are, and Thursday next the day appointed.

Another petition against Sir Henry Martin, for converting a great part of the personal estate of one Browne, who died worth 50,000*l.* This referred to the Committee of Justice.

Sir Henry Martin reports, how that Mr. Recorder sent no warrant for the reprieve of the priest condemned, but my Lord Chief Justice had a warrant from the King's mouth immediately.

But moved by Mr. Stroud that my Lord Chief Justice was to answer this, and that he should have had more than words but a warrant.

Mr. Chancellor of Duchy said that it was no new thing for a judge to reprieve any man, much more for the Lord Chief Justice, and having the King's direction. But he thought that he had reprieved him upon a declaration of Star Chamber that judgment should be given, and then to be sent to Wisbech to be there imprisoned.

Sir Francis Seymour reports what answer Mr. Attorney gave them who were to examine him. But first they went with Mr. Long, who showed them a letter from Mr. Attorney that he should prosecute those men at sessions, viz., against those three, viz. Weden, Moore, and Parr as priests only, and to tender the other the oath of allegiance, and if they denied to proceed to their conviction.

And going to Mr. Attorney to his house, he, upon questions made, answered thus;—that he had a warrant from Council Board for the prosecuting against those priests, but that warrant appeared to be against them as priests or Jesuits. And for the bonds which he took for their appearance he had them, but he could not deliver them till he had acquainted the King with it.

Mr. Long, being examined, saith that he offering at the sessions to the bench to give in evidence, by papers which he conceived would much induce to give the court and jury satisfaction that they were priests, and that would prove that this was *domus probationis*, and that my Lord Richardson asked him if he had anything to prove priest or no priest, he might speak to it, if not it was but discourse.

Mr. Secretary Coke observes that these evidences were denied, and so they were cleared, but these afterwards being given in evidence for the seizing them for the King, they were found guilty, and the goods seized.

Mr. Selden said that a replevin was grantable out of the Exchequer.

17th [February].

My Lord Chief Justice, being examined, said that he doth not remember any further evidence offered by Mr. Long against the priests which was refused; but he remembers that Mr. Long had certain papers in his hand, but whether it concerned this matter or no he knew not.

My Lord Richardson saith that no papers were read or pressed to be read by Mr. Long that he remembers; but it may be he did not hear all that that was spoken.

Mr. Justice Jones saith being demanded, that Mr. Long offered papers to be read, but whether they were or not he doth not know, but one of the Judges said that if it was not to prove them priests it were not material.

Justice Whitlocke likewise saith under his hand, that there were no papers offered by Mr. Long after I came.

Justice Crook saith the same.

19th [February].

Mr. Dawes examined, confesseth that he knew Mr. Rowles to be a parliament man, but he never heard that a parliament [man] was freed for his goods for duties to the King, and he had a commission for the taking of those duties which was paid in King James his time. And for his exposition what he meant by duties he had directions from the King by mouth that he should make no explanation what was intended by this.

Disputed whether those customers shall be proceeded with to be censured for delinquency.

The Chancellor moves that it may be weighed for a time; for I fear since they had the King and Council's command for this, if we censure them it may be thought it is censuring the King's command, which if it be said *actum est de imperio;* which he being called to explain said, that no man will obey the King's command hereafter. Said on the other side, that this doth not reflect upon the King. And resolved upon question, that the further consideration shall be taken of it.

23rd [February].

The House resolved into a Committee, Mr. Herbert in the chair. The question to be disputed was, whether Mr. Rowles being a member of this House was to have privilege for his goods which were taken for duties to the King : but upon proof that the King, if he had any right, had granted over by lease to the customers rendering 150,000*l.* per annum, and though there was a covenant under the signet manual that what wanted of that the King should bear the loss, yet this did no ways take the interest of the customers if the King had any ; and so the question was properly betwixt one subject and another, and did no ways reflect whether a subject should have privilege for his goods against the King, (though as afterward it may appear it was conceived one might, though this question was declined.)

First Mr. Littleton. That Mr. Rowles shall have privilege for his goods as well as for his person, appears by divers authorities both ancient and modern.

And first ; the ground of all privilege is for the general good, and the great respect that is of it appears by 31 Hen. VI, that the Judges thought it too high a thing to give their opinion in.

And for authority in it, in 18 Edw. I, that both lands and goods are privileged ; and so it is in 18 Ric. II, upon a petition in the parliament house that one might distrain for rent, it was denied, as it is said, quia inhonestum videtur.

Vide 7 Edw. II. close roll, membrane [*blank*].

17 Edw. IV, parliament roll, articulo 35. That no man being a member shall be touched in person or goods,· in coming, staying, or going to or from parliament.

5 Edw. IV, rotuli parliamenti, numero 78. Cheder's case, it was petitioned that if any man killed a parliament man or his servant it might be treason, and for striking or suing other penalties (" q̄ le inferance del c ").

9 Hen. IV. f. 1°. And in rotuli parliamenti, numero 71, in " un " petition q̄ leur serauts ne poᵗ estre arest pʳ dett accōupt &c., Le " answer fuit p le Roy, q̄ fuit remidie denᵗ."

8 Hen. VI, 31 Hen. VII, Thorpe the Speaker " fuit arest in temps " del progation del plᵗent," and was not delivered upon petition because he was arrested without time of privilege of parliament.

· 34 Hen. VIII, et 36 Hen. VIII, " q̄ pʳ un coudemnation in dett " &c. denᵗ le plement, ne serra trouble ou arrest pʳ c."

1 Car., Sir Edward Coke " ad p̄vilidge del plᵗeꞑt, mes est. q̄ in temps " del vacation, null home ad privilidge mes pʳ les Joʳˢ del vacation q̄ sont " 16 joʳˢ all myens."

" Mes nota q̄ in 29 Eliz. in le case del un Martine le reasonable temps del privilidge fuit reduce all 20 jours."

36 Hen. VIII; " le case del Carꭎs, q̄ serra privilidge pur byens vers " le Roy, et fuit dit q̄ pʳ un rᵗ dew all Roy, ne serra un distreese pʳ c. " durᵗ le temps del plement."

In 12 Jac. "suites in le Starchamber q̃ sont les suites del Roy serra
" staye p' privilidge; ut in le case del Senior Clare, et S' Symiond
" Steward et est valde frequent."

12 Eliz. " Le case del Johnes ad sou privilidge p' byens, q̃ fueron
" deliu a lui apris seisure."

" Et fuit le darien plement adjudge in le house de Seniors q̃ un del
" leur servants auera privilidge p' son byens."

" Et in le case in question Selden dit q̃ Icy home nad privilidge les
Seniors nad ascun privilidge p plement, car leur psons sont privilidge
sans c̃ ; q̃ fuit absurd.

2ndly. Cest case est enter subject et subject (et issent le privilidge p'
byens vers le Roy est wave in cest question q̃ᵈ nota) p' c̃ cy le Roy ad
intrest in les coustomes c̃ passa p les leases cy monstre avant, et null
covenant q̃ est add q̃ ills ne serra lousers prendera leur intrest ; et cy
le Roy nad powre all faire leases, donq ills sont trespassers.

3rdly. Le warant fuit all collect et levie, et q̃ᵗ ills prise c̃ q̃ est pluis
q̃ 20 temps le value c̃ nest un leviinge."

25th [February].

At the Committee. Disputed whether the first dispute shall not be
how the goods of the merchants shall be restored, or whether we shall
not dispute what punishment shall be inflicted upon those customers.

Upon a message from the King by Secretary Coke that the King had
taken notice of the debate on Saturday, and with what care they had
endeavoured to distinguish the King's command from their acts, but
the King doth avow what they did was by his direction and assistance himself in person at the Council table, and considering how nearly it touched
his honour, and therefore he would not have us to proceed against
the customers to censure them, wherein it did so nearly concern him and
his honour ; and therefore he commended this to our consideration.

And this being delivered to the House, after it had been delivered
to the House, it was moved that this being of this weight that we may
adjourn the House to to-morrow, and all things may cease in the
meantime."

[1629. Account of a Journey into Scotland : *a 12 mo Volume.*]

" C. LOWTHER. } OUR JOURNAL INTO SCOTLAND
  MR. R. FALLOW. } A.D. 1629, 5TH OF NOVEMBER,
  PETER MANSON. } FROM LOWTHER.

From Carlisle.

From Carlisle to the river Leavens 4 miles, in that space is wet
moorish mossy ground all but a little by the river side, which is good.
From Leavens to the river Esk 2 miles, all this space is plain very good
ground, most corn ground, all betwixt these two rivers are of Barronet
Grame land and the debateable land which is divided appertaining to
England ; the whole length of Sir Rich. Grame's purchase is some 16
miles down to Sarkfoot it is some 6 or 7 miles broad for 14 miles some
2 or 3 miles broad towards Sarkfoot : it is most of it good. There is
betwixt Esk and Leavens, the church of Arthuret built by a stock
gathered through the whole kingdom of England, being about 1500
pounds, Mr. Curwen parson of the same procurer of it. By this church
is the Howe end where the thieves in old time met and harboured. From
over passing from Esk to Dunedale Dike or Sike along Esk is almost
2 miles, which Dike is the division of the debateable land first agreed on

in Hen. VI's time, but now gotten exemplified in Scotland by Barronet Grame *sed plus vide de eo.* From Carlisle they use stacking of corn, on forward into Scotland. The houses of the Grames that were are but one little stone tower garretted and slated or thatched, some of the form of a little tower not garretted; such be all the leards' houses in Scotland. The Good man of Netherby in the Wood is the chief of the Greames. The debateable land is 3 miles long and 3 broad, Soleme moss is on debatable land beyond Esk in Arthuret parish. Within a mile of the Erix Stond beside Moffat in Annandale rise the three great rivers, Annan running W. through Annandale; Clyde, north ; Tweed, east.

From Dunedale Sike to against Canonby some 4 miles, and from this Dunedale Sike to Langham almost on both sides of Esk which is 8 miles is L. Bucplewes land all; and on the east side of Esk to Selkerigg which is 4 miles along the river Esk, from Canonby to Langholm be good woods on the E. side, Helliwcarekoog and Langham wood on the W. side, and Hollow-wood through which is our way to Langham, and 3 miles from Langham, over Langham wood is my L. Bucp: colepits. Along the river of Eske is very good grounds, on the height is waste but good ground, and the most part beyond Esk towards Berwick is waste.

Langham is my Lord Maxfeild's but my Lord Buckpleugh hath it and all his land there mortgaged and is thought will have it. My Lord Maxfield hath gotten it to be a market within this 5 years, and hath given them of Langham and Erkenholme land to them with condition to build good guest houses within a year. We lodged at John a Foorde's at my Lord Maxfeild's gate where the fire is in midst of the house ; we had there good victuals, as mutton, midden fowle, oat bread cakes on the kirdle baked the 5th part of an inch thick ; wheat bread, ale, aquavitæ. Robert Pringle : Courts Barons and Burghs may hang and order any other causes, hang if offenders be taken with the manner of the deed, but it must be within 24 hours, but if after then there must be a commission gotten that they may have a jury which consisteth of 15, the first of which is called the chancellor and hath two voices, they go by votes, and the jury is to be elected out of the whole sheriffdom.

At Langham, Arche my Lord Maxfeild's steward, bestowed ale and aquavitæ ; we laid in a poor thatched house the wall of it being one course of stones, another of sods of earth, it had a door of wicker rods, and the spider webs hung over our heads as thick as might be in our bed. Mr. Curwen, parson of Arthuret sent his man over to Langham to get Arche to get us a lodging in Lord Maxfeild's house because of the outlaws in the town at that time, but the keys were at Arche's house 4 miles off so that we could not otherwise. We had my uncle Fallowfield [who] could not sleep the night for fear of them, neither would he suffer us the rest of his company to sleep ; that night also did Mr. Robert Pringle hearing my uncle Fall. was going to Edinburgh come after him, bestowed beer and acquavitæ of us and writ commendatory letters for us to Sir James Pringle sheriff of Ethrick, and to Edinburgh, and of all there we were kindly used, and Mr. Pringle the next day set us a great part of the way to Selkrig. At the Langham the river Eues where we come into Eusedale runneth into Esk.

The Saturday being the 7th of November anno dni. 1629 went we to Eskerigg, the way is most of it a valley, rivers all the way till we be almost to Selkerig, along the which rivers is excellent good ground, the mountains on both sides the river be very green good sheep pasture, and many places of them very good long grass. All the churches we see

were poor thatched and in some of them the doors sodded up with no
windows in almost till we came at Selkrig, a sheep grass here abouts
and about Langham is 1s. 6d. a year, a beast grass 2s. or 2s. 6d., butter
is some 6s. a stone, they have little or nothing enclosed, neither of corn
ground, woods, or meadow, they have very little hay unless at a knight,
leard, or lord's house some very little. They use all or most part over
Scotland (except in Murray land which is the finest country in Scotland
for all kinds of fruit, corn, and of trees, and all other necessaries, it
being most part enclosure) no enclosure but staff herding each man though
he have but one beast whether of his own or of others taken to grass
night and day. They used too in these parts to cut off the wool of the
sheep's bellies that they may go better among the ling to feed, and their
sheep skins of flayne or dead sheep they spelke them and hang them up
in their lire houses to dry, partly because they will sell better, but chiefly
because they sell them by a great company together to sell them and
hanging them so will keep them. A sheep greaser will grease some 40
sheep a day ; some use for sheep instead of tar the gilly which cometh off
broom sodd in water, and make salve of it with butter, as they do tar,
and grease with it, this learned I of Sir James Pringle of Gallowsheilds,
and because I was treating of sheep I thought good to put it in this day's
travel, being Friday. The distances from Langham to Eus Church
beside Micledale Holle 4 miles, betwixt Langham and this place was
it that my Lord Buckpleugh did wapp the outlaws into the dubb. From
thence to the Frosterly burne head, after the crossing of which we enter
into Tuidale, where the way that leadeth to Hawick called the Read road
on the right hand meeteth with the way that leadeth to Edinburgh, on
the left hand. From thence to Milcinton my Lord Bodwell's where the
coal pits be on the hill side beside Teat river. From thence to the
Burn foot 4 miles, from thence to Askerton Kirk one mile along the
river Ayle, at which kirk we drank at the vicar's house taken by an alehouse keeper, from thence to an old gentleman's house a mile on this
side of Selkrigg where we enter into Etherikke forest, 2 miles. Just on
this side is there a fair lough half a mile long, about 340 yards broad,
much fish in it, and a boat on it ; at the end of it a fair house which the
Leard of Riddall purchased it of Sir Robert Scott of Havin the name of
the house purchased.

From Selkrigge to Sir James Pringle on Sunday in the morning the 8th
of November. At Selkerigg we lodged at goodman Riddall's, a burgess
of the town, the which town is a borough regal, for antiquity the 15 in
the kingdom of Scotland ; it is governed by two bailiffs, they keep courts
of themselves and may hang and punish according as their custom is.
They have a very pretty church where the hammermen and other tradesmen have several seats mounted above the rest, the gentlemen below
the tradesmen in the ground seats ; the women sit in the high end of
the church, with us the choir, there is one neat vaulted porch in it, my
Lord Bucplewgh's seat is the highest in the church and he hath a proper
passage into it in at the outside of the vaulted porch. On a corner of
the outside of the choir is fastened an iron chain wit (sic) at a thing they
call the Jogges, which is for such as offend but especially women
brawlers, their head being put through it, and another iron in their
mouth, so abiding foaming till such time as the bailiffs please to dismiss
them, it being in the time of divine service. The form of it is a cross
house, the steeple fair, handsomely tiled as the Royal Exchange at
London, it having at each corner 4 pyramidal turrets, they call them
pricks; my Lord Maxfeild's house at Langham being of the form of
the steeple. For the repair of the churches, their presbyteries impose

taxation on the parishioners, the parson of the church looketh that accordingly they be repaired and if any pay not his tax he is put to the horne. The church was tiled upon close joined boards and not lats. In the town there were many fine buildings for hewn stone but thatched, it is as great as Appleby. The women are churched before the service begins; through Scotland the people in church when the parson saith any prayers they use a hummering kind of lamentation for their sins. The inhabitants at Selkrig are a drunken kind of people. They have goods victuals throughout the kingdom, unless it be towards the South-West, but cannot dress it well. Here had we a choking smoky chamber, and drunken unruly company thrust in upon us called for wine and ale and left it on our score. About this town and all the way to Edinburgh is good ground, but nearer Edinburgh the better and still more spacious.

From Selkeriggo to   2 miles, Ettrick and Yarrow, 2 rivers, running through Ettrick Forest, which is a sheriffdom (as Richmondshire in Yorkshire) in Tividale. There be yet some woods of Ettrick Forest along the two rivers remaining. Yarrow runneth into Ettrick about half a mile or more from Selkrige, and about a mile lower runneth Ettrick into Tweed, and about half a mile beneath that we take coble over Tweed, the form of it is as it were half of one of our barks. From to Gallowsheilds, 2 miles, to which place is excellent good ground, and to Sir James Pringle his house did we go and there were we wondrous courteously entertained, he is one of the best husbands in the country as appeareth by his planting and suffering his tenants to hold on him by planting 6 fruit trees or 12 other trees, and if they fail, to pay for every tree not planted 4d., he also finding two fullers mills and two corn mills. The town is a borough-barony, he himself is the sheriff of Ettrick and hath been these three years together, he is also a commissioner in the same sheriffdom, of which there be divers in all the sheriffdoms of Scotland, they being of the nature of our justices of assize in their circuits, above justices of peace; he is also a convener of justice, a justice of peace, he is a great man in his country. There are of the Pringles for some 8 miles up Gallowater, gentlemen all of pretty seats and buildings. On the Sunday as soon as we came to the town we alighted and went to the church to him, he took us into his own seat, the one of the one side of him, and the other of the other side, we heard a good sermon the fore and afternoon, there was the finest seats I have anywhere seen, and the orderliest church. Beside him is the Meageld hill, which word Meageld was a watch word to gather those of a company when they were dispersed in war. He hath a very pretty park, with many natural walks in it, artificial ponds and arbours now a making. he hath neat gardens and orchards, and all his tenants through his care, he hath abundance of cherry trees, bearing a black cherry, some of which I see to be about 30 yards high, and a fathom thick, great store of sycamores, trees he calleth silk trees, and fir trees. He gave very great respect, and said he heard of my father's fame. I see there the finest gun I ever beheld which was the King of Spain's. In Scotland the wives alter not their surnames. They served up the dinner and supper with their hats on before their master, each dish covered with another, then was there a bason withheld for to wash our hands before we sat down, then being seated Sir James said grace. Their cheer was big pottage, long kale, bowe or white kale, which is cabbage, 'breoh sopps,' powdered beef, roast and boiled mutton, a venison pie in the form of an egg goose, then cheese, a great company of little bits laid on a pewter platter, and cheese also uncut, then apples, then the table-cloth taken off and a towel the whole breadth of the table and half the length of it, a bason and ewer to wash, then a green carpet laid on, then one cup of beer set on the carpet, then a little long lawn serviter, plaited up a shilling or little more broad, laid cross over the corner of the table and a glass of hot water set down also on the table, then be there three boys to say grace, the 1st the thanks-giving, the 2nd the pater noster, the 3rd a prayer for a blessing to God's church, the good-man of the house, his parents, kinsfolk, and the whole company, they then do drink hot waters, so at supper, when· to bed, the collation which [is] a doupe of ale ; and also in the morn and at other times when a man desireth to drink one gives them first beer holding him the narrow serviter to dry his mouth with, and a wheat loaf and a knife, and when one hath drunk he cutteth him a little bread in observance of the old rule, *Incipe cum liquido sicco finire memento.* When we came away in the morn having walked abroad into park, gardens, and other places, and having very well with rost &c. (*sic*) Sir James set us 2 miles, and his 2nd, his eldest son better than 4, and writ us letters to Edinburgh. The Pringles glory in that they were never but on the King's part in all the troublesome times, and they therefore of the states were envied, for they never ' lowped' out with any of the lords nor were attainted.

Sir James told us of a man that said to king James when he was hunting that he would show him a buck that would let him take him by the banes, stones, speaking jestingly. At Sir James' house they have a thing called a palm in nature of our ferula, but thicker, for blasphemers. England and Scotland wooed roughly before they wedded. Sir John Scott one of the secret council is his son's wife's father.

Gallow water runneth into Tweed about a mile beneath Gallowsheilds and a little beneath its meeting with Tweed on Tweed there hath been a very strong fortified bridge having the tower yet standing which was the gate to the bridge in old time. 3 miles over the hills side on Gallowsheilds is Lauderdale, Lauder itself being one of the ancientest burghs there abouts who will take toll on the King. In it dwell many of the Lauders, one of whose houses is very fine one, there running a river hard by it called Lauder. Of this Lauderdale Viscount Metlin or Matlin is viscount. The gentlemen and gentlewomen call their men and maids Misters and Mistresses.

From Gallowshields to Windeleys, one of the Pringles, 2 miles, it stands in a dale up which dale is a pretty wood on our left hand ; within the sight of the same side another of the Pringles, his house is called Torretleys on the other side of the water on the right hand is another of them, his house is called Buckholme, and by the water side he hath a wood called the Buckholme. From thence to Herret's houses, a guest-house where we alighted, is 8 miles, in which space we crossed the Gallowater some 20 times. From thence to Fallow Burne where we enter into Lowden one mile, from the Fallow Burne to Borthwicke Castle 1 mile, from thence to Stobhill 2 miles, where all the coal pits are of the Leard of Erniston, a Seton, and Stonuobiars a lord's seat that was standing in a wood along a river side, all which now Seton the leard of Erniston hath bought of the Lord of Steanbiars, which Erniston for his wealth might buy out· a lord or two. From the Stobhill in view on our left hand some 4 miles off is Erniston, a fine seat, from the Stobhill to Dawertey upon the river Keeth and a stone bridge over it, my Lord Ramsey's house seated on a rock, a fine building ; 1 mile from thence down the river Keeth not in sight and out of our way my lord of Newbattell who sticked himself. From my Lord Ramsey's in our way to Laswade a market town one mile, it is seated on a goodly river and a stone bridge over it called the South river. From the Laswade to Liberton church 2 miles, from Liberton to Edinburgh 2 miles. The hemisphere's circumference from Edinburgh is mountains, as is Westmoreland from about Lowther, but something plainer, and their mountains not so high. In view from Edinburgh 4 miles southwards is Keeth, a borough where all the witches are burned, and Earl Morton's house is.

There is also in view from Edinburgh's craggs Musselburgh upon the Frith's side some 4 or 5 miles off where the famous battle was fought betwixt the Scotch and English. From Edinburgh about a mile eastwards is Leith, the chief haven, having belonging to it 150 sail of ships holding about 200 tons. The lords, merchants, and gentlemen join in putting out ships to take prizes, of which we saw some 3 or 4 French and Flemings they had taken, there is a pretty harbour. This town was taken and burnt by the Frenchmen in Queen Elizabeth's time, and she sent the English which did remove them, some houses we saw which were burnt but not yet re-edified; before that time it was walled about, but now it is yet better than Carlisle, having in it two fairer churches for inwork than any I saw in London, with two seats-royal in either. There be also two hospitals one of which the sailors built, the other the tradesmen, there is a stone bridge over the river Leith here, hard by the town be oysters dragged which go to Newcastle, Carlisle and all places thereabouts, they being under 3d. the 100. All their churches be lofted stage wise about Edinburgh, Leith, &c., the women at Leith in one church had loose chairs all along before the men's seats. It is governed by two bailiffs. Eniskeith an isle in the Firth, a mile or two by water from Leith is famous for a fort on a rock in the same which the Frenchmen took when they took Leith (the English built it), and left a remembrance of their being there written in latin on stone. At Leith dwelleth my Lady Lincey who married her 6 daughters to 6 knights. On our right hand as we go to Leith is the castle of Stenick, old and ruinated; the town of Leith is a borough, but holding on Edinburgh as Kingston-upon-Hull on York. The fort in Eniskeith hath yet command of the sea if it be well manned it will hold a thousand men. The passage in at the harbour at Leith is dangerous by reason of sprtes (sic) and shelves, they cannot lash in but at a full sea. The harbour is compassed in with wooden fabrics 3 fathoms high and about 2 broad, strengthened by great stones thrown into the frame all but where the ships enter in at being but narrow. White wine was there at 3d. the muskin, which is a pint.

Beyond the Frith in the sight of Edinburgh is Bruntelin, a harbour, town, and borough of regality, governed by a provost, who knoweth my Lord of Bruntelin a Melvin, (sic) dwelling there and 2 bailiffs, and 2 officers and sergeants. Their provost in Scotland is in nature of our mayor, bailiffs in nature of our sergeants-at-mace, or rather chosen to aid them, the officers they arrest if the bailiffs give them but warrant by word bid them, they are in nature of our bailiffs, and bear halberds. Here is a church square built, and it hath a seat-royal in it, there are no more churches in it, but yet they have a pretty 'towbeoth.' The Frith betwixt Leith and Bruntelin or Kengoren 7 miles, a mile or two above Bruntelin is Aberdour a   the water running through it, one side my Lord of Morton's, the other side my Lord Murray's, a mile down from Bruntelin towards the main sea is Kengoren, a haven for boats and barks, all within the view of Edinburgh crags, and a borough regal, one Lyon is earl of it, one church; hard by it is there a spawewell.

A mile beneath Kingorin is a borough regal and haven as big as Leith called Kirkaldy a borough regal, one church one towbeoth.   -

A mile beneath **Kirkaldy** is there another harbour for boats and barks as Kingoren called **Dysart** the **wealthiest and biggest** of that coast. Kirkaldy and this have markets every day in the **week**, Brunt-elin and Kingoren but one day, it is a borough regal, a mile beneath it is Weemes, a borough and barony on the sea coast, no haven, and Colinn is lord of Weemes.

Now having gone about the circumference I will come to the centre videlicet—Edinburgh, whither we came on the 9th of November; there dismounted we ourselves at Mrs. Robertson's the stabler in College-wind where during our abode our horses were, and fed with straw and oats no hay straw, 24 hours 3d.—oats 3d. a capp which is a hoop. From thence we went to our lodging at Mrs. Russell's in Bell-wind an agent who is in nature of our English attorney's and three of us paid for our chambers tire and bedding 10d. 24 hours which [is] 5s. 10d. the week, ordinary we had none but paid for what we called. That night being wearied we rested ourselves, the next day viewed we their castle which is mounted on stately rocks, having the whole town of Edinburgh, Leith, and the sea in its eye; there is a fair pair of gates with stone cut work but not finished, the porter had our swords to keep until we came back again out of the castle, there were about some 20 pieces of ordnance ready mounted, brass and iron, one piece of ordnance there was bigger than any else either in the munition house or any other which I saw to be about 4 yards long, and the diameter 20 inches, there being a child gotten in it as by all it was reported, the bullet of stone she shooteth is of weight 19 stone 4 pounds 3 ounces, after the troy-weight 20 pounds to the stone; there be great many of vaults some 6 yards by which the castle keepers say would contain 1000 men. The building is no bigger than Appleby castle,.within it is a powder mill, corn mill, &c. There is also a hewn stone well 30 fathoms deep, the water is drawn up with a wheel which one goeth in, it is hewn so deep through a rock of blue-stone; there be little wooden watch-houses, to watch in every night.

From the castle we went to the Courts where we saw all the 14 Lords sitting in the inner house in their robes, being a violet colour faced with crimson velvet of the fashion of our Judges, the 15th Lord sitteth in the outer house. The chief of these 15 is the Chancellor, the 2nd the Lord President, the 3rd the Lord Advocate, the other 12 sit in council in the outer house each third week, beginning at the ancientest, [1st of the inner house and 15th of the house itself, then of the laws and order of the house, then so of the outer house]* and of the commissary's court, and of the force of the presbyteries, &c.

[The Inner House.]

The Courts.

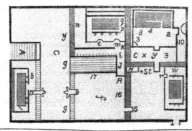

* The passage in brackets is struck out in the original.

a, the stairs up into the Courts; *b*, the commissary court; *d*, the door into it; *c*, a void place to walk in; *g*, a wainscot partition; *e*, a door which a maser keepeth; *f*, the place where those in readiness which have business; 16, a wall crossing over-thwarte; *h*, a door through the high wooden partition into the outward house the 2nd court; *g*, stagewise seats into which any may go out of the void place; (sc. *c*,). *i.g.* a pale to forlet any to go off from the stagewise seats into the Court; *k*, a long backed seat for lawyers and expectants to sit on; *m*, the door in at which the Macer and Judges, &c., go within the bar; *l*, another door on either side of which the advocates, defendant, and pursuant, plead; *n*, a place for the idle advocates to chat and walk in *o*, a seat where the Registers sit at the table; *p*, the two ascending seats on the lowest of which other clerks and registers sit, on the highest the single Judge; *q*, a wall; *r*, a door out of the outer house into a walking place before the inner house over which hangeth a bell the string of which goeth into the inner house by the judges' heads; *s*, another door into the inner house retiring place; *s*, a partition wall; *t*, the door into the inner house; *v*, a door into a severed place for any man's private dispatch, as for writing of letters or other things, conferences &c.; *w*, the seats and table; *x*, a vacant place for clients and other concourse during the advocate's pleading or motion before the Judges; *z* and ×, the bar on both sides of the door, those for the defendants and their advocates the other for the pursuers &c.; *y*, the entrance for the Judges and Registers; 5, the table with 3 sides about the outside of which, on 8, sit the Judges, my Lord Chancellor in the midst and in a black gown, the President of the sessions on his right hand in a purple gown faced with red velvet, and so the rest of the lords except the Lord Advocate, who is in black, and sitteth in the corner 3, and in degree is next the President; he is in nature of the King's Attorney at London, and pleads for the King when anything toucheth him, and also for other persons and still with his hat on if so it please him; 4, the form before the table on which the Registers sit, being men of good esteem, but bare-headed; 2, the door to the chimney; 10, the chimney, over the head is it fine fret plaister work, and in the windows behind the Judges are there the volumes of their law. Under part of these Courts is there another court called the Court of Justice, and hard by is the Lord Provost's Court, and first of the Commissary's Court beginning *ex minimis*, to it belongeth 4 Judges which formerly have been advocates, they be, as I perceived not much respected, the matter of the court be legacies, wills and testaments, debts under 40*l.* sterling, yet one may have a man for 1000 or more, but then it must be in general debts, never one amounting to above 40*l.* Their trials are wholly by oath and witnesses. Next, of the outer court, which doth but as it were prepare things for the inner house, here doth sit always but one judge, and he is one of the 12 of the 15, which 12 according to their seniority sit here each their week in course, the other 3, *sc.* the Chancellor, President, and Lord Advocate are exempted. In the morning still before the Judge comes in be all the parties called into court which that day shall have any business, then entereth in the judge, and all trivial civil matters he judgeth and likewise all great matters he handleth and at leastways prepareth if not judgeth it himself and if any like not of the judgment of this court they may have it to the inner house, but if the judges of the inner find the judgment to be good, the party which troubled the inner house with it will be punished, the process of the court being 1st a summons, attachments, &c., then a Ditte which

is in nature of our declaration, to which the Defender most commonly
answereth by word himself and not by way of replication in writing,
and if it be about a Horning matter which is in nature of our out-
lawing, then there goeth forth a caption and upon that a Horning,
which Horning is publicly read on the market cross at Edinburgh.
Now a Horning is a writing setting forth the whole matter and
cause of it, with the reasons why so, and this Horninge pronounceth
him a rebel, and yet notwithstanding this Horning may be reversed,
as our outlawry. In this court is always great noise and confusion,
but the inner house very orderly as shall appear, it only medleth
with things not determined or where his judgment is disliked. When
they are all set the door is shut and none but themselves there they
will ring a bell (and then openeth the Maser the door) when they have
any business, and the Maser as they bid him will call the parties
and their advocates whom they would have which go in thereupon with
their cause; at which time the Maser will suffer any stranger to go in
and hear the cause pleaded upon acquaintance. The form of their pleading is 1st the advocates and their clients stand each on either side of the
door through the bar, at the bar, and the advocates plead in Scotch
before them, and in the then time of their pleading their clients will put
a double piece or more, with an ordinary fee with the poorest, and will
say to their advocates ' thumb it thumb it,' and then will the advocates
plead accordingly as they feel it weigh. Their pleading is but a kind
of motion, and especially the first 6 weeks in the session for then is
there nothing else but motions. Most of their law is Acts of Parliament
and Regiam majestam, and their judgments given in court which we
call reports, only they corroborate their cause with civil arguments and
reasons. After their motion which is but short, they are all dismissed,
the door shut, and then it is voted amongst the judges and according
to the number of votes it is carried, and then the Chancellor, if present,
if not, the President, and if not he, in order to next, giveth sentence
accordingly, it still remaining hidden to the parties the carriage of the
matter; and so when this matter is done to the next, but note that the
parties with their advocates will acquaint the Judges with their case
before it comes to hearing, which they say maketh quicker dispatch,
and note further that advocates will commonly have a ' kowe ' or such like
thing sent them to make way unto them for their clients beside their
fees, by which exorbitant kind of fees they become the greatest purchasers in the kingdom. They have most of them been travellers and
studied in France, but whether they have studied at home or in France
they thus proceed, advocates, sc. :—they first get a petition to the
Judges that they may not be hindered by the Masers, but have free
access to the Courts, [and] hear their manner of pleading, from which time
till they be advocates they are called Expectants. Now as soon as they
think themselves fit and dare venture to undergo trial, they will further
petition to have a lesson, to dispute a question before the Judge,
upon which if they be thought sufficient they are admitted and sworn
advocates. A story—One being to [be] made Judge of the Session not
long ago, there being in his oath not to be partial, he excepted to his
friends and allies. Another—A borderer in a Jury gave amongst
his fellows wittingly a false verdict, and being asked why he did it,
said it is better to trust God with one's soul than their neighbour
with their geere. The poor clients say there be great delays in actions
some 7 years, some 12, 20, 27, &c., but the advocates shuffle it off
and deny it, yet I heard of one who offered the one half to recover the
other, and for an advocate or other to lay an action depending in suit

it is common with them, and they hold it reason that when a man cannot defend his own cause that he sell to another who can. Forgery is death with them, perjury the loss of their hand or ears, as the quality of the persons requireth. If a clerk do but miswrite anything it is death. Hereditaments descend, conquests(?) purchases ascend, as from the son to the father, dower and conjunct fee, jointure is as in England, almost. The form of their writings are almost the same with ours, their dignities, wards, reliefs, and marriages as with us ; but note the form of marriages, they are asked in the church as with us, the priest will appoint what company they shall have at church, but after marriage there will be continual feasting and mirth for some 4 or 5 days together, during all which time there will be presents offered to them, as all kinds of household stuff, feather beds, pots, pans, &c., and goods, as sheep, oxen, horses, kine, &c., often to the value of 500l. sterling, but according as the parson is more or less for offerings in the church they do not use. Men seldom change their servants ; the gentlemen and knights, &c., usually do ride with trumpets. The last year, 1628, the Judges went circuits, but it is doubted whether they will hereafter do so or not. The Scotch nobility do dilapidate their estates and impoverish their own kingdom by frequenting the English Court, their trading is almost wholly with England, their wines excepted which they buy in France, custom free in regard of their old league with them. Their own chief commodities are grain, sheep, and runts, salt and coal, and of coal it is observed that there is none but between Trent in England and Tay in Scotland, which cometh from a great lough so called, and glideth by Perth and Dundee. Lough Nesse beside Murray-Land and the river which runneth from it is so fierce that it never freezeth and though I saw [ice] come out of another river into it yet it instantly thaweth and becometh water. That of Lough Mirton, Lough Lomond, the Deaf stone, and the Cleke geese is reported for truth as Holingshead writes it. There be at this time three of the greatest men in the kingdom papists and their eldest sons protestants, which is remarkable, *sc.* Argyll, Hamilton, and Huntley whose eldest son is esteemed the ablest man of body in the kingdom, and will familiarly go in the mountains after the deer 80 miles a day. But I am afraid I have digressed and therefore I will return to the courts. The sheriffs be now most of them annually chosen, and the sheriff of Lothian this year, 1629, is my cousin Sir Lewis Lowther who was very glad to see me. He keepeth his court twice a week, in the afternoon, Wednesday and Friday in the outer court, at which times the 4 Lord Justices sit upon criminal matters in their own court, and their criminal offenders may have advocates to plead for their lives before the Judges. Over the Lords of the session be there 4 other lords of the Secret Council, which may sit and give their votes amongst them if they will, and they be but as spies over the rest to mark their doings, and inform the king of it. The general Justice which is through the Kingdom is by the conveners of justice at Quarter Sessions Commissioners when it pleaseth them, and sheriffs at their courts when they appoint them, but the Judges of the session bear such a hand over them as they will call in question almost every thing they do, let them do the best they can. When one is out of the Borders, and especially the further North-east is very safe travelling, safer than in England ; and much civiller be they, and plainer English, yea better than at Edinburgh. Their tillage like ours they use much liming of their ground, and they plough their ground all in winter, and in the spring then only harroweth it and soweth it. Their mason and joiner work is as good if not better than in England, most of their wear is

English cloth. They have very good meat, fish, flesh, and fowl great store, but dress it not well; in the South it is as dear as in the South of England, but in the North, about Dumbarton and thereabouts wondrous cheap, a goose for 4*d.*, and so proportionably of other things. Their drink is almost altogether ale and hot waters, and in the North most hot waters, wine is 6*d.* a quart, sack 1*s.* 1½*d.*

Now having passed through the Courts we will enter the town, in which there is but one street of note called the High Street, beginning at the Castle and going down to the Neitherbowe which is one of the bars or gates of the city, and strait on to the Abbey which is the King's Palace, but the street from the Netherbowe to the Abbey is called the Cannongate, the one side of which is a liberty of itself, the other side belongeth to Edinburgh, as Holborn one side to London the other to Westminster. They have a fine Towheooth and prison in it, this street and the High Street are but one street called by strangers, the next street is Cowgate within the city as long as either of them but narrower, the rest but winds and closes some 2 yards broad. The Abbey is a very stately piece of work uniform, and a dainty neat chapel in it, with a pair of organs in it, and none else in the city, they being puritans. There be fine prisons of a great height, and fine hewn stone buildings. There be 5 churches, of which St. Giles' is chief because of the stately steeple, before Bowbells church in London, having in it one great bell which they do not ring but tolls at 10 o'clk at night, and 4 others. At Grey Friars their tombs be in the church-yard walls but none in the church, there is one hospital within the walls, another without, which Herret the King's jeweller at his decease gave money to build it. There is one college which King James founded, being governed by a primate and other sub-regents to read to the several years which follow here in order, there be 5 classes or seats in it, 1st of Humanity, the 2nd of Greek, 3rd of Logic, the 4th of Natural philosophy, the 5th of Mathematics, and Arist de calo(?) The 1st year of students be called scholars, the 2nd Semibijani, the 3rd Semibijani, the 4th bachelors, the next degree, Laureates or Masters of Arts, and no further, tutors they call pedagogues. We supped with Mr. Addamsonn, primate of the same on Thursday at night, and much made on were we. There is one part of the college built by the Senate and people of Edinburgh, which is better than any part of the college beside, with this inscription. *Senatus populusque Edenburgensis has ædes Christo musique struendas curarunt:* there are some 300 students in it, the primate is severe, he hath a little dog following him, and 2 fair daughters, and an unhappy lad said he would wish nothing but to stick his dog and move his daughters and lye carnally with them. At the end of every year they analyze their whole year's work, when they go out Laureats they repeat their last 4 years analyses and they then be their own tutors. There is a place which they call the Society of Brewers, where the beer and ale is brewed to serve the city and they be Englishmen, they called us into their butteries and made us drink gratis, there they have wondrous fair brewing vessels and a fair kiln. There is also the Custom house not far from St. Giles' church with 3 fair arched entrances, over it is the place where butter is sold. The town is governed by a Provost which is [in] nature of our mayor, they not having any in Scotland, by 4 bailiffs and 36 of his council, in nature of our aldermen, the mayor's brethren and other under officers; the bailiffs arrest, and the officers may also if the baliffs bid. There is an officer they call the Danegeld which disburseth money for the town before the bailiffs, they call him lord. At 4 o'clk in the morning and at 8 at night goeth a drum about the town and so in other boroughs, the nobles have to carry up the supper, a trumpet sounding. All their gentlemen be courteous and affable, but hosts and the country clowns be careless and unconscionable in their usage to strangers.

On the 10 of November being Tuesday at 12 of the clock see we 3 heralds standing on the public cross which is in form of a turret but not garretted, and a wood beam standing up in the middle, the unicorn crowned on the top of it, there is a door up into it. These 3 heralds one after another did proclaim an edict concerning the papists of Scotland, reciting them by their names which get if possible, both before and after they proclaimed 3 trumpeters sounded, and so still they do if it be from the King or his council, but if some common proclamation not so in state. On this cross be all noble men hanged and headed, as about 9 years since, 1619 or thereabouts, the Earl of Orkney headed, his son hanged, and others, for the keeping a castle against the King being treason ; on this cross be citations read, denunciations, and hornings denounced.

On the 14th of November I went to Leeth whereof more before, crossed the Firth to Bruntelin, which is 7 miles from thence to beside the Leard of Dowhill, a Lincey, 8 miles, 2 miles before we came thither is the river of Ore, narrow but deep and fierce we rid it the height of the horse's mane and the fierceness of it turned the horse off his feet. From Dowhill to Geaney Priggle which parteth Fife and Kinross-shire one mile, from thence to Kinross at the West end of Lough Leven, a borough barony, 2 miles, it is a market town, the Lough Leven is 4 miles square, which is 16 miles about. So far is the land good, but here and there many high rocks and hills, in this lough is fish every day in the year gotten for store, none in Britain like, and consider the bigness of it, as also for fowl. The general kinds of fishes be these—the pikes of which many [be] as big as a man, eels, gelltoughes, chars, perches, camdowes, a kind of trout which have not scales, grey trouts, gelletough is the high char, sysbinge the she. There is a river they call the Leven running out of it 8 miles into the sea, and in it is salmons. In the midst of this lough is a castle of my Lord of Morton's, well fortified with good ordnance, the walls some 3 yards thick, a ship might sail in it, there [be] great store of almost all kinds of wild fowl, of wild geese there being continually seen 3000 or 4000, and swans many, the swans will not suffer any foreign swan to be with them, in stormy weather the old swans will carry the young ones on their wings off the water. King James desired to dwell in it, and did with the Queen only for his pleasure. The town of Kinross at the foot where I lodged on Saturday at night which is also my Lord of Morton's, he having another house there too that they dry them in their chimneys like red herrings (sic). It [is] governed by one bailliff, 2 officers, one church they have and a Towbooth, it is the head town of the shire, and that after which the shire is named, Robert Crenyam my host of this place, one of the elders of the church, told us he saw some 30 years since on a ship which was come from the East Indies shells which in that 3 years' space had grown to the ship have the forms of fowl in them, as in an egg. In Stirling, not far from the sea side some 15 miles there is a gentleman's estate much harmed by a strange outbreaking of the water on Christmas day in the afternoon, 1628, in a moss some 3 miles compass cast up and laid on good ground which hath spoiled the gentleman that mossy ground now covering their arable so thick as to the tops of the trees; and the 3 miles compass out of which it was cast suddenly up became a great lough which before was a dry moss.

The bleaching of linen.

A good spinster will spin 2 bauks a day of that which will be 4s. 6d. the yard, and when the linen is in varne they seeth it half a day and

more in the ashes of any green wood, and after that let it stand in it a
day or more, they wash it by trampling it in hot water and then battling it
in cold, some use raw daike (?) small wourt, and this is before it be in
cloth, and when it is in cloth they take sheep dung and make it small,
put it into hot water and steep the cloth in the same 4 or 5 days, they
then wash it in hot water, battles it [in] cold water and after lies it by
the water side by 8 days together casting water on it and never suffer it
to dry, then they steep in the sheep dung and all more as before.

The Scottish dialect.

Ingle, Fire; Spence, boor in a country house: twill yee, will ye,
t'wadd ye, would yow. Bigge, corne: Bearve, a glutte of water a
draught of &c.: excamen, exchange: lumant, chimney: through of paper,
sheet of paper: gigget of mutton and a spald of mutton, but that's
commonly a shoulder: an oval pannier: a creel, a boat: a stand of beer,
a stand, a barrel set end ways: my dowe, my wife: pantry, buttery:
chop, strike: aught, dighte: what hours, what a clock: wappe, throw:
burne, water: serviter, a table napkin: a kealle pie, a pie with pieces
of cut mutton and pruned: a chair, chare: a brase, chimney beam:
chaule, a candlestick: a coase or leed garan, a kitte: a piele or keoren
of wool is 100 stone of &c.: a gritte is all above a hundred stone.
Their 100 stone of wool at Selkirk is 150 stone in England, their 14 is
our 21. Report .George Ribcall, burgess: sile (sic) min, bedtester:
pendicle or paine. vallance of a bed: head codes, pillows: a drink of ale
or beer, some ale or beer: penyells or drawers, curtains: close, courte:
a manager as called, a tenies: scriver, a writer: vote, voice, opinion:
drite, shite: dung, shite: a lough, tarn or mere: blith, glad.

Measures of liquids.

A bilder, a gill: a mushkin, a pint: a choppin, a quart: a pint, two
quarts or a pottle: a quart, a gallon or 4 quarts, this at Langholm
and Selkirk.

Measure of corn.

[At] Langholm their bushel is 6 peeks of Carlisle, the 4th part of
one of their peeks is called a cappe, the price, 3d.; a bushel of oats, 4s.;
at Selkirk so called also, and there a beat . . or a   is the same with
a cappe or a heappe, the same at Selkirk, but there measure is less and
at Edinburgh their forlet is our 6 pecks or thereabouts, 4 forlets is their
bow, 16 bows is their chaldron, a bow of wheat is 10l. Scotch: bigge,
8l. Scotch: oats 6l. Scotch. A horse will bear a bow 40 miles.

Avoirdupoise—16 pounds to the stone, and troy weight 20 pounds to
the stone is all through Scotland, and none other.

Wixe him of, drink him of: please, sike: no, not: woursill, change:
partrick is the best peasant fuel in the Brittany: creen, rabbit: shanks,
stockings: pantol, pantables: mores, hills: bangister, wrangling:
collation, a drink when one goeth to bed: diswynes, breakfast: smeringe,
greasing: heartsome, delightsome: wilecoate, waistcoat: waterpot pots,
chamber-pots: cracklike, a hand-gun, a phrase applied to those who be
bravado talkative folks; a health used at Langholm taking one by the
hand, the Lord's blessing light on your hand, yourself, and all your body
beside: a sponnge, a brush: locky, an old woman: a wind, a lane, or
rather an alley, as Ram alley at the Inner Temple at London; a close,
the same: a capp, a dish: a k . . ., a clock: skeith, damage: slay and
thow the beer, warm: tue, lease: orelayer, a bawd.

Their coins.

A Scotch penny the 12th part of an English penny: a turnamoure *aliter*, a 2odwell or a black dog, the 6th part of an English penny: a placke, the 3rd part of an English penny: an atclinson the 3rd part of 2 pence: the dollar is with them 5s. wanting 2d., it being most of their money. Their 20s. is our 20d., their shilling our d., our cross dagger in gold is 11s. with them, our 22s. piece, 22s. 3d.

Necke, band; hands, cuffs: heugh, a little hill: moyne, money: dole weed, mourning apparel: sibb, akin or allied: clans, kindred: beosse, a box: shuts, the oval holes in galleries: conjunct fee, jointure: chestons, chestnuts: a geene tree, black cherry tree: a powle foule, a turkey: a coler, a pair of snuffers: turnpike, turn stayre: anent, concerning: a fell spirit, a wise man: crackiuge, drinking a while, or talking: ford, wath: rests, rents: holders, tenants: government, etc.

On the 15th day of November from Kinross to Millsforth, better than a mile on the right hand, a quarter of a mile thence is my Lord Burley's house (a very pretty little one). From thence to my lord of Ballmannoe and Aughchinfleck 6 miles, from thence to Erne brigge, the toll of it belongeth to Perth, St. Johnstowne, St. John being patron of it. The sea floweth up so high, the bridge is four bowes long, the river runneth into Teath a mile and a half beneath the bridge. Beneath the bridge by the river side is my Lord of Munchreth, a Muncreeth, a bowdrift lower eastwards is Sir John Muncreth of East Muncreeth, now deputy sheriff, whom they call my lord during the time of his office, (and so are the provost and bailiffs of Perth, being 4, and their Council being 12, if it please your wisdom, King James during his life was provost of it, and my Lord of Scone his deputy, but since his death they choose one each year.) Beneath East Muncreeth is Kellmoneth, a seat of Sir John Muncreeth's, beneath it a mile Phingaske, my Lord Phingaske's a baron, his name is Dundas, it is at the meeting of Teath and Erne, there is great store of fruit, and good grounds; a mile beneath on the river Teath is West Weemes castle, my Lord of Weemes, it is fine ground, and he hath salmon fishing. From Erne brigges to St. Johnstown 2 miles. St. Johnstown is walled and moated on 3 sides, on the 4th the river Teath, over which there was a bridge of 11 bowes, and 1621 or thereabouts was driven down by the water, the water is very rough and dangerous, boats go on it. Besides the lay government before spoken of there be deacons 9, as many as craftsmen, *videlicet*—hammermen, carpenters, scriners, gardiners, websters, wakers, fleshers, backsters, millers, under which all other trades are contained. Each of the deacons do receive apprentices, and redress all faults in trades belonging to them, and are termed lords, they are chosen every year; every trade sitteth in the church by themselves. There be 2 churches in the town, the one called St. John's church having 7 great bells, 4 little, and chimes, the finest in Scotland, the church is hung with many candlesticks. Here I saw a woman sit on the stool of repentance and the parson admonish her, adulterers here do stand bare foot, some half an hour at the church door, then at the beginning of the sermon they go into the church [and] sit on the stool of repentance; this they do at St. Johnstown for the space of a year, and they have a white sheet on during all those ceremonies for the first adulteries committed. For the 2nd being Wednesday having crossed the Frith with much danger we went to Edinburgh and the weather keeping, Thursday and Friday we were taking leave of our friends, Mr. Primate, Advocate Fletcher, and my cousin Sir Louis Lawder, sheriff of Loudon, who made much of me.

We were offered acquaintance to my Lord Chancellor, my Lord of Underpeter, and others of the nobles, but we weighed more our own pains in going down the street than their countenance. On Saturday to Gallowsheilds, half a mile from Liberton **as** we went is the oil well, which is like the fat in the beef pot, it is a present cure for scalded heads. A mile beyond Borthwick is a town called Middleton. At Gallowsheilds we stayed all night and Sunday, and in the morning went away by 3 of the clock to Mr. Robert Pringle's at Baytingbush, from thence the next morning to Barronet Graham's at the Folde 2 miles whence back again we went after supper to Mr. Curwen parson of Arthuret, thence the next day at noon to Bleckhell where we dined whence home the next night.

1639, April 8.   Whitehaven.

" May it please you to take notice that the 6th instant I being with my Lord Clifford at Workington, and all of us rayzed out of our bedds with an Alarum that the Citye of Carlisle was burnt and the Irish souldiers all slaine by the Scotts, insomuch that the Beacons were lighted, and the Contrye arose, which putt my Lord and all men into such an amazement, that he had given me comaundment to rayse what strength about me as was possible for our defence at Whitehaven, and to send for the trayned band of Lancashire to be readye at Lancaster, but God be praysed the Alarum being false, and all safe I sent after the Alarum and stayd it, and the same day I received one of these letters inclosed from my Lord wherein I doubt not but that he hath better certified yow of all, which makes me shorter.   And yesterday I received another letter from him to your Lordship and another to myselfe with a warrant to the Captain or Master of your Lordshipp supposing that she had bene ungone from hence, yett I tould my Lord Clifford that both his Majesty's pinnace the *Confidence*, and your honour's pinnace the *Phœnix* were gone, but it seemes multitude of business caused his Lordship to forget and therefore I have likewise sent you the warrant to the Captain and his Lordship's letter to me, that your honour may be better informed ; I expedited this barque away of purpose for the speedye conveyance of these letters.   My Lord Clifford departed yesterday imediately after dinner towards Carlile, and since this morninge came a warrant from my Lord Marshall to stay all Scotch shippinge till further order, which here I have done.   My Lord Clifford and all the Contrye are much affraid of this port of Whitehaven being the best landinge place for the Enemie, if they should come with force by sea, wherefore I have bought two peeces of ordinance (2 sacres) of Captain Bartlett, and his brother, and tenn musketts with furniture from Newcastle all at my owne charge, and I desire that your honour would be pleased to send me two peecs of ordinance more to these two I have, and I shall with thanks either pay for them, or when these troubles are quieted send them back againe for I will presently make a fortification for them on the peere.   And if your Lordship will be soe pleased to send me them I doe intreat yow that I may have some powder shott and other materialls belonging to them."

1644, July 20.—Kirby Lonsdale. Petition of Sir John Lowther Knight Baronet to Prince Rupert. " Who humbly sheweth that albeit your Petitioner bathe showne all loyalnes and obedience to his Majestie and hath used all his endeavours in promoteinge his Majesties service, And your Petitioner haueinge a Commission granted for the goverment of Browham Castle wherein your Petitioner had both bestowed cost and laide in sume provision of corne and fireinge at his owne charge, for preventinge an enemie from possessinge the same. Yet soe it is that Sir Phillip Musgrave Barronet without any cause knowne unto your Petitioner hath set a centry upon the Castle and endeavoureth as it seemeth to possesse himselfe thereof to the greate disrepute and discouragement of your Petitioner and the Country therebouts where your Petitioner's regiment is raysed.

May it therefore please your highnesse to grant unto your Petitioner redresse herin, whereby he may be the better inabled to serve his Majestic and your Highnes, and the Country satisfied and your Petitioner vindicated, and your Petitioner shall be ever obliged to remayne your humble and devoted servant."

" I think it most just that Sir John Lowther be continued in the custody of the Castle of Browham according to his Comission, without any lett or interruption from Sir Phillip Musgrave or any other person and that convenient allowance be made for the support of the Garrison in the sayd Castle from tyme to tyme out of such estate as is belonging therunto.

Kirby Lonsdall,   RUPERT."
20th of July, 1644.

THE PROTECTOR CROMWELL to LORD MONTAGUE. [*Copy*].

1657, August 11th. Whitehall.—" You haveing desired by severall letters to knowe our minde concerninge your weighinge Ancho and sayleing with the Fleet out of the Downes, wee have thought fitt to lett you knowe, that wee do very well approve thereof, and that you doe cruse up and down in the Chanell, in such places as you shall judge most convenient, takeinge care of the safetie, interest and honour of the Comonwealth.

I remayne Your very lovinge Friend.
OLIVER P."

Directed :—For Generall Mountague on board the *Naseby* in the Downs.
Endorsed :—His Highnesse letter August 11th, 1657. To command mee to sayle.

QUAKERS.

1661-2, March 17. Morland.—Warrant signed by Thomas Sandford and Edward Nevinson, justices of the peace, for the apprehension of Timothy Robarts, incumbent of Barton church, Westmoreland, for refusing to read and make use of the Book of Common Prayer, and to administer sacrament.

1664, May.—Certificate of William Smith, rector, and Christopher Holm, churchwarden, of Lowther parish, that John Wilkinson, *alias*

Crag of the Parkfoot, had not been to church for the four Sundays last past. They "desire that the Statute in that behalf provided may be executed upon him."

1664, July 20, Woodside.—" Sir John Lowther, Baronet, John Dalston, Richard Braithwait, and Edward Nevinson, Esquires, four of his Majesty's Justices of Peace for said County, &c.

" Forasmuch as it hath been made appear to us, by the oaths of credible and sufficient witnesses, that Anthony Bownas of Shapp, William Whitehead of Hardingdaile, John Barwick of Shapp, Richard Barwick of the same, James Fallowfield of Great Strickland, Edward Winter of Morland, Robert Bowman of Bampton, William Bland of Newby, Robert Robinson of the same, John Bolton of Bongait, and William Hebson of Sleagill, the third day of July last, and John Smith of Sleagill, the tenth of July last, have met together, under the preteuce of the exercise of religion, contrary to the Liturgy of the Church of England and contrary to the Act, made the last session of Parliament intituled, An Act to prevent and suppress seditious conventicles. Do therefore adjudge and declare the aforesaid persons to be convict, and so to stand convict, according to the power given unto us by the said Act ; and in pursuance thereof have putt our hands and seals."

1664, Sept. 5. Appleby.—Edward Guy to " my much respected friends John Lowther and Philip Musgrave." Defending himself in vague language from various charges brought against him.
Endorsed : " Nedd Guy the Quaker's letter."

1664, November 28.—" From my prison house at Appleby." Michael Langhorne to " John Lowther of Lowther, justice of peace." Complaining of the wrong done him by his imprisonment, and that Guy Coperthwait and another had most rudely taken away his goods, no fine having been inflicted upon him ; and abused the people of Askham, shaking their staves over their heads and threatening to hang them (the Askham people) by their necks, &c.

1665, 7 August.—" The names of those who have been imprisoned upon the second offence, whose time is long since expired.

> Edmond Robinson of Newby.
> Eliza. Holme of Sleagill.
> John Bolton of Bongate.
> Richard Barwicke of Shapp.
> Wm. Hebson of Sleagill.
> John Barwick of Shapp.
> Edward Winter of Morland.
> Robert Winter of the same.
> Anthony Bownas of Shapp.
> Margaret Fallowfeild of G. Strickland.
> Eliza. Morland of Milflatt.
> Dorothy Arey of Shapp, and
>   attached upon the third.

The names of the persons who are now in custody upon the second offence whose time is not yet expired.

> Lancelote Fallowfeild of G. Strickland.
> James Fallowfe:ld of the same.
> Janet Smith of Sleagill.
> Frances Lawson of G. Strickland.
> Mary Robinson of Cleburne.
> Eliza. Gibson of G. Strickland."

1665, August 7.—" The names of the Quakers which met at Strickland Head the 7th day of August.

Imp. Rich. Arey of Shapp.
    Rob. Winter of Morland.
    Lanclot Fallowfeild of Great Strickland.
    Jennat Smith of Slegill.
    Ann Robinson of Newby.
    Elinor Winter of Morland.
    Francis Lawson of Great Strickland.
    Margarat Fallowfeild of the same.
    Anna Holme of Slegill.
    Ann Licake of

Item the 14th of August.

    Lanclot Fallowfeild de Great Strickland.
    Rob. Winter of Morland.
    Rob. Hebbson of Litle Strickland.
    Ann Smith of Shapp.
    Dorety Arey of the same.
    Margarat Arey of the same.
    Catheren Clarke of the same.
    Elinor Winter of Morland.
    Margarat Fallowfeild de Great Strickland.
    Ann Robinson of Newby.
    Mary Richardson of Great Strickland.
    Elizabeth Holme of Slegill.
    Jennat Smith of Slegill.
    Elizabeth Morland of Millflatt.

Item the 21st of August.

    Rich. Arey of Shapp.
    Rob. Winter of Morland.
    Hugh Gibbson of Shapp.
    Rob. Bowmen of Bampton.
    Edw. Robinson of Newby.
    Lanclot Fallowfeild of Great Strickland.
    Tho. Smith of Slegill.
    Mary Arey of Shapp.
    Elizabeth Morland of Millflatt.
    Francis Lawson of Great Strickland.
    Margarat Fallowfeild of the same.
    Ann Smith of Slegill.
    Jennatt Smith of the same.
    Jane Winter of the same.
    Jennat Atkinson of Shapp.
    Eliza Dent of King's Meaberon.
    Ann Holme of Slegill.
    Ann Licake.

Again the 4 of September.

    Lanclot Fallowfeild of Great Strickland.
    Rob. Hebbson of Litle Strickland.
    Edw. Winter of Morland.
    Will. Hebbson of Slegill.
    Rob. Winter of Morland.
    Ann Robinson of Newby.

Margarat Fallowfeild of Great Strickland.
Mary Holme of Slegill.
Mary Richardson of Great Strickland.
Jennat Smith of Slegill.
Dorety Arey of Shapp.
Margarat Arey of the same.
Jennat Atkinson of the same.
Grace Wattson of Thrimby.
Sarah Whitehead of Shapp.
Elinor Cloudsdaile of the same.

The 28th day of August.

Lanclot Fallowfeild of Great (*blank*).
Tho. Langhorne of Helton.
Dorety Arey of Shapp.
Margarat Arey of the same.
Margarat Fallowfeild of Great Str[ickland]."

Undated.]

" A calendar of all the Quakers now in gaol at Appulby.

John Boulton.
Anthony Bownass.
Thomas Langhorne.   } Committed by order of Sessions
Robert Bowman.   upon the third offence.
Elizabath Holme.

Richard Barrick.   } Committed for five months upon
Edmund Robinson.   the second offence and remained
Robert Winter.   2 months more than their time for
Edward Winter.   the Clerk of the Peace fees.

John Robinson.   { Committed upon a Sessions Ut-
John Thompson.   lawry and refused to submit or tra-
William Scaife.   verse to the Indictment and pay the
                        Clerk of the Peace fees.

Kendall Quakers.

William Cartmell.
Elizabeth his wife.   } Committed by Allan Bellingham
Edward Burrow.   Dan. Fleemeinge James Duckett
William Mansergh.   and Nicholas Fisher, Esquires, for
Robert Atkinson.   refusing either to submit or traverse
Rowland Warriner.   to these Indictments.

                        { Committed by Sir John Lowther,
Michaell Langhorne.   Baronet, for refuseinge to find secu-
                        rity for his appearance and good
                        behaviour.

Francis Howgill and William Hebson upon an other account."

SIR JOHN ARMITAGE to ——— (*copy*).

1663, Monday, 12 o'clock forenoon. Kirklees.—"I am commanded by the high sheriff of our county and the Deputy Lieutenants of the West Riding, to give you notice that the fifth monarchy men, the Anabaptists, Independents, Presbyterians, and a great many of the old soldiers, are resolved upon a rising, the day appointed is the 12th instant, the rebellion is to be general throughout the kingdom, if not in Scotland too. Therefore I thought it was my duty to acquaint you that all loyal subjects in the county may have notice to be in readiness if possible to prevent the horrid design, for they are resolved to destroy all which doth not come in unto their assistance. I am afraid I have been too tedious so shall only trouble you with the subscribing of myself," &c.

SIR PHILIP MUSGRAVE to SIR JOHN LOWTHER, at LOWTHER.

1664, December 24.—"I do give you thanks for the account you are pleased to give me of your proceedings against the quakers concerning which matter I did a few days ago speak with my Lord Chancellor who told me (as Mr. Secretary Bennet had done formerly) that from all parts of England they heard of their insolent behaviour, and did desire as quick a course might be taken for suppressing of them by imprisonment and transportation as the law will allow, I shall before the end of Christmas give you what I can learn for the way appointed for their transportation : The country will have a loss of Sir Patricius Curwen having a long time lived with much reputation among them and loved just ways. A writ for a new election is granted and I perceive Sir William Dalston intends to stand, and your nephew Sir John Lowther doth the like. They are both my very good friends and I will be accountable to you for my carriage in this matter.

The loss of our fort, and all the merchandise, and merchant ships at Guine taken by the Dutch, I suppose will be sent you in more particular manner then I have it, it is a sad story : I wish you a good Christmas.

P.S.—If you have not (by the authority of an umpire) put an end to the dispute betwixt my cousin William Musgrave and his son in law Mr. Simpson, I do beseech you do it, for it is an act of charity and Mr. Simpson's designs very disagreeable to ingenuous dealing especially with a father."

DR. THOMAS BARLOW to SIR JOHN LOWTHER BART. at LOWTHER.

1670, April 5th. Q[ueens] Coll[ege] Oxon.—"I receaved yours, and returne my respects, and harty thanks for your kindnes to the Colledge and me ; and for your good opinion of both ; which appears in this, that you are pleased to trust us with the education of your Grand-child, the heire and hopes of your ancient and worthy family. Sir, whenever you shall be pleased to send him hither, he shall be very welcome, and you may be sure, he shall have the best accommodation the Colledge can give him. For placinge him in the Colledge be pleased to know, that we have two ranks of Gentlemen in the Colledge. 1. Those we call *Communars*, which are Gentlemen of inferior quality usually (though many times men of higher birth and fortune, will have their sonnes and beires in that ranke). 2. *Upper Communars*, which usually are Baronetts or knights sonnes, or Gentlemen of greater

fortunes; these have some honorary privileges above ordinary *Communars*, but are not (as in all other Houses generally) freed from any exercise the meanest gentlemen undergoe : soe we conceave, and (by experience find and) know it to be true, that to exempt them from any beneficiall exercise, is not a priviledge, but indeed an injury and losse to them : seeinge it is really a depriveinge them of the just means of attaininge learninge, which is the end they and we should aime att. I doe (with submission to your prudence) thinke it most convenient to make your Grandchild *Upper-Communar*; it is some more honor, and benefitt to him, seeinge he will be ranked amongst Gentlemen of better birth and fortune, and soe (in reason and probabilytie) of most ingenuous breedinge and civility. For a Tutor, in case you know any in our Colledge to whom you would commend him, lett me know it, and your commands shall be obeyed ; otherwise if you shall be pleased to referr it to me, I shall commend him to such a one, as shall carefully indeavor to direct and instruct him in the grounds of Religion and Literature. But whoever be his Tutor, I shall (God willinge) diligently oversee and take care of both, and assist them in attaininge the end they aime att (piety and learninge). Though my imployments here are neither few nor little; yet (if you give me leave) I shall at convenient times (privately) read over the grounds of Divinity to him, that soe he may have a better understandinge and comprehension of the reason of that Religion, which alone is, or can be a just foundation of true comfort here, and of our hopes of a better life hereafter. . . . .
Lastly, to send a servant to attend him, will be some charge (though, to you, that be inconsiderable) and indeed (which is considerable) to noe purpose : for he must have a boy (assigned by his Tutor) to be his servitor, who must be a gowne-man and a scholar, and will be able to doe all his little businesses for him; and he may chuse such a servitor as is a very good scholar and sober Student, and soe be helpfull to him in his studies. Very few Gentlemen (though heires to very great fortunes) keepe any men to attend them here ; and these few which sometimes doe, those servants haveinge nothinge to doe themselves commonly make their Maisters most idle. But I referre this (as all other things) to your prudence."

DR. THOMAS BARLOW to [SIR JOHN LOWTHER BART.].

1670, May 26th. Queen's College, Oxon.—" I receaved yours, and 'tis true, I understood your meaninge, (when you mentioned sendinge a man to waite on your grandchild here) to be of a *Clocke-man;* and such persons (haveinge usually little or noe buisines with bookes) beeinge commonly idle themselves, concurre many times to make their maisters soe too. But, it seemes, I misunderstood your meaninge, for you intended to send a younge man, a scholar, who might waite on him as his servitor : and (as to this) my Cosin Dr. Smith, said truely, that such a person will be very convenient to come with him ; for a servitor, who is a gown-man, he must have ; and 'twill be much better that he have one of whose fidelity and industry he is (by experience) assured, then a stranger ; besides that boy (if borne in our country) will be capable of any preferment in our Colledge, and if (by his civility and proficiency in good literature) he prove worthy, he shall not want it."

LANCELOT LOWTHER to SIR JOHN LOWTHER BART.

· 1670, July 23rd, New Castle.—About the price and supply of alum, estimated to be worth about 25*l.* a ton.

HENRY DENTON to SIR JOHN LOWTHER BART.

1670-1, January 17th.   Q[ueens] C[ollege], Ox[ford].

"Your Grandchild continues his application to his studies not onely with diligence, but delight. Onely he has by an accident common to men who are in the vigour of their youth in jesting with an other Gentleman sprained his legge. But without any further hurt then some five dayes confinement to his chamber, which to him that can entertain himself all day with his book is no punishment. I am very well satisfyd with your intentions of making him his own purse bearer, · because as I do not distrust his discretion, so will it ease mee."

SIR THOMAS OSBORNE to LORD ——.

1671, October 3rd, London.— . . . . "Your Lordship was pleased in that to oblige mee with your ' commands to indeavour Sir John Finch his being one of the Commissioners for the Customes, and I must assure your Lordship itt was so much my desire that his Majestic should choose the best men for that place, and so much my inclination to serve so worthy a Gentleman, that I had proposed him to the Duke of Buckingham before I received your letter, and his Grace did not only approve the choice, but recommended him to his Majestic, whose answer was that hee had pitch't upon the men already, and I can assure your Lordship further, that the King depended wholly upon my Lord Ashley and Sir Thomas Clifford for the choice of all those Commissioners. Could I have pleased myselfe with a more satisfactory answer according to my desire, your Lordship should not have staid so long for it, and though I cannott take upon me to answer all the queries in your second letter, viz :—what qualifications are necessary to a Pretender, yett I dare bee confident to say my Lady Mary Bertie is in no way ingaged and when she is, I should thinke itt one great step to her happinesse that her Gallant could bee accompanied with your credentialls."

The EARL OF DANBY to the EARL OF CONWAY.

1680, August 21st.—" I know itt is pitty to interrupt you in your great pleasure of building, but besides that I can bee no longer silent without inquiring after your health (which no man is more concernd in then myselfe) I desire to partake of some of the pleasure by knowing what advances you have made in your work and whither you have made any progresse in the fencing of the Park. If itt please God that ever I have liberty to go where I .please I resolve to make my first visitt to Ragley and I am sure I shall not want your Lordship's assistance for that liberty when the time comes. I am glad therefore for my owne sake that a certain day is now sett for the meeting of the Parliament.

I suppose you heard that Mr. Hyde is sworne a Gentleman of the bed-chamber and I find every body wondring att itt and guessing that itt portends some great alteration in the Treasury. I heare my Lord

Grauard is in towne and that some would find an imployment for him to Tanger, but I imagine those are not his best friends. I intend to write to my Lord Brooks to thank him for his civility in the last Parliament and to desire the continuance of itt in this, but I have not yett learnt how to direct my letter to him."

ANNE WHARTON to [HER HUSBAND] the HON. THOMAS WHARTON.

1681, April ²⁸⁄₁₀, Paris.— . . . . "I here your poore house of commons were very roughly dealt with, they have noe vertue left (that I know of) but patiance, to make use of, and they say that is the coward's vertue, but yet I hope they will practise it in their affliction, which I cannot be very sory for, because I am the more likely to see you heare; you see how publick misfortuns bring private satisfactions."

THOMAS LOWTHER to SIR JOHN LOWTHER BARONET.

1688, August 22nd. Preston [or Purston Jacklin, near Pontefract].— I delayed till this post, to give you an accompt what was done at our meeting at Pontefract. Wee mett an houre or two before the questioners came where we agreed on the Answers; as on the other side there were but three that differed from us that were protestants, (viz) Sir J. Bointon, Mr. Hammon, and Mr. Towneley, the two former we expected would doe soe, and what their auswers were we know not, but they looked sneakingly on't. Now shall acquaint you what a fatall day had like to have beene to me; in the morning the stewart of my Colepitts fell downe the Pitt 34 yards deep, and a piece of timber after him, yet by God's mercie was not killed; and other two at the same time had like to have beene kild that should have lett him downe. Tom Widdop is onely lamed but recovers fast, and was able in two days to ride downe. That day Tanckard and his two Red Coats came and dined with me, after dinner Tanckard quarrelled with my son Tom and challenged him. Tom stole out of the house and mett them betwixt [here] and Swillington, made Charles the butler follow him with two swords. Tom and the other two charged theire pistoll as they went; Charles got to my son before they did, they threatened to pistoll my son for not bringing a gentleman, but Tom and Tanckard drew where after 4 or 5 passes they closed and fell into a ditch. Tanckard would not fight without he had the higher ground; at Tom's last pass he bent his sword neare to his hand either against his belt or buckle. The souldier went to Charles whilst the other 2 were ingaged and swore he would pistoll him if he did not lie down his sword, which he did, the other taking it up and broak it; then the two souldiers run to the other two who were strugling and disarmed Tom, and cut Charles twice across his head. As soone as I mist my son I got upon a hors without sadle or bridle and came just as all was done. You may believe I was in great confusion yet had that command when I see him well not to ingage further. I thank God he had noe hurt but a butt in his head which the souldier gave him."

THOMAS BRATHWAIT, J.P., to SIR JOHN LOWTHER.

1688, August 23rd. Kendal.—"I did really designe to waite on you tomorrow night att Lowther (as Cousin William Fleming will acquainte you,) but I am so confined with endless and bottomless business concerning Clipping, daily examining and bindeing over, that I have not been master of myselfe a good while, nor am yett, that fatigue not being yett over."

—— to Sir John Lowther at Lowther.

1688, September 22nd. London.— . . . "The wind has been so long westerly that we know not what the Dutch Fleet design, but all agree 'tis for something extraordinary. Several towns are said to be beseiged by the French but no certainty."

—— to Sir John Lowther.

1688, September 29th. London.—" I suppose before the post goe the proclamation wil`be out for recalling the Parliament writs ; whether they will be revived I know not. I writ (as in my last) to my Lord Thanet concerning my son but have no answer; Mr. Musgrave also writ to him the same post, not having determined before to stand, but apprehending some new measures, as he thought, begun then to think on it, but he told me he believed that his father would stand both for Westmoreland and Carlisle, and if so there would be room at Carlisle upon his waiving one of them.

We cannot tell what to think of the Invasion ; the King said he thought the Prince of Orange would goe on board as Munday next, letters last night say on Thursday or Friday, the Merchants' letters are wholy silent and all other news is from our Envoy in Holland, onely all agree in great preparations."

Jos. Reed to Sir John Lowther at Lowther.

1688, December 6, Carlisle.—"It's now discoursed here by Sir Christopher's friends that he intends to be governor here, and that soon, and they talk it publicly, the reason, because he and Sir George refused to sign a petition or to join with your Honour in anything. This Mr. B. F[eilding] told young Mr. Warwicke that your Honour dined at Sir Christopher's with Sir George, and that they absolutely refused to join with you but would stick by the King, as if your Honour were otherwise, I hope my Lord Carlisle or your Honour may expect to be served as soon as he, for I am confident both the other, as plainly appears by their actings, that profit is preferred before religion (sic) ; yet they must go still by the people here for the only loyal men and the upholders of the Church of England. Sir John I do all that possibly I can yet cannot get up the rents."

[J. Aglionby] to Sir John Lowther at Lowther.

1688, December 10, Carlisle.—" I delivered your letter to Captain C. and had a long discourse with him upon it, wherein I represented to him the untenableness of their post for want of men, provisions, &c., and the little grounds they had to hope for any assistance, insinuating also some designs upon them from their old enemies which (as I am since credibly informed) is very true. He seemed at first to be thoughtful, yet told me they had an assurance from the Lord Chancellor of Scotland of what men they needed which I scarce believe though I know they hold correspondence with him and have had some expresses from him of late. At the last he told me he would confer with the governor and the lieutenant colonel (who rules all) and that I should have an answer, but though I have purposely stayed in town and have seen them all since several times, and that the last post brought them very unwelcome news (which I heard them read), yet they say nothing to me, so that I conclude they will take no counsel but in extremity and that nothing further is to be attempted that way. Mr. Fielding hath been very busy in misrepresenting your proposals to Sir C. M[usgrave] and Sir G. F[letcher], and would have it believed here that you signed ill things, but that Sir C. M. and Sir G. F. (being firm in their loyalty) would not join. Sir C. M. speaks confidently of his interest in Westmoreland and gives out he will not spare money in the business of elections there. On Wednesday last Sir C. M. sent in great diligence to Carlisle, and a common council being called a letter of his was read wherein he recommended himself or his son ('tis said his younger son) to serve them in parliament, proposing the privy purse for another, but the privy purse being rejected with contempt he immediately joined Captain Bubbe who stands also for a member. Before I got to town they had given a great treat to the most considerable men of the corporation and 'tis said have carried on their business a great way so that by what I can yet learn it will be a matter of much difficulty and expense to prevail for a new man. However I have sent out some of the most considerable men here to observe and take measures of the strength of our adversary, and also to try how the common people stand affected to my Lord C., and till I have an account from them how things are like to go I have suspended the making any public or direct proposal, although I have declared that I intend to do so if the thing appears feasible. You shall hear from me in a week's time, otherwise you may conclude that matter at an end. Sir G. F. wrote in behalf of the privy purse, undertaking for him (as he had for himself) that he would be for the support of the Protestant religion and property, but all was to no purpose. Mr. Fielding tells the people here that my Lord C. makes no pretensions to recommend any to them, but that what is said by me is by your direction only in opposition to Sir C. M. and Sir F. G.

[P.S.]—There was a sham story spread abroad last week that the garrison under the pretence of making an alarm designed some ill thing upon the townsmen here, in so much that the people sat up in their houses one whole night, and Captain Bubb having done something in favour of the town hath gained some interest by it, though the wiser sort ridicule the whole matter."

Jos. Reed to Sir John Lowther at Lowther.

[1688, Dec.] 15th instant.—" On Sunday morning last I went for Durham having business to do that required my being there and at Newcastle. I got home last night and was presently sent for to the Governor, who asked me where I had been, I told him, he asked me if I had not seen your Honour, I told him not, however it's believed otherwise. Honoured Sir, having this safe bearer, have writ this till I see your Honour to beg that you will have a care of your person, for I believe the seizing of those arms hath exasperated some here, that it's good to guard against. But I hope you need no premonishing, for the news from York I know you have. Here came some more papists in here last night from Berwick but I know not their names."

Jos. Reed to Sir John Lowther at Lowther.

[1688, December 16] 7 o'clock Sunday morning.—" Not hearing of anything till just now that one comes and tells me the town is surrendered to Sir Christopher [Musgrave], who came in it seems last night by consent, for he had the word and so went into the castle and, as I am told, the Governor told him he might yield and would give it to him sooner than any, so delivered up all the keys and everything. I cannot but admire the proceedings of the last night and to hear Sir Christopher and all those officers in the garrison before to be so gracious and kind now. I know not how they will use me, but I expect no good treatment from them however will see something further ; they will certainly write by to morrow's post to give an account of the great feats done in taking the garrison. I cannot tell how to add further, though a great deal might, but I am, &c.

[P.S.]—It seems the mayor and all men was forthwith sent for by Sir Christopher and much joy expressed on both sides.

The gate is but now opening and the Mayor and his brethren the aldermen are waiting at Mr. Basyll Feilding's where two sentries are, for Sir Christopher laid there last night, and now they are for going to church. I am further certainly told just now that they are at Captain Bubb's lodgings, first I mean Sir Christopher to signify to the Prince by an express that Captain Bubb betrayed the town into Sir Christopher's hands, and with much ado they took it, and so to know the Prince's further pleasure what to do, when now it's certainly known that Sir Christopher was sent for yesterday morning ; but they must say something to clear the Governor and to make Sir Christopher great. This was told me after I had writ the other side."

J. Aglionby to Sir John Lowther.

1688, December 16.—" This morning I received yours and immediately went to Carlisle, but when I came there I understood the garrison was delivered up to Şir C. Musgrave the night before at one o'clock. 'Tis certain the Governor hath not dealt well with you and that he and Sir C. M. had concerted their matters before and made haste lest you should take the place by force. The late governor with all the popish officers retired this morning to Corby, but 'tis said they return to morrow morning the governor's family being still in the castle. On Saturday in the evening Captain Bubb went to Rose where Sir C. M. met him ; they came to Carlisle together and were received at the gate by the Lieutenant Colonel, who gave Sir C. M. the word and advancing thence to the castle was met at the gate there by the late governor, who immediately delivered up the keys of the garrison, and after a small treat Sir C. M. retired to his lodging. ·Basil Fielding hath treated you here with the worst language imaginable, and amongst others he used this expression of you, viz., ' God damn him for a whig, he pretends to do great things, but never did any good yet.' This was after you had seized the arms. Sir G. F[letcher] came to town this morning and this day is to be a day of rejoicing, preparations being making for that purpose. On Tuesday I intend to be at Lowther and shall acquaint you with what further occurs."

Jos. Reed to Sir John Lowther at Lowther.

[1688] December 17, Carlisle.—" Now at 10 o'clock some of the papists are 'going out of this town, and no body so great as they and our new governor Sir Christopher and Sir George, who talks very big. I send my man purposely to signify that they are now going to Corby, and as their men tell me will be at Appleby this night; for Sir Christopher has given them a pass, and as they say hath directed them to his mayor's, Mr. Atkinson, who he says will let them pass and assist them. If you think to stop it may do well, for all this town is so dissatisfied with Sir Christopher and Sir George that they should let them go, so that the are almost mad; and not only that but those of the officers as Booth and others that could not pay their debts they put them out yesterday that nobody could arrest them. I am sure if your Honour cause your men to stop it will oblige all here except the governor and our mayor and 2 or 3 more. Our late governor has dealt very dirtily with those that had been kind to him here. They posted away for Squire Dacre's, and he just now came to town.

[P.S.]—There will be 5 or 6 of those men, they have I believe 200*l.* with them and very good horses, they have a guide with them and will certainly be at Appleby this night at Atkinson's, but believe it may be late if they stay anything at Corby."

Tho. Addison to [Sir John Lowther].

1688-9, January 1, Whitehaven.—" I am heartily troubled and ashamed that a parcel of inconsiderate hot-headed men should give your Honour (the only aid, support, and defence of our country) so unreasonable a charge and disturbance in sending men and arms to join them in a project not in your power to carry on. All the world sees your worth in complying with all things that may tend to the public good. This might easily have been accomplished if the town had been consulted therein and the true plot laid Mr. Sandforth and Mr. Simpson who have sufficiently acted their parts will give your Honour a full relation of the failure, to which I beg leave to refer you, with this faithful assurance that if I had been a party to the letter sent to your Honour or advised the thing, or if I had received your Honour's commands for carrying it on, I would have hazarded my life and fortune to have perfected the project.

When your Honour has an answer to what was written when I had the satisfaction to wait on you at Lowther, I beg the favour of a line.

Most heartily wishing that my good Lady may present your Honour with a son and heir for your new-year's gift, and that you may all live in all imaginable happiness for many and many years is the hearty prayer of," &c.

The Earl of Shrewsbury to Sir William Rawlinson.

1688-9, March 4.—" The Commission for the great Seale being to be layd before his Majesty tomorrow morning, att his returne from Hampton Court, to be sealed in his presence, I desire you would attend then with the Great Seal at the Council Chamber about nine of the Clock."

The Earl of Nottingham to the Lords Commissioners of the Great Seal.

1689, April 20th.—The King being informed that a great number of the Irish Clergy being driven over hither, many of them are in a starving condition, and being desirous to give them all the relief he can for their support and maintenance ; his Majesty commands me to acquaint your Lordships that he would have you forbear bestowing some of the lesser preferments in the Church, which are in your gift, for some convenient time, that a present provision may be made by sequestration for such of those clergymen, who shall be judged worthy by those whom his Majesty shall employ to that purpose.

The Earl of Shrewsbury to the Lord Chief Justice [Holt].

[1689 ?] May 4.—The King being informed that the prisons here in town are so full that great inconveniences are like to ensue if a Gaol Delivery be not speedily held, his Majesty thinks it reasonable that it should be done, which I am commanded to signify to your Lordship. And if there be anything to be done here in order to it, you will please to let me know it.

The Earl of Shrewsbury to the Lords Commissioners of the Great Seal.

[1689 ?] June 13th.—The King commands me to enquire of your Lordships whether you have yet had any returns of the names of those put into the commissions of the peace who have taken the oaths, as also whether you have had an account that any of them have either refused taking the oaths, or having taken them decline to act, which it imports his Majesty to be informed in, and therefore if your Lordships are not already prepared to satisfy the King in these particulars, he would have you do it with all the dispatch that may be, and (if it be possible) before the Judges begin the Circuit; and an immediate account is expected into whose hands the severall commissions of the peace for each county were delivered. I send your Lordships inclosed a list of persons presented to his Majesty by my Lord Lucas to be on the commission of the peace for the liberty and precincts of the Tower.

William III. to Sir John Lowther Baronet First Commissioner of the Treasury.

1690, June 11th. Gayton near Hoylake.—" We are just going to embarque but considering how necessary it will be to have the rest of the money dispatcht unto us, we recommend this matter to your particular care. In like manner we expect that Provision be made to enable the Lord Ranalaugh to pay all those Bills which will be drawn upon him from Holland."

Signed.

William III. to the Same.

1690, June 18th. Belfast.—" We lately directed you to hasten to us the remaining 70,000*l.* with all convenient speed; as also to enable the Earle of Ranelagh to answer all such Bills as should be drawn upon him from Holland, which again we remind you of. And whereas we directed you to advance onely a third part of the money desired for the supply of the Vaudois, we now understand from the Earle of Nottingham that the whole sume is very impatiently expected from us; and therefore our Order is, that you go on furnishing the same in such methods, as our present service, and other occasions will permitt.

By his Majesties Command,
(*Signed*) Robert Southwell.."

SIR ROBERT SOUTHWELL to SIR JOHN LOWTHER.

1690, July 4th. From his Majesty's Camp near Goulding Bridge.—" It was on the 27th past that I layd before his Majesty yours of the 22nd, wherein his Majesty tooke notice of your extreame concerne for his Supply here, which was alsoe the argument of your former. He has since ordered me to acquaint you that he hopes the money promised to be lent in London would be made effectuall, in which case he expects that what hath been diverted by publick necessity from the supply of Ireland should thereout be made up. As alsoe timely provition thought on for the future support of this great Body which may yett possibly be putt on some seiges and difficult attempts.

We have just now advice that the Jersey Frigott is arrived in Dublin with 30,000*l.* and his Majesty is in care how to have it soone here where tis wanted enough, and indeed the Country feeles in consequence the smart thereof.

I know you partake of all I write to my Lord Nottingham. See that I will not trouble you with a repitition of our particulars here."

SIR ROBERT SOUTHWELL to SIR JOHN LOWTHER.

1690, July 17. The Camp at Wells.—" On receipt of yours of the 7th which I had on the 14th, I lost no time to lay it before his Majesty. He read it with satisfaction, and yesterday sent orders to the *Jersey* frigate to hasten to Chester for the fifty thousand pounds which you hoped might be there on the 19th instant, and Mr. Cunningsby wrote by your conveyance. I will not presume to touch on our affairs here since his Majesty now writes when you are to partake."

SIR JOHN TREVOR to SIR WILLIAM RAWLINSON, LORD COMMISSIONER.

1690, August 18th.—" I did this day acquaint my Lord Nottingham with the Circuite Pardon and some of the reasons why wee could not passe it: his Lordship said that the Queene and himself were surprized in it, and did much wonder that such a pardon should bee tendered, and his Lordship desired that you would come to him some time with the pardon, that his Lordship (with you) might peruse it. Pray my Lord spare some time to góe to him as soone as you cann, that he may see what carefull and reforming Judges wee have, that would with most religious eyes have hanged you and myselfe for passing such a Pardon when time was, which time I hope will ncaver be againe. These men, that make such a noise about Blood, and yett are without any difficulty pardoning persons attaincted of Murder and by that name too " (*sic*).

MEMORANDA ON TRADE AND PLANTATIONS.

1690, September 11th.

" Affrican Companie.

They cannot return in time :—the Plantations ill supplied with Negroes the last year :—they therefore desire Convoy :—the Castles and Planta.

tions will be in danger:—betwixt 30 and 40 Ships to be employed, and about 40 Men a peece :—they would send before the end of October 16 sail :—12 are the ffewest they ought to send in October.

the Levant Marchants.

They desire the Convoy may goe the middle of October, that it may be att Messina the middle of Jan[uary] to meet the Turkey ships thence to goe to Leghorn, thence call att the several Ports of Spain :—there are about 16 may return of the Turkey ships from Messina by that time :— there are 6 Men of War of ours and 2 Dutch there to convoy them.

20 Days the usuall voyage betwixt Smyrna and Leghorn.

East India Companie.

Would send six ships would take up 600 men, 3 to be sent in Sept[ember] the other 3 in March. they have 2 in Milford haven, and expect 2 more dayly.

Spanish Marchants.

That there ships will be readie the last of October and may return the middle of March, there are no concealed seamen.

Presse warrants to be concealed.

a third Land men   } List of Ships to goe.
a positive time to return } Commissions to be given earlie.

That as to this trade there may be a Publication by the Commissioners of the Customs, that the ships that are to goe may enter their Names Number of men and Burthens may be there registred by a certain Day.

6 Ships to goe to Leghorn with 40 men each that cannot return, and about 5 to Venice and Zant.

Canarie Marchants.

If they goe out the 20th of Octo[ber] may be back the the latter end of Feb[ruary].

the Number 30 or 40. Men 600.

Bilboa.

If they goe the 31 of Octo[ber] they will return in Jan[uary] 8 Ships. 150 Men. One Man of War, to attend them.

Eastland.

50 Ships 400 Men in Ap[ril] next :—one 4th and one 5th Rate.
the Marchants would take the Marine men.
a ffith Land men.
the Convoy to return by a certain day.
a List of the Ships to be entered at the Customhous.
Bond to be given by the Marchants for their return.
Commissions to be earlie given out.

Endorsed :—" Trade and Plantations."

THE EARL OF NOTTINGHAM to SIR JOHN LOWTHER.

1690, November 11th, Whitehall.—" I send you enclosed an extract of the Treaty with the Swisses, as far as relates to the payments that are to be made, and I desire you will lay it before his Majesty for his directions, that the Messenger may be dispatched by the next post, and I should be glad if you could let me have the Bills on Thursday next.

The Swisse Troops are to be 4000 men comprehending Officers.

The pay is 7 crownes per month for each man, counting 58 sols of french money to the crowne.

The Plat de Colonel 1160 } livres tournois } per
The Estat Major   800 } and 8 sols   } month

One month's pay to be advanced for the levys.

The first month's pay to be made at the first Muster on the frontiers of Swisserland.

The Pay to the severall Companys commences from the day they respectively march in entire Companys.

6000 livres tournois per month to the Protestant Cantons, but no time specifyed in the Treaty for the commencement of this payment, and therefore most reasonably to be computed from the day of the Ratification, viz :—November 6, 1690."

(LORD COMMISSIONER) SIR GEORGE HUTCHINS to SIR WILLIAM RAWLINSON.

1690–91, March 7th.—"I have spoken with Mr. Dodson in reference to the warrants touchinge the 2 priests and truly am satisfied that as the matter now stands he ought to keepe the warrants and the rather for that the Chiefe Justice of the Common Pleas is out of towne and will not be here till next Satturday, wherein I think Mr. Dodson is just to his trust, I have therefore proposed this expedient, that Mr. Dodson make copyes of the warrants attested by himselfe with an acknowledgment that he had the originalls which he will not deliver out of his custody without other order, which I question not his performance of, and that hee'll be equally just to us as well as to the Judges, which I submit to your Lordship's consideration."

THE EARL OF NOTTINGHAM to the LORD COMMISSIONER RAWLINSON.

Wednesday.—The King would have one of the Lords Commissioners of the Great Seal to attend him at my Lord Shrewsbury's office at 4 of the clock this afternoon ; and your Lordship being in the best state of health I trouble *you with this notice of his Majesty's pleasure.*

THE EARL OF NOTTINGHAM to the LORD COMMISSIONER RAWLINSON.

1691, May 5.—Before the King went from Kensington his Majesty appointed Mr. Serjeant Powell to be Judge of the Common Pleas in Judge Ventris's place. But I am told that his Majesty at Harwich nominated Sir William Pulteney, for which reason I delay the warrant for Mr. Powell : and I desire your Lordship to send me word whether you have heard of any fresh warrant for Sir William Pulteney and what you know of the matter and to take no notice of what I now write.

SIR JOHN LOWTHER to SIR WILLIAM RAWLINSON.

1693, April 5.—"I am sorrie I can now give you so certain and so ill an account off the affair, ffor being tired off the delays and uncertainties I daylie mett with upon the account, I presumed this day to speak to the Queen herself concerning it, she told me that notwithstanding shee had assured My Ld Cheif Baron that tho he might now have the money yet he must expect it no more att anie other time, yett he still desires to continue ffor two terms, which to me is the same thing as if he had said always. As to the other tis certain he doth desire to keep it, tho it were but ffor a year, yett the King being resolute that he should not, he now saith that he hath it ffor life, but will submit it to the King's pleasure if he pleas to command it, which no doubt he will, but in the meantime it stays till the King's answer come. Thus Sir you see the unavoidable delay, and that it is not the King nor Queen's fault but others, who will always be to blame."

The Duke of Leeds to Sir John Lowther.

1694, August 9th, London.—"I am but lately returned hither from the North, and have mett with no pleasing news since I came, but what Sir Henry Goodrich told mee this day, of your family being strengthned by another son to support itt. I assure you I partake doubly with you in the satisfaction, both as itt is an addition to your comfort, and that I think the Nation cannot have enough of your breed, and I doubt not but my Godson is secure from any diminution of your kindnesse by the increase of younger brothers.

The Fleet under my Lord Berkeley is going before Dunkirk, and that in the streights was att Barcelona when the last letters came from itt. I am not able to informe you whither itt will winter in those parts or not, that being left to Mr. Russell's discretion, but the Admiralty and Navy board have said they can provide all things necessary for it's stay there if itt shall bee judged convenient.

The Armys in Flanders remaine in their Station att Mont St. André, and there is not any likelyhood of an engagement, which gives us hopes of seeing the King back sooner then formerly.

In my late Progresse I visited 18 severall considerable houses, and am sorry that the distance would nott permitt mee to make yours the 19th, both because I heare itt is as well worth seeing as any of them, and more because I should have had the satisfaction of paying you my respects."

The Earl of Nottingham to Sir John Lowther.

1694–5, January 1st, London.—"I was very unhappy that my businesse here obliged me to come from Exton, when you designed me the honour of your company there: and should be very glad that the health of your Lady would allow you to return hither before I leave the town, for I long to talk with you to whom I can most freely impart my thoughts, and my sorrow too for the losse [of] the Queen who on earth had not her equall: But I will not dwell on so melancholy a subject, with which I am so affected that I could not help mentioning it, though I intended onely to beg the favour of you to send the enclosed to Mr. Swingler, to whom I did not know how to direct it: t'is in answer to one I lately received from him, which I have sent to you open that, if you will trouble yourselfe to read it and seal it, you may see his scruples, to which I think the articles were not lyable, and you will oblige me, if he has yet any doubts, to remove them, which none can so effectually do as yourselfe, because the measures you took with him in your building shall be my rule to decide the differences if there should be any, which I can't foresee, between us."

Lord Godolphin to Sir John Lowther, Bart.

1695, May 13th.—"One may well bee throughly ashamed for having been soe long without thanking you for the favour of your letter and at the present you sent mee, I took them both extream kindly from you, and it was a great pleasure to mee to receive any mark of your remembrance. I have endeavoured lately to deserve them by remembring the comands you left with mee in relation to Mr. Serjeant Rawlinson whom I earnestly recomended to the place of chiefe Baron, and made bold to putt the King in mind of your concerning yourselfe for him, which I am very sure has a great deale of weight with his Majesty, but Mr. Sollicitour, hee said, must bee Attorney Generall, and no argument was able to resist that; however I have given the King a hint of another thing just now upon his going away, which hee seemed to relish well enough, and which I am willing to hope may please Sir W. Rawlinson. At his returne, I shall watch it as well as I can, upon your account."

LORD GODOLPHIN to SIR JOHN LOWTHER AT LOWTHER.

1695, June 20th.—" When the King gave the reversion after Queen Dowager of some lands in your Country to my lady Fitzharding I remember it was his desire and intention that, in case she found her selfe obliged to part with it, you might have the refusal, I know the King will still bee of the same mind, and my Lady Fitzharding having acquainted mee she is offered 3200ll. for her Grant, I could not but give you this notice of it, and shall bee very glad to receive your commands, if you have any on this occasion."

LORD GODOLPHIN to [JOHN] VISCOUNT LONSDALE.

[*Top torn off.*]
" Your Lordship will perhaps wonder that I should trouble you with a letter from this place but the subject of it is not altogether improper. I have been told that your Lordship has bred for some time of a stallion that wee here in the South have in very slender esteem, and I have at this time a horse called Honeycom punch that I hope would bee very proper for your use. He is a perfect good horse, and of a competent speed, gott by a barb, and extreamly well shaped and very well limbed; if hee bee acceptable to your Lordship it would bee a great pleasure to mee that you should make use of him, and I will bring him to London this winter that you may send him from thence at the proper season of the year."

LORD GODOLPHIN to THE SAME.

[16—] May 5th.   *   *   *   *   *
" Your Lordship being soe good natured as to bee concerned for the Duke of Shrewsbury's health, I can now tell you that he is in hopes again that the quiett of his body and mind in the country may at last enable him to gett the better of his distemper; there's no discourse at present of filling his place, or the Lord Chamberlain's.
I am glad to hear for your own sake that you are grown soe great a philosopher, though in the country that's not of soe much use to you, as I think it would bee if you were here.
The King has been 10 days at Windsor and returns this night to Kensington."

TENISON, ARCHBISHOP OF CANTERBURY to THE SAME.

1696, July 14, Whitehall.—" Ever since your Lordship's leaving this town I have been inquiring after such a scholemaster as might be fitt for the carrying on your great and good design ; but I have not yet bin able to find one perfectly to my mind. The fittest I have mett with is one Mr. Coe of St. Giles's, who is a Northern man and known (as he saies) to the Archbishop of York. But he has a schole here and some boarders, and a wife and children ; and perhaps he may have great expectations upon removing. Your Lordship may, therefore, be pleased to acquaint me with your Lordship's terms, and how farr you may approve of a man in such circumstances. If I am capable of serving you here in this or any other matter, there needs only an intimation to (My Lord) Yours faithfully,

Tho : Cantuar.

Mr. Lock has brought up your Lordship's papers about coin with some notes upon them which I have by me. No other persons have seen them."

John Lowther to The Same.

1697, June 9th, Dublin.

" I suppose your Lordship has heard already that our new Lord-Justices are landed, and the Chancellor with them. There is none here who pretend to any acquaintance or knowledge of him, but he has behaved him selfe soe well these four days he sat in Court, that there is great hopes of him. On fryday at night Sir Rich[ard] Lovings landed, who was at first feed in my cozen's case, and was wellcomd to barr on Munday with twenty guineas as retaining fees, soe that I hope to send a good account of his tearm's proceedings." . . .

Lord Massereene to The Same.

1697, August 2nd, Dublin. . . . .

" I shall allways acknowledge, your Lordship's favour, in sending me such good horses, whose reputation shall not be lessened by my care, to make them as famouse as any ever was in this Kingdome, especially the .young Chestnut, which is the most improved horse, that I ever saw, for the time ; he is now matched for two hundered Guinys, each horse, halfe forfit, against Jolly Backus ; they are to run in Aprill, 1699, and I only feare they will pay me the forfit." . . .

The Duke of Leeds to The Same.

1697, December 18th, London.—" I am sorry your Lordship's friends are forced to give you this trouble att a time when wee all hoped to have inioyed your company, and when I doubt not but you have been told from Court that your presence would bee usefull. For my owne part I was so greived to hear of your intentions not to come to towne this winter, that I was not willing to beleeve Sir William Low-ther when hee pretended to mee to have your Lordship's directions to desire mee to make your excuse to the King. But I did not do itt notwithstanding his desire, having no commands from yourselfe about itt. If I have done amiss I have told you my reasons, and hope you will pardon mee, but I will rather yett hope to see your Lordship in towne before the end of this Session. I can send your Lordship no publick newes but what you have from more knowing hands so that I will only make inquiry after my Godson's health, and conclude with much respect."

The Earl of Portland to The Same.

1697, Dec. ²⁄₁₃. Kensington.—" Je vous asseure que jay une joye tres
sensible de me voir tousjours si fort dans vostre souvenir, et que me
vous continuez tousjours lhonneur de vostre amitié, que jestime infiniment, et sur la quelle je fais fonds, je vous remercie de vos felicitations
sur le peu de part que jay a eu contribuer a la Paix, le bon Dieu nous
la coserve longtemps en sa grace. la presence dun aussi honeste homme
et si capable que vous est si necessaire ici durant cette Session dans
laquelle il ue sagira de rien moins que destablir cette Paix et nostre
repos et celui de la nation, avec la Religion protestante par toutte
lEurope, que si jamais vous avez fait un effort sur vous mesme pour
cela, vous le devez asteur pour pouvoir estre en tranquilité a ladvenir,
ainssi vous pouvez juger que moy, ni personne qui vous cognoist, et
qui est bon Anglois, ne peut travailler pour vous faire demeurer chez
vous dans un temps si critique, je puis vous asseurer que quant vous
auriez des ennemis que je ne cognois pas qui voulussent vous mettre mal
avec le Roy ils i travailleroit inutilement, car il a pour vous les sentiments que vous pourriez desirer, et quant je lui ay montre vostre lettre,
il ma ordonné, de vous escrire quil conte absolument sur vous pour les
raisons que je viens de vous dire, et de vous presser autant quil est
possible pour vous faire venir au plustost, croyant que vous lui estes
aussi utile pour son service que qui que ce soit le puisse estre, apres quoy
je suis scur quil nen faut pas davantage pour que jaye bientost lhonneur
de vous voir ici, et de vous réiterer les asseurances dune veritable
amitié, et de la veritable estime et veneration dont je scray toutte
ma vie," &c.

The Duke of Leeds to The Same.

1697-8, January 1st, London.—" I have received the honour of your
Lordship's of the 23rd December, and am very much pleased
to find there is hopes of seeing your Lordship in some short
time. I have been confined to my chamber 8 or 9 daies by a severe
cholick, and have not yett dared to go out of my house, so that I have
had no late opportunity of waiting on the King, but I heare hee is not
easy under the vote of reducing the army to so small a number ; but
that vote is so uncertaine in the meaning of itt, that there may be roome
both to preserve that vote and to comply with that number which was
said in the house of Commons that the King would bee contented with,
vizt., 15,000 men ; but whither the Country Gentlemen will bee brought
to consent to that number I am not able to foretell, and I rather doubt
itt under the management of the present Leaders, who are not very
acceptable unlesse the withdrawing of my Lord Sunderland sweeten
some of their tempers who suspected that Minister to bee apt to give
such advice as would need the argument of a standing force to support
itt. The weather hath been so fine here as makes mee hope itt has
incouraged your Lordship to begin your iourney before this can gett to
you, and I shall attend you here with great satisfaction."

The Earl of Portland to The Same.

[1697-8 ?] Jan. ¹⁷. Kensington.—" Je vous asseure que ce mest
une sensible joye de recevoir des nouvelles dun ami, que j'estime et que
j'honore si fort, quoy que je sois faché de loccasion qui vous la fait escrire,

dans lestat ou estoit nos affaires je croy que nous aurions peu a appre-
hender les menaces at les vains desseyns des gens mal intentionez. Mais
considerant lestat ou la nation va estre reduitte par le Bill qui se forme
dans la maison basse, laquelle nous prive de toutte defense, et nous
expose a tous les malheurs, nous avons raison de craindre puis que
nous n'aurons pas les moyens de nous opposer au mal que lon voudra
nous faire, et que cette occasion en fera naistre lenvie, mesme a ceux
qui n'osoit pas i songer auparavant, je regrette vostre esloignement, vos
sentiments sont si bons, vous avez tant a perdre, et vostre zele pour la
conservation de la Liberté et la Religion de cette nation est si cogneue,
que vostre presence ici j auroit fait grand bien, cette consideration vous
fera peutestre encore haster de venir, comme je le souhaitte, cependant
le Roy m'a ordonné de vous prier, danimer lhoneste homme qui vous a
donné cest advis, de continuer a veiller sur les desseyns que nos ennemis
pourroit avoir, et de vous en donner cognoissance, je me flatte de ce
qu'une occasion aussi pressente me pourra donner loccasion de vous voir
et que vostre santé vous permettra de venir ici je vous suplie de croire
que je suis tousjours du fonds de mon coeur," &c.

The EARL OF PORTLAND to THE SAME.

[1697–8], Feb. $\frac{9}{19}$. Kensington —" Il n'importe gueres gueres de
quels sentiments je suis a vostre esgart, ne pouvant vous estre bon a
rien, cependant vous me ferez justice en estant persuade de ma veritable estime, et de ma sincere amitié, Mais vous pouvez conter sur
ce qui est plus estimable, cest les bons sentiments que le Roy retient
tousjours pour vous, il me semble que cette consideration, et celle du
zele que vous avez tousjours temoigné pour le bien de S. Mté., et du
publicq, suffit pour vous donner du chagrin de vous reprocher un peu a
vous mesme de n'avoir pas este ici, Mr. le Prince de Conty ma envoye
deux Barbes, si vous le voulez bien accepter pour vostre haras, je vous
en destine un et je vous prie de donner la commission a quelqu'un ici
de choisir pour vous et de vous lenvoyer, a moins que vous ne voeuillez
envoyer un palfrenier expres pour le chercher je vous prie de me faire
scavoir vostre reponee au plustoit, parce que plusieur mont de-
mandéz le second, je vous prie de me croire de tout mon coeur," &c.

LORD GODOLPHIN to THE SAME.

1698, April 17th, St. James's.—" I was really in pain till I received
the honour of your Lordship's letter, at my return from Newmarket
last night, because I expected the horse while I was there from what
you had said to mee, and knowing how exact you love to bee I was
heartily afraid of some worsé accident than it proves to bee. I am of
the same mind to have him thàt I was when wee talked of it at London
and will send one down about the middle of next month to fetch him
away, provided always that if you find an opportunity of disposing of
him to your liking in the mean time, you would not lose such an
opportunity on my account.

Wee have had the Duke of Shrewsbury at Newmarkett in my house,
but in soe uncertain and, I doubt, dangerous an estate of health, that to
mee there seems but little hopes of keeping him long, which, considering what other prospects wee have to supply the want of him, is a
subject too disagreeable to speak of, and as unfitt to bee spoken of to

you, who are apt enough to indulge **your own melancholly thoroghly
to the** prejudice of the publick, of your self, **and of your friends."**

The Earl of Portland to The Same.

[1698], $\frac{\text{pril } 28}{\text{May } 9}$, Windsor.—"Je minteresse si fort en vostre santé
que je ne saurcis me dispenser de vous prier de men donner des **nou-
velles,** j'espere encore quelle ne vous, empechera **pas de venir encore**
bientost ici, et cela pour plusieurs raisons, la princip'ale est que **je suis**
persuade que cest air contribueroit a vostre restablissement et **me**
donnerois les occasions de vous confirmer combien je suis," &c.

The Earl of Portland to The Same.

[1698 ?], May 1, Windsor park.—"Je vous prie de me donner des
nouvelles de vostre santé, vous savez combien je mi interesse, j'espere
quelle vous permettra bien tost daccomplir vostre promesse, cependant
je vous prie de me permettre que je lasse mettre vostre nom dans les
escrits que vous savez pour mon trustee ne me refusez pas cette faveur
car je nay point dami au monde auquel je me confie comme a vous,
Mandez moy un peu comment vont les changements car j'en suis tout a
fait ignorant, croyez moy tousjours sans reserve," &c.

M. Ld. Pr. Seal.

Lord Godolphin to The Same.

1698, May 17th.—" Since I had the favour of your Lordship's last
letter I have had another from the Duke of Shrewsbury with the confirmation of his health's being in a very hopeful posture, but at the
same time, hee imputes it wholly to the quiett and idlenesse which he
now enjoys.

There's a great project depending before the House of Commons at
present which I find people are willing to flatter themselves may shorten
the Sessions, but I must own myself not sanguine enough to expect
the publick will have any great advantage by it. I shall not faile to
attend very carefully the bill your Lordship was pleased to mention ;
some of the northern Lords in our house seem to think it against their
particular interest, but surely the making a river navigable in any county
has a face of being for the good of the publick. There has been endeavours to delay it, but it is to bee heard at the bar of our house either
tomorrow or next day."

Lord Godolphin to The Same.

1689, June 23rd.—" I should sooner have acknowledged the favour of
your Lordship's last letter if I had had any thing worth that trouble,
it's expected the Sessions should end presently and yett the 2 millions
are not passed in the house of Commons, though ther's a great majority
of their small number for the bill; nor is the dispute arisen between **the**
2 houses upon the forme of carrying over the impeachments at **an end,**
but I incline to think one day more will agree that matter."

LORD GODOLPHIN to THE SAME.

1698, July 19th . . . . " The king went away this morning as soon as 'twas light ; the Lords Justices are the same as last year, except my Lord Marlborough and Mr. Montague in the room of my Lord Shrewsbury and Lord Sunderland, no Chamberlain nor Secretary of State made. His Majesty as I am told has left abundance of orders at the Treasury and elsewhere sealed up with particular directions not to bee opened, till hee was embarqued ; there have past since I had the honour to see you many incomparable things of severall kinds, the particulars of them are not very proper for a letter, but I shall not forgett them, I hope, before I have the happynesse to see you again. I hear of severall new titles given but no Dukes made, to the no small disappointment of a noble Lord of our acquaintance which perhaps may afford some diversion next winter, to you, I hope, as well as to my Lord."

VISCOUNT WEYMOUTH to THE SAME.

1698, July the last, Drayton. . . . . " I have already told my sister how prosperously wee performed our whole journey, and now wee begin to provide for another to L[ong] Leat, which I would bee glad might bee the last of this yeare, for the prospect of frequent removes is not very pleasant to a crasy old man.

My son and daughter have bin with me some time, but are going to see his estate in Shropshire, to return hither, before wee leave this place. They are neither of them soe fat as when I last sawe them, but when the losse of my dear boy will bee repeired God onely knowes."

LORD LUCAS to THE SAME.

1698, November 1st, Tower :— . . . . " Wee have set up a fourteen stone Plate at Newmarket, the first horse One hundred pounds valew in Plate besides the fashion, the Second Horse fifty pounds, the subscriptions are almost full." . . . .

LORD CONINGSBY to THE SAME.

1698–9, January 21st, ... " I can't tell you how much you are wanted heer att this time of difficulty, and yett I love you to well to wish you from the quiett you injoy in the middle of soe much uneasiness as I am sure you would find heer. I can see noe hopes of any advantage towards you from my great relation . . for whilst his extravaguancyes increas att the rate they doe I supose his own debts enterteyn him sufficiently."

LORD GODOLPHIN to THE SAME.

[1698–9, January.]—" I have the honour of your Lordship's letter, and am always sorry that you should ever receive a mortification, but I hope this may not prove soe great a one to your Lordship as it will bee to your friends not to have the pleasure of seeing you here ; severall of the Lords to whom letters have been written by order of the house, as to your Lordship, have written answers to my Lord Chancellor that they have been hindred by the gout, or other indisposition [top of page worn off] faile to doe it, as soon as they had recovered their health. These excuses have been received, and your Lordship's I make no doubt will goe too, but it must cost you the trouble of a letter to my Lord Chancellour and that letter must be red in the house, from which a rise will bee taken to excuse you; but I was in hopes that an Appeal lodged against you in the house yesterday, upon which a month's time was given to putt in y . . . . [*torn off*] pen to have come amongst us again, though if you find it inconvenient in other respects, I beleive you need not doubt the justice of the house, nor the attendance of your friends upon that occasion.

The bill for disbanding the Army is at last committed in the house of Lords and I beleive will passe, not but that the force maintained by it is generally thought too small, but that soe great a division and distraction as the losse of that bill would have proved of worse consequence, and harder to bee retrived again."

M[ary] Lowther to The Same.

1698-9, February the 16th, [London].— . . . .

Our Parliament is nothing but a nest of strife and contention. God knows how they will end, for they have don no good yet nor none seems likely. . . . .

The Earl of Portland to The Same.

[1698-9?], March $\frac{9}{18}$, Kensington.—" Jay recen vostre tres agreable lettre du 13me passé, jay choisi pour vous, de mes deux barbes ce qui est assez aise, car il me semble quil i a grande difference de lun a lautre, celuy que j'ay donné lannee passée au Roy est mort, je vous remercie de ce cheval que vous voulez menvoyer, mais devant touttes choses nous devons nous mettre en peine de faire en sorte que nous puissions nous en servir en paix, ce que nous ne pourrons certainement pas faire si les affaires continuent sur le piet quelles vont asteur et pour cest effect il faut que les honestes gens mettent la main a l'oeuvre, jespere que vostre sante vous permettra de venir ici au plustost, car jay ordre du Roy de vous escrire de le vouloir faire sans perdre du temps, pour estre employé a vostre contentement et satisfaction, je ne vous en diray pas davantage par cette lettre esperant d'avoir bientost lhonneur de vous voir, je vous prie seulement de me faire reponce au plustost, et de croire que je seray toutte ma vie avec sincerité," &c.

Lord Somers to The Same.

1698-9, March 11th.—" Tho I had very great reason to make my farther acknowledgments of your Lordship's repeated favours in respect to the clamours very unjustly endeavourd to be raisd upon the account of the Fee farm Rents, yet I was scrupulous of giving you the trouble of a letter meerly upon that account. But I am very glad to lay hold on this occasion to do it, which Mr. Wybergh has given mee by petitioning the House of Peers yesterday against your Lordship, because your answer to his appeal did not come in within the time given by their Lordships. The House have given ten days farther time to your Lordship, but I think myself obliged to intimate to you, that it seemed not to be very well taken that the first time was not complyed with, and therefore I hope your Lordship will give orders to your Agents to take care the answer be in before the ten days bee past. I had hopes we should have seen your Lordship in town before this time that I might have had means of expressing this personaly to you.

I am assured that such effectual care is taken for payment of the Pensions for the future that there never shall be any just occasion of complaint. I perceive by Mr. Heyhurst's case, which he shewd mee, (and came to mee, as he said, by your Lordship's command), that some letters between him and the Auditor gave occasion to the obstruction which was given. One or both of them, and they only, were in fault."

The Duke of Leeds to The Same.

1699, May 19.—" This is in the first place to wish you as much joy as your own heart can desire of the high station [Lord Privy Seal] of which your Lordship is now in possession, and I must pray your Lordship that you will please to give the inclosed memorial to his Majesty and receive his answer to it.

I do likewise pray to know his pleasure about Hull, and the lientenancy of Yorkshire, and in case he intends my removal from those, I pray that I may also receive my arrears as governor, which are due for a great while, and, unless his Majesty's displeasure reach to every branch of my family, I pray my brother Osborne may be continued in his place of lieutenant governor, who hath been a thorough voter always for the court in parliament, and to whom heretofore the King promised a compensation for his remove from the place of a riding surveyor in the Custom-house. This is too much to charge so good a friend with all but I hope hereafter to be as little troublesome to your Lordship."

William, Marquis of Halifax, to The Same.

1699, May 31, Rufford.—"I am to return your Lordship thanks for the honour of your letter of the 27. I was in hopes it would have told mee, I should have seen you here which would please mee so much, that your Lordship must permit mee still to expect you,—and indeed I could not persuade myself to desire it, if I thought it were any inconvenience or hindrance to you in your journey. My coach shall not onely waite upon you to Sir William Ramsden's, but shall meet you at Grantham or Newark if you please to command it. In the meantime pray, my Lord, do not allow such a melancholy consideration to take place that your freinds what are at a distance should bee unreasonably weighty as to overload business. I do rather suspect those who are at present the nearest to you will bee the more dangerous, and give less quarter."

The Earl of Bath to Lord ———.

1699, July 1, St. James's.— . . . . " I send enclosed a copy of the last warrant I received from the late Queen of blessed memory, to whom the King during her said Majesties life left intirely the ordering and governing St. Jameses Parck, as I conceave is not unknown to your lordship, and since her Majesties death hath declared that the same orders shall be still observed untill his Majesties pleasure be signifyed to the contrary ; and on this occasion it may not be improper to informe your lordship with a particular passage relating to one of your predecessors in your office of Justice in Eyre, the late Lord Lovelace, who, sending his warrant for killing a buck in St. Jamses Parck, which being refused, came the next day in person there and killed the said buck, whereat the Queen was much offended and gave that Lord a seveere reprimand, but afterwards upon his submission and further application to her said Majesty she was pleased to order by her personall command that the said Lord Lovelace, or the Justice in Eyre for the time being, should enjoy the same priviledge in the said Parck, as in the former reignes of her Royall unckle and grandfather, when Phillip Earle of Pembroke and George Duke of Albemarle were Rangers of St. Jameses Parck, commanding me to signify the same to the said Lord Lovelace, as I did in the words following, *videlicet* That it was her Majesty's pleasure the Justice in Eyre for the time being should have every yeare a buck and doe of each season for his owne use, not by his warrant but by his verbali intimation to the Keeper, which course and noe other hath been observed by the Earle of Abbington as well as the Lord Lovelace, your two best predecessors in the said office, with mutuall satisfaction on all sides without any dispute."

MR. SECRETARY VERNON to LORD LONSDALE.

1700, May 23, Whitehall.—" You will see by the inclosed letter from his Majesty that I have received your Lordship's of the 20th instant, and have layd it before the King, who has commanded mee to acquaint you, that hee gives you leave to go into your owne country for the recovery of your health, and as to the Seale hee would have you take the same method for the dispatch of the business that you used when you went into the country the last year, or if you have thought of any other way that is more convenient his Majesty will readily comply with it, so as it dos not import a resignation, since his Majesty hopes for your recovery and is very unwilling to remove the Seale into any other hand."

WILLIAM III. to THE SAME, LORD PRIVY SEAL.

1700, May 23rd, Hampton Court. — " J'ay este extrement marri d'aprendre par la lettre que vous aves escrit au Secretaire Vernon que vous avez trouve si peu de soulagement en vostre sante au bains, que vous estes oblige de songer d'aller ches vous en esperance d'y trouver plus de soulagement, ce que je vous souhaite de tout mon cœur, et suis tres content que vous y allies, quoy que j'aurois extrement souhaite de vous avoir aupres de moy en cette conjuncture ou j'ay plus besoin que jamais des personnes en qui je me fie autant qu'a vous, et pour que j'ay autant d'estime. J'espere que le bon Dieu vous rendra bientost vostre sante et que vous reviendres le plustost qu'il vous sera possible ; cependant vous poures faire avec les prevy ceaus, comme vous aves fait l'anne passe quandt vous esties ahsens, ou de telle autre maniere que vous trouveres convenable, mais j'espere que vous ne songes pas a quitter mon service, fut tout a present que j'eu ay plus besoin que jamais, et que je n'y poures point consenti, ayent autant d'estime et d'amitie que j'ay pour vous, dont je seres tresnise de vous donner des marques en toute sorte d'occasions." WILLIAM R.

Holograph.

SIR G. ROOKE to THE SAME.

1700, May 25, *Shrewsbury* off the Maes.— . . . . " I have beene att the Hague by the King's direction to conserte matters relating to the execution of my Orders, and I think everie thinge adjusted, but the poynts of Salutes of the Flagge and Command, in case we joyne the Swedish fleete ; which I find must be left a little too much to me, though I am sure whatever I suffer the honoure of the Flagge of England shall never be exposed under my direction.

On this, and another occation that I had of conversing with the Pentioner, I cannot but thinke him in my poore opinion an able minister and a verie honest man. I have beene att sea, but putte backe againe by contrarie winds and bade weather, in which I mett with some of those ill accidents I always apprehended from our stay on this Coast, tho' happily nothing more than we can repaire heare, and I hope I shall be readie to prosecute my Orders upon the first favourable opertunitie of a winde, tho' I have noe more then nine Dutch shipps of the line yett joyned me, in which number are the Admirall and Reare-Admirall, and what I am further to expect is the Vice-Admirall with three ships besids himselfe, which makes theire squadron thirteene of the line ; soe that if our appearance disposes the Northern Crownes to an accommodation, I must conclude they are not veric intent upon quarreling. If your Lordship's curiositie inclines you to know what was concluded at the Hague, Mr. Secretarie Vernon will informe you, to whome tho' I wrott in hast, I thinke I gave a full account of everie particular."

. . . .

Mr. Secretary Vernon to The Same.

1700, May 28, Whitehall.—I have the honour of your Lordship's letter of the 25th and have presented the inclosed to the King who is very well satisfied that your Lordship will take the Seals with you to your owne house and I have orders to speak to Sir Robert Cotton and Sir Thomas Frankland, that your pacquets should bee conveyed backward and forward free of charge. I shall see them to morrow and advise with them how they would have the King's pleasure signified in this behalf. . . . . I am sorry Mr. Wandesford's business has failed at least as to the height of his expectations. My Lord Keeper I find is grown uneasy at this gentleman's being recommended to him, having as I hear a brother of his owne to put into the employment of Purse Bearer, which hee says is so great a trust that hee can't think of putting it into the hands of any one that is a stranger to him. Besides speaking of it to me with some concern when I waited on him upon Saturday last, his Lordship writ about it the next day to my Lord Jersey, who I suppose has let him know that though the King would have been glad this gentleman had been more agreable to him, yet hee did not intend to impose any one upon him whom hee might have exceptions against." . . .

The Earl of Portland to The Same.

1700 [June 16].—Whitehall. "Vous ne pouvez pas me croire vostre ami et serviteur autant que je le suis et me laisser si longtemps sans me donner des nouvelles de vostre santé, pour laquelle je m'interesse plus qu'homme du monde, Mr. Flemming ma dit avoir ouy dire que vous vous portiez un peu mieux, je le souhaitte de tout mon coeur, vous supliant que durant mon absence du pais, vous ne me laissiez pas dans lincertitude, mais que quant vous ne mescririez pas vous mesme vous fassiez savoir a Mr. Flemming comment vous vous portez, il ma promis de mescrire en Hollande, pour ou jespere de partir demain, et je vous suplie de me faire la justice destre bien persuadé quil nest pas possible destre avec plus de passion ni de sincerité que je seray tousjours," &c.

WILLIAM III. to THE SAME, LORD PRIVY SEAL.

1700, July 2nd, Hampton Court.—"Je fais estat de partir apres demain pour la Hollande, je gene tres marri que votre saute ne vous a pas permis d'estre aupres de moy pendant mon cejour icy, j'aprens avec bien de la joie qu'elle commence a se remettre, jespere qu'elle vous permessera bien tost de revenir pour assister nu gouvernement en mon absence, ou du moins qu'a mon retour j'aures la satisfaction de vous trouver en parfaite sante, ce que je souhaite avec beaucoup d'ardent et que je puisse avoir bien des occasions a vous donner des preuves de mon amitie."

WILLIAM R.

Holograph.

THE DUKE OF LEEDS to THE SAME.

1700, July 6th, Thorp-Salvin.—"I am informed that you are gott safe to Lowther, and that you find your selfe much better in your health then you were at the Bathe. I heartily wish itt bee so, but I cannot bee satisfied till I have itt from your selfe. I trouble your Lordship therefore with this to pray that I may know how itt is with you, and if you bee well enough to write newes, I should be glad to heare what you thinko of the state and temper of your neighbours the Scotts, and whither you thinko wee are in any danger of trouble from them. I am sorry my distance from your Lordship is too far for mee to make a visitt, but I have found my journey from London hither very uneasy, and have not had any good health since my coming hither. My blessing I pray to my Godson. [P.S.] If your Lordship gives your selfe the trouble of writeing hither you may please to direct your letter for me att Thorp-Salvin by Doncaster bagg, and I do not know whither this have a right direction to your Lordship."

LORD SOMERS to the REVD. ———.

1702, April 4, Saturday.—"I had the favour of your letter last night. I think the most usefull answer I can make to it is to lay before you the matter of fact relating to the Bill for settling Sir Thomas Cook's charity. The Bill was reported from the Committee on Thursday last and was then ordered to be ingrossed, and to be read the third time on Fryday next. The Earl of Winchelsea desired it might be read in a full house and that the House might be summoned for that purpose, because he knew there would be opposition made to it, and that was readily consented to.

I have communicated your letter to several Lords who were of the Committee, and they all said that the Committee being now at an end they could propose nothing thereupon, but that you would instruct such Lords as you think most proper to trust with the reasons of your dislike of the Bill, that so they may be prepared to speak' against it at the third reading; which is all that is now left to be don in the House of Lords. As to what relates to my self I will not fail to acquaint the House with the letter you were pleased to send mee. I shall only add that no man does more truly wish the prosperity of the University or would be more glad to contribute to it in any manner than myself."

——— to ———.

1703-4, February 10th, London.—"I was ordered to goe to Portsmouth in so much haste that I had not time to give you any account 'of it having only had notice the afternoon before I went. [*Here follows a passage in shorthand or cipher.*] My chief business was to deliver arms and tents, &c., to the ten regiments that are going to Portugall. The King of Spain was all the while in the town of Portsmouth and I went every day to his dinner and supper where I used to meet the Duke of Sommersett and Duke Schombergh and all the English and Dutch Generall Officers. I became very well acquainted with both the Dukes, who present their service to you. I used to be talking French every day with the King of Spain's Gentlemen of the Bedchamber and other Officers, and the Emperours and the Portugall Ambassadour. The Prince of Lichtenstein is cheif Minister and Governour. The King is a very pretty gentleman, about 19 years old, pretty tall and slender, his face long, fresh coloured, dark brown eyebrows, very good eyes, of an easy and obliging behaviour, he talks high Dutch, Italian, Spanish and French very well, understands Mathematicks and Musick, he is certainly a young Gentleman of a great deal of spirit and a very hopefull Prince, he has about 300 Germans with him of all sorts." . . . .

Thomas, Lord Wharton to ——

1705, April 24.—" I have the favour of yours of the 19th of this month. It hath been all along a trouble to me to find that Sir Richard Sandford and yourself have not had that mutual confidence in one another that I should have thought you reasonably might have had. I wish to God I could have credit enough with both of you, to prevail with you both to stand and fall together; 'tis what I have often said to him here, when he hath complained of your not having mentioned him, as you sent round the country, and 'tis what I can, therefore, with the more freedom now say to you; and I will hope, that now you are both in the country together, you will both join heartily, and in good courage, in serving one another, to serve the public by opposing the common enemy: This is what I heartily wish, and would endeavour to bring about, had I the honour to be with you: But as I am all this distance, I can only tell you my honest thoughts, and be as good as my word to you both, in endeavouring to serve you both, to the best of my power; which I have directed, and will do to the best of my power."

[P.S.]—" The Queen ordered the writs last night in Council, to bear Testé the 2nd of May next."

H. M. to ——.

[1705, Nov.]   Saturday night, 10 o'clock.

" I have scarce time to tell you this day's debate, it began about one o'clock, Mr. Baylay spoke first, and extremely well, and concluded with a motion, that for the future there shall be but one Councell in Great Brittain : it was opposed by Montgomery and severall others, who all agreed that it was very reasonable hereafter, tho' not att this time, and desired att least further time to consider of it. There was att least a dozen spoke, before any of us South Brittons interposed, and I believe it would have ended in a further consideration, had not the Secretary, the Speaker, the Attorney Generall and the chearful Admirall spoke; but after that, the Question for leaving the chair could not prevail, and the main question being putt, it was carried by a vast majority, there being no division, there being scarce twenty Negatives : wee had a

Gallery full of Peers, where some of the Northern ones were handled by their countrymen very familiarly : the Torys were very silent, and left all the play to us : The last bell rings, so my Humble service to everybody, from my sober cozen, to Boozy Mrs. Coll."

THO. HOPKINS to [LORD WHARTON].

1705, November 29th, Whitehall.—" The house of Commons were this day in a Committee upon the Scotch affairs. The Question before them was, that there should be but one Privy Councill for Great Britain. The debate was carry'd on for near two hours, only by our new Northern Brethren ; and they seem'd to be pretty equally divided ; but the Southern Tories, and a great body of the Whigs joyning for the Question, it was carryed by an infinite majority without a division. It is impossible for me to give you any particulars of the debate, not haveing mett with any one member, that had either patience or parts to inform me, but only thus much I'me told ; Sir Simon Harcourt was against the Question and Sir James Montague for it. Walpole (who will always be either laughing or talking) was against it ; tall Sir Richard and Peter for it ; the Chancellor mumm, and fought cunning the arguments pro and con. I am sure your Lordship has often heard in other places, so that it's needless to trouble you with the few I have heard." . . . .

The EARL OF SUNDERLAND to LORD ———

[1706 ?] April 2, , London.—" Lord Orford has spoke to Mr. Doddington about his being Secretary to the Scotch Commission, who made severall objections to it, but Lord Orford would nott take a deniall, but desired him to consider of it ; I fancy he will accept of it at last. I have nothing more, worth troubling you with, but to wish you a great deal of success at Newmarkett, now and then a little walk on the Bowling green.

I hope you remember our Sunday appointment and that you will be in town time enough."

CH. ——— to [LORD WHARTON].

[1706], May 6. Campe att Matick.— . . .
" This day Monsieur Hope mett us on the march and told us the good news that Barcellona was certainly releived, which after our bad success in Italy comes very seasonably. We are to join the Duke of Marlborough after to morrow att the camp near Slonger, and it is not improbable but you may soon have good news from us, since I beleav it will be necessary for us to make our attempt before their troopes return from Germany ; I am mighty glad to hear your Lordshipe has settelled such harmony amongst the Comissioners for the Union, and I hope it is a good step towards the rest." . . . .

——— to the EARL OF WHARTON.

[1709], July 13, Dublin.—My letter of yesterday was sent in great hast to the office for fear the Packet should begone, but the Lord Lieutenant having stopt it till this morning I have time to add that the Lords voted a letter of thanks to the Queen for sending over (some say the word is for restoring) the D[uke] of Ormond to the

Government of this Kingdom. Against this vote the Lord Santry in particular entred his protest. That the Torys had a majority of 10 in the house of Commons, but they being most of em in town and a great many of the Whig members in the country 'tis hoped that the latter will soon be able to make a very good stand. That yesterday the Convocation voted a letter of thanks to those Bishops that stood by the Protestors in the case of Dean Lambert and the late Provost relating to the papers that the Provost left in your Lordship's hands, and that this day they voted another letter of thanks to the two Bishops of Killaloe and Ossory who were sent over Embassadors in the same cause.   *   *   *

J. Forster to the [Earl of Wharton].

1709, October 11, Dublin.—" In my last to your Excellency I gave you an account that Mr. Blyth had a second time returned Mr. Ash as Portreeve, since which time he has committed such outrages in the towne that the people looke on themselves to be in a state of warr as by the inclosed examinacons will appeare. I thought it my duty by this post tho' very late at night before the papers came back to my hand to send your Excellency the earliest account of this matter, because there are not people wanting heere to misrepresent these proceedings ; tomorrow the Council meet on this affaire. Considering how the majority of the Board incline I shal propose to have the matter relating to the force referred to the examination of judges of the Queen's Bench, who properly are the conservators of the Peace, and when they report the truth of the fact I don't see how Mr. Blyth's friends can avoyd comeing to a censure of him or makeing an order to restrain his exorbitant proceedings. At present nothing can be more agreeable to the towne than to find Mr. Blyth removed from the trust and power which he has used in violating instead of preserving the publique peace. This inactive part of the world affords noe news, tho' it abounds with fals and reflecting accounts not worth your Excellency's notice. Pray let my lady know I wil use my best endeavors to preserve her right in the burrough of Trim."

J. Dawson to Mr. [Joseph] Addison.

1709, October 18, Dublin Castle.—" The Councill having met yesterday according to appointment, the affaire of Trim came againe under consideration, and the Petition of Mr. Fox against Mr. Bligh, and the Petition of Mr. Bligh against Mr. Fox, complaining of force and breach of the peace on both sides having bin read, and a great number of examinations to justifie and prove their Petitions having bin produced, the Board considered how farr the matter of complaint was cognizable before them, and my Lord Chancellor proposed that the examinations should be sent to the Judges of the Queen's Bench, with directions to them to take care that the peace be preserved and an order was accordingly signed to that purpose. Mr. Bligh then stood up and moved that he might have the order of the Board to quiet him in the possession of the Magistracy untill it should be determined at law who had the right, that was opposed by my Lord Chancellor as a thing very improper for the Board, when they had signed an approbation for another man to be Portrieve. My Lord Abercorn then declared what the sense of the Board was, and the reason that induced him to signe that approbation was, that it was not intended that Mr. Fox should by that approbation be put into the possession of the office, but onely to put him into a capacity to try his title which otherwise he could not doe without it, and appealed to the Board whether that was not their generall sense, which they all declared to be soe except the Bishop of Kildare. Mr. Bligh urged againe that Mr. Fox was no magistrate, not being legally sworne before the Portrieve or his Deputy according to the directions of the Charter; that matter of fact being averred, and the Charter being produced to justifie it, my Lord Chiefe Justice Doyne gave his opinion that Mr. Bligh was not legally superceded and therefore was still in the possession of the Magistracy. This matter was long debated, and all the Board agreed with my Lord Chiefe Justice Doyne that Mr. Bligh was not legally superceded, except the Bishop of Kildare who dissented from the rest when it was put to the vote. The Lords Justices gave noe voice nor opinion in the case. It was then moved that this opinion of the Board should be entred in the Minutes of the Councill Bookes, but it was strongly opposed by my Lord Chancellor, and after some debate it was let fall. At last to put an end to the matter it was agreed that Mr. Fox and the rest of the Burgesses in his interest should be called in and told that it was the sence of the Board that Mr. Bligh was not legally superceded, and that they should have a care not to breake the Queen's peace on any account, and accordingly they were called in and my lord Chancellor told them that it was the sense of the greatest part of the Board that Mr. Bligh was not legally superceded, and therefore it was the direction of the Board that they should take care not to comitt force, but to keep Her Majesty's peace, and then they were dismissed. This is a true account of what passed as near as I can remember, and soe it is quite taken from the Councill Board, and I hear the Judges of the Queen's Bench have bin upon it to day, and are to be soe againe to morrow.

Mr. Prat has bin applyed to about the entertainment to the Lords Justices who used to be paid monthly, and he made answer that my Lord Lieutenant had given him no directions in that matter. I onely acquaint you with this because I believe his Excellency did not think of it.

Wee want three Pacquets from your side of the water, soe that wee have no letters to answer."

T. Southwell to the Earl of Wharton.

1709, December 17, Dub[lin].— . . . . "by the last Pauquetts are gone of for London his Grace of Dub[lin] and the Chancellor of the Exchequer with whom was to goe my Lord Havercorne, but the latter has thought better on't. The first is very full of the Palatine Settlement, and the other as I am told to complain of me for not signeing a warrant to pay him some fees I did not think his due. There being but three and I refusing the matter, itt coud not be done, so that the whole Party have fallen on me as if I had executed some commands of resentment for his late behaviour in Parliament, which I am sure I shoud have as much scorned to have obeyed for that reason, as you woud have despised to have given them, though justly enough provoked as I am told in particular by him. 'Tis to long to trouble your Lordship with the detail of the whole matter especially since Sir William St. Quintin is on the spot, and if itt be not to troublesome, can give you a full account of itt, and since I have done nothing but my duty and for the service of the Revenue I cannot doubt of your Excellency's protection in this or anything els."

The DUKE of RICHMOND to the SAME.

1710, 29th ——, Limerick.—" I had the satisfaction of receiving your letter a day after I came heither I am very glad you was received so well. I hope wheu I come into England (tho' a staunche Whig) I shall be received so tow. I am going back to Dublin aud shall stay theire as little as I can. I hope your Lordship aud the rest of my freinds are persuaded I will make all the hast I can. I have done all my business here effectualy for all the tenants have attorned to me, which if I had not come in person not one of them would."

LORD DARTMOUTH to the SAME.

1710, June 20, London.—" The Queen haveing been pleased to make me Secretary of State, in the room of my Lord Sunderland, and to assigne me the Southerne Provinces, I thought it my duty to acquaint your Excellince with it."

The EARL OF SUNDERLAND to [LORD LONSDALE].

1710, September 30, Althorp.—" This is nott to condole with you upon your being out, I think the Public and your friends are onely to be condol'd with upon that accouut, butt to putt your Lordship in mind of the hopes you gave me, that I should have the honour of seeing you here, which I will hope for, if you can spare so much time from elections; I think by all we hear we are like to have very good ones, and if so, a good Parliament, and our success in Spain, will effectually retrieve everything; I hope Apulby is secure, since you have had time for a new Mayor."

FRAN. HARRISON to LORD——-

1711, July 7, Dublin.— . . . . " I make bold to inclose you our Recorder's Speech to the D[uke] of O[rmonde] which has not only incenced him, but all his friends very much ; there uot being that flattery in it, that he has been accustomed to; I finde they are resolved to be very warm, and will endeavour to cast reflections, but I am of opinion they finde a very hearty number, that will make them a just returne, that we shall be persecuted is most certain; but as we shall have the greater satisfaction when affairs take another face, we shall bear all with resolution.

On Monday our house meetts, and as soon as his Grace has made his Speech I will make bold to send it you. Our Citty are still resolute in relation to their choice of a lord Mayor, what the event will be I cannot yett tell ; but in a very few days it will be over." . . . .

HENRY, VISCOUNT LONSDALE, to [JAMES LOWTHER].

1717, July 21st, Byrom.—" I was very much surprised at the receipt of your's the last night, to find that such a mark of honour is designed me, as you say the King intends. I believe you know me so' well as to be convinced that this cou'd not be of my seeking, and I hope that nothing has dropped from you to any of the Ministers, which might induce them to believe that this or any other proffer was either expected by me or might be acceptable. I am afraid that a Court employmeut will require more attendance, than I (who am att present very fond of the country) can have inclination to give, this single consideration wou'd I believe have hindered me from accepting this offer, were it not for the unhappy divisions that are amongst us. I fear that if I should refuse any mark of honour that is proffered me by the King, it wou'd seem as if I had greater expectations from another sett of people and had listed my self in their ranks, which as it is the farthest that's possible from my intentions, I shou'd be very sorry to have it appear so to the world. You know that I voted several times the last year against the Court, I am sure I need not to tell you, that the only reason for my doing so was because I thought it right, I hope I shall have no more occasion to oppose them, but whenever I have the same reason I shall always do the same thing." . . . .

ALAN CHAMBER of KENDAL, Agent, to JAMES LOWTHER.

1719, August 27th, [Kendal].—. . . . "I impute the general dissaffection:—1, to the too necessary continuance of land and malt taxes, which bear hard upon the circumstances of 10 in 12 partes as to number of the freeholders:—2, to the three partes in 4 of the pulpits from whence and their conversation out of the church too much discontenting matter is vented. But how these two fountains can be dried up is I fear above the reach of any human power. Two Assise Sermons, to wit at Newcastle and Appleby, were vented to such purposes in the last circuit, but were excellently refuted &c. by the Judges in the proems to their charges to the grand Jurys, to wit by Baron Mountague at Newcastle, and Baron Page at Appleby. I may add a 3d cause of the continuance of discontents, that is the visible unconcernednesse of private gentlemen (the hearty well wishers to the publick) and who by their daily conversation with their inferior freeholders &c. might easily demonstrate the necessity of taxes as a lesser evill then loseing our all, might as easily explode all sermons and discourses that are levelled against the publick administration. But it being the practice of the Tories when in power to prefer to the utmost all such usefull under agents in their interest, and of the whigs· to neglect such their under agents, it necessarily folows that the Tory interest is generally better cultivated, their chiefs not so wholly ingrossing all places &c. like the other chiefs, but allso takeing care of their subalterns so much despised by, tho' so absolutely necessary to, the other party the which three sources of our evills are submitted to your consideration." . . . .

[SIR ROBERT] WALPOLE to VISCOUNT LONSDALE.

1720, July 24th, Whitehall.—" I had the honour of your Lordship's commands relating to Mr. Pennington and do assure your Lordship, that if I had at all apprehended, that it would have been agreeable to Mr. Pennington to be sent into Scotland, I would most readily have recommended him to the King to be one of the new Commissioners, but I always understood that a sinecure of about 300l. or 400l. per annum was his only view, and that no employment of business or personal attendance was at all agreeable to his life or circumstances, and had your Lordship been so free as to mention this to me, when, as I remember, I talked to your Lordship upon this subject, with regard to Mr. Lanson, I promise you, my Lord, you would have had no occasion to complain. It would be too great a happiness for men in high stations to have the opportunities of obliging gentlemen as fre-

quent as their wants and occasions, but I' can with great truth assure
your Lordship, that your recommendation shall always be a command
to me and I am so far from wanting an inclination to serve Mr. Pennington, that I will certainly take the first opportunity of doing it."

ANTHONY LOWTHER to his brother VISCOUNT LONSDALE.

[1721-2] February 6th, [London]. . . . . "There was last Saturday such a Flame in the House of Lords that the like can not be remember'd; one wou'd have thought that they wou'd have unanimously
agreed to have sent the Chancellor and all the Ministers to the Tower;
it was occasion'd by the Chancellor not attending them till near four
a clock, before he came they named the Duke of Somerset for Speaker,
but the moment he heard of it he run out of the House, then they
named Lord Lechmere, and he hid him-self. When the Chancellor came
in (who had been detained all this time at a Cabinet Councell) some
body moved that they might adjourn ; upon which Lord Sunderland
got up and said that their adjourning at that time he thought might be
of ill consequence, that it wou'd be said without doors that it was done
out of rage and resentment, then he advised them to have temper, and
told them that if they wou'd but have patience for half an hour, that
he himself wou'd then move to adjourn, however the Question was
put and passed in the Negative by the usual majority, wanting five.
        The same day a pritty remarkable thing happened in the House of
Commons; a Judge was accused of having . attempted to corrupt a
Burrough. Sir John Cope accused Baron Page for having offer'd a
considerable sum of money to the town of Banbury, to elect a friend
of his the next election ; he is to be hear'd at the Burr by his Councell
next Tuesday."

VISCOUNT LONSDALE to [his Cousin] JAMES LOWTHER.

1723, September 26th, Lowther.—. . . . . "There is a story
has been very currently reported in this country, which if it be true,
you may very likely be better informed of att London, since in all
probability it must have come to the knowledge of the Government, but
as the matter was transacted a good distance from hence, and my
intelligence of it is not very certain, I can only lett you know how it is
told here. The Duke of Wharton went about ten days ago to his
estate in Swaledale near Richmond, and Sir C [hristopher] Musgrave
went along with him; when they were there the Duke took an occasion
of treating about threescore of the country people, and after they had
drank a good deal, the Duke and Sir C. Musgrave pulled of their coats
and waistcoats fell down upon their knees and drank the Pretender's
health by the name of James the 3rd of England and 8th of Scotland
and obliged all the people who were with them to do the same. The
noise of this was quickly spread, and the wives and daughters of the
people who were in company came immediately crying to fetch their
husbands away. Some of the men being frightened themselves went
to make information of this to a Justice of Peace, but the Justice in all
(probability not caring to meddle with so great a man, told the people
who came to him, that if they would bring the offenders before him, he
would do as the law directed, but he would grant no warrant.
Whether any part of this story be true or no, I can't pretend to say, but
as I am told it was brought into this country by several people of that
neighbourhood, and many of them were such as said they were present

themselves. If this be really as it is represented, I don't see how the Government can avoid takeing notice of it, for as it was done so openly and before such numbers of people it will be generally known, and every body who has ever lived in the country and are friends of the Government must certainly know the very bad consequences that will attend the not punishing so flagrant an action as this."

HENRY, VISCOUNT LONSDALE to JAMES LOWTHER.

1725. September 11th, Lowther.—. . . . "I am not at all displeased that the Mayoralty of Appleby has fallen to Mr. Tufton for this year, it would have been more difficult for me to have regulated the expenses of it, if it had lit upon me now, than it will be when it comes to my turn the next year."

THE DUKE OF NEWCASTLE to LORD LONSDALE.

1733. July 21st, Claremont.—"I make use of the leave your Lordship has given me, to acquaint you with what should pass during your absence in the country. Nothing has happened in our domestick affairs worth writing to you; and as to our foreign affairs, you left us engaged in a Negociation with the Imperial and the Spanish Ambassadors, to find out if possible a new expedient for accommodating the disputes about Don Carlos in Italy, and we have at last agreed upon what seems to be the most probable method of doing it, which they have both sent to their respective Courts, and there is great reason to hope it will be approved by them, at least if one can judge by the opinion of their Ministers here.

The affair of the Polish Election, which is what most deserves attention, has not as promising an aspect as one could wish. It looks as if the Oath of Exclusion of Foreigners would be generally confirmed by the Dietines, and the French have worked so successfully for Stanislaus, that without force be used by the Emperor or Muscovy, the Elector of Saxony seems to have but a small chance for it. We hear the Treaty between the Elector of Saxony, the Emperor and the Czarina is as good as concluded, whereby Saxony guarantys the Pragmatick Sanction; how far the Emperor may think himself engaged by that to use forcible means in favour of the Elector, or at least for the exclusion of Stanislaus, is yet uncertain; he has indeed ordered some troops to advance to Glogaw, nearer than they were before to the Frontiers of Poland; yet this may be only to intimidate the Poles; but if force be used at all, it looks as if the Czarina was to begin. We have indeed sent orders to Robinson to dissuade the Emperor from it, but what effect that will have is also uncertain. The French still continue to talk big, and declare that the moment the Emperor, or the Czarina, which they understand to be the same thing, enters Poland with troops, they will attack the Emperor; and in this I doubt they will be too much encouraged by the behaviour of the Dutch. Five of the seven provinces have agreed to a neutrality for Flanders, that is, in case the French will agree not to attack the Low Countries, they will not concern themselves on what they may do any where else. This resolution they have taken without previously communicating any thing to us; and may lay us under difficulties.

We have reason to think, that France intends to find some way to insinuate to us their desire, that we would come into such an agreement for a neutrality; but I believe it will not be thought advisable on any account. France would then have it in their power to over-run the Emperor and the Empire, on engaging only not to attack Flanders, and when they have succeeded elsewhere, they would undoubtedly do afterwards what they pleased in Flanders. The Actions in France, upon the rumour of a war, are fallen from 1800 to 1200. This is a circumstance that may make their Court think twice, before they venture upon it.

Our situation is in one respect very happy. We have no engagements but those that are publickly known, and consequently shall be at liberty to act just as the interests of this Nation shall make it advisable, and in that case whether it be Peace or War, I doubt not but we shall have the concurrence of the Nation. We have already, but that is a secret, and I beg may remain so, endeavoured to dissuade the Emperor from pushing things to extremities, and shall equally use our instances to prevent France from attacking the Emperor in case he should ; if we succeed in either, the thing is over, if in neither, we must then consider what part is right to take, for the interests of this Nation and the preservation of the general Balance of Power.

I have now given you a sketch, tho' not a very short one, of our present situation, and as anything material occurrs, I shall not fail to trouble you with it."

" My dear Lord, you allowed me to make use of another hand, which I only shall do for our Foreign Affairs. There is att present little stirring att Court. Sir Robert is expected this night, which will put things in motion. I conclude the G   of B   will soon hear of us. The King and Queen are in as good a way as possible, and as determined as we can wish. They talk of nothing but Elections, and show all that come to Court, how desirous they are of a Whigg parliament. Our accounts from the Country are in the main very good. Sir Robert has been prodigiously well received in Norfolk, which is a good thing on many accounts. In Gloucestershire, they have sett up two Whiggs, and I hope will carry it.

I go on Tuesday next to Sussex for a fortnight, when I beleive we shall find things pretty well. I shall not fail to give you an account of all that passes, but in return I shall expect sometimes to have the pleasure of a letter from you. Pray my kind compliments to Lowther. Albemarle and Arundel dine here to-day, and we will not fail to drink your healths."

THE DUKE OF NEWCASTLE.

1745, April 8th.—" Minute by the Duke of Newcastle of an interview of his brother (Mr. Pelham) with George II., and sent probably to the Chancellor."

[*Note at top in a different hand.*]

" To my B[rother ?]

The King has been worse than ever.

He had been promised the Parliament should rise in a fortnight.

Damn *it* and *you,* I shall be obliged to strike a strong stroke. My Brother replied very properly desiring him to do it, to which no answer.

The Duke's affair seems suspended.

That must be determined.

Lord Harrington is very impatient to give the King a final answer about the —

We all think we must meet this night.

At what hour ? "

WALTER LUTWIDGE and others to SIR JAMES LOWTHER.

1745, November 25th, Newcastle.—Gentlemen. We received your Express late last night and waited upon Marshall Wade according to your desire early this morning, who returned for answer, He was to march next day in pursuit of the Rebells, that he could not spare a sufficient body to drive them from Carlisle, and that he tho't the best effectuall method of doing it would be to beat the Rebels, and then of course they must evacuate Carlisle, which we dare say we all heartily wish may soon be the case.
Monday 12 a clock forenoon.

1745, December 1, Whitehaven.—Honourable Sir, Some of the Gentlemen of this country sent an Express to generals Howard and Mordaunt to pray some assistance from Marshall Wade to reduce the Rebells at Carlisle; and above we send you a coppy of the answer. The county is in the utmost distress from the Rebell garrison, and you would hear of an excursion of 18 or 20 of them to Lowther Hall, who were gallantly defeated by the Penrith gentlemen, but as we apprehend this garrison to be a resort for the disaffected Scots we are in hopes the Government will take care to rout them out immediately, and we apprehend that a few regular forces from Ireland assisted by our seamen and countrymen and a few of our large cannon from this place woud as yet easily destroy them, or a party of the troops from Edinbrough, but you will judge what is best, and are assured of our utmost endeavours for this Country. We make this application by desire of the Gentlemen of the County, as well as for our own safety. We are, Sir, your most humble Servants

<table>
<tr><td>WALTER LUTWIDGE.</td><td>PETER HOW.</td></tr>
<tr><td>J. PATRICKSON.</td><td>R. GILPIN.</td></tr>
<tr><td>WILLIAM [HICKS].</td><td></td></tr>
</table>

HENRY, VISCOUNT LONSDALE to —————

1745, December 11th, Byrom.— . . . . "The Rebels having proceeded as far as Derby are returning Northwards, I hear they came to Manchester last night, and as they are three days march before Marshal Wade (who left Ferrybridge this morning and lyes at Wakefield to night in the way to Hallifax) I don't think it possible he can overtake them. Tis likely they will stay at Carlisle. How long God knows, but while they are there unmolested the countys of Cumberland and Westmorland must be subject to contributions and pillaging." . . . .

MRS. KATHARINE LOWTHER to MR. JAMES WATSON [her steward].

1745, December 22nd [Warter].—"I have received your letters and was glad to find by the first that you all got safe home and have been under great anxiety to hear what would become of poor Westmorland. I think you acted very prudently in leaving Meaburn till the Rebells were gone by, but am glad to find both you and your wife happened to be got back before the King's Officers came there as I don't doubt but you would make them the best accomodatiou you could and to be sure it was very right not to take any thing for the hay, &c. I hope the next post will bring us better news, I fear the main body of the Rebells had escaped, as you don't seem to think the number at Clifton to be above 500, I beg you would continue to let me hear every post; as you know the letters from York are very imperfect."

Viscount Lonsdale to— ——

1747, July 14th, Lowther.—"I received yesterday the favour of your two letters of the 10th and 12th, the latter confirming what I believed before, that Sir Richard Hylton had no intention of standing for Cumberland. If there is not some mistake in respect of the Duke of Somerset's orders to his agents at Cockermouth, Mr. Simpson will certainly feel the effects of his resentment; for there is nobody more punctual in requiring a strict compliance with his directions from those that are employed under him, and as this character is so generally known, it is difficult to account for the different behaviours of Sir T. Booth and Mr. Simpson with regard to this Election, but as I hear there are complaints already sent to the Duke against Mr. Simpson this intricate matter will shortly be explained. I don't find that if the Duke's interest had gone in the manner you expected that it would even then have been an easy matter to have turned out B. (*sic*) Mordaunt. There are many Gentlemen of the country zealous for him, and the town's people of Cockermouth are afraid and unwilling to have the power of Election taken out of their hands. The buying a few Burgages for some years past, has given them the alarm, and though this attempt is now become impracticable from the excessive prices that have been lately offered for several Burgages of little or no value in themselves, yet the people's apprehensions will not suddenly be removed. I find this contest has made a good deal of noise, and bred ill blood, which must require some time to cool again, but as far as relates to Elections, I hope the mischief is over for the present and may by good management be retrieved."

Henry Fox to Sir James Lowther.

1755, February 12th.—"I have laid your request before His Royal Highness the Duke, who, with all his inclination to oblige you, cannot think of giving the L[ieutenan]t Govern[men]t of Carlisle to Sir William Fleming who sold out, and therefore has certainly no pretence to a favour of this kind."

Henry Fox to Mrs. Katherine Lowther.

1755, March 21st, War Office.—"I have the favour of your letter of yesterday's date, with the therein enclosed Representation, from three of His Majesty's Justices of the Peace for the County of Westmorland, that the road from Kendal to Penryth, through Shap, is made turnpike and that they will take care that the carriages be changed at Shap, by which means the troops may without any great inconveniency march from Kendal to Penryth without halting at Orton and Shap. I thereupon send an Order to meet Lieutenant Generall Skelton's regiment at Carlisle directing them to march through in a day from Penryth to Kendal, notwithstanding Orton and Shap is mentioned in the route waiting their arrival, at Carlisle. And I shall take care that no troops or companys do halt at Orton and Shap in their march between Kendal and Penryth as you are pleased to desire."

[The foregoing is in a clerk's hand.]

"I hope, Madam, You will excuse me that in this very busy time, I have wrote this by another hand, and believe me, with the greatest respect, Madam, &c."

Henry Fox to [Mrs. Katherine Lowther].

1755. August.—" The Marines are out of my Department, and entirely under the Lords of the Admiralty, who countersign all their commissions and with whom I dare believe your recommendation will have great weight. But Lieutenant Moore being Quarter Master as well as Lieutenant in Colonel York's, and so very near the top of the Lieutenants, I cannot but wonder he should desire a company of Marines, I think he is very ill advised. If he remains where he is, it may be in my power to be of service to him, and you may command whatever is so."

Henry Fox to Mrs. [Katherine] Lowther.

1755. September 29th.—" I flatter myself you will not think me impertinent nor be sorry when I acquaint you, that the King has declared his intention to make me Secretary of State and give me charge of his affairs in the House of Commons. I must not take the Seals till after the House meets because a debate is expected on the first day. You will immediately see the consequence of my having a numerous attendance of friends in this my first essay of Administration. I therefore beg, Madam, that you would be so good as to prevail on your friends to shew themselves mine, the night before the Parliament meets, at the Cockpitt to which place I shall have the Honour to invite them.

The good opinion of persons of your character and rank is the only support I am ambitious of in my new station, and indeed I will endeavour to deserve it.

[P.S.] Sir Thomas Robinson will go to his old place the Wardrobe, with 2,000l. a year pension for 31 years, or Ireland, and Lord Barrington will succeed me."

Henry Fox to Sir James Lowther.

[N.B.—From a copy in Sir James Lowther's own hand.]

1756, January 18th, Sunday one o'clock. —" Send me word how you do. I have heard last night, and this morning from good intelligence so much as makes it my duty to advise you to compromise this Election for one and one this Parliament, and stop there. It is my belief that we shall lose it if we go on. Upon my word of honour nobody knows or shall know, that I have given you this advice. And I will assist you with the utmost interest I can make, or service I can do you. I have no reserve about it. The Torys, the Scotch, are so much against you, so many will stay away, and give what they unjustly call your obstinacy as a reason for it, and my interest where it would otherwise be very strong is so broke in upon by Honeywood among the officers who are Members, that I fear you risk too much by persevering. I am so unwilling to give this advice that nothing but that the thinking it might be deceiving you or letting you deceive yourself if I did not should make me venture at it.

I beg nobody may know I give it, but Mrs. Lowther and Sir John Ramsden to whom I beg you to show this letter, and to whom, as well as to you I beg leave again to repeat, that I have spoke, and will speak earnestly in your favour both in publick and private, being indeed with as much zeal, tho from many cursed circumstances not with so much power as I coud wish to serve you.

[P.S.]—"You see the consequences of mentioning this advice from me. It would take away your merit with h[is] M[ajesty] in doing it, and if you do not, increase the clamour so industriously raised against you. Wherefore again I promise you nobody shall know from me that I ever gave it, though I would have Sir J. Ramsden, for whom I have the greatest respect, acquainted with it."

HENRY FOX to SIR JAMES LOWTHER.

1756, January 20th.—I am really very sorry you are ill, and you have chosen an ill time to be sick, but you must not let your business make you come and risk your health, of much more worth than even Appleby.

JOHN ROBINSON to [SIR JAMES LOWTHER].

1757, April 24th, Whitehaven.—" Sir George Dalston and I got here this day about 1 o'clock where we flattered ourselves with having some account of you or further directions from you—Nothing being come, we were obliged to go on in settling matters as well as we could upon consultation with Mr. Spedding, &c., for the Election, since it was necessary to give directions to provide to-night, and have fixed things upon the following plan, which is much after that followed in the last; 'except that in this, we have laid down more restrictions to prevent fraud and the great abuses committed by the mob on these occasions—There are 7 Houses fixed for the entertainment of your friends, vizt the Globe, Mr. Dixon's, *unlimited*, the House late John Lucock's, Ordinarys 130. —Wine 10 Dozen. Punch and ale proportionable—Two others at 50. ordinarys each— one of them allowed 4 dozen of Wine, and punch and ale, and the other punch and ale proportionable. Those provide for 350. at 1s. each besides the Globe which perhaps may be 500 and was the last 638, and we hope will do, though far within the No. at Sir William F[lemin]g's election charged to us, but as there will be more inspectors. fixed, some other rules laid down, and the innkeepers are told they will be paid for no more, hope it may be managed to answer. It is proposed also to have 13 other houses, for taking off the lower class as much as. may from the better houses, and small sums at not exceeding 4 guineas a house, many less, and in the whole 40 guineas, besides likewise some ale from other houses for the mob. These means it is hoped may lessen the expense at the great houses where it used to run high by the rabble getting in and stealing and carrying off all the liquor they could, and that we shall be at no greater expense than the last election, it so much. as we shall endeavour to take all prudent means to retrench.

We flatter ourselves we shall have some letters with your orders. tomorrow's post, if you will not be down, and shall endeavour to do the best we can in every respect, and I hope to give you joy by the next letter of your seat, as there is not the lest appearance of any rub in the way. Sir George gave a ball at Carlisle the night after the entertainment and purposes to do the same here; As also to have several of the Gentlemen to dine tomorrow Tuesday."

JOHN ROBINSON to [SIR JAMES LOWTHER].

1757, April 30th, Appleby.—"I hope you have many hours since received the return of yourself as Member for Cumberland and my letter therewith with some account of the election. I have little to add to what then and before I mentioned relating it, except that Sir George gave a ball on Monday night to the Ladies at Whitehaven, entertained the Gentlemen at dinner Monday and Tuesday at the Flatt, and after a publick breakfast at the Flatt as usual was accompanied to the election.

I am sorry to say our shew at the Flatt and from Whitehaven on this occasion was but very poor, and indeed I was never so much mortified with the appearance of the Lowther interest before, though really was then much so. There was not above 30 at breakfast and not 40 I think accompanied, instead of 3 or 4 times the number as usual. Indeed there was two ways of accounting for it. One that the Gentlemen of the Williamite Society which takes in all the young ones almost had the night before, as on the Duke of Cumberland's Birth day, had a meeting, sat up all night and were left at 5 o'clock that morning unbroke up, as such incapable of attending. The other, a notion that had obtained credit, that people were invited, and it was not general. This had arose entirely unknown to us, and contrary to our declarations."

WILLIAM PITT (the Elder) to SIR JAMES LOWTHER.

1760, January 15th, St. James's Square.—"Having in consequence of the honour of your letters just before you left London acquainted Lord Barrington that you was ready to agree that the subsistence should commence from the days on which such individual shall enlist, and having also desired his Lordship's opinion with regard to the other parts of your proposal, Lord Barrington sent me the enclosed letter [*missing*], to which I beg leave to refer you, as this contains all the points of objection to which the Secretary at War thinks the plan liable. I would submit it to you how far you may judge it proper to render the terms conformable to those of Colonel Hale's corps, as contained in the papers delivered to you.

In case you shall approve of the same for the body you may raise, there remains only to transmit a proposal, on that foot, to Lord Barrington through whose department alone it can pass. I beg leave to repeat here the real sense I have of the zeal and spirits for the King's service, which you have testified on all occasions, and to assure you that I always remain with perfect truth and consideration," &c.

HENRY FOX to SIR JAMES LOWTHER.

1760, January 16. Pay Office.—"Mr. Vaughan has, since you left town made an offer, which has been accepted, to raise five companies of 100 men each. One of which is given to my nephew Cornet Digby whom I had the honour to recommend to you.

It is my duty to inform you of this, and to thank you, as I most sincerely do, for your kind intentions in his favour, had your proposal taken effect. I am not the less obliged to you, and shall esteem it an honour on all occasions to acknowledge myself," &c.

SIR GEORGE SAVILE to SIR JAMES LOWTHER.

1760, February 5, London.—"If what I am going to trouble you with can be of no use to you or the person who is the subject of it, you will I dare say nevertheless excuse me for the intention's sake.

It is said you are about to raise a regiment and that the officers will be, as is indeed probable, of your own nominating. If this be true I will beg leave to mention to you a person who by the knowledge I have of him would, I really believe, be of real service to any young corps. He is a Lieutenant in the Duke of Richmond's, to which rank he was raised from Sergeant Major in an old corps at a time they wanted some experienced persons to fill the subaltern parts of some new regiments, and though these Sergeant Lieutenants, as they are called, have certainly no claim to an extraordinary share of preferment, yet their farther advancement to companies is not unprecedented I believe.

I was very desirous of obtaining his assistance in my militia regiment but could not obtain it; but his readiness to give me what assistance he could, together with the particular talent he seems, to my little judgment, to have for military matters made me unwilling to refuse him this testimony.

His name is Atkins and he is I think oldest Lieutenant in the Duke of Richmond's."

The DUKE of NEWCASTLE to SIR ROBERT WILMOT.

1762, November 13th Claremont, Saturday Morning.—" It is absolutely necessary, that I should have a safe conveyance to the Duke of Devonshire's sometime on Monday next. If none can be found, or you have none ready, I must send a person on purpose. Pray let me know what you have heard of him, if any thing, since I had the pleasure of seeing you at Newcastle. I must insist upon his coming soon to town. I see nothing will, or can be done without him. I am going to work with his Book, and wish I may find it, as it is there stated."

The EARL of BUTE to SIR JAMES LOWTHER, Bart.

1762, November 17th, London.—" I am extremely oblig'd to you for your kind and friendly letter; the Peace is at last sigu'd, and such a one as this nation never saw before ; but war seems to be declared at home with the utmost virulence; I am the mark for the party watch word, but the whole is a reality aim'd at the King himself, whose liberty is to be now decided on, liberty that his poorest subject enjoys, of choosing his own menial servants; the happy conclusion of the Peace has however drawn the teeth of faction, but they have made themselves desperate, and must persist in their presumptuous folly. . . . . My friends tell me, the House of Lords is to be the principal scene of action, where I am to be arraign'd, for the King's preferring the Duke of Marlborough a Tory, to the Duke of Devonshire à Whig, for making the Peace and being an Anti-German."

The Earl of Bute to Sir James Lowther.

1763, February 3rd.—London. . . . .

" Hitherto the Junto have ventur'd on no overt act, and content themselves with the little despicable arts of sowing lies, perverting well intention'd people; and tearing from me any little merit I can acquire; which to say the truth (as things are situated) is small enough; in short, in the midst of triumph any good act I am able to do, is so traduc'd, so many infamous falsehoods publish'd concerning things I never thought of, such inveteracy in the enemy, such lukewarmness (to give it no harsher a name) such impracticability, such insatiable dispositions appear in those *soi-disant* friends; that if I had but 50*l*. per annum, I would retire on bread and water, and think it luxury, compar'd with what I suffer.

The army rate, and the bill for increasing the Irish army, seem the only things likely to open the least opposition till the treaty comes over sign'd which we hope will be in a few days; when I hear, they are to make a last effort; much good may it do them; for the little plausibility they had will then vanish, by two great events, the offer made by us to Prussia to deliver up to that Scourge of Mankind Wezel, Gueldres, &c,; indeed the peace, I believe, already sign'd between him and Vienna, and 2ndly, the French abandoning all America and giving up their Louisiana to the Spaniards which is an undoubted fact; so much for politicks." . . . .

Thos. Worsley to Sir James Lowther.

1763, February 5th.—"I have had your horse at Mr. Hall's this week, have seen him ride him, and rode him myself every day, he went extreem pleasantly, and gently, and we both like him extreemly. I mounted him yesterday before the King and Queen, who thinks him a very fine horse, but not strong enough to carry his weight. I have only to add his Majesty expressed very graciously his sense of your kind intentions.'

Lord North to Sir James Lowther.

[1763]. February 21, Downing Street.—"Although Mr. Stanhope has called more than once at my house, I have not yet seen him, but he has been with Mr. Robinson, and fully stated his request to him. I understand that he proposes to be at my house on Thursday, and am unwilling to determine positively upon his application before I have had an opportunity of speaking with him. Nothing can in general be more inconvenient than the practice of permitting Officers of Revenue to resign their offices to their friends, and I have resolved never to consent to such resignations except upon very particular occasions. I wish Mr. Stanhope may be able to shew that his case ought to be an exception to the general rule.

When I had the honour of seeing you here, I fully explained to you my situation with respect to the office of Patent Customer at Whitehaven. I mentioned to you, if I remember right, that the Patent Offices in the Customs were about the only places which a first Lord of the Treasury could bestow upon his own relations, and his private friends, [and] that I had never disposed of any of them in any part in Great Britain at the recommendation of those, who, on account of their interest in the neighbourhood, might be thought well intitled to recommend to the other offices of the place."

The EARL of BUTE to SIR JAMES LOWTHER.

1763, May 13, Knaresborough.—"Thank you a thousand times, my dear Sir James, for the curious enclosures you have sent me, on my word I expect to hear of the Standard of Rebellion being rais'd before I reach town, and that sedition once more takes the field in this country; Parliament alone can now restore vigour to the laws, and secure our Constitution, and I shall wait with unusual impatience for its meeting, in the mean time I struggle hard for health; and shall certainly reap some advantage from my house and exercise, but little from the waters ; I heard by chance of your visit to Lord Halifax; and took a method that I hepe will prove effectual, tho' I can by late experience answer for nothing."

GEORGE GRENVILLE to SIR JAMES LOWTHER, Bart.

1763, May 27th, Downing Street.—" I have this moment received the favor of your letter, and as it will always be a real pleasure to me to do any thing agreable to you, I shall be desirous whenever the vacancy happens to comply with your recommendation in behalf of your friend R^t Stanhope if I possibly can, but as there are always a multitude of applications from the gentlemen of the county upon this subject, I have laid it down as a rule never to make an absolute promise till the vacancy happens and I am fully apprized of the state of it."

HORACE WALPOLE to the REV. HENRY ZOUCH, SANDAL, near WAKEFIELD.*

1764, February 21st, Arlington Street.—" You will have heard of the severe attendance which we have had for this last week in the House of Commons. It will, I trust, have excused me to you for not having answered sooner your very kind letter. My books, I fear, have no merit over Mr. Harte's Gustavus, but by being much shorter. I read his work, and was sorry so much curious matter should be so ill and so tediously put together. His anecdotes are much more interesting than mine ; luckily I was aware that mine were very trifling, and did not dwell upon them. To answer the demand, I am reprinting them with additions, but must wait a little for assistance and corrections to the two latter as I have had for the former.

You are exceedingly obliging, Sir, to offer me one of your Fergusons; I thank you for it as I ought, but in truth I have more pictures than room to place them ; both my houses are full and I have even been thinking of getting rid of some I have. That this is no declension of your civility, Sir, you will see, when I gladly accept either of your medals of King Charles; I shall be proud to keep it as a mark of your friendship; but then I will undoubtedly rob you of but one.

* There are many other letters at Lowther Castle from Walpole to H. Zouch, but, with the exception of the short one which follows on the next page, they are all printed in Cunningham's edition.

I condole with you, Sir, for the loss of your friend and relation, as I heartily take my share in whatever concerns you. The great and unmerited kindnesses I have received from you will ever make me
Your most obliged and obedient humble Servant."

George Grenville to Sir James Lowther, Bart.

1764, April 8th, Downing Street.—" Mr. Jenkinson informs me that you wrote to him about a proper arrangement of R^t How's affairs for the benefit of the public, and of his private creditors. The Commissioners of the Customs were immediately directed to make a report upon it which they have now done, and it shall be taken into consideration to morrow at the Board, and I hope this affair will be ended in some shape or other that may be agreable to you. I will give directions that for the future you shall have as little trouble as is possible with regard to offices upon incidents in the two Counties of Westmorland and Cumberland. I shall be extremely glad upon this and every occasion to show the real regard I have for you and my sense of the friendship and kindness you have allways expressed towards me."

Horace Walpole to the Rev. Henry Zouch.

1767, April 6th, Strawberry hill.—" Your letter has lain here a few days, while I was in London, or I should certainly have obeyed your commands sooner. I will leave word with my housekeeper, as I am not settled here yet, to admit Sir Thomas Wentworth and your friends whenever they shall call to see my house.
I am much obliged to you, Sir, for your kind inquiry after my health. I was extremely ill the two last summers, but have had no complaint since Christmas last. I should have been very glad if you had given me as good an account of your own health, which I most sincerely desire "

The Countess of Bute to Sir James Lowther, Bart.

[1768], Saturday.—" I am sensible you converse with many who will be extremely glad to see you plunge yourself much deeper in opposition, than (by what you said to me) is your present intention; they have views of their own advantage, and very little consider your character or figure in the world. It appears to me in the strongest manner, that you will injure yourself much more by this measure than it is possible for you to hurt any other person, and this I own is what gives me the greatest uneasiness; I am very positive in the opinion that Sir George Macartney's seat would in every light be far more eligible, and much more conformable to my Lord's intention when he ask'd the favour of your bringing Sir George into Parliament. Forgive me my dear Sir James for my earnestness in this matter, but I foresee the consequences too well not to endeavour to avert what will cause great vexation to my Lord, and what I am sure you will repent of when too late."

George Johnstone, M.P. for Appleby, to [Sir James Lowther].

[1775], January 20th.—" If you have not communicated your intentions to Major Gowland I still presume to bring an image to your mind that has disturbed me all night. Genius, generosity, fortitude, and affability, are painted on his mien, loving and beloved by all men of worth and real virtue. Known and esteemed by the first characters for the extent of his knowledge, 'with an elocution capable of enforcing his opinions. Talbot raised Thompson. Hertford, David Hume. Rockingham, Burke. But you have a prize in your power superior to all three and your glory and advantage would be in proportion. You have laid me under so many obligations that you cannot add to them. I have therefore only to beg forgiveness if my solicitation has no success and that you will believe if I am again importunate that it is as much from thinking the measure for your interest as for the sake of him I love. The most perfect of human characters without any exception as far as my knowledge of mankind goes, try him on any one quality or all united."

George Johnstone to Sir James Lowther, Bart.

1775, June 7th, London.—"I did not answer your letter expecting you would have been in London immediately, from your conversation the last time we parted. As I now suppose something has detained you, I acknowledge with great pleasure the account of your success. I was indeed very anxious because I considered the circumstance of this election as a loop-hole in your political situation which if not secured might have run things into great confusion. The late news from America makes me wish very much you was on the spot. Government have as yet received no accounts, and pretend there is not the least grounds for believing an open rupture and some assert the whole has been fabricated. I can venture to assure you the essentials are true and the spirits of the Public are much affected by it. Lord Chatham is generally looked up to, though most people agree he could not form an administration without the Rockinghams. He is very ill, but recovering. Much will depend on a good intercourse by intermediate friends and some communication with the Closet. I see nobody better qualified to effect both than yourself, but alas Lowther is 300 miles distant from St. James's; both must be attended to, the interest in the one gives tone to operations in the other, and human powers can hardly undertake both. Leaving Lowther to descend to this hot nasty town is like a flight from Heaven, so that without calculating all your necessary attentions for securing your interest, I should not be surprized if human frailty yielded to such temptation.

If any change takes place on this American storm, it must be quickly, for although the matter is very nice, and people in power will find a thousand expedients before they quit their hold, yet the affair is sufficiently serious to startle the most intrepid and there will be no correcting the evil by a change of system, if much more blood is spilt or at least if it should afterwards be attempted. The blood of the advisers must cement the breach between the two Countries."

The Rev. Thomas Zouch to William Lowther, of Swillington (afterwards Earl of Lonsdale).

1775, Dec. 28, Wycliffe.—Letter of advice on the occasion of his commencing residence at Trinity College, Cambridge, after leaving Westminster School, and undergoing a course of study with the writer.

The Duke of Rutland to Sir James Lowther.

1779, July 27th, Chevely.—"Lord Chatham's son, Mr. Pitt, a particular of friend of mine, having declared himself a candidate for the

University of Cambridge, I cannot forbear at his desire from requesting your interest in his behalf. The great situation of Sir James Lowther in this county must naturally give him an essential weight with every description and body of men; and I trust that Mr. Pitt's principles founded on those by which his father so long upheld this country will give force to this application. It is upon this ground and the many civilities I have so frequently received from you that I venture to trouble you with this letter.

[P.S.].—I had the satisfaction of seeing Lord Shelburne this morning. He has no fever or any symptom to cause alarm. A few *old Letters*, in his waistcoat pocket—impeded the force of the ball. I need not say, that his conduct in *the Business* was highly honourable.

Men in these times must stand prepared for strange events. How necessary *General Union* is become."

The MARQUIS OF ROCKINGHAM to the Rev. HENRY ZOUCH.

1780, March 23rd, Thursday evening. Grosvenor Square.—"I am much grieved to be unable to attempt to be present at York at the ensuing County meeting. I have been much hurried and fatigued with variety of business, and though I feel anxious beyond measure, that the decisions at York should be such as would redound to the honour of the County and the good of the nation, I can not undertake to throw my little *mite* in the scale by my personal attendance and by the opportunity it might give one of suggesting my thoughts on the spot.

I can not nevertheless refrain from communicating some of my opinions on the matters, which you and those who are there will have to consider and on which you will have to act.

I am under some uneasiness at not having received any answer from Mr. Milnes. I find by the letter which I had the pleasure to receive from you, that he had got my *long letter*. I trust there was nothing in it, which went so much against his ideas, as that he should rather decline answering it, and leave it to future conversation, than to send me his objections at once—against any part or sentiment which I had conveyed. I indeed hope that Mr. Milnes' not writing has proceeded from his expectation of seeing me soon in Yorkshire.

A variety of incidents have happened in regard to the conduct and in regard to what has passed among the Deputies in London—which at this time it would be both unnecessary and too long to enter into. I shall therefore hasten to the actual state of what has been concluded here among the Deputies, and which is to become the subject matter of consideration for the *County Committees* in the first place—and for *the County Meetings at large* in the second place.

I enclose to you the Printed Paper which contains what is to be laid before you, and I must particularly call your attention to the concluding part—viz.—*Mr. Wyvill's* circular letter which is ordered—by the Meeting of Deputies—to be annexed to the Resolutions.

I must observe to you—that the occasion of this circular Letter being annexed—arose from the *very great doubts* which *many* entertained in regard to *two* of the *four* Resolutions which the Deputies at a Meeting *last week* had agreed to. *Very many indeed* will by no means admit—as *an Article* to which they will bind themselves—*that the Members* of the House of Commons *be annually* elected to serve in Parliament. I verily think—that that Article will not be adopted by any *one of the Counties* whose Deputies were in London, *if the County of York* are not led into that decision. *Perhaps* if the County of York doth, some

Counties may follow, but I will venture to foretell that they will be few in number. I am convinced that nothing but confusion will arise, if this measure is enforced. Surely the impracticability of the measure of Annual Parliaments—must strike the bulk of the thinking part of the subjects of this country. The whole fabrick of the idea is entirely built on vague theories. You will have seen by my letter to Mr. Milnes—that I am, (and I really have been) inclined for some time past —to shorten the duration of Parliament. *Septennial* is too long a Term. *Triennial* was the term of duration fixed at the *Revolution*. I have examined the number of *Petitions* on contested elections presented—on several *New Parliaments*. I see both before and since Mr. Greenvile's Bill, the Number of Petitions on undue elections, have been so great, that they have not been decided in the *first Session*. On the General Election in 1768—prior to Mr. Greenvile's Bill—the number of Petitions were 38, whereof 5 *were left undecided*. Many of those which were decided, were not decided till just in the end of the first Session.

Mr. Greenvile's Bill, rendering the *Trials* more equitable, admits and requires more fair and *strict* examination into the justice of each election, and of course the Trials are more *formal* and take longer time in deciding. It appears on the General Election in 1774, there were 50 Petitions on undue elections at the different towns, counties, &c. *All the* Committees who could set could only decide 34 out of the 50 in the course of the first Session of that Parliament. So that 16 remained over for *another Year*. Most of these 50 were two members each—some few were only *Single Members* who contested. Upon the whole I imagine 80 Members sat during *great part of the Session,* when no body could say they were *certain* to be the *real* and *fairly chosen* representatives.

I hope Mr. Wyvill will not press the *Annual Parliament* as a specific Article on which men are to associate. If it is pressed at York I hope a majority will by no means adopt it. I think it may, and should be stopped in the *Committee* on Saturday next at York.

I shall now proceed to state shortly some doubts I have in regard to the other Article relative to there being sent not less than *One Hundred* new Members of Parliament to be chosen—*in a due proportion*—by the several Counties of Great Britain. I like exceedingly the principle on which this measure stands, but it is a proposition, as *yet crude* and *unascertained* in regard to the *Specific Proportions* for each County, &c.— and I must think it not ripe for an *Article* of Association.

I must observe—that though any alteration in regard to the Boroughs —which are called the Rotten Parts of the Constitution—doth not *now* appear to be *directly* in contemplation, yet it must be understood as a matter *hereafter* to be reformed. I think Yorkshire sends 32 Members, 16 of which may be deemed to come from what are called *Rotten Boroughs. There is a Circumstance*—which though *zealous men* for *Liberty* may be angry with me for mentioning, yet I think a *little attention* to the *Security of Property* is not beneath the consideration of the Gentlemen Freeholders in Yorkshire. I dare say you know very well that the Counties, &c. which are *low rated to the Land Tax* have found some security from their being very *numerously* protected by having a pretty large proportion of Members of Parliament chosen for the Counties or *Boroughs* within the Counties which are low rated to the Land Tax. As *no certain* proportion of the 100 new Members, *or*, indeed any *Line* is stated by which an idea can be formed how they are to be *allotted*, is as yet digested, it rather appears to me in a light as·

that we *may be dashing* away and *committing* to some danger the real property of many individuals, who are neither apprized, perhaps have not the *least Idea, of what* they are consenting to.

I am quite in haste to send off this-letter to you and also *one* which I have wrote to Mr. Crofts. I would wish them to be communicated to many friends who may attend at the Committee on Saturday and also to many more who may be at the General Meeting on Tuesday next.

I by no means presume to *dictate*, but I do earnestly wish that I may not be included as a *Tacit Assenter* to the propositions on which I have expressed *doubts.* My conduct in political life has ever been regulated by one fixed principle in regard *to Reforms*, I *never* have nor *never will* commit myself as a supporter of propositions which in my conscience according to the best of my judgement are *not evidently* likely to turn out *beneficial* to every object which can secure the freedom and happiness of this Country. I *dare* not assent to *doubtful Propositions.* I hope you and many of the gentlemen of your neighbourhood will attend at the Committee on Saturday. This letter to you as well as the letter which I send to Mr. Crofts—I wish may be communicated to those gentlemen who you and he may think proper. Indeed I care not *how generally* they *are shewn*, for though I hate altercations and don't doubt that able and artful men might even catch at. some of my expressions and might pervert the meaning, yet I would venture everything in following the impulse of my mind, and while I retain content in my own mind I shall little value the discontents of others. I trust indeed, that those who I love and honour—though they may differ with me—will do me the justice of thinking, that though we may differ in the modes we do not differ in the object."

The MARQUIS OF ROCKINGHAM to the Rev. HENRY ZOUCH.

1780, September 11th, Monday morning, Wentworth.—" Mr. Pemberton Milnes and you disappointed us very much in not coming to Tolston Lodge on Thursday night. I believe the fact was, that you both of you were suspicious, that I should have made rakes of you and kept you up to a late hour. We certainly should have talked a great deal, but that can be done in a short time.

The election business for the City of York afforded an opportunity for *some Gentlemen* to play *some Pranks.* But they *availed* not.

I shall say no more at present upon that subject.

The business of the County election is important, Mr. Henry Duncombe *offering himself* as a candidate, and *the grounds* he *puts* it upon in *his letter to* me, which I received on Thursday night, is well judged. He says he is induced to offer himself as a necessity appears in the situation of the affairs of this County that *two* members for the County should be chose who might *be depended upon* as *opposers* to the present *Ruinous Administration.*

I have long known his way of thinking on the *Measures* which have brought on all the calamities of this country. *Particularly*—the horrid, wicked, and abominable *American War.* His words *include a positive declaration* on that subject, though not in a manner which might make *some gentlemen* who heretofore were abettors of it take offence. Mr. Henry Duncombe *must stand on general ground*—that *all real friends* of their country may support him. Mr. Lascelles has been at Sheffield—and I understand is going about into different parts of the County. He has also published a Hand-Bill—to desire *his friends* to meet on *Saturday next* at York. A good, full meeting on

Thursday would have the best effects and might prevent much bustle and confusion. ⁽⁾

I am very much hurried, as I have several letters to write."

The MARQUIS of ROCKINGHAM to the Rev. HENRY ZOUCH.

1780, December 23rd, Saturday night, Grosvenor Square :—

" I *thank you* much for the Pamphlet you enclosed to me, and *am sorry* to send you in return, an authentic document, *which too fully proves* that *those* who rule the councils of this unhappy country are decided to continue on, in the same mad pursuits, even though every step they take, increases the difficulties, the distresses, and the calamities, under which this country labours.

I intend to write to you soon by a safe conveyance, I shall say therefore the less in this letter. I have had thoughts of coming in to Yorkshire for some weeks last past, but partly the weather, and partly some business, and partly from not being *well* in *health* and still less so in spirits—I have not been able to undertake the journey.

I intend to go on Monday next to Wimbledon and if I should find myself well after some days rest there, *I possibly* may make an excursion to Wentworth—so as to be there in the first week in January. I much wish to be able. I long to have some conversation with *some good Friends.*

Surely a war with Holland—must be attended with the *utmost ill Consequences* to the export trade of the *Woollen Manufactures* of the *W[est] R[iding] of Yorkshire.*"

The DUKE OF RUTLAND to SIR JAMES LOWTHER, Bart., Charles Street.

1780, November 27th, Arlington Street.—" The Duke of Rutland presents his compliments to Sir James Lowther, and if he will give him leave he will introduce Mr. Pitt to him to-morrow morning at any hour which may suit his convenience."

The DUKE OF RUTLAND to SIR JAMES LOWTHER, Bart.

[1780, November] 30th, Arlington Street.—" The Duke of Rutland presents his compliments to Sir James Lowther. He will be very happy to have the honor of seeing him in Arlington Street, and will take care that Mr. Pitt shall meet him."

The DUKE OF RUTLAND to [SIR JAMES LOWTHER, Bart.].

1781, March 2nd, Belvoir Castle.—" I must take the liberty of congratulating you on the success of Mr. Pitt's first appearance in the House of Commons. The satisfaction I have felt in his having fulfilled all the encomiums made of him is very great, and I trust, Sir, yours will not be less in the thoughts of having placed him in that situation where his abilities may operate with utility to his country. I cannot conclude this with (*sic*) assuring you that I shall ever remember the obligations I have received from you with the sincerest gratitude and affection. I hope this letter will find you recovered from the disorder with which you have been attacked."

SIR MICHAEL LE FLEMING, M.P. for Westmoreland, *to* SIR JAMES [LOWTHER, Bart.].

[1781.] Tuesday Morning.—"In case you should not be visible when I call—I have wrote this to tell you we had an exceeding animated debate, and that Mr. Pitt your member was beyond anything I could have had an idea of—indeed the whole House seemed astonished and the greatest part very much pleased—I wish you had been there, as I am sure you would have had great pleasure in attending to him—I hope to God you are free from pain and that you will get out."

WILLIAM PITT to [SIR JAMES LOWTHER, Bart.].

[1783] February 27th, Thursday evening, Downing Street.—" I cannot help being anxious to give you the earliest information, that I have, upon full reflection, thought myself under the necessity of declining the offer made me; and have consequently asked the King's permission to resign my present office. I hope soon for an opportunity to have the honour of explaining to you more at large my motives."

CHARLES JAMES FOX to SIR JAMES LOWTHER, Bart.

1783. August 22nd, St. James's Palace.—" Mr. Fox presents his compliments to Sir James Lowther and will be extremely happy to meet him upon any day or at any hour that he will be so obliging as to name. If Mr. Fox has not the pleasure of hearing from Sir James Lowther before Wednesday next, he will take the liberty of calling in Charles Street at twelve o'clock on that day, when he does not doubt but that he shall be able to give him satisfaction upon the several public points alluded to in his letter, and to convince him how desirous he is upon all occasions to obey Sir James's commands to the utmost of his power."

WILLIAM PITT to SIR JAMES LOWTHER, Bart.

[1783] November 16th, Sunday evening.—" I am very much concerned at your indisposition, and truly sorry to have occasioned your having the trouble of writing; still more so, to add to it now that of a second letter, but I rely on your goodness to pardon it. Mr. Mansfield by being appointed Solicitor General, vacates his seat for the University of Cambridge, and I have reason to believe that there are strong inclinations to oppose his re-election. I am in hopes Lord Euston will stand, but if he should not, it may perhaps be very difficult for me under all the present circumstances not to offer myself, and I should on many accounts be strongly tempted to make the trial, if I may flatter myself that my vacating my. seat for Appleby would not be inconvenient to you and that you would allow me again to become indebted to the friendship with which you have honored me. I feel how much I rely upon it, when I take the liberty of mentioning this circumstance to you. I am extremely mortified not to be able to pay my respects to you to morrow morning, but it is essential for me to be at Cambridge without loss of time; and being obliged to be in town again on Tuesday I must set out early."

WILLIAM PITT to SIR JAMES LOWTHER, Bart.

[1784], April 3rd, Saturday night. Pembroke Hall.—"I am this moment returned for the University by a great majority, and Lord Euston is my colleague. I am impatient to communicate this to you, as I need not now avail myself of the assistance to which I have been so much indebted."

WILLIAM PITT to SIR JAMES LOWTHER, Bart.

[1784, March], Sunday morning ½ past 9, Downing Street.—"I have this moment an express from .York. Mr. Duncombe and Mr. Wilberforce are to be nominated for the county against Mr. Foljambe and Mr. Weddel. The meeting for the nomination is Friday April 2nd. Our friends expect a majority of two to one, if a sufficient subscription can be raised to carry on the contest. I have a list of names in town who are thought likely to subscribe. If you should be induced to give it the countenance of yours the example will I dare say have effect. You will I am sure forgive my troubling you, as this is a struggle in which the honour of our cause is so much concerned, and which will certainly influence others."

[There are many other letters of Pitt to Sir James Lowther, made Earl of Lonsdale in May 1784, making appointments or of a complimentary character, some undated.]

WILLIAM PITT to JAMES EARL of LONSDALE.

[1785,] February 21st, Monday, Downing Street.—"Mr. Pitt presents his compliments to Lord Lonsdale, and thinks himself greatly obliged by the honor of his Lordship's notes. Mr. Pitt is under the necessity of attending a Cabinet Council at Lord Carmarthen's office at one o'clock to-day, and cannot be certain at what hour precisely he shall be released: he will not therefore give Lord Lonsdale the trouble of coming to Downing Street, but will do himself the honor of waiting upon his Lordship the moment he leaves the Council."

WILLIAM PITT to [WILLIAM] LOWTHER.

1787, February 23rd, Downing Street.—"The place of Register of Wine Licences, which is an easy employment, and worth about 100l. per annum is just vacant. If this will suit the person you wish to recommend, be so good as to send me his name, and I shall have great pleasure in immediately appointing him to it."

WILLIAM PITT to JAMES EARL of LONSDALE.

1788, December 13th, Saturday. Downing Street.—"Mr. Pitt presents his compliments to Lord Lonsdale. He is extremely sorry to learn that his Lordship is so much indisposed, and is fearful that he could hardly with convenience allow Mr. Pitt the honor of seeing him at present; but being particularly anxious to have as early an opportunity as he can of having some conversation with his Lordship, he will be much obliged to him if he will have the goodness to name any day or hour for Mr. Pitt to wait upon him, when he is enough recovered to make it not improper."

The PRINCE of WALES to the EARL of LONSDALE.

1788, December 13th, Carlton House.—"As it is possible that the unfortunate circumstance of Your Lordship's indisposition may prevent my having the pleasure of seeing you before Tuesday, I take this method of expressing my earnest hope that Your Lordship's friendship to me will induce you to discountenance any proposition which may be brought forward with a view *to insult and arraign my character and conduct.*

It is in this light I most seriously assure Your Lordship I regard Mr. Pitt's determination to press for a decision *in a claim I have not preferred* and the discussion of which is both painful and injurious to me, and wholly unnecessary if not detrimental to the public good."

The PRINCE OF WALES to JAMES EARL OF LONSDALE.

1788, December 14th, Carlton House.—"The Prince of Wales considers Lord Lonsdale's suggestion as an additional proof of his attachment and feels the highest satisfaction in the reflection that he can rely firmly on the friendship of a person of his great consideration in the country.

With respect to the plan proposed it appears to the Prince that in substance, it is full of good sense and propriety, but if Lord Lonsdale had not been confined to his house, he would have been witness this week past to such a spirit of misconstruction in regard to every step the Prince takes that he would see infinite hazard in any direct communication from the Prince to either house of Parliament. In this view it was thought proper that His Royal Highness's sentiments should be conveyed to the House of Lords, by a speech from the Duke of York rather than by message.

If Lord Lonsdale is of opinion that Mr. Pitt would consent to the opening of a communication between His Royal Highness and the House of Commons, The Prince sees no objection, and would be particularly pleased with the motion coming from Sir William Lowther both on account of his consequence in the Country and because it would be an indication of Lord Lonsdale's attachment on which he sets so high a value. If Mr. Pitt disapproves of the measure, the Prince would wish it to be well considered, before it is moved, in order to know how far it would meet the opinion of some persons in the House of Commons who support the Prince on the present occasion. His Royal Highness does not mean Mr. Fox and his friends who he is sure will perfectly approve the substance of Lord Lonsdale's Plan. At any rate His Royal Highness flatters himself that Lord Lonsdale will see the necessity of preventing the discussion, much more the decision, on the abstract point which Mr. Pitt is to bring on to-morrow, as it would throw infinite difficulty on the Plan proposed."

WILLIAM PITT to JAMES EARL of LONSDALE.

1788, December 16th, Tuesday, Downing Street.—"Mr. Pitt presents his compliments to Lord Lonsdale, and takes the liberty of troubling him with the enclosed Resolutions which he proposes to move to day in the Committee on the State of the Nation, and shall be peculiarly happy if they coincide with his Lordship's sentiments."

Enclosure in preceding letter.

" 1st.—That it appears to this Committee that His Majesty is prevented by his present indisposition from coming to his Parliament, and from attending to Public Business, and that the personal exercise of the Royal Authority by His Majesty is thereby for the present interrupted.

2nd.—That it is the Right and Duty of the Lords Spiritual and Temporal and Commons of Great Britain now assembled and lawfully fully and freely representing all the Estates of the People of this Realm to provide the means of supplying the defect of the personal exercise of the Royal Authority arising from his Majesty's said indisposition, in such manner as the exigency of the case may appear to them to require.

3rd.—Resolved that for this purpose, and for maintaining entire the Constitutional Authority of the King, It is necessary that the said Lords Spiritual and Temporal and Commons of Great Britain, should determine on the means whereby the Royal Assent may be given in Parliament to such Bill as may be passed by the two Houses of Parliament respecting the exercise of the Powers and Authorities of the Crown in the name and on the behalf of the King during the continuance of His Majesty's present indisposition."

WILLIAM PITT to JAMES EARL of LONSDALE.

1788, December 31st, Wednesday, ½ past 4 p.m., Downing Street.— " Mr. Pitt presents his compliments to Lord Lonsdale. He had the honor of calling at his Lordship's door, to day, to enquire after his health, and in hopes that he might be enough recovered to allow him the opportunity of conversing with him. But having the mortification to find that Lord Lonsdale is still so much indisposed, Mr. Pitt takes the liberty of enclosing, for his perusal the Heads of the Plan which he proposes to open to the House of Commons, for supplying the defect of the exercise of the King's Authority. Mr. Pitt regrets much that Lord Lonsdale's health prevents his having the satisfaction of a personal communication with him on so important a subject, but will be extremely happy if the general outlines he has stated coincide with his Lordship's sentiments."

Enclosed in preceding letter.

" That His Royal Highness the Prince of Wales should be empowered to exercise the Royal Authority in the name and on the behalf of His Majesty, during His Majesty's illness and to do all Acts which might legally be done by His Majesty; with Provisions nevertheless that the care of His Majesty's Household, and the appointment and direction of the Officers and Servants of the same, should be in Her Majesty the Queen, under such Regulations as may be thought necessary.

That the Power so to be exercised by His Royal Highness the Prince of Wales should not extend to the granting the real or personal property of the King (except as far as relates to the renewal of leases)—to the granting any Office whatever in reversion—or to the granting for any other term than during His Majesty's pleasure, any Pension, or any Office whatever, except such as must by law be granted for life, or during good behaviour. Nor to the granting any Rank or Dignity of the Peerage of this Realm, to any person except His Majesty's Royal Issue who shall have attained the age of twenty one years."

CAPTAIN PAYNE to JAMES EARL 'OF LONSDALE.

[1789], January 6th, Tuesday.—"Captain Payne presents his compliments to Lord Lonsdale, and was sorry to learn that his Lordship is still confined, when he did himself the honour of waiting on him by the Prince of Wales's direction to deliver to him the enclosed paper, as well as to express his Royal Highness's wish that his Lordship would give every support to his cause, which is this day to be agitated, and which he only feels as directed against him for the purpose of attaching suspicion and jealousy on his character."

(Enclosure.)

" The Prince of Wales learns from Mr. Pitt's Letter, that the Proceedings in Parliament are now in a train which enables Mr. Pitt, according to the intimation in his former letter, to communicate to the Prince the outlines of the Plan which His Majesty's confidential servants conceive to be proper to be proposed in the present circumstances.

Concerning the steps already taken by Mr. Pitt the Prince is silent —Nothing done by the two Houses of Parliament can be a proper subject of his animadversion—but when previously to any discussion in Parliament the outline of a scheme of government is sent for his consideration in which it is proposed that he shall be personally and principally concerned and by which the Royal Authority and the Public Welfare may be deeply affected the Prince would be unjustifiable were he to withhold an explicit declaration of his sentiments.—His silence might be construed into a previous approbation of a Plan, the accomplishment of which every motive of duty to his father and Sovereign, as well as of regard to the public interest obliges him to consider as injurious to both.

In the state of deep distress in which the Prince and the whole Royal Family were involved by the heavy calamity which has fallen upon the King and at a moment when Government, deprived of its chief energy and support, seemed peculiarly to need the cordial and united aid of all descriptions of good subjects, it was not expected by the Prince that a Plan should be offered to his consideration by which Government was to be rendered difficult if not impracticable in the hands of any Person intended to represent the King's authority, much less in the hands of his eldest Son, the Heir-Apparent of his Kingdoms, and the Person most bound to the maintenance of His Majesty's just Prerogatives, and Authority as well as most interested in the happiness, the prosperity, and the glory of his People.

The Prince forbears to reason on the several Parts of the Sketch of the Plan laid before him—he apprehends it must have been formed with sufficient deliberation to preclude the probability of any argument from him producing an alteration of sentiment in the projectors of it ; but he trusts with confidence to the wisdom and justice of Parliament when the whole of the subject and the circumstances connected with it shall come under their deliberation.

He observes therefore only generally on the heads communicated by Mr. Pitt, and it is with deep regret the Prince makes the observation, that he sees in the contents of that Paper, a project for producing weakness, disorder and insecurity, in every branch of the Administration of Affairs—A Project for dividing the Royal Family from each other —for separating the Court from the State, and disjoining Government from its natural and accustomed support. A Scheme for disconnecting the Authority to command Service, from the Power of animating it by reward, and for allotting to the Prince all the invidious duties of Government, without the means of softening them to the People by any one act of grace, favour, and benignity.

The Prince's feelings on contemplating this Plan, are also rendered still more painful to him, by observing that it is not founded on any general principle, but is calculated to infuse jealousies, and distrust, wholly groundless he trusts, in that quarter, whose confidence it will ever be the first pride and object of his life to receive and to merit.

With regard to the motive and object of the limitations and restrictions proposed, the Prince can have but little to observe—no light or information whatever is afforded to him by His Majesty's Ministers on these points—they have informed him what the powers are which they mean to refuse to him, not why they are to be withheld.

The Prince however—holding as he does that it is an undoubted and fundamental Principle of this Constitution that all the Powers and Prerogatives of the Crown are vested there a trust for the benefit of the People, and that they are sacred only as they are necessary to the preservation of that poise and balance of the Constitution which experience has proved to be the true security of the liberty of the subject—must be allowed to observe, that the plea of public utility ought to be strong, manifest and urgent which calls for the extinction, or suspension of any one of these essential rights in the supreme Power or its Representative, or which can justify the Prince in consenting that in his Person an experiment shall be made to ascertain with how small a portion of the Kingly Power the executive Government of this Country may be carried on.

The Prince has only to add, that if security for His Majesty's repossessing his rightful Government, whenever it shall please Providence in bounty to the Country to remove the calamity with which he is afflicted, be any part of the object of this plan, the Prince has only to be convinced that any measure is necessary or even conducive to that end, to be the first to approve and urge it as the preliminary and paramount consideration of any settlement in which he would consent to share.

If attention to what is presumed might be His Majesty's feelings and wishes on the happy day of his recovery be the object, it is with the truest sincerity the Prince expresses his firm conviction that no event could be more repugnant to the feelings of His Royal Father than the knowledge that the Government of his son, and representative had exhibited the Sovereign Power of the Realm in a state of degradation, of curtailed authority, and diminished energy—a state hurtful in practice to the prosperity and good Government of his People, and injurious in its precedent to the security of the Monarchy and the rights of his Family.

Upon that part of the plan which regards the King's real and personal property, the Prince feels himself compelled to remark that it was not necessary for Mr. Pitt, nor proper, to suggest to the Prince, the restraint he proposes against the Prince's granting away the King's real or personal property—The Prince does not conceive that during the King's life he is by law entitled to make any such grant; and he is sure that he has never shewn the smallest inclination to possess any such power—but it remains with Mr. Pitt to consider the eventual interests of the Royal Family and to provide a proper and natural security against the mismanagement of them by others.

K

The Prince has discharged, an indispensible duty in thus giving his free opinion on the plan submitted to his consideration.—His conviction of the evils which may arise to the King's interests, to the peace and happiness of the Royal Family, and to the safety and welfare of the Nation, from the Government of the 'Country remaining longer in its present maimed and debilitated state, outweighs in the Prince's mind every other consideration, and will determine him to undertake the painful trust imposed upon him by the present melancholy necessity (which of all the King's subjects he deplores the most) in full confidence that the affection and loyalty to the King, the experienced attachment to the House of Brunswick, and the generosity which has always distinguished this Nation, will carry him through the many difficulties inseparable from this most critical situation with comfort to himself with honor to the King, and with advantage to the Public."

The PRINCE OF WALES to JAMES, EARL OF LONSDALE.

[1790, June?], Carlton House, six o'clock.—"I am this instant arrived in London having left it for a few hours since I met Hamilton this morning and just as I returned into Pall Mall I met Morris who informed me, that the information you had heard as well as that I had heard relative to Braddyll was equally true in both cases, as Braddyll stands upon the Duke of Norfolk's interest both for Horsham as well as Carlisle, I therefore thought it a duty incumbent upon me instantly to acquaint you by this note of the intelligence I had gained, as otherwise I might appear though innocently to have misled you which I never could in any case have intended to have done."

WM. PITT to SIR WILLIAM LOWTHER, Bart.

1791, January 13th, Burton Pynsent.—"I was so much engaged till I left London, as to make it absolutely impossible for me to write to you. I have less pleasure in doing it now, as the renewal of a very urgent application from Duncombe will, I fear, not allow me to comply with your wishes respecting Catterick. I am not without hopes however that if any other living of equal value, and in the gift of the Crown should become vacant in that part of the world, I might be able to manage an exchange and open Catterick for Mr. Zouch, which I should have great pleasure in doing. I return to town on the 17th, and shall not be farther than Hollwood between that time and the meeting of Parliament. I shall be happy to see you at any time that suits you best, and you will be sure of finding me at Hollwood if I am not in town. I will then return you the curious letter you were so good to send me, which I beg your pardon for having kept so long."

ROBERT THOROTON to SIR WILLIAM LOWTHER, Bart., Cottesmore, Stamford.

1796, February 19th, Dublin. — "Politics may be said to go on smoothly here, so far as relates to the ordinary proceeding of Government little can be done by Opposition, deserted, dwindled, and dispersed as they are, and the independent part of Parliament being determined from the late alarming outrages, to give the most effectual support to Administration. There is a spirit of sanguinary ferocity, and implacable discontent, among the lower order of the People, that threatens the most formidable consequences, under the style of defenderism. This cause was first set on foot by the Catholics, and has since been encouraged by assurances of assistance from France, which has carried the feelings of the lower order of the People (naturally desperate from their poverty) to an extent of violence, that nothing but the bayonet can keep down. The most cruel murders and atrocious outrages are daily committed, and as you will read in the papers, last week, a party came from the country, and murdered two men, who were placed for protection in a lodge, in the park of Lord Carhampton, within four miles of Dublin, in order to give their testimony upon a trial, which was to have been brought on in a few days. There was something peculiarly barbarous in their manner of treating these unfortunate men, one of whom had concealed himself; upon their finding him, they formed a circle, and danced round him; and then discharged five shots, and mangled him in a dreadful manner. The consequence of these outrages is, that the country in the parts where they prevail is entirely deserted by those who can remove, either into the country towns or to the metropolis, and even in the quiet parts of the kingdom, the gentlemen apprized of the disposition of the People, are not very anxious to reside at their country seats. Were it not for these internal disturbances Ireland would actually have profited by the war. Her trade, manufactures, and revenue, having been encreased, and no deficiency having arisen from want of grain or dearness of provision, nor any taxes imposed that affect the lower order of the People. Lord Camden therefore, with these disturbances quelled, and an opposition consisting but of 16, with no measures of difficulty to bring forward, is not likely to encounter any embarrassment this Session; the next Session (I think) will require most strenuous exertion to keep *The Cart upon its wheels.*" . . .

LORD BELLENDEN to the EARL OF LONSDALE.

1794, April 21st.—"Although I have not the honour to be known to your Lordship, I had the pleasure to be known to Sir William Lowther and his two sons, who I boarded with many years ago in Dean's Yard, Westminster, I am sorry to inform your Lordship that I am one of those exigent mortals, who having but a slender income of two or three hundred a year to live upon, am often liable to be thrown into embarrassment, and as it has been the decree of fate that I should be so singularly distinguished by the caprice of fortune, and the innumerable difficulties and disappointments she has thrown before me, I have no other resource at present than to make application to those characters who I hope will deign to compassionate a nobleman in distress. If your Lordship could find it convenient to render me the smallest assistance per bearer, I will take the earliest opportunity of waiting upon you for which to return the obligation conferred upon me, and do assure your Lordship that nothing could have induced me to make application to you but the greatest distress, and most pinching necessity."

WILLIAM PITT to [SIR WILLIAM LOWTHER, Bart.]

1796, September 24th, Downing Street.—" At a moment so important as the present, you would oblige me very particularly if you would undertake seconding the Address at the opening of the Session. It is to be moved by Lord Morpeth. The task is becoming fortunately every day less disagreeable than it promised to be, by the good news from the Continent, but the Crisis is still one which calls for all the zeal and exertions of the country. We shall have to announce every step taken on our part towards Peace that any reasonable man I believe will desire. Whether our overtures are accepted or rejected, the chance of obtaining good terms, or the means of prosecuting the War will equally require vigorous and effectual support from Parliament and the country. You will I am persuaded not be adverse to shew your concurrence in these sentiments ; and on this ground as well as from your kindness and friendship at all times, I flatter myself you may be induced to comply with my wishes. The King's Speech will be deferred till after the members are sworn, and therefore will not take place till Tuesday sen'night, but the choice of the Speaker will be Tuesday next. I shall be happy to see you at any time in the interval that suits you."

Sir William Lowther to [James, Earl of Lonsdale].

1798, October 26th, Apethorpe.—" I am very much ashamed of Major Zouch's behaviour, and extremely sorry that I yielded so far to his very pressing importunities, as to recommend him to Your Lordship's protection. He has frequently shown some peculiarities in his conduct, but I never supposed he would have acted with so much impropriety as he has done on this occasion.

I am very sorry to hear of your Lordship's indisposition. I hope you will not venture on so long a journey at this season of the year, till your health is reestablished. Lord Westmorland understands that the meeting of Parliament is to be postponed to the 20th or thereabouts, and is much surprized that he has not received any notification of it, as it was not Mr. Pitt's intention that it should meet before that time— at all events I shall be in London at the meeting of Parliament, but if that does not take place till the 20th I shall be ready to wait on your Lordship at the time you mention, if you will have the goodness to direct some one to communicate your wishes to me.

Lord Clare is expected here tomorrow. An Union betwixt this Country and Ireland, I have some reason to think, is in agitation."

William Pitt to James Earl of Lonsdale.

1798, September 4th, Hollwood.—" I was honored yesterday with your Lordship's letter, and shall be happy to lay before His Majesty so valuable a proof of your zeal for the public service. The arrangements, however, which are already made for sending to Ireland reinforcements to the full extent authorized by Parliament, will necessarily preclude the acceptance of this liberal and spirited offer."

(" A copy from a copy.")

William Pitt to I. Hawkins Browne, Esq.

1799, February 7th, Downing Street.—Private. " I felt greatly obliged to you for communicating to me the idea which you entertain of proposing to accompany the measure of the Union by a reduction of the number of members for English boroughs, equal to the additional number from Ireland. The reasons you allege are those most likely to represent the proposal in a favourable light ; but the first of them, in the extent in which you state it, I confess does not seem to me justified by experience, and I must fairly confess that everything which has passed for the last ten years convinces me more and more, of the little advantage, and the infinite danger, which must attend the agitation in any mode of the principle of Parliamentary Reform. This is in my mind an insuperable objection, and you will I am sure excuse my taking the liberty of stating it to you, as I do without reserve."

Endorsed : " The original of this letter in Mr. Pitt's writing was put into Lord Farnborough's hands by the Rev. Dr. Wordsworth, Master of Trinity College, Cambridge, who allowed Lord Farnborough to take a copy of it."

SIR JOHN BECKETT to ——.

1800. November 17th, Leeds . . . . . " The most striking circumstance which arises out of the subject on which you have honoured me with your correspondence is the present state of men's minds, not one in an hundred admitting there is any real scarcity but contending and preaching loudly there is plenty of corn, but that it is unfairly withheld from the poor for the purpose of keeping up the price—that the poor have now patiently borne their distress long enough and if they shall have recourse to violent measures who can blame them—or who would interfere—this and such like is the language which I find held by the best informed part of society ; and what is likely to be the consequence considering the actual distress of the poor, God only knows, but looking forwards to the winter I tremble when I think of it— The crop of the present year in this part of Yorkshire has been in general pretty good and therefore it cannot or will not be admitted it has been bad any where, yet in that part of Lincolnshire where I resided the crops of 1799 and 1800 added together fell far short of the single year 1798 and in several other parts of the country I am credibly informed it has been the same, indeed considering the seed time for wheat in 1799 it could hardly be otherwise, for it lasted from October to the end of February and went into the ground very badly the whole time. I believe the Duke of Portland to be very near the truth in his statement and if the present crop be only $\frac{3}{4}$ or perhaps $\frac{2}{3}$ of an average crop, considering too that it is a second bad year, I think it sufficiently accounts for the present high price without recurring to monopolizing, or hoarding, or any such silly stuff. On this point I admire the good sense of a Representation of the Privy Council dated the 8 March 1790, from which I will give you an extract as you may not perhaps have the Pamphlet—" In other countries magazines of corn are formed by their respective Governments as a resource in times of scarcity—this country has no such institution—The stores of corn are here deposited in the barns and stacks of wealthy farmers and in the magazines of merchants and dealers in corn who ought to be by no means restricted but rather encouraged in laying up stores of this nature, as after a deficient crop they are thereby enabled to divide the inconvenience arising from it as equally as possible through every part of the year and by checking improvident consumption in the beginning of scarcity prevent a famine which might otherwise happen before the next harvest. The inland trade of corn therefore ought to be perfectly free—this freedom can never be abused—*To suppose that there can be a monopoly of so bulky and perishable a commodity dispersed through so many hands over every part of the country is an idle and vain apprehension* "—what good sense, I say, is this compared with the popular tales of the present moment!

I forget whether I mentioned to you
price of wheat which is that before the
all for
labour
cheese
within

almost every other article preserves its relative value. No longer ago
than the year 1774 when I begun housekeeping I paid for my butchers
meat 3½d. a lb. the year round, for butter about 7d. or 8d., for cheese
5d., for milk 6d. a gallon, for wheat about 6s. a bushel. Wheat
till the year '99 was not higher than 6s. a bushell on an average of
almost any number of years, yet for every other article I have mentioned the price is double. From this circumstance I have been led
to suspect that the price of wheat has been improperly depressed
by the corn laws and in addition to bad years may have had some
effect in increasing the present scarcity, for as the produce of grass
land has been continually increasing in value 'till now it is more than
double what it was even within the last 40 years, and wheat remains
stationary, it seems cause enough to suspect a general tendency to convert arable land to grass and so lessen the quantity of the former in
comparison with the latter. The object of the last general Law for
regulating the price of wheat seems to have been to keep it at 6s. a
bushell, a price that it had borne for many years before, which was
ridiculous enough considering that 6s. of that day was worth no more
than 3s. of 40 years before, nor would buy more of the produce of grass
land than 3s. of the 40 years before, and may probably therefore have
had the effect I suspect. If it was now in the power of the Legislature
to govern circumstances and absolutely to fix the price of wheat, it
would be a question sooner asked than ably answered what sum would be
advisable to fix it at, should it not however be such as to make it as well
worth the farmers' while to grow corn as grass, otherways land will run
to grass too much—then at what period did the produce of the two sorts
of lands bear the best proportion to each other? Probably I should
think when we grew as much Corn as served ourselves and a little at
least to spare for exportation, that was when the price of wheat was
from 5s. to 6s. a bushell and the produce of grass land at half its
present price—to give wheat then its natural price as compared with
the produce of grass land now (I mean before '99) it ought not to have
been less than 10s. a bushell and though that price seems extravagantly
high in common times I really see no reason or good policy in making
laws endeavouring to keep it at a lower price.

The comparative advantages of labour bestowed upon land or manufactures I hope I shall some day have the pleasure of discussing with
you personally, and I hope of convincing you if you can have any doubts
on the subject, that no policy is so wise, no patriotism so true (particularly in men who hold the lofty situation in which you are placed
in the country, allow me to say I think very deservedly), as to turn
their thoughts and exertions to improvements in agriculture." . . . .

The Rev. Thomas Zouch to Sir William Lowther.

1801, February 16th, Sandal.—. . . "A Petition to the King for
Peace has been subscribed by many of the Wakefield manufacturers,

consisting principally of Presbyterians, and men of republican principles, while a Protest against their proceedings has appeared in some of the provincial papers from the merchants, clergy, and others. In the meantime the distresses of the poor are daily increasing; all trade is nearly at an end; and provisions of every kind rapidly advance in price. The Aire and Calder Navigation flourishes exceedingly. This is attributed to the vast quantities of corn brought up the river, Wakefield being the greatest corn market in the north of England."

The Rev. THOMAS ZOUCH to SIR WILLIAM LOWTHER.

1801, September 29th, Sandal.—Encloses a letter of Dr. Parr, in which his "late accomplished brother," Henry Zouch, is praised in the highest terms; and refers to the Doctor's recent Spital Sermon, in which he defended the system of modern education against a French writer "who reprobates every plan of early instruction as productive only of prejudice and error."

The Rev. THOMAS ZOUCH to SIR WILLIAM LOWTHER.

1802, April 26th, Scrayingham . . . "On reading two letters of Sir Henry Sidney to his son it struck me that the reprinting of them at this time might be an useful undertaking. I have gradually collected some materials for the Life of Sir Philip, whose character the more I consider it, the more I admire. Some notes also, illustrating the letters, have suggested themselves, particularly from comparing them with the lessons of admonition given by Sir Matthew Hales to his children. These letters are included in the Papers of the Sidney family published by Collins. There is also a copy of them annexed to Archbishop Usher's Letters edited by Dr. [Richard] Parr in 1692 (sic), but that copy is mutilated, and imperfect in many places . . .

It is said that Dr. Milner exerted every effort to change his Deanery of Carlisle for that of York; and that all the evangelical Preachers, as they insolently style themselves, were much disappointed on this occasion.

Mr. Maltby, chaplain to the Bishop of Lincoln, has published his long expected work. To eke out the volume he has added a Latin Thesis, and a Latin sermon. He refutes the arguments brought against Christianity by Mr. Chubb and Lord Bolingbroke, men whose writings sleep on the shelf undisturbed, and whose objections have been repeatedly answered."

WILLIAM PITT to WILLIAM VISCOUNT LOWTHER.

1802, June 7th, Thursday, Park Place.—"I am very sorry that I missed you when you were so good as to call to-day, and that I cannot have the pleasure of meeting you at Euston's at dinner. I wished much to have the opportunity of thanking you for the note you sent me with the account of Lord Lonsdale's death; as well as to assure you, (what I hope you cannot doubt) how much I partook in the pleasure which I believe was very generally felt when the destination of his property was known."

WILLIAM PITT to VISCOUNT LOWTHER.

1802, June 25th, Walmer Castle.—"I am very sorry that circumstances have prevented me from telling you with certainty for whom I wished to avail myself of your kind offer. One day's additional delay will not I hope produce material inconvenience, as I shall be in town on Sunday, and shall by that time have received the answer I am now expecting."

WILLIAM PITT to VISCOUNT LOWTHER.

1802, June 28th, Pembroke Hall.—Tuesday. "The answer which I expected unfortunately did not reach me before I left town yesterday, but I have received it by to-day's post. The person whom I was anxious to recommend to you, is most desirous of accepting the seat. His name is Ward. He is a near relation of Lord Mulgrave's, and is at the Bar, and of such promising talents, that I hardly think he can fail to distinguish himself. Notwithstanding this impression, I should not, however, wish to avail myself of your kindness in his favour, after knowing that our friend [Meeke ?] has been in your thoughts, if I had not some time since undertaken, that if anything happened to put it in my power, I would endeavour to procure him a seat. I hope this long delay has not been materially inconvenient to you."

[P.S.] " My friend's address is Robert Ward, Esq., No. 48 Lincoln's Inn Fields."

The Rev. THOMAS ZOUCH to VISCOUNT LOWTHER.

1802, July 3rd. Sandal.—Respecting the progress he is making in the Collection of materials for a history of the Lowther family. [Many other letters from Dr. Zouch about this date refer to the same subject.] Solicits his lordship's interest to procure for him some ecclesiastical dignity—"though I am not unconscious of my own merit, I entirely acquiesce in what you think best."

WILLIAM PITT to VISCOUNT LOWTHER.

1803, March 22nd, Walmer Castle.—"I am quite ashamed of not having sooner answered your letter, and told you how glad I am to be able to furnish Colonel Lowther's son with the recommendation you wish. Lest my delay should prevent my letter being in time for him to carry with him, I have begged Colonel Lowther in that case to send it to Mr. W. Dundas who will I know forward it by the first opportunity. The slight attack which I felt of gout has left me much the better for it, and the sea breezes have hitherto exempted this place from the complaints which have infected London. I am not without some thoughts of making a visit to Bath during Easter, and hope to have the pleasure of meeting you in town soon afterwards, as I imagine you will probably be there in the course of the spring."

WILLIAM PITT to VISCOUNT LOWTHER.

1804, April 12th, Thursday. Walmer Castle.—"I trouble you with two lines only to say that I shall be in town on Monday next, chiefly for the purpose of attending Yorke's Bill for suspending the Army of reserve, the second reading of which I find is to be fixed for Tuesday; and also to take my chance of being in time to object to the third reading of the Bill for augmenting the Irish Militia, if it should be deferred till Monday. I think it material to object to both as parts of the only system which Government has brought forward, and which in all its parts I consider as most inefficient and objectionable. We shall hardly be able to have a full muster of our force till the end of the week, but I have desired Long to endeavour to obtain as good an attendance as he can on Monday and Tuesday, and shall be much obliged to you if you will give a hint to any of your friends to whom you think it necessary."

WILLIAM PITT to VISCOUNT LOWTHER.

1804, May 3rd, Thursday. York Place.—"I shall be happy to dine with you on Monday, and also on Wednesday, supposing as is most probable that both days remain free from business in either House. Something will probably pass at the House of Lords to day respecting a further delay of Lord Stafford's motion, and you will probably be there, in which case I will meet you; and I will try in the mean time to put down some names as you desire for Wednesday."

WILLIAM PITT to VISCOUNT LOWTHER.

1804, November 14th. Downing Street.—"In spite of *bad habits* I have just time to thank you for your letter to me and that to Bourne, which arrived this morning. Lord Villiers is I am persuaded perfectly well disposed, and would be a very creditable accession to our list of friends; but as in addition to votes (of which we have certainly not too many) it is very desirable to reinforce our line of debaters, the person for whom I should most wish to procure a seat is Gibbs (the Chief Justice of Chester); and as I find from Rose, that on account of a candidate on a new interest having already started, the Duchess of Bolton is anxious to settle her recommendation as soon as possible, I have ventured to desire him to propose Gibbs immediately to her, in order to avoid the delay which must arise if she waited to hear from you again upon the subject. I was very sorry that the renewal of an application from Lord Coventry (on which he had received great encouragement twelve or fourteen years ago) made it impossible for me to take care of Mr. Zouch, on the last vacancy at Worcester. But either there or elsewhere you may be assured that he shall be thought of at the earliest possible opportunity."

WILLIAM PITT to [VISCOUNT LOWTHER].

1804, November 23rd. Downing Street.—"Since I wrote last I have been enabled to make some arrangement respecting ecclesiastical preferment; and am happy to find it in my power to assure you, that I shall recommend Mr. Zouch for the next vacancy which may take place at Worcester, or the next but one in any other Stall. Every thing is satisfactorily arranged with respect to Mr. Gibbs's election, and there seems nothing to apprehend from the Opposition. If I can find any mode of making a provision for poor Penn, I shall be very glad if you will allow me to make use of your kind offer, in order to introduce some other useful recruit. We are expecting every day to receive the account of our being decidedly at war with Spain; an event which as things now stand will rather improve than embarrass our situation."

The Rev. THOMAS ZOUCH to VISCOUNT LOWTHER.

1805, January 7th. Sandal.—I have read the MS. poem [Wordsworth's?] with attention. It is certainly an extraordinary performance

and discovers a singular originality of poetic genius, an exuberance of
invention and sentiment, and great powers of description. The scenery
which he exhibits on Skiddaw and its adjacent mountain Saddle-back or
Blencathara is truly grand. I have marked with a pencil in the margin
the passages which appeared to me incorrect, and drawn a line under
the expressions and words which seemed exceptionable. The terms
green and *bowers* are used too often, and there are some rhymes which
occur too frequently and which I have noticed.

WILLIAM PITT to VISCOUNT LOWTHER.

1805, February 20th, Wednesday, Downing Street.—" It gives me
great pleasure to find that the arrangements in the Church will give me
an immediate opportunity of acquitting myself of my engagement to
you in favor of Dr. Zouch. The particular preferment which I have
in view to offer him is the Precentorship of Lincoln ; but I am not yet
certain whether it will be that or some other Stall, as it depends on the
decision of Dr. Pretyman (brother to the Bishop) to whom I have
offered the Prebend of Durham, and whose acceptance would vacate
both the Precentorship and a Prebend of Norwich. Should Dr. Pretyman decline, I shall have no difficulty in making some other arrangement which will open a situation of the description you wished for
Dr. Zouch. Whatever it may be, I wish it to be considered only as a
step towards the Bishoprick of Carlisle which I shall reserve for your
recommendation, whenever an opportunity arises of promoting the
present Bishop. I should add that the Precentorship of Lincoln is
worth, as I understand, between seven and eight hundred pounds per
annum."

WILLIAM PITT to VISCOUNT LOWTHER.

1805, March 2nd, Downing Street.—" After so many years of uninterrupted friendship, during which I have received from you the
strongest proofs of personal kindness, and of zealous and honorable
support, it is certainly a severe mortification to me to find that what
has lately passed has given you so much dissatisfaction. I regret
extremely that I had not the opportunity of seeing you while you were
in town, and of explaining to you fully all the grounds on which I have
acted ; because I cannot help still flattering myself that on a knowledge and consideration of all the circumstances your judgment would
be different. At all events it will be a great satisfaction to me, if
whenever you return you will allow me to converse fully with you on
the whole subject. In the mean time the knowledge of your present
sentiments, cannot make the smallest change in the desire I feel both
to acquit myself of an engagement, and to mark the sense I shall
always retain of your cordial and effectual support, without the smallest
view in doing so, to what may be your future conduct. I shall therefore lose no time in endeavouring to compleat the arrangement, which
may enable me to place Dr. Zouch in such a situation as will answer
your views for him. Unluckily a few days may still elapse before I can
name the precise preferment, as I find that it would not be convenient
to Dr. Pretyman to vacate the preferments he now holds in exchange
for the Prebend of Durham."

WILLIAM PITT to VISCOUNT LOWTHER.

1805, August 21st, Downing Street.—" Dr. Monkhouse called here
to-day to deliver your letter, and brought at the same time the account

of the living of Wakefield being actually vacant. The knowledge I before had of your wishes had determined me to recommend him as the successor, and I have accordingly given directions for his appointment."

"CORRESPONDENCE RELATING TO MR. PITT'S DEATH.'

The EARL of ESSEX to VISCOUNT LOWTHER.

1806, January 14th, Wycombe Abbey. (*Private.*)—"Friendship of long standing as Dr. Johnson said (most wisely) ought to be' kept in repair and therefore I feel that in any event wherein I am at all interested it is my duty as well as inclination to communicate most confidentially with those for whom I profess the real and true regard that I do for yourself. After so long a preface something of greater consequence ought to follow than the simple event of my moving the address on Tuesday next in the House of Lords. Two nights ago I received a letter from Lord Camden at Lord Hawkesbury's request, desiring that I would undertake a task which I feel unequal to, but at the same time I think I ought not to refuse. To say no more on this subject on my own part I will now tell you what I hear of Pitt. He came to Putney as you probably know on Saturday. I hear that he is very weak, and you will perhaps better judge of his real situation when I tell you that all idea of his attending Parliament at first is at an end. The letter I got from Lord Hawkesbury last night has in these words—' I am sure you will be gratified by hearing that Dr. Reynolds and Dr. Baily who have been called in to attend Mr. Pitt are of opinion with Sir W. Farquhar that there are no serious or unpleasant symptoms in his complaint, that it is principally weakness owing to the very severe attack of the gout which he has experienced and that by attention and quiet he will in a short time recover his strength, his attendance in Parliament for a fortnight after the meeting will be however impossible'—on this account of our friend you will make your own comments on this statement. The place from which this is dated will certainly furnish me with the last accounts, and Lord Mahon who is in London writes to his wife that he met Farquhar going to Putney yesterday, that he states Mr. Pitt as having had two attacks of the gout since he came home, and that he shook his head as if he did not like what was going on. Perhaps he may make more of this from other medical advice being called in; here you have all we know on this important subject. My private opinion is that nothing can be worse, a general debility with gout constantly flying about, and his pulse I know to have been as high as 130, only upon the common and ordinary exertion of dressing himself, are symptoms too alarming not to make us anticipate the worst. I cannot have an idea that with the present state of his weak frame and living solely as I hear he does upon milk, that it can last long, frequent attacks of gout must shew there is no strength to throw it out, and at last end in the falling upon some vital part. I have now told you all I know and I trust you will consider that the part I am about to take proceeds from those just feelings that I ought to possess towards our friend. We are of the same opinion as to many circumstances respecting his conduct of late years, but if he is in the utmost need he must not be deserted even by those who have as little support as myself to give him. I have a thousand other things to say but they are too much to put into a sheet of paper, the times are become now so extraordinary and interesting and so much more so from the probability of Pitt's health being upon the decline that of course great

and important changes must be looked for even if no other circumstances
produce them that I take it for granted you will come up. I go from
hence to-morrow and shall be in town Tuesday and have a little chicken
establishment in town for the next week, therefore if you do come up
pray recollect that you will find a manger in John Street when you
are reduced to a mutton chop. Excuse this *pen, ink, paper,* and
writing, the *first, second* and *third,* are Lord Carrington's, the *last*
your &c.

Of course say nothing of Tuesday till you have it in the newspapers
the Duke of Rutland had accepted . . . . refused; why this just
now. What say y[ou] . . . . . ."

The Earl of Essex to Viscount Lowther.

(Private.)

1806, January 16th, John Street.—" I am this moment come to
town and will tell you all I hear on that subject which most interests us
at this moment as any public event, for such is the health of Mr. Pitt.
Farquhar slept at Putney last night, and does so again to-night. A
friend of mine met him this morning and he shook his head saying that
Mr. Pitt might get over it. This is a sort of language that I know
Farquhar often holds *pour se faire valoir*, and I should have attributed it
to that motive had I not met Lord Chatham a few minutes afterwards
who I think gave me a very bad account indeed by saying that Mr. Pitt
was seized in the night with a violent sickness (a bad symptom in his
state) and that the Bishop of Lincoln who was with him had just written
Lord Chatham word that he thought Mr. Pitt had rather lost ground
than gained it since Monday last. The King I hear is very low, and I
do not see much comfort for us in the political world unless some more
favourable events arise. You shall hear from me to-morrow if anything
arises."

" P.S.—I have this moment a line from Lord Henry, who says the
Physicians do not perceive any alarming symptoms, but that his recovery
was not as rapid as they expected."

The Earl of Essex to Viscount Lowther.

[Undated.] *(Private.)*—" I fear I cannot send you a better account
to day though they say there is a shade of difference for the better, a
letter Lord Henry read us from the Bishop of Lincoln this morning
written at 7 o'clock last night mentions the extreme debility of Mr. Pitt
and that it would be necessary to lift him from his bed for a moment to
his couch that the former might be made, thus you see his state of weakness is terrible, the account this evening is that he had taken an egg
yesterday which he had kept upon his stomach and had had a tolerable
night and that he asked for some food this morning which they thought
proceeded from a wish to keep himself up more than from any natural
inclinations to eat, but he said it was really from an inclination to take
sustenance and he was to try some chicken broth. The Physicians, and
Baillie in particular, still say that no symptoms of real alarm shew themselves, so that although we may hope that his life may yet be preserved,
his political life is at an end for the present. What the result will be
God knows, a few days must determine. If you do not come up you
shall hear from me constantly whilst I am in town. The Duchess's
friends are again talking of him as sure of returning to power. The
King's eyes worse I believe.

Burn this.

I have yours of the 15th. I find Lord Carrington is to second the Address."

The EARL of ESSEX to VISCOUNT LOWTHER.

1806, January 18th, London. (*Private.*)—" Pitt is certainly ¦better to-day, he took chicken broth three times yesterday and had very little return of his sickness, but I hear Baillie has pronounced that he cannot attend even to any common business for these next 10 or 12 weeks. There is much cabal going on. I have no more to say now on the subject but will write more fully if possible to-morrow and tell you all that I know, so that on Tuesday you shall be *au fait*. I am just come from the Birthday, it was thin, and the Prince of Wales there in high spirits."

The EARL of ESSEX to VISCOUNT LOWTHER.

1806, Sunday evening, January 20th. (*Private.*)—" I fear you must expect to hear the worst to-morrow if I write. The accounts to-day are sad from Putney, and Pitt is in the utmost danger, probably to-night will decide everything. God grant that a change may take place. The account from the physicians is that the symptoms are unpleasant and his situation dangerous. A letter from Charles Stanhope says the consultation is over, and Mr. Pitt is in great danger. The Bishop of Lincoln's letter says to Pitt's private secretary—Mr. Pitt is worse than yesterday and the symptoms most alarming—I fear we must expect the worst. Pray if this melancholy event should happen come up directly. There are sorts of cabals going on, and such men as yourself should be here and become *landmarks* to those who like myself wish to do the best. I will write to-morrow of course.

Baillie said this morning he was in the greatest danger, and this very publicly, his pulse was 130, and in moving him last night in a blanket from his bed to the couch he fainted away, his voice I understand is too feeble to be heard; what can be worse and how hurried it is ? "

The EARL of ESSEX to VISCOUNT LOWTHER.

1806, January 22nd, London.—" It is for me amongst many others I have no doubt to undertake the painful task of telling you that Mr. Pitt died about 2 o'clock to-day. I am too oppressed with grief to say more, what will be done I know not ; you shall hear from me to-morrow if I know anything, pray come up, if you do so on Friday or Saturday you will find me at Cashiobury. I shall return here Sunday."

LORD MULGRAVE to VISCOUNT LOWTHER.

1806, January 23rd.—" During the anxious suspense of our excellent friend's illness I knew not how to write to you lest I should create fears or hopes that might mislead you. At half-past four this morning the world was deprived of its greatest ornament and the country of its best protector. I know you will feel this most unhappy event as I do, in the general affliction ; I have the aggravated sorrow of paternal feelings, my affection for him was that of a brother."

JOHN STONARD to VISCOUNT LOWTHER.

1806, January 23rd, Chertsey.—" I write immediately and shall send the letter to town by the coach, which will save a day, because I plainly perceive that you are not aware of the very alarming nature of Mr. Pitt's illness. By what I gathered from Stanhope when I was in town a fortnight since, I was convinced that we might wish rather than hope for Mr. Pitt's restoration. This morning has confirmed my worst apprehensions. I have received a letter from poor Stanhope evidently written in the greatest distress and agony of mind. He tells me emphatically ' All is not yet over and that is all I can say, I fear there are no hopes remaining.' Your Lordship therefrom will judge how near one of the worst calamities that can overtake this country is now taking place.

Most likely your Lordship will have heard the truth before you receive this letter. But I think it right to let you know in case you should not. I shall be very happy to see Henry again. Mr. Drummond's [   ] comes on Saturday."

John Stonard to Viscount Lowther.

Thursday afternoon, Chertsey.—" I have written to you before to-day but take the liberty of writing once more. I have this moment received a letter from Stanhope who stopped at Staines in his way down to South Hill with Mr. Canning. The intelligence is indeed most melancholy. Mr. Pitt departed this life at ½ past 4 this morning. Stanhope sat up with him and to use his own words he burnt out quietly and went off without a groan or struggle. Probably I shall not be the first bearer of these most unwelcome tidings, but having a moment's time for the post I write lest others should forget to do it."

The Earl of Essex to Viscount Lowther.

1806, January 23rd, London. (*Private*.)—" I was premature only, in my melancholy intelligence, which was owing to Lord Castlereagh having told Lord Rivers positively at 3 o'clock that Mr. Pitt was dead, the last scene did not close till ½ past 4 o'clock this morning, and with that last breath expired the last hopes of this country. That he will hereafter meet the just rewards due to a character who had devoted itself to his country's service I have no doubt. I never saw more heartfelt grief and sorrow in the countenance of every honest man. I will however hope for the best and not suppose that this country can be lost although it is deprived of the services of such a man whose like we shall never look upon again. I will not close this till after I have been up with the Address and know what is likely to be done in the House of Lords or Commons in consequence of this event. Lord Carrington and myself were at Lord Hawkesbury's for a moment last night at 12 o'clock, the account then was as bad as possible, he was sensible and Farquhar had allowed him in the course of the day to see any one he might wish to speak to but he declined it and I beheve did not see Lord Chatham or any one but the Bishop of Lincoln with whom he had prayed, and poor fellow, I hear he made a will, but God knows can have had little to leave of anything. How melancholy is this event. We found Lord Castlereagh and Wallace, that great man, with Lord Hawkesbury. I hear Lord Sidmouth was seen with the Prince of Wales in close conference. My friends are kind enough to say that everything went off tolerably well with myself on Tuesday.

5 o'clock.

I have yours and quite agree with you as to what you say respecting a wish to have seen Pitt more out of office during his life. I am just come home from the address to the King, he seemed affected and I hear was

very much so at the account of that event we have all so to lament. I hear
no particulars about what is likely to happen. Every man has his own
speculation, and a thousand lies are abroad, some say Lord Hawkesbury
is to be at the head of everything, others, Lord Sidmouth, he and Lord
Henry and Castlereagh have been with the King in private this morning,
and the former gave me a hint that the King would make up his mind
upon what was to be done in the course of 48 hours. I hardly think
anything can come on in the House of Lords or Commons till Pitt
is buried. Lord Grenville is gone to Dropmore to-day and I find
more afflicted than can be described. I shall probably go out of town
very early to-morrow morning, in that case shall not be able to write. I
shall stay till something is likely to come on in Parliament, having
nothing to do with the present cabals and wishing to be absent from
them. Let me know when you mean to come.

[P.S.] They talk of the King sending to Lord Spencer to talk to him.
Lord Henry Petty and Lord Althorp are gone down to Cambridge to
stand."

The EARL of ESSEX to VISCOUNT LOWTHER.

[1806], January 24 (*Private*.)—" I did not leave London early as I intended this morning. I believe all you see in the papers is correct about
our poor dear friend's death except that he did not see Lord Chatham or
any one except the Bishop of Lincoln and Lord Charles Stanhope at
8 o'clock on Wednesday evening, after which time I believe he was
insensible till his death. No blisters were applied to his feet.

I hear nothing certain except that Lord Hawkesbury is decided to
remain firm in not making up any patched administration; this I am
assured of, and if so the others will come in I conclude, and all Pitt's
friends will remain entire and judge which way they ought to give
their support or to withhold it. I suspect Lord Sidmouth will lean to
Fox and the Prince of Wales. Lord Grenville is gone to Dropmore
they say more afflicted than can be described. I have just seen
Lord Camden, nothing will be done in Parliament till the funeral is
over. I hear the Cabinet are determined one and all to give up. The
King is to know this on Saturday."

LORD CAMDEN to VISCOUNT LOWTHER.

1806, January 24th, Arlington Street.—" I had meant to have written to you on the sad and melancholy prospect which has presented
itself for some days respecting Mr. Pitt's health, but I heard you were
coming to town. I should not have given you the pain of hearing from
me that his last breath is gone or myself the pain of writing it—had I
not learnt you were not expected in town for 2 or 3 days.

Upon the event itself I am sure our public and private feelings are
in unison. The political crisis is of importance and I should conceive
you will think it right to come to town. Indeed myself and many of
Mr. Pitt's friends are very desirous you should. It seems to me the
Government cannot proceed and there is great temper in the King and
amongst his ministers on the occasion."

LORD MULGRAVE to VISCOUNT LOWTHER.

1806, January 25, Harley Street.—" I am sure you will think
that the remnant of our dear friend's government have taken the step

best suited to the unhappy state of affairs which the melancholy catastrophe has produced by resigning their offices and advising his Majesty to form a new Government. Lord Grenville will be sent [for] to-morrow, and I trust and hope that such measures will be adopted in the conduct of public affairs as may produce that unanimity in Parliament which is at this moment so essential. Nothing but unanimity and moderation on all sides can give a hope of mitigating the loss which the world and the country has sustained.

With respect to your coming to town I know but one point which might make it particularly desirable to you to be present. You will have seen in this day's paper the notice given by Lascelles of a motion for a public funeral, I do not apprehend that any opposition is likely to be made in the House of Lords, but your situation in life and above all your long steady and well known friendship for the departed object of those public honours would I think render it desirable that you should have a share in the proposal or discussion of such a tribute to his memory.'

The EARL of ESSEX to VISCOUNT LOWTHER.

1806, January 26th, Cashiobury.—"I well know what your feelings must be on the late melancholy event, the newspapers will tell you all that is doing in Parliament, and others of your friends can give you better information than myself as to political arrangements about to take place, but I believe that Lord Hawkesbury and the others remain firm in their determination not to continue the government with only replacing the Chancellor of the Exchequer, that would never do and it is unlikely that Lord Grenville will take in many of the present persons at the head of affairs, so that an entire new administration becomes the most likely thing to take place. You will know when any business is likely to come on and probably will be up for it. Henry Lascelles' motion will I believe only go to the funeral of Mr. Pitt which ought to be equal at least to what his father's was. I shall go up on Thursday for a day or two. I dread all this oversetting the King, if he stands the shock all may yet not be so bad, though the loss of our dear friend can never be replaced as long as we live."

The EARL of WESTMORLAND to VISCOUNT LOWTHER.

1806, January 26th.—"You of course hear a hundred stories—all that can be known is, that the King sent to Lord Grenville to-day to desire him to form an administration. The result of the conversation I have not yet heard.

[P.S.]—House of Lords, 5 o'clock.

Lord Grenville is to go to the King on Thursday "

The EARL of EUSTON to VISCOUNT LOWTHER.

[1806], January 27th, Margaret Street.—"I should have written to you before this time if any event political or other worth notice had occurred since the fatal termination of our much lamented friend's illness.

Lascelles moves this day in the House of Commons that his remains should have a public funeral, and that a monument should be erected to his memory. Most of his most intimate friends are averse to any proposition being made in Parliament respecting his debts, I cannot say that I think they have judged wisely. With regard to new arrangements nothing has as yet transpired. Lord Grenville went to the King (being sent for) at about one o'clock to-day. You shall hear from me again when more is known."

The Earl of Euston to Viscount Lowther.

[1806], January 28th.—" Nothing has transpired but that Lord Grenville received yesterday the King's commands to form an administration which will be laid before his Majesty to-morrow."

Charles Long (afterwards Lord Farnborough) to Viscount Lowther.

[1806], January 28th, 30 Hill Street.—(*Most private and confidential*). " I arrived in town from Ireland last night and sent to your house this morning in the hope of seeing you. I will not attempt to express to you the affliction I feel at this moment. The country has sustained an irreparable loss, but I confess whatever sensations I feel on that consideration are absorbed in my own private feelings.

I am anxious at this moment to perform a duty I owe towards you. You will remember having placed in my hands a sum to be employed for a particular purpose. I looked immediately into the state of the debt to which this was to he applied and I found it so considerable (at that time above 20,000), that it would have done very little towards its liquidation. Under the circumstances I thought I could not better carry into effect your kind intentions than by reserving it for such pressing occasions as unfortunately had but too often occurred. I was enabled by so doing to prevent the most unpleasant consequences by the advancement of two sums at different times, one of 200*l.* and the other of 500*l.*, and last September the remainder was directed to be employed for the purpose of removing an execution. But I was in the country at the time and I found on my arrival in town that other means had been found and the execution taken out of the house. I am therefore to return you this sum of 800*l.* which I will do when you return to town.

I have only to hope that in acting on this as I did on every occasion in the manner most conducive (to the best of my judgment) to the welfare and happiness of my friend I fulfilled your kind intentions towards him."

W. Spencer Stanhope to Viscount Lowther.

1806, January 29th, Grosvenor Square.—" What you conjectured to me on Sunday appeared last night very likely to come to pass, namely, that the two parties of Grenville and Fox were likely to disagree even at the outset. From a hint that Fox let fall last night it appeared that no arrangement was then made, and from the ill-temper shown both by him and Grey to Lord Castlereagh, and above all the offensive speech of Windham on Monday, there seems to be little disposition to conciliate the friends of Pitt. They surely must or ought at least to wish for a strong and popular administration, but the party feelings, and demeanour and language of the Foxites seem to me to be as violent and bitter as ever, and that they would prefer a dissolution of the present Parliament before the trouble of obtaining its good will. I could not help writing these few lines and will not close my letter till near the time of the post's going out.

All I have been able to learn in my morning's walk is that there has been a great struggle whether the Duke of York or Lord Moira should be commander-in-chief, but which is to have it I cannot tell. The result of all this scramble we shall probably know more of to-morrow."

The Earl of Westmorland to Viscount Lowther.

1806, January 30th, London.—" I have nothing of any authority to tell you. There seem doubts whether Grenville as auditor can be first Lord of Treasury, and Lord Spencer is talked of. I have some reason to believe Mansfield is to be Keeper or Chancellor and Erskine Chief Justice of Common Pleas.

Grenville has not been able to make out his plan to go to the King to-day.

We have to our other hopes to add that of Lord Cornwallis."

The Earl of Westmorland to Viscount Lowther.

[1806], January 31st, Friday, ¼ before six.—" Lord Grenville went to the King to-day. I do not hear very particularly their arrangements. It is said their Cabinet is to consist of nine Foxites and four Grenvilles, but this cannot be. All that seems quite certain is that Lord Sidmouth has made terms with them, and is to be either President or Privy Seal. There is some talk of Grant being Chancellor. The story in circulation of Lord Melville's death is unfounded. Lady Chatham is exceedingly ill."

[P.S.] " Lord Buckinghamshire is to have an office, I believe not in the Cabinet."

The Earl of Westmorland to Viscount Lowther.

Saturday, February 1st.—" I can add very little to what I did yesterday. The seals seem at last intended for Erskine, which is shocking. I do not suppose we shall resign before Tuesday. I have just been with the King who seems very quiet, but much hurt. Lady Chatham continues very ill.

Supposed to be

Lord Grenville	1st Lord.
Lord Spencer	Secretary for Home.
Fox	Foreign.
Wyndham	War.
Grey	Admiralty.
Erskine	Chancellor.
Sidmouth	Privy Seal.
FitzWilliam	President.
Moira	Ordnance, or Ireland.
Ellenborough	of Cabinet."

The Earl of Westmorland to Viscount Lowther.

[1806], February 3rd, London.—" A violent rumour prevailed at the Opera circulated by all the party that the arrangement for the new ministry was off. That Lord Grenville had been bowed out by the King, saying he should reconsider the subject. What the exact state was I cannot tell you, nor is, but I believe something proposed respecting the military command, either to remove his Royal Highness or to take away his powers, and in addition to the appointment of Erskine to be Chancellor, which seems to give universal disgust. It was rumoured last night that this hitch was to be got over, whether by his Majesty's submission or by some alteration on the part of their High Mightinesses I cannot say, for l do know no more of the matter than the town reports. If anything should come to my knowledge before six I will add," &c.

"By the accounts stuck up, the King has in a degree yielded. Grenville was to go to him again this evening. Our troops from the Continent are embarking and may soon be expected home."

LORD CAMDEN to VISCOUNT LOWTHER.

1806, February 3rd, Arlington Street.—"You will have seen the list of the new administration in the newspapers and will be somewhat surprised after the professions of forming an administration upon a broad basis, that not a single word has passed from Lord Grenville to any man connected with Mr. Pitt, but that the honourable connexion with Lord Sidmouth was immediately resorted to. There have been some difficulties but I believe they will all be overcome and that the government will be formed. Although I cannot avoid making the observation I have done, I am the last person who is inclined to begin to oppose the Government, and if they do not fall upon our measures I should wish to give a real support to their measures. Though it is quite impossible to give one's confidence to the men, for Lords Grenville and Spencer are the only persons in whom one can have any confidence. Whenever the discussion takes place on the subject of the Continental conduct of the late Government (as I may now term it) I hope you will be able to be in your place. There was no part of our dear and respected friend's conduct on which he conceived himself so well entitled to commendation or any part of it on which he more entirely deserved it."

W. SPENCER STANHOPE to VISCOUNT LOWTHER.

1806, February 4th, Grosvenor Square.—"You may very possibly know more of the new arrangements than I do, but whatever they are they are to take place immediately, as the King has we are told consented to a military Council which I heartily approve. Last night after the payment of Pitt's debts had been carried unanimously, Fox gave notice of a Bill to be passed this day to enable Grenville to hold the office of First Lord of the Treasury with that of Auditor. The last office was given him by Pitt, who never thought of keeping it himself, and the return he makes to his memory is to turn out every man in office who supported him, and instead of acting as the leader of Pitt's friends, and who were so long his own, I fear it is true though hardly credible that he spurns them from him. I met Lord Glastonbury yesterday morning and *entre nous* he says he cannot conceive what his cousin is driving at, that he does not approve at all of his present arrangements, and that he considers Lord Grenville and Lord Spencer to be the only two in the Cabinet that can strictly be held to belong to them. Think of Lord Ellenborough, the first criminal Judge, being of the Cabinet, a   and unprecedented breach of the constitution, and for what is it? That he may have the pleasure of ordering an arraignment for high treason in Council and giving sentence upon it in Court, and so become both judge and party in causes of life and death.

Erskine too is to be Chancellor, and what at this moment appears to me worst of all, Grey is to go to the Admiralty. Is not all this cast of parts like forcing Mrs. Siddons into a comic, and Mrs. Jordan into a tragic character. I feel very differently now from what I did at Cottesmore last week, I then hoped that Lord Grenville would have selected the fittest men for the higher departments from all parties, and by forming a strong and popular Administration, and it cannot be the one without being the other, have afforded the best chance to save the state: as it is, God send us a good deliverance. To go into opposition now would only insure our destruction, but I see no ground for confidence and much for most gloomy prognostic.

I have this moment heard that Lord Grenville wrote a handsome letter to Lord Bathurst to request him to keep the mastership of the Mint, which he peremptorily declined."

GEORGE CANNING TO VISCOUNT LOWTHER.

1806, Sunday, February 9th, Somerset House.—" I think it right to let you know that within a short time after my return home from Charles Street yesterday, the Attorney General (Perceval I mean), and Lord Castlereagh called on me for the express purpose of asking what sentiments I and those who felt with me in respect to Mr. Pitt, entertained, and what part we were inclined to take in the present situation of affairs, and of expressing on their own part and that of those with whom they had acted, an earnest desire that Mr. Pitt's friends of all descriptions should, if possible, come to some general understanding, and concert so far as circumstances may admit a common line of conduct.

It always appears to me so much the best policy, as well as the'fairest mode of acting, to state openly whatever one has in one's mind—when one is called upon to state anything—that I had very little hesitation in confessing to them the extent and nature of the difficulties (such as your Lordship and I had considered them) which seemed to be in the way of any such concert and understanding between two sets of men, who agreeing in the point from which they set out might yet differ widely as to that to which they were to direct their proceedings. I took for granted that we should all agree as to the propriety of beginning with general professions of support to this, or to any Government which his Majesty had been pleased to form, so long as it conducted the affairs of the country upon principles such as we had been accustomed to profess and to uphold, &c., &c. But when the time should come (as it must come) for finding out that departure from those principles which would justify one taking a part against the Government, then I expressed my apprehension that those who had belonged to the Government which Mr. Pitt succeeded, would probably look to Lord Sidmouth's influence with the King as the best means for forming a new administration, and would shape their conduct in the way best calculated to give him support in such an undertaking. Whereas I, and those in whose sentiments I shared certainly considered Lord Grenville as the direct and lawful inheritor of the support of Mr. Pitt's friends, provided he continued to maintain Mr. Pitt's system, and provided he shewed himself disposed to call for our aid. We should therefore look for his separation from his present colleagues as the best chance for the formation either of a new administration (in the event of Lord Grenville's getting the better in the struggle and having a new administration to form) or (in the event of his being obliged to resign) of such an opposition as might afford an effectual protection to the country against a system the reverse of Mr: Pitt's, and a solid resource to the King whenever he might be disposed to avail himself of it.

I was not a little surprised when Lord Castlereagh immediately answered that I had spoken exactly their opinions, and upon my observing that there were others who had been more personally opposed to Lord Grenville and more intimately connected with Lord Sidmouth whose sentiments I imagined must be different, he said that he was authorised to declare on behalf of Lord Hawkesbury that he also agreed in these opinions, and that he was ready to co-operate precisely on the grounds, and for the objects, which I had described.

I then proceeded to mention the second difficulty which your Lordship and I had talked of in the morning—that arising out of questions connected with Lord St. Vincent and his naval administration—I said that the part of the new arrangements which gave most offence to me, and to most others, I believed, who felt as I did about Mr. Pitt, and which at the same time I did conscientiously believe to be most detrimental to the public service, was the revival of the St. Vincent system throughout all the naval departments. It was impossible that many questions should not come before Parliament in which the merits of this system would be necessarily subject of discussion. Mr. Jeffery's motion alone, which no power on earth could keep back, would force such a discussion upon us. Were we like to agree as to the part to be taken in it ? Would the former colleagues and defenders of Lord St. Vincent against Mr. Pitt, take the same part as those who then held and now hold Mr. Pitt's opinions upon the subject ? If not we should split upon the point, perhaps the most personally connected with Mr. Pitt's name, and certainly the best calculated to make impression against the Government.

Lord Castlereagh answered for himself and Lord Hawkesbury that they should have no difficulty in conforming their conduct rather to the opinions of Mr. Pitt, than to any notion of tenderness for their former colleague, Lord St. Vincent, and Perceval said that he would examine the grounds of Jeffery's motion with the utmost impartiality, and if he found them to be as strong as I believed them to be, he certainly should not feel a less strong inclination to give that motion, or any measure of the same sort, his warmest support in the House of Commons. Upon the general character of the new naval arrangements they professed to feel just as we do.

Unquestionably these concessions (for such they are) remove the chief impediments which we thought might be in the way of an union between the two different classes of Mr. Pitt's friends. Whether upon any other ground such an union would be inexpedient, is a point upon which I confess I have not been able fully to make up my own mind since my conversation with your Lordship yesterday. It is a point which I wish to leave open until I shall have had an opportunity of conversing with you again, and I have therefore only agreed, as the result of what passed with Lord Castlereagh and Perceval, that there may safely be a general intimation to different individuals of both classes that an understanding is likely to take place, without specifying of what description or to what extent. Thus much was thought to be absolutely necessary to prevent people from committing themselves at once to the new Government under the notion that there was no alternative open to them. And this will, I trust, be quite sufficient for a week or ten days, by which time I suppose there is a probability of your Lordship's being in town.

[P.S.]—You will observe that the changes go on in a way which shews that they set all interest, even Lord Grenville's, at defiance. W. Pole, Lord Wellesley's brother, and Hammond, Lord Grenville's under-secretary, are among the last dismissals."

The Earl of Westmorland to Viscount Lowther.

[1806], February 14th, London.—"We have had nothing of notice since you left us, and I think rumours have not been very numerous. One that has been in circulation can hardly be true, that Fox has a mind to a trial of another India Bill. I should think he would be very glad to remove the present direction of the India House. Another story is that they mean again to get a draft from the Militia. After the violent manner in which this was opposed last year, they can hardly have the face to propose it, nor would it in truth add any efficient strength as our present object is defence at home, and indeed I think we have force nearly enough. However as they have talked so much they must propose something, and they will look very mean in the first instance to copy what they so abused, and so I cannot believe this. Fox's speech to the electors of Westminster was careful enough, but when he got to the whig club, the cloven foot seemed to shew in his toasts, viz.,— 'The cause of liberty all over the world,' which was always drank as a sentiment of the French revolution."

The Earl of Chatham to Viscount Lowther

1806, February 17th, Dover Street.—"Notwithstanding your kind injunctions to the contrary yet painful as the subject is I cannot resist writing you a few lines as I should be sorry you should learn from any other hand than mine when the last sad ceremony is to take place, and the arrangements made concerning it. The day which I find the Lord Chamberlain has fixed is the 22nd instant. I cannot I assure you find words to express how deeply I feel the sentiments contained in your letter. I can with great truth say that I know the feelings of uninterrupted friendship and affection were most truly and sincerely returned on the part of my poor brother towards you, and nothing can be more gratifying to me than that you as one of the nearest of his friends should attend among the six assistant mourners selected for this painful duty."

George Canning to Viscount Lowther.

1806, February 19th, Somerset House.—"It is a very great satisfaction to me that your Lordship sees the present situation of things, and the motives of objects which ought to govern the conduct of Mr. Pitt's friends in the same light in which I had occasion to represent them in the conversation which I reported to you last week.

Nothing material has taken place since that time, except that I think one finds reason every day to be satisfied that there are a much greater number of individuals than one had imagined, waiting and wishing for an opportunity of concerting and co-operating in some general understanding, while on the other hand the government, but especially the Foxite part of it, are said to spare no pains and no promises to draw people to themselves.

I shall be very glad if when you come to town you can conveniently make such a stay here as would enable you to collect the opinions of that description of persons (mentioned in your letter) who were most nearly attached to Mr. Pitt, out of office, as personal friends or political admirers.

So highly do I rate the importance of such opinions, that I have been from the beginning and am still entirely persuaded that nothing can be done or attempted (even if opportunities the most provokingly favourable were to offer themselves) unless some persons of that description shall consent to lend their names, influence, and character to give weight and consistency to the connexion which we have in view.

I need hardly say that I look to your Lordship (and I am not singular in doing so) as one of the persons the most peculiarly qualified from long known disinterested attachment to Mr. Pitt, from personal weight, and from the very circumstance of never having hitherto taken any active share in party politics—to give that countenance to such a plan, and to take that lead among any combination of Mr. Pitt's friends, which can alone rescue many of us from the obvious imputation of being actuated by no other motive than a desire to scramble for our offices.

It is on this account particularly that I very earnestly wish it may not be inconvenient to you to remain for a short time in London."

George Rose to Viscount Lowther.

[1806, February.]—"From the time the melancholy stroke was inflicted upon us by the loss of Mr. Pitt, I hardly ever went out except to the House of Commons (where I felt it a duty to go) and once to call on you, till I came here to be free from an interruption I felt painful to me. As I found your Lordship was going out of town the morning after I was at your door I did not then make any further attempt to see you, but I shall be very glad if you will allow me to have a little quiet conversation with you on your return.

Avoiding intercourse with persons on the present state of things as much as possible, I have talked with only two friends at all confidentially on the subject, to whom I found it necessary to express myself strongly and freely respecting the course of proceeding at first proposed. The one which seems now to be thought of appears a much more desirable one. My appetite for political concerns is by no means keen, and I stated to the persons before alluded to an earnest wish to know how far Mr. Pitt's friends can have your Lordship's protection and countenance before I commit myself in the remotest degree. It will therefore be a real comfort to me to have an early opportunity of suggesting to your Lordship my view of public matters at present.

A line directed to Old Palace Yard will find me there any time after Wednesday evening, and I will wait on your Lordship at any time on Thursday or Friday."

George Rose to Viscount Lowther.

1806, February 21st, Old Palace Yard.—"Next to an opportunity of seeing you for a quarter of an hour nothing could be so satisfactory as your letter, it has afforded me real comfort, and I shall wait without impatience for an opportunity entirely convenient to yourself to have some conversation with you. My only anxiety has been that nothing should be done hastily or unadvisedly, of which there does not now appear to be the remotest danger. I trust there will be no difficulty in keeping Mr. Pitt's friends together, which I am sure is essential to the public interest. I return to Buckden with the Bishop on Tuesday for a week, after which I shall settle here."

John Stonard to Viscount Lowther.

1806, February 23rd, Chertsey.—"Yesterday, I understand you assisted in committing to their last earthly mansion the mortal remains of the greatest of statesmen and your friend. It was the discharge of a very awful and affecting duty. In the course of the morning I often thought of your Lordship and poor James Stanhope. It must have been to him a most heart-rending day. He parted with his best friend beneath the sun, from his guardian, his father. He may however be sure of all the consolation that sympathy can afford. The whole nation, I may say the whole world, suffers with him, and a great portion of both mourns also. . . . . In Lord Nelson we lost a right hand of the kingdom, but in Mr. Pitt we have lost the acting soul, the presiding reason of the state, that which employed its wealth and directed its force to the best and wisest ends. I think there are marks to [be] discerned of astonishment and terror even among his adversaries. For after all their opposition I suspect they reposed more confidence in him than themselves. They felt that he was made for command. They knew by experience that he was neither to be driven or diverted from his purpose, and they knew that the whole country reposed their firmest trust and their highest hopes in his talents, his integrity and his firmness. Nothing but the fanatical folly of Sir Francis or the diabolical malevolence of Mr. Windham can hesitate to acknowledge and deplore the greatness of our loss. Indeed we cannot yet estimate its total amount. I hope we shall not be made to feel it. Mr. Pitt seemed to have been given by heaven to the nation in order to save it, and he has performed that high office in more instances than one. But we need him still ; we need him more than ever. May God therefore have mercy on us and make his own divine power and protection more evident and more glorious in this our state of weakness. His late servant lived, though not, we fear enough for us, yet enough for himself, for his own fame and happiness. For though his life was short in number of years, yet it was very long, longer than the days of man, in activity and honour. In the welfare of his country he yet lives, and we trust will continue to live. The impression of his mighty hand is fixed indelibly upon it, and let us pray that neither the imprudence of his successors nor the efforts of our enemies may overthrow the fabrick that is thus impressed.

We need not wait I think for history to do him justice.

The present age is every day becoming more sensible of his deserts, and though ' the memorials of his friendships and his enmities have not yet perished,' yet his decease has, except in some few breasts of more atrocious malignity than ordinary, already damped the fiery spirit of party violence and will speedily make us regret that he was not when living valued as he deserved to be. The breath of posthumous admiration will soon swell to its proper note the trump of true glory.

I was truly sorry to learn from your Lordship's letter that Lord Grenville is disposed to show so little attention to the friends of Mr. Pitt. It is I think not more inconsistent with humane and honourable feelings than with sound policy. His Lordship cannot consider Lord Sidmouth as better than a broken reed, and surely he cannot look to Mr. Fox and his party, however connected by present interest, for any sure support in the hour of need, upon motives either of agreement in political principles or of personal attachment. Mr. Pitt's friends were his friends and he ought to be sensible of their value.

Henry conducts himself entirely to my satisfaction. He is certainly improving, and I think is more attentive than he used to be. But patience is absolutely necessary. It must be ' line upon line, precept upon precept.' He agrees vastly well with Drummond. Indeed it would be wonderful if he did [not],£ or they are both as good-tempered lads as ever it was my lot to see."

LORD CAMDEN to VISCOUNT LOWTHER.

1806, February 25th, Arlington Street. —" You will have seen in the newspapers that notice has been given of a motion in each House of Parliament for Monday next by Lord Bristol in the House of Lords and by Spencer Stanhope in the House of Commons. These notices have been given without the slightest communication with any of those who are inclined to take a more moderate line and seem at once to show that it is determined by the new opposition not to wait for events which may call for observation, but to seek for them. That the appointment of Lord Ellenborough to a seat in the Cabinet is a measure I disapprove. I do not deny but to make it the matter of a specific motion strikes me as very unjudicious even to their own views, as the defence of the measure will more closely unite Lords Grenville and Sidmouth, and plausible arguments will be given for this appointment. But the reason of my writing to you is in consequence of the conversation we had, and, as Spencer Stanhope has given notice of the motion, you will probably be supposed to be more eager and more engaged in this sort of measure than by your language to me you seemed inclined to be. You will of course take whatever steps you think right, but I thought it right to give you this intimation as well as to repeat that these notices have been given without any communication with me, the Duke of Montrose, Lord Chatham, Lord Bathurst, Long, and others."

LORD MULGRAVE to VISCOUNT LOWTHER.

1806, February 25th, Harley Street.—" The important object which you have suggested is but a continued proof of the uniform feeling of paternal affection which has marked the whole course of your long and uninterrupted friendship for the great, amiable, and interesting object of our regret. I will lose no time in consulting with Lord Camden and others of his real friends upon the most effectual mode of collecting ample and authentic materials for putting posterity in possession of the solid and extensive ground on which his great reputation rests. It will be still more difficult to fix upon any professed author capable of doing any justice to the subject, but to this also I will turn my enquiries.

It appears to me also desirable to revive the intention of erecting his statue, for the execution of which very large sums were subscribed amongst the many persons who admired and regret him. It appears to me (perhaps erroneously) that there are few who feel the loss of him as an individual as deeply as I do. You are one of those who do as much justice to his merits and to his memory as I can pretend to do. I do not mean by this to impute any neglect of either, to any of his friends, nor do I know how I happened to express the sentiment, except from a feeling that I shall be most happy to co-operate with you at all times in any course which you may feel to be most conducive to the honour of his memory, either with a view to the greatness of his public, or to the faultless excellence of his private character.

Lord Bristol has given notice of a motion on Monday next on the subject of Lord Ellenborough having a seat in the Cabinet. I have not seen his motion nor do I know either the substance or form of it. I doubt much whether any legal or technical imputation can be fixed upon the appointment, or rather upon the summons to Council. The general principles laid down both by Blackstone and Montesquieu certainly militate against it. There is something, however, in objections to the formation of the ministry which may have too much the appearance of regret at not having made a part of the administration, to be a desirable line for those who have withdrawn from the Government, and themselves proposed the formation of a new administration. At the same time it appears to me that when a great constitutional question is brought into discussion, any person who has held an high office in the state and has taken an active part in parliamentary debates ought not to shrink from the discussion or at least from being present at it. There are other branches of the government of which I should be more jealous—though this arrangement may be more calculated to startle the national jealousy upon the unbiased administration of criminal justice. I think the individual in question to be of a coarse and violent disposition, but at the same time I do not entertain any very serious apprehension that he will in fact exercise any extraordinary injustice or tyranny on the Bench in consequence of his seat in the Cabinet. I should therefore have been as well satisfied if nothing had been said about it, unless the conduct of the chief justice at any future period should have rendered it necessary. I feel nevertheless that many strong objections in point of responsibility and coercion in parliament present themselves. It is no unusual thing (and we have indeed a very recent instance) for parliament to address the King to remove a minister of state whom they think culpable as such, from his presence and councils for ever. It is at the same time held by many that a judge cannot be removed from the bench but for his misconduct as a judge, and yet it would be an awkward state of things to have a chief justice sitting in the King's Bench who should have been dismissed from the King's presence and council for ever, for having advised an impolitic peace, or any other ministerial measure which might bring upon him the censure of the Houses of Parliament. If in answer it is said that under such censure of the Houses of Parliament the address would be sufficient to remove him from the bench also. The obvious inconvenience arises of rendering the judge's tenure of his judicial office liable to the fluctuation of political parties. I agree so entirely in the opinion which you stated when I saw you in Charles Street, that systematic opposition to every measure of a government is neither wise nor dignified that I was desirous of touching upon some of the points which occurred to me upon this question which I have not stirred. I conclude you have had a little share in the step taken by your friend Spencer Stanhope, as I have in the course adopted by my cousin, Lord Bristol. The appointment is certainly the more objectionable as they cannot want a common law adviser in the Cabinet if the present Chancellor be good for anything.

I hear rumours of great alterations in the military system of the country. I shall not be disposed to object to any tolerably rational measures and shall content myself with upholding the merit of those already adopted under the influence of the great statesman who proposed them, and with resisting any injurious comparisons which may be attempted between those and such as are to be brought forward to replace them. I have given you a political sermon, little short of the usual length of essays which bear that name, but it is impossible to consider any point relating to Pitt without being led on to other subjects connected with his pursuits and with the course and conduct which he would have approved in those whom he knew to be his friends."

LORD MULGRAVE to VISCOUNT LOWTHER.

1806, March 1st, Harley Street.—" In pursuance of the object of your letter I called upon Rose to enquire what materials he possessed or could procure for the life of Mr. Pitt, he assured me that he had very numerous and important papers relating to the principal points of his public conduct and character, and that the Bishop of Lincoln has much with respect both to his private and public life which will afford a most material and satisfactory addition to what he (Rose) can supply. He mentioned a Mr. Mackenzie as likely both from his talents and warm attachment to our friend to do justice to his memory. He also suggested the Bishop of Lincoln as likely to execute the work with zeal and fidelity. I however expressed to him my doubt of the Bishop giving to the work the necessary brilliancy and animation of style which should distinguish the biography of so illustrious a character, a striking feature of which was that splendour of language which should at least not be neglected in describing him. On the subsequent day Rose informed me that he had received a letter from the Bishop gratuitously stating his own disposition to undertake such a work. This is rather embarrasing as from consulting Lord Camden on the subject he does not seem to entertain any hope of a very spirited history from that quarter, and it is highly important that there should be something in the manner of telling the facts which may keep alive to a late period the desire and pleasure of perusing them. The negociation of the transfer of the materials into other hands if it can be undertaken must be attempted by those who are most intimate with the Bishop.

I have just received your letter of the 28th February. I will enquire of Mr. Angerstein, who was one of the principal promoters of the subscription for the colossal statue, how much money was actually deposited. The subscription certainly was very great and the order for the execution of the statute was only delayed out of consideration to the British inhabitants in India that they might have the opportunity of gratifying their feelings by adding largely to the sums already engaged.

You will see by this day's papers that there is still grace enough in the city to spurn at any illiberal attempt to retract the honours which have been voted to the memory of the national benefactor, the motion for revising the order for this statue in Guildhall has been rejected by a majority of near two to one."

GEORGE ROSE to VISCOUNT LOWTHER.

1806, March 4th, Old Palace Yard.—" My intention of returning to Buckden was defeated, which prevented my receiving your letter till yesterday. The Bishop is gone to Bury for a few days, to whom I have written respecting the wish you expressed, and I am quite confident he will do all in his power towards the gratification of it ; of Lord Chatham being so disposed I need give you no assurance. I think the Bishop mentioned the Princess of Wales having requested to have the bust of the late Lord Chatham, but I do not know whether she had any assurance of it. In any event I am persuaded some way will be found of complying with your anxious wish.

I delayed one post writing to your Lordship in order to communicate to you anything interesting that might pass in either pass (sic), you will however learn nearly all from the newspapers that I could tell you. I had not the remotest idea of a division in the House of Commons, and saw so little appearance of a possibility of it that I actually wrote to some friends to say they need not come to town. You will see that not one half of the House of Commons was present. Of Mr. Pitt's friends, Mr. William Dundas was in the majority, and I think Sir Evan Nepean and one other of the ministers; some absent under the impression I have mentioned, with whom I had no communication, Mr. Cartwright, Sir Henry Mildmay, and others."

JOHN STONARD to VISCOUNT LOWTHER.

1806, March 3rd, Chertsey.—"I received your very obliging letter yesterday morning and perfectly agree with your Lordship that Mr. Pitt's character as a statesman never soared to a higher pitch than it had attained at the moment of his death. A sense of truth and justice has extracted that honourable testimony from the hostile lips of General Tarleton. Even the capture of the Cape, the fruit of his counsels, though an event of great importance and advantage to the country, loses its merit and value by comparison with the so much 'higher glory of that alliance in which his singular wisdom and dexterity had contrived to link together such jarring materials by bonds of particular interest and general good. To form opinions merely by events is the common idolatry of fools. The man who believes and adores the wisdom of the supreme Providence in the production of final good, respects the wisdom by which inferior agents aim at a more immediate improvement of their condition. Their merit he sees lies not in the process but in the sagacity of their plans.

Nothing can be more just than your Lordship's observation upon the necessity of some person immediately undertaking a history of Mr. Pitt's administration and believe me my good lord I feel in full force the very high honour you are pleased to confer in proposing to me to undertake it. But I hope you will allow me a week to deliberate. It will be a work of no common extent and importance. The subject is among the greatest and the noblest that the world can offer to exercise the understanding of man. When I consider what a field it opens to the utmost reach of comprehension, what an exercise of judgment in all its offices, and of taste in various branches it will demand, I am ready almost to blame your Lordship for making me the proposal, and myself for entertaining one thought of accepting it. When I lift up my eyes to the supreme elevation at which Mr. Pitt stood in the scale of human genius, and think of approaching near to scan the lineaments as it were of his greatness and to present to the world the form and figure of his mighty mind, I seem to be repelled by feelings of more than diffidence, of awe rising almost to terror. It seems to me that none but himself could be a worthy historian of his fame.

My friend Hugh Cholmondeley, the new dean of Chester, having been here for a few days, I have consulted him on the subject and he gives his voice for my undertaking the labour. He has just now left me and I have desired him to send down Heber immediately that I may consult him too. Your Lordship will I trust excuse me for having mentioned this matter to these friends as it shall not for the present go any further, and I really wish much for the advice of judicious friends. Your Lordship will permit me also I hope to suggest the propriety of writing not merely a history of Mr. Pitt's administration but of his life, that not only the greatness but the amiableness of his character may be presented to public view. I have reason to think that I can obtain some very interesting anecdotes of his earlier years, which I am sure will be denied to some persons. This is from my friend Cholmondeley."

JOHN STONARD to VISCOUNT LOWTHER.

1806, March 6th, Chertsey.—" From mv answer to your last letter though I requested an interval to deliberate upon the subject of your proposal, yet it must have been pretty evident that I have at least no repugnance to the undertaking proposed. My hesitation arises from nothing but doubts of my own ability to do justice to so exalted a theme, and of my finding leisure for the necessary application to such a laborious task as I conceive it will be. I expect, though not with certainty, my friend Heber to day and I am disposed to yield myself to his direction. Certainly if the work shall be committed to my hands I shall proceed to it *con amore*. My admiration of Mr. Pitt has been from my earliest years and is now as high as any human object can raise it, and I feel not only that high regard for his memory which every true lover of his country ought, but even the nearer ties of personal attachment. Stanhope has informed me that the day before he died Mr. Pitt recommended him to return to me if his military duties would permit. What a heart then must I have if I were not sensible of the value of such a man's approbation at such an hour. I perceive that Lord Mulgrave proposes what I took the liberty of suggesting to your Lordship, a Life of Mr. Pitt. Ever since his death I have thought it highly probable that the Bishop of Lincoln would undertake it, and if he should, I own that I shall entertain the same apprehension with Lord Mulgrave and Lord Camden. Besides in a piece of biography which should include the whole of Mr. Pitt's life, the history of his earlier years would form a most interesting feature. But by far the principal part of the memorials necessary to illustrate these is in the hands of Mrs. Wilson or her family, and I am well assured that the Bishop of Lincoln is the last man in the world to whom they would communicate these materials. The dean of Chester, as I before hinted to your Lordship, has promised to use all the influence he possesses (and I believe that is considerable) to procure everything of this kind in the power of Mrs. Wilson or her family, in case I shall be engaged in this important and honourable employment. This however your Lordship will perceive must be kept a secret from the Bishop, who may perhaps in his turn refuse to communicate to those who may be favoured by the Wilsons. The Bishop of Lincoln I am informed (and your Lordship will know whether I am rightly informed or not) though called Mr. Pitt's tutor, was in fact only his college tutor, *pro formâ*. Mr. Wilson having remained at Cambridge with his illustrious pupil and had the whole and sole care of his education. The Bishop therefore could not have had any intimate connexion with him till he became his private secretary. I might say more to your Lordship on the subject of this life, but I fear lest when I enclose Lord Mulgrave's letter the packet should become over weight. There is one thing however which I much desire, that whoever shall undertake the life, it may not be made or considered as a party work. As such it will never go down to distant posterity. Let those who still retain their former spirit of malevolence to the dead know that his friends are animated by the purer genius of those heavens to which we trust he is gone through the divine mercies, a meritorious and immortal guest."

GEORGE ROSE to VISCOUNT LOWTHER.

1806, March 7th, Old Palace Yard.—" The subject of your letter is, you will easily believe a highly interesting one to me. While I was at Buckden I had repeated conversations with the Bishop upon it,

whose anxiety about it must **also be unquestionable. We talked of**
undertaking the work jointly, but nothing was decided, and are agreed
to delay a final determination till he shall be in town the latter end of
this month. Your Lordship will probably be up also about that time,
when we may have an opportunity of coming to some settlement on the
point. I have no hesitation in saying that I have so much confidence
in your Lordship's judgment that I shall feel entirely disposed to waive
the part I thought of taking, and to give the best aid in my power to
the gentleman you have in view, and I think the Bishop will have as
little hesitation in acquiescing in your suggestion as I have. He had
Mr. Pitt with him as you know from fourteen years of age, or thereabouts, and never quitted him till he left the University, the interval
between that and his coming into office was not a very long one, and
from that time I was not separated from him six weeks in any one
year; both of us in the closest confidence during the periods with the
incomparable creature. I assure you my Lord with perfect sincerity
that so far from feeling in the smallest degree uncomfortable at giving
up the intention (by no means a fixed one) of executing the work in
the whole or in part, it is a real gratification to me that you have
thought of it in the manner you have. I write this in great haste
because I would not lose a post. I may perhaps wish from the intimate
knowledge I have of our late friend's character, to express what I really
had experienced of it in a few pages, which may be adopted or rejected
as shall hereafter be thought right."

The Earl of Essex to Viscount Lowther.

1806, March 10th, Berkeley Square.—"The hope and expectation
of seeing you in London has prevented my writing which I wished to
do with a view of communicating to you most openly the result of my
own reflections and considerations upon all that has been going on *dans
le monde politique*, and though I may be mistaken in my conjectures
yet I feel inclined to think that from all I see and hear there is very
little chance of that degree of unanimity or close connection being kept
up between what was called Mr. Pitt's party which we thought might
be likely to take place, but I fancy amongst that party there are too
many jarring interests and political speculations, and animosity towards
many now in power to make it possible that those who might wish to
hold together could do so with any effect unless it was *sub auspice* of
some one who does not at this moment appear as a leader. It is evident
that Lord Castlereagh and Lord Hawkesbury, and Lord Mulgrave
consider themselves as decided enemies to Fox and Lord Grenville, and
the former I suspect has no small influence over Lord Camden, not the
most decided character in public or private matters. Lord Bathurst I
have always thought very hostile to Fox, personally, and the Duke of
Montrose evidently shews strong marks of discontent, at least he expressed himself so at not being consulted upon Lord Bristol's motion,
whereas he could [not] be so, because Lord Bristol had not even communicated his intentions to Lord Hawkesbury. It was an idea of his own
and I believe he wrote only to Lord Sidmouth on the subject. I therefore think that his private friendship for Lord Grenville will very
shortly outweigh all ideas of scruple, and that the living friend will beat
the departed one hollow. In the House of Commons there are per-
turbed spirits enough, and though Canning and many others of that
description are labouring hard to create an opposition I do not think
they are likely to succeed, as many are inclined to watch the measures

of the present men, but few I believe think it wise or prudent to commence a system of opposing upon all occasions ; as far as related to that question the other day it was evident that no plan was acted upon as ought to have been the case. I was at Windsor on the Saturday as was Charles Long who wished to see the King and whom I knew the King wished also to see, and his sentiments and feelings are such as they ought to be, he is not at all pleased at his present government being opposed whilst they conduct themselves upon principles such as governed their predecessors. He said he was too old to change his principles and was much pleased when Long signified to him that he thought Lord Grenville was of the same opinion, and that he might be sure of not being deserted by him, and he is evidently alarmed at those who now appear inclined to act in opposition, thinking that such conduct may be imputed to secret influence on his part and give rise to mistrust and jealousy on theirs, and it has that effect from a conversation Lord Lauderdale held with Long at the Duchess of Gordon's two nights ago when he expressed his opinion on some act of Lord Sligo's who had given his proxy I believe to Lord Bristol or Lord Hawkesbury. Lord Camden whom I met yesterday again repeated, upon my asking what was to be done should any business come on soon, that we ought to hold back. It is then from these circumstances and others perhaps of a more trifling nature and yet connected with the general system that I allude to, that I feel very anxious to know your sentiments. I have endeavoured, I assure you, to weigh all these matters, divesting myself of every prejudice and of every degree of partiality which is equally (as to individuals) divided between those in and those out of power, and though I sincerely wish that Mr. Pitt's friends had formed a part of the present government, yet I cannot see that the country is likely to suffer any injury from the loss of the abilities of those who were in high situations under Mr. Pitt. To those who were hostile to any idea of junction with Mr. Fox at the last period of Mr. Pitt's coming into power the present administration cannot be agreeable, but were we of that opinion ? I think the contrary. On what grounds then should we abstain at this moment from giving support to those measures which are not in opposition to those rules and principles upon which Mr. Pitt acted ? And in giving our support to those measures are we precluded at any moment when those principles are broken in upon from opposing such measures in the strongest possible manner ? Are we not more likely to shew Lord Grenville that it is to him we look up, by an open support than by absence which may bear the doubtful combination of concurrence or dissatisfaction ? Will he not be more apt to rate his own strength higher from such support ? and thus feel less dependent on Mr. Fox and his party when he knows that he has a strong party of his own that is inclined to rally round him if he should differ in any degree with those he now acts. And I confess I have less expectation of those differences being so near at hand than many others who I know think that such must be the case very shortly ; it may be so, but are we then at all more pledged or less independent than we were before from having given support to the government ? And may it not enter into the calculation of many of those who think themselves as obnoxious to the present leaders of government as they are to those leaders, that if they can keep away certain respectable and independent persons from giving support to the administration it will enable them to take advantage of the events that may take place and so make their own terms by transferring their slaves as the proprietor of one West India plantation does to another. Whilst

Mr. Pitt's friends and supporters had a prospect of being kept really together, and a leader had arisen for that purpose, allegiance to him should have been sworn. No such leader exists, but every one who wishes to be so and knows he cannot, forms his own plan and acts upon it. One stays away, one opposes, and one supports and thus none act together, and I cannot put this more strongly than by saying that on the question of last Monday relating to Lord Ellenborough, when I arrived in town I accidentally met Lord Bathurst who was in pursuit of the Duke of Montrose to tell him that Lord Eldon had been in pursuit of him to express his dissatisfaction that he had not had any communication on this subject. Lord Camden went to Wilderness, and I met Lord Bridgewater a few minutes after (this being 5 o'clock) in Berkeley Square like a dog in a fair who had lost his master, seeking out for some one to direct him to the proper road which he could not find ; and Charles Long, who came to town decided not to vote at all, remained in the house, having previously communicated with those who were supposed to act in concert, and had agreed not to divide but did so as he was shut in and forced to divide. Now my dear Lowther after all this, where is the party ? Where are the persons to whom one is to look on this occasion ? I confess I am bewildered in all these nice and secret schemes, I see one plain way of acting and I wish you may do the same, and I cannot perceive that the taking no part at all amounts to anything short of waiting to take a more decided part whenever events may arise, that may justify subtle and crafty politicians, but cannot nor ought it to influence those who really wish to see this country extricated from its difficulties by the efforts of a united and strong Government. The King is with his Government. Lord Grenville seems to court all parties and some seem averse to accepting those attentions which he offers so constantly, and I suspect as I have before said he feels himself sure of many. You will perhaps say that all this proceeds on my part from having on Saturday partaken of the good things of his table. I did not dare risk writing this the next day, but as the fumes of the Burgundy and champagne are by this time evaporated, and the recollection of the *entrées and entremets* in some measure passed away, I may be considered as rather less interested in any speculations, and which are likely to be done away entirely if you differ from us in opinion, as I shall be more inclined to lean to yours than to adhere to my own, though I think they are not much if at all at variance with Long's, who in a great measure sees things as I do and promised to write to you and tell you all he knew. When have we a chance of seeing you ? "

LORD MULGRAVE to VISCOUNT LOWTHER.

1806, March 10, Harley Street.—" Nothing can be more promising than the style and zeal of Mr. Stonard's letter. I saw Rose yesterday who seems cordially disposed to give every assistance in his power by furnishing important materials for the history. I communicated your views and the letter of Mr. Stonard to Lord Camden, Long and Canning, they are all as well satisfied as I am with the prospect of his success in this important work.

I have called twice at Mr. Angerstein's, but he was not in town, I learn however from Long (who has seen him) that there are seven thousand pounds for the statue which will be sufficient to execute it as it ought to be done.

I know of nothing in the way of news worth telling you."

JOHN STONARD to VISCOUNT LOWTHER.

1806, March 11th, London.—"I came to town yesterday to advise with my friend Heber. He concurs with the Dean of Chester in wishing me to undertake this great task. I therefore commit myself entirely to your Lordship with the highest sense of the honour you do me and the favourable opinion you are pleased to entertain of me. The Dean has seen Mrs. Wilson and she has kindly promised that all the papers in her possession shall be at my service. They are of a very interesting nature indeed and of great extent.

I cannot, however, free my mind from serious apprehensions as to the time and labour that must be bestowed on the work, which I fear will meet with great impediments from the attention due to my two pupils."

CHARLES LONG to VISCOUNT LOWTHER.

1806, March 13th, Hill Street.—"I called upon you the day after I had the pleasure of seeing you here, and have since often wished to have some conversation with you upon our political state. However right it might have been to discuss the question of Lord Ellenborough's appointment, we certainly did not do wisely in dividing upon that question, for it was generally understood that no division was to take place, and in such circumstances a division is always most unwise. It had the effect of attempting to shew the strength of party upon a question which was not of a party nature, and upon which that strength had not been collected, but we seem to have among us the *enragés*, and the *moderés*, I am much disposed to class myself among the latter, and in that character I think there is neither good sense, fairness, nor good policy in attempting anything like opposition unless some measure should be brought forward by the government inconsistent with those principles which we have maintained. Our bond of union at present is the defence of the principles and the protection of the memory of Mr. Pitt, so that it seems to me best to confine ourselves till new events justify another course, but while many of us are agreed that Lord Grenville is the fittest person to be placed at the head of the Government it is surely most inconsistent to go into direct opposition to that Government until it is found that he cannot carry his own measures, or until those measures shall appear to be different from what we have reason to expect.

I heard lately to my great satisfaction that you had proposed Mr. Stonard as a fit person to write the life of Mr. Pitt. I had some thoughts of employing the leisure I shall probably have in this way, but so many jealousies from those who could furnish the necessary information would attach to me that would not to him. And besides from what I have heard of him he would do it so infinitely better in every respect that I was delighted to hear you had suggested him. Rose I understand was anxious the Bishop of Lincoln should do it, but I should hope that is quite out of the question.

I had written so far when Lord Essex called upon me with your letter. It is almost unnecessary for me to say that I coincide very much in your views. I confess myself mortified that Lord Grenville should have preferred in his arrangement Lord Sidmouth &c., to those of Mr. Pitt's friends whose assistance he probably might have obtained. I think it in every point of view most injudicious, and I could not help conveying to him what I felt upon that subject. But however unjust or impolitic I may think this it is no patriotic ground of opposition. Windham is to propose shortly his new military plans, there has been much doubt upon this subject I believe among the ministers, and I really think with all its imperfections he will not produce a better than that which is to be abandoned, and which has lately been productive to the extent of 300 men per week.

I am going into the country on Saturday to stay till after Easter. If we should not otherwise meet I will come up any day and have a *causer* with you when you are settled in town, or perhaps you will take a ride to Bromley Hill where I can give you a bed whenever it may be convenient to you."

John Stonard to Viscount Lowther.

1806, March 16th, Chertsey.—"I was detained in town by business longer than I expected and did not arrive here till Thursday evening when I found your Lordship's letter of the ninth, and this morning brought me that of the 12th. I feel very sensibly my obligations to your Lordship for having mentioned me in such favourable terms to Mr. Rose and others of Mr. Pitt's friends as you must have done to engage their approbation of my undertaking. *Talibus auspicibus nil desperandum est.* Yet I cannot but consider that I have much to read and much to learn before I can begin to enter upon the active part of such a life as Mr. Pitt's. It is not indeed to be expected that his biographer should be able entirely to descry and to comprehend every part of the vast circuit embraced by his sublime and comprehensive genius, if this were necessary I believe his life must remain unwritten. Yet upon the various subjects that such a work will comprise, it will be requisite that the writer should possess some previous knowledge and some capacity to judge, or he will never express himself with elegance, with force, or with perspicuity. I have therefore, let me repeat, a great deal to learn, and some time must elapse before I can be properly qualified even to examine every part of the materials that may come to my hands.

To your Lordship I will freely confess that I think a life of Mr. Pitt by the Bishop of Lincoln and Mr. Rose would not be likely to meet with a favourable reception from the world, and that I think chiefly on Mr. Rose's account. He has been an actor in the scenes he would have to describe and many would be inclined to impute to him not only a partiality for his friend but a desire to vindicate himself. I mention this circumstance because when in town I heard it mentioned that Mr. Canning was a likely person to undertake this subject, but the idea was condemned by several judicious men upon the grounds which I have above stated as objectionable to Mr. Rose's undertaking. At the same time Mr. Rose must not only possess materials of the highest value in letters &c., but from the stores of his own memory and judgment must be able to afford ample instruction and satisfaction to all who are interested in his friend. The aid therefore which he so kindly and liberally offers will be accepted by any biographer with the heartiest thanks. His wish to express what he has experienced of his friend's character will of course meet with the readiest acquiescence, and the pages which he may devote to his labour of love, if from difference of style or any other reason they may be thought likely to appear to less advantage in the body of the work, must certainly afford great assistance to the full delineation of Mr. Pitt's character, and ought to stand whole and unaltered among other important documents in an appendix.

I perceive that I was mistaken about the Bishop of Lincoln, which indeed I discovered while in town. Yet I do understand that Mr. Wilson was Mr. Pitt's tutor for some time after he went to college. But it is very likely that some confusion may have arisen from the circumstance mentioned by your Lordship, that Mr. Pitt did not reside much for two years after he entered at college. Probably Mr. Wilson continued to be his tutor during that time. I am only sorry that the claims of the Bishop and Mr. Wilson to the honour of educating their illustrious pupil should have produced so much ill-will, as I am sure it has. The Bishop must I conceive have it in his power to communicate the most interesting details of Mr. Pitt's private life and private thoughts for the principal part of his life. Cholmondeley has seen several of the papers in Mrs. Wilson's possession. He did not specify, to me any letters of the late Lord Chatham's, but in all probability there are some in her hands. He mentioned to me many letters of Mr Wilson's writing containing most interesting anecdotes of the family. There are also two plays in which the young people wrote the parts they were to take, with many other juvenile compositions of Mr. Pitt. It will be a very curious and most interesting task to trace the progress of such a genius from the first dawn of his faculties to their consummation in manhood. Indeed I am inclined to think that to the majority of readers his private life will be the most attractive part of his history. In that not only is he less known to the public, but his character has no opposition to expect from political enmity, his greatness being reduced, to a standard which common minds can comprehend he becomes as it were accessible and tangible. His lustre though not obscured, assumes a milder cast, as the sun appears to the eye through a fleecy cloud. How far it may be practicable to blend his public and his private life together, or with what propriety and elegance transitions may be made from the one to the other, it is at present impossible to judge. But I think it would give the performance a stiff and formal appearance if they should be always treated under distinct and separate heads. But these things must be reserved for further consideration. Lord Chatham must have a great deal of valuable matter relative to his brother, and I should suppose Lord Melville possesses many important memorials. Mr. Canning probably has something considerable to contribute, and I will write to Lord Frederick Campbell for whatever he may have, as I know his Lordship was on very intimate terms with Mr. Pitt, and I am sure he will grant me anything that I can reasonably request.

Towards the end of this month I conjecture your Lordship and family will be coming to town when I shall hope to have the honour of a little conversation on the subject.

Mr. Windham's malevolence towards the illustrious dead has not (as your Lordship justly conjectured) been of any service to him at Oxford. Several of his votes I know are come over to Heber. Such is the due reward of political enmity carried beyond the precincts of the grave."

The Earl of Chatham to Viscount Lowther.

1806, March 16th. Dover Street.—" I received your very kind letter of the 8th instant on a subject most interesting to my feelings. As yet I have had but few opportunities of talking with any friends on the subject, but as far as I have gone, and the more I have revolved it in my own mind the more I am induced to think that such a work as you allude to, must involve in it many questions (at so early a period) of a most delicate nature and which will therefore require the utmost consideration before any decision can be come to respecting it. This of course leads to some delay, and which will give me the opportunity of talking over the proposal with you in all its different points of view, and which I shall be extremely anxious to do whenever you come to town. I had not heard from the Bishop of Lincoln of any idea of his undertaking the task you allude to. He returns however to town again on the 26th of this month."

The EARL OF ESSEX to VISCOUNT LOWTHER.

1806, March 18th, Berkeley Square.—" I have intended every day to thank you most sincerely for your letter and should have done so had not the gout laid an embargo upon my right foot on Saturday last which however was taken off (that is, the embargo and not the foot) on the following day so as to leave me free from pain and I am now getting quite well though a little weak in the fetlock joint. I dread the return after an attack so short, and wish it may not turn out the blossom of good living only which is to be succeeded by the fruit.

It is impossible for any one to feel more satisfaction than I have derived from the contents of your letter, because every sentiment and intention as to future conduct upon the existing circumstances as they now stand so completely meets my ideas and wishes. If I disagree with you in any part of your letter, and in one I certainly do so most entirely wherein you declare that you do not think yourself fit to be a leader of a party, no one surely could be more properly placed in that situation provided those who formed that party had less ardent minds, more moderation, and above all a greater chance of real unanimity and harmony in their proceedings than at present seems likely to exist. I communicated your sentiments to Long whom I found in the act of writing to you. I am persuaded that the prevailing ideas in his mind are nearly in unison with yours, though perhaps if he did act he would be rather more inclined to oppose than to support, thinking that by keeping away entirely the same end may be accomplished and by means more preferable this could do if a general plan on that subject could be adopted, but as you justly observe, the difficulties that have arisen of keeping Mr. Pitt's friends together is too obviously the result of every day's debate in the House of Commons. Therefore the consequence must be either support or the contrary, it is very well to talk of *moderés* and *enragés*, the former seldom exist, and the latter always do mischief. I think many of our friends have acted hastily by those meetings at dinners which are in direct contradiction to their general language as to moderation and keeping aloof with a view to watch.

Lord Bathurst's dinner last week consisting of Duke of Montrose, Castlereagh, Mulgrave, Hawkesbury, Perceval, Canning, &c., astonished C. Long, as he said he came up for the dinner from Bromley and thought it an even chance that he met Lord Grenville there. I know not what part Lord Camden takes, I think his ideas agree more with ours than others, though Lord Castlereagh will not suffer him to decide otherwise than he wishes. Lord Hertford I am told is very inimical and it is certainly extraordinary that Lord Grenville should suffer all the patronage to go one way which hitherto it has done invariably almost, excepting Lord Stafford who is to be invested next Saturday. The King I hear was on Wednesday peevish and low. Canning, Burne, Rose, Lord Binning, Mildmay, Robert Dundas, and about eight or ten more names are up at White's for dinners every fortnight and yet they say there is no idea of opposition as a system, but the cloven

foot appears in all these measures whatever they may say, and I fear
what I before stated that personal animosity to certain characters is the
leading principle upon which they oppose, and I think not the just or
proper use upon which any respectable opposition should be formed.
No one I am sure ought either to offer unconditional support to Lord
Grenville, or determine to oppose without knowing what the measures
will be, nor can qualified support engage any of Mr. Pitt's old friends to
countenance in the slightest degree any proposition that may tend to
cast the most distant reflection on the memory or conduct of our
departed friend and leader. I wish Lord Sidmouth had not formed any
part of the present Government, but his doing so does not operate so
strongly in my mind as to make me think Lord Grenville may not have
been unavoidably over-ruled in a measure not at all congenial to his
own wishes or intentions ; this act I know is what most affects those
who have so recently lost their places, and I imagine the present return
of winter has made them feel out of office the sharp influence of that
inclemency of political weather which the warmth of office protected
them from. On the whole personal animosity should not regulate political
conduct, it may to a degree influence the mind a little, and will do so,
beyond that no credit will be gained by it. You will know what
measures are likely to come on, and I shall be most anxious to hear
your sentiments respecting them, and still more desirous to regulate
mine accordingly. I know Lord Grenville's anxiety to preserve the
good opinion of Mr. Pitt's friends, and possibly I may betray too great
a degree of faith on this subject after what he has done, by giving too
much credit to those professions and in supposing that under all circumstances he has now no other line to take, and that he looks forward to
having those friends who must be his *really* ones(*sic*) again acting in strict
concert and friendship with him. You shall hear from me whenever I
feel that I can write anything worthy your attention, and I will always
do so most openly and ingenuously, never disguising my sentiments,
which may be the part of a politician, but is not the conduct of an
honest man or a gentleman. I hear Reeves is to be displaced from the
Alien Office, and Perry of the *Morning Chronicle* placed there. Lord
Holland I fancy goes to Berlin, it was offered to Lord St. John, who
refused. In all these touches we see the pencil of Fox, &c., and not a
stroke of Grenville's brush, which ought in fact to cover the canvas.
Why these things are so I know not. Time will develope these
mysteries, violent opposition will not I think do so, perhaps exactly
the contrary. I have bored you enough, my future reveries shall be
shorter. I heard of Sheridan appearing before the Bank Directors to
open his Navy office account, the joke is that they all ran out of the
room carrying away their books and papers, &c.
[P.S.] I hear from Long to day that you do not mean to . . . .
till after Easter. Have mercy upon the 'b——h foxes, I beseech you."

GEORGE CANNING to VISCOUNT LOWTHER.

1806, April 8th, Berkeley Square.—" After the communications with
which I have been honoured by your Lordship of your opinions upon
the state of things which have arisen in politics, and in Parliament
since our irreparable loss at the beginning of the year, I feel it in some
degree necessary, and I trust your Lordship will at least think it not
impertinent in me, to trouble you with a very few lines upon the
present occasion.

"The opening of Mr. Windham's military plan leaves us no longer in doubt that it is the intention of Government to do away with every vestige of Mr. Pitt's system upon that subject, particularly the volunteers, whom it must be the effect of the present measures to discontent, and in a great degree to disband, and still more directly the Additional Force Act, to which Mr. Pitt attached the greatest importance, and to substitute in its room projects, of which (to say the least) the practicability or advantage is very questionable, and perhaps the very experiment of them, in many views, highly inexpedient and hazardous.

"The points upon which—as I understood your Lordship's sentiments, and so far as I have been able to collect those of others of Mr. Pitt's friends—all persons of that description were agreed, were these—1st That whenever a direct attack should be made by the Government upon any system of Mr. Pitt's, resistance should be made to it in Parliament by all those who had looked up to him in his life time, and who considered the defence of his memory as a sacred duty. 2nd. That whenever the Government brought forward any measure of their own manifestly objectionable in principle or dangerous in practice, there should be no delicacy or difficulty about declaring an opinion in Parliament upon that particular measure, and that it would be highly desirable that Mr. Pitt's friends should on any such occasion act together upon an opinion common to them all.

It is the strong feeling and persuasion of those who have taken, or are likely to take part in the House of Commons, and of very many who have never yet shown themselves there, that the second of these cases does arise upon the military plan—that the first of them has arisen, is matter, not of opinion, but of fact.

I apprehend, therefore, that after the holidays an opportunity will be taken, probably not later than the 2nd reading of the Bill for repealing the Additional Force Act, to make a decided stand, and to take the sense of the House of Commons against this demolition of Mr. Pitt's favourite system, a demolition attempted at a moment when it is just beginning to realize his views, and without anything like an adequate substitution for the advantage which it promises to the country.

It is probable, that this struggle may take place on or about Monday the 21st instant.

I have thought it incumbent upon me to make this communication to your Lordship, and in consideration of your distance from town, to make it with as little delay as possible, but without in any degree presuming to anticipate your Lordship's judgment and determination."

WILLIAM WILBERFORCE to VISCOUNT LOWTHER.

1806 Wednesday, May 21st. House of Commons.
Most private.
Your Lordship will have the goodness to consider all this as strictly confidential.

"Every man is open to requests which he cannot well refuse, and which he yet feels a little awkward about granting. This reflection is called forth by a note which I have received this morning from Mr. Brougham, and which after a little consideration I take the liberty of transmitting to you. You probably know the family and character of Mr. Brougham, he is the son of a gentleman, as I have been, told of old family, the proprietor of a seat called Brougham Hall by the river near Penrith, who settled in Edinburgh many years ago, and marrying a near relation of Dr. Robertson the historian, has resided there ever since, and has brought up this son at the Edinburgh University. The latter, the writer of the note, is about 25 or 26 years of age, and a man of very extraordinary talents and qualifications and knowledge for his time of life. He published about two years ago a work on Colonial policy of two vols. 8vo., and though there is much in it on which your Lordship I believe, as well as I myself should not agree with him, yet it is certainly for the years of the writer a wonderful publication. He has written also many of the best pieces in the *Edinburgh Review.* In Edinburgh I understand he was always regarded as the champion of Mr. Pitt's party against a numerous and active host of the partizans of the opposition in the University, and that he was regarded as *inter primos* appeared from his having been chosen as the commander of a large corps of volunteers to consist of the members of the University, which corps, owing to some misunderstanding with Lord Hobart, was never however accepted or embodied. He came up about two years ago to reside in London and entered himself of the Temple as a student of the Law, and having known Lord Henry Petty very well at Edinburgh, he has, I believe, renewed the acquaintance here. I wish (because I think I ought considering that you honoured me so kindly with your friendly regard and confidence) to tell you all I know or even think about him, and therefore I ought to add that I have heard from common fame that he is the author of a pamphlet lately published on the state of the Nation, and though the censures. it passes on the late administration's conduct chiefly respect (I speak from having very hastily and cursorily run over it on its first coming out) the management of foreign (Continental) affairs, in the formation and carrying on of the late Confederacy, yet I cannot but say that the language in which it speaks is not such as one should have expected from any warm admirer of Mr. Pitt. I ought however to do Mr. Brougham the justice to say that having been a good deal abroad last summer but one, he became deeply impressed with a sense of the mismanagement of our affairs on the Continent, and spoke of several of our agents abroad in terms of strong censure. This general opinion was expressed in some letters I had from him myself, and which I shewed to Lord Harrowby then Secretary of State, who had given him very particular letters of recommendation.

I understand from some of his young friends who have belonged to a literary society with him, that he is an extremely good public speaker, and I have rather understood that he has for some time been desirous of coming into Parliament.

He was of material use in a matter in which I was much interested which gave him a claim to a return of civilities on my part, that is the reason of my troubling your Lordship with his note, and I thought that in justice to you I ought to accompany it with all the intelligence I could convey. You will allow for a letter written at the Committee table amid constant distraction of mind from my being obliged to attend to other business at the same time and while liable to incessant interruptions. Lord Muncaster has told me in confidence your Lordship's kind and liberal offer to him, and I think he has judged well in accepting it, if he was not absolutely resolved against entering again at all into public life. That circumstance of course in some degree may seem to supersede the necessity of putting the question to your Lordship. However lest I should seem to act ungratefully to Mr. Brougham in refusing such a request (for I undertake for no more than that) I think it best to transmit his note and you will I trust receive it with your accustomed kindness."

[P.S.]—" I ought to have said that our poor friend who is no more (who as you know as well as I, was unjust to himself by a failure in the common minor attentions of life) was not so civil as he ought to have been to Mr. Brougham, which though he never intimated anything of it to me, I rather suspect wounded his *amour propre*, he having been considered by his Edinburgh friends (some of whom came to reside in London at the same time, and were from the first opposition men) as the advocate of Pitt's party, and therefore being liable to the imputation of not being treated with respect by his own connections. I am quite ashamed of the length of my letter."

[Enclosed with the above.]

HENRY BROUGHAM, junior, to MR. WILBERFORCE.

—— Tuesday, —— Temple.—" You have of course heard of poor Sir M. le Flemming's death. I wish you would do me a favour by asking Lord Lowther the following question, either in writing or personally— ' Supposing Government were to give their warmest and effectual support to a candidate, and that Lord Thanet were to lend his assistance with several others whose personal influence is considerable—and supposing that candidate were personally unobjectionable and a man attached to no party exclusively—would Lord Lowther lend his support to bring him in for Westmoreland, or, bringing in some friend of his own for the county, would he name the Government candidate for one of his boroughs?'

By obtaining an answer to this enquiry you would confer a great obligation on me, as well as on several other friends.

[P.S.]— Should you prefer transmitting the Query in another (manner?) you would confer an equal obligation by simply communicating this note to Lord Lowther."

VISCOUNT LOWTHER to MR. WILBERFORCE (copy).

1806, May 21st, Charles Street.—" Wishing on all occasions to give the fullest and kindest consideration to any matter in which you take an interest, I feel some concern that I am under the necessity of returning to you Mr. Brougham's note without answer or observation.

The subject he has thought proper to introduce to me through your intervention is one which under no circumstances, either from the respect due to the county of Westmoreland or with regard to my own interest in it, can I presume to discuss in the way he proposes."

W. WILBERFORCE to VISCOUNT LOWTHER.

1806, Thursday morning, May 22nd, Palace Yard.—" Excuse my troubling you for a few moments to assure you how much I respect the principles contained in the letter I have just received from you, and the spirit which it breathes. Were I less personally interested for your Lordship than I trust you give me credit for being, I should on public and general grounds rejoice that in your instance great power and influence were likely to be used as they ought to be in a free and enlightened country. So used, power is softened into influence, and while the sphere of influence is extended, it becomes a pleasure to be subject to its effects. Forgive this effusion," &c., &c.

JOHN STONARD to VISCOUNT LOWTHER.

1806, July 24th, Chertsey.—" I had begun an answer to your Lordship's former letter when I was favoured with that of the 19th instant. Henry has written to Charles Street, and if a place can be had in the mail he will set off on Friday, if not, on Saturday, for as I intend going to town with him, if he should not get a place on the former day, he shall sleep at the house of a friend of mine where I intend to be.

Last week I wrote to Lord Melville and directed the letter to Wimbledon, but his Lordship must then have been at Lowther, whither perhaps it has followed him. I will trouble your Lordship with a copy of the principal part of it, as I mentioned that I would do so in my last, though from the little consideration I have hitherto given to the subject, there can be little worthy of notice in it. I am still at a loss to know whether the Bishop of Lincoln has abandoned or perseveres in his design, though I am inclined to think from the steps your Lordship has taken with Lord Melville and Mr. Rose that at least you do not consider his approbation of my undertaking to be requisite. Yet since from his great intimacy with Mr. Pitt, and his office of executor, he must be in possession of many valuable documents and much interesting information, will it be more than politic, if not necessary, ceremony and attention to consult his opinion and request his consent ? If he should not persist in his intention of writing the life he will probably accommodate me with papers, which if he should refuse to do we may conclude that he has determined to proceed, and I suppose your Lordship will hardly wish me to write in opposition to the Bishop.

I am infinitely obliged to Mr. Rose for the generous confidence he would have reposed in me, and to your Lordship for what you must have said to induce that confidence. You will see my Lord from what I have said to Lord Melville that my sentiments upon the subject of delicate papers and transactions are entirely conformable with your own. In relating some events it may perhaps be desirable to trace with some minuteness the secret motives and views of the actors. But still generosity and honour are not to be sacrificed to any consideration, nor can it be wished that the just fame of Mr. Pitt himself should be promoted by a breach of that confidence and delicacy, without which any more than without truth, no private intercourse can subsist between men. Mr. Rose therefore and every other friend of Mr. Pitt, who may indulge me with the loan of private and confidential papers, may be assured that not the least use shall be made of them which either their prudence or honour may forbid. It will certainly be highly desirable to talk the matter over with Mr. Rose on many accounts. His great intimacy with Mr. Pitt, together with his long experience and extensive knowledge of affairs, have given him such a clear and full sight and comprehension of the subject as few others can have attained, and he may also direct me in the readiest way to the acquisition of such materials as he may not himself be possessed of.

A life of Mr. Pitt, it appears to me, should exhibit to the world a full delineation of his character and conduct, both in his political station and private life, equally amiable in the one as great in the other. As a man he has been so much less known than as a statesman, that every information and anecdote that can be collected as to his manners, habits, temper, and opinions on literature, philosophy, and religion, will be not less interesting than they are likely to prove entertaining and instructive. General readers are likely to be most attracted by this part of the work, and they will the more readily admit the claims of splendid talents and illustrious actions, the more sensibly they feel the force of private virtue. They like also to enter into the closets of the great. They hope to see them there divested of extrinsic honours, beings of a less elevated caste and order, accessible and tangible to men of meaner mould. Besides, the fine and exquisite touches of character, which as your Lordship well knows, are lost in the rude bustle of public affairs display themselves to the eye of friendship and tenderness in the hour of domestic retirement and social converse.

Let me however assure you my Lord that I am not like some late biographers, so maddened with the love of anecdote as to be desirous of "drawing from their dread abode" every little flaw and frailty that may have been discernible in the character of the mighty dead. To friends indeed such disclosures may be made without danger, but it would ill become those who revere the memory of Mr. Pitt to hold up the little specks of mortal imperfection to the curiosity and scorn of enemies who seem not to have enough of humanity to recognise even the failings of man. But the private life of Mr. Pitt is not likely to have contained any undue proportion of the alloy of human weakness. Here therefore he may appear divested of his greatness and descended from his elevation without any injury to his fame. A monotonous and affected gravity of deportment may be necessary to support the vain formality of stately dulness, which when it once sinks rises no more, but the lively sallies and the sportive mirth of genius may be pursued and may be related with no other effect than to heighten by their contrast the dignity of its more serious occupations.

Through the interest of my friend the Dean of Chester I have a promise from Mrs. Wilson of some very interesting materials for the history of his most early years, till he went to the University. Much probably may be obtained from his college associates for the time between that period and his first appearance as a public character, while for the relaxations and amusements of his later years, the public must be indebted to your Lordship and other friends who were the chosen companions of his leisure hours.

But the life of Mr. Pitt, consecrated as it was to the good of his country and consolidated with the national history, may be collected in some degree from public journals, parliamentary debates, and other printed sources of information, to the best and most authentic of which I would solicit your Lordship's goodness to direct my attention. From these however the public gain little more than a knowledge of events, the mere consequences of counsels. The motives whence those counsels spring, the reasons on which they are founded, the facilities that may invite to their adeption and the difficulties that may impede their execution, are for the most part unknown to the world, and therefore the general judgment formed of them must often be inadequate to their merits. There are many circumstances too I am aware that act with considerable effect on the minds and on the conduct of statesmen. The nature of the intercourse they maintain with their prince, with foreign ministers, and with one another, their various characters, and their mutual opinions of each other, their different political principles, connections and dependences, their inclinations and aversions, suspicions and jealousies, are necessary to be known previous to the attainment of a full and perfect comprehension of political measures and events. But these are points of high delicacy and secrecy, which the respect justly due to persons of high station and great virtues will in many cases prevent from being disclosed for at least a number of years, if ever. Much of this, I presume, my Lord, you will find applicable to yourself. The high stations you have held and the unreserved communications you must·have had with the King, with your late lamented friend, and other persons of high rank, have doubtless rendered you party and privy to many designs and to many affairs and master of many secret springs of actions, which though they might tend to elucidate the history of Mr. Pitt's administration yet cannot be made public without violating some of the best principles of the mind and best feelings of the heart.

But without the least wish to publish what may be so prudently and honourably concealed the writer of Mr. Pitt's life will indulge the hope of receiving from your Lordship in consideration of your known friendship for that greatest of statesmen, whatever may tend to a full development of his political principles, views, and measures, with whatever may help to explain the characters of his friends and of his adversaries, together with his own private opinion of them and of their proceedings, as far as may be thought consistent with the dictates of justice, honour, and generosity. Perhaps, too, he will be bold enough to expect that communications may he made to him that must. he withheld from the world ; and that not from a motive of vain curiosity, but because he must collect from particular details what he is to give to the public in general terms, and because in order to convey to his readers that degree of satisfaction which it is desirable they should feel, he ought to write with that vigour and decision which can arise from nothing but full conviction in himself.

The matchless powers of Mr. Pitt's eloquence, the support which in the most trying circumstances he often derived and the ascendency in parliament which he acquired from its exertions, as well as the impulse which he thereby gave to the public mind, form a part of his history which the author will be expected to distinguish by a double portion of spirit and accuracy. But it is to be feared however it may be admired, that those stupendous efforts of oratory which 'fulmined' over Europe were perfectly extemporaneous and that what he orally delivered he had never previously committed to writing. Still it is to be hoped that in addition to what may be collected from Parliamentary debates, his friends have preserved in notes some valuable fragments of his noblest speeches, perhaps corrected by himself, part of which possibly your Lordship may have in your possession, and to others may have access. These will be of the highest consequence in taking a critical view of his eloquence and will impart immense value to the work, whether dispersed in proper order through its pages or collected in an appendix at the end.

I do not conceive it possible to submit to your Lordship at present any sketch of the arrangement that must be adopted in this important work. The mode of digesting it by annals or sessions of parliament is indeed easy but dry and uninteresting in the extreme, and the mind of the reader would find it rather a series of annual histories than one continuous whole. Yet a certain *lucidus ordo* must be established and observed, and this is likely to be best attained by fixing on proper epochs for the grand and subordinate divisions of the subject, each of which should comprise the narrative of some considerable event or some great design with the accessory concomitant and consequential circumstances. Some difficulty may be found in determining these points, and considerable variations in the mode of arrangement may be admitted with advantage to the book. But I do not see that anything of this nature can be resolved upon till the materials have been accurately examined and a comprehensive view taken of the whole.

The extent of the work is an object of serious consideration. The most active of lives spent in the most active of stations, in circumstances and times of the greatest variety, importance, and danger, cannot be comprised in a small compass. But as the work is intended to be not a record laid up in dusty archives, but a history to be read, care must be taken that it be not oppressed by its own weight. Mr. Coxe has filled three quarto volumes with his life of Sir Robert Walpole, and it should seem hardly possible to contract that of Mr. Pitt within the limits of four, but should it exceed four, its bulk and its price together will prevent its being generally read. Hence will arise the necessity of exercising a certain rigour in the admission of historical details. It must be remembered that the public are to expect a life of Mr. Pitt, not a history of his times, and therefore while nothing should be excluded that can give light or interest to the subject, nothing should be allowed a place that does not tend to the exaltation of Mr. Pitt's character, to the development of his motives and counsels, the vindication of his measures or the establishment of truth.

A life of Mr. Pitt published under the sanction of his friends, the world will expect to find written in the spirit of zealous attachment to his memory. The warmest and highest expressions of praise and admiration, as every day more clearly shews, will not be so much endured as demanded by the public sentiment itself. At the same time all appearance of the *partium judicem* must be carefully kept down. The suspicion of its being written with party views would turn the tide of prejudice against the work, and would prevent its descending with credit to posterity. Of Mr. Pitt's opponents indeed and of their mode of opposition the honourable calls of truth and justice will require the author to speak with openness and manly decision, but though he may find it difficult to avoid the severe language prompted by indignation he must refrain from all expressions that may be supposed to indicate personal or political malevolence. Long, indeed, ere the publication of the intended life, the great probability seems to be that Mr. Pitt's chief antagonist will be also called to give in a longer account of time far differently spent, and talents far differently employed. That difference will be seen and felt though charity will not dwell upon it.

It can hardly be till after much consideration and many efforts that the author will be able to satisfy himself as to the proper style of his work. But since his object should be to present to the public a portrait of Mr. Pitt, he must be careful not to obscure the features by too gaudy a dress. He must therefore studiously avoid all inflated and affected writing, all incumbrance of ornament and strained attempts at elegance. If he regard the style of them whose eloquence he is to record, he will be correct without elaboration, perspicuous without diffusiveness and nervous without asperity, and if he suffer his feelings to direct his pen, he cannot on suitable occasions fail of attaining grandeur and sublimity.

The above contains everything material in the letter I have addressed to Lord Melville. Your Lordship will see that I have spoken my sentiments freely and at some length on the points that have occurred to me, and though I have not detailed anything that can be called a plan or even a sketch, yet I hope I have expressed with sufficient clearness my general, but very crude and imperfect, ideas of what the life should be, of the materials that may [be] necessary for the undertaking, and of the use that will be made of them. If what I have said be in any degree satisfactory to your Lordship and Lord Melville, it will make me very happy. But I shall be still better pleased to receive from both such suggestions as may turn my mind to those parts of the subject towards which it has not been at all or not sufficiently directed. I have doubtless omitted many important considerations and in particular it has occurred to me that it will be an object of the greatest consequence to detail with all the accuracy and clearness possible the state of the country at the period when the reins of government were happily confided to the hands of Mr. Pitt."

VISCOUNT MELVILLE to VISCOUNT LOWTHER.

[1806], July 25th, Raehills. —"I received the enclosed at Feather-stone and send the perusal of it to your Lordship as the best mode of conveying to you the extent of the difficulties which Mr. Stonard perceives in the execution of the work which his friends are desirous he should undertake. I confess I have always felt the same difficulties as often as I have revolved the subject in my mind, and the letter tends strongly to confirm the doubts I have always entertained as to the possibility of writing such a comprehensive view of Mr. Pitt's life as the world would wish to see before a very considerable time shall elapse. Such a history of his life must in truth be the history of the times in which he lived, and I don't see it possible to execute such a work with any degree of authenticated materials so long as the King lives, and there may be even difficulties existing after that period, if the present apparent heir of the Crown should live to occupy it. To write a mere biography of the education or anecdotes of his early life would be uninteresting and much beneath the dignity of the subject, and besides his public exertions burst forth at so early a period of life little time was left for any other, and in fact except the short intervals of relaxation which he passed among his friends, there was not a day of his life from his first entering into the bustle of the world that was not devoted to the service of his country. I don't recollect amidst the many years in which we lived almost unremittingly together that I ever had a walk or a ride with him that a very considerable part of the time was not occupied in discussions of a public concern, and for the same reason it is that most of the most useful knowledge I possess of his sentiments either as to men or measures does not exist in any written documents, but rests upon my memory and recollection, and must die with myself. What I do possess I shall certainly at my leisure endeavour to collect together, and so far as may be proper leave behind me for future use, but I am positive that even of that a great portion cannot now or perhaps ever be brought before the public, without disclosures of which if alive he would disapprove, and of course a similar restraint must impose itself on those to whom his memory is dear. The result of what I have observed is an opinion that any such history of his life in general as the eager curiosity of the public might wish to peruse cannot with propriety be undertaken at the present moment. There is one view of his conduct as a public man which I think may and ought to be given in order to impress and keep alive on the memory of the present age some of the leading important transactions of his administration. For example, his struggle to preserve the constitution at the time he came first into power, particularly in the contest respecting the India Bill, in which it could be shown that India was completely redeemed from the ruin which was represented as impending over its affairs without having recourse to the violent extremities which his opponents and rivals at that time proposed. A second topic would be his immediate attention to the distracted state of the revenues of the country in which the measure of the sinking fund and its various improvements and consequences could be detailed. Thirdly, the interposition in favour of Holland, the benefits of which to that country were only lost by their folly and supineness in not effectually resisting in conjunction with this country the tyranny and encroaching revolutionary principles of France. Fourthly, the Commercial Treaty with France. Fifthly, the maintenance of the national pride and honour of the country in the contest with Spain respecting Nootka Sound. Sixthly, the noble support given to the constitution and the sovereignty during the King's illness, and all the questions respecting the Regency. Seventhly, the vigour of his exertions which became unremittingly necessary for a tract of years to save the constitution of this country from the revolutionary principles of France. Eighthly, although the last years of his life and administration was a state of war and adverse to the prosperity of the various wise pacific measures with which his public life began, these wars were not of his seeking, they were inevitable and in fact a state of war was perhaps the only one in which it would have been practicable to have adopted the measures necessary for the preservation of the constitution and the internal peace of Great Britain. If other nations failed in preserving the security of their own kingdoms it was owing to their own jealousies, supineness, and imbecility, and not to the want of a powerful support from this country. Our own separate interests never suffered by the wars in which we became necessarily involved, but on the contrary were prosperous and successful in every quarter of the world.

Each of those heads I have alluded to would branch out into various other topics connected with them, and even the general heads I have enumerated would admit of extensive additions. I have only thought it necessary to specify those in illustration of the idea I mean to convey, and your Lordship will observe that a sketch of Mr. Pitt's public life, in which all those topics and eminent services might be detailed with ability and brilliancy, could be compiled without increasing in any material degree the difficulties stated in Mr. Stonard's letter, and in which I have stated that I perfectly participate. They are all public transactions resting on public documents upon which the most forcible and striking features of his public character and the vigour of his mind could be portrayed, and by a connected view of the whole collected together, a just though not an adequate representation of his public services could be given, even to the present age, and tend to keep alive in their memories that veneration for him and the deep sorrow for his loss, which in some of us can only end with our lives.

I should apologize for troubling your Lordship with so long a letter but I have been led into the intrusion by my anxiety to impress upon you what my genuine sentiments are, and which I shall trust to your goodness to convey to Mr. Stonard, as it is unnecessary to trouble him with a similar detail. At your leisure return to me his letter which I have sent under a separate cover. I leave this to-morrow for Melville Castle, and after a few days' residence in the neighbourhood of Edinburgh, I shall proceed to the Highlands."

JOHN STONARD to VISCOUNT LOWTHER.

1806, August 28th, Hodnet Hall, Shrewsbury.— "Your letter reached me at this place three days ago. It was not my intention originally to remain so long a time here, but the wishes of my friends who are rather numerous in the neighbouring county of Chester have induced me to prolong my stay. Next week I shall certainly return home, but as I have some business awaiting me in town I shall not be ready to receive Henry till the close of the week following. I hope this will not be inconvenient to your Lordship or injurious to Henry as he has the benefit of Mr. Brown's instructions.

I had not an opportunity of meeting the Bishop of London before my journey to this place or I would have asked him what he knew of the Bishop of Lincoln's intentions Heber and myself have conversed upon the subject and are disposed to conclude that it will be the best way to suspend all inquiries as to his Lordship's views. If he is really employed in writing he will doubtless be as speedy as possible and will endeavour to silence all competition by communicating his intentions to the public. If not, I have little doubt that I shall be able to learn the truth from the Bishop of London in the course of the winter. If his friend is writing, he is likely to be wary and circumspect on the subject, if not he will probably be open and unreserved.

As I am on the point of setting off for Chester, your Lordship I hope will excuse an abrupt conclusion."

"Negociations with the Grenville Party, 1806."

Earl Bathurst to Viscount Lowther.

1806, June 11th.—" I wrote a no'e to Lord Grenville as soon as I left you, and he desired me to call at four o'clock : On my return from thence I called on you and was very sorry I missed seeing you. He expressed himself very particularly gratified with my intention of *not opposing* this measure, and the ground on which I told him I could alone assign for so doing : viz., my personal good will towards him.

We had some general conversation, in which he wished to impress me with an idea that he was fully convinced of Mr. Fox's sincerity of good faith, as far at least as Mr. Fox was personally concerned, at the same time expressing a very great desire of seeing more of, and having more communication with, Mr. Pitt's friends, who are not embarked in opposition. He told me, and as I understood him not as a secret, that there was no intention, and never was an intention, of an India Bill."

George Rose to Viscount Lowther.

1806, June 15th, Old Palace Yard.—" The communication you had the kindness to make to me yesterday gave me (as I expressed to you) much concern at the moment, which has not lessened on reflection ; and as the subject is deeply interesting to my feelings I trust I shall have your excuse for troubling you with some observations upon it : I am the more desirous of doing so as I have a real anxiety to stand well in the judgment of one so valued by Mr. Pitt as your Lordship was. You know my Lord, as well as any one, the rule of conduct I prescribed to myself on Mr. Pitt's death—left by that deeply lamented event, as much alone in the political world as ever a human being was, I determined to act as I thought Mr. Pitt would have wished me to do if he had been living in a state to prevent his mixing in public affairs.

' 'After his loss I looked to Lord Grenville as the person on whom the King and the country could more safely rest their hope ; under a persuasion that if His Majesty should place him at the head of his

councils, we should have the fairest prospect of good
adopted, and of any that could have a mischievous
avoided. With that impression strong on my mind I gave assurances
both publicly and privately of high personal respect for Lord Grenville.

Having prescribed to myself the line of conduct, and entertaining the
opinion above mentioned, I certainly cannot feel very comfortable in
having it imputed to me that I am actively resisting a measure that Mr.
Pitt would have seen the necessity for and would himself have brought
forward if he had been living. The matters cannot have been properly
explained to Lord Grenville : I oppose the West India Commissioners'
Bill because I know Mr. Pitt would not have taken the same course ;
I am perfectly sure he would not : I say that confidently because his
measure for discovering and punishing abuses in the West Indies
originated with me ; and the whole subject respecting public account-
ants was discussed by us at Cuffnells so lately as in September last,
when further measures were agreed on, not similar exactly to those now
coming forward : his decided opinion, as well as mine, was that frauds
and all breaches of trust committed in the West Indies could only be
detected effectually there ; and that any proceeding here (which in most
instances could be little more than formal) might be conducted by the
Commissioners for auditing the public accounts, whose number he had
recently increased and is now about to be further augmented. With
that view of the subject, his Act was passed in 1801 *for sending Commissioners to the Islands,* followed by another in 1802 to enable the
trying persons here for offences committed out of Great Britain. The
latter was defective in provision not having been made in it for
punishing perjury here that was committed abroad ; for which a remedy
might have been provided in a single clause in a Bill to *continue* Mr.
Pitt's Act : Instead of that however a new Bill was pompously introduced by Lord Henry Petty to *repeal* the former one, with pointed
remarks on the inefficiency of that : In the Preamble of his Lordship's
are two offensive recitals founded on those remarks, but not a new
power in it of the smallest importance for detecting and punishing
frauds : On the contrary, instead of providing that a certain number of
Commissioners *shall be appointed to go to the West Indies,* the new
Bill enacts that a Board of five Commissioners *here* shall be named :
who *may* with the consent of the Treasury send out two of their number—three of course always to remain at home, to do what may be
done just as expeditiously and effectually by the auditors in Somerset
Place, especially with the additions lately made to their strength, with
the further intended increase before mentioned, whose ultimate fiat is
rendered necessary by this Bill as well as by Mr. Pitt's, notwithstanding one of the recitals alluded to.

In addition to these reasons I will fairly own that connecting this
measure with the more general one of Lord Henry Petty for auditing
the public accounts (as applauded in a most marked manner by Mr.
Wickham on his first attendance for some months) with remarks imputing very culpable negligence to the former Government and conveying strong insinuations of losses sustained by the public therefrom, I
felt some anxiety to prevent the House being misled by specious statements, and to protect the memory of Mr. Pitt from suffering in the
public estimation. Your Lordship is I know aware how extensively, in
consequence of Lord Henry's speech, an opinion prevailed of the injury
that had been sustained by gross neglect, (if nothing worse) of Mr.
Pitt, as well as of the hopes that were raised from the promised activity
of his Lordship ; and I am confident *you* will not blame my conduct
in attempting to put the matter in a true point of view.

It is not however merely of repeated attacks on Mr. Pitt's memory, and of insinuations unfavourable to it, that I have to complain ; it is really impossible for any one not present at the discussions to conceive the want of information of the Chancellor of the Exchequer on subjects he brings forward; he insisted on Friday night, in which he was strenuously supported by Mr. Wickham, that the accounts of the Commissary General in the West Indies were retarded by the Bank account not having been brought forward, with which they have no more to do than with the Archbishop of Canterbury's private account, except the drafts being examined as vouchers for the payments made.

Another Bill is now depending in the House of Commons to do away in effect all that I was labouring to accomplish during the whole time I was Vice-President of the Committee for Trade, with Mr. Pitt's entire approbation, and for the success of which he was more than ordinarily solicitous: And there is a third lately sent up to the House of Lords which will undoubtedly be attended with mischievous consequences ; neither of these two called for from any quarter though the first is now sanctioned by the West India Planters ; not one of whom has a greater interest in those colonies proportioned to their whole property than myself and my son, and indeed almost all my nearest connections. Can it therefore my dear Lord be justly imputed to me by any one that I am acting inconsistently with the professions of respect I made for Lord Grenville. I am sure I need not ask you whether I am acting inconsistently with the reverence I have for the memory of our late invaluable friend. Nothing has occurred to abate my respect for Lord Grenville ; in professing which, when I did it, no selfish motive could possibly be suspected, accompanied as it was by a letter I wrote to his Lordship on his coming into office. I have not the remotest ground of complaint of any sort against his Lordship ; I attributed to Lord Henry Petty and to one or two persons about him the sort of attacks that have been made from time to time on Mr. Pitt's measures, which I have endeavoured earnestly though feebly to vindicate.

There are other matters that I should have been desirous of referring to, but this letter is already a much longer one than I meant it should have been when I began it, I could not however compress more narrowly what I wished to put you in possession of clearly and distinctly. Having done that, if an opportunity should offer of your Lordship vindicating me on any future occasion I am satisfied I may safely rely on your good nature for your doing so."

LORD GRENVILLE to VISCOUNT LOWTHER.

1806, June 16, Downing Street.—" I am much obliged to you for the communication of Mr. Rose's letter and if my view of what has passed does not entirely coincide with that in which he sees it, I am at least gratified by the obliging solicitude he expresses on the subject. I have not the smallest claim upon him to act or speak otherwise than as his own mind shall suggest to him. I felt much satisfaction (at the outset of the Government) from the favourable disposition he expressed, and from the grounds on which he rested that disposition. If our measures, and particularly those more immediately under my own direction, have since altered that disposition I may regret the change but I have no right to complain of it.

It would however be unjust to Lord Henry Petty to leave him charged with faults which, if they are such, belong to me nor would it be just to myself to let any of my friends believe that any attack has been intended (or as I think made) against the memory of my oldest and dearest friend.

What would have been Mr. Pitt's measures on the subject it is difficult to discuss, and I can only conjecture them from knowing what their principle would have been. He would most assuredly have done what I have done, that is, have adopted those measures which appeared to him most effectual for pursuing the investigation of abuses and securing the speedy liquidation of public accounts, both of them objects which he had peculiarly at heart.

That the preamble of the West India Bill can be considered injurious to him or his measures, I know not how to conceive. That it was not so intended I have the best reason to know, having drawn it myself, and drawn it as far as I can recollect in the same words in which he and I together have drawn I dare say not less than an hundred preambles to Bills for giving farther efficacy to our own measures.

So as to *repealing* his Bill—when fresh regulations are to be made on any subject it is often more convenient to consolidate the whole into a new Bill than to superadd new matter to the existing law. In all other respects than those of convenience it seems to me perfectly indifferent which is done, and he and I have repeatedly done both in the case of our own measures, sometimes by choice and sometimes by accident.

But can any friend of his believe that if he were now alive he would wish his successors, especially those whom he loved and esteemed to refrain from doing in their time what he had done in his, and following up to the best of their judgment those objects which he partly provided for, but did not live to accomplish.

As to the expediency of the particular regulations proposed in this case opinions may differ. It is even possible (though I think very improbable) that his opinion and mine might have differed. It is more probable that they might have done so on the other questions to which Mr. Rose adverts, those of West India trade, because on that subject there always was between us a shade of difference in our general systems, which we have frequently and confidentially discussed.

But surely there is nothing in any one or all these points which could naturally have led me to expect from any persons whose dispositions had continued favourable to me, an opposition carrying with it so many indications of the most decided hostility.

One word more I must add on the subject of Mr. Wickham, a gentleman well known to be connected with me in a situation of the most intimate confidence, and in habits of very early friendship, and whose conduct in Parliament can not well be assigned as the *cause* of any thing that has passed, since he never has appeared there this session (but once in support of Lord Wellesley) till he was in his absence brought forward by name into public notice, in a manner that seemed to call upon him indispensably to defend himself, and in that defence to defend both Mr. Pitt and me.

You have seen how much trouble you have brought upon yourself by your kindness and friendship towards me. I never meant to complain of a conduct which I had no right to control, and even now if I have entered so much into the subject it has been partly in the hope of satisfying you that the view I had taken of what has passed was neither unfounded nor captious; but much more in order to vindicate myself from an imputation cast on measures which are entirely and immediately my own, and for which I trust Mr. Rose himself will no longer think there is any foundation, that of their being either in intention or in effect contrary to the system which I have uniformly pursued both in public and in private with respect to the character of a person whose memory is naturally as dear to me as it can be to any man now living."

VISCOUNT LOWTHER to LORD GRENVILLE (*Copy*).

1806, June 17th, Charles Street.—"Could I have foreseen the trouble I have occasioned you I should scarcely have ventured to send you Mr. Rose's letter, with the hope, however, that you will forgive this intrusion, I beg to thank you for your kind attention and at the same time to assure you that if Mr. Rose has misconceived Lord Henry Petty's statement either as to the manner or the matter of it, that misconception was not peculiar to himself but was felt I believe by every person who heard him, and has been felt also in the most remote parts of the Kingdom. You will not infer from this that I have the smallest intention of imputing to you the knowledge that any expressions having a tendency to depreciate the character of Mr. Pitt were ever employed by the Chancellor of the Exchequer, but I am satisfied you would have heard them with the same impression they have excited in others who are not disposed to contend with you in anything but in their love and admiration of that much lamented person.

Of Mr. Wickham I have not the slightest knowledge, but I will not disguise from you that he is not considered by those of Mr. Pitt's friends with whom I am most acquainted as particularly inclined to indulge a very favourable consideration of Mr. Pitt's character. With what motive this is conjectured, I really have not the slightest reason to know, having never till within the last few days heard his name mentioned; but as it has been introduced, I should have thought it unfair to you to have withheld from you what I am sorry to find is a prevailing opinion with many persons who stand high in your regard."

GEORGE ROSE to VISCOUNT LOWTHER.

1806, June 26th.—"The accompanying letter was meant to have been left at your house yesterday in the afternoon, in the event of the American Intercourse Bill coming on.

I am sure Lord Grenville must be ignorant of Mr. Wickham saying within two or three weeks after Mr. Pitt's death (in the House of Commons) 'he did not think human credulity could go the length of leading ministers to believe the Austrians could bring forward such a force as Mr. Pitt justified his continental measures upon' and of that gentleman *loudly* applauding Lord Henry Petty's direct suggestions of neglect and gross inattention on the part of Mr. Pitt. I am sure the friends of the latter will think the vindication of his measures may be in better hands than Mr. Wickham's."

CHARLES LONG to VISCOUNT LOWTHER.

1806, July 19th, Bromley Hill.—"If any thing at all interesting had passed and had come to my knowledge you should have heard from me before but as little of any thing of this kind has come to Bromley Hill as to Lowther, and I have very little indeed worth communicating, and a long letter from Lord Essex, who you know is the Prince of Gossips, does not contain a report except that Mrs. Fitzherbert has renounced the errors of Popery and eats meagre no more.

I hear from better authority however that peace is not nearer than when you left us, and ministers complain that upon more than one point Bonaparte after bringing things near to a conclusion changed his mind suddenly. It is said, and I believe with truth, that he insists upon our assent to the sovereignty of Holland being recognised by us in the person of his brother Louis, and that of Naples and Sicily in the person of his brother Joseph, and he is willing upon that to leave us in possession of Malta and the Cape and restore Hanover, he has also I hear talked of our guaranteeing to him, Holland and Naples and Sicily, the latter of which he insists upon if we are to retain Malta, and upon this latter point it is supposed all the demur has taken place, still I think we shall have peace because I believe both parties are anxious to conclude it. Fox has on some days been free from pain, but from what I hear he is not materially better.

The Report respecting the Princess was made to the King on Sunday they are much puzzled what to do in it, the principal evidence is that of Lady Douglas, and from what I hear I believe it is the only one of consequence. I shall write to you whenever I hear any thing more precise upon any of these, or upon any other, points that may interest you."

George Rose to Viscount Lowther.

1806, July 23rd, Old Palace Yard —" I am unwilling to leave London without writing a line to you although I have really nothing interesting to tell you.

You will receive by this post my pamphlet, which records the state of the country when Mr. Pitt came into office, and when this country and the world had the misfortune to lose him; exhibiting the wonderful increase of our commerce, navigation and revenues under his fostering care; in that view the publication is an important one, and should induce future ministers not rashly to pull down the fabric raised by that great man.

I hear of no charges, except Mr. King quitting the Secretaryship of the Treasury, to be succeeded by Mr. Fremantle, Deputy Teller of the Exchequer under the Marquis of Buckingham; a gentlemanlike man but as new to business as a child.

Respecting a dissolution of Parliament I can form no probable conjecture : I am persuaded no decision is yet taken about it, and the inclination of my opinion *now* is that we shall not be turned adrift.

Of Mr. Fox's health I know nothing with any degree of certainty ; but I continue to believe he will never be in business again. I do not indeed meet with anybody who thinks he will."

Earl Camden to Viscount Lowther.

1806, July 23rd, Arlington Street.—" I am here in my way into Wales and set out to-day. The intelligence I have learnt is that Fox is certainly worse, that his ever appearing again as a public man in Parliament is quite out of the question and that it is probably a question of how many months he may live. There has not been the slightest allusion to any wish on Lord Grenville's part to have any union with Mr. Pitt's friends, and I thought from the tone taken on Lord Melville's motion it did not appear likely that there would.

It is imagined that peace is probable, and that the messenger who arrived yesterday, and in consequence of which the prorogation of Parliament was delayed, brought a more peaceful answer from France than has yet been received.

I shall return into this part of the world in about two months."

LORD GRENVILLE to VISCOUNT LOWTHER.

1806, July 23rd, Downing Street.—"I am very sorry that I have been deprived, by your absence from town, of the pleasure of seeing you, as I wished to converse with you again on the subject of the expected vacancy for Lancaster. I find from Lord Douglas that he does not wish to engage himself or Duke Hamilton in any contest there, and that he would, if I understood him right, prefer supporting any proper candidate whom you would recommend so that there might be no danger of seeing that place represented by any person whose character or political principle might be adverse to both your wishes. I feel that in such a case, especially when I am speaking the sentiments of another person, there is some awkwardness in writing, and that a few minutes' conversation might have arranged with great facility what cannot so well be settled or even stated by letter. But if you would have the goodness to mention to me anybody that you think might be a proper candidate on such an occasion, and who would be willing and able to meet the possible expence of a contest, (which however I trust would not be likely to take place) I feel little doubt that Lord Douglas would be disposed to assist him with his interest; and I am very anxious that the matter should be so settled before the vacancy takes place as that the choice may fall upon a person agreeable to you."

CHARLES LONG to VISCOUNT LOWTHER.

1806, August 5th, Bromley Hill.—"It is generally understood that Lord Lauderdale has a few unsettled points to determine and is then to sign the peace, but it is still possible that Bonaparte may again change his mind and undo all that he appears to have agreed to during the negotiation. There is another circumstance which may avert from us a most disadvantageous peace, which is that since Fox has become worse he has made over to Grenville all his papers and has put the state and conduct of the negotiation entirely into his hands—at Paris I know they look upon peace as certain and conceive that Bonaparte is to dictate it. General Abercrombie who is just come from thence says nobody entertains a doubt of it being concluded—and a letter I saw written from thence yesterday mentions Bonaparte as having said that he should celebrate at the same time (in September) the victory of Austerlitz and the peace with England.

The account of Fox in London yesterday was that he had increased in size and had become more lethargic—and that the operation of tapping was to be performed tomorrow. Vaughan I hear despairs, but Pitcairn thinks rather better of his case.

If we have peace of course a dissolution of Parliament will follow; if not the present determination I have reason to think is not to dissolve—and yet without it or without some new arrangement the Treasury Bench will not be the pleasantest seat in the House of Commons next year.

The Report of the Privy Council respecting the Princess, it is now said is not to be made public. The story of her having had a child is now disbelieved even by the Prince's friends and the real father and mother (poor peasants near Blackheath) have been ascertained. The report contains evidence of many acts of indiscretion and levity (perhaps not unfounded); but the lady's answer I understand to all this is that these things are told by persons who had a personal prejudice against her—and that their evidence (and particularly that of Lady Douglas) is the effect of resentment.

The *Committee of Taste* are called upon to prepare inscriptions for the different public monuments which have been or are to be erected. Perhaps Mr. Stonard or some of your friends would give us one for that of our much lamented friend.

I know not whether our news at Bromley Hill is likely to be more authentic than yours at Lowther, but if I hear of anything worth your knowing, from being nearer the scene of action, you shall hear from me."

Lord Grenville to Viscount Lowther.

1806, August 5th, Downing Street.—"I am very sorry to hear that Mr. Morritt has declined offering himself for Lancaster on the expected vacancy. He would have been I think in every respect a most unexceptionable candidate. If any other person occurs to you I will thank you to let me know it, and in the mean time whenever I see Lord Douglas I will endeavour to persuade him to let the matter rest till a proper candidate has been found."

Viscount Melville to Viscount Lowther.

1806, August 17th, Dunira.—"I have received your Lordship's stating the anecdote respecting our political Chief Justice. It is certainly a very striking one unless he can give a satisfactory explanation of it. The more one thinks of it, the more astonished must he be at the absurdity and impropriety of placing Lord Ellenborough in the Cabinet. If it had even been customary to admit other Chief Justices into the Cabinet, the character, temper, and vulgarity, of his Lordship would have afforded good reason for making him an exception from a general rule, but to select a person for the situation against whom there lay so many objections is quite inexplicable.

It cost me a week's time to get from my friends in the neighbourhood of Edinburgh. I have now been here near a fourth night (*sic*), enjoying good health, good weather and good sport, of this last I take a moderate share, but my son and his friends who have encamped on the hills have been very successful, and the weather highly favourable. I hope you have been enjoying yourself in the same way."

Charles Long to Viscount Lowther.

1806, August 24th, Bromley Hill.—"The negotiation is not at an end though the alarm of peace has nearly subsided. Lord Auckland who called here yesterday and who affects to be in the secret tells me that Bonaparte totally changed his mind and receded from his own propositions after he had concluded his peace with Russia—and that Lauderdale had been hitherto trying in vain to bring him back to his original proposals—and yet it is said that no pains were taken to prevent the Russians concluding their separate peace. I hear also from Lord Auckland that though Fox is much better than was expected after the operation, that it is not thought he can again ever venture upon active business, and he intimated that it would be necessary (and that Lord Grenville he had reason to think was satisfied of the necessity) to make proposals to some of the present opposition to strengthen the ranks of Government in the House of Commons in the next session, but as I thought all this was mentioned rather to hear what I had to say than to give me any information, I leave you to put your own construction upon it.

It is generally understood that the Report respecting the Princess is not to be made public—the rumour of her having had a child is totally discredited, but the commissioners after stating the evidence speak of the *irregularity and indecency* of her conduct. These are hard words and I should think she will hardly remain quiet under such a charge unless she has given ground for it.

Lauderdale is supposed to have left Paris yesterday, but the gentle-men at Lloyd's, I hear, take odds that Bonaparte sends for him back before he embarks."

LORD GRENVILLE to VISCOUNT LOWTHER.

1806, September 9th, Downing Street.—" I am very much obliged to you for your letter of the 3rd inst. I fear from the statement which it contains that there is not much hope of procuring a candidate such as would have been to be wished, both for the interest of Government and for the credit of the place.

I should be very much obliged to you for your advice what in these circumstances it might be best to do. Whether the thing must be left to its own course or whether there would be any chance of success for any person of commercial connections either in London or Liverpool supposing any such could be found, who would be disposed to incur the expense of an election now, on any engagement to receive the same support on a dissolution.

I have no particular person of this description in my view, but if you think it worth trying possibly such a person might be found."

CHARLES LONG to VISCOUNT LOWTHER.

1806, September 22nd, Bromley Hill.--" I thought it possible that Fox's death might have changed Lord Grenville's dispositions, and that some overture might have been made to form the administration upon a more extended basis—but I believe no such intention exists, and I just hear that Lord Howick is certainly to be the successor of Mr. Fox at the Foreign Office—and that this is fixed after some attempt on the part of Lord Grenville to appoint his brother. Lord Spencer it is supposed goes to the Admiralty, and T. Grenville to the Home Department. During Fox's illness Lord Grenville I understand communicated through the same channel, and to the same person from whom you before heard of the communication, a readiness to extend the offer which had been before made; but the proposal seemed, as I understood it, to be as indefinite as before, and to refer not to a party but to individuals. It seems therefore at present Lord Grenville's determination to endeavour to go on as he is—those who have the battle to fight in the House of Commons for the Government will certainly not have a very easy time of it, and the bed will not be so full of roses as it has been. The King I believe is heartily fond of his shackles, but we have no head to the party and nobody to advise him to shake them off. Before Parliament meets, which we understand will be the end of October, we must arrange things better than in the last session.

Sheridan I hear still hopes to be forced (?) to represent Westminster."

GEORGE CANNING to VISCOUNT LOWTHER.

1806, September 26th, South Hill.—"I have not hitherto troubled your Lordship upon the subjects on which we conversed before we left town; because there has been no period, till the present, at which I have had any thing precise to communicate, and I have not thought myself at liberty to report, without a distinct object, what has passed between Lord Grenville and myself since that communication which I mentioned to your Lordship and to others in July.

Since that time Lord Grenville has expressed more than once, through the same confidential channel, his wish for a renewal of the connection which formerly subsisted between him and me; and his readiness to find the means of making such an opening for me in office, as would certainly have left to me personally, in that respect, nothing to desire.

Knowing, as you do, my sentiments towards Lord Grenville, you will readily judge in what way my inclination would have led me to meet such a disposition on his part, had I acted upon the impulse of those sentiments alone, without reference to other considerations.

But I declined listening to any separate overture. And Lord Grenville was not prepared, at that time, to give to such an overture any farther extension, than that of some law arrangement which should comprehend (but exactly in what manner was not explained) Perceval and the Master of the Rolls.

In this state things continued till the day before Mr. Fox's death. It had indeed been mutually agreed that any farther discussion should be deferred till after the decision of the two important events then depending—that of Mr. Fox's recovery, and the question of peace with France.

Mr. Fox's death, happening before the negotiation had terminated, was of itself a source of new difficulty. On the one hand, it was hardly to be expected that any man would enter at hazard into a connexion with the Government, while the nature and result of so important (and in the view of those out of office, so questionable) a measure was yet unascertained. And on the other hand this event appears to have made it necessary for Lord Grenville to proceed to the making his arrangements without delay.

Upon that occasion it is but justice to Lord Grenville to say, that I believe he did seriously turn his thoughts to the possibility of comprehending a larger proportion of Mr. Pitt's friends than he had hitherto had in contemplation. But he uniformly avowed the determination of not displacing for that purpose any one of the persons who had come into office with him.

Upon comparing the number of openings which Lord Grenville could have to offer, consistently with this determination, with the number of persons acting with us, who had not put themselves out of question as to office; and with what I had been able to collect of the pretensions and expectations of some of them, and particularly of some of those whom I met at your house in July—it was obvious that any proposal which could be founded on so narrow a basis, must be insufficient for its purpose. And as the whole of Lord Grenville's communications with me on this subject were professedly directed to the single object of ascertaining my opinion as to the probable success of any such overture as he might find himself enabled to make—with the intention (if I should encourage him to believe that it was likely to be accepted) of submitting it for the approbation of his colleagues in office, previously to its being communicated by me to those with whom I was acting, as a distinct and formal proposal; I felt myself bound, in fairness to Lord Grenville, not to give him an opinion more encouraging than I really had reason to entertain. The discussion, therefore, terminated, without ever having assumed the shape of a regular negotiation; but with the expression of a strong wish on my part, that if Lord Grenville should think fit to make any proposal of the sort which he appeared to have had in contemplation, he would do so rather through somebody less personally interested in it than myself and I took the liberty of naming the Duke of Portland as the person who, I thought, would be considered by all parties as the most unexceptionable channel for such a communication.

I have thus given your Lordship an account of a transaction, the result of which I know you will regret.

It is indeed a mortifying circumstance (in our view of the situation of the Government and of the country) that Lord Grenville should, from whatever sense of his actual engagements and obligations, have lost so favourable an opportunity of obtaining that ascendency to his own power and principles in the administration, which we have all along lamented that he has not appeared to possess, and which a connexion with Mr. Pitt's friends would have secured to him. But while I regret this result, I really cannot accuse myself of having in any degree contributed to it, by omitting any thing on my part which could have led to a general or comprehensive arraugement."

Viscount Lowther to Lord Grenville (copy).

1806, October 2nd, Lowther.—"My correspondent at Lancaster has not enabled me to answer your enquiries in the manner I could wish. He seems to think, that unless the probability of a vacancy in the representation of that place was more immediate than it appears at present to be, it would be difficult to form an opinion on the question I stated to him, as to the probable success of a person of commercial connections or of any other respectable man not connected with the place. The Duke of Hamilton having never ceased to express his disapprobation of his son's acceptance of a foreign mission, as well as of his desire to be called to the upper House induces a belief at Lancaster that neither of these events will take place.

I hope I may be excused for taking this opportunity, after condoling with you, which I very sincerely do, on the death of Mr. Fox, to express my sincere regret that your arrangements, in consequence of that event, have been such as to preclude all expectation of your desire to form any connection with the members of the late Government. On every account this circumstance is particularly painful to me. On public grounds it appears to me that the co-operation of all parties at this juncture is as important to the national interests as it was at the time when our ever to be lamented friend formed his last administration—and when he had difficulties to contend with in carrying his own views into execution, which do not present themselves to your Lordship. For private reasons I lament this state of things inasmuch as the greater part of the persons who were connected with the last administration, are those with whom I have acted during almost the whole course of my political life, and who I am sure have no desire to alienate themselves from you, if they saw any disposition on the part of your Lordship to conciliate them.

With many apologies for intruding this subject upon you again."

GEORGE CANNING TO VISCOUNT LOWTHER.

1806, October 7th, South Hill.—" Before I received your Lordship's letter of the 29th of September I had written to you an account of some communications which had taken place between Lord Grenville and myself in the course of the summer, the result of which (as you may well judge from the arrangements which have actually taken place) was not altogether satisfactory ; though the substance and the intention of them was, in the first instance, to me personally as kind and flattering as possible, and with respect to others (between whom and Lord Grenville there subsists less private acquaintance or personal regard) certainly of a conciliatory nature.

This letter you would have received about the time at which you were writing to me, had it not struck me that in giving an account of the result of many detached conversations, it would be satisfactory to myself to be quite sure that I was not mistaken in any material part, and that the general impression which I retained of the transaction was such as the person with whom I had been in direct intercourse admitted to be just. I therefore thought it right to transmit my letter to that person (the same who had been the channel of that communication which I formerly related to your Lordship) and by some accident it has happened that I have not received it back from him. It is even possible that some days may yet elapse before I receive it. In the mean time, it may be quite sufficient to say to your Lordship that when you have that letter you will see that its contents are by no means of a nature to require, or even to justify, any very general communication of them. With respect to myself I do not wish to have the appearance of assuming any extravagant credit for having declined, under the circumstances of the case, to take advantage of any disposition, that might exist, to a separate arrangement. And as to any arrangement on a more comprehensive scale, as all that passed on that subject was in the nature of an amicable and confidential inquiry on the part of Lord Grenville as to what would, or would not in my opinion, be likely to be thought acceptable to those with whom I was acting, but never came to anything like a distinct proposal. I do not think myself at liberty in fairness to Lord Grenville to say more on this part of the subject than may suffice to shew that Lord Grenville entertained a wish to open the way to the making of some such proposal, if he had found that he had the means of making it with a prospect of its being well received.

With regard to the state of things, as we now see them, I entirely agree with your Lordship. And as no option appears to be left as to the course which we have to pursue, I feel it to be a great advantage that while the arrangements which have been made are not of a sort to do away in any quarter with the objections that were felt to the original formation of the Government, the array of the Treasury Bench in the House of Commons has certainly received no alteration that can much embarrass us in our pursuit of the course to which we are driven. The triumvirate of Lord Howick, Tierney, and Whitbread has nothing in it less offensive, though I think it is perhaps less powerful, than the dictatorship of Fox. I should have been sorry, from old habits and personal feelings, that the lead of the House of Commons should have been in T. Grenville's hands. But having taken the Admiralty, which does not leave time for a constant parliamentary attendance, I take for granted that we shall see him very little in the heat of the battle.

I have not heard from any authority when Parliament is likely to meet, certainly not now before the middle of November and how soon after that time I suppose can hardly be yet decided. The decision must probably wait for that of the negotiation at Paris. I have never yet believed in the possibility of peace; and even Lord Lauderdale's unaccountable stay does not shake my incredulity. I hope Morpeth will succeed in blowing the fire faster than Lord Lauderdale has been able to extinguish it. But it seems strange that both operations should be going on at the same time. The course to be taken in Parliament must depend so much upon the issue of the events now passing, that it would be difficult to settle at this moment what are the points most likely, or most fit, to be brought into discussion.

In the event of the continuance of the war, I apprehend it would be our policy, as well as our duty to the country, to give that question the most unqualified support. And I doubt whether it would be desirable in that case, however inviting the opportunity might be, to go back, with a very critical examination, into the errors or mischiefs of the negotiation.

As to a peace, it is utterly impossible that any one should be made in the present circumstances, that would not call for abundant discussion.

In either case, we have Windham just where he was, with some defalcation of absurdity (it may be feared) by the loss of Craufurd, but covered with laurels from the only expedition which he has yet sent forth, that from the Downs against Plymouth.

I am glad to hear so good an account of Lord Melville's health and spirits, though I doubt a little whether it be desirable for him to come forward until some great occasion calls for him. Indeed I have been considering (but as yet with myself only) whether an attempt might not *now* be advantageously made to prepare the way for him, by rescinding the resolutions of the 8th of April. Last session it certainly would have been unwise to try it. But perhaps circumstances are changed. I should like to know how it strikes you."

LORD GRENVILLE to VISCOUNT LOWTHER.

Private and confidential.

1806, October 8th, Downing Street.—"I am not aware of any probable change in those circumstances which are likely to create a vacancy at Lancaster, and I sincerely regret that so much difficulty seems to occur in finding an acceptable candidate there.

You cannot more sensibly oblige me than by the openness with which you have had the goodness to communicate to me the impressions produced on your mind by the late arrangements. It is precisely on that footing of open and unreserved communication that I wish to be allowed to cultivate and maintain your friendship.

If I had the advantage of conversing with you in that manner on the circumstances which led to that form of arrangement, I am very sure I could have little difficulty in satisfying your mind that instead of wishing to exclude the persons whom you describe I was anxiously desirous to admit, and even to induce them, to take a part in those arrangements. And that the exclusion, as far as it is such, can be attributed only to their having formed themselves into a body for the purpose of maintaining pretensions so extensive as not to admit of any possibility of their being satisfied without my being guilty of the most dishonourable conduct towards those with whom I am actually joined in office, and who having been placed there at my own re-commendation I never could consent to remove from their situations without their having given me any cause to do so.

I do not ask how far the pretensions to which I refer were reason-able in themselves. I am ready to do the fullest justice to the abilities and characters of persons whom I had much rather consider as friends than as opponents, all I contend for is that no man of honour placed in my situation could have done that which was required from me as an indispensable condition and price of their friendship.

It is difficult to write at all on these subjects, and still more to do it in reference to communications which are in their own nature confidential. But let me beg of you that I may not suffer in your good opinion on this account until I have the opportunity of speaking to you freely upon it."

CHARLES LONG to VISCOUNT LOWTHER.

1806, October 14th, Bromley Hill.—"I am anxious to communicate to you what I have this moment learnt, and from a quarter on which I can rely, that it is the intention of the Government to dissolve the Par-liament at the end of the present month ; lest it should expose my friend who gives me the information (and who seems very anxious upon this point), I have only to request that you will not mention that you heard this from me.

You ask what I think we should do at this meeting, the circum-stance above mentioned may possibly vary what might otherwise be determined upon, but at all events the first thing to be determined upon, is to have some head to the party without which we shall soon be no party at all. I have understood that previous to the late new arrangements the same proposition, and through the same channel of which we heard at your house was renewed but upon a more extended scale—the answer I believe was that nothing could be listened to unless the proposition was made to the *party*. I have reason to think (though I do not know it positively) that Lord Grenville's observation was, that there was no person who could treat for the party ; though I do not believe he showed any readiness to do so, if there had had been such a person, but the necessity of some leader is quite evident. You probably know that Lord Melville has been very ill, his secretary writes to me that he had had a bilious fever for twelve days and does not say that he was better ; previous to his illness he wrote to me and gave me what he called his political creed, in which I very much agree—he says (upon Fox's death) that it will be in vain to attempt to force out the Government while it is upheld by the King and supported by the heir apparent, but that the former has the power of forming a more respectable Government than the present if he chooses so to do. This I think too, but before he attempts it he ought to try what could be done by a union of parties, for war is now certain, the diffi-culties will be great, and every energy and all the ability of the country should be exerted. How Lord Grenville, who would not join Pitt without Fox because it would be a Government of exclusion when the country required a union of parties, can now justify the exclusion of the most respectable party in the country, is beyond any ingenuity I possess to conceive.

I returned from Suffolk, last from Rendlesham two days ago where I had most excellent sport, I hope the mountains have afforded you the same in Cumberland."

CHARLES LONG to VISCOUNT LOWTHER.

1806, October 15th, Bromley Hill.—"I wrote to you yesterday and had little more to add when I closed my letter that I might not be too late for the post, what I mentioned to you is again confirmed by letters I have received this morning—it was decided upon at the Cabinet on Monday, and I hear the proclamation for the dissolution is to be out in the course of a fortnight.

Lord Spencer has I hear been prevailed upon whenever Lord Grey dies to return to the Admiralty, and T. Grenville is to take the Home Department and to have the management of the House of Commons, but unless the Government get some able speakers in a new Parliament, I do not think all this promises very powerful and triumphant debate on the part of the administration in the House of Commons.

The Duke of York has some letters mentioning further successes of the British in Calabria, which he believes to be authentic, and I hear also there are letters from Vienna which state that on account of a formidable insurrection at Naples King Joseph had retired to Florence.

I do not know whether the Royal journey which was supposed in some degree to be a canvassing one has had any great effect, but it is supposed to have had great influence upon the politics of the noble possessor of Ragley. I do not hear that any progress was made in any other quarter."

GEORGE ROSE to VISCOUNT LOWTHER.

1806, October 15th, Christchurch.—"It is hardly within the remotest probability that you should not hear of the certainty of a dissolution of Parliament in the course of this month, before you learn it through me; but I am not willing there should be a possibility of your being ignorant of anything that I can be useful in communicating. The account came to Cuffnells yesterday from a quarter I can perfectly rely on, but happening to be here I have only just received it The measure at this moment is utterly unaccountable to me; not having taken place at the close of the harvest I persuaded myself it was given up for this year at least; it is not conceivable that anything can have happened in the interval to account for the proceeding; the breaking off the negotiation, however popular, cannot obtain much credit for ministers, as Lord Lauderdale remained at Paris till he was actually *sent off* by the French Government.

There have been further negotiations through Canning, but they were not of a nature or rather did not open such a prospect as he thought would justify him in making any communication of particulars to friends on the subject. Lord Grenville therefore strengthened himself with Mr. Bragge Bathurst and Mr. Tierney.

We are hard pressed in this county to meet the expense of protecting Mr. Chute again t a proscription for no assignable or possible cause but his consistency in supporting some measures of Mr. Pitt's, which induced me to write a begging letter yesterday to Lord Camden; we are raising *all we can* within the county, but without contributions of good and loyal subjects without it I fear we shall not be able to save him. However the matter may be explained it is a plain, positive and direct attack on the part of Government; threats and persuasions are most abundantly held out in a manner unexampled, from all Departments. Without presuming to entertain an expectation that your Lordship can think of anything but immediate claims upon you (which I am persuaded are sufficiently numerous) I trust you will have the goodness my merely mentioning (*sic*) our anxious and unprotected state."

George Canning to Viscount Lowther.

1806, October 15th, South Hill.—" I am infinitely obliged to you for the communication of the letter, which you have had the goodness to send me, and which I have read with a surprise, in which I think you will share, when you are in possession of my statement of what has passed between Lord Grenville and me this summer.

The cause of your not being yet in possession of that statement is solely the desire which I have felt to make it as accurate as possible. In pursuance of this object I had sent it, as I mentioned when I last wrote to your Lordship, to the person through whom the communications with Lord Grenville had passed. He returned it to me with a variety of observations, the main (and laudable) tendency of which was to remove or soften every thing that might look like asperity, though there was, as I need hardly say, nothing intentional of that sort, or that by any possible misconstruction might create ill blood among our friends, and especially to sink altogether all mention of individual claims and pretensions on either side. All these observations I cheerfully adopted, and returned the letter altered in conformity to them. So altered, it was pronounced to be correct and unexceptionable in every part, and as such was returned to me this day sen'night, but with an intimation that it had not been shewn to Lord Grenville and a desire that if I thought it fit that Lord Grenville should see it, I would return it again. I did so. I sent it back as well the original as the corrected copy, and with it the observations, in compliance with which the corrections had been made on Thursday last. The person to whom I sent it was then in London. I am of course in daily expectation of receiving it from him again, after having been submitted to Lord Grenville. And the moment that it reaches me I will forward it to you.

But you may form some conjecture from what I have now said, as to what my surprise must have been, to find that while I have been, from the 26th of September (for that is the date of my letter to you) to this time, delaying the communication of my statement of the transaction, in order to make it as exactly as possible comformible to the views of Lord Grenville and his mediator, Lord Grenville has not thought himself precluded on his part from such a statement as that which you have transmitted to me, a statement which puts prominently forward the very topic, which, at the earnest desire of the person employed by him, I had consented to keep back as unnecessary to the giving a fair view of the general character and substance of the transaction, and as liable to create unpleasant feelings on both sides.

Undoubtedly Lord Grenville cannot have seen my letter to your Lordship, or his friend's observations upon it, when he wrote that letter which I have now before me. But I should have thought, and I did think, that in those observations the person who made them spoke, and knew he was speaking, Lord Grenville's wishes and sentiments. And as the whole communication between us was understood to be carried on in the strictest confidence we had either of us an unquestionable right to say how much of it was to ·be disclosed· (beyond the general result, which practically discloses itself) to · the friends of either· ·party. · But then, whatever one of us stipulated with the other not to make public, he who exacted the stipulation was surely bound to adhere to it on his own part.

This transaction, like all others in which the names of individuals have of necessity been introduced, is capable of being represented to those individuals in either of two ways (without deviating from the truth in either) ; in a way to conciliate, by stating what would have been granted, or in a way to alienate, by dwelling upon what would have been refused them. My sincere wish is that if the discussion has done no great good, it should at least have done as little mischief as possible.. But with this view, and if Lord Grenville shares in this wish (as I have hitherto understood him to do) it will certainly be necessary that any communication to be made by either of us to our friends should be rather in the tone of that letter of mine which your Lordship is to receive (and which it would be only useless and troublesome to anticipate) than in that of Lord Grenville's letter to you.

It is as Lord Grenville says ' very difficult to write upon this subject at all, and still more to do it in reference to communications which are in their own nature confidential,' but this difficulty is increased tenfold, whether for written or verbal communication, if the rule laid down by mutual agreement for the extent of the communication to be made by one party is to be at pleasure transgressed by the other.

I will therefore not attempt to enter into any further explanation now, nor until I receive back my so much considered and commented letter with Lord Grenville's additional observations, which I think I can not fail to do in a day or two. I keep Lord Grenville's letter for this short time in order that I may compare the two statements, but you may depend upon my keeping it in the confidence in which your Lordship is so good as · to intrust it to me ; and returning it faithfully with my other letter.

I must just add, for fear of the possibility of a misconception on that point, that nothing that passed in any part of the transaction was, or could be, felt, or could by any mistake be represented, as otherwise than perfectly cordial, and friendly between Lord Grenville and myself personally, nothing on his part but what was flattering to me and kind in the highest degree, nothing on my part towards him but what I hope carried my sense of those dispositions, and my wish that circumstances *on both sides* had not rendered them, for the present, unavailing. Where we have differed it has been with reference to those with whom we are respectively connected. Could any thing be less judicious than to let those persons know precisely on what points with respect to them those differences have turned? I should think not. And why is *my* connection with others to be represented as the *only* impediment, when *his* is at the same time avowed to be *indissoluble in all its parts?* "

LORD GRENVILLE to ——— (*copy*).

1806, October 16th, Downing Street.—" I return the papers you sent me, they afford ample proofs of the fairness of the intention with which Canning's letter has been drawn, and it is impossible for me not to feel highly gratified by his expressions of personal kindness towards myself, which indeed I never doubted and which are met on my part by feelings perfectly reciprocal. I also concur entirely with him in the propriety, for his sake as well as for my own, of our being enabled to make to our respective friends some statement on this subject. I have indeed already had occasion to say something on the subject to the very person to whom Canning's letter is addressed. In answer to some observations of his I felt myself at liberty to say that I had had the means of ascertaining that the persons with whom he wished to see me connected had determined not to treat for that purpose but as a body, and to maintain pretentions which (whether reasonable or not in themselves) were inconsistent with what I felt I owed as a man of honour to those whom I myself had so recently recommended to the stations they now hold in Government.

This is the substance, and [I] believe not far from the words which I used, and I confess I think it is only in some such short statement of the leading facts that the respective parties to such a transaction can ever be brought to concur. I cannot but agree with you that the draft of Canning's letter, even as now amended, is much too long, and too detailed for such a purpose. In a narrative of that length and particularity no man can avoid that species of colouring which every one naturally gives in telling his own story, and which would be found to be perfectly different on two such representations of facts precisely the same. The slightest change of the turn of an expression will as you well know lead to different inferences in matters of so much delicacy. And in guarding the impression of my conduct, as I endeavoured to guard my conduct itself, against the two extremes of which I am liable to be suspected by different persons of too great or too little facility, on this occasion I never could concur in and adopt a representation of the details drawn by a person who probably does not feel exactly as I do, as to all the motives which regulated my decision. In such cases I cannot but think that the leading facts are those which can alone be stated by the common consent of both parties; and that the rest must be left to the fairness and mutual good faith of persons honourably and kindly disposed to each other, and who certainly have no intention to misrepresent the particulars.

In this view I think our joint statement might be shortly thus—

1. That nothing passed on either side but with reference to communications to be subsequently made to the respective friends of each, as the proper foundation of any distinct and regular discussion or treaty.

2. That Lord Grenville and Mr. Cruntnelly expressed a desire that circumstances might lead to a renewal of their former connection.

3. That Mr. Cruntnelly described himself as bound by engagements which prevented him from acting otherwise than in concurrence with the body of the opposition, whom he also described as bound by similar engagements to each other.

4. And that it appeared almost immediately that the pretensions of that body were such as could not be satisfied by such facilities as Lord Grenville was likely to find himself enabled to furnish from actual or probable openings, but would require a departure from the determination which he uniformly avowed of not forcibly displacing for that purpose any of the persons who had come into office with him. And that on this ground the whole terminated without ever having assumed the shape of a regular negotiation.

This of course (if anything like it be adopted as a joint statement) will not preclude either Canning or myself from stating our own views and impressions as to minute details—but these will be stated as our own, and consequently by just and reasoning minds will be received as such.

Had a more particular statement by common consent appeared to me necessary or proper I should have had to thank you much for your observations in all which I concur thinking some of them also extremely material, particularly those which relate to Windham and Lord Melville.

I should indeed be sorry to be thought to have admitted a discussion of which Windham's removal formed a part; nor could I acknowledge what was said about Lord Melville to be in any degree a just representation of my sentiments.

Nothing of course can now be said as to future intentions, but speaking of the past, even up to this very moment, I must say that if there be one individual in this country to whom I conceive myself to have shown the *greatest kindness*, and that too with much embarrassment and difficulty to myself, that individual is Lord Melville.

I also think it most essential, that all that passed on my part should be clearly stated as having had reference to future communication, and concert with my friends, before it could assume a binding form. I have no pretensions to be (as is stated) the *master* of the Government I act with, the station I do hold was, as you know, forced upon me by them against my wishes, and I have no desire to carry its pretensions at all higher than necessity requires; much less could I think of acting in such a matter as this, without full communication with them, and a determination not only to ask their advice, but to abide by it as far as a man can honestly sacrifice his own judgment to that of others."

George Canning to Viscount Lowther.

(*Most private.*)

1806, October 17th, South Hill.—"To my great surprise I have not yet received back, from the person to whom I sent it for the purpose of being communicated to Lord Grenville, that letter to your Lordship which has been so long due to you. It cannot, I should think, be withheld much longer. But I feel that I have already detained too long that letter of Lord Grenville which you had the goodness to send me, and which I kept back to compare it with the observations which I may probably receive with mine when returned to me. And tomorrow not being a post day, I think it absolutely necessary to return it to you to day. I keep, however, an extract of the two or three material passages; pledging my word of honour to you that I will destroy that extract, as soon as I have had an opportunity of comparing it—and will preserve it in the mean time as sacredly as I have the original.

I have marked with pencil two passages in Lord Grenville's letter which appear to me peculiarly inaccurate, I think I may say *unfair*. I do not know precisely *who* are included in the description of the words '*the persons whom you describe.*' But if the word ' persons' is indeed to be taken in the plural number, it is itself inaccurate for the ' desire' and ' inducement' mentioned by Lord Grenville were expressed, and related (in the first instance) to *myself alone*. Afterwards a disposition *was* expressed to make a Law arrangement to include Perceval and Sir W. Grant—though how Sir W. Grant was to be bettered in *his* condition *except by the Great Seal* (which was never hinted at) I think would be difficult to explain. And this was the utmost extent to which there ever appeared to be the smallest desire or intention to go—until the very day before Fox's death—when, for the first time, a willingness was expressed to take into consideration the ' pretensions' of other persons;

and they were found (as must naturally have been expected) on a first view, too numerous to be satisfied, consistently with the adherence to Lord Grenville's determination 'not to remove' any person 'actually joined with him in Office.'

But surely there is no more ground for saying that 'the persons described by you had *formed* themselves into a body *for the purpose* of maintaining pretensions, &c.' than there would be for my asserting of Lord Grenville that he had connected himself with his colleagues in Office *for the purpose* of resisting those pretensions. His connexions, and ours, are equally the result of the circumstances in which we are respectively placed—and there are undoubtedly difficulties arising out of them, with respect to any arrangement, which can only be gotten the better of by mutual concession.

Had there been time for a reference, and had I been furnished with any such proposal on Lord Grenville's part as I could lay before the body of our friends, possibly the pretensions which I could not but bring forward in the first instance might have been considerably reduced—provided there had appeared on the other side a disposition to recede in some degree from the strictness of the rule of 'moving nobody.' Possibly I might think, myself, that those 'pretensions' (as stated at your house in July) were capable of being lowered, without disparagement to the body or to individuals ; but I could not possibly undertake beforehand that they should be lowered to such a degree as to come within the limits which Lord Grenville had prescribed. And still less could I undertake for this, or for any thing like it, without communication with those concerned, from which communication I was precluded not only by want of time, but by a distinct understanding that all that passed between us on the subject of other person's pretensions was not to be taken as '*a proposal* to the body' nor was it to be communicated, unless I could in some degree undertake that it should be found acceptable. Accordingly I have not to this hour communicated it to any one of them—excepting to Perceval so much as related personally to himself, which being in every respect flattering to him, could do no harm.

Lord Grenville therefore is certainly not warranted in the implication, conveyed in the words which I have marked, that his good dispositions were foiled only by the extravagant pretensions of the body of Mr. Pitt's friends.

The second passage, which I have pencilled, I really do not distinctly understand. I am not aware of any 'indispensable condition' that was attempted to be prescribed to him. Unquestionably the finding offices for some who have them not *implies* the necessity of making room, but how the room was to be made was Lord Grenville's business. And though in talking this matter over amicably and confidentially I may (for it is possible I may) have pointed out different openings and facilities which I saw, or thought I saw, it in his power to contrive—though I may even have mentioned one or two, but one in particular which would be of itself not only a facility in arrangement, but a means of conciliation (I have no scruple in saying what I meant—the removal of Windham from his present office), yet neither this nor any other suggestion respecting individuals was pressed, or stated as a 'condition,' or was talked of in any other way than as half a dozen other names and things may have been mentioned between us, with remarks which, though perfectly harmless in intention, it would certainly be a violation of confidence to report. But what makes this part of Lord Grenville's letter more extraordinary is, that I had in the original draft of *my* letter to you (of the 26th September) made particular mention of this suggestion of mine respecting Windham—and I have since *struck it out* at the express desire of the person with whom the whole transaction passed—as tending to bring individual pretensions and points of honour into question unnecessarily. And yet it must be to this, if to any thing specific, that Lord Grenville's observation alludes—for I protest I recollect nothing else that bore the most distant resemblance to a desire of having ' that done which Lord Grenville could not do as a man of honour.' You will observe too that even on this subject, and in this confidential way, the utmost extent of my suggestion was *not* a removal of Windham from office altogether, but a change from that particular office in which all the world agrees as to the expediency of a change.

I could not return Lord Grenville's letter without remarking upon these most prominent points of difference between us; but I must again refer you to my letter which you *are* to receive, for my statement of the substance of the whole transaction."

CHARLES LONG to VISCOUNT LOWTHER.

1806, October 20th, 31, Hill Street.—" I write chiefly to say that as I shall be in town or within ten miles of it if I can be of any service I beg you will command me. I confess I wish you were in this part of the world, because it seems to me that the present state of things requires a meeting of those who think alike to determine what steps are to be taken—such a meeting must at all events take place before the Parliament assembles. It is understood that the Proclamation for the dissolution will be out Friday or Saturday next. I did not know till to-day precisely what had taken place respecting the proposition from Lord Grenville which I before referred to—not having seen Canning during the recess till within this half hour, and I understand he writes to you by this post detailing the whole of it."

VISCOUNT MELVILLE to VISCOUNT LOWTHER.

1806, October 20th, Dunira.—" I received yours and also the Duke of Portland's information as to the dissolution of Parliament two days ago, and I have made the proper use of them. I have been so unwell for these three weeks past I am not in a very good state to encounter the bustle of a new election, and on account of my own immediate interests and friends I have no occasion to be at any trouble, but I propose going to Edinburgh for a fortnight in order to be at hand to aid and advise our friends who may stand in need of my advice and assistance.

At the same time that I thank your Lordship for the communication of the intended measure, I cannot refrain from expressing the sincere concern I feel that His Majesty should have been induced by any consideration to listen to those who counselled him to adopt such a measure. To save myself the trouble of more writing than necessary, I send you enclosed a copy of my answer to the Duke of Portland which contains my genuine sentiments on that subject."

(*Enclosure.*)

VISCOUNT MELVILLE to the DUKE of PORTLAND.

1806, October 19th, Dunira.—" I received your Grace's letter last night, together with several others giving me the same information, I sincerely regret it, not from any personal injury it can do to any political interest of mine—for it can do none—but upon serious public grounds. I have, from its formation, considered a Government formed by a sturdy faction, acting under the auspices of the apparent heir of the crown against the wishes and influence of the legitimate sovereign on the throne, as placing the monarchy of the country in a more disgraceful and dangerous predicament than any other circumstances could have done. Of course I felt a deep anxiety that such an attempt should not be crowned with permanent success. On these grounds I have for many months rejoiced at the conviction that the King had it in his power to get rid of such an administration, and to form another perfectly adequate to the service of the country, and which would, both in its original construction and its subsequent conduct, maintain the dignity of the crown and the personal independence of the existing sovereign, and would, above all, protect him against the intrigues of his own family. The only difficulty which seemed to stand in the way was a pending negotiation. That being at an end, I was sanguine that His Majesty would be relieved from all embarrassments in acting agreeably to what I conceived to be equally his wishes and his interest. A dissolution of Parliament was certainly not the measure which under those impressions I either wished or expected. I always fixed my eye on that point as the standard by which I should judge, how far the King was in truth his own master or how far he was either gained or subdued by his present servants who had seized on the reins of Government in so inauspicious a manner. Deeply impressed with these sentiments, your Grace will be enabled to judge how sincerely I lament the measure about to be carried into execution. I can have no pleasure in detailing the various evils I foresee progressively awaiting us. One reason is sufficient for me to deplore the dissolution of Parliament while the present administration subsists. With the sentiments of duty, loyalty and grateful attachment I feel and ever must feel for the person of my sovereign, I cannot fail to lament that he should have listened to an advice for the adoption of a measure which to my conviction will enslave him and aggrandize his son at his expense during the remainder of his reign."

GEORGE CANNING to VISCOUNT LOWTHER.

(Most private.)

1806, October 21st, Berkeley Square.—" I am at length enabled to transmit to you my long promised letter of the 28th of last month, after having submitted it to the repeated revisal of the person with whom my intercourse took place, and through him to that of Lord Grenville himself. And in another cover I transmit a copy of a letter from Lord Grenville to the person employed between us, which accompanied his return of the different papers which had been sent to him— viz.—The original draft, and amended copy, of my letter—and the observations of that person upon it and my reply to them. These papers it would only be unnecessary trouble to you to read. The original draft of my letter indeed I have destroyed. And the observations and the answers to them are not worth your perusal, as the result of them is incorporated in my letter as it now stands. Some slight alterations I have made in it, since the receipt of Lord Grenville's letter of the 16th, in order to conform it as exactly as possible (consistently with my impression of the fact) to *his* views and impressions. There is indeed hardly a shade of difference between us: and if I agreed with him (which I do not) as to the necessity of a *joint* statement of the sort which he suggests, I should not have much more than verbal objections to offer to any part of that proposed by him. In No. 2 for instance I should require that our 'mutual expressions' should be stated in their order of *time*, that Lord Grenville 'expressed' first and that I answered his expression. In No. 3 I should have to soften a little the phrase 'bound by engagements'; I certainly felt an honourable obligation not to accept a separate overture, and acted upon it, but I did not feel, nor describe myself as '*bound*' or as having 'engagements' but such as arose out of a liberal construction of those relations which belong to concert and co-operation. In No. 4, Lord Grenville falls into the obvious mistake, which he points out as unavoidable in 'telling one's own story' that of stating what is really *his own* impression, as that which was common to us both. He speaks of 'actual *or* probable openings'—as if they were equally known to me, as to himself. Whereas *I* could know nothing but of the '*actual*' ones—which were precisely *two* and no more. If all that have since been and are now said to be 'probable' had been mentioned to me, *perhaps* my view of their sufficiency might have been altered.

These are however very trifling and, I am persuaded, unintentional inaccuracies — and are only worth remarking, as they prove that Lord Grenville's observation with respect to the 'species of colouring which every man naturally gives in telling his own story' is applicable also to what he intended, I am sure, as a perfectly *impartial* statement.

You will find the truth of this observation still further exemplified in the account which he gives in *this* letter of the contents of that letter of his to your lordship, which you were so good as to communicate to me. The substance is pretty fairly related—but the 'colouring' certainly was higher than he represents it.

You will have the goodness to return me the copy of Lord Grenville's letter. Mine you will use according to your discretion, only have the goodness to let me know that it reaches you safely.

What says Lord Westmorland to the late event? Surely they promised us too much."

CHARLES LONG to VISCOUNT LOWTHER.

1806, October 21st, Bromley Hill.—"After I had written to you yesterday I received yours on my return to this place written from Carlisle. I can go to Haslemere at any time and shall wait for further instructions from you upon this subject. The Dissolution has taken our friends very much by surprise; I hear of the unprovided, in all quarters. The appointment of the day for the meeting of Parliament for the dispatch of business, together with a strong doubt whether such. a preposition would be acquiesced in seems in various instances to have thrown our friends off their guard. Sir H. Mildmay and Chute through. the assistance of Lord Temple are likely to succeed in Hampshire. Lord Camden does not give so favourable an account as I could wish. of his progress at Bath, and unless Castlereagh who is his candidate arrive soon I fear his prospect will be a bad one. You shall hear from me when any thing occurs worthy your notice."

CHARLES LONG to VISCOUNT LOWTHER.

(*Most private*).

1806, October 24th, Bromley Hill.—" I imagine you have by this time received the letter a copy of which Canning shewed me a few days ago. I am sorry to see from the nature of his transaction as well as from other circumstances the little disposition there appears to be in Lord Grenville to connect himself with those who were the friends of Mr. Pitt, or rather the determination there appears to be in his mind to prefer all others of a different description. It is very intelligible why he should have no great inclination to those who he supposes to have stood in the way of a junction between himself and Mr. Pitt and Mr. Fox, but there are others who were anxious for such a junction and to whom I do not think he appears to have shewn more favourable dispositions. If he says that he could not treat with the present opposition as a party because they have no leader, that ought not to have prevented his considering them according to their respective merits—particularly as he gave as a reason why he would not join Mr. Pitt without Mr. Fox, that he would not be a party to a Government of exclusion—but precisely such a Government he appears to me to have taken pains to form.

In all this I think Lord Grenville has acted most unwisely for himself, he would have found opinions much more congenial with his own in Mr. Pitt's friends than in those either of Mr. Fox or of Lord Sidmouth. The question for us is, what is now to be done—what is best for the country and most honourable for ourselves, and upon this point I am very anxious to know your opinion. Lord Grenville appears to have lost the opportunity which Fox's death gave him of making any thing like a general arrangement unless what passed with C——— can be called an attempt to make it. His new allies are Lord Holland, Mr. Bragge, Mr. Tierney and (whenever General Fitzpatrick chooses to retire, which he will do whenever one of the three best military governments becomes vacant) Mr. Whitbread. It seems therefore that there is no prospect of admission for any of the late government unless Lord Grenville should quarrel with any of his present colleagues—all this I lament because I cannot help thinking Lord Grenville the fittest person in point of talents and weight to be the first minister, and this opinion together with old habits of friendship would have naturally led me to wish to have connected myself with him if I could honourably have done so. I cannot help therefore being concerned at a conduct the tendency of which has been to drive the friends of Mr. Pitt into opposition to him.

With respect to those who acted together in opposition last year I see great probabilities of more than shades of difference between them—first I imagine there are those among them who think the only object worth contending for is that of turning out the present Government by force and substituting another, and who if they do not avow this opinion, at least act upon it. I have never acquiesced in the practicability, or if it were practicable, in the policy of such a measure and recent circumstances have rendered its practicability still more doubtful than formerly—but of this opinion I believe are Lord Eldon, Hawkesbury, Castlereagh, and I fear Perceval—there are others who have always thought 'fair compromise was most advisable, among which I believe are yourself, Lord Camden, Lord Bathurst, Canning, myself and many others. It is probable also that since a certain person (as it will be considered) has shewn no disinclination at least to the present Government by agreeing to the Dissolution there may be others who will not be of either of the opinions above stated, but who may think they are now at liberty to make their own separate terms, and who supposing there is more affinity between their opinions and Lord Grenville's than those of any other persons, will therefore be disposed to unite with him, in the hope of inducing him gradually to admit more of Mr. Pitt's friends as opportunities arise, and Canning who has always been disposed to compromise threw out several things lately to me which seemed rather to favour this latter opinion. Unless we have a head to the party opinions may still be more various even than I have supposed—for that situation the persons whom I have heard suggested are yourself, the Duke of Portland, Lord Camden, and Lord Hawkesbury. I am sure you would unite the greatest numbers under your banners, but I doubt your inclination to be troubled with all that belongs to this troublesome office.

I have thrown out all this for your consideration and have insensibly been led almost to exceed the fair bounds of a letter—let me know something of what is the tendency of your opinion—there is none for which I have a higher respect, and none which will so much guide my own.

By a letter from Canning this morning I find he is totally unprovided with a seat unless he has what he does not expect, a favourable answer from Ireland. I have heard of ten or twelve of our friends in the same predicament—Wallace, Holford, Lord Rendlesham, Mr. Thellusson, two Scotts, Moreland, Lord Binning, Lord Clancarty, &c. Lord Castlereagh who I fear has little chance at Bath has secured a seat at Plympton.

There is every prospect of a contest here as Sir E. Knatchbull it [appears ?] means to offer himself in opposition to [Sir William] Geary."

VISCOUNT LOWTHER to GEORGE CANNING (*copy*).

1806, October 26th, Lowther.—"If I knew in what way to repre-sent it to Lord Grenville with the smallest chance of making any impression, or of awakening in him a sense of that danger which seems to threaten us, I would detail to him some of the proceedings which have taken place during the progress of a certain person in the north. Political intrigues seem to have been the chief object—and those intrigues have all been carried on with a view to strengthen the old Foxite party, in so much that all the new candidates whom this visitation has produced are every one of them men who went into all the excesses into which the most decided revolutionary principles could carry them—should these efforts succeed I will venture to say that Parliament will be composed of men who will have no difficulty in assenting to any measure which a certain person may countenance, and as we know what has already been attempted, we may guess under such auspices what may be accomplished. I am really full of indignation and alarm at the probable success of this delusion which seems to prevail. For the county of Durham the two candidates have been expressly nominated after dinner at Raby, and the two for the city likewise, and sent forth upon their canvas with the assurances of support that the P——'s personal influence could give them. I have great reason to believe that money has been supplied to Cawthorne at Lancaster—and the two persons Lord Darlington has selected for one of his boroughs are two officers of his militia. The formality of Castle Howard will probably not be broke in upon by an inundation of country visitors—particularly as I suppose Wentworth will be the grand scene of action in Yorkshire. To what can all this tend but to place the King under the command of his son, voting with a sturdy faction during the remainder of his reign. The game he is playing is a deep one, and when it is constantly on his lips that Charles the 2nd was the only gentleman who ever sat on the throne of England, we have only to compare the two characters and then tremble at the issue of this conflict—for unless there is more servility and meanness than I trust in God there is, it must come to this at last. If Lord Grenville could be apprized of all this—if he could but be persuaded that all that remains of the Foxite party is now led on by a person who will stop at no point till he gains his purpose, and that this faction will heartily go along with him, I think he would rouse himself from the security in which I think he has already slept too long. Excuse this hasty scrawl, which I have written under the strong impression of the moment—but under impressions which I think will grow stronger on reflection."

VISCOUNT LOWTHER to CHARLES LONG (*copy*).

1806, October 27th, Lowther. — "Whatever may have been the obstacles in the way of accommodation previous to the dissolution of Parliament I fear they will be greatly increased by this measure. Numberless difficulties present themselves which ever way I consider the questions you have proposed, and like all others much may be said on all sides. My general wish not only from its object being the most just and reasonable, but because, on that account perhaps, most easily attainable, was such a share in the Government as our friends from their relative strength had fair pretentions to expect. Supposing Lord Grenville to have been disposed to enter on a treaty on this principle, I should have taken, as the basis of it, the terms on which it was understood Mr. Pitt last year was disposed to have granted to the parties of Lord Grenville and Mr. Fox. Perhaps you will say in adopting this I carry our pretensions too high, perhaps it may be so, but I can see no better way of bringing those pretensions into discussion than by taking this precedent, as parties do not enter on a negotiation of this kind without being disposed to mutual concessions. The accession of strength which it is to be feared Lord Grenville will derive from the election of a new Parliament must necessarily alter our situation very materially, and were he more disposed to conciliation on fair terms than I conceive them to be at this moment, I am afraid these terms would become too low to be the object of consideration for a party denominating as rash all who act in concert together. To oppose openly and to place some person at the head of the party to direct its motions seems to afford a still more hopeless prospect. Without any reason to presume that the King is dissatisfied with his servants, and seeing that the heir apparent not only supports him, but is creating all the influence his rank and station give him to turn the elections in their favour (and which shall be the subject of a separate examination) what chance is there of raising any force to conduct such an array ? You will ask then what course we have to pursue ; my great alarm at present arises from the predominance of the Foxites without his great mind to sway them. We know that his adherents, most of whom acted on the worst of his principles, have placed themselves under another leader illustrious in rank, but I will not add what I was going to say. That some steps will be attempted to be taken, which no honest man can assent to, I firmly believe, and I am afraid the King will find himself in a situation he has never before experienced. If the admission of a few of our friends into the Government would afford some security for the due maintenance of the royal authority and place, a sufficient guard to resist the encroachments of the P——, I for one should feel no difficulty in acceding to such terms. What Lord Grenville means by not forcibly removing any one whom he has recommended I do not exactly understand, any more than his holding his present situation in consequence of being forced into it by his colleagues to whom he seems to think so much deference is owing; I can only understand it as a civil way to putting by the question. So far therefore from being able to relieve your difficulties I am afraid I have only contributed to increase them. I think the Duke of Portland the properest person to defer to on this occasion; I feel myself unequal to the situation and I am afraid should be hunting at Cottesmore when you wanted me to be speaking in Parliament, and as I can do one better than the other you may guess which I should prefer. As this matter of an union has been proposed to Lord Grenville I should have no objection at all, if the Duke of Portland will not undertake it, to become the mediator, and if the discussion breaks off in a question of terms I hope we shall have such a case to show as will do no discredit to us. If Lord Grenville is in earnest, a great deal of the formality with which he proposes to encumber this treaty might be removed and a plain intelligible statement submitted to him on which his precise opinion might be taken. I can readily understand the line he would wish to draw, and I think it will be to persons rather than to numbers he will object. But still all or most of this will chiefly depend on the turn the elections take, of which I find but little doubt can be entertained. Admitting all this there are at the same time so many other points for consideration and so many remote causes operating to defeat any plan that may be proposed I find myself in a situation rather to follow others than to point out any line for them to pursue, and being so far removed from all communication with you and those whom I should most wish to advise with, I am incapable of suggesting anything which should have any weight in deciding you. At all events let me hear from you again and tell me what, or if anything, you think ought to be done. I should be glad to support Lord Grenville's Government but I feel it impossible to do so whilst all our friends are proscribed."

CHARLES LONG to VISCOUNT LOWTHER.

1806, October 29th, Bromley Hill.—" I have just received your letter, and agree with you in the observations it contains entirely, what I threw out was much more for consideration than decision, for I do not think it possible to decide upon these points without a good deal more communication between those who have been in the habit of acting together; but I mentioned the different views of things which I had discovered in different persons because in any meeting which may take place whenever you return to town, I am sure you will see these different views operating and influencing the opinions which may be given. Lord Camden writes to me that he has lost Bath by one vote, from what I hear I believe we shall lose by the new elections, for the Parliament could not have been dissolved at a moment more disadvantageous to us, our friends were taken by surprise, they were dispersed, and at a distance, and the dissolution followed the report of it so soon, that they had no time to arrange their plans, the Grenvilles from what I hear will gain, the Foxites and the Sidmouths will lose, at least this is the complexion of things at present.

I have arranged everything with Mr. Denton, and am just going to set out for Haslemere, where the election comes on to-morrow.

[P.S.] Lord Camden has just called, he has succeeded in the county of Brecon."

CHARLES LONG to VISCOUNT LOWTHER.

1806, November 1st, Hill Street.—" Every thing passed off at Haslemere as pleasantly as possible—the inhabitants in general expressed a
great wish to see you, and all agree that the place is very much improved since it has been in your possession—all that related to the election was very well managed by Mr. Denton. You will see by the
papers that the French are at Berlin, and as far as I can judge by the
map, affairs there appear almost irretrievable, for the King by going to
Magdeburg seems to have put himself out of the assistance of the
Russians and to have abandoned every thing. I imagine we shall see
Bonaparte erecting Saxony into a kingdom after making the Elector
pay for his title, which he is very well able to do—and we shall probably see all the work of the Great Frederick undone and Prussia reduced to insignificance—all this is very bad. You shall hear from me
in a day or two upon the subject of your last letter."

GEORGE CANNING to VISCOUNT LOWTHER.

1806, November 3rd, South Hill.—" I happened to have an opportunity of communicating to Lord Grenville the letter of the contents of
which you expressed your wish that he should be apprized. I cannot
do better than enclose to you the note with which he returned it to
me." [See enclosure.]
" P.S.—I have given to Long a copy of my letter of the 26th of
September—as the shortest and most authentic way of conveying to
such persons as would naturally expect some information on the subject, the substance of what passed between Lord Grenville and me in
the summer. It would be endless to make a separate statement for
every person, who might require it. And the slightest variation in
expression upon a subject of so much delicacy is (as we have had
occasion to see in the course of some correspondence which has taken
place upon this very letter) capable of giving, or of being understood to
give an impression different from what is intended."

(Enclosure.)
LORD GRENVILLE to GEORGE CANNING (copy).

1806, October 30th, Downing Street.—" I return you Lord Lowther's
letter, upon its contents I can only say that I have changed none of my
principles, and shall always be ready to act upon them, whenever any
occasion shall seem to me to require it; and that I am very sensible of
Lord Lowther's kindness in writing the letter and of yours in communicating it."

CHARLES LONG to VISCOUNT LOWTHER.
(Private.)

1806, November 11th, Bromley Hill.—" From an expression in your
letter I fear that I may have explained myself very ill, or possibly the
expression to which I allude may have arisen from something you may
have heard in another quarter—you seem to think it probable that Lord
Grenville may make some new proposal. Now I have no reason to think
he has this in contemplation, if he has however I hope he will refer to

you, and his not having referred on the former occasion either to yourself or to some other person who would like yourself have given the
subject a fair consideration, makes me say that he did not give the
avowed intention a fair chance of success and makes me doubt much
whether he really wished that it should succeed. Lord Stafford I hear
wrote to T. Grenville expressing his surprise and concern that some of
Mr. Pitt's friends were not admitted into the administration on Mr.
Fox's death, and I hear also that T. Grenville's answer was in substance that their demands were too unreasonable to be admitted.

The contested elections have not upon the whole gone favourably
for Government among our friends. I lament much Lascelles' defeat in
Yorkshire. I hear Lord FitzWilliam and the Duke of Norfolk were
determined to go all lengths to keep him out. We have a strong contest
here, I am doing what I can for Sir E. Knatchbull and I hope we shall
carry his election. Lord Camden, who has just been here, is obliged from
old friendship (though very reluctantly) to give his interest to Sir
W. Geary. As soon as I received your letter I called upon Dr. Smith—
but I found he had just set off to Oxford to vote for Heber, so that I
have no merit in persuading him—he has since told me that he and
Mr. Fox his curate voted in that way, on hearing that it was your wish.
I have just sent him into Hampshire to vote for Sir H. Mildmay and
Chute.

Of the two, Lord Morpeth is certainly much better than Sir R.
Fletcher, but Wallace who called here yesterday says you might have
carried both members without difficulty—which would have been still
better. I do not however give implicit credit to him on this point.

There is a report that it is the intention of ministers to put the
Scotch representative Peers upon the same footing as the Irish—to elect
them for life—if this is to be done it should have been by a decision of
Parliament previous to the election—it would be a strong measure to
consider those who may be chosen for the Parliament, as representative
Peers for life. I am sorry to hear that Lord Temple is to have the
support of Government as one of them.

Canning you will see is returned for Newtown. He has put a copy
of the letter he wrote to you into my hands, and in a note which accompanied it, he says he acted under the *instructions* he received at your
house, and I think pretty strongly implies that if he had acted upon his
own inclinations, he should have been disposed to have accepted Lord
Grenville's proposal—but under the idea that it would have led to a
more extensive admission of Mr. Pitt's friends in a short time."

GEORGE CANNING to VISCOUNT LOWTHER.

1806, November 12th, South Hill.—"I have this moment received
your letter of the 8th and I hasten to thank you for the very kind and
flattering offer which it conveys to me.

It is true that I have been kept in uncertainty as to my re-election
in Ireland. And at the time when, I suppose, Long must have mentioned the circumstance to you, I had been disappointed in several
attempts to secure a seat elsewhere.

Since that time, however, I have found one in the Isle of Wight;
for which I am returned.

My not having occasion to avail myself of your kindness does not,
however, make me feel it the less sensibly. And I cannot better express
the value which I set upon it, than by assuring you, which I do with
perfect sincerity; that there are very few persons indeed from whom I

should not have hesitated to accept a similar obligation; but that, after the intercourse which has taken place between us since the beginning of this year, I should have received it at your Lordship's hands not only without scruple, but with the utmost satisfaction and acknowledgment."

GEORGE CANNING to VISCOUNT LOWTHER.

1806, November 13th, South Hill.—" I wrote in such haste, to save the post, yesterday, that I omitted to notice that part of your letter of the 8th which relates to the communication of your former letter to Lord Grenville.

Undoubtedly I thought that the whole of that letter, not in substance only, but in the form and manner of expression, was calculated to do good and to awaken Lord Grenville, if any thing could do so, to a sense of some of the dangers which he has to apprehend from those with whom he is connected; and more likely to produce this effect, from the very circumstance of its not being conceived in those measured terms which you might probably have used in writing upon such a subject directly to Lord Grenville himself.

But even with this persuasion I should not have thought myself at liberty to make such a communication on my own judgment, if I had not understood parts of your letter, particularly the beginning of it, as distinctly intimating your wish that such a communication should be made. And the opportunity, which happened to be afforded me on the very day on which your letter reached me, I thought too advantageous to be lost.

Fortunately I have not destroyed your letter, and can therefore return it to you that you may satisfy yourself how free it is from any thing that you could wish to be kept back from Lord Grenville. His answer which I also re-enclose, compared with it, will shew you that no part either of your meaning in what you wrote, or of mine in communicating it, has been misapprehended."

VISCOUNT MELVILLE to VISCOUNT LOWTHER.

1806, November 19th, Dunira.—"Nothing but the very peculiar anxiety I feel on the subject which creates to you the trouble of this letter could justify me to myself for the liberty I take. Lord Binning has failed in all his attempts to obtain a seat in Parliament. He was under the peculiar protection of Mr. Pitt who provided him a seat in the last Parliament, and if he had been now alive I should have had no occasion to make any attempt on the goodness of others. Mr. Pitt had a sincere attachment to him, and there never was a more enthusiastic worshipper of Mr. Pitt's memory than Lord Binning is. He is unhappy in being out of Parliament, and I am satisfied his chief cause for being so is his being deprived of that means of manifesting his respect for the character and memory of Mr. Pitt. As the eldest son of a Scotch peer he is ineligible for any seat in Scotland, and I have no interest any where else. In this dilemma if the death of Lord Galloway could make any opening for the wishes of Lord Binning I should feel it a most lasting and serious obligation, as probably the wishes of the present Lord Galloway may form a subject of attention in the present vacancy of his seat, I have taken the liberty of bringing the subject under his view, and as I have lately I hope materially aided his political objects, and have the prospect hereafter of doing it more effectually, I trust that on the present occasion his Lordship will not be indisposed to forward an object I have so much at heart."

ROBERT WARD to VISCOUNT LOWTHER.

1806, November 23rd, Hyde Lodge.—"The death of so worthy a man, as I believe Lord Galloway was, is a much greater cause of concern than any I could feel from a much longer absence from Parliament than will be occasioned by the delay of a new writ. But even if this were not so, I beg to say that your Lordship's answer to Lord Garlies is precisely what I should have returned myself, could I have had a right to return any answer at all. At the same time I hope you know me too well not to be certain that any feeling of yours upon the subject must also be mine. As I consider myself now as entirely belonging to the Lowther *party*, I shall be glad to know by any opportunity who is to be my honourable friend for Cockermouth when Mr. J. Lowther makes his election. What I should like to know still more is, whether Miss Mary's partiality for a young and handsome member for Cumberland, instead of an old worn out India Captain, goes at all beyond mere favour to a young and handsome man; that is, whether any political consequence is to be attached to the active canvass which she says she made for Lord Morpeth. The state of parties is surely interesting, critical and important; and the next session I should think would instantly call for a declaration of sentiment in the different members, much more pronounced and extensive than that which has yet been made since Mr. Pitt's death. I am therefore naturally anxious to understand explicitly the views and opinions of one in whom I so much confide as your Lordship. With all their concentration of weight and talents, the ministry have hitherto done nothing but imitate Mr. Pitt's measures or attack his friends. At the same time I cannot help thinking that Lord Grenville himself has a very warm regard for his memory, and may have permitted much of what has been done in resentment for the personal opposition of last session, which though chiefly directed against Windham and Fox, was, I always thought, too violent. This, added to the high consideration which he enjoys and deserves for ability and experience, induces me to think it would be difficult to say that any other person ought to be at the head of the Government or that a personal, systematic opposition ought to be resolved upon. There are no doubt many instances during the course of the elections, of attacks from the Grenvilles, as well as the Foxites, and when their history comes to be known in detail, it may probably make a great difference in one's feelings; but the question is I apprehend still open, whether the whole body of Mr. Pitt's friends are to *engage* to make war *ad internecionem* upon the present Government? Without such an engagement, any war of theirs would be of little consequence; and as it is the dignified design of keeping and acting together with force, is altogether frustrated by the conduct of many of the leading men of his party, I mean such as Lord Bathurst, and Lord Camden, not to say Lord Carrington who is a decided deserter. No one has a right to blame them, but they have completely broken down our power as a *party*, whether to embark in actual hostility, or to preserve an armed demonstration. Considering these things therefore, I own I am anxiously desirous of knowing your Lordship's sentiments at large upon a matter so important as to conduct. Perhaps I may be a little swayed by a good deal of personal respect for Lord Grenville, from whom I

have received at least a good deal of civility; but I confess, though
alive to his conduct towards Mr. Pitt, in his late administration, I gave
him credit for the sincerest and deepest grief at his death ; I have not
seen the proof on his part, of an attempt to persecute his memory, but
the contrary, and he is at least the man whom we all of us wanted to
see in the lead of affairs. If then, we add to this, that we cannot call
ourselves *exclusively* the friends of Mr. Pitt, while so many of those he
most loved and trusted are either neuter, or supporters of Government
(Lord Euston for instance) and that we must therefore engage to one
another as *individuals*, I own I think it yet to be decided whether in
your Lordship's opinion we are to become an embodied and systematic
opposition; or whether your former sentiment is not still to be acted
upon, that though there is abundant cause for private dissatisfaction,
direct hostility may yet be avoided. Many of us indeed have put the
matter out of doubt, by their marked and most able conduct last summer,
and to them I feel attached by every personal consideration of esteem
and regard; but I was induced not less by my own feeling on the
subject, than your Lordship's determination, to stand aloof as I did from
the sort of contest they courted, and I confess I do not see that we are
either strong, or the ministry bad, enough to attempt their destruction
by regular war. To hold together with a view to honourable independence, and to resist all attack, either upon ourselves or the constitution,
would be a thing much to be coveted; but at any rate, the time is come
when something explicit should be known. I am aware how terribly
I am trespassing upon you, and how little perhaps it was your intention
(when you did me the honour you have done) of making a member who
would so plague you with his thoughts. But as consistency and even
honour may depend upon future Parliamentary conduct, the present
leaders of opposition will no doubt expect to know upon what they may
depend; and it would be unmanly in me if I avoided to declare myself
freely to those whom I much love and honour, and with whom I have
generally acted, though I have sometimes, and may now differ with
them in opinion. I trust therefore you will not think me very prag-
matical in bringing a subject of such magnitude before the person in
the world whose sentiments upon it are to me of the most importance.
It is with the greatest truth that I repeat, that a seat in Parliament is
nothing in comparison with the thought that I have enjoyed your
confidence, and shared, as well as acted upon your opinions. It is one
of my proudest wishes to continue to do so, and you must not therefore
wonder, if I seek with some little degree of anxiety to know them with
accuracy in a juncture so critical as the opening of a new Parliament.
The same motive will I hope be my excuse with you for this invasion
of your time, by the liberty I have taken in mentioning my own sentiments so much at length. I rejoice that Wharton has not been forced
to put your kindness to all the expense to which it was willing to go for
him, as well as that he has had the happiness of knowing Lowther.
We have no news except that the Prince has taken it into his head
that he is in love with Lady Hertford, and that she has taken it into
her head that it would be right to run away to Ireland as the best
protection for her modesty."

GEORGE CANNING to VISCOUNT LOWTHER.

(*Private.*)

1806, November 23rd, South Hill.—" I am very happy to find that it
will not be inconvenient to you to be in town a short time before the

meeting of Parliament. The present state of things requires a much more intimate and particular communication between those whose general views and principles of action agree than it would be possible (if it were prudent) to enter into by letter.

I could not even answer one single sentence in your Lordship's last letter (that in which you state your impression as to the situation in which we now stand with respect to the issue of the late transaction between me and Lord Grenville) without going into a detail, which I should feel the utmost difficulty in committing to paper. I can only say generally, upon that subject, that I retain all the opinions which your Lordship and I have entertained in common since our first intercourse at the beginning of the year; that after all that has passed, and *in spite* of much that Lord Grenville has done or suffered, or left undone, I still think him the fittest man for the situation which he fills, perhaps from the fact (a melancholy and not very creditable one for the country) that he is the *only* man fitted for it in any eminent degree; that I still think him, *in spite* of many things which in this view are to be lamented even while they are forgiven, the natural head of an administration of which Mr. Pitt's friends should form a part; that such an arrangement still appears to me an object to be pursued *by all honourable means;* and that, unpromising as appearances are at present, and perplexed as is the whole state of parties and of public affairs, I still think such an arrangement not altogether unattainable—differing only in a slight degree from what seems to be your impression, as to the mode, or rather perhaps as to the moment of taking any steps directly towards it.

The grounds of this slight difference (and it is much less than even in statement it may appear to be) I have no doubt of explaining to your entire satisfaction when we meet.

In the mean time (which is a point of more immediate practical importance) I am most decidedly convinced that, *with a view to this object,* active exertion and zealous attendance in parliament are more than ever necessary; that any abatement either of vigour in our attack, or of numbers in our support, would so far from facilitate the accomplishment of the object, that it would in fact render it impossible for Lord Grenville, however desirous he might be, to do any thing effectual towards it.

In this view, I am particularly glad to receive such accounts, as have been sent me by some of our friends skilled in such mystical matters, of the numerical effect of the new elections. From one quarter I hear that the gain of new strength to Government is no more than 29—and that to opposition 22—that 5 more are to be considered as *hopeful* for *us,* and 14 as *doubtful*—'all but three of whom' (I do not quite understand whether all the *hopefuls and doubtfuls,* or all the *doubtfuls* only) 'supply the places of determined enemies. If therefore they were *all* with Government they would swell their balance only from 7 (the difference between 22 and 29) to 10. If *half* only are with us, they turn the balance in our favour.'

This calculation is made exclusive of Ireland and Scotland—in the latter of which I suppose the turn will be rather against the Government in the former I should apprehend rather in its favour. But upon the whole it seems clear that they cannot have gained *in numbers* any thing that can compensate them for the trouble, the expense, and the unpopularity of the Dissolution—and for the rashness of having thrown away, when they wanted it but little, a measure which they might by possibility wish to have recourse to hereafter. Nothing could be more

satisfactory *to us* than the complete rout of the Doctor's forces. I have
a list of *sixteen* of his men, who are slain outright; and I trust they are
not likely to revive in other places.

There are, however, *other* views in which the Dissolution certainly
gives strength to Lord Grenville's Government. These, I think, will
not have failed to strike your Lordship, as they have me; and as I find
they have struck Long, and a few others with whom I happen to have
had an opportunity of talking. While others of our friends, however,
resist (as I am told) the conviction which appears to me irresistible.

The considerations arising out of this point must be reserved for discussion when we meet. They bear directly (as it appears to my mind)
upon the subject of the former part of this letter; and may not impro-
bably make it necessary to have a very unreserved and distinct communication upon that subject with many of those with whom we have
been acting.

I shall be very glad to hear that my opinions (so far as I have been
able to explain them) have the advantage of your Lordship's concurrence;
and I shall be equally glad of an opportunity to enter fully and confidentially into an explanation of any parts of them, and of the
circumstances with which they are connected."

CHARLES LONG to VISCOUNT LOWTHER.

1806, November 24th, Bromley Hill.—" I hear it is the intention
of the ministers to meet Parliament on the 15th next month to give a
certain time for swearing in the members and to proceed to business
with as short a Christmas holiday as possible—this information comes
from Hatsell, who says he knows it to be so determined.

It is impossible not to feel as you do respecting Lord Grenville's offer
—he has not made it as if he considered the success of his proposal of
any consequence, and it is unfair to state the pretentions of Mr. Pitt's
friends as unreasonable without precisely ascertaining what those pretentions were, which he never has done—putting every other consideration out of the question. I think he has acted more unwisely for himself—he will have difficulties enough to struggle with, and in rejecting
persons who would have given him important assistance he has not
taken the means he had in his power of encountering them.

The issue of the Westminster Election is just what one would have
wished. I should have been sorry that such a person as Paull had
succeeded, and yet I should have been sorry that anything had appeared
like a general approbation of Sheridan, in truth the whole transaction
must be mortifying enough to him—he owes his success entirely to the
popularity of his colleague, and to exertions and expense, the half of
which would have carried the election of almost any other candidate.
If any assistance had been given to Paull by the opposition he certainly
would have beat Sheridan, it is to their credit that they did not do so—
and yet there was nothing which was factious (not to say occasionally
treasonable) which the Foxites did not let loose against the Government of Mr. Pitt. That Mr. Whitbread and others should discover
that Sir F. Burdett's principles (now that he has declared against them)
are hostile to the constitution, of which his connection with O'Connor
and Despard could not formerly even raise a suspicion, is a circumstance which ought not to pass without a good deal of observation.

I have no news to communicate—the Government do not give up the
Prussian game as lost yet—such at least is the tenor of the language

they hold. The Prince I hear was very unwell upon his second tour as well as on his first—he is said now to be recovered.

Webb who I met lately at Lord Bridgwater's was the person, if I recollect right, who mentioned Smirke's plan—and he spoke very well of it. I heartily hope Cawthorne may not be suffered to sit among us."

[P.S.]—"Prince Hohenlohe's surrender seems to put an end to all hopes of Prussia, and I believe it is certain that the King has sued for peace on any terms he can obtain."

VISCOUNT MELVILLE to VISCOUNT LOWTHER.

1806, November 28th, Dunira.—" I have this morning received your very obliging letter. I must go to town for a few days next week to aid my friends the candidates for the representation of the Peerage, which comes on next Thursday. I shall then have an opportunity of explaining to Lord Binning the *chance* which your Lordship's goodness presents to his hope. I hope I need say nothing to convince your Lordship of the deep sense I entertain of your kind feelings to myself in this business. I trust your Lordship will never see cause to repent it, or the motives which dictate it. What you say of Mr. Pitt's memory is truly gratifying, the more so as some who had every cause to have felt the same sentiment, seem to feel very little of the active operation of that sentiment."

LORD MULGRAVE to VISCOUNT LOWTHER.

1806, November 30th, Mulgrave Castle.—" I did not trouble you with an answer to your letter, in the midst of your election arrangements, because I was persuaded that every day's letter bag must have brought you an heavy task of reading and writing, and I take some degree of merit for my forbearance as my curiosity was much excited by many things to which you alluded and of which in this remote and retired corner I had heard nothing—I mean the transactions at Ruby and the visit to Sir John Lawson—and though they must now be considered by you as old stories, I still feel rather inquisitive after any circumstance of the conduct of the great, or rather high, personage in question, which can be supposed to create surprise.

With respect to Lord Grenville I confess I have been much disappointed and surprised at the course he has pursued, not only since the death of Pitt, but even previous to it—from the period of the peace of Amiens he began to *set up for himself*, and to endeavour to collect as many as he could detach from Pitt on that question into a body of which he should be the leader and oracle, and I have no doubt that he considered himself from that period, as the head of a distinct party, with which to stipulate and negotiate, and upon the great struggle to turn out the Doctor he united himself so closely with Fox to balance the great weight and popularity of Pitt, that he would not and I believe could not separate himself from him—how far the conduct which he pursued afterwards was formed upon broad principles, or upon ambitious speculation, his junction with Addington, the object of his contempt and reprobation and the ostensible cause of his political separation from his political benefactor, his great intimacy with Lord Auckland, and his vehement and strenuous endeavours to force Lord Lauderdale into a situation of unbounded power and uncontrolled discretion, may be sufficient to prove without minor though numerous instances of a similar description. But how any degree of passion or prejudice, should ruin itself in this stoical endurance of all former objects of hatred, contempt and disgust—and should without any provocation to excite it, become so strong as to set aside the steady pursuit of supreme power which might have been confirmed by a moderate and very limited encouragement of a few of Pitt's friends and a decent forbearance towards his leading principles, and favourite measures, I cannot take upon me to guess, it can only be attributed to one of those strange inconsistencies in human nature which no sagacity could foretell and no reason can explain. As his conduct has been inexplicable, so also has the result of his scheme been more unfavourable to the character and estimation of his Government, than could have been supposed possible, with a man at its head confessedly the first of the surviving statesmen of the country, for though he has not the universal and transcendent powers of mind which rendered Pitt a prodigy, nor the brilliant talents and large compass of intellect which distinguished the wonderful but ineffective understanding of Fox, yet he has a clear and confident mind and a strong and laborious understanding; but with all this his administration is neither popular nor respected, nor indeed enjoys much more credit with the country for wisdom, vigour, and activity than that of the Doctor himself. And this because he is not alone sufficient to create an opinion of talent and principle in a Cabinet where they cannot elsewhere be sought for in the same person. Lord Spencer is a most respectable worthy and honest man, but splendour of talent he would probably not himself affect—what are the qualities of the rest of the Cabinet, give them the epithets which should belong to the situations they hold, and see how they will fit them, the mild temper, conciliatory manners, and tried partiality to the ancient order of things in Europe of the foreign secretary of State—the universal popularity amongst all the descriptions of armed force of the Kingdom, the judicious and popular selection of commanders, prompt and steady decision of military operations, and calm laborious attention to business in trade and colonial policy of the Secretary of State for War and Colonies. The dignified, constitutional, and deliberate disposition of the Chancellor on political subjects, his just and temperate estimate of law and constitution, and above all the perfect propriety of his private life and conduct. The Lord Privy Seal's just estimate of the power of 'this country as opposed to France, and lastly the great financial talents and powerful influence in parliamentary debate of the Chancellor of the Exchequer. These elements of the Cabinet, together with the great measures which they have omitted and the petty papers which they have published have completely obscured with their Bœotian Fog whatever the country formerly esteemed as brilliant and great in the character of the favourite *Elève* and most distinguished associate of Pitt. I beg your pardon—I find I have been severely inflicting the arrears of my silence, and have run imperceptibly into something very near as bad as a party pamphlet or parliamentary speech—when I only intended to have observed that the inveterate attack of every friend and supporter of Pitt in the elections all over the country, not merely where there was a probable chance, but wherever there was the possibility of entertaining any hope of success, seems to mark a determined disposition to force even the most unwilling into hostility, and as far as politics are concerned we may say for Pitt, what Henry the 4th says to the Prince, 'Your life did manifest you loved me not, and you would have me die assured of it.' It only remains to hope that the occasion may create men, and that the new Parliament may produce some great light to guide us, some one willing to lead and worthy to be followed; I heartily wish that any way there were a strong Government. By strong Government, I do not mean merely a great majority, but an administration formed of persons whose political principles the people do not suspect, whose characters they can venerate, whose talents and wisdom they can respect, and in the vigour and patriotism of whose measures they can place an implicit confidence, unmixed with fear. I for one should be well satisfied to sit quietly by my fire side, under the care and protection of such a Government."

GEORGE CANNING to VISCOUNT LOWTHER.

1806, December 3rd, Berkeley Square.—"I very much hope that it will not be inconvenient to you to be in town by the beginning of; the week next. As though no business of importance can come on for some days, the debate on the Address, which is expected to take place on the Thursday or Friday, the 18th or 19th, is of itself very important.

I should be sorry not to have an opportunity of communicating fully with you before that debate. And the rather, as I am afraid I shall be under the absolute necessity of leaving town (on private business) as soon as it is over, for ten days, or perhaps a fortnight.

It is certainly much best to defer any more particular discussion till our meeting.

[P.S.] I have not seen Long very lately, but when last we met I found his impressions of the state of things very much the same as my own. I shall be in town the 13th."

CHARLES LONG to VISCOUNT LOWTHER.

1806, December 3rd, Bromley Hill:—"You may possibly not have heard what is to be the course of proceeding in Parliament, it is intended to meet the 15th, Monday, to choose the Speaker, on Tuesday, to have the Speech and the Address on Friday, and to have two or at most three days holiday at Christmas.

I have received a letter from Lord Melville giving an account of his success in the elections in Scotland, where he seems to have been very triumphant, he is particularly happy at Pitfour's [James Ferguson's] election of which he had despaired. You will see on the papers the resolution of the Hampshire meeting to petition Parliament in consequence of the interference of Government, they certainly have interfered more openly and I believe more grossly than ever was done before, but unless the case is very strong indeed, all this is better as a topic of debate than as a parliamentary question. My late colleague is the great promoter of this measure, and as I cannot rate his judgment very high, I doubt a little the policy of this measure, he had intended making a similar complaint respecting the interference at Christchurch, but he was dissuaded by those whom he consulted and who expressed their surprise to me that upon the case stated he should ever have thought of bringing it forward.

The capture of Hamburgh has thrown the city into the greatest consternation, several failures it is supposed will be the consequence, where shall we hear of this disturber of nations next? The King's speech will not be able to hold out any thing consolatory.

Shall you be up for the meeting or do you spend the Christmas at Lowther?"

Robert Ward to Viscount Lowther.

1806, December 3rd, Hyde Lodge.—" I owe you all my thanks for your answer to my last, and the manner in which you are so as to permit the communication of my feeling with respect to its subject. I never expected, nor even wis large upon it by letter, but am very glad soon meet you in town. As the Cockpit shows no indication of sitting, and I cannot take my seat in Parliament till after the recess, I had not till then intended to have stirred from my shepherd's cot; but I shall fly with pleasure to the meeting you are so good as to announce, and am only sorry to beg another letter from you to tell me when you expect to arrive in town.

Mean time, though my fair enemy misrepresents me (which I am very glad of, because it serves to shew her wit and vivacity), I hope your Lordship does not, with her, believe that Brennus the Gaul has lost his noble spirit. I trust I may not be quite so great a savage as is necessary to please Atalanta, and yet hate His Majesty's Government with a sufficient degree of virtue. As your Lordship is so good as to enter upon the subject, I will just add a few words that I may not misrepresent myself, and own that there is nothing which appears to me so disgusting in the history of parties, as that there should scarcely ever have been a resting place between a relinquishment of office and a violent opposition. It always seemed to me, that the true independent and dignified character is much better preserved by a firm and discriminating moderation. I was always struck with that honourable part of Lord Townshend's life, when, though he had separated from Walpole with every sentiment of mortification and disgust, he utterly refused to embark in a party contest against him. Perhaps (on the same principle) no public sentiment of our great and lamented friend ever did him more honour than his hope (when driven out of office by the coalition in 1783) never to be found in an undiscriminating opposition. I add to this, that Lord Grenville was the person whom every one of the late administration called to the helm; and that all, or nearly all, of us were prepared to approve of an union with every man of the present administration. The wrongs of Lord Grenville towards us as a party, and as old friends, are indeed great; but on that very account one would be cautious not to begin an opposition on personal motives, not to fall into the very fault of which we so justly accused the Grenvilles themselves when they opposed Mr. Pitt. These sentiments lose none of their weight from the dreadful approach of a storm from without, which may extinguish both party and the nation itself in one general wreck. But though these are my sentiments, such as they are, you may suppose they are merely speculative, and submitted to be corrected by your Lordship and other friends, and above all to be controlled by events; nor will it be necessary I trust seriously to observe that nothing can be more widely different from these opinions than to engage in the support of an administration that attacks us as a party, and takes every occasion to blast the reputation of the late ministry. It is this which, as your Lordship remarks, in language not more pointed than deserved, makes Lord Carrington's desertion appear of the meanest and basest kind; a sentiment which I have not refrained from indulging here, within the pale almost of his private society. Whatever I might think, I was quite sure you would forgive my mentioning it, particularly at a time when it was so necessary to discuss things preparatory to conduct and decisive action. I was thus sure because your

Lordship knows me to be attached to you, not merely from a sense of personal obligation, but from regard (if you will allow me to say so) both as a private man and a political leader. Need I add the instances of kindness and confidence upon which such regard is founded. I was however most tempted to enter so much at large into the subject, because from any thing that had hitherto passed, I did not know exactly how your Lordship meant to act yourself towards those gentlemen who have already drawn the sword. On the one hand I was by no means prepared to say that I was ready to go all lengths with them, either on account of my own opinions, or the knowledge of your Lordship's; on the other, from my great and known esteem for them, as well as intimacy with many of them, they have every right in the world to demand of me the precise line of conduct which it is meant to pursue. To be told that the ' bent of your own mind is opposed by many difficulties' does not diminish the interest of the subject, and only makes me more than ever wish for the pleasure of a personal communication with your Lordship.

[P.S.] You are extremely obliging on Lord Binning's subject. I learned with surprise and concern from Mr. Drake his uncle, who is my neighbour, that he was likely to be out of Parliament.

After all, I have, I believe, been wrong in troubling you with these my primitive, innocent, and (*somebody* may add) very ridiculous notions; but only wrong from the difficulty of explaining one's self in a short letter, and the *ennui* of a long one. Lord Mulgrave to whom I had written in this style quizzes me, and says such conduct will by vulgar and plain persons be deemed trimming and courting. Yet we did not. trim or court in our vote upon Lord Ellenborough's appointment, even. while we professed *not to oppose*. It is this conduct only which I meant to propose. Yet Lord Mulgrave himself says he is not determined as to the line he will pursue, and that much will depend upon the nature of the Paris negotiation, when disclosed. That much *should* depend upon it, and that we should not prejudge it in the true sharp spirit of party vehemence, is all that I mean. At the same time I beg to add that wherever my friends lead, there will I follow."

VISCOUNT MELVILLE to VISCOUNT LOWTHER.

1806, December 4th, Edinburgh.—" I met Lord Binning yesterday in this place, and communicated to him the contents of your Lordship's letter. Even the chance held out to his view overjoyed him, and short as the period of it may be, it will give him very great satisfaction if it shall suit your convenience to give him the accommodation you hold out to his hopes. I will not trouble your Lordship with a repetition of my own feelings on the subject, but I can assure you with great truth that I would rather owe the obligation to you than to any other person in England. I shall have an opportunity some future day to explain to your Lordship why I feel in that manner.

[P.S.] Our friend Pitfour has had a hard struggle against the whole power and efforts of Government, but we have carried it to his great joy and to the great annoyance of his opponents."

CHARLES LONG to VISCOUNT LOWTHER.

1806, December 8th, Bromley Hill.—" The Speaker is to be chosen on Tuesday 16th and the Speech and the Address to be on Friday

19th,' this I know is what is now determined upon, if any alteration takes place of which I am apprised in time to reach you I shall not fail to give you notice, but I do not think it likely that any new arrangement should be made.

' I shall have to shew you the state of the new House of Commons as compared with the old when we meet, it is not complete as I have not an accurate return from Scotland or Ireland, but calculating upon the probable returns from them I cannot put our loss by the Dissolution at less than 25. There is one result of the Dissolution at which I cannot grieve, Lord Sidmouth out of 30 which was his whole strength in the House of Commons loses 16, and is I understand very angry."

EARL CAMDEN to VISCOUNT LOWTHER.

1806, December 10th, Wildernesse.—"It is very long since we have corresponded, but had I not been informed by Long that he occasionally wrote to you and apprized you of the state of things I should certainly have written to you.

Lord Hawkesbury spent two days with me in his way from Walmer. He is disposed to be very moderate at present, but at the same time, to let it be understood that there are topics on which a good deal might be said at a proper opportunity. The principal thing I am anxious about, is that ministers should prepare such an address on the rupture of the negotiation as may produce an unanimous vote in favour of the spirited prosecution of the war.

I saw by Canning's desire the copy of the letter he wrote to you, the offer to him was surely much too limited, I think he appears to have acted very correctly. I learn from a source, which can be depended upon, that the Prince of Wales is   e of health and that the greatest apprehensions are entertaine   on the accuracy of this information.

Pray let me know if we are likely to see you in town at the meeting of Parliament."

CHARLES LONG to VISCOUNT LOWTHER.

1806, December 12th, Bromley Hill.—"I hope very much that you mean to be in town for the speech, which is to be Friday as I before mentioned, if you should have no particular engagement perhaps you will pass the Christmas here.

I have been looking as accurately as I could at the state of the Returns, by which I find that the gain of the Government cannot be put at less than 30, and since I have ascertained the politics of several of those whom I considered as doubtful, I find that the Foxites have gained full as much as Lord Grenville, and more if the Prince is reckoned as belonging to the former. Lord Sidmouth complains most bitterly and thinks himself ill-used, he pretends to have lost 18, I can account for only 16, which however is more than half his whole force, but he says that some of his friends were ready to purchase and that Foxites were preferred; he is doing what he can to get in some of his friends for the six double returns.

I have letters from Ireland giving a most lamentable account of the state of that country, the Thrashers have already appeared in great numbers in Mayo, Sligo, Roscommon, Cavan and Longford, and they were spreading further. The civil power has been totally ineffectual in crushing or even in intimidating them, they have murdered several witnesses, and the juries are afraid to convict, and they have applied to the Government, for regular troops, not venturing to trust the militia. This together with the disasters on the Continent presents a most dismal picture."

VISCOUNT LOWTHER to LORD GRENVILLE. (*Draft of letter endorsed* "*not sent.*")

1807; October 12th.—" Nothing can be further from my intention than to draw you into a correspondence on points which are not only most difficult to discuss in writing, but in a great degree scarcely fitting to be the subject of it. However, if I were much less sensible of the kindness I have received from you and less indifferent as to your good opinion I should feel the necessity of making my best acknowledgments for the last letter I received from you.

Nothing, you may be sure, could be further from my mind than to expect that in any communication with an opposing party, the slightest deviation from the strictest principles of honour could be admitted as the basis even of a negotiation. The character of the nation can only be supported by the private honour of individuals. I have ever held in abhorrence those easy and fluctuating principles which can bend themselves to the service of any party, and though I will not speak with disrespect of any of your colleagues, I am sure you will excuse me if I tell you that the only point on which I ever differed with my late friend was on the subject of his union with Lord S.; which I thought after what had already passed was incompatible with the dignity of his character and with the opinions I heard him express. The purity of his mind was as conspicuous as the splendour of his talents, and though I had never any opportunity of hearing from his own lips the explanation which he frequently promised me, I am led to believe, having his assurance for it, that he could satisfactorily account for the whole of that transaction. You will easily see how I mean to apply this example. There is nothing in principles of difference betwixt you and the friends to whom I allude. That they have now connected themselves as a party is precisely what was to be foreseen, and though I have reason to believe at the time you allowed me to speak to you on this subject in June last, no pretensions should have been set up by them as a collective body, I am afraid the great events of the session have made it almost impossible to detach them, were ever those circumstances to be desired. Being entirely ignorant of the pretensions on which you have had to decide, I can only judge of the extent by the light in which you consider them. Knowing a little of the scheme which it was Mr. Pitt's intention to submit to the consideration of the King last year, and which perhaps he did submit to it, it is difficult for me to conceive how any party standing as that does, which you allude to, could assume to themselves more consequence than Mr. Pitt gratuitously attached to his opponents at that time. That the present opposition is neither deficient in talents and consequence, in character or in numbers, I am sure you will readily allow. You will admit likewise that on no great constitutional question is there any material difference of opinion. I would, therefore, beg to ask if fair and reasonable concessions can be made on both sides, supposing that the project as it is now understood to be capable of some modification, for I am in entire ignorance on the subject, would you feel disposed to enter on the discussion, his Majesty's permission for that purpose being previously obtained? There is one duty you owe to your colleagues, and there is another you owe to the public should the exigency of the times produce events which may render them incompatible with each other. Should the sense of Parliament and that of the House of Commons in particular and of the public appear in favour of that union which appears to me so important to effect, is it to be understood that no recognition of the persons with whom you negotiate, as a party, is to be the basis of that treaty. The terms of such a treaty must in a great degree be governed by the relative strength of the contracting parties, but any disparity of that strength in my opinion should make that conduct fair and honourable that would not be equally so under all circumstances, and in all situations. To require impossibilities is to shut the door against communication—but it may be a question whether the mode in which the vacant offices have been filled has not increased the difficulties in the way of an union—under similar circumstances Mr. Pitt's arrangements were evidently calculated to meet a different state of things, and to facilitate the admission of new persons into the Government. With this view of it, you will, I am sure, forgive the freedom I use in saying that I see no signs of such a disposition on your part in what has taken place since Mr. Fox's death. From motives of personal regard towards some and with the highest respect for the talents of others I cannot but feel most anxious to see this union effected. I am persuaded it is for the benefit of the country, and I should have hoped likewise it might have become most grateful to yourself.

The arrangements which have taken place in consequence of Mr. Fox's death seem to preclude all hope of your having it in contemplation to extend your political connections. No one can regret the necessity which has suggested this measure more than I do, [being?] sincerely attached to your Lordship, as well from the high estimation I have ever had for your character, as from a knowledge of the value our late most excellent friend entertained for you. With no very pleasing reflections I look to the events of the approaching session. When all those with whom I have ever been connected and have acted with in public life are ranged in opposition to your Lordship, an opposition which it seems might have been easily conciliated when the very system which was almost all that was ever objectionable in the conduct of my late revered friend, is acted upon by you—and when it is known that he had difficulties to encounter which made his adoption of that system, almost involuntarily, consistent with his own idea of the duty he owed to a high authority, difficulties which do not present themselves to your Lordship, I would ask your Lordship how it is possible for myself and many who think as I do to reconcile their duty with their inclination should they support the measures of the present Government constituted as it now is. The conduct of the last session can not have given your Lordship, as I am sure it has not the country, a very mean opinion of those members of the late Government who have distinguished themselves most in the House of Commons, and with whatever confidence your colleagues may enter the lists this year, I fear the country will suffer, as I have no idea that its difficulties or dangers are in any degree diminished."

Dr. Thomas Zouch to the Earl of Lonsdale.

1808, Jan. 16, Durham.—"The Duke of Portland was certainly incorrect when he asserted that the annual value of Carlisle was nearer 4,000 than 3,000 pounds a year. Dr. Douglas held the Deanery

of Windsor along with Carlisle, and Dr. Law held his Mastership
of Peter House along with the living of Graystock. His Grace by
disposing of my living with my prebend would have taken from me
nearly what he would have given me. My character is, I find, much
higher in the world than what I ever thought it to be: and a
prime minister would not have disgraced himself by being a patron
of merit. Instead of that he has shewn himself as a factor, making
the best bargain that he can. Dr. Goodenough is glad to mount the
Bench on any terms, because he expects to rise higher, and will be
restless until he obtains in due time a translation . . . . . I mention
these things, not that I am dissatisfied, but just the reverse. My
situation is perfectly grateful to me, and the congratulations I have had
on declining the mitre convince me that I have not lost any honour by
that measure."

Dr. THOMAS ZOUCH to the EARL OF LONSDALE.

1808, March 4, College, Durham.

" Lord Lonsdale's History of the Reign of James II. will be printed
off in the end of next week or the beginning of the week after. I think
that 200 copies were to be printed.

I am informed that in the gallery of Mr. West's house at Windsor
is a picture of the Death of Sir Philip Sidney, and also a drawing of
Sir Philip Sidney ordering the water to be given to the wounded
soldiers—both by Mr. West. It would be an acquisition to my work
to have a description more particular of these two pieces . . . .
The Life of Sir P. S. will be printed off very soon. I am extremely
anxious lest it should not be received by the public according to my
wishes. An engraving of Sidney will be executed by Mr. Warren.
It is from a fine picture at Wentworth Castle given by Horace
Walpole to his friend Lord Strafford. But Mr. Vernon, who now
resides there, gives so vague an account of it, that I fear little dependence can be had upon what he says."

Dr. THOMAS ZOUCH to the EARL OF LONSDALE.

1808, April 21, College, Durham.—" I have just received from York
a packet containing twelve copies of Lord Lonsdale's Memoir. The
work is most beautifully printed. Fifty copies are forwarded to
Lowther, a certain number to Swillington, and the remainder will be
sent to Cottesmore in the course of a few days."

·Dr. THOMAS ZOUCH to the EARL OF LONSDALE.

1808, June 20, Sandal.—"I am very happy to know that the
Memoir [of James II.] is read with much satisfaction. Indeed I
did not doubt but that it would be generally approved. It has
frequently occurred to me that the publication of it would be very
useful, and a very proper antidote against Mr. Fox's History, which I
have read with much attention. In many passages of this long expected
work the language is coarse, and the style slovenly in the extreme.
Every writer of an English History should surely endeavour to improve
his native language. I say nothing of those political principles or
sentiments in Mr. Fox's volume, which are very objectionable."

THOMAS HOLCROFT to the EARL OF LONSDALE.

1808, Dec. 1, Clipstone Street, 30, Fitzroy Square (sic); and Dec. 7.
—Two letters asking assistance, and giving some particulars of his life,
which will be found in the dramatist's *Memoirs*.

The Hon. H. C. LOWTHER to the EARL OF LONSDALE.

The Hon. H. C. LOWTHER to the EARL OF LONSDALE.

1808 Dec. 4, Astorga.—"It is quite out of my power to send you any news from this country, although we are upon the spot, everything is kept quite silent from us, and there are so many different reports, we do not know which to give the most credit to, nothing even is to be heard from the Spaniards.

I saw an English paper yesterday dated the 12 of last month, it mentioned that the army was treated with the greatest civility possible; it is quite the contrary, they do not like us in the least, and they tell us very often (to please us) that they had rather see the French than us, I do not know how our generals get on, but I suppose it is they that receive the civility, as they are always at a nobleman's (if they may be so called) house, but one of their houses is not half so comfortable, or one tenth part so clean as an English cottage. It is impossible for anyone who has not been to Spain, to conceive how the Spaniards live in their filth and dirt, they have no amusement whatever, you never by any chance see one with a book in his hand (but that is the case with a great many of our English gentlemen); the way they pass their day is I believe in sleeping and smoking, for that is the only way we see them pass it, they are quite ignorant of everything that is going on, they think they have three different armies in Spain, amounting to three hundred thousand men, and their whole force in Spain does not amount to more than than 25,000, and 80 cavalry (sic) that we can hear of, and they say they could mount 80 more if they could get horses, I have given you a short account of the inhabitants of Spain and now I will give you one of the country. The principal part of our march has been through the mountains, in short, I may say the whole way except the last day. It is a most beautiful country, and numbers of uncommon fine rivers and bridges. We are going in a few days to undergo a long and tedious march to Lisbon, and I am afraid a very cold one as we have to pass a great number of snowy mountains."

Dr. THOMAS ZOUCH to the EARL OF LONSDALE.

1809, July 19. Durham.—"Mr. Southey, whose usual place of residence is at or near Keswick, has been upon a visit to his brother, a physician of this place. He is pretty well known by his Works, his prose and poetical compositions making no fewer than twenty volumes. He dined with me one day. His conversation is very interesting and full of anecdote. He is now engaged in writing the History of Portugal. The fertility of his imagination is such that he will never find any difficulty in furnishing materials for the employment of his pen.

The prospect of affairs on the Continent assumes a more pleasing appearance, but it seems impossible to terminate the horrors of war so long as the ferocity of the Corsican is allowed by Providence to exercise its relentless rage with impunity."

The Hon. H. C. LOWTHER to the EARL OF LONSDALE.

1813 Sept. 1, Bilbao.—"Part of our regiment arrived in the entrance of the river Durango (which is the river that runs through Bilbao) when we disembarked the next day, and marched into the town of B———. It is a tolerable good town, but a very mountainous country around it. I have not heard anything respecting the army since my arrival, nor can I learn any particulars respecting St. Sebastian. We had a tolerable good passage, we were on board twelve days, and we have not had a wet day since we left London. Three of our transports have not yet arrived in the river, and it is supposed that they are gone to St. Andero which is about 40 or 50 miles W. from Bilboa. I hope they have not put into St. Antona by mistake, for the French have possession of it, and it is garrisoned by 2,500—at least those are the numbers that the Spaniards say they have there—however it is an amazing strong place, it is a small island about 2 or 3 miles in circumference, with very strong batteries surrounding it, and they have also very heavy guns upon the mount which lays nearly in the centre of the island, and which is very high and commands the whole island. The Spaniards are blockading them and prevent them getting fresh provisions, but I am afraid they will annoy our transports very much for they have a corvette and several privateers, which are constantly on the watch to catch any straggling vessels. They succeeded one night in cutting out a store ship from the river, that is the only one I believe they have as yet taken. Our ships cannot get at them, for they run into their harbour the moment they see any of our armed vessels, and there they are safe, for they are under the protection of a 20 gun battery. It is situated rather in an unfortunate place for our transports, for it lays about half way between this town and St. Andero, and our store ships are constantly employed in going from one place to the other.

. I have not heard when we are likely to march from hence, but I should not think that we shall remain in our present quarters for this fortnight, for they are not in any want of cavalry at present. The Spaniards from what I have as yet seen are not the least improved in respect to their civility towards you. But I always understood that the Biscayans were the worst conditioned people in Spain. The army is employed in making breast works, and strengthening the passes over the Pyrenees as much as possible.

There are an immense number of wounded lying at this town, I should think to the amount of nearly four thousand, I believe there is nearly the same number at St. Andero. I believe that I mentioned to you that Capt. Gordon of the *Magicienne* was so good as to give me a passage in his frigate. We had rather a large party, for he brought Col. Kerrison and Elphinstone also. You will hear of the fate of St. Sebastian long before I can send you any account of it, for there is very little communication with the army from hence, since we have got possession of Passage which is between six and seven miles E. of. St. Sebastian."

The Hon. H. C. LOWTHER to the EARL OF LONSDALE.

1813, Sept. 6, Bilbao.—"There are an immense number of French prisoners going through here daily to be embarked for England, they are chiefly young men and a great many young boys with them, they are very sick of war and complain most bitterly against Bonaparte. There were several French officers on their parole in this town when we arrived, waiting for a passage to England, one of whom is a French colonel whose regiment which consisted of 5,000 men were all killed or wounded to a man ; he himself was wounded in the shoulder ; they had to cover the retreat after the battle of Busaco. Lord Wellington wished to get him exchanged as he behaved so well, but Soult had received strict orders from Bonaparte not to exchange a man, and this has

enraged the French colonel and his account of the proceedings of
Bonaparte and his government is horrible. He states the south of
France to be in a state of rebellion against his government, but he says
it is so drained of men that it would be impossible to muster any men
to rise against it. He says also that he should not be the least
surprised at their joining the English if they were to march into their
country."

The Hon. H. C. Lowther to the Earl of Lonsdale.

1813, Oct. 1, Bilbao.—" We are to march from hence in the morning to Durango which is 20 miles distance from hence, and there remain
until Sir Stapleton Cotton has inspected us, and then we proceed on our
march to Olite, which will most probably take us eight or ten days, as
the roads I understand are very bad and mountainous. Col. Vivian
returned from head quarters yesterday, but he has not brought any
news with him, he says the army is in capital condition and very
healthy, and the numbers amount to upwards of 100,000 men. He
says that he should not be the least surprised at the army advancing.
They are kept at work the whole of the day in fortifying the passes in
the Pyrenees. Lord Wellington has placed a Spanish garrison in St.
Sebastian, and he has set them to work to rebuild the walls of the town
and castle, and I understand that it will be made uncommonly strong.
The French Army does not amount to more than 36,000 men. Of course
you have received the accounts of the retreat of Lord W. Bentinck's army.
I am afraid Suchet is in too great a force to allow Lord W. B. to drive
him out of the country. Our route to Olite is a very circuitous one,
but it is on account of getting supplies. The principal places in which
we pass are Bergara, Tolosa, and then we come back to Irurzun, and
Noain, which you will see by the map is within half a league of Pampeluna and from thence we shall go to Olite, and there remain until
there is a movement in the army. One of our officers saw young Chaplin
three days ago, he was then going on very well and out of danger. The
Spaniards seem very anxious for an advance into France, they expect
to regain their losses again, but I think they will find themselves very
much mistaken. We have had uncommonly fine weather since our
arrival, and very little rain, considering we are in so mountainous a
country."

The Hon. H. C. Lowther to the Earl of Lonsdale.

1813, Oct. 17, Olite.—" We arrived last Friday at Olite which is to
be our winter quarters, if Lord Wellington does not make any further
advance into France. We passed Pampeluna on the 15th inst., and it
had not then surrendered, we halted that night at a small village called
Noain which is between one and two miles from thence; there was a
constant firing that day, and the following morning when we marched
we heard the firing commence again. The garrison are now living
upon four oz. of horse-flesh and three oz. of bread, and Don Carlos who
commands the Spanish Army in front of Pampeluna says that he thinks
they will be able to hold out a week or ten days longer. The French
general attempted to send 3,000 of the inhabitants out of the town last
week, but Don Carlos sent to him to say, that it would go very much
against his inclination to fire upon his countrymen, but if he did send
them out of town he would fire upon them instantly. However the
French persisted in sending them out and Don Carlos fired upon them,
and the French were obliged to admit them into the town again. The
Spanish general also sent word to the commandant of the garrison, that

if he heard of any Spaniard whatever being starved to death, that he should give orders, when the town surrendered, to have the commandant hung. And I believe Don Carlos will be as good as his word, for a greater savage I believe never lived, at least that is his character in this part of the world. We have come through a most beautiful country and capital roads. We halted one night at a small village called Irurzun, which is about 14 miles N. of Pampeluna, and about 45 miles E. of Vittoria. I have mentioned this, as it was the village in which Lord Wellington dated his 2nd despatch after the battle of Vittoria, and it is also where the French lost their last gun. It is a very small village, situated at the foot of several very high mountains, and which mountains are called the Gates of Biscay. The pass in which the road runs, which is the high road from France to Spain, appears as if the rocks had been cut away for the purpose of making a road, and the valley which the road runs through is upwards of three miles long, and I am sure not above 20 yards wide. It is the most singular thing I ever saw for it would be impossible to pass over any part of the mountains, they are so steep and craggy. Since writing the above I have just heard a report, that they expect the French to make a sortie from Pampeluna, and endeavour to make their escape to France. If that is true, we shall in all probability have a gallop after them, for we are not more than 25 miles from them at present. Sir Thomas Graham of course has arrived with the news of Lord Wellington having passed the Bidassoa and taken up his quarters in France in front of St. Jean de Luz. It is reported to have been the most complete attack that ever was made. The French were attacked at every point, and I suppose they have not forgot the lickings they have received from us in Spain, for they ran from every point they were attacked. Lord Wellington has now got possession of the position he was so anxious of obtaining, and what is of still more advantage to him he will be able to get his supplies up the Bidassoa instead of having to cross those very high mountains. The commissariat have lost upwards of 5,000 mules, since the army has been upon the mountains.

Will you tell my mother that I received her letter dated the 23 of September, and it has given me great pleasure to hear of your all being so well. We are going on uncommonly well in this country, we find it very different to what it was the last time we were here. And I have been as comfortable every day as if I was marching through England. We are ten times better off both for men and horses than we were in Ireland. You must not tell Pat so, or he will never speak to me again. The country we are quartered in at present, is very flat and not a fence for miles and miles, a delightful country for cavalry to act."

The Hon. H. C. LOWTHER to the EARL OF LONSDALE.

1813. Nov. 3, Musquz.—" We marched from Olite the moment Pampeluna fell into the hands of the Spaniards, which was on the 1st of this month. They surrendered upon conditions of being prisoners of war, and I am sorry to say that the Spaniards behaved to them in the most infamous way possible. They plundered every man the moment they lay down their arms and even stripped them as naked as when they were born. They were not even content with that, but the savages (for you cannot call them anything else) murdered, I am under the mark when I say thirty, because the prisoners retaliated at being treated in that manner. I should not have believed it, had I not seen the bodies lying upon the road, and upon enquiries the Spaniards told me this story, and they spoke of it at the same time, with such enthusiasm as if it was the bravest act that ever was done by Spanish troops, which will ever make me hate the name of Spaniard as long as I live. I am at present quartered at Musquz, which you will see in the map, it is about 15 miles N. of Pampeluna, and about 6 miles E. of Irurzun. It is a very small village consisting of 7 or 8 houses, and in the very centre of the mountains, and I believe we shall remain here until Lord Wellington decides whether he enters France or not. It is the general opinion throughout the army that he intends attacking the French lines and making a rapid march into France, for he has a sufficient force with him for so doing, and his army is in high condition. I went into Pampeluna as our regiment passed under the walls, I think it is by far the finest town I have seen in Spain, and kept beautifully clean; how long it will remain so now the French have left it I cannot say. The French held out until the very last moment they were able. They lived for the last three weeks upon nothing but 4 oz. of bread and 3 oz. of horse-flesh. A great many of the Spaniards were starved to death, one of whom was the Grande of the town. It is an amazing strong place, on the north side it is bordered by the river Agra, and a steep rock of at least 80 feet arising from the foot of the river, the north-west side is by nature falling ground, of at least 60 feet, and the Spaniards long before the French ever had possession of it, built a perpendicular wall on that side, so that it made an amazing strong place on that angle, especially as the ground on that angle of the town falls to the river, which you will see by the map is some distance from that angle of the town, as the river takes a bend after it has passed the north end of the town. The south side there is not any means of approaching with artillery, as the river winds nearly three parts round the town, and the ground upon which the town is built, falling so steep upon the river, and at a distance of at least 3 quarters of a mile. The S.W. end of the town, is the citadel and commands the whole of the city. It is built upon the highest ground, and it commands the whole country around it, as the ground falls so directly from it, and there is not a single rise, for at least 2 miles, so that it would be perfectly ridiculous ever attempting to storm it at least as far as I can see, and from what people say who understand these things. It is of vast importance to our army, for in case Lord Wellington retires (which I hope is not likely) the French cannot advance as long as we have possession of it, and they knew well before they surrendered, of what importance it would be to us, and that they kept Lord Wellington's army in check as long as they held out. No further movements I believe have been made in the army since I last wrote, but we are all anxiously looking forward to spending our winter in France."

The Hon. H. C. LOWTHER to the EARL OF LONSDALE.

1813, Nov. 11, St. Esteran.—" Lord Wellington made his attack upon the French lines yesterday, and I am happy to say with great success, but I am sorry to add with severe loss. The action commenced about 5 o'clock in the morning upon the centre and right of the French army. The French began their retreat about 11 o'clock and continued it I understand, as far as a league in rear of Bayonne. They suffered immensely, two of their divisions in the centre of their army were nearly cut to pieces, with the loss of two French generals and another wounded. Lord Wellington's head-quarters are at a small village, distant of about two miles from Bayonne. The French lost an immense number of guns. No British officer has yet arrived in this town, and these accounts are only picked up from wounded Spaniards who have come to this town. We are not above nine or ten miles from where the action commenced, and·yesterday morning we heard the firing, which was very heavy indeed, until 11 o'clock, and then it began to be very faint, and at about 4 o'clock we could not hear a shot. The wind was in the same quarter the whole day, so that the army must have advanced, or we must have heard the firing in the evening. It was as fine a day as could possibly be yesterday. I went up upon a very high mountain in the morning, just above the town, in hopes of being able to see part of the army, but I was disappointed. I saw an immense way into France, and I saw also part of the smoke rising from the left of our line, but the country being so very hilly prevented my seeing anything of thé lines. We are waiting in expectation of being called upon every moment, as Lord Wellington wrote to Lord Edward Somerset (who commands our brigade) the night before the action, saying that the frontiers of France were too hilly for cavalry to act, and desired him to keep us here until he made a further advance into France, so that I have no doubt we shall soon be called upon as the French are retiring so fast."

The Hon. H. C. LOWTHER to the EARL OF LONSDALE.

1813 Nov. 17, Sare.—"Our regiment is now quartered at Sare; it is about 6 miles from the frontiers of Spain, and it is where Lord Wellington first commenced his attack upon the French lines. I have been over the greatest part of the ground where the centre and left of our army was engaged, and from the very strong positions the enemy held, you would not have thought it possible for troops to have got possession of the heights, so strongly fortified as they were, in so short a space of time. The French, ever since they took up that position, have been strengthening themselves by fortifications, breast-works, &c., and from Sare to St. Jean de Luz (where Lord Wellington has taken up his head-quarters), which is upwards of twelve miles, their works are innumerable and immensely strong, and for many miles in rear of where the attack commenced, the ground was in every way favourable in affording them the greatest resistance against our troops, by a chain of hills which are scarcely more than seven hundred yards apart, and at the top of each hill were strong batteries. The French by all accounts seem to have premeditated their retreat, for they took care to have a good road from each of their batteries, and thus retreated in the greatest order possible, and abandoned several of their positions long before our troops reached them. One position in particular, which was full a league in rear of where the attack commenced, and which was an eleven gun battery and garrisoned by six hundred picked men, chiefly Grenadiers, and what seems more extraordinary they had upwards of four days' provisions in it, surrendered without firing a shot. The fact was I believe that the British advanced so rapidly, that they were surrounded before they had the least conception of our troops being so near them. Our loss compared with the French is very great, but that must have been foreseen from the nature of the ground, our troops upon all occasions having to attack them in their redoubts. The French prisoners I believe amount to nearly 1,000, and they lost also 52 pieces of artillery. St. Jean de Luz surrendered, their troops making but a slight resistance. The French set fire to the bridge, but the inhabitants extinguished it, before it did any damage. A great number of the inhabitants fled from the town but have since returned, and others are coming back to the town daily: They are uncommonly civil to our troops, they treated our wounded with the greatest kindness possible, and gave them every assistance that lay in their power. The French

villages I have been in are nearly deserted, and a great number who
have returned, all agree in saying that they were forced by their own
troops to quit their houses, with the threat that if they did not, their
houses should be burnt and they themselves hung. The only dread the
inhabitants have is that of the Spaniards being quartered upon them.
Wherever a Spanish soldier entered a house, he destroyed every article
in the house and even pulled the roofs from the houses. Lord
Wellington hung seven on the 10th inst. and I have heard of several
more since that have been executed for plundering. He has sent the
whole of the Spanish army to the rear as far as Tolosa and Villa Franca.
I never saw people more civil or more attentive then the French are to
our soldiers. We have marched through a most beautiful country since
I last wrote to you, over the very tops of the Pyrenees, which makes
France look very flat, although it is a hilly country; what little I have
seen is very pretty and resembles Yorkshire. Two sergeants of the
Gens d'Armes deserted to our army on the night of the 16th inst., and
they informed the officer whom I met the following morning that great
discontent prevailed in the French army, they not having received a
farthing of their pay for these last five years, and the troops since they
have been in their own country have scarcely drawn any provisions.
They also stated that they had heard three weeks ago (for the first time)
the result of Bonaparte's campaign in Russia, and that now it was
generally spoken of throughout the whole army. They also stated that
papers had arrived from Paris, stating that no accounts had been received
from Bonaparte for three days and the report was that he was missing.
I hope he never will be found again. They also said that the French
army had not the least confidence in the commanding officer (Soult) and
that the British would defeat them whenever they chose to attack
them; and I am sure you would believe it if you were to see the positions they left without even thinking of making a stand. Our light
divisions suffered severely, the 54th which forms one of the brigade lost
nearly 300 men, and the 95th also had upwards of two-thirds of their
men killed and wounded."

The Hon. H. C. LOWTHER to the EARL OF LONSDALE.

1813, Nov. 22nd, Echauri.—" Since I last wrote to you we received
orders to retreat to this part of the country, there not being a sufficiency
of forage for our horses in France, which has disappointed us all very
much, as we expected to spend our winter quarters in France, and being
marched over the Pyrenees at this time of year, we little thought of
being sent back again in so short a space of time. Our regiment is now
quartered on the banks of the Agra, in seven different villages, my
troop at present is at Echauri, it is but a small place, but we have a
sufficiency of forage in it to last our troops the whole winter, it is about
2 leagues and a half from Pampeluna, and about 6 leagues from Estella,
and lays in a direct line between these two towns. Lord Wellington
has taken up his winter quarters at St. Jean de Luz, and all our troops
have been allowed to put up in villages and houses for the first time
these six months and it is generally supposed that Lord Wellington
does not intend making any further movement until the spring. Two
of our generals were wounded on the 19th inst. reconnoitering; General
Vachleur is one and General Wilson the other, the latter general was
shot through the lower jaw, and the ball was extracted from the roots
of his tongue." Asks his father to use his influence to procure him
promotion to a majority in one of the West India regiments, which he
would not be compelled to join as long as he remained in Parliament.
[The writer was member for Westmorland.]

The Hon. H. C. LOWTHER to his brother VISCOUNT LOWTHER.

1813, Dec. 2. Echauri.—" We are now under orders to go to the front again, which I am not sorry for in the least, as I am quite tired of remaining still in this country, and as France is far more preferable to any part of Spain, we expect now to have comfortable winter quarters, although we shall have the outpost duty, but that will not come to our turn more than once in four or five days, as there is a fine river between the two armies. The French are uncommonly civil to our troops. St. Juan de Luce is a very good town and as good a market as in any town in England. There were upwards of two thousand people returned to the town last week. The peasants are also returning to their cottages daily, and it is generally supposed that in the course of a few weeks, that they will nearly all be returned. They talk of Lord Wellington remaining in his present quarters during the winter, I cannot say how far this is true, but one thing I know, that he is collecting all his force together and orders have been given repeatedly to all the surgeons of hospitals not to keep a man a day after he is fit to do his duty, so that by that he wishes to have as strong a force with him as possible. Lord Wellington has sent the whole of the Spanish army to the rear, they behaved so infamously to the inhabitants, they were not content with plundering the different houses, but in many places they broke the limbs of the poor unfortunate people. And even the inhabitants of Spain came for miles and miles, when they heard of the advance of the army into France, and they returned with their mules laden with plunder. When Lord Wellington heard of this, he ordered our regiment to send out patrols and catch these plunderers and search their mules, and in the course of four or five days, I believe we sent in upwards of eight hundred of these rascals to head-quarters. They soon found out what our men were always patroling the country for, and for the last two or three days we were in France, the moment they saw a man of our regiment coming, they used to set off across the country as fast as they could."

The Hon. H. C. LOWTHER to the EARL OF LONSDALE.

1814. Feb. 3rd, Hasparren. " Every person seems to think that Lord Wellington will advance very shortly, and I should conceive it very probable that he would, for he cannot remain much longer in his present quarters unless he wishes to starve the inhabitants, for they are all crying out for bread, and they all agree in saying that they have not above a fortnight's consumption left in their houses, and that they must either leave their homes and houses or starve. I believe it to be the case, for when the army first came into this country, both infantry and cavalry took every morsel of grain they could find in the houses for their horses and mules, and I know myself that our regiment has been in every house within ten miles of their present quarters, and that they could not find a grain of corn in any one of them, so that we must either advance to allow the inhabitants to get provisions, or on the other hand, if we remain in our present quarters these poor unfortunate people must remain at home and starve. The country now is nearly drained of everything, and there is scarcely a thing to be got but what comes from England. Our horses have been living these last three weeks upon nothing but chopped furze and about once a week we get about 10 lbs. of corn, every bit of hay and straw being consumed in the country. I am very sorry for the fate of these poor unfortunate inhabitants, for they are the best tempered race of people I ever met with,

Q

and will do anything in the world you ask of them. I should conceive this country in time of peace, to be one of the richest and most beautiful countries in the world. There is not an inhabitant that does not possess a capital house, and as for anything like a poor cottage [it] is quite unknown in this country, and what is more surprising, there is not a single beggar to be met with, which is very different to Spain, for you cannot move in that country without having eight or ten at your heels.

Some Spanish officers who arrived at this place two days ago, and who were sent from the interior to be exchanged, state that about 2C0 miles from hence they met two divisions of infantry and 2,500 cavalry marching towards Paris. The inhabitants informed us three weeks ago, that two divisions of Infantry had left Soult's army, but very little credit was given to them as they bring in so many false reports. However their report is confirmed now, so that Soult's army at present must be very weak, Their whole army is under arms every morning an hour before daylight and remains so until 11 or 12 o'clock, for they expect to be attacked every day. The Spaniards have had a good deal of skirmishing with them lately, but the Spaniards run away in a most shameful manner."

The Hon. H. C. LOWTHER to the EARL OF LONSDALE.

1814, Feb. 18th, Oregue, 2 leagues on the Hasparren side of St. Palais.—"The army advanced on the 14th of this month, and the French retreated making but very little defence. Sir R. Hill had the command of the right of the army which advanced on that day about one mile beyond Hellette which you will see by the map is about 12 miles distant from St. Jean Pied de Port. The French retreated after dark to a height about 3 miles in front of St. Palais, where our army overtook them about 2 o'clock on Tuesday. There was skirmishing until dark and at 7 o'clock the British troops attacked them. They were taken quite by surprise as our troops advanced during the time our artillery kept a heavy fire upon the spot where the French were observed to take their position before dark. The English, Portuguese, and Spaniards, advanced at the same time in three different columns upon the height, and it being perfectly dark, the enemy were panic struck at the approach of the troops, and as they had not the slightest expectation of an attack, they were not prepared for the reception of the allies, and from what I can learn they lost about 300 prisoners, a great number of officers. The slaughter on the enemy's side was immense. They retreated that night beyond St. Palais, and are moving upon Peyrehorade as fast as they can. The advance of the British have crossed the river which runs by St. Palais, and falls into the Adour and the following day the army crossed the river at St. Palais and Came, and what advance we have made since I am quite in the dark. Our regiment is now turning out to advance to a village about 6 miles beyond Came called Arraute."

The Hon. H. C. LOWTHER to the EARL OF LONSDALE.

1814, March 7th, Barcelona.—"I have been ever since the 15th of last month wishing that we might halt a day that I might be able to send you a few lines to let you know how we were going on, but ever since that day until now we have not had an hour to ourselves. So what has been done in this country lately, I must refer you to his lordship's despatches, for we never know what is passing on in the army excepting at the spot in which we are. I am happy to say, and you

will also be glad to hear that our regiment received thanks in general
orders the day after the battle of Orthes for their steady and gallant
conduct on that day. We charged the infantry twice, the first time
was early in the day, the second was about 5 o'clock in the evening,
when we took twelve officers, and upwards of seven hundred men. We
had three officers wounded and our loss was about thirty men killed and
wounded. Thornhill I am sorry to say was badly wounded, he has
joined us since and is recovering fast. I was very much afraid that his
wound was worse than it now appears to have been, for it was a thrust
from a standard just below the ribs, the only standard that was taken on
that day. He attributes his life being saved by my tumbling over his
opponent, for I saw the perilous situation he was in, and galloping up to
the man, my horse fell with me about two yards before I reached him,
which knocked him over, and we all lay sprawling upon the ground
together. However in the scuffle Monsieur lost his standard, and I had
my sword fast round my wrist, which made him then very civil, and beg
for mercy, which I was glad to give him, for I should not have relished
a poke from such a weapon in the least. The allies' loss on that day
was severe, owing to the strong position they had to drive the enemy
from. Soult is said to have declared to his officers and men, that the
British with whatever force they could bring against him, could not
drive him from those heights in three days. However, he was egre-
giously mistaken and his loss on that day is estimated at 10,000 men,
including deserters after they were driven from their position, which
was late in the evening, for our attack did not begin until past twelve
o'clock. Their whole army was in confusion in a valley near Sault (*sic*)
Sever, about one league and a half from Orthes, and if the country had
been open, and not so very much enclosed as it was, their whole army
must have been cut to pieces by the British cavalry. For the French
troops were so tired they could not run, but were moving off as fast as
they were able without looking behind them to see whether any troops
were following them. They have retreated by St. Sever, and were
making for Bordeaux, but hearing Sir J. Hope had crossed the Adour
and might get there before them, they altered their course and are supposed to be making their way to Toulouse, to join Suchet at that town.
They have blown up every bridge on the road, which has impeded us
very much, and by which means they have got several days start of us,
and unless Suchet's army joins M. Soult, I do not believe we shall ever
see his army again, for deserters are coming in every hour and there is
scarcely a day passes without twenty or 30 arriving. Our regimen at
present is about a league in front of Barcelona on the Auch road. I
believe we shall halt a few days for the weather has been very wet
lately, which has overflowed the rivers, so that we expect to remain in
our present quarters until the weather gets more settled.

Sir Rowland Hill gave the French division which was on the south
side of the Adour a good drubbing the other evening. I was on picquet
on the opposite side of the river close to the town of Air and saw the
whole affair. They drove the French in every direction and took a great
many prisoners. Our loss was 150 killed and wounded. There is a
report circulated that the allies have entered Paris without a shot being
fired, but whether it is the case or not we are quite ignorant."

The Hon. H. C. Lowther to the Earl of Lonsdale.

1815, August 23rd, Beauvais.—" I have to thank you for your letter
I received a few days ago. I have been to Paris for this last week.
Marshal Ney is arrived there, he came last Thursday, and his trial is

to come on in a very few days. He was taken in Switzerland at a relation's house, by the Gens d'Armery, who followed him so close that he had been but a very few hours in the house before they came up with him. Labédoyère was shot near Paris by a company of Grenadiers, on the very day that Ney arrived, and I hope he will have the same fate. He deserves it richly. Troops are arriving in this country daily, and the general opinion seems to be that the army will not return home until near Christmas. The Duchess of Rutland passed through here on her way to Paris about a fortnight ago. The Prussians have taken a great number of pictures from the gallery and would have taken a vast number more, had not the other Powers interfered. I did not hear until a few days ago, the particulars of poor major Hodge's death. The man who informed me was a private in the regiment, who had been wounded at the same time, and was passing through this town on his way to join the 7th. The facts are these, that Hodge charged on the 17th at the head of his squadron, against the enemy's Lancers, who were formed up in the high road, in which charge his horse was killed and himself badly wounded, having a sabre cut across the head, and his bridle hand nearly cut in two. He was taken prisoner with two privates of the 7th who had their horses killed also, before they had gone 100 yards to the rear, the 7th charged the Lancers a second time and obliged them to retire, at which period the Lancers conceiving they were defeated, put to death their prisoners. Hodge was piked in two places through the neck and back, and he expired instantly. The soldier who told me this was within two yards of Hodge the whole time and was wounded himself in three places, having two pike wounds in his side and one on his head. This man was in hospital at Brussels at the time Mrs. Hodge was there, she went to see him, and asked him if he knew anything concerning her husband's death, he gave her the whole account, but she would not believe a single word of it. Alas ! I am afraid she will find it too true."

II.—MANUSCRIPTS AT WHITEHAVEN CASTLE.

Roger Kirkby [M.P. for Lancaster] to his brother-in-law Christopher Lowther, High Sheriff of the county of Cumberland.

1641, July 5, [London] . . . . . . " The House of Commons has declared that it is not fit that so much luxury should be used by sheriffs in their entertainments and attendants, and that no sheriff should give any entertainment to the judges, nor fees or gratuities to the judge's men ; and this declaration the Lord Keeper is to acquaint the judges withal before they go in their circuits ; and the House is resolved to proceed to make an Act for the prevention of such inconveniences for the future. However this is a sure opportunity to do both yourself and the country right. This I thought good to give you notice of as timely as possible, it being but the motion of yesterday, and so you may fit your occasions."

. . . . " Yesterday I must tell you there appeared a little rub in our proceedings which is much feared by many and what effects it may produce is to be feared in-

deed. It was this, we had prepared two bills, one for the extirpation of the Star Chamber, and regulating the Council board; and another for the taking away the High Commission Court. These we hoped should have passed, with the great bill of Poll money: but his Majesty gave his assent to the Poll bill, and took time to consider of the other two. This has begotten very much discontent amongst men especially in the City, so as it is thought the money will not be paid unless those bills pass; but what will be the end no one knows. This great sum is to be received by all the sheriffs of England, and some are to return the money to York and some to London . . . . .
The want of money for the disbanding of the services, and the jealousies amongst men begotten by these plots and conspiracies and discontents about the Court, have put a delay and a stand in all other business; and yet we have sitten every day both forenoon and aftereven till 8 or 9 of the clock at night. The business now in band is the charges against the Bishop (*sic*) of Canterbury, and the judges, the disbanding of the army, and the further discovery of Perlies (*sic*) plot, which by some men is much more feared than by others, being verily thought by many it will end in nothing.
This day the King hath passed the two bills and all are well pleased, so that now there is no talk but of great disbanding, and the King's going into Scotland."

Roger Kirkby [M.P. for Lancaster] to his brother-in-law Christopher Lowther, High Sheriff of the county of Cumberland.

1641, July 10.—"The House of Commons continue in their resolution concerning the entertainment of judges and the exorbitant fees and gratuities challenged by their men. There is a bill in the House which has been twice read against this abuse, and for the present there is a Committee appointed to draw a declaration to that purpose whereof I am one; this day we are to meet about it. . . . For the judges we hear of none spoken of yet for our circuit but Serjeant Whitfeeld alone . . .
For news I must refer you to the last, only this, the King has made his manifesto concerning the Queen of Bohemia, his sister, and her children; and the House of Commons has approved of it. . . For the Bishops' bill, which is now the great work in agitation, and it is a great work indeed, for the settlement of the government of the Church doth depend upon it, is as yet but under commitment in our House and hath many rubs, going with much difficulty on; so that if it pass as it is thought it will go off with much opposition; and then what will be be done in the Lords' house may be easily imagined."

The Same to the Same.

1641, August 12. . . . "For the judges Sir Robert Heath is to be your only judge. He will come from York to Appleby, and so to Carlisle, which will be the 2nd of September. I was with him, and did present your service to him, but for matter of his entertainment did not meddle because the House of Commons was still in hand with their declarations concerning these things, but was not finished when I came down."

The Same to the Same.

1641, Aug. 15.—On private matters.

PROTESTANT DISSENTERS of WHITEHAVEN.

1694, July 6, Whitehaven.—Memorial of the Protestant Dissenters to Sir John Lowther for the grant of "so much ground as might serve the good intent and purpose of your humble servants who would not desire more in front than twenty yards and thirty yards backwards, in Hodgson's Croft near the rivulet."

About 60 signatures attached—only 3 or 4 by mark.

[1694, Nov. 5.] and 1694-5, March 20, Whitehaven.—Letters of thanks, signed by Elisha Gale and others, for the great favour conferred upon them by the grant of the above.

WILLIAM PENN to Sir JOHN LOWTHER.

1701, June 16 ("16·6ᵐ"), Pennsberry.—" Honored Friend, I would not but have thought my selfe lost in thy country entertainments but I finde that Whitehaven is much kinder than Whitehall to Pennsylvania, for the one sends it good wishes and the other suffers itselfe to be mislead to crush such prosperous beginings. I return my most hearty acknowledgements for thy obligeing remembrance and beg the continuance of thy good word and wishes for our prosperity; for whatever interested men suggest, we are an approved experiment what sobriety and industry can do in a wilderness against heats, colds, wants and dangers. The Crown gets best by us, but its officers less than by other Governments, and that's our crime; but time will sett truth in a better light, to which I adjourn my resentments. We thrive, our town, I think, too much for the country, not keeping a ballance in all things in Government is (perhaps) the hidden but sure cause of visible obstructions and entanglements in administration. I finde the country 70 miles back, the best land, Sasquehanah a glorious river boatable upon freshes. We are planted 170 miles upon Delaware, and in some places 16 miles back into the woods. Our staple corn and tobacco ; we are trying for rice, converted timber for shipping and hemp. Returns for England is what we want, and either we must have less from thence or better ways of making them. Barbado's and those Islands are our market and we are too hard for our neighbours in our flowr and bread, being the whitest and preferred ; we spare much of both to our neighbour colonys also, as New England, Maryland, Virginia, and Carolina, where wheat will hardly grow, but rice to perfection, and silk is got to a good pitch, and will certainly be a commodity. We have had a good share of health since our arrival and my family encrease by a little son, and if ill treatment call us not home are like, if God please to prolong life, to pass away a year or two at least. Only my privat affairs could make me leave it any more, but they will compel it once again, and then it would not displease me to lay my bones where I have layd my labour, mony, and solicitation, in Pennsylvania.

I shall close with this assurance that I am with great esteem and affection

thy very faithfull Friend
WM. PENN."

NICHOLAS LECHMERE to [JAMES LOWTHER].

1713, Sept. 17.—I am very sensible how much I am obliged to you for the success of my election. Your presence and favour was a balance to the good will of your brother Lawson, of which I had some account. By all the computations I have heard of distinguishing between Whig and Tory, the latter are least 3 to 1 ; but on the Court test, which is, for or against the Bill of Commerce, 'tis believed the Bill has lost ground.

[There are two or three letters previous to this touching Lechmere's election for Cockermouth.]

HENRY NEWMAN to the Honble. JAMES LOWTHER, member of Parliament, at Whitehaven.

1713, October 8.—Young man's Coffeehouse [London].

"The Guardian was laid down this day senight and the Englishman is rise up to supply its place. The subject of it this day is what I have often heard you bewail, the loss of public spirits (*sic*); and therefore I have sent it for your meditation, it being some satisfaction to find others of the same sentiments with our selves tho' upon a melancholy theme. That Mr. Steele is the author of this as much as he was of the other I believe I need not tell you, because his style discovers him in whatever he writes. He is very much threaten'd to be voted disqualified to serve this Parliament, but I hope with the help of you and some other of his. friends he will be able to keep his seat . . . . . General Cadogan is come over and has had a gracious reception as is said by the Government, and my Lord Tr——r said t'other day at his levée *we expect the Duke over in a little time*, but whether he means anything or nothing by saying so time will unfold. I am sorry General Stanhope miscarried at Cockermouth, but 'tis hoped he will be chose at Sarum, where Mr. (Fox ?) since his election is dead . . . Things abroad look as ever. M. Villars is besieging Fribourg, and if Pr. Eugene can't give him battle must in all likelihood carry it, and then nothing but a general battle can hinder his marching into Bavaria. There will be a great struggle in the City election next Monday, and 'tis thought the contest will end in choosing 2 W—gs and 2 T's."

HENRY NEWMAN to the Honble. JAMES LOWTHER, member of Parliament, at Whitehaven.

1713, October 20.—Whitehall. . . . . . .

The Poll (in the City) began yesterday se'night and is not yet ended, unless they have closed it by consent this evening when the Poll books yielded the following numbers :—

Ward, 3,654.	Hoare, 3,667.
Scawen, 3,552.	Withers, 3,587.
Heysham, 3,665.	Cass, 3,633.
Godfrey, 3,604.	Newland, 3,655.

Considering the great influence the magistracy, Common Council, and Lieutenancy have over the City 'tis a wonder the W—gs have been able to make such a shew on this occasion as they have.

HENY NEWMAN to the Honble. JAMES LOWTHER, member of Parliament, at Whitehaven.

1713, Nov. 3.—Whitehall. . . . . . .

Mr. St——le under the title of Englishman continues to write very freely and 'tis hoped will open some men's eyes.

HENRY NEWMAN to the Honble. JAMES LOWTHER, member of Parliament, at Whitehaven.

1713, November 21, Whitehall.— . . . . .

The Treasury writers begin to be out of breath, and the W—gs to take heart, and if you'll believe the Examiner of Monday last there are great prognostications that the present M——y will not be of long duration, though he trembles to think what will be the consequences of the W——gs getting into the saddle again ; one of which he says will be to involve all Europe abroad in a Civil war. His Paper of yesterday says nothing on this head but gives notice of a voluntary resignation he is about to make of his paper, and to acknowledge that some of his adversaries have acted their parts pretty well, the Medley especially.

. . . . . .

The Englishman of last Thursday dissected the Jacobite folio about Hereditary Right, &c. so as to spoil effectually the market of the book, and to open the eyes of many people.

HENRY NEWMAN to the Honble. JAMES LOWTHER, member of Parliament, at Whitehaven.

1713, December 26, Whitehall.—My last was since the 10th of this month, but what day exactly I cannot tell. The subject of it was to give you an account of the meeting of some of your friends at the Leg tavern in Fleet Street the 9th, with a few of their acquaintance to the number of 21 English to give a dinner to the 10 French confessors that were then in town of those lately set at liberty from the galleys. The appearance was what I am sure would have pleased you, their modesty and behaviour was so moving, that after dinner a collection being promoted there was collected what you find a particular account of in the Paper accompanying this [*missing*] and 'tis hoped a considerable addition will be made to it by some gentlemen in the City who would gladly have given their company at the entertainment, but it was fear'd their appearance would have been thought too ostentatious.

[There are a few other letters of the same writer in 1718 and 1729, dated from the Middle Temple and Bartlett's Buildings.]

BISHOP (NICHOLSON) OF CARLISLE to JAMES LOWTHER at Whitehaven.

1714, October 9, Rose . . . We continue here in the most profound quiet as to matters of election, every one taking it for granted there's no room for the disturbers of our peace to fix a foot amongst us. Brigadier Stanwix has been happily instrumental in carrying one great point for Sir R. Sandford at Appleby. His brother Nevinson seem'd resolved to accept of the mayoralty, notwithstanding the due election (according to Charter) of Mr. John Baynes. But the late mayor was at last persuaded to consider the hazard which he would be in by countenancing such illegal pretensions, and therefore resigned his staff to Baynes.

BISHOP (NICHOLSON) OF CARLISLE to JAMES LOWTHER at Whitehaven.

1714, Oct. 20. . . . " You hear of Sir Con. Phipp's commencing. Dr. of Laws at Oxford, on the Coronation Day, and the reasons given for their conferring that mark of respect. They were—for his wise conduct in Ireland *et propter insignem defensionem Herois nostri Oxoniensis*, an improper day for the playing of Champion Sacheverell against Champion Dimock."

BISHOP (NICHOLSON) OF CARLISLE to JAMES LOWTHER at Whitehaven.

1714, Dec. 4, Rose . . . What comforts I am to promise myself from my new brethren on the Bench I cannot yet tell. Dr. Wyn has the reputation of being a learned and good-tempered person. But my Lord of Cant. seems not to hope for the like respects in him, as in the

Bishop of Glocr. His promotion is chiefly owing to the E. of N., who (after his refusal of the see of St. A. for one or both of his own brothers) had the favour allow'd him of giving his third option to his son Mostyn's friend. The good old man at Lambeth is not quite satisfy'd with this motley succession in the prelates of his province, since it affords no sure prospect of having any end put to his synodical squabbles.

Whether Dr. Phipps (as they call him) will have any further distinguishing mark of the University's favour for his heroic defence of their champion, time must shew. The fore-mentioned advancement of their Margaret Professor has so far transported some of the most sanguine advocates for the Irish Chancellor that they make use of it as a sure argument of the Court's inclining to that party of men, as the only stanch supporters of monarchy. A few months more, it is hoped, will convince them of their mistake . . .

I am sorry that Mr. Yates's bodily infirmities have no due effect upon his mind. His picking up young (and loose) curates to call down fire from above on lukewarmness here below, shows what manner of spirit he is of. You are not, sir, to wonder at these intemperances amongst our country zealots; since those of the city are yet more inflamed. They do not only print and preach ; but pray in their pulpits, against the growth of the *Lutheran Heresy*, and 'tis not difficult to guess what's meant by that behaviour. This forwardness will do good in the end."

BISHOP (NICHOLSON) OF CARLISLE to JAMES LOWTHER at Whitehaven.

1714–5, Feb. 19.—The inclos'd comes down from so good a hand that I cannot doubt of its being very just. I am also able to acquaint you (from the same hand) that the little misunderstandings, which seem'd to be arising amongst the great ones above are pretty well blown over.

Enclosure.—Paper headed " State of Elections, Feb. 9."

Tories	151	Tories in posts at court	11
Whigs	244	Whigs for Tories	117
Queries	2	Tories for Whigs	3
		Whigs in two places	3
	397 whereof		

BISHOP (NICHOLSON) OF CARLISLE to JAMES LOWTHER at Whitehaven.

1714–5, Mar. 3. Rose.—About the election of members to Convocation—the old Proctors, Mr. Chancellor Tullie and Mr. Benson returned.

" I can honestly assure you that my nephew Rothery was not advised by Mr. Y[ates] in the preaching against slander ; for he gave us that sermon in my chapel, and 'twas I who wished him to take it with him to Whitehaven." Alludes to the new church at Whitehaven.

INDEX.

R.

s 2

O.

P.

LONDON: Printed by EYRE and SPOTTISWOODE,
Printers to the Queen's most Excellent Majesty.
For Her Majesty's Stationery Office.

HISTORICAL MANUSCRIPTS COMMISSION.

Date.	—	Size.	Sessional Paper.	Price.
				s. d.
1870 (Reprinted 1874.)	FIRST REPORT, WITH APPENDIX - Contents :— ENGLAND. House of Lords; Cambridge Colleges; Abingdon, and other Corporations, &c. SCOTLAND. Advocates' Library, Glasgow Corporation, &c.	f'cap	[C. 55]	1 6
1871	IRELAND. Dublin, Cork, and other Corporations, &c. SECOND REPORT, WITH APPENDIX, AND INDEX TO THE FIRST AND SECOND REPORTS - - - - - Contents :— ENGLAND. House of Lords; Cambridge Colleges; Oxford Colleges; Monastery of Dominican Friars at Woodchester, Duke of Bedford, Earl Spencer, &c. SCOTLAND. Aberdeen and St. Andrew's Universities, &c. IRELAND. Marquis of Ormonde; Dr. Lyons, &c.	„	[C. 441]	3 10
1872	THIRD REPORT, WITH APPENDIX AND INDEX - - - - - Contents :— ENGLAND. House of Lords; Cambridge Colleges; Stonyhurst College; Bridgewater and other Corporations; Duke of Northumberland, Marquis of Lansdowne, Marquis of Bath, &c. SCOTLAND. University of Glasgow; Duke of Montrose, &c. IRELAND. Marquis of Ormonde; Black Book of Limerick, &c.	„	[C. 673]	[Out of print.]
1873	FOURTH REPORT, WITH APPENDIX. PART I. - - - - - Contents :— ENGLAND. House of Lords; Westminster Abbey; Cambridge and Oxford Colleges; Cinque Ports, Hythe, and other Corporations, Marquis of Bath, Earl of Denbigh, &c. SCOTLAND. Duke of Argyll, &c. IRELAND. Trinity College, Dublin; Marquis of Ormonde.	„	[C. 857]	6 8
1873	DITTO. PART II. INDEX - - -	„	[C.857i.]	2 6
1876	FIFTH REPORT, WITH APPENDIX. PART I. - Contents :— ENGLAND. House of Lords; Oxford and Cambridge Colleges; Dean and Chapter of Canterbury; Rye, Lydd, and other Corporations, Duke of Sutherland, Marquis of Lansdowne, Reginald Cholmondeley, Esq., &c. SCOTLAND. Earl of Aberdeen, &c.	„	[C.1432]	7 0
	DITTO. PART II. INDEX - - -	„	[C.1432 i.]	3 6

Date.	—	Size.	Sessional Paper.	Price.
				s. d.

1877	SIXTH REPORT, WITH APPENDIX. PART I. -
	Contents :—
	  ENGLAND. House of Lords; Oxford and Cambridge Colleges; Lambeth Palace; Black Book of the Archdeacon of Canterbury; Bridport, Wallingford, and other Corporations; Lord Leconfield, Sir Reginald Graham, Sir Henry Ingilby, &c.
	  SCOTLAND. Duke of Argyll, Earl of Moray, &c.
	  IRELAND. Marquis of Ormonde.
		f'cap	[C.1745]	8 6

	DITTO. PART II. INDEX - - -	„	[C.2102]	[*Out of print.*]
1879	SEVENTH REPORT, WITH APPENDIX. PART I. - - - - - - Contents :— House of Lords; County of Somerset; Earl of Egmont, Sir Frederick Graham, Sir Harry Verney, &c.	„	[C.2340]	[*Out of print.*]
	DITTO. PART II. APPENDIX AND INDEX - Contents :— Duke of Athole, Marquis of Ormonde, S. F. Livingstone, Esq., &c.	„	[C. 2340 i.]	[*Out of print.*]

1881	EIGHTH REPORT, WITH APPENDIX AND INDEX. PART I. - - -
	Contents :—
	  List of collections examined, 1869–1880.
	  ENGLAND. House of Lords; Duke of Marlborough; Magdalen College, Oxford; Royal College of Physicians; Queen Anne's Bounty Office; Corporations of Chester, Leicester, &c.
	  IRELAND. Marquis of Ormonde, Lord Emly, The O'Conor Don, Trinity College, Dublin, &c.
		„	[C.3040]	8 6

1881	DITTO. PART II. APPENDIX AND INDEX - Contents :— Duke of Manchester.	„	[C.3040 i.]	1 9
1881	EIGHTH REPORT. PART III. APPENDIX AND INDEX - - - - - - Contents :— Earl of Ashburnham.	„	[C.3040 ii.]	1 4
1883	NINTH REPORT, WITH APPENDIX AND INDEX. PART I. - - - - Contents :— St. Paul's and Canterbury Cathedrals; Eton College; Carlisle, Yarmouth, Canterbury, and Barnstaple Corporations, &c.	„	[C.3773]	[*Out of print.*]

1884	DITTO. PART II. APPENDIX AND INDEX -
	Contents :—
	  ENGLAND. House of Lords, Earl of Leicester; C. Pole Gell, Alfred Morrison, Esqs., &c.
	  SCOTLAND. Lord Elphinstone, H. C. Maxwell Stuart, Esq., &c.
	  IRELAND. Duke of Leinster, Marquis of Drogheda, &c.
		„	[C.3773 i.]	6 3

1884	DITTO. PART III. APPENDIX AND INDEX - - - - - - Contents :— Mrs. Stopford Sackville.	„	[C.3773 ii.]	1 7

Date.	—	Size.	Sessional Paper.	Price.
				s. d.
1883	CALENDAR OF THE MANUSCRIPTS OF THE MARQUIS OF SALISBURY, K.G. (or CECIL MSS.). PART I. - - - -	8vo.	[C.3777]	[*Out of print.*]
1888	DITTO. PART II. - - -	„	[C.5463]	3 5
1889	DITTO. PART III. - - -	„	[C. 5889 v.]	2 1
1892	DITTO. PART IV. - - -	„	[C.6823]	2 11
1885	TENTH REPORT - - - - This is introductory to the following :—	„	[C.4548]	0 3½
1885	(1.) APPENDIX AND INDEX - - - Earl of Eglinton, Sir J. S. Maxwell, Bart., and C. S. H. D. Moray, C. F. Weston Underwood, G. W. Digby, Esqs.	„	[C.4575]	[*Out of print.*]
1885	(2.) APPENDIX AND INDEX - - The Family of Gawdy.	„	[C.4576 iii.]	1 4
1885	(3.) APPENDIX AND INDEX - - Wells Cathedral.	„	[C.4576 ii.]	2 0
1885	(4.) APPENDIX AND INDEX - - Earl of Westmorland ; Capt. Stewart ; Lord Stafford ; Sir N. W. Throckmorton, Stonyhurst College ; Sir P. T. Mainwaring, Misses Boycott, Lord Muncaster, M.P., Capt. J. F. Bagot, Earl of Kilmorey, Earl of Powis, Rev. T. S. Hill and others, the Corporations of Kendal, Wenlock, Bridgnorth, Eye, Plymouth, and the County of Essex.	„	[C.4576]	3 6
1885	(5.) APPENDIX AND INDEX - - - The Marquis of Ormonde, Earl of Fingall, Corporations of Galway, Waterford, the Sees of Dublin and Ossory, the Jesuits in Ireland.	„	[C. 4576 i.]	[*Out of print.*]
1887	(6.) APPENDIX AND INDEX - - -- Marquis of Abergavenny, Lord Braye, G. F. Luttrell, P. P. Bouverie, W. B. Davenport, M.P., R. T. Balfour, Esquires.	„	[C.5242]	1 7
1887	ELEVENTH REPORT - - - - This is introductory to the following :—	„	[C. 5060 vi.]	0 3
1887	(1.) APPENDIX AND INDEX - - H. D. Skrine, Esq., Salvetti Correspondence.	„	[C.5060]	1 1
1887	(2.) APPENDIX AND INDEX - - House of Lords. 1678-1688.	„	[C. 5060 i.]	2 0
1887	(3.) APPENDIX AND INDEX - - Corporations of Southampton and Lynn.	„	[C. 5060 ii.]	1 8
1887	(4.) APPENDIX AND INDEX - - Marquis Townshend.	„	[C. 5060 iii.]	2 6
1887	(5.) APPENDIX AND INDEX - - Earl of Dartmouth.	„	[C. 5060 iv.]	2 8

Date.	—	Size.	Sessional Paper.	Price.
				s. *d.*
1887	(6.) APPENDIX AND INDEX - - - Duke of Hamilton.	8vo	[C. 5060 v.]	1 6
1888	(7.) APPENDIX AND INDEX - - - Duke of Leeds, Marchioness of Waterford, Lord Hothfield, &c.; Bridgwater Trust Office, Reading Corporation, Inner Temple Library.	,,	[C.5612]	2 0
1890	TWELFTH REPORT - - - This is introductory to the following :—	,,	[C.5889]	0 3
1888	(1.) APPENDIX - - - - Earl Cowper, K.G. (Coke MSS., at Melbourne Hall, Derby) Vol. I.	,,	[C.5472]	2 7
1888	(2.) APPENDIX - - - - Ditto. Vol. II.	,,	[C.5613]	2 5
1889	(3.) APPENDIX AND INDEX - - - Ditto. Vol. III.	,,	[C. 5889 i.]	1 4
1888	(4.) APPENDIX - - - The Duke of Rutland, G.C.B. Vol. I.	,,	[C.5614]	3 2
1891	(5.) APPENDIX AND INDEX - - - Ditto. Vol. II.	,,	[C. 5889 ii.]	2 0
1889	(6.) APPENDIX AND INDEX - - - House of Lords, 1689-1690.	,,	[C. 5889 iii.]	2 1½
1890	(7.) APPENDIX AND INDEX - - - S. H. le Fleming, Esq., of Rydal.	,,	[C. 5889 iv.]	1 11
1891	(8.) APPENDIX AND INDEX - - - The Duke of Athole, K.T., and the Earl of Home.	,,	[C.6338]	1 0
1891	(9.) APPENDIX AND INDEX - - - The Duke of Beaufort, K.G., the Earl of Donoughmore, J. H. Gurney, W. W. B. Hulton, R. W. Ketton, G. A. Aitken, P. V. Smith, Esqs. ; Bishop of Ely ; Cathedrals of Ely, Glouces- ter, Lincoln, and Peterborough ; Corporations of Gloucester, Higham Ferrers, and Newark; Southwell Minster; Lincoln District Registry.	,,	[C. 6338 i.]	2 6
1891	(10.) APPENDIX - - - The First Earl of Charlemont. Vol. I. 1745-1783.	,,	[C. 6338 ii.]	1 11
1892	THIRTEENTH REPORT - - - This is introductory to the following :—	,,	[C.6827]	0 3
1891	(1.) APPENDIX - - - The Duke of Portland. Vol. I.	,,	[C.6474]	3 0
	(2.) APPENDIX AND INDEX - - - Ditto. Vol. II.	,,	[C. 6827 i.]	2 0
1892	(3.) APPENDIX. J. B. Fortescue, Esq. Vol. I. -	,,	[C.6660]	2 7

Date.	—	Size.	Sessional Paper.	Price.
				s. *d.*
1892	(4.) APPENDIX AND INDEX - - - Corporations of Rye, Hastings, and Hereford. Capt. F. C. Loder-Symonds, E. R. Wodehouse, M.P., J. Dovaston, Esqs., Sir T. B. Lennard, Bart., Rev. W. D. Macray, and Earl of Dartmouth (Supplementary Report).	8vo.	[C.6810]	2 4
1892	(5.) APPENDIX AND INDEX - - - House of Lords, 1690–1691.	,,	[C.6822]	2 4
1893	(6.) APPENDIX AND INDEX - - Sir William FitzHerbert, Earl of Ancaster, &c.	,,	[C.7166]	1 4
	(7.) APPENDIX AND INDEX - - - The Earl of Lonsdale.	*In the Press.*		
	(8.) THE FIRST EARL OF CHARLEMONT - Vol. II. 1784–1799.	*In the Press.*